"This wonderful collection offers readers an opportunity to explore the deep interdisciplinary nature of urban history through topics ranging from migrants and immigrants to the environment and transportation. The essays, like cities themselves, unfold in layers: there are documents offering insight in cities, classic essays on urban history and studies, as well as the latest scholarship. While providing a wide-ranging introduction to cities, the volume also encourages thoughtful consideration of gender, race, and class across American history."

–Ann Keating, Dr. C. Frederick Toenniges Professor of History, North Central College, co-editor of the *Encyclopedia of Chicago*

"An outstanding single-volume reader, incorporating a richly diverse array of primary and secondary sources from the pre-Colombian period to the present. The second edition further enriches the content of the first with inclusion of the newest scholarship and primary-source materials you won't find anywhere else. Carefully curated and thoughtfully introduced, this is an essential resource for anyone wanting to better understand America's urban past."

–Margaret O'Mara, Howard & Frances Keller Professor of History, University of Washington, author of *Cities of Knowledge*

"As the planet's population moves into growing megacities, a more just and sustainable future depends upon understanding the social, environmental, and political complexities of human settlement. The essays and documents in the second edition of *The American Urban Reader* provide valuable historical perspectives on contemporary problems of cities in the United States. This volume will generate productive classroom discussion about the roots of the systems we rely upon, as well as the inequities that divide us."

–Carl A. Zimring, Professor of Sustainability Studies, Pratt Institute, author of *Clean and White: A History of Environmental Racism in the United States*

D1220663

THE AMERICAN URBAN READER

The American Urban Reader, Second Edition, brings together the most exciting and cutting-edge work on the history of urban forms and ways of life in the evolution of the United States, from pre-colonial Native American Indian cities, colonial European settlements, and western expansion, to rapidly expanding metropolitan regions, the growth of suburbs, and post-industrial cities.

Each chapter is arranged chronologically and thematically around scholarly essays from historians, social scientists, and journalists, and is supplemented by relevant primary documents that offer more nuanced perspectives and convey the diversity and interdisciplinary nature of the study of the urban condition. Building upon the success of the First Edition, and responding to increasingly polarized national discourse in the era of Donald Trump's presidency, *The American Urban Reader*, Second Edition, highlights both the historical urban/rural divide and the complexity and deeply woven salience of race and ethnic relations in American history.

Lisa Krissoff Boehm and Steven H. Corey, who together hold forty-five years of classroom experience in urban studies and history, have selected a range of work that is dynamically written and carefully edited to be accessible to students and appropriate for anyone seeking a deeper understanding of how American cities have developed.

Lisa Krissoff Boehm is Dean of the College of Graduate Studies at Bridgewater State University. She is the author of *Popular Culture and the Enduring Myth of Chicago* and *Making a Way out of No Way: African American Women and the Second Great Migration*.

Steven H. Corey is Dean of the School of Liberal Arts and Sciences and Professor of History at Columbia College Chicago. He has written for *Environmental Ethics*, *PS: Political Science and Politics*, *Journal of Urban History*, and was research curator for *Garbage! The History and Politics of Trash in New York City*.

Together they are also co-authors of *America's Urban History* (Routledge, 2015).

ROUTLEDGE READERS IN HISTORY

CV 07.11.2023 0849

The Postmodern History Reader
Edited by Keith Jenkins

The Postmodernism Reader: Foundational Texts
Edited by Michael Drolet

The Public History Reader
Edited by Hilda Kean and Paul Martin

Renaissance Thought: A Reader
Edited by Robert Black

The Slavery Reader
Edited by Gad Heuman and James Walvin

The Terrorism Reader
Edited by David J. Whittaker

The Twentieth Century Russia Reader
Edited by Alistair Kocho-Williams

The Victorian Studies Reader
Edited by Kelly Boyd and Rohan McWilliam

The Witchcraft Reader
Edited by Darren Oldridge

The World War Two Reader
Edited by Gordon Martel

The American Urban Reader
Edited by Lisa Krissoff Boehm and Steven H. Corey

THE AMERICAN URBAN READER

HISTORY AND THEORY

SECOND EDITION

Lisa Krissoff Boehm and Steven H. Corey
EDITORS

Routledge
Taylor & Francis Group

NEW YORK AND LONDON

Second edition published 2020
by Routledge
52 Vanderbilt Avenue, New York, NY 10017
and by Routledge
2 Park Square, Milton Park, Abingdon, Oxon, OX14 4RN

Routledge is an imprint of the Taylor & Francis Group, an informa business

© 2020 Taylor & Francis

The right of the Lisa Krissoff Boehm and Steven H. Corey to be identified as the authors of the editorial material, and of the authors for their individual chapters, has been asserted in accordance with sections 77 and 78 of the Copyright, Designs and Patents Act 1988.

First edition published by Routledge 2010

Library of Congress Cataloging-in-Publication Data
Names: Boehm, Lisa Krissoff, 1969- editor. | Corey, Steven H., editor.
Title: The American urban reader : history and theory / edited by Lisa Krissoff Boehm
& Steven H. Corey.
Description: Second edition. | New York : Routledge, 2020. |
Series: Routledge readers in history; 29 | Includes bibliographical references and index.
Identifiers: LCCN 2019029842 | ISBN 9781138041059 (hardback) |
ISBN 9781138041066 (paperback)
Subjects: LCSH: Urbanization–United States. | Cities and towns–United States. |
Sociology, Urban–United States.
Classification: LCC HT123 .A66644 2020 | DDC 307.760973–dc23
LC record available at https://lccn.loc.gov/2019029842

ISBN: 978-1-138-04105-9 (hbk)
ISBN: 978-1-138-04106-6 (pbk)
ISBN: 978-0-429-43797-7 (ebk)

Typeset in Sabon
by Swales & Willis, Exeter, Devon, UK

Visit the companion website: www.routledge.com/textbooks/9781138041066.

For the boys
David Krissoff Boehm, Peter Krissoff Boehm,
and Alexandros X. F. Corey

CONTENTS

PART III. FROM BRITISH TO AMERICAN CITIES

PART IV. WAYS OF CITY LIFE, 1820s–1920s

PART V. FROM PARTY BOSSES TO FEDERALISM: THE EVOLUTION OF URBAN GOVERNMENT

Documents

Illustrations

PART VIII.   URBAN MIGRATIONS, RACE, AND SOCIAL MOBILITY

ACKNOWLEDGMENTS

We spent over three years working on the Second Edition of *The American Urban Reader: History and Theory* and it is wonderful to see the volume come to fruition. We want to thank all of those who supported this work. Routledge's history editor Kimberly Guinta helped the first edition come to life, and editor Eve Mayer assisted with the second. Zoë Forbes at Routledge and Megan Symons at Swales & Willis aided us in the process of bringing the myriad pieces to typesetting.

Many librarians, archivists, and administrators gave their time and expertise to the work. We would like to thank the staffs of the American Antiquarian Society, the Kheel Center at Cornell University, the Brookings Institution, the Oklahoma Historical Society, the Newberry Library, the University of Georgia Libraries, the Canal Corridor Association, the Gilder-Lehrman Institute, Minnesota Public Radio, and the Kentucky Historical Society. Thank you also to the staffs of the Brown University Libraries, the Goddard Library at Clark University, the Department of Health and Human Services, the Library of Congress, the Congress for the New Urbanism, the Newberry Library in Chicago, the New-York Historical Society, the New York Public Library, the North Kingstown Free Library, the Oklahoma Historical Society, the University of Rhode Island Library, the Worcester State University Library, the *Worcester Telegram and Gazette*, *Curbed*, the Columbia College Chicago Library, and the Bridgewater State University Library. Thank you to the authors here for allowing their works to be included, and for the hard-working permissions staffs of their publishers. Thank you also to families of Wayne Andrews, Harriette Arnow, Arthur M. Schlesinger, Sr., and Richard C. Wade.

The framework of this book was born at key conferences where we discussed teaching urban history. At the 122nd Annual Meeting of the American Historical Association in Washington, D.C., January 3–6, 2008, we served on a panel with historians Amy Howard (University of Richmond), Michael Lewis (Salisbury University), and Gregory Wilson (University of Akron). At the request of editor David Goldfield, our remarks evolved into papers that we published as the January 2010 version of the *Journal of Urban History* (*JUH*), the first ever edition of that journal devoted to teaching. Since graduate school, we have both fought against the all-too-frequent hesitancy to discuss teaching. It was refreshing to start a conversation with Howard, Lewis, and Wilson online and watch it blossom into a thorough dialogue at the conference and through the writing of articles for the *JUH*. The thought process continued on through the 2009 Urban History Association conference in Houston, where we spoke on a panel with Janice Bedarneck (University of Dayton). We put together a first version of the updated table of contents for this Second Edition while at the meeting for the American Studies Association in Denver in 2016.

We benefitted greatly from conversations with scholars including Adam Arenson, Clifton Hood, Lizabeth Cohen, Russell Chabot, Tom Conroy, Jared Day, Corey Dolgon, Maura Doherty, Amy Finstein, Charlotte Haller, Tona Hangen, Sean Holmes, D. Bradford Hunt, Dennis Judd, Joyce Mandell, Martin Melosi, Erin McCarthy, Mark Motte, Dominic Pacyga, Dick Simpson, Emily Straus, Jo-Ann Della Guistina, Joel Tarr, Kristin Waters, Carl Zimring, and Lisa's various writing group cohorts at Brandeis University and Bridgewater State University. Bridgewater State University graduate assistant Jonathan Louis provided his unflappable organizational effort to the volume. Lauren Lamothe assisted with scanning of newly read articles with good cheer. At Bridgewater State University, Lisa wishes to especially thank Provost Karim Ismaili, the Provost's Council, and the stellar Leadership Team and staff of the College of Graduate Studies. At Columbia College Chicago, Steven wishes to especially recognize the support of Christie Dal Corobbo, Robin Whatley, Sandra Chapman, Erika Roditis, Dok Kang, Regina Wellner, Suzanne Blum Malley, Stanley Wearden, and the entire Provost Office.

Families and friends of course provided the backbone of the practical support and encouragement necessary to complete the daily labors involved with writing and editing. Steven Corey thanks Alexandra Filindra, Alexandros Corey, Lori Corey, Keith Corey and Katie Minihan, Xanthi Pappa, Eugenia Filindra, George Tsipras, Melina Tsipra, Eric Freedman, Ryan Ratliff, Deborah Holdstein, Jay Boersma, Greg Jacobson, David Kieffner, Mark Pesce, Stephen Beganyi, Melissa Devine, Noah Kaplan, Kate Boulay, Shannon Chandley, and Thomas Silvia. Lisa Krissoff Boehm would like to thank Chris Boehm, David and Peter Krissoff Boehm, Madelon and Joel Krissoff, Jonathan and Nikolette Krissoff, Sarah Krissoff and Andy Boss, Suzan and Wayne Ushman, Gina Lavallee, Joyce Mandell, and George and Becky Pins. Friends, too numerous to name here, listened to updates on the book progression with utmost patience and didn't complain about the negative social consequences of weekends devoted to writing and editing rather than fun.

FOREWORD

The majority of Americans have lived in cities now for nearly a century. The fact that the United States began as a nation with a largely agrarian population and evolved into a country of city dwellers is well known. Less understood is what this momentous transformation meant to the nation's history and how it was understood by the people who lived it. The distinctive contribution of this innovative reader by Steven H. Corey and Lisa Krissoff Boehm is its recovery of the vast scale of this story—both its analytical and personal sides—and the powerful impact the growth of cities made on the lives and minds of so many citizens. This book makes it clear that Americans not only settled in cities but thought about them a great deal.

The American Urban Reader offers a particularly powerful view of the residents of metropolitan areas and the trials and tribulations they faced. As city spaces became more crowded with migrants of various ethnic and racial backgrounds, Americans expended an enormous amount of time to identify who they wanted to live near them in their neighborhoods and who they did not. Cities became cauldrons of ethnic and racial accommodation and tension. Neighbors rendered assistance to some and erected barriers to keep out those who appeared alien or threatening. And they did so over the entire course of our urban experience—a point that the editors make well by extending the story of immigration and race from the nineteenth century into contemporary times.

American cities—as documented here—were not only sites of conflict and social disorder, however, but also laboratories where citizens attempted to work out solutions to enormous social problems, a point that has not been readily appreciated. It was on city streets and in urban universities that reformers, scholars, and political leaders fashioned solutions to the vexing problems of modern American life such as public health, charity and welfare, transportation, and education.

Even more striking was the degree to which citizens funneled so many aspects of city life into their imaginations. Corey and Boehm explain well how a preoccupation with urban growth actually helped to initiate a number of academic specialties in history, economics, and sociology. Historians have published a considerable number of studies—many sampled here—that identify colorful urban types that moved through the city such as pickpockets, boarders, and prostitutes. Pioneering works in sociology were authored by social workers like Jane Addams and sociologists like W.E.B. Du Bois. Novelists never tired of creating characters who moved from rural regions to city streets and thinking out loud regarding the impact of this change on the ordinary person. *The American Urban Reader* is exceptional in the way it captures not only the conditions of city life but the massive impact of the urban landscape on the American cultural imagination.

Finally, the book takes due note of the fact that the urban transformation of America is not simply a historic or completed process. It reveals the rise of suburban and exurban regions and the emergence of new cities with reasons for being that could not even be imagined in the nineteenth century. Thus, the growth of an industrial city like Chicago is contrasted with the dynamic entertainment driven metropolis of Las Vegas. One can only wonder near the end of this story what will come next.

John Bodnar[i]

NOTE

i John Bodnar is Chancellor's Professor, Indiana University, and his latest book is *The "Good War" in American Memory* (Johns Hopkins University Press, 2010).

PREFACE

The essays in this anthology, *The American Urban Reader: History and Theory* (AUR), Second Edition, are examples of the finest scholarship in U.S. urban history and urban studies. We have assembled works that convey the richness and strikingly broad breadth and depth of the various subfields of social history and related humanities and social science disciplines which deal with urban life. We have also attempted to balance time and geographic space in sampling the spectrum of the American (which for this volume means the United States) urban experience from pre-colonial settlements to contemporary post-industrial cities, as well as many other configurations in between, from coast to coast. We have supplemented the essays with documents from actual observers of and participants in the events, movements, and social conditions covered in the larger themes found within each part of the anthology.

Given the abundance of writing on urban, metropolitan, and suburban affairs, selecting articles and primary documents for this volume was no easy task. Due to the space constraints, we have omitted many wonderful and insightful contributions that we had hoped to include. Our original list of articles and documents could have filled multiple volumes. This attests to the richness of recent scholarship on the city.

The themes we have chosen to anchor each chapter are at once chronological and thematic. We start with selections that probe into various definitions of and competing viewpoints on the urban condition. We follow with historical overviews on city growth, beginning with the colonial period and proceeding on to the modern day. Urbanists writing for roundtables published in the *Journal of Urban History* and those taking part in discussions on the H-Urban list on H-Net, have commented on the modern focus (late nineteenth to twentieth century) of the bulk of new urban history. But without the added perspective of scholarship on the colonial era through the early nineteenth century, we cannot truly understand contemporary urban places. We follow with primary documents related to the readings that provide chronological, geographical, and social diversity and the kinds of nuances only this type of source offers. We expect the document sections will give readers a more interactive experience, and that they will open the themes up nicely for classroom discussions. Researchers could rely on these documents as a starting point for class assignments, and students of urban history also may want to draw on the book-length works in which the essays were originally published. Note, whenever possible, we have retained the original spelling and grammar of the documents. We have also included a bibliography of recommended works, divided by theme, in the back matter of the volume. We expect that professors utilizing the book in the classroom will pair the *AUR* with one or more of these works depending on the focus of the class.

The book highlights persistent themes in urban history, including immigration, migration, industrialization, urban politics, transportation, environmental concerns, the growth of the modern "ghetto," suburbanization, post-industrialization, and the carceral city. The volume emphasizes the role of race as a salient theme throughout the history of the American metropolis. We devote substantial space to issues of class, race, gender, sexual orientation, and ethnicity. For an expanded exploration of suburbanization, we recommend Becky Nicolaides's and Andrew Weise's *The Suburb Reader*, Second Edition (New York: Routledge, 2016). For reasons of space and consistency, we consider the impact suburbanization from the point of view of the central city, but do not delve into the creation of a suburban way of life to a considerable extent. We ultimately did not have the space to deal extensively with the connected themes of architecture or urban art, although architecture makes more than a passing appearance here in some articles.

Students love urban studies, urban sociology, and urban history, although, in the case of the latter, at times they do not know it. Students regretfully often arrive at college associating history with the rote memorization of dates and facts. History professors have to dispel these preconceptions in the first few days of class. As practiced today, urban history is a very interdisciplinary field. This book is not simply urban history, however. This book comes from our collective forty-five years of higher education experience teaching urban studies, history, geography, American studies, education, and women's studies courses at our previous home institution of Worcester State University in Worcester, Massachusetts, our previous teaching positions at Indiana University, University of Michigan-Dearborn, Emmanuel College, Manhattanville College, University of Rhode Island, and Yeshiva University, and our current positions at Bridgewater State University and Columbia College Chicago respectively. We owe a debt to the historians and social scientists that have taught us over the years. For example, the innovative historian John Bodnar, who penned our Foreword, was a large influence on our thinking. Without forward-thinking professors, we would not have been able to find the comfort level necessary to take on the modern city in an interdisciplinary way. Both of the editors pursued interdisciplinary master's degrees before we entered our history Ph.D. programs. The field of urban history provided a good fit for the type of social history we were doing by the time we completed our graduate studies.

The historiography of American cities has grown considerably since Arthur M. Schlesinger's publication of *The Rise of the City, 1878–1898* in 1933. By that point, urban sociology was well underway and held sway over how academics and many college-educated people dealt with issues connected to the urban setting. The growth of social history during the twentieth century, as is discussed at length in our revised essay, "Examining the Urban Landscape: From Social Reform to Social History, and Back" in Part I of the volume, gave weight to the scholarly value of viewing the world from "the bottom up." Urban history often views the city right from street level, which offers an intriguing view, indeed. Urban history is social history with an urban focus. In the modern day, when most Americans reside or work in metropolitan settings, and cities provide the backdrop for the nation's tense interplay regarding issues of race, class, gender, and sexuality, the importance of understanding urban life cannot be overestimated.

PART I

PLACE MATTERS

Definitions and Perspectives

This part of *The American Urban Reader* provides an overview of how scholars and social commentators have conceived of cities and assessed the nature of urban life in the United States. It begins with our own original essay that examines the origins of the field of urban history and the ways in which urban reformers and academics have framed investigations of cities. We argue that in an effort to understand the weighty issues associated with industrialization, immigration, and explosive metropolitan growth, social reformers influenced academics and contributed to the growth of urban history.

Sociologists and other social scientists who drew heavily from the work of urban activists were decades ahead of historians in assessing life in the American city. The myopic view of cities within the historical profession began to change in the 1930s and 1940s, when a small group of social historians published cutting-edge works on colonial and nineteenth century cities. Leading the pack was noted American historian Arthur M. Schlesinger, Sr., who argued that the city, no less than the frontier, shaped the course of U.S. history. We are pleased to include one of Schlesinger's clearest syntheses of urban history with the selection, "The City in American Civilization" from his 1949 book *Paths to the Present*.

While historians were just beginning to explore the history of cities systematically, sociologists were well under way with their work of formulating comprehensive theories on urban life. At the forefront of this movement were members of the Chicago School, who sought to examine the city as an object of detached analysis. The Chicago School, known for such luminaries as Robert Park, Ernest W. Burgess, and Louis Wirth, set the stage for future generations of social scientists and public policy makers seeking to understand the city.

One of the most important works of the Chicago School was Ernest W. Burgess' "The Growth of the City: An Introduction to a Research Project," published in 1925. [**See Illustration I.2.**] The sustained influence of the Chicago School can be noted in essays across *The American Urban Reader*. In the selection "Urbanism and Suburbanism as Ways of Life: A Reevaluation of Definitions," originally published in 1962 and updated with a postscript three decades later, renowned sociologist Herbert Gans questions whether it is possible to formulate a sociological definition of the city. In the essay by William H. Frey, we move forward to examine the American city in the twenty-first century. Frey points to the continued salience of racial discord as a defining characteristic of the American city, and, increasingly, a prominent source of disruption within suburban America. The United States was formed by colonial efforts detailed in the early portions of this reader. The colonial effort relied on cities. Cities constituted the building blocks of colonial economic success, and ultimately served as the building blocks of states and nations. Yet the question of who was included and excluded within urban spaces, and who had access to power and economic opportunity has remained a point of debate in the nation since its earliest days. Frey unflinchingly takes on the issue of race, class, space, and power in his important work. As the Chicago School knew from the outset, place matters.

The documents in this part explore the interplay of social investigation, fear, and safety in cities. The first, **Document 1.1**, is an excerpt from John H. Griscom's 1845 report *The Sanitary Condition of the Laboring Population of New York*. The report provides an overview of the work of sanitary reformers and Protestant ministers regarding the living conditions of the working poor. The work of Jane Addams and Ellen Gates Starr is detailed in **Document 1.2**. In 1890 the pair launched Hull-House, the first social settlement of its kind in the United States. Inspired by European models, Addams and Starr brought urban reformers into a struggling neighborhood on Chicago's West Side, where they administered programs for poor immigrants and studied the urban condition. We see a work by a formidable urban scholar of the late 1800s in **Document 1.3**. W.E.B. DuBois paved the way for sociologists and urban historians to come with his examination of turn-of-the-century Philadelphia's black neighborhoods. DuBois' cutting-edge research is still carefully studied by urban historians and urbanists within other disciplines.

The large gulf that existed between modern industrial cities and the agrarian countryside during the late nineteenth and early twentieth centuries is depicted in the once infamous "Tillman's Allegorical Cow" cartoon. [**See Illustration I.1.**] Although it was drawn to show how capitalists who supported the gold standard lived off the hard work of farmers, it also summarized the distrust many rural people held toward Wall Street and wealthy people in Eastern cities.

ESSAY 1.1

Examining America's Urban Landscape: From Social Reform to Social History, and Back

Steven H. Corey and Lisa Krissoff Boehm

Source: Steven H. Corey and Lisa Krissoff Boehm, "Examining America's Urban Landscape: From Social Reform to Social History, and Back." Copyright © 2010 and 2019 by Steven H. Corey and Lisa Krissoff Boehm.

EDITORS' INTRODUCTION

An earlier version of this essay opened the First Edition of *The American Urban Reader: History and Theory*. In this new edition, we take time to ponder how the hopes of the late twentieth century for a more unified America devolved into sharp division surround the 2016 presidential elections. Urban history as a field has much to teach us about the way in which cities have contributed to the growth of the nation. Perhaps it will be in urban communities that we find the strength and wisdom to cut through resilient class, racial, and ethnic divides and to truly realize the great potential of the American experiment.

Steven H. Corey is Dean of the School of Liberal Arts and Sciences and Professor of History at Columbia College Chicago, Illinois. He has written for *Environmental Ethics*, *PS: Political Science and Politics*, and the *Journal of Urban History* and was research curator for the noted public history exhibit *Garbage! The History and Politics of Trash in New York City*. With Lisa Krissoff Boehm, he is co-author of *America's Urban History* and co-editor of *The American Urban Reader: History and Theory*.

Lisa Krissoff Boehm is Dean of the College of Graduate Studies at Bridgewater State University in Massachusetts. She is the author of *Popular Culture and the Enduring Myth of Chicago* and *Making a Way out of No Way: African American Women and the Second Great Migration*. With Steven H. Corey, she is co-author of *America's Urban History* and co-author of *The American Urban Reader: History and Theory*. She has served as guest editor of and written for the *Journal of Urban History*.

EXAMINING AMERICA'S URBAN LANDSCAPE: FROM SOCIAL REFORM TO SOCIAL HISTORY, AND BACK (2010, 2019)

The United States is an urban nation. As such, it is impossible to understand American civilization without studying and appreciating its cities. Arguably, the social diversity, cultural vitality, and economic innovation of the United States are largely the products of urban life. Although urbanization in North America predates European exploration and settlement of the continent, the contemporary importance of cities is not surprising in light of their prodigious growth and development during the nineteenth and twentieth centuries in concert with the equally dramatic rise of industrialization, immigration, and internal migration in the same period. Indeed, since 1920, the majority of Americans have lived in urban settings. The year 2008 marked the first time that the majority of the world population resided in cities, and this demographic change prompted renewed interest in urban history and urban studies.

Even during the American colonial era, cities, or more accurately towns, exerted a disproportionate influence over the overwhelmingly rural landscape. Given the prominence of cities in colonial America and the United States, it is not surprising that many social observers and academics have attempted to chronicle the evolution of urban spaces and analyze a host of issues associated with urban life. This essay, and this Second Edition of *The American Urban Reader: History and Theory* in its entirety, highlights selected trends in this rather voluminous literature on American cities.

It is of course impossible to make mention of every genre of writing on the urban condition within a single essay, or even one anthology. Our training as social historians and experience as professors in an interdisciplinary social science department led us to concentrate on how ordinary men and women have lived in, perceived, and responded to urban surroundings, as well as the ways in which social and political elites have interpreted and attempted to shape urban growth and development. Therefore, we have framed *The American Urban Reader* as a collection of scholarly essays from social historians and social scientists, supplemented with primary documents that provide a broader view of leading issues, trends, and opinions on urban life throughout American history.

This Second Edition also reflects the heightened salience of race in American politics and culture since the release of the First Edition, published shortly after the election of Barack Hussein Obama as the 44th President of the United States. Since then, naive assertions that the United States had entered a "post-racial" society have been challenged by seemingly countless examples of racial division and race baiting. Among the most high profile are the shootings of young black males and subsequent demonstrations and protests, such as those in Ferguson, Missouri in 2014, and campaigns against systematic racism such as the Black Lives Matter movement. Racialized politics has unfortunately become mainstream with the gerrymandering of state and local voting districts and voter identification laws

meant to suppress and dilute urban and minority political power, as well as outright anti-immigrant sentiment, the racist Unite the Right rally in Charlottesville, Virginia in 2017, and attempts by President Donald J. Trump to build a unpopular wall on the U.S./Mexican border. As such, within each part of this volume we have selected scholarly essays and/ or documents that demonstrate the role race has played in the development of cities and suburbs.

This essay itself has a much narrower focus than the volume as a whole. Here, we investigate the relationship between the evolution of urban life since the nineteenth century and the establishment of and transformations within some of the academic disciplines that study the American city. More specifically, the essay considers how issues associated with urban life spawned an array of social commentaries and reform efforts that influenced sociologists and, subsequently, historians, and a broad assortment of other academicians. In an attempt to consider the evolution of the field of urban history, we examine how a wide range of scholars, journalists, and social activists have framed their understanding of American cities. Beginning with a discussion of urban social reform, the essay moves on to cover the early work of new urban-oriented subfields within sociology, history, and other social sciences.

Cities and the quest to understand and transform them played a direct role in the establishment of sociology as an academic discipline in the late nineteenth and early twentieth centuries. Urban themes also fundamentally shaped the writing of American history in the latter half of the twentieth century, although urban history was not fully developed as a subfield. In fact, during the 1960s and 1970s, the study of urban history ignited the American historical profession, both as a discrete area of scholarly inquiry and as a means to understand and address contemporary social policy concerns. In higher education today, social historians largely outnumber other types of historians (much to the consternation of some of their colleagues in other subfields). Urban history, which may be considered the social history of particular places, urban groups, urban movements, or urban phenomenon, has become so ubiquitous that it is often difficult to recognize as a distinct historical subfield.

Some urban historians, as well as scholars from other disciplines who utilize urban history, bemoan the field's under-theorization and absence of a canon. As this essay argues and *The American Urban Reader* demonstrates, though, the state of urban history is both vibrant and in keeping with the long-standing interests and diversity of urban research. By tracing the roots of urban sociology and its offspring—urban history—through both popular and scholarly inquiry, this essay contextualizes these approaches by historicizing select theories on, and historiographic trends concerning, the growth and development of American cities. In addition, we would assert that historically-based urban scholarship has become bolder, more intellectually challenging, and even more influential. New works in the field demonstrate how the study of race and ethnicity, immigration and citizenship, gender and sexual identity, and social class may help readers understand and affect change in American communities.

The Rise of the City

In the manner of many introductory urban studies, urban sociology, and urban history courses, we first need to ask what at first appears to be seemingly simple questions: What is a city? What is urban? Perhaps not surprisingly, answers have changed considerably over time, in response to the context within and the age when they are asked. For social observers and academic investigators over the last two centuries, definitions fall into one or more of three categories: urban as a place, urban as a process, or urban as a way of life. Below we will examine the evolution of all three approaches simultaneously as they emerged by those beginning to understand the relative newness, complexity, and scope of rapidly developing cities.

Beginning in the early nineteenth century, American cities and their inhabitants became the subject of intense investigation by social

and political reformers, later joined by a fervent new brand of change-oriented journalists (often referred to as muckrakers). After the 1860s, scholars in the social sciences and humanities entered the discussion. The backdrop for this intellectual activity was the dramatic increase in the number and size of cities. The large metropolitan regions had significant weight in popular culture, those that became associated with anti-urban sentiments were known as "shock cities." In particular, the outsized growth of Chicago, redolent with crime, flooded with immigrants, and intriguingly located in America's rural-identified heartland, fueled growing scholarly contemplation of urban life, and birthed the Chicago School of urban sociology in the gothic-styled halls of the University of Chicago.

Statistics on nineteenth century urban growth can only hint at the difficulties facing the United States as the nation transformed from an overwhelmingly agrarian society to one on the verge of becoming evenly divided between the country and the city. Even though the United States Bureau of the Census began to count the nation's population in 1790, the relative newness of rapidly growing cities, and the emerging field of statistics itself, made it difficult to determine exactly how many people, or how large a physical area, should denote an area as urban. In fact, actual definitions of urban, based on a certain threshold of people in any incorporated area, did not emerge until the second half of the nineteenth century. Even then, the Bureau of the Census used varying figures, such as 8,000 people in the 1870s, 4,000 inhabitants in the 1880s, and just 2,500 people beginning in 1910. In the 1930s, the Bureau of the Census set 2,500 as the urban threshold. The Bureau then recalculated the size and number of cities in the country since the first census in 1790. Today, the 2,500 figure is the most commonly cited by scholars examining change in American urbanization over time.[1]

Using the United States norm of 2,500, the very first census of the U.S. population revealed that the fledgling country contained just twenty-four urban places. By the standards of their day, these urban areas, which contained just over 5 percent of the nation's total population, were equivalent to cities. These sites obviously had far fewer people in them than today's urban centers; only two of them had more than 25,000 people, while exactly half held between 2,500 and 5,000 inhabitants. They served, nonetheless, as conduits of growth for the new nation. By 1900, there were 1,737 urban areas containing almost 40 percent of the nation's population—with eighty-two cities containing between 25,000 and 50,000 people, another seventy-two between 50,000 and 500,000 inhabitants, three between 500,000 and one million, and another three (New York City, Chicago, and Philadelphia) with populations over one million.

Cities were epicenters of unprecedented social and economic change. Each year thousands of migrants from the countryside and immigrants from foreign countries poured into cities and competed with each other and native-born residents for jobs, housing, and other vital resources. At the same time, a variety of new and expanding commercial activities, such as industrial manufacturing and real estate speculation, challenged traditional urban enterprises and folkways. Small-scale craft production and the unabashed use of public spaces to raise plants and livestock went on without planning or regulation, thus leading to social and political conflicts over acceptable civic behavior and basic political rights such as taxation, suffrage, and representation. These disagreements and challenges caught the attention of social commentators who, more often than not, viewed them as negative consequences of the newly emerging urban way of life.

Famously, Thomas Jefferson, writing to Benjamin Rush in 1800, exclaimed, "I view great cities as pestilential to the morals, health and liberties of man."[2] Jefferson is often cited as the champion of the yeoman farmer and the morally invigorating life found by spending the bulk of one's time out-of-doors. Anti-urban attitudes such as Jefferson's transcended the early years of the Republic. In their influential, yet often disputed book, *The Intellectual Versus the City:*

From Thomas Jefferson to Frank Lloyd Wright, historians Morton and Lucia White argue, "enthusiasm for the American city has not been typical or predominant in our intellectual history. Fear has been the more common reaction."[3] **[For more on the origins of anti-urban attitudes and fear and American cities, see "The Forgotten City" by Benjamin Carp in Part III.]** Thomas Bender, in *Toward an Urban Vision: Ideas and Institutions in Nineteenth Century America*, however, offers a nuanced view, exploring the ways in which the producers of high culture may have expressed more favorable attitudes towards the urban than once understood.[4]

We can see by examining popular attitudes in the nineteenth and twentieth centuries, however, that our national conception of cities, especially in terms of their effect on morality or psychological health, remains at best a contested one. Historian Andrew Lees notes that beginning in the 1820s, a wide range of authors in Europe and the United States began to deal specifically with urban issues in the course of their work; most notably the clergy who served city parishes, doctors and public health officials, writers of descriptive books, and essayists. Not all observations of American cities were critical. Many individuals expressed excitement about the new opportunities for economic, social, and personal advancement found in urban settings. In fact, Lees argues that "Americans were just as favorably disposed toward their cities as Europeans were toward theirs, and that a good case can be made that the balance of opinion was more favorable in the United States than it was anywhere else."[5] However, the tenor and tone of the works that most influenced the academic tradition routinely placed cities in an unfavorable light, especially when compared to more traditional rural life.

Not surprisingly, middle and upper class individuals who engaged in religiously based social activism experienced firsthand the substandard living arrangements and working conditions of the urban poor. While many ministers and their followers sympathized with the underprivileged, many still attributed the plight of the destitute to individual depravity. Yet a new brand of social research and activism, emerging in Europe and the

United States in the early to mid-nineteenth century, slowly chipped away at notions that the impoverished or sick held all responsibility for their own suffering. While commentators on both sides of the Atlantic, particularly England's Herbert Spencer (1820–1903), began to popularize Social Darwinism and its "survival of the fittest" mentality to justify social inequality, a small but influential number of reformers went beyond simply identifying problems and condemning individual behavior by documenting in detail the very conditions they sought to fix and providing specific solutions. These efforts represented the earliest systematic studies of urban life, setting the stage for subsequent academic efforts.

In the United States, this newer way of thinking predated the progressive and social survey movements of the late nineteenth and early twentieth centuries, although it constituted less of a national phenomenon. Nor were the links between social and political reform activities throughout this period necessarily direct. Indeed, when assessing the connections between the social survey movement, made famous by the *Pittsburgh Survey* undertaken between 1907 and 1908 (see below), and the rise of empirical social research methods, sociologist Martin Bulmer argues, "Various traditions in the history of social investigation may have coexisted, or followed one another in time, but there were no necessary connections between them."[6] However, the prodigious growth of cities in the nineteenth century did lead social reformers and government officials to take note of a series of problems common to many cities. In the areas of public health, housing, immigration, and politics, those working to improve urban conditions began to follow similar trajectories and occasionally borrowed directly from one another. These activities were an attempt to understand and control a wide variety of conditions associated with rapid urbanization. They also shaped the course of social science. In time, many academics became less interested in advocacy and reform as a means of understanding and influencing society, and more interested in the development of rigorous scholarship.

The first round of urban investigations came in the field of public health, most notably with the work of sanitary reformers in the 1830s–1860s. Cities in this period faced unprecedented overcrowding and unpleasant living conditions, primarily from the interaction of manufacturing and the extraordinary influx of new people, which served to intensify preexisting class inequality, poverty, malnutrition, and physical squalor. These circumstances promoted the spread of disease and shortened the average life span. Reformers began their work by compiling statistics on births, marriages, and deaths in order to track larger public health trends. Throughout the 1830s and 1840s, a veritable "statistical movement" emerged in Great Britain and the United States around health and other social concerns, which led in part to the establishment of the Royal Statistical Society in 1834, the American Statistical Association in 1839, and government agencies on both sides of the Atlantic charged with collecting data and protecting the welfare of the general public.[7]

A small cadre of health officials and medical professionals also altered the way people viewed the relationship between poverty, disease, and the physical environment, particularly in cities. Before the advancement and acceptance of the germ theory in the latter half of the nineteenth century, a wide variety of theories competed as to the cause of sickness and epidemics. Not surprisingly, many explanations focused on the lifestyles and activities of victims, especially those perceived as living immoral lives. Beginning in the 1840s, though, health reformers advanced the so-called "sanitary idea" that ill health caused poverty and that disease had decided environmental origins. People came to consider disease a product of an individual's interaction with his or her surroundings rather than sinful habits.

Leading this sanitary movement were England's Edwin Chadwick (1800–1890) and New York City's John H. Griscom (1809–1874). In 1842, Chadwick had published the groundbreaking *Report on the Sanitary Condition of the Labouring Population of Great Britain*. Three years later, Griscom published *The Sanitary Condition of the Laboring Population of New York: With Some Suggestions for Improvement.* [**See Document 1.1.**] Both volumes documented the wretched living conditions faced by the urban poor and emphasized the physical sources of sickness. By stressing the need for proper sanitation to prevent illness, these two landmark studies galvanized reformers and contributed to the widespread association between a clean environment, good health, and the escape from poverty.[8]

Frederick Engels' *The Conditions of the Working Class in England in 1844*, published in 1845, became the work that perhaps most solidly connected the concerns of the sanitary movement with the academic scholarship explored in the second half of this essay. Writing up his observations of Manchester, England, a city ravaged by the industrial revolution and the resulting overcrowding of workers and their families, Engels (1820–1895) startled readers and prompted scholars to examine cities at street level, gleaning knowledge from the seemingly mundane details of everyday life. Engels' work directly or indirectly inspired the members of the legendary Chicago School, detailed below, generations of realist American urban novelists such as Upton Sinclair, Theodore Dreiser, Ann Petry, and Nelson Algren, and influential social commentators ranging from Jacob Riis to Alex Kotlowitz.

The most dramatic and comprehensive survey of an American municipality during the nineteenth century was the 1865 *Report of the Council of Hygiene and Public Health of the Citizens' Association of New York Upon the Sanitary Condition of the City*. By mid-century, New York was not only the nation's largest urban area, but it also bore the reputation for being the filthiest city in the western world. Physicians and other members of the Citizens' Association of New York worked as a team to map and compare every dwelling and parcel of property in New York City against a checklist of twenty-two criteria, ranging from street cleanliness to the presence of overcrowding, sickness, and high mortality. The results were nothing short of staggering, revealing a city in decay where thousands of people died each year from preventable disease. Like Manchester, New York was a city divided by class, with its filthiest and deadliest sections housing the poor. Wealthy and middle class residents, though, were not immune from the deadly effects of "offensive nuisances" such as slaughterhouses, manure yards, and fat rendering plants located near their homes or commuter routes. [**See Illustration VI.2, "Encroachment of Nuisances Upon Populous Up-town Districts."**] The report generated such an intense public outcry that the following year the New York state government created the Metropolitan Board of Health, the first modern health department in the United States, in order to clean up New York City.[9]

The year 1865 also witnessed the formation of the American Social Science Association (ASSA) in Boston, Massachusetts. This powerful group and its publication, the *Journal of Social Science* (which commenced in 1869) provided a conduit between the study of cities and advocacy for fixing urban problems. Additionally, the ASSA fostered fledgling formal academic disciplines, especially economics, history, political science, and sociology. At the request of the Massachusetts Board of State Charities, prominent Boston area reformers organized the ASSA in the model of the British National Association for the Promotion of Social Science to better understand and address statistical and philanthropic matters, including sanitary conditions, employment, education, crime, and mental illness. Throughout the 1870s–1890s, the nation's most influential social reformers and academics gathered at ASSA annual meetings, held in cities throughout the United States, to exchange information and formulate plans of action. The *Journal of Social Science* published pieces by such public intellectuals as Frederick Douglass, Florence Kelley, Charles Loring Brace, and W.E.B. Du Bois. Members of the ASSA also spun off a number of more specialized social reform organizations including the National Prison Association (established in 1870), the National Conference of Charities and Corrections (established in 1874), and the American Health Association (also established in 1874). ASSA members routinely engaged social concerns directly, speaking out about the dire conditions faced by the urban poor and becoming well-known outside academia for their efforts. Social science professors even brought their students into the streets to study conditions first-hand.[10]

The marriage between social activism and the traditionally conservative university curriculum did not last. While social reformers sought to influence the behavior of others through moral suasion and government regulation, academics were more concerned about establishing legitimacy and authority within their own newly emerging disciplines, as well as avoiding conflict with administrative officials and wealthy donors who might object to politically charged activism. As such, the various divisions of ASSA fractured, and ASSA members contributed to the founding of the American Historical Association (established in 1884), the American Economic Association (established in 1885), the American Political Science Association (established in 1903), and the American Sociology Society (established in 1905). By 1912, ASSA ceased to exist and what little remained of the body eventually folded into the National Institute of Social Sciences. Nonetheless, cities and their residents remained the subject of inquiry and reform.

Two areas in particular that generated investigations and activism were the effects of widespread immigration on the cultural life of the nation and the rise of political machines led by party bosses, many of whom rose to power by securing the loyalty of newly naturalized immigrants residing in cities. Following the influx of people during colonial settlement, the first great wave of immigration to the young United States occurred in the 1840s–1850s, with some 4.3 million people arriving largely from Ireland, Germany, Great Britain, and Canada. Many of these immigrants settled in cities and joined the large numbers of native-born Americans who had moved from the countryside in search of economic opportunity. By 1860, almost 20 percent of the total U.S. population was urban. Immigration leveled off in the 1860s–1870s to about 2.5

million each decade, and then shot up again to 5.2 million in the 1880s. By 1890, almost 15 percent of the total U.S. population was foreign born, the highest percentage during the nineteenth century. Nearly 3.7 million more immigrants came in the 1890s and total immigration numbers peaked at 8.7 million in the decade between 1900 and 1910, with two-thirds of these people coming from Southern and Eastern Europe. The foreign-born and their children comprised a sizable portion of the urban population, and in some cities made up a majority or more of the local residents by the late 1890s. For example, immigrants and their children comprised 79 percent of the population of Chicago in 1890. In 1920, just over 13 percent of all Americans were foreign born and more than half (51.2 percent) lived in cities.

The settling of so many people in urban spaces resulted in chronic overcrowding. In the tradition of the Citizens' Association and the ASSA, journalists, housing reformers, and officials representing government commissions documented and assessed the reasons for such wretched conditions, often recommending specific steps to bring about change. Perhaps the most famous of these investigations was journalist and Progressive Era reformer Jacob Riis' 1890 work, *How the Other Half Lives: Studies Among the Tenements of New York*. [**See Document 4.4, Jacob Riis, The Mixed Crowd (1890).**] Riis (1849–1914), himself a Danish immigrant, spent years as a police reporter and worked closely with charity aid workers, public health officials, and others interested in assisting New York's poor. Although steeped in denigrating stereotypes of ethnic groups, the book did provide the city's privileged classes with unforgettable stories and heart-wrenching insights into the daily life of immigrant New Yorkers. Riis's work encouraged the passage of the Tenement House Act of 1901, which required improved light and ventilation in multifamily properties and called for the establishment of New York City's Tenement House Department.

Riis was part of a much larger national reform movement during the so-called

Progressive Era of approximately 1889–1920. Progressives attempted to reign in abuses of power; they brought business-like practices to notoriously corrupt city government. Many progressives turned away from the idea of Social Darwinism, coming to believe that immigrants, the impoverished, and others in need within the city were deserving recipients of their efforts. With the development of social services, progressives believed, these once marginal urban dwellers could themselves become society's leaders. Social settlement house workers spearheaded this movement within the city by moving directly into immigrant neighborhoods to provide assistance. Settlement house workers contributed to the creation of the academic study of sociology, informing generations of academics with their findings and their methodologies.

Jane Addams (1860–1935) and Ellen Gates Starr (1859–1940) arrived in Chicago in 1889 and established the nation's most influential settlement house, Hull-House, on the city's Near West Side. [See Document 1.2, *Hull-House, A Social Settlement* (1894).] Jane Addams and Ellen Gates Starr were both graduates of Rockford Female Seminary in Rockford, Illinois. Starr spent much of her life working on labor issues and leading programs at Hull-House, where she expressed a special interest in bookbinding and taught the skill to students of all ages. Hull-House offered a broad-range of programs to the newly arrived immigrants and their families living in the surrounding area. The services included health care, kindergarten, literature courses, and clubs for young working women. Addams' and Starr's 1888 visit to London's Toynbee Hall had led to the creation of Hull-House. Jane Addams achieved acclaim for her work on behalf of the poor and her international peace advocacy. Addams, perhaps the best known woman of her day, inspired like-minded people in other cities; by 1900 there were approximately five hundred settlement houses in the United States. Addams' many books include *Hull-House Maps and Papers* (1895), a thoroughly researched edited collection complete with multi-colored maps indicating wage, ethnicity, and other neighborhood differentials. *Hull-House Maps and Papers* and Addams' work *Twenty Years at Hull-House* (1910) are still taught at colleges and universities, which demonstrates how advocates for social reform can influence academic pursuits. Addams has direct links with a number of influential academics, including John Dewey (1859–1952), who taught at the University of Chicago between 1894 and 1904 and founded the Chicago School of Pragmatism there. Dewey challenged generations of educators to rethink the structure of higher education and the public school.[11]

Fighting government corruption was another area of interest for urban reformers. By the middle of the nineteenth century, explosive population growth, economic expansion, and the physical transformation of urban space brought about increasing demands by citizens for new government regulations and municipal services. As the nature of local and state government shifted in emphasis from touting individual responsibility to support for providing employment for individuals and lucrative contracts for private sector companies, opportunities for graft and malfeasance blossomed. At the center of this transformation of government were political parties and their bosses, who oversaw the election of politicians and the distribution of patronage (i.e.: jobs) and other spoils of office for loyal party members. One of the most notorious of these bosses was New York City's William M. Tweed (1823–1878). Tweed used his connections as a member of Tammany Hall—the political machine associated with the Democratic Party which manifested influence from the 1790s to the 1960s—to swindle millions of dollars from city coffers. Political bosses operated in other locations and in other eras, although the heyday of the political boss was between the Civil War and the Great Depression. Well-known bosses include Democrat Daniel P. O'Connell in Albany (who wielded party power between approximately 1921–1977), Democrat Richard J. Daley in Chicago (1953–1976), Republican George Cox in Cincinnati (approximately 1880s–1911), and Democrat Thomas Pendergast in Kansas

City (approximately 1925–1936). [See Document 5.1, "William Tweed's Confession" (1878).]

Tweed's nefarious activities, and similar antics by Democrat and Republican politicians in communities all across the country, led to citizen reform organizations, and investigations by journalists and state legislative bodies. Such corruption placed cities in a precarious position since, as legal creations of their state government, they could and often did find their right to self-government revoked or severely restricted. Reactions to political machines within Boston, Chicago, Cleveland, Kansas City, New York City, Philadelphia, St. Louis, and other cities inspired an array of municipal reforms during the Progressive Era that called for adherence to "good government" and sound business practices. Progressives promoted the implementation of civil service programs, whereby public employees were hired and promoted on the basis of merit rather than party affiliation.

A new style of journalism, muckraking, provided commentary on the changing city and offered practical direction for emerging public policy. English newspaper editor William T. Stead's *If Christ Came to Chicago!*, imagined what Christ would have thought about Chicago if he had visited at the time of the city's momentous World's Fair of 1893. Stead (1849–1912) concluded that Christ would have found Chicago a reprehensible city, its values steeped in base concerns. Stead wrote, "This vast and heterogeneous community, which has been collected together from all quarters of the known world, knows only one common bond. Its members came here to make money. They are staying here to make money. The quest of the almighty dollar is their Holy Grail."[12] Another muckraker journalist, Lincoln Steffens (1866–1936), writing in the pages of *McClure's Magazine* alongside his notable colleagues Ida Tarbell and Ray Stannard Baker, focused on ineffectual and unethical city governments. Steffens' opinions inspired a generation of urban political reformers and a collection of his essays, published as *The Shame of the Cities* (1904), remains a staple in urban

studies, history, urban planning, and political science courses to this day. [See Document 5.2, Lincoln Steffens, *Philadelphia: Corrupted and Contented* (1903).] Arguably, the most famous and influential of these writers was Upton Sinclair (1878–1968), whose novel *The Jungle* (1906) sought to expose the destitute life of the working class life in Chicago and the brutality of the American wage labor system. Rather than responding to his indictment of capitalism, the public reacted with outrage to his depictions of unsanitary practices within the meatpacking industry. Sinclair lamented in his autobiography, "I aimed at the public's heart, but by accident I hit it in the stomach."[13] As a result of intense public pressure, and sagging sales of processed meats, the federal government enacted the Meat Inspection Act and the related legislation, the Pure Food and Drug Act, in mid-1906.

At the same time that these campaigns against urban problems fueled actual political reform, they also inspired academics. While critics of higher education commonly deride the professoriate as being ensconced in an ivory tower, a place wholly separate from the real world, leading scholars have long been aware of and influenced by the challenges of their local, national, and global surroundings. Urban historians, sociologists, and theorists must, of necessity, grow ties with the "real world" rather than hiding from it. Although academics busied themselves with establishing their disciplines during the 1880s and 1890s, they still did not ignore the plight of cities around them. Many promising young scholars joined their friends and colleagues in social settlements and various reform movements, conducting surveys of communities all across the United States.

British businessman and social investigator Charles Booth (1840–1916) led the way by inspiring a new generation of researchers to investigate cities firsthand. Despite a lack of formal academic training, Booth directed a group of scholars gathering data on private households throughout London, England. Booth's team gathered information on social conditions, religion, wages, and occupations for what would become the multi-volume

Life and Labour of the People of London, in surveys for multiple editions conducted between 1886 and 1903.[14] Heavily laden with statistics, charts, and richly-detailed colored maps, *Life and Labour* harkened back to the work of the sanitarians in the early half of the nineteenth century and heavily influenced the social survey movement of the 1890s–1920s. *Life and Labour* was also quite similar to Jane Addams' *Hull-House Maps and Papers* (1895) and other investigative works published by settlement house workers. Booth's study was so well-received that in 1892 the Royal Statistical Society awarded him their first Guy Medal (named for the British statistician William Guy) and elected him to serve as their president between 1892–1894.

Although not necessarily confined to cities, the survey movement resulted in thousands of separate studies on the social structure, economic characteristics, and leading problems of municipalities throughout the United States. The most famous of these was the Pittsburgh Survey, conceived in 1906 as the first major attempt within the United States to investigate the social life of one place by a research team. Seventy-four people conducted the field research, including social reformers from Pittsburgh, Hull-House's Florence Kelly, South End (Boston) House's Robert Woods, and other settlement house leaders from across the country. These social reformers were joined by academics, such as University of Wisconsin's John R. Commons and his student, John Fitch. The Pittsburgh Survey examined housing conditions, the way in which gender effects work, the ethnic and racial composition of the workforce, union issues, and the multifaceted influence of manufacturing—particularly the power and influence of the steel industry—in six volumes published from 1909–1914. Excerpts from these volumes also appeared as articles in the widely read periodical *Survey* (formerly *Charities and the Commons*).

Although the Pittsburgh Survey was widely publicized, some contemporary scholars argue it had little initial impact on the development of empirical research methods in academic social science. Such methods, particularly in the field of sociology, were evolving

independently in the early twentieth century. Sociologist Martin Bulmer posits that the Pittsburgh Survey, like much of the social survey movement in the United States, was ultimately more akin to the journalism of Riis and Steffens. According to Bulmer, the content of the Pittsburgh Survey lacked integration, although it was factual and systematic in scope. The survey remained, however, undeniably important for bringing a wide range of middle-class professionals from settlement houses "into the orbit of social investigation."[15]

Another innovative contribution to social science research was *The Philadelphia Negro: A Social Study* (1899) by the African American sociologist W.E.B. Du Bois (1868–1963). Du Bois studied at Fisk University, Harvard University (where he earned his Ph.D.), and the University of Berlin. Du Bois' work was related to that of Charles Booth and Jane Addams. Du Bois moved to Philadelphia in 1896 with his wife and lived above a cafeteria in that city's Seventh Ward, well known for its large black population. Du Bois conducted in-depth interviews, compiled statistical data, and used maps to describe the living and working conditions of black Philadelphians. [See Document 1.3, W.E.B. DuBois, *The Philadelphia Negro* (1898).] Trained primarily as a historian, Du Bois' outlook included a broad sweep of the social sciences, and his published work contributed in a direct way to the field of sociology. As sociologist Elijah Anderson argues, Du Bois represents an essential link in the empirical chain between academic social science and the settlement house movement. Anderson notes that Du Bois' studies are seminal not just for their investigations of the urban poor, but also for being among the first to formally consider race in urban America. However, as Bulmer notes, because Du Bois was black and taught for a lengthy time at a black institution of higher education (Atlanta University—now Clark Atlanta University), his work initially had less impact than it should have within the white social science community.[16]

Sociologists and the City

The evolution of mainstream academic research on cities began in Europe. The establishment of the modern university and the emergent academic disciplines and professions paralleled the rise of the industrial city. German theorists in particular paved the way for work done in the United States. The 1887 publication of sociologist Ferdinand Tönnies' treatise on societal change, *Gemeinschaft und Gesellschaft* (*Community and Society*), remains a watershed moment in urban scholarship. In this volume, Tönnies (1855–1936) theorized that the modern world was transitioning away from communities built upon kinship relations (*gemeinschaft*), to the multivalent, urban society (*gesellschaft*), in which everyday life was defined by contracts and non-familial connection. Modern commentaries typically portray Tönnies as saddened by this movement towards *gesellschaft* community, but this interpretation of his stance may be overdrawn.[17]

French sociologist Emile Durkheim (1858–1917) was clearer in his classic work, *The Division of Labor in Society* (1893). Durkheim differentiated the mechanical solidarity of the rural village with what he termed the organic solidarity of urban life, where everyone in a functioning society had a particular role to fill. At its face, this theory appeared to give a more positive coloration to the urbanization of modern life than did Tönnies' argument, but Durkheim also famously introduced the concept of *anomie*, or disorientation based on the challenges and multiple stimuli of urban life. Durkheim theorized that the pressures of *anomie* can lead ultimately to increased suicide levels. This idea was brought to fruition in the writing of George Simmel (1858–1918), especially in his essay "The Metropolis and Mental Life" (1905).[18]

The influence of German scholars on urban theory in the United States came through the establishment of graduate programs in the social sciences, most notably at Johns Hopkins University and the University of Chicago, in the late nineteenth century. Sociologists at Chicago in particular took the lead in urban research by adding empirical evidence from direct field research to the ideas of their German counterparts. Adherents of the so-called Chicago School sought to examine the city as an object of detached analysis and, as such,

abandoned the nineteenth century tradition of merging urban investigations with social activism. In the process they laid the intellectual framework for how most American social scientists, and even many urban historians, viewed cities.

Robert E. Park (1864–1944), a student of Georg Simmel and John Dewey, is widely regarded as the founder of the Chicago School. Park's collection of essays, *The City: Suggestions for the Study of Human Nature in the Urban Environment*, written with his colleagues at Chicago, Ernest W. Burgess (1886–1966) and Roderick D. McKenzie (1885–1940), forever changed scholarly research on urban environments. In addition to finding inspiration from German sociologists, the Chicago School also borrowed liberally from the sciences, especially biology, and perceived the city in ecological terms, akin to a living organism. The concept of social ecology sought to explain patterns of urbanization with models that could be applied universally to all cities. The most famous was Ernest W. Burgess' concentric zone model, which laid out a physical outline of a typical industrial American city in the 1920s. [See **Illustration I.2, Ernest Burgess, Urban Areas (1925).**]

Members of the Chicago School took to the streets and neighborhoods of America's Second City, producing an impressive number of case studies that made it the most studied city in the country, if not the world. Influential students of Robert E. Park used his views in their case studies. Harvey Zorbaugh's 1929 work, *The Gold Coast and the Slum*, followed the idea of city as organism and highlighted the interdependency of wealthy and poor Chicagoans. William I. Thomas and Polish sociologist Florian Znaniecki's *The Polish Peasant in Europe and America* (published in separate volumes between 1918 and 1920) was heralded as one of the most important works of sociology in the period.

Beyond Chicago, sociologists also explored the nature of urban life in smaller cities. This was an important development and one worth reviving today; too often modern urban studies focuses only on mega-cities (cities of ten million or more residents), ignoring the smaller, and perhaps more representative, locales. The most famous work on smaller-sized cities was Robert S. and Helen Merrell Lynd's study of Muncie, Indiana published in 1929 as *Middletown: A Study in American Civilization*. (Robert S. Lynd lived 1892–1970 and Helen Merrell Lynd from 1896–1982.) As is common to the social survey movement, the Lynds sought to study everything they could about one community. The Lynds examined paid work, home, schools, leisure, religious, and community activities within the anonymous community they referred to only as Middletown. Only in later years was Middletown revealed to be Muncie. *Middletown* established a scholarly model for community sociology. *Middletown* was also very popular with a general audience. During the 1930s, the Lynds returned to Muncie to study the impact of the Great Depression. The result was *Middletown in Transition: A Study in Cultural Conflicts* (1937) that further theorized social and economic change in urban America. Since then, numerous other studies of Muncie have been undertaken, making it the most thoroughly documented small city in the United States. The complete collection of documents gathered on Muncie now comprises the Middletown Studies Collection & Digital Archives administered by Ball State University.[19]

Urban theory advanced further in 1938 when another member of the Chicago School, Louis Wirth (1897–1952), published "Urbanism as a Way of Life" in the *American Journal of Sociology*. Wirth refined the distinctions put forward by the German theorists regarding the differences between urban and rural life when he argued that the size, density, and heterogeneity of an urban area influenced the outlook and behavior of its inhabitants. As one of the definitive statements of the Chicago School, "Urbanism as a Way of Life" remains one of the most important and widely read essays in all of urban sociology. Wirth's work influenced generations of social scientists and social workers eager to understand life in cities and reform urban problems. Building from Wirth, many of these professionals focused on negative aspects of urban life, especially perceptions of family decline, the breakdown of primary groups and ties, the concept of *anomie*, and social deviance.[20]

However, in 1962, sociologist Herbert J. Gans challenged Wirth's argument in his book chapter "Urbanism and Suburbanism as Ways of Life" in which he argued that there was no single urban, or even suburban, way of life. [See Essay 1.3, "Urbanism and Suburbanism as Ways of Life: A Reevaluation of Definitions" (1962, 1991).] Gans examined five major types of inner city residents, the "cosmopolites," the "unmarried and childless," the "ethnic villagers," the "deprived," and the "trapped and downwardly mobile" and found that residential instability, rather than population size, density, and heterogeneity of cities caused the social features of the urbanism identified by Wirth. Drawing on his own study of suburban Levittown, New Jersey, Gans expanded the focus of urban inquiry beyond the inner city to the outer city, i.e. residential neighborhoods and adjacent suburbs, where he found relationships between people to be "quasi-primary," or more intimate than secondary ties, yet more guarded than primary. For Gans, socioeconomic class status and lifecycle stage were more important than settlement type, and this conclusion led him to assert that a sociological definition of the city, as was formulated by Wirth, could not be made.

Enter the Historians: The City as Frontier

While sociologists were busy conducting field research, theorizing the nature of urban life, and formalizing the vibrant subfield of urban sociology, historians were just beginning to contemplate the impact of cities on America's development. This tardiness led noted urban scholar Richard C. Wade (1921–2008) to muse in retrospect that, "Historians have arrived at the study of the city by slow freight."[21] Beginning in the early 1930s and 1940s, Arthur M. Schlesinger, Sr. (1888–1965) and a small number of historians commenced the first wave of scholarly interest in American urban history. In 1933, Schlesinger's *The Rise of the City* appeared as part of the multivolume A History of American Life series published by Macmillan and edited by Schlesinger and his colleague Dixon Ryan

Fox (1887–1945). The June 1940 edition of *The Mississippi Valley Historical Review* carried Schlesinger's seminal article "The City in American History" which signaled the emergence of urban history as a vibrant and viable field of study within the larger historical profession. [See the updated version of this essay, Essay 1.2.][22]

Historians had not completely ignored cities before Schlesinger. A few acknowledged and even briefly commented upon urban growth when writing about related themes such as industrialization, immigration, labor, capital accumulation, and regional difference. In the main, though, historians concerned themselves with political and economic narratives which stressed American distinctiveness. Cities, commonly associated with Europe and its ills, did not fit neatly into this script, and were left to social scientists for rigorous inquiry. It is no surprise then to find that early in Schlesinger's career, while a professor of history at Iowa State University in 1921, he turned to the *American Journal of Sociology* to publish his article "The Significance of Immigration in American History."[23] Other historians also recognized the importance of the city and in 1932, a committee of the American Historical Association (AHA) formally concluded that cities and urbanism needed further study. That same decade, Carl Bridenbaugh, Constance McLaughlin Green, Robert Albion, Sidney Pomerantz, and of course, Schlesinger, published on on colonial and select nineteenth century cities.[24]

The backdrop for this first round of heightened interest in cities was the conclusion of the U.S. Census Bureau in 1920 that, for the first time in history, that the majority of Americans lived in urban areas. The shift from a majority rural to a majority urban nation was not only a significant turning point in America's evolution, but it also influenced the writing of American history. This paradigm shift paralleled the finding three decades earlier by the Census Bureau that the line of frontier settlement had ceased to exist. The demise of the frontier led a young history professor at the University of Wisconsin named Frederick Jackson Turner (1861–1932) to deliver what would become his most famous work,

"The Significance of the Frontier in American History" at the meeting of the American Historical Association concurrent with the World's Columbian Exhibition in Chicago during July 1893. Turner's argument that the abundance of "free land" on the frontier had shaped America's uniquely democratic institutions did not immediately take hold. However, Turner's clarity and ability to synthesize large periods of time and space while extolling the perceived virtues of American exceptionalism, propelled his interpretation of national development into the forefront of the historical profession during the early twentieth century.

Ever perceptive to social transformations, Turner—by the early 1920s a Harvard professor in the twilight of his scholarly career—knew that an urban reinterpretation was near. He even made notes for a paper outlining the significance of the city in American history. Although he never finished this work, Turner did express concern to his eventual replacement in the Harvard history department, Arthur M. Schlesinger, Sr., that any such revaluation must lie squarely in the American rather than European political and historical tradition.[25] Schlesinger's 1940 work "The City in American History" did just that by weaving in the narrative synthesis of U.S. history trumpeted by Turner and Charles Beard (1874–1948) into the history of cities. Schlesinger stated that the themes of the frontier and economic conflict were central organizing concepts behind the growth of cities. In bold strokes, Schlesinger argued that the city, no less than the country, was responsible for shaping American culture. He also bridged the long standing divide between urban and rural ways of life by arguing that, in the end, the distinction between city and country blurred as each became more and more like the other.

Almost immediately, though, there were those who cautioned against such revisionist history without the development of a corresponding theory of urbanism to provide a framework. In 1941, William Diamond argued that while Schlesinger's essay did much to advance Turner's call for an urban reinterpretation, it still lacked clear definitions of central terms, especially "urban" and "city," which have multiple meanings. Diamond pointed out that historians could learn much from urban sociologists, such as those at the University of Chicago, particularly in terms of creating categories of classification and analysis. Even urban sociologists had not advanced far enough for the demanding Diamond, who asserted that little effort had been made to formulate a comprehensive theory of urbanism. He did deign to label Louis Wirth's 1938 essay "Urbanism as a Way of Life" an "exceedingly interesting attempt" at theorization.[26]

In what would become a familiar pattern in American urban historiography, Diamond's critique had little impact on the production of scholarly monographs, the majority of which continued to be case studies of individual communities that were, as historian Michael Frisch notes in 1979, "idiographic" in approach, devoid of generalizations about the nature of urban life. In 1960, Eric Lampard suggested a new direction for urban historians and urban sociologists, when he called for rigorous examination of urbanization as a societal process and an end to the traditional focus on the perceived "problems" or deviance of cities in contrast with romantic notions of rural life. Although he was critical of the sociological conception of "ideal types," he did advocate the "ecological complex" model advanced by sociologists in the field of human ecology such as Amos H. Hawley and Leo F. Schnore, that defined community structure as the interplay between population and environment, mediated by technology and organization.[27]

Lampard found his attempt at theorization largely ignored. Part of the reason lies in the longstanding reluctance of American historians in general to engage in rigid structural analysis, Marxist or otherwise, or highly theoretical approaches which are the hallmark of sociology and other social science disciplines. In fact, many contemporary historians do not even consider themselves social scientists and instead stress a narrative approach more common to the humanities. As Michael Frisch argues, analytical power implied descriptive weakness for those American urban historians

who were "committed to the more traditional goal of the fullest possible historical explanation...rather than a framework of conditions necessary to such explanation."[28] In practice then, most urban historians followed Blake McKelvey's reasoning that there should be "no qualms about writing local history," since the goal of the historian, in contrast to the sociologist, is to "trace the forces and directions of human social movement through time and place [rather] than to define inflexible patterns."[29]

A mild undercurrent of debate persists as to whether history is really a social science or a humanistic discipline. Urban historians, who draw overtly and covertly from sociology, geography, psychology, and other social sciences, most often take advantage of the growing acceptance of interdisciplinarity within history, and may label themselves social scientists. This tendency is supported by the high number of urban historians with membership in the Social Science History Association, formally organized in 1974, that features a network devoted to urban concerns. On the other hand, urban historians with a deep connection to the humanities are also easy to find within the field. Oral history, a growing methodology within urban history and urban studies, shares obvious methodological connections with English and American Studies, for oral history transcripts and recordings are carefully parsed just like poems, short stories, or novels would be within literary and cultural studies.

The 1960s and 1970s witnessed a second round of interest in American urban history, set against the backdrop of the tremendous political and social change that swept the nation and transformed the historical profession. Leading this wave of new scholarship was Richard C. Wade, who influenced an entire generation of urban scholars with his noteworthy 1958 article "Urban Life in Western America, 1790–1830," and the books *The Urban Frontier: The Rise of Western Cities, 1790–1850* (1959) and *Slavery in the Cities: The South, 1820–1860* (1964).[30] [See Essay 3.3, Richard Wade, "Urban Life in Western America, 1790–1830."] Wade, a former graduate student of Schlesinger's at Harvard, set Turner on his head by proclaiming that the establishment of towns spearheaded the American frontier. Wade traced this line of reasoning all the way back to Josiah Strong. In 1885, Strong had surmised that western growth was launched by the presence of the railroads, solidified by the growth of towns, and, finally, bolstered by the farms that followed town development.[31]

Another pathbreaking work in this period was Sam Bass Warner's *Streetcar Suburbs: The Process of Urban Growth in Boston, 1870–1900* (1962), which demonstrated how urban sprawl preceded the automobile. [**See Essay 7.1, Sam Bass Warner, "From Walking City to the Implementation of the Street Railways."**] *Streetcar Suburbs* provided a conceptual framework for the evolution of urban physical space and differentiation by class within a single Boston case study. *Streetcar Suburbs* has shaped how scholars across numerous disciplines understand suburban growth and the impact of transportation on American cities. Warner, whose collective body of work comes as close as any urban historian to fulfilling the promise of understanding urbanization as a process, was widely influential in shaping the so-called "new urban history" along with his colleague Stephan Thernstrom, author of *Poverty and Progress: Social Mobility in a Nineteenth Century City* (1964). Thernstom, in particular, is credited with a move toward quantification within social history, which led to a long-lived debate regarding the relative reliability of quantitative versus qualitative data. The resonance of this particular infighting has considerably lessened over the decades. Together Warner and Thernstrom provided models of scholarship that broke with traditional ways of presenting America's past, frequently referred to as "consensus history." So-called consensus history stressed the common unity of the American political, social, and cultural experience and held little room for tension and conflict, especially for those often found on the margins of power, like working people, minorities, and women.

The promises of quantitative research and the new urban history began to be realized with the work of Theodore Hershberg, who founded and directed the Philadelphia Social History Project between 1969 and 1981. Through generous federal funding, a team of scholars and their assistants gathered and processed census returns and other quantifiable material on the city of Philadelphia, forming a database suited for interdisciplinary and multidisciplinary research. Hershberg conceived of the city in active terms, fulfilling Eric Lampard's call for scholars to think of the city as a process, rather than simply as a place. While the results of the Philadelphia Social History Project were impressive, resulting in a treasure trove of databases, several scholarly books, sixteen doctoral dissertations, and at least one hundred articles and papers, it was not enough to sustain the promise of the new urban history. Like Thernstrom and Warner before him, Hershberg grew tired of working within the confines of the new urban history label.[32]

Other fields of historical inquiry have also profoundly shaped the course of urban scholarship. Immigration history is one such subfield, although it commonly lacks proper recognition for its direct relation to urban history. Books that set forth an urban take on immigration, including Oscar Handlin's *Boston's Immigrants, 1790–1965* (1941) and *The Uprooted* (1951), John Bodnar's *The Transplanted: A History of Immigrants in Urban America* (1985), and Bernard Bailyn's *The Peopling of North America: An Introduction* (1986), all had enormous influence on the future of urban history. Case studies of the immigrants in particular cities, for which works like Kathleen Neils Conzen's astute commentary, *Immigrant Milwaukee, 1836–1860: Accommodation and Community in a Frontier City* (1976), set the standard, also strengthened the connections between urban and immigration history.

The historical narrative of regional migrants also rounded out the understanding of urban populations. Joe Trotter, Jr.'s *Black Milwaukee: The Making of an Industrial Proletariat, 1915–1945* (1985), Nell I. Painter's *Exodusters: Black Migration to Kansas after Reconstruction* (1977), and James R. Grossman's *Land of Hope: Chicago, Black*

Southerners, and the Great Migration (1989) told the story of black migration to cities. White migration, especially the story of the millions of white southern migrants who flooded into the Midwest, aptly captured by Chad Berry's *Northern Migrants, Southern Exiles* (2000), is less often placed in the context of urban history, yet it is a vital component of the story. [See Part VIII for excerpts from Chad Berry's book (Essay 8.3) and also Lisa Krissoff Boehm's *Making a Way out of No Way: African American Women and the Second Great Migration* (2009) (Essay 8.2).] The study of migrants can be enhanced by examining gender and sexual orientation. Cities proved to be especially alluring to single females, as Joanne Meyerowitz documents in her first book, *Women Adrift: Independent Wage Earners in Chicago, 1880–1930* (1988). And the impact of George Chauncey's *Gay New York: Gender, Urban Culture and the Making of the Gay Male World, 1890–1940* (1994), is difficult to overstate.[33] [See Essay 4.4, George Chauncey, "Urban Culture and the Policing of the 'City of Bachelors'" (1994).]

While many of these works share themes and settings common to the new urban history, they compose part of a much larger movement within the American historical tradition, called the "new social history." The new social history grew out of interest in and concern over social and political issues facing the United States in the 1960s and 1970s, especially those affecting groups of people traditionally outside of mainstream historical research. This "history from the bottom up" has encouraged an explosion of scholarship that, in essence, has resulted in the dominance of social history within the American historical profession over the last few decades. As Thomas Bender notes, though, this new American history is much more than the triumph of social history, it is a broader transformation in which "the domain of the historical has been vastly extended, inherited narratives displaced, new subjects and narratives introduced."[34]

Urban history cannot help but have an overlapping agenda with urban geography. Geographer John W. Reps's *The Making of Urban America: A History of City Planning in the United States* (1965) remains essential reading for serious urban historians. James T. Lemon's *The Best Poor Man's Country: A Geographical Study of Early Southeastern Pennsylvania* (1972) and *Liberal Dreams and Nature's Limits: Great Cities of North America Since 1600* (1996) relates key facts about the growth of American cities since colonial settlement. William Cronon introduced a generation of historians to the basic tenets of geography, including the way in which cities relate to their hinterlands, with his widely read *Nature's Metropolis: Chicago and the Great West* (1991). Cronon segues neatly into environmental history and environmental studies, fields which continue to influence, and be influenced by, urban history. Additionally noteworthy in the cross-pollination of urban and environmental history are the works of Samuel P. Hays, Martin V. Melosi, Christine M. Rosen, and Joel A. Tarr.[35] [See Essay 6.3, Martin Melosi and Joseph Pratt, "Houston: The Energy Metropolis" (2007).]

Another trend that began in the 1960s and gained speed in the 1970s was the establishment of urban studies programs at colleges and universities across the nation. Tumultuous and geographically widespread riots took place in American cities during the 1960s. They combined with a host of other social, political, and economic trends to produce a so-called "urban crisis" that seemed to threaten the viability of cities. Institutions of higher education sought to offer new curricula, majors, and programs to promote the understanding and management of this extensive social change. [See Parts V, VIII, and IX for essays and documents on various aspects of the "urban crisis."] These programs differed greatly in their structure and approach. Some offered graduate or undergraduate courses through stand-alone departments, while others were fed by faculty located in a variety of departments. Emphasis varied widely, including professional or academic tracks and interdisciplinary or multidisciplinary focuses. Some programs highlighted public policy analysis, while others had strengths in social work, public administration, nonprofit management, education, or planning. Very few of the urban studies programs boasted of strengths in urban history. In 1969, a group of leaders from these urban studies programs formed the Council of University Institutes for Urban Affairs in Boston, Massachusetts. In 1981, this body became the Urban Affairs Association (UAA). The UAA remains as one of the leading professional organizations for urban scholars.

The present-day practice of urban studies often centers upon the question of whether or not a Los Angeles School of Urbanism—popularly identified, like the city itself, as simply the L.A. School—has come to replicate the influence had by the Chicago School during the early twentieth century. Allen J. Scott and Edward W. Soja's *The City: Los Angeles and Urban Theory at the End of the Twentieth Century* (1996) perhaps best approaches the debate over whether L.A. typifies the contemporary city or is a place without precedents or antecedents. What does L.A.'s history tell us about other American cities, if anything? The Huntington Library, the University of California-Los Angeles, and the L.A. School of Urbanism at the University of Southern California all promote the L.A. School at an institutional level. They question whether or not Los Angeles, the city that first comes to mind when one discusses urban sprawl and automobile-based congestion, has something to tell us about American cities generally. The University of Southern California's website states, "In a nutshell, the difference between Chicago and L.A. is this: whereas traditional Chicago-based concepts of urbanism imagine a city organized around its central core, in L.A. urbanism, the urban peripheries are organizing what is left of the center. For many, this difference is emblematic of a shift toward postmodern urbanism."[36]

The L.A. School owes quite a bit to writer, activist, and academic Mike Davis, whose innovative works, including *City of Quartz: Excavating the Future in Los Angeles* (1990) and *The Ecology of Fear: Los Angeles and the Imagination of Disaster* (2000), brought new focus to the impact of the city. Perhaps the most important lesson of L.A. is not its sprawling landscape but the extent of its global connections, especially the influence of Asian capital, Asian immigrants, and Mexican and South American immigrants within the city. The L.A. School asks if Los Angeles is *the* city of the *world*, and not just the United States. The possibility that the rest of the world might become more like L.A. frightens many urbanists. Imagining more of the world's cities being consumed by an L.A.-style sprawl worries more than the likes of pessimistic pundits. Greater world reliance on the automobile and fossil fuels would bring staggering ramifications. Here again Mike Davis offers a possible picture of our global future through the nexus of rapid urbanization and capitalist globalization in *Planet of Slums* (2007). Another vision of the future where the rest of the world catches up to trends set in motion in the urban United States is Fareed Zakaria's *The Post-American World* (2008). While not an urbanist in his academic training or other writings, Zakaria's book has raised calls for a rigorous examination of the implications of the new global and highly urbanized economy."[37]

The depth and breadth of urban scholarship has come a long way from the streets of London and Manchester, in the United Kingdom, and New York, Chicago, and Pittsburgh within the United States. In 1988, the Urban History Association (UHA) was formed by 264 charter members in order to stimulate scholarship on world cities in all periods of history. Richard C. Wade served as the UHA's first president; the organization now holds biennial meetings and awards prizes for books, articles, and dissertations. Despite this progress, many urban historians believe there are unresolved theoretical issues. For example, in 1990, approximately two hundred and fifty urban historians gathered in Chicago to commemorate the fiftieth anniversary of Schlesinger's article, "The City in History." The event proved bittersweet, for it revealed that urban historians remained divided about the success of their chosen field. Some lamented the lack of coherence within the field, which seemed not to have a real sense of a canon. Yet the more upbeat found the widespread impact of urban history an exhilarating challenge. Margaret Marsh attempted to explain this duality by pointing out how the goals of "new urban history" were not always complementary:

> The first was a passionate commitment to find in history a set of keys that would enable policy makers to gain a more enlightened perspective on contemporary urban problems. In this quest, for so it must be defined, scholars drew much of their inspiration from an earlier group of activist scholars, the social ecologists of the Chicago school of the 1920s. Another influence on the "new" urban historians came from a more recent empirical trend in the social sciences, particularly political science and sociology.[38]

Marsh concluded by stressing the importance of agency as way of successfully rejuvenating urban history. Continued focus on agency would add the voices of the marginalized to the historical story. She urged scholars to "develop a research agenda that, in illuminating issues central to the human experience, makes our own contributions both larger and more compelling."[39]

Sixteen years later, however, many of the same themes continued to reverberate in a lively exchange on the state of urban history between noted academics Clay McShane, Carl Abbott, and Timothy Gilfoyle. McShane conducted a thorough review of trends in urban history by examining five separate databases, which included analysis of the field's leading scholarly publication, the *Journal of Urban History,* and book prizes awarded by the Urban History Association. McShane concludes that there is no urban history canon, contested or otherwise. This results in a serious disconnect between urban history and the rest of the history profession. More intriguingly, McShane argues that given the large number of works with an urban theme that have been recognized by historical societies outside of the UHA, it is quite possible that urban history has simultaneously triumphed among the profession at large, while much of the scholarly output has been disregarded by urban history's own practitioners. Abbott and Gilfoyle, however, see the state of the field in more positive terms. In fact, they argue that the presence of urban themes in other historical subfields is an indication of strength, not weakness, for the field. In a summation of the dialogue, McShane acknowledged that where he sees fragmentation, Carl Abbott sees vitality. For McShane, "the two are not incompatible."[40] Given the long and winding evolution of the field of urban history within the United States, perhaps this is the most astute and judicious assessment that can be made.

Scholars whose work focuses on American cities have greatly contributed to the mission of understanding the nation's past, and helped clarify the contemporary state of affairs within major metropolitan areas and the nation as a whole. Urban history is particularly good at shining light on how we live within our communities, and helping us grapple with the longevity and power of the themes of race and conflict within our nation. If, as it has been argued, social history makes up one of the most influential elements of today's historical studies, and urban history proves to be one of the central themes within social history, urban history ought to be a component of history courses taught at all levels of the educational system. All too often, however, when urban historians explain their subfield to a lay audience, they are first met with puzzled looks and many questions. History, as presented in middle schools and high schools across the nation, has too often devolved into rote memorization of dates and facts for standardized tests. A fixation on dates and facts may make for easier accountability through politically mandated assessments, but the reliance on this tired practice allows little room for innovative theories and thinking. And a preference for teaching factoids and historical "firsts" dwindles opportunities for relaying the moving stories of immigration, migration, and the varied reasons for the establishment and growth of cities. Urban history, urban sociology, and urban geography comprise an inherently compelling building block of knowledge, essential for all learned persons.

The field has evolved from the work of social reformers to become one of the most vital aspects of the academy. Relevant to all those who live in or are affected in any way by cities, urban history and urban studies proves to be an engaging field with resonance far beyond the classroom.

NOTES

1. For definitions of "urban" and the evolution of a numerical threshold for "urban" by the United States Bureau of the Census see, Lisa Krissoff Boehm and Steven H. Corey, *America's Urban History* (New York: Routledge, 2015), 1–16.

2. Barbara B. Oberg, editor, *The Papers of Thomas Jefferson*, Volume 32 (Princeton: Princeton University Press, 2005), 167.

3. Morton and Lucia White, *The Intellectual Versus the City: From Thomas Jefferson to Frank Lloyd Wright* (Cambridge, MA: Harvard University Press and the M.I.T. Press, 1962), 1.

4. Thomas Bender, *Toward an Urban Vision: Ideas and Institutions in Nineteenth Century America* (Baltimore: Johns Hopkins University Press, 1991).

5. Andrew Lees, *Cities Perceived: Urban Society in European and American Thought, 1820–1940* (Columbia University Press, 1985): 103.

6. Martin Bulmer, "The Social Survey Movement and Early Twentieth-Century Sociological Methodology," in Maurine W. Greenwald and Margo Anderson, editors, *Pittsburgh Surveyed: Social Science and Social Reform in the Early Twentieth Century* (Pittsburgh: University of Pittsburgh Press, 1996), 15.

7. Andrew Lees uses the term "statistical movement" in reference to Great Britain, although it certainly applies to activities within the United States as well. See Lees, *Cities Perceived*, 20.

8. Edwin Chadwick, *Report…From the Poor Law Commissioners, on an Inquiry into the Sanitary Condition of the Labouring Population of Great Britain; With Appendices* (London: W. Clowes and Sons, 1842; John H. Griscom, *The Sanitary Condition of the Laboring Population of New York: With Some Suggestions for its Improvement* (New York: Harper & Brothers, 1845; reprint, Arno & *The New York Times*, 1970). For the influence of Chadwick and Griscom's reports see Martin V. Melosi, *The Sanitary City: Urban Infrastructure in America from Colonial Times to the Present* (Baltimore: The Johns Hopkins

University, 2000), 43–48 and 60–62. An assessment of public health activities on emerging urban environmental values is discussed in Christopher J. Preston and Steven H. Corey, "Public Health and Environmentalism: Adding Garbage to the History of Environmental Ethics," *Environmental Ethics* 27 (Spring 2005): 3–21.

9. Citizens' Association of New York, *Report of the Council of Hygiene and Public Health of the Citizens' Association of New York Upon the Sanitary Condition of the City*, 2d ed. (New York: D. Appleton and Co., 1866; reprint, New York: Arno Press, 1970), xxii-xxx, xxxix-xlvii, lxi-lxvii, and xcii-xcvi. A brief summary of the *Report of the Council of Hygiene* and its impact is discussed in John Duffy, *A History of Public Health in New York City, 1625–1866* (New York: Russell Sage Foundation, 1968), 558–566; Gret Brieger, "Sanitary Reform in New York City: Stephen Smith and the passage of the Metropolitan Health Bill," in Judith Walzer Leavitt, *Sickness & Health in America: Readings in the History of Medicine and Public Health* (Madison: The University of Wisconsin Press, 1985), 339–413; James C. Mohr, *Radical Republicans and Reform in New York During Reconstruction* (Ithaca: Cornell University Press, 1973), 61–69.

10. F. B. Sanborn, "Mother of Associations. A History of the American Social Science Association," *Journal of Social Science*, 46 (December 1909): 2–6; Dorothy Ross, "The Development of the Social Sciences," in James Farr and Raymond Seidelman, *Discipline and History: Political Science in the United States* (Ann Arbor: University of Michigan Press, 1998), 85; Betsy Jane Clary, The Evolution of the Allied Social Science Associations," *American Journal of Economics and Sociology* 67, no. 5 (November 2008): 987.

11. Charlene Haddock Seigfried, "Socializing Democracy: Jane Addams and John Dewey," *Philosophy of the Social Sciences*, vol. 29, no. 2 (1999): 207–230.

12. William T. Stead, *If Christ Came to Chicago!: A Plea for the Union of All Who Love in the Service of All Who Suffer, 1894* (Chicago: Chicago Historical Bookworks, 1990), 123.

13. Carl S. Smith, *Chicago and the American Literary Imagination, 1880–1920* (Chicago: University of Chicago Press, 1984), 170.

14. There are several editions of this work published with various titles by Macmillan and Company in London between 1889 and 1903. For Booth's impact see Harold W. Pfautz, *Charles Booth on the City: Physical Patterns and Social Structure* (Chicago:

University of Chicago Press, 1967) and Bulmer, "The Social Survey Movement and Early Twentieth-Century Sociological Methodology," 15–18.

15. Bulmer, "The Social Survey Movement and Early Twentieth-Century Sociological Methodology," 18.

16. Elijah Anderson, "Introduction to the 1996 Edition of *The Philadelphia Negro*," in W. E. B. Du Bois, *The Philadelphia Negro: A Social Study* (Philadelphia: University of Pennsylvania Press, 1899, 1996), xviii-xix. Bulmer, "The Social Survey Movement and Early Twentieth-Century Sociological Methodology," 22. For a more extensive treatment of Du Bois and his contribution to sociology see, Aldon D. Morris, *A Scholar Denied: W. E. B. Du Bois and the Birth of Modern Sociology* (Berkley, CA: University of California Press, 2015).

17. Mathieu Deflem, "Ferdinand Tönnies (1855–1936)," in the Edward Craig, ed., *Routledge Encyclopedia of Philosophy* (London: Routledge, 2001).

18. See Hans Polis, "Anomie in the Metropolis: The City in American Sociology and Psychiatry," *Osiris*, 2nd Series, 18 (2003): 196 and 198.

19. Robert S. and Helen Merrell Lynd, *Middletown: A Study in American Culture* (New York: Harcourt, Brace, and Company, 1929) and Robert V. Kemper, "Middletown," *Encyclopedia of American Urban History*, David Goldfield, editor, Volume 2 (New York: Sage, 2007), 475–476.

20. Louis Wirth, "Urbanism as a Way of Life," *American Journal of Sociology* 44, no. 10 (July 1938): 1–24; Hans Polis, "Anomie in the Metropolis: The City in American Sociology and Psychiatry," 200–201; J. John Palen, *The Urban World*, 8th Edition (Boulder, CO: Paradigm Publishers, 2008), 16 and 151–152.

21. Richard C. Wade, "An Agenda for Urban History," in Herbert J. Bass, ed., *The State of American History* (Chicago: Quadrangle Books, 1970), 43.

22. Arthur M. Schlesinger, *The Rise of the City, 1878–1898* (New York: Macmillan, 1933) and Arthur M. Schlesinger, "The City in American History," *Mississippi Valley Historical Review* 27 (June 1940): 43–66.

23. Arthur Meier Schlesinger, "The Significance of Immigration in American History," *American Journal of Sociology* 27, no. 1 (July 1921): 71–85.

24. The AHA committee is mentioned in Bayrd Still, *Urban America: A History With Documents* (Boston: Little, Brown, and Company, 1974), 543. Writing in 1941, William Diamond cited a "vast number of books" written on cities and urbanization in the 1930s. See William Diamond, "On the Dangers of an Urban reinterpretation of History," in Eric F. Goldman, ed., *Historiography and Urbanization: Essays in American History in Honor of W. Stull Holt* (Johns Hopkins University Press, 1941, Kennikat Press, 1968), 67. For a sampling of urban monographs in the 1930s see, Robert Albion, *The Rise of the Port of New York, 1815–1860* (New York: Charles Scribner's Sons, 1939); Carl Bridenbaugh, *Cities in the Wilderness: The First Century of Urban Life in America, 1625–1742* (New York: Ronald Press, 1938); Constance McLaughlin Green, *Holyoke, Massachusetts, A Case Study of the Industrial Revolution in America* (New Haven: Yale University Press, 1936); and Sidney Pomerantz, *New York, An All American City 1783–1803* (New York: Columbia University Press, 1938).

25. For Turner's notes on the significance of the city in American history see Bayard Still and Diana Klebanow, "The Teaching of American Urban History," *The Journal of American History* 55, no. 4 (March 1969); 843. The letter from Turner to Schlesinger is reprinted in Wilbur R. Jacobs, *The Historical World of Frederick Jackson Turner: With Selections From His Correspondence, Narrative by Wilbur R. Jacobs* (New Haven: Yale University Press, 1968), 163–165; on Schlesinger replacing Turner see Ray Allen Billington, *Frederick Jackson Turner: Historian, Scholar, Teacher* (New York: Oxford University Press, 1973), 386–387.

26. Diamond, "On the Dangers," 81, 90 (footnote 64), and 100.

27. Eric E. Lampard, "American Historians and the Study of Urbanism," *The American Historical Review* 67, no. 1 (October 1961): 58–60.

28. Michael Frisch, "American Urban History as an Example of Recent Historiography," *History and Theory* 18 (October 1979): 355.

29. Blake McKelvey, "Urban History Today, *The American Historical Review* 57, no. 4 (July 1952): 920; Frisch, "American Urban History as an Example of Recent Historiography," 920.

30. Richard C. Wade, "Urban Life in Western America, 1790–1830," *The American Historical Review*, 64, no. 1 (October, 1958): 14–30; Richard C. Wade, *The Urban Frontier: The Rise of Western Cities, 1790–1850* (Cambridge, MA: Harvard University Press, 1959); and Richard C. Wade, *Slavery in the Cities: The South, 1820–1860* (New York: Oxford University Press, 1964).

31. Wade, "An Agenda for Urban History," 60.

32. Theodore Hershberg, ed., *Philadelphia: Work, Space, Family, and Group Experience in the Nineteenth Century* (New York: Oxford University Press, 1981), v–xvi and 3–35; Bas van Heur, "New Urban History," *Encyclopedia of American Urban History*, David Goldfield, ed., volume 2 (New York: Sage, 2007), 538–539; and "Theodore Hershberg, Biography," Center for Greater Philadelphia, http://www.cgp.upenn.edu/th_bio.html, accessed September 28, 2009.

33. See Joe Trotter, Jr., *Black Milwaukee: The Making of an Industrial Proletariat, 1915–1945* (Urbana: University of Illinois Press, 1985); Nell I. Painter, *Exodusters: Black Migration to Kansas after Reconstruction* (New York: Knopf, 1977); James R. Grossman, *Land of Hope: Chicago, Black Southerners, and the Great Migration* (Chicago: University of Chicago Press, 1989); Chad Berry, *Northern Migrants, Southern Exiles* (Urbana: University of Illinois Press, 2000); Lisa Krissoff Boehm, *Making a Way out of No Way: African American Women and the Second Great Migration* (Jackson: University Press of Mississippi, 2009); Joanne Meyerowitz, *Women Adrift: Independent Wage Earners in Chicago, 1880–1930* (Chicago: University of Chicago Press, 1988); and George Chauncey, *Gay New York: Gender, Urban Culture and the Making of the Gay Male World, 1890–1940* (New York: Basic Books, 1994).

34. Thomas Bender, "Strategies of Narrative Synthesis in American History," *The American Historical Review*, 107, no. 1 (February 2002): 129.

35. John W. Reps, *The Making of Urban America: A History of City Planning in the United States* (Princeton: Princeton University Press, 1965); James T. Lemon, *The Best Poor Man's Country: A Geographical Study of Early Southeastern Pennsylvania* (Baltimore: Johns Hopkins University, 1972); James T. Lemon, *Liberal Dreams and Nature's Limits: Great Cities of North American Since 1600* (New York: Oxford University Press, 1996); and William Cronon, *Nature's Metropolis: Chicago and the Great West* (New York: W. W. Norton, 1991). Joel A. Tarr provides an overview of the works of Cronon, Hays, Melosi, and other urban environmental scholars in Joel A. Tarr, "Urban History and Environmental History in the United States: Complimentary and Overlapping Fields," http://www.h-net.org/~environ/historiography/usurban.htm, accessed April 7, 2009. For further insights on urbanization as a process see also Samuel P. Hays, "From the History of the City to the History of Urbanized Society," *Journal of Urban History* 19, no. 4 (August 1993).

36. See University of Southern California's L.A. School at http://college.usc.edu/la_school/.

37. Mike Davis, *Planet of Slums* (London: Verso, 2006); and Fareed Zakaria, *The Post-American World* (New York: W.W. Norton, 2008). In October 2009, the New England Studies Association organized their annual meeting around Zakaria's work with the theme, "The Post-American City."

38. Margaret Marsh, "Old Forms, New Visions: New Directions in United States Urban History," *Pennsylvania History*, 59, no. 1 (January 1992): 21.

39. Marsh, "Old Forms, New Visions: New Directions in United States Urban History," 26.

40. Clay McShane, "Response to Abbott and Gilfoyle," *Journal of Urban History*, vol. 32, no. 4 (May 2006): 606. See also Clay McShane, "The State of the Art in North American Urban History," *Journal of Urban History*, vol. 32, no. 4 (May 2006): 582–606; Carl Abbott, "Borderland Studies: Comments on Clay McShane's 'The State of the Art in North American Urban History,'" *Journal of Urban History*, vol. 32, no. 4 (May 2006): 598–601; and Timothy Gilfoyle, "Urban History: A Class Half Full or Half Empty? Comments on Clay McShane's 'The State of the Art in North American Urban History,'" *Journal of Urban History*, vol. 32, no. 4 (May 2006): 602–605.

ESSAY 1.2

The City in American Civilization

Arthur M. Schlesinger, Sr.

Source: Arthur M. Schlesinger, Sr., *Paths to the Present*
(New York: Macmillan, 1949).

EDITORS' INTRODUCTION

In stark contrast to sociologists and academics in other related disciplines, American historians arrived at the study of urban life, in the words of the late Richard C. Wade (1921–2008), "by slow freight."[i] Not until the publication of Arthur M. Schlesinger's book *The Rise of the City* in 1933, and his seminal article "The City in American History" in 1940, did an actual subfield of urban history begin to emerge.[ii] Although a few academically trained historians dealt with issues and themes related to urbanization, notably immigration and industrialization, amateur and booster historians were responsible for the bulk of city histories written at the local level.

The following essay from *Paths to the Present* (1949) is one of Schlesinger's clearest and most comprehensive calls for an urban reinterpretation of American history. He begins by citing Professor Frederick Jackson Turner's "frontier thesis," arguably the most influential piece in American historical writing, which placed the "Great West" at the center of the nation's unique social evolution and democratic achievement. Turner presented his thesis, which explained the significance of the closing of the American frontier, at a special meeting of the American Historical Association held at the 1893 Columbian Exposition in Chicago. The Columbian Exposition, otherwise known as the Chicago World's Fair, was designed in large measure to celebrate the progress of Western civilization. Although not widely accepted at first, Turner's thesis became ubiquitous and largely self-evident to many American historians by the early twentieth century. However, criticism of Turner's emphasis on the frontier was inevitable, and not all together unexpected. Writing to his friend and colleague Arthur Schlesinger in 1925, Turner himself stated that an alternative "urban reinterpretation" of American history seemed likely.[iii] In the following selection, Schlesinger boldly outlines such an approach by carefully balancing the influence of the city with the frontier. Schlesinger concentrates on the origins and manifestations of the rural-versus-urban discord prominent throughout much of the nineteenth and early twentieth centuries and argues that, in the end, the distinction between city and country eventually blurs, as each becomes more and more like the other.

---

i Richard C. Wade, "An Agenda for Urban History," in Herbert J. Bass, ed., *The State of American History* (Chicago: Quadrangle Books, 1970), 43.

ii Arthur M. Schlesinger, *The Rise of the City, 1878–1898* (New York: Macmillan, 1933); "The City in American History," *Mississippi Valley Historical Review* 27 (June 1940): 43–66.

iii Wade, 46; Wilbur R. Jacobs, *The Historical World of Frederick Jackson Turner: With Selections From His Correspondence* (New Haven: Yale University Press, 1968), 163–165. While Turner's frontier thesis has long lost its luster, it is still serves as a convenient point of departure for understanding much of American history including urbanization. For example, see William Cronon, *Nature's Metropolis: Chicago and the Great West* (New York: W. W. Norton, 1991), 46–54.

Arthur Meier Schlesinger was born in 1888 in Xenia, Ohio. He received his bachelor's degree from The Ohio State University and doctorate from Columbia University where he studied under noted historians Charles Beard and James Harvey Robinson. Schlesinger taught at the University of Iowa before moving to the history department at Harvard University in 1924, where he replaced the newly retired Frederick Jackson Turner (at Turner's request) and remained there for the rest of his career. In addition to *The Rise of the City* and *Paths to the Present*, Schlesinger was the author of *New Viewpoints in American History* (New York: Macmillan, 1922), several monographs on colonial history, and coeditor with fellow social historian Ryan Dixon Fox of the widely influential A History of American Life series published by Macmillan from the 1920s through 1940s. He died in 1965 and that year Harvard University formally named the Woman's Archive at Radcliffe College after him and his wife, Elizabeth Bancroft Schlesinger, who were strong supporters of women's rights. Their son, the late Arthur M. Schlesinger, Jr. (1918–2007), was also a noted historian and member of the history department at Harvard University and the Graduate Center of the City University of New York (along with Richard C. Wade), as well as special assistant to President John F. Kennedy.

THE CITY IN AMERICAN CIVILIZATION

"The true point of view in the history of this nation is not the Atlantic Coast," declared Frederick Jackson Turner in his famous essay of 1893, "it is the Great West." Professor Turner, writing in Wisconsin, had formed his ideas in an atmosphere of profound agrarian unrest, and the announcement of the Superintendent of the Census in 1890 that the frontier line could no longer be traced impelled him to the conclusion that "the first period of American history" had closed. His brilliant paper occasioned a fundamental reappraisal of the mainsprings of national development.

Today, however, it seems clear that in the zeal to correct older notions he overlooked another order of society which, rivaling the frontier even in the earliest days, eventually became the major force. The city marched westward with the outposts of settlement, always injecting exotic elements into pioneer existence, while in the older sections it steadily extended its dominion over politics, economics and all the other interests of life. The time came, in 1925, when Turner himself confessed the need of "an urban reinterpretation of our history." A true understanding of America's past demands this balanced view—an appreciation of the significance of both frontier and city. The broad outline of the particular role of the city are here suggested.

I

The Atlantic shore constituted the original frontier. Though the great bulk of colonists took up farming, the immediate object of the first settlers was to found a village or town, partly for mutual protection and partly as a base for peopling the near-by country. Other advantages presently gave these places more lasting reasons for existence. There persons could enjoy friendly intercourse with their neighbors as in Europe and there, too, ply a variety of occupations. These communities, besides taking in farm produce for consumption and export, developed local manufactures, arts and crafts and carried on fisheries and an active overseas trade. Without the articles so provided—hardware, firearms, medicine, books and the like—the colonial standard of living would have greatly suffered.

In time the coastline became beaded with towns, many of them so well situated with respect to geographic and trading advantages as to grow into the great cities of today. The establishment of settlements like Albany, New York, and Lancaster, Pennsylvania, moreover, foreshadowed the rise of urban communities inland. If colonial towns seem small by modern standards, it is well to remember that this was also true of contemporary English provincial towns, for industrialization had not yet concentrated populations in the home-land. Philadelphia with thirty thousand people on the eve of Independence was one of the metropolises of the British Empire.

From the outset townsfolk were plagued with what would today be called urban problems. There were disadvantages as well as advantages in living closely together, and as these disadvantages became flagrant, the citizens were moved to action. Though they seldom assumed community responsibilities willingly, their record compares favorably with that of provincial cities in the mother country. To combat the increase of crime the public-spirited in some places maintained night watches out of their own purses, while in others the city fathers required persons to take turns guarding the streets by night on pain of fines. Sooner or later, however, the taxpayers accepted such policing as a normal municipal charge. The fire hazard early prodded the authorities to regulate the construction of chimneys, license chimney sweeps and oblige householders to keep water buckets; and when these measures fell short of the requirements in the eighteenth century, the people formed volunteer companies which, long after the colonial period, continued to be the chief agency of fire fighting. The removal of garbage generally devolved upon roving swine and goats, while drainage remained pretty much an unsolved problem, though occasional individuals laid private sewers. The pressure of urban needs also fertilized American inventiveness, producing Franklin's lightning rod and the fireplace stove.

Thanks to the special conditions of town life, the inhabitants developed a sense of collective responsibility in their daily concerns that increasingly distinguished them from the individualistic denizens of the farm and frontier. Other circumstances served to widen the distance. As cities grew in size and substance, they engaged in economic rivalry with one another which tended to ignore the interests of the intervening countryside. Boston, New England's metropolis, possessed special mercantile advantages which enabled her for nearly a century to maintain a position of primacy in British America, with New York, Philadelphia and lesser centers hardly more than

commercial satellites. These other ports, however, contended as best they could for their share of ocean-borne traffic and briskly cultivated their local trading areas. [...]

Happily for America's future independence, Britain's new revenue policy after 1763 struck deeply at the roots of urban prosperity. The business classes rallied promptly to the defense of their interests and, heedless of the dangers of playing with fire, secured the backing of the artisan and mechanic groups. Throughout the decade of controversy the seaports set the pace of resistance, supplying most of the militant leaders, conducting turbulent demonstrations at every crisis, and mobilizing farmer support when possible. Even in rural commonwealths like Virginia and Maryland the most effective steps of opposition were taken when the colonists consulted together at the provincial capitals while attending legislative sessions. Boston's foremost position in the proceedings may well have arisen from the fact that, having recently fallen behind Philadelphia and New York in the commercial race, she was resolved at any cost to stay the throttling hand of Parliament. [...]

The colonial town, however, was more than an embodiment of political and economic energies or a means of gratifying the gregarious instinct. Cities, then as now, were places where one found a whole gamut of satisfactions. Ports of entry for European settlers and goods, they were also ports of entry for European thought and standards of taste. At the same time their monopoly of printing presses, newspapers, bookstores and circulating libraries exposed the residents to a constant barrage of mental stimuli. Hence the spirit of innovation expressed itself quite as much in intellectual as in commercial undertakings. It was townsfolk who led in founding schools and colleges. The protracted battle to establish inoculation as a preventive against smallpox was fought out in the cities. The first great victory for freedom of the press was won by a Philadelphia lawyer defending a New York editor. Besides, mere numbers of people made it possible for the professions to become more clearly differentiated, so that a merchant need no longer plead cases before the courts nor a clergyman practice medicine. Before the colonial period ended, bar associations and medical societies were flourishing in New York, Boston and elsewhere, and medical schools were drawing students to Philadelphia and New York. [...]

The city, both in its internal life and external relations, deeply affected colonial society politically, economically and culturally. Though in 1776 only about one in twenty-five Americans dwelt in places of eight thousand or more, the urban influence, thanks to its concentrated character, carried far greater weight than its fractional representation in the population indicated. Moreover, city residents evolved a pattern of life which not only diverged from, but increasingly challenged, that of countryside and frontier. These restless, aspiring urban communities foreshadowed the larger role that cities would play in the years ahead.

II

That role townsfolk began to assume in the struggle for a strong central government following the Revolution. [...] The framing and ratification of the Constitution represented in considerable degree their triumph over the debtor groups and small farmers of the interior. In the circumstances the first Congress under the new instrument was greeted with petitions from Philadelphia, New York, Boston and Baltimore for a tariff to protect American manufactures.

The underlying strife between city and country led also to the formation of the first national parties under the Constitution. Hamilton's famous financial plan, intended to benefit urban capitalists and thus indirectly the nation, formed the rallying point of the Federalists, while Jefferson, imbued with physiocratic notions, organized the Republican opposition. The Virginia planter, unlike the New York lawyer, dreaded the growth of a powerful moneyed class, and in the spread of cities he foresaw a repetition of the social miseries of the Old World. "For the general operations of manufacture," he declared, "let our workshops remain in Europe." He could even regard calmly the destructive yellow-fever epidemics in Philadelphia and other ports in the 1790's, since the pestilence might teach people to avoid populous centers. [...]

III

The westward surge of population beginning shortly after the Revolution has obscured the fact that the leading Atlantic cities, though hard hit by the war, soon resumed their growth, and that with the coming of the nineteenth century the rate of urban development in the nation at large far surpassed that of rural development. Between 1800 and 1860 the number of townsfolk increased twenty-four times while the rural population merely quadrupled. By 1810 one out of every twenty Americans lived in communities of eight thousand or more, by 1840 one out of every twelve, and by 1860 nearly one in every six.

Paradoxically enough, westward migration itself helped to bring this about, for the transappalachian region bred its own urban localities. Serving at first chiefly as distributing centers for commodities from the seaboard, these raw settlements quickly developed into marts where local manufacturer and farm dweller exchanged products. Pittsburgh early began to make glass, shoes, iron castings, nails and textiles, and already in 1814 the *Pittsburgh Gazette* was complaining of the sooty atmosphere. By that time Cincinnati, farther down the river, boasted of two woolen mills and a cotton factory, and its meat-packing business was winning it the sobriquet of Porkopolis. Emboldened by such achievements, apparently every cluster of log huts dreamed of equal or greater eminence. The Indiana pioneers, for example, hopefully named their forest hamlets Columbia City, Fountain City, Saline City, Oakland City and Union City or, setting their sights still higher, called them New Philadelphia, New Paris, Rome City and even New Pekin.

Meanwhile, in the East, scores of cities sprang into being, generally at the fall line of the rivers, where water power was available for manufacturing. As the budding industrialists looked about for new worlds to conquer, they, together with the Eastern merchants and bankers, perceived their El Dorado in the settling West. Soon New York, Philadelphia and Baltimore were racing for the trade of the transappalachian country. This clash of urban imperialisms appeared most strikingly perhaps in the rivalry for transportation routes to the interior. The Baltimoreans led off by building a turnpike to tap the eastern terminus of the Cumberland Road, which the federal government by 1818 had completed as far as Wheeling on the Ohio. In order to counter this move, Pennsylvania promoted Philadelphia's wagon trade with the West by subsidizing a chain of roads to Pittsburgh. New York City, utilizing her natural advantages, now secured state backing for an all-water artery through upstate New York from the Hudson to Lake Erie. [...]

Middle Western towns, following the Eastern example, meanwhile entered upon a somewhat similar struggle, each seeking to carve out its own economic dependencies and spheres of influence and to profit from the new ties with the seaboard. By 1840 a network of artificial waterways joined Cleveland and Toledo on Lake Erie with Portsmouth, Cincinnati and Evansville on the Ohio. As in the East, however, the arrival of the steam locomotive changed the situation. Now every up-and-coming municipality strove by hook or crook to become a railroad center, sometimes plunging heavily in debt for the purpose. And looking to the commercial possibilities of the remoter West, Chicago, St. Louis, Memphis and New Orleans concocted rival plans for a Pacific railroad—a maneuvering for position that had political repercussions in Congress and contributed to the passage of the Kansas-Nebraska Act in 1854, which it was thought would facilitate the building of a transcontinental line from St. Louis. This law, by authorizing slavery by "popular sovereignty" in a region hitherto close to it, helped to set the stage for the Civil War.

The progress in transportation facilities, confined largely to the North, spurred urban development throughout that part of the country. The Erie Canal, reinforced by the rail arteries to the West and the magnificent harbor at the mouth of the Hudson, established conclusively New York's preeminence on the seaboard and in the nation. From only sixty thousand inhabitants in 1800 its population (not counting Brooklyn) climbed to eight hundred thousand by 1860, outdistancing Philadelphia and placing it next to London and Paris in size, while Philadelphia with more than half a million was in 1860 larger than Berlin. Brooklyn, Baltimore and Boston came next in size. Indicative of the westward movement of the urban frontier was the fact that at the latter date all the other places of over hundred thousand—New Orleans, Cincinnati, St. Louis and Chicago— were in the heart of the country. Chicago, though the smallest of these cities in 1860, had already gathered the economic sinews which would make it New York's chief rival before the century closed. Anthony Trollope, observing the Midwest in 1861, remarked that except for a few river and lake sites "settlers can hardly be said to have chosen their own localities. These have been chosen for them by the originators of the different lines of railway." Urban communities greatly augmented the demand for farm products, accelerated the invention of labor-saving implements like the steel plow and the reaper and thus furthered commercial agriculture, which in turn speeded city growth.

To master the new complexities of urban living demanded something more than the easygoing ways of colonial towns. Enlarged populations called for enlarged measures for the community safety and welfare, whether by government or otherwise. As might be expected, the bigger cities set the pace. After the lethal yellow-fever visitations of the 1790's frightened Philadelphia into installing a public water works, other places fell into line, so that more than a hundred systems came into existence before the Civil War. Unfortunately, ignorance of the yet to be discovered germ theory of disease fastened attention on clear water instead of pure water, thus leaving the public health still inadequately protected. To cope with the growing lawlessness the leading cities now supplemented night watches with day police. In 1822 Boston instituted gas lighting and in 1823 set the example of a municipally owned sewerage system. About the same time regular omnibus service was started on the streets of New York, to be followed in the next decade by horsecars running on tracks.

Fire fighting, however, continued generally in the hands of volunteer companies. Though Boston organized a paid municipal department in 1837 and Cincinnati and other Western towns greatly improved the apparatus by introducing steam fire engines in the 1850's, New York and Philadelphia, thanks to the political pull of volunteer brigades, resisted changes in equipment and waited respectively till 1865 and 1871 to municipalize their systems. The cities did nothing at all to combat the evil of slums, an unexpected development due to the great inrush of foreign immigrants into the Atlantic ports in the forties and fifties. Even more serious for the ordinary citizen was the growth of political machines, rooted in the tenement-house population, the fire companies and the criminal classes, and trafficking in franchises for the new public utilities. Appointments to government office for partisan services, first practiced in Eastern cities, preceded and led directly to the introduction of the spoils system into state and national politics.

The "diversities of extreme poverty and extreme wealth," which Edwin H. Chapin etched so sharply in *Humanity in the City* (1854), distressed the tenderhearted and gave rise to most of the reform crusades of the pre-Civil War generation. Compact living facilitated the banding together of such folk and also the collection of funds. Never before had America known so great an outpouring of effort to befriend the poor and the handicapped. Under urban stimulus arose the movement for free schools, for public libraries, for married women's property rights, for universal peace, for prison reform, for a better deal for the insane. The new conditions of city life begot a social conscience on the part of townsfolk which would be lasting of effect and which increasingly differentiated them from their brethren on the farm and frontier. [...]

Whatever the attractions of town life, the eleven fold leap in urban population between 1820 and 1860 aroused increasing dismay and foreboding among rural folk who saw their own sons and daughters succumbing to the lure, "Adam and Eve were created and placed in a garden. Cities are the results of the fall," cried Joseph H. Ingraham, a popular religious novelist. Country preachers joined in denouncing these human agglomerations "cursed with immense accumulations of ignorance and error, vice and crime," while farm journals implored the young not to sacrifice their manly independence in order "to fetch and carry" and "cringe and flatter" for a miserable pittance. Political attitudes further mirrored the deepening distrust.

IV

In the generation following the Civil War the city took supreme command. Between 1860 and 1900 the urban population again quadrupled while the rural merely doubled. With one out of every six people inhabiting communities of eight thousand or over in the earlier year, the proportion rose to nearly one out of four in 1880 and to one out of three in 1900. Considerably more than half of the urban-moving throng gravitated to places of twenty-five thousand and upwards. Since every town dweller added to this effectiveness by association with his fellows, even these figures understate the city's new role in the nation. Nevertheless the sheer growth of particular localities is amazing. By 1890 New York (including Brooklyn) had about caught up with Paris, while Chicago and Philadelphia, with over a million each as compared with New York's two and a half million, then outranked all but five cities in Europe. In the Far West, Los Angeles jumped from fewer than 5,000 in 1860 to more than 100,000 in 1900, and Denver from nothing at all to 134,000, while in the postwar South, Memphis with a bare 23,000 in the former year surpassed 100,000 in the latter. "The youngest of the nations," wrote Samuel L. Loomis in 1887, "has already more large cities than any except Great Britain and Germany." Thanks to the progress of settlement in the West and the burgeoning of industry in a South emancipated from slavery, the city had at last become a national instead of a sectional institution.

As urban centers grew in size and wealth, they cast an ever stronger spell over the American mind. Walt Whitman, returning to Greater New York in September, 1870, after a short absence, gloried in the "splendor, picturesqueness, and oceanic amplitude of these great cities." [...] Conceding that Nature excelled in her mountains, forests and seas, he rated man's achievement equally great "in these ingenuities, streets, goods, houses, ships—these hurrying, feverish, electric crowds of men." Little wonder that the young and the ambitious yielded to the temptation. "We cannot all live in cities, yet nearly all seem determined to do so," commented Horace Greeley, adding that with "millions of acres" awaiting cultivation "hundreds of thousands reject this and rush into the cities."

The exodus from the older countryside was especially striking. While the cities of Maine, Vermont, Massachusetts, Rhode Island, New York, Maryland and Illinois gained two and a half million people between 1880 and 1890, the rural districts of these states lost two hundred thousand. The drain of humanity from backwoods New England left mute witnesses in deserted hill villages and abandoned farms. In the nation as a whole, 10,063 townships out of 25,746 in thirty-nine states and territories shrank in population during the decade. Some of the rural decline was due to the shifting of agriculturists from older regions to the free unworked lands of the trans-Mississippi West, but the phenomenon was so widespread—and, indeed, as characteristic of Europe during these years as of America—as to evidence the more potent and pervasive influence of the city. True, the 1880's merely climaxed a historic trend. In the century from 1790 to 1890 the total population had grown 16-fold while the urban segment grew 139-fold. Hence the celebrated announcement of the Superintendent of the Census in 1890 that a frontier line no longer existed can hardly be said to have marked the close of "the first period of American history." Rather it was a tardy admission that the second period was already under way. [...]

These civic advances, however, came at a price already beginning to be evident before the Civil War. Americans had developed their political institutions under simple rural conditions; they had yet to learn how to govern cramped populations. Preyed upon by unscrupulous men eager to exploit the expanding public utilities, municipal politics became a byword for venality. As Francis Parkman wrote, "Where the carcass is, the vultures gather together." New York's notorious Tweed Ring denoted a sickness that racked Philadelphia, Chicago, St. Louis, Minneapolis and San Francisco as well. "With very few exceptions," declared Andrew D. White, "the city governments of the United States are the worst in Christendom—the most expensive, the most inefficient, and the most corrupt."

Through an irate citizenry succeeded now and then in "turning the rascals out," the boss and the machine soon recovered control. Nevertheless, the good-government campaigns ventilated the abuses of municipal misrule and aroused the humane to the worsening plight of the urban poor. Under reform prodding, the New York legislature from 1865 onward adopted a series of laws to combat the slum evil in America's metropolis, though with disappointing results. More fruitful were the steps taken by private groups in Manhattan and elsewhere to establish social settlements and playgrounds and to replace the indiscriminate almsgiving of earlier times with a more rational administration of charity. Religion, awakening to the social gospel, helped out with slum missions and institutional churches. In the city, too, trade-unions made a new start, organizing the swelling army of urban workers on a nationwide basis, joining with the reformers in securing factory legislation and gradually winning concessions from the employing class. Occasional voices with a foreign accent advocated socialism or anarchism as the remedy for the city's gross disparities of wealth and want, while Edward Bellamy in *Looking Backward* offered a home-grown version of communism in his fanciful account of Boston as it would be in the year 2000.

The increasing tension of living was evidenced in a variety of ways. Masses of people reared in a rustic environment had suddenly to adapt themselves to the frantic urban pace. One outcome was a startling growth of neurasthenia, a word coined by Dr. George M. Beard of New York in his work *American Nervousness* (1881), which traced the malady to the hurry and scurry, the din of the streets, the frenzied struggle for existence, the mental excitements and endless distractions. From the ranks of the high-strung, Mary Baker Eddy gathered most of her converts to the new religion of Christian Science, and for much the same reason townsfolk now gave enthusiastic support to organized sports. Flabby muscles unfitted most persons for direct participation, but they compromised by paying professional contestants to take their exercise for them. If, as a magazine writer said, nervousness had become the "national disease of America," baseball, partly as an antidote, became America's national game.

The stress of existence seemed only to enhance creative powers, however. The cities, re-enacting their role of the "fireplaces of civilization"—Theodore Parker's phrase—provided compelling incentives to cultural achievement, multiplying colleges, public libraries and publishing houses and founding art museums, art schools and conservatories of music. [...] Civic pride prompted the holding of two great expositions, one at Philadelphia in 1876 and the other at Chicago in 1893. That the second and grander took place in an inland metropolis revealed how decisively urbanization had altered the face of traditional America.

The new age of the city rested upon an application of business enterprise to the exploitation of natural resources such as mankind had never known. The city, as insatiable as an octopus, tended to draw all nutriment to itself. Railroads, industrial combinations, investment capital, legislative favors, comprised the means. There arose a complex of urban imperialisms, each striving for dominion, each battling with rivals and each perforce yielding tribute to the lord of them all. "Every produce market, every share market," observed James Bryce, "vibrates to the Produce Exchange and Stock Exchange of New York."

As the city forged ahead, imposing its fiat on less developed regions, the rift between country and town widened portentously. [...]

This feeling of rural inferiority, this growing sense of frustration, underlay the political eruptions in the farming regions: the Granger movement in the 1870's, the Farmers' Alliances of the eighties and the Populist conflagration in the nineties. Each time specific economic grievances like steep freight rates, high interest charges and low crop prices stirred the smoldering embers into blaze. These were tangible hardships which the farmers demanded the government remove by such measures as railroad regulation and silver inflation. It fell to the greatest of the agrarian champions, addressing the Democratic national convention in 1896, to hurl the ultimate challenge at urban imperialism. "Burn down your cities and leave our farms, and your cities will spring up again as if by magic," cried William Jennings Bryan of Nebraska in a speech that won him the nomination, "but destroy our farms and the grass will grow in the streets of every city in the country." In the election that followed, the big cities in the East and Midwest, including New York which for the first time went Republican, responded by casting decisive majorities against the Democrats and free silver. [...]

V

Urban dominance was further enhanced by the emergence of great metropolitan districts or regions. These "city states" had begun to form in the nineteenth century as swifter means of transportation and communication flung the inhabitants outward into the suburbs, but it was the coming of the automobile and motor truck and the extension of electricity and other conveniences into the surrounding territory that gave these super-communities their unprecedented size and importance.

Each consisted of one or more core cities with satellite towns and development rural areas, the whole knit together by economic, social and cultural ties. The hundred and thirty-three metropolitan regions in 1930 grew to a hundred and forty by 1940, when they contained almost half the total population. [...]

Of all the new trends in urban development, however, none had such profound effects as the altered relationship of country and city. Historians generally attribute the decline of the free-silver movement in the late nineties to the discovery of fresh sources of gold supply and an uptrend of crop prices, but probably the more fundamental cause was the amelioration of many of the social and psychological drawbacks of farm existence. The introduction of rural free delivery of mail after 1896, the extension of good roads due to the bicycle craze, the expanding network of interurban trolleys, the spread of party-line neighborhood telephones after the basic Bell patents expired in 1893, the increase of country schools—all these, coming shortly before 1900, helped dispel the aching isolation and loneliness, thereby making rustic life pleasanter.

Yet these mitigations seem trifling compared with the marvels which the twentieth century wrought. The automobile brought farm families within easy reach of each other and of the city; the motorbus facilitated the establishment of consolidated schools with vastly improved instruction and equipment; while the radio introduced new interests and pleasures into the homes themselves, shedding its benefits impartially on country and town. At the same time the mechanical energy used in agriculture grew eightfold between 1900 and 1935, thus lightening the husbandman's toll and adding to his opportunities for leisure. [...]

Just as rural life became more urbanized, so urban life became more ruralized. Wooded parks, tree-shaded boulevards, beautified waterfronts, municipal golf courses, athletic fields and children's playgrounds multiplied, while an increasing army of white-collar workers and wage earners piled into motorcars and buses each night to go farther and farther into the suburbs. Within the metropolitan regions population actually grew faster in the rustic outskirts between 1930 and 1940 than in the central cities. Retail trade too felt the centrifugal tug, and even factories showed a tendency to move into outlying villages where taxes, rent and food cost less. The extension of giant power will doubtless speed the trend, affording more and more townsfolk a chance to live and work and bring up their children in country surroundings. The dread specter of atomic-bomb attacks may operate to the same end in the interests of national military security.

Thus the twentieth century has been spinning a web in which city and country, no longer separate entities, have been brought ever closer together. When the city encroaches sufficiently on the country and the country on the city, America may hope to arrive at a way of life which will blend the best features of both the traditional ways. [...]

From humble beginnings in the early seventeenth century the city thus traced a varied course. In Europe the modern urban community emerged by gradual stages out of the simple town economy of the Middle Ages; by comparison, the American city leaped into being with breath-taking speed. At first servant to an agricultural order, then a jealous contestant, then an oppressor, it now gives evidence of becoming a comrade and co-operator in a new national synthesis. Its economic function has been hardly more important than its cultural mission or its transforming influence upon rural conceptions of democracy. The city, no less than the frontier, has been a major factor in American civilization. Without an appreciation of the role of both the story is only half told.

ESSAY 1.3

Urbanism and Suburbanism as Ways of Life: A Reevaluation of Definitions

Herbert J. Gans

Source: Herbert J. Gans, *People, Plans, and Policies* (New York: Columbia University Press and Russell Sage Foundation, 1991). Originally published in Arnold M. Rose (editor), *Human Behavior and Social Processes: An Interactionist Approach* (Houghton Mifflin, 1962).

EDITORS' INTRODUCTION

Is there a distinctly urban way of life? If so, what accounts for the differences between the actions and attitudes of people in cities versus rural areas? Noted sociologist Louis Wirth, part of the University of Chicago's influential "Chicago School," contended that such distinctions existed and in 1938 published "Urbanism as a Way of Life," one of the most important and widely read essays on cities, in which he argued that the size, density, and heterogeneity of an urban area influences the outlook and behavior of its inhabitants. As one of the definitive statements of the Chicago School style of urban inquiry, "Urbanism as a Way of Life" influenced generations of urban sociologists, social scientists, and social workers eager to understand urban life and/or reform problems that they tended to associate with cities. Building on Wirth, many of these professionals focused on negative aspects of urban life, especially perceptions of family decline and the breakdown of primary group ties. Many urbanists performed studies related in some way to the concept of *anomie* (a term popularized by sociologist Emile Durkheim), which can be defined as the absence of social norms and disassociation from others in the community, and social deviance, especially in the form of mental illness, vice, and crime.[i]

In 1962, sociologist Herbert J. Gans reassessed Wirth's argument in "Urbanism and Suburbanism as Ways of Life: A Reevaluation of Definitions." Gans asserted that there was no single urban or even suburban way of life. Gans examined five major types of inner city residents, the "cosmopolites," the "unmarried and childless," the "ethnic villagers," the "deprived," and "trapped and downwardly mobile" and found that residential instability, rather than number (or size), density, and heterogeneity of cities caused the social features of the urbanism identified by Wirth. Drawing on his own study of suburban Levittown, New Jersey, Gans expanded the focus of urban inquiry beyond the inner city to the outer city, i.e. residential neighborhoods and adjacent suburbs, where he found relationships between people to be "quasi-primary," or more intimate than secondary ties yet more guarded than primary. For Gans, socioeconomic status class and lifecycle stage were more important than settlement type, which led him to assert that a sociological definition of the city, as formulated by Wirth, could not be made.

---

i Louis Wirth, "Urbanism as a Way of Life" *American Journal of Sociology* 44, no. 10 (July 1938): 1–24; Hans Polis, "Anomie in the Metropolis: The City in American Sociology and Psychiatry," *Osiris*, 2nd Series, 18 (2003): 200–01; J. John Palen, *The Urban World*, 8th edition (Boulder, CO: Paradigm Publishers, 2008), 16 and 151–152.

Looking back at his essay in 1991, Gans added a postscript (included in the essay) where he notes the ways in which his original article was time bound. Although he underestimated the potential of suburban growth and failed to consider the increasing polarity between the rich and the poor in American cities, Gans contends that the main tenets of his essay concerning the relationship between social structure and the physical environment were still sound after almost three decades. Widely regarded as one the nation's preeminent sociologists and the leading proponent of "public sociology," Herbert J. Gans retired in 2007 as the Robert S. Lynd Professor of Sociology at Columbia University. He is the author of hundreds of scholarly articles and a dozen books including *The Urban Villagers* (Glencoe, NY; Free Press, 1963), *The Levittowners* (New York: Pantheon, 1967), *People and Plans: Essays on Urban Problems and Solutions* (New York: Basic Books, 1968), *People, Plans, and Policies: Essays on Poverty, Racism, and Other National Urban Problems* (New York: Columbia University and Russell Sage Foundation, 1991), from which this essay is taken, *The War Against the Poor: The Underclass and Antipoverty Policy* (New York: Basic Books, 1995), and *Democracy and the News* (New York: Oxford University Press, 2003).

URBANISM AND SUBURBANISM AS WAYS OF LIFE

A Reevaluation of Definitions

The contemporary sociological conception of cities and of urban life is based largely on the work of the Chicago School and its summary statement in Louis Wirth's essay "Urbanism as a Way of Life."[1] In that paper, Wirth developed a "minimum sociological definition of the city" as "a relatively large, dense and permanent settlement of socially heterogeneous individuals." From these prerequisites, he then deduced the major outlines of the urban way of life. As he saw it, number, density, and heterogeneity created a social structure in which primary-group relationships were inevitably replaced by secondary contacts that were impersonal, segmental, superficial, transitory, and often predatory in nature. As a result, the city dweller became anonymous, isolated, secular, relativistic, rational, and sophisticated. In order to function in an urban society, he or she was forced to combine with others to organize corporations, voluntary associations, representative forms of government, and the impersonal mass media of communications. These replaced the primary groups and the integrated way of life found in rural and other preindustrial settlements.

Wirth's paper has become a classic in urban sociology, and most texts have followed his definition and description faithfully.[2] In recent years, however, a considerable number of studies and essays have questioned his formulations.[3] In addition, a number of changes have taken place in cities since the article was published in 1938, notably the exodus of white residents to low- and medium-priced houses in the suburbs and the decentralization of industry. The evidence from these studies and the changes in American cities suggest that Wirth's statement must be revised.

There is yet another and more important reason for such a revision. Despite its title and intent, Wirth's paper deals with urban-industrial society, rather than with the city. This is evident from his approach. Like other urban sociologists, Wirth based his analysis on a comparison of settlement types, but unlike his colleagues, who pursued urban-rural comparisons, Wirth contrasted the city to the folk society. Thus, he compared settlement types of pre-industrial and industrial society. This allowed him to include in his theory of urbanism the entire range of modern institutions which are not found in the folk society, even though many such groups (for example, voluntary associations) are by no means exclusively urban. Moreover, Wirth's conception of the city dweller as depersonalized, atomized, and susceptible to mass movements suggests that his paper is based on, and contributes to, the theory of the mass society.

Many of Wirth's conclusions may be relevant to the understanding of ways of life in modern society. However, since the theory argues that all of society is now urban, his analysis does not distinguish ways of life in the city from those in other settlements within modern society. In Wirth's time, the comparison of urban and preurban settlement types was still fruitful, but today, the primary task for urban (or community) sociology seems to me to be the analysis of the similarities and differences between contemporary settlement types.

This paper is an attempt at such an analysis; it limits itself to distinguishing ways of life in the modern city and the modern suburb. A reanalysis of Wirth's conclusions from this perspective suggests that his characterization of the urban way of life applies only—and not too accurately—to the residents of the inner city. The remaining city dwellers, as well as most suburbanites, pursue a different way of life which I shall call "quasi-primary." This proposition raises some doubt about the mutual exclusiveness of the concepts of city and suburb and leads to a yet broader question: whether settlement concepts and other ecological concepts are useful for explaining ways of life.

The Inner City

Wirth argued that number, density, and heterogeneity had two social consequences which explain the major features of urban life. On the one hand, the crowding of diverse types of people into a small area led to the segregation of homogeneous types of people into separate neighborhoods. On the other hand, the lack of physical distance between city dwellers resulted in social contact between them, which broke down existing social and cultural patterns and encouraged assimilation as well as acculturation—the melting-pot effect. Wirth implied that the melting-pot effect was far more powerful than the tendency toward segregation and concluded that, sooner or later, the pressures engendered by the dominant social, economic, and political institutions of the city would destroy the remaining pockets of primary group relationships. Eventually, the social system of the city would resemble Tonnies *Gesellschaft*—a way of life which Wirth considered undesirable.

Because Wirth had come to see the city as the prototype of mass society, and because he examined the city from the distant vantage point of the folk society—from the wrong end of the telescope, so to speak—his view of urban life is not surprising. In addition, Wirth found support for his theory in the empirical work of his Chicago colleagues. As Greer and Kube[4] and Wilensky[5] have pointed out, the Chicago sociologists conducted their most intensive studies in the inner city.[6] At that time, it consisted mainly of slums recently invaded by new waves of European immigrants and rooming-house and skid-row districts, as well as the habitat of Bohemians and well-to-do "Gold Coast" apartment dwellers. Wirth himself studied the Maxwell Street Ghetto, a poor inner-city Jewish neighborhood then being dispersed by the acculturation and mobility of its inhabitants.[7] Some of the characteristics of urbanism which Wirth stressed in his essay abounded in these areas.

Wirth's diagnosis of the city as *Gesellschaft* must be questioned on three counts. First, the conclusions derived from a study of the inner city cannot be generalized to the entire urban area. Second, there is as yet not enough evidence to prove—or, admittedly, to deny—that number, density, and heterogeneity result in the social consequences which Wirth proposed. Finally, even if the causal relationship could be verified, it can be shown that a significant proportion of the city's inhabitants were, and are, isolated from these consequences by social structures and cultural patterns which they either brought to the city or developed by living in it. Wirth conceived the urban population as consisting of heterogeneous individuals, torn from past social systems, unable to develop new ones, and therefore prey to social anarchy in the city. While it is true that a not insignificant proportion of the inner-city population was, and still is, made up of unattached individuals,[8] Wirth's formulation ignores the fact that this population consists mainly of relatively homogeneous groups, with social and cultural moorings that shield it fairly effectively from the suggested consequences of number, density, and heterogeneity. This applies even more to the residents of the outer city, who constitute a majority of the total city population.

The social and cultural moorings of the inner-city population are best described by a brief analysis of the five major types of inner-city residents. These are: 1. the "cosmopolites"; 2. the unmarried or childless; 3. the "ethnic villagers"; 4. the "deprived"; and 5. the "trapped" and downward-mobile.

The "cosmopolites" include students, artists, writers, musicians, and entertainers, as well as other intellectuals and professionals. They live in the city in order to be near the special "cultural" facilities that can be located only near the center of the city. Many cosmopolites are unmarried or childless. Others rear children in the city, especially if they have the income to afford the aid of servants and governesses. The less affluent ones may move to the suburbs to raise their children, continuing to live as cosmopolites under considerable handicaps, especially in the lower-middle-class suburbs. Many of the very rich and powerful are also cosmopolites, although they are likely to have at least two residences, one of which is suburban or exurban.

The unmarried or childless must be divided into two subtypes, depending on the permanence or transience of their status. The temporarily unmarried or childless live in the inner city for only a limited time. Young adults may team up to rent an apartment away from their parents and close to job or entertainment opportunities. When they marry, they may move first to an apartment in a transient neighborhood, but if they can afford to do so, they leave for the outer city or the suburbs with the arrival of the first or second child. The permanently unmarried may stay in the inner city for the remainder of their lives, their housing depending on their income.

The "ethnic villagers" are ethnic groups which are found in such inner-city neighborhoods as New York's Lower East Side, living in some ways as they did when they were peasants in European or Puerto Rican villages.[9] Although they reside in the city, they isolate themselves from significant contact with most city facilities, aside from workplaces. Their way of life differs sharply from Wirth's urbanism in its emphasis on kinship and the primary group, the lack of anonymity and secondary-group contacts, the weakness of formal organizations, and the suspicion of anything and anyone outside their neighborhood.

The first two types live in the inner city by choice; the third is there partly because of necessity, partly because of tradition. The final two types are in the inner city because they have no other choice. One is the "deprived" population: the emotionally disturbed or otherwise handicapped; broken families; and, most important, the poor white and especially the nonwhite population. These urban dwellers must take the dilapidated housing and blighted neighborhoods to which the housing market relegates them, although among them are some for whom the slum is a hiding place or a temporary stopover to save money for a house in the outer city or the suburbs.[10]

The "trapped" are the people who stay behind when a neighborhood is invaded by nonresidential land uses or lower-status immigrants, because they cannot afford to move or are otherwise bound to their present location.[11] The "downward-mobiles" are a related type; they may have started life in a higher class position, but have been forced down in the socioeconomic hierarchy and in the quality of their accommodations. Many of them are old people, living out their existence on small pensions.

These five types may all live in dense and heterogeneous surroundings; yet they have such diverse ways of life that it is hard to see how density and heterogeneity could exert a common influence. Moreover, all but the last two types are isolated or detached from their neighborhood and thus from the social consequences that Wirth described. [...]

Wirth's description of the urban way of life fits best the transient areas of the inner city. Such areas are typically heterogeneous in population, partly because they are inhabited by transient types who do not require homogeneous neighbors or by deprived people who have no choice or may themselves be quite mobile. Under conditions of transience and heterogeneity, people interact only in terms of the segmental roles necessary for obtaining local services. Their social relationships may thus display anonymity, impersonality, and superficiality.[12]

The social features of Wirth's concept of urbanism seem, therefore, to be a result of residential instability, rather than of number, density, or heterogeneity. In fact, heterogeneity is itself an effect of residential instability, resulting when the influx of transients causes landlords and realtors to stop acting as gate-keepers—that is, wardens of neighborhood homogeneity.[13] Residential instability is found in all types of settlements, and presumably its social consequences are everywhere similar. These consequences cannot, therefore, be identified with the ways of life of the city.

The Outer City and the Suburbs

The second effect which Wirth ascribed to number, density, and heterogeneity was the segregation of homogeneous people into distinct neighborhoods[14] on the basis of "place and nature of work, income, racial and ethnic characteristics, social status, custom, habit, taste, preference and prejudice."[15] This description fits the residential districts of the *outer city*.[16] Although these districts contain the majority of the city's inhabitants, Wirth went into little detail about them. He made it clear, however, that the sociopsychological aspects of urbanism were prevalent there as well.[17]

Because existing neighborhood studies deal primarily with the exotic sections of the inner city, very little is known about the more typical residential neighborhoods of the outer city. However, it is evident that the way of life in these areas bears little resemblance to Wirth's urbanism. Both the studies which question Wirth's formulation and my own observations suggest that the common element in the ways of life of these neighborhoods is best described as *quasi-primary*. I use this term to characterize relationships between neighbors. Whatever the intensity or frequency of these relationships, the interaction is more intimate than a secondary contact, but more guarded than a primary one.[18] [...]

Postwar suburbia represents the most contemporary version of the quasi-primary way of life. Owing to increases in real income and the encouragement of home-ownership provided by the F.H.A., families in the lower middle class and upper working class can now live in modern single-family homes in low-density subdivisions, an opportunity previously available only to the upper and upper-middle classes.[19]

The popular literature of the 1950s described the new suburbs as communities in which conformity, homogeneity, and other-direction are unusually rampant.[20] The implication is that the move from city to suburb initiates a new way of life which causes considerable behavior and personality change in previous urbanites. My research in Levittown, New Jersey, suggests, however, that the move from the city to this predominantly lower-middle-class suburb does not result in any major behavioral changes for most people. Moreover, the changes which do occur reflect the move from the social isolation of a transient city or suburban apartment building to the quasi-primary life of a neighborhood of single-family homes. Also, many of the people whose life has changed report that the changes were intended. They existed as aspirations before the move or as reasons for it. In other words, the suburb itself creates few changes in ways of life.[21]

A Comparison of City and Suburb

If outer-urban and suburban areas are similar in that the way of life in both is quasi-primary, and if urban residents who move out to the suburbs do not undergo any significant changes in behavior, it is fair to argue that the differences in ways of life between the two types of settlements have been overestimated. Yet the fact remains that a variety of physical and demographic differences exist between the city and the suburb. However, upon closer examination, many of these differences turn out to be either spurious or of little significance for the way of life of the inhabitants.[22]

The differences between the residential areas of cities and suburbs which have been cited most frequently are:

1. Suburbs are more likely to be dormitories.
2. They are further away from the work and play facilities of the central business districts.

3. They are newer and more modern than city residential areas and are designed for the automobile rather than for pedestrian and mass-transit forms of movement.
4. They are built up with single-family rather than multifamily structures and are therefore less dense.
5. Their populations are more homogeneous.
6. Their populations differ demographically: they are younger; more of them are married; they have higher incomes; and they hold proportionately more white-collar jobs.[23]

Most urban neighborhoods are as much dormitories as the suburbs. Only in a few older inner-city areas are factories and offices still located in the middle of residential blocks, and even here many of the employees do not live in the neighborhood.

The fact that the suburbs are farther from the central business district is often true only in terms of distance, not travel time. Moreover, most people make relatively little use of downtown facilities, other than workplaces.[24] Many downtown stores seem to hold their greatest attraction for the upper-middle class;[25] the same is probably true of typically urban entertainment facilities. Teenagers and young adults may take their dates to first-run movie theatres, but the museums, concert halls, and lecture rooms attract mainly upper-middle-class ticket buyers, many of them suburban.[26]

The suburban reliance on the train and the automobile has given rise to an imaginative folklore about the consequences of commuting on alcohol consumption, sex life, and parental duties. Many of these conclusions are, however, drawn from selected high-income suburbs and exurbs and reflect job tensions in such hectic occupations as advertising and show business more than the effects of residence.[27] It is true that the upper-middle-class housewife must become a chauffeur in order to expose her children to the proper educational facilities, but such differences as walking to the corner drugstore and driving to its suburban equivalent seem to me of little emotional, social, or cultural import.[28] In addition, the continuing

shrinkage in the number of mass-transit users suggests that even in the city many younger people are now living a wholly auto-based way of life.

The fact that suburbs are smaller is primarily a function of political boundaries drawn long before the communities were suburban. This affects the kinds of political issues which develop and provides somewhat greater opportunity for citizen participation. Even so, in the suburbs as in the city, the minority who participate routinely are the professional politicians, the economically concerned businesspeople, lawyers, and salespeople, and the ideologically motivated middle- and upper-middle-class people with better than average education.

The social consequences of differences in density and house type also seem overrated. Single-family houses in quiet streets facilitate the supervision of children; this is one reason why middle-class parents who want to keep an eye on their children move to the suburbs. House type also has some effects on relationships between neighbors, insofar as there are more opportunities for visual contact between adjacent homeowners than between people on different floors of an apartment house. However, if occupants' characteristics are also held constant, the differences in actual social contact are less marked. Homogeneity of residents turns out to be more important than proximity as a determinant of sociability. If the population is heterogeneous, there is little social contact between neighbors, either on apartment-house floors or in single-family-house blocks; if people are homogeneous, there is likely to be considerable social contact in both house types. One need only contrast the apartment house located in a transient, heterogeneous neighborhood and exactly the same structure in a neighborhood occupied by a single ethnic group. The former is a lonely, anonymous building; the latter, a bustling microsociety. I have observed similar patterns in suburban areas: on blocks where people are homogeneous, they socialize; where they are heterogeneous, they do little more than exchange polite greetings.[29]

Suburbs are usually described as being more homogeneous in house type than the city, but if they are compared to the outer city, the differences are small. Most inhabitants of the outer city, other than well-to-do homeowners, live on blocks of uniform structures as well; for example, the endless streets of row houses in Philadelphia and Baltimore or of two-story duplexes and six-flat apartment houses in Chicago. They differ from the new suburbs only in that they were erected through more primitive methods of mass production. Suburbs are, of course, more predominantly areas of owner-occupied single homes, though in the outer districts of most American cities home-ownership is also extremely high.

Demographically, suburbs as a whole are clearly more homogeneous than cities as a whole, though probably not more so than outer cities. However, people do not live in cities or suburbs as a whole, but in specific neighborhoods. An analysis of ways of life would require a determination of the degree of population homogeneity within the boundaries of areas defined as neighbourhoods by residents' social contacts. Such an analysis would no doubt indicate that many neighbourhoods in the city as well as the suburbs are homogeneous. Neighborhood homogeneity is actually a result of factors having little or nothing to do with the house type, density, or location of the area relative to the city limits. Brand new neighborhoods are more homogeneous than older ones, because they have not yet experienced resident turnover, which frequently results in population heterogeneity. Neighborhoods of low- and medium-priced housing are usually less homogeneous than those with expensive dwellings because they attract families who have reached the peak of occupational and residential mobility, as well as young families who are just starting their climb and will eventually move to neighborhoods of higher status. The latter, being accessible only to high-income people, are therefore more homogeneous with respect to other resident characteristics as well. Moreover, such areas have the economic and political power to slow down or prevent invasion. The demographic differences between cities and suburbs cannot be questioned, especially since the suburbs have attracted a large number of middle-class child-rearing families. The differences are, however, much reduced if suburbs are compared only to the outer city. In addition, a detailed comparison of suburban and outer-city residential areas would show that neighborhoods with the same kinds of people can be found in the city as well as the suburbs. Once again, the age of the area and the cost of housing are more important determinants of demographic characteristics than the location of the area with respect to the city limits. [...]

A Reevaluation of Definitions

The argument presented here has implications for the sociological definition of the city. Such a definition relates ways of life to environmental features of the city qua settlement type. But if ways of life do not coincide with settlement types, and if these ways are functions of class and life-cycle stage rather than of the ecological attributes of the settlement, a sociological definition of the city cannot be formulated.[30] Concepts such as "city" and "suburb" allow us to distinguish settlement types from each other physically and demographically, but the ecological processes and conditions which they synthesize have no direct or invariate consequences for ways of life. The sociologist cannot, therefore, speak of an urban or suburban way of life.

Conclusion

Many of the descriptive statements made here are as time bound as Wirth's.[31] In the 1940s Wirth concluded that some form of urbanism would eventually predominate in all settlement types. He was, however, writing during a time of immigrant acculturation and at the end of a serious depression, an era of minimal choice. Today, it is apparent that high-density, heterogeneous surroundings are for most people a temporary place of residence; other than for the Park Avenue or Greenwich Village cosmopolites, they are a result of necessity, rather than choice. As soon as they can afford to do so, most Americans head for the single-family house and the quasi-primary way of life of the low-density neighborhood, in the outer city or the suburbs.[32]

Changes in the national economy and in government housing policy can affect many of the variables that make up housing supply and demand. For example, urban sprawl may eventually outdistance the ability of present and proposed transportation systems to move workers into the city; further industrial decentralization can forestall it and alter the entire relationship between work and residence. The expansion of urban-renewal activities can perhaps lure a significant number of cosmopolites back from the suburbs, while a drastic change in renewal policy might begin to ameliorate the housing conditions of the deprived population. A serious depression could once again make America a nation of doubled-up tenants.

These events will affect housing supply and residential choice; they will frustrate, but not suppress, demands for the quasi-primary way of life. However, changes in the national economy, society, and culture can affect people's characteristics—family size, educational level, and various other concomitants of life-cycle stage and class. These in turn will stimulate changes in demands and choices. The rising number of college graduates, for example, is likely to increase the cosmopolite ranks. This might in turn create a new set of city dwellers, although it will probably do no more than encourage the development of cosmopolite facilities in some suburban areas.

The current revival of interest in urban sociology and in community studies, as well as the sociologist's increasing curiosity about city planning, suggests that data may soon be available to formulate a more adequate theory of the relationship between settlements and the ways of life within them. The speculations presented in this essay are intended to raise questions; they can be answered only by more systematic data collection and theorizing.

Postscript

When I reread this essay again after many years, I was struck by how much the first sentence remains largely true. While no single school, including the ecological school, is now dominant in urban sociology, Louis Wirth's "Urbanism as a Way of Life" remains the most often cited article and probably the most often read one as well. It still supplies the simplest and seemingly most accurate definition of the city, and a rationale, not to mention an outline, for studying urban sociology—all the research and writing questioning Wirth's ideas notwithstanding. In fact, although over half of all Americans now live in the suburbs; urban sociology courses remain resolutely urban, although often because they deal with the urban sociology of the poor and the minorities who remain stuck in the city. Whatever the merit of that approach (which I use myself), we still do not have a sociology of the suburbs or even a respectable sociological literature on suburbia.

I pointed out in my article, originally published in 1962, that it was as time bound as Wirth's, and I was by and large right. Even though I seem to have predicted the yuppies in my penultimate paragraph, I did not consider the possibility that someday suburbia would be the majority form of residence, and that it would then be inhabited by people of all ages and households of all types, rather than mainly young families with young children. I did mention the decentralization of industry, but did not think that it might one day become a flood. Now, about two-thirds or more of those living in the suburbs also work there, and even fewer than a third need to come to the city's central business district, except perhaps for high culture, since museums and concert halls have by and large not decentralized (yet). Professional sports teams have, however, even if they are still called by the name of the city nearest to where they play.

I should also have thought about the possibility that when the suburbs became more popular, the mainly urban essayists and intellectuals who criticized them—and by implication their middle-American residents—for undue conformity, homogeneity, and other sociocultural diseases would have to end the suburban critique. This they did, shortly after I published this article, but they found new targets with which to continue the cultural class war. Such targets are always available, however, beginning and still ending with television viewing and television programming.

Having underestimated the extent of the suburban move, I also failed to consider the likelihood of a city inhabited increasingly by the very rich and the poor. Nor did I consider that black ghettos would also be found in what I called the outer city, even if they are ghettos of the black working class and lower middle class more than of the black poor, and are thus not altogether different than when they were inhabited by the white working and lower middle classes. It did not even occur to me that housing might one day become expensive, so that most American home buyers could no longer afford either a new or a secondhand single-family house, that suburbia would be filling up with row houses and condominiums—and that the major housing problem of the poor was the inability to pay high rents, which was one cause of the tragic increase in homelessness exacted by the Reagan administration on the poor, the cities, and even many suburbs.

Actually, my prediction of the yuppies was partly luck, for while I expected more young people to come into the inner city after college, some having done so already in the 1950s, I did not expect the large number who came and for whom old neighborhoods near the central business district and elsewhere were gentrified. They have come largely because of the dramatic increase in *professional* service employment in the central business districts of many cities, although because they spend so much time on the streets and in expensive "boutiques," their visibility is greater than their actual number. Moreover, that number could decline sharply in the 1990s, not only because when they marry and have children many move to the suburbs, but also because if the boom times in professional service employment end, their number—and visibility—will shrink quickly and considerably.

I could list other ways in which the 1962 article was time bound; for example, it paid no more attention than Wirth's article to the various political battles—about race, or class, or just property values—that take place in cities and suburbs, and thus could

not consider that as all resources became scarcer, these battles would increase in number and intensity. Still, in its basic conception, the article remains accurate as I write this postscript in the spring of 1990. The basic differences are not between city and suburb, but between the inner city and the rest of the metropolitan area, and the major reasons are more or less as I stated them.

NOTES

1. Louis Wirth, "Urbanism as a Way of Life," *American Journal of Sociology* (July 1938), 44:1–24; reprinted in Paul Hatt and Albert J. Reiss, Jr., eds., *Cities and Society* (Glencoe, Ill.: Free Press, 1957), pp. 46–64.
2. Richard Dewey, "The Rural-Urban Continuum: Real but Relatively Unimportant," *American Journal of Sociology* (July 1960), 66:60–66.
3. I shall not attempt to summarize these studies, for this task has already been performed by Dewey, Reiss, Wilensky, and others. The studies include: Morris Axelrod, "Urban Structure and Social Participation," *American Sociological Review* (February 1956), 21:13–18; Dewey, "The Rural-Urban Continuum;" William H. Form et al., "The Compatibility of Alternative Approaches to the Delimitation of Urban Sub-areas," *American Sociological Review* (August 1954), 19:434–440; Herbert J. Gans, *The Urban Villagers* (New York: Free Press of Glencoe, 1962); Scott Greer, "Urbanism Reconsidered: A Comparative Study of Local Areas in a Metropolis," *American Sociological Review* (February 1956), 21:19–25; Scott Greer and Ella Kube, "Urbanism and Social Structure: A Los Angeles Study," in Marvin B. Sussman, ed., *Community Structure and Analysis* (New York: Crowell, 1959), pp. 93–112; Morris Janowitz, *The Community Press in an Urban Setting* (Glencoe, Ill.: Free Press, 1952); Albert J. Reiss, Jr., "An Analysis of Urban Phenomena," in Robert M. Fisher, ed., *The Metropolis in Modern Life* (Garden City, N.Y.: Doubleday, 1955), pp. 41–49; Albert J. Reiss, Jr., "Rural-Urban and Status Differences in Interpersonal Contacts," *American Journal of Sociology* (September 1959), 65:182–195; John R. Seeley, "The Slum: Its Nature, Use, and Users," *Journal of the American Institute of Planners* (February 1959), 25:7–14; Joel Smith, William Form, and Gregory Stone, "Local Intimacy in a

Middle-Sized City," *American Journal of Sociology* (November 1954), 60:276–284; Gregory P. Stone, "City Shoppers and Urban Identification: Observations on the Social Psychology of City Life," *American Journal of Sociology* (July 1954), 60:36–45; William F. Whyte, *Street Corner Society* (Chicago: University of Chicago Press, 1955); Harold L. Wilensky and Charles Lebeaux, *Industrial Society and Social Welfare* (New York: Russell Sage Foundation, 1958); Michael Young and Peter Willmott, *Family and Kinship in East London* (London: Routledge and Kegan Paul, 1957).

4. Greer and Kube, "Urbanism and Social Structure," p. 112.

5. Wilensky and Lebeaux, "Industrial Society," p. 121.

6. By the *inner city* I mean the transient residential areas, the Gold Coasts and the slums that generally surround the central business district, although in some communities they may continue for miles beyond that district. The *outer city* includes the stable residential areas that house the working- and middle-class tenant and owner. The *suburbs* I conceive as the latest and most modern ring of the outer city, distinguished from it only by yet lower densities and by the often irrelevant fact of the ring's location outside the city limits.

7. Louis Wirth, *The Ghetto* (Chicago: University of Chicago Press, 1928).

8. Arnold M. Rose, "Living Arrangements of Unattached Persons," *American Sociological Review* (August 1947), 12:429–435.

9. Gans, *Urban Villagers.*

10. Seeley, "The Slum."

11. *Ibid.* The trapped are not very visible, but I suspect that they are a significant element in what Raymond Vernon has described as the "gray areas" of the city in his *Changing Economic Function of the Central City* (New York: Committee on Economic Development, Supplementary Paper No. 1, January 1959).

12. Whether or not these social phenomena have the psychological consequences Wirth suggested depends on the people who live in the area. Those who are detached from the neighborhood by choice are probably immune, but those who depend on the neighborhood for their social relationships —the unattached individuals, for example —may suffer greatly from loneliness.

13. Needless to say, residential instability must ultimately be traced to the fact that, as Wirth pointed out, the city and its economy attract transient—and, depending on the sources of outmigration, heterogeneous— people. However, this is a characteristic of urban-industrial society, not of the city specifically.

14. By neighborhoods or residential districts I mean areas demarcated from others by distinctive physical boundaries or by social characteristics, some of which may be perceived only by the residents. However, these areas are not necessarily socially self-sufficient or culturally distinctive.

15. Wirth, "Urbanism as a Way of Life," p. 56.

16. For the definition of *outer city*, see note 6.

17. Wirth, "Urbanism as a Way of Life," p. 56.

18. Because neighborly relations are not quite primary and not quite secondary, they can also become *pseudo-primary*, that is, secondary ones disguised with false affect to make them appear primary. Critics have often described suburban life in this fashion, although the actual prevalence of pseudo-primary relationships has not been studied systematically in cities or suburbs.

19. Harold Wattel, "Levittown: A Suburban Community," in William M. Dobriner, ed., *The Suburban Community* (New York: Putnam, 1958), pp. 287–313.

20. Bennett Berger, *Working Class Suburb: A Study of Auto Workers in Suburbia* (Berkeley: University of California Press, 1960). Also Vernon, *Changing Economic Function of the Central City.*

21. Berger, *Working Class Suburb.*

22. Wattel, "Levittown." They may, of course, be significant for the welfare of the total metropolitan area.

23. Otis Dudley Duncan and Albert J. Reiss, Jr., *Social Characteristics of Rural and Urban Communities, 1950* (New York: Wiley, 1956), p. 131.

24. Donald L. Foley, "The Use of Local Facilities in a Metropolis," in Hatt and Reiss, *Cities and Societies*, pp. 237–247. Also see Christen T. Jonassen, *The Shopping Center versus Downtown* (Columbus: Bureau of Business Research, Ohio State University, 1955).

25. Jonassen, "The Shopping Center," pp. 91–92.

26. A 1958 study of New York theatergoers showed a median income of close to $10,000, and 35 percent were reported as living in the suburbs. That year, the median U.S. family income was $5,087. John Enders, *Profile of the Theater Market* (New York: Playbill, undated and unpaged).

27. A. C. Spectorsky, *The Exurbanites* (Philadelphia: Lippincott, 1955).

28. I am thinking here of adults; teenagers do suffer from the lack of informal meeting places within walking or bicycling distance.

29. Herbert J. Gans, "Planning and Social Life: Friendship and Neighbor Relations in

Suburban Communities," *Journal of the American Institute of Planners* (May 1961), 27:134–140.

30. Because of the distinctiveness of the ways of life found in the inner city, some writers propose definitions that refer only to these ways, ignoring those found in the outer city. For example, popular writers sometimes identify "urban" with "urbanity," that is, "cosmopolitanism." However, such a definition ignores the other ways of life found in the inner city. Moreover, I have tried to show that these ways have few common elements and that the ecological features of the inner city have little or no influence in shaping them.

31. Even more than Wirth's they are based no data and impressions gathered in the large eastern and midwestern cities of the United States.

32. Personal discussions with European planners and sociologists suggest that many European apartment dwellers have similar preferences, although economic conditions, high building costs, and the scarcity of land make it impossible for them to achieve their desires.

ESSAY 1.4

Melting Pot Cities and Suburbs

William H. Frey

Source: William H. Frey, *Diversity Explosion: How Racial Demographics Are Remaking America* (Washington, D.C.: Brookings Institute Press, 2018).

EDITORS' INTRODUCTION

The 1968 *Report of the National Advisory Commission on Civil Rights* speculated that the future of U.S. urban areas was one of two increasingly separate Americas; an African-American society mainly concentrated in large central cities, and a white society located in the suburbs, smaller central cities, and peripheral areas of large central cities.[i] **[See Document 9.1, Watts Riots, 1965.]** Over the last half-century, this racial dichotomy has been a central focus of inquiry and thematic organization for urban scholarship, as middle-class whites increasing left the incorporated limits of cities for the suburbs, while poorer whites, African-Americans, and other racial minorities moved to and/or remained in city centers and bordering neighborhoods. **[See Parts IX and X of this volume.]** The racialized city-suburban divide has also been a popular social and cultural trope, occasionally summarized in variations of the expression "chocolate cities and vanilla suburbs," drawn from lyrics to the song "Chocolate City" by the musical funk group Parliament.[ii]

However, as demographer William H. Frey documents in *Diversity Explosion: How Racial Demographics Are Remaking America* (2015, updated 2018), contemporary cities and suburbs in the United States reflect a far more multiracial country. In fact, during 2011, more minority than white babies were born in the United States, and by 2050, whites will constitute a minority of all Americans. Even now, there is clear evidence that an increasingly diverse, even globalized population, has replaced the white middle-class baby boom culture that dominated the suburbs and defined the urban divide during the second half of the twentieth century. Although there are remnants of minority-city-white-suburb residential divisions, largely confined to the Heartland region of the United States., the stereotype of white-only flight to the suburbs is a thing of the past. By 2010, for the first time, in the largest metropolitan areas of the nation, more African-Americans lived in the suburbs than in the cities.

In this essay, Frey describes how racial minorities dominate both city and suburban growth in the nation's 100 largest metropolitan areas. Building from the long-standing metaphor of America as a melting pot, wherein waves of European immigrants originally clustered in gateways cities like New York and Chicago and then gradually dispersed to other parts of the country where they fused with the larger population to form a more homogeneous population, Frey identifies four demographic trends that have created diverse cities and suburbs across the United States. First is the rise of "black flight" from some of the nation's largest cities, resulting in the diminishing presence of blacks in communities where they have been a backbone of the population for generations. Second is significant decline in white population growth, with

---

i U.S. National Advisory Commission on Civil Disorders, *Report of the National Advisory Commission on Civil Disorders* (Washington, D.C.: U.S. Government Printing Office, 1968), 407.

ii B. Worrell, G. Clinton, and W. Collins, *Chocolate City*, Casablanca-NBLP 7014 (June 1975).

approximately one-third of all large metropolitan suburbs showing decreases in the overall number of white residents. Third is the dramatic growth of Hispanic and Asian population growth, with Hispanics (defined by Frey as racial group like blacks and Asians), as the largest agents of growth in both cities and suburbs. And finally, with more minorities in the suburbs than cities within the country's large metropolitan areas, Frey contends that suburbs have become and will continue to be a microcosm for America's diversity, with little resemblance to the white vanilla stereotype.

Dr. William H. Frey is a sociologist and demographer who has authored numerous books, book chapters, articles, and research reports on migration, population redistribution, the U.S. Census, and the demography of metropolitan areas and American politics. He serves as Senior Fellow with the Metropolitan Program at the Brookings Institution and also a Research Professor at the Population Studies Center, Institute for Social Research at the University of Michigan, where he directs the Social Science Data Analysis Network (www.SSDAN.net) that creates demographic media for educators and policy-makers.

MELTING POT CITIES AND SUBURBS

Perhaps the most visible demographic impact of America's diversity explosion is occurring within urban areas. The classic image of an American metropolis was that of a polyglot city surrounded by mostly white suburbs—the "chocolate city/vanilla suburbs" of the 1950s and 1960s, when white-dominated suburban-ization left largely black minority populations stranded in many of the nation's largest cities.[1] The black city/white suburb paradigm has almost entirely broken down. Only in slowly growing northern parts of the country does this stereotype partially hold, and even there changes are afoot as newly arriving His-panics and Asians contribute to population gains. The old dichotomy stands in sharp con-trast to residential patterns in the Melting Pot region of the country, where suburbs and cities alike are receiving large waves of immi-grant minorities, often within the context of declining white populations. The old path of white flight to the suburbs is now followed by Hispanics, Asians, and, to a greater degree than ever before, blacks—all aspiring to achieve the suburban American Dream. This essay explores how America's diversity explo-sion is playing out within the nation's largest metropolitan areas, especially in the suburbs.[2]

Minorities Dominate City and Suburban Growth

The rise of new minority populations, the sharp slowdown of white population

growth, and the economic gains and increased residential freedom of new gener-ations of blacks are rapidly changing the classic image of suburbanization. Together these trends paint a picture of population growth dynamics in the nation's cities and suburbs that is very different from the one etched in the minds of pollsters, political consultants, and the public at large. [...] About one-half of the nation's suburban population gain is attributable to Hispanics, both native born and immigrant. In the cities, Hispanics account for the lion's share of gains, more than making up for cities' loss of white and black residents.

The national picture, then, is one in which the new minorities, Hispanics and Asians, are now the main contributors to city population growth and each of the major minority groups—Hispanics, Asians, and blacks—con-tributes more than whites to suburban gains. This stands in stark contrast to the white-dominated suburbanization that was a signa-ture trend of the last half of the twentieth cen-tury. Of course, the national picture varies greatly across regions of the country [...]. This is especially the case for Hispanics, who originally settled in mostly coastal gateway cities in the nation's Melting Pot region and often expanded to their suburbs. Today immigrant as well as native-born Hispanics are dispersing to New Sun Belt suburbs in the Southeast and Mountain West.[3]

The suburbs of all 100 metropolitan areas experienced Hispanic population gains in 2000–10. Areas with the largest numeric gains were Riverside, New York, Houston, and Miami. Yet the fastest Hispanic *growth rates*, all more than 150 percent, are found in the suburbs of the New Sun Belt cities of Nashville, Charlotte, Raleigh, and Provo as well as the Heartland cities of Indianapolis and Scranton. Although overall Hispanic populations are small in the latter areas, their rapid growth indicates where the shifts are trending.

Each central city of the 100 largest metropolitan areas also saw Hispanic gains. As with the suburbs, numeric gains were largest in Melting Pot cities such as Dallas, Houston, and Los Angeles, while growth rates were fast in all parts of the country, including rapidly growing Florida cities such as Cape Coral, Lakeland, and Palm Bay. Hispanics contributed to city population gains (or reduced city losses) more than any other racial group in 76 of the 100 largest metropolitan areas. Asians also contributed to city and suburban population gains in each of the 100 largest metropolitan areas. Asians made substantial contributions to suburban gains in Los Angeles, New York, San Francisco, and Washington, D.C. They contributed more than other racial minorities to city gains in San Francisco, New York, and San Jose. Hispanics and Asians already were responsible for nearly all of the population gains in central cities nationwide in 2000–10. Moreover, these new minorities and their later generations are poised to become the backbone of future suburban growth in ways that will transform the nation.

The Diminished Role of Whites in Twenty-First-Century Suburbanization

[...] On the national level, white population loss is projected to occur in less than a decade. This diminished white role is now beginning to play out in U.S. suburbs as well as cities. White population losses in cities are not new. Many of the nation's large older cities showed white losses beginning in the 1950s, during the peak period of white migration to the suburbs.[4] Today, the slowdown in national white population growth is driving white losses in cities more broadly. Nearly three-quarters (72) of central cities in

the nation's 100 largest metropolitan areas lost whites between 1990 and 2010. Still, the magnitude of those losses has diminished somewhat—a consequence of the renewed attraction of cities for some whites. Fifty of these 72 cities lost fewer whites during the first decade of the 2000s than the decade before, including New York, Los Angeles, Chicago, Boston, and St. Louis. As a group, cities lost one-half as many whites in 2000–10 as in the 1990s.

What is new and likely to be a long-term trend is the slowdown in white population gains in the suburbs. As the white population ages and the childbearing population increasingly consists of minorities, the traditional attraction to the suburbs will be felt more by the latter groups. In addition, the "new white flight" [...] has directed whites away from the cities *and the suburbs* of many large metropolitan areas in both coastal areas and interior metropolitan areas, especially in the Heartland.

Nearly one-third of large metropolitan areas experienced absolute declines in their white suburban populations over 2000–10. The greatest white suburban losses occurred in large coastal metropolitan areas like New York, Los Angeles, and San Francisco as well as northern industrial areas such as Detroit, Cleveland, and Buffalo. Nationally, whites contributed only 9 percent to the growth in the suburban population during this decade. [...] More than one-quarter of the 100 largest metropolitan areas experienced white losses in both cities and suburbs. Yet 23 areas recorded white gains in both cities and suburbs. These areas—which include Austin, Denver, Atlanta, and Las Vegas—are located primarily in the New Sun Belt region, and they have been attracting whites from parts of the country that either are more expensive or are in a state of economic decline. There also are 45 metropolitan areas that exhibit the traditional patterns of white flight, including Midwest areas such as Columbus, Kansas City, and Minneapolis–St. Paul. Whites still dominate population gains in a few suburban areas, including Des Moines, Provo, Louisville, and Omaha, but in 78 metropolitan suburbs, such as those of Los

Angeles, New York, San Francisco, and Chicago, minorities accounted for most or all of the population gains. In addition, among the 77 cities that gained population during the past decade, minorities contributed to all or most of the gains in 71 of those cities. As new minorities, particularly Hispanics, continue to diffuse across the country, they will increase their presence in suburban communities and cities.

Black Flight

An important counterpoint to slowing white flight in recent decades is the emergence of "black flight" from major cities with established black populations. Black population losses have been occurring in some cities since the 1970s.[5] However, the magnitude and pervasiveness of black losses in cities during the first decade of the 2000s were unprecedented. [...] There was a total decline of 300,000 blacks in the central cities of the 100 largest metropolitan areas, the first absolute population decline among blacks for these cities as a group.

Thirteen of the 20 cities with the largest black populations (including nine of the ten largest) registered declines in their black populations in 2000–10. Among central cities of the 100 largest metropolitan areas, 33 cities experienced declines in their black populations and 68 showed first-time losses, larger losses, or smaller gains among blacks than in the 1990s. Clearly, the black presence, which has been the mainstay of many large city populations, is diminishing.

Three cities with large black declines— Detroit, Chicago, and New York—were among the primary destinations for blacks during the Great Migration out of the South in the first part of the twentieth century. However, black losses were not confined to northern cities. Southern and western cities such as Atlanta, Dallas, and Los Angeles were also among those losing blacks in 2000– 10. Much of that population is shifting to the suburbs of these metropolitan areas.

The sharp rise in black suburbanization can be attributed in part to the black population's economic progress in recent decades, especially among younger people aspiring to

the suburban lifestyle that eluded their parents and grandparents. Among blacks ages 25 to 34, 19 percent were college graduates in 2010; in contrast, 12 percent were graduates in 1990 and only 6 percent in 1970. Also, a half century has now elapsed since the 1968 Fair Housing Act outlawed racial discrimination in the housing market and made suburban developments open to blacks who have the economic means to move. [...] Segregation between blacks and whites is now diminishing gradually but consistently across metropolitan areas, with the growing southern and western parts of the country exhibiting the least segregation. Metropolitan areas in these less segregated, growing parts of the country are registering the greatest numeric gains in the suburban black population. The suburbs of Atlanta, Houston, Washington, D.C., and Dallas experienced the largest increases in black population during 2000–10, although Detroit and Chicago also make the list, due in part to large black losses from their central cities [...]. Among the largest 100 metropolitan areas, 96 showed gains in their suburban black populations. Of those, more than three-quarters had larger increases in 2000–10 than in the 1990s. While delayed for decades, the full-scale suburbanization of blacks is finally under way.

Minority White Cities, Melting Pot Suburbs

The new demographic dynamics affecting the nation's metropolitan areas—substantial Hispanic and Asian population gains, unprecedented slowdowns and losses in white population growth, and an emerging black flight from the city—have already affected city and suburban populations, sometimes dramatically. Two benchmarks tell the story. First, it is now Hispanics, not blacks, who constitute the largest minority group in cities. Second, the white share of the suburban population, 65 percent, in 2010 was nearly the same as the white share of the national population. From a racial standpoint and in other respects, the suburbs are becoming a microcosm of the general American population.[6] Both cities and suburbs are being transformed because of these shifts.

Minority White Cities Are the Norm

Minority white cities are not new. Some major cities, including Washington, D.C., and Atlanta, had fewer whites than blacks by 1960, and several others, such as Baltimore and Detroit, became majority black by 1980.[7] By 2000, with continued white suburbanization and increased Hispanic and Asian gains, central cities in 42 of the nation's 100 largest metropolitan areas had minority white populations. By 2010, more than one-half (58) of the central cities were minority white [...]. Among the 16 cities that shifted to minority white status in 2010, Hispanics were responsible for 14 of the shifts, including those in rapidly diversifying areas such as Phoenix, Austin, and Las Vegas.

Because of the long history of city segregation and white flight, blacks are still the dominant racial minority in more cities than Hispanics and Asians are, but the latter groups are catching up. In 1990, blacks were the largest minority in 68 of the central cities in the 100 largest metropolitan areas. By 2010 they dominated in only 54 of them, with Hispanics dominating in 41 and Asians in 5. Chicago, a long-standing "white-black" city, has become about one-third white, one-third black, and one-third Hispanic or other races, with an even greater Hispanic presence in the offing. [...] Hispanics dominate all minorities with respect to the nation's city population as a whole, due to their large numbers in Los Angeles and other large cities in the Melting Pot region. Yet changes are occurring elsewhere. The rise of Hispanics as the "major city minority" foreshadows tomorrow's urban America. Their rise will affect education, the workplace, commercial life, and patterns of civic engagement.

The Rise of Melting Pot Suburbs

More than ever, major metropolitan suburbs reflect the rest of American society. A growing number of suburban areas are achieving what might be termed "melting pot" status. In 36 of the 100 largest metropolitan areas, minorities represented at least 35 percent of the suburban population in 2010, approximately the same as their share of the national population. Within those areas, 16 have majority-minority populations, up from just 8 in 2000. With a few exceptions, such as suburban New York and Chicago, these "melting pot" suburbs are located in the South and West [...]. Hispanics are the predominant racial minority in most of these suburban areas, an edge that they already held by 1990 and continue to hold despite the increasing share of blacks in the suburbs. Hispanics represent the largest minority group in 25 of these 36 highly diverse suburbs while blacks are the largest group in 9 suburbs and Asians in 2.

Five of the metropolitan suburbs that tipped into majority-minority status in the 2000s were in California: San Francisco, San Jose, Riverside, Sacramento, and Modesto. Others are Houston, Las Vegas, and Washington, D.C. In each of these eight areas, the white share of the population dropped by at least 9 percent. In suburban Las Vegas, the drop was even more dramatic, from 61 percent white in 2000 to 48 percent white in 2010. The racial transitions giving rise to newly majority-minority suburbs also were evident in suburbs nationwide. In the suburbs of all 100 large metropolitan areas, the white share of the population declined over 2000–10. Still, there are wide variations in suburban racial profiles across the country, mirroring regional demographic patterns. For example, the suburbs where Hispanics constitute the largest part of the population—more than 50 percent—are on the Texas border, including the areas of El Paso and McAllen, in addition to the interior California areas of Fresno and Bakersfield. Those with highest black percentages are in the Deep South: Jackson, Mississippi; Virginia Beach, Virginia; and Columbia, South Carolina. The largest Asian shares of suburban populations are in Honolulu and San Jose.

In many cases the racial mix in the suburbs closely resembles the mix in the cities. This is especially the case in Melting Pot metropolitan areas such as Los Angeles [...]. Other areas, epitomized by Atlanta, showed brisk black suburban gains following considerable white suburban growth, creating a sizable black suburban presence.

For many southern and western areas, the city-suburb minority gaps are declining as suburbs become a magnet for all racial groups. At the other extreme are northern metropolitan areas like Detroit, where decades of nearly exclusive white suburban growth have only recently been accompanied by a breakthrough in black suburban growth. Detroit shows a substantial city-suburb/black-white disparity that is unlikely to be erased soon, despite new minority growth. Other areas that show similar city-suburb disparities are located primarily in the North. They include Milwaukee and Cleveland—areas with a tradition of high black-white neighborhood segregation that continues today.

Of course, racial shifts are constantly occurring within the suburbs, especially in recent decades and in the inner and middle rings of suburbs. Racial minorities constitute approximately two-fifths of the population of inner and middle suburbs in the nation.[8] Other exurbs, which constitute only about 10 percent of the metropolitan population, are four-fifths white and are driven largely by white growth. So while Hispanics, Asians, and blacks are now main players in the suburbanization movement, they do not yet have a substantial presence in the outer suburbs and show some clustering in same-race communities, in many cases as a result of quasi-legal exclusionary practices.[9]

Still, demographic forces will continue to diversify the nation's cities and suburbs, with important implications for both policy and politics. Both suburbs and cities face increasing demands for the services needed by new populations, particularly those of different economic circumstances and cultural and linguistic backgrounds. Increasing suburban diversity may cause suburbs to become more "purple" than their traditional red in local and national elections, making them less reliable bases for either Republicans or Democrats, who have depended on demographically homogeneous voting blocs. Similarly, the changing demographics of big cities indicate that success for urban politicians may hinge on cultivating growing Hispanic and Asian constituencies along with traditional black voters and gentrifying whites. The historically sharp racial divisions between cities and suburbs in metropolitan America are more blurred than ever. The shifting social, economic, and political structures of these places will challenge leaders at all levels to understand and keep pace with the consequences.

Achieving the Suburban Dream

For generations, young adults of all backgrounds, but especially racial minorities, viewed a residence in the suburbs as both a means and an end toward achieving the classic American Dream. As far back as the 1920s, when the widespread use of the automobile enabled the development of early suburbs, a move away from the city was associated with upward mobility—a larger, more spacious house, a less crime-ridden community, and a greater distance from neighborhoods composed of disadvantaged and lower-status minority segments of the population.[10] By the end of World War II, many of the nation's older industrial cities already showed sharp city-suburb gaps in their racial profiles as well as in their predominant family types and socioeconomic attributes. Those gaps became far more pronounced after the massive, largely white suburbanization that took place in the immediate postwar years, making the suburbs an even more alluring destination for whites.[11] In contrast, Asians, Hispanics, and particularly blacks dispersed from cities far more gradually. For them, the suburban American Dream was still a goal rather than a given. Hispanics and Asians initially settled primarily in the city's racially circumscribed communities, and until recently, most blacks resided in largely segregated neighborhoods.

As recently as 1980, less than one-half of metropolitan minorities resided in the suburbs.[12] Only beginning in 1990 did more than half of metropolitan Asians become suburban residents, while more than half of Hispanics did not do so until 2000. Moreover, it was not until 2010 that more than half of metropolitan blacks became suburban residents [...]. Thus, an important milestone was passed when the 2010 census became the first to show a majority of each of the nation's largest racial minority groups residing in the suburbs. These recent trends were fueled by increased suburban development, especially in growing southern and western parts of the country, and the desire among new minorities to follow the broader postwar trend toward suburban living. For blacks, the substantial rise in suburbanization countered decades of concentration in urban residential neighborhoods fostered by housing discrimination in suburban communities and previously sharp economic disparities with whites.

While suburbs today are far less homogeneous in many respects than in the immediate postwar decades, a suburban residence is still a goal for many American households and, for minorities especially, a symbol of "making it" in America. Sociologists have treated the suburban residence of racial and ethnic groups as an outcome commensurate with their achievement of certain other levels of economic and social status.[13] This is consistent with the earlier experience of whites, who were most likely to be suburban residents if they were well educated, had higher incomes, and were raising children.[14] Of course, by now a supermajority of whites resides in the suburbs. White households of all types are far more likely to live in suburbs than cities. But among minority groups, selective suburbanization is still taking place [...]. Among each minority group, more than one-half of college-graduate metropolitan residents reside in the suburbs. The likelihood of suburban residence decreases with declining level of education. In fact, among blacks, a suburban residence is likely only for those who achieve at least some post-high school education. Furthermore, although Asians overall are the most suburbanized of the three minority groups, those without a high school diploma are more likely to reside in the city than in the suburbs.[15]

Suburbs also have been the prime destination for families, especially married couples with children, in keeping with the long-held view that the suburbs are better for child-rearing. Among Asians, Hispanics, and blacks, married-with-children families are more likely to reside in the suburbs than any other household type. This is significant in light of the fact that minorities will constitute an increasing portion of the nation's child population. From now on, suburban schools and other child-related services will need to become more tailored to a far more diverse child population than in the past. From blacks in particular, there is a sharp difference between married-couple households (with or without children) and other household types with respect to suburban residence. For them especially, there appears to be a clear dividing line between "suburban" middle-class attributes, such as education and marriage, and "urban" attributes associated with lower education levels and other types of households.

Living in the suburbs does not, of course, guarantee a middle-class lifestyle. Communities that develop within the broad "suburban" category can take many forms. Studies on early black and immigrant minorities who were suburban pioneers show that in many cases, their places of residence were only barely an upgrade from the city neighborhoods that they left behind.[16] The experiences of recent minority suburbanites are more mixed, with some residing in racially stable mainstream suburban communities and others in largely minority, less advantaged communities vacated by the new white flight.[17] This pattern will play out as melting pot suburbs proliferate, increasingly in the New Sun Belt and eventually in the Heartland region of the country.

In sum, the first decade of the twenty-first century has set the table for a very different city-suburban racial dynamic, one that stands in stark contrast to what existed in the past. The new minorities, Hispanics and Asians, and others are becoming primary engines of growth in the nation's cities and suburbs in an era when the aging white population will be barely holding its own. There will be hurdles to overcome, including continued racial segregation at the neighborhood level. [...] But for the first time, more of the minority population in the nation's largest metropolitan areas lives in the suburbs than in the city. That is surely an important milestone on the road toward becoming a central part of the American mainstream.

NOTES

1. Reynolds and Farley and others, "Chocolate City, Vanilla Suburbs: Will the Trend toward Racially Separate Communities Continue?," *Social Science Research*, vol. 7, no. 4 (1978), pp. 319–44 (http://deepblue.lib.umich.edu/bitstream/handle/2027.42/22472/0000013.pdf?sequence=1); William H. Frey and Alden Speare Jr., *Regional and Metropolitan Growth and Decline in the United States* (New York: Russell Sage Foundation, 1988); William H. Frey and Elaine L. Fielding, "Changing Urban Populations: Regional Restructuring, Racial Polarization, and Poverty Concentration," *CityScape: A Journal of Policy Development and Research*, vol. 1, no. 2 (1995), pp. 1–38 (www.huduser.org/Periodicals/CITYSCPE/VOL1NUM2/ch1.pdf).

2. The cities and suburbs discussed in this chapter are those within the nation's 100 largest metropolitan areas. Cities pertain to the major city or cities within each metropolitan area and the suburbs pertain to the territory in the rest of the metropolitan areas. These definitions vary slightly from census definitions and are discussed in the following report, on which some of the material in this chapter is based: William H. Frey, "Melting Pot Cities and Suburbs: Racial and Ethnic Change in Metro America in the 2000s" (Brookings Metropolitan Policy Program, 2011) (www.brookings.edu/-/media/research/files/papers/2011/5/04%20census%20ethnicity%20frey/0504_census_ethnicity_frey.pdf).

3. Audrey Singer, Susan W. Hardwick, and Caroline B. Brettell, *Twenty-First Century Gateways: Immigrant Incorporation in Suburban America* (Brookings, 2008).

4. William H. Frey and Alden Speare Jr., *Regional and Metropolitan Growth and Decline in the United States* (New York: Russell Sage Foundation, 1988), appendix table E8B; Campbell Gibson and Kay Jung, "Historical Statistics on Population Totals by Race, 1790 to 1990, and by Hispanic Origin, 1970 to 1990, for Large Cities and Other Urban Places in the United States," Population Division Working Paper 76 (U.S. Census Bureau, 2005) (www.census.gov/population/www/documentation/twps0076/twps0076.html).

5. Frey and Speare, *Regional and Metropolitan Growth and Decline in the United States*, appendix table E8A; William H. Frey, "Minority Suburbanization and Continued 'White Flight' in U.S. Metropolitan Areas: Assessing Findings from the 1990 Census," Research Report 92–247 (University of Michigan Population Studies Center, 1992) (www.frey-demographer.org/reports/R1992-7_MinoritySuburbanizationWhiteFlight.pdf).

6. For example, suburban shifts in age structure and household type are discussed in William H. Frey, "The Uneven Aging and 'Younging' of America" (Brookings Metropolitan Policy Program, 2011) (www.brookings.edu/-/media/research/files/papers/2011/6/28%20census%20age%20frey/0628_census_aging_frey.pdf); William H. Frey, "Households and Families," in "State of Metropolitan America: On the Front Lines of Demographic Transformation" (Brookings Metropolitan Policy Program, 2010), pp. 90–107 (www.brookings.edu/-/media/Research/Files/Reports/2010/5/09%20metro%20america/metro_america_report.pdf).

7. Frey and Speare, *Regional and Metropolitan Growth and Decline in the United States*, appendix table E8C.

8. These statistics are based on a typology of metropolitan counties based on density and developed by the Brookings Metropolitan Policy Program. The "inner and middle suburbs" discussed in the text refer to the typology types "high-density counties" and "mature suburban counties." For definitions, see "State of Metropolitan America: On the Frontlines of Demographic Transformation," pp. 16–19.

9. Myron Orfield and Thomas Luce, "America's Racially Diverse Suburbs: Opportunities and Challenges" (University of Minnesota Law School, Institute on Metropolitan Opportunity, 2012) (www.law.umn.edu/uploads/e0/65/e065d82a1c1da0bfef7d86172ec5391e/Diverse_Suburbs_FINAL.pdf).

10. R. J. Johnston, *Urban Residential Patterns* (New York: Praeger, 1971).

11. Frey and Speare, *Regional and Metropolitan Growth and Decline in the United States*, chapters 7–11.

12. Frey, "Minority Suburbanization and Continued 'White Flight' in U.S. Metropolitan Areas.

13. Richard D. Alba and John R. Logan, "Variations on Two Themes: Racial and Ethnic Patterns in the Attainment of Suburban Residence," *Demography*, vol. 28 (1991), pp. 431–53.

14. Frey and Speare, *Regional and Metropolitan Growth and Decline in the United States*, chapters 8–10 and appendix tables E9B, E9D, and E10D.

15. Of all Asian-origin groups, Asian Indians, the group with the highest education

attainment, have the highest share of suburban residents, at 70 percent.

16. Mark Schneider and Thomas Phelan, "Black Suburbanization in the 1980s," *Demography*, vol. 30 (1993), pp. 269–79; John R. Logan, Richard D. Alba, and Wenquan Zhang, "Immigrant Enclaves and Ethnic Communities in New York and Los Angeles," *American Sociological Review*, vol. 67 (2002), pp. 299–322 (http://isites.harvard.edu/fs/docs/icb.topic.868440.files/Logan%20Immigrant%20enclavbes%20and%20thnic%20communities.pdf).

17. Orfield and Luce, "America's Racially Diverse Suburbs: Opportunities and Challenges."

DOCUMENTS FOR PART I

1.1 *THE SANITARY CONDITION OF THE LABORING POPULATION OF NEW YORK* (1845)

John H. Griscom

Source: John H. Griscom, *The Sanitary Condition of the Laboring Population of New York. With Some Suggestions for Improvement* (New York: Harper & Brothers, 1845).

EDITORS' INTRODUCTION

Along with religious missionaries, medical and civic leaders who sought to prevent epidemics by improving public health were the first to address the living conditions of the urban poor. Dr. John D. Griscom conducted the research for *The Sanitary Condition of the Laboring Population of New York* in 1844 with the assistance of other physicians and ministers throughout the city. This work was the first sanitary survey of the city, modeled after Edwin Chadwick's *Report on the Sanitary Condition of the Labouring Population of Great Britain* (1842).

The sanitary reform movement of the early nineteenth century advanced the idea that ill-health caused poverty and that disease had decidedly environmental origins. Sanitarians held that filth and decaying waste products generated miasmas or poisonous effluvium that spread illness. The solution for a healthier city was to clean sources of dirt and foul odors, particularly from damp cellars and other forms of substandard housing. Although sanitarians failed to accurately explain the origins of disease—that would happen later in the century with germ theory—they did advance the modern association between cleanliness and good health.[i]

Sanitarians also pioneered the use of social statistics as evidence to justify reform, and linked environmental factors to social behavior. In the following report, Griscom provides an explanation as to why the city's poorest residents, especially immigrants, women, and children, were its sickest. He describes in detail the specific danger of tenement houses, or multiple unit residential dwellings, which spread disease and compromised personal virtue. Griscom's recommendations for stricter sanitary and housing laws, to be enforced by a sanitary police, were decades ahead of their time. In fact, only after the formation of the Metropolitan Board of Health in 1866 was sanitation a priority for the city, and not until the Tenement House Act of 1901 did the average New Yorker experience significant improvements in their day-to-day living conditions.

THE SANITARY CONDITION OF THE LABORING POPULATION OF NEW YORK (1845)

Objects Briefly Stated

Of the three objects contemplated in the Declaration of Independence as necessary to be secured by government, the first named is "Life." Higher purposes cannot be conceived for which government should be instituted.

[...]

As upon the individual, when sick, falls an increased pecuniary burden, with (in general) a suspension of income, so upon the state or city, must rest, not only the expense of removing an unsound condition of public

---

i For an overview of the sanitary movement see, Martin V. Melosi, *The Sanitary City: Urban Infrastructure in America from Colonial Times to the Present* (Baltimore: Johns Hopkins University Press, 2000), 43–48 and 60–62.

health, but also, from the attendant loss of character, a diminution of its resources.

When individuals of the pauper class are ill, their entire support, and perchance that of the whole family, falls upon the community. From a low state of general health, whether in an individual or in numbers, proceed diminished energy of body and of mind, and a vitiated moral perception, the frequent precursor of habits and deeds, which give employment to the officers of police, and the ministers of justice.

[...]

The objects of this communication, briefly stated, are these;—1st, to show that there is an immense amount of sickness, physical disability, and premature mortality, among the poorer classes;—2d, that these are, to a large extent, unnecessary, being in a great degree the results of causes which are removable;—3d, that these physical evils are productive of moral evils of great magnitude and number, and which, if considered only in a pecuniary point of view, should arouse the government and individuals to a consideration of the best means for their relief and prevention; and 4th, to suggest the means of alleviating these evils and preventing their recurrence to so great an extent.

[...]

Distinction between Public Health and Individual Health

At all seasons of the year, there is an amount of sickness and death in this, as in all large cities, far beyond those of less densely peopled, more airy and open places, such as country residences. Even in villages of small size, there is an observable difference over the isolated country dwelling, in the proportionate amount of disease prevailing; proving conclusively that the congregation of animal and vegetable matters, with their constant effluvia, which has less chance of escape from the premises, in proportion to the absence of free circulation of air, is detrimental to the health of the inhabitants.

These circumstances have yet to be investigated in this city, as they should be. Our people, especially the more destitute, have been allowed to live out their brief lives in tainted and unwholesome atmospheres, and be subject to the silent and invisible encroachments of destructive agencies in every direction, without one warning voice being raised to point them to the danger, and without an effort to rescue them from their impending fate.

[...]

It is of course among the poorer labouring classes that such knowledge is most wanted. The rich, though they may be equally ignorant of the laws of life, and of the best means of its prevention, live in larger houses, with freer ventilation, and upon food better adapted to support health and life. Their means of obtaining greater comforts and more luxuries, are to them, though perhaps unconsciously, the very reason for their prolonged lives.

[...]

The investigations...so necessary and desirable for this city, have been carried on in other countries, with a degree of enthusiasm, sustained by talent and learning, which does honor to Philanthropy. No one can rise from the perusal of the works of Edwin Chadwick of London, or of Parent Du Chatelet of Paris, or of many others who have laboured in this field of humanity, with out feeling a portion of the ardor which inspires them, and wishing he had been thrown into the same pursuit, that some of the leaves of the same laurel might encircle his own brow.[1] It is in the cause of Humanity, of the poor, the destitute, the degraded, of the virtuous made vicious by the force of circumstances, which they are now investigating, and exposing to the knowledge of others.

It is often said that "one half of the world does not know how the other half lives." The labor of raising the veil which now separates the two halves, by which the misery and degradation of the one, have been concealed from the view of the other, has been theirs and their associates. Howard,[2] called by distinction *the Philanthropist*, revealed to the gaze of the astonished multitude the interior of the prisons of England, and straightaway the process of reform commenced in them, and continued until the prison system of the present day, has become one the most striking examples of the spirit of the times. But Chadwick and Du Chatelet, especially the former, are diving still deeper into the subject of moral and physical reform. They are probing to the bottom the foul ulcers upon the body of society, and endeavoring to discover the causes of so much wretchedness and vice, which fill the prisons and the work-houses. Howard's labours tended to *cure* the disease, Chadwick's to *prevent* it.

[...]

System of Tenantage of the Poor

The tenements, in order to admit a greater number of families, are divided into small apartments, as numerous as decency will admit. Regard to comfort, convenience, and health, is the last motive... These closets, for they deserve no better name, are then rented to the poor, from week to week, or month to month, the rent being almost invariably required in advance, at least for the first few terms. The families moving in first, after the house is built, find it clean, but the lessee has no supervision over their habits, and however filthy the tenement may become, he cares not, so that he receives his rent.

[...]

In these places, filth is allowed to accumulate to an extent almost incredible. Hiring their rooms for short periods only, it is very common to find the poor tenants moving from place to place, every few weeks. By this practice they avoid the trouble of cleaning their rooms, as they can leave behind them the dirt which they have made. The same room, being occupied in rapid succession, by tenant after tenant, it will easily be seen how the walls and windows will become broken, the doors and floors become injured, the chimneys filled with soot, the whole premises populated thickly with vermin, the stairway, the common passage of several families, the receptacle for all things noxious, and whatever of self-respect the family might have had, be crushed under the pressure of the degrading circumstances by which they are surrounded.

[...]

Ventilation—Amount of Air Necessary for Each Person

We now naturally come, in the course of this inquiry, to two important questions, preparatory to the suggestion I intend to make, of remedy for these evils.

1. What is the effect of this degraded and filthy manner of life upon the health of the individuals, and the duration of their lives?
2. What is the influence upon their morals, their self-respect, and appreciation of virtue?

The answers to these queries must have an important bearing upon the moral obligations, the pecuniary expenses, and the order and character of the City Government. If it can be shown that much sickness and many premature deaths are the results of these residences, it will be evident that the care of the sick, and the support of the widows and orphans, must add greatly to the expenses of the city; and it can be proved that degraded habits, bad associations, and immoral practices (through the results only of circumstances, and not of education) are their consequences, it will be equally apparent, there will thus be continued, a class in the community more difficult to govern, more disposed to robbery, mobs, and other lawless acts, and less accessible to the influences of religious and moral instruction.

With regard to the first question, an argument can hardly be necessary. Almost everyone can recall to mind, some proof of the effects of nauseous odors, of the inhalation of foul air, or of sleeping in a small confined apartment, upon his own health and feelings. These effects may have only been temporary, but they serve to show that a prolonged continuance of them, must, in reason, produce permanently bad results upon the continuance of mental and corporeal powers.... Every city resident who takes a stroll into the country, can testify to the difference between the atmosphere of the two situations:—the contrast of our

out-door (to say nothing of the in-door) atmosphere, loaded with the animal and vegetable exhalations of our streets, yards, sinks, and cellars—and the air of the mountains, rivers, and grassy plains, needs no epicurean lungs to detect it.
[...]

Number of Sick Paupers—Greater Proportion Females

If the habitations of damp, dark cellars, and of narrow alleys and courts, and the breathing of a vitiated atmosphere, are *rightly* asserted to be promotive of disease, then the most subject to these causes should be sick in the greatest numbers. Now the *male* part of this class breathe a totally different air throughout the day, and their labors in the streets, along the rivers, or upon buildings, and *only at night* are they subject to the worse atmosphere.... One the other hand, *the females, both day and night*, inhale the polluted atmosphere of the dwellings, and are more continually under all the other bad influences of their unfortunate situations.

Do the official results correspond with these premises?

It will be seen upon examining the Dispensary[3] returns, that in some years the proportion of female to males, prescribed for at the Dispensaries, has been 12 to 10 1/2 –in others, 12 to 8 1/2, and in one instance 19 to 11. This comparison is rendered more striking when we take into account the greater amount of intemperance among the males.

The Annual Reports of the City Inspector[4] show that nearly one-half the deaths caused by consumption[5] are of the *foreign part of the population*, and that more than *one-third* the whole number of deaths are of foreigners. Such an immense disproportion can only be accounted for on the supposition that some extraordinary cause of death prevail among the strangers who come to reside among us. Now it is pretty well ascertained fact, that a large majority of the cellar and court population of this city consists of persons of foreign birth and their children. Of the Dispensary patients, about 60 *per cent* are natives of other countries, and if it were possible to ascertain the parentage of the children receiving aid from these institutions, we should find a larger portion than this directly dependent upon foreigners.
[...]

Answer from Reverend Isaac Orchard

In one of these houses, in a garret, with sloping roof and low ceiling, one small, broken window, no bedstead, nor other bedding than a few bundle of rags upon the floor, I have found three families of men, women, and children: there they lived, and there they all slept. Now, if a woman accustomed to humble life, or decent poverty, be constrained to remove to such a place, what must be the effect on her mind, morals, and her habits? At first, she will recoil from undressing in the presence of a strange man, but soon she will do it without a blush. Is she a wife? There are other wives and their husbands in the room, without even a curtain to hide the most private transactions. That which transpires cannot be unobserved, though seeking the darkest recess, and soon it will be imitated without secrecy and without scruple. Children too will see them, and think, and imitate—and thus become depraved in their thoughts, desires, and practices. Can any one doubt that there must be a rapid declension in morals, in both parents and children?
[...]

Suggestion of a New Arrangement for, and Proper Duties of a Sanitary Police

From what has been related respecting the effects of the habitations of the poor, upon their health, viz., 1st, the living in damp, dark, underground, and other ill-ventilated apartments. 2d. The dirty and injured condition of the floors, walls, yards, and other parts of the premises. 3d. The crowding too many persons in single rooms of inadequate size and accommodations. To correct the first of these evils, there appears but one way, and that is to place all the dwellings of the city under the inspection of competent officers, who shall have the power *to enforce the law of domiciliary cleanliness*. For this purpose, those places known or suspected to be kept usually in improper condition, should be visited periodically, say once in one, two, or three months. The law should be so arranged as to make cleaning bear upon the owner or lessee, and not upon the tenant directly, who is generally so poor, as to be unable to perform the necessary purgation and rectification of the premises.

[...]

The effect of such a law upon the habits of the tenant would not be *direct*,—his personal condition can only be reached by moral law,—but the landlord, under this compulsory process, urged by the fear of having his premises out-lawed would, in letting them, stipulate with his tenants to keep them clean, to whitewash the walls and ceilings, wash the floors, remove the collections of dirt and garbage, and keep the yards and cellars in good order. And knowing that the health officer will pay them frequent visits, armed with the power of the law, it is altogether reasonable to suppose that the tenants themselves would be stimulated to maintain a better appearance of person and domicils—that many would feel a pride in a good and cleanly aspect—that the smothered feelings of self-respect, love of praise, and desire for the comforts of cleanliness, would, in hundreds of bosoms, be re-awakened into life and energy.

NOTES

1. Edwin Chadwick was an English sanitary reformer who also advocated for changes in Britain's poor laws. Alexandre Parent Duch-âtlet, was a French public health theorist who worked on the sewers of Paris and prostitution.
2. John Howard (1726–1790), noted British reformer who toured Europe examining prisons and advocating for the single-cell method of incarceration. His most famous work, *The State of the Prisons* was originally published in 1777.
3. Dispensaries were clinics that provided health care for people at little or no cost. Griscom uses numbers from the Northern, Eastern, and New York Dispensaries.
4. The City Inspector was New York's chief public health officer until the creation of the Metropolitan Board of Health in 1866.
5. Common nineteenth century term for tuberculosis.

1.2 *HULL-HOUSE, A SOCIAL SETTLEMENT* (1894)

Jane Addams and Ellen Gates Starr

Source: Jane Addams and Ellen Gates Starr, *Hull-House, A Social Settlement at 225 Halsted Street, Chicago: An Outline-Sketch*, 1894. Courtesy of the Newberry Library, Chicago, Illinois.

EDITORS' INTRODUCTION

In 1894, Jane Addams (1860–1935) and Ellen Gates Starr (1859–1940), published a slim volume to explain the settlement house they had founded in Chicago in the fall of 1889. The authors related the settlement concept itself and the activities of the house in great detail. The booklet discusses the extension classes offered at the house, the working people's chorus, working girls club, on-going lectures, women's club, children's dinner club, medical services, labor bureau, and a host of other activities. Jane Addams, a graduate of Rockford Female Seminary (Illinois) was a noted progressive-era reformer and perhaps the best known woman of her day. Addams and Starr's 1888 visit to London's Toynbee Hall inspired them to found Hull-House, wherein people interested in social change lived within the neighborhood they hoped to change in the United States, and Hull-House provided a model for other communities. Addams' numerous articles and well received books, including *Hull-House Maps and Papers* (1895), *Democracy and Social Ethics* (1902), *Newer Ideals of Peace* (1907), *Spirit of Youth and the City Streets* (1909), *Twenty Years at Hull-House* (1910), *A New Conscience and an Ancient Evil* (1912), *The Long Road of Women's Memory* (1916), *Peace and Bread in Time of War* (1922), and *The Second Twenty Years at Hull-House* (1930), brought her ideas and reflections on her experiences to an eager audience. Jane Addams was awarded the Nobel Peace Prize in 1931.[i]

HULL-HOUSE, A SOCIAL SETTLEMENT (1894)

The two original residents of Hull-House are entering upon their fifth year of settlement in the 19th Ward. They publish this outline that the questions daily asked by neighbors and visitors may be succinctly answered. It necessarily takes somewhat the character of a report, but is much less formal. It aims not so much to give an account of what has been accomplished, as to suggest what may be done by and through a neighborhood of working people, when they are touched by a common stimulus and possess an intellectual and social centre about which they may group their various organizations and enterprises. This centre or 'settlement' to be effective must contain an element of permanency, so that the neighborhood may feel that the interest and fortunes of the residents are identical with their own. The settlement must have an enthusiasm for the possibilities of its locality, and an ability to bring into it and develop from it those lines of thought and action which make for the 'higher life.'

The original residents came to Hull-House with a conviction that social intercourse could best express the growing sense of the economic unity of society. They wished the social spirit to be the undercurrent of the life of Hull-House, whatever direction the stream might take.

All the details were left for the demands of the neighborhood to determine, and each department has grown from a discovery made through natural and reciprocal social relations. [. . .]

Ward Book and Maps

A ward book has been kept by the residents for two years in which have been noted matters of sociological interest found in the ward. Many instances of the sweating evil and child labor have been recorded as well as unsanitary tenements. A resident has charted the information collected during the slum investigation in the form of two sets of maps, one set on the plan of Charles Booth's wage maps of London and one set showing the nationalities of the district. The latter indicates nineteen different nationalities within the third of a square mile lying east and south of Hull-House. Arrangements have been made for the publication of these maps with a series of papers written by the residents.

After the passage of the factory and workshop bill, which includes a clause limiting women's labor to eight hours a day, the young women employés [sic] in a large factory in the near neighborhood of Hull-House formed an EIGHT HOUR CLUB for the purpose of encouraging women in factories and workshops to obey the eight-hour law.

---

i Victoria Bissell Brown, "Jane Addams," 14–22, and Jennifer L. Bosch, "Ellen Gates Starr," 838–842, in Rima Lunin Schultz and Adele Hast, eds., *Women Building Chicago, 1790–1990* (Bloomington: Indiana University Press, 2001).

1.3 THE ENVIRONMENT OF THE NEGRO (1899)

W.E.B. DuBois

Source: W.E.B. DuBois, *The Philadelphia Negro: A Social Study* (Philadelphia: The University of Pennsylvania Press, 1899).

EDITORS' INTRODUCTION

Published in 1899, *The Philadelphia Negro: A Social Study* was a pioneering work in the scholarly documentation and analysis of cities. Its author, William Edward Burghardt (W.E.B.) Dubois, was trained in social science at the University of Berlin and became the first African American to earn a Ph.D. from Harvard University. Part social history, part urban ethnography, and part statistical portrait, *The Philadelphia Negro* was one of the first reports to employ what were then cutting-edge methods of social research. While today *The Philadelphia Negro* is widely regarded as an important contribution to the evolution of social science, and its author one of the founders of American sociology, the work did not have an immediate or as large an impact as it should within the white dominated academic community. **[See Essay 1.1, Steven H. Corey and Lisa Krissoff Boehm, "Examining America's Urban Landscape; From Social Reform to Social History, and Back."]**

The Philadelphia Negro covered the overall condition of the roughly 40,000 African Americans who resided in that city at the end of the nineteenth century, most especially their geographic distribution, occupations, daily life, residences, organizations, and relation to the more populous white citizens. DuBois saw segregation as the central problem for blacks in Philadelphia and other U.S. cities, given that they were excluded from the larger social group. In this respect, he compared blacks to other unassimilated groups, notably Jews and Italians. However, the segregation of African Americans was more conspicuously interwoven within the long history of the United States. As is contended throughout *The American Urban Reader*, racial issues have played a central role in the evolution of the American nation and its cities. A product of its time, DuBois used the term "Negro" to denote all persons of African ancestry. In a precursor to his later years as an activist, he chose to capitalize the word as matter of principle.

The purpose of the study was to provide a "safe guide" towards solving many so-called "Negro problems" facing American cities. DuBois intended the results of his survey to constitute the scientific basis of further study and practical reform. In terms of methodology, DuBois conducted house-to-house canvasing of the Seventh Ward, a center of Philadelphia's black community where he and his wife temporarily resided. He created a series of schedules (uniform questionnaires) asking residents about place of birth, family size, conjugal state, employment status, and wages. As noted in the document, DuBois also discussed the residential movement of Philadelphia's black population within the city, and the layout and conditions of their housing.

THE ENVIRONMENT OF THE NEGRO (1899)

Houses and Rent

[...] The rents paid by the Negroes are without doubt far above their means and often from one-fourth to three-fourths of the total income of a family goes in rent. This leads to much non-payment of rent both intentional and unintentional, to frequent shifting of homes, and above all to stinting the families in many necessities of life in order to live in respectable dwellings. Many a Negro family eats less than it ought for the sake of living in a decent house.

Some of this waste of money in rent is sheer ignorance and carelessness. The Negroes have an inherited distrust of banks and companies, and have long neglected to take part in Building and Loan Associations. Others are simply careless in the spending of their money and lack the shrewdness and business sense of differently trained peoples. Ignorance and carelessness however will not explain all or even the greater part of the problem of rent among Negroes. There are three causes of even greater importance: these are the limited localities where Negroes may rent, the peculiar connection of dwelling and occupation among Negroes and the social organization of the Negro. The undeniable fact that most Philadelphia white people prefer not to live near Negroes[1] limits the Negro very seriously in his choice of a home and especially in the choice of a cheap home. Moreover, real estate agents knowing the limited supply usually raise the rent a dollar or two for Negro tenants, if they do not refuse them altogether. Again, the occupations which the Negro follows, and which at present time is compelled to follow, are of a sort that makes it necessary for him to live near the best portions of the city; the mass of Negroes are in the economic world purveyors to the rich—working in private houses, in hotels, large stores, etc.[2] In order to keep this work they must live nearby; the laundress cannot bring her Spruce Street family's clothes from the Thirtieth Ward, nor can the waiter at the Continental Hotel lodge in Germantown. With the mass of white workmen this same necessity of living near work, does not hinder them from getting cheap dwellings; the factory is surrounded by cheap cottages, the foundry by long rows of houses, and even the white clerk and shop girl can, on account of their hours of labor, afford to live further out in the suburbs than the black porter who opens the store. Thus it is clear that the nature of the Negro's work compels him to crowd into the center of the city much

more than is the case with the mass of white working people. At the same time this necessity is apt in some cases to be overestimated, and a few hours of sleep or convenience serve to persuade a good many families to endure poverty in the Seventh Ward when they might be comfortable in the Twenty-fourth Ward. Nevertheless much of the Negro problem in this city finds adequate explanation when we reflect that here is a people receiving a little lower wages than usual for less desirable work, and compelled, in order to do that work, to live in a little less pleasant quarters than most people, and pay for them somewhat higher rents.

The final reason of the concentration of Negroes in certain localities is a social one and one peculiarly strong: the life of the Negroes of the city has for years centred in the Seventh Ward; here are the old churches, St. Thomas', Bethel, Central, Shiloh and Wesley; here are the halls of the secret societies; here are the homesteads of old families. To a race socially ostracised it means far more to move to remote parts of a city, than to those who will in any part of the city easily form congenial acquaintances and new ties. The Negro who ventures away from the mass of his people and their organized life, finds himself alone, shunned and taunted, stared at and made uncomfortable; he can make few new friends, for his neighbors however well-disposed would shrink to add a Negro to their list of acquaintances. Thus he remains far from friends and the concentred social life of the church, and feels in all its bitterness what it means to be a social outcast. Consequently emigration from the ward has gone in groups and centred itself about some church, and individual initiative is thus checked. At the same time color prejudice makes it difficult for groups to find suitable places to move to—one Negro family would be tolerated where six would be objected to; thus we have here a very decisive hindrance to emigration to the suburbs.

It is not surprising that this situation leads to considerable crowding in the homes, i.e., to the endeavor to get as many people into the space hired as possible. It is this crowding that gives the casual observer many false notions as to the size of Negro families, since he often forgets that every other house has its sub-renters and lodgers. It is however difficult to measure this crowding on account of this very lodging system which makes it very often uncertain as to just the number of rooms a given group of people occupy.

Sections and Wards

The historic centre of Negro settlement in the city [... is] at Sixth and Lombard. From this point it moved north, as is indicated for instance by the establishment of Zoar Church in 1794. Immigration of foreigners and the rise of industries, however, early began to turn it back and it found outlet in the alleys of Southwark and Moyamensing. For a while about 1840 it was bottled up here, but finally it began to move west. A few early left the mass and settled in West Philadelphia; the rest began a slow steady movement along Lombard street. The influx of 1876 and thereafter sent the wave across Broad street to a new centre at Seventeenth and Lombard. There it divided into two streams; one went north and joined remnants of the old settlers in the Northern Liberties and Spring Garden. The other went south to the Twenty-sixth, Thirtieth and Thirty-sixth Wards. Meantime the new immigrants poured in at Seventh and Lombard, while Sixth and Lombard down to the Delaware was deserted to the Jews, and Moyamensing partially to the Italians. The Irish were pushed on beyond Eighteenth to the Schuylkill, or emigrated to the mills of Kensington and elsewhere. [...]

This migration explains much that is paradoxical about Negro slums, especially their present remnant at Seventh and Lombard. Many people wonder that the mission and reformatory agencies at work there for so many years have so little to show by way of results. One answer is that this work has new material continually to work upon, while the best classes move to the west and leave the dregs behind. The parents and grandparents of some of the best families of Philadelphia Negroes were born in the neighborhood of Sixth and Lombard at a time when all Negroes, good, bad and indifferent, were confined to that and a few other localities. With the greater freedom of domicile which has since come, these slum districts have sent a stream of emigrants westward. There has, too, been a general movement from the alleys to the streets and from the back to the front streets. Moreover it is untrue that the slums of Seventh and Lombard have not greatly changed in character; compared with 1840, 1850 or even 1870 these slums are much improved in every way. More and more every year the unfortunate and poor are being sifted out from the vicious and criminal and sent to better quarters.

And yet with all the obvious improvement, there are still slums and dangerous slums left. Of the Fifth Ward and adjoining parts of the Seventh, a city health inspector says:

"Few of the houses are underdrained, and if the closets have sewer connections the people are too careless to keep them in order. The streets and alleys are strewn with garbage, excepting immediately after the visit of the street cleaner. Penetrate into one of these houses and beyond into the back yard, if there is one (frequently there is not), and there will be found a pile of ashes, garbage and filth, the accumulation of the winter, perhaps of the whole year. In such heaps of refuse what disease germ may be breeding?"[3]

To take a typical case:

"Gillis' Alley, famed in the Police Court, is a narrow alley, extending from Lombard Street through to South Street, above Fifth Street, cobbled and without sewer connections. Houses and stables are mixed promiscuously. Buildings are of frame and of brick. No. — looks both outside and in like a Southern Negro's cabin. In this miserable place four colored families have their homes. The aggregate rent demanded is $22 a month, though the owner seldom receives the full rent. For three small dark rooms in the rear of another house in this alley, the

Some Alleys Where Negroes Live.

	Govett's Court.	Hines' Court.	Allen's Court.	Horstman's Court.	Lombard Row.	Turner's Court.	Alley off Carver Street.	McCann's Court.	Cross Alley.
General Character....	Poor.	Poor.	Very Poor.	Squalid.	Fair.	Wretched.	Fair.	Poor.	Bad.
Width, in feet	3	3–6	6	12	9	3–12	6	12	12
Paved with	Bricks.	Bricks.	Bricks.	Bricks.	Bricks.	Bricks.	Bricks.	Bricks.	Asphalt.
Character of Dwelling ...	Poor.	Back Yard Tenements	Back Yard Tenements	Back Yard Tenements	Fair.	Old Wooden Houses.	Old Brick Tenements	Old Brick Tenements	Wood and Brick.
Number of Stories in Houses	3	3	3	2 and 3	3	1 to 3.	3	2 to 3.	2 to 3.
Inhabitants	All Negroes.	All Negroes.	All Negroes.	All Negroes.	Negroes and Jews.	All Negroes.	Jews and Negroes.	All Negroes.	Jews and Negroes.
Cleanliness, etc......	Fair.	Fair.	Dirty.	Dirty.	Fair.	Fair.	Fair.	Fair.	Dirty.
Width of Sidewalk ..feet.	4	5	6	None.	None.	None.	None.	None.	None.
Lighted by	No Lights.	No Lights.	No Lights.	1 Gas Lamp.	1 Gas Lamp.	1 Gas Lamp.	1 Gas Lamp.	1 Gas Lamp.	No Lights.
Privies in Common or Private	Common.	2 for whole Alley.	½ for each House.	5 in open Court.	Private.	Common.	Common.	Common.	Common.
Remarks.		Emigrants from 5th Ward slums.	Poor and Doubtful Characters.	Very Poor People.	Respectable Homes mingled with Gamblers and Prostitutes.	Many Empty Houses; Poor and Doubtful People.	"Blind" Alley; Fairly Respectable.	Poor People and some Questionable.	Some Bad Characters.

tenants pay, and have paid for thirteen years, $11 a month. The entrance is by a court not over two feet wide. Except at midday the sun does not shine in the small open space in the rear that answers for a yard. It is safe to say that not one house in this alley could pass an inspection without being condemned as prejudicial to health. But if they are so condemned and cleaned, with such inhabitants how long will they remain clean?"[4]

Some of the present characteristics of the chief alleys where Negroes live are given in the [...] table [see p. 62].

The general characteristics and distribution of the Negro population at present in the different wards can only be indicated in general terms. The wards with the best Negro population are parts of the Seventh, Twenty-sixth, Thirtieth and Thirty-sixth, Fourteenth, Fifteenth, Twenty-fourth, Twenty-seventh and Twenty-ninth. The worst Negro population is found in parts of the Seventh, and in the Fourth, Fifth and Eighth. In the other wards either the classes are mixed or there are very few colored people. The tendency of the best migration to-day is toward the Twenty-sixth, Thirtieth and Thirty-sixth Wards, and West Philadelphia.

NOTES

1. The sentiment has greatly lessened in intensity during the last two decades, but it is still strong.
2. At the same time, from long custom and from competition, their wages for this work are not high.
3. Dr. Frances Van Gasken in a tract published by the Civic Club.
4. *Ibid.*

Illustration I.1 Senator Tillman's Allegorical Cow, 1896 (revised 1913). Source: Congressional Record: The Proceedings and Debates of the *Sixty-Third Congress, First Session* (Washington, D.C.: Government Printing Office) 50-Part 6 (October 1913).

The deep distrust between rural and urban America during the late nineteenth and early twentieth centuries is reflected in this cartoon conceived by the outspoken United States Senator Benjamin R. Tillman (Democrat, South Carolina). In 1896, Tillman commissioned artist Tom Fleming to depict Wall Street bankers symbolically milking a cow fed on the produce of southern and western farmers. Supporters of William Jennings Bryan, who was both the Democratic Party and Populist Party nominee for president in 1896, handed out millions of copies of the allegorical cow during the election. Republican William McKinley won the election in large measure due to the support of urban industrial voters. The cow cartoon reappeared when Bryan ran for president again in 1900 and 1908; making it one of the most widely circulated cartoons in American history.

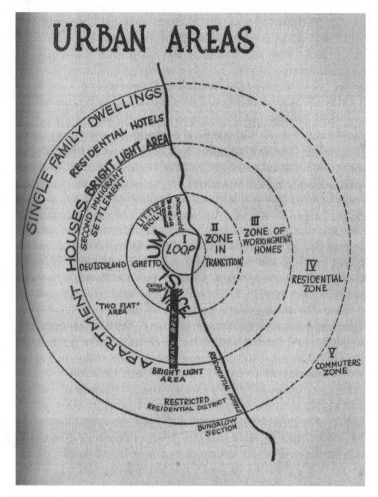

Illustration I.2 Ernest W. Burgess, Urban Areas, 1925. Source: Robert E. Park, Ernest W. Burgess, and Roderick D. McKenzie, *The City* (Chicago: The University of Chicago Press, 1925).

Perhaps the most famous diagram in social science, Ernest W. Burgess' "Urban Areas," known more commonly as the concentric zone model, accompanied his seminal chapter "The Growth of the City: An Introduction to a Research Project," in the 1925 book *The City* co-authored with his colleagues from the University of Chicago. "The Growth of a City" sought to explain the relationship between social growth and the physical expansion in the typical industrial American metropolitan region. To illustrate the process of city expansion, Burgess superimposed five zones (identified within the concentric rings) over the rough borders and principle features of the city of Chicago and outlying suburbs. Burgess argued that as cities grow, a distribution process sifts, sorts, and relocates people by residence and occupation. The main characteristic of this expansion is the succession process—a concept borrowed from plant ecology—wherein inner zones expand into and invade each bordering outer zone. The result is a differentiation in urban areas based on "natural" economic and cultural groupings that give cities their unique character (as identified in the model above with labels like "The Loop," "The Black Belt," and "Chinatown" in locations specific to Chicago).

PART II

PRE-COLUMBIAN AND EUROPEAN FOUNDATIONS

EDITORS' INTRODUCTION TO PART II

The United States was a product of urbanization long before the majority of its people lived in cities. From the beginning of colonial settlement, people lived in and depended upon urban configurations of all sizes for protection as well as economic, political, and social interaction. Even before the arrival of Europeans, some Native Americans lived in urban settlements. Although the highest percentage of colonial settlers living in an urban area peaked at just ten percent in 1690, cities played a critical role and exerted a disproportionate influence over European and American settlement of the North American continent. The essays and documents in this part describe principle features of city building and characteristics of urban life during this foundational colonial period, with first-hand accounts and innovative scholarship by historians writing in the twentieth century.

This part begins with an excerpt from our 2015 book, *America's Urban History* (New York: Routledge, 2015). In this narrative urban history of the pre-colonial, colonial, and national history of the United States, we place new importance in understanding the history of Native American settlements in North America. Etzanoa and Cahokia alter our conception of Native American life. Because these cities were not known to most European explorers (with notable exception of the Spanish example) [see Document 2.1], the impressively-sized communities did not make their way into urban history until now.

Fittingly, we then examine the history of Spanish colonization, as the Spanish were the first group to create European-style urban settlements in North America. San Juan, Puerto Rico was founded in 1521 and St. Augustine, Florida, in 1565. The Spanish established their way of life and world view in new places by using these colonial cities as cultural, political, and religious anchors. The approach they took to colonialism is still evident on the physical and cultural landscape. David J. Weber's engaging selection works as a corrective to the colonial history that many of us were taught, which typically seemed to start and stop with English settlers and focused on New England.

The First Earl of Shaftesbury, Ashley Cooper, decreed that the English way of life be established in the colony of Carolina via city building, and he commanded the settlers in his colony to "plant in towns." Historian Emma Hart presents the story of Charleston and the city's importance as a key colonial city in the South. Remember the Native American urban story, the Spanish cities, and the establishment of southern urban centers when addressing the documents in Part III, "From British to American Cities."

The documents in this part reflect the urban attitudes and assumptions of European and American-born white men. In 1601, Spanish colonial Governor Don Juan de Oñate encountered a large Native American settlement made up of approximately 2,000 dwellings, each housing families of an estimated ten people. Spanish guides and a captured Native American known only as Miguel both documented the existence of this large

Indian settlement. The written records seemed the stuff of myth until recent archaeological findings and clearer translations of the Spanish documents have led scholars to rethink earlier assumptions. Another traveler's impressions, this time of the remains of ancient Indian mounds of Cahokia, east of modern-day St. Louis, are provided in the form of a letter by Henry M. Brackenridge to Thomas Jefferson in 1813. Though abandoned long before the first European explorers and settlers arrived in the region, Cahokia was at one time the heart of an expansive Native American trading network that archeologists estimated contained 35,000 or more people. The third document is an excerpt from John Winthrop's "A Model of Christian Charity"—better known as the "City Upon A Hill" sermon —given in 1630 to fellow Puritans migrants on their way to settling Boston in the Massachusetts Bay Colony. Next is a description of Philadelphia's early years by Dr. Benjamin Bullivant, who traveled from Boston to Delaware and back in 1697. "An Act for Establishing Ports and Towns" (1705) examines a portion of the General Town Acts and the importance of creating urban areas in the colonial Chesapeake.

ESSAY 2.1

Pre-Colonial and Seventeenth-Century Native American Settlements

Lisa Krissoff Boehm and Steven H. Corey

Revised from the original essay. Source: Lisa Krissoff Boehm and Steven H. Corey, *America's Urban History* (New York: Routledge, 2015), 17–41.

EDITORS' INTRODUCTION

In 2015, Lisa Krissoff Boehm and Steven H. Corey published a narrative history of American cities, from pre-colonial times to the present. This essay, which is the first chapter in the book, has been updated to take into account more recent archaeological and scholarly findings regarding settlements built by Native Americans prior to the European colonization of North America.

Lisa Krissoff Boehm is Dean of the College of Graduate Studies at Bridgewater State University. She is the author of *Popular Culture and the Enduring Myth of Chicago* and *Making a Way out of No Way: African American Women and the Second Great Migration*. With Steven H. Corey, she is co-author of *America's Urban History* and co-author of *The American Urban Reader: History and Theory*. She has served as guest editor of and written for the *Journal of Urban History*.

Steven H. Corey is Dean of the School Liberal Arts and Sciences and Professor of History at Columbia College Chicago. He has written for *Environmental Ethics*, *PS: Political Science and Politics*, and the *Journal of Urban History* and was research curator for the noted public history exhibit *Garbage! The History and Politics of Trash in New York City*. With Lisa Krissoff Boehm, he is co-author of *America's Urban History* and co-editor of *The American Urban Reader: History and Theory*.

PRE-COLONIAL AND SEVENTEENTH-CENTURY NATIVE AMERICAN SETTLEMENTS

Introduction: Indigenous Footprints

Urban settlements in the continental United States date back at least fourteen hundred years, and the fundamental relationships and processes that comprise urbanization even longer. Traditional American history survey textbooks and even urban history narratives, though, rarely mention Native American communities or relegate them to a few preliminary pages in order to contrast indigenous ways of life with dramatic transformations brought about by contact with Europeans.

Our understanding of American urban history is enriched when we consider in more detail the story of populous Native American settlements such as the city of Cahokia in the American Midwest, the Iroquois and Algonquin longhouses in the Northeast, and the canyon dwellings of the Southwest. This essay argues that Europeans did not encounter a land unencumbered by its own history—a land shaped by diverse peoples living in varying patterns of settlement. In fact, Europeans benefited greatly by launching their colonial ventures in regions in which Native Americans had already cleared ground, established fruitful patterns of interaction with natural resources, and forged economic partnerships. This Native American community building provided colonialists with an infrastructure that later begat immense mercantile wealth.

Although urban communities created by American Indians (we use the terms Native American and American Indian interchangeably throughout this essay) did not evolve in a straightforward manner, without interruption, into present-day cities, examining their history informs the evolution of the built environment in the United States. In terms of physical appearance, Native American settlements were often dissimilar, having been constructed by different peoples over different periods of time, and in regions as physically dissimilar as the rocky, arid landscape of the Southwest and the dense forests of the Northeast. The most populous communities, though, shared certain characteristics common not only with each other, but also with urban forms found throughout the world regardless of historical epoch. And while pre-colonial or pre-Columbian (meaning before European contact) settlements are interesting and historically important in their own right, they also resonate in contemporary American culture. U.S. cities and suburbs are grounded, literally, in the society and physical landscape fashioned from the interaction of European and native peoples.

Historian Coll Thrush finds Seattle, Washington to be a prime example of how American cities have historical roots in Native American places. As Thrush asserts, "Every American city is built on Indian land, but few advertise it like Seattle." Thrush notes that Seattle is reputedly a haunted city, with stories circulating about how a white settler, Joshua Winfield, built his home directly on top of a Native American cemetery and later died of fright from ghosts in 1874. For Thrush:

> in Seattle, visitors and residents alike tell and are told stories about this city: that it is built on Indian land, that that land was taken to build a great metropolis, and that such a taking is commemorated by the city's Native American imagery. These stories in and of place, these place-stories, define Seattle with an indigenous pedigree.[1]

Millions of Native Americans perished post-European contact, a fact we will explore at length later in the essay. Yet Native Americans and their culture, while mightily reduced in numbers, persisted post-European contact, albeit not with the same access to land and undoubtedly effected by prevailing cultural forces. American Indians did not disappear the moment Europeans arrived and appropriated their land; they have remained a part of the cultural, economic, political, and social fabric of villages, towns, cities, suburbs, and rural communities scattered throughout North America. Native Americans responded to change brought about by contact with Europeans by modifying their physical surroundings and social structure in order to preserve as much agency over their way of life as possible. Such adjustments also included the adaptation, to one degree or another, of European commodities, religion, and standards of living. During the seventeenth century, some Native Americans even joined so-called "praying Indian towns" or villages in New England organized by Protestant ministers and laid-out like English settlements. These praying towns ultimately failed to convert and assimilate large numbers of American Indians into Christian culture or to protect those who did join from English colonists who coveted their land. These praying communities, like indigenous ones before them, gave way to subsequent generations of European settlers and their descendants who built modern towns and cities over the foundations of a Native American past.

Academics and the Origins of Urbanization in the New World

There was a time when even preeminent of American historians argued that since there were no written documents from pre-contact Native Americans, their history could not be told. In 1965, Samuel Eliot Morison noted in *The Oxford History of the American People* that, "When we try to tell the story of man in America from the beginning, the lack of data quickly brings us to a halt.... Thus what we mean by the history of the American People is the history in America of immigrants from other continents."[2] Fortunately, with the evolution of Native American history as a subfield within the historical profession and the rise of interdisciplinary studies throughout academia in general, American history surveys now begin with a discussion of those inhabitants who were native to North America by the time of Columbus' arrival in the "New World." Contemporary scholars use several terms to describe indigenous North Americans and their descendants, the most common being Native Americans, American Indians or Amerindians, aboriginals, indigenous or first peoples, and, in the case of Canada, even more specified terms such as members of the First Nations. European explorers and colonists, though, still enter the story in history textbooks very quickly. This brief reference to native people and their culture is what Native American scholar Vine Deloria, Jr. terms the "cameo theory of history."[3]

The tendency to dash past American Indians in history surveys is changing. Historians are now more comfortable in drawing upon the conceptual framework and methodologies of scholars outside their discipline to discuss aboriginal cultures. Archaeologists and anthropologists in particular have been useful for historians in addressing the formation and structure of pre-Columbian American Indian communities. In addition, new trends in historical research methodologies, including an increasing reliance on oral history to capture otherwise untold tales, the use of folklore, and the integration of visual artifacts within traditional scholarship, have allowed all scholars to move past the exclusive use of written records.

The intellectual underpinnings informing the study of Native Americans and their culture have also changed significantly over the last few generations to enhance our understanding of an indigenous urban past. Not surprisingly, scholars in the nineteenth and early twentieth centuries commonly viewed American Indians and their communities as "exotic" and "different," ranking these cultures several notches below the "civilization" created by white Europeans; and hence unlikely to have ever established advanced urban centers and ways of life. Attitudes in the academy progressed after the Second World War, particularly during the 1960s and 1970s alongside the "Red Power" movement in the United States that was analogous to the better-known fight for civil rights for African Americans. What came to be known as the "new Indian history" sought to recast Native Americans on their own terms rather than as victims of abuse who suffered genocide at the hands of Europeans and their descendants. This new history emphasized that native peoples were motivated by their own unique cultural patterns that adapted to change over time.[4]

As with pre-colonial American Indian culture, historians also rely upon the work of scholars outside their discipline to determine what makes a place urban. In terms of classifying ancient settlements as "cities," the most influential line of reasoning remains that set forth by V. Gordon Childe, an Australian archaeologist, in his seminal 1950 *Town Planning Review* article, titled "The Urban Revolution." Childe conceived of human development in four distinct stages: Paleolithic, Neolithic, urban, and industrial. Childe's four stages are bridged by three revolutions—the Neolithic, which brought settled agriculture, the Urban Revolution, which saw the concentration of population in the first cities and the rise of manufacturing and trade, and the Industrial Revolution, in which human and animal power were replaced by alternate sources of energy that fueled complex machines. Childe traces the earliest cities to the settlements around the Tigris and Euphrates Rivers in what is commonly termed the "Fertile Crescent" in modern day Iraq around 4000 BCE ("before the common era," also known as BC for "before Christ"). However, other arguments can be made that trace cities back even further to places like Çatalhöyük in what is now the modern nation of Turkey, which housed about 6,000 people in 6500 BCE.[5]

Some urban theorists, most notably Jane Jacobs and Edward Soja, have even questioned Childe's trajectory that settled agriculture must predate urban settlement and instead postulate whether the desire for humans to settle together in villages led to advances in agriculture. Archaeologists by and large, though, contend that a society must possess sufficient excess in its agricultural harvest to support specialized urban workers who do not farm. The existence of these nonagricultural laborers is therefore a key component in differentiating a true urban settlement from a large village. According to Childe, several other factors that help define a location as urban are: population size, density, monumental public buildings, a ruling class, a system of writing and predicative sciences, artistic expression, trade, and a society built on residence rather than familial ties.[6]

While Childe's list provides considerable guidance in defining what is, and in some cases what is not, urban, there is considerable leeway amongst academics as to what are the most essential criteria. Attempting to categorize American Indian settlements is a case in point. Should we look for physical signs of urbanization left on the landscape? Iroquois and Algonquin longhouses in the American Northeast were large enough to contain two hundred members of an extended familial network. Dense clusters of longhouses were typically surrounded by substantial palisades like the massive fortifications of ancient walled cities found in the Middle East. Other American Indian communities built extensive irrigation systems that could also be classified as elements of an urban infrastructure. However, does physical infrastructure equate to urban cultural achievement? And must Native American ways of life and divisions of labor be similar to Mesopotamia or even Çatalhöyük in order to be considered urban? These questions attract, beguile, and ultimately may even confound urbanists (those who study and/or appreciate cities and the processes and characteristics of urbanization), yet they must be considered when studying and attempting to identify early America cities.

So when and where did the earliest American Indians live? Even with advancements in research methodologies and a greater appreciation of Native American history and culture, scholars still remain uncertain about the details of the process of populating the North and South American continents. The most popular theory holds that a land bridge provided a connection between Asia and North America, although recent academic works reveal a growing skepticism of this explanation. According to the land bridge hypothesis, Asia and North America were joined by a 1,000-mile-long landmass known as "Beringia," which was exposed when glaciers extended in size and the water level dropped. Somewhere between 10,000 and 80,000 years ago, conditions could have been cool enough to foster a 150-foot drop in the sea level that would have allowed people to travel the 150 miles between the two continents.[7]

Migrants from Asia eventually moved eastward from the Pacific coast of North America to the area called the American Bottom; a floodplain along the Mississippi River in what is now southern Illinois and eastern Missouri, created by a melting glacier at the end of the Ice Age.[8] Newer data prompts scholars to ask if some early settlers used boats to come to the New World, even though it is generally thought that seafaring techniques did not arise until 10,000 years ago. Findings in South America have now pushed the date of the first marine voyages as far back as 50,000 years ago. While much has yet to be determined, the remaining physical evidence does indicate that there was migration to the North American continent as early as 13,000–18,000 years ago, although there were no semi-permanent settlements during this early period.[9]

According to historian Daniel K. Richter, semi-permanent settlements emerged in the Northeast around 1200 BCE, when native peoples involved in pre-farming techniques began to rely on storage pits and pots for storage of excess food. These Northeast cultures are among the first that the English colonists would encounter when they began to arrive in North America in 1497. (All years and centuries in the contemporary period known as CE "of the common era" or AD "anno Domini" are provided without such a specific notation within this essay.) By the late sixteenth and seventeenth centuries, the Iroquois in upstate New York lived in three types of communities–camps, hamlets, and semi-permanent towns. Towns were the largest arrangements, containing as many as two thousand people apiece and averaging about two hundred people per acre. With this concentration, argues Daniel K. Richter, Iroquois towns "were the most densely settled places in the European or native Northeast before the nineteenth century."[10] In the region of American Bottom, though, there had once been an even larger and more permanent Native American settlement.

The (Once) Overlooked City of Cahokia

In contrast to the Northeast, American Indians built several impressive and long-lasting cities in the Midwest and West, although they ceased to function as thriving centers by the time European explorers and settlers arrived. One of the most astonishing of these urban achievements was Cahokia, situated east of present day St. Louis, Missouri and inhabited between approximately 700 and 1400 A.D. Cahokia was built by the Later Mississippians people, and drew on the relative largesse of a strong maize-based agricultural system. Although unknown to Europe at the time, and thus not included in the canon of Western knowledge, Cahokia was actually one of the largest cities in the world. In fact, it was likely the first most populous pre-contact settlement north of what would become the nation of Mexico.

Cahokia arose out of the rich soils of the American Bottom, next to the Mississippi River at the juncture of Cahokia Creek and Canteen Creek. At its height around 1100, Cahokia was home to as many people as the European cities of London or Florence during the same period, albeit perhaps at a lesser density. The Cahokia region consisted of two hundred mounds, with at least 10,000 people dwelling in the center and an additional 20,000–30,000 people spread-out within a fifty-mile radius. Archeologist Timothy R. Pauketat argues that while it is difficult to determine the exact boundaries of sprawling Cahokia, the heart of the city contained as many people as an average city-state in ancient Mesopotamia. In comparison with modern cities, Pauketat notes that Cahokia was more than double the size of Washington, D.C. when it became the nation's capital in 1800.[11]

Amerindians did not call the city "Cahokia"; modern scholars have labeled it that after the name of the Native American group that lived in the region beginning in the 1600s. Despite its size and, as we shall see, its political and economic dominance of a huge swath of the continental United States, the history of Cahokia as an urban center is obscured by the absence of stories about it within Native American culture. While the settlements of Chaco Canyon in the arid Southwest, discussed below, were commemorated and remembered in Native American song, no such folklore exists regarding Cahokia.[12] The physical manifestations of settlement are the primary sources used to glean the story of this once massive American city that Biloine Whiting Young and Melvin L. Fowler argue in their book, *Cahokia: The Great Native American Metropolis* (2000), was "the most complex and elaborate achievement of Native Americans in what is now the United States of America."[13]

In terms of geography, Cahokia was a logical site to make a river portage (i.e. the place to carry canoes from one river to another) and confirms sociologist Charles Cooley's assertion that "population and wealth tend to collect wherever there is a break in transportation."[14] In the center of the large mounds that dominated the landscape was an open space referred to by archaeologists as the Grand Plaza, which was, in turn, surrounded by several lesser plazas. At the northern edge of the Grand Plaza stood Monks Mound (named after a group of French Trappist Monks who lived there in the early nineteenth century), the largest pre-Columbian earthen construction in the entire Western Hemisphere, covering about fifteen acres and containing more than twenty-five million feet of landfill. Experts have debated how long it would have taken to amass and shape such great quantities of soil, especially given the fact that the Native Americans in the region lacked draft animals, vehicles, or iron tools. Perhaps one thousand people, laboring for five years, were involved with building this monumental structure. To command this kind of labor force, the leaders of Cahokian society exerted impressive power and influence. Remarkably, though, very little is known about Cahokia's social and political structure. It is even unclear who settled in the area, and which native groups can trace their ancestry back to the city.[15]

Cahokia's roots appear to lie within a variety of Native America communities since it most likely served as a religious center, open to those from different backgrounds. The city's physical features certainly reveal it was the center of spiritual and celebratory functions, and affirm one of Childe's urban identification criteria: monumental public buildings (or in this case massive structures). Perhaps the people who constructed Cahokia had visited the earthworks of Mexico, or drew their inspiration from the forty to fifty foot mounds of Toltec, near Little Rock, Arkansas. At the top of Monks Mound stood a temple, while at its base the pageantry of ancient Cahokia unfolded within the Grand Plaza. The location of each mound, and the juxtaposition of wooden poles, or woodhenges, set about the city's courtyards, may also relate to the appearance of a cosmic supernova in 1054, which undoubtedly made an impression on the philosophy and religious practices of American peoples. Perhaps the woodhenges even constituted a pre-Columbian observatory.[16] In her work *Cahokia: Mirror of the Cosmos* (2002), art and architecture professor Sally A. Kitt Chappell argues, "With its plazas aligned on the cardinal directions and the mound of greatest height at the crossing of the plazas, it is clear that Cahokia is a landscape cosmogram."[17]

Archaeologists have unearthed an assortment of artifacts at Cahokia, complete with some grisly findings, both of which confirm Childe's urban criteria of a ruling class, trade, and artistic expression. At one particular ridge-top—a site known as Mound 72—archeologist Melvin Fowler discovered human sacrifices, including mass graves of women who were pregnant at the time of death and, at the lowest level, thirty-nine men and women who appeared to have been killed on site. The victims had been decapitated as part of ceremonial violence, and this points to Cahokia being a highly stratified and formalized society. Although other indigenous communities on the North American continent performed ritualized killings, Cahokia's were the most extensive north of what is now Mexico. A figure with a long nose, perhaps a god, seems to be associated with Cahokia rituals and his likeness is found in earpieces and in paintings at this and other Amerindian sites. Other compelling items from excavations include copper awls, needles, artistic pieces resembling turtle shells, a distinctive form of Cahokian pottery featuring elongated necks, numerous buffalo teeth, and seashells that were carried to the city through impressive long-distance trade routes.[18]

Perhaps the most compelling evidence of the power and influence of Cahokia is the extent to which evidence of a popular game called "chunkey" can be found from present-day Montana all the way to South Carolina. Chunkey is the name indigenous peoples used during the early centuries of contact with Europeans and American settlers to describe a hurling stone similar to a modern hockey puck that was rolled on its side on a clay-packed field. Scholars are in disagreement as to how the game was played, and it may have varied regionally. Some posit that players threw sticks, some as long as nine feet, at the chunkey and points were awarded according to how close they came to the stone. Others contend two players from opposing teams engaged on the field, one rolling the stone on its edge and the other trying to stop the roll with a long wooden implement. Like contemporary sporting events, chunkey games were public spectacles, complete with intense community rivalries; chunkey arguably constituted the most popular form of entertainment for Native Americans. Yet, as Miranda Yancey and Brad Koldehoff argue, was more than a game, it was a community affair that commonly "involved gambling, and when played between two different clans or communities, was perhaps used at times as a substitute for warfare."[19]

At the center of the chunkey world stood Cahokia. Everything about the game was connected to the cosmology and diplomatic agenda of the city; Cahokians even dictated its rules and produced the most desirable form of hurling stones. Discoidals (game stones) of Cahokian origin, decorated with symbols for the sun, crosses indicating the four cardinal directions, and oblong shapes for eyes, have been unearthed in wide-ranging locations throughout North America. The most revealing evidence of Cahokia's dominance is the fact that in regions north and west of the city (in present day Minnesota, Wisconsin, and Iowa) there are no local varieties of chunkey dating from the height of Cahokia's political and economic power between 1050 and 1200.[20]

While archeologists now know a great deal about what was buried at Cahokia, and how far the city's influence stretched by analyzing unearthed chunkey, there are many unanswered questions surrounding the community's decline. Cahokia's fortunes began to erode around 1300 and the city disappeared completely a century or so before Columbus ran into the New World. Perhaps the settlement grew overpopulated and could not subsist on the available foodstuffs. Or maybe the city faced political or physical challenges from outlying populations, or drought and/ or disease ravaged the community. What is clear is that without a stable and centralized political system, Cahokian society fragmented, resulting in occasional mass violence and social chaos. One result was a Cahokian diaspora (from the Greek word meaning dispersion) and population exchange as people left the city along the Mississippi and Missouri River basins and were replaced by newcomers who made their homes in the footprints of the once massive city.[21]

Since Cahokia ceased to be thriving social, cultural, economic, and political center by the time of European exploration, it failed to make an impression upon generations of white explorers and settlers. Nor did they recognize the soaring mounds, after some time covered over with trees and thick brush, for the human achievement that they were. An important factor for this oversight has to do with the European conception of continued historical progress. The French, English, Spanish, and Dutch explorers imagined that they had arrived at the apex of Native American cultural achievement and did not guess that great communities such as Cahokia had already peaked and fallen away.

The earliest documented European travelers to Cahokia were Father Jacques Marquette and Louis Joliet, who set off in two birch bark canoes from St. Ignatius of Michilimackinac with five other men on May 17, 1673 for an epic, 2,500-mile exploration of the Mississippi River. As Marquette and Joliet plunged into what was for them an unknown world, they became some of the first to fashion a European understanding of native peoples. Although they traveled in the area of the Cahokia mounds, they made no mention within the chronicles of their exploration of any abandoned city, although they did make note of a large village of Illinois Indians, consisting of a full three hundred cabins. When they did encounter signs of advanced civilization, Marquette expressed his incredulity that native peoples could have produced them. One such example were decorated rocks upon which, Marquette declared, "...two monsters are so well painted, that we could not believe any Indian to have been the designer, as good painters in France would find it hard to do as well."[22]

For generations, such condescending attitudes toward Amerindians flourished. One of the first people to recognize that a great indigenous civilization could have existed at Cahokia was Henry Marie Brackenridge, who in July 1813 sent a letter outlining this prospect to then former President Thomas Jefferson, who took a special interest in history, and that of American Indians in particular. Brackenridge had commenced a concerted study of Native American antiquities in his hometown of Pittsburgh when just a boy. By the time he wrote Jefferson, Brackenridge was in his late 20s and had explored numerous indigenous mound sites located throughout the Ohio and Mississippi River Valleys, from Pittsburgh, Pennsylvania to Baton Rouge, Louisiana. In his letter to Jefferson, Brackenridge noted that Cahokia's mounds, or "tumuli," were not well understood by the contemporary Native Americans who dwelled in the region. Unafraid to think in unconventional ways, Brackenridge offered his own interpretation of Cahokia and the numerous American tumuli, noting that:

> I have been sometimes induced to think, that at the period when those mounds were constructed, there existed on the Mississippi, a population as numerous as that which once animated the borders of the Nile, or of the Euphrates, or of Mexico and Peru.[23]

Insightfully, Brackenridge also asserted that those who used the term "New World" helped to erase the possibility that such grandeur existed in Native American antiquity. In other words, for the colonizing peoples of Europe, North American history was not deemed to have commenced until their ships landed.

Brackenridge's letter was subsequently reprinted in journals and magazines, such as the *Transactions of the American Philosophical Society*, yet it did not contribute to the rewriting of the history in his own age. There were those, however, who later joined Brackenridge in considering the Cahokia site of importance to American history. In 1831, Monks Mound was purchased by T. Amos Hill who established a home and dug a well on the summit, thus uncovering human bones. In 1860, archeologists, including Charles Rau of the Smithsonian, visited the site and in 1883, William McAdams published *Antiquities of Cahokia, or Monks' Mound in Madison County, Illinois*, in which he extolled, "The greatest mounds in the United States are here, and it is really the Egypt of America with its pyramids and tumuli looming up."[24] Cahokia even made a cameo appearance as part of an exhibit at the Columbian Exposition in Chicago in 1893, curated by the widely acclaimed Dean of American Archeology, Warren King Moorehead. And in 1922, Moorehead sought to draw further attention to the importance of the mounds with his pamphlet, *Help Save Cahokia Mounds*, published by the University of Illinois.[25]

Only rushed archaeological surveys conducted during the 1960s in the face of impending highway construction finally uncovered the elaborate ceremonial burial grounds located in the area, as well as the sites of hundreds of homes, and the wide array of goods traded in and out of Cahokia. These "salvage archaeology" endeavors, conducted under great time pressures due to the construction calendar, provided a tantalizing, although not procedurally correct, record for scholarly work. Drawing on recreations of notes on early digs in the area, including the rushed "salvation archaeology," and some relatively recent research, archaeologists are now able to grasp the significance of this site.[26]

The fact that it took so long to recognize the importance of Cahokia as an Amerindian city, despite its proximity to one of the most important urban centers in the United States —St. Louis, Missouri—again tells us a great deal about the power of intellectual assumptions and prejudice. Many nineteenth and early twentieth century scholars believed that Native Americans were unsophisticated and lacked the work ethic to create massive cities. Writing in a 1907 issue of the *American Anthropologist*, ethnologist Cyrus Thomas articulated this perspective in no uncertain terms when he stated: "That no tribe of Indians ever did, would, or could devote five years of constant labor to the erection of a single tumulus, will probably be admitted by everyone acquainted with Indian character."[27]

More contemporary scholars have also underplayed the remarkable urban achievement that was Cahokia by attempting to ascribe to Native Americans moral values and environmental ethics that run counter to those of Europeans and their descendants. Categorizing American Indians as immune from the same impulses that guided white explorers and settlers, such the desire to accumulate material wealth and power, leaves little room for explaining war, human sacrifice, and even the popularity of chunkey. The failure to include Cahokia in the history of the American city also draws from the pervasive myth that Native Americans lived in harmony with nature. As Timothy R. Pauketat explains, the findings on Cahokia:

call into question some long-held beliefs—for instance, that ecologically sensitive, peaceful, mystical, and egalitarian peoples freely roamed the North American continent, never overpopulating or overexploiting their environments; or that these peoples were not subject to such base emotions as avarice, greed, and covetousness and thus could not have built cities or allowed power to be concentrated in the hands of elites.[28]

Etzanoa

Cahokia was not the only Native American settlement of significant proportions. The latest research posits that the settlement known as Etzanoa may have had a population of 20,000. Etzanoa was not, however, overlooked by the historians crafting the traditional narrative of American urban history, because it remained only the stuff of myth until very recently. Although archaeologists had been studying the sites near Arkansas City, Kansas since the 1930s, it was only with a new, more thorough translation of historical documents produced by the University of California, Berkeley in 2013 that archaeologist Donald Blakeslee of Wichita State University began putting the pieces together.

Blakeslee employed the new translations to view the Arkansas City sites through new eyes. He wondered if the Kansas dig sites lined up with the newly clarified archival records. If so, he had quite a find on his hands. Blakeslee writes, "Previous attempts to decipher the map have not used all of the ancillary documents and have depended on early translations with errors of both transcription and translation. Information from witness accounts from the 1601 Oñate expedition show that the place called Etzanoa and the great settlement is located at Arkansas City, Kansas."

The Spanish colonial governor Juan de Oñate led his followers on a 1601 exploration of lands within what is now the western United States. Upon the journey the men came across a large Indian city, reports of which, until now, had been considered exaggerated. According to their reports, they had encountered a city made up of approximately 2,000 grass-thatched, bee-

hive shaped homes clustered in communities around agricultural fields. As each dwelling was of sufficient size to shelter ten people, the explorers estimated the population of the city was 20,000. The adventurers did not encounter the Etzanoan population, however. Apparently, upon seeing the Spanish advance, the city inhabitants had fled. The Etzanoan enemies, the Escanxaques, attacked the Spanish before they left the region.

A kidnapped Native American, who the Spanish named Miguel, drew a map of the settlement and other key aspects of the city of Etzanoa, and his own homeland, Tancoa. Miguel's Map, produced in 1602, constitutes the oldest cartographic study produced by a Native American. Relying on Miguel's Map, Juan Rodriquez, one of Miguel's interviewers, and royal cartographer Enrique Martinez produced a more traditional European rendering of the space. This map, known as The Martinez Map, marks Etzanoa as the "town of new discovery."[29]

What is extremely exciting to urbanists in Blakeslee's findings lies in the existence of the written documents. Historians of course are trained to rely on written documents, and in this case they appear to align with the archeological findings. Miguel's Map, alongside the Martinez Map, Blakeslee's new interpretation of the physical landscape at Arkansas City, and notes from Oñate's journey provide us with far more documentation about pre-contact Native American settlements than we ever had before. Etzanoa helps to buttress the argument that the North American continent was far more settled than the colonists believed or admitted.

Chaco Canyon

Stories about Chaco Canyon and the Anasazi peoples of the Four Corners area of the United States (the meeting place of Utah, New Mexico, Colorado, and Arizona), who also built impressive cities, persisted in Native American folklore. When combined with academic research on the physical remains of Anasazi achievements, as well as those of the neighboring Hohokam people in the Lower Gila Valley of Arizona who created extensive irrigation networks, a clearer picture emerges of the diversity and even longevity of Native American urban forms that predated colonial America.

Chaco Canyon lies in the northwest portion of New Mexico and was the site of a thriving Anasazi culture for about six hundred years between the seventh and twelfth centuries. Like Cahokia, the Anasazi sites of Chaco Canyon were only known to European explorers and settlers as ruins. However, even though the Anasazi lived in smaller urban settings than Cahokia, as scientist and best-selling author Jared Diamond notes, they did build from stone the largest and tallest buildings in North America until the steel girder skyscrapers of Chicago in the late nineteenth centuries. Remarkably, these Anasazi cities are located in what is today an arid landscape that seems both inhospitable and improbable as an urban center.[30]

As Jared Diamond argues, Native Americans in the Four Corners area employed three main settlement strategies to grow crops given the region's limited and often inconsistent amount of annual rainfall. The first was to live in high elevations that received more rainfall; this was the case of the Anasazi peoples at Mesa Verde in southern Colorado who tended to their crops atop plateaus. Popular today as the site of the spectacular Cliff Palace, Mesa Verde is a United Nations Educational, Scientific, and Cultural Organization (UNESCO) World Heritage Site under the jurisdiction of the United States National Park Service. Over six hundred cliff dwellings, comprised of sandstone and mud mortar, have been discovered at Mesa Verde, with those at the Cliff Place constructed directly into the side of a canyon and ranging in size from small one-room storage structures to those with as many as 150 rooms. As no corridors or obvious stairs exist at Cliff Palace, it appears that its residents walked between one roof and the other to transverse the neighborhood.[31]

The second and third approach to coping with low annual rainfall consisted of building settlements in areas with groundwater close to the soil surface, such as at the bottom of a ravine, or collecting water and distributing it through an irrigation system. Both of these methods were employed with considerable success at Chaco Canyon. In fact, during the first few centuries of Amerindian habitation at the site, the physical landscape resembled a veritable oasis of abundant flora and fauna. However, as the process of urbanization intensified over time, the dense concentration of the people living at Chaco Canyon became dependent upon an extensive network of neighboring satellite communities to import foodstuffs and other natural resources from as far away as sixty miles. By the early eleventh century, Chaco Canyon may have been the home to some 5,000 or more people (population estimates for the region at that time are hotly debated). The physical remains of Chaco Canyon reveal stone building techniques that allowed for early one story structures to evolve into five or six stories in height, resembling a modern-day apartment complex, with as many as 600 rooms. While Anasazi builders originally drew timber for roofs and support beams from nearby forests, over time they too had to import materials from long distances in order to continue construction in the face of a dwindling, and then nonexistent, local wood supply.

By 1050, Chaco Canyon functioned as a thriving cultural, economic, and political center, linked to subordinate outlying settlements through a network of roads that totaled hundreds of miles in length, and an extensive catch basin and dam irrigation system. The physical layout of Chaco Canyon's built environment indicates that it may have also served as a gathering place for rituals and that the Anasazi people worshipped according to the sun, moon, and/or a celestial calendar. Chaco Canyon itself was a highly stratified society with a comfortable elite and a peasant class. A network of one hundred and fifty multi-story buildings, constructed in part from two hundred thousand timbers imported to the area during the eleventh century, housed the Anasazi in densely populated quarters. The largest of these structures, called great houses, consisted of outer walls, inner rectangular rooms, and round kivas (chambers for worship). The earliest or "classic-style" great houses, faced southeast as opposed to those built later (the so-called McElmo great houses), which were oriented along a southwest axis. The classic-style great houses contain a gendered space in the form of communal grinding rooms, which were isolated and protected from other chambers, where women prepared maize, a staple of the Anasazi diet. Public cooking, probably of turkey, took place in large, public masonry-lined fire pits, enabling ceremonial group feasting.[32]

Chaco Canyon's demise remains the subject of academic discussion, although a significant number of scholars have identified economic collapse due to drought and the resulting agricultural crisis of 1090–1100 as the primary cause. Much of what we know about what happened at the site comes directly from the study of middens (waste deposits) made by packrats (or woodrats) who lived contemporaneously with the Anasazi. Food intake appears to have declined over time, and inhabitants ate fewer deer and more mice, which they appeared to decapitate and swallow whole. There are even signs of cannibalism within the community, as human muscle residue shows up inside pots left at the site, as well as in dried human feces. Drought and environmental imbalances contributed to the ultimate failure of the community. Between the years of 1150 and 1200, the Anasazi left Chaco Canyon after having inhabited the canyon for six hundred years.[33]

Unlike the Cahokians, the Anasazi people did not disappear, as their descendants dispersed into several Native American communities, particularly the Hopi and Zuni who make up the Pueblo Indians of the Southwest. Navajo Indians also claim a familial relationship with the ancient Anasazi people of the region, inspiring contentious debates that place academic scholars in the middle of a high-stakes political battle. Oral history, rather than archeological or genetic data, links the Navajo to the Anasazi. The Navajo tell the tale of the magician named Gambler, who enslaved the Navajo people and relied on their labor to construct the great houses of the area. In 1999, the National Park Service publicly declared that the Navajo and eighteen Pueblo tribes have an ancestral link to Chaco Canyon.[34]

Besides the Anasazi, the Hohokam people who lived not far from Chaco Canyon in central and southern Arizona during the seventh to fifteenth centuries also built dense urban centers. The Hohokam created the most extensive irrigation system in pre-colonial North America, which spread out like spider webs over their fields and enabled the cultivation of foodstuffs in an otherwise arid landscape. Near the Gila River, at a spot known as Casa Grande, archaeologists have discovered roughly eighty-five miles of canal, and they also determined that approximately seventy-five more miles of networked waterways lay in Los Muertos, a community near present day Tempe, Arizona. Native American canals even run beneath the streets of modern-day Phoenix. As with Cahokia, excavation of Hohokam settlements occurred in areas destined for road and other construction so the sites were not preserved for future study. In the excavation of one particular site slated to become a freeway, La Ciudad, two hundred homes and one hundred trash pits were unearthed, along with seven hundred thousand artifacts.[35]

Despite the sophisticated nature of the Hohokam irrigation system, Native Americans are rarely connected to technological advances of this kind within the historical record. Writers and scholars alike have been far more likely to make note of what technological advances the Native Americans did not have—the wheel, metal tools, horses, guns—rather than those they crafted to help support urban ways of life. Like the Anasazi, though, the Hohokam civilization eventually declined for reasons that remain unclear. Climatic change is a leading theory, so too the paradox that perhaps the Hohokam's own irrigation system may have drawn in highly salted water that ultimately contaminated their fields and led to agricultural collapse. The legacy and influence of the Hohokam peoples, though, can be seen in the ways in which their irrigation system was later adopted and reworked by the Mormon settlers of the American Southwest beginning in the nineteenth century.

Contact with Europeans

Europeans sought to transplant their urban worldview and ways of life onto the North American continent. The colonists imposed order upon nature and created their version of a civilized society. The colonial English, and to some extent other European colonists, considered underdeveloped land to be a squandered resource. Natural areas should be platted into towns and cities, prepared for agriculture, or used for hunting. Lakes, rivers, and oceans should be fished. The English thought that contact with the uncontrolled wilderness could transform even the godliest Christians into barbarians. The fact that the English did not encounter familiar farming techniques or cities in North America reinforced their view of American Indians as uncivilized. However, once the English began to inhabit North America, a counter narrative emerged that they had discovered a veritable Eden of flora and fauna. Remarkably, the English, and Europeans in general, failed to give credit to Native Americans for transforming, or at least acting as wardens of, the physical environment. For example, the "swidden" or slash and burn agriculture practiced by many native groups created the lush meadows that Europeans considered tailor-made for hunting small game. What the colonists read as an untended landscape ready for their settlement was actually an environment already influenced by thousands of years of native settlement and husbandry.[36]

Native Americans forcibly lost their land through a lethal combination of war and other forms of violence, intimidation, persuasion, and exposure to viruses at the hands of Europeans. Depopulation, brought on by the ravages of disease, enabled colonists to settle directly onto large swaths of

lands formerly inhabited by native peoples. Historian Alfred W. Crosby has termed the transference of people, culture, plants, animals, and even bacteria between Europe, Africa, and Asia with the Americas as the Columbian Exchange. As Europeans arrived with their set of microbes, Native Americans, especially those in the prime of their lives, succumbed to unfamiliar diseases.

Traditional American Indian treatments for illness, like sweating, purging, and fasting, actually strengthened the devastating toll of smallpox and other maladies. As indigenous populations dwindled, fewer people were able to care for others and the incidence of secondary issues, like hunger, rose. Not yet cognizant of germ theory, and primed to consider their settlement of the New World as blessed by a Christian god, European colonists considered the fact that American Indians succumbed to disease in such high numbers as divine will. When bubonic plague struck the Indians of the Northeast, Pilgrims deemed this the "good hand of God" weighing in on their behalf and enabling swifter settlement of the land. Between 1600 and 1900, at least twenty major smallpox epidemics ravaged Native American groups. Indians also faced virulent outbreaks of influenza, measles, typhus, cholera, and whooping cough (pertussis).[37]

Scholars remain divided on how many native peoples lived on lands that now constitute the United States and Canada prior to contact with Europeans, with estimates as low as 500,000 and as high as eighteen million. The most common baseline approximations range between five and twelve and a half million, with the most frequently cited figures at four to seven million people. Even with moderate estimates, it is clear that millions of indigenous people perished—as high as 80 to 90 percent of the total population—from disease, malnutrition, or war as a result of colonization and the Columbian Exchange. Even before contact, Amerindian communities were far less dense than those in Europe, with fewer people living in the New World than in the Old. As Shepard Krech III documents, the most densely populated regions of North America by 1500 were California, the

Pacific Northwest, the Southwest, and the Southeast, followed by the Northeast. Although California and the Pacific Northwest enjoyed densities of 194 and 140 persons per 100 square miles respectively, densities in Europe were literally in the thousands per 100 square miles. By 1700, there were about ninety two million people on the European continent, and just two million in North America.[38]

Despite what at first glance appears self-evident, that one group of people with overwhelmingly superior numbers would impose their will on those with substantially fewer, none of the outcomes of European colonization ought to be considered inevitable, nor should the culture and accomplishments of Native American peoples be overlooked. Migration flows from the Old to New World occurred in fits and spurts, and varied considerably between regions and decades. Heightening the chance of success for European colonists and later generations of settlers was the fact that from coast to coast, they saved time developing land and extracting resources by utilizing spaces previously cultivated by Native Americans. Therefore, contrary to longstanding historical tropes, Europeans encountered a landscape that was anything but "virgin." Given the fact that American Indians could not defend their territory and way of life due to war, death, and disease, a more appropriate metaphor for North American land should be "widowed." Once they gained firm possession of a new territory, though, Europeans made dramatic modifications to the landscape such as the felling of forests for household fires and the production of charcoal for metallurgy, the draining of marshes, and the destruction of wildlife habitats, most especially those of passenger pigeons, wolves, beaver, buffalo, deer, and elk.[39]

The existence of Native American towns and cities confound modern students of history because urban growth is so highly conjoined with the idea of acquiring personal material wealth, as well as the creation of permanent settlements and large agricultural surpluses. Not all native groups lived in one location for an extended period of time,

some established semi-permanent villages. The lack of permanency, however, does not discount the people's desire to live and work side-by-side. Communities were built in quite elaborate ways despite their lack of physical continuity. Algonquin peoples lived in a semi-nomadic existence in the region between the Carolinas in the Southern United States all the way north to Labrador in what is now the nation of Canada. Algonquins dwelled within homes fashioned of bent saplings and bark, which they took down and relocated when they set up new camps. The Iroquois, grouped together in what is now New York State, formed the League of Five Nations in order to better confront the challenges of colonization. The Iroquois, known as the "people of the longhouse," lived within family groups, or clans, each occupying a longhouse as discussed above. The Iroquois relied on a single physical location for as long as ten to twenty years. The Creek Confederacy, which linked tribes from northern Florida, the Carolinas, and Georgia, constructed settlements around elaborate ceremonial plazas that featured a central meetinghouse close to which they played sporting events.

By the turn of the seventeenth century, Native Americans in the Northeast built settlements on high ground and/or clustered together, with small hamlets close to larger towns, for better protection from enemy attack. In what is now upstate New York, approximately 20,000 to 30,000 Native Americans of the Five Iroquois Nations lived in ten towns and numerous hamlets. As historian Daniel K. Richter details: the Mohawks lived in up to four towns and adjacent hamlets south of the Mohawk River; the Cayugas in three towns near lakes Owasco and Cayuga; the Senecas in two towns and two hamlets east of the Genesee River and north of the Finger Lakes; the Onondagas in a town and a hamlet southeast of modern Syracuse; and the Oneidas in a town and hamlet in what is now Madison County, New York.[40]

English and Dutch colonists referred to fortified Native American communities as Iroquois castles given their size, from two to sixteen acres, and the large surrounding palisades, twelve to twenty feet in height with stakes angled inward at the top for maximum defense. Inside the castles were thirty to fifty structures, the majority of which were longhouses measuring twenty feet wide and forty to two hundred feet long, built from bent saplings, bark, and tree fibers. Longhouses themselves were divided every twenty feet by an individual family fireplace, with central corridors and sleeping quarters set against the outer walls. Movable panels allowed inhabitants to let smoke from the fires out and sunshine in. Longhouses could easily be expanded when growing populations called for more space. Residents stayed in one town for twelve to twenty years, moving to a new location when pests invaded the storage sheds, available firewood dwindled, and the soil grew worn from repeated plantings.[41]

In these Native American communities, some of which traced family heritage through female ancestors, women provided the majority of the foodstuffs, including beans, squash, and maize fashioned into soups and breads. Towns were inhabited year-round primarily by women and children as men often hunted and traveled. Reciprocity marked most transactions between peoples and those who displayed the most generosity, and gave the most away, gained considerable status. While all goods were allocated to a family or single person, as Richter argues, American Indians believed that "unused items should be free for anyone who needed them, and hospitality required owners to yield them to those without."[42]

Trade with Europeans, though, fundamentally changed Native American communities. At first, American Indians considered European goods scarce commodities and used them in a manner that varied from their original intent. For instance, copper cooking kettles were cut up and used to tip arrows or serve as jewelry. After the 1610s, though, American Indians began to utilize items made by Europeans and then colonists of European descent for their designed function. Once exposed to European commodities, Native Americans began to rely increasingly upon them and eventually lost the means to produce their own wares. European contact complicated the traditional structure of Amerindian communities with more than just trade. War and disease intensified the Amerindian system of enslaving members of competing or neighboring tribes, for either ritual sacrifice or adoption as a means of replacing lost community members, thus fragmenting Native American culture even further.[43]

Seventeenth-Century Native American Towns

Another phenomenon of European contact was the establishment of religious-centered settlements for the conversion of Native Americans to Christianity. Catholic missions were founded throughout New Spain and, to a lesser degree, New France in the South, Midwest, and Southwest of the United States, and the St. Lawrence River and Great Lakes regions in Canada. In British North America, more than a dozen so-called "praying Indian towns" or villages were built in the New England region. Praying towns offered those Native Americans who had survived years of conflict and disease an opportunity to band together for survival.

In 1632, English colonist John Winthrop (author of the infamous "Modell of Christian Charity" sermon) traveled fifteen miles westward from the coast on the Charles River, clambered up a rock, and looked westward upon the Native American settlement of the Nipmuck. Winthrop and his Puritan followers, having only recently relocated to the New World in 1630 had not yet traversed the westward terrain of the region in large numbers. Spreading Christianity among native peoples had not been the main goal of settling in the colony and it took some time for the English to adopt the task. Once underway, however, the Christianizing of the Indians gave the English immigrants an added justification for the acquisition of native lands.[44]

The Reverend John Eliot, soon known as "the apostle to the Indians," personally took up the work of proselytizing to the native peoples living in Natick. Born in England in 1604, Eliot attended Cambridge and came to America with twenty-three barrels of books in November 1631. Eliot served as a pastor to English colonists in Roxbury. He learned the native dialect of the region, and commenced preaching to the native peoples, much to the chagrin of other local religious leaders within the English colony. In his zeal, he also recruited Indians to preach among their own people. In 1654, the General Court, following Reverend Eliot's petition, ruled that Indians who converted to Christianity would receive land grants. Eliot worked with native people to establish Punkapoag and Natick in 1647, within the area that would become the state of Massachusetts.

In 1660, a third town, Hassanamesit, meaning "place of small stones," was formally established, consisting of twelve Nipmuck families, numbering about sixty people. These settlers adopted a formalized code of conduct, common to all of Eliot's "praying Indian towns," that reflected Puritan values and a nascent mercantile work ethic:

1. If any man be idle a week, or at most a fortnight, he shall pay five shillings.
2. If any unmarried man shall lie with a young woman unmarried, he shall pay five shillings.
3. If any man shall beat his wife, his hands shall be tied behind him, and he shall be carried to the place of justice to be severely punished.
4. Every young man, if not another's servant, and if unmarried, shall be compelled to set up a wigwam, and plant for himself, and not shift up and down in other wigwams.
5. If any woman shall not have her hair tied up, but hang loose, or be cut as men's hair, she shall pay five shillings.
6. If any woman shall go with naked breasts, she shall pay two shillings.
7. All men that wear long locks shall pay five shillings.
8. If any shall kill their lice between their teeth, they shall pay five shillings.[45]

For Eliot, who clearly had passion for his work and the people he believed he was helping, the establishment of praying towns offered Native Americans protection from whites who might want to seize their land. Settlers built English style houses at Hassanamesit and grew corn planted on hills at convenient distances from their homes, and cultivated apples that they converted into cider. Cattle and pigs were abundant and local craftspeople fashioned handicrafts such as baskets and brooms. Religious services took place in a central meetinghouse with a Bible written in the native language published by Eliot.

Despite its early success, those living in Hassanamesit dispersed during the skirmishes of King Phillip's War (1675–1676), a bloody European-Native American conflict that destroyed dozens of English and praying Indian towns, and killed hundreds of English settlers and thousands of Native Americans throughout New England. Some Nipmuck returned to Hassanamesit after the conflict, but in 1726, most of those who remained sold their land, about seventy-five hundred acres, for £2,500. By 1728, nine English families settled in town. They erected a meetinghouse in 1730 and a school a year later; the school allowed Indians to attend for free in perpetuity. Finally, in 1735, the town was incorporated and given its current name of Grafton, Massachusetts. Some of the original Native Americans also retained familial plots of land and at least one hundred acres for their heirs and assigns forever. Today, about three and a half acres of the original town is now operated as the Hassanamisco Indian Museum.[46]

Nearly a century and a half after the incorporated town's founding, the author Frederick Clifton Pierce wrote in his celebratory *History of Grafton* (1879):

In reviewing the past, nothing strikes us so forcibly as the change which has taken place since this town was first known to the English. We have seen that Eliot, nearly two hundred years ago, came here, and first preached the gospel to the Indians. That race, then free and conscious of their rightful possession of the soil, had no suspicion that the day of their extinction was so near at hand...and that their hunting and fishing places would be occupied by the habitations and improvements of the white man.... The groves that had sheltered them from the burning sun and the driving storm, they thought would remain forever.... But in these anticipations they were mistaken. Two centuries have passed—and they have vanished.[47]

Pierce, however, was mistaken. Native Americans did not evaporate into thin air. While they were indeed vanquished, small numbers of American Indians remained in Massachusetts, and elsewhere in the colony. Native Americans remained in North America long after Europeans and their descendants assumed physical and numerical superiority. So what do we make of these praying Indian towns? To what extent can they be seen as an experiment in town building by native people? And to what extent does their history reveal a level of coercion?

Not surprisingly, Puritan leaders saw praying Indian communities as a worthwhile endeavor. The experience of English immigrant Daniel Gookin, who served as Superintendent of the Indians in the Commonwealth of Massachusetts between 1654 and his death more than thirty years later, in 1687, is a case in point. Gookin viewed himself as a great champion of the native people. The Commissioners of the United Colonies of New England, in writing to the English Corporation for Propagating the Gospel Among the Indians in New England during the 1670s in support of paying Superintendent Gookin, said it plainly:

We have spoken with Mr. Eliot and others, concerning Mr. Gookin's employment among the Indians, in governing of them in several plantations, ordering their town affairs (which they are not able to do themselves), taking account of their labor and the expense of their time, and how their children profit in their learning, with many things of a like nature, and find it is to be of much use and benefit to them, and therefore could not but desire him to go on with that work, and have ordered £15 to be paid to him for the work of the year past.[48]

Historian Kenneth M. Morrison finds the praying Indian towns to be a symptom and product of the radical disruption of the Native American world soon after the dawn of colonial settlement. The native peoples of the area had been decimated by an epidemic outbreak from 1616–1619 and another (smallpox) in 1633–1634. They formally submitted to the English powers in February 1644 and the coercion grew more pronounced with the outbreak of King Phillip's War in 1675. As Morrison aptly argues, "the Indians joined the praying towns because they were no longer economically or politically independent; the towns failed because the Indians could not understand an impersonal religious or economic system—one which did not arise from bonds between family, friend, and tribe."[49] Ironically, since Native Americans lacked a written history, and relied on the oral tradition of interaction with others for maintenance of their culture, it was actually difficult to *be* Native American without a strong community of other native peoples.[50]

When the Native Americans succumbed to disease in great numbers, they were unable to sustain strong and vital communities. Even with the protective cloak of Protestant Christianity, which provided the native peoples of the praying Indian towns with a lifestyle similar to that of the colonists, Native Americans were not easily able to grow and thrive as neighbors to the English settlers. The praying Indian towns did not develop into long-running communities. Without settlement in towns, Native Americans had no hope of co-existing in high numbers alongside the English, for the English and Native American ways of using the land—one relying on the English model of ownership of land and long-term residency, and one that had no practice of enclosing fields to claim ownership and tended to favor the establishment of separate summer and winter residences, as well as the shifting of field locations—were incompatible.

Conclusion: Indigenous Legacies

The story of Hassanamesit repeated itself across North America all the way to Seattle,

Washington, and beyond, as people of Old World origin settled into the community foundations left by Native Americans. Roads forged and fields cleared by Native Americans became those traveled and cultivated by English, Dutch, French, Spanish or other migrants to the New World. The land was anything but virgin, being home to complex communities fashioned over thousands of years of settlement and cultural accretion. To persist in the mythology that the Native Americans had not left signs of their culture upon the land, according to historian Richard White, "demeans Indians. It makes them seem simply like an animal species, and thus deprives them of culture."[51]

NOTES

1. Coll Thrush, *Native Seattle: Histories from the Crossing-Over Place* (Seattle: University of Washington Press, 2007), 3–4.
2. Samuel Eliot Morison, *The Oxford History of the American People*, Volume 1 (New York: Plume, 1995), 31. This is a republication of the original 1965 work, with some edits.
3. Daniel K. Richter, *The Ordeal of the Longhouse: The Peoples of the Iroquois League in the Era of European Colonization* (Chapel Hill: University of North Carolina Press, 1992), 1. See also Vine Deloria, Jr., *Red Earth, White Lies: Native Americans and the Myth of Scientific Fact* (Golden, Colorado: Fulcrum Publishing, 1997).
4. R. David Edmunds, "Native Americans, New Voices: American Indian History, 1895–1995," *American Historical Review* (June 1995): 717–740. A significant step in solidifying the field of Native American Studies was the establishment of the D'Arcy McNickle Center for American Indian and Indigenous Studies at the Newberry Library Chicago in 1972.
5. V. Gordon Childe, "The Urban Revolution," *The Town Planning Review* 21, no. 1 (Apr., 1950): 3–17; William Carl Eichman, "Catal Huyuk: the Temple City of Prehistoric Anatolia," *Gnosis Magazine* (Spring 1990); and Jason Ur, "Settlement and Landscape in Northern Mesopotamia: The Tell Hamoukar Survey 2000–2001," *Akkadica* 123 and 57–88.
6. Childe, "The Urban Revolution," 9–16; Jane Jacobs, *The Economy of Cities* (New York: Random House, 1969), 3–48; and Edward W. Soja, "Putting Cities First: Remapping the Origins of Urbanism," in

Edward W. Soja, *Postmetropolis: Critical Studies of Cities and Regions* (Hoboken, NJ: Wiley-Blackwell, 2000), 19–47.
7. Shepard Krech III, *The Ecological Indian: Myth and History* (New York: W.W. Norton, 1999), 31–32.
8. Biloine Whiting Young and Melvin L. Fowler, *Cahokia: The Great Native American Metropolis* (Urbana: University of Illinois, 2000), 16–17.
9. Jon M. Erlandson and Todd J. Braje, "From Asia to the Americas by boat? Paleogeography, Paleoecology, and Stemmed Points of the Northwest Pacific," *Quaternary International* 239 (2011): 28–37; and E. James Dixon, "How and When did People First Come to North America?" *Athena Review*, vol. 3, no. 2 (2002).
10. Richter, *The Ordeal of the Longhouse*, 17. For more on Iroquois settlement patterns and the longhouse see 13–20.
11. Tertius Chandler, *Four Thousand Years of Urban Growth: An Historical Census* (Lewiston, NY: St. David's University Press), 111, 187, and 241; Timothy R. Pauketat, *Cahokia: Ancient America's Great City on the Mississippi* (New York: Viking: 2009), 26.
12. Pauketat, *Cahokia*, 159.
13. Young and Fowler, *Cahokia*, 39.
14. Charles Cooley, *The Theory of Transportation* (Baltimore: Publications of the American Economic Association, 1894), as quoted in Sally A. Kitt Chappell, *Cahokia: Mirror of the Cosmos* (Chicago: The University of Chicago Press, 2002), 23.
15. Pauketat, *Cahokia*, 26; and Cyrus Thomas, "Cahokia or Monk's Mound," *American Anthropologist*, vol. 9, no. 2 (April-June 1907): 364.
16. Pauketat, *Cahokia*, 8–20, 63, and 127.
17. Kitt Chappell, *Cahokia*, 55.
18. Pauketat, *Cahokia*, 64, 66, 75–81, and 89; William McAdams, *Antiquities of Cahokia, or Monk's Mound in Madison County, Illinois* (Edwardsville, Illinois: W. R. Brink, 1883), 4 and 8. From the Collections of the American Antiquarian Society, Worcester, Massachusetts.
19. Miranda Yancey and Brad Koldehoff, "Rolling Icons: Engraved Cahokia-Style Chunkey Stones," *Illinois Archaeology*, 22, no. 2 (2010): 491–501; and Pauketat, *Cahokia*, 40–50. See also Steward Cullin, *Games of the North American Indians* (New York: Dover, 1975) and "Discoidals," accessed at www.ohiohistorycentral.org/w/Discoidals. The discoidal game may be spelled chunkey, chunky, or chungke'.
20. Pauketat, *Cahokia*, 42–47.
21. Pauketat, *Cahokia*, 168.
22. John Gilmary Shea, *Discovery and Exploration of the Mississippi Valley: With Original*

Narratives of Marquette, Allouez, Membre, Hennepin, and Anastase Douay (Albany: Joseph McDonough, 1903), 8, 26, and 42.

23. Henry Marie Brackenridge, "On the Population and Tumuli of the Aborigines of North America. In a Letter from H. H. Brackenridge, Esq. to Thomas Jefferson—Read October 1, 1813," *Transactions of the American Philosophical Society*, Vol. 1, New Series (1818): 154; a excerpted version of the letter is included in Steven H. Corey and Lisa Krissoff Boehm, *The American Urban Reader: History and Theory* (New York: Routledge, 2011), 99–102.

24. McAdams, *Antiquities of Cahokia*, 1.

25. Young and Fowler, *Cahokia*, 23–24, 29, and 33. Incidentally, like the "Dean of Urban History," Arthur Schlesinger, the "Dean of Archaeology" Warren King Moorehead hailed from Xenia, Ohio.

26. Young and Fowler, *Cahokia*, 15.

27. Thomas, "Cahokia or Monk's Mound," 364.

28. Pauketat, *Cahokia*, 3.

29. Donald J. Blakeslee, "The Miguel Map Revisited," *Plains Anthropologist*, vol 63, no. 245 (February 2018): 67; David Malakoff, "Searching for Etzanoa," *American Archaeology* (Spring 2016): 26–31; Michael D'Estries, "Native American City Unearthed in Kansas," *Mother Nature Network* blogs, accessed at www.mnn.com/lifestyle/arts-culture/blogs/lost-native-american-city-unearthed-kansas; Connie Kachel White, "Etzanoa: The Great Settlement," *Wichita State University Alumni Magazine* (Spring 2016): 1–3; "Dr. Donald Blakeslee Delivers Presentation on Etzanoa at Cowley College," accessed at www.cowley.edu; Beccy Tanner, "Mysterious 'Lost City' of Etzanoa in south-central Kansas now open to tours," April 21, 2018, 1–4; David Malakoff, "Searching for Etzanoa, *Archaeological Conservancy* (March 2016): 1—3; Jacqui Goddard, "Lost Native American city of Etzanoa opens its Gates to Tourists," *The Times* (London) (August 21, 2018): 1–8.

30. Jared Diamond, *Collapse: How Societies Choose to Fail or Succeed* (New York: Penguin, 2005), 116 and 143–144.

31. Diamond, *Collapse*, 140–143; United States Department of the Interior, National Park Service, "Mesa Verde National Park, Colorado, Cliff Dwellings," http://www.nps.gov/meve/historyculture/cliff_dwellings_home.htm (accessed May 1, 2014); "UNESCO World Heritage List, "Mesa Verde National Park," http://whc.unesco.org/en/list/27 (accessed May 1, 2014); and *The Mystery of Chaco Canyon* at http://video.pbs.org/video/1966617792/.

32. Diamond, *Collapse*, 147–150; Keith Kloor, "Who were the Anasazi," *Archaeology* 62, issue 6 (November–December 2009): 18–69.

33. Diamond, *Collapse*, 144–156.

34. W.H. Wills, "Cultural Identity and the Archaeological Construction of Historical Narratives: An Example from Chaco Canyon," *Journal of Archaeological Method Theory* 12 (2009): 285, 287, 292, 295, and 299; Krech, *The Ecological Indian*, 77; and Keith Kloor, "Who were the Anasazi," 18–69. Many archeologists, however, argue that the Navajo arrived in the Four Corners area in the 1500s, after the height of Chaco Canyon.

35. Krech, *The Ecological Indian*, 45–46, 53, and 47.

36. William Cronon, *Changes in the Land: Indians, Colonists, and the Ecology of New England* (New York: Hill and Wang, 1983), 50–51; Kretch, *The Ecological Indian*, 73–75.

37. Alfred W. Crosby, Jr., *The Columbian Exchange: Biological and Cultural Consequences of 1492* (Westport, CT: Greenwood Press, Inc., 1972); Richter, *Ordeal of the Longhouse*, 59; Krech, *The Ecological Indian*, 79, 80, 89, and 90.

38. For estimates on the size and density of the Native American populations see Krech, *The Ecological Indian*, 83–96; John D. Daniels, "The Indian Population of North America in 1492," *The William and Mary Quarterly*, Third Series, 49, no. 2 (April 1992): 298–320.

39. For the concept of North American land prior to Europeans and their descendants as being "virgin" see, Henry Nash Smith, *Virgin Land: The American West in Symbol and Myth* (Cambridge: Harvard University Press, 1950 and 2007); Krech, *The Ecological Indian*, 95–99.

40. Richter, *The Ordeal of the Longhouse*, 17.

41. Ibid., 18 and 23–24.

42. Ibid., 22.

43. Ibid., 52 and 76.

44. Richard W Cogley, *John Eliot's Mission to the Indians Before King Philip's War* (Cambridge: Harvard University, 1999), 3 and 4.

45. Frederick Clifton Pierce, *History of Grafton, Worcester County, Massachusetts. From Its Earliest Settlement by the Indians in 1647 to the Present Time, 1879* (Worcester: Press of Charles Hamilton, 1879), 21. Collections of the American Antiquarian Society, Worcester, Massachusetts.

46. Pierce, *History of Grafton*, 20–47; and Richard W Cogley, *John Eliot's Mission to the Indians Before King Philip's War* (Cambridge: Harvard University, 1999), 5 and 46. The Hassanamisco Indian Museum

presence is largely virtual, see http://www.nipmucmuseum.org.

47. Pierce, *History of Grafton*, 79.

48. Daniel Gookin, "Doings and Sufferings of the Christian Indians in New England in the Years 1675–1677," *Transactions of the American Antiquarian Society*, Vol. II (Cambridge: Printed for the Society at the University Press, 1836), 426–427.

49. Kenneth M. Morrison, "'That Art of Coyning Christians': John Eliot and the Praying Indians of Massachusetts," *Ethnohistory* (January 1974): 80 and 89.

50. Morrison, "'That Art of Coyning Christians'...," 77; Cogley, *John Eliot's Mission*, 29–30 and 38; and John Gorham Palfrey and Francis Winthrop Palfrey, *History of New England*, Vol. 3 (Boston: Little Brown and Company, 1899), 199.

51. William Cronon and Richard White, "Indians in the Land," *American Heritage* 37 (August 1986) 18–25, as quoted in Krech, *The Ecological Indian: Myth and History*, 26. See www.AmericanHeritage.com for the full article by Cronon and White.

ESSAY 2.2

Frontiers and Frontier Peoples Transformed

David J. Weber

Source: David J. Weber, *The Spanish Frontier in North America*, Brief Edition (New Haven, CT: Yale University Press, 2009).

EDITORS' INTRODUCTION

The Spanish were the first Europeans to establish permanent settlements in North America, and did so a full century before their English, French, and Dutch counterparts. Europeans viewed the physical and social landscape of North America as uncivilized and there for the taking. These colonizers sought to impose order on the unknown by replicating their way of life which, in its most idealized form, was urban. Success for the Spanish was measured, in part, through the discovery of prosperous Native American cities, and the establishment of new ones. **[See Essay 2.1, Lisa Krissoff Boehm and Steven Corey, "Pre-Colonial and Seventeenth Century Native American Settlements" and Document 2.1, "The 'Lost' Native American City of Etzanoa (Kansas)," 1602.]** The earliest Spanish settlements, however, were irregular in layout and underwhelming in terms of population size and urban amenities. The oldest Spanish city under the sovereignty of the United States is San Juan, Puerto Rico founded in 1521, with St. Augustine, Florida the oldest continuously occupied city in the continental United States, organized in 1565. By the time of the founding of St. Augustine, the Spanish had settled hundreds of communities from Mexico south through Central and South America and the Caribbean. To improve urban conditions, in 1573 King Phillip II Spain issued the earliest of what are now called the Laws of the Indies, which evolved into a series of social, political, and economic measures that guided the founding, design, and governance of municipalities throughout the Spanish Empire.

The selection in this essay, by historian David J. Weber, is an assessment of just how effective the Spanish were in replicating their European urban worldview in the Spanish borderland of North America. As Weber argues, while the Spanish and Europeans in general succeeded in transforming the North America environment to a greater extent than the region changed them, the Spanish were limited in transplanting their social and culture institutions and only modified them when they clearly had no viable alternative. Spanish municipalities remained relatively small in population compared to other European settlements in the colonial era, and, in general, failed to nurture thriving commercial economies. And while the Spanish were more likely to borrow from Native American ways of life, there was no true synthesis of elements from Iberian and indigenous civilizations on the Spanish frontier. Indeed, Spanish culture undeniably prevailed over those of Native Americans, and to this day it remains salient in those portions of the modern United States that were settled, occupied, and administered by the Spanish. Not only have place names like Santa Fe, San Francisco, San Diego, and San Antonio endured, but so have Hispanic communities and townspeople.

David J. Weber (1940–2010) was an award-winning historian and noted scholar of Spanish borderland history in North America. He taught at San Diego State University and later as the Robert and Nancy Dedman Professor of History and Director of the Clement Center for Southwest Studies at Southern Methodist University. Weber authored more than two dozen books on Spanish and Mexican America; the most noted of Weber's books, *The Spanish Frontier in North America*, won the Carr P. Collins Award for best nonfiction book in 1992 from the Texas Institute of Letters and the *Premio Espana y America* award from the Spanish Ministry of Culture. In 2002, King Juan Carol I of Spain awarded Weber membership in the Real Orden de Isabel la Catholica (Order of Isabela the Catholic), and in 2005 the government of Mexico gave him their highest honor awarded to foreigners, the Order of the Aztec Eagle.

FRONTIERS AND FRONTIER PEOPLES TRANSFORMED

In March 1762, as she lay dying in her bed following a sudden illness, Juana Luján prepared her last will and testament. The pious and prosperous widow, who owned the sprawling Rancho de San Antonio near Santa Cruz de la Cañada in New Mexico, affirmed her faith in "everything that is upheld, believed and preached by our mother, the Holy Roman Catholic and Apostolic Church." She left instructions for her burial in the mission chapel of the Indian pueblo of San Ildefonso and for prayers for the repose of her soul. Juana Luján itemized her property, which she bequeathed to her three children, all of them illegitimate. The size of her estate, valued at some six thousand pesos, and the nature of her possessions suggest that she was among the province's more affluent residents. She had owned a twenty-four-room home with its furniture, kitchenware, religious paintings and images, jewelry of gold, silver, and pearls, clothing made of fabrics imported from Europe, China, and Mexico, and land with its pastures, planted fields, garden, walled orchard, stable, corrals, livestock, and farm and ranching implements.

Although they effected remarkable changes in the natural and native worlds, Spaniards had come to the frontiers of North America hoping to change little in their lives except to enhance their wealth and status. Like other Europeans in America, they succeeded remarkably well—they transformed their environment far more than it transformed them, and they built new societies that owed more to inheritance from the Old World than to experience in

the New World. As the will of Juana Luján suggests, Spaniards of means on the North American frontier lived by Spanish law and custom and surrounded themselves with traditional Spanish amenities. They organized the North American landscape into familiar shapes and measures, and they bestowed recognizable names on the land in order to incorporate it into their cosmos. They maintained time in familiar modes, marking their days by the Christian calendar and their hours by the bells of their churches. Within familiar time and space, they also reconstructed the hierarchical and patriarchal institutions of their homeland. One of those institutions was the household, where men held authority over wives and children but where married women like Luján owned separate private property and could pass it on to their heirs—a right not enjoyed by English women. Throughout their lives, they engaged in familiar routines of work and play and gave obeisance to the orthodoxies that characterized life in Christian communities in Iberia. When they grew ill, they turned to Iberian medical knowledge and medicines. When they died, they were buried by tradition, as was Juana Luján, in a simple shroud in emulation of Christ but in a place in or near the church that corresponded to their status. Social distinctions followed Spaniards to the grave.

On North American frontiers, however, Spaniards never reconstructed Spanish culture and institutions in unadulterated forms. First, Spanish civilization crossed the Atlantic in simplified forms that never reflected its full variety and complexity. Second, many

Hispanic settlers did not come to the frontiers directly from metropolitan Spain, but from peripheral areas such as Minorca, the Canaries, the Antilles, or New Spain, where Spanish culture had already been filtered through other distinctive environmental, economic, and social settings. Then, too, however much they wished to conserve the familiar, Spaniards' scanty numbers and resources left them no choice but to make concessions to their strange new environment and, on occasion, to learn from Natives, who understood local conditions better than they. Like Indians and other Europeans, Spaniards resisted change unless it offered distinct benefits and did not challenge cherished beliefs or offend their sense of identity. Only when it seemed necessary did they make modest adjustments in their material culture—in dress, diet, medicine, tableware, homes, and communities, which further transformed Hispanic culture on the frontier.

From the outset Spaniards went to great lengths to maintain appearances, for dress signified status and distinguished Spaniards from Indians as well as from one another. Setting off to conquer New Mexico with Juan de Oñate, for example, Capt. Luis de Velasco packed a wardrobe that included such items as linen handkerchiefs, numerous Cordovan leather boots and shoes, fancy hats, and six elegant suits—two of satin, one of silk, and one of "blue Italian velvet ... trimmed with wide gold passementerie, consisting of doublet, breeches, and green silk stockings with blue garters with ... gold lace." In day-to-day life, however, and especially in the more isolated areas, only the upper and middle strata of society could afford stylish dress. From California to Florida, when the shoes and boots of ordinary Hispanics wore thin, for example, they donned locally made, Indian-inspired leather moccasins or moccasin-like shoes.

Necessity also drove Spaniards to adopt strange New World foods because few places in North America proved ideal for cultivating all of the staples of the Mediterranean diet, and bulky foodstuffs could not be shipped economically to remote North American outposts. After failing in their attempts to raise wheat, olives, and grapes at St. Augustine and Santa Elena, Spaniards turned to indigenous cultigens—maize, beans, and squash—and supplemented them with adaptable foods from the Old World like peaches, melons, and watermelons and New World crops such as squashes, chili peppers, and lima beans. Because sheep, Spaniards' preferred source of meat, did not thrive in their Atlantic colonies, Spaniards depended on fishing and on hunting deer, birds, and turtles while they husbanded their imported pigs, chickens, and cattle.

By eating native foods as well as European imports, Hispanics probably enjoyed a richer, more varied diet than they would have had in Spain. Nonetheless, with wheat bread, olive oil, wine, and other familiar foods in short supply across much of the frontier, Spaniards at first believed themselves deprived—reduced to "herbs, fish and other scum and vermin," as one soldier in St. Augustine complained in 1573. As they grew more accustomed to native foods, however, the colonists' sense of privation may have diminished. In the Southeast, Hispanics quaffed the highly caffeinated native black tea, *cacina*, to the point of addiction. In the Southwest, *chocolate, atole*, and *pinole* became favored drinks, and other Mesoamerican foods with Nahautl names and corn as the principal ingredient—*elotes, posole, tamales*, and *tortillas*—became mainstays of the Hispanic diet. Hispanics at all social levels altered the traditional Iberian diet in order to survive, but those at the lowest level made the greatest adjustments. "There is little difference between the food of the Indian and that of the common Spaniard," a German-born Jesuit noted in Sonora.

Spaniards adopted techniques and implements of food preparation from Native Americans—most directly from Indian women who worked in Hispanic kitchens as servants, mistresses, or wives—to a much greater extent than did their English counterparts on the Atlantic coast. It was in "female activities with low social visibility," anthropologist Kathleen Deagan has suggested, that Spaniards allowed themselves to fall most readily under indigenous influences, including perhaps the use of Indian-made baskets, mats, and cloth for work regarded as suitable only for women. In the patriarchal Hispanic world, the high status associated with Spanish culture militated against an easy acceptance of native influences in such visible male activities as warfare and construction.

In constructing new homes and public or ecclesiastical buildings in North America, Spaniards may have depended on Indian labor, but beyond some decorative touches, Indians had little influence on building techniques or the styles of Hispanic architecture. On the contrary, Spanish churches, government buildings, and fortifications followed European conventions, and Spanish-built homes in North America resembled those of different regions of Spain. Poverty and shortages of skilled artisans and metal tools on the frontier, however, usually resulted in a simplification of styles for both public and private structures. With few exceptions, such as the ensemble of neoclassic residences built by the elite in New Orleans after the fires of 1788 and 1794 destroyed the old French structures, even the homes of the well-to-do seemed austere compared to those of the aristocracy in Spain or Mexico City. Most Hispanic frontiersmen lived in small, unadorned, functional houses with a few multipurpose rooms in which they cooked, ate, entertained, and slept.

Simplification to the point of austerity also characterized the interiors of most public buildings and private homes. A few churches, such as San Xavier del Bac with its ornate, gilded baroque altarpiece, had elaborate decor, and late in the colonial era California mission chapels had bright motifs painted on their interior walls, but most church interiors seemed plain. As fray Francisco Atanasio Domínguez wrote of the parish church at Santa Fe in 1776, "Its furniture, or adornment, is the absence of any." The twenty-four-room house owned by the affluent Juana Luján had no moveable wooden furniture other than her plank bed, a cabinet, a chest, two chairs, two benches, and a writing desk, and her walls were unadorned except for a mirror and religious paintings on elk hides. Those less well off than Luján had more spartan furnishings; they slept and sat on mats on the floor, as did the lower classes in Spain.

Spanish attempts to reorganize urban space also bumped up against frontier realities. More than any other colonial power, Spain attempted to impose a uniform urban design on newly founded municipalities, which it regarded as central to colonization. Royal regulations promulgated in 1573 required officials throughout the empire to lay out new town sites in orderly grids, reflecting Renaissance ideal that most of the labyrinthine medieval communities in Spain itself never achieved. Municipalities such as St. Augustine, Pensacola, San Antonio, El Paso, Santa Fe, Los Angeles, and San José were to reckon their boundaries at four leagues square. At the heart of each community would stand a principal plaza laid out to the points of the compass, rectangular in shape to accommodate equestrian events, and faced by government and ecclesiastical buildings and shops. Beyond the plaza, surveyors generally divided the town into straight streets, designating uniform blocks and lots for houses and gardens. Still farther from the plaza, yet still within the municipal boundaries, stood private fields, municipal lands, and common pastures and woodlands.

Wherever Spaniards formed municipalities in the western hemisphere, they repeated the general principles of this urban template with remarkable consistency. On the frontier, however, municipalities displayed organic as well as geometric elements. Indeed, to the dismay of Spanish officials, who regarded urban life as the ideal, Hispanic frontiersmen from Florida to California often preferred to live in the countryside, close to herds, watercourses, fields, and Indian laborers. One traveler in 1754 noted that he had passed through Albuquerque, "or I might say the site of the villa of Albuquerque, for the settlers, who inhabit it on Sunday, do not live there. They must stay on their farms to keep watch over their cornfields."

Spanish municipalities in North America lacked the most basic urban amenities. The cosmopolitan "new city" of New Orleans, rebuilt in the classic Spanish mode following the devastating fires of 1788 and 1794, stands as an exception. As the hub of a prosperous plantation economy and entrepôt for the Mississippi River trade, New

Orleans grew from 3,000 in 1777 to over 8,000 in 1803 and could support sophisticated urban life. Places with more modest populations at the end of the colonial era, such as Los Angeles (850), Santa Fe (6,000), San Antonio (1,500), and St. Augustine (1,500), on the other hand, could not boast of impressive cathedrals or public buildings, convents, seminaries, universities, libraries, theaters, newspapers, or presses, as one might have found in Mexico City.

Many Spaniards on the frontier lived not in or near formal municipalities but at military bases. In contrast to the westward-moving Anglo-American frontier, where the government usually established military posts to protect an advancing line of settlers, many of Spain's North American fortifications anchored territory so remote that it had little prospect of attracting significant numbers of Hispanic settlers. Presidial communities such as San Diego, Santa Barbara, Monterey, San Francisco, Tucson, San Fernando (Memphis), and Nogales (Vicksburg) took on the characteristics of small villages as soldiers, their families, and nonmilitary personnel settled around them, but they did not develop into municipalities until long after the Spanish era ended. Nor did they enjoy more than the essentials of Hispanic life.

Tucson is a case in point. Ranchers and farmers who lived on the outskirts of the fort paid no taxes or tithes, but neither did they derive benefits from a town government or a parish church (they used the military chapel). As a condition of owning land within a five-mile radius of the presidio, settlers were obliged to take up their own arms and mounts to campaign against Apaches. The community, the post commander, José de Zúñiga, reported in 1804, had no weaver, saddlemaker, or hatmaker, and "desperately needs a leather tanner and dresser, a tailor, and a shoemaker." The artisans who had recently completed the monumental baroque church of San Xavier del Bac just south of the presidio, "out here on the farthest frontier," as Zúñiga put it, had received double pay "because of the consequent hazard involved." [...]

On the frontier, then, as in other parts of Spain's colonial empire, Hispanic society and culture never fully replicated Iberian models. Instead, material culture, institutions, social structure, and family life underwent modest transformations as tenacious Spaniards contended with native peoples and with one another to try to rebuild the old order in the New World. Hispanic colonists owed much more to the influence of Indians than did their English counterparts along the Atlantic coast, but Hispanic frontier culture and society did not represent a true synthesis of elements from native and Iberian worlds. Sustained by the technological, economic, and political strength of a large state society, Spanish culture has clearly prevailed over the cultures of native American tribal groups.

However much Spaniards might eat Indian foods, wear Indian footwear, take Indian wives or concubines, produce *mestizo* children, learn Indian languages, and live beyond the civility of Spanish urban life, the core of Hispanic frontier culture and society had remained recognizably Hispanic and intact. If Spanish political, economic, cultural, and social institutions seemed pallid all across the frontier, it was because Hispanic settlers suffered from isolation, poverty, sparse immigration, low imperial priorities, and Indian resistance, not because they had embraced the ways of native Americans. In contrast, those Indian societies impinged upon by influences from the more powerful and complex Spanish state had been deeply transformed—frequently beyond recognition.

Wherever Hispanic communities developed in North America, they left an enduring legacy. As Anglo Americans moved into the former Spanish possessions, they found institutional and cultural patterns so well established that it made more sense to adapt to them than to change them. From St. Augustine to San Francisco, not only Spanish names endured (however badly pronounced), but so too did the Hispanic communities and townspeople. With changes in transportation, "new towns" grew up at San Diego, Albuquerque, and San Antonio, but the "old towns" remained. In the countryside beyond the towns, Spanish private and communal land grants determined the shape of the land for years to come. Meanwhile, those Hispanics who remained in the former colonies passed their specialized knowledge on to Anglo-American newcomers—knowledge of local arts, architecture, foods, language, literature, laws, music, and the management of water and livestock in arid lands.

Until the large immigrations from Mexico and the Caribbean in the twentieth century, the Hispanic legacy in North America remained strong along the continent's southern rim, less because of the power of Spain's presence than because Hispanics had made the initial European imprint on the region. Cultural geographer Wilbur Zelinsky has explained this phenomenon; "The first group able to effect a viable, self-perpetuating society are of crucial significance for the later social and cultural geography of the area, no matter how tiny the initial band of settlers may have been." But because Spanish North America never moved beyond the frontier stage in size or sophistication and because it remained linked to a declining Spain, it stood vulnerable to its modernizing and predatory neighbor. Anglo Americans enjoyed not only demographic and economic advantages, but also a mercantile ethos and certitude in what they believed to be the superiority of their race, religion, and political institutions. Those conceits served Americans as a rationalization for conquering and transforming the lands of their former Spanish neighbors, much as Spaniards' ethnocentric values had facilitated their domination of indigenous Americans several centuries before.

ESSAY 2.3

"To Plant in Towns": Charles Towne at the Founding of Carolina

Emma Hart

Source: Emma Hart, *Building Charleston: Town and Society in the Eighteenth-Century British Atlantic World* (Charlottesville: University of Virginia, 2010 and Columbia: University of South Carolina, 2015), 17–27.

EDITORS' INTRODUCTION

Urban history constitutes a very important part of American history. Colonial America relied on the creation of cities to establish and spread the Europeanization of the continent. In New England, Massachusetts grew as a conglomeration of Boston and smaller communities. Massachusetts' government was completely structured around cities and towns; its town meeting structure continues to this day. Rhode Island relied upon Newport and Providence. Pennsylvania flourished due to William Penn's Philadelphia. The southern colonies had been thought to have grown in a different manner, with a reliance on plantations. Yet there was an exception. Unlike the colonies established in Maryland and Virginia which had rural roots, South Carolina grew like its New England sister-colonies. Charleston, relying on the Fundamental Constitutions designed by Ashley Cooper, the first Earl of Shaftesbury, anchored South Carolina in place and helped the colony spread inland.

Cooper insisted that the settlers "plant in towns," or quite literally plant the seeds of a new way of life in the soil of this conquered land. Shaftsbury had watched as London had risen from the ashes of the Great Fire of 1666. Sometimes fires that rage in wooded areas foster clearing that leads to important regrowth. Where there once had been dense forest, the tree canopy blocking the sunlight from reaching the forest floor, low bushes and wild-flowers moved into the cleared area, flourishing in the unblocked access to sun.

Principles of good government and religious freedom motivated South Carolina's founders. The adherence of tolerance brought Catholics, like the French Huguenots, to settle in the region. Yet the European colonists soon turned to worship commercialism.

Freedom and tolerance did not extend to native peoples, and clashes between new-comers and native peoples shaped the creation of the colonial cities. We cannot study the creation of these new places without recognizing the way of life that was lost in their wake. The cities both created new places and destroyed old ones.

Hart celebrates the societal energy cities generate, an energy that is more than the sum of its parts. She explains, "with their extraordinary concentration of people, their shared closed spaces that force inhabitants of different colors, classes, and nationalities to collide with one another, and their plethora of commercial and cultural possibilities, cities have often made a special contribution to the character of societies." Hart discovers Charleston's "middling sort," a proto-middle class not thought to have thrived in the American colonies until a later date. Simultaneously, Charleston developed a cadre of the poor and created a special southern brand of upper class, a provincial gentility.[i]

Emma Hart is a lecturer in the Department of Modern History at the University of St. Andrews, Scotland.

"TO PLANT IN TOWNS": CHARLES TOWNE AT THE FOUNDING OF CAROLINA

The narrative of Carolina's early colonization is a familiar one in the context of England's New World settlements. Although the colony took an unusually long time to achieve stability, the events, people, and processes behind its founding followed the usual trajectory of the Old World's move westward to the "empty" lands of America. Profit slowly triumphed over principle, and whites gradually accumulated control over blacks and Native Americans. Two groups of white adventurers were chiefly responsible for initiating the occupation of Carolina. The first group, an assemblage of eight Lords Proprietors who had been granted land by Charles II, was behind the logistics of settlement and the drawing up of the territory's template for government, the Fundamental Constitutions. With most of these Proprietors never visiting Carolina, however, it was up to a second collective of Europeans —mostly consisting of Englishmen with Barbadian connections, and a party of French Huguenots—to people the new colony.[1]

These early white claimants to the territory of Carolina shared the initial motivations of others who led Europe's settlement of North America. Like their compatriots, they embarked on their New World project to implement beliefs and principles that they had been unable to realize in their Old World. For Carolina's eight Proprietors, such principles, embodied by the Fundamental Constitutions, centered on emerging ideas of governance too radical to implement in England. For the colony's Huguenot settlers, arriving in waves toward the end of the seventeenth century, it was the religious

toleration endorsed by the Constitutions that drew them from an intolerant Catholic France to a colony in which they could freely establish their own churches.[2]

However, those settlers with ties to the British Caribbean island of Barbados—settlers often known collectively as the Goose Creek men—were less devoted to the political or religious principles of their co-colonists. Leaving the Caribbean from a lack of economic opportunity, the Barbadians arrived in the Carolina Low Country intending to recreate the lucrative commercial society familiar to them in the empire's southernmost reaches, and also characteristic of the nearby colony of Virginia. The exclusive commitment of these men to profit clashed with the more ideological stance of the Lords Proprietors, and it was this long-running conflict that lay behind Carolina's troubled early history. Contravening the system of land distribution so that they might grab the best territories, the Goose Creek men relentlessly pursued their own agenda of settlement.

Also ignoring the Proprietor's policies and regulations concerning the Indian trade, the Barbadians chased profits through such commerce to the degree that armed conflict broke out between the two parties, reaching its zenith during the 1715 Yamassee War. Finally, the Goose Creek faction objected to the dissenting principles embodied by the Constitutions, instead seeking the primacy of their religious institutions. Receiving little support from metropolitan authorities, who were of course supportive of the Church of England, the embattled Proprietary government gradually lost ground to its opponents. With most of the original Proprietors either dead or disengaged from their colonizing project, Carolina eventually became a royal colony in 1729, with a standard system of

i Emma Hart, *Building Charleston: Town and Society in the Eighteenth Century British Atlantic World* (Charlottesville: University of Virginia, 2010 and Columbia: University of South Carolina, 2015), 1, 7 and 14.

British colonial rule through governor, royal council, and a Commons House of Assembly. Over the first half century of Carolina's settlement, principles of political experimentation and religious freedom had largely lost out to the profit motive and the might of England's official church.[3]

The quest for riches also triumphed when colonists confronted the need for labor on their extensive new plantations. With the experience of previous English settlers in New England, the Caribbean, and the Chesapeake at hand, Carolina's Proprietors had planned for a colony built on long-term settlement and cultivation of the land rather than on the easy extraction of mineral wealth. Thus, on arrival, the majority of the colonists got down to the business of commercial agriculture. In this task, the Barbadian settlers found particular success, not only because they brought with them knowledge about cultivating crops in a hot climate, but also because they imported the enslaved Africans necessary to undertake the hard project of improving the "wilderness." Quite unusual in the British American context, Carolina was a colony based on slave labor from its very beginning, and, as successive historians have documented, Africans were critical component of Low Country society from founding onwards. As expert keepers of livestock, and as essential hands in the production of naval stores such as tar, pitch, and staves, slaves were central to the range of economic activities that kept the colony afloat in its first decades. While their precise role is hotly debated, it is also clear that slaves were critical to the successful cultivation of rice—the crop that after 1700 made Carolina a success despite the political instability that had initially threatened to destroy the enterprise.[4]

Although the narrative of Carolina's settlement had its particularities, in the end the precedence of profit over principles placed the colony in the mainstream of colonial British American society. And along with this triumph of materialism came a familiar power dynamic between Carolina's European settlers and the nonwhite people with whom they shared their new world. Initially, Native Americans proved to be more than a match for white settlers. However, disease, faltering supplies of deerskins, and indebtedness to traders meant that, following the Yamassee War of 1715, Europeans in the Low Country were able to pursue their economic goals with less heed to the wishes of Catawbas or Cherokees. As Native Americans retreated westward, African slaves came to be the predominant nonwhite presence. With their knowledge of rice cultivation and their perceived ability to thrive in a subtropical climate, blacks were condemned to a lifetime of bondage so that their white masters might enjoy the status of mainland America's wealthiest residents. Slaves nevertheless managed to carve out areas of economic and cultural autonomy for themselves, in 1739 even mounting the sizeable Stono Rebellion. Reaction to the uprising by the government in Charles Towne, however, resulted in a new slave code and the brutal repression of any transgressions of whites' authority. As had already occurred in many other coastal regions of colonial America, the English soon found themselves in better control of their domain.[5]

What was unusual about Carolina throughout these first decades of its existence were the many different milieux that influenced the nature of the colonizing enterprise. In most of England's territories the natural environment proved to be the principal force acting upon the settlers, since (in contrast to the Iberian model of colonization) the metropolitan government did not direct the actions of colonists or insist upon the creation of urban settlements. In the Low Country, the "virgin" territories claimed by the Lords Proprietors as their own when they received their charter from Charles II in 1663 played a major part in dictating the direction of the enterprise. This potential agricultural land held a powerful attraction for those settlers who had made the journey to these southern reaches of England's New World. The process of acquiring that land from its Native occupants then figures largely in white-Indian conflicts and, once secured, these tracts proved to be the route to wealth for those Carolinians able to survive the ravages of the environment long enough to develop their plantations.

A second influence, the Old World background of England's first adventurers, was also vital to the nature of their initial colonizing efforts. In Virginia, the economic expectations of the metropolitan Virginia Company directed the pursuits of Jamestown's inhabitants. In New England and Pennsylvania, ideologies and ideas formed by founders in the Old World were highly influential to the colonies' first decades. And as L. H. Roper has recently highlighted, events on both sides of the Atlantic influenced the decisions made by Carolina's Proprietors about their new territory. Both the claustrophobia and the competition of life in the Court and Parliament of the kind, and the imagined tracts of empty, fertile, lands loomed large for the Earl of Shaftesbury and his fellow Proprietors as they shaped their colonial enterprise.[6]

More unusual in the English context, however, there was yet another backdrop for the opening acts of Carolina's history: the urban setting of Charles Towne.[7] This town—or, rather, village, in the decades before 1700—struggled as much as Carolina's first plantations. Once relocated to its final home at Oyster Point, it has streets and squares but few people willing to make a home on them. It had a harbor, but few ships arrived to weigh anchor in it. However, Charles Towne was the center of the Goose Creek men's political power in the young colony, and also the hub of the small amount of trans-atlantic and domestic trade being conducted in these early years. When new settlers arrived, they came to Charles Towne. Early on, the town would also be home to the first churches established by Anglicans, Huguenots, and Congregationalists. The urban environment continued to increase in importance as it received support from certain groups of settlers and, eventually, encouragement from a strengthening economy. Together, these stimuli colluded to make Charles Towne a central force in the colony of South Carolina by the 1740s.

Although there was much that was typical about Carolina's founding, the colony was thus distinctive because its beginning featured a triangle formed by rural New World, town, and mother country. Right from the start, all three of these locations would interact—as would the humans who moved through them—to create the character of Carolina. The conflict between English Proprietors and New World settlers is well documented, as are the processes by which these settlers established a rural plantation economy. Less understood is Charles Towne's place in the narrative of Carolina's founding and of the colony's growth.

Laying the Groundwork for Urbanism

How did South Carolina end up with a town at its heart, when its close neighbors, the Chesapeake colonies of Maryland and Virginia, had remained predominantly rural? The answer did not lie solely with the nature of the colony's staple economy. Before an economic raison d'être had been found for Carolina, an urban aspect to the seventeenth-century colony was secured by the beliefs and preferences of its founders. Responsibility lay, first, with the most enthusiastic Proprietor, Anthony Ashley Cooper, the first Earl of Shaftesbury. Shaftesbury had taken less interest in the enterprise at its inception, but toward the end of the 1660s he proved himself to be its strongest cheerleader, hoping that a successful colonization project might become his legacy. The major manifestation of Shaftesbury's rejuvenated enthusiasm was his authorship of a founding document for the colony. When they drew up their Fundamental Constitutions in 1669, the Earl of Shaftesbury and John Locke set in motion a second beginning for Carolina. Although moves toward settlement had begun in 1663, the Constitutions offered a new template for the basic structures of government and society in the colony. Among early America's more idealistic founding documents, the Constitutions were used by Shaftesbury and Locke to test out radical ideas of governance. Designed to promote an ordered, yet enlightened, society of nobles and commoners, of the sort endorsed by the neo-Harringtonians, the document envisaged a social structure that had proved unrealizable in England, even through civil war. However, Shaftesbury's Fundamental Constitutions were innovative for another, less commented on, reason: they were the first English colonial founding documents to make secular urban settlement an obligatory feature of a society. The Constitutions thus became the vehicle by which their authors might impose their belief in the importance of the modern town on an entirely rural New World.[8]

Shaftesbury's commitment to urban settlement, and the reasons behind it, emerged first in his private letters. There, the earl explicitly stressed that Carolina adventurers should "plant in towns," a form of settlement that, he believed, would immediately make his colony into a more successful and civilized society than Virginia, which he judged inferior to New England precisely because it lacked urban places. As he wished his towns to serve both a social and an economic purpose in an otherwise "uncivilized" New World, Shaftesbury further expressed the desire that urban settlement should conform to the model offered by the classical town, which at this time was believed to be the most advanced example available. Thus, when mulling over his plans for Charles Towne, the earl thought carefully about the width of the streets and alleys, and the size of house plots, explaining that although buildings would be "never so mean and thin at first yet as the town increases in riches and people the void spaces will be filled up and the buildings will grow more beautiful."[9]

The Fundamental Constitutions then elaborated on Shaftesbury's privately articulated wishes. In a departure from other such documents of the era, which were preoccupied with the simple establishment of settlement or the achievement of a specific religious goal, the Constitutions stipulated that it was of "great consequence to the plantation that port-towns should be built and preserved." This regulation was given economic support by the granting of an urban monopoly on the landing of imported goods, with further authority stemming

from a structure of incorporated government for each town. Every settler who was granted a rural tract would also receive a piece of urban land in Carolina's chief town. At the same time, the colony's High Steward's Court was given the power for "setting out and appointing places for towns to be built on in the precincts, and the prescribing and determining the figure and bigness of the said towns, according to such models as the said court shall order; contrary or differing from which models it shall not be lawful for anyone to build in any town."[10] In short, the creation of classical, regular towns with political and economic importance was a central element in the vision of the Fundamental Constitutions' authors. Because Shaftesbury believed that the cooperation of farmers and city traders was the recipe for a successful Carolina, he was determined to legislate against an entirely rural settlement that would only serve as a "hindrance to towns."[11]

A primary motivation for Charles Towne's creation, Shaftesbury's strong interest in towns was continually reinforced by his metropolitan experiences. Until the summer of 1666, keeping a place at court and handling its many intrigues were foremost in Shaftesbury's mind. In the autumn of that year, however, other preoccupations of Londoners were suddenly eclipsed by the devastation caused by the Great Fire. The effects of this inferno, and of the plague that accompanied it, are legendary in the annals of English history. Thirteen thousand buildings burned, leaving many homeless and destitute. Preachers bemoaned Charles II's profligate ways, blaming him for provoking God into punishing his kingdom. It comes as no surprise, therefore, that the Great Fire had direct consequences for Shaftesbury's personal situation. The earl was entirely caught up in the circumstances created by the disaster, and in the immediate aftermath he was kept busy drafting in laborers to eradicate dangerous hot embers. With fears circulating that the conflagration had been a Papist conspiracy, Shaftesbury also devoted a portion of his time to protecting a servant to the Portuguese ambassador who had been accused of starting the fire.[12]

However, it was the events following the Great Fire that really propelled Shaftesbury's urban vision: in subsequent months and years, he witnessed the creation of a brand new, modern London that transformed metropolitan society. One of the most visible benefits of reconstruction was the creation of a more classical townscape to replace the ramshackle, timbered buildings that had been destroyed by the fire. Legislated into existence by the 1667 "Act for Rebuilding the city of London" (subsequently followed by a further act of 1670), this classical vision was an improvement already accessible to Shaftesbury as he drew up his Constitutions. The London Act boldly declared, "in regard that building with brick is not only more comely and durable, but also more safe against future perils of fire," that all edifices should henceforth be made from "brick or stone." Finishing with detailed instructions on the desired mathematical relationship between house and street, the act was replete with the precise guidelines needed to achieve the symmetry and uniformity required by the classical home and townscape.[13] Before London's rebuilding had even begun, the English statute books revealed to Shaftesbury the nuts and bolts of a "modern" city. It was in the light of such developments that Shaftesbury elaborated on his initial 1669 urban ideal for Carolina with the 1680 implementation of his "Grand Modell," a town plan whose regularity clearly drew on the principles guiding the capital's Act for Rebuilding and the work of its chief supervisor, Sir Christopher Wren.

Shaftesbury's continued commitment to urbanism was also a reflection of the fact that the reconstruction of London had proven to be a dramatic stimulus to economic growth and development in the metropole. In order to raise the new types of building enumerated on his statute book, Charles II was forced to end the monopoly of some of the London guilds, thus setting in motion major economic change among the capital's building trades. Seeing a free market opportunity, tradesmen flooded into London, refashioning themselves as construction entrepreneurs by buying leaseholds on mortgage, then developing the land with housing on a speculative basis. Led by these "general contractors," core working practices among all of England's building artisans began to change. Whereas landowners had previously called in individual bricklayers, carpenters, and plasterers on discrete accounts, master craftsmen made themselves into the managers of extensive projects at their own financial risk, and ultimately for their own profit.

By the first decades of the eighteenth century, contemporaries lavished praise on the new urban landscape. Laid out before Shaftesbury's eyes was the stimulation that an expanding town could bring to an economy.[14]

Between the settlement of Virginia, New England, and Jamaica, and that of Carolina, the Great Fire helped in England's transformation from a struggling postwar society into a cultural and economic leader. Such transformations encouraged Shaftesbury to transfer an idea to the New World that was already being successfully realized in the Old. In the belief that towns might do for his society what they were doing for Restoration England, the Proprietor wished to extend to his Carolina the benefits of the revivified urban environment that surrounded him in London. Hence, rather than pursuing the example of his predecessors, Shaftesbury set an example for his successors, Most notable among his followers was William Penn, whose 1681 "Charter for the Province of Pennsylvania" showed a parallel concern for towns as political and economic centers in his own, Quaker enterprise. A wealthy Londoner, Penn had also experienced the Great Fire and witnessed firsthand the revival of the city following the destruction, and although urban development in his Pennsylvania colony ultimately followed a different trajectory, the roots of town settlement there were embedded in a similar background.[15]

Shaftesbury's idea of an urban Carolina was critical to the creation of Charles Towne, but the Proprietor's distance from his New World territory meant that he lacked the ability to take practical steps toward his vision. Fortunately, there were others among the colony's early settlers who were willing to lend their support to the urban project. Early on, the arrival of the dynamic Governor John Archdale in 1695 resulted in the implementation of new policies to encourage urban growth through "sobriety and vertue as well as trade," an aim clearly founded on Shaftesbury's earlier ideas that towns were not merely central to the economy, but also to society.[16] At the same time, Carolina's initial colonists were also ready to see the logic and the necessity of urban settlement. Although few among these early settlers were familiar with recent developments in London, they had experienced the effects of growing towns in their own colony or country.

Carolina's Barbadian immigrants, for example, came from a society that was home to one of the British New World's largest towns. In 1680, Bridgetown had 3,000 residents, but it was subsequently to experience its major period of growth, and by 1712 its inhabitants numbered over 10,000. In the course of three decades, the town had become Barbados's primary commercial entrepôt, hosting a large community of merchants, maritime workers, and service providers. It was thus little surprise that Carolina's Goose Creek men further guaranteed Charles Towne's future when, rather than allow the deerskin trade to be conducted in the rural parts of the colony, they pushed through a 1707 act to concentrate it in the colonial capital. This act had the effect of privileging the role of specialist urban merchants who could mediate between the town and the colony's interior to collect and ship skins, thus securing the fortunes of a notable proportion of Charles Towne's population. As a result, over half a million skins left the colony through the town between 1706 and 1715.

Numbers in the town were also dramatically boosted by the arrival of a large number of French Huguenot refugees. With many urban-dwelling craftsmen and merchants in their number, the Protestants began arriving as early as 1679. However, the largest influx came in 1687, when six hundred arrived in Charles Towne. Some settlers targeted the French Santee area some sixty miles north of the town, drawing up detailed plans for their own urban settlement—Jamestown—on the river's edge. Most Huguenot merchants and tradesmen, though, chose to base themselves in an existing urban environment where opportunities for trade were more established.[17]

Soon, the French Protestant community had built their principal place of worship in Charles Towne and had begun to achieve prominence on the commercial scene. Tradesmen like Huguenot watchmaker and jeweler Nicholas de Longuemare placed their faith in the young urban economy, setting up some of the town's earliest businesses. De Longuemare's records of his work between 1698 and 1707 show that he labored alone repairing the clocks and watches of the Low Country's residents, making sets of mourning rings, gold buttons, and brass weights, and fashioning the occasional set of cutlery. Work came into his shop only sporadically, with a "busy" month yielding four customers and a quiet one none at all. De Longuemare dealt with this low demand by also establishing himself in the business of silk importation and by developing a cattle ranch on a nearby suburban tract. Although demand for his luxury services obviously remained weak, De Longuemare nevertheless stayed on in Charles Towne. Many of these early townspeople further demonstrated their commitment to the urban environment when they invested in the lots marked out in Shaftesbury's Grand Modell. Early records show that 161 settlers purchased 236 lots before 1700. The largest investor was politician, merchant, and Barbados man, Jonathan Amory, who owned seven of the town's more than three hundred tracts. Huguenot settlers also showed themselves to be eager buyers, with at least seven investing in town lands.[18]

Through the actions of the Proprietors, and the predilections of settlers who subsequently came to the colony, urbanism was a reality in South Carolina from the first decades of its history. Before a successful staple economy existed, Shaftesbury had conceived of a society civilized by the presence of towns. Working in line with a growing urban movement in England, and implementing his ideas in the light of the experiences of previous New World settlement enterprises, the Proprietor was successful in ensuring that his beloved Carolina would have an urban character to complement its rural focus. Very early on, Shaftesbury's plans were supported by the choices of those French and Barbadian settlers who came to Carolina, and even though both groups of incomers found little to their liking in the Fundamental Constitutions, they were nevertheless sympathetic to Shaftesbury's urban vision. [...]

In all of these places, urban growth was underwritten by a strong economy. Bridgetown's rapid ascent had come in the wake of Barbados's sugar revolution, the increase in trade of the staple through the port prompting the expansion of the urban service sector. A lively trading economy meant that Philadelphia had garnered almost 8,000 inhabitants by 1734, climbing to 9,500 by 1741. At the same time, between 1650 and 1750, the urban population of England increased by some 5 percent as the early stages of industrial revolution and the expansion of the empire stimulated town and city economies. In particular, western coastal cities like Glasgow and Liverpool were beginning to forge ahead on the back of the tobacco and slave trades, and Manchester flourished as its textile industries grew. In both Britain's provinces and in colonial America, strong economies firmly rooted in international trade or domestic manufacturing had proved to be the key to urban growth.

NOTES

1. The fullest recent account of Caroline's proprietary period is Roper, *Conceiving Carolina*, 4–5. See also Weir, "Shaftesbury's Darling," and Clowse, *Economic Beginnings*.
2. On the French Huguenot experience, see Hirsch, *Huguenots of Colonial South Carolina*, and McClain and Ellefson, "A Letter from Carolina, 1688."
3. On the Barbados connection, see Greene, "Colonial South Carolina and the Caribbean Connection"; Coclanis, *Shadow of a Dream*, 21–23; Sirmans, *Colonial South Carolina*, 19–128; and Roper, *Conceiving Caroline*, 51–67.
4. On the importance of Africans to early economic activity in South Carolina, see Wood, *Black Majority*, 96–130; Littlefield, *Rice and Slaves*; Carney, *Black Rice*; and Edelson, *Plantation Enterprise*, 53–91.
5. On the experiences of Native Americans and Africans in the early years of South Carolina, see Merrell, *The Indians' New World*,

1–91; Wood, *Black Majority*, 271–330; and Littlefield, *Rice and Slaves*, 74–114.
6. On early settlement in Virginia, see Kupperman, *The Jamestown Project*, 210–328. For details of Pennsylvania's early decades, see Nash, *Quakers and Politics*. On Carolina's first years, see Roper, *Conceiving Carolina*, 16–49.
7. The spelling of Charleston underwent a number of changes before 1790. It was first named Charles' Towne but, as the eighteenth century progressed, the "e" was dropped and the apostrophe disappeared, leaving it as Charles Town, and sometimes CharlesTown. After the Revolution, the name was formerly changed to Charleston. For the purposes of clarity, this book will use Charles Towne to discuss the town's early years in this first chapter, and then will switch to Charleston.
8. On the Fundamental Constitutions, see Roper, *Conceiving Carolina*, 29–50. For discussion of James Harrington and his seventeenth-century followers, see Pocock, *Machianvellian Moment*, 361–422. In Maryland and New York, the manorial system was deployed as a unit of settlement. For a history of manorial settlement, see Kim, *Landlord and Tenant*. New England towns were mentioned in charters but not legislated into existence. See, for example, Connecticut's "Fundamental Orders of 1639."
9. As quoted in Haley, *First Earl of Shaftesbury*, 249. For a contemporary discussion of the benefits of the classical urban plan, see Wren, *Parentalia*, 267.
10. "The Fundamental Constitutions of Carolina: March 1, 1669," Article 44.
11. As quoted by Roper, *Conceiving Carolina*, 48.
12. Haley, *First Earl of Shatesbury*, 186. The most comprehensive contemporary accounts of the fire's impact on London's elite and upper-middling sorts are available in Latham and Matthews, *Diary of Samuel Pepys*, 7, and in *Diary of John Evelyn*, 3.
13. Great Britain and Pickering, *Statutes at Large*, vol. 8, Article 7 and Article 5, 235.
14. McKellar, *Birth of Modern London*, 31. McKellar's discussion of London's rebuilding is the most recent, and definitive, treatment of the process and its impact. For the continuing repercussions of new urban construction in the eighteenth century, see Corfield, *Impact of English Towns*, and Chalklin, *Provincial Towns of Georgian England*. The rebuilding also had an impact on the New World, as in part it was responsible for the diminished supply of white indentured labor to the Chesapeake. See Menard, "From Servants to Slaves."

15. "Merchandise and trade unto the said Province, or out of the same shall depart, shall be laden or unladen only at such Ports as shall be erected and constituted by the said William Penn, his heires and assignee, any use, custome, or other thing to the contrary notwithstanding" ("Charter for the Province of Pennsylvania—1681"). For discussion of William Penn's urban plans, see Nash, *Quakers and Politics*, 38–39, as well as Nash, "Framing of Government in Pennsylvania," 187–88.

16. Clowse, *Economic Beginnings*, 96.

17. Welch, *Slave Society in the City*, 53 (table 3.1); Clowse, *Economic Beginnings*, 165–66; and Hirsch, *Huguenots of Colonial South Carolina*, 47; Bertrand van Ruymbeke has estimated that 54 percent of Huguenot settlers were either artisans or merchants, while only 14 percent were yeomen. Further, he shows that most tradespeople chose to establish themselves in an urban setting. Ruymbeke, "Huguenots of Proprietary South Carolina," 32–39.

18. Account book of Nicholas de Longuemare, 1703–1708, Charleston Museum. List of initial buyers of Charleston Grand Modell lots, misc. ms., SCHS.

DOCUMENTS FOR PART II

2.1 THE "LOST" NATIVE AMERICAN CITY OF ETZANOA (1602)

Source: "Official Hearings Conducted by the Crown's Fiscal Agent Don Francisco de Valverde by Order of the Viceroy Count of Monterrey, Concerning Governor Don Juan de Oñate's Recent Explorations in the Northern Territories beyond the Provinces of New Mexico" (1602). Reproduced in: Jerry R. Craddock and John H. R. Polt, "Juan de Oñate in Quivira, 1601: the "Relación cierta y verdadera" and the Valverde Interrogatory," University of California, Berkeley Cibola Project, https://escholarship.org/uc/item/7162z2rp (May 21, 2013): 143–152 and 185–189.

EDITORS' INTRODUCTION

In the summer of 1601, Governor Don Juan de Oñate, one of the founders of the Spanish colony of New Mexico, led over sixty soldiers and many more camp followers, along with several cannons, on an expedition within what is now the United States. The explorers ventured into "Quivira," a name the Spanish gave for the Great Plains area in and around the present state of Kansas, to look for possible survivors from an earlier unauthorized excursion into the region. On their way to what is now the Kansas-Oklahoma border, Oñate's party encountered enormous herds of American bison and other abundant forms of fauna and flora, as well as several different Native American Indian tribes that spoke distinct languages and resided in configurations of various sizes and degrees of permanence. One group the Spanish identified as the "Escanxaques" lived in a rather large encampment, comprised of tents made of branches and dressed hides, some as much as ninety feet wide, and containing an estimated 5,000 people. Another group, labeled the Quivirans, lived in a series of permanent settlements with the largest, Etzanoa, reportedly including at least 2,000 dwellings. It took the Spanish three days to traverse the length of the settlement on foot. Even by today's standards, both of these residential configurations were remarkably urban in terms of population size, density, and function.

Oñate's group spent only a brief period in one sector of Etzanoa and never returned, since they became embroiled in conflict between the Escanxaques and Quivirans. Oñate's party escaped an attack by the Escanxaques—who had originally befriended the Spanish—only by use of *cannon*. There is no further record of the Spanish ever formally revisiting Etzanoa, and by the time the French explored the region in the eighteenth century, the city became one of legend, all but lost to history. However, in 2015 Adam Ziegler, then a high school student working with Donald Blakeslee, an archeology professor at Wichita State University, found one of the Spanish cannon balls and a functioning water shrine. When combined with new translations of official inquiries into Oñate's expedition (quoted in part in the document), and a reproduction of an actual map drawn from the testimony of a Native American named Miguel, who Oñate's men had captured, Blakeslee concluded that present day Arkansas City, Kansas is the site of the great settlement of Etzanoa. Blakeslee and other scholars confirm that Etzanoa could have been home to as many as 20,000 people between 1450 and 1700, making it one of the largest urban areas in what becomes the United States from the peak of Cahokia's population in the thirteenth century, to and the rise of Philadelphia on the eve of the American Revolution in the eighteenth century.[i] **[See Document 2.2, Henry Marie Brackenridge, "Envisioning Great American Indian Cities" (1813).]**

The excerpt in this document is a first-hand account of Etzanoa from four Spanish guides who took part in Oñate's expedition, and the Indian Miguel, recorded as part of an official interrogation conducted under the auspices of Don Francisco de Valverde y Mercado, the royal fiscal agent of New Spain in 1602. The questions raised by Valverde and answered by Miguel and the guides provides unique insight into sedentary indigenous urban formations and population size. Of note in their testimony is the uniform way in which the guides describe the location, design, and construction of dwellings, as well as the domestic spaces, culinary characteristics, dress, and appearance of those who lived in Etzanoa. In addition, Miguel's perspective represented the only recorded Native American testimony on Quivira. Although Miguel did not speak Spanish—his testimony was an interpretation of his Plains Indian sign language—his map was accurate enough to allow Blakeslee to identify the city four centuries later.[ii]

THE "LOST" NATIVE AMERICAN CITY OF ETZANOA (1602)

Witness, Baltasar Martínez, King's Bailiff for the Expedition, Age 23.

In the city of Mexico on the 23d day of the month of April of the year 1602, Don Francisco de Valverde y Mercado, His Majesty's fiscal agent for this realm of New Spain, in virtue of His Lordship's charge that he investigate the most recent exploration carried out by Governor Don Juan de Oñate in the provinces of New Mexico, caused to appear before him a man who declared that his name is Baltasar Martínez and that he is a native of the municipality of Budia in the kingdom of Toledo and diocese of Sigüenza and that he is the King's bailiff for the commander Captain Bernabé de las Casas, who led a relief expedition into the said provinces of New Mexico in the year 1600; and this man he placed under oath by God and by the sign of the cross as prescribed by law, and [the man] promised to tell the truth.
[. . .]

Layout of the Large Town They Saw, Where They Started Back, Etc.

Upon being asked whether this witness entered the said town and its houses, whether he saw and examined them, how many houses there might be and of what configuration, and what the Indians kept in the said houses, he said that this witness along with the whole army entered the said town and its houses, which said town lies on the shores of a small river that flows into the large one, on both banks of the said small river, and the houses are set about 20 or 30 or 40 paces apart and they form something like districts, with 30 or 40 houses in each district, and between one district and another there are open spaces of 200 or 300 paces; and the houses are made of thin sticks set very close together in the ground that come together above like a tent, and at their base they are round, with a circumference of some 70 or 80 feet, with doors so low that you must get on your knees to enter, and they close them with little sticks covered with straw; and inside, from one side to the other, occupying about a half or a third of the house, they have

---

i Donald J. Blakeslee, "The Miguel map revisited," *Plains Anthropologist* 63, no. 245 (February 2018): 67–84; David Malakoff, "Searching for Etzanoa," *American Archeology* (Spring 2016): 26–31; and David Kelly, "Archeologists explore rural field in Kansas, and a lost city emerges," *Chicago Tribune* 19 August 2018, http://www.chicagotribune.com/la-na-kansas-lost-city-20180819-htmilstory.html (accessed 2 October 2018).

ii For a copy of the map, see Jerry R. Craddock and John H. R. Polt, "Juan de Oñate in Quivira, 1601: the "Relación cierta y verdadera" and the Valverde Interrogatory," University of California, Berkeley Cibola Project "Appendix I: The Maps," https://escholarship.org/uc/item/7162z2rp, page 206.

some horizontal poles on which they set up beds the size of the rope beds in Castile, with some sticks lying across them, which is where it seemed to this witness that they slept; and at about a quarter of the height of the house, [there were sticks] stretching from one side to the other so as to make something like a loft, which they reached by means of a wooden ladder outside; and this witness and the others thought that this arrangement was for hot weather, and in the lower part of the houses there were so many fleas that they felt distressed if they had to go inside; and this is how all the houses were that this witness saw, and outside they were covered from top to bottom with straw.

[...]

How Far beyond the Large Town the Adelantado Went, and What Planted Fields They Saw, Etc.

Upon being asked how far the said Don Juan de Oñate advanced through the said towns, and what fields of corn they saw within them, and whether they saw any other kind of foodstuffs that the said Indians customarily use for their sustenance, he said that it seems to him that the said governor and his men advanced for almost two leagues[1] along one side of the houses of the said town, where the carts could go, and it seemed to him that the said town ended there, and all of it consisted of districts as he has said; and he remembers hearing that four soldiers counted the houses and found about 2,000; and that in all of the said town the fields and cleared lands form the space between houses, and some stretch out from the sides of the said houses, although always within sight of them; and they also saw a few beans and small squash, and nothing else, nor fruit trees, except some plum trees and trellises that hold the wild grapes that he has mentioned, and this without any cultivation.

[...]

Testimony of the Witness Juan de León, a Soldier on the Expedition.

[...]

Layout of the Large Town They Saw, Where They Started Back, Etc.

Upon being asked whether this witness entered the said town and saw it, that he should describe the form and layout of the houses and say how many there might be and of what configuration and what there was inside the said houses, he said that this witness entered the said town and some of its houses, and the houses are made of poles the thickness of an arm, and in the center they have another heavier one at which they are all joined, and they are similar to tents and large, though constructed as explained, all with beds of woven sticks inside, and outside they have wooden ladders whereby they climb up to a loft that they make of wood to store corn, because in many of these lofts they saw the said corn, and inside the said houses they found grinding stones like the *metates* with which the Indian women grind corn here, and they did not find the pestles of the said stones with which they grind, and they found pots and jars of dark clay, and in the said town and its houses they did not find any chickens or chicken feathers or dogs or cats or any other animal; and the Indians of the said town whom this witness saw were of very dark complexion and all were scantily clothed, some of them wearing deerskin that covered them to the knees, and he saw none of them wearing any cloth garment of any kind, and he did not see any women, because all those who showed themselves were men; and this witness could not see more than 700 or 800 of the said houses because the troops, in order to be able to take the carts across the river, detoured from the said town, and four or five Indians whom the governor had ordered seized from among the Escanxaques to serve as guides said that the said town would go on for three days' journey.

[...]

Witness Diego de Ayardia, Soldier on the Expedition.

[...]

Layout of the Large Town They Saw, Where They Started Back, Etc.

Upon being asked whether this witness saw the said town and entered its houses and saw what was in them, and that he describe their configuration and what was in them, he said that the said houses were all made of poles stuck into the ground, covered with straw, and closed on top like tents, some larger than others, and inside [there were] some beds made of sticks and straw, and outside they had some lofts with some moveable ladders, and inside the said houses in some holes in the ground they kept the corn and beans and some squash, and they had some stones the length and width of three bricks, along with other small stones, that seemed to be for grinding, and they had some clay pots and some gourd vessels, and there was no sign of chickens or chicken feathers, and he saw some small dogs, and he saw no other kind of animal; and the said people of the said town whom he saw were sturdy and handsome and all went naked but for some small pieces of deerskin and dressed cowhide, and he did not see any of them wear any cloth, and he did not see any woman; and the said Indians, both these and the Escanxaques and the Apaches and those pacified and settled in San Gabriel, men and women, all use footwear similar to boots covering half their legs, with the shaft made of deerskin and the sole of thick leather of the cattle or elk; and this witness thinks he saw as many as 2,000 houses in the said town, and other soldiers told him they had seen many more, because they went ahead with the colonel, and all the Indians said by signs that the town stretched on for three days' journey.

[...]

Witness, Miguel Montero, Ensign on the Expedition.

Layout of the Large Town They Saw, Where They Started Back, Etc.

Upon being asked to tell and declare what he saw and what occurred in the large town that they discovered, he said that before the troops could explore the said town, the Indians of the large encampment had gone ahead without their being able to stop them and, being enemies of the Indians of the said large town, had challenged and alarmed them, and thus they came forth armed, and as soon as they sighted the Spaniards they stopped; and the said governor called them peaceably, and a large number of Indians began to draw near the army, all bearing bows and arrows, and it seems to this witness there might have been some 20,000 Indians; and they all stayed on the other side of the river, and some came into the camp and brought ears of corn and large loaves and offered and gave this to the governor and to his soldiers, who gave them tobacco and other things; and all the time signs of peace were displayed toward the Spaniards, which consisted of raising their hands toward the sun and then placing them on their breasts; and the Indians of the large encampment told the said governor by signs that those Indians had killed the Spaniards and that they were holding one of them alive; and when the said Indians of the said town were asked about the said Spaniard, they said they knew nothing of him and that they had not killed the Spaniards; and the said governor decided that some Indians should be seized to be exchanged for the said Spaniard, and the next day they seized two Indians for the said purpose, and the night of the day of their capture they escaped from a soldier who was guarding them; and the said Indians of the large town withdrew from their houses and left them empty, and the Indians of the encampment entered them and sacked them and set fire to some of them, and the said governor sent some men to stop it and drive the said Indians of the encampment out of the town, as was done; and the said governor with his troops entered the said town and camped among the houses.

[...]

Procedures Followed with Miguel, an Indian...

[...]

The Indian, Who Spoke Only by Means of Signs, Was Brought in.

And then the said agent [Don Francisco Valverde y Mercado] ordered Ambrosio de Rueda, executive bailiff of the royal treasury, to go to the lodgings of Baltasar Mejía Salmerón, chief bailiff of this city, where the said Indian Miguel is being held, and ask for him and bring him to his presence in order to follow the said procedure, and the said bailiff went and brought the said Indian Miguel before the said agent and to his lodgings, which Indian is well built and handsome, of a complexion somewhat darker than that of the Mexican Indians; and with the said Indian the said agent employed the following procedures and by means of signs asked the following questions, in the presence of the physician Dr. Contreras and the said interpreter Juan Grande and the bailiff Ambrosio de Rueda and Don Juan Bautista, governor of Santiago.

Miguel Drew His Country on a Sheet of Paper…

First the said agent ordered the said Indian Miguel by signs that on a sheet of paper that was placed before him on a table he draw with pen and ink the towns of his country, and the said Miguel proceeded to make some circles like o's on the said sheet of paper, some larger than others, and all of it in such a way that the meaning of each circle was quite clear; and by order of the said agent, I, the present notary, wrote on each of the said circles what the said Indian said they were, so that one might understand them; and then he drew some lines, some of them winding and others straight, which he said by signs were rivers and roads, and on them also was written what they are as the said Indian gave us to understand.

[…]

That between Where He Was Born and Where He Was Held Captive There Are a Great Many People.

And in the towns where he was born and raised and captured by the Spaniards there are many people, stressing that they are many.

And he said by the said signs that having been born in Tancoa, he was captured in a battle that the Indians of his country had with those of Aguacane when he was a boy, and he was captive there until the said Indians of Aguacane and its district went to war, now that the Spaniards had come; and having fought against the said Spaniards near the large town, he was captured by them and brought to San Gabriel and to this city by Colonel Vicente de Zaldívar.

And he said that the Indians of the large town that Governor Don Juan de Oñate discovered and the Indians of the towns where he was raised are enemies and fight against each other.

NOTE

1. Editors' note: A league is a unit of measurement for distance that varied between countries and time-periods; the editors of this document use the estimation that one league equals roughly three miles.

2.2 ENVISIONING GREAT AMERICAN INDIAN CITIES (1813)

Henry Marie Brackenridge

Source: *Transactions of the American Philosophical Society*, Vol. 1, New Series (1818): 151–159.

EDITORS' INTRODUCTION

Just east of St. Louis, Missouri, across the Mississippi River, are numerous earthen mounds that comprise the remains of the ancient American Indian city of Cahokia. At one time, more than 200 of these mounds or pyramids radiated twenty miles or so from the center of Cahokia, the largest such concentration in North America, with more than half arranged within a five-square-mile area around vast open plazas. During its height in the twelfth century (AD or CE), Cahokia was the center of an extensive Indian nation whose influence extended throughout the Mississippi and Missouri River Valleys as far north as the Dakotas, east to present day New York and Florida and south and west to Mexico. Cahokia was the largest Native American city north of Mexico, with 10,000–20,000 or more people at its center, and another 30,000 or so in surrounding communities stretching out in a fifty-mile radius. At its height, Cahokia was as large as the city of London and, until the rise of Philadelphia in the late eighteenth century, the largest city in the territory that would become the United States.

Cahokia collapsed by the time of European exploration, leaving subsequent generations to speculate on the purpose of the mounds, their composition, and the people who built them. The following document is one such assessment from the writer Henry Marie Brackenridge (1786–1871) who presented his ideas to former President Thomas Jefferson (1743–1826) in the form of a letter written in 1813 and subsequently reprinted in several journals and magazines of that era. Brackenridge envisioned Cahokia (his original spelling of "Cohokia" and other words are retained in the document) as part of a series of large ancient cities with high populations located throughout the Mississippi and Ohio River Valleys. Seeing this area through an urban lens was not uncommon in the early nineteenth century, as Richard C. Wade illustrates in his essay, "Urban Life in Western America, 1790–1830" in Part III (**Essay 3.3**). However, while many nineteenth-century settlers and investors envisioned an urban future, Brackenridge sought to stake out a past in which ancient American cities and their inhabitants compared favorably to other civilizations of the ancient world including the celebrated Teocalli—or Mesoamerican pyramids—of Mexico.[i]

ENVISIONING GREAT AMERICAN INDIAN CITIES (1813)

On The Population and Tumuli of the Aborigines of North America. In a letter from H.M. Brackenridge, Esq. to Thomas Jefferson.

Baton Rouge, July 25, 1813.

Sir,

From a knowledge that research into the history of the primitive inhabitants of America, is one of your favourite amusements, I take the liberty of making this communication. My attention to the subject, was first awakened on reading, when a boy, the observations contained in the "Notes on Virginia," and it has become, with me, a favourite theme of speculation. I often visited the mound, and other remains of Indian antiquity in the neighbourhood of Pittsburgh, my native town, attracted by a pleasing interest, of which I scarcely knew the cause, and afterwards read, and heard with delight, whatever related to these monuments of the first, or rather earlier, inhabitants of my native country. Since the year 1810 (without previously intending it) I have visited almost every thing of this kind, worthy of note on the Ohio and Mississippi; and from examination and reflection, something like hypothesis, has taken the place of the vague wanderings of fancy. The following is a sketch of the result of those observations.

I Throughout...the valley of the Mississippi, there exist the traces of a population far beyond what this extensive and fertile portion of the continent, is supposed to have

---

i For more on Cahokia, see Timothy R. Pauketat, *Cahokia: Ancient America's Great City on the Mississippi* (New York: Viking, The Penguin Library of American Indian History, 2009) and Bilonie Young and Melvin Fowler, *Cahokia: The Great Native American Metropolis* (Urbana: University of Illinois Press, 2000).

possessed: greater, perhaps, than could be supported of the present white inhabitants, even with careful agricultural practiced in the most populous parts of Europe.

[...]

II In the valley of the Mississippi, there are discovered the traces of two distinct traces of people, periods of population, one much more ancient than the other. The traces of the last are the most numerous, but mark a population less advanced in civilization; in fact, they belong to the same race that existed in the country when the French and the English effected their settlement on this part of the continent.

[...]

III The first and most ancient period, is marked by...extraordinary tumuli or mounds. I have reason to believe that their antiquity is great. The oldest Indians have no tradition as their authors, or the purpose, or which they were originally intended; yet they were formerly, I might also say instinctively, in the habit of using them for one of the purposes for which they were at first designed, to wit, as places of defence [sic]... These tumuli as well as the fortifications, are to be found at the junction of all the considerable rivers, in the most eligible positions for towns, and in the most extensive bodies of fertile land. Their number exceeds, perhaps, *three thousand*; the smallest not less than twenty feet in height, and one hundred in diameter at the base. Their great number, and the astonishing size of some of them, may be regarded as furnishing, with other circumstances, evidence of their antiquity. I have been sometimes induced to think, that at the period when those mounds were constructed, there existed on the Mississippi, a population as numerous as that which once animated the borders of the Nile, or of the Euphrates, or of Mexico and Peru.

IV The most numerous, as well as the most considerable of these remains, are found precisely in the part of the country where the traces of a numerous population might be looked for, to wit, from the mouth of the Ohio (on the east side of the Mississippi) to the Illinois river, and on the west side from the St. Francis to the Missouri. I am perfectly satisfied that cities similar to those of *ancient Mexico*, of several hundred thousand souls, have existed in this part of the country. Nearly opposite St. Louis there are the traces of two such cities, in the distance of five miles, on the bank of the Cohokia, which crosses the American bottom at this place. There are not less than one hundred mounds, in two different groups; one of the mounds falls little short of the Egyptian pyramid Mycerius... The following is an enumeration of the most considerable mounds on the Mississippi and on the Ohio; the greater part I examined myself with such attention as the short time I had to spare would permit.

1. At Great Creek, below Wheeling.
2. At Pittsburgh.
3. At Marietta.
4. At Cincinnati.
5. At New Madrid—one of them 350 feet diameter at the base.
6. Bois Brulie bottom, fifteen miles below St. Genevieve.
7. At St. Genevieve.
8. Mouth of the Marameck.
9. St. Louis—one with two stages, another with three.
10. Mouth of the Missouri.
11. On the Cohokia river—in two groups.
12. Twenty miles below—two groups also, but the mounds of a smaller size—on the back of a lake, formerly of the bed of the river.
13. Near Washington (M.T.) 146 feet in height.
14. At Baton Rouge, and on the bayou Manchac—one of the mounds near the lake is chiefly composed of shells—the inhabitants have taken away great quantities of these for the purpose of making lime.
15. The mound on Black River, of two stages, with a group around it.

At each of these places there are groups of mounds; and at each there probably existed a city. On the other considerable rivers which are tributaries to the Ohio and Mississippi, in Kentucky, Tennessee, state of Ohio, Indiana territory, &c. they are equally numerous. But the principle city and center of the population was between the Ohio, Mississippi, Missouri, and Illinois.

[...]

Such are the appearances of antiquity in the western country, which I consider as furnishing proof of an ancient and numerous population. The resemblance to those of New Spain would render probable the existence of the same arts and customs; perhaps of an intercourse. The distance from the large mound on Red River, to the nearest in New Spain, is not so great but that they might be considered as existing in the same country.

[...]

The antiquity of these mounds is certainly very great; this is not inferred from the growth of trees, which prove an antiquity of a few centuries, but from this simple reflection; a people capable of works requiring so much labour, must be numerous, and if numerous, somewhat advanced in the arts; we might therefore look for works of stone or brick, the traces of which would remain for at least eight or ten centuries. The great mound of Cohokia, is evidently constructed with as much regularity as any of the Teocalli of New Spain, and was doubtless cased with brick or stone, and crowned with buildings; but of these no traces remain... Some might be startled if I should say that the mound of Cohokia is as ancient as those of Egypt! The Mexicans possessed but imperfect traditions of the construction of their Teocalli; their traditions attributed to the Toultees, or to the Olmess, who probably migrated from the Mississippi.

Who will pretend to speak with certainty as to the antiquity of America—the races of men who have flourished and disappeared—of the thousand revolutions, which, like other parts of the globe, it has undergone? The philosophers of Europe, with a narrowness and selfishness of the mind, have endeavoured to deprecate everything which relates to it. They have called it the *New World*, as though its formation was posterior to the rest of the habitable globe. As few facts suffice it to repel this idea:—the antiquity of her mountains, the remains of volcanoes, the alluvial tracts, the wearing away of cataracts, &c. and the number of primitive languages, greater perhaps than in all the rest of the world besides.

2.3 A MODEL OF CHRISTIAN CHARITY (1630)

John Winthrop

Source: Samuel Eliot Morison, ed., *Winthrop Papers*, Volume II, 1623–1630 (Boston: The Massachusetts Historical Society, 1931). Courtesy of the Massachusetts Historical Society, Boston, Massachusetts.

EDITORS' INTRODUCTION

In April 1630, the Reverend John Winthrop led a group of Puritans from England on eleven ships bound for the Massachusetts Bay Colony. Their goal was to create a model for how to reform and purify the Church of England. Prior to landing in Massachusetts, Winthrop delivered his famous "A Model of Christian Charity" sermon aboard the ship *Arbella* in which he reminded his fellow Puritans of the importance of their undertaking. Although the sermon revolved around the themes of justice and mercy, it is most remembered for Winthrop's concluding remarks where he draws from biblical verse (Matthew 5:14) in arguing that in their New England efforts they will be as "a City upon a Hill" with the eyes of all people upon them.

This theme has become one of the most influential and enduring self-reflections in all of American history and forms the underpinning for much of U.S. foreign policy.

Winthrop and his followers eventually settled on the Shawmut Peninsula in Massachusetts and renamed it Boston after a town in Lincolnshire, England where many Puritans once lived. Boston was a covenanted community, composed of individuals in a special compact with one another and God. The Puritans adopted the town or township form of government, also transplanted from England, with a congregation of believers at the center. The Puritan form of settlement became the archetype American municipality, replicated with each generation throughout New England and portions of the Middle Atlantic and Midwest.

The following version of Winthrop's sermon is from a manuscript printed in the seventeenth century for mass circulation. The twentieth century editors of the *Winthrop Papers* who worked with the Massachusetts Historical Society (which included Samuel Eliot Morison and Arthur M. Schlesinger, Sr.), retained the original seventeenth-century spelling, grammar, and inconsistent capitalization, and supplemented it with select biblical references in the citations. The contemporary reader will note the common inversion of the letters "u" and "v" in certain words, the use of "c" instead of "t" and the addition of the letter "e" in several places.

A MODELL OF CHRISTIAN CHARITY

Written

On Boarde the Arrabella

On the Attlantick Ocean.

By the Honorable JOHN WINTHROP, Esquire.
In His passage (with the great Company of Religious people, of which Christian Tribes he was the Brave Leader and famous Governor;) from the Island of Great Brittaine, to New-England in the North America.

Anno 1630.

CHRISTIAN CHARITIE.
A MODELL HEREOF.
God Almightie in his most holy and wise providence hath soe disposed of the Condicion of mankinde, as in all times some must be rich and some poore, some highe and eminent in power and dignitie; others meane and in subieccion.
THE REASON HEREOF.
1. REAS: *First*, to hold conformity with the rest of his workes, being delighted to shewe forthe the glory of his wisdome in the variety and differance of the Creatures and the glory of his power, in ordering all these differences for the preservacion and good of the whole, and the glory of his greatnes that as it is in the glory of princes to haue many officers, soe this great King will haue many Stewards counting himselfe more honoured in dispenceing his guifts to man by man, then if hee did it by his owne immediate hand.

2. REAS: *Secondly*, That he might haue the more occasion to manifest the worke of his Spirit: first, vpon the wicked in moderateing and restraineing them: soe that the riche and mighty should not eate vpp the poore, nor the poore, and dispised rise vpp against theire superiours, and shake off theire yoake; 2ly in the regenerate in exerciseing his graces in them, as in the greate ones, theire loue mercy, gentlenes, temperance etc., in the poore and inferiour sorte, theire faithe patience, obedience etc:

3. REAS: Thirdly, That every man might haue need of other, and from hence they might be all knitt more nearly together in the Bond of brotherly affeccion: from hence it appeares plainely that noe man is made more honourable then another or more wealthy etc., out of any perticuler and singular respect to himselfe but for the glory of his Creator and the Common good of the Creature, Man... There are two rules whereby wee are to walke one toward another: JUSTICE and MERCY.
[...]
When God giues a speciall Commission he lookes to haue it strictly obserued in every Article... Thus stands the cause betweene God and vs, wee are entered into

Covenant with him for this worke, wee haue taken out a Commission, the Lord hath giuen vs leaue to drawe our owne Articles wee haue professed to enterprise these Accions vpon these and these ends, wee haue herevpon besought him of favour and blessing: Now if the Lord shall please to heare vs, and bring vs in peace to the place wee desire, then hath hee ratified this Covenant and sealed our Commission, [and] will expect a strickt performance of the Articles contained in it, but if wee shall neglect the observacion of these Articles which are the ends wee haue propounded, and dissembling with our God, shall fall to embrace this present world and prosecute our carnall intencions, seekeing great things for our selues and our posterity, the Lord will surely breake out in wrathe against vs be revenged of such a periured people and make vs knowe the price of the breache of such a Covenant.

Now the onely way to avoyde this shipwracke and to provide for our posterity is to followe the Counsell of Micah, to doe Justly, to loue mercy, to walke humbly with our God,[1] for this end, wee must be knitt together in this worke as one man, wee must entertaine each other in brotherly Affeccion... wee shall finde that the God of Israell is among us, when tenn of vs shall be able to resist a thousand of our enemies, when hee shall make vs a prayse and glory, that men shall say of succeeding plantacions: the lord make it like that of New England: for wee must Consider that wee shall be as a Citty vpon a Hill,[2] the eies of all people are vppon vs; soe that if wee shall deale falsely with our god in this worke wee haue vndertaken and soe cause him to withdrawe his present help from vs, wee shall be made a story and a by-word through the world, wee shall open the mouthes of enemies to speake euill of the ways of god and all professours for Gods sake; wee shall shame the faces of many of gods worthy seruants, and cause theire prayers to be turned into Cursses vpon vs till wee be consumed out of the good land whether wee are goeing...

Therefore lett vs choose life,
that wee, and our Seede,
may liue; by obeying his
voyce, and cleaueing to him,
for hee is our life, and
our prosperity.

NOTES

1. Micah, vi. 8.
2. Matthew, v. 14.

2.4 PHILADELPHIA IN 1697

Benjamin Bullivant

Source: Benjamin Bullivant, *A Journall with Observations on my Travail from Boston in N.E. to N.Y. New Jersies & Philadelphia in Pennsylvania* A.D. 1697, as excerpted by Wayne Andrews, "The Travel Diary of Dr. Benjamin Bullivant," *New-York Historical Society Quarterly* 60, no. 1 (January 1956): 69–71. Courtesy of the New-York Historical Society, New York, New York and the estate of Wayne Andrews.

EDITORS' INTRODUCTION

William Penn founded Philadelphia in 1682 as a commercial port between the Delaware and Schuylkill Rivers for the new colony of Pennsylvania. Philadelphia and the colony as a whole grew quickly as large numbers of Quakers, Scotch-Irish, and German immigrants settled the region. In 1760, less than a century later, Philadelphia was the largest town in British North America and one of the largest urban areas in the entire British Empire except for London. William Penn laid out the streets of Philadelphia in a grid pattern that became a model for other cities as the colonies and later the United States expanded. **[See Essay 3.3, Richard Wade's essay "Urban Life in Western America, 1790–1830."]**

The following description of Philadelphia, made by Benjamin Bullivant just fifteen years after its founding, reflects the quick growth and vibrancy of the port. Bullivant, born in England, worked as a physician and apothecary. He also served as Attorney General under Royal Governor Edmund Andros during the short-lived Dominion of New England (1686–1689), which also included the provinces of New York, East Jersey, and West Jersey. Between June and August 1687, Bullivant traveled south from Boston to Newcastle (Delaware) and back, visiting and describing the principle port towns along the way. The excerpt in this document, edited by Wayne Andrews, retains its seventeenth-century spelling and grammar. Andrews served as the curator of manuscripts for the New-York Historical Society in 1956 and later Archives of American Art Professor at Wayne State University in Detroit from 1964 to 1983.

PHILADELPHIA IN 1697

Philadelphia in Pensylvania is seated on Delaware River 150 myles from the Sea, it is now but 15 yeares since they begann to Build, and yet do all ready shew a very magnificent City. The Streetes are regularly layd out along the Delaware, & thwarting Into the Land, Broad, & even, Leadeing forth into smooth roades, that carry you into the Country, & at about 2 myles distance from ye River delaware, direct from the City, is another Large River, called Schuilkill beyond which some are building & this is the extent of ye City bounds to the Land from Delaware, and it is probable enough the Vacancy betwixt the 2 Rivers may in time be made into fayr streetes, & Joyned into one City as is designed & layed out by the Proprieto^r, & Surveyed [by] m^r Penn in his printed draught of ye City of Philadelphia which when finished, will be almost a square in forme. The Delaware is fresh & good water so are they^r pumps & wells, here is also sundry sort of fish, Sturgeon & flesh of all sorts plenty enough. There are some few large and stately dwellings of some eminent Merchants, But ordinarily theyr houses exceeded not our second rate buildings in London, and many Lower. But generally very pretty with posts In the streets as in London and shops after the English mode they have a market twice a week with butchers stalls, & Blocks, and a market Bell, Rung also att certain howres of the day by a woman to give the time of the day. Here is a very large, tall, Brick meeteing house for the quakers neare ye market place, & not fair distant a Neate little church for ye Ch of England, English fashion, handsomely pailed in, and a sufficient decent buryall place annexed to itt. Philadelphia hath somewhat upwards of 500 families dwelling now in itt, & very many Buildings goeing forw^d it seems allready to exceede most shire towns in England, it hath no fortifications, though very capable of it (on ye River side) being so farr distant from ye sea, & mostly quakers they say it is not they^r practice to trust in carnall weapons & find by good usadge of the Indians they are a safeguard to them, & rather seeke shelter amongst the english than annoy them wth a warr being at a greate distance from all European enemies. I was presented at Philadelphia wth sundry Nosegayes of as large & beautifull flowers as are ordinarily in the London gardens. The gouuerno^r of this province is the Honb^le Coll Markham,[1] who lives in a small, but very Neate dwelling, and is a person of much Courtesie, and Learned, he hath his Lady with him, and some children. here is gathered the Black stone in which is found the Salamanders wool, so called because it will not burn, thought it may be spunn into thread for service.[2] Philadelphia hath the purest bread and strongest beere in America the Beefe, Veale & pork tollerable but short of England mutton & Lamb indifferent, but scarce at some times of ye yeare. Butter and cheese very good. They have two markets a weeke, wednesdays and

Saturdays, and the most like an old England market of any in this part of the world, it is at this Instant very hott weather, which obliges people to go very thinly habited of the Negros & Indians I saw many quite naked, except what covered the Secrets of nature. Vessells of 500 tunns lay theyr sides to the wharfes, & unlode by theyr own takle. The Quakers are very generous in they[r] Entertainments and furnish they[r] houses very Neatly and stick not to give theyr daughters to men of the world, and indeed they are many of them prettey women, here are apples, peares, peaches, apricots, mulberries, & cherries in abundance. They pay little or no taxes of any Sort whatsoever nor any Customes or Excise have no militia, only a Night watch in Philadelphia, Justices & Constables County Courts, Provinciall Courts and assemblies.

NOTES

1. William Markham (c. 1635–1704/5), Lieutenant-Governor or Governor of the Province and the Lower Counties 1693–99.
2. Asbestos.

2.5 AN ACT FOR ESTABLISHING PORTS AND TOWNS (1705)

Source: William Waller Henning, *The Statutes at Large; Being a Collection of All the Laws of Virginia, From the First Session of the Legislature, in the Year 1619*, Volume III (Philadelphia; Printed for the Editor by Thomas Desilver, 1823), 404–405 and 415–517.

EDITORS'S INTRODUCTION

In contrast to European colonies in New England, only a few settlements of any notable size arose during the first century of English occupation in the Chesapeake. Such a situation was not for a lack of trying. English royal authorities, the Virginia Company of London, the joint stock venture that oversaw the initial English settlement of the Chesapeake, and legislative bodies of both the Virginia and Maryland colonies all sought to create principle urban centers. A series of so-called General Town Acts—six in Virginia and ten in Maryland—specified the locations of anticipated cities, their primary function as a port and/or country seat, their initial physical size, their use of public lands, the obligatory construction of churches, and the mandated operations of marketplaces. The development of the Chesapeake urban centers was to be paid for through tobacco taxes.

The following excerpt is from a 1705 Virginia act that explicitly articulates the underlying assumption that urbanization is vital to well-organized commerce. All trade in and out of the colony is mandated to flow through one of the ports or inland towns enumerated in the legislation. Even the days of the week for public markets in each town and days of the month for annual fairs spelled out within the act. Despite the legislation of urbanization, Virginia remained largely rural in this period. The cultivation and distribution of the Chesapeake's primary economic commodity, tobacco, did not support urban growth. Tobacco plantations, and the extensive waterways that penetrated deep into the colony, rendered regional towns and city centers unnecessary for commercial growth. The lack of strong urban growth undermined the colony's ability to collect tobacco revenue. Tobacco taxes were unpopular with tobacco planters and merchants who lobbied, often successfully, to repeal specific town acts. As with *A Model of Christian Charity* (1630) **[see Document 2.2]**, this early nineteenth-century reprint of the 1705 act retains original spelling, grammar, and inconsistent capitalization. It has also been edited to remove margin notes.

AN ACT FOR ESTABLISHING PORTS AND TOWNS (1705)

CHAP. XLII.

An act for establishing ports and towns.

WHEREAS her most sacred majesty, Queen Anne, out of her princely care of this her colony and dominion of Virginia, by instructions to his excellency Edward Nott, Esq. her majestys lieutenant and governor-generall here, has been pleased to take notice that the building of towns, ware-houses, wharfs and keys, for the more expeditions lading and unlading of ships at proper places in this colony, exclusive of others, will be particularly usefull and ser-viceable to her majesty, in bringing our people to a more regular settlement and of great advantage to trade, and has therefore caused it to be recommended by her said governor to this generall assembly to pass an act for that purpose, suitable to the interests and conveniencys of this colony.

Be it therefore enacted, by the Governor, Council, and Burgesses of this present Gen-eral Assembly, and it is hereby enacted, by the authority of the same, That from and after the twenty-fifth day of December, which shall be in the year of our Lord 1708, all goods, wares and merchandises which shall be imported into this colony by water (servants, slaves and salt, excepted) shall be entered, allowed and landed at some one or other of the ports, wharfs, keys or places hereafter mentioned and appointed in this act, and at none other place whatsoever until they shall have been first landed at one of the ports or wharfs aforesaid, and a certificate thereof obtained from the officer of the port, appointed or to be appointed by his excellency the governor or the governor and commander in chief of this colony for the time being, by advice of the councill of state here for collection of the Virginia dutys, upon pain of forfeiture and loss of all such goods, wares and merchandises.

And be it also enacted, That from and after the said twenty-fifth day of December, 1708, all servants, slaves and salt, which shall be imported into this colony by water, shall be reported and entered at some one or other of the ports, wharfs, keys or places by this act appointed as aforesaid, and a certificate thereof obtained as aforesaid, before they shall be landed, bought or sold upon pain of forfeiture and loss of every such servant and slave so landed, sold, or put to sale.

And be it also enacted, That from and after the said twenty-fifth day of December 1708, all goods, wares and merchandises of what nature and kind soever, to be exported out of this colony by water, coal, corn and timber excepted, shall, before they be put on board any ship or vessell for exportation, be landed or cleared at some one or other of the ports, wharfs, keys or places, as aforesaid, upon pain of forfeiture and loss of all such goods, wares and merchandises.

And because there will be an absolute necessity of ware houses and other conveni-ent buildings for reception of all sorts of goods and persons, at these ports,

Be it therefore enacted, That a township or burgh be established at each of the places hereinafter appointed by this act for ports, and that from and after the said twenty-fifth day of December, 1708, all goods, wares and merchandises whatsoever, which shall be imported for sale into this colony (servants, slaves and salt, excepted) shall be bought and sold in one or other of these towns hereinafter appointed, or not within five miles of any of them water born or on the same side the great river the town shall stand upon, except such persons as are all ready inhabited, and their heirs and such other persons as having been for the space of three years inhabitants of this colony...
[...]

And be it enacted, That the places herein-after named, shall be the ports meant and intended by this act, and none other place or places whatsoever (vizt.)

On James river, Hampton, James City, Flower de Hundred.

On Elizabeth river, Norfolk Town.

On York river, York town and Tindals point one port, and West point.

On North river in Mockjack Bay, at Blackwater on Hills land.

On Rappahanoch river, Corrotomen upon the town land formerly appointed in Lancaster county.

Middlesex upon the town land formerly appointed Hobbshole.

On Wicocomoco river upon col. Coopers land in Potomack district.

On Potomack River.

Yohocomoco upon the land of Richard Tidwell in Westmoreland.

Potomack creek at the town land in Stafford.

On Easterne Shore.

The mouth of Kings creek in Northampton county, upon the land called the secretarys land.

Orancocke upon the town land formerly appointed in Accomack.

[...]

That at Hampton in Elizabeth City county to be called Hampton, and to have Wednesday and Saturday in each week for market days, and the tenth day of October and four following days, exclusive of sundays, annually for their fair

That at Norfolk town to be called Norfolk, and to have Tuesday and Saturday in each week for market days, and the third day of October and four following days, exclusive of Sundays, annually their fair.

That at Nansemond town to be called Nansemond, and to have Mundays and Thursdays in each week for market days, and the fifteenth day of October and four following days, exclusive of Sundays, annually their fair.

That at James City to be called James City, and to have Tuesdays and Satturdays in each week for market days, and the twentieth day of October and four following days, exclusive of Sundays, annually their fair.

That at Flower de Hundred to be called Pohatan and to have Tuesday and Satturdays in each week for market days, and the first Tuesday in November and four following days annually their fair.

That at York Town to be called York, and to have Wednesdays and Satturdays in each week for market days, and the first

Tuesday in October and four following days annually their fair.

That at Black Water to be called Queensborough, and to have Tuesdays and Thursdays in each week for market days, and the last Tuesday in November and four following days annually their fair.

That at West Point to be called Delaware, and to have Tuesdays and Satturdays in each week for market days, and the second Tuesday in September and four following days annually their fair.

That at Corrotomen to be called Queens town, and to have Tuesdays and Satturdays in each week for market days, and the third Tuesday in October and four following days annually their fair.

That at Middlesex to be called Urbanna, and to have Tuesdays and Frydays in each week for market days, and the second Tuesday in March and four following days annually their fair.

That at Hobbs Hole to be called Tappahannock, and to have Tuesdays and Satturdays in each week, for market days, and the fifth day of October and four following days, exclusive of Sundays, annually their fair.

That at Wicocomoco to be called New-Castle and to have Mundays and Frydays in each week for market days, and the second Tuesday in October and four following days annually their fair.

That at Yohocomoco to be called Kingsale, and to have Tuesday and Satturday in each week for market days, and the nineteenth day of October and four following days, exclusive of Sundays, annually their fair.

That at Potomac Creek to be called Marlborough, and to have Munday and Fryday in each week for market days and the twenty-fifth day of September and four following days, exclusive of Sundays, annually their fair.

That at Kings Creek in Northampton county to be called Northampton, and to have Tuesday and Saturday in each week for market days, and the twenty-sixth day of September and four following days, exclusive of Sundays, annually their fair.

That of Orancock to be called Orancock, and to have Munday and Fryday in each week for market days, and the second

Tuesday in October and four following days annually their fair.

[...]

And be it further enacted, That where any port is by this act appointed to be at a place that hath land already purchased and laid out for a town, such land so laid out, is hereby declared to be the land where the ports and towns appointed by this act shall be settled and built, and where a port or town is appointed by this act at any place not having land purchased for that purpose, the county court is hereby impowered and required to purchase fifty acres of land for the uses in this act mentioned...

PART III

*F*ROM BRITISH TO AMERICAN CITIES

EDITORS' INTRODUCTION TO PART III

In the modern United States, over 80 percent of all Americans live in an "urban" area, defined by the United States Bureau of the Census as an incorporated municipality or designated counting district containing 2,500 or more people, which includes cities of all sizes and their outlying areas, plus many towns, villages, and boroughs (suburban or otherwise). In the colonial period, American cities constituted ten percent of the population. The United States government did not have a set figure for what constitutes urban until about 1910 when it designed the 2,500-population threshold. In projecting that figure back to the time of the very first federal census in 1790, most people lived in much smaller agrarian communities that are classified as "rural."[i] In fact, the first census counted only five cities (New York, Philadelphia, Boston, Charleston, and Baltimore) with more than 10,000 inhabitants, and just 5 percent of the total national population (200,000 out of 3.9 million people) living in urban areas. It was not until 1830 that the overall urban population of the United States reached the 10 percent level of the colonial era again. Three decades later, the 1860 census revealed that the nation's total urban percentage reached 20 percent, or 6.2 million people, with 392 urban areas, 93 of them containing more than 10,000 people, 9 of which had 100,000 or more inhabitants. Finally, by 1920 the census revealed that for the first time in the nation's history the majority of the population, 51 percent, lived in any one of 2,722 urban areas, 68 of which were cities with 100,000 or more people, and 3 of them (New York, Chicago, and Philadelphia) serving as a home to over 1 million residents.

The first essay in this part by Pauline Maier speculates on the role of distinction and variance in shaping characteristics of American-versus-European urbanization. To make her argument she compares and contrasts eighteenth century Boston and New York City. Benjamin Carp, in his 2007 work, concludes that urban colonists were the first residents of the colonies to develop identities as Americans. The urban setting provided the infrastructure for cultural interchange that enabled a new national ethos. Carp's important work not only provides a fresh look at the American Revolution, but also the place of cities in this key historical moment. Finally, Richard C. Wade's classic 1958 essay "Urban Life in Western America, 1790–1830" provides an overview of city building along the Ohio and Mississippi River Valleys in the late eighteenth and early nineteenth centuries. More than any other historian, Wade directly confronts the anti-urban bias of traditional historiography by asserting that cities, in the form of frontier towns, first settled the American West and paved the way for later agricultural successes.

The first document reinforces arguments made in Part I of this volume, by bringing the focus back to the high level of colonial racial discord and class-based divide that unfortunately continues to plague the United States in the twenty-first century. A 1741 arson plot was purportedly developed via a conspiracy between poor whites and enslaved blacks. As in other historical moments, popular discourse ran far ahead of factual evidence; no actual plan was even revealed. The allegations led to the deaths of approximately thirty-four people, the majority black, and the banishment of others. In the second document, railroad engineer and visionary T.D. Judah calls for the building of a transcontinental railroad, and in the third document, *New York Tribune* editor Horace Greeley urges his friend to go west to take advantage of opportunities. These documents can be used in combination with the Richard C. Wade article to consider the importance of westward movement and settlement in the creation of the young United States.

In the illustrations section, a map of Savannah in 1800, and two illustrations, one of Boston in 1768 and the other of New Orleans in the 1850s, provide an artistic glimpse into the way people organized and viewed their urban surroundings. Tom Willcockson's illustration of a packet boat on the Illinois and Michigan Canal demonstrates the immense infrastructure and labor intensive work needed for the establishment of cities in the United States during its phase of western expansion. Finally, Joseph Smith's Plat of Zion illustrates that some of the new urban settlements had complex religious drivers, just like some of the colonial cities on the Atlantic and Pacific coasts.

NOTE

i. "Rural" is defined by the U.S. Bureau of the Census as anything not "urban." The Census Bureau has modified the definition of urban several times since the late nineteenth century, most notably after the 1940 census in order to include large and densely settled areas outside of an incorporated municipality. Starting with the 2000 census, the Bureau defines "urban" as all territory, population, and housing units specifically within an urban area (UA) or urban cluster (UC). For more detail see United States Bureau of the Census, *Historical Statistics of the United States: Colonial Times to 1970*, Bicentennial Edition, Part 1 (Washington, D.C., 1975), 2–3; U.S. Census Bureau, Geography Division, "Census 2000 Urban and Rural Classification," created April 30, 2002, revised December 30, 2008 (www.census.gov/geo/www/ua/ua_2k.html). See also, Lisa Krissoff Boehm and Steven H. Corey, *America's Urban History* (New York: Routledge, 2015), 4–5.

ESSAY 3.1

Boston and New York in the Eighteenth Century

Pauline Maier

Source: The Proceedings of the American Antiquarian Society 91,
Part 2 (October 1981), 177–195.

EDITORS' INTRODUCTION

Although cities were an essential component of European colonization, the Euro-American population was overwhelmingly rural and agrarian during the colonial era. No more than 10 percent of the entire population lived in urban areas, more accurately towns, by the end the seventeenth century and by the time the colonies achieved independence from Great Britain, the percentage had fallen in half. In fact, just five cities contained more than 10,000 people by the time of the American Revolution, with Philadelphia, Pennsylvania leading at roughly 25,000, New York 22,000, Boston, Massachusetts 16,000, Charleston (Charles Town), South Carolina at 12,000, and Newport, Rhode Island with 11,000. As urban historians Carl Bridenbaugh and Gary Nash have shown us, urban areas were few in number and relatively small by today's standards, both in terms of population and geographic size, they exerted a considerable amount of influence over the countryside, especially in political, economic, and cultural affairs.[i] What accounts for this urban hegemony? What functions did American cities perform, and were they unique from each other and their European counterparts?

In this essay, historian Pauline Maier addresses the issue of what constituted a city in the colonial era by comparing and contrasting eighteenth-century life in Boston and New York. She explores the major characteristics and functions of these two seaports with an eye to how they developed separate economic, political, and intellectual spheres of influence and personalities which went on to define each city in the nineteenth and twentieth centuries. Maier even speculates on the larger meaning of urbanism in the United States versus Europe by stressing that differences between cities are as important as commonalities. Such variance helps to account for America's diversity and resilience to major economic and political crises throughout history.

Pauline Maier was the William R. Kenan, Jr. Professor of American History at the Massachusetts Institute of Technology. She is the author of *From Resistance to Revolution: Colonial Radicals and the Development of American Opposition to Britain, 1765–1776* (New York: Knopf, 1972), *The Old Revolutionaries: Political Lives in the Age of Samuel Adams* (New York: Knopf, 1980), *American Scripture: Making the Declaration of*

---

i Population figures are averaged from a variety of sources, James A. Henretta and Gregory H. Nobles, *Evolution and Revolution: American Society, 1600–1820* (Lexington, MA: D.C. Heath, 1987), 75–76; Carl Bridenbaugh, *Cities in the Wilderness: The First Century of Urban Life in America, 1625–1742* (New York: Ronald Press, 1938; New York: Oxford, 1964), 143–144; Carl Bridenbaugh, *Cities in Revolt: Urban Life in America, 1743–1776* (New York: Alfred Knopf, 1955), 216–217. For urban influence see also Henretta and Nobles; Bridenbaugh, *Cities in the Wilderness* and *Cities in Revolt*; Gary B. Nash, *The Urban Crucible: Social Change, Political Consciousness, and the Origins of the American Revolution* (Cambridge, MA: Harvard University Press, 1979); and Gary and Benjamin L. Carp, *Rebels Rising: Cities and the American Revolution* (New York: Oxford University Press, 2007).

Independence (New York: Knopf, 1997), and notable articles in the *William and Mary Quarterly* and the one reproduced here from the *Proceedings of the American Antiquarian Society*.

BOSTON AND NEW YORK IN THE EIGHTEENTH CENTURY (1981)

My title was inspired by George Rudé's *Paris and London in the Eighteenth Century*, though my concerns were not his. In the course of working on urban politics in the Revolutionary period I became aware of how remarkably different were Boston and New York—different not just in their people and politics but in feeling, in character, in that wonderfully all-encompassing thing called culture. Their differences were neither incidental nor ephemeral: to a remarkable extent the distinctive traits each city had developed by the end of the eighteenth century survived into the nineteenth and even the twentieth century. And so I propose to consider those differences, how they began and persisted over time, and their more general importance in American history.

Any such exercise assumes that the subjects of inquiry were comparable, that is, that they had some essential identity in common upon which distinctions were grafted. The existence of such a common identity for two early American ports on the Atlantic seaboard is in part obvious. But there remains a problem relevant to their comparability that is worth beginning with, one that has troubled me and, I suppose, other students of the period since first encountering Carl Bridenbaugh's pathbreaking books *Cities in the Wilderness* and *Cities in Revolt*. That is, by what right do we classify together Boston, New York, and similar communities as 'cities' before 1800?

Consider the gulf between Rudé's subjects and mine. He wrote about two of the greatest cities in the Western world, population centers that no one hesitates to call urban. Paris already had over a half million people in 1700. It grew only modestly over the next century, while London expanded at a quick pace—from 575,000 people in 1750 to almost 900,000 fifty years later. By contrast Boston's population stood at 6,700, New York's nearer 5,000 when the eighteenth century began. One hundred years later New York had over 60,000 and Boston almost 25,000 people.[1] It takes no very sophisticated statistical analysis to suggest that a 'city' of 6,700 was something very different from one of a half million, that New York at its eighteenth-century peak was still in many ways distinct from London, whose population was some fifteen times greater. If 'city' denotes a community's size, Boston and New York would not qualify.

The word 'city' has not, however, distinguished places by size so much as by function. Historically it designated independent communities that served as centers for surrounding countryside and as points of contact with the outside world. The word derives from the Latin word *civitas*, which the Romans used, as it happens, for a colonial situation—for the separate states or tribes of Gaul, and then for their most important towns. There were also *civitates* in Roman Britain, but the Angles and Saxons used instead the word *burh* or *borough*, adopting *city* in the thirteenth century for foreign or ancient cities, for large indigenous communities such as London, and later for the chief boroughs of a diocese, those that became cathedral towns.[2]

Cities perform their centralizing function in many ways, most of which were exercised by Boston and New York. Like other major colonial cities, they were provincial capitals as well as important cultural centers where newspapers and pamphlets were published, discussed, and distributed. But above all they were commercial centers, Atlantic coastal ports where the produce of the countryside was collected and shipped to the West Indies, Africa, or Europe and exchanged for goods of foreign origin needed by colonists in both city and country. Later cities became the merchandising centers for manufactures of either rural or urban origin, whose 'reach' and therefore whose volume of business grew with the development of more advanced transportation systems; they became the homes of banks, of insurance companies, or stock exchanges.[3] As they did so, they drew upon the efforts of increasing numbers of people. But it was not the size of their populations that made them cities so much as the functions Boston and New York shared with Paris and London even when their people were counted in thousands, not tens or hundreds of thousands.

From the beginning, moreover, colonial cities had a cosmopolitan character that distinguished them from more rural towns, of whose people it could be said, as George Homans wrote of thirteenth-century English villagers, that they 'had upon the whole more contact with one another than they had with outsiders.'[4] While their ships traded at ports-of-call in the Caribbean and the larger Atlantic world, the cities played host to numbers of transients of 'strangers,' whether in the laboring force or among the more substantial persons of affairs who found business to transact at Boston or New York. Already in the seventeenth century Boston merchants found themselves in conflict with their colony's Puritan leaders, whose effort to isolate Massachusetts from Old World contamination proved incompatible with the demands of commerce. 'The well-being of trade,' Bernard Bailyn has observed, 'demanded the free movement of people and goods.'[5] In the end the merchants won, but their victory was never such as made Boston altogether hospitable to new immigrants, particularly those of non-English origin. Only the French Huguenots—the Faneuils, Bowdoins, Rivoires, and their like—found a welcome there and were easily assimilated.

New York's population was more diverse in origin, including persons of Dutch as well as of French and English origin along with lesser numbers of Germans, Irishmen, Jews, and other Europeans as well as substantial numbers of Africans. Manhattan and the nearby countries of Long Island had the largest concentration of blacks anywhere in North America above the plantation colonies.

The city also absorbed substantial numbers of migrants from New England.[6]

The diversity of New York's peoples has, however, often been exaggerated, for they were, like Boston's people, predominantly Northern European Calvinists who shared, out of diverse historical experiences, a militant hostility to 'papism' and to Catholic Absolutism in France and Spain. Even Manhattan's Sephardic Jews shared in some measure this 'Protestant' culture, for they had suffered from the same forces that the Dutch had fought in their long struggle for national independence—the Spanish monarchy and the Catholic Church.[7] With people already so alike, the 'melting pot' could melt: by the mid-eighteenth century, Peter Kalm noted, younger persons of Dutch descent, particularly on Manhattan, spoke mostly English, attended the English church, 'and would even take it amiss if they were called Dutchmen and not Englishmen.' French Huguenots who first arrived at New York in the seventeenth century also gradually became Anglicans,[8] helping to make the city by the late eighteenth century far more culturally unified than it had been on hundred years earlier or would be a century later when Italian Catholics, the Ashkenazic Jews of Eastern Europe, and other decidedly alien people were added in great numbers to the older 'native stock.'

In the course of the eighteenth century, Boston and New York also gave evidence of a new anonymity among their people that reflected the growth of their populations. That development was slow in coming. Certainly there remained much of the small town about Philadelphia, the largest of American cities in 1771 when Ester DeBerdt Reed reported to her father in London that 'the people must either talk of their neighbors, of whom they know every particular of what they both do and say, or else of marketing.... We hardly dare tell one another our thoughts,' she added, 'lest it should spread all over town; so, if anybody asks you how we like Philadelphia, you must say very well.'[9] The newspapers published in colonial cities in their very dearth of local news also testify to the way eighteenth-century urban people knew their news without reading about it. There were, however, signs of change. Thomas Bender cites the appearance of craftsmen's ads in New York newspapers of the 1750s as evidence that artisans were finding it necessary to announce their existence to townsmen who might in an earlier day have known of it without such formal notice. The publication of city directories at New York in 1786 and Boston in 1789 attests again to an increasing unfamiliarity of city people with each other.[10] Soon thereafter authorities addressed themselves to the problem of locating people within the increasingly anonymous urban masses. In 1793 New York's Common Council ordered that buildings along the streets be numbered according to a prescribed method. From that regulation it was but a short step to the 1811 report of a New York commission that surveyed the island and planned the expanse of practical if monotonously regular numbered streets that would in time stretch from the old and irregular colonial city on the lower tip of Manhattan up toward the Harlem River, and which has been logically taken as the beginning of New York's emergence as a 'modern' city.[11]

In all these ways—in the functions that marked them as cities, in their relative cosmopolitanism and common Protestant culture, in the gradual development by the late eighteenth century of a social anonymity that has since become so much a part of urban life—Boston and New York were almost interchangeable. And yet they had acquired, like children, distinctive traits that they would carry with them into later life. The appearance of differences early in the cities' histories is striking, their persistence over time the more so. Both need to be explained. Their reasons lie, I suggest, in the ideals of purposes of the cities' founders, and in the peculiar, unpredictable way those early traditions were reinforced by eighteenth-century circumstances.

Boston's Puritan fathers came to America with a mission defined against the avarice and corruption of contemporary England. They sought to establish close-knit communities where love of God and concern for neighbor took precedence over selfish gain.

Their ideology proved well suited to the business of colonizing. Because the Puritans sought to found permanent homes in America, whole families migrated, not the men alone. The population of New England therefore grew naturally at a far faster rate than elsewhere in seventeenth-century North America.[12] The Puritans' commitment to their 'callings' and their emphasis on industry also contributed to the cause of success in this world as much as in the next, and Boston became the premier city of British North America.

Its early achievement proved impossible to sustain, however, and as the eighteenth century proceeded Boston gradually yielded its leadership to Philadelphia and New York. It is commonplace to say that geography determined Boston's destiny: the proximity of the Appalachian mountains to the Atlantic coast in New England, the rocky quality of soil along the coastal belt, the course of its rivers, which too often ran on a north-south axis and so provided no ready path to the interior, all these limited the extent and the richness of that hinterland upon which Boston's importance depended. But its fate, we now know, is not so simply explained. An 'almost biblical series of misfortunes' afflicted Boston in the mid-eighteenth century, most of which were related to the series of colonial wars that brought disaster to Boston even as they blessed with prosperity the artisans and merchants of New York and Philadelphia. [...]

It is too much to say that Boston never recovered, but its record in the late colonial period was overall one of decline. And hard times served the cause of tradition, for the Spartan ideals of the founders could ennoble necessity by calling it virtue. New England's ministers continued to cite the first generation of settlers as a model of achievement, as they had done from the late seventeenth century, and to chastise the children failing to take up their fathers' 'Errand into the Wilderness,' explaining the calamities that fell upon them as punishments for the sinful shortcomings of those who had inherited that New World Israel. The ideals of the fathers provided, in short, a way of understanding and of organizing experience, of ordering history, and so continued to influence the life of the region and of its major city.

New York was founded instead as an outpost of the Dutch West India Company in its search for profit. No greater mission brought the Dutch from Holland: indeed, the Dutch were on the whole unwilling to migrate, finding their homeland hospitable as the English Puritans did not. The Dutch West India Company therefore turned elsewhere for settlers—to the oppressed Protestants of France, to Africa—in the hope that they might help make New Netherland economically viable. The commitment to material gain that marked Company rule continued after the British conquest. The financial needs of the later Stuart kings, the hopes of greater fortunes that motivated the governors appointed by them and their successors, the ambitions of colonists who flattered royal officials in a quest for land grants, contracts, or lucrative appointments, all these only enhanced New York's materialistic bent. The city became a nest of those after profit however won—of pirates and privateers, of slave traders and smugglers—a community whose spokesmen on into the Revolutionary era emphasized interest while those of Boston cultivated virtue.[13]

New Yorkers did well—and then did better. The city sat at the mouth of the great Hudson River, which, with the Mohawk, provided ready access to a rich and extensive market even before the canal era added the trans-Appalachian West to Manhattan's 'back yard.' It benefitted also from wartime contracts and privateering returns, and except for occasional years of recession continued the ascent that would in time make it the foremost American city. [...]

Politics moderated the distance between rich and poor in Boston. There the governing town meeting brought together persons of different station and blessed persons of different station and blessed men with power for their eloquence, reason, and character as well as their wealth. Boston had a board of selectmen and a series of other municipal officers who were chosen by the town meeting, and those who sought

such preferment learned, if they did not instinctively know, that respect was a prerequisite of political support. New York was governed differently. By terms of the Montgomery Charter of 1731, the governor and provincial council named the city's mayor, recorder, clerk, and treasurer. Municipal ordinances were passed by a Common Council that consisted of the mayor and recorder along with the city's aldermen, who were elected by voice vote within the several wards into which New York had been divided. Qualified voters also chose a set of assistants, several minor officials, and the vestry-men who cared for the poor. But they had no continuing, direct voice in governing the city as in Boston. [...]

The existence of a wealthy upper class with a taste for European ways had, however, some cultural advantages, for its patronage set eighteenth-century New York on its way toward becoming an American center for the performing arts. Manhattan claimed two playhouses in 1732; by the time of the Revolution it had as many as seven. Not that all New Yorkers were free from scruples born of their Protestant heritage. William Hallam's London Company of Comedies, which came to the city in 1753, was denied official permission to perform until after it issued assurances that its members were 'not cast in the same Mould' as their 'Theatrical Predecessors,' that 'in private Life' and 'publick Occupation' they were of a different moral order. In retrospect, however, it seems more important that the company went to New York because people in Virginia predicted a 'genteel and favourable Reception' in Manhattan, where 'the Inhabitants were generous and polite, naturally fond of Diversions rational, particularly those of the Theatre,' and that Hallam's company finally enjoyed a successful and profitable run in the city. New York also saw occasional musical performances, as in January 1737 when the *New-York Gazette* advertised a 'consort ... for the benefit of Mr. Pachebell, the harpsicord parts performed by himself.' And two years later an advertisement announced 'A New Pantomine Entertainment.... To which will be added an Optick,' which was a primitive predecessor of motion pictures. Cockfighting was also popular, as was horse-racing, with wagers part of the event—all of which remained far from Boston, a city less open to such forms of commercial entertainment. Indeed, theatre was introduced at Boston only during the 1790s, having been earlier outlawed by an act of 1750.[14]

Boston was distinguished instead by its traditional respect for learning and for the printed word. Before the Puritan fathers were more than a decade in America they founded Harvard College and established a printing press in Cambridge.[15] New York City was settled in 1626—four years before Boston—but had no press for almost seventy years, until William Bradford was lured to Manhattan in 1693. Even a casual survey of the Evans bibliography of early American imprints testifies to the immense and continuing superiority of eighteenth-century Boston as a place of publication. Few book and pamphlets came out of New York, and those were heavily weighted toward the official publications of the provincial government. As for newspapers, the first to be published on a continuous schedule in British North America was the *Boston News-Letter*, begun in 1704. And Boston had two other papers, the *Boston Gazette* (1719) and the *New-England Courant* (1721) before the *New-York Gazette* began publication in 1725.[16]

New Yorkers' sense of a good education apparently differed from that of Bostonians: the City of New York was 'so conveniently Situated for Trade and the Genius of the people so inclined to merchandise,' wrote the Rev. John Sharpe in 1713 after some twelve years on Manhattan, 'that they generally seek no other Education for their children than writing and Arithmetick. So that letters must be in a manner forced upon them not only without their seeking, but against their consent'—a proposal unlikely to meet with success. [...]

New York was, quite simply, a different kind of place than Boston, shaped by different values that were sustained by economic success. [...] These distinctions were reflected in John Adams's perceptions of New York, which he visited on the way to the Continental Congress in Philadelphia, with eyes fully open and with Boston as a constant standard of comparison. Like all travellers, Adams was impressed by New York's beauty, for it was in ways long since lost a garden city whose clean and spacious streets were lined with trees and where the noise of frogs, especially on hot nights when rain was expected, provided a major annoyance.[17] He remarked on the striking views or 'prospects' the city offered of the Hudson and East Rivers, of Long Island and what he called the 'Sound River,' and of New Jersey. He found New York's streets 'vastly more regular and elegant than those in Boston, and the houses are more grand, as well as neat.' [...] Adams was struck, too, by the evidence of wealth, as in the costly accoutrements of John Morin Scott's breakfast table, which he inventoried lovingly ('rich plate, a very large silver coffee-pot, and a very large silver tea-pot, napkins of the very finest materials'), or the 'rich furniture' at the home of Isaac Low. Still, the continuous socializing he found 'very disagreeable on some accounts.' It seems never to have crossed the New Yorkers' minds that a Bostonian might be more anxious to see the twenty-year-old King's College, or the city's churches, printers' offices, and bookshops. And 'with all the opulence and splendor of this city,' Adams reported that there was 'very little good breeding to be found.... I have not seen one real gentleman, one well-bred man, since I came to town.' There was, moreover, 'no conversation that is agreeable' at their 'entertainments': there was 'no modesty, no attention to one another,' for the New Yorkers of that still-pastoral island had already acquired the conversational style of the modern metropolis. 'They talk very loud, very fast, and altogether,' Adams observed. 'If they ask you a question, before you can utter three words of your answer, they will break out upon you again, and talk away.'[18]

There are in these observations testimony not merely to style, but to the pace, the bewildering restlessness that already possessed New Yorkers long before the nineteenth century. Even the sleighs they rode in the winter to friends' homes out of town or to 'Houses of entertainment at a place called the Bowery ... fly with great swiftness,' Madam Knight notes on her visit there in 1704, 'and some are so furious that they'll turn out of the path for none except a Loaden Cart.' What was the hurry? And why were New Yorkers always building, tearing down, rearranging, reconstructing their city, leaving not even the bones of their ancestors in peace? They seem forever to have done things with what struck outsiders as excess: convinced that 'merchandizing' was a good employment, they went into trade in such numbers, reported the visitor John Miller in 1695, 'that whosoever looks on their shops would wonder'—like a modern stroller down Madison Avenue —'where there are so many to sell, there should be any to buy.'[19] The monumental energy of colonial New Yorkers prefigured that of later Americans, who within a century of winning independence built from thirteen modest colonies a nation whose western boundary had pushed from the Appalachians to the Pacific. The enterprise of New Yorkers contributed generously to that development. Indeed, the very physical circumstances of New Yorkers identified them with the nation in 1776: they were concentrated within the lowest mile of a thirteen-and-a-half-mile-long island much as their countrymen were settled along the eastern edge of a vast continent whose expanses of empty land invited and even demanded expansion. People such as these had no time to celebrate the past. They were too engrossed with inventing the future.

How different the situation of the Bostonians, housed on a modest peninsula already fully settled by the time of the Revolution, suffering from a generation of decline, a people convinced that the model of their future lay in the past. In fact, nineteenth-century Boston, true to its colonial origins, became the literary capital of the new nation and also a financial center whose importance yielded to New York only in the 1840s. Meanwhile New Englanders, fleeing the rural poverty of their native region, settled and populated much of the West. These remains considerable irony nonetheless in the fact that Boston served for the generation of 1776 as a model for the new republic. Its democratic politics, tradition of disinterested public service, and modest style, inculcated by Puritanism and continued through hardship, coincided neatly with the demands of classical republicanism—so much so that Samuel Adams could see in the United States a final realization of New England's historic mission.[20] New York played a far more ambiguous role in the politics of the Revolution than did Boston, and the city never took on a similar symbolic importance—perhaps because infinite possibilities are more difficult to comprehend than the limited values of an established and well-defined historical tradition. New York has in fact remained difficult to grasp, to summarize. 'By preference, but also in some degree by necessity,' Nathan Glazer and Daniel Patrick Moynihan observed in *Beyond the Melting Pot*, 'America has turned elsewhere for its images and traditions. Colonial America is preserved for us in terms of the Doric simplicity of New England, or the pastoral symmetry of the Virginia countryside. Even Philadelphia is manageable. But who can summon an image of eighteenth-century New York that will *hold still in the mind*?[21] And yet the importance of openness, optimism, opportunity, and energy, even of materialism and of visual over literary entertainments to the nation that emerged from the American eighteenth century is undeniable.

Neither Boston nor New York had an enduring importance for the United States like that of London for Britain or of Paris for France. The United States was too diverse, too dynamic to allow any one economic, political, and cultural center to emerge on the European model. Even the economic dominance New York achieved in the early nineteenth century gave way or was shared with Chicago and Los Angeles, which themselves took on qualities that distinguished them from each other and from their 'parent cities' on the Atlantic coast. Students of the city have been more interested in the attributes that distinguish urban from rural life and in those traits that cities share than in the differences that distinguish one city from another. But in a nation predominantly urban, whose people are geographically mobile, differences are at least as important as commonalities. They mean that American cities provide homes for persons of widely different styles and interests, who serve to reinforce the traits that originally attract them. The differences between cities have also shaped the way they responded to major economic and political crises in American history, not least of all the Revolution itself. The characteristics that separated Boston from New York in the eighteenth century were therefore part of an important urban pattern, and contributed to the texture and complexity that came to characterize the nation they helped to found and to build.

NOTES

1. George Rudé, *Paris and London in the Eighteenth Century* (London, 1970), pp. 7, 35–36; Carl Bridenbaugh, *Cities in the Wilderness: The First Century of Urban Life in America, 1625–1742* (New York, 1964), p. 143n; Douglass C. North, *The Economic Growth of the United States, 1790–1860* (New York, 1961), p. 49 (table 5).

2. *The Oxford English Dictionary*, 2 (Oxford and London, 1961): 443–45. I am here bypassing the narrow and more legalistic meaning the word assumed in North America, where it was applied to separately incorporated communities governed by the traditional English mayor and court of aldermen. [...] The definition was not, however, respected in common usage. Boston was, for example, commonly referred to as a city in the eighteenth century, and by a man no less learned than Cotton Mather. See Samuel G. Drake, *The History and Antiquities of the City of Boston* (Boston, 1851), p. 569n.

3. For a still-useful treatment of urban economic development, see N. S. B. Gras, *An Introduction to Economic History* (New York and London, 1922), esp. ch. 5, pp. 181–269.

4. Homans, *English Villagers of the Thirteenth Century* (Cambridge, Mass., 1941), p. 403, cited in Tomas Bender, *Community and Social Change in America* (New Brunswick, 1978), p. 61.

5. Bailyn, *New England Merchants in the Seventeenth Century* (Cambridge, Mass., 1955), pp. 105–6.

6. Robert V. Wells, *The Population of the British Colonies in America before 1776: A Survey of the Census Data* (Princeton, 1975), pp. 114–15; Edgar J. McManus, *A History of Negro Slavery in New York* (Syracuse, N.Y., 1966), p. 25; and Gov. Robert Hunter, Aug. 11, 1720, in Stokes, *Iconography of Manhattan Island*, 4:493.

7. See Israel Goldstein, *A Century of Judaism in New York: B'Nai Jeshurun 1825–1925, New York's Oldest Ashkenazic Congregation* (New York, 1930), p. 8.

8. Peter Kalm, *Peter Kalm's Travels in North America: The English Version of 1770* (1937; repr. New York, 1966), 1:142; and Robert M. Kingdon, 'Why Did the Huguenot Refugees in the American Colonies Become Episcopalian?' *The Historical Magazine of the Protestant Episcopal Church* 49 (1980): 317–35, esp. p. 317, where he comments on the 'unusually rapid' assimilation of Huguenots, who 'seem to have lost the use of their language and other cultural traits,... to have dropped the custom of inter-marrying among themselves,' and 'even ... stopped using distinctively French names, more rapidly than members of other non-English groups of immigrants,' and also pp. 325–26 on the gradual defection of Manhattan's Huguenots to the Church of England's Trinity Church.

9. Reed to Dennys Deberdt, Philadelphia, January 17, 1771, in [William B. Reed,] *The Life of Esther DeBerdt, Afterwards Esther Reed, of Pennsylvania* (Philadelphia, 1853), p. 166.

10. Bender, *Community and Social Change*, p. 74.

11. Stokes, *Iconography of Manhattan Island*, 1:387, 407–8.

12. The importance of sex ratios to relative population growth was discussed first by Wesley Frank Craven in *White, Red, and Black: The Seventeenth-Century Virginian* (New York, 1971), esp. pp. 26–27.

13. *The Urban Crucible: Social Change, Political Consciousness, and the Origins of the American Revolution* (Cambridge, Mass., 1979), pp. 304–5, and Pauline Mair, *The Old Revolutionaries: Political Lives in the Age of Samuel Adams* (New York, 1980), esp. pp. 97–100.

14. Mary C. Henderson, *The City and the Theatre, New York Playhouses from Bowling Green to Times Square* (Clifton, N.J., 1973), esp. pp. 8–9, 14; Stokes, *Iconography of Manhattan Island*, 4: 639–40, 641, 544 (and also 546), 558–59, 545, and passim. Samuel Eliot Morison, *Harrison Gray Otis, 1765–1848: The Urbane Federalist* (Boston, 1969), pp. 59–61.

15. Drake, *History and Antiquities of ... Boston*, pp. 241–42.

16. Stokes, *Iconography of Manhattan Island*, 1:184; Frank Luther Mott, *American Journalism: A History, 1690–1960* (New York, 1962), pp. 11, 15, 30.

17. See esp. *Peter Kalm's Travels in North America*, 1:131–32.

18. Madam Knight's comments on the city and its sociability are in *The Journal of Madam Knight*, introduced by George Parker Winship (New York, 1935), pp. 54–56. Adams's diary for August 20–26, 1774, in Charles Francis Adams, ed., *The Works of John Adams*, 2 (Boston, 1850): 345–55, esp. pp. 345–47, 349, 352, 353.

19. *The Journal of Madam Knight*, pp. 55–56; John Miller, *A Description of the Province and City of New York; with Plans of the City and Several Forts as they Existed in the Year 1695*, ed. John Gilmary Shea (New York, 1862), p. 35.

20. Maier, *The Old Revolutionaries*, pp. 4–45, 49.

21. Glazer and Moynihan, *Beyond the Melting Pot* (Cambridge, Mass., 1963), p. 2. Emphasis mine.

ESSAY 3.2

The Forgotten City

Benjamin L. Carp

Source: Benjamin L. Carp, *Rebels Rising: Cities and the American Revolution* (New York: Oxford University Press, 2007).

EDITORS' INTRODUCTION

Cities were crucial to the founding and development of British North America. They also played a pivotal role in forging the political independence from Great Britain of the thirteen colonies that became the United States of America. At the eve of the American Revolution, though, most residents of the thirteen colonies lived in rural areas (defined as communities with fewer than 2,500 people), and only five cities contained a substantial population of over 9,000 inhabitants. These five cities were: Boston, Massachusetts; Newport, Rhode Island; New York, New York; Philadelphia, Pennsylvania; and Charleston, South Carolina. Although small by today's standards, these urban seaports held a disproportionate influence over the surrounding countryside since they served as the social, political, economic, and cultural hubs of their respective colony. Urban areas were also more connected to the British Empire than their rural counterparts, experiencing wars, commercial trends, and flows of information, culture, and people from all over the Atlantic World earlier and on a grander scale. As such, imperial British economic policies tended to primarily impact cities in a negative manner, resulting in mass political discontent and demonstrations that encompassed a wide spectrum of inhabitants. In fact, as historian Benjamin L. Carp argues, it was the political mobilization of urban residents against imperial British authority that made the American Revolution possible.[i]

However central cities were to the start of the revolution, the ensuing armed conflict and independence from Great Britain destroyed their status at the pinnacle of American society. The war itself saw cities as the primary target of, and base for, the British military, forcing American patriots to abandon them for the countryside. As Americans recovered from the war and built their new nation, they worked to restore cities to the forefront of civic and political affairs. This essay by Benjamin Carp explains the fall of cities from their former dominance by examining the rise of anti-urban attitudes and key characteristics of a new republican form of government in which national political factions replaced some key functions of urban mobilization. Distrust of cities and their residents was yet one factor in the decision to permanently move the nation's capital from its original location in New York City to the rural banks of the Potomac. Anti-urban attitudes and suspicion of city dwellers underscored and reinforced political and social tensions between agrarian regions and booming industrial cities in the nineteenth century, and have echoed since then in a variety of public policy and cultural debates over the role of government, race relations, economic policies, and national identity. **[See Part V, "From Party Bosses to Federalism: The Evolution of Urban Government."]**

---

i Benjamin L. Carp, *Rebels Rising: Cities and the American Revolution* (New York: Oxford University Press, 2007), 5.

Benjamin L. Carp is an Associate Professor and Daniel M. Lyons Chair of History at Brooklyn College, the City University of New York. Prior to joining Brooklyn College, he taught at the University of Edinburgh and Tufts University. He is the author of *Defiance of the Patriots: The Boston Tea Party and the Making of America* (Yale University Press, 2010), which won the triennial Society of the Cincinnati Cox Book Prize in 2013; *Rebels Rising: Cities and the American Revolution* (Oxford University Press, 2007); and co-editor with Richard D. Brown of *Major Problems in the Era of the American Revolution, 1760–1791: Documents and Essays*, 3rd ed. (Cengage Learning, 2014).

THE FORGOTTEN CITY

Urban Americans had previously cherished their cities, but during the war many were able to give them up. How did Patriots justify their shift in sentiment? In many cases they did so by devaluing their cities. Benjamin Franklin wrote that cities were places where Americans "generally import only Luxuries and Superfluities," and if Great Britain stopped this commerce it would "contribute to our Prosperity." Ezra Stiles wrote in his diary, "It is a right[e]ous & holy thing with G[o]d to bring the Severest Calamities of this civil War upon the maritime Towns, because [they are] most abounding with Vice & Wickedness." After the burning of Charlestown (fig. E.I) and Falmouth, Abigail Adams asked, "Are we become a Sodom?" As she pondered the Lord permitting "Evil to befall a city," she wrote, "We have done Evil or our Enemies would be at peace with us. The Sin of Slavery as well as many others is not washed away." It was foolish to be too attached to cities, wrote Lovell: "We act as if Commerce and not Acres was our Foundation."[1] Over the course of the war, many Patriots came to see the countryside as worth defending, but deliberately set the cities aside as stinking dens of commerce and corruption.

From a psychological standpoint, abandoning the cities was probably for the best. Outmatched by amphibious British forces, the Americans had garnered few laurels during their fights over seaport cities—only surrenders, retreats, and smoldering ruins. For Americans, commemoration of the stirring victories at rural Trenton, Saratoga, Cowpens, and Yorktown would yield greater satisfaction. The cities and their scenes of revolutionary action were slipping away, not just in terms of their political importance but in American memory as well.

The cities did not fare well under British occupation, and their sad fate was difficult to absorb. With the Patriots evading blockades, attacking ships, repulsing raids and forage expeditions, and retreating into the countryside, the British garrisons were sullen and frustrated. Soon after the battle of Bunker Hill, Gage complained, "I wish this Cursed place was burned," and British soldiers expressed similar frustrations about the cities they occupied. When the British occupied Philadelphia, Adams predicted, "They will hang a Mill stone about their Necks." Adams was correct: by the time the British evacuated the city in 1778, British officers were complaining, "We have possessed it, at the expence of a whole Campaign, to very little purpose." When the British were forced to withdraw from cities, they sometimes expressed regret that they had not burned these places to the ground. Weeks after the evacuation, Lieutenant Loftus Cliffe wrote, "I believe our Troops left Philadelphia extreamly dissatisfied that it was not consumed."[2] If the British stopped short of burning the occupied cities to the ground, they still did extensive damage to the urban landscape. Even with the best of intentions, an occupying army is often ham-handed, and the British army was no different. Patriots returning to the cities after the British evacuations were shocked at what had happened to private residences, churches, and public buildings. Economic hardship also plagued the cities, leading to riots over food, wages, and prices, with women, sailors, and militiamen at the forefront.[3]

Many city dwellers demonstrated questionable patriotism during the war—all had supported substantial Loyalist populations, augmented by the migration of refugees (including blacks hoping to obtain freedom) from the countryside. When the British evacuated Philadelphia in 1778 and took many Loyalists with them, Benjamin Rush wrote, "Our city has undergone some purification, but it still too much resembles the Ark which preserved not only the clean, but the unclean beasts from the effects of the deluge." Many more city dwellers selfishly pursued neutrality and trade with the British in the interest of safety and survival.[4]

In the spring of 1779, Charlestonians almost collapsed in fear and panic as Major General Augustine Prévost and the British army approached the town. Governor John Rutledge sent out a flag of truce and asked Prévos for terms. When the British general demanded surrender and oaths of loyalty to the Crown, Rutledge and the majority of his Privy Council proposed "a neutrality, during the war between Great-Britain and America," with South Carolina's allegiance to be determined by the eventual peace treaty. When Prévost demurred answering such terms, the Patriot general William Moultrie took charge of the situation and refused to surrender. With reinforcements arriving, Prévost lifted the siege, and the British postponed their capture of Charleston for another year.[5] No doubt a series of fire scares and persistent fears of slave revolts in the city had contributed to Charleston's timidity.[6]

When the war ended, the cities were in a difficult position. Their populations had undergone dramatic upheaval [...], with Patriots fleeing during the British occupation and Loyalists fleeing when the British left. The economic effects of British blockades, commercial collapse, military appropriation and corruption, uncollected rents, and deteriorated property had been devastating. Loyalism, neutrality, and riots had poisoned the cities in many Americans' minds. The war was particularly devastating to Newport, which never recovered its economic importance or its demographic dominance.

In 1783, a mutiny exacerbated the cities' declining reputation. On June 21, 1783, a few hundred Continental soldiers protested outside the State House in Philadelphia, demanding not to be disbanded until the government had settled their accounts. The delegate Alexander Hamilton of New York favored calling up the Pennsylvania militia, but state authorities (who had jurisdiction) refused. The incident exposed the weakness of the federal government, and an indignant Congress used the mutiny as a pretext to leave Philadelphia. As they decamped for Princeton, New Jersey, congressmen reflected that Pennsylvania's interference, alcohol-fueled mob action, the Loyalist presence, and commercial influence had all made a large city like Philadelphia a threat to decentralized government and unfit as the seat of a republic. At the end of 1783, after news of the Treaty of Paris arrived, the British evacuated New York City. Americans gleefully watched the backs of the British soldiers recede into the distance, yet many Americans were turning their backs on the cities as well.[7]

The cities themselves, of course, survived. The golden age of Newport and Charleston was in the past. Merchants went looking elsewhere for these ports' principal products, the slave trade legally ended in 1807, and neither city had the resources to open new avenues for growth. In Newport, there was almost no one left to remember its revolutionary legacy after the war, and its prominence gave way to Providence. Charleston remained the state's principal port (though it never became a railroad hub), and cotton sustained the state until it exhausted the soil. Charlestonians of the early nineteenth century celebrated their local Revolutionary heroes, but became increasingly defensive about slavery (and against slave uprisings). As their economy faltered, their voices rose. By the 1840s and 1850s, their vigorous campaign of sectionalism had absorbed their revolutionary contributions. By then, neither Newport nor Charleston could look upon the Revolution and its effects with much fondness.[8]

After their postwar economic setbacks, Boston, New York City, and Philadelphia roared into the nineteenth century with new markets, new financial institutions, a cosmopolitan cultural outlook, and plenty of potential to nourish new manufacturing sectors. What the cities lost, ultimately, was their ability to feel that they were leaders in America's political mission. Provincial legislatures had acquired a taste for the relative safety of the countryside, and they sought more central locations away from the coast, amidst a westward-moving population. New York City and Philadelphia each served temporarily as the nation's capital (though New Yorkers had little use for Congress during its stay), and then the federal hub went elsewhere. By the century's end, both cities had relinquished their positions as state capitals. South Carolinians voted to move their state capital inland in 1786, and almost every other state in the nation made similar decisions in the ensuing decades. Rhode Islanders continued to rotate the seat of government. Only Boston remained the center of government, economy, and society for Massachusetts, though it often invited resentment and distrust from the countryside and the rest of the nation, a far cry from the outpouring of sympathy and support it had enjoyed in 1774. The cities would be places of economic rather than political leadership.[9]

Critiques of the cities and urban politics during the late eighteenth century arose from many sources. First, the country itself was still mostly rural: on the eve of independence, 7 or 8% of Americans lived in towns of over 2,500. By 1790, this number had fallen to 5.1% and remained below 7% until 1810. In America, city dwellers were a small minority.[10]

Second, being a city dweller was anathema to agrarian visions of the new nation's political economy. Many Americans, particularly rural southerners, challenged the mercantile interests who represented northern cities. These agrarian champions preferred to lionize the self-sufficient yeoman farmer. As republicans, they distrusted the financiers, foreign traders, courtiers, and bureaucrats that had corrupted the metropolises of Europe and would defile American

cities as well. The regional divisions of the early republic helped to define party disputes over foreign policy, debt, tariffs, constitution making, and other issues—and such divisions often led to national policies that favored the rural south over the more urbanized sections of the country.[11]

Third, many Americans—especially the elite—had a strong distaste for the urban crowds, urban problems, and dependent urban poor who were thought to arise from a nation's insufficient attention to agriculture. Americans of the early republic observed the rioting, labor actions, fires, filth, diseases, crimes, irreligion, ethnic mixing, and vice that plagued the cities and saw ample proof for their prejudices. From a political standpoint, the "mobs and tumults, so naturally incident to great cities," were particularly threatening to republican government. These "mobs and tumults," though they had been crucial to political mobilization before the war, were now anathema. Many leaders of the new republic strove to limit the influence of politics out of doors. As Christopher Gadsden had written in 1778, "I am afraid we have too many amongst us who want again to be running upon every fancy to the Meetings of [the] liberty tree," which was a "disease amongst us far more dangerous" than the Loyalists had been.[12]

This anti-urban bias, combined with a suspicion of the metropolises of centralized governments, helped shape the decision to locate the national capital at a sparsely populated bend of the Potomac River rather than in an existing urban center. Those who distrusted a federal city conjured up fearsome images of its power, its privileges, and its threats to civil rights, states' rights, and slavery. Congress chose to build Washington, D.C., on the Maryland-Virginia border as a concession to the rural south and with rural, pastoral notions of classical virtue in mind. The new capital city kept urban values, urban vices, and urban commercial ventures at arm's length, and remained moribund as a city for a hundred years. The founders of the nation's capital sought to escape from cities rather than engage with their disorderly bustle and intrigue. The four Virginians among the country's first five presidents were content with this arrangement. For its first forty years, the United States would largely be a nation led by Virginia, for Virginia, and (all but) from Virginia.[13]

In the new republican government, many city dwellers had a new outlet for political action at the voting booth. Yet even a representative government could frustrate city dwellers' desire for wider political participation, and both of the national political parties that emerged in the 1790s appeared disinclined toward broad-based urban politics. The Federalist Party was the party of urban mercantile interests that detested the French Revolution and its excesses of political mobilization. Though the cities were natural rallying points for the Federalists, the party leaders' elitist attitudes kept them at arm's length from democratic mass politics. In 1791, President Washington wrote, "The tumultuous populace of large cities are ever to be dreaded." His treasury secretary, Alexander Hamilton, distrusted urban tumults as well. When arguing for the Constitution, he had expressed similar fears of "the depredations which the democratic spirit is apt to make on property." Congressman Fisher Ames of Massachusetts railed against the "self-created societies" that sprang up in American cities in the 1790s—in a republic, that sort of political mobilization was unnecessary and dangerous.[14]

Such attitudes, combined with anti-British and pro-French sentiment, drove more city dwellers into the arms of these Democratic societies (which were explicitly modeled on revolutionary organizations) and the Republican Party. The Republicans earned urban support with their canny local alliances and their promises of broader social and economic opportunity. Yet any party with Thomas Jefferson at its head was bound to have mixed feelings toward cities. Jefferson, a rural Virginia slave-owner; made little secret of his distaste for cities and his vision for an agrarian republic. "Those who labor the earth," he wrote,

"are the chosen people of God," while "the mobs of great cities" were "sores" on the body politic. "The great mass of our people are agricultural," he wrote during his presidency, "and the commercial cities, though, by the command of newspapers, they make a great deal of noise, have little effect on the direction of the government." Jefferson even called city dwellers a distinct people under a "foreign influence" who were "clamorous" against the "agricultural interest" and its virtuous "country people." Jefferson and his disciple, James Madison, acknowledged a need for commercial and manufacturing centers, but they feared the actions of city people who (economically speaking) were still under the thumb of the British Empire. In Jefferson's mind, the worst institutions of countermobilization (aside from foreign states, armies, and navies) were American countinghouses, banks, and their puppet newspapers. Jeffersonian Republicans may have had electoral success in the cities, but a national story written by Republicans would not be one that celebrated the cities' role in the spirit of 1776. Jeffersonian dismissal of the cities would become painfully clear when the Embargo of 1807 and the War of 1812 disrupted urban commerce. During the Age of Andrew Jackson, Democrats with a backcountry slaveholder at their head would similarly recruit city dwellers while denigrating the cities. Following Jefferson's lead, most Americans located the nation's soul in the countryside.[15]

If the American narrative seemed to be bypassing the cities, they nonetheless remained important sites for political mobilization. The mechanisms of revolutionary mobilization—newspapers, crowd action, parades, voluntary associations, tavern toasts, and organized meetings—largely endured and helped draw together the city and countryside, though these mechanisms also developed in ways that would have rendered them unrecognizable to colonial city dwellers. The nineteenth century was to be an age of wage labor and slave labor, immigration and westward migration, manufacturing and rapid transportation, interest groups and corporations, individualism and party politics. Many of these new phenomena encouraged new mechanisms of mobilization, such as broader suffrage, workers' associations, reform movements, nationalist festivals, party conventions, and the partisan press. In other ways, the changes of the nineteenth century discouraged political mobilization by atomizing the cities and divorcing individualist striving from civic duty. Where revolutionary radicals had claimed to mobilize the people, nineteenth-century city dwellers were mobilizing money, interests, and party. Colonial conflicts had been divisive, and the resistance to Great Britain had given city dwellers (and their rural neighbors) grounds for unity, but after the Revolution new crises appeared to divide Americans much more often than they encouraged broad coalitions.[16]

The Revolution had reshaped American politics, and cities no longer served the same function in the early republic as they had in the colonial era. Postrevolutionary Americans split into partisan camps and splintered into numerous other factions and interest groups with different perspectives on local and national issues. Slavery, labor, foreign policy, race, government, taxation, vice, and immigration all continued to make the cities fertile ground for political action. Coalitions formed and disbanded, just as they had done immediately before the Revolution. Sometimes a broad urban coalition trumped narrower interests; at other times, interests fractured the cities.[17] Of course, at the end of the day, all these mobilizing city dwellers called themselves Americans—and that had been the purpose of the Revolution. American nationhood and the nation's thriving nineteenth-century political culture were the principal legacies of urban political mobilization.

As the nineteenth century progressed, the nature of urban places changed. The richest city dwellers owned most of the wealth and real estate; they were increasingly separating themselves into their own neighborhoods; they kept to themselves in elite voluntary

organizations (and helped cement their position through philanthropy); and they controlled city government. The waterfronts retained their potential as hotbeds of political action, but the merchants abandoned them, and the workers who remained were politically weaker and more divided than they had been before the Revolution. As strikes became increasingly common, the urban workplace was often the forge of political protest. Taverns were still vital places for gathering and politics. Yet the loose hierarchy of colonial urban taverns was becoming more stratified, giving way to respectable upper-class hotels and pleasure gardens and rowdy, violent lower-class saloons that were the founts of working-class politics and the targets of temperance forces and local peacekeepers. Church adherence remained spotty, flexible, and pluralistic in the cities, and the variety of religious groups grew even more during the nineteenth century. Churches retained their towering (and increasingly refined) presence in the urban landscape, and they remained powerful sources of mobilization for their congregations. Differences in religious belief continued to play a role in politics, and religion infused debates over slavery, temperance, and nativism. Urban households ceased to be the main sites of production for working men, while household authority, consumption, and virtue persisted as urgent concerns, with new implications for public health and welfare. Popular protests still focused on civic buildings and the squares around them, but these spaces also changed to suit the needs of contemporaries. To encourage order and uniformity, city authorities promoted grid streetscapes, compartmentalized buildings, and court-houses dominated by increasingly professional judges and lawyers. To discourage rioting and out-of-door politics in the streets, cities introduced new prisons and municipal police forces.[18]

Americans had redrawn the boundaries of political mobilization, but some traditional hierarchies persisted. Cities were magnets for free blacks and runaways in cities north and south. In southern cities, blacks found themselves excluded from public life, yet free blacks (and sometimes slaves) engaged in crowd action or pursued their limited freedom in churches and associations, as well as the shadow landscape of the waterfront (and waterborne) community, grogshops, groceries, and illegal schools. Nevertheless, every rumor of slave disobedience or revolt resulted in even tighter restrictions for urban blacks. Emancipated from slavery in the north, blacks nevertheless faced oppression, exclusion, racism, poverty, and violence in nineteenth-century cities. Concentrated populations of urban black men and women found their own political voice in the northern cities, and developed their own sites of political mobilization, especially in churches, schools, and voluntary associations, but also in newspapers, vigilance committees, and public celebrations. As they sought inclusion, equality, and independence, black Americans understood that further political mobilization would be necessary.[19]

Women of the early republic ran up against a prevailing ideology that sought to confine them to the "separate sphere" of the household. Still, men reached out to women for support—though they sometimes co-opted their efforts. White women took their own initiative to congregate, to mobilize, and to escape the confines of the Victorian household. Politicized women took advantage of cosmopolitan cities and their churches, voluntary associations, communication networks, street culture, and print culture for their own purposes and for the public good. In addition to using these old mechanisms of revolutionary mobilization in new ways, women also helped create new sites of political action, such as the theater and the salon.[20]

After the Revolution ended, Americans never fully embraced the urban political mobilization that had preceded it. Rural Americans had numerous reasons to ignore or disclaim the cities, yet urban Americans also forgot their cities' role as cradles that had nursed the resistance to Great Britain. The Sons of Liberty began bowdlerizing the resistance movement as soon as crowds had gotten out of hand in 1765. After the war was over, Boston's Federalist leaders emphasized commemorative celebrations that were orderly, staid, compartmentalized, and hierarchical. As they mobilized the past for purposes of national unity, they robbed the Revolution of its complex, dynamic history. Occasionally city dwellers would explicitly revive and recall the political mobilization of the 1760s and 1770s by hoisting liberty poles or staging new mass meetings at Boston's Faneuil Hall or Philadelphia's State House Yard. Yet these tended to be the acts of radical groups like supporters of the French Revolution, nascent unions, and (paradoxically) both pro-slavery secessionists and the antislavery movement. Local and national leaders refused to sanction such acts—conservative elites understood the risks involved in opening the door to unfettered political mobilization. As a result, most Americans continued the process of forgetting. Developments of the nineteenth century encouraged city dwellers to withdraw into their private domains, and the growing apparatus of local, state, and national governments threatened to insulate itself from the people's input. At moments of crisis, city dwellers remembered their history of popular mobilization and resisted new encroachments on their rights, but this was often an uphill battle.[21]

City dwellers still engaged in political action, and they continued to redefine the boundaries of political mobilization. Their cities persisted as vibrant, dynamic, and cosmopolitan places that fostered diversity and innovation. Radical groups commemorated and celebrated the urban political mobilization that had nourished the American Revolution, even when leading politicians and writers declined to do so. As city builders leveled hills and paved the way for commerce, they erased substantial portions of their revolutionary landscapes. Older forms of political mobilization that had made the cities essential to the revolutionary movement likewise disappeared. The cities had changed since the days of the Stamp Act resistance and the signing of the Declaration of Independence, for better and for worse. The outbreak of the

Revolutionary War diminished the cities' importance. Yet the Revolution had begun, not on Paul Revere's lonely road to Concord or amid floating chunks of ice in the Delaware River, but on the waterfront and in the streets, squares, and meeting places of the cities. These were the places that made the Revolution possible.

NOTES

1. Benjamin Franklin to Jonathan Shipley, July 7, 1775, *PBF*, 22:95; Stiles, *Literary Diary*, 1:624; Abigail Adams to John Adams, October 25, 1775, in *Adams Family Correspondence*, 1:313; James Lovell to Oliver Wendell, May 3, [1775], in Upham, "Occupation of Boston," 172; see also John Adams to Abigail Adams, June 2, June 14, August 23, 1777, in *Adams Family Correspondence*, 2:253–54, 262, 326.

2. General Thomas Gage to Lord Viscount Barrrington, June 26, 1775, in *Correspondence of General Thomas Gage*, 2:686–87; John Adams to Abigail Adams, June 4, 1777, in *Adams Family Correspondence*, 2:262; *Diary of Frederick Mackenzie*, 1:297–98; Loftus Cliffe to [Charles Totten], July 5, 1778, Loftus Cliffe Papers, WLCL; see also Lieutenant William Feilding to Basil Feilding, sixth Earl of Denbigh, April 28, 1776, in Balderston and Syrett, *Lost War*, 76–77; *Journal of Ambrose Serle*, 300–302; "Letters of Robert Biddulph," 101: Kwasny, *Washington's Partisan War*; Mackesy, *War of America*, 65–66, 97–102, 150–51, 154–57, 172–73, 185–86, 198 n2, 220–21, 254–56, 269–71, 405–10.

3. On Boston, see Carr, *After the Siege*, chap. 1; Frothingham, *History of the Siege of Boston*, 327–28; on New York City, see Barck, *New York City*, chaps. 4, 8; Burrows and Wallace, *Gotham*, 249–55, 266; on Newport, see Crane, *Dependent People*, epilogue; Withey, *Urban Growth*, chap. 5; on Philadelphia, see Jackson, *With the British Army in Philadelphia*, esp. chap. 16; on British depredations, see Conway, "Great Mischief"; Conway. "To Subdue America"; on rioting, see Rosswurm, *Arms, Country, and Class*, chaps. 5–7; Schultz, *Republic of Labor*, 51–68; Foner, *Tom Paine*, chap. 5; Smith, "Food Rioters"; Walsh, *Charleston's Sons of Liberty*, 77–87, 100–105.

4. Benjamin Rush to Abigail Adams, August 15, 1778, in *Adams Family Correspondence*, 3:74; see also Lambert, *South Carolina Loyalists*. esp. chaps. 11, 14: McCowen, *British Occupation of Charleston*; Van Buskirk, *Genero us Enemies*; Barck, *New York City*, chaps. 5–6, 9; Burrows and Wallace, *Gotham*, 245–49; Hodges, *Root and Branch*, chap. 4; Jackson, *With the British Army in Philadelphia*, esp. chaps. 8. 11, 14; Doerflinger, *Vigorous Spirit of Enterprise*, 218–23; Irvin, "Streets of Philadelphia," 22–32; Schultz, *Republic of Labor*, 48–51.

5. Haw, "Broken Compact"; Moultrie, *Memoirs of the American Revolution*, 1:402–35; Borick, Gallant Defense, chap. 1; Godbold and Woody, *Christopher Gadsden*, 192–95.

6. John Wells Jr. to Henry Laurens, January 23, 1778, *PHL*, 12:332–35; Hart, Memorandum," 393–97; Kennett, "Charleston in 1778," 109; "Journal of Ebenezer Hazard," 181–83; Henry Laurens to John Laurens, March 1, 1778, Henry Laurens to John Lewis Gervais, March 11, 1778, Henry Laurens to John Laurens, June 7, 1778, *LDC*; *South-Carolina and American General Gazette*, January 29, February 5, 1778; *Pennsylvania Gazette*, May 23, 1778; Stoney, "Great Fire of 1778," 23–26; Olwell, *Masters, Slaves, and Subjects*, 228–43.

7. Bowling, "Philadelphia Mutiny"; Bowling, *Creation of Washington*, chap. 1.

8. Crane, *Dependent People*, epilogue; Withey, *Urban Growth*, chap. 6, conclusion; Coclanis, *Shadow of a Dream*; Goldfield, *Cotton Fields and Skyscrapers*, 76–78; McInnis, *Politics of Taste*, esp. chap. 5; Travers, "Paradox of 'Nationalist' Festivals."

9. Aggarwala, "Seat of Empire"; Doerflinger, *Vigorous Spirit of Enterprise*, chaps. 7–8; Burrows and Wallace, *Gotham*, esp. 306, 354; Spaulding, *New York in the Critical Period*, 113, 163; Zagarri, "Representation and the Removal of State Capitals"; Zagarri, *Politics of Size*, chap. 1; Thomas Jefferson, Notes concerning a Bill for the Removal of the Seat of Government of Virginia, [November 11, 1776?], *Papers of Thomas Jefferson*, 1:602–3; Formisa no, *Transformation of Political Culture*, 150, 160–61; Onuf, *Jefferson's Empire*, 121–29: Meinig, *Shaping of America*, 1:400–403; Waldstreicher, *In the Midst of Perpetual Fetes*, 251–62.

10. McCusker and Menard, *Economy of British America*, 250.

11. Cress, "Whither Columbia"; Bowling, *Creation of Washington*; McCoy, *Elusive Republic*; see also Olton, *Artisans for Independence*, chaps. 8–9; Foner, *Tom Paine*,

chap. 6; Burrows and Wallace, *Gotham*, 30 0–302.

12. Cress, "Whither Columbia," quote 592; Walsh, *Charleston's Sons of Liberty*, quote 87 [...]; McCoy, *Elusive Republic*; Bowling, *Creation of Washington*; Gilje, *Road to Mobocracy*; Burrows and Wallace, *Gotham*, esp. pp. 266–70, 322–25, 350–52, 413–14, chaps. 23–25, 29–33, 35–37.

13. Elkins and McKitrick, *Age of Federalism*, chap. 4; Cress, "Whither Columbia"; Bowling, *Creation of Washington*.

14. George Washington to the Marquis de Lafayette, July 28, 1791, *PGW: Presidential Series*, 8:378; Hamilton quoted in Young, *Democratic Republicans*, 59; Ames quoted in Elkins and McKitrick, *Age of Federalism*, 486; see also Morgan, *Inventing the people*; Gilje, *Road to Mobocracy*, 71, 103–4. 107; Rock, *Artisans of the New Republic*, esp. chaps. 1–2; Kerber, *Federalists in Dissent*, esp. chap. 6.

15. Jefferson, *Notes on the State of Virginia*, 197; Onuf, *Jefferson's Empire*, 69–72, 90–93, quote 204 n57, 224 n37; Thomas Jefferson to Thomas Mann Randolph Jr., May 6, 1793, in *Papers of Thomas Jefferson*, 25:668; Elkins and McKitrick, *Age of Federalism*, chap. 5; Berg, *Remembered Gate*, chap. 2; Murrin, "Great Inversion"; Link, *Democratic-Republican Societies*; Young, *Democratic Republicans*; Young, "Mechanics and the Jeffersonians"; Rock, *Artisans of the New Republic*, chap. 3. pp. 123, 176, 280; Miller, *Philadelphia*; Koschnik, "Political Conflict and Public Contest"; Shankman, "Malcontents and Tertium Quids"; Shankman, *Crucible of American Democracy*; Kornblith, "Artisan Federalism"; Bender, *Toward an Urban Vision*, 3; McCoy, *Elusive Republic*; Aggarwala, "Seat of Empire," chap. 5; White and White, *Intellectual Versus the City*, esp. chap. 2.

16. Gilje, "Rise of Capitalism"; Nash, "Social Evolution"; Salinger; *Labor and Indentured Servants in Pennsylvania*, epilogue; Ryan, *Civic Wars*; Neem, "Freedom of Association": Bridges, *City in the Republic*; Appleby, *Inheriting the Revolution*; Gunn, *Decline of Authority*; Greenberg, *Cause for Alarm*; Waldstreicher, *In the Midst of Perpetual Fetes*; Newman, *Parades and Politics*; Travers, *Celebrating the Fourth*; Davis, *Parades and Power*; Brooke, "Ancient Lodges and Self-Created Societies"; Koschnik, "Democratic Societies of Philadelphia"; Bullock, *Revolutionary Brotherhood*, esp. chap. 8; Pasley, *Tyranny of Priners*; Rock, *Artisans of the New Republic*; Wilentz,

Chants Democratic; Gilje, *Road to Mobocracy*, esp. chap. 8.

17. Ryan, *Civic Wars*; Teaford, *Municipal Revolution*; see, for example, Young, *Democratic Republicans*, 100–102, 201–2, 405–7, 495.

18. Nash, "Social Evolution"; Ryan, *Civic Wars*; McInnis, *Politics of Taste*; Bushman, *Refinement of America*; Burrows and Wallace, *Gotham*; Gilje, *Road to Mobocracy*; Wilentz, *Chants Democratic*, esp. 53–54, 77–87; Stott, *Workers in the Metropolis*; Rosenberg, *Religion and the Rise of the American City*; on the elite, see Pessen, *Riches, Class, and Power*; Jaher, "Politics of the Boston Brahmins"; Jaher, *Urban Establishment*, chaps. 2–4; but see also Gough, "Philadelphia Economic Elite"; Kornblith and Murrin," Making and Unmaking"; on the waterfront and workplace, see Gilje, *Liberty on the Waterfront*; Laurie, *Working People of Philadelphia*; Schultz, *Republic of Labor*; on taverns, see Thompson, *Rum Punch and Revolution*, epilogue; Salinger, *Taverns and Drinking*, conclusion; Kaplan, "New York City Tavern Violence"; but see also Shankman, Malcontents and Tertium Quids," 57–58; on churches, see Bilhartz, *Urban Religion*; Appleby, *Inheriting the Revolution*, chap. 7; Butler, *Awash in a Sea of Faith*, chap. 9; Laurie. *Working People of Philadelphia*; on households, see Stansell, *City of Women*, esp. 11, 22, 30–37, 41–42, 63–68, 92–94, 163–64, 187–88, chap. 10: Lyons, *Sex among the Rabble*; Blackmar, *Manhattan for Rent*; Herman, *Town House*; McCoy, *Elusive Republic*; on public spaces, see Upton, "Another City"; Mires, *Independence Hall*, esp. 60; McNamara, *From Tavern to Courthouse*, chap. 4: Davis, *Parades and Power*, esp. 30–36.

19. Wade, *Slavery in the Cities*; Powers, *Black Charlestonians*, chaps. 1–2; McInnis, *Politics of Taste*, esp. chaps. 3, 6, 8; Egerton, *Gabriel's Rebellion*; Nash, *Forging Freedom*; Horton and Horton, *Black Bostonians*; Curry, *Free Black in Urban America*; Bolster, *Black Jacks*; Newman, "Protest in Black and White"; Perlman, "Organizations of the Free Negro"; White, *Somewhat More Independent*; Hodges, *Root and Branch*, chaps. 5–8; Gilje, *Road to Mobocracy*, chap. 6; Waldstreicher, *In the Midst of Perpetual Fetes*, esp. chap. 6.

20. Crane, *Ebb Tide in New England*, 96–97, chap. 6; Cott, *Bonds of Womanhood*; Zagarri, "Women and Party Conflict"; Lebsock, *Free Women of Petersburg*, chap. 7;

Branson, *These Fiery Frenchified Dames*; Waldsreicher, *In the Midst of Perpetual Fetes*, esp. 232–41; Berg, *Remembered Gate*; Boylan, *Origins of Women's Activism*; Stansell, *City of Women*; Ryan, *Women in Public*.

21. Young, *Shoemaker and the Tea Party*, pt. 2; Young, "Mechanics and Jeffersonians," 276; Schoenbachler, "Republicanism in the Age of Democratic Revolution," 243, 256–57; Newman, *Parades and Politics*, 94, 123–26, 129–30, 144, 148, 172–76; Gilje, *Road to Mobocracy*, 110; Mires, *Independence Hall*, esp. 28–29, 120–21; Carp. Nations of American Rebels"; Teaford, *Municipal Revolution*; Ryan, *Civic Wars*.

ESSAY 3.3

Urban Life in Western America, 1790–1830

Richard C. Wade

Source: *The American Historical Review*, 64, no. 1 (October 1958): 14–30.

EDITORS' INTRODUCTION

The settlement of the American "West" began with towns, several of which grew into great cities. Many of the towns existed on paper and in the minds of speculators long before the arrival of their first inhabitants. From the small towns, and the cities which evolved from some of them, the agrarian countryside emerged. Historian Richard C. Wade made this argument in his landmark 1958 essay from *The American Historical Review*, reprinted as this essay. With these fundamental insights, Wade, a graduate student of Arthur M. Schlesinger, Sr., turned Frederick Jackson Tuner's famous "frontier thesis" on its head and ignited a new wave of interest in urban history in particular and urban studies in general during the 1960s and 1970s.

In this selection, Wade contemplates the founding of towns and cities along the Ohio and Mississippi River Valleys and their contribution to defining the qualities and nature of life in the tramontane West region. By West, Wade is referring to the trans-Allegheny West, the region beyond the Appalachian Mountain Range that served as the official western border of the American colonies under the British Proclamation Line of 1763. Today, of course, these same cities typically are considered part of the Midwest, the Middle Atlantic region, and the upper South.

The location of each town derived from a combination of perceived natural advantages and anticipated trade routes. These settlements, however, did not arise in a vacuum. Commercial agents, military officials, and land speculators surveyed and planned each town after pre-existing models, principally the city of Philadelphia with its checkerboard pattern of streets crossing at right angles, regardless of the actual physical characteristics and limitations of the natural terrain. Eastern capital, travelers' accounts, and exaggerated newspaper promotion fueled a process that predicted a future sprawling metropolis at almost every river bend. While few of these envisioned great cities actually emerged, the pattern of urban promotion and "city making mania" took root and moved further west with each generation.[i] Civic leaders in the West also looked eastward, again primarily to the "mother city" of Philadelphia, to recruit physicians, teachers, and ministers, as well as to adopt best practices in municipal government. Over time, two distinct types of society, one urban and one rural, emerged in tandem to define Western life in the United States.

Richard Clement Wade, widely regarded as the father of American urban history, was the founder and first president of the Urban History Association. He was born in Des Moines, Iowa in 1921 and raised in Winnetka, Illinois, a northern suburb of Chicago. He taught at Washington University in St. Louis in the early 1960s. Wade moved to the

---

i For more on city making in the Great Lakes region and other parts of the expanding "Great West," as well as the reinterpretation of Turner's frontier thesis, see William Cronon, "Dreaming the Metropolis," chapter one in *Nature's Metropolis: Chicago and the Great West* (New York: W. W. Norton, 1991): 23–54.

University of Chicago until 1971, when he became Distinguished Professor of History at the Graduate Center of the City University of New York. More than any other historian, Wade influenced generations of urban studies scholars with his emphasis on the interdisciplinary examination of urban life. His classic works include *The Urban Frontier: The Rise of the Western Cities, 1790–1830* (Cambridge, MA: Harvard University Press, 1959), *Slavery in the Cities: The South, 1820–1860* (New York: Oxford University Press, 1964), and *Chicago: Growth of a Metropolis* (Chicago: University of Chicago Press, 1969) with Harold M. Mayer. Wade also enjoyed public service and taking part in Democratic Party politics. He served as a member of the Chicago Housing Commission from 1967–1971, the manager of Robert F. Kennedy's upstate New York campaign for the United States Senate in 1964, and as an advisor to Senator George McGovern's 1972 presidential campaign. He died at his home in New York City in 2008.[ii]

URBAN LIFE IN WESTERN AMERICA, 1790–1830 (1958)

The towns were the spearheads of the American frontier. Planted as forts or trading posts far in advance of the line of settlement, they held the West for the approaching population. Indeed, in 1763, when the British drew the Proclamation Line across the Appalachians to stop the flow of migrants, a French merchant company prepared to survey the streets of St. Louis, a thousand miles through the wilderness. Whether as part of French and Spanish activity from New Orleans or part of Anglo-American operations from the Atlantic sea-board, the establishment of towns preceded the breaking of soil in the transmontane West.

In 1764, the year of the founding of St. Louis, settlers made the first plat of Pittsburgh. Twelve years later and four hundred miles down the Ohio, Louisville sprang up at the Falls, and the following decade witnessed the beginnings of Cincinnati and Lexington. Before the century closed, Detroit, Buffalo, and Cleveland were laid out on the Great Lakes. In fact, by 1800 the sites of every major metropolis in the old Northwest except Chicago, Milwaukee, and Indianapolis had been cleared and surveyed.

Furthermore, these urban outposts grew rapidly even in their infant decades. By 1815 Pittsburgh, already a thriving industrial center, had 8,000 inhabitants, giving it a slight margin over Lexington. Cincinnati estimated its population at 4,000 at the end of the war with Great Britain, while farther west Louisville and St. Louis neared half that figure. [...]

Not all the towns founded in the trans-Allegheny region in this period fared as well, however. Many never developed much beyond a survey and a newspaper advertisement. Others, after promising beginnings, slackened and settled down to slow and unspectacular development. Still others flourished briefly then faded, leaving behind a grim story of deserted mills, broken buildings, and aging people—the West's first harvest of ghost towns. Most of these were mere eddies in the westward flow of urbanism, but at flood tide it was often hard to distinguish the eddies from the main stream. Indeed, at one time Wheeling, Virginia, St. Genevieve, Missouri, New Albany, Indiana, and Zanesville, Ohio, were considered serious challengers to the supremacy of their now more famous neighbors.

Other places, such as Rising Sun, Town of America, or New Athens, were almost wholly speculative ventures. Eastern investors scanned maps looking for likely spots to establish a city, usually at the junction of two rivers, or sometimes at the center of fertile farm districts. They bought up land, laid it out in lots, gave the place a name,

ii For more on Wade's influence and career see his obituaries by William Grimes in *The New York Times* 25 July, 2008 and Kenneth T. Jackson in the Organization of American Historians' *OAH Newsletter* 36, no 4 (November 2008): 27.

and waited for the development of the region to appreciate its value. Looking back over this period one editor called it a "city-making mania," when everyone went about "anticipating flourishing cities in vision, at the mouth of every creek and bayou."[1] This speculation, though extensive, was not always profitable. "Of the vast number of towns which have been founded," James Hall declared, "but a small minority have prospered, nor do we think that, as a general rule, the founders of these have been greatly enriched by their prosperity."[2]

Despite many failures, these abortive attempts to plant towns were significant, for they reveal much about the motives of the people who came West in the early period. Many settlers moved across the mountains in search of promising towns rather than good land, their inducements being urban opportunities rather than fertile soil. Daniel Drake, who was among the earliest urbanites of the frontier, later commented on this process:

It is worthy of remark, that those who made these beginnings of settlement, projected towns, which they anticipated would grow into cities.... And we may see in their origins, one of the elements of the prevalent tendency to rear up towns in advance of the country which has ever since characterized Ohio. The followers of the first pioneers, like themselves had a taste for commerce and the mechanic arts which cannot be gratified without the construction of cities.[3]

[...] The West's young cities owed their initial success to commerce. All sprang from it, and their growth in the early years of the century stemmed from its expansion. Since the Ohio River was the chief artery of trade and travel, the towns along its banks prospered most. Pittsburgh, where the Allegheny meets the Monogahela, commanded the entire valley; Cincinnati served the rich farm-lands of Kentucky and Ohio; Louisville fattened on the transshipment of goods around the Falls; and St. Louis, astride the Mississippi, was the focus of far-flung enterprises, some of which reached to the Pacific Ocean. Even Lexington, landlocked in a country of water highways, grew up as the central mart of Kentucky and Tennessee.

Though these cities were firmly established by the first decade of the century, the coming of the steamboat greatly enhanced their size and influence.[4] By quickening transportation and cutting distances, steam navigation telescoped fifty years' urban development into a single generation. The flow of commerce down river was now supplemented by a northward and eastward movement, giving cities added opportunities for expansion and growth. "The steam engine in five years has enabled us to anticipate a state of things," a Pittsburgher declared enthusiastically, "which in the ordinary course of events, it would have required a century to have produced. The art of printing scarcely surpassed it in beneficial consequences."[5] The "enchanter's wand" not only touched the established towns but created new ones as well. A French observer noted that "in the brief interval of fifteen years, many cities were formed ... where before there were hardly the dwellings of a small town.... A simple mechanical device has made life both possible and comfortable in regions which heretofore have been a wilderness."[6]

As these commercial centers grew, some inhabitants turned to manufacturing. Indeed, this new interest spread so rapidly in Pittsburgh that in 1810 a resident likened the place to "a large workshop," and already travelers complained of the smoke and soot.[7] Between 1803 and 1815 the value of manufactured goods jumped from $350,000 to over $2,600,000, and the city's iron and glass products became known throughout the new country.[8] Watching this remarkable development, the editor of *Niles' Register* exclaimed: "Pittsburgh, sometimes emphatically called the 'Birmingham of America,' will probably become the *greatest manufacturing town in the world*"[9] Lexington also turned increasingly to industry, her rope walks and textile mills supplying the whole West. Beginnings were more modest in other places, but every city had at least a few ambitious enterprises.

Some of this urban expansion rested on a speculative base, and the depression of 1819 brought a reckoning. Lexington, already suffering from its land-locked position, received fatal wounds, while Pittsburgh, the West's foremost city, was crippled for a decade. Elsewhere, however, the setback proved only momentary and the mid-twenties saw the old pace renewed. Population growth again provides a convenient index of development. Cincinnati quickly overtook its faltering rivals, the number of its residents leaping from 6,000 in 1815 to over 25,000 in 1830. By the latter date the census recorded Pittsburgh's recovery. Though the figure had dropped to 7,000 during the depression, it rose to 13,000 in 1830. Farther west Louisville and St. Louis enjoyed spectacular expansion, the former boasting over 10,000 inhabitants at the end of the period, while the Mississippi entrepôt passed the 6,000 mark. Lexington alone lagged, its population remaining stable for the next two decades.

Even these figures, however, do not convey the real growth. In most places municipal boundaries could no longer contain the new settlers, and many spilled over into the suburbs. For instance, Allegheny, Bayardstown, Birmingham, Lawrenceville, Hayti, and East Liberty added nearly 10,000 to Pittsburgh's population, bringing the total to 22,000.[10] The same was true of Cincinnati where 2,000 people lived in the Eastern and Northern Liberties.[11] In Louisville, Preston's and Campbell's "enlargements" and Shipping-port and Portland swelled the city's total to 13,000.[12] Ultimately, the urban centers annexed these surrounding clusters, but in the meantime local authorities grappled with early manifestations of the suburban problem.

As the cities grew they staked out extensive commercial claims over the entire West.[13] Timothy Flint calculated that Cincinnati was the central market for over a million people, while a resident asserted that its trade was "co-extensive with steamboat navigation on the western waters."[14] Louisville's economic penetration was scarcely less impressive. As early as 1821, a local editor declared that "the people of the greater part of Indiana, all Kentucky, and portions of Tennessee, Alabama, Illinois, Missouri, now report to this place for dry goods, groceries, hardware and queensware."[15] St. Louis' empire touched Santa Fe on the south, Canada on the north, and the Pacific on the west. "It is doubtful if history affords the example of another city," wrote Hiram M. Chittenden, "which has been the exclusive mart for so vast an area as that which was tributary to St. Louis."[16]

In carving out these extensive dependencies, the young metropolises overwhelmed their smaller neighbors. The rise of St. Louis destroyed the ambitions of Edwardsville across the Mississippi, which once harbored modest hopes of importance. Pittsburgh's recovery in the late twenties condemned Wheeling and Steubenville to minor roles in the upper Ohio region. And Louisville's development swallowed two Kentucky neighbors while reducing Jeffersonville and New Albany on the Indiana side of the river to mere appendages.

Not satisfied with such considerable conquests, the cities reached out for more. Seeking wider opportunities, they built canals and turnpikes and, even before 1830, planned railroads to strengthen their position. Cincinnati, Pittsburgh, and St. Louis tried to tap the increasing trade on the Great Lakes by water links to the North. Pennsylvania's Iron City also hoped to become a major station on the National Road, and for a decade its Washington representatives lobbied to win that commercial bond with the East. Lexington, suffocating in its inland position, frantically strove for better connections with the Ohio River. A turnpike to Maysville was dashed by Jackson's veto, technical difficulties made a canal to the Kentucky River impractical, but some belated hope rose with the possibility of a railroad to Louisville or Cincinnati.

The intensive search for new advantages brought rivalry and conflict. Though the commerce of the whole West lay untouched before them, the cities quarreled over its division. Thus Louisville and Cincinnati fought over a canal around the Falls of the Ohio. The Kentucky town, feeling that its strength depended upon maintaining the break in transportation, obstructed every attempt to circumvent the rapids. Only when Ohio interests threatened to dig on the Indiana side did Louisville move ahead with its own project. Likewise, harsh words flew between Wheeling and Pittsburgh as they contended for the Ohio River terminus of the National Road. Smaller towns, too, joined the struggle. Cleveland and Sandusky, for instance, clashed over the location of the Ohio Canal, the stake being nothing less than control of the mounting trade between the Valley and the lakes. And their instinct to fight was sound, for the outcome shaped the future of both places.

Urban rivalries were often bitter, and the contestants showed no quarter. In the late twenties when only the success of Transylvania University kept Lexington's economy from complete collapse, Louisville joined the attack which ultimately destroyed the school. In a similar vein Cincinnatians taunted their upriver competitor as it reeled under the impact of the depression of 1819. "Poor Pittsburgh," they exclaimed, "your day is over, the sceptre of influence and wealth is to travel to us; the Cumberland road has done the business."[17] But even the Queen City found her supremacy insecure. "I discovered two ruling passions in Cincinnati," a traveler remarked, "enmity against Pittsburgh, and jealousy of Louisville."[18] This drive for power and primacy, sustained especially by merchants and articulated by editors, was one of the most consistent and striking characteristics of the early history of Western cities.

As they pursued expansive policies, municipalities also ministered to their own growing pains. From the beginning, urban residents had to contend with the problems of living together, and one of their first acts was to petition the territory or state for governing authority to handle them. The legislatures, representing rural interests and generally suspicious of towns, responded with charters bestowing narrow grants of power which barely met current needs and failed to allow for expansion. As localities grew, however, they developed problems which could be met only with wider jurisdiction. Louisville's charter had to be amended twenty-two times before 1815 and Cincinnati's underwent five major changes

between 1815 and 1827. Others, though altered less often, were adjusted and remade until finally scrapped for new ones. Reluctantly, and bit by bit, the states turned over to the cities the responsibility of managing their own affairs, though keeping them starved for revenue by strict tax and debt limitations.

Despite inadequate charters and modest incomes, urban governments played a decisive role in the growth of Western cities. Since these were commercial towns, local authorities paid special attention to mercantile requirements. They not only constructed market houses but also extended municipal regulation over a wide variety of trading activity. Ordinances protected the public against adulterated foods, false measurements, and rigged prices. Some municipalities went even farther and assumed responsibility for seeing that "justice is done between buyer and seller."[19] In search of this objective, officials fixed prices on some goods, excluded monopolies from the market, and tried to equalize opportunities for smaller purchasers. To facilitate access to the exchange center, they lavished time and money on the development of wharves and docks and the improvement of streets.

Municipalities also tackled a wide variety of other problems growing out of urban life. Fire protection, at first casually organized, was placed on a more formal basis. Volunteer companies still provided the manpower, but government participation increased markedly. Local councils legislated against many kinds of fire hazards, and public money furnished most of the equipment. Moreover, some places, haunted by the image of Detroit's disaster in 1805, forbade the construction of wooden buildings in the heart of the city, a measure which not only reduced fire risks but also changed the face of downtown areas. The development of adequate police was much slower. By 1830 only Lexington and Louisville had regular patrols, and these were established with the intent more of control of slaves than the general protection of life and property. In other towns law enforcement was lax by day and absent at night, though the introduction of gas lighting in

Pittsburgh and Cincinnati in the late twenties made the after-dark hours there less dangerous than before.

Congested living created new health hazards and especially increased the likelihood of epidemics. Every place suffered, but none like Louisville, which earned a grim reputation as the "Graveyard of the West" because of the constant visitations of yellow fever and malaria.[20] Cities took preventive measures, such as draining stagnant ponds and clearing streets and lots, and also appointed boards of health to preside over the problem. Municipal water systems, introduced in Pittsburgh and Cincinnati before 1830, made life healthier and certainly more comfortable, while the discussion of installing underground sewers pointed to still more extensive reform in sanitation.

In meeting urban problems, Western officials drew heavily on Eastern experience. Lacking precedents of their own, and familiar with the techniques of older cities, they frankly patterned their practice on Eastern models. There was little innovation. When confronted by a new question, local authorities responded by adopting tested solutions. This emulation characterized nearly every aspect of development—from the width of streets to housing regulations. No major improvement was launched without a close study of established seaboard practices. St. Louis' council, for example, instructed its water committee to "procure from the cities of Philadelphia and New Orleans such information as can be obtained on the subject of conveying water and the best manner of clearing it."[21] When Cincinnati discussed introducing underground sewers, an official group was designated to "ascertain from the city authorities of New York, Philadelphia, Baltimore and Boston, how far the sinking of common sewers is approved in those cities."[22] Pittsburgh undertook gas lighting only after exhaustive research and "very full enquiries at New York and Baltimore."[23]

Though the young towns drew upon the experience of all the major Atlantic cities, the special source of municipal wisdom was Philadelphia. Many Western urbanites had lived or visited there; it provided the new country with most of its professional and cultural leadership; it was the model metropolis. "She is the great seat of American affluence, of individual riches, and distinguished philanthropy," a Pittsburgh editorial declared in 1818. "From her ... we have everything to look for."[24] Newspapers often referred to it as "our mother city."[25]

From street plans to cultural activity from the shape of market houses to the habits of people, the Philadelphia influence prevailed. Robert Peterson and John Filson, who had a hand in the founding of Louisville, Lexington, and Cincinnati, borrowed the basic grid pattern of the original plats from the Pennsylvania metropolis.[26] Market location and design came from the same source, as did techniques for fire fighting and police protection. Western towns also leaned on Philadelphia's leadership in street lighting, water-works, and wharving. Even the naming of suburbs—Pittsburgh's Kensington and Cincinnati's Liberties—came from the mother city. The result was a physical likeness which struck many travelers and which Philadelphians themselves recognized. Gideon Burton, for instance, remembered his first impression of Cincinnati in the 1820's: "How beautiful this city is," he remarked, "how much like Philadelphia."[27]

The Quaker City spirit, moreover, went beyond streets, buildings, and improvements, reaching into a wide range or human activity. Businessmen, yearly visitors in the East, brought marketing and promotion techniques from there;[28] young labor movements lifted their platforms from trade union programs in the mother city; employment agencies were conducted "principally on the Philadelphia plan."[29] The same metropolis trained most of the physicians of the West and a large share of the teachers and ministers. Caspar Wistar's famed Sunday evening gatherings of the intelligentsia provided the idea for Daniel Drake's select meetings of Cincinnati's social and cultural elite. Moreover, Philadelphia furnished the model of the perfect urbanite, for the highest praise that Western town dwellers could bestow upon a fellow citizen was to refer to him as their own "Benjamin Franklin."[30] In short, Philadelphia represented the highest stage of urban development, and progress was measured against this ideal. [...]

As transmontane cities developed they created societies whose ways and habits contrasted sharply with those of the countryside. Not only was their physical environment distinct, but their interests, activities, and pace of life also differed greatly. In 1811 a farmer near Lexington expressed the conflict as contemporaries saw it in a dialogue between "Rusticus" and "Urbanus." The latter referred to the "rude, gross appearance" of his neighbor, adding: "How strong you smell of your ploughed ground and corn fields . How dismal, how gloomy your green woods. What a miserable clash your whistling woodland birds are continually making." "Rusticus" replied with the rural image of the town dweller. "What a fine smooth complexion you have Urbanus: you look like a weed that has grown up in the shade. Can you walk your streets without inhaling the noxious fumes with which your town is pregnant? ... Can you engage in calm contemplation, when hammers are ringing in every direction—when there is as great a *rattling* as in a storm when the hail descends on our house tops?"[31] [...]

Urban ways were further distinguished from rural habits by the collective approach to many problems. City living created issues which could not always be solved by the highly individualistic methods of agrarian society. Local governments assumed an ever wider responsibility for the conduct of community affairs, and voluntary associations handled a large variety of other questions. Merchants formed chambers of commerce to facilitate cooperation on common problems; professional people organized societies to raise the standards of their colleagues and keep out the untrained. Working people, too, banded together in unions, seeking not only greater economic strength but also fraternity and self-improvement. Religious and philanthropic clubs managed most

charity and relief work, while immigrants combined to help new arrivals. In addition, other associations grew up to promote literature and music, encourage debating, advocate social innovations, support public causes, and conduct the welter of amusements which larger cities required. Just as conditions in the countryside placed greatest emphasis on individual effort, so the urban situation made cooperative action seem more appropriate.

Rural and metropolitan West were also separated by distinctive social and cultural developments. The towns very quickly produced a surprisingly rich and diversified life, offering opportunities in many fields similar to those of Eastern cities but lacking on the farm or frontier.[32] They enjoyed a virtual monopoly of printing presses, newspapers, bookstores, and circulating libraries. Theaters sprang up to encourage local players and traveling troupes, while in larger places museums brought the curious and the scientific to the townfolks.[33] In addition, every week brought numerous lectures and debates on all kinds of topics, keeping urban residents abreast of the latest discoveries and developments in every field. By 1815 these amenities had already lost their novelty. Indeed, some thought the civilizing process was getting out of hand. "Twenty sermons a week—," a Cincinnatian wearily counted, "Sunday evening Discourses on Theology—Private assemblies—state Cotillion parties—Saturday Night Clubs, and chemical lectures—... like the fever and the ague, return every day with distressing regularity."[34]

Of course, the whole transmontane region matured culturally in this period, but the towns played a strategic role. "Cities have arisen in the very wilderness...," a St. Louis editor noticed in 1821, "and form in their respective states the *foci* of art and science, of wealth and information."[35] A Cincinnatian made a similar observation. "This *city*, in its growth and cultural improvements has anticipated the western country in general."[36] The hinterland, already bound to urban communities by trade, readily admitted its dependence. The *Pittsburgh Gazette* merely stated the obvious when it remarked in 1819 that the surrounding region "looks up to Pittsburgh not only as a medium through which to receive the comforts and luxuries of foreign commodities, but also a channel from which it can most naturally expect a supply of intellectual wealth."[37] Thus while the cities' merchants staked out markets in the countryside, their civic leaders spread a cultural influence into the same area.

This leadership extended into almost every field. For example, the educational opportunities of town children greatly exceeded those of their rural neighbors. Every municipality developed a complex of private tuition schools topped by an academy and, in every place except Louisville, a college. Moreover, the cities organized the movement for public schooling. Ohio's experience is illustrative. The movement for state legislation started in Cincinati, received its major impetus from the local press, and was carried in the Assembly through the efforts of representatives from Hamilton county. It is also significant that the first superintendent of common schools in Ohio was Samuel Lewis of Cincinnati. Nor was this urban leadership surprising. The cities, as the great population centers, felt the educational pressure first and most acutely. In addition, they alone had the wealth needed to launch ambitious projects for large numbers of children. Hence the towns were ready for comprehensive public programs long before the countryside.

The most striking illustration of the cultural supremacy of the cities, however, was Lexington's unique reign as the "Athens of the West."[38] The area's largest town until 1810, it was early celebrated for its polish and sophistication and was generally conceded to be the region's capital of arts and science. But the coming of the steamboat and the depression of 1819 combined to undermine its economic position. To offset this commercial and industrial decline, Lexington's civic leaders inaugurated a policy of vigorous cultural expansion.[39] They built schools, subsidized Transylvania University, and advertised the many opportunities for advancement in learning and letters in the metropolis. Throughout the twenties this campaign was a spectacular success. The

town became the resort of the most talented men of the new country. Educators, scientists, painters, lawyers, architects, musicians, and their patrons all flocked there. Transylvania University attained national eminence, attracting most of its faculty from the East and drawing students from better than a dozen states. Like a renaissance city of old Italy, Lexington provided the creative atmosphere for a unique flowering that for a decade astonished travelers and stimulated the best minds of the West.

The graduating class of the medical school in 1826 demonstrated the extent of the university's reputation and influence. With sixty-seven degrees granted in that year, twenty-eight of the recipients came from Kentucky, ten from Tennessee, five each from Virginia, South Carolina, and Alabama, three from Ohio, two each from Mississippi, Illinois, and Louisiana, and one each from North Carolina and Georgia. During the twenties the college trained many of the West's most distinguished people. In politics alone it turned out at least seventeen congressmen, three governors, six United States senators, and the president of the Confederacy. In the same decade the school produced scores of lawyers, clergymen, and physicians, who did much to raise professional standards in the new country. Few universities have left such a clear mark on a generation; in its heyday Transylvania fully deserved its title of the "Harvard of the West."[40] [. . .]

The glitter of this city drew young people from all over the transmontane region, including many from the countryside. In doing so, it provoked a familiar lament from the rural areas whose children succumbed to the bewitchment of Lexington. "We want our sons to be practical men," wrote a Kentucky farmer, "whose minds will not be filled with those light notions of refinement and taste, which will induce them to believe that they are of a different order of beings, or that will elevate them above their equals."[41] Later, agrarian representatives in the legislature joined the attack on Transylvania by voting to cut off state financial assistance.

No less striking than cultural cleavages were the differences in rural and urban religious development. Progress in the cities was steadier and more substantial—though less spectacular—than in the back country. Traveling ministers might refer to Pittsburgh as "a young hell, a second Sodom,"[42] and Francis Asbury might complain in 1803 that he felt "the power of Satan in those little, wicked western trading towns,"[43] but both churches and membership multiplied rapidly in urban centers. Furthermore, the growth owed nothing to the sporadic revivals which burned across the countryside at the beginning of the century. These movements were essentially rural, having their roots in the isolation of agricultural living and the spiritual starvation of people unattended by regular services. The city situation, with its constant contacts and settled church organizations, involved neither of these elements. Instead, religious societies proliferated, sects took on such additional functions as charity and missionary work, and congregations sent money back East to aid their seminaries. Far from being sinks of corruption, Western cities quickly became religious centers, supplying Bibles to the frontier, assisting foreign missions, and, in the twenties, building theological schools to provide priests and ministers for the whole region.

Political life also reflected the growing rural-urban division. Though the rhetoric of the period often obscured them, differences existed from the very beginning. Suspicion of the towns led states to avoid economic and cultural centers when locating their capitals. Nearly all these cities sought the prize, but none was successful. The *Missouri Gazette* candidly stated the issue in 1820. "It has been said that St. Louis is obnoxious to our Legislature—that its growth and influence ... are looked on with a jealous eye, and its pretensions ... ought to be discouraged."[44] The same clash had earlier occurred in Kentucky, where state leaders virtually invented Frankfort to keep the capital away from Louisville or Lexington. [...]

The cities' political influence rested on their ability to produce leadership. As the economic and intellectual centers of transmontane life they attracted the talented and

ambitious in all fields. Politics was no exception. Nearly all the great spokesmen of the West had important urban connections and their activity often reflected the demands of their town constituents. Henry Clay was one of Lexington's most prominent lawyers when he went to the United States Senate in 1806. Thomas Hart Benton held local offices in St. Louis before moving on to the national scene, and William Henry Harrison, though he lived in nearby North Bend, had deep roots in Cincinnati affairs through most of his long public life. Moreover, all were alive to the interests of their city. Benton's successful attack on government factories in the Indian territory culminated a long and intense campaign by St. Louis merchants to break federal trade control on the Missouri. Clay's enthusiasm for an ample tariff hemp derived at least as much from the pressure of Lexington's manufactures as from that of the growers of the Blue Grass. And Harrison, as state senator, led the campaign for public schools in Ohio largely at the behest of his Cincinnati supporters. These were not isolated cases; an examination of the careers of these men demonstrates the importance of their urban connections.

By 1830, then, the West had produced two types of society—one rural and one urban. Each developed its own institutions, habits, and living patterns. The countryside claimed much the larger population and often gave to transmontane affairs an agrarian flavor. But broadcloth was catching up with buckskin. The census of 1830 revealed the disproportionate rate of city growth. While the state of Ohio had four times as many inhabitants as it counted in 1810, Cincinnati's increase was twelvefold. The story was the same elsewhere. Louisville's figure showed a growth of 650 per cent compared with Kentucky's 50 per cent, and Pittsburgh tripled in size while Pennsylvania did not quite double its population. By 1830 the rise of these cities had driven a broad wedge of urbanism into Western life.

Though town and country developed along different paths, clashes were still infrequent. The West was large enough to contain both movements comfortably.

Indeed, each supported the other. The rural regions supplied the cities with raw materials for their mills and packinghouses and offered an expanding market to their shops and factories. In turn, urban centers served the surrounding areas by providing both the necessities and comforts of life as well as new opportunity for ambitious farm youths. Yet the cities represented the more aggressive and dynamic force. By spreading their economic power over the entire section, by bringing the fruits of civilization across the mountains, and by insinuating their ways into the countryside, they speeded up the transformation of the West from a gloomy wilderness to a richly diversified region. Any historical view which omits this aspect of Western life tells but part of the story.

NOTES

1. *Missouri Republican* (St. Louis), Aug. 29, 1825.
2. Hall, *The West: Its Commerce and Navigation* (Cincinnati, 1848), p. 227.
3. Drake, "Dr. Drake's Memoir of the Miami County, 1779–1794," Beverley Bond, Jr., ed., Historical and Philosophical Society of Ohio, *Quarterly Publications*, XVIII (1923), 58.
4. Louis C. Hunter, *Steamboats on the Western Rivers, An Economic and Technological History* (Cambridge, Mass., 1949), pp. 27–32.
5. Morgan Neville, "The Last of the Boatmen," *The Western Souvenir for 1829* (Cincinnati, Ohio, n.d.), p. 108.
6. [Jean Baptiste] Marestier, *Mémoire sur les Bateaux à vapeur des États-Unis d'Amérique* (Paris, 1824), pp. 9–10.
7. Zadock Cramer, *Pittsburgh Almanack for the Year of Our Lord 1810* (Pittsburgh, Pa., 1810), p. 52.
8. Pittsburgh's industrial foundations are discussed in Catherine Elizabeth Reiser, *Pittsburgh's Commercial Development, 1800–1850* (Harrisburg, Pa., 1951), pp. 12–21.
9. *Niles' Register*, May 28, 1814.
10. *Pittsburgh Gazette*, Nov. 16, 1830.
11. *Cincinnati Advertiser*, Aug. 18, 1830.
12. United States *Census*, 1830, pp. 114–15.
13. For an appreciation of the economic importance of the cities in the growth of the West, see Frederick Jackson Turner, *Rise of the New West, 1819–1829* in *The American Nation: A History*, A. B. Hart, ed., XIV (New York, 1906), 96–98.
14. Flint, "Thoughts Respecting the Establishment of a Porcelain Manufactory at Cincinnati," *Western Monthly Review*, III (1830), 512; Benjamin Drake and Edward W. Mansfield, *Cincinnati in 1826* (Cincinnati, Ohio, 1827), p. 71.
15. *Louisville Public Advertiser*, Oct. 17, 1829.
16. Chittenden, *The American Fur Trade of the Far West* (2 vols., New York, 1902), I, 99.
17. *Pittsburgh Gazette*, Dec. 18, 1818.
18. *Pittsburgh Gazette*, Feb. 5, 1819.
19. *Pittsburgh Gazette*, Mar. 9, 1810.
20. Benjamin Casseday, *The History of Louisville from Its Earliest Settlement till the Year 1852* (Louisville, Ky., 1852), p. 49.
21. St. Louis City Council, Minutes, Court House, St. Louis, June 12, 1829.
22. Cincinnati City Council, Minutes, City Hall, Cincinnati, Oct. 6, 1827.
23. Pittsburgh City Council, City Council Papers, City Hall, Pittsburgh, May 10, 1827.
24. *Pittsburgh Gazette*, Oct. 27, 1818.
25. For example, see *Pittsburgh Gazette*, June 23, 1818.
26. For example, see Rufus King, *Ohio First Fruits of the Ordinance of 1787* (Boston, 1888), p. 209.
27. Burton, *Reminiscences of Gideon Burton* (Cincinnati, Ohio, 1895). The strategic location of Western cities in the life of the new country reminded some visitors of the regional supremacy of Philadelphia. Lewis Condict, for example, referred to Lexington as "the Philadelphia of Kentucky." "Journal of a Trip to Kentucky in 1795," *Proceedings of the New Jersey Historical Society*, n.s., IV (1919), 120.
28. *Cincinnati Enquirer*, Apr. 22, 1923.
29. *Pittsburgh Mercury*, Aug. 7, 1827.
30. The phrase was constantly used in characterizing John Bradford of Lexington and Daniel Drake of Cincinnati, but it was applied to others as well.
31. *Kentucky Reporter* (Lexington), July 2, 1811.
32. For a day-to-day account of the cultural offerings of a Western city between 1820 and 1830 see the highly informative but unpublished diary of William Stanley Merrill in the library of the Historical and Philosophical Society of Ohio (Cincinnati).
33. The development of the theater in Western cities is outlined in Ralph Leslie Rush, *The Literature of the Middle Western Frontier* (New York, 1925), I, 352–400. For a detailed study of a single town see William G. B. Carson, *The Theatre on the Frontier, The Early Years of the St. Louis Stage* (Chicago, 1932), pp. 1–134.
34. *Liberty Hall* (Cincinnati), Dec. 9, 1816.

35. *Missouri Gazette* (St. Louis), Dec. 20, 1820.
36. *Liberty Hall* (Cincinnati), June 29, 1819.
37. *Pittsburgh Gazette*, Apr. 30, 1819.
38. For Lexington's growth and brief supremacy see Bernard Mayo, "Lexington, Frontier Metropolis," in *Historiography and Urbanization*, Eric F. Goldman, ed. (Baltimore, Md., 1941), pp. 21–42.
39. See, for example, *Kentucky Reporter*, Oct. 4, 1820.
40. The reputation of Lexington in Cincinnati is charmingly portrayed in the letters of young Ohioans attending Transylvania University to their friends back home. See especially the William Lytle Collection in the library of the Historical and Philosophical Society of Ohio (Cincinnati).
41. *Kentucky Reporter* (Lexington), Feb. 16, 1824.
42. *Pittsburgh Gazette*, Sept. 23, 1803.
43. Francis Asbury, *Journal of Rev. Francis Asbury, Bishop of Methodist Episcopal Church* (n.p., 1821), III, 127.
44. *Missouri Gazette* (St. Louis), Dec. 6, 1820.

DOCUMENTS FOR PART III

3.1 CONSPIRACY... FOR BURNING THE CITY OF NEW YORK... (1744)

Source: Recorder of the City of New-York, *A Journal of the Proceeding in the Detection of the Conspiracy Formed by Some White People, in Conjunction with Negro and Other Slaves, For Burning the City of New-York in America, and Murdering the Inhabitants.* (New York: James Parker, at the New Printing-Office, 1744).

EDITORS' INTRODUCTION

In the spring of 1741, New York City's leaders were gripped with fear that a multi-racial conspiracy to burn down the city and kill all of its residents was underway. A series of suspicious fires, insubordinate acts, and criminal behavior by free residents, indentured servants, and slaves followed a long period of bad weather, a poor economy, and the threat of invasion from an ongoing war between Great Britain and Spain. While the threat of fire was omnipresent for all urban dwellers at the time (and would remain so into the twentieth century), white fears of a slave rebellion were intensified by recent events in South Carolina, specifically the Stono Rebellion in 1739 and a November 1740 plot to burn Charleston. Roughly 2,000 slaves lived in New York at the time, representing just under 20 percent of the population, the second largest number and percentage of any city in North American behind Charleston.

After a fire in early April 1741 resulted in the arrest of a slave named Cuffee, seen near the conflagration, mobs of white vigilantes rounded up other blacks and put them in jail. Despite little to no evidence, Daniel Horsmanden, the city's recorder and justice on the province's Supreme Court, led an investigation of recent events. His first target was John Hughson, a white tavern keeper, who was known to sell liquor to blacks and allow mixed race patronage of his establishment by poor whites, soldiers, free blacks, and slaves. The court found that Hughson fenced stolen property and allowed members of the so-called Geneva Club (a group of slaves who stole Geneva, or Dutch Gin) to meet and conspire at his tavern. Hughson's sixteen-year-old indentured servant Mary Burton testified against him in exchange for a promise to free her from her indenture. Hughson was found guilty and executed on June 12, 1741. In total, just over 180 people were taken into custody—23 whites, 154 free blacks and black slaves, and five Spanish sailors recently captured and sold into slavery. In the end, four whites were hanged, thirty-one free blacks and slaves were either burned at the stake or hanged, while another thirty-one suffered "transport" or banishment from the colony. The transported were and sent to Newfoundland, Portugal, the Portuguese island of Madeira, and other colonies in the West Indies.

This document contains excerpts from the Supreme Court proceedings as recorded (most likely) by Horsmanden and published several years later. The publications stemmed in part as a response to political allegations that Horsmanden had fabricated events, if not the entire conspiracy. The event became known over time by such names as "Hughson's Plot," "Negro Plot of 1741," "Great Negro Plot of 1741," and "The New York Conspiracy." The proceedings are presented here not as conclusive proof of anyone's guilt or innocence, or even to provide evidence of an actual plot, but rather to illustrate the heightened climate and multifaceted nature of the fear that engulfed the city. Indeed, the colony's attorney general asserted in one trial session that the conspiracy to incite the city's slaves was the most horrible and destructive such collaboration ever known in the northern parts of America. The proceedings also illustrate how anyone who stood out from perceived norms became an easy target of suspicion. Of particular note is the fate of a white man named John Ury who had recently arrived in the city. Ury was a tutor and schoolmaster who also knew Latin, and Horsmanden drew on this difference to target him as a Roman Catholic priest sympathetic to Spain. Ury did admit to being a dissenter from the Church of England but did not admit to being a Catholic or a priest. A warning from Georgia's governor James Oglethorpe that the Spanish were moving north to attack English colonies arrived just before his Ury's trial started. Ury was found guilty and executed on August 29th. The first selection is Ury's last words declaring his innocence, while the remainder of the document is summation of event asserting a conspiracy. **[For another urban slave rebellion see Document 4.1, "Vesey Slave Revolt, Charleston, South Carolina (1822)."]** The text contains much of the original spelling, grammar, and capitalization from Horsmanden's 1744 publication, with modification from an 1810 reprint for purposes of clarity.

CONSPIRACY… FOR BURNING THE CITY OF NEW YORK… (1744)

The last Speech of JOHN URY.

Fellow Christians, I AM now going to suffer a Death attended with Ignominy and Pain; but it is the Cup that my Heavenly Father has put into my Hand, and I drink it with Pleasure; it is the Cross of my dear Redeemer, I bear it with Alacrity; knowing that all that live godly in *Christ Jesus*, must suffer Persecution; and we must be made in some Degree Partakers of his Sufferings, before we can share in the Glories of his Resurrection: For he went not up to Glory before he ascended *Mount Calvary*; did not wear the Crown of Glory before the Crown of Thorns. And I am to appear before an awful and tremendous GOD, a Being of infinite Purity and unerring Justice; a God who by no Means will clear the Guilty, that cannot be reconciled either to Sin or Sinners: Now this is the Being at whose Bar I am to stand; in the Presence of this God, the Possessor of Heaven and Earth, I lift up my Hands, and solemnly protest, I am innocent of what is laid to my Charge: I appeal to the great God for my Non-knowledge of *Hewson* [Hughson], his Wife, or the Creature that was hanged with them; I never saw them living, dying or dead; nor never had I any Knowledge or Confederacy with White or Black, as to any Plot: And, upon the Memorials of the Body and Blood of my dearest Lord, in the Creatures of Bread and Wine, in which I have commemorated the Love of my dying Lord, I protest that

the Witnesses are perjured; I never knew the perjured Witnesses but at my Trial. But for a Removal of all Scruples that may arise after my Death, I shall give my Thoughts on some Points.

First, I firmly believe and attest, That it is not in the Power of Man to forgive Sin; that it is the Prerogative only of the Great God to dispense Pardon for Sin; and that those who dare pretend to such a Power, do in some Degree commit that great and unpardonable Sin, the Sin against the Holy Spirit; because they pretend to that Power which their own Consciences proclaim to be a Lie.

Again, I solemnly attest and believe, That a Person having committed Crimes that have or might have proved hurtful or destructive to the Peace of Society, and does not discover the whole Scheme, and all the Persons concerned with them, cannot obtain Pardon from God: And it is not the taking any Oath or Oaths that ought to hinder him from confessing his Guilt, and all that he knows about it; for such Obligations are not only sinful, but unpardonable, if not broken: Now a Person firmly believing this, and knowing that an eternal State of Happiness or Misery depends upon the Performance or Non-performance of the above mentioned Things, cannot, will not triffle with such important Affairs.

I have no more to say by Way of clearing my Innocency, knowing that to a true christian unprejudiced Mind, I must appear guiltless; but however, I am not very sollicitous about it. I rejoice, and it is now my

Comfort (and that will support me and protect me from the Crowd of evil Spirits that I must meet with in my Flight to the Region of Bliss assigned me) that my Conscience speaks Peace to me.

Indeed, it may be shocking to some serious Christians, that the holy God should suffer Innocency to be slain by the Hands of cruel and bloody Persons (I mean the Witnesses who swore against me at my Trial) indeed, there may be Reasons assigned for it, but as they may be liable to Objections, I decline them; and shally only say, that this is one of the dark Providences of the great God, in his wise, just and good Government of this lower World.

In fine, I depart this Waste, this howling Wilderness, with a Mind serene, free from all Malice, with a forgiving Spirit, so far as the Gospel of my dear and only Redeemer obliges and enjoins me to, hoping and praying, that JESUS, who alone is the Giver of Repentance, will convince, conquer and enlighten my Murderers Souls, that they may publickly confess their horrid Wickedness before God and the World, so that their Souls may be saved in the Day of the Lord JESUS.

And now a Word of Advice to you, Spectators: Behold me launching into Eternity; seriously, solemnly view me, and ask yourselves severally, how stands the Case with me? die I must: Am I prepared to meet my Lord, when the Midnight Cry is echoed forth? shall I then have the Wedding-Garment on? Oh Sinners! triffle no longer; consider Life hangs on a Thread, here To-day and gone To-morrow; forsake your Sins e'er ye be forsaken forever: Hearken, now is God awfully calling you to repent, warning you by me his Minister and Prisoner, to embrace JESUS, to take, to lay hold on him for your alone Saviour, in order to escape the Wrath to come; no longer delay, seeing the Summons may come before ye are aware, and you standing before the Bar of a God who is a consuming Fire out of the Lord Jesus Christ, should be hurled, be doomed to that Place, *where their Worm dies not, and their Fire is never to be quenched.*
[...]

The Conclusion

BY the Course of the Evidence, it appears. That a Design was conceived to destroy this City by Fire, and massacre the Inhabitants: That Fire was to be put to several Quarters of the Town, at one and the same Time: That the *English Church* was to be set on Fire, at a Time when 'twas most likely there would be the fullest Congregation, and the Avenues from the Church were to be guarded by these Ruffians, in order to butcher those that should attempt to escape the Flames: This Part of the Scheme, it seems, *Ury* the *Priest*, had particularly at Heart.—The Winds were consulted which would be most proper to attempt the Fires with: They were to begin at the East End of the Town with a strong Easterly Wind, which (as it was projected) according to the Course of its Situation, would probably destroy the whole Town; but the King's *Fort* was *first* to be burnt, because most likely to annoy these *Furies*, when their hellish Devices were putting in Execution The Negro Confederates were each of them to set Fire to his Master's House, and proceed to the Assassinating their respective Masters and Families; and these Fires were calculated for the Night—*St. Patrick's* Night was the Time appointed. Accordingly we find, as a Proof that they were in earnest, the Attempt upon the *Fort* was made on *St. Patrick's Night*, tho' through the Providence of GOD, the Fire did not take Effect until the next Day at Noon, when the Villain who first put it, had renewed his Effort, by blowing up the same Brand that he had placed for the Purpose the Night before.
[...]

By the Evidence of this Girl [Mary Burton], it appears, that her Master *Hughson* was a Principal, Engine, Agent and Instigator of these Deeds of Darkness amongst the Slaves here, ever since she came into his Service; and by the Evidence of others, Whites and Blacks, it also appears, that he having kept a publick House for some Years, had long since made it a Practice to entertain Numbers of Negroes, often 20, 30, 40 or 50 at a Time, and by Degrees deluded them to engage in the Conspiracy, upon his Promises, that they should all be Freemen, and that other fine Things should be done for them; that upon their consenting, *Hughson* always bound them to their Engagements by *horrible Oaths*, not only to perform what they undertook to do, *viz.* to *burn and massacre*, but also to keep *all secret*, though they were to die for it; that these Oaths were reiterated at all future Meetings in order to confirm them; and for their Encouragement, *Hughson* often swore himself over again, and had sworn his Wife and Daughter into the Confederacy also That *Hughson* provided Arms and Gunpowder, further to convince these deluded Wretches, how much he was in earnest; but the Butchery to be executed by the Negroes after they had set Fire to their Masters Houses, was calculated to be done with Knives; for those Weapons, it seems they judged, would make no Noise: This the whole Current of Negro Evidence agrees in, and 'tis corroborated by Whites.—That a Knife designed for this Purpose was actually found in the Chest of one of the Negro Conspirators, and most others of them were provided with Knives.

That *Hughson* employed some of the Head Negroes as Agents under him, to decoy other Negroes, and their Instructions were not to open the Conspiracy to any but *those* that were of their *own* Country (as they are brought from different Parts of *Africa*, and might be suppos'd best to know the Temper and Disposition of each other) and when they brought a Convert to *Hughson*, or one likely to become such, *Hughson* always gave them Drams 'til they were intoxicated, and then the Conspiracy was proposed to them; and they generally consented without much Difficulty, upon his specious Promises, and sometimes upon the bare Proposal; but if they were unwilling to engage, they were terrified by Threats of being murdered, 'til they complied then all such were constantly *sworn*, invited to *Hughson*'s Feasts, and these commissioned to seduce others.

[...]

The White Conspirators were sworn by *Ury* the *Priest* in chief, and the Negroes sometimes by *Hughson*, and sometimes by *Ury* in a Ring surrounded by them, and *he*, while the Oath administering, holding a *Crucifix* over their Heads. They were persuaded that *the French and Spaniards* were soon to come and join them, and if they did not come in a set Time, they were to begin and do all themselves.—Further to encourage the Town Negroes, they were told the Confederates had many Whites and Blacks to come out of the Country to their Assistance, particularly from *Long-Island*, and *Hughson* was to give the Word when they were to begin. The Negroes were flattered they were to be formed into Companies, several Officers of them were named for the Purpose, Captains, *&c.* and the Town was divided into Districts. Thus all was to be their own, and if any of them were squeamish, *Ury* the *Priest* could forgive Sins, and did forgive them all they had committed, or should commit, *provided they performed* what they had engaged in, and kept all secret to their last Breath.

[...]

But we may remember, that the principal Witness in this *shocking* Case, and happy Instrument of this Detection, was *Mary Burton, Hughson's* indentured Servant; who (however it was) no one so much as insinuated to have been sworn of the Confederacy. As she was the prime Cause of the Discovery, as before related, their envenom'd Arrows have been chiefly pointed at her; and no Doubt, say they, she must be the Wickedest of Mortals, to bring so many Innocents to this shameful, miserable and untimely End.

[...]

The Girl doubtless must be under terrible Apprehensions when her Life was thus endangered, both from *Blacks and Whites*, if she made Discovery; this must have been a matter of great Restraint to her, and, in her Hurry and Confusion; of Thought, might occasion her to utter that through Inadvertency, which upon calm Reflection, she became conscious was wrong, though at the time, it might be an involuntary

Suppression only of Part of the Truth, arising from an Over-hastiness in answering, and want of due Recollection; which therefore perhaps, after making all candid and ingenuous Allowances, will not be rigorously construed a wilful and deliberate Falsehood.

[...]

The other White People executed, as well as *Ury*, like true *modern Romanists*, pretended to maintain (and did protest) their Innocence to their last Breath; though *Hughson* himself, soon after his Conviction, seemed to betray strong Symptoms of his Inclination to confess his Guilt, and make Discovery; but if he was in earnest to have done so, in Hopes of saving his own Life, his Mind was soon changed (as 'twas conjectured) by the Persuasion of his Wife; yet *Kerry* left such Proofs behind her of many of the Particulars of this Conspiracy, and of her own Guilt, as add great Force to the aforegoing Accounts of it; and her recanting afterwards, is another irrefragable Instance, how these Wretches do prevaricate, even in their last Moments!

That a Plot there was, and as to the Parties and bloody Purpose of it, we presume there can scarce be a Doubt amongst us at this Time; the Ruins of his Majesty's House in the Fort, are the daily Evidence and Memento of it, still before our Eyes: If the other Frights and Terrors this City was alarmed with, to their great Consternation, are, as to some amongst us, so soon slipt into Oblivion, yet surely others will think we ought once a Year at least, to pay our Tribute of Praise and Thanksgiving to the Divine BEING, that through his merciful Providence and infinite Goodness, caused this inhumane horrible Enterprize to be detected, and so many of the wicked Instruments of it to be brought to Justice, whereby a Check has been put to the execrable Malice, and bloody Purposes of our Foreign and Domestick Enemies, though we have not been able entirely to unravel the Mystery of this Iniquity; for 'twas a dark Design, and the Veil is in some Measure still upon it!

3.2 A PRACTICAL PLAN FOR BUILDING THE PACIFIC RAILROAD (1857)

T.D. Judah

Source: T.D. Judah, *A Practical Plan for Building the Pacific Railroad* (Washington, D.C.: Henry Polkinhorn Printers, 1857).

EDITORS' INTRODUCTION

Theodore Dehone Judah, a surveyor and engineer, served as a strong proponent of the Central Pacific Railroad and the conglomeration of routes that came to make up the First Transcontinental Railroad. The First Transcontinental Railroad, known also as the Pacific Railroad, was primarily constructed between 1863 and 1869. At the outset, most railroads were local, meant to support existing business. The dream of a transcontinental route was of another scope altogether, and required risk and vision. The transcontinental would create business rather than just serve existing need. The Central Pacific, which was part of the First Transcontinental Railroad, predated the Pacific Railroad Act of 1862, which established the Union Pacific line. The Central Pacific ran from Sacramento, California to Promontory Summit in the Utah territory, while the Union Pacific ran from Council Bluffs, Iowa (near Omaha) to Promontory. In addition to his roles building the Central Pacific Railroad, Judah also served as clerk of the House subcommittee working on the Pacific Railroad Bill and later as secretary of the Senate Committee on the Pacific Railroad. Judah proposed routing the transcontinental route through the daunting terrain of the Sierra Nevadas. Judah persuaded wealthy business leaders known as the Associates, including Leland Stanford, Collis Huntington, Mark Hopkins and brothers Charles and Edwin Crocker to fund the Central Pacific Railroad through private means. (Edwin had a stroke and had to curtail his involvement in the project.) The group also build a toll road for wagon traffic alongside the railroad, hedging their bets on the railroad's success. In 1863 President Abraham Lincoln declared Omaha, Nebraska the eastern terminus of the Union Pacific Railroad. On May 10, 1869, Leland Stanford drove the symbolic last spike into the railroad tracks at Promontory Summit using a silver hammer.

A PRACTICAL PLAN FOR BUILDING THE PACIFIC RAILROAD (1857)

The project for construction of a great Railroad through the United States of America, connecting the Atlantic with the Pacific ocean, has been in agitation for over fifteen years.

It is the most magnificent project ever conceived.

It is an enterprise more important in its bearings and results to the people of the United States, than any other project involving an expenditure of an equal amount of capital.

It connects these two great oceans.

It is an indissoluble bond of union between the populous States of the East, and the undeveloped regions of the fruitful West.

It is a highway which leads to peace and future prosperity. An iron bond for the perpetuation of the Union and independence which we now enjoy.

Many projects for the prosecution of this enterprise have been presented.

Various schemes for the fulfillment of these projects have been devised.

Our wisest statesmen, most experienced politicians, scientific engineers, and shrewdest speculators, have each and all discussed the subject in nearly every point of view, and given the results of their wisdom and experience to the world.

Yet—

Their projects have proved abortive.

Their schemes have failed

The world has listened with attentive ears to the words of eloquence and wisdom, from the lips of great and wise men.

Yet—

This project has not been consummated.

The road has not been finished.

Its practicability has not been established.

A survey has not been made.

It has simply been made the subject of reconnaissance.

Still—

During the first twenty-five years, twenty-five thousand miles of Railroad has been constructed in the United States, and a thousand million of dollars expended thereon.

This road is but two thousand miles in length, and its cost not over, say $150,000,000.

As many as eight or ten great avenues of transit between the present East and West (three of which, in the State of New York alone, cost one hundred million of dollars) have been constructed.

This highway, the greatest and most important of them all, remains unbuilt, it may be said unsurveyed, simply reconnoitered.

Why is this?

Its popularity is universal.

Its importance admitted.

Its practicability believed in

Its profitableness unquestioned.

1. It is because these projects have been speculative in their nature; and the people are disposed to look with distrust upon grand speculations.
2. There are different routes, advocated by diverse interest, each eager that the road be built to subserve its own particular interest, but unwilling to make common cause upon a common route.

3. From the lack of confidence in private capitalists, dissuading them from investing in any project, through which they cannot see their way clear.

This plan assumes to obviate these objections; and,

1. To build the Pacific Railroad.
2. To accomplish the same in ten years.
3. To raise the capital therefore.

And suggests practical means for the accomplishment of its object by means of private capital.

It assumes that, without confidence of the people, the road cannot be built.

Therefore,

It proposes to divest the project of its speculative features, and thereby endeavor to inspire the public with confidence.

To do this, therefore, its direction and destiny must not be controlled by a grand stock jobbing company, whose united aggregate wealth will not pay once per cent. upon their magnificent subscriptions.

2ndly. To divest it of the difficulties consequent upon sectional prejudices.

It is proposed to ask aid of no kind whatsoever from the General or any State Government, but to combine the interest of either the Northern or Southern States, upon their favorite route; to ask for private capital, and confine the sphere of action entirely to one or the other of these sections.

This insures unity of action.

3.3 HORACE GREELEY, LETTER TO R.L. SANDERSON, NOVEMBER 15, 1871

Source: **Courtesy of the Gilder Lehrman Institute.**

EDITORS' INTRODUCTION

Horace Greeley, born into poverty in New Hampshire in 1811, apprenticed as a printer and worked his way into the world of magazine and newspaper publishing. He adhered to phrenology and vegetarianism, and supported ideas like feminism and temperance. The 1837 Depression furthered his political theories. He wrote pieces urging the unemployed, immigrants, and under-paid government workers to move West to seek a secure living. There, he theorized, they would escape the problems of the city.

Greeley is improperly credited with coining the phrase, "Go, West young man," but he does seem to have contributed to the popularization of the saying, and the ideas behind it.

Greeley was at one time associated with the Whig party, then helped found the Republican Party. Horace Greeley ran for president of the United State in 1872 as a Liberal Republican, a party formed by Senator Carl Schurz. During Greeley's failed run for the presidency, Greeley's wife died, and he followed soon thereafter.

HORACE GREELEY, LETTER TO R.L. SANDERSON, NOVEMBER 15, 1871

New York, Nov. 15, 1871.
dear Sir:

So many people ask me what they shall do; so few tell me what they **can** do. Yet this is the pivot wherein all must turn.

I believe that each of us who has his place to make should go where men are wanted, and where employment is not bestowed as alms. Of course, I say to all who are in want of work, Go West!

But what can you do? and how can your family help you? Your mother, I infer, is to be counted out as an effective worker. But what of the rest? And you – can you chop? Can you plow? Can you mow? Can you cut up Indian corn? I reckon not. And in the west it is hard to find such work as you have been accustomed to. The conditions of living are very rude there.

On the whole I say, stay where you are; do as well as you can; and devote every spare hour to making yourself familiar with the conditions and dexterity required for the efficient conservation of out-door industry in a new country. Having mastered these, gather up your family and Go West!

Yours,
Horace Greeley
R.L. Sanderson,
Duxbury, MA

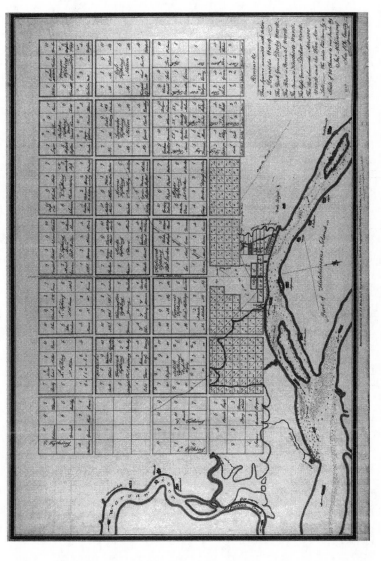

Illustration III.1 John McKinnon, City of Savannah, Georgia (circa 1800). Source: Courtesy of the Hargrett Rare Book and Manuscript Library/University of Georgia Libraries.

General James Oglethorpe and 112 other colonists founded the city of Savannah, Georgia on February 12, 1733. Oglethorpe envisioned the colony of Georgia as a haven for British debtors and persecuted Protestants in continental Europe. He established Savannah as the colonial capital and laid it out in a gridiron pattern modeled after Philadelphia, with residential lots in groups of ten to twelve, often with a trust lot for public buildings. Each ward featured an open square in the center. The pattern was easily expandable and by the middle of the nineteenth century, there were twenty-four squares in the city. This rare map by John McKinnon details the development of the city's squares circa 1800.

Illustration III.2 Paul Revere, "A View of Part of the Town of Boston, in New-England and British Ships of War: Landing Their Troops! 1768." Source: Clarence S. Brigham, *Paul Revere's Engravings* (Worcester: American Antiquarian Society, 1954). Courtesy of the Center for Historic American Visual Culture at the Antiquarian Society.

Paul Revere (1734–1818) was a noted silversmith and patriot during the American Revolution. He was also an engraver who established a successful printmaking business that won acclaim for the depiction of political events, such as the Boston Massacre of March 1770. The engraving above portrays the landing of British troops on the Long Wharf in Boston on October 1, 1768. In addition to the military presence, the engraving shows a city crowded around its economic lifeline, the harbor, dominated by churches and mixed use residential and commercial buildings.

Illustration III.3 Tom Willcockson, Packet Boat on the Illinois and Michigan Canal. Source: Courtesy of the Canal Corridor Association.

VIEW OF NEW ORLEANS.

Illustration III.4 Bernhard Dandorf, "View of New Orleans Taken from the Lower Cotton Press" (circa 1850–1855). Source: Bernhard Dandorf, "View of New Orleans Taken from Lower Cotton Press," (Louis Schwarz, Publisher, circa 1851–1855). Courtesy of the Center for Historic American Visual Culture at the American Antiquarian Society.

The French founded New Orleans in May 1718 and named it after Phillippe II, duc d' Orleans and regent of France. Spain took over in 1762 and it remained in their hands until 1801 when the French resumed control before selling it to the United States in 1803. The export of southern cotton helped make New Orleans the fourth largest port in the world by 1840. During the 1850s, German lithographer Bernhard Dandorf (1809–1902) made this print of commercial activity along on the Mississippi River (the modern-day Press Street area). Cotton presses used steam power to pack cotton into bales for shipment to northern and European factories.

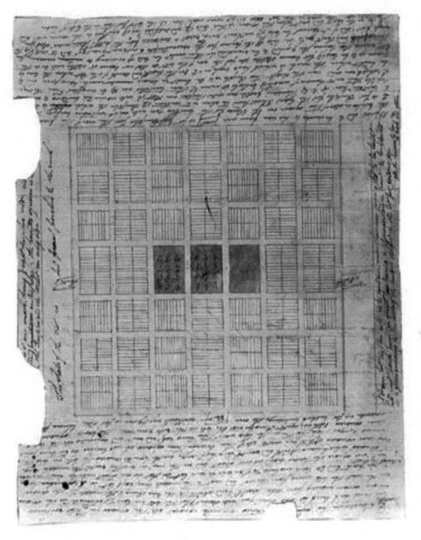

Illustration III.5 Joseph Smith, Plat of Zion, 1833. Source: The Joseph Smith Papers, Church History Department of The Church of Jesus Christ of Latter-day Saints.

PART IV

Ways of City Life, 1820s–1920s

EDITORS' INTRODUCTION TO PART IV

The study of the city's past—the field of urban history—evolved in the twentieth century alongside the general discipline of history, and reflected changes in the parent field. As explored in **Essay 1.1** by Steven H. Corey and Lisa Krissoff Boehm, "Examining America's Urban Landscape: From Social Reform to Social History, and Back," the formal study of history grew increasingly open to interdisciplinary ideas and also included far more quantitative work than in the past. The cultural environment of the mid-twentieth century, including the civil rights, women's rights, anti-war, student, and other social movements, irrevocably altered academic life. Heretofore, the so-called ivory tower, and particularly the professorate, was predominated by a group of people who were both wealthier and whiter (and more often males and Protestants) than the American population in general. With the growth of economic opportunity in the twentieth century, college education became an option open to more Americans, including the working class, immigrants and the children of immigrants, and women. Some decided to stay permanently within the hallowed halls of academia, and located jobs as professors. The viewpoints of these newcomers transformed formal study by bringing in a host of diverse concerns, particularly in regards to the study of a wider range of American experiences. Peter Stearns, writing in the *Journal of Social History*, summarizes, "The fundamental twin premises—that ordinary people not only have a history but contribute to shaping history more generally, and that a range of behaviors can be profitably explored historically beyond (though also including) the most familiar political staples—are still valid."[i]

What became known as the "new social history," and is now regarded simply as social history, considered the American past from a new vantage point. As Stearns points out, the methodology also relied on new sources. Where once historians solely had tackled such documents as the papers of presidents, the archival holdings of corporations, and the letters of statesmen when crafting their studies, they now redefined "primary source" and read a wider range of materials. Popular works, advertisements, oral histories, the letters and diaries of everyday people, union minutes, and city directories, once of suspect historical value, all became suitable fodder for respectable historical study. Instead of viewing history "from the top down," the new social historians looked at history "from the bottom up." This shift in directional focus changed almost everything.

Four of the historical essays featured in this part written by Christine Stansell, Timothy Gilfoyle, Ronald T. Takaki, and George Chauncey, offer unforgettable examples of history from the bottom up. So too does **Document 4.7** by John Hope Franklin and Scott Ellsworth on the 1921 Tulsa Race Riots. However, historian Clifton Hood presents life from the other direction—the viewpoint of the urban elite. Readers rarely have access to this rarified world.

Timothy Gilfoyle, using a memoir penned by a petty thief as his starting point, creates a wide-ranging narrative of the life of the poor and criminal classes of New York City. He takes his readers from the hardscrabble streets of Five Points, to the opium dens, and through the nightmarish prison system. Pickpocketing ranked among the most prevalent of crimes nineteenth-century cities, as evidenced in *The National Police Gazette*'s illustration from 1857 of such criminals at work. The danger of the streets extended beyond petty crime, as shown in the open passages of Theodore Dreiser's iconic *Sister Carrie* (1900) in **Document 4.5**. Carrie Meeber, a naïve country migrant, was led astray by two men quickly after she arrived in Chicago. George Chauncey relates the little-known story of gay New York, broadening our understanding of life in America's largest metropolis. Chauncey demonstrates that the big city proved alluring for homosexuals from small town America, as it did for young women like Sister Carrie.

Conditions in American cities were far from ideal. As immigration grew, housing failed to keep up with demand and conditions deteriorated. Many Americans lived in poverty generation after generation. As Christine Stansell demonstrates in **Essay 4.1**, "Women in the Neighborhoods," women carved out their own worlds within the city as part of a cash and barter economy of necessity that swirled about the teeming tenements. Castle Garden and Ellis Island were immigration processing centers in New York City that channeled millions of newcomers into the country. Increased diversity challenged Americans. Thousands flocked to join the American Protective Association, founded in 1887 and focused on limiting the number of Catholics entering the United States, and the Immigration Restriction League, founded in 1894. Many Republican political leaders, fueled by the strong anti-immigrant leanings of their constituents, promoted literacy tests for all newcomers, as well as physical examinations for immigrants traveling to America in the least-expensive steerage cabins of ships.

The Chinese found themselves in the center of the anti-immigrant debate, particularly on the country's west coast, where they were more numerous. The Chinese Exclusion Act of 1882 cut off most of the immigration from China; all Asian immigration was reduced by law until late in the twentieth century. These debates are covered in **Document 4.3** in which Senator Aaron Sargent of California and an anonymous defender of Chinese immigration present arguments for and against restrictions. The case of the Chinese demonstrates how American immigration fears were heightened with racial difference. Although a very small minority, the Chinese sojourners soon experienced a thunderous wave of discrimination. Economic and cultural exclusion limited immigrants from China to niche labor opportunities and isolated Chinatowns into ethnic islands as discussed by Ronald T. Takaki in his essay for this part. Japanese immigrants went through similar trials, faced with the exclusionary Gentlemen's Agreement of 1908, and the subsequent Ladies' Agreement of 1922, which ended the immigration of Japanese wives (many of them the well-known picture brides) from joining husbands in the United States.

It is important to note that slavery existed in cities as well as plantations and in the North as well as South. In **Document 4.1**, the "Vesey Slave Revolt, Charleston, South Carolina (1822)," we learn about the lengths that white Charlestonians would go to maintain order in their city city and in **Document 4.2** the uproar of white factory workers over the use of slave labor in a manufacturing facility in Richmond, Virginia. Anti-immigration sentiment and discomfort over changing economic realities also played out in nineteenth century cities. The popularity of Jacob Riis' *How The Other Half Lives* (1890) demonstrates the centrality of the immigrant question for the nation. The social and ethnic diversity of immigration is reflected in **Document 4.4**, which is a chapter from Riis' landmark book, and in the lives of those lost due to the tragic 1911 Triangle Shirtwaist Fire in **Document 4.6**.

NOTE

i.   Peter Sterns, "Social History Present and Future," *Journal of Social History*, 37 (1) (Fall 2003): 9.

ESSAY 4.1

Women in the Neighborhoods

Christine Stansell

Source: Christine Stansell, *City of Women: Sex and Class in New York, 1789–1860*
(New York: Knopf, 1986).

EDITORS' INTRODUCTION

This selection, drawn from the two opening chapters of Christine Stansell's ground-breaking work, *City of Women*, introduces readers to the history of urban women. Stansell examines the world of working-class New York City between the late 1700s and the Civil War, concluding that women, while subject to the pressures of their low economic status and a patriarchal culture, were far from victims. In contrast to New Englanders, who turned to large-scale factories when farming faltered, New Yorkers relied on commercial ports, expanding national and international trade, and entrepreneurship for its economy. The highly organized craft system established in colonial New York City eroded in the face of the pressures of the world market and left many families without assurance of an adequate living. Small production houses were hurt by increased competition and low-priced, factory-produced goods. The erstwhile artisans lost the opportunity for advancement with this reduced need for highly trained workers. Middle class families foundered, and more women needed to contribute to their household incomes in order to make ends meet.

Stansell's book, which established a common starting point for the scholars who study urban women, offers innovative arguments. She makes a keen observation regarding the lack of privacy in these women's lives; so many of their daily tasks—and the tasks of their children—took them outside of their own dwellings. Women and children did the work that modern urban residents pay their utility companies to perform today. Women and children brought in water to their households, gathered wood for cooking, and purchased or scavenged coal to warm their lodgings. Women contributed in a monetary way to their households by working outside the home for wages, caring for boarders, or producing goods out of raw supplies brought to their homes by middlemen. This latter practice, known as "outwork," constituted a popular choice, although caring for children and performing household chores while trying to keep up with the time demands of outwork proved daunting. The urban women also pawned household goods for ready cash, or sell homemade food or even alcohol. The women moved easily in and out of their neighbors' apartments, and claimed the stoops of their tenements as their own by their constant presence there. While men were slightly more obvious to city visitors, with their regular business taking them frequently into the streets, Stansell has demonstrated the existence of a public female realm, which formed, quite literally, a city of women. Urban women were not invisible, they were simply overlooked by many academics prior to the publication of this important study.

Stansell, a former professor at Princeton University, retired from the University of Chicago, where she served as the Stein-Freiler Distinguished Service Professor. Stansell is the author of *Powers of Desire: The Politics of Sexuality* (co-authored with Ann Snitow and Sharon Thompson, New York: Monthly Review Press, 1983) and *American Moderns:*

Bohemian New York and the Creation of a New Century (New York: Henry Holt, 2000). Stansell served as a Radcliffe Institute Fellow 2006–2007.

WOMEN IN THE NEIGHBORHOODS (1986)

By the 1820s, men and women of the urban bourgeoisie were coming to see households as more than just lodgings. The "home," their own term for the domestic setting, had become for them a pillar of civilization, an incubator of morals and family affections, a critical alternative to the harsh and competitive world of trade and politics. The home was based on a particular configuration of family members: woman at home, man at work, children under maternal supervision or at school. In its psychological form, it embodied the emotional self-sufficiency of the conjugal family and the suitability of women to private life; as a material setting, it elaborated the physical elements of the household into an embellished inner space cut off from the public world.[1]

In this sense, the home was absent from the lives of urban laboring women, who observed no sharp distinctions between public and private. Rather, their domestic lives spread out to the hallways of their tenements, to adjoining apartments and to the streets below. Household work involved them constantly with the milieu outside their own four walls; lodgers, neighbors, peddlers and shopkeepers figured as prominently in their domestic routines and dramas as did husbands and children. It was in the urban neighborhoods, not the home, that the identity of working-class wives and mothers was rooted. ...[...]

The particular kind of urban neighborhood which so disturbed civic-minded bourgeois New Yorkers was different from earlier forms. One new element was the extensive community of women that developed within the transient and disruptive circumstances of urban migration. Of course, the most visible inhabitants of the neighborhoods were men. They were the preponderance of drunken brawlers and street loungers and the most noticeable workers, as they trudged to and from the docks or labored at the open doors of the craft shops that dotted the streets. Another, less noticeable round of female activity, however, went on around this masculine sphere, a cycle of pinching and saving, of cleaning and borrowing and lending, of taking—and of being taken. With unremitting labor, wives, mothers and female neighbors kept the "tenement classes" going from day to day—whether stitching shirts for the clothing shops or bargaining down street peddlers. Out of the precarious situations into which immigration, poverty and (for many) the erosion of male support thrust them, women formed particular attachments to each other and to their children that made the neighborhoods important resources in the negotiations and battles of daily urban life.

Industrialization and Working-Class Formation

The residents of these gregarious neighborhoods helped to transform New York into what was, by 1860, the largest manufacturing city in America and the capital of the country's finance and commerce.[2] Its small workshops, stacked floor by floor in the new cast-iron warehouses that lined the narrow, crowded streets, were as important to America's Industrial Revolution as the better-known mills of New England. Between 1820 and 1860, the population quadrupled to over 800,000; the city's border moved a mile and a half north from City Hall to Forty-second Street. "How this city marches northward!" marveled diarist George Templeton Strong after a walk in 1850. "Wealth is rushing in upon us like a freshet."[3]

New York's spectacular rise began in the 1820s. The disruption of shipping in the war had seriously damaged the port, but recovery was steady, and by 1820 the maritime economy was sturdy and thriving. In the next few years, in a series of remarkable leaps, its merchants gained control of the American import/export economy. In 1825, the completion of the Erie Canal, the final step to preeminence, linked the city to the Great Lakes and secured its position as an entrepôt for the enormous hinterland the canal penetrated.[4] "Not a tree will be felled which does not necessarily operate to increase the trade and riches of New York," a contemporary observed in 1819.[5]

These commercial developments stimulated a phenomenal growth of the small manufacturing sector that had appeared in the 1790s. The opening of the Erie Canal, with its profitable possibilities for new inland markets, alerted many more craftsmen to the advantages of mass production and the entrepreneurial-minded began to expand their operations. The steady flow of people into the city allowed ambitious master craftsmen to restructure and enlarge their work forces and to cut labor costs by hiring unskilled and semiskilled immigrants and women as wage laborers rather than journey-men who had served regular apprenticeships. When skilled workers faced this competition they, too, accepted lowered wages and intermittent work.

The genius of the city's entrepreneurs, its favored situation in trade and, above all, its cheap labor brought about New York's Industrial Revolution. In contrast to the pattern usually associated with industrial development—the mechanization of work in factories—New York employers generally did not adopt new machines but rather incorporated handicraft workers into wage-labor arrangements. With the exception of a few trades where journeymen continued to craft custom goods for a luxury market, wage labor and its attendant insecurities came to affect most New York laboring people in the years after 1820. Metropolitan industrialization greatly reduced the chances that journeymen might own their own shops, and greatly enlarged the scale of proletarian dependency: the state in which workers own no means of a livelihood other than their own ability to labor. The distinction between skilled and unskilled, artisan and laborer had been meaningful in the eighteenth century when chances were good that a journeyman might in due time become a proprietor of his own shop. It became far less so in the nineteenth century, as craftsmen and laborers alike were pulled into the working class, and as proprietorship itself became a shaky business. [. . .]

Between 1820 and 1860, the working class became largely immigrant: English, German and (most of all) Irish. The foreign-born population soared from 18,000 in 1830 to more than 125,000 in 1845, a proportional increase from 9 percent of the city's residents to 35 percent; by 1855, the Irish accounted for 28 percent of New York's populace, the Germans for 16 percent.[6] Before 1846, the newcomers tended to be poor but not necessarily penniless: The Irish, for instance, were often Protestant farmers and skilled craftsmen from the North, although canal and railroad construction projects also drew thousands of Catholic peasants and cottiers who ended up as day laborers in the States. After the first crop failures of the potato famine in Ireland in 1845, however, distress became desperation, and Irish refugees began to arrive bereft of all but the clothes on their backs. Depression in the grain-exporting regions of northern Germany also sent a small, steady flow of poor German peasants into the tide of pauperized Irish. In 1855, an estimated three-quarters of the work force were immigrants.[7] [. . .]

A small black population also figured in the ranks of the working poor. Strictly speaking, slavery did not altogether end in New York until 1827. It had long been declining in the city, however, and beginning with the Revolution (when the British occupying the city had announced a general emancipation), the black community consisted primarily of freed men and women. As in other Northern cities, racial segregation was marked. Although blacks lived in pockets scattered throughout the whole city (a pattern of dispersal among whites that accounts for the frequency of interracial domestic feuds in the court records), they were often denied the use of public conveyances and almost always barred from working in the crafts. Black men worked as seamen, day laborers, waiters, barbers and whitewashers, generally in menial, ill-paid and casualized situations.[8]

The political economy of the city of women was distinct, although not unrelated to that of race, ethnicity and occupation. Family situations propelled women into the working class, and the relations of gender gave a distinct shape to the female experience of proletarianization. A woman's age, marital status, the number and age of her children and, above all, the presence or absence of male support determined her position in working-class life. Any woman, whether the wife of a prosperous artisan or a day laborer's daughter, was vulnerable to extreme poverty if, for some reason, she lost the support of a man. With the expansion of manufacturing employment after 1830, young single women might earn some kind of a living for themselves, but married women with children experienced the loss of men's wages, either through death or desertion, as devastating. The seasonal moves that men made to find work enhanced their women's vulnerability. Tramping artisans and migrant laborers could die on the road or take advantage of the moment to abandon their families, and even loyal husbands could find it hard to get news and money back to children and wives in New York. The frequency of occupationally related accidents and disease in men's employments contributed to a high rate of male mortality, which also left many women as the breadwinners for their families.[9] Men, too, suffered when their wives died or left them. The loss of women's housekeeping services, along with whatever income they contributed, created hardships for widowers and deserted husbands. Nonetheless, a woman's absence alone was not sufficient to imperil a husband's livelihood, while a wife cast on her own faced the specter of the Almshouse.

Domestic Labor in the Tenements

For all laboring women, native-born and immigrant, black and white, wives of skilled men and daughters of the unskilled, working-class life meant, first and foremost, the experience of living in the tenements. The tenements were remote from the middle-class home, and they were also different from the households of the urban laboring classes in the late eighteenth century. The difference was not in standards of living, although there has been great historical debate over whether the material conditions of the laboring classes improved or declined with industrial capitalism. Certainly, eighteenth-century New York, as compared to the nineteenth century, was no golden age of prosperity for working people. What did distinguish the industrial metropolis from the eighteenth-century port was not the existence of poverty but rather its context and scale, as the uncertainties of wage work spread out from the lowest ranks of laborers to artisans accustomed to some measure of domestic security, and encompassed multitudes of immigrants who arrived each decade.

Women experienced this partly as a change in the nature of housekeeping. We have seen that after the Revolution urban domestic production had become the privilege of a minority of prosperous artisans' wives; after 1820 it virtually disappeared along with its symbols, the peripatetic pigs and cows who trotted about the streets. Even those women still prosperous enough to carry on household production, the wives of successful artisan entrepreneurs, largely abandoned it for commercial goods. Poorer women lacked the steady income, the space or the facilities to engage in household crafts. Another pattern took hold in the tenements, the catch-as-catch-can struggle to make ends meet. A ceaseless round of scraping, scrimping, borrowing and scavenging came in some measure to dominate the housekeeping of all working-class women.

Tenement life overrode distinctions between ethnic and occupational groups and played an important role in the creation of a metropolitan working-class culture. Tenements were one response to the acute housing shortage that began in New York with the surge in immigration in the 1820s and lasted unabated through the mid-1850s. Tenements differed from earlier housing for the poor in that they were constructed or refurbished specifically for multiple occupancy. Before 1850, landlords had generally subdivided existing buildings, usually single-family houses, into "reconstructed" tenements to accommodate more people and generate more rents[10]—"dilapidated, crazy old houses," one urban reformer called them.[11] Landlords rented out hives of subdivided space, packing people into attics, outlying stables and sheds, and damp basements. In 1842, a public health survey found that more than 7,000 people lived in cellars, and by mid-century, the number had grown to 29,000.[12] The old wooden tenements stood for decades. The infamous Old Brewery, a five-story tenement in the heart of the Five Points, supposedly housed more than 1,000 people in its labyrinth of rooms, cellars, subcellars and hidden passageways.[13] Several families might occupy a large room; it was common for one family to crowd into a single room. In 1839, for instance, an evangelical tract distributor in lower Manhattan visited six families living in a garret. A sick woman lay on a few rags on the floor. "The place where she lay was so low that the shingles of the roof could be reached by the hand," he related.[14] In another tenement in 1845, a reporter for a *Tribune* series on labor found a shoemaker living with his family in a room in which a man could not fully stand. The furnishings were his workbench, a cradle made from a dry-goods box, one pan and a few broken chairs.[15]

In the early 1830s, a few speculators erected buildings specifically for occupancy by the poor. In the next decade, builders began to construct working-class tenements divided into standard units of space. Recalling the English model of workers' block housing, regimented lines of the bare brick buildings appeared in the upper reaches of the east side in the newly settled wards above Fourteenth Street. The typical apartment in a new tenement had a front room, which served as kitchen and parlor, and one or two sleeping cubicles, often windowless.[16] Even so, the new construction did not meet the demand: Lodgers and whole families doubled up in the back rooms, "space filtered from within working class neighborhoods," as Elizabeth Blackmar has put it.[17] Lodgings in the standardized tenements could be even worse than the odd-size crannies of the reconstructed tenements, since builders often erected tenements in the centers of blocks, nearly flush with the back walls of those that fronted the streets, thus blocking off light and air. The rear buildings themselves lacked direct light and cross-ventilation. Often adjoining the privies, the rear tenements were the recourse of the very poor and became the scenes of some of the worst horrors of metropolitan housing.[18]

In the worst tenements, there was little that went on that visitors from charitable organizations could recognize as housekeeping. The households of the poorest people—the day laborers, free blacks, underpaid craftworkers and single mothers who crowded into the back rooms of their neighbors and into basements and attics—were packed with people but bare of domestic effects. There was no furniture to speak of, few clothes to wash, little food to prepare. The reports of social investigators at mid-century described an overwhelming domestic inertness in the tenements. The poor "crowded beneath mouldering, water-rotted roofs, or burrowed among rats in clammy cellars," observed one; another exclaimed that tenement dwellers "exist almost comfortably in conditions which others of refinement would find intolerable."[19] The Irish seemed especially bad housekeepers: "accustomed in their own country to live like pigs, they can stow themselves away into all sorts of holes and corners, and live on refuse,"[20] noted a sardonic journalist. What such observers could not see was that despite the odds against them, most women, no matter how poor, took pride in neat and clean lodgings. Even the Irish, commented an English workingman with all the prejudices of his countrymen, were proud of their domestic amenities, their "'bits of carpits on their flures.'"[21] A well-swept hearth and scoured floor were symbols of self-esteem still within the reach of even the very poor: The *mise en scène* of many a charity visitor's account is a bare room where a woman or child is scrubbing the floor.

Slightly more prosperous working people were likely to win bourgeois encomiums as the "respectable" poor; especially if they approximated the family patterns of the prosperous: father at work, mother at home, children in some apprenticed position or at school. "Their habitations, though generally small and crowded, and in very unpleasant situations, nevertheless present the appearance of neatness and order, which widely distinguishes their occupants from the more wretched portion of society," a tract-distributing minister reported in 1834. "Their children are many of them decently clad and sent to school, and when they arrive at a suitable age, are generally apprenticed to some mechanical art."[22] Respectable families could maintain furnished interiors which also garnered the charity visitors' approval: chairs, bedsteads and icons of decency like clocks and prints on the wall.[23] [...]

What the charity visitors were unable to see was that keeping house in the tenements in any circumstances was hard work. Dirt and trouble abounded.[24] [...] For all the lack of substantial household effects, domestic labor in these tiny rooms absorbed the energies of women morning to night. The poorer the family, the heavier was woman's work. Cleaning was only a small part of complicated and arduous family economies. The major effort went into acquiring necessities—food, fuel and water —a task that took up hours of the day and entailed scores of errands out of the house. This work was by nature public, knitting together the household with the world of the streets. It generated its own intricate network of exchange among neighbours and between parents and children and created the material basis for a dense neighborhood life.

Women and children spent a great deal of time on work that, in the twentieth century, utilities would perform. Although by the 1840s the privileged classes were beginning to enjoy the first fruits of domestic technology—running water, piped gas and water closets—the tenements had no utilities.[25] Privies were in the back courts; light came from candles and kerosene lamps; water, from rain barrels, street-corner pumps and, for a fortunate few, sinks in downstairs hallways. New York completed its much-touted Croton water system in 1842, and gas was introduced in the early 1830s, but tenement landlords seldom went to the expense of piping either into their buildings; the few who purchased water only ran it to the first floor. The burden of "the almost entire absence of household conveniences" usually fell on young children not otherwise employed; like their peers in rural America and Ireland, they toted water up the stairs and hauled slops back down (less fastidious mothers tossed their slops right out the window). Children also ran the many errands required when there was never enough money in hand for the needs of the moment. Mothers sent them out to fetch a stick of wood for the fire, thread for their sewing, potatoes for dinner. Purchases were necessarily piecemeal, "by the small," and often on credit: one candle, an ounce of tea, three cents' worth of Godfrey's Cordial for a colicky baby.[26]

Children's street scavenging also produced objects for domestic use. Scavenging seems to have been a widespread practice among the laboring classes in the eighteenth century, but after 1820, those who could afford to probably began to desist from sending children out to the streets, since child scavengers were liable to be arrested for vagrancy, and the habit of mixing scavenging with petty theft and prostitution had become common. The poor, however, had no choice. For them, scavenging was an essential way to make ends meet, even if the chore might lead their children into thieving or illicit sex. Scavenging was the chore of those too young to earn income through wage work or street selling.

Six- or seven-year-olds were not too small to set out with friends and siblings to gather fuel for their mothers. Small platoons of children scoured the docks for food—tea, coffee, sugar and flour spilled from sacks, barrels and wagons. Streets, shipyards and lumberyards, building lots, demolished houses and the precincts of artisan shops and factories held chips, ashes, wood and coal to take home or peddle to neighbors.[27] As children grew more skilled, they learned how to pillage other odd corners of the city. "These gatherers of things lost on earth," a journalist called them in 1831. "These makers of something out of nothing."[28]

Street scavenging has probably been a practice of the urban poor for centuries, but this was a specifically nineteenth-century form, which depended on a demand for raw materials from an urban manufacturing system where commercial lines of supply were not fully in place. Besides taking trash home or peddling it to neighbors, children sold it to junk dealers, who in turn vended it to manufacturers and artisans to use in industrial processes. On the waterfront, children foraged for loose cotton, which had shredded off bales on the wharves where the Southern packet ships docked, as well as for shreds of canvas and rags; junk dealers bought the leavings and sold them to manufacturers of paper and shoddy (shoddy, the cheapest kind of cloth, made its way back to the poor in the form of "shoddy" ready-made clothing). Broken bits of hardware—nails, cogs and screws—went to iron and brass founders and coppersmiths to be melted down; bottles and bits of broken glass to glassmakers. Old rope was shredded and sold as oakum, a fiber used to caulk ships. The medium for these exchanges was a network of secondhand shops along the waterfront. In 1850, public authorities made some efforts to close down the junk trade, but police harassment seems to have had little effect. [...]

Pawning was also a feature of domestic work. Through pawning, women made use of less-needed goods in the service of procuring necessities. The traffic was especially heavy toward the end of the week, since rent was usually due on Saturday morning. "Sunday clothes are put in pawn during the week, and redeemed again on Saturday night" when wages were paid.[29] Clothes were the most common pledge—winter clothes in summer, extra clothes in winter, Sunday clothes any time. A substantial wardrobe was one edge against adversity. The pawning cycle functioned fairly smoothly as long as income was steady enough for a woman to redeem the possessions when she needed them—shoes, for instance, when the cold weather came. In hard times, however, women gave up absolute necessities, a sign a family was in trouble: pots, pans, bedding and treasures of respectability like watches, clocks and books. [...]

In the tenements, even laundry was a feature of public life, strung up high above the streets and alleys. The solitary housewife would not emerge within the urban working class until the late 1920s, when cheap utilities first became available in the tenements. In the first half of the nineteenth century, the boundaries between private and public life were fluid and permeable. Laboring women made their lives as wives and mothers on the streets as much as by their hearthsides.

NOTES

1. Cott, *Bonds of Womanhood*, pp. 63–100; Ryan, *Cradle of the Middle Class*, pp. 14–15.
2. Carl N. Degler, "Labor in the Economy and Politics of New York City, 1850–1860; A Study of the Impact of Early Industrialism" (Ph.D. diss., Columbia University, 1952), pp. 3–4.
3. *The Diary of George Templeton Strong*, ed. Allan Nevins and Milton Halsey Thomas, 4 vols. (New York, 1952), 2:24 (entry for October 27, 1850).
4. For discussions of economic change in the city, see Albion, *The Rise of New York Port*; David T. Gilchrist, ed., *The Growth of the Seaport Cities 1790–1815; Proceedings of a Conference Sponsored by the Eleutherian Mills-Hagley Foundation* (Charlottesville, Va., 1966); Ernst, *Immigrant Life*; Flick, *History of the State of New York*, 5:327–28.
5. John M. Duncan, *Travels Through Part of the United States*, 2 vols. (New York, 1823), 1:25.
6. Ernst, *Immigrant Life*, pp. 23, 192–93; Stott, "Worker in the Metropolis," pp. 54–60.
7. Another estimate places the number of foreign-born in the *nonclerical* work force at 85 percent in 1855. Stott, "Worker in the Metropolis," pp. 58–60.

8. On Germans, see Ernst, *Immigrant Life*, pp. 84–92. On blacks, see Leo H. Hirsch, Jr., "The Negro and New York, 1783 to 1865," *Journal of Negro History* 16 (October 1931): 382–473; Ottley and Weatherby, *The Negro in New York*, 1–91.

9. Richard Stott stresses that the city's male labor market was *regionally* based, thus necessitating that men travel frequently outside the city for work. "Worker in the Metropolis," p. 101. Contemporary testimony about the mobility of male laborers can be found in the Society for the Reformation of Juvenile Delinquents, *Fifteenth Annual Report* (New York, 1850), p. 9; Matthew Carey, "Essay on the Public Charities of Philadelphia," *Miscellaneous Essays* (Philadelphia, 1830), pp. 172–73.
   Both Sally Alexander in "Women's Work in Nineteenth Century London: A Study of the Years 1820–50," in *The Rights and Wrongs of Women*, ed. Juliet Mitchell and Ann Oakley (Harmondsworth, Eng., 1976), p. 80, and Barbara Taylor in *Eve and the New Jerusalem*, pp. 203, 244, 336, note the growing instability of male support among British laboring people. See also the general comments on the numbers of women in New York bereft of male support in the Association for the Asylum for Lying-In Women (AALW), *Sixth Annual Report* (New York, 1829) and Commissioner of the Almshouse, *Annual Report* (New York, 1847), p. 39. On male mortality see Carol Groneman Pernicone, "'The Bloody Ould Sixth': A Social Analysis of a New York City Working-Class Community in the Mid-Nineteenth Century" (Ph.D. diss., University of Rochester, 1973), p. 29.

10. The best account of tenement development is Blackmar, "Housing and Property Relations," pp. 169–492. Richard Stott points out that by 1864, 70 percent of New York's population lived in multiple family dwellings; in 1859, two-thirds of the city's families lived in buildings occupied by three or more other families. "Workers in the Metropolis," p. 305.

11. Association for the Improvement of the Condition of the Poor (AICP), *Fourteenth Annual Report* (New York, 1857), p. 18. Blackmar gives an interesting account of the evolution of multiple occupancy. "Housing and Property Relations," pp. 184–88.

12. City Inspector, *Annual Report of the interments ... in New York ... and a Brief View of the Sanitary Conditions of the City* (New York, 1843), p. 163; AICP, *Sixteenth Annual Report* (1859), p. 46; Ernst, *Immigrant Life*, p. 49.

13. A sensational account of the Old Brewery and similar tenements is in Herbert Asbury, *The Gangs of New York* (New York, 1927), pp. 12–17; the *Daily Tribune* (New York), June 19, 1850 contains a contemporary account. See also Groneman Pernicone, "The 'Bloody Ould Sixth,'" pp. 39–40.

14. New York City Tract Society (NYCTS), *Thirteenth Annual Report* (1839), p. 25.

15. *Daily Tribune*, September 9, 1845.

16. Blackmar, "Housing and Property Relations," pp. 436–37; Smith Rosenberg, *Religion and the Rise of the American City*, pp. 176–77.

17. Blackmar, "Re-Walking the 'Walking City': Housing and Property Relations in New York City, 1780–1840," *Radical History Review* 21 (Fall 1979): 131–48.

18. Ernst, *Immigrant Life*, pp. 49–51; Stokes Collection Typescript, passim, NYPL; New York Assembly, *Report*.

19. Ibid., p. 13; AICP (1862), quoted in Groneman Pernicone, "'The Bloody Ould Sixth,'" p. 15.

20. George C. Foster, *New York Naked* (New York, 1850), p. 118.

21. James Dawson Burn, *Three Years Among the Working Classes* (London, 1865), p. 15; see also Stott, "Worker in the Metropolis," pp. 313–14.

22. George B. Arnold, minister-at-large, in 1834, quoted in Stokes Collection Typescript, p. 593.

23. Catharine Maria Sedgwick describes the interior of a respectable artisan household where pawning had not taken its toll in *The Poor Rich Man, and the Rich Poor Man* (New York, 1839), p. 105, and in *Clarence; Or, a Tale of Our Own Times* (New York, 1849), p. 320. See also Stott, "Worker and the Metropolis," pp. 311–13 for the cheap furniture market.

24. This account of tenement conditions is drawn chiefly from John H. Griscom, *The Sanitary Condition of the Laboring Population of New York* (New York, 1845); New York Assembly, *Report*; Citizens' Association of New York, *Report of the Council of Hygiene and Public Health ... Upon the Sanitary Condition of the City* (New York, 1865).

25. Susan Strasser, *Never Done: A History of American Housework* (New York, 1982), pp. 6, 67–72, 85. On the absence of utilities, see Duffy, *History of Public Health*, pp. 209, 275, 524; New York City Inspector, *Annual Report ... and a Brief View of the Sanitary Condition of the City*, p. 201; New York Assembly, *Report*, p. 35; Citizens' Association, *Report*, passim.

26. Griscom, *Sanitary Condition*, p. 8; [Sedgwick], *Poor Rich Man*, pp. 99, 157; Foster,

New York in Slices; By an Experienced Carver (New York, 1849), p. 82; Matthew Carey, *A Plea for the Poor* (Philadelphia, 1837), p. 12. The reference to Godfrey's Cordial comes from Records of the County Coroner, case #414 (1855), NYMA; tea, from New York Assembly, *Report*, pp. 25–26. On throwing slops see Duffy, *History of Public Health*, pp. 361, 364–65.

27. As early as 1823, the SPP had denounced chip picking along the waterfront. SPP, *Report of a Committee ... on the Expediency of Erecting an Institution for the Reformation of Juvenile Delinquents* (New York, 1823), p. 17. For other references see Joseph Tuckerman's comments on similar patterns in Boston in *An Essay on the Wages Paid to Females* (Philadelphia, 1830), p. 22; Samuel I. Prime, *Life in New York* (New York, 1847), p. 87; [Sedgwick], *Poor Rich Man*, p. 87; Virginia Penny, *The Employments of Women* (Boston, 1863), pp. 122, 435, 444, 467, 484–85; Solon Robinson, *Hot Corn: Life Scenes in New York Illustrated* (New York, 1854), p. 207; *Daily Tribune*, March 16, 1850; William H. Bell Diary, NYHS; Phillip Wallys, *About New York: An Account of What a Boy Saw on a Visit to the City* (New York, 1857), pp. 43–44.

28. *New York Mirror*, quoted in Stokes Collection Typescript, p. 461.

29. *Jonathan's Whittlings of War* (New York), May 24, 1854.

ESSAY 4.2

The "Guns" of Gotham

Timothy Gilfoyle

Source: Timothy Gilfoyle, *A Pickpocket's Tale: The Underworld of Nineteenth Century New York* (New York: W. W. Norton, 2006).

EDITORS' INTRODUCTION

Timothy Gilfoyle, a professor of history at Loyola University in Chicago, is the author of the well-regarded work, *City of Eros: New York City, Prostitution, and the Commercialization of Sex, 1790–1920* (New York: W. W. Norton, 1992). With that work, Gilfoyle introduced many readers to the seedier side of New York City streets and the elaborate social systems that grew up around the sex industry. In *A Pickpocket's Tale*, Gilfoyle takes readers deeper into the urban underworld by revealing the life of George Appo, a petty-thief born in 1856 to an Irish mother and a Chinese father. Appo penned a slim memoir, a selection of which begins Gilfoyle's essay. Using George Appo's life as a jumping off point, Gilfoyle launches into a thorough and compelling history of the world of crime in the late 1800s.

Crime history tends to quickly veer off into stories of prurient interest rather than items of true historical importance. Gilfoyle deftly avoids this issue in his writing, bringing forth readable books and articles of true social history. In the wider work from which this selection is taken, all of the institutions George Appo becomes acquainted with during the course of his life are discussed in depth, including the famed Five Points neighborhood, the Five Points House of Refuge, the *Mercury* packet ship (a veritable prison with sails for wayward youth), Sing-Sing, Clinton State Prison, the city's network of opium dens, the Eastern Penitentiary, the Tombs, Blackwell's Island, and the New York County court system. The work also details the inner-workings of the crimes themselves. Here we see the methodology of the pickpocket. The crowded streets, full-to-bursting streetcars, and the loose clothing of the period gave pickpockets ample opportunities. The reliance on cash heightened temptation, for a single score could bring in quite a few dollars. Prior to the Civil War, lawmakers and cultural observers treated pick pocketing as a minor crime, and even occasionally deemed this crime "romantic," part of the compelling atmosphere of the city. In the 1860s, attitudes changed, and prosecutors punished pickpockets more harshly than they did those enacting violent crimes.

A Pickpocket's Tale is an excellent example of what became known as "the new social history," for here we literally see the street from its basest level. Where once the word history meant only the tales of warfare, the biographies of kings, the building of nations, or the lives of presidents, historians began to consider the history of the masses. The change in viewpoint accompanied sweeping cultural changes outside academia; with the civil rights movement, the women's movement, and the empowering of the working and middle class, more Americans received an education and different types of people entered the professorate. These professors' personal views of the world influenced the kinds of questions they asked of the past. Even those who were not themselves working class or members of a minority group were often made more aware of the struggles of those who were. Sensitivity towards issues related to gender and sexual orientation also grew with time. Everyday urban life held fascination for scholars, and they gleaned from the available documents a much more nuanced understanding of American life. Gilfoyle demonstrates that we can learn a lot from a short memoir; gaining access to the viewpoint of a small-time thief, we take front row seats at a theatrical show on nineteenth century life.

A Pickpocket's Tale received the Dixon Ryan Fox Prize from the New York State Historical Association, was a Book-of-the-Month Club selection, and was included in the Chicago Tribune and the London Times' Best Books of 2006 lists. City of Eros also won the Dixon Ryan Fox Prize and the Allan Nevins Prize from the Society of American Historians. Gilfoyle is a former president of the Urban History Association, book review editor for the Journal of Urban History, the author of Millennium Park: Creating a Chicago Landmark (Chicago: University of Chicago Press, 2006), co-author (with Patricia Cline Cohen and Helen Lefkowitz Horowitz) of The Flash Press: Sporting Male Weeklies in 1840s New York (Chicago: University of Chicago Press, 2008) and author of The Urban Underworld in Late-Nineteenth Century New York: The Autobiography of George Appo (New York: Bedford/St. Martin's, 2013).

THE "GUNS" OF GOTHAM (2006)

When I was released from Sing Sing Prison [on 2 April 1876], I had to go to St. Luke's Hospital to be operated on by Professors Otis and Peters. After nearly three months under good medical treatment, I left the hospital. As I had no means or way to obtain the necessities of life, I naturally went back to stealing for a living. But the two years in state prison made me wiser than before so I left New York and went to Philadelphia, where I remained about four months and then returned to New York looking very prosperous.

The year was the Centennial Year, 1876, and near to a close, the time being November. New York City was full of strangers from all parts of the world, and the crooks were all doing well, in general, at their business. In fact, New York was overrun with crooks from the West.... I soon became intimately acquainted with the crooks and learned many ways and means to earn money dishonestly with not so much risk as picking pockets, but I could not read nor write and my mode of talking was too slangy. Therefore, I could not operate with safety and success as my general appearance was against me, so I had to continue picking pockets.[1]

The second half of the nineteenth century was the era of the "gun"—the pick-pocket— in American cities. "Of all the departments of crime as now practiced," admitted America's most famous private detective, Allan Pinkerton, in 1884, "there is not one which contains a larger number of adept operators than that of pickpockets." As regards New York, Pinkerton was right. From 1861 to 1863 the municipality successfully convicted only 74 individuals for larceny. But a decade later, from 1873 to 1875, 519 felons landed in the state penitentiary for the same offense. The period from 1866 to 1887 might better be described as the age of larceny. During those two decades larceny comprised between one-third and one-half of all crimes in New York State. In the words of one pickpocket, the decades following the Civil War were "the halcyon days for us."[2]

Yet pickpocketing was a poorly defined crime. Although the act was among the most common and frequently mentioned transgressions in the nineteenth-century city, it never appeared in any criminal code. Picking a pocket or snatching a purse was larceny, "one of the primordial crimes of Western culture," according to the legal historian George Fletcher. Larceny, however, was never authoritatively defined until the twentieth century. Judges punished such acts on the simple assumption that they knew what it was—taking the goods of another. Hence no clear boundaries separated larceny from burglary and robbery.[3]

Similarly the precise dimensions of the pickpocket's world remain impossible to measure. Purloined goods were rarely recovered, and even smaller proportions of pick-pockets were ever prosecuted. In the seventeen known years in which George

Appo worked as a pickpocket, for example, he was arrested for and convicted of larceny four times. To the average law-abiding citizen, four convictions were considerable. But Appo picked hundreds—quite possibly thousands—of pockets *without* being apprehended. Once, while working a county fair outside Toronto, Appo pickpocketed approximately twenty-five different individuals.[4] His four arrests for pickpocketing quite likely account for less—maybe much less—than 1 percent of all his thefts.

Pickpockets like Appo were part of a distinctive criminal order. Numerous observers described pickpockets as "professional thieves" and "artists," part of a social underground fraternity with hidden rules and practices. Allan Pinkerton believed that criminal subcultures replicated the American middle class by dividing into specialized professions, each concerned with their own particular status and reputation. Petty crooks operated in social isolation, noted writer James D. McCabe, Jr., but pickpockets were different: They "have certain habits, attitudes, haunts; they act in certain ways when placed in certain positions." For George Appo such people were "good fellows," individuals who refused to cooperate with law enforcement authorities, who eschewed testifying against enemies. "What constitutes a Good Fellow in the eyes and estimation of the underworld is a nervy crook, a money getter and spender," wrote Appo. A good fellow valiantly accepted the consequences and punishment of an arrest, even if the crime was committed by another.[5] A good fellow was a member of a fraternity of thieves.

This fraternity shared a distinctive, arcane language. One reporter confessed that he found pickpockets impossible to comprehend, sounding as if they spoke a foreign tongue. Pickpockets referred to their accomplices (numbering two to six) as "mobs." The streets, parks, or trolleys where they worked were "beats." Pocketbooks were "leathers," and money was a "roll." The actual larceny was a "touch," which was performed by a "wire," a "pick," a "bugger," or a "tool," while

"stalls" distracted or jostled the victim. The "cover" made sure the theft took place unobserved. The novelist Herman Melville described the underworld vocabulary as "the foulest of all human lingoes, that dialect of sin and death, known as the Cant language, or the Flash."[6] [. . .]

When necessary pickpockets went on a "jump-out," traveling to fairs, circuses, race-tracks, sporting events—in essence, any large assembly or festivity in a nearby town. Swarms of pickpockets followed traveling circus shows as they moved about the country. Some concentrated on certain types of public gatherings, such as funerals, weddings, and parades. Such "rovers" literally roamed the United States in search of such gatherings, forcing police officials to take special precautions. For example, before the ceremonies surrounding Ulysses S. Grant's funeral, the opening of the Statue of Liberty, and the Centennial of the Constitution, New York's chief detective, Thomas Byrnes, ordered the summary arrest of all known pickpockets, including Appo. The practice—known as "caging"—was "truly a bold one," admitted Byrnes, "but the ends certainly justified the means." Detectives literally waited at the city's railway stations and arrested suspects on their arrival. The policy continued into the twentieth century.[7]

Pickpocket mobs working in specialized locations were probably the most successful in the fraternity. Arrest records indicate that individuals working alone—like Appo—were more likely to get caught. More than three-quarters of those prosecuted labored by themselves, and most were simply "working the street." Quite likely arrested pickpockets like Appo enjoyed no relationship with a "percentage copper"—a police officer who tolerated their pilferings for a bribe or "percentage" of their haul. Still, many ignored the danger. "If I needed a dollar quick I'd take any risk," admitted one pickpocket. "I'd jump on a car, and tackle the first sucker I saw."[8]

Streetcars—with more than 90 million annual riders nationwide by the 1880s—were among the most favored workplaces for pickpockets. Riders complained that the cars were so bumpy and crowded that it was impossible to feel the arms or hands of adjacent passengers. By the 1860s, New York streetcars conspicuously posted signs warning BEWARE OF PICKPOCKETS! Many passengers felt their pockets immediately on reading the warning, allowing conscientious thieves to determine which ones to pick. Nearly a decade later, a state assembly report admitted that well-known pickpockets routinely boarded streetcars, "hustled" passengers with ease, and made "scarcely any concealment of the matter." If a conductor resisted or warned passengers, pick-pockets simply took "the first opportunity to knock him on the head." Conversely, sympathetic drivers frequently worked in league with pickpockets.[9]

Pickpockets did not often knock people on the head, however. The craft attracted individuals who avoided violence. "Knock-down pickpockets"—individuals who physically assaulted pedestrians, snatched the object, and immediately ran away—were rare.... Pickpocket dress and fashion placed a premium on blending into the general populace. Law enforcement officials like George Washington Walling argued that leading pickpockets were "stylishly dressed, easy in their manners and correct in speech." Pick-pockets like Jim Caulfield confirmed as much, emphasizing that they always tried to be neat, clean, and as fashionable as possible. An attractive personal appearance, he admitted, was part of "the capital of a grafter."[10]

Pickpockets may have differed over precisely where and how they worked, but they shared certain demographic characteristics. First, picking pockets was a young man's game. More than three-quarters (80 percent) of those arrested were male, more than half (56 percent) being fifteen to twenty-four years of age. Like Appo, however, many pickpockets continued working well into adulthood. (Appo's final conviction occurred when he was twenty-six.) Fully a quarter of all arrested pickpockets during these years were twenty-five to twenty-nine years old, and another 17 percent continued their stealthful ways throughout their thirties. Less than 4 percent were forty or over.[11] [...]

Females were part of this criminal fraternity. Detective Allan Pinkerton, for example, believed that female thieves were as successful as their male competitors. His counterpart and rival detective, Thomas Byrnes, even considered female pickpockets to be more dangerous. Like their male counter-parts, many women worked in "mobs" and directed their pirating toward men. Most significantly female pickpockets tended to be poorer than men, the majority occupying the lowliest wage-labor positions, such as servants and prostitutes; more than half were associated with a brothel, concert saloon, barroom, or boardinghouse. Sex was the lure.[12] Michael Springer, for example, agreed to treat several females in an East Tenth Street restaurant. After ordering wine and sitting down beside one young woman, Springer suddenly felt her hand in his pants. "What are you doing with your hand in my pocket?" he asked. Sexual stimulation was not her purpose—Springer was missing $273.[13]

Pickpockets prospered in nineteenth-century New York and other urban centers for many reasons. First, the forced, physical intimacy of the new, densely packed industrial city made picking pockets easy. "It's only a big city that can furnish one of this craft with his daily supply of purses and pocketbooks, jewelry and small wares," declared one observer. Moreover, fashion encouraged pickpocketing. For most of the nineteenth century, men tended to carry valuables in their coats, not their pants. Before the Civil War frock coats tended to be long, extending to the midthigh, if not the knee, and providing a protective cover for the front pants pocket. But after 1860 the shortened length of frock coats facilitated pick-pocketing. Although overcoats were longer, they included external pockets with no flaps. By midcentury many New Yorkers argued that a majority of the city's pickpockets were newsboys and bootblacks who learned the technique during cold weather when pedestrians wore overcoats with external change pockets.[14]

During the final decades of the century, frock coats were replaced by the popular sack coat. "Every man in America, multimillionaire as well as laborer, wears a sack coat," wrote one designer. "It is the great American business coat, and in other countries is recognized as the badge of the American." Sack coats were short, extended to the waist, included a small collar, and offered comfort and easy movement. Most important, with a plentiful number of pockets, the sack was a coat waiting for a pickpocket.[15] [...]

Female clothing was even easier to pilfer. Nineteenth-century women generally wore layers of clothing, some with long skirts and hoops underneath, making it difficult to detect the touch of a pickpocket. On street-cars and other forms of public transit, the dresses of seated women frequently fell over the legs of passengers sitting beside them. Pickpockets then simply slid a hand underneath the dress and cut out the pocket.[16]

A third contributing factor to the rise of pickpocketing was tolerance by law enforcement officials. "The old system," wrote journalist Lincoln Steffens, "was built upon the understood relations of the crooks and the detective bureau." "Professional" criminals were allowed to operate "within reason." For pickpockets specific blocks or streetcars were divided among themselves, each of whom had a "monopoly." In return for such privileges, pickpockets reported on others who violated such agreements, and were expected to return stolen goods on police request.[17] [...]

But the greatest incentive for pickpockets was the exorbitant amount of cash in people's pockets. Nineteenth-century businessmen, bank messengers, and ordinary pedestrians routinely carried large quantities of money and other valuables on their persons. This was especially true in the Wall Street area before 1880. "It is remarkable," concluded another detective, "how careless business men are about their watches, however valuable they may be." Some cases involved extraordinary sums. In 1866 a Williamsburg Bank messenger was picked clean on his way to the Park National Bank of New York with a satchel containing fourteen thousand dollars in cash and checks.... Appo himself admitted that it was easy to get rich quick. After a few days of pickpocketing, he usually accumulated six to eight hundred dollars. [...]

Necessity demanded that pedestrians carry significant sums of money. (Credit cards did not become a financial instrument until the twentieth century.) Only a minority of Americans entrusted their money to banks, so few people rendered payments with personal checks. Even then, many merchants refused such forms of payment, especially from strangers. Hence to purchase most goods—expensive or cheap—shoppers had to carry cash. This reality made the streets of New York and other American cities pickpocket heaven.

The perception that pickpocketing was an increasingly common urban experience produced a hostile public reaction. Prior to the Civil War, pickpockets evoked little public fear. Novelists like George Thompson treated such thievery as a unique urban adventure, while George Foster portrayed the best pickpockets as "genteel." Even the detective Thomas Byrnes described pickpockets as "an interesting class of thieves." One newspaper openly acknowledged that "a tinge of romance [was] connected with the profession of picking pockets."[18]

The romance disappeared after 1870. In that decade, New Yorkers were besieged with numerous publications warning residents of the dangers presented by pickpockets and other criminals. Charles Loring Brace's *The Dangerous Classes of New York and Twenty Years Among Them* (1872) and Edward Crapsey's *The Nether Side of New York; or, the Vice, Crime and Poverty of the Great Metropolis* (1872) were but two examples reflecting a new consciousness of the city's criminal dangers. The New York State Assembly even created a special select committee in 1875 to investigate and address Gotham's growing crime rate. [...]

Criminal prosecutions of pickpockets reflected this growing fear. Between 1859 and 1876 the number of pickpockets brought to trial by the district attorney nearly quintupled, increasing from 52 to 242. Since no systematic sentencing policy existed in New York's criminal courts, judges enjoyed wide discretion to crack down whenever and on whomever they wanted. Examples abound reflecting the judicial intolerance of street crime. One thirty-four-year-old pickpocket received a five-year sentence for picking $210. A twenty-two-year-old stole ten cents; the judge sentenced him to two and a half years in the penitentiary. Upon learning that a thirty-five-year-old female was an experienced pickpocket, the judge sentenced her to five years in prison, specifically "to protect the community from pickpockets." Even pleas of poverty and contrition fell upon deaf ears. Young, unemployed men begged judges for mercy, only to be sent to Sing Sing for terms ranging from two to five years.[19]

Youthful mischief likewise engendered little judicial sympathy. One fourteen-year-old Irish immigrant was convicted of stealing one dollar; for that he was sent to the House of Refuge for a year. When two teenagers, in separate cases, were convicted of pilfering fifty cents, they each received three-year sentences. Similarly one nineteen-year-old was sent to Sing Sing for five years for stealing eighty cents; another was given four years for absconding with five cents.[20]

These harsh punishments reflected a new conception of larceny. During the second half of the nineteenth century, Anglo-American courts expanded the law of larceny to encompass a broader range of cases and common law. Whereas earlier larceny law was based on "stealthful or forcible conduct," new interpretations of such criminal behavior encompassed taking that was outwardly innocent. As criminal law increasingly protected social interests, police and courts intervened prior to the occurrence of harm. Hence larceny came to be defined as a crime against property, and police began arresting suspects as soon as they simply touched another with the intent to steal.[21]

In fact larceny (and hence pickpocketing) was treated more severely in New York City than in the rest of New York State. In 1860 the legislature passed a law applicable only to the city whereby any "stealing, taking and carrying away" of property from a person was to be treated as grand larceny, even if the property was less than twenty-five dollars in value. Simply touching a potential victim, or even his or her clothing, now constituted an assault with intent to steal, irrespective of whether any violence was inflicted. One judge later remarked that these statutes deliberately addressed a defect in criminal law that previously rendered pickpocket convictions difficult if not impossible.[22] [...]

In general the New York nineteenth-century judiciary was extraordinarily lenient in meting out punishments from 1830 to 1880. Violent crimes like assault and battery were punished with fines, probation, and indeterminate sentences 25 percent of the time. Serious offenses like rape and man-slaughter were rarely penalized with prison terms approaching the available statutory maximum. In the most comprehensive examination of New York City's 1,560 murders from 1800 to 1875, the historian Eric Monkkonen found that only 10.7 percent of all murderers were caught, tried, and convicted. Of those convicted 75 percent were sentenced to seven or fewer years in prison; only 2 percent (thirty-one total) were executed.[23]

Not so with pickpockets. After 1870 New York's judges punished such convicts not only with increasing severity but with more rigor than murderers. Of the twenty-one convicted pickpockets sentenced in the Court of General Sessions in 1859 and 1864 for stealing one hundred dollars or more, only two, or 10 percent, received sentences of three years or more. By contrast after 1871 54 percent of pickpockets convicted of stealing one hundred dollars or more received such stern sentences. Meanwhile, two-thirds of those convicted of stealing one dollar or less were sentenced to one or more years, and nearly half drew sentences in excess of two years. Perhaps most significant was that sentences longer than four years were rare before 1870, but thereafter 12 percent were given such punishments.[24]

Appo confronted this changing judicial reality on multiple occasions. Recorder John

K. Hackett, for example, was well known for his unremitting hatred of pickpockets. Once, while sitting on the bench, he proclaimed "that the law ought to condemn them to be shot." On another occasion Hackett instructed a jury that simply because a purloined watch was not found in the possession of a pickpocket was no reason to acquit, because "pickpockets generally went in couples." The jury rendered a verdict of guilty; Hackett happily sentenced him to five years in Sing Sing.[25] This was not unusual. Between 1871 and 1874 Hackett issued harsh sentences to a variety of pickpockets.... And on 3 April 1874, Hackett sentenced seventeen-year-old George Dixon, better known as George Appo, to two and a half years in Sing Sing.[26]

NOTES

1. Appo, 8–9.
2. Allan Pinkerton, *Thirty Years a Detective* (Chicago, 1884), 36; Hutchins Hapgood, ed., *The Autobiography of a Thief* (New York, 1903), 13–49 (pervasive pickpocketing), 35 (halcyon days); Josiah Flynt, *Notes of an Itinerant Policeman* (Boston, 1900), 67–68; Flynt, *The World of Graft* (New York, 1901), 2–15; Lawrence M. Friedman, *Crime and Punishment in American History* (New York, 1993), 108–10. Nearly half (48 percent) of all crime in 1866–67 was some type of larceny, and never dropped below 36 percent until after 1887. In 1927 robbery (25 percent) surpassed larceny (24 percent) for the first time. See NYSS, *Proceedings Before the Special Committee of the New York State Senate* (Albany, 1876), 1192a (statistics before 1876); and table no. 1 in NYSCC, *Report to the Commission of the Sub-Commission on Penal Institutions—1928* (Albany, 1928), 33. "Gun" was reportedly an abbreviated form of the Yiddish word for "thief," or *gonnif*. See Edwin H. Sutherland, *The Professional Thief: By a Professional Thief* (Chicago, 1932), 44.
3. George F. Fletcher, *Rethinking Criminal Law* (Boston, 1978), 3–5 (primordial), 30–42, 90, 100–12.
4. Appo, 29.
5. Appo, 81, 84, 94–96; James D. McCabe, Jr., *The Secrets of the Great City* (Philadelphia, 1868), 359–60; Allan Pinkerton, *Professional Thieves and the Detective*

(New York, 1880), 69; *NPG*, 29 Apr. 1882 (artist).
6. Hapgood, *Autobiography*, 51–53 (special part); Pinkerton, *Thirty Years*, 33–39, 48–50; Herman Melville, *Pierre, or The Ambiguities* (New York, 1852; reprint, 1984), 281; McCabe, *Secrets*, 358 ("foreign tongue"), 359 ("bugger"), 369 ("beats"); A. E. Costello, *Our Police Protectors: History of the New York Police* (New York, 1885), 417; *Tribune*, 2 July 1883, 25 Dec. 1887. For lists of underworld slang, see Timothy J. Gilfoyle, "Street-Rats and Gutter-Snipes: Child Pick-pockets and Street Culture in New York City, 1850–1900," *Journal of Social History* 37 (2004), note 28. For examples of street gang or group organization of pickpockets, see People v. Charles Cassel, 9 July 1869; People v. Witt and Malloy, 8 Aug. 1876, both in DAP; unmarked clipping, 8 July 1889, vol. 62, DAS; Thomas Byrnes, *Professional Criminals of America* (New York, 1886), 36–37; Phil Farley, *Criminals of America* (New York, 1876), 202–3. For examples of married and heterosexual couples working as pickpockets, see People v. John Williams and Bella Williams, 16 Sept. 1864; People v. Bridget McGuire, 19 Dec. 1859; People v. Ellen Wilson, 5 Sept. 1872, all in DAP; *World* clipping, 2 Aug. 1885, vol. 13, DAS.
7. Hapgood, *Autobiography*, 53 (jumps out), 78–82; Munro, *New York Tombs*, 172; *Flynt, Graft*, 39 (jump out); Pinkerton, *Thirty Years*, 31–37; Benjamin P. Eldridge and William B. Watts, *Our Rival, the Rascal* (Boston, 1897), 16; McCabe, *Secrets*, 366–70; NPG, 27 May 1882; *Tribune*, 25 Dec. 1887. On preventive arrests, see *Tribune*, 7 Aug. 1885; World, 8 Aug. 1885; unmarked clipping, 22 Apr. 1889, vol. 60, DAS; Byrnes, *Professional Criminals*, 34–35; Helen Campbell, Thomas W. Knox, and Thomas Byrnes, *Darkness and Daylight: or, Lights and Shadows of New York Life* (Hartford, Conn., 1891), 704 (rovers). On preventive arrests of Appo, see *World*, 6, 7 Aug. 1885; *Brooklyn Eagle*, 2 May 1889.
8. Hapgood, *Autobiography*, 51; People v. Charles Cassell, 8 July 1869; People v. John Riley, 21 Nov. 1864; People v. John Brown, 13 Dec. 1864. For pickpockets in churches, see People v. Maria Anderson, 2 June 1874; People v. Henry Maler, 8 June 1876; People v. John Danaker, 17 Feb. 1869; People v. James Watson, 8 Apr. 1869; People v. Maria Brown, 19 Apr. 1869, all in DAP. Arrest and prosecution statistics in this chapter are based on the sampling of 1,176 individuals arrested

for pickpocketing from 1859 to 1876 and described in chapter 2, note 20; and Gilfoyle, "Street-Rats and Gutter-Snipes," notes 19 and 20. Of 1,176 individuals prosecuted, trial and other testimony revealed that at least 279 (24 percent) worked with one or more accomplices, 51 percent worked on the street, 14 percent in a concert saloon or restaurant, and 13 percent on a street-car or other form of public transit.

9. People v. Henry Gibson, 6 Dec. 1871; People v. John McClane, 9 July 1872; People v. James Carson, 5 Dec. 1876, all in DAP; *Harper's Weekly*, 20 May 1871 (in league); *Increase of Crime*, 24 (hustle passengers); McCabe, *Secrets*, 367 (Beware); Sutherland, *Professional Thief*, 44 (warning signs). On crowded streetcars, see *Herald*, editorial, 2 Oct. 1864; *Tribune*, editorial, 2 Feb. 1866.

10. *Star* clipping, 8 Oct. 1883 (delicately); unmarked clipping, 8 Aug. 1895, vol. 144; *Times* clipping, 7 July 1890 (knockdown pickpockets), vol. 75, all in DAS; Hapgood, *Autobiography*, 39–40; George W. Walling, *Recollections of a New York Chief of Police* (New York, 1887), 330; NPG, 27 May 1882; Byrnes, *Professional Criminals*, 34; *Tribune*, 25 Dec. 1887; Farley, *Criminals of America*, 202. Only 11 percent (114 in number) of those arrested in the sample were "knockdown pickpockets."

11. Of 1,176 individuals prosecuted for pickpocketing, 940 were male (80 percent) and 236 female (20 percent). The breakdown by age was:

Ages	Total	Percentage of Total	Percentage of Adults
10–14	57	5	–
15–17	109	9	–
18–19	179	15	18
20–24	372	32	37
25–29	203	17	20
30–34	110	9	11
35–39	57	5	6
40–44	22	2	2
45–49	11	1	1
50 and above	5	0.4	0.5
Unknown	51	4	5

For examples of pickpockets identifying themselves as "gentlemen" and "entrepreneurs," see People v. Charles Gibbons, 7 Apr. 1876; People v. James O'Brien, 17 Jan. 1876, both in DAP. To categorize the occupations given by prosecuted pickpockets, I relied on the classification scheme devised by Michael B. Katz in *The People of Hamilton, Canada West: Family and Class in a Mid-Nineteenth-Century City* (Cambridge, Mass., 1975), 343–48; and "Occupational Classification in History," *Journal of Interdisciplinary History* 3 (1972), 63–88. With roman numeral I identifying occupations with high socioeconomic ranking to roman numeral V for those with low socioeconomic ranking, pickpockets fell into the following categories: [See table below].

Roman numeral VI includes "unclassified occupations." Newsboys and bootblacks were not included in Katz's classification, and I recategorized servants and laundresses from "unclassifiable occupations" to category V.

12. Campbell, *Darkness*, 705–6 (Byrnes); Pinkerton, *Thirty Years*, 37 (female thieves); Byrnes, *Professional Criminals*, 35–36; Farley, *Criminals of America*, 206–7. On female mobs, see People v. Ellen Daley and Mary Ann Williams, 5 Aug. 1859, DAP; unmarked clipping, 30 June 1885, vol. 13; unmarked clipping, 11 Aug. 1895, vol. 144, both in DAS. Among the 241 females prosecuted for larceny or grand larceny, 43 percent were arrested in a panel house (a house of prostitution where male clients were systematically robbed), brothel, saloon, or concert saloon. Another 22 percent were arrested in the street.

13. People v. Catharine Smith, 25 Nov. 1864; People v. Catherine Columbus, 16 Nov. 1864; People v. Josephine Thompson, 9 Mar. 1869, all in DAP.

14. *Star* clipping, 8 Oct. 1883 (big city), DAS; *Tribune*, 12 Aug. 1876; Slick, *Snares of New York*, 39; *Tribune*, 12 Aug. 1876.

15. R. I. Davis, *Men's Garments, 1830–1900: A Guide to Pattern Cutting* (London, 1989), 54, 60 (decline of frocks); H. Matheson, *H. Matheson's Scientific and Practical Guide for the Tailor's Cutting Department* (New York, 1 871), 14 (popular garment); Frederick T. Croonberg, *The Blue Book of Men's Tailoring* (1907; reprint, New York, 1977), 14–15 (Every man; plenty of pockets); R. L. Shep, "Introduction" in Louis Devere, *The Handbook of Practical Cutting on the Centre Point System* (London, 1866, 1868; reprint, Lopez Island, Wash., 1986).

16. Hapgood, *Autobiography*, 34; *Sun*, 4 Mar. 1861; Munro, *New York Tombs*, 41.

17. Steffens, *Autobiography*, 222–26, 288.

18. *Star* clipping, 8 Oct. 1883, DAS; NPG, 27 Dec. 1845, 3 Jan. 1846, 10 Jan. 1846, 4 Apr. 1846; George Thompson, *Adventures of a Pickpocket; or Life at a Fashionable Watering Place* (New York, 1849); George G. Foster, *New York by Gas-Light*

(New York, 1850), 85; Campbell, *Darkness*, 704.

19. On the sample from the DAP and related methodology, see note 9 above; People v. Joseph Brunner, 17 Nov. 1876; People v. John McGrath, 17 Nov. 1876; People v. Hoy, 17 June 1879; People v. Ellen Wilson, 5 Sept. 1872, all in DAP. For cases involving unemployed men pleading for mercy, see People v. James Delany, 6 July 1876 (2.5 years); People v. Joseph Carroll, 29 June 1876 (4.5 years), both in DAP. On judges issuing severe penalties against "knockdown pickpockets" to deter others, see *Times* clipping, 7 July 1890, vol. 75, DAS.

20. People v. Henry Ducketts (14 years old), 24 June 1879; People v. John Kelly (19 years old), 16 Mar. 1871; People v. John Golden (17 years old), 14 Jan. 1874; People v. Alfred Johnson (19 years old), 3 June 1874; People v. Lawrence Dixon (19 years old), 6 Feb. 1874, all in DAP. For an earlier charge against Ducketts when he was nine, see People v. Henry Ducketts, 21 Apr. 1874, DAP.

21. For statutes defining pickpocketing and various forms of larceny, see Laws of 1860, chapter 508, sections 33, 34; revised in Laws of 1862, chapter 374, sections 2, 3 (assault with intent to steal); revised in Laws of 1882, chapter 410, sections 3 (attempted larceny), 63 (grand larceny), 531 (larceny in the second degree), 686 (punishment for unsuccessful attempt), 1447. Grand larceny was the felonious taking and carrying away of another's personal property valued in excess of twenty-five dollars. Larceny in the second degree included unlawful appropriation of property of any value from a person. Courts upheld convictions of attempted larceny even if nothing was in the victim's pocket or the perpetrator gained control of no property. See *Commonwealth of Massachusetts v. McDonald*, 5 Cush. 365; *People v. Jones*, 46 Mich. 441; *State of Connecticut v. Wilson*, 30 Conn. 500; 1862 LEXIS 24; *Rogers v. Commonwealth of Pennsylvania*, 5 Serge. & Rawle 463; *People v. Bush*, 4 Hill 133. For examples of the above statues and cases, see *People of the State of New York v. Thomas Moran*, 123 N.Y. 254; 25 N.E. 412; 20 Am.St.Rep. 732; 1890 N.Y. LEXIS 1730; Fletcher, *Rethinking Criminal Law*, 4–5.

22. Unmarked clipping, 10 June 1883, DAS; Board of Police Justices of the City of New York, *Second Annual Report for the Year 1875* (New York, 1876), 9; NPG, 31 Dec. 1881.

23. William Francis Kuntz II, *Criminal Sentencing in Three Nineteenth-Century Cities* (New York, 1988), 358–59, 370; Monkkonen, *Murder in New York City*, esp. 167; Monkkonen, "Racial Factors in New York City Homicides," 113 (2 percent); Monkkonen, "The American State from the Bottom Up," 521–31.

24. The data and information below are based on the sample in DAP, 1859–74, described in chapter 2, note 20. In 1871, 1872, and 1874, 101 individuals were convicted of larceny, 54 of whom were sentenced to three or more years in prison. Court of General Sessions indictments in 1859 and 1864 frequently did not include the final punishment on convicted defendants. Only twenty-one indictments and convictions involving individuals who stole $100 or more in valuables provided a final sentence.

25. *Truth*, 4 June 1883, DAS (shot); Matthew Hale Smith, *Sunshine and Shadow in New York* (Hartford, Conn., 1868), 569; People v. John Smith, 25 Nov. 1872, DAP. For other examples of long sentences, see People v. John Jackson, 17 Nov. 1876; People v. Henry Lee, 15 June 1876, all in DAP.

26. Entry for 20 Mar. 1874, 475–76, First District, PCDB (Appo); entry for "George Dixon," 15 Apr. 1874, 396, vol. 11, SSAR; entry for 13 Apr. 1874, vol. 3, Sing Sing admissions, 1842–1874 (n.p.), Executive

Total in Category	I	II	III	IV	V	VI	Unknown
1,176	14	90	406	249	265	69	69
	(13M/1F)	(85M/5F)	(390M/16F)	(228M/21F)	(142M/123F)	(13M/56F)	
Total % (of 1,107)	1.3	7.6	37	23	24	6	1
Male % (of 871)	1.5	9.7	49	26	16	1.5	
Female % (of 222)	–	2.3	7	9	55	25	

Register of Commitments to Prisons, NYSArc; People v. John Williams, 15 Sept. 1871 (5 years for a $60 watch); People v. Emma Wilson and Catherine Love, 16 Oct. 1874 (3 years for a $6 watch); People v. Jane Crane, 20 Oct. 1874 (3 years for $2.30); People v. Jane Loughlin, May 1876, all in DAP; *Morning Journal* clipping, 20 Dec. 1886 (25 years), vol. 29, DAS. For other examples of lengthy Hackett sen-

tences to teenagers, see entry for George Smith, age nineteen (2.5 years), 11 Sept. 1875, 56; entry for John McCauly, age eighteen (2 years), 17 Sept. 1875, 80, both in vol. 13, SSAR. Near the end of his career, Hackett allegedly became insane and issued even heavier sentences.

Percentage Breakdown of Prison Sentences

Year	Total Cases	Total Sentenced	<1 year	1–1.9	2–2.9	3+	Suspend.	H. of Ref.
1859	54	26	35	8	31	27	0	0
1864	118	40	35	8	28	3	0	0
1869	91	47	9	15	30	38	0	9
1871	144	84	12	7	14	52	11	4
1872	144	74	9	16	38	31	9	5
1874	316	245	14	12	42	20	1	11
1876	301	219	10	20	33	27	0	11
TOTAL	1,168							

ESSAY 4.3

Ethnic Islands

The Emergence of Urban Chinese America

Ronald T. Takaki

Source: Ronald T. Takaki, *Strangers from a Different Shore: A History of Asian Americans*
(Boston: Little, Brown, 1989).

EDITORS' INTRODUCTION

The late Ronald T. Takaki (1939–2009), Emeritus Professor of Ethnic Studies at the University of California, Berkeley, is responsible for introducing a great many Americans to a revised history of the United States that honors the nation's diverse past. For far too long, American history has been recounted through stories of Jamestown, Plymouth, and frontier settlements, featuring only Americans of white, European descent as historical actors. Takaki's landmark work, *A Different Mirror: A History of Multicultural America*, has been in demand as a college textbook since it was first published by Little, Brown in 1993. Takaki's *Strangers From a Different Shore* introduces readers to an extended history of Asian Americans, many of whom, like the Chinese featured in this essay, made homes in urban settings.

Arriving on America's Pacific coast, Asian immigrants often passed through Angel Island, the immigration processing center for the western United States which operated between 1910 and 1940. A large group of Asian immigrants also settled in Hawaii. Asians who settled in cities on the mainland of the United States often found themselves living in "ethnic islands," settlements composed of people from their own background who were isolated culturally and economically from the dominant American culture. The Chinese Exclusion Act of 1882 coalesced nativist and racist sentiments with worries about labor competition into a landmark law. The Chinese Exclusion Act became the first federal law to prohibit the immigration of one specific group of people based on nationality. Chinese settlers composed only 2 percent of the American population at this time, yet they were subject to a disproportionate share of American anti-immigrant preoccupation. The law specifically restricted Chinese immigrants who were seeking wage labor positions, although there were exceptions for Chinese businessmen. Some resourceful immigrants found ways to immigrate despite restrictions. When earthquakes ripped through San Francisco in 1906, and the resulting fires destroyed the city's legal records, some Chinese then claimed to have been born in San Francisco. As citizens, they could bring their wives and children into the United States. Chinese communities had suffered greatly due to the lack of women immigrants. Legal loopholes, such as those created by the loss of San Francisco records and the creation of "paper sons" that Takaki describes in this essay, helped the Chinese American community stabilize. By 1920, the Chinese had settled in cities from Los Angeles to Boston. Yet 40 percent of all Chinese lived in just two major cities: San Francisco and New York. Chinese urban dwellers crowded into limited housing and carved out economic opportunity in service industries. Chinatown itself became a commodity, sold to curious whites as a tourist attraction, and creating a long term market for an Americanized version of Chinese food.

ETHNIC ISLANDS: THE EMERGENCE OF URBAN CHINESE AMERICA (1989)

The Chinese had been forced to retreat into ethnic islands — their own separate economic and cultural colonies. During the early decades of the twentieth century, the Chinese became increasingly urban and employed in restaurants, laundries, and garment factories. Isolated from American society, their communities in the cities became places of curiosity for white tourists, and a new industry began to develop in Chinatowns. Tourism became a new "necessity," reinforcing both the image and condition of the Chinese as "strangers" in America.

Angel Island

"Rather than banish the Chinaman," Jacob Riis recommended in 1890 in *How the Other Half Lives,* "I would have the door opened wider — for his wife; make it a condition of his coming or staying that he bring his wife with him. Then, at least, he might not be what he now is and remains, a homeless stranger among us." But the door to Chinese immigration had been closed by the government here, creating an isolated, predominantly male community. The exclusion law and the *Ah Moy* court decision had prohibited the entry of Chinese women, including the wives of Chinese laborers already in the United States.[1] [...]

The women had become "widows" of men living in America. They sent the stranded sojourners, their husbands, "letters of love, soaked with tears." One Chinese migrant in Oregon responded, writing a letter that began, "My Beloved Wife":

> It has been several autumns now since your dull husband left you for a far remote alien land. Thanks to my heart body I am all right. Therefore stop your embroidering worries about me.
>
> Yesterday I received another of your letters. I could not keep tears from running down my cheeks when thinking about the miserable and needy circumstances of our home, and thinking back to the time of our separation.
>
> Because of our destitution I went out, trying to make a living. Who could know that the Fate is always opposite to man's design? Because I can get no gold, I am detained in this secluded corner of a strange land. Furthermore, my beauty, you are implicated in an endless misfortune. I wish this paper would console you a little. This is all what I can do for now....

This letter was never finished and never mailed, left in a desk drawer of the Kam Wah Chung Store in Oregon.[2]

What happened to the nameless writer of this unmailed letter might have paralleled the life stories of the owners of the Kam Wah Chung Store — Lung On and Ing Hay. They had come to America as sojourners in the 1880s. They worked first as wage earners and then opened their own merchandise store. Gradually, over the years, as they built their business and developed personal and social ties to their new community, they felt a detachment from their homeland and their families. In 1899, Lung's father instructed his son in a letter: "Come home as soon as you can. Don't say 'no' to me any more.... You are my only son. You have no brothers and your age is near forty.... You have been away from home for seventeen years, you know nothing about our domestic situation.... Come back, let our family be reunited and enjoy the rest of our lives." In a letter to "My Husband-lord," Lung's wife scolded her absent mate: "According to Mr. Wang, you are indulging in sensuality, and have no desire to return home. On hearing this I am shocked and pained. I have been expecting your return day after day.... But, alas, I don't know what kind of substance your heart is made of.... Your daughter is now at the age of betrothal and it is your responsibility to arrange her marriage." Her appeal must have moved her husband, for Lung wrote to his cousin Liang Kwangjin on March 2, 1905: "We are fine here, thank you. Tell my family that I will go back as soon as I accumulate enough money to pay the fare." But a few weeks later, Lung learned from a letter written by his cousin, dated March 4, that certain events in the life history of his family in China had already passed him by: "Two years ago your mother died. Last year your daughter married. Your aged father is immobile. He will pass away any time now. Your wife feels left out and hurt.... Come back as soon as you receive this message." Meanwhile, Ing's father had also written to his son in 1903: "Men go abroad so that they might make money for support of their families, but you have sent neither money nor a letter since you left."[3]

Separated from their families in China, the men missed the company of their own small children — their sounds and laughter. Perhaps this was why Lung On and Ing Hay regularly saved pictures of children cut from calendars, advertisements, and newspapers and placed them safely in a box. Discovered decades later in one of the desk drawers of the abandoned store, this box of pictures told sad tales of Chinese-immigrant fathers living far away from their children. The two shopkeepers also pampered the white children in the neighborhood. Years later, one of them, Mrs. John W. Murray recalled: "Doc Hay always gave us children Chinese candy, oranges and other goodies."[4]

Back home, Chinese women fingered and studied old yellowing photographs of their men, so young and so handsome. Look at these dreamers and the twinkle in their eyes, filled with possibilities and promises, they said proudly. But, aiya, what did they look like now, after twenty years in *Gam Saan*? [*Gam Saan* means "Gold Mountain," the name Chinese immigrants gave to the United States.] [...]

Desperate to be reunited with their loved ones, some men looked for loopholes in the law. Aware Chinese merchants were permitted to bring their families here, Chinese laundrymen, restaurant owners, and even common laborers sometimes tried to pose as "paper merchants." A Chinese who had sworn in his oath to the immigration authorities that he was a "merchant" turned out to be a hotel cook; another was actually a gardener. Other Chinese would bribe merchants to list them as partners or would buy business shares in order to claim they were merchants. "A number of the stores in the cities are organized just for that purpose," explained an immigration commissioner. "They are organized just to give the Chinese a chance to be a merchant."[5]

Most Chinese men, however, believed they would never be able to bring their wives to America. Then suddenly a natural disaster occurred that changed the course of Chinese-American history. Early in the morning of April 18, 1906, an earthquake shook San Francisco. "*Aih yah, dai loong jen, aih yah dai loong jen,*" residents of Chinatown screamed, "the earth dragon is wriggling." In terror, they jumped out of their beds, fled from collapsing buildings, and ran down buckling streets. [...]

The fires destroyed almost all of the municipal records and opened the way for a new Chinese immigration. Chinese men could now claim they had been born in San Francisco, and as citizens they could bring their wives to the United States. Before the earthquake, the number of women had consistently remained at 5 percent or less of the Chinese population. In 1900 there were only 4,522 Chinese females in America. Only handfuls of them entered the country each year: between 1900 and 1906, their numbers ranged from twelve to 145 annually. But after the catastrophe in San Francisco, they began arriving in increasing numbers — from 219 in 1910 to 356 in 1915 to 573 in 1920 to 1,050 in 1922 and 1,893 two years later. One out of every four Chinese immigrants was female during this period, compared to only one out of twenty during the nineteenth century. Some 10,000 Chinese females came between 1907 and 1924. But this immigration was halted suddenly by that year's immigration act. One of the law's provisions prohibited the entry of aliens ineligible to citizenship. "The necessity [for this provision]," a congress-man stated, "arises from the fact that we do not want to establish additional Oriental families here." This restriction closed tightly the gates for the immigration of Chinese women. [...] The provision applying the restriction to wives of citizens was repealed in 1930. By then, women represented 20 percent of the Chinese population, pro-viding the beginning of a viable base for the formation of Chinese-American families.[6]

Meanwhile, Chinese sons had also begun coming to America. According to U.S. law, the children of Americans were automatically citizens of the United States, even if they were born in a foreign coun-try. Thus children fathered by Chinese Americans visiting China were American citizens by birth and eligible for entry to their country. Many young men came to the United States as sons of American citi-zens of Chinese ancestry. Others came as imposters: known as "paper sons," they had purchased the birth certificates of American citizens born in China and then claimed they were citizens in order to enter the United States. [...] Exactly how many Chinese men falsely claimed citizenship as "paper sons" will never be known, but it was later calculated that if every claim to natural-born citizenship were valid, every Chinese woman living in San Francisco before 1906 would have had to have borne eight hundred children.[7]

But the purchase of a birth certificate did not mean entry, for the "paper sons" were detained at the immigration station on Angel Island in San Francisco, where they had to pass an examination and prove their American identity. To prepare for the examination, they studied "crib sheets," or *Hau-Kung,* and memorized information about the families of their "fathers": they had to remember "everyone's name, the birthday, and if they passed away, when." When they approached the Golden Gate, they tore up their crib sheets and threw them overboard. [...]

By the thousands, Chinese had begun entering the United States again. After sail-ing through the Golden Gate and disem-barking on Angel Island, the newcomers

were placed in the barracks of the immigra-tion station. Their quarters were crowded and unsanitary, resembling a slum. "When we arrived," said one of them, "they locked us up like criminals in compartments like the cages in the zoo. They counted us and then took us upstairs to our rooms. There were two to three rooms in the women's section [...]. Each of the rooms could fit twenty or thirty persons." The men were placed in one large room. There were 190 "small boys up to old men, all together in the same room," a visitor reported in 1922. "Some were sleeping in the hammock like beds with their belongings hanging in every possible way ... while others were smoking or gambling." The days were long and tedi-ous, and "lights went out at a certain hour, about 9 P.M." But their "intestines agi-tated," many could not fall asleep. The inmates could see San Francisco to the west and Oakland to the east; they had jour-neyed so far to come to America and yet they had not been allowed to enter. [...]

But the newcomers were not released until they had convinced the authorities their papers were legitimate. And not every-one passed the examination. Approximately 10 percent of all the Chinese who landed on Angel Island were forced to board oceangoing ships and sent back to China. [...]

The lucky ones were allowed to hurry onto ferries and to sail happily to San Fran-cisco. By 1943, some 50,000 Chinese had entered America through Angel Island. But they did not then go to the California foot-hills to become miners, the Sierra Nevada Mountains to work on the railroad, or the valleys of San Joaquin and Sacramento to join the migrant farm laborers. Unlike the earlier pioneers from China, they went to the cities, seeking shelter and employment in Chinatowns.

Gilded Ghettos: Chinatowns in the Early Twentieth Century

The geographical distribution of the Chin-ese in America changed significantly during the early decades of the twentieth century. By 1940, of the 77,504 Chinese on the mainland, 43,987, or 57 percent, resided in the Pacific states and 16,404, or 21 percent, in the Middle Atlantic states. Between 1900 and 1940, Chinatowns in the mountain and western regional cities like Butte, Boise, Rock Springs, Denver, and Salt Lake City were in decline. While the percentage of the Chinese population residing in cities with 100,000 or more inhabitants was only 22 percent in 1880 and 33 percent in 1900, it rose rapidly to 56 percent within twenty years and to 71 percent by 1940. Predominantly a rural people in the nineteenth century, the Chinese became mainly an urban group. By 1940, 91 percent of the Chinese population, compared to only 55 percent of the Japanese (and 57 percent of the total U.S. population), was classified by the Census Bureau as "urban."[8]

The urbanization of the Chinese population reflected several different developments. A Chinatown could survive, as Rose Hum Lee noted, only in a city with a population of at least 50,000, in an area with a diversified rather than a single industry, and in a state with a Chinese population of at least 250. Most of the Chinatowns in small western towns did not have these requirements. Secondly, the decline of the small Chinatowns was a consequence of the immigration exclusion laws and the absence of Chinese women. [...]

Pushed from the small towns, the Chinese were pulled to the metropolitan cities where employment was available in an ethnic-labor market. In the nineteenth century, Chinese laborers could be found in every sector of the American economy — agriculture, mining, manufacturing, and transportation. By 1920, they had virtually vanished from these areas of employment. The mainstay of California agriculture in the late nineteenth century, Chinese farm laborers did less than one percent of the harvesting in 1920. By then, there were only 151 Chinese miners, compared to 17,609 in 1870; only one hundred Chinese workers in cigar making and boot and shoe manufacturing, compared to more than 2,000 in 1870; only 488 Chinese railroad workers, compared to over 10,000 Chinese employed by the Central Pacific Railroad in the 1860s.

The Chinese were located in a different sector of the labor market from whites. By 1920, 58 percent of the Chinese were in services, most of them in restaurant and laundry work, compared to only 5 percent for native whites and 10 percent for foreign whites. Only 9 percent of Chinese were employed in manufacturing, compared to 26 percent for native whites and 47 percent for foreign whites. [...]

Explaining why so many Chinese had entered the laundry business, one of them said: "It is a very hard job, sure enough. But there is nothing else to do. This is the kind of life we have to take in America. I, as one of the many, do not like to work in the laundry, but what else can I do? You've got to take it; that's all." The Chinese laundryman personified the forced withdrawal of the Chinese into a segregated ethnic-labor market. They had not always been laundrymen; in fact, in 1870 of the 46,274 Chinese in all occupations, only 3,653, or 8 percent were laundry workers. By 1920, of 45,614 gainfully employed Chinese, 12,559, or 28 percent (nearly one out of three) were laundry workers. The number of Chinese laundries soared in the first half of the twentieth century. In Chicago, for example, there were 209 of them in 1903 and 704 twenty-five years later. In New York City by 1940, 38 percent of all gainfully employed Chinese were engaged in laundry work; Chinese laundries were "located on almost every street corner." Chinese laundrymen had to spread themselves out, to Chicago, New York, Baltimore, Los Angeles, and other cities and to different districts within a city, where there were not too many laundries.[9] [...]

Once he had secured his loan and opened his business, the Chinese laundryman found himself working long hours. During his visit to a Chinese laundry, sociologist Paul Siu recorded the activities of the day. Like most laundrymen, Tong and his partners lived in the back of the shop, and they woke early in the morning. At 8:00 A.M., Tong went out to collect the laundry. Hong and Wah worked inside, attending the steam boiler and washtub. Ming sorted and marked laundry in the office. The noise of the washing machine drowned out their conversation. Tong returned with a load of dirty laundry in a wooden trunk and left again. The first wash was done, and Hong and Wah rinsed and wrung it then hung it to dry. About ten Tong was back, bringing a second load with him. It took an hour and a half to wash, rinse, wring, and then hang the clothes in the drying rooms. Around ten-thirty, Hong began to cook lunch. For lunch on busy days, they had cold meats and cakes with coffee. In the afternoon, they turned to the next set of tasks: Hong and Ming did most of the starching work, while Wah and Tong did the damping and ironing. Afterward Hong set the collars and cuffs on a machine, a chore that took him the whole afternoon and deep into the night. At eleven thirty, all the men ate their dinner. After supper, they all sat in the yard to cool off before they went to bed, and they finally were able to fall asleep at one in the morning.[10] [...]

Isolated in white neighborhoods, Chinese laundries were connected to larger segregated ethnic islands in American cities — the Chinatowns. In 1920, concentrations of Chinese were present in Los Angeles, Oakland, Chicago, Seattle, Portland, Sacramento, and Boston. Forty percent of all Chinese lived in two cities — San Francisco and New York. The metropolitan Chinatowns developed a different character and purpose from the initial nineteenth-century Chinatowns. They were no longer way stations to service single-male workers in transit to the gold fields, farms, and railroads. While they remained a place of refuge for a bachelor society, Chinatowns became residential communities for families, Chinese economic enclaves, and tourist centers.[11]

In Chinatown in 1934, 276 families lived in 652 rooms, or cubicles, or 2.4 rooms per family. They had seventy bathrooms, or four families per bathroom, and 114 kitchens, or 2.4 families per kitchen. The average number of persons per bathroom was 20.4 and per kitchen 12.3. Six years later, 15,000 Chinese lived in a confined area only five blocks by four blocks in size, their residential spaces wedged between, above, and below shops, restaurants, and stores. Of the 3,830 dwelling units in Chinatown, a city housing authority report revealed, approximately 3,000 had no heating. "Buildings constructed after the fire to house single men on a bare existence basis — that is, containing tiny windowless rooms with hall toilets and kitchens and often no bath facilities anywhere — now housed families." Chinatown was a slum. Eighty-two percent of Chinese dwellings were substandard, compared to only 20 percent for the rest of the city's population. The tuberculosis rate in Chinatown was three times higher than the rate for the other residential areas of San Francisco. The children were forced to play in the streets, for Chinatown had no parks.[12]

A ghetto, Chinatown confirmed views of the Chinese as unhealthy, unassimilable, and undesirable immigrants, yet this same negative imagery opened the way to the development of Chinatown as a tourist center — a "quaint" and "mysterious" section of the city, a "foreign colony" in America. There, advertisements promised, white tourists could experience the "sounds, the sights, and the smells of Canton" and imagine themselves in "some hoary Mongolian city in the distant land of Cathay." They could "wander in the midst of the Orient while still in the Occident" and see throngs of people with "strange faces" in the streets and also "a few Ah Sins, bland and childlike as Bret Harte's immortal hero," sitting in restaurants and eating "chop suey."[13]

NOTES

1. Jacob Riis, *How the Other Half Lives: Studies Among the Tenements of New York* (rpt. Cambridge, Mass., 1970), p. 69.
2. Chinese rhyme, Hom (ed. and trans.), *Songs of Gold Mountain*, p. 124; letter by unknown Chinese migrant, in the Kam Wah Chung Company Papers, John Day, Oregon.
3. Chu-chia to Lung On, July 1899; wife to Lung On, n.d.; Lung On to Liang Kwanjin, March 2, 1905; Liang Kwan-jin to Lung On, March 4, 1905; Ing Du-hsio to Ing Hay, April 9, no year, translations by Chia-

Lin Chen, Kam Wah Chung Company Papers.

4. Mrs. John W. Murray to Chia-Lin Chen, October 30, 1971, reprinted in Chen, "A Gold Dream in the Blue Mountains: A Study of the Chinese Immigrants in the John Day Area, Oregon, 1870–1910," unpublished M.A. thesis, Portland State University, 1972, pp. 123–124.

5. Esther Wong, "The History and Problem of Angel Island," March 1924, pp. 7–8, Survey of Race Relations, Stanford University, Hoover Institution Archives; "Interview with Mr. Faris, Deputy Commissioner of Immigration in Seattle," ibid., pp. 2–11.

6. Eliot G. Mears, *Resident Orientals on the American Pacific Coast* (Chicago, 1928), p. 408; Helen Chen, "Chinese Immigration into the United States: An Analysis of Changes in Immigration Policies," unpublished Ph.D. thesis, Brandeis University, 1980, p. 105; Nee, *Longtime Californ'*, p. 25; R. D. McKenzie, *Oriental Exclusion: The Effect of American Immigration Laws, Regulations, and Judicial Decisions upon the Chinese and Japanese on the American Pacific Coast* (Chicago, 1928) pp. 46, 94, 192, 194; S. W. Kung, *Chinese in American Life: Some Aspects of Their History, Status, Problems, and Contributions* (Seattle, 1962), pp. 92, 100, 192–195; Wen-Hsien Chen, "Chinese Under Both Exclusion and Immigration Laws," unpublished Ph.D. thesis, University of Chicago, 1940, pp. 28–29. In a note to the author, July 1988, H. M. Lai points out that Chinese from remote areas like Grass Valley were also able to secure forged birth certificates.

7. Richard Kock Dare, "The Economic and Social Adjustment of the San Francisco Chinese for the Past Fifty Years," unpublished M.A. thesis, University of California Berkeley, 1959, p. 54.

8. Fuju Liu, "A Comparative Demographic Study of Native-Born and Foreign-Born Chinese Populations in the United States," unpublished Ph.D. thesis, Michigan State College, 1953, pp. 96, 97. "Urban area," as defined by the 1940 census report, "is made up for the most part of cities and other incorporated places having 2,500 inhabitants or more." *Sixteenth Census of the United States, 1940, Population*, vol. 2, part 1, p. 8.

9. Siu, "Chinese Laundryman," pp. 25, 146; Kung, *Chinese in American Life*, p. 57; Peter Kwong, *Chinatown, N.Y.: Labor & Politics, 1930–1950* (New York, 1979), p. 61; Wong Wee Ying, interview, May 7, 1982, Chinese Women of America Research Project, Chinese Culture Foundation of San Francisco, p. 4.

10. Siu, "Chinese Laundryman," pp. 88–89.

11. Lee, "Decline of Chinatowns," p. 428; Nee, *Longtime Californ'*, p. 62.

12. Lim P. Lee, "The Need for Better Housing in Chinatown," *Chinese Digest*, December 1938, p. 7; Carey McWilliams, *Brothers Under the Skin* (rpt. Boston, 1964, originally published in 1942), pp. 108–110; "The Life Story of Edward L. C. as written by himself," circa 1924, p. 5, Survey of Race Relations, Stanford University, Hoover Institution Archives.

13. Herman Scheffaner, "The Old Chinese Quarter," *Living Age* (August 10, 1907) pp. 360, 362; "Historic Chinatown," *San Francisco Chronicle*, October 1, 1917 and December 24, 1917.

ESSAY 4.4

Urban Culture and the Policing of the "City of Bachelors"

George Chauncey

Source: George Chauncey, *Gay New York: Gender, Urban Culture, and the Making of the Gay Male World, 1890–1940* (New York: Basic Books, 1994).

EDITORS' INTRODUCTION

George Chauncey joined the faculty of Columbia University in 2017; he previously had taught at Yale and the University of Chicago. *Gay New York* was an instant success when published in 1994, winning the Merle Curti Prize for the best book in social history from the Organization of American Historians and the organization's Frederick Jackson Turner Prize for the best first book in history, as well as the *Los Angeles Times* Book Prize and the Lambda Literary Award. This book profoundly influenced thinking about gay men in urban settings. Chauncey also served as a legal witness, testifying on the history of anti-gay discrimination for the Supreme Court's *Romer v. Evans* in 1994. The case had broad implications that involved the question of the legality of gay rights statues within Colorado communities. Chauncey also served as lead author in a legal brief for *Lawrence v. Texas* (2003) which led to the overturning of the majority of the nation's remaining sodomy laws. In 2004, Chauncey published *Why Marriage: The History Shaping Today's Debate Over Gay Equality* on Basic Books.

Gay New York is important not only for the detailed story it reveals about gay spaces and places within New York, but also for its reception by academic and mainstream audiences. Chauncey was not the first to broach the subject of homosexuality in a historical study. Martin Duberman, John D'Emilio, Carol Smith-Rosenberg, Vern L. Bullough, Michael Sherry, and a host of independent scholars have provided much insight on this aspect of the American past. But Chauncey's work caught the attention of those inside and outside academe in a way that no other work had yet accomplished.

Gay New York is also a fine work of American urban history. Chauncey deftly connects his narrative of gay Americans migrating to cities with concurrent migrations of other rural or small-town Americans and the immigrants flowing in from other countries. All of these newcomers headed for urban areas in order to take advantage of economic and cultural opportunities. Chauncey marks the outbreak of the First World War as a watershed moment in this history; with mobilization for war and the increasing diversity of urban populations came a heightened interest in urban morality. In his descriptions of the organizational response to these perceived moral threats, Chauncey concludes that scrutiny of gay behavior, which was termed "male perversion," grew out of worries over prostitution and the sexual behavior of servicemen, who were perceived as "innocents abroad," under *in loco parentis* care of President Wilson and the armed services. The paradigm of the day defined homosexual encounters between servicemen and urban dwellers as incidents in which vulnerable people were led astray by unscrupulous urbanites. Chauncey places the history of homosexual America in the context of broader American urban history. With the influx of people from the American countryside, prosaic small towns, and varied global communities, the great city of New York was irrevocably changed. Chauncey writes, "This reconstitution of the population had vast ramifications for the city's politics and for the social organization and culture of class, nationality, and sexuality."[i]

URBAN CULTURE AND THE POLICING OF THE "CITY OF BACHELORS" (1994)

The men who built New York's gay world at the turn of the century and those who sought to suppress it shared the conviction that it was a distinctly urban phenomenon. "Only in a great city," declared one man who had moved to New York in 1882, could an invert "give his overwhelming yearnings free rein *incognito* and thus keep the respect of his every-day circle. ... In New York one can live as Nature demands without setting every one's tongue wagging."[1] In his hometown he had needed to conform at all times to the social conventions of the community, for he had been subject to the constant (albeit normally benign and unselfconscious) surveillance of his family and neighbors. But in the city it was possible for him to move between social worlds and lead a double life: by day to hold a respectable job that any queer would have been denied, and by night to lead the life of a fairy on the Bowery.

This freedom was precisely what troubled the Committee of Fifteen, an anti-vice society established in 1900 to suppress female prostitution in New York's saloons. It noted ominously that in the city

> the main external check upon a man's conduct, the opinion of his neighbours, which has such a powerful influence in the country or small town, tends to disappear. In a great city one has no neighbours. No man knows the doings of even his close friends; few men care what the secret life of their friends may be. ... [T]he young man is left free to follow his own inclinations.[2]

The Committee was particularly concerned about the ease with which men developed liaisons with female prostitutes in New York, but it was distressed as well by other, more unconventional manifestations of such "freedom." Its agents visited saloons primarily in search of female prostitutes, but they repeatedly stumbled upon resorts where fairies gathered, such as Paresis Hall on the Bowery and Billy's Place on Third Avenue, which they believed would never have been tolerated in smaller communities.

To some observers, sympathetic and hostile alike, the fairy became an emblem of modernity and of the collapse of traditional forms of social control. Doctors who studied the problem of inversion inevitably associated it with the growth of cities and sometimes attributed it either of the cities' increasingly alien character or to the nervous exhaustion (or "neurasthenia") produced by the demands of urban industrial culture. In 1895, for instance, the American translator of a French article on inversion claimed that the "forms of vice" the article described were "as yet familiar [to Americans], at least so far as concerns [our] native-born population." But he warned that "the massing of our population, especially the foreign element, in great cities" would inevitably lead to an increase in inversion and similar vices.[3] Some theorists in the first generation of American urban sociologists, who echoed many of the concerns of the reformers with whom they often worked, expressed similar anxieties about the enhanced possibilities for the development of a secret homosexual life that urban conditions created. Urbanization, they warned, resulted in the breakdown of family and other social ties that kept an individual's behavior under control in smaller, more tightly organized and regulated towns. The resulting "personal disorganization," the sociologist Walter Reckless wrote in 1926, led to the release of "impulses and desires ... from the socially approved channels," and

---

i. George Chauncey, *Gay New York: Gender, Urban Culture, and the Making of the Gay Male World, 1890–1940* (New York: Basic Books, 1994), 137.

could result "not merely in prostitution, but also in perversion."[4]

As the early sociologists suspected, the emergence of an extensive and multifaceted gay male world was made possible in part by the development of distinctive forms of urban culture. But the gay world was shaped as well by the efforts of those sociologists, the Committee of Fifteen, its successor, the Committee of Fourteen (established 1905), and a host of other authorities to understand and discipline that broader culture. The making of the gay world can only be understood in the context of the evolution of city life and the broader contest over the urban moral order.

Like the first generation of sociologists, many subsequent analysts have focused on the supposed anonymity of the city as the primary reason it became a center of unconventional behaviour. To be sure, the relative anonymity enjoyed in Manhattan by gay tourists from the heartland—and even from the outer boroughs—was one reason they felt freer there than they would have at home to seek out gay locales and behave openly as homosexuals. But to focus on the supposed anonymity of the city (a quality that is, in any case, always relative and situational) is to imply that gay men remained isolated from (or "anonymous" to) one another. The city, however, was the site not so much of anonymous, furtive encounters between strangers (although there were plenty of those) as of an organized, multilayered, and self-conscious gay subculture, with its own meeting places, language, folklore, and moral codes. What sociologists and reformers called the social *disorganization* of the city might more properly be regarded as a social *reorganization*. By the more pejorative term, investigators actually denoted the multiplication of social possibilities that the massing of diverse peoples made possible. "Disorganization" also evoked the declining strength of the family, the neighborhood, the parish, and other institutions of social control, which seemed, in retrospect at least, to have enforced other patterns of social order in smaller communities.[5] But it was ignored, or was incapable of acknowledging, the fact that new forms of social order were emerging in their place. Although the anonymity of the city was important because it helped make it possible for gay men to live double lives, it was only a starting point. It will prove more useful to focus on the ways gay men utilized the complexity of urban society to build an alternative gay social order.[*]

The complexity of the city's social and spatial organization made it possible for gay men to construct the multiple public identities necessary for them to participate in the gay world without losing the privileges of the straight: assuming one identity at work, another in leisure; one identity before biological kin, another with gay friends. The city, as the sociologist Robert Park observed in 1916, sustained a "mosaic of little [social] worlds," and their segregation from one another allowed men to assume a different identity in each of them, without having to reveal the full range of their identities in any one of them. "This [complexity] makes it possible for

---

[*] Whether the processes described here should be regarded as an effect of urban culture or of industrial capitalism has been subject to debate. Both positions have merit. It clearly was not the massing of people of the spatial expansion of cities alone that facilitated the emergence of gay subcultures. Changes in urban social organization and in the role of particular cities in the broader economy were also critical. The decline of the system of household-based artisanal production in New York City in the nineteenth century, which resulted in a breakdown in preindustrial modes of social control, was equally significant, for instance. Thus there is considerable merit to the argument made by some urban theorists that "urban culture" is a misnomer for the forms of social organization characteristic of industrial capitalist culture. The latter conceptualization of the phenomenon, however, fails to account fully for the social and spatial complexity peculiar to cities even in an industrial capitalist society. Although limited gay social networks developed in rural areas, and even small towns usually had a handful of surreptitious gay meeting places by the early twentieth century—hotel men's bars, bus stations, and certain street corners or blocks, most commonly, as well as the homes of a few of the town's "confirmed bachelors"—only large cities had the social and spatial complexity necessary for the development of an extensive and partially commercialised gay subculture.[6]

individuals to pass quickly and easily from one more milieu to another," Park mused, which "encourages the fascinating but dangerous experiment of living at the same time in several different contiguous, but otherwise widely separated, worlds ... [and] tends ... to produce new and divergent individual types."[7] Though Park's model overestimated the cohesiveness and isolation of each "little world"—and underestimated the degree to which they were mutually constitutive and to which dominant social groups intervened in the social worlds of the subordinate—it captured some of the significance for gay men of the complexity of the city's social organization. [...]

It is impossible to determine how many men moved to New York at the turn of the century in order to participate in the gay life merging there, but gay men and other contemporary observers believed the numbers were large. Case histories of "inverts" published in medical journals early in the century were peppered with accounts of men who came to New York because they were aware of homosexual interests they had to hide in their hometowns or because they were forced to flee when their secret was discovered. Numerous doctors not only identified inversion as a distinctly urban phenomenon but commented especially on the number of inverts in New York. As early as the 1880s, George Beard thought that many male inverts lived there, and in 1913 the psychiatrist A. A. Brill confidently estimated there were "many thousands of homosexuals in New York City among all classes of society."[8] Two researchers investigating homosexual life in the late 1930s found that most of the men they interviewed who had moved to New York from smaller towns had done so because "their local communities frowned upon homosexuality, and New York [seemed to them] to be the capital of the American homosexual world."[9] The researched noted that

many such migrants had indeed been able to find "work, a homosexual circle of acquaintance, [and] a definite social life."[10]

Whatever the numbers, gay men's migration was clearly part of the much larger migration of single men and women to the city from Europe and rural American alike. A disproportionate number of the people who moved to the cities were young and unmarried, and while for many of them migration was part of a carefully considered strategy designed to address the broader economic need of their families, for many it also provided a welcome relief from family control.[11] The city was a logical destination for men intent on freeing themselves from the constraints of the family, because of its relatively cheap accommodations and the availability of commercial domestic services for which men traditionally would have depended on the unpaid household labor of women.

"For the nations' bachelors," the *New York Times Magazine* declared in 1928, "this city is the Mecca. Not only is it the City of Youth, but it is the City of the Single," with some 900,000 unmarried men and 700,000 single women counted among its residents. "It is certain," the article continued, "they are not all in a [Madison Square] Garden line-up waiting for admission to the next fight, neither are they all concentrated in speakeasies and along the docks. ... The city has something for every kind of bachelor."[12] Some of those bachelors were working-class immigrants crowded in the tenement districts and waterfront; others were American-born rural youths barely marking enough to rent a furnished room; still others were successful entrepreneurs living in the city's luxurious new apartment hotels. Together the bachelors constituted 40 percent or more of the men fifteen years of age or older living in Manhattan in the first third of the century.[†]

---

† The number of unmarried men and women in the city increasingly distinguished it from the nation as a whole. Immigrants were disproportionately young and single, but even the native-born Americans of the city were much less likely to marry than their rural counterparts. Only a third of the native-born white men aged twenty-five to thirty-four with American parents were unmarried in the nation as a whole in 1900, compared to half of those in

The existence of an urban bachelor sub-culture facilitated the development of a gay world. Tellingly, gay men tended to gather in the same neighborhoods where many of the city's other unmarried men and women clustered, since they offered the housing and commercial services suitable to the needs of a nonfamily population. Gay male residential and commercial enclaves developed in the Bowery, Greenwich Village, Times Square, and Harlem in large part because they were the city's major centers of furnished-room housing for single men. Lesbian enclaves developed for similar reasons in the 1920s in Harlem and the Village, then the city's two primary centers for housing for single women. Rooming houses and cafeterias served as meeting grounds for gay men, facilitating the constant inter-action that made possible the development of a distinctive subculture. To the horror of reformers, many small entrepreneurs ignored the "disreputable" character of their gay patrons precisely because they were patrons. A smaller number actively encouraged the patronage of openly gay men because it attracted other customers.

The expanding bachelor subculture in the city's furnished-room and tenement districts precipitated a powerful reaction by social-purity forces, which would have enormous consequences for the development of the gay world. The emerging bachelor subcul-ture was only one of the ominous features of a changing urban landscape that many native-born middle class Americans found increasingly threatening. The rapid growth in the number and size of cities in the late nineteenth century was itself a source of concern, but even more anxiety-provoking was their increasingly "alien" character. As America's greatest port, New York City had always been an immigrant metropolis. Even as early as 1860, Irish Catholic immi-grants constituted a quarter of the city's white population, and the nineteenth cen-tury was punctuated by nativist reactions to them. Beginning in the 1880s, the national

background of the immigrants began to shift from northern and western Europe—the historic source of the so-called old-stock Americans—to southern and eastern Europe. Germans and the Irish continued to migrate in large numbers, but by the 1890s the majority of people immigrating to New York, in particular, were from Italy or Russia (the latter primarily Russian Jews). Almost a third of Manhattan's residents in 1910 were foreign-born Jews or Italians and their children.[14]

This reconstitution of the population had vast ramifications for the city's politics and for the social organization and culture of class, nationality, and sexuality. The grow-ing number of immigrants and their cultural difference from the northwestern Europeans who had already settled in the States led many Americans of "older stock" to fear that they would lose control of their cities and even the whole of their society. This provoked a generation of struggle over urban political and social power. These conflicts became inextricably linked to the class conflict of the late nineteenth century, for, to an astonishing extent, the industrial working class forged in the later-nineteenth-century United States was an immigrant class. The peasants and laborers who left their European homelands became the workhorses of the second industrial revolu-tion in the United States. The sharp class conflict of the later nineteenth century, then, was construed in ethnic as well as class terms, and conflicts over political and cultural power became inextricably inter-twined with conflicts of class, ethnicity, and race. The Anglo-American middle class increasingly defined its difference from immigrants in the interrelated—and mutu-ally constitutive—terms of race and class. As immigrants seemed to overwhelm the nation's cities, growing numbers of Anglo-American middle-class families fled to sub-urbs such as Brooklyn. They increasingly feared, as the historian Paul Boyer has shown, that the city posed a threat not just

Manhattan; only 15 percent of those aged thirty-five to forty-four were unmarried in the nation, versus 30 percent of those living in Manhattan.[13]

to the morality of individuals but to the survival of American society as a whole.[15]

In the closing decades of the nineteenth century and the opening decades of the twentieth, an extraordinary panoply of groups and individuals organized to reform the urban moral order. Although their efforts rarely focused on the emerging gay world, most of them nonetheless had a significant effect on its development. Some sought to reconstruct the urban landscape itself in ways that would minimize the dissipating effects of urban disorder: reforming the tenements, putting up new residential hotels in which single men and women would lead moral lives, creating parks to reintroduce an element of rural simplicity and natural order to the city, building playgrounds and organizing youth clubs to rescue young people from city streets and gangs, and constructing grand boulevards and public buildings that would inspire a new order in the city itself and command respect for an orderly society.[16]

Other reform efforts had a more coercive edge. Native-born Americans usually controlled the state legislatures in which smaller towns and rural districts were disproportionately represented, but they could not count on locally controlled urban police forces to enforce the vision of moral order they had codified in state law. Indeed, the integration of New York City's police force into the local political structure, the subordination of individual officers to local ward bosses, and their role in enforcing the elaborate system of extortion and profiteering that allowed the Bowery resorts to exist were continuing sources of outrage and frustration to the reformers.[17]

Beginning in the 1870s, they responded to this problem by organizing a host of private anti-vice and social-purity societies to enforce the law themselves and to institutionalize a new regime of surveillance and control. Sometimes working together, sometimes highly competitive, each society claimed the authority to combat a different threat to the city's moral order. At the height of its powers under the leadership of the Reverend Charles Parkhurst in the 1890s, the Society for the Prevention of Crime, founded in 1877, worked to compel the police to enforce anti-vice laws by exposing the links between police corruption and the vice resorts of the Bowery and Tenderloin. In later decades it focused its more limited resources on studying criminal behaviour. The Society for the Suppression of Vice, which Anthony Comstock founded in 1872 under the auspices of the Young Men's Christian Association of New York and led until his death in 1915, fought to suppress stage shows and literature it deemed obscene. The Committee of Fourteen, founded in 1905, took the lead in the fight against prostitution; it was the largest and most effective of the groups until its demise at the onset of the Depression. The Society for the Prevention of Cruelty to Children, founded in 1872 by Eldridge Gerry as an offshoot of the Society for the Prevention of Cruelty to Animals, sought to protect children in general. It concentrated its efforts on "saving" children from immigrant parents who they thought neglected or abused them. In immigrant neighborhoods, as the historian Linda Gordon notes, it was known simply as "The Cruelty" because of its agents' reputation for taking children from homes it deemed undesirable.[18]

The policing of gay culture in the early twentieth century was closely tied to the efforts of these societies to police working-class culture more generally. The societies' efforts to control the streets and tenements and to eliminate the saloon and brothel were predicated on a vision of an ideal social order centered in the family. The reformers' targets reflected their growing anxiety about the threat to the social order posed by men and women who seemed to stand outside the family: the men of the bachelor subculture who gathered without supervision in the "dissipating" atmosphere of the saloons; the women whose rejection of conventional gender and sexual arrangements was emblematized by the prostitute; the youths of the city whose lives seemed to be shaped by the discordant influence of the streets rather than the civilizing influences of the home; and, on occasion, the gay men and lesbians who gathered in the niches of the urban landscape constructed by those groups. The reform campaigns constituted a sweeping assault on the moral order of working-class communities, and especially of single women and rough working-class men, although middle-class entrepreneurs and intellectuals also became their targets at times. The Anti-Saloon League, for instance, mounted a frontal attack on one of the central institutions of male sociability in many working-class neighborhoods. Similarly, the Committee of Fourteen defined "prostitution" more broadly than many working-class youths did. As the historian Kathy Peiss has shown, the Committee frequently regarding working-class conventions of treating as a form of prostitution, for it labeled women who were willing to offer sexual favors (of any sort) to men in exchange for a night on the town, or even as part of an ongoing relationship, as "amateur prostitutes."[19] Thus their campaign against "prostitution" led the reformers to attached not just brothels but saloons, cabarets, and other social venues where men and women transgressed Victorian gender conventions by interacting too casually.

The social-purity activists were also keen to prevent the violation of racial boundaries, which they imagined inevitably had a sexual element. W. E. B. Du Bois learned as much in 1912, when the Committee tried to close Marshall's Hotel on West Fifty-third Street, because, according to the Committee, it tolerated "that unfortunate mixing of the races which when the individuals are of the ordinary class, always means danger [that is, interracial sex]."[20] Similarly, the Society for the Suppression of Vice's definition of indent literature was not limited to erotic photographic or written depictions of sexual acts, which even most opponents of suppression agreed were "indecent." Their targets also included birth control literature, medical studies of homosexuality, and plays and short stories with lesbian or other unorthodox sexual themes, which other people might classify as "scientific," "artistic," or "serious."[21] The reform societies' campaigns against "prostitution" and other "social evils," in other words, actually constituted much broader campaigns to

reconstruct the moral world by narrowing the boundaries of acceptable sociability and publish discourse.

Some of the organizations secured quasi-police powers from the state legislature in order to pursue their objectives; others used their connections with the city's business leaders to put economic pressure on tenement landlords, hotel operators, and the brewing companies to close clubs and saloons where men and women worked as prostitutes. Reformers hired agents who put the immigrants neighborhoods under surveillance: visiting the saloons, streets, and tenements where men and women gathered; reviewing the moral tenor of the files, stage shows, burlesque routines, and club acts seen by New Yorkers; attending the masquerade balls and other social events organized by the city's immigrant, bohemian, and gay social clubs to regulate the kinds of costumes worn and dancing allowed. They also monitored the police and devised elaborate administrative mechanisms to force them to uphold moral regulations they otherwise would ignore. Ironically, the records of the anti-vice societies serve as one of the richest sources for this study. Although requiring careful interpretation, they constitute some of the most comprehensive surveys available of the social and sexual life of the city's working-class districts from the 1870s (and especially the 1890s) until the 1920s, after which state agencies began to take greater responsibility for regulating the urban moral order.

The role of the anti-vice societies in enforcing the state's sodomy law in emblematic. A legacy of English statutes, laws against sodomy and the "crime against nature," had existed since colonial days, but the state had done little to enforce the sodomy law in the first century of independence. As the scholars Timothy Gilfoyle and Michael Lynch discovered, only twenty-two sodomy prosecutions occurred in New York City in the nearly eight decades from 1796 to 1873. The number of prosecutions increased dramatically in the 1880s, however. By the 1890s, fourteen to thirty-eight men were arrested *every year* for sodomy or the "crime against nature."

Police arrested more than 50 men annually in the 1910s—more than 100 in 1917—and from 75 to 125 every year in the 1920s. Although the dramatic increase in arrests resulted in part from intensified concern among the city's elite about homosexuality and a new determination on the part of the police, much of it stemmed from the efforts of the Society for the Prevention of Cruelty to Children, which involved itself in the cases of men suspected of sodomy with boys in order to ensure their indictment and successful prosecution by the district attorney. The fragmentary court records available suggest that at least 40 percent—and up to 90 percent—of the cases prosecuted each year were initiated at the complaint of the SPCC. Given the SPCC's focus on the status of children in immigrant neighborhoods, the great majority of sodomy prosecutions were initiated against immigrants in the poorest sections of the city; in the 1940s and 1950s, African-American and Puerto Ricans would become the primary targets of sodomy prosecutions for similar reasons.[22]

The role of the SPCC in the prosecution of men for sodomy exemplified the role of the other moral-reform groups in the policing of homosexuality before World War I. Although the SPCC had a tremendous impact on the number and character of sodomy prosecutions, it did not make homosexuals a special target. It was only in the course of its more general campaign to protect the city's children from assault that men were arrested for having sex with boys. The other societies also contributed substantially to the policing of homosexuality, but they, too, usually did so only in the course of pursuing some other, more central mission, and rarely focused on homosexuality per se. The Society for the Prevention of Crime and its allied organization, the City Vigilance League, investigated and denounced the male prostitutes of Paresis Hall in 1899, for instance, but only as part of their general campaign against the police corruption that allowed prostitution to flourish in New York. The superintendent of the Society reported to his board of directors in 1917 that one of its agents had been solicited by "a man of unnatural sexual desires" near its offices on Union Square and that "evidence of many such cases could probably be got." In response, the board instructed him to proceed against such cases only on an individual basis when they came to his attention and not to "enter upon [a] campaign against such vice."[23] Similarly, the sporadic efforts of the Committee of Fourteen to prevent men's use of the streets and saloons for homosexual trysts and social gatherings, while not insignificant, usually were only an incidental aspect of its more general effort to regulate the streets and commercial amusements that served as sites for sexual encounters or unchaperoned meetings between young men and women.[24] Until World War I, the societies did not identify homosexuality as a social problem so threatening that it merited more than incidental attention.

World War I and the Discourse of Urban Degeneracy

World War I was a watershed in the history of the urban moral reform movement and in the role of homosexuality in reform discourse. The war embodied reformers' darkest fears and their greatest hopes, for it threatened the very foundations of the nation's moral order—the family, small-town stability, the racial and gender hierarchy—even as it offered the reformers an unprecedented opportunity to implement their vision. It also led them to focus for the first time on homosexuality as a major social problem. For the Committee of Fourteen and other social-purity groups, which had monitored New York's sexual underworld closely since the turn of the century, were convinced that the war had resulted in a substantial growth in the scale and visibility of gay life in the city.

Military mobilization had an enormous impact on New York, the major port of embarkation for the European theater. Hundreds of thousands of servicemen passed through the city during the war; one official estimated that five thousand to ten thousand soldiers from two camps on Long Island alone visited New York every day and twice that many came on weekends.[25] The streets were filled with soldiers and sailors. "They were to be seen singly," one of the Committee of Fourteens' investigators reported in 1917, "or (and mostly) in couple, trios and quartettes walking about the streets either soliciting girls or being solicited by the girls and women. ... There were many thousand ... in the proportion of three soldiers to ten ... civilians."[26] They congregated especially in the Union Square area, on Fourteenth Street near Third and Fourth Avenues, at Times Square, and on MacDougal Street in the Village, as well as in Riverside and Battery Parks and other waterfront areas—places known as cruising areas for gay men as well as prostitutes.[27]

The presence of so many soldiers from rural backgrounds in New York and other cities augured to purity crusaders a moral crisis of alarming proportions. The war to make the world safe for democracy threatened to expose hundreds of thousands of American boys from farms and small towns to the evil influences of the big city. The manner in which the reformers construed this crisis was profoundly shaped by the discourse of urban degeneracy that had been central to their moral vision throughout the Progressive Era. Indeed, the social disorganization, anomie, and unraveling of family ties associated with urbanism colored the responses to the way on every side, from the solemn pledge President Wilson made to the mothers of America that Uncle Sam would act in loco parentis, protecting their sons from urban evils, to the gleeful taunt of urban musicians (who viewed the change altogether more positively), "How You Gonna Keep 'Em Down on the Farm After They've Seen Paree?" The dominant wartime discourse portrayed American troops as naive rural boys, "innocents aboard," and depicted New York itself as a seductive big-city woman who threatened to infect those small-town boys with venereal diseases and unwholesome city ways. As a longtime social-purity activist warned at the moment of American entry into the war, soldiers who were not protected from temptation "not only will ... bring back into the social structure a vast volume of venereal disease to wreck the lives of innocent women and children, but they will bring back into it other attitudes and practices which will destroy homes, cause misery, and degenerate society."[28] Urban immorality was considered by activists to be a virulent plague threatening to invade the bodies and minds of the nation's youth, and, through them, the nation itself.

NOTES

1. Paraphrased in Ralph Werther, *The Female-Impersonators* (New York: Medico-Legal Journal, 1922), 200–201. It is entirely possible that Werther was the source of these sentiments, rather than the person to whom he attributed them, but that would not undermine my point that gay men viewed the city in these terms.

2. Erwin R. A. Seligman, ed., *The Social Evil: With Special Reference to Conditions Existing in the City of New York* (1902; New York: Putnam's, 1912), 8. On the Committee of Fifteen, see Jeremy P. Felt, "Vice Reform as a Political Technique: The Committee of Fifteen in New York, 1900–1911," *New York History* 54 (1973): 24–51.

3. C. Judson Herrick, note concerning his translation of Marc André Raffalovich, "Uranism, Congential Sexual Inversion," *Journal of Comparative Neurology* 5 (March 1895): 65. G. Frank Lydston also commented in 1889 that there was "in every community of any size a colony of male sexual perverts; they are usually known to each other and are likely to congregate together" ("Sexual Perversion, Satyriasis and Nymphomania," *Medical and Surgical Reporter* 61 [1889]: 254); see also James Kiernan, "Classification of Homosexuality," *Urologic and Cutaneous Review* 20 (1916): 350.

4. Walter C. Reckless, "The Distribution of Commercialized Vice in the City: A Sociological Analysis," in *The Urban Community*, ed. Ernest W. Burgess (Chicago: University of Chicago Press, 1926), 192, 202.

5. The major proponent of this alternative view of urbanism is Claude Fischer, *To Dwell Among Friends: Personal Networks in Town and City* (Chicago: University of Chicago Press, 1982), especially 64–66; idem, *The Urban Experience* (New York: Harcourt Brace Jovanovich, 1976), especially 35–39.

6. Contributors to this debate include Fischer, *The Urban Experience*, 25–36, and Manual Castells, "Is There an Urban Sociology?," *Urban Sociology: Critical Essays* (New York: St. Martin's, 976). On the breakdown of social control in nineteenth-century cities upon the decline of artisanal modes of production and the increasing class segregation of cities, and the related decision of employers and reformers to establish professional police forces in New York and other cities in the 1840s–60s, see John C. Schneider, *Detroit and the Problem of Order, 1830–1880: A Geography of Crime, Riot, and Policing* (Lincoln: University of Nebraska Press, 1980), 83–86 and passim; for a detailed study of this process in New York City, see Sean Wilentz, *Chants Democratic: New York City and the Rise of the American Working Class, 1788–1850* (New York: Oxford University Press, 1984).

7. Robert Park, "The City: Suggestions for the Investigation of Human Behavior in the Urban Environment" (1916), as reprinted in *Classic Essays on the Culture of Cities*, ed. Richard Sennett (New York: Meredith, 1969), 126.

8. George M. Beard, *Sexual Neurasthenia*, ed. A. D. Rockwell (New York: E. B. Treat, 1884), 102; A. A. Brill, "The Conception of Homosexuality," *Journal of the American Medical Association* 61 (1913): 335. For an account of a man forced to flee his home, see Douglas C. McMurtrie, "Some Observations on the Psychology of Sexual Inversion in Women," *Lancet-Clinic* 108 (1912): 488.

9. Martin Goodkin to author, Aug. 3, 1988; Maurice Leznoff, "The Homosexual in Urban Society" (master's thesis McGill University, 1954), 40–49.

10. George E. Henry and Alfred A. Gross, "Social Factors in the Case Histories of One Hundred Underprivileged Homosexuals," *Mental Hygiene* 22 (1938): 602.

11. See, for example, Joanne J. Meyerowitz, *Women Adrift: Independent Wage Earners in Chicago, 1880–1930* (Chicago: University of Chicago Press, 1988).

12. "The Bachelors of New York," *New York Times Magazine*, Sept. 9, 1928. Although the *Time* was probably not thinking of gay bachelors in particular, some of its gay readers seem to have understood the article in such terms. Alexander Gumby, a black gay man who ran a famous salon frequented by Harlem's intellectuals, many of them gay, in the 1920s, clipped the article and put it in a scrapbook he titled "Odd, Strange and Curious," now part of the Alexander Gumby papers at the Columbia University Library.

13. James Ford, *Slums and Housing: With Special Reference to New York City: History, Conditions, Policy* (Cambridge, Mass.: Harvard University Press, 1936), 336; *Twelfth Census of the United States Taken in the Year 1900, Vol. II, Population, Part II* (Washington, D.C.: United States Census Office, 1902), 254, 333; see also *1890 Census, Part 1*, 883; *1910 Census, Vol. I*, 630; *1920 Census, Vol. II*, 504; *1930 Census, Vol. II*, 962; *1940 Census, Vol. IV, Part III*, 683.

14. *Thirteenth Census of the United States Taken in the Year 1910, Vol. I, Population 1910, General Report and Analysis* (Washington, D.C.: Government Printing Office, 1913), 948.

15. An immense number of historical studies document and analyze these trends. The major points are usefully summarized and argued in Paul Boyer, *Urban Masses and Moral Order in America, 1820–1920* (Cambridge, Mass.: Harvard University Press, 1978), 123–32; see also, to cite just three other studies, John Higham, *Strangers in the Land: Patterns of American Nativism, 1860–1925* (New Brunswick, N.J.: Rutgers University Press, 1855); Kenneth T. Jackson, *Crabgrass Frontier: The Suburbanization of the United States* (New York: Oxford University Press, 1985); Thomas Kessner, *The Golden Door: Italian and Jewish Immigrant Mobility in New York City* (New York: Oxford University Press, 1977).

16. A number of historians have analyzed this process. See, for example, Boyer, *Urban Masses*; Daniel M. Bluestone, *Constructing Chicago* (New Haven, Conn.: Yale University Press, 1991); David Scobey, "Empire City: Politics, Culture, and Urbanism in Gilded Age New York" (Ph.D. diss., Yale University, 1989).

17. For an overview of the role of the police, see Samuel Walker, *A Critical History of Police Reform* (Lexington, Mass.: Lexington Books, D. C. Health, 1977).

18. My comments on the general character of the societies are based on my research in their organizational records (as described in the Note on Sources) and on Timothy J. Gilfoyle, "The Moral Origins of Political Surveillance: The Preventive Society in New York City, 1867–1918," *American Quarterly* 38 (1986): 637–52; idem, *City of Eros: New York City, Prostitution, and the Commercialization of Sex, 1790–1920* (New York: Norton, 1992), 185–96; Boyer, *Urban Masses*; Mary Ryan, *Women in Public: Between Banners and Ballots, 1825–1880* (Baltimore: Johns Hopkins University Press, 1990), ch. 3; John D'Emilio

and Estelle Freedman, *Intimate Matters: A History of Sexuality in America* (New York: Harper & Row, 1988), ch. 7 and 9; and Linda Gordon, *Heroes of Their Own Lives: The Politics and History of Family Violence* (New York: Viking, 1988).

19. Kathy Peiss, "'Charity Girls' and City Pleasures: Historical Notes on Working-Class Sexuality, 1880–1920," in *Passion and Power: Sexuality in History*, ed. Kathy Peiss and Christina Simmons (Philadelphia: Temple University Press, 1989), 57–69.

20. W. E. B. Du Bois to the Committee, letter dated Sept. 23, 1911 (the actual year must have been 1912); Frederick H. Whitin to Du Bois, Oct. 11, 1912, Du Bois folder, box 11, COF. Du Bois wrote to protest the Committee's campaign against Marshall's, which had once been a popular nightspot when many of Manhattan's African-American residents had lived in the midtown area, because it was "about the only place where a colored man downtown can be decently accommodated." The Committee continued to worry that illicit sexual intentions offered the only explanation for the social mingling of blacks and whites; see, for example, their investigator's observation in 1928 that Small's Paradise, a famous Harlem nightspot on Seventh Avenue, "was rather crowded with white and colored people, dancing and drinking. ... Mixed couples are allowed to enter this place," he noted ominously (report on Small's Paradise, 2294 1/2 Seventh Ave., basement, July 24, 1928, 2 A.M., box 36, COF).

21. Linda Gordon, *Woman's Body, Woman's Right: A Social History of Birth Control in America* (New York: Penguin, 1976); David J. Pivar, *Purity Crusade: Sexual Morality and Social Control, 1868–1900* (Westport, Conn.: Greenwood, 1973). I discuss the attacks on scientific books on homosexuality, lesbian plays and short stories, and the like in chapters 9, 11, 12.

22. I have not offered more precise figures here because the sources are dismayingly vague and contradictory. The number of sodomy cases between 1796 and 1873 is based on the comprehensive survey of the Manhattan district attorney case files conducted by Timothy Gilfoyle in the course of his research on prostitution in nineteenth-century New York, and is reported in Michael Lynch, "New York City Sodomy, 1796–1873," as cited in D'Emilio and Freedman, *Intimate Matters*, 123. The immense number of cases prosecuted in the twentieth century made a comprehensive survey of the case files impossible, so I have relied instead on published reports and a sampling of the manuscript case files. The annual reports of the Board of City Magistrates and Board of Police Justices give figures for the number of arrests and convictions for sodomy in New York for the late nineteenth and early twentieth centuries, but those numbers often conflict; one reports that thirteen men were arrested for the crime against nature in 1896, for instance, while the other reports thirty-eight arrests. (I have based my estimates on the lower figure given, so they should be taken as conservative estimates.) It is even more difficult to determine the percentage of cases in which the SPCC played a role, since that is not noted in the annual reports. My estimates are based on my review of actual district attorney case files concerning sodomy prosecutions from 1890 to 1940 (see the Note on Sources for more information about those files). Because the district attorney did not index cases by charge, I reviewed his alphabetical list of all cases prosecuted for every year surveyed and then ordered the cases identified as sodomy cases. Only a fraction of the sodomy cases were identified as such in the docket books, however, so my estimate could not be based on a full survey of the sodomy prosecutions. There is no reason to believe that the two hundred sodomy cases I did review were unrepresentative, but given the limitations of the evidence I have not attempted to offer more precise or "definitive" figures for the percentage of cases initiated by the SPCC. It is clear that the SPCC played an active role and that men who had sex with boys were the primary targets of sodomy prosecutions, but precise figures are unavailable.

23. Superintendent's Report to the Board of Directors, n.d. [Apr. 9, 1917], and Minutes of a regular meeting of the Board of Directors, Apr. 9, 1917, box 13, Society for the Prevention of Crime papers, Rare Book and Manuscript Library, Columbia University.

24. My comments on the role of the moral-reform societies in policing homosexual matters are based on my review of the manuscript records of the Society for the Prevention of Crime (most of which are held at the Rare Book and Manuscript Library, Columbia University) and the Society for the Suppression of Vice (Library of Congress). The particular actions taken by the societies are documented later in this chapter [...].

25. T. S. Settle to Raymond Fosdick, chair, War Department Commission on Training Camp Activities, Sept. 4 1917, box 24, COF.

26. J. A. S., report on street conditions, Nov. 17, 1917, box 25, COF.

27. See the hundreds of reports submitted by Committee of Fourteen investigators during the war.

28. M. J. Exner, "Prostitution in its Relation to the Army on the Mexican Border," *Social Hygiene* 3 (April 1917): 205, as quoted in Allan M. Brandt, *No Magic Bullet: A Social History of Venereal Disease in the United States Since 1880* (New York: Oxford University Press, 1985), 57. My characterization of World War I discourse is based primarily on the accounts provided by Brandt's superb study, as well as David Kennedy's *Over Here: The First World War and American Society* (New York: Oxford University Press, 1980). I have, however, stressed the continuity between the Progressive Era depiction of urban immorality and wartime moral discourse more than these authors have.

ESSAY 4.5

A Dynamic Businessman's Aristocracy: The 1890s

Clifton Hood

Source: Clifton Hood, *In Pursuit of Privilege: A History of New York City's Upper Class and the Making of a Metropolis* (New York: Columbia University Press, 2017).

EDITORS' INTRODUCTION

Many studies have been made of the urban poor. But the great disparity in American cities contains two distinct groups—the very poor and the very rich. Few historians have studied the lives of the very wealthy, and none have done so as clearly and thoroughly as Clifton Hood. His research explores the creation of the upper class in New York, from its earliest days to well into the twentieth century.

A tradition of anti-urbanism in the United States followed European colonists from their original continent. Comingled with the anti-urbanism were theories that luxuries tainted the soul. Rich New Yorkers, however, reveled in the connections created by city life and the conspicuous consumption of luxury products available to urban shoppers with ample finances. But, as Hood warns, we must consider the social elite and economic elite as two distinct categories.

An increased overlap between the social and economic elite occurred over time. At first wealth could not break down the barriers preventing entry to the social elite. John Jacob Astor, born into poverty in Germany, symbolized this new economically elite American. Coming from nothing, he was the richest man in America in 1840. His vast fortune was made in the American Fur Trading Company. His initial attempts to enter upper class society were met with stern rebukes, even when he abandoned Lutheranism for the Episcopalian church.

Over time, the number of wealthy persons in New York grew, as did the subgroups within it. The selection included in this volume concentrates on the infamous Gilded Age. Throughout the 1850s, Moses Y. Beach published multiple editions of the book, *Wealth and Pedigree of the Wealthy Citizens of New York City*, in which he published the names of New Yorkers with fortunes he believed to be worth $100,000 or more. Hood argues that this book marks the formal beginning of the American fascination with those who had accumulated wealth. In this period, lineage began to matter far less than the size of one's pocket book in terms of entrance into New York's social elite. Giving precedence to wealth over ancestry was a very American sort of choice; no longer would Europe's royal titles reign, but those with commercial or industrial networks. These were the people of new money, the *nouveaux riche*. As Hood points out, the relatively impious New York embraced the attitude of accepting the newly rich earlier than did Boston and Philadelphia.

New York's elite created their own culture and commanded their own urban spaces. The Union Club, explored in this piece, typifies this kind of upper class space. Here we encounter the lived experience of the very rich as well as the changes that were befalling their community. These rarified spaces were also often distinguished by gender—wealthy men and wealthy women claiming their own club rooms. They created a culture that continues to leave its mark today; even in the twenty-first century, upper class New York more openly display signs of wealth than do the wealth of Boston and Philadelphia. With today's gap between the wealthy and other Americans, what do we make of the cultural divide? Do we envy the lives of the rich? Do we consider it morally challenged? Is American democracy challenged by the existence of spaces and organizations that exclude others?

Clifton Hood is George E. Paulsen '49 Professor of American History and Government at Hobart and William Smith Colleges where he teaches American history courses on cities, immigration, industrialization, and the environment. He authored *722 Miles: The Building of the Subways and How They Transformed New York* (Baltimore: Johns Hopkins University Press, 2004), *In Pursuit of Privilege: A History of New York City's Upper Class and the Making of a Metropolis* (New York: Columbia University Press, 2017) and essays for *The Journal of Urban History, The Journal of Social History,* and *Reviews in American History.* Hood was Senior Fulbright Lecturer at Seoul National University in 2001. [**See Essay 7.3 for Hood's essay on the New York subway.**]

DYNAMIC BUSINESSMAN'S ARISTOCRACY: THE 1890S (2017)

Broken Barriers

The Union Club was caught in a dilemma. In the 1870s and 1880s it had a membership ceiling of 1,000, with a waiting list that usually had several hundred names on it. Starting in 1885, a small group of members tried to raise the limit to 1,100 or 1,200, but their proposals kept being voted down, in order, insiders revealed, to block the rising "income men" from gaining admission.

As the population of the city grew, the club's 1,000 members represented a smaller and smaller proportion of the upper class, and even of the social elite, but men's clubs that had tight membership restrictions were viewed as being more exclusive and prestigious, and the Union Club was proud of its preeminence as the oldest in the city. Its members worried that becoming too big and impersonal would undermine its standing as an "association of gentlemen." Their emphasis on status and exclusivity also meant excluding nouveaux riches who had made fortunes in the booming Gilded Age economy. Having come out of nowhere, without family antecedents, close relationships with others in the upper class, or social graces, the income men had only their wealth. An etiquette manual said scornfully of "our newer millionaires and pluto-crats" that "it is undeniable that many of these captains of industry—however strong and virile their natures—become utterly helpless and panic-stricken at the mere sight of a gold finger bowl, an alabaster bath, a pronged oyster fork, or the business end of an asparagus."[1]

But the Union Club had to abruptly change its policy in 1891, when J. Pierpont Morgan and some others became disgusted by the black-balling of several of their acquaintances and decided to form their own club. Morgan, a member of the Union Club since 1865, was apparently also irked that he had never been elected to its ruling body, the august Governing Committee. Morgan's new Metropolitan Club became known as the "millionaires' club" for its openness to new money and its sumptuous clubhouse on upper Fifth Avenue and threatened to overshadow the Union Club. Confronted with this unexpected challenge, and needing more revenue to replace the obsolete building it had occupied since 1855 with a modern structure that could restore its competitive position, the Union Club increased its membership limit by 30 percent, to 1,300, later in 1891 and eventually to 1,500 by 1894. Although some of the men who filled these extra slots were the relatives of established members who had been on the waiting list for years, the club also made room for "income men" like Samuel L. Rea of the Pennsylvania Railroad. In accommodating the social changes caused by the supercharged urban economy, the Union Club absorbed the kind of members it had tried to exclude earlier and became a larger and less intimate place than some of its leaders had wanted it to be.[2]

A similar powerlessness to control the boundaries of polite society beset the preeminent arbiter of social exclusivity, the *Social Register*. When first published as the definitive "record of society" in 1887, the *Social*

Register consisted almost entirely of the names of descendants of seventeenth- and eighteenth-century Dutch and English merchants. The *Social Register* sought to create a space that would be theirs alone, one that would enclose them behind walls that newly rich and middle-class people could not breach. The 1904 edition accordingly contained the expected complement of Old New Yorkers from distinguished families such as the Beekmans, De Peysters, and Stuyvesants, along with a smattering of members from the second generation of families of newer wealth, like the Vanderbilts. Yet it also included Andrew Carnegie and John D. Rockefeller, the embodiment of rags-to-riches social mobility. Carnegie and Rockefeller clearly fell outside the *Social Register's* conventional definition of "society," but excluding them would have seemed peculiar to many established upper-class New Yorkers who sat on charitable boards, socialized, did business with, or lived near the two multimillionaires, and it would have seemed outlandish to ordinary Americans who by now equated wealth with upper-class status. Like the Union Club, the Social Register Association had been forced to adjust to the realities of economically dynamic New York City, and it had become more open, more accommodating of diversity, and larger than it had initially intended.[3]

The combined enlargement and enrichment of the city's elites represented the single most momentous change facing the upper class during the Gilded Age. These pressures had existed to a degree before the Civil War, but rapid economic growth heightened their intensity and made them the central feature of upper-class life in the second half of the nineteenth century. Families like the Vanderbilts and Rockefellers accumulated fortunes that dwarfed those of the Astors and Lorillards from earlier in the century, widening the income gap within the upper class as well as between it and middle- and lower-class New Yorkers. As a result of the structural instabilities caused by the dynamic urban economy and the lack of a titled American ruling class, along with the cultural strains caused by the nation's democratic ethos, the upper class

of New York City has throughout its existence been prone to thoroughgoing social and cultural changes.[4] Since rapid urban development began in the early nineteenth century, it has re-formed and then re-formed again as it gained new sources of wealth, grew larger and more powerful, and became infused with outsiders. The intensification of these demographic and economic pressures in the second half of the nineteenth century raised concerns within that upper class about the sources of its legitimacy and the need for more coherent and restrictive social and cultural codes.

The Gilded Age is the single most important period in the history of the New York City upper class; upper-class New Yorkers were at their maximum in terms of wealth, power, and showiness during the Gilded Age, and afterward this era would serve a yardstick for measuring other American urban upper classes. This is why historians and biographers who have studied the upper class of New York City have concentrated on the late nineteenth century.[5]

The banks, exchanges, and corporate headquarters that went up in lower Manhattan as Wall Street became a financial center of world significance in the late nineteenth century were the primary symbol of elite wealth and influence. In fact, elites in New York City were at the peak of their wealth, prestige, and authority in this period. Yet urban economic growth had also let loose centrifugal forces that unsettled and destabilized the upper class by expanding its size, infusing it with fresh blood, and normalizing the possession of immense wealth. These developments alarmed upper-class New Yorkers who had absorbed lessons from Victorian culture about the necessity of defending genteel society against outsiders who were uncivilized, crude, unsophisticated, and materialistic.

The reality is that the reciprocal relationship between economic development and the preoccupations of the upper class was never more evident than in the Gilded Age. As the urban economy produced more and more people with wealth, members of the established upper class and newcomers alike became increasingly aware of their identities as elites. Compared to its counterparts in other big American cities, the upper class in New York was larger, more open to outsiders, quicker to pursue the main chance, and less constrained by stuffy tradition. These traits in and of themselves raised concerns within that upper class about the degradation of its social standards and the porousness of its boundaries. Upper-class New Yorkers thus went in pursuit of privilege to separate themselves from the middle-class and new-money swarms. They identified with Europe and with European social institutions, art forms, and aristocracies for similar reasons. They did not want to be aristocrats but wanted to use associations with the aristocracy and similar markers of taste to distinguish themselves.

In the end, however, upper-class attempts to draw boundaries around their businessman's aristocracy and to confirm its elegance and refinement broke down under the erosive effects of the city's own economic dynamism, in a process of abrasion.

The upper class between its self-aggrandizement and the genuine contributions it made to the growth and welfare of the city. Even though this upper class was becoming much more conscious of itself as an elite, it was not entirely self-focused. In unprecedented ways, upper-class New Yorkers supplied the crucial leadership that allowed New York City to reach for greatness. They played a decisive role in launching economic projects like the Grand Central Terminal and the IRT subway and in founding cultural institutions such as the Metropolitan Opera, the Metropolitan Museum of Art, and the New York Public Library, enhancements that helped New York become a metropolis of the first rank and improved the lives of its residents. Ironically, an upper class that embraced aristocratic forms and disdained ordinary people wound up ennobling the public sphere.

New York Ascendant

By 1900, New York City ranked as the second-largest city in the world, surpassed only by London. Fifty years earlier, New York had been comparable to four other major North Atlantic ports in terms of the size of its population and the structure and functions of its economy. But its population had continued to surge between 1850 and 1900, almost quintupling with the arrival of hundreds of thousands of Irish, Germans, Eastern European Jews, and Italians. It had reached a new level of urban complexity, finally becoming the equal of the great European capitals.

Commerce remained the chief economic sector in this period, but manufacturing and, in particular, finance were strengthened. As the commercial, manufacturing, and financial nucleus of a nation that sustained phenomenal economic growth after the Civil War and would soon succeed Great Britain as the world's preeminent industrial nation, New York served as a principal node in the urban network that bound Europe and North America.[6]

Sinews of this urban network threaded the metropolis. After the Civil War, the core of the port shifted from the East River to the Hudson River to accommodate the freight and passenger traffic moving through the rail and ferry terminals being constructed on the New Jersey side of the harbor. New York became the busiest port in the world shortly after 1900 and retained that position for more than fifty years. Wharves and docks lined the shores of the East and Hudson Rivers and much of the cavernous Upper Bay.[7]

In the early 1890s, the headquarters building of the Western Union Company on Broadway in lower Manhattan was the single busiest telegraph station in the world.[8] In 1891, journalist Richard Harding Davis captured the significance of that communications activity for the financial district it served:

I never pass Wall Street but that I am filled with wonder that it should be such a narrow, insignificant street. One would think it would need more room for all that goes on there, and it is almost a surprise that there is no visible sign of the fortunes rising and falling, and of the great manœuvres and attacks which emanate in that two hundred yards, and which are felt from Turkey to Oregon. But it seems just like any other street, except for the [telegraph and telephone] wires that almost roof it over.[9]

"Wherever the electric wires have penetrated," an investment banker marveled, "the Wall Street broker has followed."[10] The telecommunications revolution embodied in the telegraph and later the telephone allowed financiers to enormously expand their reach and tighten their control of remote business operations [...].

"Information makes money in Wall street," the *Wall Street Journal* declared in 1896 in promoting subscriptions to the news bulletins of its parent Dow Jones & Company. "People who trade in Wall street naturally seek those offices which have the best information and the most of it."[11] A prime source of that knowledge was the Dow Jones Industrial Average of leading industrial stocks, inaugurated in 1884. Similarly, by introducing the telegraph in the mid-1840s, the stock ticker in 1867, and the telephone in 1878, the New York Stock Exchange enabled brokerage offices anywhere in the country to immediately learn the price and volume of shares being traded and to participate in these transactions. For the first time, the New York Stock Exchange became a genuinely national financial market.[12]

With improved transportation and communications facilities better integrating its North American hinterland and strengthening its linkages to Europe, South America, and other zones of a globalizing world economy, New York acquired added importance as a relay station for the movement of trade, capital, ideas, and people and as a business headquarters where decisions were made. That gave it unparalleled wealth and influence; it was the sole American national metropolis at a time when the small size and limited portfolio of the federal government afforded the private sector a relatively free hand in the economy. As a center of unbridled finance capitalism, New York benefited from the weaknesses of federal regulation, which meant that there were no countervailing institutions to prevent its businessmen from exercising their muscle nationwide. Relatively speaking, New York City was probably at the zenith of its wealth and power around the turn of the century, causing many people to express fear and resentment about its clout.

Complaints about the "money power" radiated from virtually everywhere, including New York City itself. Daniel T. Rogers has shown that the epithet "robber baron" that journalist Mathew Josephson popularized in his 1930s exposé of Gilded Age financiers and industrialists had not originated with midwestern populists in the 1880s, as Josephson had supposed. Instead, the phrase was already being employed several decades earlier (and may have been coined) by Boston-born patricians Charles Francis Adams Jr. and Josiah Quincy Jr. and then came into widespread use in the critiques that New Yorkers and other easterners made of the takeover that Jay Gould engineered of the Western Union Company in 1881. As Richard R. John concludes, Josephson's error of attribution fostered the mistaken impression that the antimonopoly movement began in the countryside rather than in the urban east and that it appealed chiefly to farmers rather than the urban middle class or, for that matter, the social elite.[13] From its eastern urban origins, antimonopoly had spread quickly to the small towns and rural areas in the hinterland where there was anxiety about being crushed by larger forces and left behind. Many critics conceived of Wall Street in terms of conspiracies. In 1900 the *Adair County News* in central Kentucky blasted Standard Oil, the City National Bank, the United Trust Company, and other Wall Street companies for colluding with the McKinley administration and taking the nation to the brink of financial panic, a state of affairs that it characterized as "this gigantic and almost inconceivable assault upon the country's prosperity."[14] Newer sources of concern had also arisen, with stories about the villainy of J. Pierpont Morgan and about trusts becoming staples.[15]

From this perspective, New York City was like a giant oak tree whose extensive root system robbed other plants of moisture they needed to thrive and whose outsized canopy kept them in a perpetual shade.

"Business is King"

"Business is king."[16] That was the conclusion that British statesman and historian James Bryce reached in an article he wrote for *Outlook* magazine in 1905, surveying the changes that had occurred in the United States since the publication of his *The American Commonwealth* (1888). In the tradition of works like Fanny Trollope's *Domestic Manners of the Americans* (1832) and Alexis De Tocqueville's *Democracy in America* (1835) that offered magisterial examinations of the United States from a respected European standpoint, *The American Commonwealth* had become a classic. In his 1905 piece, Bryce said that what most struck him about the American society of the day was "its prodigious material development" with the growth of commerce, industry, and finance.[17] According to Bryce, businessmen had gained prestige and power from that economic expansion and had begun "to overshadow and dwarf all other interests, all other occupations."[18] He thought that financiers and manufacturers were becoming more important and landowners, professional men, and men of letters less so.[19]

Cultural values had shifted profoundly from the time earlier in the century when John Jacob Astor had been pilloried for his wealth and business methods and when Washington Irving had been unable to burnish Astor's tarnished reputation. Now popular magazines like *McClure's* and *Outlook* ran fawning portraits of industrialists like Cornelius Vanderbilt and Philip Armour, and *Harper's Bazaar* and *Century* published reverential descriptions of the New York Produce Exchange, the Chamber of Commerce, and the New York Stock Exchange. This journalism echoed the famous defense of great wealth and business competition as a source of social progress that Andrew Carnegie made in his 1889 essay, *The Gospel of Wealth*.[20] In 1899, for instance, *Outlook* informed its readers that Cornelius Vanderbilt II was not just a millionaire railroad king: no, he was "a Christian philanthropist who gave liberally of his wealth and of what was more valuable, his time and energy, to a great variety of philanthropic and Christian enterprises."[21] *Outlook* extolled Vanderbilt as "a man of great simplicity of character, easily approached, but strong, even to sternness, when necessary, and yet withal as gentle as a woman."[22] The magazine emphasized that Vanderbilt possessed his money not for himself but for others: he regarded his wealth "not simply as something personal, but as a great and sacred trust, which it was his duty to administer ... with a wise and discriminating conscientiousness, for the benefit of his fellow-man."[23] Now the *Wall Street Journal* could respect even the reptilian Jay Gould for having built railroads, telegraphs, and elevated railways that had improved the country, even as it acknowledged his unethical business conduct and indifference to charity.[24]

New York City exemplified (and drove) many of the changes in economic productivity and the status hierarchy that James Bryce spoke of in his article. At the end of the century, commerce remained an important sector of the urban economy and a key source of upper-class wealth. Yet manufacturing, in keeping with its meteoric growth nationwide, had become far more significant than it had been at midcentury and now supplied more jobs than commerce did.[25] In 1900 New York City ranked as the nation's top manufacturing city. Unlike archetypal industrial cities like Pittsburgh or Lowell that specialized in a single product, manufacturing in New York City was highly diversified. And while factories in prototypical manufacturing cities were good sized and capital intensive, the extraordinarily high cost of land, the availability of cheap immigrant labor, and the proximity of large consumer markets discouraged concentration in New York. Instead, its factories generally occupied relatively little space, had small workforces, and were labor intensive. In 1900, its top three industries were women's clothing; men's clothing; and tobacco, cigars, and cigarettes.[26]

The distinctive structure of manufacturing had consequences for urban elites. The kinds of great industrialists who arose and exerted so much power in other U.S. cities—for instance, Philip D. Armour, Gustavus F. Swift, and George Pullman in Chicago; Andrew Carnegie, Henry Clay Frick, and H. J. Heinz in Pittsburgh; and the Pillsbury and Washburn families in Minneapolis—were uncharacteristic of New York City. There were, to be sure, exceptions: the Lorillard family made its fortune from manufacturing tobacco, the Havemeyers from refining sugar, and the Steinways from building pianos. In New York City, however, the main sources of great wealth have been commerce, real estate, finance, and business services, not manufacturing. And while many wealthy industrialists lived in New York City, most of them had relocated there after having made their money elsewhere, as with Carnegie and Frick from Pittsburgh and John D. Rockefeller from Cleveland.

A second consequence was that the strikes and industrial violence that broke out in New York City typically did not directly involve upper-class New Yorkers. It was the Homestead strike outside of Pittsburgh that ensnared Carnegie and Frick and the Ludlow massacre in Colorado that besmirched Rockefeller's reputation, not anything that took place in Manhattan or Brooklyn. By contrast, the worst labor incident of this period in New York City, the Triangle Shirtwaist fire of 1911, involved a small company owned by a pair of Russian Jews (Max Blanck and Isaac Harris) that had subcontracted much of the work to other immigrants. They were decidedly not part of the upper class. A similar ownership pattern typified the garment companies that were caught up in the massive strikes led by the International Ladies' Garment Workers Union before World War I. In New York, upper-class people could stay aloof from the most unsavory elements of American industrialization and affirm their elegance and their affinity for the European aristocracy all the more naturally. They were several cuts above those grubby manufacturers, or so they could believe.[27]

The single most important aspect of this urban economic growth is that between 1880 and 1914, New York City took its place with London, Paris, and Berlin on the top shelf of international financial centers. Although London remained the world's financial capital and Paris was a strong second, New York City, according to one scholar, had become "the rising star."[28] That occurred because phenomenal industrial development enlarged the capital needs of the United States in the late nineteenth century and made Wall Street the gateway for the pounds, marks, and francs that bankrolled American manufacturing.[29]

Investment banking became the nucleus of the financial sector. The investment banks that proved to be most successful either had offices in Europe or cultivated alliances with European banks that helped them place American stocks and bonds overseas. Two clusters of paired institutions arose, both along family and ethnoreligious lines. One was Anglo-American and Protestant and included firms like Bliss & Company (which worked closely with Morton, Rose & Company, of London), Henry Clews & Company (connected to Clews, Habicht & Company, London), and J. P. Morgan & Company (long an agent for London's J. S. Morgan & Company). By the 1890s J. Pierpont Morgan was the most powerful investment banker in the United States, restructuring and refinancing railroads such as the New York Central and directing mergers for U.S. Steel and General Electric. The second cluster of investment banks was German Jewish. August Belmont & Company was the American agent for the Rothschilds; J. & W. Seligman & Company had houses in London, Paris, and Frankfurt; Kuhn, Loeb & Company, formed in New York in 1867, cultivated a relationship with M. M. Warburg of Hamburg; and Speyer & Company joined forces with Deutsche Bank. Two other notable German-Jewish investment banks were Goldman Sachs, founded in New York in 1869, and Lehman Brothers, a former cotton brokerage in Montgomery, Alabama, that moved its headquarters to New York City after the Civil War and entered the railroad securities market.

Large financial institutions that could procure domestic capital for the investment banks also emerged in New York after the Civil War. Trust companies and insurance companies grew tremendously, as did commodity exchanges such as the New York Produce Exchange. Even more important were the national banks. From the passage of the National Banking Act of 1863 until the creation of the Federal Reserve System in 1913, commercial banks in New York City functioned as the nation's central reserve and assumed special responsibilities for managing the money supply, particularly during the panics of 1873 and 1907. By 1910, six big banks in New York accounted for three-fifths of the capital and surpluses of all U.S. national banks. Their throttlehold on the national credit structure led the Pujo Commission of 1912 to crusade against the "money trust" and contributed to the formation of the more decentralized Federal Reserve System.[30]

The New York Stock Exchange (NYSE) ballooned in the late nineteenth century, with the number of its listed stocks and bonds more than tripling and with the volume of shares traded annually increasing by a factor of five from 1871 to 1900. Securities trading had lost its previous grubby reputation, and the sale of securities became central to a burgeoning corporate capitalism. By 1900 the membership list included titans such as John D. Rockefeller, J. Pierpont Morgan Jr., George J. Gould, Edward H. Harriman, Collis P. Huntington, and Russell Sage. A seat on the exchange could now bestow or at least denote social status, and the scions of Old New York families such as the Beekmans, Delafields, Haights, and Suydams joined it.[31]

New York City also became a corporate center in the 1880s and 1890s, a development that initially stemmed from business efforts to curb competition via tighter combination and centralization. Trying to control the ruthless competition that made the price of a barrel of crude oil alternately spiral downward and upward, John D. Rockefeller resorted to the "trust," a legal mechanism that allowed rival operators to come together in a cartel that could force hundreds of small-fry producers to stabilize prices. This device also enabled Rockefeller's Standard Oil to absorb some of its adversaries. To give this huge endeavor a legal and administrative framework, a New York City attorney named Samuel C. T. Dodd created the Standard Oil Trust in 1883, whereby shareholders of its forty separate companies exchanged their stock for shares in the trust, which thereupon gained supervisory control over the enterprise from a centralized office in New York City. After moving the home offices of Standard Oil from Cleveland to New York, Rockefeller began to assemble properties in lower Manhattan for the site of a new headquarters, a ten-story building at 26 Broadway that became the most famous business address in the world when it opened in 1885.

Impressed by this achievement, ten other processing industries adopted trusts, with eight of them situating their home offices in New York City. Henry O. Havemeyer consolidated seventeen metropolitan sugar refining companies into a "Sugar Trust" that ultimately controlled 97 percent of national sugar production, and tobacco maker James B. Duke relocated his head office from North Carolina to New York City and formed the American Tobacco Company. Trusts proved to be unwieldy and unstable, however, and soon gave way to forms of combination that were tighter and more permanent. During the great merger movement of 1895 to 1904, more than 1,800 firms disappeared into consolidations, many of which—like American Can, Crucible Steel, and International Paper—controlled more than 70 percent of the markets in which they operated. In 1917, of the 500 largest corporations (in terms of gross revenues) in the United States, 150 were headquartered in metropolitan New York; the second leading corporate center, Chicago, housed only 32. This high degree of concentration persisted well into the twentieth century. In 1957, of the Fortune 500 firms, 144 were based in the

New York region, a net loss of only six from 1917.[32]

As the availability of capital and financial expertise from Wall Street banks and exchanges made New York City an attractive corporate location, firms that provided corporations with professional and business services also sprang up in lower Manhattan: law firms, such as Cravath, Swaine & Moore, Cadawalader, Wickersham & Taft, and Sullivan & Cromwell (to use their current names), became proficient in antitrust, mergers and acquisitions, bankruptcy, and real estate law; advertising agencies, like J. Walter Thompson, devised national campaigns to promote the consumer products being introduced by Colgate-Palmolive and Nabisco; and accounting firms, such as Haskins & Sells (now Deloitte Touche Tohmatsu), devised auditing procedures that made it possible to evaluate complex transactions. By increasing the number of office jobs and by further separating administrative work from factory employment, this corporate headquarters complex fostered a distinctive white-collar world. Increasingly, it became a place where economic elites made their careers and fortunes.[33]

The Chamber of Commerce had developed into a pivotal institution in the new political economy that came into being with the expansion of heavy industry and finance after the Civil War. The most powerful nonprofit body in New York City, it was the driving force behind the consolidation of Manhattan, Brooklyn, the Bronx, Queens, and Staten Island into Greater New York in 1898 and the impetus for the planning and construction of the city's first subway, the 1904 line of the Interborough Rapid Transit Company. The heart of this new political economy was the interdependence of government and business leaders on all levels who acted together in using state intervention to promote national expansion.[34]

The New York Stock Exchange unveiled its own landmark classical revival building in 1903. To handle the expanding volume of trading and to integrate new communications technologies that were revolutionizing securities transactions, the Stock Exchange had enlarged and modernized its space on three separate occasions between 1869 and 1887. In 1901, needing still more room, the Exchange decided to erect a heroic new structure on its existing site near the corner of Broad and Wall Streets that would herald its coming of age as an important—and trustworthy—national institution. A broker had once lauded its old headquarters as "a fine, solid structure, devoid of anything showy, pretentious or decorative."[35] That could not be said of the new Stock Exchange, which matched the architectural grandiosity and imperial ambition of the Chamber of Commerce and suggested age and stability and importance.[36] During its dedication, Rudolph Keppler, the president of the Stock Exchange, extolled the national significance and solidity of the financial sector, quoting the observation of an unnamed New York City clergyman that "the great things for which Wall Street exists are not gambling: they are legitimate and in every way necessary to carry on the processes of modern civilization."[37]

Thanks in large measure to the peculiar structure of manufacturing in New York City, it was Wall Street that was the chief source of the city's expanded national influence. A Presbyterian minister put it this way in 1901: "Wall Street is one of the longest streets in the world. It does not begin at the foot of Trinity Church ... and end at the East River, as many suppose. It reaches through all our American cities and across the sea."[38] This was clearly true: when J. Pierpont Morgan conferred in his office at 23 Wall Street about the Federal Steel Company, the Lake Shore Railway, or the Mexican Telephone Company, the reverberations from his decisions could affect jobs, wages, and prices in distant locations.[39] Wall Street accordingly became a flashpoint for conflicts over the pursuit of wealth, monopoly power, the limits of democracy, and business ethics. Industrialization had created a social crisis, and the newfound capacity of financiers and industrialists to utterly transform the lives of people in remote places, for good or for ill, gave rise to opposed positions about the role of Wall Street, with some applauding it for rewarding the talented and enterprising and contributing mightily to national progress, and others seeing the financial district as rapacious and socially divisive.

Wall Street: Our Fathers' True Heirs

This period of U.S. history was thus replete with protests against the financial center. This opposition elicited responses from apologists who drew on American nationalism to uphold the financial district's integrity, and it would be their ideas that eventually became embedded in popular understandings of Wall Street. Moreover, as the financial sector became more and more important as a source of wealth and prestige for the high-status population in New York City, representations of Wall Street would increasingly shape the meanings that they and others gave their work and lives.

Political radicals were one source of censure. John Swinton's Paper, a labor organ, rebuked "our ruling swashbucklers" for trying to subdue workers by brandishing the raw military power available to the upper classes.[40] Socialist leader Eugene V. Debs railed against the corporate plutocracy and prayed for the arrival of "the final hour of capitalism and wage slavery."[41]

Another assault came from within the two-party political system, in the form of the crusade that William Jennings Bryan made against the gold standard during the 1896 presidential election. At the National Democratic Convention that July, Bryan secured the presidential nomination by delivering a spellbinding speech condemning the business interests in the great cities on the East Coast as "the few financial magnates who in a backroom corner the money of the world."[42] He staged the acceptance of the nomination in New York City—venturing, he told his supporters, "in[to] the heart of what now seems to be the enemy's country but which we hope to occupy before the campaign is over."[43] In his acceptance speech at Madison Square Garden, Bryan rebuked "the money changers" who ruled the nation from New York City and declared that the biblical commandment "Thou shall not steal" must apply to the strong as well as the weak.[44]

Bryan's nomination sent Wall Street into a frenzy. Business leaders resented his demagoguery and insisted that his policies would wreck the financial system. More than that, they saw Bryan as a harbinger of social revolution, with some fearing a violent working-class uprising on the order of the New York City draft riots or the Paris Commune. Inside the Stock Exchange, traders reacted to news of the nomination of the Great Commoner with a display of nationalism. A half hour before the close of trading, a broker held up a large American flag and paraded it around the boardroom, as cheering traders denounced secessionists, revolutionists, populists, and anarchists. NYSE governors later claimed that they had planned on closing the Exchange indefinitely had Bryan won the general election.[45]

Protestant clergy joined the attack against the elite financiers of Wall Street. The Protestant clerical opponent of Wall Street special privilege who had the broadest social impact was Reverend T. De Witt Talmage, pastor of the Central Presbyterian Church in Brooklyn, widely regarded in his day as the best preacher in America. Talmage was a social conservative, and while deeply suspicious of the working class, his concern that mounting labor violence threatened to exacerbate social divisions led him to take aim at business. For the next decade, he berated Chicago "grain gamblers" for driving up the price of bread and compounding the desperation of the urban poor; reprimanded Wall Street stock speculators for being in league with Satan; and censured bankers and trust officers for enriching themselves with other people's money. For Talmage, the danger of business practices that promised instant wealth lay in their encouragement of luck, impulsiveness, and desire that would undermine the Victorian virtues of industry, self-discipline, and perseverance.[46]

Wall Street's defenders were quick to reply to these assaults. A particularly influential response came from Henry Clews, a prominent investment banker and civic leader later dubbed the "dean of Wall Street." In 1887, Clews published a rebuttal to Talmage in the *North American Review* expressing his dismay that the Presbyterian minister had employed "his flashy wit and mountebank eloquence" to equate the financial district with brothels and gaming dens and to defile the reputations of Wall Street men who for the most part were "paragons of personal honor."[47] What made Talmage dangerous, Clews wrote, was his sure grasp of middle-class Victorian culture. Clews was concerned about respectability, the core Victorian virtue, not about religiosity per se. According to Clews, Talmage mistook constructive entrepreneurialism for mindless destruction and greed and did not comprehend that the financial center served as a "great distributor" by supplying money to start-up ventures and allowing industries to grow and the nation to prosper.[48] For Clews, who had been an agent for the sale of Treasury bonds during the Civil War and an early member of the Union League Club, the strongest evidence of the importance of Wall Street was that its financiers had raised the funds that let Union armies defeat the Confederacy. He acknowledged that swindlers and confidence men occasionally fleeced investors and injured the reputation of the Street, but these malefactors were the exception, and the great mass of Wall Street bankers and brokers were continuing the work of Washington, Jefferson, Madison, Franklin, and Hamilton.[49]

This powerful idea had received tangible expression four years earlier, when the Chamber of Commerce arranged for a statue of George Washington to be erected on the front steps of the U.S. Sub-Treasury, at the corner of Wall and Broad Streets, where Washington had taken the oath of office as the first president of the United States in 1789.[50] By 1883 this street corner had become the axis of the financial district, with the renowned investment house of Drexel, Morgan & Company located across from the Sub-Treasury on one side of Broad Street and the U.S. Custom House and the New York Stock Exchange on the other. If the accident of this spatial proximity was not enough for people to link the founding of the nation to the operation of the financial district, then the myriad centennials that were held between 1875 and 1889 of events from the American Revolution conditioned them to think in terms of historical memory. Covering themselves in patriotism, business apologists used this history to deflect battering from the likes of Talmage.

In wider popular memory the notion that there was a relationship between the nation's first capital city and its modern financial center was still sufficiently novel and unfixed in 1883 for the detractors of Wall Street to offer their own interpretations of J. Q.A. Ward's monument, as one skeptic did in concluding that the colossal bronze figure of "the Father of his Country ... dwarfs and belittles its surroundings."[51] His point was obvious: children do not always meet the expectations of their parents, some fathers are more demanding than others, and perhaps the "Father of his Country" could be counted on to be the sternest taskmaster of all. This cynic swore that Washington looked "morose and disdainful" and that his countenance bore "a singularly disagreeable grimace": "The immortal George appears to look across at the Stock Exchange and raise his right hand in horror at the financial performances that obtain there, while his face betokens the most vivid disgust."[52]

By repeatedly driving these patriotic associations home, however, Wall Street supporters ultimately gave this new understanding the stability and continuity of meaning to resist further redefinitions and to be experienced as part of the normal scheme of things. In 1889, the Chamber of Commerce, the New-York Historical Society, and the Sons of the Revolution, a leading patriotic hereditary association, orchestrated a jubilee to memorialize the centennial of Washington's inauguration as president. The members of these organizations came from the city's social and economic elites, and the committee that planned the fête included Wall Street titans J. Pierpont Morgan, Cornelius Vanderbilt, and Jesse Seligman and wealthy Old New Yorkers Theodore Roosevelt, S. Van Rensselaer Cruger, and Rutherford Stuyvesant. In celebrating the enormous progress that the United States had made in its first century, these organizers emphasized that a line of descent ran from Washington, who had launched the new nation by taking the oath of office on Wall Street, to the heads of the financial institutions that now occupied the area.[53]

This link between the nation's origins and the financial district was reinforced by the plethora of New York City guidebooks produced in the late nineteenth and early twentieth centuries. Guidebooks typically put the financial district high on the list of locations that tourists had to visit while they were in New York, often devoting fifteen or more pages to its places of interest. Their portrayal of the neighborhood blurred the line between past and present and used history to ex alt the financial center—reminding readers, in the words of *Pictorial New York and Brooklyn* (1892), that Wall Street "retains something descriptive of its ancient character or use in its modern designation."[54]

The World of Elites

The new order was synonymous with colossal personal wealth. In 1892 greater New York had 1,265 millionaires, nearly one-third of the total for the entire United States and a number that would have been inconceivable before the Civil War. John D. Rockefeller, the richest man in the world, was worth $1 billion in 1913, the equivalent of $22.3 billion today. Andrew Carnegie had a personal fortune of $150 million—about $3.2 billion today.

High salaries for elite businessmen were commonplace. In the early 1900s, when laborers on a major New York City construction project earned $600 to $675 a year if unskilled and $750 if skilled, the president of the Delaware & Hudson Railroad ma de $75,000 per year and the presidents of other large railroads between $35,000 and $60,000. At New York Life, the president received a salary of $100,000, and three senior vice presidents, $75,000, $40,000, and $25,000, respectively. Charles M. Schwab, head of U.S. Steel, reportedly took home $100,000. These salary figures underestimate total compensation, because they exclude stock options and bonuses. According to the *Wall Street Journal*, Schwab was entitled to buy a sum of U.S. Steel stock equal to 5 percent of his salary at a guaranteed price every year. For many years, the president of a leading New York City commercial bank collected a bonus of $50,000 that duplicated his annual salary, while J. P. Morgan & Company gave its employees bonuses that ranged from 20 to 100 percent of their salaries, depending on how profitable the firm had been in a given year.[55]

With the thriving economy enriching many people, the urban elite grew much larger. Although the category "elite" is too imprecise in American society (and the social structure of New York City too complex) to permit anything like an exact count, it seems reasonable to estimate that by 1900 somewhere between seventy thousand and one hundred thousand people had achieved the social or economic standing to be considered part of the elite. (Both figures amount to less than 4 per cent of the total city population.) By this rough estimation, the elite was four or five times larger in 1900 than it had been in the 1850s. No organization was more affected by the tensions caused by the enlargement of the high status population th an the Social Register Association. But the economy and population of New York City continued to boom, and in 1904 the *Social Register* contained the names of more than twenty-five thousand individuals.[56] It was simply impossible to know everyone or maintain real exclusivity anymore. Exclusivity had become an ideal; it was part of a story that elite New Yorkers told about their lives and tried to make come true.

In the face of this relentless growth, and bolstered by the Victorian penchant for erecting barriers that sought to preserve the pure and exemplary by excluding the unworthy and degraded, upper-class New Yorkers tried to tighten the boundaries and screen out the ordinariness of the middle class and the baseness of the newly moneyed. There was a new awareness about the need to bolster upper-class privilege.

"Club World"

In the 1880s and 1890s, a distinctive social space called "Club World" or "Clubdom" took shape in New York City.[57] The site of most of the city's exclusive men's clubs, Club World centered on Fifth Avenue from about Twenty-First Street to Thirty-Ninth Street but also spilled over onto nearby streets and avenues. A few institutions, like the Metropolitan Club at Fifth Avenue and East Sixtieth Street, were situated beyond it.

The area merited its special name because private clubs reached their zenith in the late nineteenth and early twentieth centuries, when they became essential to how upper- and upper-middle-class New York men organized their lives. There were many different kinds of clubs: social clubs like the venerable Union Club and the Knickerbocker Club, politically oriented social clubs such as Union League Club and the Manhattan Club, special-purpose clubs (the New York Yacht Club and the American Jockey Club), clubs devoted to a single profession or occupation (the Lawyers', the Grolier, and the Lotos), ones with a cultural slant (the Authors' Club and the Century Association), athletic clubs (the Racquet Club and the New York Athletic Club), college alumni clubs (the University Club and the Harvard Club), and ethnonational clubs (the Progress Club, for German Jews, and the Caledonian Club, for Scots). This proliferation indicates the importance these clubs had for elite male New Yorkers.

In 1890 the *New York Times* estimated that there were 350 private men's clubs in New York City that had their own quarters, but that only 25 to 30 of them could be considered socially prestigious. The paper calculated that these first-rank institutions—such as the Union, the Union League, the Knickerbocker, the Calumet, and the New York Yacht—had an aggregate membership of about twenty-five thousand. Since men usually belonged to multiple organizations, the number of individuals who comprised Club World was probably no more than fifteen thousand.

Initiation fees and annual dues varied widely as well. For instance, the Nassau Boat Club, a New York City—based rowing association with modest facilities that did not profess to be socially exclusive, charged an initiation fee of $10 and annual dues of $25. By contrast, membership in top-flight clubs involved substantial costs that were beyond the means of middle-class New Yorkers and—since multiple memberships were the norm—also put a crimp in the budgets of upper-class people with more social than economic capital. The New York Athletic Club, the St. Nicholas Club, and the Century Association set their initiation fees at between $100 and $150; the University, Lotus, Calumet, and Manhattan Clubs at $200; and the Metropolitan, Union, Union League, and Knickerbocker at $300. The Union Club charged annual dues of $75 and the Metropolitan Club of $100.[58]

The most salient attribute of Club World was that it was entirely male. This gender exclusivity became a source of complaint on the part of some members and their families, and a few people urged the creation of mixed clubs where men and women would join as equal members. They were ignored. Instead of granting membership to females, club leaders expanded their hours and areas of access. The Lawyers' Club and the Commercial Club regularly opened their reading, dining, and dressing rooms to the wives and daughters of members, while the Manhattan Club and the Authors' Club instituted ladies' days and held ladies' receptions in the evening or late afternoon hours for wives and daughters.[59] These were obviously trifling measures, and in fact these clubs did not and could not admit women because the male-only policy was central to their very being. In explaining why women should be excluded, club defenders cited the supposed differences between male and female temperament. *Harper's Bazaar* maintained that women were "too exclusive, too eclectic, not sufficiently impersonal in their relations to one another, too much affected by each other's 'sphere' to meet in the club-room, discuss business, eat at a common set of club tables, and lead the life that men do."[60] As a result of their emotional makeup, women could not do what men did: "seek a refuge where they can enjoy the benefits of a club, read the papers and magazines daily laid out for them, eat an easily ordered meal, find a place to write their letters, in fact, enjoy all the comforts of a clubhouse."[61]

But if men's clubs were a refuge, what exactly were they a refuge from? The supporters of the clubs were not entirely clear on this point. Some wanted to escape the undifferentiated social mixing that made public space in New York City discomfiting by establishing semiprivate places where like-minded men of the same social station could congregate, while others prized the clubs for offering a respite from the demands of the marketplace. Most of all, however, the clubs provided a retreat from the place that dominated late Victorian culture, the home. Upper- and middle-class Americans regarded the home as a primary site to nurture families and children, teach morals and religion, entertain friends and relatives, enjoy fine music and literature, and conduct courtships. These activities were considered to be the purview of women, and in terms of its design and furnishings and social functions, the Victorian home was a feminized environment. The cultural ideals associated with the home also inspired a number of social reforms in the late nineteenth century, as tens of thousands of women sought to apply the moral virtues of the domestic sphere to the larger society by campaigning for the prohibition of alcoholic beverages, the elimination of prostitution, and the passage of mandatory school attendance laws.

All that could be suffocating—and men's clubs provided an asylum from the womanly home. It was easier for men to smoke (particularly cigars) and drink alcohol in the clubs. In offering a manly haven, however, they unwittingly confirmed the centrality of the home to late Victorian culture. By the 1890s the memberships of most New York City clubs had grown so large that their clubhouses no longer bore any resemblance to single-family dwellings, as they once had. With their massive bulks and imposing façades, these buildings evoked semipublic and public institutions such as hotels, banks, department stores, and libraries [...]. It was another story, though, with their interiors, which of necessity were given over to the same everyday activities—eating, reading, socializing, and sleeping—that took place inside private houses. To be sure, the interiors featured oversized fireplaces, stairways, and great rooms, had heavy tables, chairs, and sofas, and were adorned in dark hues that imparted a masculine atmosphere. They also had special rooms for manly pastimes like billiards. But the greatest part of the interior spaces open to members consisted of dining rooms, libraries, and bedrooms that were not so different from their counterparts in private houses and that were identified by the same names, with their main reception rooms, for instance, generally known as "parlors." Men's clubs were less an alternative to the home than a continuation of it. As a third place that provided venues for informal and voluntary gatherings beyond the realms of home and business, men's clubs could not admit women without crossing the line and becoming entirely too homelike.[62]

Upper-class men made the clubs a significant part of their lives. Take Harper S. Mott, a graduate of Columbia College and Columbia Law School who had received a sizable inheritance of money and Manhattan real estate that enabled him to lead a leisurely existence. In the mid-1880s, Mott regularly took the 8:25 a.m. train from his home in upper Manhattan to his office in Wall Street, where he managed his properties, and returned home on the 3:35 or the 4:35, in plenty of time to take his carriage out for a drive or pursue his interest in local history. Mott usually went to the New York Athletic Club or the Lawyers' Club in the early afternoon to eat lunch, see friends, and conduct business. Club World was even more important to James N. De R. Whitehouse, the head of a family-owned stockbrokerage house. He and his wife, Vera, were socialites who went to Newport for the season in July and August and then spent late August in the Adirondacks. In New York City, James Whitehouse took his meals at the Union Club, the New York Athletic Club, or Delmonico's Restaurant on workdays; went to the Whist Club many weekday nights; and spent his Saturdays at the Badminton Club and the Players Club. The Whitehouses also patronized the Westchester Country Club and the Morris Park Cricket Club.[63] Altogether, James N. De R. Whitehouse belonged to about ten clubs.

The clubs were a priority for the very rich and powerful, too. J. Pierpont Morgan regularly dined at the Union Club and frequented the Century Association, the New York Yacht Club, the Union League Club, the Whist Club, and the New York Jockey Club, among others. Morgan also made time for club business: in his annual engagement diaries, appointments to plan the new headquarters of the New York Yacht Club or to review the Union League Club balance sheet share space with corporate and nonprofit board meetings and sessions to organize mergers and acquisitions. Morgan navigated urban public space by treating his clubs, home, and office, the meeting rooms at Grand Central Dépot and the Chamber of Commerce, and Delmonico's Restaurant as private and semiprivate preserves. Like other upper-class individuals, he was constantly hopping from one of these islands to the next.[64]

For Mott, Whitehouse, and Morgan, these clubs were important for imposing a protective wall around men of financial and social position and allowing them to interact freely and informally, while excluding outsiders. Especially for newcomers, membership was a way to demonstrate one's bona fides and learn how to conduct and value oneself in rarefied company. All that raised the caliber of the elite category and made the clubs critical elite institutions. The *New York Times* defined the club ideal this way in 1891:

> A club is presumably an association of gentlemen, in which there can be no distinctions as

to wealth, social standing, or anything else. The members of any given club meet on a common footing in their clubhouse, however different may be their several positions in the world outside. Anything which elevates one member above his fellow-members or procures for him superior advantages in the clubhouse is clearly antagonistic to the ground principles of club life, and must be prevented.[65]

To succeed as an "association of gentlemen," a club had to have a sociable environment that fostered strong bonds and open intercourse, and achieving that goal, longtime clubmen knew, depended entirely on the character and commitment of its members. They had to be "clubbable." "Clubbability" was an ambiguous term that could be stretched and manipulated as need be, but most members knew what it meant. The creation of a brotherhood required that the men be willing and able to *be* brothers: they had to get to know one another individually and develop loyalty to each other and the group. If they hoped to bring out the best in themselves and the other members, they could not drop in for a meal every few weeks and then nonchalantly go on their way. Nor should they be preoccupied with moneymaking, either. Top-notch clubs banned or limited business activities to ensure a sociable atmosphere; without a doubt these restrictions were impossible to enforce, and clubs were places to make business connections and meet clients, but the ideal remained.[66]

An 1896 obituary of one John L. Lawrence defined the model club-man. The son of a carriage maker who had made a fortune, Lawrence had closed the business after the death of his father and pursued a leisurely life. He belonged to the Riding Club and the Larchmont Yacht Club, but was proudest of his almost twenty-five-year association with the Union Club. According to the *Times*, Lawrence made the Union Club "virtually his home during the daylight hours for most of the year," daily occupying a window seat that looked onto Fifth Avenue.[67] He not only knew every member of the Union Club, but his engaging personality, ability to converse on a range of subjects, knack for putting other people at ease, handsome looks, and success at games perfectly suited this "association of gentlemen." The *Times* conceded that Lawrence's temper and quickness to resent an affront kept him entangled in personal squabbles, including a spat that had ended in a fistfight one summer in Newport, but a little eccentricity could be forgiven, and perhaps even esteemed as a mark of the value that a man put on himself. At any rate, the *Times* felt that Lawrence "probably was better known in the club world of New-York than any other man of his age."[68]

But sentimental portrayals of men's clubs as intimate gathering places were misleading. The continued economic development of New York City put even the most prestigious clubs under pressure to expand their memberships in the late nineteenth century. As the size of the economic elite grew, there was a corresponding increase in the number of men with the financial resources to be admitted to these clubs and the inclination to think about their identities and their relationships in a new light. While clubs could have chosen to remain small and exclusive by retaining low membership ceilings, they competed with one another for status and were forever jockeying to maintain or improve their position with respect to their rivals, another indication of the importance of social and business networking in the club system. Top-flight clubs, cherishing their lofty ranking, felt this strain acutely. Significantly, in the 1880s, the Union League Club began to consider dispensing with its guiding principle of screening applicants for their political views, and by the 1890s had become an exclusively social club that paid lip service to its previous stress on national and municipal policy making.

An added complication was that a club's standing depended as much on its reputation with the general public as it did on its reputation with upper-class New Yorkers. That was not the case in Boston and Philadelphia, where the upper classes were small and relatively self-contained and elites could ignore popular reputation, but the rapid growth of New York made for greater social instability and competitiveness within the upper class and led many to seek affirmation outside their circles. Beyond that, there was also a difference in social ethos. A belief that status depended on celebrity prevailed in New York City but not in Boston and Philadelphia, where members of the social elite went out of their way to dress and live inconspicuously. New Yorkers were showier and more ostentatious. Since popular status reflected the extensive coverage that mainstream newspapers and leading magazines devoted to Club World, the concern was that a club might be too small to attract public notice. A further peril was that a club that barred the newest tycoon might appear to be odd to ordinary people or might risk having a rival club admit him—and gain the benefit of his resources to build a new clubhouse or improve its facilities. In dynamic New York City, public reputation conflicted with selectivity, and prestige was ambiguous and unstable.[69]

The evidence, while fragmentary, suggests that elite men's clubs in other American cities were not under the same pressures. By the 1890s men's clubs had become a critical institution for urban business and social elites and existed in virtually every U.S. city. However, cities such as Philadelphia, Boston, and Baltimore that had well-entrenched social elites were not growing fast enough or generating hordes of income men for their clubs to accommodate, while an instant city such as Chicago that was developing rapidly did not have an old social elite that was being crowded out. Compared with other U.S. cities, the upper class in New York City was singular in its openness to newcomers, its readiness to shed traditions, and its aggressive approach to moneymaking.

The proclivity of the Victorian cultural system for social partition and hierarchy exerted its influence everywhere, but the large size and the quick expansion of the New York City elite made it a special case. We have seen how these strains led the Union League to expand its membership in the early 1890s. Nearly all of the city's other leading clubs experienced the same tensions and took the same course of action. By 1891 the Union League Club had about 1,700 members; the Manhattan Club, 1,500; and the New York Athletic Club, 2,300. However, two prominent clubs, the Knickerbocker and the Calumet, chose to buck this trend, maintaining their small sizes and confining their membership to "men of good name and position." In 1891 the Knickerbocker had 500 members and the Calumet 400. The small size of the Calumet Club may have been a sign of weakness: it was beginning to lose members to the Metropolitan Club and would soon experience serious financial troubles.[70] That was not the case with the Knickerbocker Club, which had a long waiting list and was thought to stand first among all New York City clubs "in terms of exclusiveness and social standing."[71] Thus, *Town Topics*, the gossip sheet of the upper class, complained that too many governing officers of the Union Club lacked the quality of birth and family to warrant their eminent positions, yet praised the leaders of the Knickerbocker Club for combining wealth and social position and being "representative fashionable men of New York."[72] But even though the Knickerbocker was highly selective, almost nobody outside the upper class had ever heard of it, whereas the Union Club had a *public* reputation for being exclusive, and from an institutional perspective, that was what counted.

Clubs had similar admissions procedures. These rules required that a prospective member be proposed and seconded by established members, sometimes with written testimonials, and that the names of the candidate and the members who had proposed and seconded him be posted in the club's rooms for as long as three weeks, so that other members could review them. The candidate then had to be approved by the ruling body of the club or by an admissions committee. The Union Club gave its Governing Committee sole authority to admit new members, and the Down-Town Club entrusted decisions to its twenty-man board of trustees, with one adverse vote in five being grounds for exclusion. The Union League Club and the Harvard Club put

candidates who passed an initial screening to a secret vote of the entire membership. Unsurprisingly, these gateways had the intended effect of reproducing the ethnoreligious character and the personal relationships of the social elite.[73]

Even for the wellborn, though, gaining admission could be nerve-racking. In February 1888, Harper S. Mott embarked on an elaborate campaign to join the Union League Club. He started by asking Frederick Law Olmsted, one of its founders, to sponsor him. After Olmsted agreed to help, he and Mott met on at least seven occasions to plot strategy, with the key step being the selection of the other members who would second his candidacy and write letters on his behalf. As soon as his name was posted, Mott lunched at the Union League Club to meet more members and let them take his measure. Meanwhile, he provided the same assistance to friends and acquaintances who wanted to join two of his clubs, the Lawyers' Club and the New York Athletic Club. This system of mutual obligations created strong bonds among upper-class men, helping to tie together and give shape to an upper class that was becoming large and formless.

Not only were admissions procedures labyrinthine, but rejections became common knowledge and, at times, public sensations. In 1893 the Union League Club blackballed Theodore Seligman, a son of longtime club member Jesse Seligman, because he was Jewish. If Jesse Seligman's prominence in the Republican Party had aided his own admission to the Union League Club in 1868, the club's deemphasis of political considerations in the late nineteenth century, coupled with the intensification of anti-Semitism, contributed to its rejection of his son. Jesse Seligman angrily resigned from his old club, leaving it with only one Jewish member, who also eventually quit in protest.

This "housecleaning" brought the Union League Club into line with the other top men's clubs. *Town Topics* reported approvingly that leading clubs had a tacit understanding that Jews were not to be proposed as members. As justification for this anti-

Semitic policy, *Town Topics* cited the case of an unnamed Jewish publisher who had somehow slipped through the screening procedures of the Century Association, to the point that he was actually certified as being a Gentile.[74] With "the peculiar effrontery of his race," this newcomer then offended the sensibilities of regular members by inviting other Jews to the club as his guests and acting as if he had the same rights and privileges as anyone else, conduct so brazen that *Town Topics* demanded that this "undesirable incursion" of clubdom must be stopped in its tracks.[75] An upper-class New Yorker later recalled the casual anti-Semitism of his set: "It simply seemed to be accepted that [Jews] were to be avoided at all costs in terms of social mixing. It was as if they carried some easily contractible and unattractive, though not necessarily dangerous, ailment."[76]

Applicants could be blackballed for other reasons than "the Jew question." In 1891 the governing committee of the Union Club turned down Austin Corbin, the president of the Long Island Rail Road; John King, the president of the Erie Railroad; and W. Seward Webb, the president of several rail companies. While it is not possible to discern the reasons for decisions that were made in secret, contemporaries believed that these snubs were driven by the resentments that some old-guard New Yorkers felt toward the new wealth. Webb came from an Old New York family, but his marriage to a daughter of William K. Vanderbilt had catapulted him into the presidency of a number of companies in the Vanderbilt system—and made him a punching bag for the family's detractors. Corbin and King had been proposed by J. Pierpont Morgan, and their rebuffs may have been calculated to cut the investment banker down to size.[77]

More than any other Gilded Age institution, Club World was used by upper-class men to regulate their relationships with one another and define suitable conduct. Club World reified a masculine version of social hierarchy, promoted upper-class networking, and punished nonconformity. It stood for stability and tradition and upheld gentlemanly standards. It became a place where upper-class men pursued privilege by policing their boundaries and celebrating their prerogatives. However, the struggles that club leaders experienced when trying to restrict the size of memberships and exclude inappropriate outsiders points to the powerful effect that economic vitality had in encroaching on upper-class life in New York City.

Upper-class women faced their own social pressures and developed their own networks.

Upper-Class Women's Networks

Among the subscribers who contributed large gifts of money in the 1890s to create the New York Botanical Garden were three upper-class women: Helen M. Gould, a daughter of robber baron Jay Gould and a leading philanthropist in her own right; Esther Herrman, a Jewish philanthropist and suffragist; and Melissa P. Dodge, widow of the president of Phelps Dodge. Yet neither they nor any other women served on its board of managers or in other leadership positions. This was the norm: in this period, the governing bodies of major New York City cultural institutions did not include women.[78]

Upper-class women found other means to network and exercise power. One way they did so was by patrolling the gateways of high society. This role acquired greater importance as the growth of the upper class in the late nineteenth century intensified social competition. Upper-class social affairs in this period included weddings, teas, receptions, holiday musicals, charity balls, young people's dances, and children's parties, and upper-class women organized virtually all of them—selecting the dates and venues; creating the guest lists; sending invitations; deciding on decorations, refreshments, and seating plans; handling newspaper and magazine announcements; and supervising the attendants. By restricting access to these activities, New York society women "brought control to the exceedingly fluid social situation of the post-Civil War period."[79] They also monitored the guests to ensure that conversation flowed and adhered to appropriate topics and that bachelors and children stayed in check.[80] According to the author of an 1896 etiquette manual, "The graces and courtesies of life are in [women's] hands. It is women who create society."[81]

A scrapbook that an upper-class New York City woman named Pauline Robinson kept from 1894 to 1912 reveals the significance of these female-arranged events in creating social spaces where upper-class people could come together. For instance, Robinson stayed with friends on Jekyll Island, Georgia, for three weeks in February and March 1904; then visited another set of friends in Latrobe, Pennsylvania; traveled to Boston at the end of April; spent time in June on the Main Line of Philadelphia; celebrated the Fourth of July in Shelburne, Vermont; went to Newport later that month; and stopped in Lenox, Massachusetts, and then in Winterthur, Delaware, in the fall. Almost everywhere, Robinson resided with friends or relatives rather than in hotels or inns and thus depended for her hospitality on other women (and their servants). Similarly, a young woman of marriageable age from an upper-class New York City family used dances, dinners, and parties to open a window of freedom for herself. Florence Adele Sloane was extremely frustrated by the restrictions of the respectable existence that she led, but on these special occasions she could meet new people and have lively conversations.[82]

In the late nineteenth and early twentieth centuries many women's clubs, societies, and associations sprang up in the United States. Because men participated minimally or not at all in organizations that dealt with "women's issues," these organizations became places where upper- and upper-middle-class women interacted. This was their Club World. In New York City, there were alumni groups such as the Emma Willard and Mount Holyoke Associations, literary societies like Minerva, local chapters of patriotic hereditary associations such as the National Society of Daughters of Founders and Patriots, and political organizations like the Woman's Republican Club and the Elizabeth Cady Stanton Political Equality League.

The most prestigious and influential groups were nonprofits that aided working-class and immigrant families and children, notably the Young Women's Christian Association (YWCA) and the Junior League. With an entirely female board of directors and administration, the YWCA was a complex enterprise that had ten thousand members and that operated nine branch offices and a girl's camp, all racially segregated. It offered classes in the Bible, home economics, foreign languages, and art; ran an employment bureau; and provided a residence for nurses.

Far more stylish was the Junior League, which Mary Harriman, the daughter of railroad executive Edward H. Harriman, founded in 1901 so that young New York City socialites could address the problems of urban poverty. Harriman also had a secondary objective of transforming society women's own lives, hoping that these young women would gain a serious purpose and become more independent and self-aware. Within a few years, the Junior League numbered some twenty-five to thirty young women "well-known to society" such as Gladys Vanderbilt, Beatrice Morgan, and Janet Dada, who volunteered at settlement houses and staged annual theatrical performances to raise money for their programs. The Junior League later opened a residential hotel on the East River at Seventy-Eighth Street that had rooms for 350 working-class girls.

From the start, the Junior League had a mixed reputation. The spectacle of debutantes dirtying their white gloves doing charity work in settlement houses, health clinics, and playgrounds exposed it to ridicule, and in actuality many of its volunteers dripped noblesse oblige and treated their assignments as a lark. At its best, though, the Junior League articulated an ideal of service and conscience that provided a moral corrective to the hard-nosed orientation of elite businessmen and that improved the lives of underprivileged New Yorkers.[83]

NOTES

1. Francis W. Crowninshield, *Manners for the Metropolis: An Entrance Key to the Fantastic Life of the 400* (New York: Appleton, 1908), 4.

2. *Town Topics and the American Queen*, March 28 and April 11, 1885; *Town Topics*, November 17, 1887; *New York Times*, November 13, 1875, May 28, 1885, January 17, May 26, and April 18, 1887, May 26, 1888, December 5, 1890, May 8 and 29, April 5, and December 30, 1891, December 6, 1896, May 9, 1897; M. F. Sweetser, *How to Know New York City: A Serviceable and Trustworthy Guide, Having Its Starting Point at the Grand Union Hotel* (Boston: Rand, Avery, 1888), 87–89; Paul Porzelt, *The Metropolitan Club of New York* (New York: Rizzoli, 1982), 7–32; Jean Strouse, *Morgan: American Financier* (New York: Random House, 1999), 276–77; and *Officers, Members, Constitution and By-Laws of the Union Club of the City of New York* (New York: n.p., 1894), 13–75.

3. Social Register Association, *Social Register, 1887* (New York: Social Register Association, 1886; facsimile ed., New York: Social Register Association, 1986), 2; and Social Register Association, *Social Register, New York, 1904* (New York: n.p., 1903), 11, 30–31, 74, 122–23, 135, 394, 398, 448, 476–77.

4. Sven Beckert argues that an upper class formed in New York City in the late nineteenth century, an interpretation strongly influenced by scholarship on the formation of the working and the middle classes. While these two classes were new in the nineteenth century, my view is that a self-conscious and cohesive upper class already existed in the eighteenth and the early nineteenth centuries but underwent major structural and cultural changes beginning in the first half of the nineteenth century and continuing in the Gilded Age. Sven Beckert, *The Monied Metropolis: New York City and the Consolidation of the American Bourgeoisie, 1850–1898* (Cambridge: Cambridge University Press, 2001), 1–14.

5. Examples included Beckert, *The Monied Metropolis*; Thomas Kessner, *Capital City: New York City and the Men Behind America's Rise to Economic Dominance, 1860–1900* (New York: Simon & Schuster, 2004); Eric Homberger, *Mrs. Astor's New York: Money and Social Power in a Gilded Age* (New Haven: Yale University Press, 2004); Ron Chernow, *Titan: The Life of John D. Rockefeller, Sr.* (New York: Random House, 1998); David Nasaw, *Andrew Carnegie* (New York: Penguin, 2006); David Cannadine, *Mellon: An American Life* (New York: Knopf, 2006); and Strouse, *Morgan*.

6. Population figures for New York are for Greater New York, comprising the five boroughs of Manhattan, Brooklyn, the Bronx, Queens, and Staten Island, which came into being with the consolidation of 1898. Joseph J. Salvo and Arun Peter Lobo, "Population," in *The Encyclopedia of New York City*, 2nd ed., ed. Kenneth T. Jackson (New Haven: Yale University Press, 2010), 1018–20; Campbell Gibson, *Population of the 100 Largest Cities and Other Urban Places in the United States: 1790 to 1990*, Population Division Working Paper No. 27, U.S. Bureau of the Census, Population Division (Washington, D.C.: n.p., 1998), table 14, accessed March 23, 2007, www.census.gov/population/www/documentation/twps0027; Paul M. Hohenberg and Lynn Hollen Less, *The Making of Modern Europe, 1000–1950* (Cambridge, Mass.: Harvard University Press, 1985), 11; Ira Rosenwaike, *Population History of New York City* (Syracuse, N.Y.: Syracuse University Press, 1972), 58; Tertius Chandler, *Rour Thousand Years of Ubran Growth: An Historical Census* (London: Edwin Mellen, 1987), 492; Tertius Chandler and Gerald Fox, *3000 Years of Urban Growth* (New York: Academic, 1974), 330; and U.S. Census Office, *Twelfth Census of the United States: 1900, Census Reports*, vol. 7, *Manufactures*, part 1, sect. 3, *Urban Manufactures* (Washington, D.C.: Government Printing Office, 1902), ccxxx.

7. "World's Tallest Buildings: Timeline of All Skyscrapers Holding the Title of Tallest Building in the World from 1890 to the Present," web project on Tallest Towers, Skyscraper Museum, New York N.Y., accessed June 26, 2008, www.skyscraper.org/TALLEST_TOWERS/talltest.htm; "Manhattan Timeformations," web project, Skyscraper Museum, New York N.Y., accessed June 26, 2008, www.skyscraper.org/timeformations/intro.htm#; U.S. Department of Treasury, Bureau of Statistics, *Foreign Commerce and Navigation of the United States, the Year Ending June 30, 1900* (Washington, D.C.: Government Printing Office, 1900), 50–51; Norman J. Brouwer, "Port of New York," in Jackson, *Encyclopedia of New York City*; and Clifton Hood, *772 Miles: The Building of the Subways and How They Transformed New York* (New York: Simon & Schuster, 1993), 11–18, 1022–26.

8. Western Union Company, *Annual Report, 1892* (New York: Kempster, 1892), 8; Susan B. Carter, editor in chief, *Historical Statistics of the United States: Earliest Times to the Present, Millennial Edition*, vol. 4, *Economic Sectors* (New York: Cambridge University Press, 2016), tables Dg8–21, "Domestic Telegraph Industry, Wire, Offices, Employees, and Finances, 1866–1987."

9. Richard Harding Davis, "Broadway," *Scribner's Magazine* 9 (May 1891): 588.

10. Henry Clews, "Delusions About Wall Street," *North American Review* 145 (October 1887): 412.

11. *Wall Street Journal*, January 2, 1896.

12. Lloyd Wendt, *The Wall Street Journal: The Story of Dow Jones & the Nation's Business Newspaper* (Chicago: Rand McNally, 1982), 30–42, 68; Youssef Cassis, *Capitals of Capital: A History of International Financial Centres, 1780–2005* (New York: Cambridge University Press, 2006), 75–77, 119; George Leland Leffler and Loring C. Farell, *The Stock Market*, 3rd rev. ed. (New York: Ronald, 1968), 91; and *New York Stock Exchange Directory, June 1st, 1889* (New York: Spanzenberg & Bishop, 1889), 7–40, 68–71.

13. Matthew Josephson, *The Robber Barons: The Great American Capitalists, 1861–1901* (New York: Harcourt, Brace, 1934; repr., New York: Harcourt, Brace & World, 1962), vi; Daniel T. Rogers, "In Search of Progressivism," *Reviews in American History* 10 (December 1982): 123–23; Richard R. John, *Network Nation: Inventing American Telecommunications* (Cambridge, Mass.: Harvard University Press, 2010), 156–58; and Richard R. John, "Robber Barons Redux: Antimonopoly Reconsidered," *Enterprise & Society* 13 (March 2012): 1–38.

14. *Adair County News*, January 3, 1900.

15. *Gainesville Star*, October 13, 1903; *Amador Ledger*, August 2, 1903; and *Deseret Evening News*, December 27, 1899.

16. James Bryce, "America Revisited: The Changes of a Quarter-Century: Part 1," *Outlook* 80 (March 25, 1905): 734.

17. Ibid., 733.

18. Ibid., 734.

19. Ibid., 734.

20. Arthur Warren, "Philip D. Armour: His Manner of Life, His Immense Enterprises in Trade and Philanthropy," *McClure's Magazine* 2 (February 1894): 260–81; Helen Churchill Candee, "Once Too Often," *Harper's Bazaar* 34 (February 16, 1901) 418–26; Joseph Edgar Chamberlin, "The Sleeplessness of John Colton Dow," *Century* 56 (June 1898): 308–12; Richard Wheatley, "The New York Stock Exchange," *Harper's New Monthly Magazine* 71 (November 1885): 830–53; Richard Wheatley, "The New York Chamber of Commerce," *Harper's New Monthly Magazine* 83 (September 1891): 502–13; Richard Wheatley, "The New York Produce Exchange," *Harper's New Monthly Magazine* 73 (July 1886): 189–218; Samuel Hopkins Adams, "The Realm of Enchantment," *McClure's Magazine* 23 (September 1904); 520–32; and Andrew Carnegie, *The Gospel of Wealth* (Bedford, Mass.: Applewood, 1998), 5–24.

21. "Cornelius Vanderbilt," *Outlook* 63 (September 23, 1899): 192.

22. Ibid., 192.

23. Ibid., 192.

24. *Wall Street Journal*, January 12, 1893.

25. The U.S. Census' categories of "trade and transportation" and "manufacturing and mechanical pursuits" are only approximate equivalents of commerce and manufacturing, respectively. U.S. Department of Commerce and Labor, Bureau of the Census, *Occupations at the Twelfth Census*, sect. 9, *Principal Cities* (Washington, D.C.: Government Printing Office, 1904), 457, 459.

26. U.S. Census Office, *Twelfth Census of the United States: 1900*, vol. 7, *Manufactures: States and Territories*, sect. 3, *Manufactures by States and Territories: Maine–Minnesota*, 388–90; sect. 5, *Manufactures by States and Territories: New York–Ohio*, 620–28; and sect. 6, *Manufactures by States and Territories: Oklahoma–Tennessee*, 792–95. Unlike the aggregate data cited above, these figures are for the five boroughs of Greater New York City.

27. James Bradley, "P. Lorillard and Company," in Jackson, *Encyclopedia of New York City*; Joseph Rishel, *Founding Families of Pittsburgh: The Evolution of a Regional Elite, 1760–1910* (Pittsburgh, Pa.: University of Pittsburgh Press, 1990), 1004; David Nasaw, *Andrew Carnegie* (New York: Penguin, 2006), 117, 70–118; Chernow, *Titan*, 218–23, 578–85; and Leon Stein, *The Triangle Fire* (New York: Carrol Graf, 1962), 44–46. Manufactures figure more prominently in Sven Beckert's analysis than in mine, largely because his bourgeoisie category is inclusive, while my upper class and economic elite categories are more exclusive. Beckert, *The Monied Metropolis*, 1–14, 52–55, 60–66, 242–43.

28. Cassis, *Capitals of Capital*, 114.

29. Ibid., 114–24; Mira Wilkins, *The History of Foreign Investment in the United States to 1914* (Cambridge, Mass.: Harvard University Press, 1989), 469–89.

30. Cassis, *Capitals of Capital*, 115–19; Margaret G. Myers, *The New York Money Market*, vol. 1, *Origins and Development* (New York: Columbia University Press,

1931), 234–50; Morton Rothstein, "New York Produce Exchange," in Jackson, *Encyclopedia of New York City*, 928–29; Moses Rothstein, "New York Cotton Exchange," in Jackson, *Encyclopedia of New York City*, 915; George Winslow, "New York Mercantile Exchange," in Jackson, *Encyclopedia of New York City*, 923–24; *Coffee, Sugar & Cocoa Exchanges, Inc., 1882–1982* (New York: n.p. [1982?]), unpaginated; New York Cotton Exchange, *New York Cotton Exchange, 1870–1945* (New York: n.p., 1945), 1–3; New York Produce Exchange, *Ceremony at the Laying of the Cornerstone of the New York Produce Exchange, June 6, 1882* (New York: Vaux and Roper, 1882), 4–11; Vincent P. Carosso *Investment Banking in America: A History* (Cambridge, Mass.: Harvard University Press, 1970), 18–77; Wilkins, *The History of Foreign Investment in the United States*, 469–89; Ron Chernow, *The House of Morgan: An American Banking Dynasty and the Rise of Modern Finance* (New York: Simon & Schuster, 1990), 70–161; Strouse, *Morgan*, 87–102; and Kathleen Burk, *Morgan Grenfell, 1838–1988: The Biograph of a Merchant Bank* (New York: Oxford University Press, 1989), 52–63.

31. New York Stock Exchange Archives, *Records of the New York Stock Exchange, 1817–1869* (New York: n.p., n.d.), 3, 54; George L. Leffler and Loring C. Farwell, *The Stock Market*, 3rd ed. (New York: England, 1870), 5–6, 11–12, 15, 23–24; and New York Stock Exchange, *Officers, Governing Committees, and Standing Committees, List of Members, with Their Annunciator Numbers and Addresses, Co-Partnerships, Branch Offices, Out-Of-Town Members, and Rules for Delivery* (New York: Searing and Watson, 1900), 8, 16, 18, 19, 25, 28–29.

32. Conservation of Human Resources Project (Columbia University), *The Corporate Headquarters Complex in New York City* (New York: n.p., 1977), 7–38. The figures on headquarters locations are for metropolitan areas, not cities.

33. Here I am indebted to Edwin G. Burrows and Mike Wallace, *Gotham: A History of New York City to 1898* (New York: Oxford, 1999), 1044–50. See also Chernow, *Titan*, 212–24; Kessner, *Capital City*, 234–37; Naomi R. Lamoreaux, *The Great Merger Movement in American Business, 1895–1904* (Cambridge: Cambridge University Press, 1985), 1–13; Conservation of Human Resources Project (Columbia University), *The Corporate Headquarters Complex*, 7–38; Chauncey G. Olinger Jr. and

Meghan Lalonde, "Advertising," in Jackson, *Encyclopedia of New York City*, 8–9; Kevin Kenny and Meghan Lalonde, "Lawyers," in Jackson, *Encyclopedia of New York City*, 725–27; Paul J. Miranti Jr., "Accounting," in Jackson, *Encyclopedia of New York City*, 5–6; and Olivier Zunz, *Making America Corporate, 1870–1920* (Chicago: University of Chicago Press, 1990), 1–10.

34. David C. Hammack, *Power and Society: Greater New York at the Turn of the Century* (New York: Russell Sage Foundation, 1982), 3–27; and Beckert, *The Monied Metropolis*, 1–14. See also Emily Rosenberg, *Spreading the American Dream: American Economic and Cultural Expansion, 1890–1945* (New York: Hill and Wang, 1982), 38.

35. Henry Clews, *Twenty-Eight Years in Wall Street* (New York: Irving, 1888), 88.

36. New York Stock Exchange Archives, *Records of the New York Stock Exchange*, 3, 54; Leffler and Farwell, *The Stock Market*, 91–95; *New York Times*, April 19, 22, and 23, 1903, June 10, 1904; *New York Tribune*, April 23, 1903; *Wall Street Journal*, April 23, 1903; and Margot Gayle and Michele Cohen, *The Art Commission and the Municipal Art Society's Guide to Manhattan's Outdoor Sculpture* (New York: Prentice-Hall, 1988), 26.

37. *New York Times*, April 23, 1903.

38. *Owingsville Outlook*, June 13, 1901.

39. Pierpoint Morgan's Engagement Diary for 1899, entries for March 24, June 16, 23, and 27, 1899, Archives of the Morgan Library and Museum, New York, N.Y. [hereafter MLM].

40. *John Swinton's Paper*, November 25, 1883.

41. Eugene V. Debs, "The American Movement," in *Debs: His Life, Writings, and Speeches* (Girard, Kans.: Appeal to Reason, 1908), 117.

42. William Jennings Bryan, *The Cross of Gold: Speech Delivered Before the National Democratic Convention at Chicago, July 9, 1896* (Lincoln: University of Nebraska Press, 1996), 28.

43. *New York Times*, August 8, 1896.

44. *Brooklyn Eagle*, August 13, 1896.

45. *Brooklyn Eagle*, August 21, September 25, November 8, 1896; *Columbia Register*, n. d., reprinted in *New York Times*, July 12; *New York Times*, July 12 and 13, September 23, October 23, November 3–9, 1898; *New York Tribune*, August 13, September 24, 1896; and Michael Kazin, *A Godly Hero: The Life of William Jennings Bryan* (New York: Knopf, 2006), 66–67.

46. T. De Witt Talmage, *Social Dynamite; Or, the Wickedness of Modern Society* (Chicago: Chicago Standard, 1887), 113, 123,

132, 144–60, 163, 202, 224, 338–47; May Talmage, comp. *Fifty Short Sermons by T. De Witt Talmage* (New York: Doran, 1923), 28–33; *Washington Post*, April 13, 1902; *New York Tribune*, April 13, 1902; *New York Times*, April 13, 1902; *Brooklyn Eagle*, January 9, 1882, September 15, 1884, November 1, 1886, October 13, 1888; *Berea Citizen*, June 13, 1901; *Owingsville Outlook*, June 13, 1901; *Richmond Dispatch*, February 7, 1902; *Adair County News*, April 17, 1901; and *Salt Lake Herald*, September 30, 1900. Another Protestant cleric who became a critic of corporate capitalism was Washington Gladden, a Congregationalist minister and a leader of the social gospel movement. See *New York Times*, August 27, 1899, March 31 and April 1, 26, and 28, 1905; and Chernow, *Titan*, 499–500.

47. Clews, "Delusions About Wall Street," *North American Review*, 411, 410. See also Clews, *Twenty-Eight Years in Wall Street*, 13–18. *New York Times*, February 1, 1923; and *Washington Post*, February 1, 1923. The phrase "dean of Wall Street" is from the *Washington Post* obituary.

48. Clews, "Delusions About Wall Street," *North American Review*, 410.

49. Ibid., 410–21. See also Clews, *The Wall Street Point of View* (New York: Silver, Burdett, 1900), 1–4.

50. *New York Times*, October 9, November 25 and 27, 1883; and *Brooklyn Eagle*, November 26, 1883.

51. Ibid.

52. Ibid.

53. Clifton Hood, "An Unusable Past," *Journal of Social History* 37 (Summer 2004): 883–913; "The Inauguration of Washington," *The Century* 37 (April 1889): 803–33; *Brooklyn Eagle*, November 25–26, 1883; *Souvenir of the Centennial Exhibition of Washington's Inauguration, held in New York City, April 29th and 30th, 1889* (New York: Nicholl & Roy, 1889), 3; "Editor's Easy Chair," *Harper's New Monthly Magazine* 78 (March 1889): 653–55; *Brooklyn Eagle*, April 28–29, and May 1, 1889; *New York Times*, January 12, April 30, and December 8 and 23, 1888, May 1, 1889.

54. *Pictorial New York and Brooklyn: A Guide to the Same and Vicinity* (New York: Smith, Bleakley, 1892), 25. See also Gustav Kobbé, *Kobbé's New York and Its Environs* (New York: Harper, 1891, 80–123; *The Sun's Guide to New York* (Jersey City, NJ: Jersey City Print Company, 1892), 2–12; and Cynthia M. Westover Alden, *Manhattan: Historic and Artistic* (New York: Morse, 1897), 34–35.

55. Kessner, *Captial City*, 238; Chernow, *Titan*, 344; Nasaw, *Andrew Carnegie*, 768; *New York Times*, May 28, 1901, May 26, June 30, and December 22, 1905, April 11, 1907; *Wall Street Journal*, January 3, 1903; and Moneyworth.com, accessed August 14, 2009, www.measuringworth.com/growth. Here I employ the historic standard of living as my measure of changes in relative value over time. Unskilled workers who were employed building the IRT subway earned $2 to $2.25 daily, and skilled workers made $2.50 daily. I base my calculations about their annual wages on the assumption that they put in 6 days a week and 50 weeks a year; obviously, most construction laborers could not count on such regular work. Hood, *722 Miles*, 85.

56. This statements is based on a count of every name in Social Register Association, *Social Register, New York, 1904*, 4–526. See also Social Register Association, *Social Register, 1887*, 2; and *New York Times*, January 2, 1887 and November 24, 1889.

57. Cromwell Childe, *New York: A Guide in Comprehensive Chapters* (New York: Brooklyn Daily Eagle, 1903), 29; *New York Times*, September 13, 1896.

58. *New York Times*, December 7, 1890 and March 8, 1891; *Washington Post*, November 1, 1896; *Wood's Illustrated Hand-Book to New York and Environs: A Guide for the Traveller or Resident* (New York: Carleton, 1873), 76–77; Childe, *New York*, 21; Sweetser, *How to Know New York*, 87–89; Nassau Boat Club of the City of New York, *Constitution, By-laws, Rules, and List of Members, etc.* (New York: n.p., 1892), unpaginated; and *Officers, Members, Constitution and By-Laws of the Union Club*, 88.

59. *Wood's Illustrated Hand-Book*, 76–77; Sweetser, *How to Know New York*, 87–89; *New York Times*, March 9, 1890, April 19 and March 15, 1891; "Personal," *Harpers' Bazaar* 30 (June 26, 1897): 535.

60. "Ladies' Clubs," *Harper's Bazaar* 18 (October 17, 1885), 666.

61. Ibid., 666. See also Lillian W. Betts, "The Value of Club Membership to the Individual Member," *Harper's Bazaar* 26 (April 29, 1893): 334–35; and Betts, "Club Loyalty," *Harper's Bazaar* 29 (June 20, 1896): 532.

62. Down-Town Club of Business Men's Republican Association of the City of New York, *Constitution, By-Laws, List of Members, etc.* (New York: n.p., 1889), 31–32; *Constitution, By-Laws, and Rules of the Harvard Club of New York City with List of Officers and Members* (New York: n.p., 1888), 24–27; *Officers, Members, Constitution and By-Laws of the Union Club*, 96–98; Porzelt, *Metropolitan Club*,

57–104; *New York Times*, February 12, 1886, February 13, 1890, September 6, 1891, February 25, 1894, May 9, 1897; Louise L. Stevenson, *The Victorian Homefront: American Thought and Culture, 1860–1880* (Ithaca, N.Y.: Cornell University Press, 1991), xxiii–xxxv; Jane Tompkins, *West of Everything: The Inner Life of the Westerns* (New York: Oxford University Press, 1992), 3–19, 43; and Ray Oldenburg, *The Great Good Place: Cafés, Coffee Shops, Community Centers, Beauty Parlors, General Stores, Bars, Hangouts, and How They Get You Through the Day*, 1st ed. (New York: Paragon, 1989), 16.

63. *New York Times*, June 17 and 18, 1924, March 4, 1928, October 8, 1949; Harper S. Mott Diary, 1886, entries for May 3 and 5, 1886, Library of the New-York Historical Society, New York, N.Y. [hereafter N-YHS]; Mott Diary, 1888, entries for February 3, 7, 18, and 22, March 1, 2, 7, 12, 14, and 15, 1888, N-YHS; James Norman Whitehouse Diary, 1890, entries for March 8, 15, and 19, April 12, May 26, June 20, 1890, N-YHS; Whitehouse Diary, 1892, entries for February 19 and 22, May 15, 1892, N-YHS; Whitehouse Diary, 1900, entries for August 15 and 17, 1900, N-YHS.

64. Morgan's Engagements Diary for 1899, entries for March 10, 11, 15, 16, 18, 20, and 25, April 1, May 18, June 16, June 23 and 26, July 20, September 14 and 24, October 7 and 12, November 9, 23, and 28, and December 2, 1899, MLM; Pierpont Morgan's Engagement Diary for 1904, entries for January 16, March 19 and 26, November 17, 19, 25, 26, and 29, December 10, 13, and 20, 1904, MLM; and Pierpont Morgan's Engagement Diary for 1907, entries for January 6 and 2, 1906, MLM.

65. *New York Times*, March 15, 1891.

66. Betts, "The Value for Club Membership," 334–35; "Club Loyalty," 352.

67. *New York Times*, September 13, 1896.

68. Ibid.

69. E. Digby Baltzell, *Puritan Boston and Quaker Philadelphia* (New York: Free Press, 1979; repr., New Brunswick, N.J.: Transaction, 1996), 31–55; Betty G. Farrell, *Elite Families: Class and Power in Nineteenth-Century Boston* (Albany: State University of New York Press, 1993), 1–19; Rishel, *Founding Families of Pittsburgh*, 3–13; Kathryn Allamong Jacob, *Capital Elites: High Society in Washington, D.C., After the Civil War* (Washington, D.C.: Smithsonian Institution Press, 1995), 1–13; and Frederic Cople Jaher, *The Urban Establishment: Upper Strata in Boston, New York, Charleston, Chicago, and Los*

Angeles (Urbana: University of Illinois Press, 1982), 1–13.

70. *Town Topics and the American Queen*, March 28 and April 11, 1885; *Town Topics*, November 17, 1887; *New York Times*, November 13, 1876, May 28, 1885, January 17, May 26, and April 18, 1887, May 26, 1888, December 5, 1890, May 8 and 29, April 5, and December 30, 1891, December 6, 1898, May 9, 1897; Sweetser, *How to Know New York*, 87–89; and *Officers, Members, Constitution and By-Laws of the Union Club*, 13–75. For clubs in other cities, see Alexander W. Williams, *A Social History of the Greater Boston Clubs* ([Boston?]: Barrie, 1970), 16–30; Grace Dwight Potter, "The Social Life of American Cities: Syracuse," *Town Country* (June 7, 1902): 13–19; Union League Club of Chicago, *The Spirit of the Union League Club, 1879–1926* (Chicago: The Club, 1926); Clover Club of Philadelphia, *The Clover Club of Philadelphia, 1882–1904: Souvenir of the 22d Anniversary* (Philadelphia: Burbank, 1904); Metropolitan Club of the City of Washington, *Financial History to January 1, 1897; Report of the Executive Committee* (Washington, D.C.: n.p., 1897); Martha Goode Anderson, "The Social Life of American Cities: Atlanta," *Town & Country* (December 27, 1902): 10–14; and Edwin Fairfax Naulty, "Philadelphia Fox Hunters," *Town & Country* (January 3, 1903): 10–12. See also Robert J. Brugger, *The Maryland Club: A History of Food and Friendship in Baltimore, 1857_1997* (Baltimore: Maryland Club, 1998), 33–63; and Lisa Holton, *For Members Only: A History and Guide to Chicago's Oldest Private Clubs* (Chicago: Lake Claremont, 2008), vii–23.

71. *New York Times*, March 22, 1891.

72. *Town Topics*, February 2, 1888.

73. *Officers, Members, Constitution and By-Laws of the Union Club*, 85–88, 93–93; *Constitution, By-Laws and Rules of the Harvard Club of New York City, with the List of Officers and Members* (New York: n. p., 1888), 17–18; Down-Town Club of Business Men's Republican Association of the City of New York, *Constitution, By-laws, Rules, and List of Members, etc.*: unpaginated; Porzelt, *Metropolitan Club*, 108.

74. *New York Times*, April 15, 1893, January 7, 1895; and *Town Topics*, April 19, 1888.

75. *Town Topics*, April 19, 1888.

76. Louis Auchincloss, *A Voice from Old New York: A Memoir of My Youth* (Boston: Houghton Mifflin Harcourt, 2010), 6.

77. *New York Times*, April 19, December 6 and 7, 1891, June 5, 1896, March 21, 1897, October 30, 1926.

78. New York Botanical Garden, *Bulletin of the New York Botanical Garden*, 1, no. 1 (April 15, 1896): 8–18; and *New York Times*, July 6, 1911, December 21 and 22, 1938.

79. Maureen E. Montgomery, *Displayed Women: Spectacles of Leisure in Edith Wharton's New York* (New York: Routledge, 1998), 60.

80. *New York Tribune*, January 3, 1904; and Crowninshield, *Manners for the Metropolis*, 29–36, 53.

81. Maud C. Cook, *Social Etiquette; Or, Manners and Customs of Polite Society* (Philadelphia: Keller & Kirkpatrick, 1896), 358.

82. Pauline Robinson Scrapbook, 1894–1912, entries for 1904, N-YHS; and Florence Adele Sloane, *Maverick in Mauve: The Diary of a Romantic Age*, ed. Louis Auchincloss (Garden City, N.Y.: Doubleday, 1983), 22–35, 76–84.

83. *Club Women of New York, 1904* (New York: Mail and Express, c.1904), 47, 55–57, 70–71; Mary I. Wood, *The History of the General Federation of Women's Clubs, for the First Twenty-Two Years of Its Organization* (New York: General Federation of Women's Clubs, 1912), 27–31; *The Junior League for the Promotion of Neighborhood Work, Annual Report 1913* (New York: n.p., 1913), 8–11; *The Young Women's Christian Association of the City of New York, Statement of Work for 1916* (New York: n.p., c. 1916), 5–6; and *New York Times*, February 21, 1905, May 16, 1911, November 30, 1913, September 2, 1916, May 3, 1943, March 20, 1952, February 15, 1954, July 3, 1961.

DOCUMENTS FOR PART IV

4.1 VESEY SLAVE REVOLT, CHARLESTON, SOUTH CAROLINA (1822)

Source: *An Account of the Late Intended Insurrection among a Portion of the Blacks of this City*. Second Edition. (Charleston: Corporation of Charleston, Printed by A.E. Miller, 1822). Courtesy of the American Antiquarian Society, Worcester, Massachusetts.

EDITORS' INTRODUCTION

This pamphlet, most likely written by Charleston Mayor James Hamilton, Jr., and published by the city of Charleston, was meant to inform white Charlestonians about the details of a slave uprising. According to the pamphlet, one slave reported a planned uprising of other slaves and free blacks for June 16, 1822, which led to a series of arrests (eventually numbering 131 in total). Among the free blacks arrested was Denmark Vesey who had come to the United States in 1781 as a slave and had purchased his freedom with the winnings of a lottery. Government officials executed Vesey and thirty-five others to discourage any further disturbances. At that time, the majority of people in Charleston were African American, and thus white officials remained vigilant about possible threats. Documents related to the Vesey uprising are thin, and some historians even question the existence of a conspiracy.[i] **[For another supposed urban slave rebellion see Document 3.1, Conspiracy... For Burning the City of New York... (1744).]**

VESEY SLAVE REVOLT, CHARLESTON, SOUTH CAROLINA (1822)

On Thursday the 27th, Denmark Vesey, a free black man, was brought before the Court for trial,

Assisted by his Counsel, G.W. Cross Esq.

It is perhaps somewhat remarkable, that at this stage of the investigation, although several witnesses had been examined, the *atrocious* guilt of *Denmark Vesey* had not been as yet fully unfolded. From the testimony of most of the witnesses, however, the Court found enough, and amply enough, to warrant the sentence of death, which, on the 28th, they passed on him. But every subsequent step in the progress of the trials of others, lent new confirmation to his overwhelming guilt, and placed him beyond a doubt, on the criminal eminence of having been the individual, in whose bosom the nefarious scheme was first engendered. There is ample reason for believing, that this project was not, with him, of recent origin, for it was said, he had spoken of it for upwards of four years.

These facts of his guilt the journals of the court will disclose—that no man can be

---

Sources differ as to the date of the planned uprising, and some point to an initial date of mid-July, which was moved up due to secrecy concerns. A few place Vesey's immigration to the United States in 1771 rather than 1781. Others question the existence of a conspiracy at all, wondering if the investigations, trial, and executions were staged in order to impart order in Charleston. See Richard C. Wade, *Slavery in the Cities: The South 1820–1860* (Oxford: Oxford University Press, 1967), Thomas Wentworth Higginson, *Denmark Vesey, The Atlantic* (originally published in *The Atlantic Monthly*, June 1861; Volume 7, Number 44, pages 728–744), http://www.theatlantic.com/issues/1861jun/higgin.htm (January 12, 2009), John Lofton, *Denmark Vesey's Revolt* (Kent, OH: Kent State University Press, 1983), Edward A. Pearson, editor, *Designs Against Charleston: The Trial Record of the Denmark Vesey Slave Conspiracy of 1822* (Chapel Hill: University of North Carolina Press, 1999), David Robertson, *Denmark Vesey* (New York: Knopf, 1999), Robert S. Starobin, ed., *Denmark Vesey: The Slave Conspiracy of 1822* (New York: Prentice-Hall, 1970).

proved to have spoken of or urged the insurrection prior to himself. All the channels of communication and intelligence are traced back to him. His house was the place appointed for the secret meetings of the conspirators, at which he was invariably a leading and influential member; animating and encouraging the timid, by the hopes of prospects of success; removing the scruples of the religious, by the grossest prostitution and perversion of the sacred oracles, and inflaming and confirming the resolute, by all the savage fascinations of blood and booty. [...]

He was sentenced for execution of the 2d of July.

4.2 TREDEGAR AND ARMORY IRON WORKS, RICHMOND, VIRGINIA (1847)

Source: *The Richmond Inquirer*, May 29, 1847 (including reprints from the *Richmond Republican* and *The Daily Richmond Whig*). Courtesy of the American Antiquarian Society, Worcester, Massachusetts.

EDITORS' INTRODUCTION

Historian John T. Cumbler's essay, "From Milling to Manufacturing: From Villages to Mill Towns," explores the rise of industrialization in New England. **[See Essay 6.1.]** While that region was the birthplace of American manufacturing, other sections of the country also developed factories. Even the pre-Civil War South turned to factory production in a limited scope, often with the use of slave labor. In fact, although many contemporary scholars have argued that slavery and factory work were antithetical, in some cases slavery made southern industry possible. Historian Kathleen Bruce, in her study of Virginia iron ore manufacturing, argues that it was precisely because of slave labor that the Richmond industry survived. Richmond iron manufactures hired skilled white laborers from the North, who trained slaves to work within plants. Bruce concludes that the Virginia iron industry transformed after the 1850s into an industry strictly serving the South. She writes that:

> The climax of Virginian iron manufacture came in 1861, when, though small in volume, it entered for four years upon the national stage of American history, since without it and without the allied industry of Richmond coal, which had been active from the eighteenth century, it is difficult to see how the Confederacy could have persisted.[i]

The following document contains a series of articles culled from several newspapers all reprinted on a single day in *The Richmond Inquirer*. We learn in this piece that many white factory workers had qualms about working side-by-side with slaves. Some workers had come from northern industries for the factory jobs. Free workmen balked at teaching their skill-set to men in bondage, fearing they would not be hired by other mills who might blacklist them for sharing industry secrets across racial lines. They also worried that by training less-expensive workers, they would ultimately be fired in favor of their enslaved trainees.

i Kathleen Bruce, *Virginia Iron Manufacture in the Slave Era* (New York: Augustus M. Kelley, 1968), vii–viii. There were also other factories that employed slaves. See Charles B. Dew, *Bond of Iron: Master and Slave at Buffalo Forge* (New York: W. W. Norton & Company, 1994) which chronicles the iron-making operations of Buffalo Forge, in Rockbridge County, Virginia.

TREDEGAR AND ARMORY IRON WORKS, RICHMOND, VIRGINIA (1847)

In common with our associates of the press, we deeply regret the unfortunate controversy which has recently occurred between the workmen of the Tredegar and new Armory Iron Works and their employers. We quote the publications which we find in the *Republican* of Thursday, to show the origin of a movement which our whole community must condemn:

Richmond, May 23d, 1847

Resolved, That we, the Workmen of Tredegar Iron Works, do pledge ourselves that we will not go to work, unless the negroes be removed from the Puddling Furnace, at the new mill—like-wise from the Squeezer and Rolls in the old mill.

2d. *Resolved*, further, That we, the Puddlers, will not work for less than $4.50 per ton.

(Signed by the Puddlers of Tredegar Works.)

Resolved, That we, the Puddlers of the New Mill, will act on the above resolution.

(Signed by the Puddlers of Armory Works.)

We, the Helpers of Puddling Furnaces, do act with the above resolution.

(Signed by the Helpers at Puddling Furnaces.)

Richmond, May 22d, 1847

We, the Heaters, do stand out for one dollar per ton for all sizes.

(Signed by the Heaters.)

We, the Rollers, do not intend to work until the above resolution is complied with.

(Signed by the Rollers.)

And the following note was communicated with the resolutions, to Mr. J.R. Anderson, the lessee of the Tredegar Works:

Mr. Anderson and Managers:

Gentlemen—You need not light up the Furnaces Monday, nor any time, until you comply with our resolution.

Two questions are raised in the above resolutions, viz: a demand for higher wages and the employment of negroes, but from the following additional resolution adopted on Wednesday, it is evident that the latter is the only point in issue. Indeed, it is emphatically avowed in so many words:

"At a called meeting of the Workmen of the Tredegar Iron Works,–

"*Resolved*, That whereas it has been rumored that we, the said workmen, intended to raise a mob to injury of our employers, in consequence of the difficulty that has arisen between us and the said employers, from their wishing to employ and instruct colored people in our stead in the said Tredegar Iron Works, the undersigned, workmen of the said Tredegar Works, take this method of showing to the public that we have not attempted to raise a mob, (as was rumored,) or otherwise to injure any of our employers—*having no other object in view at the time that we resolved to strike, but that of trying to prohibit the employment of colored people on the said Works.*"

On Wednesday Mr. Anderson addressed the following letter to his workmen:

To my late Workmen at the Tredegar Iron Works.

On Saturday last, I received by the hands of Gatewood Talley, information that you had determined, by a mutual combination, that you would not work for me again until I had discharged my negroes from the Squeezer and Puddle Rolls, where they had been working several years, and until the "Armory Iron Company" had discharged theirs from the puddling furnaces—and that the Puddlers and Heaters required their pay to be increased. I requested Mr. Talley to say to you, that I regretted that you had given up constant employment at good wages, always promptly paid in cash, but that I fully recognized the right of any individual to leave my employment at any time —at the same time, I had no idea of relinquishing my right to discharge or employ any one [sic] at my pleasure—that I had not designed to put negroes to puddling at the Tredegar works, but that now I should be compelled by your quitting my employment to do so, and that I had never intended to discharge any of my hands who did their duty—that in reference to the price of puddling, I had advanced the price two or three years ago when iron advanced; and when iron fell last summer, I might with propriety have reduced the wages, but have not done so to this day—that the heaters and puddlers, who complained of low wages, could earn with ordinary diligence, from $2 to $2.75, whilst the rollers may earn from $3 to $5 per day—and that I could not accede to any demand they had made. If I were to yield to your demands, I would be giving up the rights guaranteed to me by the constitution and laws of the State in which we live. This, I hope, you will never expect me to do; and having heard nothing further from you since my reply was conveyed to you on the 22d inst., I must infer that you do not intend to work for me any longer. I therefore give you notice, that I wish all who occupy my houses to give me possession of them as soon as practicable, and I have given directions for your accounts to be made out. I will waive all claim on account of the usual notice not being given, and will, in advance of the usual pay day, pay each man all that is due to him as soon as he delivers to me the possession of his house. Those who do not occupy my houses will be paid off to-morrow, and all I have to add, is, that you will bear in mind that you have *discharged yourselves*—that I gave assurance beforehand to two of your members, Henry Thomas and Lott Joy, that I would never discharge one of you who continued to do his duty to me; and now, having endeavored to do my duty as your employer, I wish that you may, one and all of you, never regret that you have given up the employment you had from me.

Your obedient servant,

J.R. Anderson

Tredegar Iron Works, May 26, 1847
These are all the facts which have been made public—and we cannot entertain the least doubt that the community, with a knowledge of what has transpired, will fully sustain Mr. Anderson in his just, liberal and proper course. As public journalists, we feel called upon to give an expression of what we deem public sentiment upon a question involving the value of slave labor and the rights and privileges of masters and employers. The principle set up in this case is not confined to Mr. Anderson or the Tredegar Works alone, but is of a general application to all kinds of business, and is, therefore, a matter of vital interest to the whole community. If it be sanctioned, it will render slave property utterly valueless, and place employers in the power of those employed, the latter dictating to the former what species of labor they shall employ in their service. We agree with the *Whig*, which says:

"It is probably that this view of the subject had not presented itself to the minds of the heretofore orderly, industrious and worthy workmen at the Tredegar works, and that they have permitted their overwrought feelings to carry them beyond the bounds of prudence and propriety. Whether this be so or not, however, it is not less certain that the claim they set up, (as we told one of them personally a few days ago, who desired us to insert an article in vindication of their position, which we respectfully declined,) is wholly inadmissible in this latitude. The right of employers to select such kinds of labor as they may prefer, is one of which the law itself cannot deprive them—much less combinations of individuals, formed either for the purpose of intimidation, or with the less criminal, though unworthy design of inducing, for other reasons, acquiescence in their demands. The sympathies of all communities are naturally and properly most generally in favor of the hard working-man, whose toils ought to be fairly requited; but in *this* community, no combination, formed for the *purpose* avowed by the authors of the recent strike, can receive the slightest toleration. We hope that better counsels and wiser determinations may prevail among the workmen—and that we may soon hear that the harmony and good feeling heretofore existing between them and their employers has been entirely restored."

4.3 DEBATES ON CHINESE IMMIGRATION (1876)

Source: *Immigration of Chinese, Speech of Hon. Aaron A. Sargent of California, In the Senate of the United States*, May 2, 1876. Courtesy of the American Antiquarian Society, Worcester, Massachusetts.

EDITORS' INTRODUCTION

During the nineteenth century, debates about immigration comprised one of the most contentious political issues, especially in cities, where immigrants congregated in high numbers. Organized labor, nativists (those with prejudice against anyone not born in the United States), and others joined the movement to curb immigration. The newcomers themselves, and those who befriended them, made repeated arguments for allowing immigration. In 1882, however, the United States passed the Chinese Exclusion Act, the first federal law targeting one particular immigrant group. Although the Chinese comprised just 0.002 percent of the United States population, racial difference and the lack of cultural understanding strengthened white prejudice. California, where just over 40 percent of the 148,000 Chinese in the United States lived, stood at the forefront of this battle. One of the charges against the Chinese was that they were working as "coolie," laborers, a type of slavery or indentured servitude. The extent of this worry far exceeded the reality, and free Chinese laborers were routinely maligned as coolies by their detractors. Chinese women were repeatedly categorized as prostitutes, and indeed Chinese prostitution constituted a rampant problem, as the majority of Chinese men arrived in the United States as bachelors or left wives behind in China.

The first item is an excerpt from a speech given on May 2, 1876 by United States Senator Aaron A. Sargent of California. The month prior, Sargent urged that President Ulysses S. Grant "cause negotiations to be entered upon with the Chinese government to effect such change in the existing treaty between the United States and China as will lawfully permit the application of restrictions upon the great influx of Chinese subjects to this country."[i] The ban against Chinese immigration was passed in 1882 and not lifted until 1943, when Chinese aligned with the Allies in the Second World War and the United States allowed Chinese immigrants into the country again in very small numbers. The second document, written under pseudonym Friends of Right, Justice, and Humanity and was attributed to Augustus Layres, and signed simply "—X."

DEBATES ON CHINESE IMMIGRATION (1876)

But when the question is as to the introduction of large numbers of people into the country whose admission is not a matter of right, but of policy, then we ought to consider whether they are a disturbing element, and whether exclusion is not the best and surest prevention against disorders which are difficult to cure when once fastened upon us.

Is the desire of the Chinese to select our country as a place of residence so clear a natural right that, rather than gainsay it, we are willing to submit to the disorders which must grow out of the prejudice known to exist against them? As to this prejudice, is it not based upon some reason? I intend to state some of the objections to their coming which account for the bitter opposition shown in California and elsewhere where they have already appeared in numbers. Are the people of the East quite certain that, if the Chinese

---

i *Immigration of Chinese, Speech of Hon. Aaron A. Sargent of California, In the Senate of the United States*, May 2, 1876.

were to land in their midst in the proportion of one in every eight of the population of several States, they would be as easy to the future as now? They should try to put themselves in our place, and deal with this question as if they too had among them this strange and dangerously unassimilative people, increasing in numbers from year to year.

GENERAL EXCLUSION ONLY REMEDY FOR EVILS

The importation of coolies is now forbidden by statute. But it is found impossible to reach the cases of violation of its provisions, because neither side will disclose the existence of cooly [sic] contracts.

The importation of females for immoral purposes is also forbidden by statute. But the law is a dead-letter, because of the impossibility of obtaining proof of its violation.

And yet it is the almost universal conviction of Californians that nine-tenths of the Chinese male immigration is in violation of the former, and ninety-nine hundredths of the female immigration is in violation of the latter statue. There can be no remedy but general exclusion; and the policy, justice, and necessity of that supreme measure I propose to discuss.

The resolution before the Senate looks to a modification of certain provisions of the existing treaty between the United States and China. Those provisions are as follows:

ARTICLE V

The United States of America and the Emperor of China cordially recognize the inherent and inalienable right of man to change his home and allegiance, and also the mutual advantage of free migration and emigration of their citizens and subjects respectively from the one country to the other, for purposes of curiosity, of trade, or to any other foreign country, without their free and voluntary consent, respectively.

ARTICLE VI

Citizens of the United States visiting or residing in China shall enjoy the same privileges, immunities, and exemptions, in respect to travel or residence, as may there be enjoyed by the citizens or subjects of the most favored nation; and, reciprocally, Chinese subjects visiting or residing in the United States shall enjoy the same privileges, immunities, and exemptions, in their respect to travel or residence, as may there be enjoyed by the citizens or subjects of the most favored nation. But nothing herein contained shall be held to confer naturalization upon citizens of the United States in China, nor upon the subjects of China in the United States.

The question of the restriction of Chinese immigration to the United States concerns at present the people of the Pacific coast more than it does Eastern communities. Our people are not always wise or deliberate in their treatment of the subject, and their irritability often leads them to extravagance of speech and exhibitions of heated prejudices which produce an effect at the East the very opposite of what they intend. The unreasonableness, or even violence, of discontented people does not, however, make the cause of their discontent any the less important. The remedy for the evils, if evils they are, of Chinese immigration lies entirely in the hands of the Federal Government. The treaty-making power must first be appealed to seek such modifications of our treaty with China as will pave the way for legislation under the power of Congress to regulate commerce. It is very desirable, therefore, that all appeals to the Federal Government should be clearly based on reason, humanity, and national interest. The Chinese are to a very limited extent the objects of hatred and prejudice east of the Rocky mountains, and all arguments against their influx must be free from the familiar cries with which place-hunting demagogues assail the ears of mobs in California. That the presence of Chinese in this country in any considerable numbers is most undesirable is my firm conviction, as I think it is of the great body of those in California who aid in the protection of them in their treaty rights. The question of national duty in the premises comes to as at the threshold of any discussion, and we are obliged to consider it.

Source: Augustus Layres (writing under the pseudonym Friends of Right, Justice, and Humanity), *Facts Upon the Other Side of the*

Chinese Question, With a Memorial to the President of the U.S., From Representative Chinamen in America, 1876. Courtesy of the American Antiquarian Society, Worcester, Massachusetts.

SUNDRY CHARGES AND CONCLUSION

We dismiss as unworthy of consideration the charges that "*The Chinese are pagans; are not a homogeneous race, do not adopt our manners, our food, our style of dress, etc.*"

It will be a sad day, indeed, for this great Republic, when it shall prescribe personal qualities of this kind as conditions to immigration. America will again become wild then, and her qualifications for simple residents as recommended by the Anti-Chinese Committee are unknown even in the most despotic countries.

The Chinese are accused of being *filthy, diseased, immoral,* and *vicious* people, who fill our prisons and crowd our hospitals.

The Report of the Board of Directors of the California State Prison, for 1875, gives the total number of prisoners as 1,083, of whom only 187 are Chinese, notwithstanding they find but little mercy in our courts. The County Hospital Report shows also but a small proportion of Chinese patients. The City Record of mortality among them is very small, and Dr. Toland has testified that they are personally clean.

But if these evils exist, why do not the Municipal Authorities remedy them? Legislation is not exhausted as it is alleged, only faithful police officers who do not accept bribes are required, as shown by the investigation.

Again, if these charges be true, how does it happen that the Chinese have "*monopolized*" as you say, a great portion of the domestic and commercial service, and in the very best houses, for nearly twenty years? Can it be that our wealthy and honored citizens will confide their households to filthy, diseased, immoral, and criminal servants? Either our citizens are not what they seem or it is not true what you say in regard to the Chinese.

But it is enough. This Anti-Chinese Crusade, started by sectarian fanaticism, encouraged by personal prejudice and ambition for political capital, has already culminated in personal attack, abuse, and incendiarism against the inoffensive Chinese. Anti-Coolie Clubs are now arming and preparing to follow the late example of the people of Antioch, who have banished the Chinese and burned their quarters.

It is high time that the Municipal, State, and National authorities, in common with law abiding citizens, should awake to the imminent danger that threatens to break the peace and to disgrace both State and nation. They must assert their authority in defense of our treaty obligations with China, for the protection of Chinese emigrants and in behalf of law and order.
—X

4.4 THE MIXED CROWD (1890)

Jacob Riis

Source: Jacob Riis, *How the Other Half Lives: Studies Among the Tenements of New York* (New York: Scribner & Sons, 1890).

EDITORS' INTRODUCTION

Jacob Riis (1849–1914), a Danish immigrant who came to the United States in 1870, documented the American immigrant experience in his short stories, muckraking journalism, and his important books *How the Other Half Lives* (1890), *The Children of the Poor* (1892), *The Making of an American* (1901), *The Battle With the Slums* (1902), and *Children of the Tenements* (1903). Riis brought critical attention to the condition of overcrowded, impoverished neighborhoods. His photographs, taken with a magnesium flash, literally and figuratively brought life to the dark side of urban life. Riis' photographs and writings allowed middle-class and upper-class Americans, not otherwise acquainted with the slums, a way to see how other Americans lived. Despite his good intentions, Riis' writing betrayed clear biases against many ethnic groups through the use of derogatory language and excessive stereotypes.

THE MIXED CROWD (1890)

Chapter III

When once I asked the agent of a notorious Fourth Ward alley how many people might be living in it I was told: One hundred and forty families, one hundred Irish, thirty-eight Italian, and two that spoke the German tongue. Barring the agent herself, there was not a native-born individual in the court. The answer was characteristic of the cosmopolitan character of lower New York, very nearly so of the whole of it, wherever it runs to alleys and courts. One may find for the asking an Italian, a German, a French, African, Spanish, Bohemian, Russian, Scandinavian, Jewish, and Chinese colony. Even the Arab, who peddles "holy earth" from the Battery as a direct importation from Jerusalem, has his exclusive preserves at the lower end of Washington Street. The one thing you shall vainly ask for in the chief city of America is a distinctively American community. There is none; certainly not among the tenements. Where have they gone to, the old inhabitants? I put the question to one who might fairly be presumed to be of the number, since I had found him sighing for the "good old days" when the legend "no Irish need apply" was familiar in the advertising columns of the newspapers. He looked at me with a puzzled air. "I don't know," he said. "I wish I did. Some went to California in '49, some to the war and never came back. The rest, I expect, have gone to heaven, or somewhere. I don't see them 'round here.

Whatever the merit of the good man's conjectures, his eyes did not deceive him. They are not here. In their place has come this queer conglomerate mass of heterogeneous elements, ever striving and working like whiskey and water in one glass, and with the like result: final union and a prevailing taint of whiskey. The once unwelcome Irishman has been followed in his turn by the Italian, the Russian Jew, and the Chinaman, and has himself taken a hand at opposition, quite as bitter and quite as ineffectual, against these later hordes. Wherever these have gone they have crowded him out, possessing the block, the street, the ward with their denser swarms. But the Irishman's revenge is complete. Victorious in defeat over his recent as over his more ancient foe, the one who opposed his coming no less than the one who drove him out, he dictates to both their politics, and, secure in possession of the offices, returns the native his greeting with interest, while collecting the rents of the Italian whose house he has bought with the profits of his saloon. As a landlord he is picturesquely autocratic. An amusing instance of his methods came under my notice while writing these lines. An inspector of the Health Department found an Italian family paying a man with a Celtic name twenty-five dollars a month for three small rooms in a ramshackle rear tenement—more than twice what they were worth—and expressed his astonishment to the tenant, an ignorant Sicilian laborer. He replied that he had once asked the landlord to reduce the rent, but he would not do it.

"Well! What did he say?" asked the inspector.

"'Damma, man!' he said; 'if you speaka thata way to me, I fira you and your things in the streeta.'" And the frightened Italian paid the rent.

Injustice to the Irish landlord it must be said that like an apt pupil he was merely showing forth the result of the schooling he had received, re-enacting, in his own way, the scheme of the tenements. It is only his frankness that shocks. The Irishman does not naturally take kindly to tenement life, though with characteristic versatility he adapts himself to its conditions at once. It does violence, nevertheless, to the best that is in him, and for that very reason of all who come within its sphere soonest corrupts him. The result is a sediment, the product of more than a generation in the city's slums, that, as distinguished from the larger body of his class, justly ranks at the foot of tenement dwellers, the so-called "low Irish."

It is not to be assumed, of course, that the whole body of the population living in the tenements, of which New Yorkers are in the habit of speaking vaguely as "the poor," or even the larger part of it, is to be classed as vicious or as poor in the sense of verging on beggary. New York's wage-earners have no other place to live, more is the pity. They are truly poor for having no better homes; waxing poorer in purse as the exorbitant rents to which they are tied, as ever was serf to soil, keep rising. The wonder is that they are not all corrupted, and speedily, by their surroundings. If, on the contrary, there be a steady working up, if not out of the slough, the fact is a powerful argument for the optimist's belief that the world is, after all, growing better, not worse, and would go far toward disarming apprehension, were it not for the steadier growth of the sediment of the slums and its constant menace. Such an impulse toward better things there certainly is. The German rag-picker of thirty years ago, quite as low in the scale as his Italian successor, is the thrifty tradesman or prosperous farmer of to-day.[1]

The Italian scavenger of our time is fast graduating into exclusive control of the corner fruit-stands, while his black-eyed boy monopolizes the boot-blacking industry in which a few years ago he was an intruder. The Irish hod-carrier in the second generation has become a bricklayer, if not the Alderman of his ward, while the Chinese coolie is in almost exclusive possession of the laundry business. The reason is obvious. The poorest immigrant comes here with the purpose and ambition to better himself and, given half a chance, might be reasonably expected to make the most of it. To the false plea that he prefers the squalid houses in which his kind are housed there

could be no better answer. The truth is, his half chance has too long been wanting, and for the bad result he has been unjustly blamed.

As emigration from east to west follows the latitude, so does the foreign influx in New York distribute itself along certain well-defined lines that waver and break only under the stronger pressure of a more gregarious race or the encroachments of inexorable business. A feeling of dependence upon mutual effort, natural to strangers in a strange land, unacquainted with its language and customs, sufficiently accounts for this.

The Irishman is the true cosmopolitan immigrant. All-pervading, he shares his lodging with perfect impartiality with the Italian, the Greek, and the "Dutchman," yielding only to sheer force of numbers, and objects equally to them all. A map of the city, colored to designate nationalities, would show more stripes than on the skin of a zebra, and more colors than any rainbow. The city on such a map would fall into two great halves, green for the Irish prevailing in the West Side tenement districts, and blue for the Germans on the East Side. But intermingled with these ground colors would be an odd variety of tints that would give the whole the appearance of an extraordinary crazy-quilt. From down in the Sixth Ward, upon the site of the old Collect Pond that in the days of the fathers drained the hills which are no more, the red of the Italian would be seen forcing, its way northward along the line of Mulberry Street to the quarter of the French purple on Bleecker Street and South Fifth Avenue, to lose itself and reappear, after a lapse of miles, in the "Little Italy" of Harlem, east of Second Avenue. Dashes of red, sharply defined, would be seen strung through the Annexed District, northward to the city line. On the West Side the red would be seen overrunning the old Africa of Thompson Street, pushing the black of the negro rapidly uptown, against querulous but unavailing protests, occupying his home, his church, his trade and all, with merciless impartiality. There is a church in Mulberry Street that has stood for two generations as a sort of milestone of these migrations. Built originally for the worship of staid New Yorkers of the "old stock," it was engulfed by the colored tide, when the draft-riots drove the negroes out of reach of Cherry Street and the Five Points. Within the past decade the advance wave of the Italian onset reached it, and to-day the arms of United Italy adorn its front. The negroes have made a stand at several points along Seventh and Eighth Avenues; but their main body, still pursued by the Italian foe, is on the march yet, and the black mark will be found overshadowing to-day many blocks on the East Side, with One Hundredth Street as the centre, where colonies of them have settled recently.

Hardly less aggressive than the Italian, the Russian and Polish Jew, having over run the district between Rivington and Division Streets, east of the Bowery, to the point of suffocation, is filling, the tenements of the old Seventh Ward to the river front, and disputing with the Italian every foot of available space in the back alleys of Mulberry Street. The two races, differing hopelessly in much, have this in common: they carry their slums with them wherever they go, if allowed to do it. Little Italy already rivals its parent, the "Bend," in foulness. Other nationalities that begin at the bottom make a fresh start when crowded up the ladder. Happily both are manageable, the one by rabbinical, the other by the civil law. Between the dull gray of the Jew, his favorite color, and the Italian red, would be seen squeezed in on the map a sharp streak of yellow, marking the narrow boundaries of Chinatown. Dovetailed in with the German population, the poor but thrifty Bohemian might be picked out by the sombre hue of his life as of his philosophy, struggling against heavy odds in the big human beehives of the East Side. Colonies of his people extend northward, with long lapses of space, from below the Cooper Institute more than three miles. The Bohemian is the only foreigner with any considerable representation in the city who counts no wealthy man of his race, none who has not to work hard for a living, or has got beyond the reach of the tenement.

Down near the Battery the West Side emerald would be soiled by a dirty stain, spreading rapidly like a splash of ink on a sheet of blotting paper, headquarters of the Arab tribe, that in a single year has swelled from the original dozen to twelve hundred, intent, every mother's son, on trade and barter. Dots and dashes of color here and there would show where the Finnish sailors worship their djumala (God), the Greek pedlars the ancient name of their race, and the Swiss the goddess of thrift. And so on to the end of the long register, all toiling together in the galling fetters of the tenement. Were the question raised who makes the most of life thus mortgaged, who resists most stubbornly its levelling tendency— knows how to drag even the barracks upward a part of the way at least toward the ideal plane of the home—the palm must be unhesitatingly awarded the Teuton. The Italian and the poor Jew rise only by compulsion. The Chinaman does not rise at all; here, as at home, he simply remains stationary. The Irishman's genius runs to public affairs rather than domestic life; wherever he is mustered in force the saloon is the gorgeous centre of political activity. The German struggles vainly to learn his trick; his Teutonic wit is too heavy, and the political ladder he raises from his saloon usually too short or too clumsy to reach the desired goal. The best part of his life is lived at home, and he makes himself a home independent of the surroundings, giving the lie to the saying, unhappily become a maxim of social truth, that pauperism and drunkenness naturally grow in the tenements. He makes the most of his tenement, and it should be added that whenever and as soon as he can save up money enough, he gets out and never crosses the threshold of one again.

NOTE

1 The Sheriff Street Colony of rag-pickers, long since gone, is an instance in point. The thrifty Germans saved up money during years of hard work in squalor and apparently wretched poverty to buy a township in a Western State, and the whole colony moved out there in a body. There need be no doubt about their thriving there.

4.5 *SISTER CARRIE* (1900)

Theodore Dreiser

Source: Theodore Dreiser, *Sister Carrie* (New York: Doubleday, 1900).

EDITORS' INTRODUCTION

The following selection comes from Chapter 1 "The Magnet Attracting—A Waif Amid Forces" of Theodore Dreiser's *Sister Carrie*, originally published in 1900 by Doubleday. In George Chauncey's essay, "Urban Culture and the 'City of Bachelors,'" one sees another example of how the city offered the possibility of economic and personal freedom to migrants from small town and rural America. **[See Essay 4.4.]** Dreiser's American classic ignited controversy upon its initial publication. Young Carrie Meeber came to the city, threw off the yoke of her sister and brother-in-law's restrictive household, and launched an out-of-wedlock relationship with Charles Drouet, whom she meets on the train to Chicago. Later on in the novel, she engages in a relationship with George Hurstwood, who seemed even more sophisticated to the naïve Carrie. The scandalous nature of this publication arises both from Carrie's nontraditional love affairs and her ultimate feat of survival. In other novels in which young women went astray in the city, the authors punished their wayward characters with an untimely death at the book's end. Dreiser allows Carrie to survive her lover Hurstwood, and even to achieve fame and monetary success in the city. In this famous scene, an anxious Carrie leaves her family behind and immediately falls under the sway of Charles Drouet.

Sister Carrie (1900)

Chapter I

THE MAGNET ATTRACTING—A WAIF AMID FORCES

When Caroline Meeber boarded the afternoon train for Chicago, her total outfit consisted of a small trunk, a cheap imitation alligator-skin satchel, a small lunch in a paper box, and a yellow leather snap purse, containing her ticket, a scrap of paper with her sister's address in Van Buren Street, and four dollars in money. It was in August, 1889. She was eighteen years of age, bright, timid, and full of the illusions of ignorance and youth. Whatever touch of regret at parting characterized her thoughts, it was certainly not for advantages now being given up. A gush of tears at her mother's farewell kiss, a touch in her throat when the cars clacked by the flour mill where her father worked by the day, a pathetic sigh as the familiar green environs of the village passed in review, and the threads which bound her so lightly to girlhood and home were irretrievably broken.

To be sure there was always the next station, where one might descend and return. There was the great city, bound more closely by these very trains which came up daily. Columbia City was not so very far away, even once she was in Chicago. What, pray, is a few hours—a few hundred miles? She looked at the little slip bearing her sister's address and wondered. She gazed at the green landscape, now passing in swift review, until her swifter thoughts replaced its impression with vague conjectures of what Chicago might be.

When a girl leaves her home at eighteen, she does one of two things. Either she falls into saving hands and becomes better, or she rapidly assumes the cosmopolitan standard of virtue and becomes worse. Of an intermediate balance, under the circumstances, there is no possibility. The city has its cunning wiles, no less than the infinitely smaller and more human tempter. There are large forces which allure with all the soulfulness of expression possible in the most cultured human. The gleam of a thousand lights is often as effective as the persuasive light in a wooing and fascinating eye. Half the undoing of the unsophisticated and natural mind is accomplished by forces wholly superhuman. A blare of sound, a roar of life, a vast array of human hives, appeal to the astonished senses in equivocal terms. Without a counselor at hand to whisper cautious interpretations, what falsehoods may not these things breathe into the unguarded ear! Unrecognized for what they are, their beauty, like music, too often relaxes, then weakens, then perverts the simpler human perceptions.

Caroline, or Sister Carrie, as she had been half affectionately termed by the family, was possessed of a mind rudimentary in its power of observation and analysis. Self-interest with her was high, but not strong. It was, nevertheless, her guiding characteristic. Warm with the fancies of youth, pretty with the insipid prettiness of the formative period, possessed of a figure promising eventual shapeliness and an eye alight with certain native intelligence, she was a fair example of the middle American class—two generations removed from the emigrant. Books were beyond her interest—knowledge a sealed book. In the intuitive graces she was still crude. She could scarcely toss her head gracefully. Her hands were almost ineffectual. The feet, though small, were set flatly. And yet she was interested in her charms, quick to understand the keener pleasures of life, ambitious to gain in material things. A half-equipped little knight she was, venturing to reconnoiter the mysterious city and dreaming wild dreams of some vague, far-off supremacy, which should make it prey and subject—the proper penitent, groveling at a woman's slipper.

"That," said a voice in her ear, "is one of the prettiest little resorts in Wisconsin."

"Is it?" she answered nervously.

The train was just pulling out of Waukesha. For some time she had been conscious of a man behind. She felt him observing her mass of hair. He had been fidgeting, and with natural intuition she felt a certain interest growing in that quarter. Her maidenly reserve, and a certain sense of what was conventional under the circumstances, called her to forestall and deny this familiarity, but the daring and magnetism of the individual, born of past experiences and triumphs, prevailed. She answered.

He leaned forward to put his elbows upon the back of her seat and proceeded to make himself volubly agreeable.

"Yes, that is a great resort for Chicago people. The hotels are swell. You are not familiar with this part of the country, are you?"

"Oh, yes, I am," answered Carrie. "That is, I live at Columbia City. I have never been through here, though."

"And so this is your first visit to Chicago," he observed.

All the time she was conscious of certain features out of the side of her eye. Flush, colorful cheeks, a light moustache, a grey fedora hat. She now turned and looked upon him in full, the instincts of self-protection and coquetry mingling confusedly in her brain.

"I didn't say that," she said.

"Oh," he answered, in a very pleasing way and with an assumed air of mistake, "I thought you did."

Here was a type of the traveling canvasser for a manufacturing house—a class which at that time was first being dubbed by the slang of the day "drummers." He came within the meaning of a still newer term, which had sprung into general use among Americans in 1880, and which concisely expressed the thought of one whose dress or manners are calculated to elicit the admiration of susceptible young women—a "masher." His suit was of a striped and crossed pattern of brown wool, new at that time, but since become familiar as a business suit. The low crotch of the vest revealed a stiff shirt bosom of white and pink stripes. From his coat sleeves protruded a pair of linen cuffs of the same pattern, fastened with large, gold plate buttons, set with the common yellow agates known as "cat's-eyes." His fingers bore several rings–one, the ever-enduring heavy seal–and from his vest dangled a neat gold watch chain, from which was suspended the secret insignia of the Order of Elks. The whole suit was rather tight-fitting, and was finished off with heavy-soled tan shoes, highly polished, and the grey fedora hat. He was, for the order of intellect represented, attractive, and whatever he had to recommend him, you may be sure was not lost upon Carrie, in this, her first glance.

Lest this order of individual should permanently pass, let me put down some of the most striking characteristics of his most successful manner and method. Good clothes, of course, were the first essential, the things without which he was nothing. A strong physical nature, actuated by a keen desire for the feminine, was the next. A mind free of any consideration of the problems or forces of the world and actuated not by greed, but an insatiable love of variable pleasure. His method was always simple. Its principal element was daring, backed, of course, by an intense desire and admiration for the sex. Let him meet with a young woman once and he would approach her with an air of kindly familiarity, not unmixed with pleading, which would result in most cases in a tolerant acceptance. If she showed any tendency to coquetry he would be apt to straighten her tie, or if she "took up" with him at all, to call her by her first name. If he visited a department store it was to lounge familiarly over the counter and ask some leading questions. In more exclusive circles, on the train or in waiting stations, he went slower. If some seemingly vulnerable object appeared he was all attention—to pass the compliments of the day, to lead the way to the parlor car, carrying her grip, or, failing that, to take a seat next her with the hope of being able to court her to her destination. Pillows, books, a footstool, the shade lowered; all these figured in the things which he could do. If, when she reached her destination he did not alight and attend her baggage for her, it was because, in his own estimation, he had signally failed.

A woman should some day write the complete philosophy of clothes. No matter how young, it is one of the things she wholly comprehends. There is an indescribably faint line in the matter of man's apparel which somehow divides for her those who are worth glancing at and those who are not. Once an individual has passed this faint line on the way downward he will get no glance from her. There is another line at which the dress of a man will cause her to study her own. This line the individual at her elbow now marked for Carrie. She became conscious of an inequality. Her own plain blue dress, with its black cotton tape trimmings, now seemed to her shabby. She felt the worn state of her shoes.

"Let's see," he went on, "I know quite a number of people in your town. Morgenroth the clothier and Gibson the dry goods man."

"Oh, do you?" she interrupted, aroused by memories of longings their show windows had cost her.

At last he had a clew to her interest, and followed it deftly. In a few minutes he had come about into her seat. He talked of sales of clothing, his travels, Chicago, and the amusements of that city.

"If you are going there, you will enjoy it immensely. Have you relatives?"

"I am going to visit my sister," she explained.

"You want to see Lincoln Park," he said, "and Michigan Boulevard. They are putting up great buildings there. It's a second New York—great. So much to see— theatres, crowds, fine houses—oh, you'll like that."

There was a little ache in her fancy of all he described. Her insignificance in the presence of so much magnificence faintly affected her. She realized that hers was not to be a round of pleasure, and yet there was something promising in all the material prospect he set forth. There was something satisfactory in the attention of this individual with his good clothes. She could not help smiling as he told her of some popular actress of whom she reminded him. She was not silly, and yet attention of this sort had its weight.

"You will be in Chicago some little time, won't you?" he observed at one turn of the now easy conversation.

"I don't know," said Carrie vaguely—a flash vision of the possibility of her not securing employment rising in her mind.

"Several weeks, anyhow," he said, looking steadily into her eyes.

There was much more passing now than the mere words indicated. He recognized the indescribable thing that made up for fascination and beauty in her. She realized that she was of interest to him from the one standpoint which a woman both delights in and fears. Her manner was simple, though for the very reason that she had not yet learned the many little affectations with which women conceal their true feelings. Some things she did appeared bold. A clever companion—had she ever had one— would have warned her never to look a man in the eyes so steadily.

"Why do you ask?" she said.

"Well, I'm going to be there several weeks. I'm going to study stock at our place and get new samples. I might show you 'round.'"

"I don't know whether you can or not. I mean I don't know whether I can. I shall be living with my sister, and—"

"Well, if she minds, we'll fix that." He took out his pencil and a little pocket notebook as if it were all settled. "What is your address there?"

She fumbled her purse which contained the address slip.

He reached down in his hip pocket and took out a fat purse. It was filled with slips of paper, some mileage books, a roll of greenbacks. It impressed her deeply. Such a purse had never been carried by any one attentive to her. Indeed, an experienced traveler, a brisk man of the world, had never come within such close range before. The purse, the shiny tan shoes, the smart new suit, and the air with which he did things, built up for her a dim world of fortune, of which he was the centre. It disposed her pleasantly toward all he might do.

He took out a neat business card, on which was engraved Bartlett, Caryoe & Company, and down in the left-hand corner, Chas. H. Drouet.

"That's me," he said, putting the card in her hand and touching his name. "It's pronounced Drew-eh. Our family was French, on my father's side."

She looked at it while he put up his purse. Then he got out a letter from a bunch in his coat pocket. "This is the house I travel for," he went on, pointing to a picture on it, "corner of State and Lake." There was pride in his voice. He felt that it was something to be connected with such a place, and he made her feel that way.

"What is your address?" he began again, fixing his pencil to write.

She looked at his hand.

"Carrie Meeber," she said slowly. "Three hundred and fifty-four West Van Buren Street, care S. C. Hanson."

He wrote it carefully down and got out the purse again. "You'll be at home if I come around Monday night?" he said.

"I think so," she answered.

How true it is that words are but the vague shadows of the volumes we mean. Little audible links, they are, chaining together great inaudible feelings and purposes. Here were these two, bandying little phrases, drawing purses, looking at cards, and both unconscious of how inarticulate all their real feelings were. Neither was wise enough to be sure of the working of the mind of the other. He could not tell how his luring succeeded. She could not realize that she was drifting, until he secured her address. Now she felt that she had yielded something—he, that he had gained a victory. Already they felt that they were somehow associated. Already he took control in directing the conversation. His words were easy. Her manner was relaxed.

They were nearing Chicago. Signs were everywhere numerous. Trains flashed by them. Across wide stretches of flat, open prairie they could see lines of telegraph poles stalking across the fields toward the great city. Far away were indications of suburban towns, some big smokestacks towering high in the air.

Frequently there were two-story frame houses standing out in the open fields, without fence or trees, lone outposts of the approaching army of homes.

To the child, the genius with imagination, or the wholly untraveled, the approach to a great city for the first time is a wonderful thing. Particularly if it be evening–that mystic period between the glare and gloom of the world when life is changing from one sphere or condition to another. Ah, the promise of the night. What does it not hold for the weary! What old illusion of hope is not here forever repeated! Says the soul of the toiler to itself, "I shall soon be free. I shall be in the ways and the hosts of the merry. The streets, the lamps, the lighted chamber set for dining, are for me. The theatre, the halls, the parties, the ways of rest and the paths of song–these are mine in the night." Though all humanity be still enclosed in the shops, the thrill runs abroad. It is in the air. The dullest feel something which they may not always express or describe. It is the lifting of the burden of toil.

Sister Carrie gazed out of the window. Her companion, affected by her wonder, so contagious are all things, felt anew some interest in the city and pointed out its marvels.

"This is Northwest Chicago," said Drouet. "This is the Chicago River," and he pointed to a little muddy creek, crowded with the huge masted wanderers from far-off waters nosing the black-posted banks. With a puff, a clang, and a clatter of rails it was gone. "Chicago is getting to be a great town," he went on. "It's a wonder. You'll find lots to see here."

She did not hear this very well. Her heart was troubled by a kind of terror. The fact that she was alone, away from home, rushing into a great sea of life and endeavor, began to tell. She could not help but feel a little choked for breath—a little sick as her heart beat so fast. She half closed her eyes and tried to think it was nothing, that Columbia City was only a little way off.

"Chicago! Chicago!" called the brakeman, slamming open the door. They were rushing into a more crowded yard, alive with the clatter and clang of life. She began to gather up her poor little grip and closed her hand firmly upon her purse. Drouet arose, kicked his legs to straighten his trousers, and seized his clean yellow grip.

"I suppose your people will be here to meet you?" he said. "Let me carry your grip."

"Oh, no," she said. "I'd rather you wouldn't. I'd rather you wouldn't be with me when I meet my sister."

"All right," he said in all kindness. "I'll be near, though, in case she isn't here, and take you out there safely."

"You're so kind," said Carrie, feeling the goodness of such attention in her strange situation.

"Chicago!" called the brakeman, drawing the word out long. They were under a great shadowy train shed, where the lamps were already beginning to shine out, with passenger cars all about and the train moving at a snail's pace. The people in the car were all up and crowding about the door.

"Well, here we are," said Drouet, leading the way to the door." Good-bye, till I see you Monday."

"Good-bye," she answered, taking his proffered hand.

"Remember, I'll be looking till you find your sister."

She smiled into his eyes.

They filed out, and he affected to take no notice of her. A lean-faced, rather commonplace woman recognized Carrie on the platform and hurried forward.

"Why, Sister Carrie!" she began, and there was embrace of welcome.

Carrie realized the change of affectional atmosphere at once. Amid all the maze, uproar, and novelty she felt cold reality taking her by the hand. No world of light and merriment. No round of amusement. Her sister carried with her most of the grimness of shift and toil.

"Why, how are all the folks at home?" she began; "how is father, and mother?"

Carrie answered, but was looking away. Down the aisle, toward the gate leading into the waiting-room and the street, stood Drouet. He was looking back. When he saw that she saw him and was safe with her sister he turned to go, sending back the shadow of a smile. Only Carrie saw it. She felt something lost to her when he moved away. When he disappeared, she felt his absence thoroughly. With her sister she was much alone, a lone figure in a tossing, thoughtless sea.

4.6 TRIANGLE SHIRTWAIST FIRE, NEW YORK CITY (1911)

Source: *The Ladies' Garment Worker*, April 1911. Permission of the Kheel Center at Cornell University.[i]

EDITORS' INTRODUCTION

On March 25, 1911, the Triangle Shirtwaist Company, located in the Washington Square area of New York City, was engulfed in flames and 146 of the 500 workers at the facility lost their lives. The majority of the victims were Italian or Jewish immigrants, mostly women and teenagers. The awful incident became a rallying point for those fighting for safer workplaces in the years to come. New immigrants often worked in highly dangerous industrial settings in the nineteenth and early twentieth centuries, and, unfortunately, sweatshop work conditions still persist in the United States and factories abroad. Frances Perkins, who would later become Secretary of Labor in the cabinet of President Franklin Roosevelt, watched the fire and the young people jumping to their deaths out of factory windows. The tragedy influenced her lifetime of work on behalf of laborers. The incident made an indelible mark in the collective memory of New Yorkers. Modern media commentators even have linked the events of 1911 to the terrorist attacks of 9/11, noting similarities in both the human tragedies and the high level of local and international attention.

TRIANGLE SHIRTWAIST FIRE, NEW YORK CITY (1911)

Notice of the Fire

When ready to go to press we learn of the awful calamity at the Triangle Waist Company. While most of the garment manufacturing establishments in New York City are not any better as far as fire protection is concerned, it is significant that the worst calamity happened at the Triangle, known among the workpeople in the trade as the "prison." The name is probably due the extraordinary discipline with poor earning for which the firm is famous.

It is not strange that in this most democratic of all countries in the world the employers can so easily use the arm of the law to protect themselves against any inconveniences which their workpeople may cause them, but the law is nowhere when the life and limb of the worker is to be protected.

The writer of these lines, when approaching the factory some two years ago in an attempt to organize the workpeople of that firm, was pounced upon by two plainclothed policemen and taken to the police cell. No one, however, knows whom to blame for this calamity.

It is evident that the worker can expect next to nothing in the way of protection from the legal authorities. Whether it is the Supreme Court or the good people who are interested in the architectural beauties of the city, nothing will be done until the workers will begin in earnest to attend to their own business. They must declare a strike at all such fire traps until adequate protection is provided.

Pickets should be posted at the entrance of such places with sign boards bearing the following inscription: *Please do not go to work in this place until proper fire protection is provided for the workpeople.*

Let the authorities find our action contrary to the Sherman Anti-Trust Laws or any other of the innumerable laws provide to safeguard the interest of the capitalists, and which the authorities are ever ready to guard jealousy. We will cheerfully go to

---

i See on-line exhibit on the Triangle Shirtwaist Company Fire at http://www.ilr.cornell.edu/trianglefire/.

prison but there will be no more fire traps. Such a strike will put an end to such a state of things within 48 hours.

There are in the same building a number of cloak shops, who before the general

strike, worked until 6 o'clock on Saturdays. Thanks to the change in hours all these left at 1 o'clock, otherwise the victims would have been more numerous.

4.7 TULSA RACE RIOTS (1921)

John Hope Franklin and Scott Ellsworth

Source: John Hope Franklin and Scott Ellsworth, "History Knows No Fences: An Overview," in *Tulsa Race Riot: A Report by the Oklahoma Commission to Study the Tulsa Race Riot of 1921*, February 28, 2001. Courtesy Research Division, Oklahoma Historical Society, Oklahoma City, Oklahoma.

EDITORS' INTRODUCTION

On May 31 and June 1, 1921, riots broke out in the city of Tulsa, Oklahoma resulting in the destruction of more than 1,000 homes, the annihilation of the black business area of the city, and an unspecified number of deaths, likely in the range of 75 to 100 people, or more. This horrible event, which historians John Hope Franklin and Scott Ellsworth declare might be better termed a pogrom or an attempt at racial cleansing than a riot, was largely forgotten by many Tulsans for decades. In 2001, the state issued a formal report which called for restitution to the riot victims and their families.

The late John Hope Franklin (1915–2009), was a native of Rentiesville, Oklahoma and professor of history at numerous colleges including Howard University, Brooklyn College, the University of Chicago, and Duke University. He was the author numerous books, including *From Slavery to Freedom: A History of African Americans* (New York: Knopf, 1947). He was the past president of the American Historical Association, the Organization of American Historians, the Southern Historical Association, and the American Studies Association. In 1995 he was awarded the Presidential Medal of Freedom by President William J. Clinton. Scott Ellsworth is a visiting lecturer in Afroamerican and African Studies at the University of Michigan. He wrote *Death in a Promised Land: The Tulsa Race Riot of 1921* (Baton Rouge: Louisiana State University Press, 1992) and worked for the Duke University Oral History Program, the Smithsonian Institution, and various national news organizations.

TULSA RACE RIOTS (1921)

History Knows No Fences: An Overview

As the centennial of Oklahoma statehood draws near, it is not difficult to look upon the history of our state with anything short of awe and wonder. In ninety-three short years, whole towns and cities have sprouted upon the prairies, great cultural and educational institutions have risen among the blackjacks, and the state's agricultural and industrial output has far surpassed even the wildest dreams of the Boomers. In less than a

century, Oklahoma has transformed itself from a rawboned territory more at home in the nineteenth century, into now, as a new millennium dawns about us, a shining example of both the promise and the reality of the American dream. In looking back upon our past, we have much to take pride in.

But we have also known heartaches as well. As any honest history textbook will tell you, the first century of Oklahoma statehood has also featured dust storms and a Great Depression, political scandals and Jim Crow legislation, tumbling oil prices and truckloads of Okies streaming west. But through it all, there are two twentieth century tragedies which, sadly enough, stand head and shoulders above the others.

For many Oklahomans, there has never been a darker day than April 19, 1995. At two minutes past nine o'clock that morning, when the northern face of the Alfred P. Murrah Federal Building in downtown Oklahoma City was blown inward by the deadliest act of terrorism ever to take place on American soil, lives were shattered, lives were lost, and the history of the state would never again be the same.

One-hundred-sixty-eight Oklahomans died that day. They were black and white, Native American and Hispanic, young and old. And during the weeks that followed, we began to learn a little about who they were. We learned about Colton and Chase Smith, brothers aged two and three, and how they loved their playmates at the day-care center. We learned about Captain Randy Guzman, U.S.M.C., and how he had commanded troops during Operation Desert Storm, and we learned about Wanda Lee Howell, who always kept a Bible in her purse. And we learned about Cartney Jean McRaven, a nineteen-year-old Air Force enlistee who had been married only four days earlier.

The Murrah Building bombing is, without any question, one of the great tragedies of Oklahoma history. And well before the last memorial service was held for the last victim, thousands of Oklahomans made it clear that they wanted what happened on that dark day to be remembered. For upon the chain-link fence surrounding the bomb site there soon appeared a makeshift memorial of the heart—of teddy bears and handwritten children's prayers, key rings and dreamcatchers, flowers and flags. Now, with the construction and dedication of the Oklahoma City National Memorial, there is no doubt but that both the victims and the lessons of April 19, 1995 will not be forgotten.

But what would have come as a surprise to most of the state's citizens during the sad spring of 1995 was that there were, among them, other Oklahomans who carried within their hearts the painful memories of an equally dark, though long ignored, day in our past. For seventy-three years before the Murrah Building was bombed, the city of Tulsa erupted into a firestorm of hatred and violence that is perhaps unequaled in the peacetime history of the United States.

For those hearing about the 1921 Tulsa race riot for the first time, the event seems almost impossible to believe. During the course of eighteen terrible hours, more than one thousand homes were burned to the ground. Practically overnight, entire neighborhoods where families had raised their children, visited with their neighbors, and hung their wash out on the line to dry, had been suddenly reduced to ashes. And as the homes burned, so did their contents, including furniture and family Bibles, rag dolls and hand-me-down quilts, cribs and photograph albums. In less than twenty-four hours, nearly all of Tulsa's African American residential district — some forty-square-blocks in all — had been laid to waste, leaving nearly nine-thousand people homeless.

Gone, too, was the city's African American commercial district, a thriving area located along Greenwood Avenue which boasted some of the finest black-owned businesses in the entire Southwest. The Stradford Hotel, a modern fifty-four room brick establishment which housed a drug store, barber shop, restaurant and banquet hall, had been burned to the ground. So had the Gurley Hotel, the Red Wing Hotel, and the Midway Hotel. Literally dozens of family-run businesses—from cafes and mom-and-pop grocery stores, to the Dreamland Theater, the Y.M.C.A. Cleaners, the East End Feed Store, and Osborne Monroe's roller skating rink — had also gone up in flames, taking with them the livelihoods, and in many cases the life savings, of literally hundreds of people.

The offices of two newspapers — the *Tulsa Star* and the *Oklahoma Sun* — had also been destroyed, as were the offices of more than a dozen doctors, dentists, lawyers, realtors, and other professionals. A United States Post Office substation was burned, as was the all-black Frissell

Memorial Hospital. The brand new Booker T. Washington High School building escaped the torches of the rioters, but Dunbar Elementary School did not. Neither did more than a half-dozen African American churches, including the newly constructed Mount Zion Baptist Church, an impressive brick tabernacle which had been dedicated only seven weeks earlier.

Harsher still was the human loss. While we will probably never know the exact number of people who lost their lives during the Tulsa race riot, even the most conservative estimates are appalling. While we know that the so-called "official" estimate of nine whites and twenty-six blacks is too low, it is also true that some of the higher estimates are equally dubious. All told, considerable evidence exists to suggest that at least seventy-five to one-hundred people, both black and white, were killed during the riot. It should be added, however, that at least one credible source from the period — Maurice Willows, who directed the relief operations of the American Red Cross in Tulsa following the riot — indicated in his official report that the total number of riot fatalities may have ran as high as three-hundred.[1]

We also know a little, at least, about who some of the victims were. Reuben Everett, who was black, was a laborer who lived with his wife Jane in a home along Archer Street. Killed by a gunshot wound on the morning of June 1, 1921, he is buried in Oaklawn Cemetery. George Walter Daggs, who was white, may have died as much as twelve hours earlier. The manager of the Tulsa office of the Pierce Oil Company, he was shot in the back of the head as he fled from the initial gunplay of the riot that broke out in front of the Tulsa County Courthouse on the evening of May 31. Moreover, Dr. A. C. Jackson, a renowned African American physician, was fatally wounded in his front yard after he had surrendered to a group of whites. Shot in the stomach, he later died at the National Guard Armory. But for every riot victim's story that we know, there are others — like the "unidentified Negroes" whose burials are recorded in the now yellowed pages of old funeral home ledgers — whose names and life stories are, at least for now, still lost.

By any standard, the Tulsa race riot of 1921 is one of the great tragedies of Oklahoma history. Walter White, one of the nation's foremost experts on racial violence, who visited Tulsa during the week after the riot, was shocked by what had taken place. "I am able to state," he said, "that the Tulsa riot, in sheer brutality and willful destruction of life and property, stands without parallel in America."[2]

Indeed, for a number of observers through the years, the term "riot" itself seems somehow inadequate to describe the violence and conflagration that took place. For some, what occurred in Tulsa on May 31 and June 1, 1921 was a massacre, a pogrom, or, to use a more modern term, an ethnic cleansing. For others, it was nothing short of a race war. But whatever term is used, one thing is certain: when it was all over, Tulsa's African American district had been turned into a scorched wasteland of vacant lots, crumbling storefronts, burned churches, and blackened, leafless trees.

Like the Murrah Building bombing, the Tulsa riot would forever alter life in Oklahoma. Nowhere, perhaps, was this more starkly apparent than in the matter of lynching. Like several other states and territories during the early years of the twentieth century, the sad spectacle of lynching was not uncommon in Oklahoma. In her 1942 master's thesis at the University of Oklahoma, Mary Elizabeth Estes determined that between the declaration of statehood on November 16, 1907, and the Tulsa race riot some thirteen years later, thirty-two individuals — twenty-six of whom were black — were lynched in Oklahoma. But during the twenty years following the riot, the number of lynchings statewide fell to two. Although they paid a terrible price for their efforts, there is little doubt except by their actions on May 31, 1921, that black Tulsans helped to bring the barbaric practice of lynching in Oklahoma to an end.

But unlike the Oklahoma City bombing, which has, to this day, remained a high profile event, for many years the Tulsa race riot practically disappeared from view. For decades afterwards, Oklahoma newspapers rarely mentioned the riot, the state's historical establishment essentially ignored it, and entire generations of Oklahoma school children were taught little or nothing about what had happened. To be sure, the riot was still a topic of conversation, particularly in Tulsa. But these discussions — whether among family or friends, in barber shops or on the front porch — were private affairs. And once the riot slipped from the headlines, its public memory also began to fade.

Of course, anyone who lived through the riot could never forget what had taken place. And in Tulsa's African American neighborhoods, the physical, psychological, and spiritual damage caused by the riot remained highly apparent for years. Indeed, even today there are places in the city where the scars of the riot can still be observed. In North Tulsa, the riot was never forgotten — because it could not be.

But in other sections of the city, and elsewhere throughout the state, the riot slipped further and further from view. And as the years passed and, particularly after World War II, as more and more families moved to Oklahoma from out-of-state, more and more of the state's citizens had simply never heard of the riot. Indeed, the riot was discussed so little, and for so long, even in Tulsa, that in 1996, Tulsa County District Attorney Bill LaFortune could tell a reporter, "I was born and raised here, and I had never heard of the riot."[3]

How could this have happened? How could a disaster the size and scope of the Tulsa race riot become, somehow, forgotten? How could such a major event in Oklahoma history become so little known?

Some observers have claimed that the lack of attention given to the riot over the years was the direct result of nothing less than a "conspiracy of silence." And while it is certainly true that a number of important documents relating to the riot have turned up missing, and that some individuals are, to this day, still reluctant to talk about what happened, the shroud of silence that descended over the Tulsa race riot can also be accounted

for without resorting to conspiracy theories. But one must start at the beginning.

The riot, when it happened, was front-page news across America. "85 WHITES AND NEGROES DIE IN TULSA RIOTS" ran the headline in the June 2, 1921 edition of the *New York Times*, while dozens of other newspapers across the country published lead stories about the riot. Indeed, the riot was even news overseas, "FIERCE OUTBREAK IN OKLAHOMA" declared *The Times of London*.[4]

But something else happened as well. For in the days and weeks that followed the riot, editorial writers from coast-to-coast unleashed a torrent of stinging condemnations of what had taken place. "The bloody scenes at Tulsa Oklahoma," declared the *Philadelphia Bulletin*, "are hardly conceivable as happening in American civilization of the present day." For the *Kentucky State Journal*, the riot was nothing short of "An Oklahoma Disgrace," while the *Kansas City Journal* was revolted at what it called the "Tulsa Horror." From both big-city dailies and small town newspapers — from the *Houston Post* and *Nashville Tennessean* to the tiny *Times* of Gloucester, Massachusetts — came a chorus of criticism. The *Christian Recorder* even went so far as to declare that "Tulsa has become a name of shame upon America."[5]

For many Oklahomans, and particularly for whites in positions of civic responsibility, such sentiments were most unwelcome. For regardless of what they felt personally about the riot, in a young state where attracting new businesses and new settlers was a top priority, it soon became evident that the riot was a public relations nightmare. Nowhere was this felt more acutely than in Tulsa. "I suppose Tulsa will get a lot of unpleasant publicity from this affair," wrote one Tulsa-based petroleum geologist to family members back East. Reverend Charles W. Kerr, of the city's all-white First Presbyterian Church, added his own assessment. "For 22 years I have been boosting Tulsa," he said, "and we have all been boosters and boasters about our buildings, bank accounts and other assets, but the events of the past week will put a stop to the bragging for a while."[6] For some, and particularly for Tulsa's white business and political leaders, the riot soon became something best to be forgotten, something to be swept well beneath history's carpet.

What is remarkable, in retrospect, is the degree to which this nearly happened. For within a decade after it had happened, the Tulsa race riot went from being a front-page, national calamity, to being an incident portrayed as an unfortunate, but not really very significant, event in the state's past. Oklahoma history textbooks published during the 1920s did not mention the riot at all — nor did ones published in the 1930s. Finally, in 1941, the riot was mentioned in the Oklahoma volume in the influential *American Guide Series* — but only in one brief paragraph.[7]

Nowhere was this historical amnesia more startling than in Tulsa itself, especially in the city's white neighborhoods. "For a while," noted former Tulsa oilman Osborn Campbell, "picture postcards of the victims in awful poses were sold on the streets," while more than one white ex-rioter "boasted about how many notches he had on his gun." But the riot, which some whites saw as a source of local pride, in time more generally came to be regarded as a local embarrassment. Eventually, Osborn added, the talk stopped."[8]

So too, apparently did the news stories. For while it is highly questionable whether — as it has been alleged — any Tulsa newspaper actually discouraged its reporters from writing about the riot, for years and years on end the riot does not appear to have been mentioned in the local press. And at least one local paper seems to have gone well out of its way, at times, to avoid the subject altogether.

During the mid-1930s, the *Tulsa Tribune* — the city's afternoon daily newspaper — ran a regular feature on its editorial page called "Fifteen Years Ago." Drawn from back issues of the newspaper, the column highlighted events which had happened in Tulsa on the same date fifteen years earlier, including local news stories, political tidbits, and society gossip. But when the fifteenth anniversary of the race riot arrived in early June, 1936, the *Tribune* ignored it completely — and instead ran the following:

Fifteen Years Ago

Miss Carolyn Skelly was a charming young hostess of the past week, having entertained at a luncheon and theater party for Miss Kathleen Sinclair and her guest, Miss Julia Morley of Saginaw, Mich. Corsage bouquets of Cecil roses and sweet peas were presented to the guests, who were Misses Claudine Miller, Martha Sharpe, Elizabeth Cook, Jane Robinson, Pauline Wood, Marie Constantin, Irene Buel, Thelma Kennedy, Ann Kennedy, Naomi Brown, Jane Wallace and Edith Smith.

> Mrs. O.H.P. Thomas will entertain for her daughter, Elizabeth, who has been attending Randolph Macon school in Lynchburg, Va.
>
> Central high school's crowning social event of the term just closed was the senior prom in the gymnasium with about 200 guests in attendance. The grand march was led by Miss Sara Little and Seth Hughes.
>
> Miss Vera Gwynne will leave next week for Chicago to enter the University of Chicago where she will take a course in kindergarten study.
>
> Mr. And Mrs. E.W. Hance have as their guests Mr. L.G. Kellenneyer of St. Mary's, Ohio.
>
> Mrs. C.B. Hough and her son, Ralph, left last night for a three-months trip through the west and northwest. They will return home via Dallas, Texas, where they will visit Mrs. Hough's homefolk.[9]

Ten years later, in 1946, by which time the *Tribune* had added a "Twenty-Five Years Ago" feature, the newspaper once again avoided mentioning the riot. It was as if the greatest catastrophe in the city's history simply had not happened at all.[10]

That there would be some reluctance toward discussing the riot is hardly surprising. Cities and states — just like individuals — do not, as a general rule, like to dwell upon their past shortcomings. For years and years, for example, Oklahoma school children were taught only the most sanitized versions of the story of the Trail of Tears, while the history of slavery in Oklahoma was more or less ignored altogether. Moreover, during the World War II years, when the nation was engaged in a life or death struggle against the Axis, history text-books quite understandably stressed themes of national unity and consensus. The Tulsa race riot, needless to say, did not qualify.

But in Tulsa itself, the riot had affected far too many families, on both sides of the tracks, ever to sink entirely from view. But as the years passed and the riot grew ever more distant, a mindset developed which held that the riot was one part of the city's past that might best be forgotten altogether. Remarkably enough, that is exactly what began to happen.

When Nancy Feldman moved to Tulsa during the spring of 1946, she had never heard of the Tulsa race riot. A Chicagoan, and a new bride, she accepted a position teaching sociology at the University of Tulsa. But trained in social work, she also began working with the City Health Department, where she came into contact with Robert Fairchild, a recreation specialist who was also one of Tulsa's handful of African American municipal employees. A riot survivor, Fairchild told Feldman of his experiences during the disaster, which made a deep impression on the young sociologist, who decided to share her discovery with her students.[11]

But as it turned out, Feldman also soon learned something else, namely, that learning about the riot, and teaching about it, were two entirely different propositions. "During my first months at TU," she later recalled:

I mentioned the race riot in class one day and was surprised at the universal surprise among my students. No one in this all-white class room of both veterans, who were older, and standard 18-year-old freshmen, had ever heard of it, and some stoutly denied it and questioned my facts.

I invited Mr. Fairchild to come to class and tell of his experience, walking along the railroad tracks to Turley with his brothers and sister. Again, there was stout denial and, even more surprising, many students asked their parents and were told, no, there was no race riot at all. I was called to the Dean's office and advised to drop the whole subject.

The next semester, I invited Mr. Fairchild to come to class. Several times the Dean warned me about this. I do not believe I ever suffered

from this exercise of my freedom of speech ... but as a very young and new instructor, I certainly felt threatened. For Feldman, such behavior amounted to nothing less than "Purposeful blindness and memory blocking." Moreover, she discovered, it was not limited to the classroom. "When I would mention the riot to my white friends, few would talk about it. And they certainly didn't want to."[12]

While perhaps surprising in retrospect, Feldman's experiences were by no means unique. When Nancy Dodson, a Kansas native who later taught at Tulsa Junior College, moved to Tulsa in 1950, she too discovered that, at least in some parts of the white community, the riot was a taboo subject. "I was admonished not to mention the riot almost upon our arrival," she later recalled, "Because of shame, I thought. But the explanation was 'you don't want to start another.'"[13]

The riot did not fare much better in local history efforts. While Angie Debo did make mention of the riot in her 1943 history, *Tulsa: From Creek Town to Oil Capital*, her account was both brief and superficial. And fourteen years later, during the summer of 1957, when the city celebrated its "Tulsarama" — a week-long festival commemorating the semi-centennial of Oklahoma statehood — the riot was, once again, ignored. Some thirty-five years after it had taken the lives of dozens of innocent people, destroyed a neighborhood nearly one-square-mile in size in a firestorm which sent columns of black smoke billowing hundreds of feet into the air, and brought the normal life of the city to a complete standstill, the Tulsa race riot was fast becoming little more than a historical inconvenience, something, perhaps, that ought not be discussed at all.

Despite such official negligence, however, there were always Tulsans through the years who helped make it certain that the riot was not forgotten. Both black and white, sometimes working alone but more often working together, they collected evidence, preserved photographs, interviewed eyewitnesses, wrote about their findings, and tried, as best as they could, to ensure that the riot was not erased from history.

None, perhaps, succeeded as spectacularly as Mary E. Jones Parrish, a young African American teacher and journalist. Parrish had moved to Tulsa from Rochester, New York in 1919 or 1920, and had found work teaching typing and shorthand at the all-black Hunton Branch of the Y.M.C.A. With her young daughter, Florence Mary, she lived at the Woods Building in the heart of the African American business district. But when the riot broke out, both mother and daughter were forced to abandon their apartment and flee for their lives, running north along Greenwood Avenue amid a hail of bullets.[14]

Immediately following the riot, Parrish was hired by the Inter-Racial Commission to "do some reporting" on what had happened. Throwing herself into her work with her characteristic verve — and, one imagines, a borrowed typewriter — Parrish interviewed several eyewitnesses and transcribed the testimonials of survivors. She also wrote an account of her own harrowing experiences during the riot and, together with photographs of the devastation and a partial roster of property losses in the African American community, Parrish published all of the above in a book called *Events of the Tulsa Disaster*. And while only a handful of copies appear to have been printed, Parrish's volume was not only the first book published about the riot, and a pioneering work of journalism by an African American woman, but remains, to this day, an invaluable contemporary account.[15]

It took another twenty-five years, however, until the first general history of the riot was written. In 1946, a white World War II veteran named Loren L. Gill was attending the University of Tulsa. Intrigued by lingering stories of the race riot, and armed with both considerable energy and estimable research skills, Gill decided to make the riot the subject of his master's thesis.[16]

The end result, "The Tulsa Race Riot," was, all told, an exceptional piece of work. Gill worked diligently to uncover the causes of the riot, and to trace its path of violence and destruction, by scouring old newspaper and magazine articles, Red Cross records, and government documents. Moreover, Gill interviewed more than a dozen local citizens, including police and city officials, about the riot. And remarkably for the mid-1940's, Gill also interviewed a number of African American riot survivors, including Reverend Charles Lanier Netherland, Mrs. Dimple L. Bush, and the noted attorney, Amos T. Hall. And while a number of Gill's conclusions about the riot have not withstood subsequent historical scrutiny, few have matched his determination to uncover the truth.[17]

Yet despite Gill's accomplishment, the riot remained well-buried in the city's historical closet. Riot survivors, participants, and observers, to be certain, still told stories of their experiences to family and friends. And at Tulsa's Booker T. Washington High School, a handful of teachers made certain that their students — many of whose families had moved to Tulsa after 1921 — learned at least a little about what had happened. But the fact remains that for nearly a quarter of a century after Loren Gill completed his master's thesis, the Tulsa race riot remained well out of the public spotlight.[18]

But beneath the surface, change was afoot. For as the national debate over race relations intensified with the emergence of the modern civil rights movement of the 1950s and 1960s, Tulsa's own racial customs were far from static. As the city began to address issues arising out of school desegregation, sit-ins, job bias, housing discrimination, urban renewal, and white flight, there were those who believed that Tulsa's racial past — and particularly the race riot — needed to be openly confronted.

Few felt this as strongly as those who had survived the tragedy itself, and on the evening of June 1, 1971, dozens of African American riot survivors gathered at Mount Zion Baptist Church for a program commemorating the fiftieth anniversary of the riot. Led by W.D. Williams, a longtime Booker T. Washington High School history teacher, whose family had suffered immense property loss during the violence, the other speakers that evening included fellow riot survivors Mable B. Little, who had lost both her home and her beauty shop during the conflagration, and E.L. Goodwin, Sr., the publisher of the *Oklahoma Eagle*, the city's black newspaper. Although the audience at the ceremony — which included a handful of whites — was not large, the event represented the first public acknowledgement of the riot in decades.[19]

But another episode that same spring also revealed just how far that Tulsa, when it came to owning up to the race riot, still had to go. The previous autumn, Larry Silvey, the publications manager at the Tulsa Chamber of Commerce, decided that on the fiftieth anniversary of the riot, the chamber's magazine should run a story on what had happened. Silvey then contacted Ed Wheeler, the host of 'The Gilcrease Story," a popular history program which aired on local radio. Wheeler — who, like Silvey, was white — agreed to research and write the article. Thus, during the winter of 1970–71, Wheeler went to work, interviewing dozens of elderly black and white riot eyewitnesses, and searching through archives in both Tulsa and Oklahoma City for documents pertaining to the riot.[20]

But something else happened as well. For on two separate occasions that winter, Wheeler was approached by white men, unknown to him, who warned him, "Don't write that story." Not long thereafter, Wheeler's home telephone began ringing at all hours of the day and night, and one morning he awoke to find that someone had taken a bar of soap and scrawled across the front windshield of his car, "Best check under your hood from now on."

But Ed Wheeler was a poor candidate for such scare tactics. A former United States Army infantry officer, the incidents only angered him. Moreover, he was now deep into trying to piece together the history of the riot, and was not about to be deterred. But to be on the safe side, he sent his wife and young son to live with his mother-in-law.[21]

Despite the harassment, Wheeler completed his article and Larry Silvey was pleased with the results. However, when Silvey began to lay out the story — complete with never-before-published photographs of both the riot and its aftermath Chamber of Commerce management killed the article. Silvey appealed to the chamber's board of directors, but they, too, refused to allow the story to be published.

Determined that his efforts should not have been in vain, Wheeler then tried to take his story to Tulsa's two daily newspapers, but was rebuffed. In the end, his article — called "Profile of a Race Riot" — was published in *Impact Magazine*, a new, black-oriented publication edited by a young African American journalist named Don Ross.

"Profile of a Race Riot" was a hand-biting, path-breaking story, easily the best piece of writing published about the riot in decades. But is was also a story whose impact was both limited and far from city-wide. For while it has been reported that the issue containing Wheeler's story sold out "virtually overnight," the magazine's readership, which was not large to begin with, was almost exclusively African American. Ultimately, "Profile of a Race Riot" marked a turning point in how the riot would be written about in the years to come, but at the time that it was published, few Tulsans — and hardly any whites — even knew of its existence.[22]

One of the few who did was Ruth Sigler Avery, a white Tulsa woman with a passion for history. A young girl at the time of the riot, Avery had been haunted by her memories of the smoke and flames rising up over the African American district, and by the two trucks carrying the bodies of riot victims that had passed in front of her home on East 8th Street.

Determined that the history of the riot needed to be preserved, Avery begin interviewing riot survivors, collecting riot photographs, and serving as a one-woman research bureau for anyone interested in studying what had happened. Convinced that the riot had been deliberately covered-up, Avery embarked upon what turned out to be a decades-long personal crusade to see that the true story of the riot was finally told.[23]

Along the way, Avery met some kindred spirits — and none more important that Mozella Franklin Jones. The daughter of riot survivor and prominent African American attorney Buck Colbert Franklin, Jones had long endeavored to raise awareness of the riot particularly outside of Tulsa's black community. While she was often deeply frustrated by white resistance to confronting the riot, her accomplishments were far from inconsequential. Along with Henry C. Whitlow, Jr., a history teacher at Booker T. Washington High School, Jones had not only helped to desegregate the Tulsa Historical Society, but had mounted the first-ever major exhibition on the history of African Americans in Tulsa. Moreover, she had also created, at the Tulsa Historical Society, the first collection of riot photographs available to the public.[24]

None of these activities, however, was by itself any match for the culture of silence which had long hovered over the riot, and for years to come, discussions of the riot were often curtailed. Taken together, the fiftieth anniversary ceremony, "Profile of a Race Riot," and the work of Ruth Avery and Mozella Jones had nudged the riot if not into the spotlight, then at least out of the back reaches of the city's historical closet.[25]

Moreover, these local efforts mirrored some larger trends in American society. Nationwide, the decade of the 1970s witnessed a virtual explosion of interest in the African American experience. Millions of television viewers watched *Roots*, the miniseries adaptation of Alex Haley's chronicle of one family's tortuous journey through slavery, while books by black authors climbed to the top of the bestseller lists. Black studies programs and departments were created at colleges from coast-to-coast, while at both the high school and university level, teaching materials began to more fully address issues of race. As scholars started to re-examine the long and turbulent history of race relations in America — including racial violence — the Tulsa riot began to receive some limited national exposure.[26]

Similar activities took place in Oklahoma. Kay M. Teall's *Black History in Oklahoma*, an impressive collection of historical documents published in 1971, helped to make the history of black Oklahomans far more accessible to teachers across the state. Teall's book paid significant attention to the story of the riot, as did Arthur Tolson's *The Black*

Oklahomans: A History 1541–1972, which came out one year later.[27]

In 1975, Northeastern State University historian Rudia M. Halliburton, Jr. published *The Tulsa Race War of 1921*. Adapted from an article he had published three years earlier in the *Journal of Black Studies*, Halliburton's book featured a remarkable collection of riot photographs, many of which he had collected from his students. Issued by a small academic press in California, Halliburton's book received little attention outside of scholarly circles. Nonetheless, as the first book about the riot published in more than a half-century, it was another important step toward unlocking the riot's history.[28]

In the end, it would still take several years — and other books, and other individuals — to lift the veil of silence fully which had long hovered over the riot. However, by the end of the 1970s, efforts were underway that, once and for all, would finally bring out into the open the history of the tragic events of the spring of 1921.[29]

Today, the Tulsa Race Riot is Anything but Unknown

During the past two years, both the riot itself, and the efforts of Oklahomans to come to terms with the tragedy, have been the subject of dozens of magazine and newspaper articles, radio talk shows, and television documentaries. In an unprecedented and continuing explosion of press attention, journalists and film crews from as far away as Paris, France and London, England have journeyed to Oklahoma to interview riot survivors and eye-witnesses, search through archives for documents and photographs, and walk the ground where the killings and burning of May 31 and June 1, 1921 took place.

After years of neglect, stories and articles about the riot have appeared not only in Oklahoma magazines and newspapers, but also in the pages of the *Dallas Morning News*, *The Economist*, the *Kansas City Star*, the *London Daily Telegraph*, the *Los Angeles Times*, the *National Post of Canada*, the *New York Times*, *Newsday*, the *Philadelphia Inquirer*, *U.S. News and*

World Report, *USA Today*, and the *Washington Post*. The riot has also been the subject of wire stories issued by the Associated Press and Reuter's. In addition, news stories and television documentaries about the riot have been produced by ABC News *Nightline*, Australian Broadcasting, the BBC, CBS News' *60 Minutes II*, CNN, Cinemax, The History Channel, NBC News, National Public Radio, Norwegian Broadcasting, South African Broadcasting, and Swedish Broadcasting, as well as by a number of in-state television and radio stations. Various web sites and Internet chat rooms have also featured the riot, while in numerous high school and college classrooms across America, the riot has become a subject of study. All told, for the first time in nearly eighty years, the Tulsa race riot of 1921 has once again become front-page news.[30]

What has not made the headlines, however, is that for the past two-and-one-half years, an intensive effort has been quietly underway to investigate, document, analyze, and better understand the history of the riot. Archives have been searched through, old newspapers and government records have been studied, and sophisticated, state-of-the-art scientific equipment has been utilized to help reveal the potential location of the unmarked burial sites of riot victims. While literally dozens of what appeared to be promising leads for reliable new information about the riot turned out to be little more than dead ends, a significant amount of previously unavailable evidence — including long-forgotten documents and photographs — has been discovered.

None of this, it must be added, could have been possible without the generous assistance of Oklahomans from all walks of life. Scores of senior citizens — including riot survivors and observers, as well as the sons and daughters of policemen, National Guards men, and riot participants have helped us to gain a much clearer picture of what happened in Tulsa during the spring of 1921. All told, literally hundreds of Oklahomans, of all races, have given of their time, their memories, and their expertise to help us all gain a better understanding of this great tragedy.

This report is a product of these combined efforts. The scholars who have written it are all Oklahomans — either by birth, upbringing, residency, or family heritage. Young and not-so-young, black and white, men and women, we include within our ranks both the grandniece and the son of African American riot survivors, as well as the son of a white eyewitness. We are historians and archaeologists, forensic scientists and legal scholars, university professors and retirees.

For the editors of this report, the riot also bears considerable personal meaning. Tulsa is our hometown, and we are both graduates of the Tulsa Public Schools. And although we grew up in different eras, and in different parts of town — and heard about the riot, as it were, from different sides of the fence — both of our lives have been indelibly shaped by what happened in 1921.

History knows no fences. While the stories that black Oklahomans tell about the riot often differ from those of their white counterparts, it is the job of the historian to locate the truth wherever it may lie. There are, of course, many legitimate areas of dispute about the riot — and will be, without a doubt, for years to come. But far more significant is the tremendous amount of information that we now know about the tragedy — about how it started and how it ended, about its terrible fury and its murderous violence, about the community it devastated and the lives it shattered. Neither myth nor "confusion," the riot was an actual, definable, and describable event. In Oklahoma history, the central truths of which can, and must, be told.

That won't always be easy. For despite the many acts of courage, heroism, and selflessness that occurred on May 31 and June 1, 1921 the story of the Tulsa race riot is a chronicle of hatred and fear, of burning houses and shots fired in anger, of justice denied and dreams deferred. Like the bombing of the Murrah Federal Building some seventy-three years later, there is simply no denying the fact that the riot was a true Oklahoma tragedy, perhaps our greatest.

But, like the bombing, the riot can also be a bearer of lessons — about not only who we are, but also about who we would like to be. For only by looking to the past can we see not only where we have been, but also where we are going. And as the first one-hundred years of Oklahoma statehood draws to a close, and a new century begins, we can best honor that past not by burying it, but by facing it squarely, honestly, and, above all, openly.

NOTES

1. For the so-called "official" estimate, see: Memorandum from Major Paul R. Brown, Surgeon, 3rd Infantry, Oklahoma National Guard, to the Adjutant General of Oklahoma, June 4, 1921, located in the Attorney General's Civil Case Files, Record Group 1–2, Case 1062, State Archives Division, Oklahoma Department of Libraries.

   For the Maurice Willows estimates, see: "Disaster Relief Report, Race Riot, June 1921," p. 6, reprinted in Robert N. Hower, *"Angels of Mercy": The American Red Cross and the 1921 Tulsa Race Riot* (Tulsa: Homestead Press, 1993).

2. *New York Call*, June 10, 1921.

3. Jonathan Z. Larsen, "Tulsa Burning," *Civilization*, IV, I (February/March 1997), p. 46.

4. *New York Times*, June 2, 1921, p. 1. [London, England] *The Times*, June 2, 1921, p. 10.

5. *Philadelphia Bulletin*, June 3, 1921. [Frankfort] *Kentucky State Journal*, June 5, 1921. "Mob Fury and Race Hatred as a National Disgrace," *Literary Digest*, June 18, 1921, pp. 7–9. R.R. Wright, Jr., "Tulsa," *Christian Recorder*, June 9, 1921.

6. The geologist, Robert F. Truex, was quoted in the *Rochester [New York] Herald*, June 4, 1921. The Kerr quote is from "Causes of Riots Discussed in Pulpits of Tulsa Sunday," an unattributed June 6, 1921 article located in the Tuskegee Institute News Clipping File, microfilm edition, Series 1, "1921 — Riots, Tulsa, Oklahoma," Reel 14, p. 754.

7. Joseph P. Thoburn and Muriel H. Wright, *Oklahoma: A History of the State and Its People* (New York: Lewis Historical Publishing, 1929). Muriel H. Wright, *The Story of Oklahoma* (Oklahoma City Webb Publishing Company, 1929–30). Edward Everett Dale and Jesse Lee Rader, *Readings in Oklahoma History* (Evanston, Illinois: Row, Peterson and Company, 1930). Victor E. Harlow, *Oklahoma: Its Origins and Development* (Oklahoma City: Harlow Publishing Company, 1935). Muriel H. Wright, *Our Oklahoma* (Guthrie: Co-operative Publishing Company, 1939). [Oklahoma Writers' Project] *Oklahoma: A Guide to the Sooner State* (Norman: University of Oklahoma Press, 1941), pp. 208–209.

8. Osborn Campbell, *Let Freedom Ring* (Tokyo: Inter-Nation Company, 1954), p. 175.

9. *Tulsa Tribune*, June 2, 1936, p. 16.

10. *Ibid.*, May 31, 1946, p. 8; and June 2, 1946, p. 8.

    The Tulsa World, to its credit, did mention the riot in its "Just 30 Years Ago" columns in 1951. *Tulsa World*. June 1, 1951, p. 20; June 2, 1951, p. 4; and June 4, 1951, p. 6.

11. Telephone interview with Nancy Feldman, Tulsa, July 17, 2000. Letter from Nancy G. Feldman, Tulsa, July 19, 2000, to Dr. Bob Blackburn, Oklahoma City.

    On Robert Fairchild see: Oral History Interview with Robert Fairchild, Tulsa, June 8, 1978, by Scott Ellsworth, a copy of which can be found in the Special Collections Department, McFarlin Library, University of Tulsa; and, Eddie Faye Gates, *They Came Searching: How Blacks Sought the Promised Land in Tulsa* (Austin: Eakin Press, 1997), pp. 69–72.

12. Feldman letter, op. cit.

13. Letter from Nancy Dodson, Tulsa, June 4, 2000, to John Hope Franklin, Durham, North Carolina.

14. Mary E. Jones Parrish, *Events of the Tulsa Disaster* (N.p., n.p., n.d.). in 1998. A reprint edition of Parrish's book was published by Out on a Limb Publishing in Tulsa.

    Tulsa City Directory, 1921 (Tulsa: Polk-Hoffhine Directory Company, 1921).

15. Parrish, *Events of the Tulsa Disaster* (rpt. ed.; Tulsa: Out on a Limb Publishing, 1998), pp. 27, 31–77, 115–126.

    Prior to the publication of Parrish's book, however, a "book let about the riot was issued by the Black Dispatch Press of Oklahoma City in July, 1921. Written by Martin Brown, the booklet was titled, "Is Tulsa Sane?" At present, no copies are known to exist.

16. Loren L. Gill, "The Tulsa Race Riot" (M.A. thesis, University of Tulsa, 1946).

17. *Ibid.* According to his thesis adviser, William A. Settle, Jr., Gill was later highly critical of some of his original interpretations. During a visit to Tulsa during the late 1960s, after he had served as a Peace Corps volunteer, Gill told Settle that he had been "too hard" on black Tulsans.

18. Scott Ellsworth, *Death in a Promised Land: The Tulsa Race Riot of 1921* (Baton Rouge: Louisiana State University Press, 1982), pp. 104–107. Gina Henderson and Marlene L. Johnson, "Black Wall Street," *Emerge*) 4 (February, 2000), p. 71.

    The lack of public recognition given to the riot during this period was not limited to Tulsa's white community. A survey of back issues of the *Oklahoma Eagle* — long the city's flagship African American newspaper — revealed neither any articles about the riot, nor any mention of any commemorative ceremonies, at the time of the twenty-fifth anniversary of the riot in 1946. The same also applied to the thirtieth and fortieth anniversaries in 1951 and 1961.

19. *Oklahoma Eagle*, June 2, 1971, pp. 1, 10. *Tulsa Tribune*, June 2, 1971, p. 7A. Sam Howe Verhovek, "75 Years Later, Tulsa Confronts Its Race Riot," *New York Times*, May 31, 1996, p. 12A. Interview with E.L. Goodwin, Sr., Tulsa, November 21, 1976, in Ruth Sigler Avery, *Fear: The Fifth Horseman — A Documentary of the 1921 Tulsa Race Riot*, unpublished manuscript.

   See also: Mable B. Little, *Fire on Mount Zion: My Life and History as a Black Woman in American* (Langston, OK: The Black Think Tank, 1990); Beth Macklin, "'Home' Important in Tulsan's Life," *Tulsa World*, November 30, 1975, p. 3H; and Mable B. Little, "A History of the Blacks of North Tulsa and My Life (A True Story)," type script dated May 24, 1971.

20. Telephone interview with Larry Silvey, Tulsa, August 5, 1999. Oral history interview with Ed Wheeler, Tulsa, February 27, 1998, by Scott Ellsworth. See also: Brent Stapes, "Unearthing a Riot," *New York Times Magazine*, December 19, 1999, p. 69.

21. Ed Wheeler interview.

22. *Ibid.* Larry Silvey interview. Ed Wheeler, "Profile of a Race Riot," *Impact Magazine*, IV (June–July 1971). Staples, *"Unearthing a Riot,"* p. 69.

23. Avery, *Fear: The Fifth Horseman*. William A. Settle, Jr. and Ruth S. Avery, "Report of December 1978 on the Tulsa County Historical Society's Oral History Program," type script located at the Tulsa Historical Society. Telephone interview with Ruth Sigler Avery, Tulsa, September 14, 2000.

24. Mozella Jones Collection, Tulsa Historical Society. John Hope Franklin and John Whittington Franklin, eds., *My Life and An Era: The Autobiography of Buck Colbert Franklin* (Baton Rouge: Louisiana State University Press, 1997). John Hope Franklin, "Tulsa: Prospects for a New Millennium," remarks given at Mount Zion Baptist Church, Tulsa, June 4, 2000.

   Whitlow also was an authority on the history of Tulsa's African American community. See: Henry C. Whitlow, Jr., "A History of the Greenwood Era in Tulsa," a paper presented to the Tulsa Historical Society, March 29, 1973.

25. During this same period, a number of other Tulsans also endeavored to bring the story of the riot out into the open. James Ault, who taught sociology at the University of Tulsa during the late 1960s, interviewed a number of riot survivors and eyewitnesses. So did Bruce Hartnitt, who directed the evening programs at Tulsa Junior College during the early 1970s. Harnitt's father, who had managed the truck fleet at a West Tulsa refinery at the time of the riot, later told his son that he had been ordered to help transport the bodies of riot victims.

   Telephone interview with James T. Ault Omaha, Nebraska, February 22, 1999. Oral history interview with Bruce Hartnitt, Tulsa, May 30, 1998, by Scott Ellsworth.

26. John Hope Franklin and Alfred A. Moss, Jr., *From Slavery to Freedom: A History of African Americans*, 7th edition (New York: Alfred A. Knopf, 1994), p. 476. Richard Maxwell Brown, *Strain of Violence: Historical Studies of American Violence and Vigilantism* (New York: Oxford University Press, 1975). Lee E. Williams and Lee. E. Williams II, *Anatomy of Four Race Riots: Racial Conflict in Knoxville, Elaine (Arkansas), Tulsa and Chicago, 1919–1921* (Hattiesburg: University and College Press of Mississippi, 1972).

27. Kay M. Teall, ed., *Black History in Oklahoma: A Resource Book* (Oklahoma City: Oklahoma City Public Schools, 1971). Arthur Tolson, *The Black Oklahomans: A History, 1541–1972* (New Orleans: Edwards Printing Company, 1972).

28. Rudia M. Halliburton, Jr., *The Tulsa Race War of 1921* (San Francisco: R and E Research Associates, 1975).

29. Following the publication of Scott Ellsworth's *Death in a Promised Land* in 1982, a number of books have been published which deal either directly or indirectly with the riot. Among them are: Mabel B. Little, *Fire on Mount Zion* (1990); Robert N. Hower, *"Angels of Mercy": The American Red Cross and the 1921 Tulsa Race Riot* (Tulsa: Homestead Press, 1993); Eddie Faye Gates, *They Came Searching* (1997); Dorothy Moses DeWitty, *Tulsa: A Tale of Two Cities* (Langston, OK: Melvin B. Tolson Black Heritage Center, 1997); Danney Goble, *Tulsa!: Biography of the American City* (Tulsa: Council Oak Books, 1997); and, Hannibal B. Johnson, *Black Wall Street: From Riot to Renaissance in Tulsa's Historic Greenwood District* (Austin: Eakin Press, 1998).

   The riot has inspired some fictionalized treatments as well, including: Ron Wallace and J.J. Johnson, *Black Wall Street. A Lost Dream* (Tulsa: Black Wall Street Publishing, 1992); Jewell Parker Rhodes, *Magic City* (New York: Harper Collings, 1997); a children's book, Hannibal B. Johnson and Clay Portis, *Up From the Ashes: A Story About Building Community* (Austin: Eakin Press,

2000); and a musical, "A Song of Green-wood," book and music by Tim Long and Jerome.

30. Oklahoma newspaper have, not surprisingly, provided the most expansive coverage of recent riot-related news. In particular see: the reporting of Melissa Nelson and Christy Watson in the *Daily Oklahoma*; the numerous non-bylined stories in the *Oklahoma Eagle*; and the extensive coverage by Julie Bryant, Rik Espinosa, Brian Ford, Randy Krehbiel, Ashley Parrish, Jimmy Pride, Rita Sherrow, Robert S. Walters, and Heath Weaver in the *Tulsa World*.

For examples for national and international coverage, see: Kelly Kurt's wire stories for the Associated Press (e.g., "Survivors of 1921 Race Riot Hear Their Horror Retold," *San Diego Union-Tribune*, August 10, 1999, p A6); V. Dion Haynes, "Panel Digs Into Long-Buried Facts About Tulsa Race Riot," *Chicago Tribune*, May 16, 1999, Sec. 1, p. 6, Frederick Burger "The 1921 Tulsa Race Riot: A Holocaust America Wanted to Forget," *The Crisis*, CVII, 6 (November–December 1999), pp. 14–18; Arnold Hamilton, "Panel Urges Reparations in Tulsa Riot," *Dallas Morning News*, February 5, 2000, pp. IA, 22A; "The Riot That Never Was," *The Economist*, April 24, 1999, p. 29; Tim Madigan, "Tulsa's Terrible Secret," *Ft. Worth Star-Telegram*, January 30, 2000, pp. 1G, 6–7G; Rick Montgomery, "Tulsa Looking for the Sparks That Ignited Deadly Race Riot," *Kansas City Star*, September 8, 1999, pp. A1, A10; James Langton, "Mass Graves Hold the Secrets of American Race Massacre," *London Daily Telegraph*, March 29, 1999; Claudia Kolker, "A City's Buried Shame," *Los Angeles Times*, October 23, 1999, pp. A1, A16; Jim Yardley, "Panel Recommends Reparations in Long-Ignored Tulsa Race Riot," *New York Times*, February 5, 2000, pp. A1, A10; Martin Evans, "A Costly Legacy," *Newsday*, November 1, 1999; Gwen Florio, "Oklahoma Recalls Deadliest Race Riot," *Philadelphia Inquirer*, May 21, 1999, pp. A1, A9; Ben Fenwick, "Search for Race Riot Answers Leads to Graces," Reuter's wire story #13830, September 1999; Warren Cohen, "Digging Up an Ugly Past," *U.S. News and World Report*, January 31, 2000, p. 26; Tom Kenworthy, "Oklahoma Starts to Face Up to '21 Massacre," *USA Today*, February 18, 2000, p. 4A; and Lois Romano, "Tulsa Airs a Race Riot's Legacy," *Washington Post*, January 19, 2000, p. A3.

The riot has also been the subject of a number of television and radio news stories, documentaries, and talk shows during the past two years. The more comprehensive documentaries include: "The Night Tulsa Burned," The History Channel, February 19, 1999; "Tulsa Burning," *60 Minutes II*, November 9, 1999; and, "The Tulsa Lynching of 1921: A Hidden Story," Cinemax, May 31, 2000.

4.8 KU KLUX KLAN INITIATION, WORCESTER, MASSACHUSETTS (1924)

Source: *Worcester Sunday Telegram*, October 19, 1924. Reprinted with permission of the Worcester Telegram & Gazette Corporation and Gatehouse Media.

EDITORS' INTRODUCTION

Millions of Americans eagerly supported the 1920s hate-mongering organization known as the Invisible Empire, Knights of the Ku Klux Klan (KKK). Unlike the previous incarnation of the group, which was southern and rural in orientation, support for the new Klan was national and heavily urban. While numerous factors account for the Klan's resurgence, its simplistic message of "one hundred percent Americanism" hit a chord with many white Protestants who felt threatened by blacks, Catholics, Jews, and immigrants who flocked to cities in large numbers. On Saturday, October 18, 1924, approximately 15,000 Klan supporters attended a "klonvocation" at the New England Fairgrounds in the Greendale section of Worcester, Massachusetts. This KKK gathering, the largest in New England during the 1920s, took place in an industrial city with a population that was heavily immigrant (over 70 percent were foreign-born or the children of immigrants). Incredibly, despite the KKK's hostility to immigrants, roughly one-third of Worcester's Klan membership was itself foreign-born. The bulk of these immigrant Klansmen were Protestant Swedes. The description is of an initiation ceremony, one of several that took place during the klonvocation, which brought 2,600 new members into the Klan.

KU KLUX KLAN INITIATION, WORCESTER, MASSACHUSETTS (1924)

Parade of Knights Colorful Scene

The evening's parade and initiation was colorful in character, with 5,000 Knights in full regalia carrying red torches and marching about the track singing "Onward Christian Soldiers."

The initiation exercises at which 1,000 new members were added to the Klan organization were conducted with elaborate ceremony. The initiates were divided into two classes at separate ends of the field and repeated the Klan oath after officers, who conducted the ceremonies from temporary stagings erected on the inner rim of the tracks.

During the exercises an airplane bearing the red cross of the Klan sailed over the grounds several times. The big cross glowing like a ruby in the sky thrilled the great crowd more than the speeches or even the constant display of fireworks had done.

Klavern yesterday was distinctly a family affair, and it seems to be largely rural in character. Many small children wearing full Klan regalia paraded about the track.

Scores of babies cried constantly during the ceremonies and the crowd was not unlike that seen at the New England fair on one of the closing days.

No reporters were observed in the press box, however. In that respect the general character of the observance was distinctly different. Newspaper men were escorted to the exits many times during the course of the afternoon.

The exhibition building was used for registration headquarters, and as an application bureau for new members. Names of all the counties in Massachusetts appeared on large placards along the wall and each county had its own clerks to assist in the new membership drive.

THE POCKET BOOK DROPPER.

Illustration IV.1 "The Pocket Book Dropper." *The National Police Gazette* May 27, 1848. Courtesy of the Center for Historic American Visual Culture at the American Antiquarian Society.

PART V

*F*ROM PARTY BOSSES TO FEDERALISM

The Evolution of Urban Government

One of the most remarkable facets of American urban life during the nineteenth century was the expansion and transformation of municipal government. During the colonial era, local communities had limited authority to manage their own affairs. After the American Revolution, individual states granted their cities and towns the right to incorporate as municipal entities. Municipal status allowed cities and towns the authority to pass local ordinances, levee taxes, enforce fines, and otherwise manage their own legal affairs. During the nineteenth century, city officials across the country used these powers to hire private contractors and public employees to meet the basic health, education, and public safety needs of a rapidly expanding urban population. As such, the actual physical and economic landscape of cities changed with the construction of schools, roads, sewers, and other forms of infrastructure, as well as the creation of new job opportunities in education, police and fire protection, sanitation, and other fields.

Concurrent with the rise of municipal governance was the extension of voting access—albeit slow and uneven—and the broadening of civil and legal rights for immigrants, racial minorities, women, and others traditionally excluded from the decision making process. In the late eighteenth century, only a minority of adults, usually propertied men, were able to vote in local elections and hold office. Only a few states allowed women to vote by the end of the nineteenth century, and working-class voters, many of them naturalized immigrants and the children of immigrants, influenced the outcome of urban elections and even held political office. The rise of the working class electorate solidified political machines and party bosses, and vice versa. While not strictly an urban phenomenon, political machines became synonymous with large cities, especially those that were able to spend vast amounts of money on public works projects. Public works projects presented opportunities for financial corruption. A handful of individuals enriched themselves through extralegal activities, which is decidedly undemocratic.

Not surprisingly, these municipal and political trends played themselves out to the extreme in New York City. As the largest metropolitan area in the nation, New York was both a trendsetter and the object of superlatives for all that was positive and negative about big city government. The construction of Central Park is a case in point. Although widely regarded as the first great public park in the United States, its design and construction reflected political and social unease within the city. As **Illustration V.1** illustrates, advocates for the park envisioned a pastoral setting where New Yorkers of all classes could benefit from tranquil vistas and peaceful social intercourse. However, the park's management became embroiled in political controversy as different constituencies vied to shape the use of public space.

Debate over Central Park highlighted a larger struggle between municipal and state officials as to whether New York City could even manage its own affairs. Adding fuel to arguments for limiting self-governance in New York City were the actions of the notorious party boss William M. Tweed, who extorted millions of dollars through the political machinery of Tammany Hall. Tammany Hall controlled the city's Democratic Party. **Document 5.1** samples the extent of Tweed's corruption as he provided city investigators with a detailed explanation of how he and others stole millions of dollars from the public between the 1850s–1870s. As **Document 5.2** demonstrates, political corruption was not limited to New York or even the Democratic Party. Noted muckraker Lincoln Steffens demonstrates the New York parallels in his investigation of Republican-dominated Philadelphia at the turn of the twentieth century. And although good government reformers who fought graft and corruption often portrayed themselves as crusaders for democracy, as political scientist Jessica Trounstine examines in her essay, they were no more interested in representing the interests of all citizens as the machine bosses they fought against.

Social reformers sought their own solutions to urban ills in this period. Following the Columbian Exposition of 1893, Daniel Burnham and Chicago businessmen set out to improve the physical infrastructure of their city. The 1909 Plan of Chicago led to great improvements within that city and simultaneously sparked a national movement for urban redevelopment. Jane Addams and Ellen Gates Starr launched Hull-House in 1889 on Chicago's Near West Side to serve the city's immigrant communities. [See Documents 7.2 and 1.2.]

State dependent cities experienced a fundamental transformation during the Great Depression. In her essay, Lizabeth Cohen explores how working class Chicagoans forged a direct partnership with the federal government. New Deal relief programs put people back to work building the urban infrastructure. The relationship between cities and the federal government further expanded following the Second World War with legislation that enabled slum clearance and public housing development. [See Document 7.3.] Nicholas Lemann's essay examines the anti-poverty programs of President John F. Kennedy's administration that lay the foundation for the federal-city partnership that evolved into the social programs of President Lyndon B. Johnson's War on Poverty. [See Document 5.3.] Despite this aid, cities still faced obstacles in rejuvenating their economic base. Some blamed the structure of the black family, a preposterous tactic that smacked of racism. Black migrants, newcomers to northern cities, were the subject of pointed criticism, although migrant families were likely to be more educated and more likely to have sustained marriages than families of more settled black urbanites. Public commentators, in the past and in the twentieth century, find it far easier to place blame than to suggest routes to success. [See Document 5.4.] For many urban critics, cities reached their nadir in the 1970s, when deindustrialization combined with decentralization and a declining tax base to create a state of urban imbalance. One of the most dramatic examples of this reversal of fortune came when New York City teetered on the verge of bankruptcy in the mid-1970s.

Despite the bad publicity, American cities proved resilient. During the 1970s–1980s, big city mayors and other civic leaders anticipated a long awaited urban renaissance. Even the unprecedented devastation of Hurricanes Katrina and Rita in August and September 2005 failed to entirely erode the resolve of the citizens and leaders of New Orleans, Louisiana. [See Document 5.5.] In the early twenty-first century, the rural-urban divide seemed to grow wider under the influence of the divisive political style of President Donald Trump. [See Document 5.6.]

ESSAY 5.1

Challenging the Machine-Reform Dichotomy: Two Threats to Urban Democracy

Jessica Trounstine

Source: Richardson Dilworth, ed., *The City in American Political Development* (New York: Routledge, 2009).

EDITORS' INTRODUCTION

Few urban history topics have generated as much interest and debate as the nature and impact of political machines. These machines took root in nineteenth-century American cities and were organized within the Democratic and Republican parties, as well as other political factions. Political machines had influence at the neighborhood and ward level, as well as in the city hall, the statehouse, and the federal government. Machines relied on reciprocal relationships between voters and party officials that provided supporters access to power in exchange for loyalty at the ballot box. Appointing loyal followers to city jobs proved an important aspect of the machine's power. Political machines deftly negotiated an ever-changing urban terrain. Rapidly growing cities offered residents unprecedented economic opportunities but also exacerbated poverty and inequality. Political machines horrified urban reformers, who saw party leaders, known as bosses, undermine previous notions of proper government and democracy and enrich themselves by plundering the public treasury and finding ways to financially benefit from government contracts. This financial gain is known as "graft." **[See Document 5.1, "William Tweed's Confession (1878)."]** In response, a cadre of reformers coalesced to combat what they considered the most egregious aspects of machine corruption. These late nineteenth century political crusaders introduced several "good government" measures, including sound business management and accounting practices and a meritocracy-based system of government hiring.

Despite the corruption inherent in the machine system of government, twentieth and twenty-first century urban historians tend to note the positive benefits of nineteenth century machine politics at the municipal level. (The term "municipal" refers to the local incorporated town and/or city.) As there was little or no direct government assistance for the needy, machines helped provide working class families with access to adequate food, shelter, and employment opportunities. Urban reformers' actions to undermine the power of machines and limit these opportunities for the urban poor often stemmed from nativist fears and a desire to implement social control of the lower class. Yet many urban scholars also acknowledge the party bosses' blatant graft and often characterize the reform agenda in the main as progressive.

For political scientists, the historical study of machine politics and reform is part of an institutionalist subfield known as American political development (APD). However, despite the presence of 19,492 municipal governments in the United States (from a 2007 estimation by the U.S. Census Bureau), political scientist Richardson Dilworth argues that "the city had been a woefully neglected topic within the recent study of American politics."[i] The following essay from political scientist Jessica Trounstine helps brings municipal government to the forefront of APD through a revisionist account of the classic machine-reform dichotomy. Trounstine examines governing coalitions in five cities dominated by machines (New Haven, New York, Philadelphia, Chicago, and Kansas City), and four by reform regimes (Dallas, Austin, San Antonio, and San Jose) and argues that once elected, both reform and machine politicians sought to alter election processes to ensure their own side's reelection and to erect defenses against future government shifts. In the process, reformers and machine politicians became increasingly unlikely to respond to the needs of their constituents, and thus limited participation in the democratic process.

Jessica Trounstine is Professor of Political Science at the University of California, Merced and a past President of the Urban and Local Politics Section of the American Political Science Association (APSA). Dr. Trounstine studies American politics with a focus on subnational politics and the process and quality of representation, primarily concentrating on large cities. She is the author of *Segregation by Design: Local Politics and Inequality in American Cities* (New York: Cambridge University Press, 2018) and *Political Monopolies in American Cities: The Rise and Fall of Bosses and Reformers* (Chicago: University of Chicago Press, 2008), winner of that year's APSA award for Best Book on Urban Politics.

CHALLENGING THE MACHINE-REFORM DICHOTOMY

Two Threats to Urban Democracy

One of the classic themes in the study of urban political history is the clash between the Boss and the Reformer. According to traditional accounts machines dominated local politics through party organizations, created corrupt and inefficient government, and were supported by immigrant masses who had been bribed into loyalty.[1] Municipal reformers on the other hand sought clean government run by experts and supported by a knowledgeable, decisive electorate, which would allow elected officials freedom to pursue growth and development.[2] Yet, despite these important differences, machine and reform coalitions shared many more characteristics than the conventional wisdom would suggest.

The machine—reform dichotomy has been a subject of debate since reformers first began penning critiques of machines at the turn of the nineteenth century.[3] In these accounts machines epitomized corrupted democracy and reformers the cities' white knights. A second generation of scholarship

challenged these early normative claims. Theorists such as Robert Merton argued that machines dominated for extended periods of time because they provided integral social functions such as the provision of welfare, the creation of informal networks between business and government, and the centralization of power.[4] Simultaneously, a new generation of scholarship on municipal reform reanalyzed the movement as an effort by businessmen and the middle class to regain governing authority. To achieve this goal reformers sought to disenfranchise poor, working class, and immigrant voters.[5] Then scholarship deriding machines reemerged while reform was reinterpreted as a complex, multifaceted movement.[6] More recently urban historians have suggested that machines dominated the minds of reformers more frequently than they dominated cities. However, even in revisionist accounts machine and reform politicians tend to be analyzed in opposition to one another and frequently at one historical moment.

Studying political machines and municipal reform side by side and over time allows us to see how alike they were. After

---

i Richardson Dilworth, "Introduction: Bringing the City Back In," from Richardson Dilworth ed., *The City in American Political Development* (New York: Routledge, 2009), 1.

coming to power, both types of coalitions sought to prevent durable shifts in governing authority by biasing political institutions in their favor.[7] In approximately 30 percent of America's largest cities the result was the elimination of effective competition and the domination of governance by a single coalition for multiple terms.[8] During periods of dominance, with reelection virtually guaranteed, machine and reform coalitions became less responsive to the populations they governed.

The development of dominance in machine and reform cities exemplifies the importance of timing and the processes of path dependence and positive feedback emphasized by scholars of American political development. The period during which a coalition established governing authority significantly affected (or attenuated) its options for biasing the system. The demographic and economic makeup of a city, the prevailing distribution of authority, and institutional setting made some strategies more attractive and successful than others.[9] Over time, dominance became self-reinforcing. The presence of biased institutions coupled with smashing electoral victories and low turnout discouraged challengers from attempting to enter the political fray at all. Ultimately though, the inflexibility in the structures and strategies of dominance undermined the ability of incumbents to maintain power as dissatisfaction became widespread among city residents and elites. Once a coalition became reliant on specific mechanisms to prevent shifts in governing authority, it became increasingly difficult for the coalition to choose any other path. In many cases a regime's inability to change its tactics ultimately led to its defeat.

In this essay I show that both machine and reform politicians sought to increase the certainty of reelection by advantaging incumbents at all stages of the voting process. The strategies that these coalitions used allowed them to maintain dominance for long periods of time while excluding large segments of the population from the benefits of municipal governance. I begin by laying out a theoretical framework for understanding the similarities between machine and reform politics. Then I provide historical evidence of the various mechanisms each type of coalition relied upon to preserve power. Finally, I explain the effects of dominance: incumbents were reelected with near certainty and large segments of the population were denied access to municipal services and benefits. The divergent characterizations scholars have offered of machine and reform politicians can be reinterpreted as alternative means to achieve the same goal—a durable shift in governing authority.

A Theory of Dominance

As is the case in the sporting world, the institutions that govern political contests have the potential to determine which contestants are most likely to win elections, what skills and strategies will be most valuable, and who gets to participate. Thus, political institutions vary in the degree to which they ensure competitive elections and responsiveness to voters. Some institutions, biased institutions, simultaneously decrease competition (increasing the probability that incumbents will retain power) and decrease the need for incumbents to be responsive to voters. We should expect politicians to favor institutions that advantage them and to select strategies that enhance their chances of victory given the context in which they run. These strategies might consist of being responsive to voters or they might be the implementation of biased institutions.

If a coalition chooses to enact or rely on bias to insulate its governing authority it selects from among a number of options that can be categorized by the decision points in a democratic electoral system—generating preferences regarding government performance (information bias), translating preferences into votes (vote bias), and converting votes into seats (seat bias).[10]

Information bias refers to a system in which the government has a systematic advantage in controlling information about its record of performance and thus, citizen's preferences. State-controlled media and low information elections (e.g. nonpartisan elections) are examples of such mechanisms. In essence, information bias suggests an advantage for incumbents in the dissemination of information about government activity and available alternatives.

Vote bias describes a systematic advantage for incumbents in the way votes are cast. When a coalition uses government resources (for example, patronage employees) to promote the organization of its supporters or inhibit the organization of its opposition, it is engaging vote bias. Mechanisms such as poll taxes, registration laws, and vote fraud are other examples of this type of bias. Additionally, this category includes barriers to competition for challengers, such as lowering officials' pay or physically intimidating candidates. Barriers to competition bias outcomes toward the governing regime because voters have no other options.

The final step in the electoral process is the translation of votes into seats. This type of bias has been extensively studied in the literature on apportionment and representation, particularly with regard to the US Congress.[11] The system's seat bias is determined by the degree to which the share of seats won exaggerates the share of votes won in favor of the incumbent coalition. Measures that create or increase malapportionment, gerrymandering, or reserved seats in the government's favor increase the incumbent coalition's probability of retaining governing authority. Additionally, the elimination of districts in legislative elections can increase incumbents' advantage when used in combination with voting restrictions. In this case at-large elections offer a substantial advantage to the incumbent coalition because all seats represent the same limited electorate. Table 5.1 displays

Table 5.1 Biasing strategies

Information bias	Vote bias	Seat bias
Media control (ownership, regulation)	Vote bribery	Annexing in government's favor
Suppression of voluntary associations	Obscure polling place sites	Gerrymandering
Control over judicial system/prosecutors	Use of government resources to prevent opponent organization or enhance incumbent organization	Malapportionment
Low information elections (e.g. nonpartisan)	Impairment of election monitoring	Decreasing size of legislature
	Disqualification of candidates	At-large elections
	Candidate requirements (signatures, thresholds)	Increasing appointed offices
	Low pay for office holders	
	Violence keeping voters from polls or forcing vote choice	
	Electoral falsification (ghost/repeat voting, inflating totals, discarding ballots)	
	Registration requirements	
	Suffrage restrictions (literacy tests, poll taxes, language or race requirements, citizens only)	
	Assassinating/threatening/imprisoning opponents	

strategies that have been used to increase the probability of incumbents maintaining governing authority in American cities.

Two bundles of strategies have been common in American history. Machine coalitions achieved control primarily through the use of government resources for political ends while reform coalitions dominated government by relying on rules that limited the opportunity for dissenters and minority populations to participate in elections.

The strategies selected and relied upon by machine and reform organizations differed because they faced different institutional constraints and political contexts. In short, the timing and location of dominance mattered a great deal. Machines lacked home rule, were frequently thwarted by state officials of opposing parties, and sought power in cities with large, diverse populations of working-class and poor voters, many of whom were first and second generation immigrants. A reliance on patronage for winning reelection made sense in this environment. Reformers benefited from flexible city charters, supportive state governments, and more homogeneous communities in which opponents to reform platforms could be excluded from the electorate through suffrage restrictions and vote dilution.

The following sections provide a more in-depth analysis of each type of bias used by governing coalitions in Chicago, New York, New Haven, Kansas City, Philadelphia, San Jose, Austin, San Antonio, and Dallas. The first five cities were dominated by machines and the latter four cities by reform regimes. The following discussion is organized by biasing category (information bias, vote bias, and seat bias) and by coalition type (machine or reform).

Controlling Information

Machines sought to control information to shape voters' preferences using a number of different mechanisms. For example they placed organization loyalists in official positions that held investigative authority such as local-level prosecutors, grand juries, or state attorneys general. When investigations

did occur, machines used control over city agencies to destroy evidence, provide extended leaves to potential witnesses, and otherwise prevent prosecutorial cooperation. The machine's relationship to the criminal underworld was sometimes utilized to kill informants.[12] Another mechanism of information control was influence over the news media. Machines attempted to achieve favorable news coverage by bribing editors or reporters, contributing heavily in advertising funds, or by offering publishers or editors public jobs. Libel suits against papers were also used to control the presentation of harmful information. In a few cases machines resorted to murdering investigative reporters.[13]

Reformers used less obviously corrupt methods for controlling information and shaping the preferences of voters in favor of their incumbent organizations. At the turn of the century, many reform organizations secured the enactment of nonpartisan local elections, arguing that parties should be irrelevant to urban administration. Because reformers argued that they had identified the most appropriate approach to good government, political institutions that made governance conflictual, such as parties, served to stymie progress. One reform leader argued the purpose of the nonpartisan movement was "to unite decent voters in an effort to take the city government out of politics."[14] By "politics" reformers meant "patronage and selfish intrigue of those who lived on the public payroll and were therefore considered hindrances to community development."[15]

In converting elections to nonpartisan contests, reformers sought to minimize divisions in the electorate and among elites. The lack of party cues to assist voters in the formation of preferences resulted in systems biased in favor of candidates with independent wealth or fame and incumbents, advantaging reform coalition members.[16] Additionally, the less structured environment for competition in a nonpartisan system served to decrease interest and knowledge among constituents, making it difficult for challengers to activate opposition to the incumbent regime.[17] Without parties to train new leaders and teach voters political skills, nonpartisan elections increased the probability that membership in the incumbent organization was the only path to access the system.

The most powerful reform weapon in shaping the preference of voters was control over the local media. Newspaper editors and owners were the leaders of the reform movement in many cities. In San Jose, San Antonio, Dallas, and Austin, reform-owned newspapers refused to report stories that challenged the dominance of the local elites.[18] The local papers in all four reform cities endorsed reform charters, and news stories about city hall tended toward unabashed editorializing. According to a review of city manager government in Dallas, the publisher of the *Dallas News* "threw the full weight of his paper behind" the movement.[19] Every day leading up to the charter election the *News* published a front-page article explaining some aspect of the proposed change and urged its adoption. On the eve of charter reform in San Jose, the *Mercury Herald* printed a front-page article that argued the election would reveal

> whether the people of San Jose want boss rule or popular rule; whether the jobs of city hall shall go to henchmen who do nothing for their pay but politics for their master, or to be clean capable men who are good citizens and are accustomed only to a fair wage for fair service.[20]

Everywhere, local news organizations shared the vision of the common good that reformers proposed to enact; but frequently only after reformers strategically purchased opposition news outlets. In Austin the leaders of the opposition owned the evening paper and reported anti-reform speeches in great detail.[21] This changed after reform leaders purchased the paper in 1924. In 1896, the San Jose Good Government League was organized to win control of the city for the forces of reform but failed in part because the city's newspapers published articles critically analyzing the reform plan. Such problems ended after reform leaders J.O. and E.A. Hayes purchased two of the city's three newspapers and ended

printed opposition to the reform charter and candidates in the newly consolidated *San Jose Mercury Herald*. The editor of the *Herald* resigned after discovering that the new owners intended to impose an editorial policy with "political implications."[22] The Hayes family completed their news monopoly in 1942 when they purchased the town's third and last independent newspaper, *The News*. Two years later the reform coalition finally achieved dominance. By coordinating the support of papers, reformers were "shielded from criticism by enthusiastic and boosterish local mass media" and successfully biased the system in their favor.[23]

Biasing Votes Using Government Resources

The second stage of the voting process requires voters to translate their preferences into votes on election day. Coalitions can take steps to ensure that incumbent office holders are advantaged when ballots are cast by limiting the ability for residents or challengers to participate in electoral contests.

In order to bias outcomes toward their organizations, governing coalitions in many political systems focus on trading divisible benefits (such as public jobs) for support, thereby using government resources to engender loyalty to the incumbent regime and pay political workers. Patronage becomes an even stronger strategy for bias when the coalition uses the benefit coercively, threatening recipients with losing their jobs if they do not perform political functions, requiring that job holders pay a portion of their salary into party coffers, and/or using political appointees to further bias the political system through practices such as vote fraud and intimidation. When workers are assured of economic security if and only if they support the incumbent coalition, they are extremely unlikely to engage in political opposition.[24] The loyalty generated by such uncertainty over maintaining one's job is likely to be even more dramatic when the employee has few options for work in the private sector. In this way, coercive patronage serves to bias the system in favor of incumbents.

Party-based coalitions in Chicago, Kansas City, New York, New Haven, and Philadelphia employed patronage coercively. In Kansas City nearly all machine leaders and workers held public jobs, some contributing up to 50 percent of their salaries to the party's campaign funds.[25] In Chicago Mayor Cermak pressured employees to contribute 1 to 2 percent of their salaries.[26] Later in the city's history, Mayor and Boss Richard J. Daley made certain that his patronage appointees would remain loyal to him by threatening their jobs and controlling which government decisions they made.[27] By using government resources to organize and maintain the coalition, machine organizations successfully biased electoral outcomes in favor of incumbent coalitions.

However, patronage was not sufficient to guarantee long-term dominance for urban coalitions because various factions and opposition parties used the same strategies. Shifting governing authority using patronage required that a coalition control *access* to patronage, often through relationships with higher levels of government. Where organizations had difficulty securing and/or controlling patronage, they did not survive without alternative electoral strategies. For instance in New York, anti-Tammany governors doled out patronage to various wings of the Democratic Party until the late 1890s. Tammany finally consolidated governing authority only after a new governor supportive of the organization channeled patronage to Tammany leaders at the turn of the century.[28]

Control over the bureaucracy through patronage workers also allowed coalitions in Chicago, Kansas City, New York, New Haven, and Philadelphia to control delivery of municipal benefits and application of city laws. New York's machine made sure that the city's attorney used the power of the office to go after political challengers or their supporters for violations of mundane city ordinances. Near election time "a general raid ... [was] made on the whole body of store keepers and others in the district, care, of course, being taken not to trouble any who are known to be of the right stripe." Storekeepers were then offered the option of settling their violations in exchange for their vote at the next election.

Any fines paid by violators were funneled into the machine's reelection fund.[29]

Legal and illegal businesses knew that they needed the machine on their side to pass inspections, secure utility extensions, ignore closing laws, sell liquor during Prohibition, run lotteries, and so on.[30] A 1917 editorial in the *New York Times* explained Tammany's system:

> Bootblacks, pushcart men, fruit vendors, soda water stand and corner grocery keepers, sailmakers, dry goods merchants, and so forth, "all had to contribute to the vast amounts that flowed into station houses, and which, after leaving something in the nature of a deposit there, flowed on higher." ... The police was a collecting agency for Tammany Hall every day of the year.[31]

Such a system ensured that businesses would organize electoral support for the machine. Incumbent politicians, reliant on their patronage work-force, could use selective application of the law to enhance their probability of reelection.

However, excessive corruption served to undermine a machine's authority if it became too offensive to voters or attracted the attention of higher levels of government. Successful machines were careful to use corruption to ensure loyalty, not to aggregate enormous wealth.[32] Properly controlled, patronage workforces could act as a strong deterrent to opposition, biasing outcomes in favor of incumbents using public funds.

Machines also profited from their skill in employing electoral fraud and repression. Stories abound of politicians at the turn of the century throwing uncounted ballots into the river, registering and voting on behalf of the dead or departed, and paying for individual votes.[33] Kansas City's Boss Tom Pendergast garnered 50,000 phantom voters in the late 1940s.[34] Between 1930 and 1934 the number of voters in the second ward went from 8,128 to 15,940 without a significant population increase.[35] In Richard J. Daley's first election for mayor, the *Chicago Tribune* published photographs of Democratic ward boss, Sidney "Short Pencil" Lewis, erasing votes cast for Daley's

Democratic opponent in the primary. Daley's Republican opponent Robert Merriam sought to have Daley disqualified because of the fraud. But, the Democratic machine controlled the Board of Elections, and the commissioner chastised Merriam rather than Lewis or Daley. The chief election commissioner charged: "Merriam is following Hitler's tactics which consisted of this—it you tell a lie often enough, people will begin to believe you."[36]

In addition to fixing the votes of people who arrived at the polls, machines preferred for their opponents to stay at home on election day, also enhancing the vote bias of the system. Gary Cox and Morgan Kousser argue that party workers turned from mobilizing supporters with illegal tactics to discouraging opponents with threats when the enactment of the Australian ballot made verifying votes too difficult.[37] Some machines avoided the problem by refusing to oil the voting machine lever for the opposition candidate. The squeak of an un-oiled lever immediately identified opposition supporters to the polling officials.[38] In other cases machines supported the passage of laws that legally limited the size of the electorate when it served their needs.[39] By constructing their ideal electorate through fraud and intimidation, machines biased the system in favor of their incumbent organizations.

Bosses also frequently frustrated their competitors' attempts to organize. Machines used threats and arrests, denial of meeting or parade permits, and selective enforcement of laws to limit insurgencies against their organizations. They relied on state laws that protected existing parties at the expense of new coalitions. For example, in Chicago, an independent needed 60,000 to 70,000 signatures to get his name on the ballot, compared with the regular party requirements of only 2,000 to 4,000. Next, the independent needed the machine-controlled Chicago Elections Board to approve the entire list of signatures.[40] In 1931 five minor candidates filed to run for mayor against the machine's founder Anton Cermak. As President of the County Board, Cermak controlled the Board of Election Commissioners, which declared the petitions of all five candidates illegal.[41] These rules

worked as barriers to entry for challengers, thus favoring the machine's incumbent candidates.

Reformers Shape the Electorate with Institutions

Where machines used informal and extra legal tactics such as patronage ties, bribery, and threats to shape election outcomes in their favor, politicians in San Jose, Austin, Dallas, and San Antonio relied on legal mechanisms of bias that determined who had the right to cast ballots. Reformers proposed, lobbied for, and supported passage of suffrage restrictions at the state and local level including literacy tests, abolition of alien suffrage, registration requirements, poll taxes, obscure polling places, and measures that decreased the visibility or comprehensibility of politics such as non-concurrent, off-year elections.[42] Reform changes to city electoral and governing institutions had the effect of limiting opportunities for opponents to voice dissent and ensured that those who cast ballots shared reformers' demographics and policy goals.

In Austin only 37 percent of adults over the age of 21 had the right to vote in 1933 because of suffrage restrictions including the poll tax and literacy test.[43] San Antonio required property ownership for bond elections until 1969 and in tax elections until 1975.[44] In California mobile and migrant workers were the focus of increased residency requirements for voters in the 1870s.[45] In 1911 the Progressive legislature established biannual registration.[46] In 1894 California's Republican-controlled state house enacted a literacy requirement that barred from voting anyone who could not write his name and read the Constitution in English.[47] The Los Angeles Times applauded the amendment saying "here is one of the greatest reforms of our age ... for the illiterate herd of voters will no longer haunt the polls on election day ... and therefore the honest voter will have a chance to carry the election."[48]

Santa Clara County, where San Jose is located, implemented an additional four dollar poll tax in the late 1890s.[49] A local populist newsletter criticized the tax for its disfranchising effects on "free white men eligible for naturalization" meaning European immigrants and low-income whites. The article made clear it was *not* concerned about "Chinamen or negroes."[50] Such barriers to registration and voting significantly decreased the size of the electorate and especially impacted participation among poor and working-class residents and people of color.

By 1900 San Jose and the Santa Clara Valley had already established their position as the agricultural heartland of California. Canneries and orchards employed large numbers of Chinese, then Japanese, and finally Mexican immigrants throughout the twentieth century. Chinese workers in particular were targeted for restriction from social and political life. Led by laborers and grangers from San Francisco, California's constitution was amended in 1879 to include a series of anti-Chinese provisions. Chinese were prohibited from voting, owning land, working in certain occupations, and municipalities were authorized to exclude Chinese from city bounds or to designate specific areas of the city where Chinese residents could live.[51]

The anti-Chinese movement found support in San Jose. The city's Chinatown was burned to the ground in 1887 and forced to relocate outside of the city. Community members largely believed the fire was a result of arson tacitly approved by the city council and mayor because the ethnic enclave stood in the way of downtown development. The fire department successfully saved every non-Chinese-owned business in the path of the fire but not a single Chinese-occupied structure. In a 1902 pamphlet entitled "Sodom of the Coast," leaders of the reform movement targeted gambling operations and graft centered in the Chinese community in an effort to overhaul the city government.[52] Throughout the first half of the twentieth century the reform-owned *San Jose Mercury Herald* printed articles in support of excluding Asian immigrants, preventing aliens from owning land, and warning of the "yellow peril."[53] Such anti-Chinese and Japanese

sentiment suggests that San Jose's leaders would have supported the state-level changes that narrowed the electorate.

In addition to state suffrage restrictions, San Jose reformers were likely aided by the fact that the laboring class worked seasonally and tended to leave the city after harvest. Elections were held when agricultural workers were not living in the city—late winter and early spring.[54] According to one source in 1939, the permanent agricultural workforce in San Jose was 3,000 people. During harvest season this ballooned to 40,000 workers.[55] Holding elections when the migrant workforce was not in residence excluded this segment of the community from direct political participation. Pickers and canners earned wages at the bottom of the city's pay scale, and given that the working class constituted the most vocal opposition to reform charters, it seems likely that reformers would have been aided by limiting their participation.[56]

Reform incumbents also benefited from institutionalized mechanisms that increased barriers to competition through charter revision and city ordinances. This legally biased the system in favor of certain types of people who were the most likely supporters of the reform agenda. Reformers decreased the pay for elected and appointed city offices and increased candidate qualifications through charter revisions. For example, in Austin council members were required to post $10,000 bonds before taking office in the early 1900s.[57]

These changes meant that office holders all worked other jobs that had flexible hours and/or had some independent source of wealth. The result was that city councils tended to be populated by upper-class professionals and small business owners, the same groups leading the reform movement. Between 1944 and 1980, a large proportion of San Jose's leadership community attended the local Jesuit high school, graduated from the local Jesuit college, and lived in one of two wealthy, white neighborhoods. They were part of a "good old boys network" of civic-minded men who "really cared about the city," but who were not representative of the entire community.[58] The changes reformers made to government erected barriers to enter the political fray, encouraged certain types of people to become active participants in governance and actively discouraged others, biasing outcomes in favor of reform candidates.

Machines and Reformers Insulate Their Seat Shares

In the final stage of the voting process, the translation of votes to seats, incumbent political coalitions often have immense power in biasing the system because they can insulate coalition members from challenges. In machine cities gerrymandering was used to bolster the chances of incumbent coalitions. For instance, during the 1920s New York's Boss Charles Francis Murphy drew district lines to dilute the votes of Italian neighborhoods. In the 1960s and 1970s, Daley's machine relied on creative district line drawing to ensure that neighborhoods with black and Latino majorities were dominated by white, machine loyal representatives.[59]

Reformers in San Jose, Austin, Dallas, and San Antonio increased incumbents' probability of retaining control using different mechanisms. They implemented at-large elections, transformed elected seats to appointed ones, and used strategic annexations. By abolishing districts and choosing citywide elections, reform charters ensured that minority preferences, even those of substantial size, remained unrepresented in the city legislature. At-large elections also had the effect of shifting representation toward voters rather than residents. In a district system, regardless of the number of voters in a given area of the city, the area is assured of representation on the council. In an at-large election this is no longer the case. Thus, in reform cities where turnout had already been decreased through suffrage restrictions and registration requirements, it became even less likely that certain areas would be represented. Given the nature of the suffrage restrictions, these areas of the city tended to be low income, working class, and communities of color.

In many reform cities, the abolition of districts or wards generated some of the most vocal opposition and contentious

argument against the reform charters. Opponents of Austin's 1908 reform charter argued that "under the aldermanic system the citizens are assured direct representation in the affairs of the municipality, and direct control over ward improvements. Ward representation is in line with the democratic doctrine of local self-government."[60] In 1924 Austin's reform charter passed by a tiny margin of twenty votes out of 4,906 ballots cast. Five of the city's seven wards defeated the charter, but the two wealthy areas of town passed it by a three to one margin. Because the election was citywide the supporters won.

San Jose reformers abolished the ward system in 1915 to reduce the influence of certain districts.[61] The coalition displaced by San Jose's reformers had been able to control city government because it maintained strong support in the city's older, central wards. Reformers came to dominate the second and third wards. According to one observer, the latter was a "traditional stronghold of the better elements, with strict moral views and continued efforts to secure a government which they believe honest and impartial."[62]

In revising the charter, San Jose reformers lost in the central wards but won large numbers of votes in the second and third wards, as well as in newly annexed territory, thereby cinching the citywide victory. According to the political editor of the San Jose Mercury News, the at-large system "served the interests of the folks who had established it, not the average person in town ... [reformers] didn't want the small, parochial interests of more narrowly based groups to have any influence in politics."[63] At-large elections required more campaign funds, more extensive organization, and bigger mobilization operations in order to win and so tended to bias outcomes in favor of reform incumbents.

Reformers also benefited from the use of strategic annexation that maintained an electorate supportive of their administrations. As they grew, cities such as San Jose, San Antonio, Dallas, and Austin selectively expanded their city boundaries and chose not to annex particular outlying communities.

San Jose's first planned annexation was a one hundred foot wide strip of land leading to the city of Alviso where San Jose hoped to build a port in 1912. Though the port was never built, San Jose did construct a technologically advanced sewage treatment plant on the site, which then became the tool by which other communities could be convinced to be annexed to the city. Given that annexation decisions were made in order to "grow and be able to pay the bill,"[64] poorer communities and undevelopable land were not priorities. San Jose reform leaders sought to "capture the cross roads which the administration told us were going to be the shopping centers of the future—where the sales tax would be."[65] Not surprisingly while San Jose had access to its treatment plant in Alviso, it did not annex the actual city, a poor agricultural community, until the late 1960s. When the annexation did occur it was in response to Alviso's attempt to annex the sewage treatment plant to its own borders.

San Jose annexed vast tracts of suburban land; incorporating 1,419 outlying areas by 1969. Yet, as of 2005 there were pockets of county land surrounded on all sides by the city of San Jose. Outside of the official city bounds, these areas have been excluded from participating in local governance. In other cities annexation decisions had a more direct and obvious political effect. San Antonio's annexation practices were challenged by the Justice Department under the Voting Rights Act in 1976 because they diluted a growing Mexican American population in the city.[66] Annexations created and maintained a community and electorate that tended to support reform goals. Had these excluded communities become part of the city, reformers might have lost elections. Thus, annexations biased the system in favor of incumbent reformers by determining whose votes translated into seats and whose views would not be counted.

Finally, reformers biased government toward the incumbent regime by transforming many elected positions into appointed offices. Reform charters eliminated popularly elected mayors or turned them into ceremonial heads and invested all executive power in city managers appointed by the council. The purpose of this change was to create a more efficient government. An editorial in the *Dallas News* urged voters to support the new charter by asking: "Why not run Dallas itself on business schedule by business methods under business men? The city manager plan is after all only a business management plan." The article goes on to explain: "[T]he city manager is the executive of a corporation under a board of directors. Dallas is the corporation. It is as simple as that. Vote for it."[67]

The elimination of elected leaders generated extensive controversy. In many cities municipal employees and labor organizations opposed reform charters and the strength of the city manager position because they did not feel that their interests would be protected. In San Jose the reform charter granted the city manager the authority to appoint all of the city's officials without approval from the council and the power to prepare the annual budget. At the same time the council served on a part-time basis, for very low pay, and was elected at-large in nonpartisan elections. The charter instructed councilors to interact with municipal employees "solely through the city manager." For further clarity, the charter explains: "[N]either the Council nor its members ... shall give orders to any subordinate officer or employee, either publicly or privately."[68] As a result the manager had an enormous information and resource advantage over the elected legislators. Even if dissenting voices were elected in small numbers to the city council, the control of the city remained tightly bound to the reformist city manager and his administration. In Austin the first council elected following the city manager charter revision was unpopular with the voters because it was not responsive to their needs. One observer noted:

The council that worked with Manager Johnson was not a representative body at all.... It was a super-managerial board. It refused to provide the type of political leadership necessary to keep the administration responsive to public opinion, and to maintain satisfactory public relations.... The council did eliminate "politics" in the sordid sense of the word by ending patronage ... it also eliminated politics in the democratic sense of the word.[69]

David Eakins explains the consequences of this drive to increase the competence of the political system: efficiency "both in theory and in practice meant heeding some citizens and not others ... [and] the cost of greater efficiency was less democracy."[70] Eliminating politics resulted in an elimination of the pressure and ability to incorporate disaffected and disgruntled constituents. Such strategies of bias effectively insulated incumbent coalitions from shifts in public sentiment and protected their governing authority.

Bias Had Electoral and Distributional Consequences

When coalitions biased the system in their favor, they won. In every year between 1931 and 1979 the same faction of the Democratic Party controlled the mayoralty and the city council in Chicago. In Philadelphia the Republican organization dominated between 1860 and 1950, at times winning more than 80 percent of the vote. Tammany Hall governed New York from 1918 through 1932; the machine's margin of victory climbing at virtually every election.

The effects of reform consolidation are similar. Like their machine counterparts, reform candidates won repeatedly, with landslide victories. In Dallas 86 percent of 182 city council members elected between 1931 and 1969 pledged allegiance to the Citizens' Charter Association. This nonpartisan slating group held a majority on the council every year except a brief period between 1935 and 1938. San Antonio's Good Government League won 95 percent of the eighty-eight council races between 1955 and 1971. Between 1944 and 1967 in San Jose seventy-five councilors were elected to office; seventy-two were members of the dominant coalition.

Additionally, turnout declined in both machine and reform cities as peripheral groups were demobilized by those in power and discouraged from participating by the lack of choices.[71] Given the long time periods governed by bias, these results suggest that outcomes were clear well in advance of election day, reinforcing the authority of the regimes. After insulating their coalitions from shifts in power, machine and reform organizations turned their attention away from a large, diverse electoral coalition.

Under machine dominance core coalitions were targeted for a disproportionate share of municipal benefits and others suffered. In Chicago African Americans were denied services, government jobs, and elected offices. Blacks made up 40 percent of the city population in 1970, but only 20 percent of the municipal workforce. In 1972 African Americans brought suit against Daley for discriminatory hiring practices and won.[72] As of 1974 Latinos made up only 1.7 percent of the full-time city payroll but composed about 10 percent of the population.[73] After 1976, when the machine was in its final stages of life, minorities' share of patronage positions grew; more than one-third of new hires were people of color.[74]

In addition to patronage, machines supported policies that benefited some groups of residents to the detriment of others. In many cities urban renewal represented the provision of benefits to core coalition members and city elites at the expense of peripheral groups. For every new building that was erected, a slum was cleared, displacing more than a million residents over the course of the federal program. These decisions were not made independent of the racial and ethnic makeup of neighborhoods. In New Haven alone Wolfinger estimates 7,000 households and 25,000 residents were moved to make way for urban renewal. As first Mayor Lee and then DiLieto pursued redevelopment, spending over $200 million of public funds, New Haven became the fourth poorest city in the country. By 1989 its infant mortality rate rivaled third world countries in some neighborhoods, and the citywide average was the second highest in the nation.[75]

While New York Italians heavily supported the Tammany machine in the 1920s they received the most menial of patronage positions—garbage men, street cleaners, and dock workers. Similarly, Chicago's African American community won few concessions from the consolidated Daley machine even after providing a large portion of the Democratic vote and the margin of victory in 1955 and 1963. Blacks demanded, but were refused, a halt to police brutality and discrimination, appointment to high-level political positions, and living wage jobs. "Mr. Mayor we would like to point out," the *Daily Defender* said, "that in comparison with other cities ... Chicago is sadly lacking in the utilization of its finest and most well-qualifies [*sic*] Negro citizens in responsible positions in your administration."[76]

Similarly, under reform dominance those excluded from the governing coalition won little from municipal leaders. Because reformers had spent much energy and many resources separating politics from government, dissent was eliminated in the very structure of the city's institutions. By unifying the executive and legislative branches of government and making council seats at-large, all of those in power were beholden to the same constituency. Such a structure made it appear as though the cities were homogeneous and unified, but many cities with reform governments had large populations of poor and minority residents who did not always share reform views. Intense debates erupted over the placement of public works, the location of new roads and freeways, the provision of parks, libraries, and schools, and the role of labor unions in municipal government.

While reform coalitions maintained agendas that promoted growth and development, benefiting business and middle-class whites, they ignored the social needs of many residents and neglected the city's burgeoning physical problems.[77] One of the clearest examples of this pattern is seen in Southwestern annexation policies. As cities such as San Jose annexed new communities at the behest of developers, poorer communities closer to the center were not provided with basic municipal services. The Latino neighborhood known as the Mayfair district in San Jose

flooded in 1952, creating a significant public health threat.[78] The same creek overflowed its banks again in 1955, 1958, and 1962. The year that the dominant coalition collapsed, 1979, the water district finally filed an application to protect the nearly 4,000 homes and businesses in the area from further damage.[79] In the early 1970s, residents of Alviso, a heavily Latino area, blocked a bridge demanding that crossers pay a toll to pay for needed repairs that the city of San Jose had refused to provide.[80]

Austin's 1969 Model Cities program first focused on paving and drainage in center city neighborhoods. Yet the predominately African American west side of Austin did not have paved streets in some areas until 1979.[81] Meanwhile, city government provided sewerage, streets, and utilities for all of the new developments. The busy annexation mill in San Antonio doubled the city's size between 1940 and 1950 but leapfrogged over older, poorer, and more heavily Latino neighborhoods. During these years reformers promised Latino leaders that they would build drainage projects in return for support in bond elections. The bonds passed and the money was allocated, but the projects were never built.[82] As late as the 1980s, Mexican American communities in San Antonio were beset by flooding due to inadequate drainage systems.

Conclusions

In both machine and reform cities coalitions selected strategies to ensure reelection that had long-term effects on the political arena. Securing dominance made governing coalitions less attentive to the broader public. When the electoral system became uncompetitive, groups outside of the dominant coalition could not easily contest the hand that they were dealt. Biased systems allowed dominant organizations to reduce the size of their electoral coalitions, conserve resources, and reward key players. Secure from threats to their governing authority, coalitions directed benefits of municipal government toward core members and coalition elites at the expense of peripheral groups. First Jews and Italians, and then blacks, Latinos, and Asian Americans were limited from participating in the political process and from receiving equal shares of government benefits. The lesson for American political development is clear—those in power can be expected to build defenses against durable shifts in governing authority, and when they succeed, as both machine and reform coalitions did, portions of the population are likely to suffer.

NOTES

1. James Bryce, "Rings and Bosses," *The American Commonwealth* (Indianapolis: Liberty Fund, 1995; originally published in 1988 by Macmillan and Company), vol. 2, chapter 63.

2. Amy Bridges, *Morning Glories: Municipal Reform in the Southwest* (Princeton, NJ: Princeton University Press, 1997).

3. Lincoln Steffens, *The Shame of the Cities* (New York: Hill and Wang Publishing, 1957; originally published in 1904).

4. Robert K. Merton, *Social Theory and Social Structure* (New York: The Free Press, 1957).

5. Samuel P. Hays, "The Politics of Reform in Municipal Government in the Progressive Era," *Pacific Northwest Quarterly* 55, no. 4 (1964).

6. On machines see Steven Erie, *Rainbow's End: Irish Americans and the Dilemmas of Urban Machine Politics, 1840–1985* (Berkeley: University of California Press, 1988). On reform see John D. Buenker, *Urban Liberalism and Progressive Reform* (New York: Charles Scribner's Sons, 1973); Kenneth Finegold, *Experts and Politicians: Reform Challenges to Machine Politics in New York, Cleveland, and Chicago* (Princeton, NJ: Princeton University Press, 1995); James Connolly, *The Triumph of Ethnic Progressivism: Urban Political Culture in Boston, 1900–1925* (Cambridge, MA: Harvard University Press, 1998).

7. By institutions I mean rules, structures, and procedures for creating, implementing, and enforcing collective action.

8. Jessica Trounstine, *Political Monopolies in American Cities: The Rise and Fall of Bosses and Reformers* (Chicago: University of Chicago Press, 2008).

9. For further explanation see ibid.

10. For a similar argument see Gary W. Cox, "Public Goods, Targetable Goods and Electoral Competition," unpublished typescript, 2001.

11. See for example Gary W. Cox and Jonathan N. Katz, *Elbridge Gerry's Salamander: The Electoral Consequences of the Reapportionment Revolution* (Cambridge: Cambridge University Press, 2002); Bernard Grofman, W. Koetzle, and T. Brunell, "An Integrated Perspective on the Three Potential Sources of Partisan Bias: Malapportionment, Turnout Differences, and the Geographic Distribution of Party Vote Shares," *Electoral Studies* 16, no. 4 (1997): 457–470; Gary King and Robert Browning, "Democratic Representation and Partisan Bias in Congressional Elections," *American Political Science Review* 81, no. 4 (1987): 1251–1273.

12. V.O. Key, "Political Machine Strategy Against Investigations," *Social Forces* 14, no. 1 (1935): 120–128.

13. Ibid.

14. "Tired of Bossism," *Los Angeles Times* June 30, 1888, p. 1.

15. Harold Stone, Don Price, and Kathryn Stone, *City Manager Government in Nine Cities* (Chicago: Public Administration Service, 1940), p. 268.

16. Charles R. Adrian, "A Typology for Non-partisan Elections," *Western Political Quarterly* 12, no. 2 (1959): 449–458; Brian Schaffner, Matthew Streb, and Gerald Wright, "Teams without Uniforms: The Nonpartisan Ballot in State and Local Elections," *Political Research Quarterly* 54, no. 1 (March 2001): 7–30.

17. Brian Schaffner and Matthew Streb, "The Partisan Heuristic in Low-Information Elections," *Public Opinion Quarterly* 66, no. 4 (2002): 559–581; Seymour Martin Lipset, Martin Trow, and James Coleman, *Union Democracy: The Inside Politics of the International Typographical Union* (New York: The Free Press, 1956).

18. Bridges, *Morning Glories*; Philip J. Trounstine, personal interview by author, 2003.

19. Stone, Price, and Stone, *City Manager Government in Nine Cities*, p. 267.

20. Quoted in Valerie Ellsworth and Andrew Garbely, "Centralization and Efficiency: The Reformers Shape Modern San Jose Government," in David Eakins, ed., *Businessmen and Municipal Reform: A Study of Ideals and Practice in San Jose and Santa Cruz* (San Jose: Sourisseau Academy for California State and Local History, San Jose State University Original Research in Santa Clara County History, 1976), p. 14.

21. Harold Stone, Don Price, and Kathryn Stone, "City Manager Government in Austin, Texas," a Report Submitted to the Committee on Public Administration of the Social Science Research Council, Washington, DC, 1937.

22. Clyde Arbuckle, *Clyde Arbuckle's History of San Jose: Chronicling San Jose's Founding as California's Earliest Pueblo in 1777, through Exciting and Tumultuous History which Paved the Way for Today's Metropolitan San Jose; the Culmination of a Lifetime of Research* (San Jose: Memorabilia of San Jose, 1985), p. 42.
23. Bridges, *Morning Glories*, p. 140.
24. Lipset, Trow, and Coleman, *Union Democracy*.
25. Lawrence H. Larsen and Nancy Hulston, *Pendergast!* (Columbia: University of Missouri Press, 1997).
26. Alex Gottfried, *Boss Cermak of Chicago: A Study of Political Leadership* (Seattle: University of Washington Press, 1962).
27. Mike Royko, *Boss: Richard J. Daley of Chicago* (New York: Signet Press, 1971).
28. Peter McCaffery, "Style, Structure, and Institutionalization of Machine Politics: Philadelphia, 1867–1933," *Journal of Interdisciplinary History* 22, no. 3 (1992): 435–452; Erie, *Rainbow's End*.
29. "Tammany Election Funds; Where Some of them Come From. How the Corporation Attorney's Office is Worked for Electioneering Purposes," *New York Times* August 27, 1877, p. 8.
30. Erie, *Rainbow's End*; Harold F. Gosnell, "The Political Party versus the Political Machine," *Annals of the American Academy of Political and Social Science* 169 (1933): 21–28; Roger Biles, "Edward J. Kelly: New Deal Machine Builder," in Paul M. Green and Melvin G. Holli, eds., *The Mayors: The Chicago Political Tradition* (Carbondale: Southern Illinois University Press, 1995).
31. "The Golden Prime of Tammany," *New York Times* October 28, 1917, p. E2.
32. Dick Simpson, *Rogues, Rebels and Rubber Stamps: The Politics of the Chicago City Council from 1863 to the Present* (Boulder, CO: Westview Press, 2001); Martin Shefter, "The Emergence of the Political Machine: An Alternative View," in Willis D. Hawley et al., eds., *Theoretical Perspectives on Urban Politics* (Englewood Cliffs, NJ: Prentice Hall, 1976).
33. A search of the *Chicago Tribune* for articles containing the words fraud, election, and mayor turned up 334 articles between 1849 and 1950.
34. Alan Reitman and Robert B. Davidson, *The Election Process: Voting Laws and Procedures* (Dobbs Ferry, NY: Oceana Publications, 1972).
35. It is likely that the surge of Democratic popularity brought many new voters into the electorate; however, this ward was predominately African American, and blacks did not abandon the Republican ticket in large numbers elsewhere until 1936. (See Larsen and Hulston, *Pendergast!*)
36. Clay Gowran, "Merriam Charges Election Board Bias: Rips Holzman as Spokesman for Opponent," *Chicago Tribune* February 27, 1955, p. 1.
37. Gary Cox and Morgan Kousser, "Turnout and Rural Corruption: New York as a Test Case," *American Journal of Political Science* 25, no. 4 (1981): 646–663.
38. Erie, *Rainbow's End*.
39. Erie argues (ibid.) that because city governments had limited resources an expanding electorate made retaining office tenuous. He provides examples in places such as New York and Pennsylvania where machine leaders supported suffrage restrict ion in order to limit demands on their organizations.
40. Royko, *Boss: Richard J. Daley of Chicago*.
41. Gottfried, *Boss Cermak of Chicago: A Study of Political Leadership*.
42. It is important to note that suffrage restrictions were not confined to states and cities where reformers came to monopolize cities. All of the states that housed political machines had at one time or another limited the right to vote to certain groups (whites, property holders, men, etc.). The point here is that reformers benefited from these restrictions because their political opponents were denied the opportunity to participate in elections.
43. Bridges, *Morning Glories*.
44. Roberts Brischetto, Charles L. Cotrell, and R. Michael Stevens, "Conflict and Change in the Political Culture of San Antonio in the 1970s," in David R. Johnson, John A. Booth, and Richard J. Harris, eds., *The Politics of San Antonio: Community, Progress, and Power* (Lincoln: University of Nebraska Press, 1983).
45. Alex Keyssar, *The Right to Vote: The Contested History of Democracy in the United States* (New York: Basic Books, 2000).
46. Progressives made registration somewhat easier in other respects. They decreased the amount of time one needed to register before the election from 3 months to 40 days, increased registration locations, and standardized the process.
47. The act included a grandfather clause that allowed anyone currently enfranchised to vote. It is likely that the generational turnover following the passage of this act aided the San Jose reformers immeasurably in the passage of the reform charter in 1915.
48. R. Garner Curran, "The Amendments. Several Very Important Questions to Be Voted on at the Next Election," *Los Angeles Times* September 29, 1892, p. 9.
49. Stephen J. Pitti, *The Devil in Silicon Valley: Northern California, Race, and Mexican Americans* (Princeton, NJ: Princeton University Press, 2003).

50. Quoted in ibid., p. 84.
51. Keyssar, *The Right to Vote*; Connie Young Yu, *Chinatown, San Jose, USA* (San Jose: San Jose Historical Museum Association, 1991).
52. Yu, *Chinatown, San Jose, USA*.
53. Tom McEnery, personal interview by author, 2003.
54. San Jose City Clerk Record of Elections and the City of San Jose Commission on the Internment of Local Japanese Americans, *With Liberty and Justice for All: The Story of San Jose's Japanese Community* (San Jose: Commission on the Internment of Japanese Americans, 1985).
55. City of San Jose, *With Liberty and Justice for All*.
56. Pitti, *The Devil in Silicon Valley*, pp. 82, 222.
57. Bridges, *Morning Glories*, p. 65.
58. Susan Hammer, personal interview by author, 2003.
59. Erie, *Rainbow's End*.
60. Austin Dailey Statemen, December 27, 1908 quoted by Bridges, *Morning Glories*.
61. Philip J. Trounstine and Terry Christensen, *Movers and Shakers: The Study of Community Power* (New York: St Martin's Press, 1982), p. 83.
62. Robert Thorpe, "Council-Manager Government in San Jose California," MA thesis, Stanford University, 1938, p. 6.
63. Trounstine personal interview.
64. Mayor George Starbird paraphrasing manager Hamann in a 1972 speech given at the San Jose Rotary Club; transcript entitled "The New Metropolis," available at the San Jose Public Library.
65. Starbird, "The New Metropolis," p. 4.
66. US Attorney General, Objection Letter to City of San Antonio. April 2, 1976.
67. Stone, Price, and Stone, *City Manager Government in Nine Cities*, p. 286.
68. San Jose City Charter, Section 411.
69. Stone, Price, and Stone, "City Manager Government in Austin, Texas," p. 24.
70. Eakins, *Businessmen and Municipal Reform*, p. 3.
71. Trounstine, *Political Monopolies in American Cities*.
72. Erie, *Rainbow's End*.
73. Joanne Belenchia, "Latinos and Chicago Politics," in Samuel Gove and Louis Masotti, eds., *After Daley: Chicago Politics in Transition* (Chicago: University of Illinois Press, 1982), pp. 118–145.
74. I.M. Pace, "Employees in Top Salary Range Jump 500 Percent in Two Years, over One Third of City Hall's New Hires are Minority in 1976," *Chicago Reporter* 6 (June/July 1977).
75. Mary Summers and Philip Klinkner, "The Election of John Daniels as Mayor of New Haven," *PS: Political Science and Politics* 23, no. 2 (1990): 142–145.
76. "Memo to Mayor Daley," *Daily Defender* June 23, 1956, p. 9.
77. Carl Abbott, *The New Urban America: Growth and Politics in Sunbelt Cities* (Chapel Hill: University of North Carolina Press, 1987).
78. Glenna Matthews, *Silicon Valley, Women, and the California Dream: Gender, Class, and Opportunity in the 20th Century* (Stanford, CA: Stanford University Press, 2003).
79. The project was completed in 2006. Santa Clara Valley Water District, Lower Silver Creek Flood Protection Project, handout. Available at www.valleywater.org/media/pdf/watershed_monthly_progress_report_pdf/11-03%20-%20LSilver3.271Handout.pdf (accessed September 12, 2006).
80. J. Douglas Allen-Taylor, "Watchin' the Tidelands Roll Away," *Metro* August 20–26, 1998. Available at http://www.metroactive.com/papers/metro/08.20.98/cover/alviso-9833.html (accessed September 12, 2006).
81. Anthony Orum, *Power, Money, and the People: The Making of Modern Austin* (Austin: Texas Monthly Press, 1987).
82. Johnson, Booth, and Harris, eds., *The Politics of San Antonio*.

ESSAY 5.2

Workers Make a New Deal

Lizabeth Cohen

Source: Lizabeth Cohen, *Making a New Deal: Industrial Workers in Chicago, 1919–1939*
(New York: Cambridge University Press, 1990), 253–289.

EDITORS' INTRODUCTION

Following the industrial revolution and up to the present day, organized labor has played a significant role in the leadership of the American city. The tangled issues of the modern city and the modern workplace proved too complex for the leadership within local communities to handle on their own. Often employers seemed more committed to the financial bottom line than to dealing equitably with their personnel. Unions filled the gap, offering a platform to the voiceless and providing a form of collective power. During the Great Depression, city leaders and union heads turned their energies to forming relationships with the federal government, largely by-passing state government. Prior to the 1930s, American cities had received little monetary assistance (or other forms of direct attention) from the United States government. Federal policies, like those of individual states themselves, favored the economic interests of rural regions. This lack of funding changed dramatically during the Great Depression of the 1930s, when municipal leaders lobbied for and secured aid from both federal and state sources to pay for a variety of relief measures that helped the unemployed, underemployed, homeless, and under-nourished citizens. President Franklin Roosevelt's New Deal offered a tripartite solution to the nation's economic woes, inviting employers, the federal government, and unions to come to the negotiating table. Workers were pleased to be recognized as players at the table.

The unions were not as radical as they might have been. Most advocated working within the capitalist system rather than overthrowing it in favor of socialism or communism. Yet veins of more leftist thought ran through most labor unions, and many unions struggled to unite in their message. Unions in many cities joined into the machine politics of the age. Political machines were local political groups, often run by a political boss, who encouraged loyalty to a political party through the generous use of patronage. Jobs and financial gains were funneled to communities and labor unions to encourage commitment to the organization. Political machines often dominated local politics for decades, and successful union leaders knew how to negotiate with these powerful bodies to achieve their own ends. Chicago grew into a strong political machine associated with the Democratic Party in the late 1920s, and the power was cemented under the leadership of Bohemian immigrant Anton Cermak in the 1931 mayoral campaign. For a short time, Cermak united the local Irish, German, Polish, Czech, and Jewish communities within the city under his leadership. Upon Cermak's assassination in 1933, the political machine in Chicago was once again dominated by Irish residents.[i] Yet the Democratic Party continued to support political issues of interest to Chicago's ethnic communities, many of which were made up of industrial

---

i Roger Biles, "Machine Politics," *Encyclopedia of Chicago* (Chicago: University of Chicago Press, 2004) 499.

workers. Black Chicagoans turned from the Republican party—the party of Lincoln—to the Democratic Party, at this time. Citizens began to believe in the power of the vote within national elections. Workers, like those Cohen describes in this piece, began to expect that the national government would build supportive programs. The welfare state of the twentieth century was beginning to form.

Lizabeth Cohen is the Howard Mumford Jones Professor of American Studies at Harvard University. Cohen is the co-author of the textbook *The American Pageant* (Wadsworth) and of the influential *Making a New Deal: Industrial Workers in Chicago, 1919–1939* (Cambridge: Cambridge University Press, 1990) and *A Consumers' Republic: The Politics of Mass Consumption in Postwar America* (New York: Random House, 2003). She is the winner of the Bancroft Prize in American History (1991), the Taft Labor History Book Award, and a finalist for the Pulitzer Prize. In 2019, she published a new book on Edward J. Logue, an influential figure in urban renewal.

WORKERS MAKE A NEW DEAL (1990)

Voting in the State

It was not at all obvious that when Chicago's working people suffered misfortunes in the depression they would turn to the federal government for protection. During the 1920s, these workers had put little faith in government, particularly at the national level. To the extent that working people's social welfare needs were met at all, they were met in the private sector, by ethnic communities and welfare capitalist employers. Many workers looked warily on the expansion of state power, as they felt it was already interfering with their cultural freedom by legislating and enforcing Prohibition.

Most indicative of their disinterest in government, large numbers of Chicago workers failed to vote. In wards with high percentages of foreign-born workers, less than one-third of the potential electorate (people over the age of twenty-one) turned out for the presidential election of 1924, in contrast to 65 percent in native, middle-class wards.[1] Many of these nonvoters could not vote because they were not citizens. Stiff citizenship requirements and a disinclination to naturalize kept them away. Others qualified to vote but did not bother to register or to vote even when registered. They simply did not find national party politics relevant to their lives. "I had cast maybe one ballot in a national election, before the mid-1930s," recalled steelworker George Patterson, an immigrant of Scottish

birth who had become a citizen easily in the twenties with no new language to learn.[2]

Even those ethnic workers who voted during the 1920s did not often identify politically beyond their local community. The kind of machine politics that flourished in Chicago during the twenties kept people dependent on a very local kind of political structure not tightly bound to any one major party. In the city at large, not only did the Democrats and Republicans fight each other, but also factions within each party warred for supporters. Alliances developed around personalities, not policies. This volatility carried over to the local level, where ethnic groups, ward leaders, and precinct captains evaluated candidates and then delivered their votes to the ones they felt would best serve their needs even if they came from a political party not usually supported. Political parties were most visible in a community right before election time and then often disappeared. There were general patterns, of course, in the voting of blacks and "new immigrant" groups who dominated Chicago's industrial work force – blacks and Yugoslavs strongly Republican; Poles, Czechs, Lithuanians, and eastern European Jews frequently Democratic; Italians often split – but no party could count on a particular group's votes, except the Republicans on the blacks. It was a rare ethnic worker in Chicago who had a strong identity as either Democrat or Republican before the late 1920s.[3]

All this changed at the end of the decade. Workers became drawn into an interethnic

Democratic machine in Chicago under the leadership of Czech politician Anton Cermak that connected them not only to a unified Democratic Party on the city level but also to the national Democratic Party.[4] The issue that made Cermak's political career, and drew Chicago's diverse ethnic communities together behind him and the national Democratic presidential candidate in 1928, Alfred E. Smith, was Prohibition. In referendum after referendum in Chicago, in 1919, 1922, 1926, 1930, and 1933, Chicago voters demonstrated that they were anywhere from 72 to 92 percent opposed to Prohibition. Sentiment in the city probably ran even higher as those workers most resentful of Prohibition were likely not voters.[5]

Ethnic populations for whom production and consumption of alcohol were central to cultural life opposed Prohibition most vehemently, and within these groups, contemporary analysts like Harold Gosnell concluded, those with lower incomes were most committed. Working-class ethnics felt discriminated against by the selective way that Prohibition was enforced in the city. A rich family could have a cellar full of liquor and get by, it seemed, but if a poor family had one bottle of home-brew, there would be trouble. To add insult to injury, workers' industrial employers embraced Prohibition as a holy cause. Indeed, employers made few efforts to hide their desire to destroy the tavern, "the workingman's club" where discontent traditionally blossomed, and to "improve" the moral habits of their employees. Prohibition served not only to unite ethnic Chicagoans around Democratic politics but also particularly to attract the workingmen and women among them. Here was a political issue that roused the masses. By 1928, Cermak had succeeded in unifying this anti-Prohibition sentiment sufficiently to make himself top Democratic boss in the city, the first foreign born and non-Irishman to run the party, whereas Smith, the party's Catholic and "wet" presidential candidate, had become the first Democrat at the top of the ticket to come close to carrying Chicago in years.[6]

The creation of a Democratic machine in Chicago under Mayor Cermak and his successor Mayor Kelly (who took office in 1933 after Cermak was killed by an assassin's bullet intended for President Roosevelt) has drawn much attention for how it paved the way for years of undemocratic rule by the Daley machine. What is lost in hind-sight, however, is how voters actually felt about joining a citywide and national Democratic Party at the time. First- and second-generation immigrants still made up almost two-thirds of Chicago's population and a large proportion of these came from eastern and southern Europe.[7] After years of having little voice in either party, new ethnic groups finally felt that they had a party that represented them. When Republican candidate "Big Bill" Thompson made an issue of Cermak's eastern European origins in the mayoral race of 1931, a multiethnic alliance for the Democrats was clinched. Thompson's taunt,

> Tony, Tony, where's your pushcart at?
> Can you picture a World's Fair mayor
> With a name like that?

and Cermak's retort ("He don't like my name.... It's true I didn't come over on the Mayflower, but I came over as soon as I could") crystallized for ethnic Chicagoans how the Democratic Party had become the only party for them.[8]

The best evidence that Chicagoans were becoming increasingly committed to the Democratic party is that the Democratic vote in both local and national elections mushroomed [...]. By 1936, 65 percent of Chicago voters favored the Democratic presidential candidate, three times as many as had in 1924. In wards with large numbers of first- and second-generation ethnics, 81 percent supported Roosevelt in 1936, in contrast to 38 percent for Davis in 1924. Even more significant, these new Democratic voters, when white, were less often converted Republicans than new recruits, ethnic working-class people who had not voted during the 1920s. In their wards, there was a two-thirds increase in voter turnout between 1924 and 1936, with essentially all of these new participants voting Democratic.[9]

Several factors explain why Chicago's ethnic workers were voting in record numbers, and overwhelmingly Democratic, during the depths of the Great Depression. To start with, more people were eligible to vote. In an immigrant district such as the one surrounding the Chicago Commons Settlement on the West Side, two-thirds of those over age twenty-one qualified to vote in 1930, in contrast to only one-third in 1920. Both the coming of age of the American-born second generation and the more than doubling of the numbers of foreign born who had become citizens, particularly women, were responsible.[10] But eligibility is one thing, actually turning out to vote quite another. Starting in 1928, Chicago's ethnic workers participated more actively in the political process, and as Democrats, because of ideology not just demography. Finally by the 1930s, they felt like legitimate players in the political game. However undemocratic the one-party rule of Chicago's Democratic machine may have later become, it began as a democratic experience for many Chicago workers, giving them for the first time the feeling that the political process worked for them.

Most crucial in explaining the commitment to federal power that Kornhauser discovered in 1937, ethnic workers were becoming invested not only in Cermak's local Democratic party. Beginning with Smith's campaign as a wet candidate in 1928 and increasing with Roosevelt in 1932 and particularly in 1936, workers felt that the policies of the national Democratic party were making a difference in their lives. Before Roosevelt, the Federal Government hardly touched your life," explained one man. "Outside of the postmaster, there was little local representation. Now people you knew were appointed to government jobs. Joe Blow or some guy from the corner."[11] For jobs, and a myriad of other services once provided by others, it soon became clear, workers looked increasingly to the state. John Mega, a worker at Western Electric who grew up in a Slovak family in Back of the Yards, watched this transformation in his own family's political consciousness: "Our people did not know

anything about the government until the depression years." His father never voted. In fact, he stated, "In my neighborhood, I don't remember anyone voting. They didn't even know what a polling place was." Suddenly with the depression, all that changed. Mega's relatives were voting to send Democrats to Washington and counting on them for relief and CCC and Works Progress Administration (WPA) jobs.[12] Because the Kelly machine identified itself so strongly with the New Deal, voters like Mega's family and neighbors did not feel they were favoring national over local government. They saw the Chicago Democrats as the conduit for Washington's largesse.

It is important to recognize, however, that the promise and impact of New Deal programs alone cannot explain workers' reorientation to the federal government. That they had personally helped put in power the Democrats in Chicago and in Washington mattered enormously. Voting was a gradual process teaching them that national politics was reciprocal. As workers took credit for electing the nation's political leadership, the state seemed less remote. Over time Chicago workers came to feel like national political actors who had earned rights by their political participation. When Celie Carradina's estranged husband refused to share his WPA pay with her in late 1935, this resident of Back of the Yards wrote to President Roosevelt for help on the grounds that "I hope you every way that I could doing election and I am going to do my best again" [sic].[13] Likewise, a WPA worker once employed by Western Electric asked Mrs. Roosevelt, "How can a worthy Democrat, with a family of 8 children and wife to support Support them civilized on $55.00 a month" [sic].[14] Many others like Mr. and Mrs. Memenga threatened the president that if relief benefits did not improve, "we will think twice the next time [we are asked to vote for you]."[15] Working-class voters in Chicago were coming to feel not only that their fate increasingly lay in the hands of New Deal officials but also that national office holders and bureaucrats owed them something for their votes. Chicago workers who ten years earlier had felt removed from the federal government would tell Professor Kornhauser by the late 1930s that they expected more from the state.

Black workers in Chicago were also voting in record numbers and more Democratic than ever before by 1936, but they arrived at this same destination via a very different route than did ethnic workers. Rather than being newcomers to the political process, blacks had participated actively in elections during the 1920s. When only a third of Chicago's ethnics were voting in 1924, over 50 percent of blacks did. At the most basic level, it was easier for blacks to vote in Chicago. The longest residency requirement they faced was a year to vote in state elections, whereas the minimum requirement for naturalization was over five years, and it usually took immigrants at least ten years to become citizens. No less important, voting mattered to blacks who had been kept from expressing their full citizenship rights in the South. Many immigrants, in contrast, were former peasants from eastern and southern Europe who had never even had the expectation of voting.[16]

Blacks not only voted more than ethnics in the twenties but also displayed a strong loyalty to one party, the Republicans. In fact, Mayor "Big Bill" Thompson built his political career on the support of Chicago's black wards. Few blacks had been in the North long enough to forget the southern lesson that the Republican Party was the black's friend, the Democratic Party his racist enemy. The National Democratic Party had done little in recent memory to alter that image. The first blacks to attend a Democratic convention were seated as alternates in 1924, whereas at the 1928 convention in Houston, black delegates were segregated behind chicken wire. In Chicago, the two major parties kept up their reputations. Thompson rewarded blacks with city and party jobs, and the Democrats tried to win white voters by appealing to their racial prejudice. As late as the 1927 mayoral election, for example, flyers circulated depicting Thompson conducting a trainload of blacks from Georgia with the warning that "this train will start for Chicago, April 6, if Thompson is elected."[17]

Yet despite Chicago blacks' unfailing loyalty to the Republicans during 1920s, by the late 1930s they were securely in the Democratic camp. Nothing demonstrates so well the extent to which working people reoriented themselves politically during the 1930s as this shift of black voters from Republican to Democrat [...]. Dependable voters in the twenties, blacks turned out in still larger numbers in the thirties. The 61 percent of eligible blacks who voted in 1932 grew to 70 percent by 1940. And blacks increasingly voted Democratic. With them as with ethnics, New Deal programs alone did not make Democrats. Local and national Democratic administrations complemented each other. Cermak, and even more so Kelly, wooed black supporters with traditional lures of the machine, like patronage jobs and benign neglect of illegal gambling, as well as with symbolic actions such as banning the film "Birth of A Nation" and ceremoniously naming boxer Joe Louis "mayor for ten minutes." In time, Kelly would even defend integrated schools and open housing, much to his own political detriment.

Blacks rewarded Kelly by filing into the Democratic Party. In fact, they demonstrated more support for the local Kelly machine in the mayoral election of 1935 than they ever did for Roosevelt, giving Kelly a record-shattering 81 percent of their vote. One year later, a slight majority of Chicago's blacks still favored the Republican presidential nominee. But what is lost in these national election results from 1936 is the magnitude of the shift nonetheless underway. Although Chicago's black national Democratic vote lagged behind other northern cities, Chicago blacks increased their support for Roosevelt 132 percent over 1932, more than blacks in any city but Cleveland. Already with the election of Arthur Mitchell in 1934, Chicago blacks had sent the first black Democrat to Congress. To the extent that black people in Chicago were slow to endorse the Democratic Party nationally, it was because of their success as Republicans in the 1920s. Blacks had enjoyed more influence in Chicago politics than in any other city, making Chicago the "'seventh heaven' of Negro political activity," according to commentator Ralph Bunche.[18]

There is no denying, however, that Kelly and Roosevelt's efforts to make Democrats out of Chicago's blacks were helped by New Deal programs. Despite charging that the NRA functioned more as a "Negro Removal Act" than a "National Recovery Act" and that relief and job programs discriminated against them, blacks found themselves dependent on whatever benefits they could wring from federal programs as they tried to cope with the ravages of the depression. "Let Jesus lead you and Roosevelt feed you" replaced "Stick to Republicans because Lincoln freed you." The following ditty, which won the thunderous applause of black audiences in Chicago during the 1936 campaign; would have been inconceivable a decade earlier[19]:

> Millions a folks got to eat and sleep;
> Millions of us settin' on the anxious seat.
> Yo'all better vote right on 'lection day
> And keep this good ole WPA
> Ain't no ifs ands about it
> How you gonna get 'long widdout it?
> How you can take a little Republican jelly,
> But I ain't messin' wid my belly.
> You got relief, ole age pensions and WPA,
> But not if the Republicans coulda had they way.

Radical Boosters of the State

Not all workers in Chicago believed electoral politics could solve the crisis of the depression. A relatively small number joined the Communist Party, and many more, particularly in the early 1930s, enlisted in radical movements of the unemployed, organized by Communists and Socialists. But these left-wing crusades taught working-class recruits the same lesson as electoral politics, to look to the state for the solutions to their problems.

Unemployed and partly employed workers were frustrated with conditions in America in the early 1930s, but few went as far as joining the Communist Party. Chicago had been the birthplace of the American Communist Party in 1919, but Communist membership in the city declined during the twenties and New York became the party's national center. By the fall of 1931, the Chicago Communist Party claimed only two thousand registered members, although it managed in the presidential election of 1932 to attract 12,000 votes for its candidate, William Z. Foster, who in 1919 had teamed with John Fitzpatrick, president of the Chicago Federation of Labor, to try to organize steel and packing workers. A report that appeared in a February 1932 issue of *The Communist*, the party's theoretical journal, lamented how poorly industrial workers, particularly ones working in large factories, were represented in the Communist membership. Those who belonged were more likely than not foreign born. Nationally in 1931 two-thirds of party members were born abroad; in Chicago 53 percent were foreign born, with only one-half of those citizens. Not surprisingly given Chicago's ethnic make-up, the party there was made up mostly of Jews, Russians, South Slavs, Lithuanians, Hungarians, and Poles.

The Communist Party went out of its way to attract blacks by consistently agitating against white racism and for black equality. Efforts ranging from sponsoring interracial dances to nominating a black man, James Ford, to run with Foster in 1932 to tenaciously defending the Scottsboro Boys – nine young blacks wrongly accused of raping two white girls on a train in Alabama – won the party black members, but uncomfortable in the party, they usually did not stay long. By the end of 1931 there were still less than one thousand black members nationwide, with half of those in Chicago. More than these five hundred Chicago blacks sympathized with the party, however. The Communists' battle against rent evictions in particular won them black votes. Seventeen percent of those who voted for Foster in 1932, over a thousand voters, came from the Black Belt's second and third wards.

As the thirties wore on, the party's influence on workers, black and white, grew, reflected somewhat in larger membership totals but much more so in the way the party cooperated with the mainstream institutions that workers most identified with, the Democratic Party and the CIO unions. Under the party's popular front strategy initiated in 1935, fascism loomed as a greater enemy than capitalism. American Communist Party members, seeking alliances with other progressive reformers, became supporters of Roosevelt and the New Deal, as well as crucial players in the CIO's drive to use collective bargaining legislation to organize America's factories. By the latter half of the thirties, workers who earlier had been wary of Communist disruption found that the party had joined the chorus exhorting the federal government to be more responsive.[20]

Although relatively few workers joined the party or voted Communist in the early 1930s, many thousands more were inspired by Communist and Socialist organizers to take to the streets in protest against the lack of jobs and relief and the prevalence of hunger and deprivation. Chicago, in fact, was an important national center for the organization of the unemployed. Here in 1930 the Communist Party held its founding convention of the National Unemployed Councils and established some of its first community councils. A year later Socialist activists affiliated with the League for Industrial Democracy founded a more moderate alternative, the Workers' Committee on Unemployment, which soon spread from Chicago to other cities. From their initiation through 1933, a period when local relief efforts were inadequate and disorganized, both groups rallied thousands of Chicago's unemployed of all races and ethnicities, along with sympathizers, to protest rent evictions, meager public relief provisions, and unfair treatment by social service agencies.[21]

Because these unemployed groups were not traditional political organizations with precise membership records, it is extremely difficult to determine how many workers belonged. In all likelihood, only a fraction of the city's population, at the most fifty thousand, considered

themselves loyal rank-and-file members in the Communist Unemployed Councils or in locals of the Socialist Workers' Committee for Unemployment. But when an event like the October 1932 hunger march through downtown Chicago took place, many more joined in. Even those who stood on the sidelines, because they were employed or wary joining a "radical" cause, were influenced by the strategies and demands of the more militant.[22]

In principle devoted to promoting Communist and Socialist alternatives to the political order, members of neighborhood locals of both organizations in practice were committed more to putting pressure on the existing system than to overthrowing it. Although famous for theatrically moving tenants and their furnishings back into apartments from which they had been evicted, unemployed groups were equally concerned with influencing the activities of the State of Illinois's Unemployment Relief Service established in the winter of 1932 to dispense the state and, by summer, federal money finally allocated for relief. Locals staged demonstrations almost daily outside relief stations but also worked tirelessly negotiating with case workers on behalf of neighborhood people with relief grievances. Securing rent and rations for someone like Mrs. Mary Brown, who had been refused relief on the false grounds that she still owned an insurance policy, was the nonsensational kind of activity that occupied a local. Some members surely participated out of ideological commitment to revolutionary politics, but with only a small number of Communist Party members in the city, these unemployed groups appealed far beyond that circle. A party organizer described honestly the attitude that was most common: "So what? Even if they are Communists, they are trying to help us help ourselves and no one else is doing that."[23]

The Communist Party learned quickly that to attract supporters to Unemployed Councils it had to subordinate its more radical agenda to the practical concerns of the rank-and-file unemployed whose dissatisfaction with capitalism tended to focus more on securing a better break today than promoting an alternative system for tomorrow. Sectarian issues like U.S. recognition of the

Soviet Union and the "imperialist war danger" had to take a back seat. Steve Nelson, secretary of the Chicago Unemployed Councils for a time, recalled how Communist organizers had "spent the first few weeks agitating against capitalism and talking about the need for socialism." They observed quickly, however, that working-class people in the communities were more concerned with their daily struggles: "We learned to shift away from a narrow, dogmatic approach to what might be called a grievance approach to the organizing. We began to raise demands for immediate federal assistance to the unemployed, and a moratorium on mortgages, and finally we began to talk about the need for national unemployment insurance."[24]

By 1932, there were an average of ten relief protests a week in Chicago. In a rare and often tense collaboration, the Unemployed Councils and the Workers' Committee together drew 25,000 in the pouring rain, while thousands more watched, to a dramatic silent march through the streets of Chicago's Loop in late October 1932 to denounce a 50 percent cut in relief grocery orders. An observer described it as the biggest parade that Chicago had seen in years: "Rank after rank of sodden men; their worn coat-collars turned up, their caps – most of them seemed to be wearing caps – pulled down to give as much protection as possible. … Eight abreast. Closely massed. Stretching as far as the eye could see through the rain." "We want bread!" "We want work!" "Don't starve; fight!" read the placards of these determined marchers; the observer assured a bystander who thought violence might erupt, "it wasn't a dynamiters' parade." Organizers claimed victory when a $6.3 million loan from the federal government's Reconstruction Finance Corporation staved off the cut. That a grant from the federal government constituted success testifies to the statist orientation of the unemployed groups.[25]

By 1934, for a variety of reasons, fewer workers were looking to these unemployed groups to express their discontent. Shrewdly, the state's Unemployment Relief Service and the Cook County Bureau of Public Welfare had centralized their grievance procedures into one public relations office in order to protect local stations from "harassment" by the organized unemployed. This action deprived locals of neighborhood targets for their protests. Locals were further neutralized through a new requirement that all complaints be submitted to a committee. Even more important, the New Deal's Federal Emergency Relief Act (FERA), in operation by the summer of 1933, channeled additional funds into the city and relieved the desperateness of the situation in a way that many of the unemployed had advocated. By the mid-1930s, the unemployed movement would itself become more centralized and bureaucratized under the aegis of a national coalition, the Workers Alliance of America. As the alliance lobbied for relief programs and represented the interests of WPA workers, who were, in effect, government employees, it increasingly forsook city streets for state legislatures and Washington.[26]

The decline of these radical groups by the mid-thirties, however, should not detract from their significance in the early years of the depression. Much more influential among workers than their small official memberships or sectarian affiliations might at first have indicated, they taught an important segment of Chicago's depression victims that being unemployed was not their fault and that they should join together to demand help, a lesson these workers would put to good use when they began to organize their factories several years later. Many organizers in the CIO would come directly out of the unemployed movement. In urging workers to ally with people of other races and ethnicities, the unemployed organizations gave a message not so different from the one delivered by Cermak's Democratic Party.

Organizers of both the Unemployed Councils and the Workers' Committee on Unemployment discovered early on that they were most successful when they structured locals around neighborhoods. Meetings could then be held in foreign languages and the memberships of ethnic organizations consistently tapped. In South Chicago, for example, a local of the Workers' Committee grew from its seven founders in March 1932 to over three hundred in a few months by drawing in members of Polish, Czech, and other national fraternal lodges and churches; it even mimicked the ladies' auxiliaries that existed in many of these organizations by establishing its own. Yet, at the same time that unemployed groups depended on narrowly defined community networks to recruit members, some locals and certainly the citywide organizations unified different racial and ethnic groups as "workers" around a common set of political goals. When the jobless from South Chicago, Back of the Yards, Little Sicily and most remarkably, the Black Belt marched shoulder-to-shoulder in October 1932 along downtown streets lined with Chicago's largest banks and corporate headquarters, they began to see with new clarity who were their allies and enemies and glimpsed as well the potential power of their collective action.[27]

Even more important than the actual relief increases and eviction suspensions that the unemployed groups won, they proved to dependent citizens that it was possible to get your way with government authorities. As one client temporarily "saved" from eviction by the "direct action" of his neighbors put it, "The Unemployed Council is built for action, not promises. The eviction was stopped. For three weeks, we could wait for recognition from a relief office. Our committee got it for us in fifteen minutes."[28] Even the police backed off in the face of organized, determined citizens.

Chicago's blacks felt particularly empowered by the movement. They were most drawn to the Unemployed Councils, where they attracted special attention from their Communist organizers. According to a study of the demographic makeup of Chicago's Unemployed Councils and Workers' Committees in 1934, blacks constituted 21 percent of the leadership and 25 percent of the membership of the Communist movement but only 6 percent of the leadership and 5 percent of the membership of the Socialist movement. Black participants gloried in standing up to landlords and police while singing the old spiritual "I shall not be moved" and in thwarting the efforts of the utility companies to turn off

gas and electricity when bills went unpaid. With pride, they asserted their rights before social agencies that had long intimidated them. "It was a period of great learning," black Communist leader William Patterson remembered.[29]

By targeting the government as the solution to people's troubles, unemployed organizations helped workers look beyond their narrow communities and beyond private industry for their salvation. In the end, despite what the labels Communist and Socialist might at first have suggested, these unemployed groups served more to make people feel that the existing government could be made to work for them if they were unified than to channel dissent into radical alternatives. Although these workers may have marched when others merely voted Democratic, all of them became more oriented toward the federal government by the mid-1930s.

From Welfare Capitalism to the Welfare State

Voting in national elections and participating in the unemployed movement gave workers greater expectations for the state. Benefiting from New Deal programs made them dependent on it. Living as we do today in a world so permeated by the federal government, it is easy to lose sight of how much people's lives were changed by the expansion of federal responsibility during the 1930s. Even the conservative politicians of the late twentieth century who repudiate a strong federal government take for granted that working people will receive Social Security benefits upon retirement, that bank accounts will be insured by the Federal Deposit Insurance Corporation (FDIC), and that anyone who works will be assured a nationally set minimum wage. A world without these protections is hardly imaginable.

Despite the indisputable expansion of federal authority engendered by the New Deal, critics at the time, and even more so historians since, have nonetheless emphasized how improvisational, inconsistent, almost half-hearted the New Deal was. The reasons were varied. The Roosevelt administration was politically cautious, more oriented toward meeting emergencies than solving long-term problems, and most importantly, ambivalent, sometimes even fearful, about the growth of federal power that it was orchestrating. Critics rightfully point out that New Deal reforms failed to make the major social transformations, like the redistribution of wealth, that many progressives hoped for.[30] The American welfare state born during the depression turned out to be weaker than that of other western industrial nations such as England, France, and Germany. But a new direction nonetheless had been set. Most significant, workers made a shift from the world of welfare capitalism, where employers and voluntary associations cared, however inadequately, for their needs, to a welfare state, a reorientation that they would not easily reverse. This transition was particularly powerful for Chicago's workers because the basic services that they had looked to their ethnic communities and bosses to provide – welfare, security, and employment – and the depression endangered were taken over by the federal government. Although the New Deal may not have gone as far as many workers hoped it would, by providing welfare services, securing their homes and life savings, and offering them new jobs or reforming their old ones, the federal government played a new and important role in the lives of Chicago's working people.

The New Deal provided workers with federally funded relief programs, and eventually a permanent Social Security system, to take the place of the welfare previously dispersed by private organizations, often sponsored by their ethnic and religious communities. Federal assistance actually had begun through loans to the beleaguered states under Hoover's Reconstruction Finance Corporation. But it was the Federal Emergency Relief Administration (FERA), one of the first and most expensive creations of Roosevelt's New Deal, that regularized the national government's role in relief. Illinois was in such dire straits by the time Roosevelt took office in March 1933 that it became one of the first seven states to receive FERA funds. By the end of 19 33, more than a third of Chicago's working population, including 44 percent of city's blacks, looked to Washington for at least some of their keep which put slightly more Chicagoans "on the dole" than was typical nationally.

It is true that FERA was designed as a shared undertaking between the federal government and the states. Of the $500 million first appropriated, half was intended to match dollars spent by the states, the other half as a discretionary fund for FERA's use wherever the need was greatest. But without a doubt, the national government shaped, and underwrote, this relief program. Between 1933 and 1935, the federal government provided 87.6 percent of the dollars spent on emergency relief in Chicago, in contrast to contributions of 11 percent by the state and 1.4 percent by the city. Even though state and local authorities administered the federal funds, everyone knew that the power lay in Washington. From the many relief recipients and unemployed organizations that lodged complaints against local relief operations directly with FERA chief Harry Hopkins or President Roosevelt to the caseworkers who feared Washington's reproof enough to beg clients not to write as it causes ... [us] a lot of trouble," it was generally agreed that the national government ruled relief. Mayor Kelly, in fact, fought efforts to return more of the administration of relief back to Chicago. The added patronage jobs were not worth the increased financial and social responsibility.[31]

NOTES

1. My analysis of voting behavior in Chicago from 1924 to 1940 depends heavily on Kristi Anderson, *The Creation of a Democratic Majority, 1928–1936* (Chicago: University of Chicago Press, 1979), pp. 83–120. I have also been helped by Dianne M. Pinderhughes, *Race and Ethnicity in Chicago Politics: A Reexamination of Pluralist Theory* (Urbana: University of Illinois Press, 1987), pp. 39–108, and John M. Allswang, *A House For All Peoples: Ethnic Politics in Chicago 18 90–1936* (Lexington: University Press of Kentucky, 1971). For an analysis of voting on the national level that comes to similar conclusions about low voter turnout in the 1920s and the mobilization of voters in the 1930s in major cities like Chicago, see Paul Kleppner, *Who Voted? The Dynamics of Electoral Turnout, 1870–1980* (New York: Praeger Publishers, 1982), pp. 55–111.

2. Interview with George Patterson, December 1970, ROHP, p. 155.
3. Anderson, *Democratic Majority*, pp. 90–2; Sonya Forthal, *Cogwells of Democracy: A Study of The Precinct Captain* (New York: William-Frederick Press, 1946); Dianne Marie Pinderhughes, "Interpretation of Racial and Ethnic Participation in American Politics: The Cases of the Black, Italian and Polish Communities in Chicago, 1910–1940" (Ph.D. dissertation, University of Chicago, 1977), pp. 171, 177–81, 194–209; Edward Mazur, "Jewish Chicago: From Diversity to Community," in Melvin Holli and Peter d'A. Jones, eds., *The Ethnic Frontier: Essays in the History of Group Survival in Chicago and the Midwest* (Grand Rapids, MI, William B. Eerdmans Publishing Company, 1977), pp. 284–5.
4. John M. Allswang, *Bosses, Machines and Urban Voters* (Baltimore: Johns Hopkins University Press, revised ed., 1986), pp. 105–16; Alex Gottfried; *Boss Cermak of Chicago: A Study of Political Leadership* (Seattle: University of Washington Press, 1962); Humbert S. Nelli, *Italians in Chicago, 1880–1930: A Study in Ethnic Mobility* (New York: Oxford University Press, 1979), p. 234; Pinderhughes, "Interpretations," p. 166; and interviews that attest to people's new Democratic identification, IC, Chicago, IL; Interview with Sylvio Petri, 8 June 1981, p. 10, and Alfred Fantozzi, 27 May 1980, p. 37.
5. Harold F. Gosnell, *Machine Politics Chicago Model* (Chicago: University of Chicago Press, 1937; Midway reprint 1968), p. 145.
6. Allswang, *House for All Peoples*, pp. 118–28; Gosnell, *Machine Politics Chicago Model*, pp. 144–9; Douglas Bukowski, "William Dever and Prohibition: The Mayoral Elections of 1923 and 1927," *Chicago History* 7 (Summer 1978): 109–18; Raymond Edward Nelson, "A Study of an Isolated Industrial Community: Based on Personal Documents Secured by the Participant Observer Method" (M.A. thesis, University of Chicago, 1929); pp. 144–50, 167–9, 233–4, 241–2, 246–7; Nelli, *Italians in Chicago*, pp. 234; Gottfried, *Boss Cermak*, pp. 115–19, 157–61; from FITZ: Mrs. Leslie Wheeler to John Fitzpatrick, 17 October 1930, Box 18, Folder 129; "What Prompted Prohibition?" n.d., Box 25, Folder 169A; John Fitzpatrick to Mrs. Glenn Plumb, 26 October 1928, Box 17, Folder 123; and from CFLPS; "The Reformers Went Too Far," *Polonia*, 7 September 1922, Box 32; "Both Sides of the Prohibition Problem: An Interesting Debate between Alder man, Anton J. Cermak and John A. Lyle,"

Denni Hlasatel, 6 March 1922, Box 1, "Italophobia," *Bulletin Italian American National Union*, April 1925, Box 21: "People's Sentiment against Prohibition," *Amerikanski Slovenec*, 17 February 1926.

Evidence abounds that drinking did not stop in Chicago's ethnic working-class neighborhoods during the 1920s despite harassment; in other words, workers and their families ignored the Volstead Act. See Marie Waite, "Prohibition Survey of the Stockyards Community Made by the University of Chicago Settlement," December 1926, MCD, Box 7; "Study of Prohibition for the National Federation of Settlements," 1926, COM, Box 24, Folder "Prohibition"; Norman Sylvester Hayner, "The Effect of Prohibition in Packingtown" (M.A. thesis, University of Chicago, 1921); Marian Winthrop Taylor, "The Social Results of Prohibition: A Study Made in the Central District of the United Charities" (M.A. thesis, University of Chicago, 1923); Anonymous, "The Lower Northwest Side," n. d. but c. 1928, Student paper for Professor Burgess, COM, Box 23, p. 24; Esther Crockett Quaintance, "Rents and Housing Conditions in the Italian District of the Lower North Side of Chicago, 1924" (M.A. thesis, University of Chicago, 1925), p. 8; John Valentino, "Of the Second Generation," *Survey* (18 March 1922), reprinted in Wayne Moquin and Charles Van Doren, *A Documentary History of the Italian Americans* (New York: Praeger Publishers, 1974), pp. 355–7; Interviews, Chicago, IL, IC, with Mario Avignone, 12 July 1979, Tape 1 (pp. 25–6), Tape 2 (pp. 15–16), and Joe LaGuidici, 21 July 1980, p. 59; Marie Bensley Bruere, *Does Prohibition Work? A Study of the Operation of the Eighteenth Amendment Made by the National Federation of Settlements, Assisted by Social Workers in Different Parts of the United States* (New York: Harper & Brothers, 1927).

For evidence that Chicago's manufacturers promoted Prohibition and let their workers know it, see *Harvester World*, July 1919, Editorial; *South Works Review*, March-April 1919, Cartoon; Taylor, "Social Results of Prohibition," pp. 108–17; Hayner, "Effect of Prohibition in Packingtown"; Eugene J. Benge, "The Effect of Prohibition on Industry from the Viewpoint of an Employment Manager," *Annals of the American Academy* 109 (September 1923): 110–20; Herman Feldman, *Prohibition: Its Economic and Industrial Aspects* (New York: D. Appleton and Company, 1927).

7. *Fifteenth Census of the United States, 1930* and *Census of Religious Bodies, 1928*, compiled by Allswang, *Bosses, Machines, and Urban Voters*, p. 93.

8. Quoted in Allswang, *Bosses, Machines, and Urban Voters*, p. 110. For more on the operation of the Democratic machine in Chicago during the 1930s and its links to Roosevelt's New Deal, see "The Kelly-Nash Political Machine," *Fortune* 14 (August 1936): 47; Paul M. Green and Melvin G. Holli, eds., *The Mayors: The Chicago Political Tradition* (Carbondale: Southern Illinois University Press, 1987), pp. 99–125; Gene Delon Jones, "The Local Political Significance of New Deal Relief Legislation in Chicago: 1933–1940" (Ph.D. dissertation, Northwestern University, 1970); William Roger Biles, "Mayor Edward J. Kelly of Chicago: Big City Boss in Depression and War" (Ph.D. dissertation, University of Illinois at Chicago, 1981).

9. Anderson, *Democratic Majority*, pp. 92–120. The elections of 1928–36 have received a good deal of attention from political scientists and historians who have tried to identify which was the "critical election" when the balance of political power was realigned. My own preference is to downplay the debate over whether 1928, 1932, or 1936 was the "critical election" and consider a "critical period" during which not only were voters converted to the Democratic party but also new people were mobilized as voters. For the debate, see Bernard Sternsher, "The New Deal Party System: A Reappraisal," *Journal of Interdisciplinary History* 15 (Summer 1984): 53–81, and Alan J. Lichtman, "Critical Elections Theory and the Reality of American Presidential Politics, 1916–40," *American Historical Review* 81 (April 1976): 317–48.

10. "Report of the Head Resident for the Year Ending September 30, 1933," COM, Box 5, Folder "Annual Reports 1933–35," p. 3. Also see Heitmann, "Report on Americanization Classes in Chicago Public Schools," 28 April 1934, MCD, Box 2, Folder 11.

11. Interview with Ed Paulsen, in Studs Terkel, *Hard Times: An Oral History of the Great Depression* (New York: Avon Books, 1971), p. 49.

12. Interview by author with John Mega, Chicago, IL, 27 January 1998. A retired sheet-metal worker, who was born in Yugoslavia but spent most of his life in Southeast Chicago, told a *New York Times* reporter right before the Illinois primary in March 1988 that by following machine boss Edward Vrdolyak into the Republican Party and voting for him for circuit court clerk and George Bush for president, he will be voting Republican for the first time since he cast his first ballot for Roosevelt in 1932. R. W. Apple, Jr. "Where the Political Vista Is Not of the White House," *New York Times*, 14 March 1988.

13. Celie Carradina to Mr. Roosevelt, 30 December 1935, WPA 693, "Illinois C-D."

14. Edward Hornbeck to Mrs. Franklin D. Roosevelt, n.d. but c. December 1935, WPA 693, "Illinois H-K."

15. Mr. and Mrs. Richard Memenga to The President, 4 December 1935, WPA 693, "Illinois M," and (Mrs.) Freda L. Smith to His Excellency Franklin D Roosevelt, 29 October 1935, WPA 693, "Illinois S-T."

16. Anderson, *Creation of a Democratic Majority*, pp. 104–6; Pinderhughes *Race and Ethnicity*, pp. 71, 86.

17. Harold F. Gosnell, *Politicians: The Rise of Negro Politics in Chicago* (Chicago: University of Chicago Press, 1935); Harold Gosnell, "The Chicago 'Black Belt' as a Political Battlefield," *American Journal of Sociology* 29 (November 1933): 329–41; Dempsey J. Travis, *An Autobiography of Black Politics* (Chicago: Urban Research Press, 1987), pp. 56–91.

18. Ralph J. Bunche, "The Thompson-Negro Alliance," *Opportunity* 7 (March 1929): 78–80. On blacks' shift from the Republican to the Democratic Party during the 1930s, see Elmer William Henderson, "A Study of the Basic Factors Involved in the Change in the Party Alignment of Negroes in Chicago, 1932–1938" (M.A. thesis, University of Chicago, 1939); Rita Werner Gordon, "The Change in the Political Alignment of Chicago's Negroes During the New Deal," *Journal of American History* 56 December 1969): 584–603; Biles, "Mayor Edward J. Kelly of Chicago pp. 154–72; St. Clair Drake and Horace R. Cayton, *Black Metropolis. A Study of Negro Life in a Northern City* (New York: Harcourt, Brace and Company, 1945), pp. 346–55, 370–7; Travis, *Autobiography of Black Politics*, pp. 92–159; Nancy J. Weiss, *Farewell to the Party of Lincoln Black Politics in the Age of FDR* (Princeton: Princeton University Press, 1983), *passim* and particularly pp. 228–9; Pinderhughes, "Interpretation," pp. 209–41; Interview with Mrs. Willye Jeffries, in Terkel, *Hard Times*, p. 461.

19. "Jelly" was slang meaning "getting by or taking advantage of an opportunity"; the inference in the poem is to a bribe. Grace Outlaw, "Folk-lore-Negro Lore," FWP, Folklore, Box A587, p. 3. For Democratic efforts to capitalize on blacks' dependence on New Deal Programs, see the Colored Division of the Democratic National Campaign Committee, "Take Your Choice: New Deal and the Negro," 1936, BAR, Box 341, Folder 1.

20. An extremely valuable source on the activities of the Communist Party in Chicago during the first half of the 1930s is Harold D. Lasswell and Dorothy Blumenstock, *World Revolutionary Propaganda: A Chicago Study* (New York: Alfred A. Knopf, 1939). On the membership of the Chicago party, see particularly pp. 47, 139–40, 196–204, 307, 391–3; also Harvey Klehr, *The Heyday of American Communism: The Depression Decade* (New York: Basic Books, 1984), pp. 162, 329–33, 469; and Harry Haywood, *Black Bolshevik: Autobiography of an Afro-American Communist* (Chicago: Lake View Press, 1978), pp. 441–66. On the party's appeal to blacks, see Michael Gold, "The Communists Meet," *New Republic* 71 (15 June 1932): 117–19; Frank L. Hayes, "Chicago's Rent Riot," *Survey* 66 (15 September 1931): 548–9; Mark Naison, *Communists in Harlem during the Depression* (New York: Grove Press, 1984), pp. 279–84. On the party's Popular Front strategy, see Klehr, *Heyday*, pp. 167–280, and Naison, *Communists in Harlem*, p. 256.

21. For background on the Communist Unemployed Councils in Chicago, see Lasswell and Blumenstock, *World Revolutionary Propaganda, passim*, but particularly pp. 170–2; Steve Nelson, James R. Barrett, and Rob Ruck, *Steve Nelson: American Radical* (Pittsburgh: University of Pittsburgh Press, 1981), pp. 70–87; Description of conditions in United Charities' district offices, 13 October 1931, and minutes of superintendents' meeting, 31 March 1931, UNCH, Box 8, Folder 1; Materials on Unemployed Council activities, 1932–4 and *The Chicago Hunger Fighter* (biweekly newspaper of the Unemployed Council of Chicago), random issues, 1932–4, Hilliard Papers, Section 2, CHS; Jack Martin, *On Relief in Illinois* (Chicago: Chicago Pen and Hammer, n.d. but c. 1935); Daniel J. Leab, "'United We Eat': The Creation and Organization of the Unemployed Councils in 1930," *Labor History* 8 (Fall 1967): 300–14. For vivid descriptions of eviction protests see Interview with Katherine Hyndman, 1970, ROHP, pp. 51–4.
    On the Socialist Chicago Workers' Committee on Unemployment, see Robert E. Asher, "The Influence of the Chicago Workers' Committee on Unemployment upon the Administration of Relief, 1931–1934" (M.A. thesis, University of Chicago, 1934); Robert E. Asher, "Chicago's Unemployed Show Their Fist," *Revolt* (December 1932): 15; Gertrude Springer, "Shock Troops to the Rescue: Chicago Settlement Houses Have Become Centers for a New Kind of Life for Those Who Must Live on 'The Relief,'" *Survey* 69 (January 1933): 9–11;

Materials on the activities of the Chicago Workers' Committee on Unemployment and *New Frontier* (biweekly newspaper of the Chicago Workers' Committee on Unemployment), 12 December 1932, Hilliard Papers, Section 2, CHS; Karl Borders, "When Unemployed Organize," *The Unemployed*, no. 5 (publication of the League for Industrial Democracy), 1931, pp. 22–3, 34; Karl Borders, "The Unemployed Strike Out for Themselves: 1. They Speak Up in Chicago," *Survey* 67 (15 March 1932): 663–5; from COM: Annual reports, 1932, 1933, 1934, Box 5 and Minute Book of Local #5, Workers' Committee on Unemployment, 1933–7 (in Italian), Box 25, and miscellaneous papers concerned with the Workers' Committee, Boxes 24–7; "Record of the Development of the Clubs for Unemployed Men and Women," 1933, University of Chicago Settlement Papers, Box 20, Folder "Adult Dept. Reports, 1922–1934," CHS; Materials on Chicago Workers' Committee on Unemployment, c. 1934, MCD, Box 3, Folder 15; Mollie Ray Carroll, "The University of Chicago Settlement, Report for January 1933, BUR, Box 18, Folder 11; Walter C. Hart, "Relief – As the Clients See It (M.A. thesis, University of Chicago, 1936); "An Urban Famine: Suffering Communities of Chicago Speak for Themselves: Summary of Open Hearings Held by the Chicago Workers' Committee on Unemployment, January 5–12, 1932," COM, Box 24, Folder "July 1931–January 1932"; Judith Ann Trolander, *Settlement Houses and the Depression* (Detroit: Wayne State University Press, 1975), pp. 91–106; Roy Rosenzweig, "'Socialism in Our Time': The Socialist Party and the Unemployed, 1929–1936. *Labor History* 20 (Fall 1979): 485–508.
    A few sources deal with both unemployed organizations within Chicago. My interpretation has been influenced particularly by Roy Rosenzweig's "Organizing the Unemployed: The Early Years of the Great Depression, 1929–1933," *Radical America* 10 (July-August 1976): 36–60 Also see Helen Seymour, "The Organized Unemployed" (M.A. thesis, University of Chicago, 1937); Mario Manzardo, "Christmas, 1934," *South End Reporter*, 11 December 1974, IC, Item 69.17; Hilliard Papers Section 2, *passim*, particularly 1932–3; Franz Z. Glick, "The Illinois Emergency Relief Commission" (Ph.D. dissertation, University of Chicago, 1939; published by University of Chicago Press, 1940), pp. 117–37, "Minutes of a Hearing for the Unemployed arranged by Miss Breckenridge of the Advisory Committee of

the County Board," 4 May 1932, Hillard Papers, Section 2, CHS; Lasswell and Blumenstock, *World Revolutionary Propaganda*, p. 273.

22. The 1932 citywide vote for Socialist, Communist, and Socialist Labor presidential candidates may be of some help in estimating membership in unemployed groups: 31,133 Socialist; 11,879 Communist; and 1,592 Socialist Labor. These numbers are four times the Socialist vote of 1928, six-and-a-half times the Communist, and two-and-a-half times the Socialist Labor. Still, however, they together only total 3 percent of the vote for president, whereas 97 percent of the vote went for the candidates of the two major parties. Philip Booth, "The Socialist and Communist Vote in Chicago: A Summary Study," 1933, MCD, Box 3, Folder 19.

    The 1932 citywide vote for Socialist, Communist, and Socialist Labor presidential candidates may be of some help in estimating membership in unemployed groups: 31,133 Socialist; 11,879 Communist; and 1,592 Socialist Labor. These numbers are four times the Socialist vote of 1928, six-and-a-half times the Communist, and two-and-a-half times the Socialist Labor. Still, however, they together only total 3 percent of the vote for president, whereas 97 percent of the vote went for the candidates of the two major parties. Philip Booth, "The Socialist and Communist Vote in Chicago: A Summary Study," 1933, MCD, Box 3, Folder 19.

23. Nelson et al., *Steve Nelson*, p. 78.

24. *Ibid.*, p. 76; Lasswell and Blumenstock, *World Revolutionary Propaganda*, pp. 91–2.

25. Paul Hutchinson, "Hunger on the March," *Christian Century* (9 November 1932): 1377–88; "The Workers' Committee and the Hunger March of October 31, 1932," MCD, Box 25, Folder "Adult Dept. 1932–1938" Trolander, *Settlement House s*, pp. 97–8; and miscellaneous papers concerning the hunger march, COM, Box 25.

26. Materials on the Illinois Workers' Alliance and the Workers' Alliance of America in Victor Olander Papers, File 157, UICC; "How to Win Work at a Living Wage Or a Decent Standard of Relief with the Workers Alliance of America," Workers Alliance of America, 1937; Rosenzweig, "Socialism in Our Time," pp. 503–8; Asher, "Influence of Chicago Workers' Committee," pp. 27–9; Frances Fox Piven and Richard A. Cloward, *Poor People's Movements: Why They Succeed, How they Fail* (New York: Vintage Books, 1979), pp. 85–92.

27. Seymour, "Organized Unemployed," p. 58.

28. On the involvement of blacks in the unemployed organizations, particularly the Communist Unemployed Councils, see Lasswell and Blumenstock, *World Revolutionary Propaganda*, p. 280; Gosnell, *Negro Politicians*, pp. 325–52; St. Clair Drake, "Churches and Voluntary Associations in the Chicago Negro Community," Report of Official Project 465-54-3-386 Conducted under the Auspices of the Works Projects Administration, December 1940, pp. 257–64; Drake and Cayton, *Black Metropolis*, pp. 86–8, 734–40; Edith Abbott, *The Tenements of Chicago* (New York: Arno Press and The New York Times, 1970), pp. 442–3; Dempsey Travis, *An Autobiography of Black Chicago* (Chicago: Urban Research Institute, 1 981), pp. 48–52; Terkel, *Hard Times*, pp. 455–62, 498–502; Elizabeth Balanoff, "A History of the Black Community of Gary, Indiana, 1906–1940" (Ph.D. dissertation, University of Chicago, 1974), pp. 205–6; "Reds! Chicago's Communists: Nothing to Lose But Their Chains," *Chicago Tribune Magazine*, 23 May 1982.

29. Annie Gosenpud, "The History of the Chicago Workers' Committee on Unemployment Local #94 Until February 1933," Paper for Social Pathology 270, February 1933, BUR, Box 144, Folder 7; Nelson et al., *Steve Nelson*, pp. 75–8. For other discussion of how unemployed groups appealed to ethnic organizations, see interviews with Mario Manzardo and Nick Migas in Alice and Staughton Lynd, eds., *Rank and File: Personal Histories by Working-Class Organizers* (Princeton: Princeton University Press, 1981), pp. 138–9, 166–7.

30. Two examples of revisionist works that stress the conservative character of the New Deal are Barton Bernstein, "The New Deal: The Conservative Achievements of Liberal Reform," in Bernstein, ed., *Towards a New Past: Dissenting Essays in American History* (New York: Vintage Books, 1969), pp. 263–88, and Mark Leff, "Taxing the 'Forgotten Man': The Politics of Social Security Finance in the New Deal," *Journal of American History* 70 (September 1983).

31. See the many letters of complaint to the president and to Harry L. Hopkins in the FERA files, particularly Mr. and Mrs. John Jerzyk to "Sir," 30 November 1933, FERA 460, "Illinois Complaints J," and Chicago Workers' Committee on Unemployment to Mr. Harry L. Hopkins, 10 May 1935, FERA 460, "Illinois Complaints C." Also, Jones, "Local Political Significance of New Deal Relief," particularly p. 145; Harry L. Hopkins, *Spending to Save: The Complete Story of Relief* (New York: W. W. Norton & Company, 1936); Arthur P. Miles, "Federal Aid and Public Assistance in Illinois" (Ph.D. dissertation, University of Chicago, 1940); Henderson, "Study of Basic Factors Involved in Change in Party Alignment of Negroes," pp. 54–6.

ESSAY 5.3

Washington

Nicholas Lemann

Source: Nicholas Lemann, *The Promised Land: The Great Black Migration and How it Changed America* (New York: Vintage Books, 1991).

EDITORS' INTRODUCTION

The 1960s saw the rise of federal anti-poverty initiatives designed to address a series of social issues that public policy analysts and elected officials saw as endemic to the plight of traditional central cities and their residents. These efforts differed from New Deal urban renewal programs and those in the immediate post-WWII era, which largely conceived of city needs in physical terms. For instance, in 1949 the term "blight" was utilized as a catch-all term for building and infrastructure decay, demanding physical solutions such as slum clearance and highway construction. The earliest of the 1960s-style anti-poverty measures involved projects designed to enhance the social and economic mobility and quality of life for inner-city residents, specifically African Americans.

The following selection from Nicholas Lemann's noted work, *The Promised Land: The Great Black Migration and How it Changed America* (New York: Vintage Books, 1991), examines the intellectual origins of anti-poverty programs that emerged during the administration of President John F. Kennedy. While many of these measures were aimed at improving the plight of African Americans, they also served as demonstration projects for much more elaborate undertakings during President Lyndon Baines Johnson's so-called War on Poverty. **[See Document 5.3, Lyndon Baines Johnson, "The Great Society," (1964).]** As Lemann notes, however, President Kennedy and his brother Robert F. Kennedy were hardly ardent supporters of the civil rights movement, at least not until such support served their political self-interest. Nor were civil rights advocates like Reverend Martin Luther King, Jr., especially trustful of the politically pragmatic Kennedys. The Kennedys did not want to ostracize white southerners who were a part of the Democratic Party base.

The impetus for identifying and addressing severe poverty in black inner-city neighborhoods came from a mix of mainstream liberal academics, grass-roots community and labor-organizers, members of the clergy, civil rights activists, and policy experts at think-tanks like the Ford Foundation. In fact, in the early 1960s, the Ford Foundation targeted select cities, such as New Haven, Connecticut discussed in the essay, to pilot the so-called Gray Areas Project. (Gray Areas was a euphemism for black neighborhoods.) The Gray Areas Project was designed to improve housing conditions, employment opportunities, education, and access to social services in order to prevent the creation of permanent slums. Another recipient of Gray Areas funding was Mobilization for Youth in New York City, which continued the work of social settlements from earlier in the century. Mobilization for Youth eventually transformed into a more direct and confrontational political activist organization following the 1964 riots in Harlem after the death of a black teenager at the hands of a white policeman.

Nicholas Lemann is the Joseph Pulitzer II and Edith Pulitzer Moore Professor of Journalism and Dean Emeritus of the Columbia Journalism School at Columbia University in the

City of New York. Lemann is the author of five books, including *Redemption: The Last Battle of the Civil War* (New York: Farrar, Straus and Giroux, 2006), *The Big Test: The Secret History of the American Meritocracy* (New York: Farrar, Straus and Giroux, 1999), and *The Promised Land: The Great Black Migration and How It Changed America* (New York: Vintage Books, 1991), which won several book prizes including the 1992 Martha Albrand Award for First Nonfiction from the PEN American Center. Lemann has written widely for such publications as *The New York Times*, *The New York Review of Books*, *The New Republic*, and *Slate*, and worked in documentary television with Blackside, Inc., *FRONTLINE*, the Discovery Channel, and the BBC.

WASHINGTON (1991)

Among public-policy experts, the idea that an important national problem was brewing in the black slums of the Northern and Western cities was not at all a part of the conventional wisdom. In fact, the book in which the term "conventional wisdom" was introduced into the discourse—John Kenneth Galbraith's *The Affluent Society*, published in 1958—mentions race only once, as a mere aside in its sweeping vision of the form that liberalism should take in the years to come. Galbraith's idea was that the United States had largely conquered the problem of poverty during World War II and the postwar boom, and that now the country should address itself to the issue of "public squalor" by increasing the government's spending and the scope of its activities. John Kennedy's campaign slogan, "Let's get America moving again," echoed Galbraith; it was a politically attractive packaging for liberalism after Eisenhower, because it tapped into the impatient energy of the veterans of the war without contradicting the reigning idea that since the Depression, the United States had become a consensus society whose citizens could go forward all together, without bitter conflicts of class and region and ethnicity.[1]

There were respectable liberals who disagreed with Galbraith, but they were well aware of being outside the mainstream of American thought. In particular, anyone working, during the late 1950s and early 1960s, on the assumption that a Northern racial crisis was on the way had ventured into daring, avant-garde intellectual territory. It wasn't just that among white intellectuals little was known about the urban

black ghettos; the very notion that an enormous racial problem existed in the North caused the whole consensual vision of American society to crumble. Segregation in the South was a regional issue with deep historical roots. The civil rights movement was, obviously, the kind of bloody conflict that the country was supposed to have gotten over, but its end result would be the bringing of the South into the healthy, rational mode of operation of the nation as a whole. Deep-seated conflict in the North was another story—it wasn't supposed to exist. The realization of it popped up in a series of places on the fringes of the government-university-foundation nexus.

After *The Affluent Society* was published, Senator Paul Douglas of Illinois, a scholarly liberal of an older generation than Galbraith's and Kennedy's, commissioned a study of poverty in the United States to see whether it was really as insignificant a problem as Galbraith had said it was. Robert Lampman, an economist from the University of Wisconsin—an institution still imbued with the legacy of the great Wisconsin Progressive politician Robert M. LaFollette—published the study in 1959, and found that the rate of "exit from poverty" had already begun to slow considerably in the late fifties.[2]

Harris Wofford, before going to work on the Kennedy campaign, was a law professor at the University of Notre Dame and a protégé of Notre Dame's president, Father Theodore Hesburgh. Hesburgh was a member of the United States Commission on Civil Rights, which undertook a major study of American race relations in the late 1950s. Wofford did some of the research for the study; when he traveled to Chicago, he was shocked to find that the conditions in which poor blacks lived there seemed to be even worse than they were in the South. The commission's report, also published in 1959, contains a mild warning about race relations in the North.[3]

Nathan Glazer and Daniel Patrick Moynihan, two young social scientists, published a book called *Beyond the Melting Pot* in 1963. Glazer and Moynihan belonged to the first generation of city-bred white ethnics to rise to the highest level in American academic life; as such, they were far more street-wise than their elders, having actually grown up in the kinds of communities that the leading sociologists of the day knew only as researchers. They put forth the notion that ethnicity, supposedly a dissolving pill in the American body politic, was remarkably persistent as an organizing principle for urban society. The vision of *Beyond the Melting Pot* is of a pluralistic, quarrelsome society, especially on the subject of race.[4]

Leonard Duhl, a psychologist at the National Institute of Mental Health, began in 1955 to assemble a loose group of experts to discuss cities. Duhl, a freewheeling character, was operating under an extremely generous interpretation of the charter of the NIMH, which directed it to look after "the mental health of the population of the United States." He was interested in creating a countervailing vision of urban life to the one that prevailed in the Eisenhower years. The urban renewal program was financing the demolition of older inner-city neighborhoods and the relocation of their (mostly black) residents, so that private developers could get rich building big, ugly new projects. The interstate highway program was encouraging the flight of the white middle class to the new, sterile, soulless suburbs, and helping another set of private developers—homebuilders—to get rich. Nobody seemed to be objecting; Duhl wanted to marshal the intellectual opposition. His idea was, in the context of the time, not so much politically radical as it was weird; on the day that the Soviet satellite Sputnik was launched, in 1957, one of his experts said, "If they think *they're* out in space, they should see us," and

thereafter Duhl's group was known as the Space Cadets.[5]

Cadging money from here and there, Duhl began to finance a series of influential research projects: Herbert Gans's book *The Urban Villagers*, which attacked the urban renewal program for destroying a vibrant Italian-American neighborhood in Boston so that a luxury high-rise apartment complex could be built on its site (Gans wrote later that "the low-income population was in effect subsidizing its own removal for the benefit of the wealthy"); Elliot Liebow's *Tally's Corner*, a depiction of the drifting life lived by "street-corner men" in a black neighborhood in Washington; and *Behind Ghetto Walls*, by Lee Rainwater, which showed how frighteningly disorganized the all-black high-rise Pruitt-Igoe housing project in St. Louis had become only a few years after it was built.[6]

Paul Ylvisaker was a mid-level official at the Ford Foundation, where he went to work after suffering a heart attack at the age of thirty-three and deciding he had better abandon for something more sedate his career as a fast-track aide to a United States senator. Ylvisaker lived in a suburb in New Jersey, and when he had to travel on Ford Foundation business, he would take a bus to the Newark airport that passed through Newark's black ghetto. "You could see the frustration," he says. "You could *read* it. You come to the North, where it's supposed to be better, and you find this!" Ylvisaker talked his superiors at Ford into letting him set up an organization called the Gray Areas Project to find ways to improve conditions in the ghettos. Gray Areas was a euphemism for black areas, necessary because the foundation's board was terrified of getting involved in anything that dealt explicitly with the subject of race. In 1954, a Ford Foundation subsidiary called the Fund for the Republic had made a $25,000 grant for a national study of housing segregation, and this set off a storm of protest; Ford automobile dealers in the South complained to Henry Ford II that they were afraid they might be boycotted. For years afterward, the foundation was willing to study racial issues only under some kind of cover.[7]

One of the Gray Areas Project's first grants was to an organization in New Haven, Connecticut, run by a former regional director of the United Auto Workers named Mitchell Sviridoff. Sviridoff was close to the mayor of New Haven, Dick Lee; they both believed that something needed to be done to help the black migrants who had been streaming into New Haven from Georgia and the Carolinas. With abundant funding from the city and the Ford Foundation—$12 million a year—Sviridoff set up a series of programs to improve education and job training in the black slums. In early 1963, there was a great controversy in the New Haven Gray Areas Project: Jean Cahn, a lawyer working in the project's legal aid department, took on the case of a black man accused (and eventually convicted) of raping a white nurse. Sviridoff was caught between the mayor, who wanted him to dissociate himself from the case, and Paul Ylvisaker, who wanted him to support it. He decided to side with the mayor, and as a result the New Haven project maintained its good relations with the local political order, but Jean Cahn's program was made a separate entity from the Gray Areas Project.[8]

Another important recipient of the Gray Areas Project's largesse was an organization on the Lower East Side of New York called Mobilization for Youth, which was the brainchild of two sociologists at the Columbia University School of Social Work, Lloyd Ohlin and Richard Cloward. Ohlin and Cloward were an unlikely-looking pair—Ohlin had the appearance of an apple-cheeked Midwestern uncle, while the younger Cloward played the part of the academic as urban hipster; their partnership represented the marriage of two great traditions in American sociology.[9]

Ohlin's Ph.D. was from the University of Chicago, which was the Olympus of sociological research. The founding fathers of the Chicago sociology department, Robert Park and Ernest Burgess, encouraged their students to roam the streets of the city, especially the slums. Park, a former newspaper reporter, dispatched his students to the funerals of the victims in the St. Valentine's Day Massacre, because he thought they'd get good stuff there. Burgess, Park's drab

and systematic partner, was Ohlin's thesis adviser (and also Saul Alinsky's, before Alinsky dropped out of academic life). There was a longstanding feud at the University of Chicago between the sociology department and the School of Social Service Administration. The social workers, strongly influenced by Freudian psychology, saw the slums as a mass of individual problems rooted in poor early-childhood development; to the sociologists, the slums were a part of a vast urban organism, and their problems were a natural part of the life of the city. Adherents of the Park-Burgess school liked to point out that certain Chicago neighborhoods always led the city in juvenile delinquency, no matter which ethnic group happened to be occupying them, because high delinquency was an unavoidable stage in each group's process of assimilation.[10]

As a part of the cleanup campaign that followed the Chicago machine's dumping of Edward Kelly as mayor, a member of the Chicago sociology department named Joseph Lohman was made head of the Illinois Parole and Pardon Board. Lohman hired Ohlin, who spent nearly a decade as a parole official, using the job, of course, as an opportunity to do studies of criminals. In one of the studies, Ohlin looked at the records of juvenile delinquents who had been paroled to serve in World War II, and found that they usually served with distinction—proving that the social workers' idea that delinquents were psychologically crippled was wrong. Another defector from the Chicago sociology department to the parole board, Richard Boone, says, "We went through the inmate 'jacket,' or file. It was all there. Every goddamn case was in the mold of psychiatric social work. 'Breast-feeding ended early.' 'An Oedipal complex.' It went on and on. It was appalling. For parole, you could just *throw* the jacket and ask the other inmates."[11]

Richard Cloward was a student of the leading theoretical sociologist of the day, Robert Merton of Columbia. Merton, who did his research at the library rather than on the streets, explained juvenile delinquency through the sociological concept of anomie: when teenage males in the success-obsessed American culture saw that it was not possible for them to achieve their goals through legitimate means, anomie set in, and they turned to the illegitimate means of crime. Cloward met Ohlin at a conference in the early 1950s, and in 1956 Ohlin left parole work to become a professor at the Columbia School of Social Work, where Cloward was teaching. Together they began working on a book that would synthesize Merton's theories with the Chicago school's field research, while also putting a slightly more positive spin on delinquency, which previously had been portrayed as an irrational and counterproductive response to difficult conditions. *Delinquency and Opportunity*, published in 1960, argued that society denies poor young men, especially blacks, any form of real opportunity, so that the ones who become delinquents are acting rationally, on the basis of a perceptive critique of society. Black delinquents did not even have the chance to get involved in profitable illegal activity, so their forays outside the law were more random and violent than those of white delinquents. It followed that if more real opportunity became available, there would be less delinquency.[12]

Even before they finished the book, Ohlin and Cloward were in touch with the Gray Areas Project, which wanted to fund an organization in New York but was looking for, as Cloward puts it, "something a little more theoretically glitzy" than the traditional approach of the old-line settlement houses of the Lower East Side—hence the appeal of creating a social welfare agency on the basis of their new line of argument. The proposal that established Mobilization for Youth was an elaborate document that was years in the making—Mobilization didn't open its doors until 1962—but the fierceness of the analytical back-and-forth among academic experts on the slums somewhat obscures the reality of Mobilization. For the most part, it was set up to do exactly what the settlement houses had been doing for years, and what the less theoretically glitzy Gray Areas Project in New Haven was doing: help speed up the assimilation process for poor migrants recently arrived in the city by providing them with special training in

the ways of industrial society. What else could Mobilization do? It was founded on the concept that American society pervasively denied opportunity to the poor, but it is beyond the power of a neighborhood social service agency to solve that problem.[13]

There was one crucial difference between the activities of Mobilization and the traditional forms of social work. Although Mobilization could hardly create more opportunity in the nation as a whole, it could at least try to create more opportunity on the Lower East Side by organizing the community to take political action. The theory here was a Marxian one: that poverty is more a political than an economic condition and that if the poor become politically "empowered," they will soon cease to be poor. Empowerment would give poor people a new spirit of community; they would run their own lives, and their neighborhoods, with renewed purposiveness and vigor, and they would learn to get things from the powers that be. As Leonard Cottrell, another Chicago-trained sociologist who was head of the Russell Sage Foundation and a close associate of Ohlin's, put it in 1960, speaking about black migrants from the South, "you get a community of people who have lost the competence to act in a community problem ... the way to attack it would be to restore the community's confidence to act...."[14]

The history of The Woodlawn Organization in Chicago was a perfect demonstration of the shortcomings of the empowerment theory in the real world of a late-twentieth-century American city: no matter how well organized a poor community was, it could not become stable and not-poor so long as the people with good jobs kept moving out and the people left behind had very little income. This lesson was not yet clear in 1962, though: along with its education and job-training programs, Mobilization began to organize rent strikes and political protests on the Woodlawn model.

The Woodlawn Organization, funded as it was by a Cardinal who had absolute power over his dominion in Chicago, did not have to worry that its protests against Mayor Daley and the University of Chicago might imperil its financial base. The same was true of the civil rights groups organizing in the South: the order they were attacking had nothing to do with their sources of funds, which were church collection plates in the South and North, and Northern philanthropists. Mobilization was in quite a different situation, though nobody seems to have recognized that in 1962. It was founded by the still fairly cautious Ford Foundation, and early in the planning stages it began to seek financial support from the federal government. This meant that it did not have anything like total independence. Confrontational tactics could imperil its existence, because it was dependent on the largesse of the power structure it intended to confront. In the New Haven Gray Areas Project, Mitchell Sviridoff perceived this problem and decided to abandon confrontational tactics, focus on education and training, and retain the support of the mayor. Mobilization went in the other direction, and soon it would suffer the consequences.

NOTES

1. John Kenneth Galbraith, *The Affluent Society* (Houghton Mifflin, 1958), p. 327.
2. Interviews with Walter Heller and Robert Lampman. The study itself is Robert J. Lampman, "The Low Income Population and Economic Growth," for consideration by the Joint Economic Committee (Government Printing Office, 1959).
3. Interview with Harris Wofford. The report is *Report of the United States Commission on Civil Rights 1959* (Government Printing Office, 1959).
4. Interviews with Nathan Glazer and Daniel Patrick Moynihan. Nathan Glazer and Daniel Patrick Moynihan, *Beyond the Melting Pot: The Negroes, Puerto Ricans, Jews, Italians, and Irish of New York City* (MIT Press, 1970).
5. Interviews with Leonard Duhl and Lee Rainwater.
6. Herbert J. Gans, *The Urban Villagers: Group and Class in the Life of Italian-Americans* (The Free Press, 1982). Quotation from Gans: "The Failure of Urban Renewal," by Herbert J. Gans, *Commentary*, April 1965, p. 30. Elliot Liebow, *Tally's Corner: A Study of Negro Street-Corner Men* (Little, Brown, 1967). Lee Rainwater, *Behind Ghetto Walk: Black Families in a Federal Slum* (Penguin, 1973).
7. Interview with Ylvisaker. On the Fund for the Republic, see Frank K. Kelly, *Court of Reason: Robert Hutchins and the Fund for the Republic* (The Free Press, 1981), pp. 63–76.
8. Interviews with Mitchell Sviridoff and Paul Ylvisaker. Peter Marris and Martin Rein, *Dilemmas of Social Reform: Poverty and Community Action in the United States* (Routledge and Kegan Paul, 1972), pp. 170–175.
9. Interviews with Richard Cloward and Lloyd Ohlin. Daniel Patrick Moynihan, *Maximum Feasible Misunderstanding: Community Action in the War on Poverty* (The Free Press, 1970), pp. 38–60, contains an extremely skeptical account of the origins of Mobilization. On the war on poverty in general, see also Allen J. Matusow, *The Unraveling of America: A History of Liberalism in the 1960s* (Harper Torchbooks, 1986), which is only partly about the war on poverty but is nonetheless the most complete work by a historian on that under-covered subject; Frances Fox Piven and Richard Cloward, *Regulating the Poor: The Functions of Public Welfare* (Pantheon, 1971); Daniel Knapp and Kenneth Polk, *Scouting the War on Poverty: Social Reform Politics in the Kennedy Administration* (Heath Lexington Books, 1971); and James L. Sundquist, editor, *On Fighting Poverty* (Basic Books, 1969), especially Sundquist's own essay, "Origins of the War on Poverty."
10. Interviews with Philip Hauser and Nicholas Von Hoffman.
11. This theory is laid out in Clifford R. Shaw, *Delinquency Areas: A Study of the Geographical Distribution of School Truants, Juvenile Delinquents, and Adult Offenders in Chicago* (University of Chicago Press, 1929). On Joseph Lohman: Interviews with Richard Boone, Richard Cloward, and Lloyd Ohlin. Quotation from Richard Boone: Interview with Boone.
12. Richard Cloward and Lloyd Ohlin, *Delinquency and Opportunity: A Theory of Delinquent Gangs* (The Free Press, 1960).
13. Interview with Cloward.
14. Quotation from Leonard Cottrell: Marris and Rein, *Dilemmas of Social Reform*, p. 170. There is useful background information on Cottrell in Matusow, *The Unraveling of America*, pp. 112–119.

DOCUMENTS FOR PART V

5.1 WILLIAM TWEED'S CONFESSION (1878)

Special Committee of the Board of Alderman and William M. Tweed

Source: Board of Aldermen, *Report of the Special Committee of the Board of Aldermen Appointed to Investigate the "Ring" Frauds Together with the Testimony Elicited During the Investigation,* Document No. 8, January 4, 1878 (New York: Martin B. Brown, 1878).

EDITORS' INTRODUCTION

William M. Tweed (1823–1878), often referred to as "Boss Tweed," was a New York City politician whose controversial career as an elected official and party boss has made him synonymous with urban political corruption. Tweed, the son of a furniture maker, won his first election as a city alderman in 1852 shortly after he became a leader in a local volunteer firefighting company. Tweed held a variety of city, county, state, and even federal offices—most notably as a member of the U.S. Congress from 1853–1855, the Board of Supervisor from 1857–1870, a state senator from 1868–1871, as well as concurrent city government titles of Deputy Street Commissioner, 1863–1870, and Commissioner of Public Works, 1870–1871.

Tweed's real political influence lay in his role as a party boss, where he was able to exchange government services and favors for money, jobs for loyal followers, and other forms of power. He was a member of Tammany Hall, the leading faction of the city's Democratic Party, which secured its control over the city by appealing to the needs of working New Yorkers, such as newly arrived immigrants. However, Tweed used his position to steal from taxpayers and extort money from those wishing to do business in the city as the head of the so-called "Ring" (also known as the "Tweed Ring" and the "Forty Thieves"), which extorted at least $30 million, and perhaps a good deal more. In 1871, a series of newspaper investigations exposed Tweed and his career came to a crashing halt. After being sentenced to twelve years in prison, Tweed escaped to Spain where authorities apprehended him. He eventually returned to New York, dying in debtor's prison in 1878.

The following document provides a remarkable account of how Tweed and his ring operated. The document comes from a report prepared for the Board of Aldermen by a special committee to account for the stolen money and the status of legal proceedings against members of the ring. In the first part, we find a review of the committee's findings, in the second actual excerpts from testimony by Tweed. Tweed, while cooperating with the committee, admitted to bribing state senators in to secure a new charter for the city under the auspices of the Charter of 1870, paying off city officials to obtain authorization and funding for the Brooklyn Bridge, and manipulating local elections at the ward level.

WILLIAM TWEED'S CONFESSION (1878)

Report of the Special Committee

THE RING IN THE BOARD OF SUPERVISORS.

According to William M. Tweed, whose evidence is in the main corroborated by that of Mr. Henry F. Taintor, the accountant who was employed on behalf of the people to work up and analyze the evidence concerning the Ring frauds; the first point of the attack of the Ring was upon the County Treasury, and as far as your Committee is able to ascertain, the first frauds were committed by a corrupt combination in the Board of Supervisors in the year 1860. This "Supervisors' Ring" existed from that time until, on account of internal dissentions, some of the members of it procured a law to be passed in 1870, by which the Board of Supervisors was abolished. The personel [sic] of this Ring changed slightly from year to year, and was composed at one time or other of the following persons: William M. Tweed, Walter Roche, John R. Briggs, Henry Smith, John Fox, James Hayes, Andrew J. Bleakley, and Isaac J. Oliver. The three first-named individuals originated the combination by agreeing to sustain each other in the Board and to vote together on bills presented for approval. Their united votes were sufficient to determine almost any question which came before the Board. In the subsequent years the other persons mentioned were from time to time added to their number and shared with them in the fraudulent gains.

HOW THE FRAUDS WERE PERPETRATED.

Almost every person who did work or furnished supplies for the county at this time were informed by some member of the Ring that, in order to insure a continuance of the public patronage, increased orders and prompt payment, it would be necessary for them to add to their bills a certain percentage in excess of their true face, which increases or percentage it was understood and agreed should be paid to the corrupt combination of members of the Board aforesaid.

The amount so added at this time was generally fifteen per cent. of the face of the bills.

[...]

BOARD OF AUDIT IN 1870.

After the Board of Audit of 1870 had been appointed in compliance with the statute [the Charter of 1870 which eliminated the Board of Supervisors], they agreed among themselves that they would require of all persons who dealt with the city in any way (except a few whom they feared to approach) to add fifty per cent. to the true face of their bills. The other fifty per cent. being intended for distribution among the members of the Board.

[...]

POWER OF THE RING.

With the City Government in their hands, the [state] Legislature under their control, and the City Treasury at their command, the Ring was now at the height of their power. They did not even hesitate to change the will of the people as expressed at elections, whenever such change seemed to them desirable. The bench of the Supreme Court ceased, under their influence, to preserve its purity, and no one who refused to submit to their dictation had the slightest chance for political preferment. To such an extent had rascality become prevalent that even in the Assembly of this State, certain members organized a band for the express purpose of selling their votes, and were known as "The Black Horse Cavalry." Persons who performed no service for the city, but who were serviceable to the Ring for purely political purposes, were placed upon the pay rolls as city and country officials and supported from the public treasury.

Several pretended attempts of self-styled reformers to expose this disgraceful combination were easily dealt with by the simple expedient of giving them fat offices.

AMOUNT STOLEN.

Mr. Taintor testifies that between January 1, 1868, and July 1, 1871, so far as he has developed the matter, $30,000,000 were fraudulently diverted from the treasury by the corrupt practices of the Ring, and that this does not include the amount stolen by the Ring in the Board of Supervisors, between 1860 and 1866. It is safe to assume that from 1860 until July, 1871, the people of the city have been robbed of fifty millions of dollars at least.

THE EXPOSURE AND DOWNFALL OF THE RING.

In the Spring of 1871, and when the operations of the Ring had reached this enormous magnitude, they were suddenly brought to light through the columns of one of the city journals, which published not only an outline of the facts heretofore recited, but also an accurate list of the principle persons who had been engaged in the frauds. Public attention was at once fixed upon this all-absorbing subject, and every possible device was suggested whereby might be assured the arrest of the thieves and the recovery of the millions stolen by them. There was a very widespread feeling of distrust manifest towards the law officers then in office, and several associations of citizens were formed, who assumed to take the prosecution of these offenders into their own hands. Committees were appointed, the most eminent counsel—selected from both political parties—were retained, accountants and detectives were employed, and a formidable campaign was commenced, having for its object the condign and speedy punishment of the thieves, and the wrestling from them their ill-gotten gains.

[...]

At present all the thieves, with one single exception, are at large, several of them are living in and near New York, in elegant ease, if not in ostentatious luxury, and all of them claim entire immunity from all sorts of suits or demands from the City or the People, on the ground that they have all been used as witnesses. Some dozen of the thieves have thus been let loose upon the community, in order that they might be used as witnesses against one or two of the others.

Nor has the pecuniary result of these suits been any more satisfactory.

The eminent counsel which had been especially retained to conduct these prosecutions originally began them in the name of the People of the State instead of the name of the Mayor, etc., of the City of New York. In those actions warrants of arrest were obtained against several of the principle members of the Ring, and bail bonds in large amounts were given by them. All of these actions failed because the Court of Appeals held that the right of action was not in the State but in the municipality.

Thereupon the Legislature passed an act—chapter 49 of the Laws of 1875—practically transferring to the State the cause of action to recover moneys fraudulently obtained from the city, and new actions were begun. Meanwhile much invaluable time had been lost, the bail-bonds taken in the original actions were, of course, not available, and the defendants had taken care to go where no new bail-bonds could be exacted of them.

[...]

An examination...shows that the energy with which these [new] suits seems to have been prosecuted at first has in very many cases entirely expended itself, and that for the last two or three years very little seems to have been accomplished in the progress of these cases, with a view either to the recovery of the stolen money or the prosecution of the thieves.

[...]

Your Committee respectfully suggests that your Honorable Board furnish the Attorney General of the State with a copy of the testimony taken in the course of this investigation, and of this report, and that you earnestly request him to take immediate and active steps to punish those of the Ring thieves who have heretofore escaped, and either to compel them to make such restitution as is now possible, or else to rid the community whom they have robbed of their presence.

Testimony of William M. Tweed

SIXTH DAY.
September 15, 1877

Q. Now, Mr. Tweed, you say that you paid money to certain members of the Senate, for the purpose of influencing their action with regard to the Charter of 1870?

A. I do say so; yes sir.

Q. Personally?

A. Yes, sir...

Q. Before it was passed?

A. Before it was passed.

Q. Well, now, will you state what members of the Senate you paid money to in this very connection, with regard to the Charter of 1870?

[...]

A. It must be told in the form of a little narrative, as there are many little points bearing on the subject... The origination of this charter was from the fact that a great many Democrats in New York had become dissatisfied... the matter became very violent among ourselves, so a meeting was called of the Tammany Hall General Committee of that year, by myself, who was then chairman of that committee... I went to Albany, I found that Mr. Hastings[1] and others, republicans, were very anxious at work to keep up this rivalry in the democratic organization... I stated my business with him, which was to ask his advice about the passage of the charter, and to get him to aid us in helping it along. After some little discussion, he finally consented to aid me, dropping his opposition to our side of the house, and suggested that the best way to do it would be that I should see certain Senators, and, if possible, have a caucus of the Republican Senators called and get them committed to our charter. We had arranged it so as to have no difficulty to pass it in the lower house. We passed it in the lower house, and at Mr. Hastings' suggestion, I saw a number of Senators, more particularly Senators Norris Winslow, William Woodin, Bowen, Minier, and Senator James Wood.

[...]

I talked the matter over with Mr. Winslow, and he thought they ought to have $50,000 apiece. I said we would pay for it, but I said we couldn't afford to pay that; finally we talked the matter over, and, in one or two days, Hastings suggested that if I got Woodin it would be well for me, as he was an influential man, a powerful speaker, and stood very high in his party.

[...]

I spoke to Woodin, and said, "I will win anyhow; I have got the thing all fixed, but I would rather win by a very large majority, and have all the Republicans go with me, and be on my side." Then I suggested the caucus, and suggested that the Republicans should resolve in the caucus to support me in this measure... finally he consented to go with the others. I said, "Shall I hand you $40,000?" He said, "Do the same with this as you are doing with the rest." I said, "I am going to hand the rest to Mr. Winslow." The Republicans held their caucus, and resolved to stand by the charter... when the bill came up every Republican voted for it except Mr. Thayer, and every Democrat voted for it except Mr. Genet. The Senate was full—thirty-two Senators; thirty of them voted for it, and only two against it.

Q. This was the charter which had been prepared by the leaders of Tammany Hall?

A. Yes, sir.

Q. Were these the only Senators whom you had dealings with in connection with this matter?

A. No, sir; I bought some of the others also.

Q. How did you buy them?

A. I bought some of the Democrats by giving them places?

Q. What Democrats, and what places? All about it.

A. I couldn't tell what places. Places—employment of men in the department, where they put their name on the pay-roll, and drew their money once a month.

SEVENTH DAY.

September 18, 1877

Q. What was your connection with the Brooklyn Bridge?

A. Well, it is a long story.

Q. Condense it; just tell me your connection with it.

[...]

A. I don't know the year... 1868, I think—Mr. Henry C. Murphy, who was a brother Senator, called on me and stated he was president of that bridge, and desired to have the Common Council authorize the Comptroller to issue the bonds, or give them money to the amount of one and a-half million dollars for the benefit of the bridge. I told him I had nothing to do with the Common Council at that time, and wasn't a member of it. "But," he said, "can't you influence them?" I told him I hadn't done any lobbying business there, but

I might, if necessary. Shortly after he called again. In the meantime I had conversed with a gentleman occupying a position in the Board of Aldermen which entitled him to credence, and he told me the appropriation could be passed by paying for it. I asked him how much was necessary... I informed Mr. Murphy of that fact. He told me to go ahead and make the negotiation. I did so, and the money was authorized to be appropriated or bonds issued...

Q. Did you tell Mr. Henry C. Murphy that you were going to get the necessary ordinance passed by paying for it?

A. That was the understanding.

Q. Did you tell him subsequently that you had done it?

A. Yes, sir.

Q. And that you had paid either fifty or sixty thousand dollars to the Board of Alderman?

A. I think it was sixty or sixty-five.

[...]

Q. Now, Mr. Tweed, with regard to elections—to the management of elections for the city and country officers—and generally, the elections for the city and county: When you were in office, did the Ring control the election in this city at that time?

A. They did, sir; absolutely.

Q. Please tell me what the *modus operandi* of that was. How did you control the election?

A. Well, each ward had a representative man, who would control matters in his own ward, and whom the various members of the general committee were to look up to for advice how to control elections.

Q. The General Committee of Tammany Hall?

A. Of the regular organization.

Q. What advice? What do you mean by that?

A. Why, what to do.

Q. What were they to do, in case you wanted a particular man elected over another?

A. Count the ballots in bulk, or without counting them announce the result in bulk, or change from one to the other, as the case may have been.

Q. Then these elections really were no elections at all? The ballots were made to bring about any result that you determined upon beforehand?

A. The ballot made no result; the counters made the result.

NOTE

1   Mr. Tweed was referring to Hugh Hastings, editor of *The Commercial Advertiser* an influential Republican newspaper.

5.2 PHILADELPHIA: CORRUPT AND CONTENTED (1903)

Lincoln Steffens

Source: Lincoln Steffens, "Philadelphia: Corrupt and Contented," *McClure's Magazine* XXI (July 1903): 249–263.

EDITORS' INTRODUCTION

Lincoln Steffens (1866–1936) is widely considered one of the foremost muckraking journalists of the early twentieth century. Steffens, the son of a banker, grew up in Sacramento, California in comfortable surroundings. He attended college at the University of California, Berkeley and studied abroad in Europe for several years before taking a position with *McClure's Magazine* in 1901. Deeply influenced by social science, Steffens contemplated the nature of political corruption in American cities. His editor, S. S. McClure, sent Steffens on a fact-finding tour, resulting in a series of six articles on St. Louis, Minneapolis, Pittsburgh, Philadelphia, Chicago, and New York. These magazine articles formed the core of his book, *The Shame of the Cities*, originally published in 1904 and still in print over a century later.

Steffens began his investigation of Philadelphia with a working hypothesis that American cities resembled each other in political structure. Through his research, Steffens determined that no matter which form of checks and balances were in place, political corruption would persist. Steffens argued that political bosses were a natural phenomenon. Steffens also found limited benefits to reforms which utilized a business model. Businesses, of course, could also be corrupt.[i] This selection on Philadelphia helps debunk a popular notion that machines were the product of cities politically dominated by immigrants and the Democratic Party. As Steffens reminded his readers, Philadelphia was a Republican city, yet political machines still reigned.

PHILADELPHIA: CORRUPT AND CONTENTED (1903)

Other American cities, no matter how bad their own condition may be, all point with scorn to Philadelphia as worse—"the worst governed city in the country." St. Louis, Minneapolis, Pittsburg submit with some patience to the jibes of any other community; the most friendly suggestion from Philadelphia is rejected with contempt. The Philadelphians are "supine," "asleep"; hopelessly ring-ruled, they are "complacent." "Politically benighted," Philadelphia is supposed to have no light to throw upon a state of things that is almost universal.

This is not fair. Philadelphia is, indeed, corrupt; but it is not without significance. Every city and town in the country can learn something from the typical political experience of this great representative city. New York is excused for many of its ills because it is the metropolis, Chicago because of its forced development; Philadelphia is our "third largest" city and its growth has been gradual and natural. Immigration has been blamed for our municipal conditions; Philadelphia, with 47 per cent of the population native born of native born parents, is the most American of our greater cities. It is "good," too, and intelligent. I don't know how to measure the intelligence of a community, but a Pennsylvania college professor who declared to me his belief in education for the masses as a way out of political corruption, himself justified the "rake-off" of preferred contractors on public works on the ground of a "fair business profit." [. . .]

Philadelphia is representative. This very "joke," told, as it was, with a laugh, is typical. All our municipal governments are more or less bad and all our people are optimists. Philadelphia is simply the most corrupt and the most contented. Minneapolis has cleaned up. Pittsburg has tried to, New York fights every other election, Chicago fights all the time. Even St. Louis has begun to stir (since the elections are over) and at the worst was only shameless. Philadelphia is proud; good people there defend corruption and boast of their machine. My college professor, with his philosophic view of "rake-offs," is one Philadelphia type. Another is the man, who, driven to bay with his local pride, says: "At least you must admit that our machine is the best you have ever seen."

All Through With Reform

Disgraceful? Other cities say so. But I say that if Philadelphia is a disgrace, it is a disgrace not to itself alone, nor to Pennsylvania, but to the United States and to American character. For this great city, so highly representative in other respects, is not behind in political experience, but ahead, with New York. Philadelphia is a city that has had its reforms. Having passed through all the typical stages of corruption, Philadelphia reached the period of miscellaneous loot with a boss for chief thief, under James McManes and the Gas Ring 'way back in the late sixties and seventies. This is the Tweed stage of corruption from which St. Louis, for example, is just emerging. Philadelphia, in two inspiring popular revolts, attacked the Gas Ring, broke

---

i Lincoln Steffens, *The Autobiography of Lincoln Steffens*, Volume 1 (New York: Harcourt, Brace, and Company, 1931), 409.

it, and in 1885 achieved that dream of American cities—a good charter. The present condition of Philadelphia, therefore, is not that which precedes, but that which follows reform, and in this distinction lies its startling general significance. What has happened since the Bullitt Law or charter went into effect in Philadelphia may happen in any American city "after reform is over." [...]

The Bullitt Law, which concentrates in the Mayor ample power, executive and political, and complete responsibility. Moreover, it calls for very little thought and action on the part of the people. All they expected to have to do when the Bullitt Law went into effect was to elect as Mayor a good business man, who with his probity and common sense would give them that good business administration which is the ideal of many reformers.

Business Men as Mayors

The Bullitt Law went into effect in 1887. A committee of twelve—four from the Union League, four from business organizations, and four from the bosses—picked out the first man to run under it on the Republican ticket, Edwin H. Fitler, an able, upright business man, and he was elected. Strange to say, his administration was satisfactory to the citizens, who speak well of it to this day, and to the politicians also; Boss McManes (the ring was broken, not the boss) took to the next national convention from Philadelphia a delegation solid for Fitler for President of the United States. It was a farce, but it pleased Mr. Fitler, so Matthew S. Quay, the State boss, let him have a complimentary vote on the first ballot. The politicians "fooled" Mr. Fitler, and they "fooled" also the next business Mayor, Edwin S. Stuart, likewise a most estimable gentleman. Under these two administrations the foundation was laid for the present government of Philadelphia, the corruption to which Philadelphians seem so reconciled, and the machine which is "at least the best you have ever seen." [...]

The machine controls the whole process of voting, and practices fraud at every stage. The assessor's list is the voting list, and the assessor is the machine's man. The assessor pads the list with the names of dead dogs, children, and non-existent persons. One newspaper printed the picture of a dog, another that of a little four-year-old negro boy, down on such a list. A ring orator in a speech resenting sneers at his ward as "low down" reminded his hearers that that was the ward of Independence Hall, and, naming over signers of the Declaration of Independence, he closed his highest flight of eloquence with the statement that "these men, the fathers of American liberty, voted down here once. And," he added, with a catching grin, "they vote here yet." Rudolph Blankenburg, a persistent fighter for the right and the use of the right to vote, sent out just before one election a registered letter to each voter on the rolls of a certain selected division. Sixty-three percent. were returned marked "not at," "removed," "deceased," etc. From one four-story house where forty-four voters were addressed, eighteen letters came back undelivered; from another of forty-eight voters, came back forty-one letters; from another sixty-one out of sixty-two; from another forty-four out of forty-seven. Six houses in one division were assessed at one hundred and seventy-two voters, more than the votes cast in the previous election in any one of two hundred entire divisions.

The repeating is done boldly, for the machine controls the election officers, often choosing them from among the fraudulent names; and when no one appears to serve, assigning the heeler ready for the expected vacancy. The police are forbidden by law to stand within thirty feet of the polls, but they are at the box and they are there to see that the machine's orders are obeyed and that repeaters whom they help to furnish are permitted to vote without "intimidation" on the names they, the police, have supplied. [...]

Bosses Appointed from the U. S. Senate

Deprived of self-government, the Philadelphians haven't even self-governing machine government. They have their own boss, but he and his machine are subject to the State ring and take their orders from the State boss, Matthew S. Quay, who is the proprietor of Pennsylvania and the real ruler of Philadelphia, just as William Penn, the great proprietor, was. Philadelphians, especially the local bosses, dislike this description of their government, and they point for refutation to their charter. But this very Bullitt Law was passed by Quay, and he put it through the Legislature, not for reform reasons, but at the instance of David H. Lane, his Philadelphia lieutenant, as a check upon the power of Boss McManes. [...]

Philadelphia Machine Upside Down

The Philadelphia organization is upside down. It has its root in the air, or, rather, like the banyan tree, it sends its roots from the center out both up and down and all around, and there lies its peculiar strength. For when I said it was dependent and not sound, I did not mean that it was weak. It is dependent as a municipal machine, but the organization that rules Philadelphia is, as we have seen, not a mere municipal machine, but a city, State, and national organization. The people of Philadelphia are Republicans in a Republican city in a Republican State in a Republican nation, and they are bound ring on ring on ring. The President of the United States and his patronage; the National Cabinet and their patronage; the Congress and the patronage of the Senators and the Congressmen from Pennsylvania; the Governor of the State and the State Legislature with their powers and patronage; and all that the Mayor and City Councils have of power and patronage;—all these bear down upon Philadelphia to keep it in the control of Quay's boss and his little ring. This is the ideal of party organization, and, possibly, is the end toward which our democratic republic is tending. If it is, the end is absolutism. Nothing but a revolution could overthrow this oligarchy, and there is its danger. With no outlet at the polls for public feeling, the machine cannot be taught anything it does not know excepting at the cost of annihilation. [...]

Making Graft Safe

But the greatest lesson learned, and applied was that of conciliation and "good government." The people must not want to vote or rebel against the ring. This ring, like any other, was formed for the exploitation of the city for private profit, and the cementing force is the "cohesive power of public plunder." But McManes and Tweed had proved that miscellaneous larceny was dangerous, and why should a lot of cheap politicians get so much and the people nothing at all? The people had been taught to expect but little from their rulers: good water, good light, clean streets well paved, fair transportation, the decent repression of vice, public order and public safety, and no scandalous or open corruption. It would be good business and good politics to give them these things. [...]

But each of these 15,000 persons was selected for office because he could deliver votes, either by organizations, by parties, or by families. These must represent pretty near a majority of the city's voters. But this is by no means the end of the ring's reach. In the State ring are the great corporations, the Standard Oil Company, Cramp's Ship Yard, and the steel companies, with the Pennsylvania Railroad at their head, and all the local transportation and other public utility companies following after. They get franchises, privileges, exemptions, etc.; they have helped finance Quay through deals: the Pennsylvania paid Boss, David Martin, Quay said once, a large yearly salary; the Cramps get contracts to build United States ships, and for years have been begging for a subsidy on home-made ships. The officers, directors, and stock-holders of these companies, with their friends, their bankers, and their employees are of the organization. Better still, one of the local bosses of Philadelphia told me he could always give a worker a job with these companies, just as he could in a city department, or in the mint, or post-office. Then there are the bankers who enjoy, or may someday enjoy, public deposits; those that profit on loans to finance political financial deals; the promoting capitalists who share with the bosses on franchises; and the brokers who deal in ring securities and speculation on ring tips. Through the exchange the ring financiers reach the investing public, which is a large and influential body. The traction companies, which bought their way from beginning to end by corruption, which have always been in the ring, and whose financiers have usually shared in other big ring deals, adopted early the policy of bribing the people with "small blocks of stock." [...]

But we are not yet through. Quay has made a specialty all his life of reformers, and he and his local bosses have won over so many that the list of former reformers is very, very long. Martin drove down his roots through race and religion, too. Philadelphia was one of the hot-beds of "know-nothingism."

Martin recognized the Catholic, and the Irish-Irish, and so drew off into the Republican party the great natural supply of the Democrats; and his successors have given high places to representative Jews. [...]

If there is no other hold for the ring on a man there always is the protective tariff. "I don't care," said a manufacturer. "What if they do plunder and rob us, it can't hurt me unless they raise the tax rates, and even that won't ruin me. Our party keeps up the tariff. If they should reduce that, my business would be ruined."

5.3 THE GREAT SOCIETY (1964)

Lyndon B. Johnson

Source: *Public Papers of the Presidents of the United States: Lyndon B. Johnson, 1963–64.* Volume I (Washington, D.C.: Government Printing Office, 1965): 704–707.

EDITORS' INTRODUCTION

Lyndon Baines Johnson (LBJ) became President of the United States during period of tremendous upheaval in the United States. In a departure from his earlier conservative political temperament, as president he embraced a pragmatic liberalism that took public policy initiatives from his predecessor John F. Kennedy's administration into to new and grander directions. Johnson built upon the legacy and promise of Franklin Delano Roosevelt and the New Deal, and the premise that government could solve pressing social issues. LBJ launched a series of domestic programs beginning in 1963–1964 called the Great Society. These programs had the intended goal of eliminating poverty and racial injustice, rejuvenating cities and the countryside, improving education from the pre-school to college levels, and providing better nutrition, improved public health, and access to the arts and humanities for all Americans.

In the very first speech in which President Johnson used the term Great Society, a commencement address at the University of Michigan in May 1964 excerpted here, he articulated the three initial areas to begin leveraging nation's vast resources to preserve the liberty and happiness of the American people—the city, the countryside, and the classroom. In fact, LBJ made it clear that the future of the nation lay in its cities, accurately predicting that in fifty years, 80 percent of Americans would live in urban areas. As such, declared President Johnson, the next forty years should be dedicated to rebuilding all urban areas in the United States. Johnson argued that American society could not be great until its cities were great.

THE GREAT SOCIETY (1964)

Remarks at the University of Michigan
May 22, 1964
[...]

I have come today from the turmoil of your Capital to the tranquility of your campus to speak about the future of your country.

The purpose of protecting the life of our Nation and preserving the liberty of our citizens is to pursue the happiness of our people. Our success in that pursuit is the test of our success as a Nation.

For a century we labored to settle and to subdue a continent. For half a century we called upon unbounded invention and untiring industry to create an order of plenty for all of our people.

The challenge of the next half century is whether we have the wisdom to use that wealth to enrich and elevate our national life, and to advance the quality of our American civilization.

Your imagination, your initiative, and your indignation will determine whether we build a society where progress is the servant of our needs, or a society where old values and new visions are buried under unbridled growth. For in your time we have the opportunity to move not only toward the rich society and the powerful society, but upward to the Great Society.

The Great Society rests on abundance and liberty for all. It demands an end to poverty and racial injustice, to which we are totally committed in our time. But that is just the beginning.

The Great Society is a place where every child can find knowledge to enrich his mind and to enlarge his talents. It is a place where leisure is a welcome chance to build and reflect, not a feared cause of boredom and restlessness. It is a place where the city of man serves not only the needs of the body and the demands of commerce but the desire for beauty and the hunger for community.

It is a place where man can renew contact with nature. It is a place which honors creation for its own sake and for what it adds to the understanding of the race. It is a place where men are more concerned with the quality of their goals than the quantity of their goods.

But most of all, the Great Society is not a safe harbor, a resting place, a final objective, a finished work. It is a challenge constantly renewed, beckoning us toward a destiny where the meaning of our lives matches the marvelous products of our labor.

So I want to talk to you today about three places where we begin to build the Great Society—in our cities, in our countryside, and in our classrooms.

Many of you will live to see the day, perhaps 50 years from now, when there will be 400 million Americans—four-fifths of them in urban areas. In the remainder of this century urban population will double, city land will double, and we will have to build homes, highways, and facilities equal to all those built since this country was first settled. So in the next 40 years we must rebuild the entire urban United States.

Aristotle said: "Men come together in cities in order to live, but they remain together in order to live the good life." It is harder and harder to live the good life in American cities today.

The catalog of ills is long: there is the decay of the centers and the despoiling of the suburbs. There is not enough housing for our people or transportation for our traffic. Open land is vanishing and old landmarks are violated.

Worst of all expansion is eroding the precious and time honored values of community with neighbors and communion with nature. The loss of these values breeds loneliness and boredom and indifference.

Our society will never be great until our cities are great. Today the frontier of imagination and innovation is inside those cities and not beyond their borders.

New experiments are already going on. It will be the task of your generation to make the American city a place where future generations will come, not only to live but to live the good life.

I understand that if I stayed here tonight I would see that Michigan students are really doing their best to live the good life.

This is the place where the Peace Corps was started. It is inspiring to see how all of you, while you are in this country, are trying so hard to live at the level of the people.

A second place where we begin to build the Great Society is in our countryside. We have always prided ourselves on being not only America the strong and America the free, but America the beautiful. Today that beauty is in danger. The water we drink, the food we eat, the very air that we breathe, are threatened with pollution. Our parks are overcrowded, our seashores overburdened. Green fields and dense forests are disappearing.

A few years ago we were greatly concerned about the "Ugly American." Today we must act to prevent an ugly America.

For once the battle is lost, once our natural splendor is destroyed, it can never be recaptured. And once man can no longer walk with beauty or wonder at nature his spirit will wither and his sustenance be wasted.

A third place to build the Great Society is in the classrooms of America. There your children's lives will be shaped. Our society will not be great until every young mind is set free to scan the farthest reaches of thought and imagination. We are still far from that goal.

Today, 8 million adult Americans, more than the entire population of Michigan, have not finished 5 years of school. Nearly 20 million have not finished 8 years of school. Nearly 54 million—more than one-quarter of all America—have not even finished high school.

Each year more than 100,000 high school graduates, with proved ability, do not enter college because they cannot afford it. And if we cannot educate today's youth, what will we do in 1970 when elementary school enrollment will be 5 million greater than 1960? And high school enrollment will rise by 5 million. College enrollment will increase by more than 3 million.

In many places, classrooms are overcrowded and curricula are outdated. Most of our qualified teachers are underpaid, and many of our paid teachers are unqualified. So we must give every child a place to sit and a teacher to learn from. Poverty must not be a bar to learning, and learning must offer an escape from poverty.

But more classrooms and more teachers are not enough. We must seek an educational system which grows in excellence as it grows in size. This means better training for our teachers. It means preparing youth to enjoy their hours of leisure as well as their hours of labor. It means exploring new techniques of teaching, to find new ways to stimulate the love of learning and the capacity for creation.

These are three of the central issues of the Great Society. While our Government has many programs directed at those issues, I do not pretend that we have the full answer to those problems.

But I do promise this: We are going to assemble the best thought and the broadest knowledge from all over the world to find those answers for America. I intend to establish working groups to prepare a series of White House conferences and meetings— on the cities, on natural beauty, on the quality of education, and on other emerging challenges. And from these meetings and from this inspiration and from these studies we will begin to set our course toward the Great Society.

The solution to these problems does not rest on a massive program in Washington, nor can it rely solely on the strained resources of local authority. They require us to create new concepts of cooperation, a creative federalism, between the National Capital and the leaders of local communities.

Woodrow Wilson once wrote: "Every man sent out from his university should be a man of his Nation as well as a man of his time."

Within your lifetime powerful forces, already loosed, will take us toward a way of life beyond the realm of our experience, almost beyond the bounds of our imagination.

For better or for worse, your generation has been appointed by history to deal with those problems and to lead America toward a new age. You have the chance never before afforded to any people in any age. You can help build a society where the demands of morality, and the needs of the spirit, can be realized in the life of the Nation.

So, will you join in the battle to give every citizen the full equality which God enjoins and the law requires, whatever his belief, or race, or the color of his skin?

Will you join in the battle to give every citizen an escape from the crushing weight of poverty?

Will you join in the battle to make it possible for all nations to live in enduring peace—as neighbors and not as mortal enemies?

Will you join in the battle to build the Great Society, to prove that our material progress is only the foundation on which we will build a richer life of mind and spirit?

There are those timid souls who say this battle cannot be won; that we are condemned to a soulless wealth. I do not agree. We have the power to shape the civilization that we want. But we need your will, your labor, your hearts, if we are to build that kind of society.

Those who came to this land sought to build more than just a new country. They sought a new world. So I have come here today to your campus to say that you can make their vision our reality. So let us from this moment begin our work so that in the future men will look back and say: It was then, after a long and weary way, that man turned the exploits of his genius to the full enrichment of his life.

5.4 THE NEGRO FAMILY: THE CASE FOR NATIONAL ACTION (1965)

Daniel Patrick Moynihan

Source: United States Department of Labor, Office of Policy Planning and Research, "The Negro Family: The Case for National Action," (Washington, D.C., March 1965).

EDITORS' INTRODUCTION

While working as Assistant Secretary of Labor during the administration of President Lyndon Baines Johnson, sociologist Daniel Patrick Moynihan crafted "The Negro Family: The Case for National Action," a white paper (an authoritative report) on what he considered the most pressing problem confronting African Americans; the disintegration of the family structure in urban ghettos. This paper caused great controversy at the time and continues to have a complicated legacy decades later. Moynihan worried that roughly half of all African Americans would be unable to climb out of cyclical poverty and into the middle class due to the increasing prevalence of female headed households. For Moynihan, the economic plight of African Americans was more than a statistical correlation between a rise in the unemployment rate and an increase in the number of claims for public assistance, often in the form of Aid to Families with Dependent Children (AFDC), know more pejoratively as "welfare." Beginning in 1960, and again in 1963 and 1964, the number of AFDC claims grew despite a decline in the nation's unemployment rate. While noting that the phenomena needed more investigation, Moynihan argued that a "tangle of pathology" would permanently trap the poorest African Americans in ghettos unless the federal government took a new and special course of action to help them overcome their situation.

Few government papers have created more intense debate over the relationship between race, poverty, and public policy as the "The Negro Family." Also known as the "Moynihan Report," the document generated a firestorm from social, political, and civil rights activists and scholars who assailed its racist and sexist assumptions, stereotypes, flaws, and its overall "blaming the victim" tone. The report downplayed ongoing systemic racism and instead stressed the need to improve the character and composition of black families. Even Moynihan's central historical premise, that the institution of slavery destroyed the black family and that three centuries of injustice crushed the will of African Americans, were not only inaccurate, but also completely ignored the agency of African Americans. While he praised blacks for the Civil Rights movement and their resilience as a people, he was unable to understand the strength of the black family. The "Moynihan Report" also failed to account for how African Americans saw themselves, their history, the plight of the inner-cities, and choices before them. **[See Document 1.3, "The Environment of the Negro (1898)"; Document 9.1, "Watts Riots (1965)"; Document 9.3, "Oakland Black Panther Party for Self-Defense, Ten Point Plan of the Oakland Black Panthers (1966)"; and Essay 8.2, Lisa Krissoff Boehm, *Making a Way out of No Way: African American Women and the Second Great Migration* (2009).]**

As a public policy document, "The Negro Family" reflected prevailing racial and paternal attitudes of government officials and the agenda of President Johnson's Great Society, specifically the War on Poverty, which sought to leverage the vast resources of the U.S. government in providing economic opportunity for the most disadvantaged. The underlying assumptions of the report also reflected the larger contours of the "culture of poverty" concept of social theory and the so-called "underclass debate" among social scientists, policy analysts, and political pundits as to whether or not the United States contained a permanent group of people trapped in poverty, and the reason for such a situation. In an ultimate case of systemic racism– converging with the "blaming the victim" mentality–in the mid-1990s opponents of AFDC, led by the Republican-controlled Congress, succeeded in eliminating the welfare program altogether after arguing that it actually created and perpetuated government dependence and poverty. Citing a need to "end welfare as we know it," President William Jefferson Clinton signed the Personal Responsibility and Work Opportunity Act of 1996 that replaced AFDC with the Temporary Assistance for Needy Families (TANF) program that limits the amount of time a person may receive government benefits.

Moynihan left the Department of Labor for Harvard University in 1966 to become a professor and director of the Joint Center for Urban Studies at Harvard and the Massachusetts Institute of Technology. He took leave from Harvard on and off over the next decade to work as Assistant to President Nixon for Domestic Policy, U.S. Ambassador to India, and U.S. representative to the United Nations. He was elected to the U.S. Senate as a member of the Democratic Party representing New York in 1976, winning re-election in 1982, 1988, and 1994, and was succeeded in this position in January 2001 by former first lady Hillary Rodham Clinton. Although long an advocate of welfare reform, as a member of the U.S. Senate Moynihan voted against the Personal Responsibility and Work Opportunity Act of 1996.

THE NEGRO FAMILY: THE CASE FOR NATIONAL ACTION (1965)

The United States is approaching a new crisis in race relations.

In the decade that began with the school desegregation decision of the Supreme Court, and ended with the passage of the Civil Rights Act of 1964, the demand of Negro Americans for full recognition of their civil rights was finally met.

The effort, no matter how savage and brutal, of some State and local governments to thwart the exercise of those rights is doomed. The nation will not put up with it— least of all the Negros. The present moment will pass. In the meantime, a new period is beginning.

In this new period the expectations of the Negro Americans will go beyond civil rights. Being Americans, they will now expect that in the near future equal opportunities for them as a group will produce roughly equal results, as compared with other groups. This is not going to happen. Nor will it happen for generations to come unless a new and special effort is made.

There are two reasons. First, the racist virus in the American blood stream still afflicts us: Negroes will encounter serious personal prejudice for at least another generation. Second, three centuries of sometimes unimaginable mistreatment have taken their toll on the Negro people. The harsh fact is that as a group, at the present time, in terms of ability to win out in the competitions of American life, they are not equal to most of those groups with which they will be competing. Individually, Negro Americans reach the highest peaks of achievement. But collectively, in the spectrum of American ethnic and religious and regional groups, where some get plenty and some get none, where some send eighty percent of their children to college and others pull them out of school at the 8th grade, Negroes are among the weakest.

The most difficult fact for white Americans to understand is that in these terms the circumstances of the Negro American community in recent years has probably been getting worse, *not better.*

Indices of dollars of income, standards of living, and years of education deceive. The gap between the Negro and most other groups in American society is widening.

The fundamental problem, in which this is most clearly the case, is that of family structure. The evidence—not final, but powerfully persuasive—is that the Negro family in the urban ghettos is crumbling. A middle-class group has managed to save itself, but for vast numbers of the unskilled, poorly educated city working class the fabric of conventional social relationships has all but disintegrated.

There are indications that the situation may have been arrested in the past few years, but the general post-war trend is unmistakable. So long as this situation persists, the cycle of poverty and disadvantage will continue to repeat itself.

The thesis of this paper is that these events, in combination, confront the nation with a new kind of problem. Measures that have worked in the past, or would work for most groups in the present, will not work here. A national effort is required that will give a unity of purpose to the many activities of the Federal government in this area, directed to a new kind of national goal: the establishment of a stable Negro family structure.

This would be a new departure for Federal policy. And a difficult one. But it almost certainly offers the only possibility of resolving in our time what is, after all, the nation's oldest, and most intransigent, and now it's most dangerous social problem. What Gunnar Myrdal said in *An American Dilemma* remains true today: *"America is free to choose whether the Negro shall remain her liability or become her opportunity."*

[...]

The Tangle of Pathology

That the Negro American has survived at all is extraordinary—a lesser people might simply have died out, as indeed others have. That the Negro community has not only survived, but in this political generation has entered national affairs as a moderate, humane, and constructive national force is the highest testament to the healing powers of the democratic ideal and the creative vitality of the Negro people.

But it may not be supposed that the Negro American community has not paid a fearful price for the incredible mistreatment to which it has been subjected over the past three centuries.

In essence, the Negro community has been forced into a matriarchal structure which, because it is so out of line with the rest of the American society, seriously retards the progress of the group as a whole, and imposes a crushing burden on the Negro male and, in consequence, on a great many Negro women as well.

There is, presumably, no special reason why a society in which males are dominant in family relationships is to be preferred to a matriarchal arrangement. However, it is clearly a disadvantage for a minority group to be operating on one principle, while the great majority of the population, and the one with the most advantages to begin with, is operating on another. This is the present situation of the Negro. Ours is a society which presumes male leadership in private and public affairs. The arrangements of society facilitate such leadership and reward it. A subculture, such as that of the Negro American, in which this is not the pattern, is placed at a distinct disadvantage.

Here an earlier word of caution should be repeated. There is much evidence that a considerable number of Negro families have managed to break out of the tangle of pathology and to establish themselves as stable, effective units, living according to patterns of American society in general. E. Franklin Frazier has suggested that the middle-class Negro American family is, if anything, more patriarchal and protective of its children than the general run of such families.[2]

Given equal opportunities, the children of these families will perform as well or better than their white peers. They need no help from anyone, and ask none.

While this phenomenon is not easily measured, one index is that middle-class Negroes have even fewer children than middle-class whites, indicating a desire to conserve the advances they have made and to insure that their children do as well or better. Negro women who marry early to uneducated laborers have more children than white women in the same situation; Negro women who marry at the common age for the middle class to educated men doing technical or professional work have only four-fifths as many children as their white counterparts.

It might be estimated that as much as half of the Negro community falls into the middle class. However, the remaining half is in desperate and deteriorating circumstances. Moreover, because of housing segregation it is immensely difficult for the stable half to escape from the cultural influences of the unstable one. The children of middle-class Negroes as often as not must grow up in, or next to the slums, an experience almost unknown to white middle-class children. They are therefore constantly exposed to the pathology of the disturbed group and constantly in danger of being drawn in to it. It is for this reason that the propositions put forth in this study may be thought of as having a more or less general application.

In a word, most Negro youth are in *danger* of being caught up in the tangle of pathology that affects their world, and probably a majority are so entrapped. Many of those who escape do so for one generation only: as things now are, their children may have to run the gauntlet all over again. That is not the least vicious aspect of the world that white America has made for the Negro.

Obviously, not every instance of social pathology afflicting the Negro community can be traced to the weakness of family structure. If, for example, organized crime in the Negro community were not largely controlled by whites, there would be more capital accumulation among Negroes, and therefore probably more Negro business enterprises. If it were not for the hostility and fear many whites exhibit towards Negroes, they in turn would be less afflicted by hostility and fear and so on. There is no one Negro community. There is no one Negro problem. There is no one solution. Nonetheless, at the center of the tangle of pathology is the weakness of the family structure. Once or twice removed, it will be found to be the principal source of most of the aberrant, inadequate, or antisocial behavior that did not establish, but now serves to perpetuate the cycle of poverty and deprivation.

It was by destroying the Negro family under slavery that white America broke the will of the Negro people. Although that will has reasserted itself in our time, it is a resurgence doomed to frustration unless the viability of the Negro family is restored.

The Case For National Action

The object of this study has been to define a problem, rather than propose solutions to it. We have kept within these confines for three reasons.

First, there are many persons, within and without the Government, who do not feel the problem exists, at least in any serious degree. These persons feel that, with the legal obstacles to assimilation out of the way, matters will take care of themselves in the normal course of events. This is a fundamental issue, and requires a decision within the Government.

Second, it is our view that the problem is so inter-related, one thing with another, that any list of program proposals would necessarily be incomplete, and would distract attention from the main point of inter-relatedness. We have shown a clear relation between male employment, for example, and the number of welfare dependent children. Employment in turn reflects educational achievement, which depends in large part on family stability, which reflects employment. Where we should break into this cycle, and how, are the most difficult domestic questions facing the United States. We must first reach agreement on what the problem is, then we will know what questions must be answered.

Third, it is necessary to acknowledge the view, held by a number of responsible persons, that this problem may in fact be out of control. This is a view with which we emphatically and totally disagree, but the view must be acknowledged. The persistent rise in Negro educational achievement is probably the main trend that belies this thesis. On the other hand our study has produced some clear indications that the situation may indeed have begun to feed on itself. It may be noted, for example, that for most of the post-war period male Negro unemployment and the number of new AFDC cases rose and fell together as if connected by a chain from 1948 to 1962. The correlation between the two series of data was an astonishing .91. (This would mean that 83 percent of the rise and fall in AFDC cases can be statistically ascribed to the rise and fall in the unemployment rate.) In 1960, however, for the first time, unemployment declined, but the number of new AFDC cases rose. In 1963 this happened a second time. In 1964 a third. The possible implications of these and other data are serious enough that they, too, should be understood before program proposals are made.

However, the argument of this paper does lead to one central conclusion: Whatever the specific elements of a national effort designed to resolve this problem, those elements must be coordinated in terms of one general strategy.

What then is that problem? We feel the answer is clear enough. Three centuries of injustice have brought about deep-seated structural distortions in the life of the Negro American. At this point, the present tangle of pathology is capable of perpetuating itself without assistance from the white world. The cycle can be broken only if these distortions are set right.

In a word, a national effort towards the problems of Negro Americans must be directed towards the question of family structure. The object should be to strengthen the Negro family so as to enable it to raise and support its members as do other families. After that, how this group of Americans chooses to run its affairs, take advantage of its opportunities, or fail to do so, is none of the nation's business.

[...]

The problem is now more serious, the obstacles greater. There is, however, a profound change for the better in one respect. The President has committed the nation to an all out effort to eliminate poverty wherever it exists, among whites or Negroes, and a militant, organized, and responsible Negro movement exists to join that effort.

Such a national effort could be stated thus:

The policy of the United States is to bring the Negro American to full and equal sharing in the responsibilities and rewards of citizenship. To this end, the programs of the Federal government bearing on this objective shall be designed to have the effect, directly or indirectly, of enhancing the stability and resources of the Negro American family.

5.5 PRESIDENT ARRIVES IN ALABAMA, BRIEFED ON HURRICANE KATRINA (2005)

George W. Bush

Source: Press Release, September 2, 2005, President Arrives in Alabama, Briefed on Hurricane Katrina.

EDITORS' INTRODUCTION

On September 2, 2005, President George W. Bush landed at the Mobile Regional Airport in Mobile, Alabama to view the destruction of Gulf Coast communities by Hurricane Katrina. At a press conference, President Bush praised the Coast Guard, the National Guard, and others involved in relief efforts. Despite the fact that much of the city of New Orleans lay under water, Bush joked with those in attendance. He commented that he looked forward to the day he could sit on the porch of U.S. Senator Trent Lott's rebuilt home. President Bush then praised the work of Federal Emergency Management Agency (FEMA) Director Michael Brown for doing "a heck of job." Although the people gathered at the news conference applauded the statement, the remark soon met with a torrent of criticism. The incident brought scrutiny into Brown's qualifications. For many, President Bush's confidence in "Brownie" underscored just how out of touch the White House and the Bush administration were with the American public.

PRESIDENT ARRIVES IN ALABAMA, BRIEFED ON HURRICANE KATRINA (2005)

THE PRESIDENT: Well, first I want to say a few things. I am incredibly proud of our Coast Guard. We have got courageous people risking their lives to save life. And I want to thank the commanders and I want to thank the troops over there for representing the best of America.

I want to congratulate the governors for being leaders. You didn't ask for this, when you swore in, but you're doing a heck of a job. And the federal government's job is big, and it's massive, and we're going to do it. Where it's not working right, we're going to make it right. Where it is working right, we're going to duplicate it elsewhere. We have a responsibility, at the federal level, to help save life, and that's the primary focus right now. Every life is precious, and so we're going to spend a lot of time saving lives, whether it be in New Orleans or on the coast of Mississippi.

We have a responsibility to help clean up this mess, and I want to thank the Congress for acting as quickly as you did. Step one is to appropriate $10.5 billion. But I've got to warn everybody, that's just the beginning. That's a small down payment for the cost of this effort. But to help the good folks here, we need to do it.

We are going to restore order in the city of New Orleans, and we're going to help supplement the efforts of the Mississippi Guard and others to restore order in parts of Mississippi. And I want to thank you for your strong statement of zero tolerance. The people of this country expect there to be law and order, and we're going to work hard to get it. In order to make sure there's less violence, we've

got to get food to people. And that's a primary mission, is to get food to people. And there's a lot of food moving. And now the—it's one thing to get it moving to a station, it's the next thing to get it in the hands of the people, and that's where we're going to spend a lot of time focusing.

We've got a lot of rebuilding to do. First, we're going to save lives and stabilize the situation. And then we're going to help these communities rebuild. The good news is—and it's hard for some to see it now—that out of this chaos is going to come a fantastic Gulf Coast, like it was before. Out of the rubble of Trent Lott's house—he's lost his entire house—there's going to be a fantastic house. And I'm looking forward to sitting on the porch. (Laughter.)

GOVERNOR RILEY: He'll be glad to have you.

THE PRESIDENT: Out of New Orleans is going to come that great city again. That's what's going to happen. But now we're in the darkest days, and so we got a lot of work to do. And I'm down here to thank people. I'm down here to comfort people. I'm down here to let people know that we're going to work with the states and the local folks with a strategy to get this thing solved.

Now, I also want to say something about the compassion of the people of Alabama and Mississippi and Louisiana and surrounding states. I want to thank you for your compassion. Now is the time to love a neighbor like you'd like to be loved yourselves.

Governor Riley announced the fact that they're going to open up homes in military bases for stranded folks. And that's going to be very important and helpful.

My dad and Bill Clinton are going to raise money for governors' funds. The governors of Louisiana, Mississippi and Alabama will have monies available to them to help deal with the long-term consequences of this storm.

The faith-based groups and the community-based groups throughout this part of the world, and the country for that matter, are responding. If you want to help, give cash money to the Red Cross and the Salvation Army. That's where the first help will come. There's going to be plenty of opportunities to help later on, but right now the immediate concern is to save lives and get food and medicine to people so we can stabilize the situation.

Again, I want to thank you all for—and, Brownie, you're doing a heck of a job. The FEMA Director is working 24—(applause)— they're working 24 hours a day.

Again, my attitude is, if it's not going exactly right, we're going to make it go exactly right. If there's problems, we're going to address the problems. And that's what I've come down to assure people of. And again, I want to thank everybody.

And I'm not looking forward to this trip. I got a feel for it when I flew over before. It— for those who have not—trying to conceive what we're talking about, it's as if the entire Gulf Coast were obliterated by a—the worst kind of weapon you can imagine. And now we're going to go try to comfort people in that part of the world.

Thank you. (Applause.)

5.6 WHY DOES DONALD TRUMP DEMONIZE CITIES? (2017)

Will Wilkinson

Source: *The Washington Post*, March 17, 2017. Reprinted with permission of Will Wilkinson and the Niskanen Center.

EDITORS' INTRODUCTION

President Donald J. Trump is the undeniable product of New York City and the economic and social opportunities found in large urban areas. Born and raised in New York, he has built his reputation as a deal maker and multimillionaire from high-profile real estate projects in New York City, Atlantic City, Chicago, Las Vegas, and other major metropolitan areas. However, as Will Wilkinson argues in the following opinion piece from *The Washington Post*, as a politician, Trump espouses anti-urban populist rhetoric more in line with the attitudes and outlook of his political base that tend to live in smaller, less dense, and economically lethargic communities. Despite evidence to the contrary, Trump and his supporters harangue large cities and their diverse multicultural populations as failures, crime ridden, and dangerous to the good of the nation.

In many respects, Trump's rhetoric is just the latest version of centuries-old anti-urban attitudes stretching back to the end of the American Revolution. **[See Essay 3.2, "The Forgotten City."]** However, there is much more to the story, given the fact that Trump did carry numerous smaller cities and metropolitan regions. The portions of the United States won by Trump in the 2016 presidential election tended to be those with lower average wages and economies more likely to be displaced rather than advanced by technology, compared to those areas taken by Hillary Clinton. Clinton received almost three million more popular votes nationwide than Donald Trump. In 2016, Republican regions, as a whole, were producing less of the nation's wealth. These regional differences, Wilkinson notes, are in line with the findings of economist Enrico Moretti, who characterizes the regional separation in education and economic productivity in the United States as the "Great Divergence," and with Bill Bishop's concept of the "Big Sort," in which like-minded people have been clustering together in the same communities. Why then, does President Trump, in the words of Wilkinson, "demonize cities?" For Wilkinson, it's because they show that the liberal experiment works. Wilkinson points out that density creates innovation and drives growth; his argument is very much aligned with the approach of urban theorist Jane Jacobs. Immigrants are an important component of this economic vitality. Their growing presence in the American population, however, plays into long standing fears of decline, disorder, and racial antipathy by those who fail to reap the benefits of economic transformations.

Will Wilkinson is the vice president for policy at the Niskanen Center and a former U.S. politics and policy correspondent for the *Economist* and Research Fellow for the Cato Institute. His writings have also appeared in a variety of on- and offline publications including *The Atlantic*, *Bloomberg*, *The Boston Review*, *Forbes*, *The Daily Beast*, *Politico*, and *Slate*.

WHY DOES DONALD TRUMP DEMONIZE CITIES? (2017)

President Trump is a big-city guy. He made his fortune in cities and keeps his family in a Manhattan tower. But when Trump talks about cities, he presents a fearsome caricature that bears little resemblance to the real urban landscape.

"Our inner cities are a disaster," he declared in a campaign debate. "You get shot walking to the store. They have no education. They have no jobs." Before his inauguration, in a spat with Atlanta's representative in Congress, he tweeted: "Congressman John Lewis should spend more time on fixing and helping his district, which is in horrible shape and falling apart (not to mention crime infested)." He makes Chicago sound like an anarchic failed state. "If Chicago doesn't fix the horrible 'carnage' going on, 228 shootings in 2017 with 42 killings (up 24% from 2016), I will send in the Feds!" he warned. His executive order on public safety claimed that sanctuary cities, which harbor undocumented immigrants, "have caused immeasurable harm to the American people and to the very fabric of our Republic."

With this talk, Trump is playing to his base, which overwhelmingly is not in cities. Party affiliation increasingly reflects the gulf between big, diverse metros and whiter, less densely populated locales. For decades, like-minded people have been clustering geographically—a phenomenon author Bill Bishop dubbed "the Big Sort"—pushing cities to the left and the rest of the country to the right. Indeed, the bigger, denser and

more diverse the city, the better Hillary Clinton did in November. But Trump prevailed everywhere else—in small cities, suburbs, exurbs and beyond. The whiter and more spread out the population, the better he did.

He connected with these voters by tracing their economic decline and their fading cultural cachet to the same cause: traitorous "coastal elites" who sold their jobs to the Chinese while allowing America's cities to become dystopian Babels, rife with dark-skinned danger—Mexican rapists, Muslim terrorists, "inner cities" plagued by black violence. He intimated that the chaos would spread to their exurbs and hamlets if he wasn't elected to stop it.

Trump's fearmongering turned out to be savvy electoral college politics (even if it left him down nearly 3 million in the popular vote). But it wasn't just a sinister trick to get him over 270. He persists in his efforts to slur cities as radioactive war zones because the fact that America's diverse big cities are thriving relative to the whiter, less populous parts of the country suggests that the liberal experiment works—that people of diverse origins and faiths prosper together in free and open societies. To advance his administration's agenda, with its protectionism and cultural nationalism, Trump needs to spread the notion that the polyglot metropolis is a dangerous failure.

The president has filled his administration with advisers who oppose the liberal pluralism practiced profitably each day in America's cities. "The center core of what we believe," Steve Bannon, the president's trusted chief strategist, has said, is "that we're a nation with an economy, not an economy just in some global marketplace with open borders, but we are a nation with a culture and a reason for being." This is not just an argument for nationalism over globalism. Bannon has staked out a position in a more fundamental debate over the merits of multicultural identity. Whose interests are included when we put "America first"?

When Trump connects immigration to Mexican cartel crime, he's putting a menacing foreign face on white anxiety about the country's shifting demographic profile, which is pushing traditional white, Judeo-Christian culture out of the center of American national identity. "The ceaseless importation of Third World foreigners with no tradition of, taste for, or experience in liberty," wrote Michael Anton, now a White House national security adviser, is "the mark of a party, a society, a country, a people, a civilization that wants to die." Bannon has complained that too many U.S. tech company chief executives are from Asia.

The Census Bureau projects that whites will cease to be a majority in 30 years. Suppose you think the United States—maybe even all Western civilization—will fall if the U.S. population ever becomes as diverse as Denver's. You are going to want to reduce the foreign-born population as quickly as possible, and by any means necessary. You'll deport the deportable with brutal alacrity, squeeze legal immigration to a trickle, bar those with "incompatible" religions.

But to prop up political demand for this sort of ethnic-cleansing program—what else can you call it?—it's crucial to get enough of the public to believe that America's diversity is a dangerous mistake. If most white people come to think that America's massive, multicultural cities are decent places to live, what hope is there for the republic? For Christendom?

The big cities of the United States are, in fact, very decent places to live. To be sure, many metros have serious problems. Housing is increasingly unaffordable, and the gap between the rich and poor is on the rise. Nevertheless, the American metropolis is more peaceful and prosperous than it's been in decades.

Contrary to the narrative that Trump and his advisers promote, our cities show that diversity can improve public safety. A new study of urban crime rates by a team of criminologists found that "immigration is consistently linked to decreases in violent (e.g., murder) and property (e.g., burglary) crime" in the period from 1970 to 2010. What's more, according to an analysis of FBI crime data, counties labeled as "sanctuary" jurisdictions by federal immigration authorities have lower crime rates than comparable non-sanctuary counties. The Trump administration's claim that sanctuary cities "have caused immeasurable harm" is simply baseless. Even cities that have seen a recent rise in violent crime are much safer today than they were in the early 1990s, when the foreign-born population was much smaller.

Yes, cities have their share of failing schools. But they also have some of the best schools in the country and are hotbeds of reform and innovation. According to recent rankings by SchoolGrades.org, the top 28 elementary and middle schools in New York state are in New York City; Ohio's top four schools are in Cincinnati, Cleveland, Youngstown and Columbus; and the best school in Pennsylvania is in Philadelphia. "The culture of competition and innovation, long in short supply in public education, is taking root most firmly in the cities," according to the Manhattan Institute researchers who run the site.

And it gets things exactly backward to think of unemployment as a problem centered in cities.

Packing people close together creates efficiencies of proximity and clusters of expertise that spur the innovation that drives growth. Automation has killed off many low- and medium-skill manufacturing jobs, but technology has increased the productivity, and thus the pay, of highly educated workers, and the education premium is highest in dense, populous cities. The best-educated Americans, therefore, gravitate toward the most productive big cities—which then become even bigger, better educated and richer.

Meanwhile, smaller cities and outlying regions with an outdated mix of industry and a less-educated populace fall further behind, displaced rather than boosted by technology, stuck with fewer good jobs and lower average wages. The economist Enrico Moretti calls this regional separation in education and productivity "the Great Divergence."

Thanks to the Great Divergence, America's most diverse, densely populated and well-educated cities are generating an increasing share of the country's economic output. In 2001, the 50 wealthiest U.S. metro regions produced about 27 percent more per person than the country as a whole. Today, they produce 34 percent more, and there's no end to the divergence in sight.

Taken together, the Great Divergence and the Big Sort imply that Republican regions are producing less and less of our nation's wealth. According to Mark Muro and Sifan Liu of the Brookings Institution, Clinton beat Trump in almost every county responsible for more than a paper-thin slice of America's economic pie. Trump took 2,584 counties that together account for 36 percent of the nation's gross domestic product. Clinton won just 472 counties— less than 20 percent of Trump's take—but those counties account for 64 percent of GDP.

The relative economic decline of Republican territory was crucial to Trump's populist appeal. Trump gained most on Romney's 2012 vote share in places where fewer whites had college degrees, where more people were underwater on their mortgages, where the population was in poorer physical health, and where mortality rates from alcohol, drugs and suicide were higher.

But Trump's narrative about the causes of this distress are false, and his "economic nationalist" agenda is a classic populist bait-and-switch. Trump won a bigger vote share in places with smaller foreign-born populations. The residents of those places are, therefore, least likely to encounter a Muslim refugee, experience immigrant crime or compete with foreign-born workers. Similarly, as UCLA political scientist Raul Hinojosa Ojeda has shown, places where Trump was especially popular in the primaries are places that face little import competition from China or Mexico. Trump's protectionist trade and immigration policies will do the least in the places that like them the most.

Yet the Great Divergence suggests a different sense in which the multicultural city did bring about the malaise of the countryside. The loss of manufacturing jobs, and the increasing concentration of the best-paying jobs in big cities, has been largely due to the innovation big cities disproportionately produce. Immigrants are a central part of that story.

But this is just to repeat that more and more of America's dynamism and growth flow from the open city. It's difficult to predict who will bear the downside burden of disruptive innovation—it could be Rust Belt autoworkers one day and educated, urban members of the elite mainstream media the next—which is why dynamic economies need robust safety nets to protect citizens from the risks of economic dislocation. The denizens of Trump country have borne too much of the disruption and too little of the benefit from innovation. But the redistribution-loving multicultural urban majority can't be blamed for the inadequacy of the safety net when the party of rural whites has fought for decades to roll it back. Low-density America didn't vote to be knocked on its heels by capitalist creative destruction, but it has voted time and again against softening the blow.

Political scientists say that countries where the middle class does not culturally identify with the working and lower classes tend to spend less on redistributive social programs. We're more generous, as a rule, when we recognize ourselves in those who need help. You might argue that this just goes to show that diversity strains solidarity. Or you might argue that, because we need solidarity, we must learn to recognize America in other accents, other complexions, other kitchen aromas.

Honduran cooks in Chicago, Iranian engineers in Seattle, Chinese cardiologists in

Atlanta, their children and grandchildren, all of them, are bedrock members of the American community. There is no "us" that excludes them. There is no American national identity apart from the dynamic hybrid culture we have always been creating together. America's big cities accept this and grow healthier and more productive by the day, while the rest of the country does not accept this, and struggles.

In a multicultural country like ours, an inclusive national identity makes solidarity possible. An exclusive, nostalgic national identity acts like a cancer in the body politic, eating away at the bonds of affinity and cooperation that hold our interests together.

Bannon is right. A country is more than an economy. The United States is a nation with a culture and a purpose. That's why Americans of every heritage and hue will fight to keep our cities sanctuaries of the American idea—of openness, tolerance and trade—until our country has been made safe for freedom again.

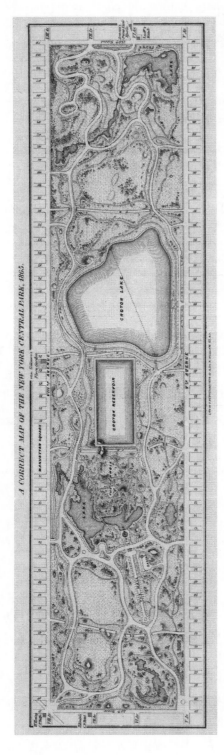

A CORRECT MAP OF THE NEW YORK CENTRAL PARK, 1865.

Illustration V.1 "A Correct Map of the New York Central Park, 1865." Source: "A Correct Map of the New York Central Park, 1865" (New York: F. Heppenheimer, 1865), Map Collection, American Antiquarian Society. Courtesy of the Center for Historic American Visual Culture at the American Antiquarian Society.

Central Park is located on 843 acres in the middle of the island of Manhattan between 59th and 110th Streets (south to north) and Fifth and Eighth Avenues (east to west). In 1858, Frederick Law Olmsted and Calvert Vaux won a contest for the park's design commission with their "Greensward" plan that called for a pastoral landscape in the English romantic tradition. This map, made while the park was under construction (it was finished in 1870), shows the open meadows, pedestrian paths, watercourses, equestrian paths, walkways, and other distinctive features of the Greensward plan.

Illustration V.2 Post-Katrina New Orleans Neighborhoods, March 2006. Photograph by Steven H. Corey.

In August and September 2005, Hurricanes Katrina and Rita wreaked havoc along the coast of the Gulf of Mexico from Florida all the way to Texas. Approximately 2,000 people in seven states died from the storm, and over a million more relocated to temporary evacuation shelters, or longer-term residential quarters, located in all fifty states, the District of Columbia, and Puerto Rico. The focal point of hurricane destruction for most people in the United States was the city of New Orleans, which at first seemed to have survived devastating winds and tidal surge. However, shortly after Katrina hit, the levee system failed, and water from Lake Pontchartrain submerged eighty percent of the city. Despite the first mandatory evacuation in the Crescent City's history, thousands of residents did not have the resources to leave, or remained by choice. As the floodwaters rose, their situation quickly deteriorated. As such, New Orleans became the focus of an intense national debate over disaster relief and recovery. These two images, taken seven months after the storm, illustrate the legacy of devastation and recovery in two very different neighborhoods. The older "shotgun style" home is from the Lower Ninth Ward, a poor and working class, predominately African American community, that arguably suffered the most extensive damage from Katrina and Rita, remaining underwater longer than any other neighborhood. Spray painted on the front of the house are multiple search and rescue markings and to the side one of the many "FEMA Trailers" distributed by the Federal Emergency Management Agency (FEMA) as temporary shelters for those rebuilding their homes. The newer home, from a more affluent community adjacent to one of the levees on Lake Pontchartrain, also has search and rescue markings, severe damage from flooding, and a "Hold the Corps Accountable" protest banner from the website www.levees.org. Formed immediately after the hurricanes in 2005 to ensure that the U.S. Army Corps of Engineers would be held responsible for failures in the city's levee system, and more broadly to educate people that the flooding of the New Orleans region was a manmade civil, and not natural, disaster. Levees.org has remains active, with five chapters across the country, and has placed a series of historical markers at each of the main levee breaks in New Orleans.

PART VI

THE URBAN ENVIRONMENT

EDITORS' INTRODUCTION TO PART VI

The alteration of the physical landscape is inherent in urbanization. American cities grew dramatically in the nineteenth and twentieth centuries as people extracted vast quantities of natural resources from the environment, and then transformed and consumed these resources to shape their living, working, and leisure spaces. The manipulation of the environment and its resources fueled the industrial revolution and the technological advancements that formed the material basis of modern urban life. Although civic and business leaders celebrated the benefits accompanying industrialization and urbanization, these processes also resulted in environmental degradation and numerous social conflicts, including the inequitable distribution of wealth and power. In the twenty-first century, these issues remain unresolved.

The intense interest in urban affairs that developed in the 1960s and the rise of the "new urban history" and "new social history" in the 1970s helped to coalesce environmental history and policy into a body of scholarship. This new work reflected contemporary popular concerns over threats to natural resources and human health. Cities were a perfect place to examine the intersection of social and environmental history.[i] The essays in this part highlight the human and environmental consequences of urbanization and reflect contemporary scholarship in urban and environmental history, public policy, and sociology. John T. Cumbler demonstrates the environmental impact accompanying the growth of small New England villages into bustling mill towns. Dominic A. Pacyga explores Chicago's economic reliance on the stockyards, an industry that strongly effected the physical environment of the city—and not for the better. Martin V. Melosi and Joseph A. Pratt trace the impact of cheap fossil fuels on the growth of cities and their surrounding metropolitan areas through a study of Houston, Texas. Sociologists David Naguib Pellow and Lisa Sun-Hee Park examine environmental inequity and racism by documenting the disproportionate association between toxic waste and hazardous manufacturing with working-class ethnic minorities in California's Silicon Valley. Andrew Needham studies the environmental impact of the growth of Phoenix, Arizona via the erection of electrical power lines. These lines ran to Phoenix through Navajo lands and the power structures revealed by the power lines proves both fascinating and vexing.

The change in attitude toward environmental protection following the Second World War forms the central theme of **Document 6.1**, "Special Message to the Congress on Conservation and Restoration of Natural Beauty (1965)," by President Lyndon B. Johnson. In this sweeping statement on the relationship between nature and the American way of life, President Johnson explains that the federal government should make cities more livable by decreasing pollution in the water, land, and air. While the subsequent environmental movement of the late 1960s and 1970s even surpassed Johnson's call to action, there were still millions of Americans overlooked by environmental regulations. As **Document 6.2**, from the United Church of Christ's landmark 1987 study *Toxic Waste and Race in the United States*, demonstrates, there is a close correlation between race and the location of environmental hazards in American cities. The release of this report was instrumental in bringing the larger issue of environmental justice into the nation's political dialogue regarding public health and social equity. Finally, in **Document 6.3** we see a recent man-made environmental disaster—the Flint water crisis. Perhaps nothing illuminates the way in which human mistakes and malfeasance can combine to shape environmental issues than the unresolved Flint crisis.

The illustrations and documents in this part highlight the often precarious relationship between human beings and their built environments. This proves especially true in terms of pollution and poor public health. As we argue in **Essay 1.1**, "Examining America's Urban Landscape: From Social Reform to Social History, and Back," beginning in the 1840s, sanitary reformers in Europe and the United States documented the relationship between the spread of disease in cities to filthy air and water, raw sewage, and the overall foul living conditions of the working poor. A graphic illustration of such conditions in 1857 is provided in **Illustration VI.1**, "Bridge Over the Monongahela River, Pittsburgh, Penn.," showing the smoky skyline of Pittsburgh. The most extensive public health study of an American city in the nineteenth century was the *Report of the Council of Hygiene and Public Health of the Citizens' Association of New York Upon the Sanitary Condition of the City* published in 1865. A map from this report, "Encroachment of Nuisances upon Populous Up-town Districts" is included as **Illustration VI.2** to illustrate how the use of mixed space in Manhattan allowed for manure yards, rendering works, and other noxious establishments to operate next to residential areas. This Manhattan landscape has similarities with the Chicago neighborhoods studied by Pacyga.

While the nineteenth century witnessed great strides in sanitation and public health, disasters such as hurricanes, floods, and earthquakes highlighted the limits of human attempts to control nature. The devastation caused the natural disasters is often augmented by human miscalculations. The San Francisco Earthquake of 1906 is one such calamity that, along with its accompanying fires, killed hundreds (if not thousands) of people and destroyed the downtown and two-thirds of all business districts and residential neighborhoods. A sample of the devastation is provided with **Illustration VI.3**, "Demolished and Tilted by the Earthquake, Homes on Howard Street at 17th, 1906 (544–7961) Kelly and Chadwick." The 1906 earthquake shares parallels with the loss of life and infrastructure devastation along the Gulf Coast region of the United States by Hurricanes Katrina and Rita. In **Illustration VI.4** we focus on air pollution in the form of smog hovering over Salt Lake City Utah in 1950. Our desire to build urban and national economies via manufacturing has an impact on our quality of life, in terms of water, soil, and air contamination. So-called "progress" has always had a price.

NOTE

i. Samuel P. Hays, *Explorations in Environmental History* (Pittsburgh: University of Pittsburgh Press, 1998), 85–86.

ESSAY 6.1

From Milling to Manufacturing: From Villages to Mill Towns

John T. Cumbler

Source: John T. Cumbler, *Reasonable Use: The People, the Environment, and the State, New England, 1790–1930* (New York: Oxford University Press, 2001).

EDITORS' INTRODUCTION

Historian John T. Cumbler blends environmental, labor, and urban history in this essay. Enormous changes occurred in the United States when investors began to establish industrial firms in the late 1790s. America's first industrial revolution followed the trend towards mechanization begun in England. The physical landscape was irrevocably changed by the early factories, which rerouted waterways to power their machines, created dams, spilled industrial waste into the water, the soil, and the skies, and drew thousands of workers to live near the factories, so that they could show up for work on time every day. As Cumbler explains here, small rural localities were transformed into industrial villages, and ultimately, cities.

These changes were not entirely unwelcomed; weary farmers were looking for a more reliable way to make a living. The highly rocky and undulating landscape of New England proved no match for the richer soils of New York State and points further west. Women and children, seeking to supplement the incomes of their families, populated the very first factories. Increasingly, men joined them, and ultimately immigrants came to America specifically to secure jobs in U.S. industry. The move away from the family farm—a move that ultimately left just two percent of Americans making their living from farming in the twentieth century—began the movement of manpower into industrial plants.

Cumbler bases his narrative in the Connecticut River Valley. The Connecticut River, the largest river in New England, flows predominantly southward through New Hampshire, Vermont, Massachusetts, and Connecticut. Other industrial firms had flowered in Rhode Island and eastern Massachusetts, along the Blackstone Valley River and its tributaries, and very well-known corporations located slightly later along the Merrimack River, flowing through Waltham and Lowell. Given the fledgling America's strained relations with its former colonial power, Great Britain, the embargo with England initiated by President Thomas Jefferson in 1807–1809, and the ravages of the War of 1812, forward thinking Americans turned their unreliable agricultural economy into one focused on industrial products. Businesses did not always prosper; after the War of 1812 and the resumption of trading relations with Great Britain, many small mills collapsed. Other firms bought out struggling businesses and buttressed their trade, growing even more profitable.

While industry brought needed jobs to displaced farmers, it wrought terrible damage on the surrounding landscape. The changes were soon noticeable. Trees were cleared for the establishment of larger towns. Lumber was used to frame new factories, utilized to erect new dwellings for the burgeoning workforce, and burned for heat. Industrial waste poured into the environment, joined by the exponential growth of human refuse and waste from the increased population. Not everyone was forward-thinking enough to imagine what further damage continued industrialization and urban growth would do to the landscape. Those who were, Cumbler argues, evolved into the very first environmental activists.

John T. Cumbler served as a professor of history at the University of Louisville. He is the author of numerous works, including *Working-Class Community in Industrial America: Work, Leisure, and Struggle in Two Industrial Cities, 1880–1930* (Westport, CT: Greenwood Press, 1979), *A Social History of Economic Decline: Business, Politics, and Work in Trenton* (New Brunswick, NJ: Rutgers University Press, 1989), *Northeast and Midwest United States: An Environmental History* (Santa Barbara, CA: ABC-CLIO, 2005), and *From Abolition to Rights for All: The Making of a Reform Community in the Nineteenth Century* (Philadelphia: University of Pennsylvania, 2008). Cumbler served as the John Adams' Distinguished Fulbright Professor in the Netherlands and held prestigious fellowships.

FROM MILLING TO MANUFACTURING: FROM VILLAGES TO MILL TOWNS (2001)

The new world of New England was one of factories and factory towns, as well as farms and forests. It was a world where farmers, looking to those factory towns for markets, plowed their fields deep and intensively managed their land. It was a world where lumbermen stripped mountainsides of their forest cover to meet the cities' growing appetite for lumber. It was a world of managed and controlled nature.[1] It was also a world of rapid change, and increasingly after 1800, the force behind that change was the coming of the manufacturing mills.

Levi Shepard's 1788 duck-cloth factory was of a different type than the traditional mills of New England. Although mills that spun or fulled cloth had long been part of rural New England, Levi Shepard had a different market in mind when he encouraged local farmers to bring him their flax. Shepard wanted to take material from the countryside and, with the help of "workers employed," "manufacture" it into a commodity for sale.[2] Shepard's decision to focus on manufacturing for distant markets represented a new world.[3]

Mills and Manufacturing

Manufacturing in rural New England began small. It grew out of, while at the same time it transformed, traditional rural society. The processing of goods of the countryside was an integral part of traditional New England life, whether in 1650 or 1800. In 1790, the *Hampshire Gazette* commented

that although "a large quantity of woollen cloth are made in private families and brought to market in our trading towns, a great part of [the woollen cloth] is not calculated for market."[4]

The shift from milling produce for local use to manufacturing occurred initially for most of rural New England with the shift of small traders, merchants, and millers from processing for local farmers to processing for external markets.[5] Edmund Taylor of Williamsburg on the Mill River, for example, at the turn of the century added carding and picking machines to his grist-mill. As he did for grain, Taylor processed the material from the countryside, keeping a portion of it as his pay. Once established, Taylor added a cotton textile factory to his enterprises, using the surplus water from his gristmill.[6]

The Bellows Falls Company of Vermont, besides running a country store, was using waterpower to run "wool carding machines" for local farmers. Like many other traditional millers and country store owners who dammed up a stream and put in a waterwheel to run a sawmill, gristmill, fulling mill, or even carding machines, the Bellows Falls Company processed produce for the local community. Customers brought to the mill products of their farm, which they had processed at the mill and then took home with them. Although the Bellows Falls Company may have kept some of the wool it carded and shipped it into the stream of commerce flowing out of the valley, the local community saw the mill's primary function as processing products for the valley's residents.[7]

In the early years of the nineteenth century, manufacturing in New England underwent a radical transformation and in doing so began the first stage of the long and complicated process of industrializing the New England countryside. When Thomas Jefferson imposed an embargo on goods coming into and going out of the United States through the War of 1812, imported manufactured goods became scarce in America. Shopkeepers and traders who found that they could no longer get finished cloth or paper began to look at the old gristmill and sawmill sites with new eyes. In 1808, Job Cotton took over Joseph Burnell's sawmill on the Mill River and brought in cotton textile spinning machines. On the Chicopee River, the Chapin brothers—William, Levi, and Joseph—built a small mill that by 1810 had two carding machines, a drawing frame, and two short spinning frames "of very rude construction." The Chapins employed eight to ten workers, who produced yarn that was put out to local women to weave. The workers had no regular payday. The company exchanged yarn and cloth at the local stores, and those it employed had credit at the stores.[8] By the time war broke out in 1812, old mill sites throughout New England were being converted into textile mills.[9] Anticipating increased demand for manufactured woolens, Stephen Cook in 1815 replaced his gristmill with a woolen manufactory, and Isaac Biglow made plans to build a cotton factory of five thousand spindles beside his gristmill.[10]

Peace with England in 1815 brought not only an end of war and of war orders for cotton and wool but also a flood of English manufactured goods to the American market. Most of the small cotton mills went under in the ensuing years. Job Cotton's mill closed its doors and stood idle, and Isaac Biglow never used his cotton factory as intended but outfitted it instead to make paper.[11] The years following the peace brought the first real depression to inland New England since Shays's rebellion. The depression may have closed Job Cotton's mill, but it did not return the valley to its more traditional past.

Although the general depression in the postwar years wiped out most of the small manufacturing operations, the better-capitalized mills with big dams, overshot waterwheels, and newer machinery weathered the depression and continued to grow. The new large dams and multistory factory buildings that utilized heavy, powered machinery to turn out woven cotton and woolen cloth needed wooden beams and flooring, machines, belts, and pulleys, candles and paper.

As New England began to manufacture goods for far-off markets, the very manufacturing process itself began consuming massive amounts of the region's resources and generated more manufacturing. Manufacturing needed machinery, and increasingly that machinery was locally produced. These mills not only gathered up massive amounts of waterpower and resources, they also gathered up hundreds and even thousands of people into new industrial cities, taking in food and water and disposing of waste.

Manufacturing along the Connecticut River Valley

At the turn of the nineteenth century, traveler Timothy Dwight noted that mill streams everywhere were giving rise to an "unusual number of works erected for various manufacturing purposes, powder, paper, glass, etc."[12] Another Dwight, Theodore, noted in 1830 that indeed New England's gristmills had given over "within a few years [to] manufactures." "On the road up the Connecticut River ... everyone must be struck with the size and number of the manufacturers which have been multiplied and magnified to such an extent all over the country."[13]

Most of these early manufacturing mills were located on small rivers and tributaries. Over the century, as engineering skill improved, technology developed, and more capital became available, manufacturers had the ability to capture more power from the larger rivers. As they did so, they moved to the falls of water on the region's great rivers. Around these falls grew industrial towns, then cities. These cities in turn reached out into the countryside, pulling more and more of it into their grasp. Included in the resources needed was water. And the Connecticut River had vast amounts of water.

Manufacturing along the southern Connecticut River Valley began early. Already by 1830, Middletown's "various manufacturers carried on with success," while Hartford had thriving paper, iron, and brass works as well as an established armaments industry. In the nineteenth century, tinware producers in Berlin, Connecticut, expanded to include brassware and hardware, and this metal-working industry spread to towns up and down the valleys between Middletown and Hartford.[14] On the west side of the river at Windsor Locks, paper mills and silk mills were built, while at Enfield, carpet making became a major industry.[15]

By the nineteenth century, Springfield's industry, led by the U.S. Armory, grew to be a crucial part of the town's activity. G. and C. Merriam bought the copyright to Noah Webster's dictionary and began to manufacture the nation's best-known reference book. Across the Connecticut River in West Springfield, along the tributary Westfield River, large-scale tannery factories transformed tanning into a huge enterprise consuming massive amounts of tree bark. The Clark Carriage and Wagon shops and several new cotton and woolen factories in Agawam village all employed large numbers of hands. The region's expanded manufacturing demanded factories and homes. New circular sawmills were built to cut lumber coming downriver. Unlike the older saw mills, these new mills were large-scale operations with dozens of workers constantly at work cutting and sawing. North of Springfield on the east side of the Connecticut, a number of manufacturing enterprises rose up along its tributary the Chicopee River. Ironworks triggered Chicopee's rise as a manufacturing center. During the early years of the century, a number of small cotton mills opened for carding and spinning cotton, although most did not survive the depression of 1816. In 1825, through the intervention of Edmund Dwight, Boston's textile investors (known to historians as the Boston Associates) began to take an interest in the waterpower of the Chicopee River.[16] The Chicopee was dammed, and the first of the huge multistory textile mills and attendant

boardinghouses were built. More mills soon followed, so that by the end of the 1830s, Chicopee had four major textile manufacturing companies that employed hundreds of workers.[17] Edmund Dwight also persuaded Nathan Ames to move his edge-tool manufacturing company to Chicopee. Ames's company prospered, and in 1845, with his connections to Dwight, Ames bought up the local machine shops and began to produce textile machines as well.[18] Upriver in Palmer, the Thorndike Manufacturing Company, again the product of Boston investment, in 1837 built a gigantic stone mill that soon employed 450 workers producing cotton ticks, denims, and stripes.[19]

At Bellows Falls, Vermont, Bill Blake obtained waterpower rights in 1802 from the Company Rendering the Connecticut River Navigable by Bellows Falls and built a paper mill there, rebuilding it in 1812. He built still another paper mill in 1814 in Wells River, Vermont. Blake's mills proved successful, and soon he had teams throughout Vermont and New Hampshire buying up rags for his paper mills, which were turning out paper for sale around the country.[20]

On the outskirts of Springfield, John Ames built an extensive paper-making factory in the early 1820s that employed dozens of local workers to cut and sort rags and work the new multistage, water-powered paper-making machines. In 1827, another Ames, David, took over a small one-vat, three-hand, screw-press paper company in Chicopee and expanded it into a major manufacturing enterprise, introducing power-driven paper-making machinery and exporting paper out of the region. By the 1840s, towns up and down the valley were turning out paper for books, newspapers, stationery, envelopes, wrapping, and collars.

Factories grew up along tributaries to the Connecticut. In the 1830s, wing dams on either side of the river north of Springfield at Hadley Falls provided power for a series of traditional mills, along with the newer cotton and woolen mills. With an initial investment of $50,000, a group of Springfield and Enfield investors formed the Hadley Falls Company in 1827 in order to build a large cotton textile mill powered by water brought in by a wing dam. By 1832, the company was running 2,700 spindles and employing forty-six women, "daughters of local farmers," and twenty-three men.[21]

North of the falls at Hadley, the tributary Mill River had a number of silk manufacturing companies, which briefly encouraged local farmers to grow mulberry trees to feed the silk worms.[22] Farther north, cotton textile and woolen factories sprang up at Bellows Falls, along with Blake's paper mills, while at Lebanon, New Hampshire, woodworking shops and factories produced tools, furniture, and agricultural implements from lumber harvested from local forests. Between 1810 and 1850, manufacturing mills, machine shops, and woodworks multiplied along the rivers and streams running into the Connecticut.[23] At Franconia, New Hampshire, a significant ironworks developed.[24] By the middle of the nineteenth century, blacksmith shops and iron foundries had shifted to waterpower for operating bellows and, in the foundries, for milling iron casting. With this shift, more ironworks were located on waterpower sites.

The expansion of sheep raising in Vermont and New Hampshire provided wool for the expanding woolen factories sprouting up around the falls of almost every northern New England river.[25] At Hartford, Vermont, Albert Dewey dammed the falls of the Quechee River and began woolen manufacturing, producing 450 yards daily.[26] Dewey's factory on the Quechee was only one of many that sprang up in northern New England in the thirty years after the War of 1812 to take wool from the region's farmers.[27] In 1811, Colonel James Shepherd opened a small woolen factory on the Mills River, where spinning and weaving was done by hand. By 1818, Shepherd had expanded and installed power spinning mules and weaving machines. By the end of the 1820s, the company was converting fleece from Shepherd's and his neighbors' large flocks of sheep into broadcloth, which was then sold throughout the country.[28]

Factories and Farms

Factories transformed the land around them from farms and fields to other factories, tenements, roads, and canals. As they produced goods for export, they also became import centers themselves, not only of food and lumber but also of people. The mills and their machines needed operatives, who came from many of those same hills that furnished the lumber for the mills.

These manufacturing and commercial centers were surrounded by commercial farmers, while poor country cousins abandoned or scraped by on overworked hill-country farms. Where once there were villages with teachers, doctors, ministers, traders, merchants, artisans, clerks, and lawyers, all with their own gardens, cows, pigs, and chickens, now there were cities with hundreds of operatives and tradespeople, very few of whom could afford the time or had the space to raise their own food. The food that fed the growing cities of New England came from the region's farms, but these were very different farms from those of the eighteenth century. New England's cities took the farm produce from farmers who specialized in feeding urban people.[29] The milk, cheese, butter, and vegetables that poured into the cities to feed the operatives came from farmers who specialized in dairy products or commercial garden vegetables.[30] In 1846, for example, Jesse Chickering noted one of the changes that had occurred in Massachusetts agriculture: The "dense state of the population in the villages" had given rise to an "increase ... of vegetables raised, such as potatoes, apples for eating, garden vegetables, and fruit."[31] New England farmers had always raised fruits and vegetables, but increasingly, nineteenth-century farmers focused their activity on perishable market produce, and the markets for that produce were local.[32] In a midcentury promotional bulletin, the Hadley Falls Company noted that "the position of a city in the midst of the splendid farms and fruitful meadows of the Connecticut Valley would be highly favorable for obtaining supplies; and the existence of such a market for their produce would be greatly beneficial to the interests, and stimulating to the industry, of the people of that part of the state engaged in agriculture."[33] As the *Hampshire Gazette* recognized in 1831, farms around the new industrial centers prospered when they shifted to sending food to feed the workers gathered to work in the mills. "Go view the manufacturing villages," it urged, "go and view the farms which surround them … see the universal prosperity which reigns there."[34] [...]

Forests and Factories

In addition to the produce from the surrounding countryside, the factory towns also consumed acres and acres of the region's forests. Hills and mountains far up the valley yielded up their forests so that dams, mills, and tenements could be built and heated, and tools and furniture could be fabricated.[35] To encourage manufacturers to build mills at their dam site, the Hadley Falls Company used a report detailing the wealth of available lumber from the valley's northern forests. The company noted in its promotional report that "there is not likely to be any lack of building materials at Holyoke. Lumber is brought greater or lesser distances down the Connecticut River from the forests on its banks."[36]

As the mills and mill towns grew in number and size, lumber floated in ever increasing volume down from the hills and mountains of Vermont and New Hampshire. The combination of burning and cutting forest land to clear farms and cutting timber for construction and fuel meant the baring of northern New England's valleys, hills, and mountains. Between 1820 and 1860, Massachusetts and Vermont went from over 60 percent forest covered to just over 40 percent, while New Hampshire went from over 60 percent to less than 50 percent.[37] [...]

Increasingly after the 1870s, New England's railroads turned to coal for fuel, and after midcentury, homes and industry in the region's cities did so too. The burning of coal eased the demand for cordwood while it increased air pollution. But the burning of coal did not end the pressure on the region's forests. It was not until the 1870s that New Hampshire's forest area stopped declining, while Vermont continued to lose forests until 1880, when only 35 percent of the state was forested.[38] [...]

On July 24, 1882, Theodore Lyman—a wealthy Boston Brahmin, Civil War veteran, Harvard Overseer, amateur scientist, Massachusetts commissioner of fisheries, and independent Mugwump candidate for Congress—in answer to a question about protective tariffs, quoted his father, who had been mayor of Boston in the 1830s. "My father use to say very truly as long as New England was overlaid by ten feet of gravel, she would have to manufacture or starve." Lyman went on to say that New England had "an extraordinary amount of manufactures and of the greatest variety.... I can hardly believe my eyes such is the enormous growth." "What would Massachusetts be like" without its industry? Lyman wondered. "You would see no mills and no dams, nothing but a few grist mills here and there and houses whose occupants raised such crops as they could from the scanty soil."[39] Of course, before the massive manufacturing establishments arrived, Massachusetts had both dams and mills, but by the 1880s, New Englanders could scarcely imagine a world without industrial enterprises; when they did, some of them viewed it as empty and miserly.

NOTES

1. Although developmental economists have argued that traditionalist farmers were more destructive to the environment than were market-oriented farmers who used more modern agricultural techniques, it is a mistake to overcredit market-oriented farmers as being more environmentally sensitive because of their long-term economic interests. Individually, traditionalists as well as market-oriented farmers may have acted in ways that were destructive to the environment. See Carolyn Merchant, *Ecological Revolutions: Nature, Gender, and Science in New England* (Chapel Hill, 1989), 154–156. See also Donald Worster, *The Dust Bowl: The Southern Plains in the 1930s* (Oxford, 1979).

2. See Christopher Clark, *The Roots of Rural Capitalism: Western Massachusetts, 1780–1860* (Ithaca, 1990). See also Timothy Dwight, *Travels Through New England and New York* (Cambridge, 1969), 4:348.

3. Although Levi Shepard represented a new focus in the valley, employing labor to manufacture goods for distant markets, his

technology was very familiar. Shepard built his factory at the back of his home lot. All the machinery was worked by hand, with a boy or girl hired to turn the wheel, yet Shepard's market was not local.

4. *Hampshire Gazette*, Sept. 29, 1790.

5. See Jonathan Prude, *The Coming of Industrial Order: A Study of Town and Factory Life In Rural Massachusetts, 1813–1860* (Cambridge, 1983), for an example of the impact of mills on the surrounding countryside.

6. Charles J. Dean, "The Mills of Mill River," manuscript, 1935, Forbes Library, Northampton, MA, 21.

7. Besides carding, fulling, sawing, and grinding, some local millers were also manufacturing tools for local farmers. Rufus Hyde and his sons built a mill dam to power a trip-hammer. The Hydes used the trip-hammer to hammer out axes and scythes. They also used the waterwheel to turn their grindstones that sharpened axes sold to local farmers. Ibid., 23.

8. Vera Shlakman, *Economic History of a Factory Town: A Study of Chicopee, Massachusetts, Smith College Studies in History*, vol. 20, nos. 1–4 (Northampton, 1934–1935), 22.

9. Dean, "Mills of Mill River," 30–33.

10. *Stephan Cook v. William Hull* (Oct. 1825), MA Reports, Pickering, 3:269; *Isaac Biglow and Others v. Mellen Battle and Others* (Oct. 1818), MA Reports, Tyng, 15:313.

11. *Biglow v. Battle*, Dean, "Mills of Mill River," 30, 31.

12. Dwight, *Travels*, 2:197, 4:342, and 4:343–346.

13. Theodore Dwight, *Notes of a Northern Traveler* (Hartford, 1831), 97, 831.

14. Ibid., 94; Dwight, *Travels*, 2:195; Alexander Johnson, *Connecticut: A Study of a Commonwealth-Democracy* (Boston, 1895), 357, 358, 363.

15. Edwin M. Bacon, *The Connecticut River and the Valley of the Connecticut: Three Hundred and Fifty Miles from Mountain to Sea, Historical and Descriptive* (New York, 1906), 430.

16. Edmund Dwight's family had been merchants and investors in the early canal projects along the Connecticut. Edmund, married to an Eliot, moved to Boston in 1816 and joined the inner circle of wealthy Bostonians just expanding into investments in textile production. See Shlakman, *Economic History*, 27–47.

17. By 1841, Chicopee had the Chicopee, Cabot, Perkins, and Dwight manufacturing corporations, employing 2,500 hands. The town also had a number of skilled workers in the Belcher Iron Works and the Ames Manufacturing Company, which produced metal tools, cutlery, knives, and swords. Shlakman, *Economic History*, 25–36; see also Bacon, *Connecticut River*, 423.

18. Shlakman, *Economic History*, 27.

19. Will L. Clark, ed., *Western Massachusetts: A History, 1636–1925* (New York, 1926), 2:946, 947, 971.

20. Lyman S. Hayes, *The Connecticut River Valley in Southern Vermont and New Hampshire: Historical Sketches* (Rutland, 1929), 290, 292, 293. See R. H. Clapperton, *The Paper Making Machine: Its Invention, Evolution, and Development* (Oxford, 1967).

21. Robert Bennett, "The Roots of the Holyoke Water Power Company" (Holyoke, 1985) manuscript, Holyoke Public Library, 2:7.

22. Silk manufacturing continued in several towns along the central and lower valleys. Bacon, *Connecticut River*, 418. Dean, "Mills of Mill River," 54–58.

23. Harold Wilson, *The Hill Country of Northern New England: Its Social and Economic History* (New York, 1967), 145.

24. On the Franconia ironworks, see Jerold Wikoff, *The Upper Valley: An Illustrated Tour along the Connecticut River before the Twentieth Century* (Chelsea, VT, 1985), 118, 119, 120; Dwight, *Travels*, 4:117. On the locating of iron works on water-power sites, see *Paul Sibley and another v. Thomas Hoar and another* (Oct. 1855) MA Reports, Gray 4:222.

25. There were almost a million and a half sheep in Vermont and over a half million in New Hampshire by the 1830s.

26. Wikoff, *Upper Valley*, 123.

27. Margaret Richards Pabst, "Agricultural Trends in the Connecticut Valley Region of Massachusetts, 1800–1900," *Smith College Studies in History*, vol. 26, nos. 1–4 (Northampton, Oct. 1940–July 1941), 53, 54. A history of Ryegate, Vermont, at the turn of the century noted that "before 1850 woolen mills could be found in [many of northern Vermont's towns]." Quoted in Wilson, *Hill Country*, 45.

28. Dean, "Mills of Mill River," 33.

29. Valley farmers continued to raise wheat and grains, but their relative importance to the region's agriculture declined after 1840, with production itself declining after 1850. Dairy products jumped in value over the first half of the nineteenth century. Pabst, *Agricultural Trends*, 54. This shift to perishable vegetables, fruits, and dairy products was encouraged after the opening up of the Erie Canal and the penetration into New England and New England's traditional markets of staple agricultural goods—

particularly grain—from central New York and the upper Midwest.

30. The impact on gender roles of the shift of vegetables and dairy products from home use to market produce is an area of research that needs more work. Carolyn Merchant's *Ecological Revolutions* explores some of these issues.

31. Quoted in Pabst, *Agricultural Trends*, 53.

32. In 1885, when Massachusetts took a census of its agricultural products, it found that for farm communities around the industrial centers, dairy products followed by garden vegetables accounted for the majority of farm income. Hampton County had a total of $175,571 in meats and game, $234,264 in cereals, $302,426 in vegetables, $950,208 in dairy, and $126,021 in poultry. Hampshire County had a total of $210,689 in meats and game, $228,341 in cereals, $266,978 in vegetables, $1,050,825 in dairy (mostly milk), and $111,843 in poultry. The produce of individual towns reflected a dramatic shift toward dairy, mostly milk, and toward vegetables, particularly cabbage, potatoes, and squashes, and to a lesser extent toward poultry. State of Massachusetts Bureau of Labor Statistics, *Census of Massachusetts, 1885, vol. 3, Agricultural Products and Property* (Boston, 1887), 568, 569, 570, 571, 216–294 (hereafter, *MBLS, Census*).

33. Hadley Falls Company, "Report of the History and Present Condition of the Hadley Falls Company at Holyoke, MA," 1853, manuscript, Holyoke Public Library, 19 (hereafter, "Hadley Falls Company Report").

34. Quoted in Pabst, *Agricultural Trends*, 26.

35. By midcentury, New Hampshire was sending almost 20 million feet of timber down the river. Wikoff, *Upper Valley*, 64; Dwight,

Travels, 2:72; Roland Harper, "Changes in the Forest Area of New England In Three Centuries," *Journal of Forestry* 16 (Apr. 1918): 443, 449. At Hartland, Vermont, David Summer erected extensive lumber mills and sent cut lumber downriver to Massachusetts and Connecticut towns, where he had lumber yards to store and sell his product. Hayes, *Connecticut River Valley*, 41.

36. "Hadley Falls Company Report" 20.

37. Harper, "Changes in the Forest Area," 447. Increasingly after 1840, railroads began consuming massive amounts of the region's lumber both for construction and for fuel. In 1846, G. B. Emerson in his classic report to the State of Massachusetts on its trees and shrubs noted that the 560 miles of railroad in the state were consuming 53,710 cords of wood annually. "Hadley Falls Company Report," 449.

38. Vermont's forests dropped from 60 to 45 percent of the state's land area between 1820 and 1850 and to 35 percent by 1880. Harper, "Changes in the Forest Area," 449; See *Henry Irvine v. Daniel Stone* (Nov. 1850) MA Reports, Cushing, 6: 508, for a case involving bringing coal to Boston to be used as a heating fuel. The cost of shipping coal from Philadelphia, where it was brought in from the mines northwest of the city, to Boston was $3.75 a ton for stove coal plus $735 freight for 202 tons of coal. At these prices, coal soon became competitive with northern cord wood. By midcentury, most New England cities had coal yards that sold to local businesses. *Common-wealth v George E. Mann* (Oct. 1855) MA Reports, Grey, 4:212.

39. *Boston Herald*, July 22, 1882; Lyman Scrapbooks.

ESSAY 6.2

Spectacle: Facing the Modern World

Dominic A. Pacyga

Source: Dominic A. Pacyga, *Slaughterhouse: Chicago's Union Stock Yard and the World It Made* (Chicago: University of Chicago Press, 2015).

EDITORS' INTRODUCTION

The association of urbanization and industry with modernity are central underpinnings in nineteenth- and twentieth-century writings that celebrate cities. In addition to stressing the natural advantages of any particular urban region, the speculative efforts of boosters and real estate developers routinely lauded a city's public works infrastructure, manufacturing prowess, and the visionary guidance of civic leaders as evidence of merit for investment and future growth. Some writers stressed the worthiness of new urban amenities, lifestyles, and diverting curiosities such entertainment venues, parks and recreational spaces, and sports arenas. With people flocking to cities for business and pleasure, new urban ways of life in general, and the distinguishing characteristics of individual cities in particular, became frequent topics of discussion and journalistic inquiry. Fascination with cities spawned growing tourism.

By today's sensibilities, many urban attractions in the nineteenth and early twentieth century seem mundane and anachronistic—such as agricultural exhibitions and fairs. They may even seem outright unsustainable, based in large measure on the manipulation of natural resources and the physical landscape that, invariably led to environmental pollution and threats to public health. Modernity, however, is more than an intoxicating glimpse into the future, it is firmly rooted in the folkways and expectations of the present. Long before tourists flocked to Chicago to see its innovative skyscrapers, or even to marvel at the acclaimed Columbian Exhibition of 1893–94, they came by the thousands each month to see one of the most fascinating marvels of modernity: Chicago's Union Stock Yard and accompanying slaughterhouses. Infamous due to Upton Sinclair's graphic depiction of unsanitary meat processing and exploitative labor conditions in *The Jungle* (1906), the stockyards and slaughterhouses fundamentally transformed the processing and consumption of meat in the United States, and throughout the world.

As historian Dominic A. Pacyga argues in the following essay, tourists confronted modernity head on with all of the technological and organizational innovation and spectacle that the stockyards and slaughterhouses had to offer. They provided a frightening sense that something basic had shifted in the age-old relationship between humans and nature. More specifically, the modern meant an increasing alienation between humans and the creation of goods (in this case food). Like *The Jungle*, Pacyga's selection is not for the faint of heart, though it dramatically demonstrates how the convergence of urban and industrial processes captivated contemporary observers, and helped reinforce Chicago as an infamous city.[i]

---

i See Lisa Krissoff Boehm, *Infamous City and the Enduring Myth of Chicago* (New York: Routledge, 2004).

Dominic A. Pacyga is Emeritus Professor of History in the Department of Humanities, History, and Social Sciences at Columbia College Chicago. In addition to *Slaughterhouse: Chicago's Union Stock Yard and the World It Made* (Chicago: University of Chicago Press, 2015), he has published *Chicago: A Biography* (Chicago: University of Chicago Press, 2009), and *Polish Immigrants and Industrial Chicago: Workers on the South Side, 1880–1922* (Columbus: Ohio State University Press, 1991; Chicago: University of Chicago Press, 2003). Dr. Pacyga is a founding member of the Packingtown Museum, dedicated to preserving, interpreting, and presenting the industrial history and cultural heritage of Chicago's Union Stock Yard and surrounding neighborhoods.

SPECTACLE: FACING THE MODERN WORLD (2015)

High above Packingtown, on the very roofs of the slaughterhouses, visitors gathered to witness the modern in all of its terrible efficiency. Thousands of hogs waited in pens. Livestock handlers drove roughly a dozen hogs at a time onto the kill floor as fascinated spectators watched the beginning of a process that helped redefine American industry and changed interactions between animals and human beings, as well as workers and management. Swift's massive plant killed thousands of hogs a day. Here animals met their fate at the hands of workers and machinery, creating a vast "disassembly" line that ended not just the lives of pigs but the age-old relationship between meat and mankind.

The "river of blood" that flowed just below the roof pen area attracted Chicagoans and tourist alike for most of the stockyard's existence. At the turn of the twentieth century, a reported five hundred thousand people visited the Union Stock Yard annually. To modern sensibilities to take a tour of the stockyard and the packing plants— even to bring small children to the hog kill— might seem repulsive, but through most of its history the Union Stock Yard and the adjacent plants were major tourist attractions. Fascination with the new drew these visitors. Here people faced the modern head on with all its innovation and spectacle. For many people, Chicago's vast livestock market and packinghouses presented a compelling if somewhat frightening window to the future.

The Chicago Stockyards helped drag the world into what I deem "the modern": the industrial culture that appeared in the years after the Civil War, which eventually gave way to the postindustrial era we inhabit today. "The modern" is the frightening sense that something basic had shifted between man and nature. The modern was terrifying in that human beings seemed to be increasingly alienated from the age-old ways of creating goods. This was nowhere more explicit than in the changing relationship between man and food as seen in what Thomas Wilson, the president of Wilson and Company, almost lovingly referred to as the "Square Mile." All of the basic themes of modern industrialization soon played out in the Square Mile; the large corporation, the factory system with its merging of human labor and machinery, the mass marketing of goods, and a transportation system that collected natural resources from a vast hinterland and distributed goods internationally.

Machinery and the emerging factory system changed the essential relationship between people and food. People have killed animals for meat since the dawn of time. For centuries, the process was an everyday event on farms, in homes, and in butcher shops all over the world. But only in the nineteenth century did meatpacking emerge as a mass production industry. While this industry made meat more widely available and cheaper to purchase, its machinery, an enormous number of anonymous workers, and a massive marketing system came to stand between consumers and their food. The modern arrived in packing plants across the country, but especially in Chicago. Instead of taking eight to ten hours to butcher a steer, Chicago's packinghouses took about thirty-five minutes; hogs and sheep took even less time. Armies of skilled and unskilled workers, men and women, operated machines and disassembled animals as they passed by on endless chains into huge refrigerated rooms. Here carcasses waited to be shipped across hundreds and even thousands of miles. The modern sped up time. Everything seemed to move more quickly, more efficiently, even if not more naturally. This proved to be part of the spectacle, the fascination with the process as it played out in the packinghouses. The speed and efficiency of these plants provided a startling look into the future for the men, women, and children who came to see the marvel of industrialization in perhaps its rawest form.

The Square Mile, first officially mapped as Section 5 of the Town of Lake, became Chicago's entry point into both the new industrial economy and the modern world as it spurred the incredible growth of Chicago and the Midwest. It was here that the connection between meat and man was altered forever. If, as historian Perry Duis has pointed out, for many people Chicago represented a window to the future, then that future could be seen most explicitly on the kill floors of Packingtown, the western section of the Square Mile, which contained many of Chicago's major packinghouses. Over the years, this would be a contested image. Some Chicagoans looked askance at the kill floors as a symbol of their city, but in the beginning the city's boosters bragged of their speed and efficiency. Visitors agreed as they came to witness the spectacle provided by the packinghouses. The Union Stock Yard showed how ingenuity, greed, science, and industrialization created the modern world.

By the time the Union Stock Yard opened, machinery had been changing the nature of work, but mass industrialization in the form that would make over the Western world had only begun to emerge. The steam engine first altered humankind's sense of time and distance with its application to shipping and railroads. Before long, the manufacturing of cloth and clothing, shoes, and other goods still dominated by skilled artisans and their helpers felt the shift of new technological advances. Soon large factories emerged creating massive cities as rural people migrated to the emerging urban centers to seek work. The relationship between human beings and machinery quickly changed, as did that between entrepreneur and worker. The factory system emerged as workers' jobs were divided into smaller and more specific tasks. Large groups of individuals had always worked together, but now with machinery they could produce more goods and do so more quickly. Technology made everything different. Mass production and the factory system became the fascination of the age and the topic of both scientific and popular inquiry.

During the almost 106 years of its existence, the Chicago Stockyards epitomized the nation's livestock industry. Even before the market reached its centennial celebration, over one billion head of livestock had passed through its pens. The massive packinghouses transformed the industry and created modern consumer culture. In those plants, man and animal not only met the modern in the form of the factory system and technological innovation that altered the process of the killing, dressing, and marketing of meat, but also shifted the relationship between worker and owner, manufacturer and consumer.

The livestock market opened on Christmas Day 1865. As a tourist attraction, the stockyard defined Chicago to a fascinated public in the post-Civil War era. The rich and the poor, royalty and rubes traveled to see the maze of pens laid out across the prairie and then to be startled by the efficiency of the "disassembly" line of the packinghouses as they turned live breathing animals into hunks of pork, mutton, and beef in mere minutes.

Beyond the fascination with the killing floors, other marvels attracted visitors to the stockyards. The simple gathering of tens of thousands of animals to be placed on the market first insured a captivated public. Then the phenomenon of horse racing, professional baseball, the immensely popular International Livestock Exposition, and the myriad entertainment, political, consumer, and sporting events housed in the International Amphitheater all brought sightseers to the Square Mile. These marvels did not distract from the kill floors, but rather added to the attraction of the Square Mile. The yards presented "spectacle" to a city and a kind of industrial pageantry to the nation. [...]

Touring the Packinghouses

After being weighed, those livestock sold to Chicago firms (like the human visitors to the stockyards) advanced to the packinghouses, driven over the huge elevated viaducts that led westward to the slaughterhouses from the pens. The French journalist Jules Huret wrote that the site of the herds of cattle, hogs, and sheep being driven to their destinies communicated "to the onlooker the melancholy like that caused by the departure of armies."[1] The 1903 *Swift & Company Visitors Reference Book* informed guests that the plant covered forty-nine acres with a floor space of over ninety-two acres and employed seven thousand men and women. The complex had a daily capacity of 2,500 cattle, 8,000 hogs, and 6,000 sheep.[2]

The tour of the Swift plant began at the "Visitor's Entrance," which included showcases of the company's finished products such as sausages, hams, and soap. Elevators then took the guests up to the roof of the pork house. Workers herded hogs, after being driven in some cases more than a mile, into holding pens on the roofs of the plants, where they rested overnight. Later this changed as it was felt that a much briefer cooling-off period was sufficient. Most packers felt that overheated hogs, or hogs overexcited after having been driven some distance, had to be allowed to "cool off" or to become perfectly quiet to prevent the meat from becoming "feverish." Swift and Company had a yard capacity of 5,000 hogs.

After the animals' night of rest, laborers washed them down and drove a dozen or so at a time into a pen where a worker, often a young boy, shackled their rear leg to the Hurford Wheel—a hoisting machine that raised the hog steadily until the shackle

hook dropped unto a sliding rail. The animal would give out a loud shriek as the device suddenly pulled it into the air, on its way to the sticker, or dispatcher, who slit its throat. A cascade of blood gushed from the open wound. The sticker, covered in blood and standing in a pool of the hog's gore, stopped for a few seconds to let the blood drain. Every ten seconds another hog appeared before the skilled slayer. To many visitors, the sticker seemed a most repellant sight. He represented the most gruesome spectacle, one that remained with the tourist long after he or she left the stock-yards. However impressed a visitor might have been by this moment, it was just part of a long day's work for the pig-sticker. The sticker, who was working rather than sightseeing, then pushed the hog carcass along the rail to the boiling vats.[3]

Men stood alongside the vat with poles to keep the hog rolling in the water until it reached the end of the vat, where an apparatus captured the carcass and dropped it on a table so that other laborers could take the hair from its ears, which was used for artists' paintbrushes and other such products. A machine then lifted the hog onto a scraper machine that removed most of its bristles, but even this process was part of the modern. The mechanical hog scraper first appeared in the 1870s. Before then, workers found the job grueling and very unpleasant as six men had to hand scrape the steaming carcasses. In 1876, William W. Kincaid of Fowler Brothers designed the first workable scraping machine. Later, in 1880, Armour and Company's Michael Cudahy and John Bouchard designed a superior scraper that adjusted itself to the size of the individual carcasses. The Cudahy-Bouchard scraper took off most of the hair, leaving the rest for workers to hand scrape. The skin was then shaved carefully, to remove remaining hair without scoring the hog. Guidebooks pointed out the fact that each of the workmen had a special duty as the hog carcass passed the army of men working in the killing department.[4]

The hog then moved to the hog-dressing department, where men opened the bodies and removed all internal organs. Some men detached the fat for the production of lard. Two men wielding cleavers cut each hog carcass into two halves, which then passed to the hog-drying room. It took the hog twenty minutes to move from the shackler to the hog-drying room. In about two hours, the carcass dried enough to be placed in coolers.

Visitors then moved to the first pork cutting station, where they observed hogs that had been in coolers kept at 32 degrees Fahrenheit for forty-eight hours. They saw the carcass subdivided into the various cuts—hams, shoulders, and sides—as demanded by the various markets across the country and overseas. Each pork cutter had his particular cut to make with a heavy cleaver. The men worked so quickly and accurately that the pork seemed to melt and vanish as it moved from block to block. As the guests progressed to the next pork cutting room, the cuts from the room above moved down chutes to be further trimmed, the pork loins removed, and those pieces to be cured and smoked prepared for those departments.

Touring groups then moved on to the smoked meat department, where they saw hams and bacon inspected, branded, and packed for shipping. The building consisted of five floors and held thousands upon thousands of hams and sausages hanging in a dense and almost blinding smoke. They had been cured in a pickle of sugar, salt, and water for thirty to ninety days. Cured meat went into the washing room where it soaked in water three minutes for every day it had lain in pickling brine. Afterward, workers thoroughly smoked the meat in rooms heated to about 140 degrees Fahrenheit. Hams prepared for the American market stayed in the smoke rooms for thirty-six hours; those for export to Europe, two days longer.

At this point, tour guides took their charges outside and passed alongside the East Beef House. At the street crossing, the guides pointed out Swift's General Offices and described the five-story building that included executive offices, a telegraph department, file rooms, the general sales departments, and the accounting department as well as a 350-seat restaurant for office employees, reading and

smoking rooms, and a barbershop. The one thousand office employees breathed air that passed through a curtain of running water warmed in the winter and cooled during the summer to maintain an even temperature. This was the first example of an early form of air conditioning for an industrial office in Chicago. Huret commented on the work ethic of the office employees: "The women were writing or working typewriting machines or attending the telephone. Some of them wrote rapidly. No one was unoccupied, not an idler in the room, not an eye raised to look at the visitors. I have never seen such an office in Europe."[5] Afterward, the tour group approached a busy loading platform. Here workers stocked a long line of wagons with the daily supply of dressed meat for retailers. Great piles of boxes, cases, and barrels containing products for shipment stood on the north end of the platform. Dressed beef in quarters wrapped in burlap for shipment swung on an overhead rail from the cooler to its destination in a wagon or a refrigerated boxcar. Men hurried along the platform to load the railcars and wagons with hand trucks filled with various Swift products. [...]

Visitors from Far and Wide

The first guidebook to the new Union Stock Yard appeared even before the livestock market opened. Jack Wing, an itinerant journalist, wrote a pamphlet describing the Union Stock Yard in December 1865, prior to the actual Christmas Day kickoff. For months, Chicago's newspapers had covered the building of the stockyard, and Wing found himself a frequent visitor to the site, in the then-suburban Town of Lake. He first went down on Friday September 1, 1865, as part of a Board of Trade excursion to see the construction firsthand. Two weeks later, he returned with a group of Englishmen, including Sir Morton Petoe, the English entrepreneur, civil engineer, railroad developer, and member of Parliament. Wing wrote an article for the *Chicago Times* based on this visit. In November 1865, James H. Goodsell, the newspaper's city editor, assigned Wing the task of writing a complete account of the Union Stock

Yard. Wing's relationship with Goodsell was strained, and he feared that he would be fired as soon as he handed in the article, so on November 24, he conceived of the idea of a tract that he could write to make extra money if he lost his job. The next day, he returned to the Union Stock Yard and pitched such a brochure, but to no avail. The reporter persisted, and on November 28, William Tucker, one of the owners of the Briggs House, a hotel on the corner of Wells and Randolph Streets, agreed to buy five hundred copies of the proposed booklet. Several railroad men also agreed to purchase one hundred copies each. Wing felt that if he could obtain some advertisements, he would be able to self-publish the piece.

The next Friday, December 1, Wing went out to the Union Stock Yard to get information on the several old stockyards that were soon to disappear. Four cattle dealers agreed to place advertisements at twenty-five dollars apiece in the proposed publication. At that point, the editor of the *Chicago Republican* offered Wing a job. That Saturday, he signed up two more cattlemen in the stockyards to advertise in his pamphlet. He then went back to the *Times* offices, took his stockyard article, and quit the newspaper.

His printer delivered *The Great Union Stock Yards of Chicago: Their Railroad Connections, Bank, and Exchange, The Hough House, Water Supply and General Features also, A Sketch of the Live Stock Trade and the Old Yards* on December 12, and Wing went about happily gathering the money promised to him by advertisers and those interested in copies. The booklet sold well, and soon another edition was needed. Colonel Rossel M. Hough, the superintendent of construction of the Union Stock Yard, said that he would take two hundred copies. Other orders poured in, and Wing put out a second edition with even more advertisements than the first edition.[6]

In the tradition of Chicago boosterism, Wing's guide lauded the great engineering feats, such as pipes to drain the swampy area, the accommodations for railroads, noting that five hundred railroad cars could be unloaded at any one time. Wing also proclaimed the market's Hough House the finest hotel in the West. The author suggested that the view from the south veranda of the guesthouse was unequaled and worthy of a landscape artist. Wing's hyperbole would not be the last time exaggeration would be used to describe both the Union Stock Yard and Packingtown.[7]

News of the Union Stock Yard spread quickly, and it became a sight to see in Chicago. In the summer of 1866, delegates from the Cincinnati City Council—the city that had only recently lost the title of "Porkopolis" to Chicago—arrived. They traveled by train to the Town of Lake where P. R. Chandler, the president of the Union Stock Yard and Transit Company, welcomed them. The Cincinnatians visited the new tunnel crib and waterworks, various breweries, and grain elevators, and called Chicago a "wonder of the world." Chandler explained the market's facilities as the visitors toured the stockyard and dined at the hotel.

The next year the Civil War hero Major General Philip H. Sheridan visited. Several notables escorted Sheridan from the Tremont House in downtown Chicago to the stockyard by carriage, where they inspected livestock along with the alleys and streets of the complex. Sheridan and his company then met with drovers and commission men in the Exchange Building. Afterward, the entourage proceeded to the Hough House for lunch before visiting Cullerton's packinghouse on Eighteenth Street to see the butchering of hogs. Sheridan saw the modern industry being born as six hogs were butchered per minute at the plant.[8]

Packers were not the only promoters of such tourism. In 1869, the *Chicago Tribune* suggested various sightseeing drives around the city and suburbs and included the Union Stock Yard. The newspaper recommended a carriage ride down Michigan or Wentworth Avenues to Forty-Seventh Street and then over to the Dexter Park racetrack adjacent to the stockyard. The "fashionable" time for driving the route was early on a Sunday morning, in order to see the horses at Dexter Park. While the new racetrack attracted the "better" classes with a day of "sport," or rather gambling, for many tourists the lure remained the adjacent livestock market.[9]

In 1871, Grand Duke Alexei Alexandrovich, the fourth son of Czar Alexander II of Russia, toured the United States. Mayor Joseph Medill, who presided over the city as it recovered from the Great Fire of 1871, called for a committee composed of Chicago's business leaders to manage the details of the Russian visit. Chandler announced that the Union Stock Yard and Transit Company would provide lunch for the visitors at the renamed Hough House, now the Transit House. The grand duke spent New Year's Day 1872 visiting the sights of Chicago, then the live-stock market and a large packinghouse. His party arrived by carriage to the horse stables adjacent to Dexter Park. Here the general manager, John B. Sherman, met them and showed off his menagerie including finely bred livestock, Mexican hogs, and other "curiosities of the animal kingdom." After visiting the stockyard, the Russians explored the Hutchinson Packinghouse. The new plant, located to the west of the stockyard, had the largest capacity in Chicago, and the packing process fascinated the Russian royalty. The grand duke's entourage then visited Dexter Park and went on to the Transit House where Sherman greeted them for lunch, with abundant toasts. Mayor Medill saluted his visitors and said, "May the rivalry between Russia and America be in the future what it has long been in the past, a rivalry to feed a hungry world." After the festivities, the party again visited Dexter Park to take part in a pigeon shoot, another stockyard tradition.[10]

American politicians soon saw a visit to the Union Stock Yard as a necessary campaign stop. Here they met average working people and paid homage to the modern as it transformed American society. It gave politicians a gritty populist appeal while endorsing modern industrialism and the new American economy. They witnessed the latest innovations in industrial production along with the vast market that brought the produce of the nation's prairies and farms to the table of the public.

Industrial capitalism along with crowds of possible voters provided an irresistible campaign stop for any politician. On October 23, 1894, Thomas R. Reed of Maine, a powerful Republican who served several terms as Speaker of the House and had presidential ambitions, arrived in Chicago and spoke at a noontime rally in the stockyards. Some five thousand people greeted Reed in the Exchange Building courtyard. Stenographers, clerks, and typists hung out of windows to watch the political spectacle. Men stood on the pen fences and waved as the party rode down Exchange Avenue. Gus Swift met Reed and took his party into his plant for a tour.[11]

While Russian royalty and American politicians might get an extensive visit and lunch, others visited the stockyard in a less formal way. In 1889, an estimated fifty thousand "transient" visitors—what we would call tourists—came to Chicago annually. The Union Stock Yards attracted many of these. Packinghouse owners invited many to inspect their plants as they fought to have their chilled beef accepted in markets across the country. Members of the Pan American Congress visited the Swift, Libby, and Armour packinghouses in 1889. In 1890, a group of businessmen, disappointed because they could not visit the yards due to inclement weather, were shown instead a papier-mâché model in the dining room of the Richelieu Hotel downtown. Large groups such as the Knights of Pythias often arranged to tour the stockyards and Packingtown.[12]

Moreover, since the Union Stock Yard was open to the public, Chicagoans and others visited the complex daily. Many sought out the advice of "Old Man" Hildreth, the caretaker of the Chicago City Railway station in the stockyards. Over the years, he directed visitors in their search for one attraction or another. Boys often led curiosity seekers on excursions. The individuals involved determined the cost, but young guides usually charged twenty-five cents for a tour of the Union Stock Yard—fifty cents for both the stockyards and packing-houses. The packinghouse owners soon opened their plants for inspection by the public, and the larger packers organized formal tours led by trained and uniformed guides, putting the young streetwise entrepreneurs out of business. Eventually, visitors would be met in elegantly appointed lounges. The large packinghouses invested in catwalks and balconies from which guests could witness their industrial operations, explicated by signs.[13]

By the early 1900s, regular tours of the stockyards and packing-houses were commonplace. In 1903, to celebrate the one hundredth anniversary of the building of Fort Dearborn, an event that signaled the American arrival in the area, Chicagoans held citywide celebrations. By that time, Swift and Company passed out its own "Visitors Reference Book" to guests, which described nineteen stations with illustrations that visitors would stop on during their tour of the massive plant. Several years later, Swift and Company handed out a well-illustrated guide, *A Visit to Swift & Company, Union Stock Yards, Chicago* as a souvenir that could be mailed off to friends describing the "Clean—wholesome—efficient" characteristics of the company's Chicago plant. The pamphlet also depicted the "system" that made the company and the industry so efficient. In addition, these souvenirs gave proof to the folks back home that one had actually made the trip and witnessed the spectacle of the modern.[14]

In August 1910, the packers prepared to receive the most visitors they had hosted since the 1893 Columbian Exposition. Ten thousand Knights Templars, in Chicago for their annual meeting, visited on August 10. Women made up more than half of the sightseers, and guides took them through the plants in groups of one hundred. Every packinghouse opened its doors, and excursions began every ten minutes. A mounted detail of stockyard employees spread out over Packingtown and provided information to the throngs.

For visitors, the spectacle contained in the Square Mile began even before reaching the main gate as the stench of the stockyards immediately affected those not accustomed to them. Chicagoans complained of "curdled" air. One description had trolley riders entering the "odor zone" and young women covering their faces with handkerchiefs as even hardened laborers attempted to protect themselves from the stench. The writer complained, "The combined smells seemed to focus in a crescendo of coagulated putridity." Grand Duke Boris, the cousin of the Russian czar, exclaimed in 1902, "I never smelled such an awful smell, but the stockyards are greater than my imagination conceived."[15] That was the smell of the modern, a modern that was paid for by Chicagoans, as they had to put up with the odor and the obvious ecological impact of this great industry.

Russian grand dukes, French journalists, Japanese businessmen and their wives, British trade unionists, Irish nationalists, Texas cattlemen, and everyday Americans all visited the Union Stock Yard and packing plants. Rudyard Kipling's account of his visit to the Square Mile remains among the most graphic. Touring the complex in 1889, he described the hog kill and its victims, "They were so excessively alive, these pigs. And then they were so excessively dead, and the man in the dripping, clammy, hot passage did not seem to care." The stockyards fascinated Sarah Bernhardt, the famous actress, who described it in vivid terms in her memoirs. She wrote of "an abominable smell" and of the "almost human cries of the pigs" being slaughtered. The German sociologist, Max Weber, visited in 1904 and also described the plants in vivid terms:

> From the moment when the unsuspecting bovine enters the slaughtering area, is hit by a hammer and collapses, whereupon it is immediately gripped by an iron clamp, is hoisted in the air, and starts on its journey, it is in constant motion—past ever-new workers who eviscerate and skin it, etc., but are always (in the rhythm of work) tied to the machine that pulls the animal past them.

For Kipling and the others, this terrifying spectacle portrayed a modern world that shattered traditional relationships and pointed to a frightening future. It stank of barbarity despite the fact that it harnessed man and machine in a new industrial economy. Chicagoans often did not feel this way. They were proud of the stockyards and Packingtown. In 1908, Mayor Busse proclaimed the Union Stock Yard as one of the "Seven Wonders of Chicago" that should be visited by any tourist and certainly by all Chicagoans. The Chicago Association of Commerce, on the other hand, in contesting the views of the mayor and much of the public tried to rid the city of its cattle town image, and attempted to direct visitors away from the stockyards, but still the square mile of packinghouses, pens, and chutes attracted tourists and Chicagoans alike. The stockyards were Chicago.[16]

NOTES

1. *Chicago Tribune*, June 23, 1905.
2. Much of the following discussion of a visit to the packing plants comes from Swift and Company, *Visitors Reference Book* (Chicago, n.d.). The author's copy of the *Visitors Reference Book* is inscribed with the date October 28, 1910—perhaps the date of the visit to the plant. Other sources give the publication date as 1903.
3. Heller and Company, *The Secrets of Meat Curing and Sausage Making* (Chicago, 1922), p. 32; *Chicago Tribune*, June 23, 1905; John O'Brien, *Through the Chicago Stock Yards: A Handy Guide to the Packing Industry* (Chicago and New York, 1907), p. 58.
4. O'Brien, *Through the Chicago Stock Yards*, p. 60; George Wm. Lambert, *A Trip Through the Union Stock Yards and Slaughter Houses, Chicago, U.S.A.* (Chicago, n.d., ca. 1890s) pp. 21–24; F. W. Wilder, *The Modern Packinghouse* (Chicago, 1905), pp. 252–72; Louise Wade, *Chicago's Pride: The Stockyards, Packingtown, and Environs in the Nineteenth Century* (Urbana, 1987), pp. 102–3.
5. *Chicago Tribune*, June 23, 1905.
6. Robert Williams, ed., *The Chicago Diaries of John M. Wing, 1865–1866* (Carbondale and Edwardsville, IL, 2002), pp. xxiv–xxvii, 34–70; *Chicago Times*, September 18, 1865.
7. Jack Wing, *The Great Union Stock Yards of Chicago: Their Railroad Connections, Bank, and Exchange, The Hough House, Water Supply and General Features also, A Sketch of the Live Stock Trade and the Old Yards* (Chicago, 1865), pp. 4–5, 24.
8. *Chicago Tribune*, December 5, 1867.
9. *Chicago Tribune*, July 18, 1869.
10. *Chicago Tribune*, December 30, 1871, January 3, 1872.
11. *Chicago Tribune*, October 24, 1894.
12. *Chicago Tribune*, February 24, 1889, August 18, 1889, October 22, 1889; *Daily Sun*, December 30, 1891.
13. *Daily Sun*, May 28, 1892; Swift and Company advertisement in *The National Provisioner*, January 5, 1907, p. 18.
14. Lambert, *A Trip Through the Union Stock Yards*; O'Brien, *Through the Chicago Stock Yards*; Swift and Company, *Swift & Company Visitors Reference Book*, Swift and Company, *A Visit to Swift & Company, Union Stock Yards, Chicago* (Chicago, n.d.). The copy of *A Visit to Swift & Company, Union Stock Yards, Chicago* is postmarked February 15, 1917.
15. *Chicago Tribune*, July 29, 1910, August 19, 1902.
16. Sarah Bernhardt, *My Double Life: Memoirs of Sarah Bernhardt* (London, 1907), pp. 400–401. Quoted in Lawrence A. Scaff, *Max Weber in America* (Princeton and Oxford, 2011), p. 45; Rudyard Kipling, "How I Struck Chicago, and How Chicago Struck Me," in Bessie Louise Pierce, ed., *How Others See Chicago: Impressions of Visitors, 1673–1933* (Chicago, 1933, 2004), p. 259; *Chicago Tribune*, August 11, 1910, November 16, 1910, June 6, 1905, September 25, 1909, April 10, 1908, October 1, 1908, March 22, 1908, July 22, 1906, August 15, 1909. Lisa Krissoff Boehm, *Popular Culture and the Enduring Myth of Chicago, 1871–1968* (New York and London, 2004), pp. 81–82.

ESSAY 6.3

Houston: The Energy Metropolis

Martin V. Melosi and Joseph A. Pratt

Source: Martin V. Melosi and Joseph A. Pratt, *Energy Metropolis: An Environmental History of Houston and the Gulf Coast* (Pittsburgh: University of Pittsburgh Press, 2007).

EDITORS' INTRODUCTION

America's dependence on fossil fuels was highlighted by the spike in gasoline prices following Hurricanes Katrina and Rita in 2005, and the subsequent worldwide speculation in oil futures. Energy remains a major public policy concern today. The first so-called "energy crisis" occurred in 1973 and the second in 1979. For better or for worse, cheap and abundant energy from coal, oil, and natural gas has shaped the American urban landscape and provided the basis for dramatic metropolitan growth during the twentieth century. No other city in the United States has been as influenced by the production, distribution, and consumption of energy as Houston, Texas. Famous for its lack of conventional zoning, Houston grew dramatically from a small frontier town in the early nineteenth century to the largest city in Texas and the fourth largest city in the United States—with a population of over 2 million people—in the early twenty-first century. In 2019 the city was the fourth largest in the nation.

Houston's story, however, is much more than that of urban sprawl. It is one of the most ethnically and racially diverse cities in America and home to world-class cultural, education, and medical institutions, impressive modern architecture, and multinational corporations. As Martin V. Melosi and Joseph A. Pratt argue, Houston is also the Bayou City. The city's setting within the Gulf Coast region of southeastern Texas is critical to understanding the interplay between energy, urbanization, and the natural environment, an area of inquiry long neglected by historians. In this selection, the introduction from their book *Energy Metropolis: An Environmental History of Houston and the Gulf Coast* (2007), Melosi and Pratt sketch the impact of energy on the evolution of American cities and explore the urbanization of the Texas Coastal Zone. Among the principle features of the interaction between human and natural forces in this region has been pollution from energy related activities and extensive urbanization. The zone is highly susceptible to tornadoes and hurricanes. Two examples of this urban fragility are Hurricane Ike, which severely disrupted Galveston, Texas in September 2008, and the great and unnamed hurricane of 1900 that all but destroyed that city.

Martin V. Melosi is the Hugh Roy and Lillie Cranz Cullen University Professor Emeritus of History and Director of the Center for Public History at the University of Houston. In addition to *Energy Metropolis*, his works include *Garbage in the Cities: Refuse, Reform and the Environment* (College Station: Texas A&M Press, 1981; Pittsburgh, PA: University of Pittsburgh Press, 2005), *Effluent America: Cities, Industry, Energy, and the Environment* (Pittsburgh, PA: University of Pittsburgh Press, 2001), and *The Sanitary City: Urban Infrastructure in America from Colonial Times to the Present* (Baltimore, MD: Johns Hopkins University Press, 2000; Pittsburgh, PA: University of Pittsburgh Press, 2008), winner of multiple awards from the American Society of Environmental History, the Urban History Association, and other professional organizations.

Joseph A. Pratt is Professor Emeritus at the University of Houston and a leading historian of the petroleum industry. Pratt has authored or co-authored nine books in addition to *Energy Metropolis* and served as a consultant for the Public Broadcasting Service (PBS) mini-series on the oil industry, *The Prize*, and for the *American Experience* documentary on the Trans-Alaskan Pipeline. He is also the founder of the Houston History Project and editor of *Houston History*, a magazine of popular history.

HOUSTON: ENERGY METROPOLIS (2007)

An Environmental History of Houston and the Gulf Coast

Cities are by their very nature energy intensive. The concentration of human and material resources for purposes of survival, construction of infrastructure for transportation and communication, and the production and consumption of goods and services are essential characteristics of communal living. As William Cronon and others have demonstrated, the connection of city and hinterland often extends the impact of urban development beyond the city's political borders while creating interdependence between the built and natural world.[1] The production and use of energy have been potent forces in driving this process of change.

The historical impact of energy reaches beyond the conversion of resources to stationary and motive power to make machines run; to illuminate streets and interiors; to move trains, cars, buses, and trucks; and to generate heat and refrigerated air. Broadly understood, energy encompasses all processes of production and consumption that allow people to function in the physical world. A key challenge in urban and environmental history is to identify and analyze the central impacts of energy production and use on the evolution of cities.

One general impact is clear: changes in energy supply and demand have greatly affected the economic context within which cities have grown. New technologies using new sources of energy have shaped the transportation and communication revolutions that have transformed the world economy in the last two centuries. The impact of new sources of energy on the American economy has been particularly pronounced in the years since the mid-nineteenth century, when the widespread use of fossil fuels encouraged the most significant transportation innovation of that century, the completion of a national system of railroads. Coal fueled the trains that transformed the American landscape, introduced a new scale of business activity, and created a much broader national market. Then oil fueled the cars and planes that extended that transformation. The burning of coal, oil, and natural gas generated the bulk of electricity and provided most of the fuel for modern industrialization. Taken together, these fossil fuels have provided far and away the most significant supplies of energy in the modern economy; their adaptation to industrial uses and transportation systems fundamentally altered the economy by broadening the scale of markets and the scope of business activities. [...]

Fossil fuels helped transform the modern city, altering the physical environment in new and significant ways. The most obvious impact was a fundamental change in land-use patterns in and around cities, which reached out and absorbed once-rural land surrounding the sprawling urban centers. The concentrated usage of energy in the production of goods brought a new scale of industrial pollution to cities. Growing energy use for transporting people and goods added another layer of pollution to the mix, particularly in cities that grew rapidly only after the advent of the automobile. In these and many other ways, as the lure of jobs and better opportunities from urban industrial growth attracted larger populations, the environmental impacts of increasing energy use also grew dramatically.

Although the strong and complex connections between energy use, urban growth, and environmental issues are intuitively obvious, they have been slighted by historians. Perhaps the connections are simply too deeply embedded to be easily analyzed. Also, the study of energy history has not yet developed as fully as the vibrant fields of urban and environmental histories. One way to begin to examine more thoroughly these related issues is to focus on extreme cases, which show most dramatically the relationship between energy, environment, and urbanization.

To more fully examine the intersection of energy, environment, and urbanization, this essay offers the example of Houston. The Bayou City is currently the nation's fourth-largest city, and it sits at the center of the seventh-largest metropolitan area in the United States. It is the home to over 100 racial and ethnic groups, making it one of the most diverse cities in the nation.[2]

As both a consumer and producer of energy, especially oil and natural gas, the city has few rivals around the world. Other parts of the nation can boast of significant oil-producing and -refining areas, most notably the original oil fields in Pennsylvania; the substantial refining complexes in Cleveland and New Jersey; southern California's concentrations of refineries, oil fields, and transportation hubs; and the refining region of southern Louisiana. None of these areas, however, matches the Houston region in its concentration of oil refining, petrochemical production, oil and natural gas transportation, and oceangoing tankers. For better and for worse, the Houston area has developed around oil and oil refining, and it provides a unique case of an energy-intensive metropolis more than other Sun Belt cities such as Atlanta, Dallas-Fort Worth, Oklahoma City, Phoenix, or Los Angeles.

Oil shaped Houston's modern economic and environmental history. In every industrial region, leading industries produce particular patterns of pollution. In the case of Houston, the production, processing, and shipment of oil and natural gas gave the city a distinctive identity within the national economy while also creating distinctive levels and forms of air, water, and ground pollution.

In every large city, the predominant fuel used in regional transportation and industry emits significant pollution. In twentieth-century Houston, oil and natural gas supplied the bulk of the fuel used to transport people and to produce and transport goods. Because petroleum was both the major industry and the major fuel for modern Houston, this self-proclaimed "energy capital of America" has also been the de facto "oil pollution capital of America."[3]

Houston's emergence as a major metropolis was shaped by fundamental changes in the national and international energy industries. Since the late nineteenth century, fossil fuels have steadily replaced wind, water, and animal power; in the process, local sources of energy have been replaced by sources supplied by an increasingly specialized and concentrated energy economy.[4] Oil and natural gas surged forward during the twentieth century to become the dominant energy source in the industrial world, and Houston, more than any other city, benefited economically from this development. Houston became synonymous with oil much as Pittsburgh was with steel or Detroit was with automobiles or the Silicon Valley became with microprocessing. It was a center for specialized activities needed by the national and international petroleum industry, one of the most dynamic industries of the twentieth century.

Nature endowed the Houston region with the abundant natural resources, innumerable sunny days, the lack of harsh winters, and the geographical location that allowed it to prosper as a center of oil production and refining. But good luck and good timing also help explain its dominant role in the development of oil and natural gas. With the discovery in 1901 of the epoch-defining Spindletop oil field in nearby Beaumont, Texas, the region's oil-related economy sprang to life. Houston and surrounding areas on the Gulf Coast quickly became the focal point for the expansion of the oil and gas industries in the southwestern United States, an area that produced the bulk of the world's oil from the turn of the twentieth century through the 1960s. Just as the nation entered the automobile age, with its surging demand for refined oil products, Houston found itself perfectly positioned to become the center for the regional and then the national petroleum industry. Even the subsequent movement of the locus of world oil production to the Middle East could not easily displace the economic advantages embedded in the region's infrastructure during the long dominance of southwestern oil. Adding strength to the regional economy after the 1930s was the spectacular growth of the natural gas industry in the United States, which was centered in Houston.

Over the course of the twentieth century, the regional economy diversified steadily to include more and more oil-related activities. The region's sturdy oil-related industrial core evolved to include the production, refining, and shipment of oil; the production and shipment of natural gas; the production and shipment of petrochemicals; management and research in oil, natural gas, and petrochemicals; specialized construction for these industries; the manufacture of tools and supplies needed by the petroleum complex; specialized technical and management services; and highway and residential construction undertaken in part to meet the needs of the workforce of the oil-related complex. From these activities came both the economic growth and the severe industrial pollution that characterized the modern history of the Gulf Coast region surrounding Houston.

The industrial heart of this oil-related complex was refining. The giant petroleum refineries and petrochemical plants that processed crude oil and natural gas into a variety of products also created tens of thousands of industrial jobs that attracted generations of workers to the region. The center of the massive refining complex that stretched from Corpus Christi, Texas, to New Orleans was the Houston Ship Channel, which reached southeastward from Houston forty miles to the Gulf of Mexico. In the mid-twentieth century, this region along the Gulf Coast produced as much as

a third of the nation's refined goods and half of its petrochemicals. Into and out of this highly specialized industrial complex flowed millions of barrels of crude oil and refined oil and tons of petrochemical products per day, and the processing and shipping of these products gave the region its identity in the national economy. Even in the late twentieth century, after automation sharply reduced the number of employees in the refineries and the Houston economy successfully diversified into other economic activities, refining remained a major contributor to regional prosperity.

The manufacturing jobs in these and other oil-related factories gave the region a distinctive industrial working-class tone to a greater extent than Dallas, Fort Worth, Austin, or San Antonio. This was a place where people from the rural hinterland of Texas and Louisiana came in search of greater opportunities for themselves and their children. Bringing with them the racial attitudes inherited from the strict and violent segregation practiced in the small-town and rural South, they helped make Houston the largest Jim Crow city in the nation by 1950. But despite segregated housing and public services and segregated workforces in the area's refineries and factories, these workers—black and white—also brought the migrants' faith that those who worked hard could create a better future for their families in Houston. This fundamental optimism that the city held opportunities for those willing to work hard floated in the air of Houston along with the fumes from the refineries. Jobs, not air pollution, remained the primary concern of millions of people who migrated to the region in the twentieth century.

Sustained growth, of course, brought a new set of challenges. Where would those who flocked to the city live? How would the urban services needed by a growing population be provided? Transportation was one key issue facing the booming region. A prototypical Sun Belt city, Houston grew up with the automobile. With no widespread investment in public transit before the coming of oil in 1901 and the opening of the Houston Ship Channel in

1914, the city expanded rapidly just as cars came into general use. It is symbolically fitting that the decade of the city's fastest growth in the twentieth century was the 1920s, when auto use took off in the region and around the nation and the ship channel refining complex boomed. In that decade, the first substantial suburbs connected to the central city by jobs and roads were the refinery towns east of the city throughout the industrial corridor along the ship channel—Pasadena, Galena Park, Baytown, Deer Park, and Texas City.

In subsequent decades, the city expanded in every other direction. Favorable state laws, such as the Municipal Annexation Act (1963), also allowed the city to aggressively annex adjoining areas and thus further enlarge its territory. By 1999, this generous annexation policy had allowed Houston to reserve approximately 1,289 square miles (excluding the areas of the city within it) for future annexation.[5] Land surrounding the city provided living space for the millions of migrants to the region; inexpensive gasoline provided the fuel needed to commute longer and longer distances; and inexpensive electricity produced primarily by abundant and low-cost natural gas allowed for the air-conditioning that made the city livable during its long, harsh summers. Local, state, and federal governments responded to citizens' demands to build more and more roads reaching farther and farther out from the city. Individuals responded by hustling up the resources to acquire cars and, if possible, homes in the suburbs. The region as a whole moved easily and with little public debate toward a "mass transit" strategy of more highways filled by more cars, often with one driver per car.

Over decades of sustained outward urban growth, both energy costs and environmental costs became embedded in regional transportation systems. Once infrastructure for the transportation of goods and people had been built, change was most difficult, in spite of shifting political calculations of economic and environmental costs. By the end of the twentieth century, most people living in a thirty-mile radius of the central city had become "Houstonians"

who were tied into the economic and cultural life of the city primarily through a sprawling system of roads and freeways. The specialized transportation system of pipelines, tanker trucks, railroads, barges, and oceangoing tankers used by the region's petroleum-related core of industries bound together the region's economy and tied it into national and global markets.

The Houston region grew from a frontier town in the early nineteenth century, to a small city of about 45,000 in 1900, and finally to an expansive metropolis of more than five million in 2006. Urban growth has been a core objective of the city from its modest start, spearheaded by John Kirby Allen and Augustus Chapman Allen in 1836, until this very day. Shipping, rail, and especially automotive and truck transportation helped push Houston's borders and Houston's influence beyond its initial location along Buffalo Bayou.

Although the region expanded geographically before oil, the booming new industry and the growing use of the automobile greatly accelerated the city's expansion out into the surrounding countryside in the twentieth century. By the turn of the twenty-first century, "Houston"—as defined by economic and commuting ties, not by political boundaries—had become one of the world's largest cities in area, spanning perhaps 2,000 square miles that stretched thirty or forty miles from downtown Houston in every direction over a broad area of the Texas Gulf Coast. Much of this land had been farmland in the early twentieth century, but by the year 2000, from Katy to Conroe to Baytown to Galveston to Sugar Land, each exit looked much the same, the homes in each subdivision merged into several generic floor plans, and all roads led into and out of Houston. The city exhibited the worst kind of urban sprawl—patternless, unplanned (Houston is the largest city in the United States without zoning), and highly decentralized. In the post-World War II years, Houston had half the population density of Los Angeles and reached into ten counties.

Of course, cars commuting around the sprawling city combined with the refineries and petrochemical plants to produce serious air and water pollution. Adding to the city's environmental woes is its susceptibility to severe weather conditions such as tornadoes and hurricanes, and a propensity to flood often and intensely. Volumes of water exacerbate nonpoint pollution problems, as all kinds of toxic materials—from lawn fertilizers to heavy metals—run into the city's extensive network of bayous and ultimately spill into the Gulf of Mexico. Severe pollution problems arose from the transportation of the millions of barrels of crude oil and refined products per day that flowed through these plants on their way through the global oil economy. In this sense, the Houston region served not only as the nation's refining center but also as one of the national economy's primary dumping grounds for oil-related and other forms of pollution.

Just as Houston earned great economic benefit from its specialized role as a center of oil-related activities, it also paid a high environmental price. Petrochemicals presented their own special set of problems from air and water emissions, along with the disposal of a variety of solid and liquid wastes. Altogether, the region suffered the triple dilemma of dealing simultaneously with mounting oil-related pollution from the exhausts of gasoline-powered automobiles, the production of oil and chemical products from local plants, and myriad urban pollutants.

Efforts to find an acceptable balance between the costs and benefits of petroleum processing and petroleum pollution proved difficult. For most of the region's history, a broadly shared societal consensus that included a majority of the population, rich and poor, favored oil development largely unrestrained by pollution controls. "Opportunity" and "economic growth" were the twin tenets of the local religion of boosterism, and the church did not have much tolerance for doubters who voiced concerns about the quality of life.

Those who called for stricter controls of pollution had to overcome more than regional attitudes favoring growth. Local politics, as well as civic leadership, were dominated by business leaders whose idea of a "healthy business climate" included low taxes, weak unions, and very limited regulation. Several scholars have provided the useful label "free enterprise city" to describe the dominance of Houston's political and civic cultures by conservative businessmen.[6] Granted such business power is hardly unique among cities in capitalist America, and further granted that much of the power and the behavior of the local elite can be explained with reference to their commitment to segregation as easily as to their commitment to free enterprise, the fact remains that business and civic leaders in Houston historically represented a strong and consistent barrier to the passage and enforcement of effective pollution controls.

Political realities also included the entrenched power in the political process at the state and federal levels of the well-organized interests of the major industries that produced the bulk of the region's industrial pollution. The basic decisions about Houston's oil-related development were made by private corporations in the global energy economy. In Houston, as around the world, price dictated the key decisions on energy use and, to an extent, the approach to pollution control. But the political process played a pivotal role in channeling government promotion and blocking government regulation. The economic importance of oil in the state of Texas, in general, and in the city of Houston, in particular, skewed political decisions toward policies that promoted the oil industry and away from policies that constrained the industry, at least until the federal government preempted much of the traditional authority of states over pollution control after the 1960s. The state's one-party political system through the 1960s also proved to be a barrier to change, as those who advocated states' rights in defense of Jim Crow had ample reason to support the states' rights arguments of those who fought against federal government involvement in pollution control.[7]

An important part of the economic/environmental history of the region has been the ongoing efforts to create more effective pollution controls while also encouraging continued economic growth. Only in the recent past have segments of the American public recognized that more efficient energy use in response to higher prices has broken the traditional coupling of growth in energy use and economic growth. Only recently have segments of the American public—including some civic leaders and grassroots organizations in Houston—recognized that high levels of pollution are not only a threat to public health and the quality of life but also can become a barrier to economic growth and the creation of jobs in the region and the nation. For most of Houston's history—in politics and in practice—there was little effort to "balance" energy and environmental needs, since pollution control was treated as distinctly secondary to economic growth. Yet there are at least tentative signs that a new balance, with greater concern for environmental quality, is politically possible.

Unlike many other oil-producing regions around the world that have been seemingly "cursed" by the problems of oil-led development, the Houston area has grown spectacularly since the discovery of oil in the region in 1901.[8] Since that time, the region has successfully absorbed the dynamic oil industry, using it as the engine of growth that transformed the city. Historically, the timing of the discovery and development of oil was fortuitous for Houston, which got in on the ground floor at the birth of the modern petroleum industry. The giant refineries built in the region in the early twentieth century could not be easily moved as oil production itself subsequently moved away from the region.

The area around Houston was a thriving regional center before the discovery of oil. The rise of shipping and commercial development along Buffalo Bayou in the nineteenth century was an essential precedent for the construction of the Houston Ship Channel and the emergence of Houston as an international focal point for oil production, refining, and petrochemicals. The business community proved well equipped to take on the new economic activities spawned by the industry. It had an established legal system capable of managing the demands of the new industry, and well-developed local corporate law firms. Most important, oil development went forward under the direction of transplanted Texans and native Texans who reinvested much of the profits from the giant new oil fields in regional developments such as giant refineries and pipelines connecting these refineries to other major oil fields outside the region.

The long-term prosperity generated by the regional economy also reflected its historical capacity to diversify away from oil production—from a regional perspective, the most difficult to retain branch of the oil industry.

In the mid-twentieth century, such diversification occurred within the expanding oil-related core, where first refining and oil-tool manufacturing, then petrochemicals, and finally the production and transportation of natural gas provided dynamic areas of economic expansion. Then in the 1960s and accelerating in the mid-1980s, after the dramatic drop in oil prices led to a devastating regional depression, diversification outside of oil bolstered the region's growth.

Yet even much of this "new, nonoil economy" in Houston had indirect ties to the oil industry. The coming of the Lyndon B. Johnson Space Center to Clear Lake, south of Houston, was orchestrated by an alliance of George Brown of Brown & Root (a construction company with many strong ties to oil industry markets), the president of Humble Oil, and Vice President Lyndon Johnson. The growth of the Texas Medical Center, which became a major employer in Houston by the 1980s, was fostered by the philanthropic support of many Houstonians who had made their original fortunes in oil, as was the growth of Rice University and the University of Houston. Even the real estate development industry that built the Houston suburbs had strong ties to the oil industry; for example, Friendswood Development, a major regional developer that built much of Clear Lake and Kingwood, originally was affiliated with Exxon and named after one of its important regional oil fields, and the Woodlands north of the city was inspired by the efforts of oilman George Mitchell. [...]

The Physical Setting

As an energy-intensive metropolis, Houston has been shaped by natural and human forces. However, to fully understand the environmental history of this urban area—including Galveston—requires attention to its physical realities, especially its location within the Gulf Coast region of southeastern Texas. The circumstance of where the metropolis is situated speaks volumes about its dynamic history.[9]

Houston is foremost a product of the Texas Coastal Zone, an area of approximately 20,000 square miles consisting of about 2,100 square miles of bays and estuaries, 375 miles of coastline, and 1,425 miles of bay, estuary, and lagoon shoreline. The shoreline itself is composed of interconnected natural waterways, restricted bays, lagoons, and estuaries with modest freshwater inflow, elongated barrier islands, and a very low astronomical tidal range.[10]

Texas actually has two shorelines—one running along the Gulf of Mexico and another along the bays. Bolivar Peninsula, Galveston Island, and Follets Island are grass-covered barrier flats and sandy beaches of one to three miles in width that separate the bay areas from the Gulf of Mexico. Galveston Island is the best known of the barrier islands, approximately thirty miles long and two-and-a-half miles wide, with no underlying bedrock and consisting of mud flats on the side facing the bay. As David McComb has noted, "Lying parallel to the coast two miles away, Galveston stands as a guardian protecting the land and the bay from the Gulf."[11]

Behind the barrier islands, Galveston Bay (composed of four major subbays: Galveston Bay, Trinity Bay, East Bay, and West Bay) and some smaller bays comprise almost 600 square miles of surface area. West Bay is a lagoon separating Galveston from the mainland. Galveston Bay and its continuation as Trinity Bay constitute an estuary. The entire Galveston Bay watershed, or drainage basin, covers 33,000 square miles of land and water from the Dallas-Fort Worth Metroplex to the Texas

coast—a substantially larger area than the water that the bay encompasses. Extensive marshy areas less than five feet above sea level extend along the landward side of West and East bays. Bolivar Roads and San Luis Pass are natural passes that connect the bays to the Gulf. Rollover Pass, extending through the Bolivar Peninsula, connects the Gulf of Mexico and East Bay.[12]

Above the bays, two major river valleys—the Trinity and the San Jacinto—and several minor valleys of headward-eroding streams—Cedar Bayou, Buffalo Bayou, Clear Creek, Dickinson Bayou, Halls Bayou, Chocolate Bayou, and Bastrop Bayou—cut into the coastal plain. The Brazos River and Oyster Creek flow through the western portion of the Texas Coastal Zone, but not within deep valleys.[13]

The Houston-Galveston area consists of approximately 2,268 square miles of land, which is a broad region of flat coastal plain situated between the coastal marshes and the areas of pine and hardwood forests along either side of the Trinity River and north of downtown Houston. The coastal plain itself inclines from the Gulf at two to five feet per mile. The maximum elevation of the coastal plain is about ninety feet above sea level in the northwestern part of the coastal zone.[14]

Situated approximately forty-nine feet above sea level on prairie some fifty miles from the Gulf of Mexico, the city of Houston is linked geographically, geologically, and climatically to the Texas coast. The coastal plain of which Houston is a part comprises gently dipping layers of sand and clay. The slope of the impermeable layers of clay, shale, and gumbo interbedded with permeable, water-bearing sands and gravel is greater than the slope of the land surface. These conditions are favorable for artesian water, and the city historically has drawn water from the Chicot and Evangeline aquifers running southeast to northwest from the Gulf Coast through the city and to its north. Extraction of the groundwater, however, can lead, and has led, to land subsidence and saltwater intrusion if water is drawn out too aggressively.[15]

On the surface, water from Houston drains into the Gulf of Mexico via an elaborate network of bayous. With an average yearly rainfall of forty-two to forty-six inches from often torrential downpours, the area is subjected to frequent flooding. Since urbanization removes much of the filtering capacity of the soil, runoff has exaggerated Houston's tendency to flood as the city continued to expand. Since the city also is susceptible to hurricanes and tornadoes, water and the pollutants it often carries have been the greatest natural threat to Houstonians and its neighbors.[16]

Along with its extensive waterways, Houston also is a heavily vegetated city. Large portions of the region are forested, with substantial tree growth along the bayous. Loblolly pine is the tree species that dominates the region. Much of the west side of the area, which contains acres of native prairie, has been converted to developed private property where trees have been planted. On the north and northeast sides, the natural land cover has densely vegetated canopies over approximately 50 percent of the area. To the south, the area is covered with a combination of prairie, marsh, forest, and abandoned agricultural lands. At the highly developed city center, however, the ground and canopy cover has diminished markedly. A "heat island" effect is most pronounced in this area. A study by the National Aeronautics and Space Administration (NASA) in August 2000 found "hot spots" of approximately 149 degrees Fahrenheit in the warmest locations and 77 degrees Fahrenheit in cooler areas.[17]

In many respects, Houston's climate is one of its most identifiable features. An ill-fated publicity campaign once used the phrase "Houston is Hot!" to promote the city. Indeed, Houston's climate is subtropical and humid, with prevailing winds bringing heat from the deserts of Mexico and moisture from the Gulf. The sun shines for much of the year, with an annual growing season of almost 300 days. The average low temperature is 72 degrees Fahrenheit in the summer and 40 degrees Fahrenheit in the winter; the average high is 93 degrees Fahrenheit in the summer and 61 degrees Fahrenheit in the winter. Humidity in June is typically about 63 percent.[18]

As one geologic study noted, "The attributes that make the Texas Coastal Zone attractive for industrialization and development also make it particularly susceptible to a variety of environmental problems."[19] The deepwater ports, intercoastal waterways, good water supplies, large tracts of arable land, and relatively mild climate have been valuable assets. In addition, the region has a variety of other exploitable resources, including timber, sulfur and salt, sand and gravel, shells for lime, abundant wildlife, shellfish and fish, and petroleum reserves.[20] The agricultural, commercial, industrial, and recreational possibilities for the region, however, have come with a price due to natural and human impacts.

Probably the most dramatic natural events have been tropical hurricanes and tornadoes. As far back as 1776, a hurricane of unknown intensity destroyed a mission in the Galveston area. In the nineteenth century, major hurricanes struck the upper coast in 1854, 1867, and 1886.[21] The "Great Storm" that hit Galveston on September 8, 1900, is the best known of the South Texas hurricanes, especially since it killed more people than any other natural disaster in the history of the United States—6,000 people in Galveston alone and probably 10,000 to 12,000 total—and devastated the city itself.[22] Although no storm since that time recorded loss of life even close to the one in 1900 (the death toll from Hurricane Katrina in 2005 exceeded 1,800 people), hurricanes and tropical storms have been regular visitors to the upper Texas coast. In recent years, powerful storms such as Hurricane Carla (1961), Tropical Storm Claudette (1979), Hurricane Alicia (1983), Tropical Storm Allison (2001), and Hurricane Rita (2005) have wracked southeast Texas.[23] Along with loss of life, property damage, and severe flooding, the storms also have contributed to substantial shoreline retreat.[24] However, human action also encourages shoreline recession. For example, until a 1970 bill was passed by the Texas legislature, beach sediments were removed for road building. Building of jetties also disrupts the normal transportation of sediment and produces recession, as in the case of the Sabine Pass jetties and jetties along Bolivar Peninsula.[25]

Human impacts on the Texas Coastal Zone are wide ranging. Extensive dredging of channels and passes has resulted in the discharge of sediment into bays, ultimately modifying natural bay circulation patterns, and affected water quality and estuarine plants and animals. Because of increased cultivation, the construction of irrigation and drainage canals and urban paving result in many streams accelerating the transport of sediment into bays as well as increasing nonpoint pollutants, including pesticides and herbicides from runoff. Straightening and lining streams with concrete—as in the case of several bayous in Houston—encourage flash flooding. Thermal effluents from various manufacturing processes and power generation can be lethal to fish. Aggressive withdrawal of groundwater causes land subsidence and saltwater intrusion, and activates faults. Discharge of organic materials, trace metals, and other materials too numerous to mention from a variety of sources—including oil production, pipelines, spills, and chemical production—adds significantly to the pollution load of all water courses.[26]

Human actions also have had significant impacts on the major habitats of the bays and environs, including oyster reefs, submerged aquatic vegetation, intertidal marsh vegetation and animal life, and freshwater wetlands. For example, between 1950 and 1989, approximately 54 percent of the freshwater marshes in the Galveston Bay watershed were lost because of draining wetlands and conversion to upland areas.[27]

Houston and other upper Texas coast cities are subject, first and foremost, to the geologic, geographic, and climatic features that help to define them in physical terms. As one observer said, "Harris County doesn't have earthquakes ... doesn't have blizzards ... doesn't have avalanches. We have flooding." The unique physical characteristics of southeast Texas go hand in hand with the human modifications to the region that define its environmental history—its potential, its shortcomings, and its

evolution. Part of what makes Houston an energy-intensive metropolis existed before people put their stamp on this part of the world—forces that resist as well as accommodate urban development.

NOTES

1. William Cronon, *Nature's Metropolis: Chicago and the Great West* (New York: W. W. Norton, 1991); Kathleen Brosnan, *Uniting Mountain and Plain: Cities, Law, and Environmental Change along the Front Range* (Albuquerque: University of New Mexico Press, 2002).

2. There is as yet no comprehensive economic history of Houston. For a general political history, see David G. McComb, *Houston: The Bayou City* (Austin: University of Texas Press, 1969). See also Marilyn McAdams Sibley, *The Port of Houston: A History* (Austin: University of Texas Press, 1968); and Lynn M. Alperin, *Custodians of the Coast: History of the United States Army Engineers at Galveston* (Galveston, Tex.: U.S. Army Corps of Engineers, 1977).

3. A pioneering work of energy, growth, and environment in a region is James C. Williams, *Energy and the Making of Modern California* (Akron, Ohio: University of Akron Press, 1997). An excellent account of the early politics of oil-led development in California is Paul Sabin, *Crude Politics: The California Oil Market, 1900–1940* (Berkeley: University of California Press, 2004).

4. For a collection of essays about energy transitions, see Lewis J. Perelman, August W. Giebelhaus, and Michael D. Yokell, eds., *Energy Transitions: Long-Term Perspectives* (Boulder, Colo.: Westview Press, 1981). For an essay on Houston, see Joseph A. Pratt, "The Ascent of Oil: The Transition from Coal to Oil in Early Twentieth-Century America," in Perelman et al., *Energy Transitions*, 9–34.

5. Martin V. Melosi, "Community and the Growth of Houston," in *Effluent America: Cities, Industry, Energy, and the Environment*, ed. Martin V. Melosi (Pittsburgh: University of Pittsburgh Press, 2001), 194–95.

6. See Joe R. Feagin, *Free Enterprise City: Houston in Political and Economic Perspective* (New Brunswick, Conn.: Rutgers University Press, 1988).

7. On the national level, see Robert Engler, *The Politics of Oil, Private Power and Democratic Directions* (New York: Macmillan, 1961). For Houston, see Feagin, *Free Enterprise City*. For Texas, see George

Green, *The Establishment in Texas Politics: The Primitive Years, 1938–1957* (Westport, Conn.: Greenwood Press, 1979). For Houston, see also Joseph A. Pratt, "8F and Many More: Business and Civic Leadership in Modern Houston," *Houston Review of History and Culture* 2, no. 1 (2004): 2–7, 31–44.

8. Short discussions of many oil-producing regions are found in Augustine A. Ikein, *The Impact of Oil on a Developing Country: The Case of Nigeria* (New York: Praeger, 1990). See also Tony Hodges, *Angola: Anatomy of an Oil State* (Bloomington: Indiana University Press, 2001).

9. I would like to acknowledge the efforts of Steven MacDonald in identifying and collecting research material for this section of the book.

10. W. L. Fisher, J. H. McGowen, L. F. Brown Jr., and C. G. Groat, *Environmental Geologic Atlas of the Texas Coastal Zone— Galveston-Houston Area* (Austin: Bureau of Economic Geology, University of Texas at Austin, 1972), 1.

11. David G. McComb, *Galveston: A History* (Austin: University of Texas Press, 1986), 6, 7–8. See also Houston Geological Society, *Geology of Houston and Vicinity, Texas* (Houston: Houston Geological Society, 1961), 3, 7; Robert R. Lankford and John J. W. Roger, comps., *Holocene Geology of the Galveston Bay Area* (Houston: Geological Society, 1969), vii, 1; and Fisher et al., *Environmental Geologic Atlas*, 7.

12. Fisher et al., *Environmental Geologic Atlas*, 7; Jim Lester and Lisa Gonzalez, eds., *Ebb and Flow: Galveston Bay Characterization Highlights* (Galveston, Tex.: Galveston Bay Estuary Program; 2001), 12; Joseph L. Clark and Elton M. Scott, *The Texas Gulf Coast: Its History and Development*, Vol. 2 (New York: Lewis Historical, 1955), 14–16; Houston Geological Society, *Geology of Houston*, 3.

13. Fisher et al., *Environmental Geologic Atlas*, 7.

14. Ibid.; G. L. Fugate, "Development of Houston's Water Supply," *Journal of the American Water Works Association* 33 (October 1941): 1769–70.

15. Planning and Development Department, *Public Utilities Profile for Houston, Texas* (Summer 1994), III-15; Fugate, "Houston's Water Supply," 1769–70. The geologic formations from which Houston obtains groundwater supplies are upper Miocene, Pliocene, and Pleistocene in origin. See Nicholas A. Rose, "Ground Water and Relations of Geology to Its Occurrence in Houston District, Texas," *Bulletin of the American Association of Petroleum Geologists* 27 (August 1943): 1081.

16. See "Houston," in *Twentieth Century Cities*, part 4 of Association of American Geographers, *Contemporary Metropolitan America*, ed. John S. Adams (Cambridge, Mass.: Ballinger, 1976), 109, 121–24; Houston Chamber of Commerce, *Houston Facts '82* (Houston: Houston Chamber of Commerce, 1983).

17. U.S. Environmental Protection Agency (EPA), *Heat Island Effect: Houston's Urban Fabric*, www.epa.gov/heatisland/pilot/houst_urbanfabric.html; U.S. EPA, *Heat Island Effect: Houston*, www.epa.gov/heatisland/pilot/houston.html.

18. U.S. EPA, *Heat Island Effect: Houston*; World Travels, Houston Climate and Weather, www.wortltravels.com/Cities/Texas/Houston/Climate.

19. Fisher et al., *Environmental Geologic Atlas*, 1.

20. Ibid., 1, 7.

21. Espey, Huston & Associates, prep., *Archival Research: Houston-Galveston Navigation Channels, Texas Project—Galveston, Harris, Liberty and Chambers Counties, Texas*, April 1993, 8.

22. McComb, *Galveston*, 121–49.

23. David Roth, "Texas Hurricane History," National Weather Service, Lake Charles, La., 2004, www.srh.noaa.gov/lch/research/txhur.php.

24. Espey, Huston & Associates, *Archival Research*, 10.

25. Eugene Jaworski, "Geographic Analysis of Shoreline Recession, Coastal East Texas," College Station, Texas A&M University, Environmental Quality Note 3, June 1971, 1–13.

26. Fisher et al., *Environmental Geologic Atlas*, 15, 20; Robert R. Stickney, *Estuarine Ecology of the Southeastern United States and Gulf of Mexico* (College Station: Texas A&M University Press, 1984), 247–80.

27. Lester and Gonzalez, *Ebb and Flow*, 9–11.

ESSAY 6.4

The Emergence of Silicon Valley: High-Tech Development and Ecocide, 1950–2001

David Naguib Pellow and Lisa Sun-Hee Park

Source: David Naguib Pellow and Lisa Sun-Hee Park, *The Silicon Valley of Dreams: Environmental Justice, Immigrant Workers, and the High-Tech Global Economy* (New York: New York University Press, 2002).

EDITORS' INTRODUCTION

Silicon Valley is located in the southern portion of the San Francisco Bay Area and includes over a dozen cities and municipalities. The valley primarily sits within Santa Clara County and includes Palo Alto, the home of Stanford University, and San Jose. The term "Silicon Valley" emerged in the 1970s due to the large number of silicon chip and semiconductor industries in the Santa Clara Valley. Although the region remains key to America's digital and information age industry, the term itself has also become synonymous with the country's entire high-tech sector. Silicon Valley enjoys immense wealth and attracts people from all over the world seeking the chance to turn their ideas and innovations into fortunes.

The high-tech industry enjoys a global reputation as an advanced form of economic development free of the industrial pollution and human exploitation of the past. However, Silicon Valley also has an underside that, as sociologists David Naguib Pellow and Lisa Sun-Hee Park argue in *The Silicon Valley of Dreams*, contains social inequality and the exploitation of workers, human suffering from preventable illnesses and premature death, and widespread ecological devastation. The transformation of the Santa Clara Valley from an agricultural area to an electronics and military-related manufacturing hub began with the building of armaments factories and the opening of the first West Coast plant for International Business Machines Corporation (IBM) in San Jose during the Second World War. Between 1950 and 1974, approximately 800 electronics businesses relocated to or opened in Santa Clara County, attracting thousands of job seekers from diverse ethnic and racial backgrounds. The region's commercial boosters hailed these and other high technology manufacturing establishments as pleasant and pollution-free enterprises in comparison to noxious, smoke-billowing factories of the Midwest and East Coast. Pellow and Park shatter the illusion of "clean" high-tech industries while at the same time linking the toxic contamination of Silicon Valley with social inequality; a combination of which, they argue, produces environmental inequalities and environmental racism.[i]

David Naguib Pellow is the department chair of environmental studies and the director of the Global Environmental Justice Project at the University of California, Santa Barbara. His research interests include environmental justice, racial and ethnic inequality, immigration,

---

i David Naguib Pellow and Lisa Sun-Hee Park, *The Silicon Valley of Dream; Environmental Justice, Immigrant Workers, and the High-Tech Global Economy* (New York: New York University Press, 2002), xi, 2, and 62.

and labor studies. In addition to *The Silicon Valley of Dreams*, his other works include *Garbage Wars: The Struggle for Environmental Justice in Chicago* (Cambridge, MA: MIT Press, 2002), *Power, Justice, and the Environment: A Critical Appraisal of the Environmental Justice Movement* (Cambridge, MA: MIT Press, 2005) co-edited with Robert J. Brulle, and *Resisting Global Toxics: Transnational Movements for Environmental Justice* (Cambridge, MA: MIT Press, 2007), and, with Lisa Sun-Hee Park, *The Slums of Aspen: Immigrants vs the Environment in America's Eden* (New York: New York University Press, 2014), *Total Liberation: the Power and Promise of Animal Rights and the Radical Earth Movement* (Minneapolis: University of Minnesota Press, 2014) and *Keywords for Environmental Studies* (New York: New York University Press, 2016), co-edited with Joni Adamson and William A. Gleason.

Lisa Sun-Hee Park is a professor of sociology at the University of California, Santa Barbara. Her interests include environmental justice, immigration and welfare policy, and Asian-American studies. In addition to *The Slums of Aspen* with Pellow, she is the author of *Entitled to Nothing: The Struggle for Immigrant Health Care in the Age of Welfare Reform* (New York: New York University Press, 2011) and *Consuming Citizenship: Children of Asian Immigrant Entrepreneurs* (Palo Alto, CA: Stanford University Press, 2005), which won the 2006 Outstanding Book Award from the American Sociological Association, Asia and Asian America Section. Park edits the book series "Asian American Experience" for the University of Illinois Press and is a member of the *Social Problems* editorial board.

THE EMERGENCE OF SILICON VALLEY (2002)

Immigrants and People of Color Seek Opportunities in the Valley of Dreams

Long an elite and exclusive private institution, Stanford University had no less stringent expectations of the firms it was allowing to locate in its industrial park. The university sought to ensure that the companies and their personnel would "blend in" with the suburban environment. They sought

> "light industry of a non-nuisance type … which will create a demand for technical employees of a high salary class that will be in a financial position to live in this area." The well-paid, well-educated worker in the industrial park made a "very desirable kind of resident" for the community, according to the president of the Stanford Board of Trustees; employers should expect the suburban environs of the park to "attract a better class of workers."[1]

The terms "desirable" and "better class" are classic *code words* that denote Stanford's wish to attract white, middle-class workers and to repel undesirables, the multiracial blue-collar "riffraff" generally associated with manufacturing industries.[2] This was a textbook pitch reminiscent of the turn-of-the-century "city beautiful" efforts by Frederick Law Olmsted and others, who were openly classist and racist in their consultations with cities regarding what a desirable citizen population might be.[3] The *San Jose News* did its part to promote Santa Clara County's clean and lily-white image when it boasted that political and business leaders were able to attract entrepreneurs to the area who used "[i]mproved production techniques and new types of industries which eliminated or reduced industrial nuisances."[4] In 1968, while the Black Panther Party, the Brown Berets, La Raza Unida, and the San Francisco State University strike were in full force, the *San Jose News* proudly proclaimed that Santa Clara "is a white collar county … and 93.6 per cent of the county population [is] white."[5] Little did the Stanford University administrators, newspaper editors, and urban planners in the county realize that the region would soon be transformed into one of the most environmentally polluted and racially and ethnically diverse in the nation.

Chicanos

The 1960s and 1970s saw the emergence of public protests in San Jose's Chicano community when activists and residents put the spotlight on police brutality, economic discrimination, and the lack of services in their neighborhoods. Punctuating some of these concerns, one Chicano activist, Sal Alvarez, told an audience at a West Valley College symposium in 1969 that "Mexicans in San Jose got cheated out of land under urban renewal ... [and] the killing of Mexican Americans by police in California is a very serious problem and a worry in San Jose."[6] Community-based and national organizations like United People Arriba, the Council on Latin American Affairs, and La Raza Unida were active in San Jose and Santa Clara County. Apartment complexes, construction companies, schools, and police departments charged with discrimination against Chicanos were the primary targets of the protest movement.[7]

A 1973 Rand Corporation study reported that while much of San Jose was experiencing prosperity, "poor [largely Latino] neighborhoods [had] deteriorated relative to better-off neighborhoods and segregation had increased."[8] Housing quickly became a social and environmental justice issue as activists linked poor housing quality and poor health with racism. The fate that befell so many African American neighborhoods around the nation during the 1950s due to urban renewal efforts also came to pass in the barrio of Sal si Puedes in east San Jose.[9] Urban renewal was the federal effort to improve municipalities by razing degraded and blighted housing and by connecting cities and states through the interstate highway system. These changes devastated and destroyed many communities, earning urban renewal the nicknames "Negro removal" and "Mexican removal." For example, most of the houses of Sal si Puedes were razed as part of an urban renewal program that included the construction of a new freeway.[10] In the 1980s, other neighborhoods populated by people of color in San Jose would fall prey to urban renewal—ironically, for the construction of the Tech Museum, the city's monument to the electronics and computer industries, and its own physical proclamation of its status as the "Capitol of Silicon Valley."[11]

The Chicano community of Alviso, in North San Jose, was also the site of many conflicts over environmental and social justice concerns. In March 1973, activists set up a tollbooth on the Gold Street Bridge, charging twenty-five cents for cars to pass—a symbolic protest to call attention to the lack of paved streets in Alviso. The streets were not paved until 1980, twelve years after Alviso was annexed by San Jose.[12]

Asian/Pacific Islander Americans and Immigrants

According to the 1980 census, an estimated 11,700 Vietnamese immigrants were living in San Jose. By 1987 that number had jumped to around 75,000.[13] During the 1980s, there was a marked rise in white resentment and hate crimes directed at the Vietnamese population in particular, and at Asian/Pacific Islander Americans and immigrants in Silicon Valley in general.[14] During this period, many manufacturing workers were being laid off in the United States and there was increased tension over the heightened competition with Japan in the auto and electronics industries. Much of this tension was channeled into scapegoating any and all Asians, regardless of their specific ancestry.[15]

At the same time, some Asian immigrants were doing well in the high-technology sector, as white-collar workers. Chinese software engineers set up many businesses by networking with firms and entrepreneurs overseas and, by 1992, Asians made up a third of the engineering work-force in Silicon Valley.[16] Very few of these upwardly mobile Asian workers broke through the glass ceiling into the ranks of management. David Lam, founder of Lam Research, a company that makes equipment used in chip making, explained, "Many Asian engineers are not being looked at as having management talent. They are looked upon as good work horses, and not race horses."[17]

As financially stable as some Asians appeared to be, most were working-class and many of them experienced plenty of setbacks. In 1983, Atari Corporation, the video game maker, announced that it was closing its Silicon Valley plant and shifting production overseas to Hong Kong and Taiwan. Most of those production employees thrown out of work were Latino, Chinese, and Vietnamese. One of these workers was Hoa Ly. In 1978, Ly escaped Saigon in a fishing boat jammed with fifty-five other refugees. He spent half a year in a Malaysian refugee camp and later moved to Silicon Valley, where he got a job in printed circuit board assembly at Atari for which he was paid $7 per hour. Since his mother and father both worked by his side at Atari, when the company closed down his whole family was suddenly out of work. The Atari case was also quite significant because it was a high-profile example of the empty "no layoff pledge" many Silicon Valley companies made during the 1970s, when business and political leaders were claiming that this industry was immune to recession.[18]

Since the 1980s, the popular sentiment regarding immigrants took at least two, perhaps contradictory, directions. The first was a continuation of the traditional nativist approach to immigration, and this anti-immigrant movement gained sanction at the highest levels, as the efforts to pass Proposition 187 (denying undocumented residents access to public services) and the implementation of the Welfare and Immigration Reform Acts of 1996 moved forward. Television commercials depicted gangs of "illegals" crossing the Rio Grande under cover of night, and presidential hopeful Pat Buchanan warned of a "foreign invasion" from Mexico. In Silicon Valley, as elsewhere, this backlash took the form of Immigration and Naturalization Service (INS) raids of workplaces. In April 1984, when the INS opened a new office in Silicon Valley, they conducted raids on two electronics firms in San Jose and the city of Santa Clara on the same day. Using classic nativist rhetoric, Harold Ezell, the INS's Western regional commissioner, stated, "Probably 25 percent of the working population in this area is here illegally, particularly in the Silicon Valley area. We intend to make our presence known. Our officers will be *freeing up jobs for U.S. citizens* and people who are here legally."-[19] Neither the newspaper article nor the INS acknowledged that, without the abundance of undocumented immigrant labor, many Silicon Valley industries would relocate overseas or south of the U.S./Mexico border. The second direction in popular sentiment was the general consensus among labor, business, and politicians that the Immigration bill of 1990 and the H1-B visa expansion in 2000 (allowing white-collar high tech workers to immigrate to work at a particular firm for a limited period) were good for the U.S. economy, because of the alleged "shortage" of skilled workers.[20] The AFL-CIO called for an amnesty for the nation's estimated 5 million undocumented immigrants and Federal Reserve Board Chairman Alan Greenspan warned that, without a new wave of skilled immigrant workers, the integrity of the U.S. economy would be threatened.[21] Soon the national and California state legislation and policy making around these questions lumped documented and undocumented immigrants together for punitive measures. This indiscriminate grouping of these populations rendered the distinctions moot in many cases and revealed the deep similarities between the racist nature of immigration policy at the turn of the twentieth century and the twenty-first.[22] One of the major differences for Silicon Valley and the state of California, however, was that, for the first time since indigenous peoples occupied the land, people of color were now the majority. Of the 1.6 million people in Santa Clara County in the year 2000, 49 percent were white, 24 percent were Latino, 23 percent were Asian, and 4 percent were African American.[23] [...]

From "Clean Industry" to the Valley of Toxic Fright

The postindustrial, post-smokestack, campus-like suburban planning made it easy for developers and industry owners to claim that the electronics sector was "clean" and "pollution free." The clean image of the electronics industry was touted by executives, politicians, and newspapers everywhere. Harold Singer, an official of the San Francisco Bay Regional Water Quality Control Board, once stated, "the horizon above San Jose is unmarred by smokestacks, and people here are proud of that. They have worked hard at making the valley a base of the computer-electronics industry and an unpolluted place to live."[24]

As recently as the year 2000, the *Smithsonian Magazine* described the "clean rooms" where microchips are made as "the most fanatically clean, most thoroughly sanitized places on the planet," where "one could eat one's oatmeal off the floor."[25] The highly toxic wafers from which microchips are cut are viewed by industry promoters as "pristine,"[26] and the chemical-laden water that washes semiconductor components in the electronics "fab" plants is described as "pure."[27] Even former U.S. President Bill Clinton rubbed shoulders with CEOs in Silicon Valley in the 1990s, publicly proclaiming that the high-tech industry "will move America forward to a stronger economy, a cleaner environment and technological leadership."[28] These accounts leave the uninformed reader with the impression that high-tech firms are the paragon of hygiene and safety, sanitation and environmental responsibility.

The history behind this image—and more importantly, the need and desire to create this image—seems to be lost on most observers of Silicon Valley's environmental problems. In the 1940s, as large defense industries such as General Electric, IBM, and Westinghouse Electric were locating and/or expanding in the Valley, the agricultural interests were quite concerned about the environmental impacts of this new form of development. In 1950, the San Jose Chamber of Commerce wrote:

> there were some sincere and intelligent people who looked askance at this industrial development. They had genuine fears that smokestacks would "encircle the city"; that "blighted areas" would spring up in industrial sections; that orchards would be torn up "by the hundreds"; and that by past standards, this accelerated trend in the establishment of a new industry might result in an unbalanced,

top-heavy economy destined to collapse at some undetermined time in the future.[29]

The author of a study of the Bay Area conducted during the 1950s described the level of accuracy of these dire predictions:

> The fears that orchards would be torn up by the hundreds were indeed well founded; and smokestacks, though they by no means encircled the city, did undeniably contribute to the development of a new problem. The Chamber [of Commerce] sought to assure the skeptical that industrial growth was not incompatible with desirable living conditions. Yet it was not long before the Santa Clara County Board of Supervisors found it necessary to designate the entire county an air pollution control district; the skies over the Santa Clara Valley were becoming a dirty gray. In March, 1950, the county health officer, declared that "smog," the murky atmospheric condition familiar to Los Angeles, was not only a Santa Clara County problem but also a "Bay Area problem." The new factories in San Jose and Santa Clara were producing air pollutants.[30]

Thus the very beginnings of the electronics and defense industries were marred by environmental problems, the greatest irony of all being that they involved "smokestacks." So it seems that in the 1950s and 1960s, when Palo Alto and other cities in the Valley demanded that new industries be smokestack-less, these concerns were rooted in the real experience of having observed this sector befoul the local environment. Whether or not the municipalities were aware of it, these expectations and claims of nonpollution were either naïve promises or lies, while the production processes internal to these corporations actually became even more toxic than before. This heavily polluted past also challenges earlier claims by Silicon Valley boosters that the region was "pollution free" prior to the electronics boom of the 1960s.[31]

The End of Innocence

In the 1960s and 1970s, a sort of amnesia fell over the Valley's residents and policy makers; they all seemed to arrive at a consensus that the new industry was somehow pristine. This image was shattered in December 1981, when it was discovered that the drinking water well that supplied 16,500 homes in the Los Paseos neighborhood of South San Jose was contaminated with the deadly chemical trichloroethane (TCA), a solvent used to remove grease from microchips and printed circuit boards after they are manufactured. Officials estimated that 14,000 gallons of TCA and another 44,000 gallons of various toxic waste materials had been leaking from an underground storage tank for at least a year and a half.[32] The responsible party was the Fairchild Semiconductor corporation.

Lorraine Ross, a resident of the neighborhood (and a mother), was catapulted into the role of environmental activist. She and her neighbors mapped out a disturbing and pervasive cluster of cancers, miscarriages, birth defects, infant heart problems, and fatalities in the neighborhood that public health authorities and the industry were forced to take seriously. Two health studies were carried out immediately, both of which confirmed the presence of higher than expected frequencies of congenital birth defects (three times the normal rate), spontaneous abortions, and heart defects. However, neither study would take the bold step of pin-pointing industrial chemicals as the cause.[33] One reason for the delayed discovery of the presence of chemicals was that at the time, state and federal regulations did not require testing for industrial chemicals. Tests were only required for viruses, bacteria, pesticides, and herbicides.[34] A painful irony here is that TCA was commonly used as a substitute cleaner for TCE (trichloroethylene). TCE is a suspected carcinogen that was nearly phased out of the industry in the late 1970s—the result of the Campaign to Ban TCE, led by occupational health advocates in San Jose.[35] This community organizing success was reversed when the industry phased out the targeted chemical and substituted a comparably hazardous one.

Back in the Los Paseos community of San Jose, Lorraine Ross was organizing against Fairchild, berating the city council that year with the question, "Fairchild or my child?": "It takes a lot of nerve for them to invade a pre-existing residential neighborhood, pour dangerous chemicals into a leaking tank, poison the surrounding environment and hide the fact from the people affected by their negligence."[36]

Ross was not alone. She was a leader of a burgeoning antitoxics/environmental justice and occupational health movement taking shape in Silicon Valley. Organizations like the Santa Clara Center for Occupational Safety and Health (SCCOSH) had prior to the contamination of Los Paseos been involved in leading community workshops on chemical solvents such as those spilled at Fairchild.[37] The Silicon Valley Toxics Coalition (SVTC), an environmental justice group that had formed in response to the Fairchild spill, was also at the forefront of the campaign to bring that company to justice. In 1983, Fairchild closed down its plant in South San Jose, a victory for Ross and the environmental justice movement. Since then, the company has spent more than $40 million on the cleanup. Similar chemical accidents and resulting toxic illness and death tolls have occurred in the communities near the IBM and Teledyne Semiconductor plants; the IBM spill is one of the largest in the county, having leaked toxics since 1956.[38] IBM had to install a more extensive chemical detection system for ground water monitoring as a result of efforts by the Silicon Valley Toxics Coalition, Communities for a Better Environment (a San Francisco–based group), the Santa Clara Valley Water District, and the County Board of Supervisors.[39] This result actually set two new precedents. The first was that the so-called "clean industry" could no longer be viewed as pristine. The second was that this industry was not trustworthy and that only the presence of a strong local environmental justice movement could ensure that necessary reforms would materialize.

Challenges to the "clean industry" image in the Valley abound. The USEPA has estimated that a large area of land, contaminated by eleven electronics plants in the Mountain View area alone (a community with a large population of immigrants, people of color, and working-class persons) will take $60 million and 300 years to clean up. [...] that site is located at Moffett Field, the old Naval base that sat on the land owned by one of the few remaining Ohlones in the area, Lope Inigo. As for the once pure water and fertile land of the Valley, 57 private and 47 public drinking wells were contaminated as of 1992, and 66 plots of land have been declared too toxic for human beings to walk on.[40]

Soon after the Fairchild spill made news headlines, various arms of the federal government also took on the charge of addressing this problem. In 1985, the Congressional Committee on Public Works and Transportation held a hearing on toxic concerns in the electronics industry in San Jose.[41] The USEPA also undertook its own study of the human health risks associated with industrial pollution in Santa Clara County. The agency released a preliminary draft of this "Integrated Environmental Management Project" in 1985, which concluded that pollution-related health risks in the area were "comparatively low."[42] Clearly elated, a spokesman for the Semiconductor Industry Association (SIA) informed the media that, based on the EPA's findings, industrial chemicals in Silicon Valley "do not pose a significant threat to human life."[43] Environmentalists and journalists immediately became suspicious and discovered that a scandal was afoot. According to one report, long before the study was released, the SIA had hired a high-ranking official of the Republican Party who lobbied the EPA into lowering risk estimates and excluding tests from the study that would indicate whether solvents caused chronic diseases, birth defects, and miscarriages.[44] This effort seems to have paid off, as it appears to have shaped the "findings" in the EPA's study. But it was a major source of embarrassment for the EPA when high-profile environmental groups and political leaders denounced the report as flawed and biased in favor of industry. The true significance of this event was that environmentalists learned that they had to remain vigilant and be wary of "scientific studies," because the USEPA and any other agency could be bought and paid for by industry to silence or "disprove" dissenting perspectives concerning the true costs of the Silicon Valley "miracle."

After testing other companies for toxins, county authorities found that sixty-five of seventy-nine (or 82 percent) had hazardous chemicals in the ground beneath their plants. Some of these included IBM, Intel, Hewlett-Packard, DEC, Tandem, Raytheon, NEC, AMD, Signetics, TRW, and many others. Today Santa Clara County is home to twenty-nine Superfund sites, more than any other county in the nation, and twenty-four of those sites are the result of pollution by electronics firms.

The earlier claims that computer/electronics was a "clean industry" rang painfully hollow, because, as the Silicon Valley Toxics Coalition's Ted Smith put it, this industry had "buried its smokestacks underground."[45] Other leaders stated similar concerns:

> Voicing the shock shared by cities that had assumed the electronics industry was nonpolluting, San Jose's mayor, Janet Gray Hayes, said, "I remember thinking about smokestacks in other industries. I didn't expect this problem in my own backyard."[46] She continued, "When I first became Mayor and we embarked on an economic development program, there was no doubt in my mind that this was a clean industry. We now know that we are definitely in the midst of a chemical revolution."[47] [...]

Environmental Inequalities

When the nature and extent of high tech's toxicity became public knowledge, a decline in the location of such industries in white communities was complemented by a shift to lower-income communities and communities of color.[48] For example, after the discovery of toxic waste in the water tables in Palo Alto, residents organized and supported new regulations so strict that some companies moved out or decided against locating there, and shifted their toxic production to less restrictive communities (with higher percentages of working-class people and persons of color) such as Mountain View.[49] Similarly, during the early 1980s in Sonoma County (north of San Francisco), citizens opposed *all* high-tech development because of the newly discovered associated pollution threats. And in 1984, a Fremont-based group, Sensible Citizens Reacting Against Hazardous Materials (SCRAM), organized to block CTS Printex's attempts to locate a plant in that town.[50] This dynamic was a stark departure from the fights and bidding wars among municipalities in their efforts to attract the "clean industry" in previous decades. But this is also a pattern we see in myriad other "environmental protection" practices that impact communities of color across the United States and around the world. In other words, immigrants and people of color bear the cost of both environmental destruction (when industry extracts or pollutes natural resources) *and* environmental protection (when white, affluent communities discover that an industry is toxic and protect themselves by shifting the burden onto lower-income neighborhoods and communities of color).[51]

However, some polluting businesses that originally located in marginal neighborhoods were forced to reform because communities of color were also organizing. For example, Lorenz Barrel and Drum was located in a working-class and Latino neighbohood in south San Jose. For forty years this company treated the electronics industry's hazardous waste. The site was located a half block away from Mi Tierra, one of San Jose's first community gardens. A local neighborhood group, Students and Community Against Lorenz Pollution (SCALP), formed and pressured authorities to take action.[52] In 1986, federal authorities shut the company down, citing criminal violations. The soil and ground water on site were found to be contaminated with at least fourteen toxic chemical compounds.[53] The site was "remediated" for a $5.2 million price tag, but was covered with an asphalt cap—the "cleanup" method of choice in low-income communities and communities of color—rather than subjected to a true abatement and restoration operation as preferred under law.[54] Even so, more than 25,000 drums containing hazardous waste and 3,000 cubic yards of contaminated soil were removed. A year later, the company's owner was sentenced to two years in jail, assessed fines of $2.04 million, and ordered to spend up to $100,000 on health monitoring for current and former neighbors and employees. So while environmental racism placed these residents and workers at risk, they were able to achieve some modicum of justice through collective action.

While residents and the general public may not have been knowledgeable concerning the hazards associated with electronics production before the 1980s, ample evidence suggests that the industry was aware of the facts early on. Years later, in 1976 (five years before the Fairchild spill was made public), a study submitted to the Santa Clara County Board of Supervisors disclosed that tons of "poisonous and explosive chemicals" were being illegally dumped in communities and into the sewer system throughout the region. These hazardous materials were from electronics firms and many of these dumps were located in communities of color and low-income neighborhoods inside the county and beyond.[55] So communities of color were being polluted well before the public outrage against the electronics industry made headlines in the early 1980s, and the industry was well aware of it.

After communities began demanding that toxic sites be placed on the EPA's Superfund list, evidence of another pattern of environmental inequality emerged. Many of these federally designated toxic Superfund sites are in communities of color and working-class neighborhoods. [. . .]

Whether from depletion or pollution, Santa Clara County industries seem always to have been intent on maintaining a dependence upon—and a lack of respect for—water, land, immigrants, and people of color. Environmental racism in the Valley meant not only that people of color were being exposed to toxics and pollutants at home and work, but also that this process was part and parcel of a broader context of general ecological degradation in the region. European contact, the missions, mining, farming and canning, and computer/electronics production each brought the promise of economic prosperity and new social liberties springing forth from the bountiful wealth of natural resources that only California could offer. But in each case, economic gains were concentrated among a few while poverty and immiseration were shared among the many; racial and ethnic cleavages reemerged and deepened; and the integrity of the natural environment suffered as yet untold assaults. Nothing is new about the latest proclamation of salvation in Silicon Valley; it is old wine in new bottles and represents only the most recent manifestation of a long history of environmental injustice, California style.

NOTES

1. Findlay 1992, 132; David Packard, President of Stanford University Board of Trustees, quoted in *Daily Palo Alto Times,* February 17, 1960.
2. See Omi and Winant (1994) for an insightful discussion of the range of racial "code words" used as proxies for more direct words like "race" or "African Americans," "Asian Americans," etc.
3. Delgado and Stefancic 1999.
4. Choate 1968a.
5. Choate 1968c.
6. Fraser 1969.
7. Hanson 1969; Larimore 1969; Flood 1968.
8. Heritage Media Corporation 1996, 215.
9. The barrio of Sal si Puedes was home to many Chicanos. The name translates to "get out if you can" and the neighborhood earned this label because of the many mud holes in its streets before they were paved and because of the preponderance of substandard housing and poverty (see Clark 1970, 35).
10. Findlay 1992, 39; Clark 1970, vii.
11. Heritage Media Corporation 1996, 229. Recent research has also begun to make links among race, environmental quality, and transportation systems. Robert Bullard and his collaborators have traced the history of America's two-tiered, racially biased transportation system, from early conflicts over "separate but equal" accommodations, through "urban renewal," to today's urban sprawl that amplifies the problems of pollution and ecological damage (see Bullard and Johnson 1997; Bullard, Johnson, and Torres 2000).
12. Alviso 2001.
13. Rios 1987.
14. Dickey 1984.
15. This tension led to the Pentagon blocking Fujitsu Ltd., a Japanese corporation, from purchasing Fairchild Semiconductor Corporation in 1987, because of the alleged "national security risk" involved (see Sanger 1987). A senior White House staff member told a reporter, "This is a test case. If Japan can come in and buy this company, it can come in and buy them all over the place. We don't want to see the semiconductor industry under Japanese control" (Kilborn 1987). Popular bumper stickers in Santa Clara County, Detroit, and other areas where competition was fiercest included those reading: "Toyota, Datsun, Honda and Pearl Harbor" or "Hungry and Out of Work? Eat a Foreign Car." Never mind the fact that Fairchild Semiconductor Corporation was already controlled by the Schlumberger company, which was itself run by a French family; or that Intel Corporation was run by Andrew Gove, a Hungarian immigrant. One writer spoke of the "Japanese domination" of the 64K random access memory (RAM) chip in the 1980s as "the technological equivalent of Pearl Harbor" (Johnston 1982).
16. Pollack 1992.
17. Ibid.
18. IBM had a fifty-year-old tradition of no layoffs before it began letting employees go (via early retirements and buyouts) in the 1980s. When, in 1993, IBM announced that it would lay off employees for the first time in its history, they planned to cut up to seven thousand jobs, ending the fifty-year legacy of "full employment" adopted by IBM founder Tom Watson Sr. One computer peripheral manufacturer boasted in a classified ad for new workers about its "Recession Proof Strategy" (see *San Jose Mercury News,* February 1, 1982, 8CL). For more on layoffs, see "Electronics Job Losses Total 55,000 so far in '92," *San Jose Mercury News,* August 26, 1992; also see "IBM Ends No-Layoff Policy," *San Jose Mercury News Wire Services,* February 16, 1993.
19. Goldston 1984.
20. Marshall 1990.
21. Freedberg 2000.
22. See Park and Yoo 2001.
23. Goodell 2000.
24. Cummings 1982.
25. Page 2000, 40.
26. Ibid., 40.
27. Ibid., 43.
28. Kadetsky 1993, 519.
29. Industrial Survey Associates 1950, 4.
30. Scott 1959, 273.
31. Mandich (1975, 41) references these early boosters' claims of a pristine Valley during the 1950s and 1960s.
32. Siegel 1984, 58–59.
33. At that time, no toxicological study had proven a link between pollution and

miscarriages or birth defects. One reason for this alleged lack of proof was the corruption and corporate bias endemic in the private laboratories and federal agencies conducting these tests (see Environmental Health Coalition 1992; Klinger 1982). For example, in one suspicious incident, of the 150 potentially toxic water samples the California Department of Health Services collected during the summer of 1980, the only one lost or destroyed was the sample from the water well Fairchild contaminated (Harris 1982). Perhaps CDHS officials were afraid of what they might find, particularly given the release of a report that very same summer revealing that the county cancer death rate had jumped 20 percent during the 1970s (see Klinger 1980). A more recent example of related corruption in environmental health testing was the indictment of employees of the Intertek Corporation for altering or falsifying some 250,000 environmental tests in 1996 and 1997. In many cases, false clean bills of health were issued for sites known to have significant environmental contamination, like the Rocky Mountain Arsenal in Denver, Colorado, and the Oakland Army Base in California (Ayres 2001).

34. Timberlake 1987, 142. Lorraine Ross and other activists in the Los Paseos neighborhood also discovered that toxicological knowledge about solvents was in its infancy during the mid-1970s, when the underground chemical storage tanks were built for Fairchild just two thousand feet from a public well (Yoachum 1982).

35. The group PHASE (Project on Health and Safety in Electronics) was at the forefront of this campaign. PHASE later changed its name to the Santa Clara Center for Occupational Safety and Health (SCCOSH), a group that continues to work closely with the Silicon Valley Toxics Coalition.

36. Timberlake 1987, 141.
37. SCCOSH 1982.
38. Champion 1988.
39. Benson 1986a.
40. Thurm 1992. Even more threatening than the contamination of the many smaller drinking wells was the pollution of the Anderson Reservoir—the county's prime drinking water source—by rocket fuel manufacturer United Technologies Corporation. In 1989, UTC spilled an estimated 10,000 gallons of groundwater contaminated with TCE into a creek that feeds into the reservoir (Calvert 1989).
41. *Hazardous Waste Contamination of Water Resources* 1985.
42. Kutzmann 1985.
43. Ibid.
44. Steinhart 1985.
45. Smith and Woodward 1992.
46. Johnston 1982, p. 470.
47. Cummings 1982.
48. Szasz and Meuser 2000.
49. *San Jose Mercury News*, April 28, 1988. Mountain View has one of the lowest median family incomes and highest percentages of people of color of any city in Santa Clara County (U.S. Bureau of the Census 1990).
50. Siegel 1984, 64.
51. With regard to solid waste, the white, affluent city of Palo Alto rejected all landfill proposals in 1976, thus shifting the burden of disposing of its own municipal solid waste to other communities.
52. Douglas 1987.
53. U.S. Department of Health and Human Services 1989a.
54. Lavelle and Coyle 1992.
55. Keller 1976. Two legally sanctioned dumps were located in the heavily African American, Latino, and Asian immigrant communities of Richmond and Martinez, north of Santa Clara County.

ESSAY 6.5

The Valley of the Sun

Andrew Needham

Source: Andrew Needham, *Power Lines: Phoenix and the Making of the Modern Southwest* (Princeton: Princeton University Press, 2014).

EDITORS' INTRODUCTION

Phoenix, Arizona is the fifth largest city in the United States behind New York City, Los Angles, Chicago, and Houston. Located in the northeastern corner of the Sonoran Desert, Phoenix was founded in 1867 by Anglo migrants who settled upon the same lands that centuries earlier the Hohokam peoples occupied and constructed a series of irrigation canals upon. **[See Essay 2.1, Lisa Krissoff Boehm and Steven H. Corey, "Pre-Colonial and Seventeenth-Century Native American Settlements."]** By 1930, Phoenix was a small city of a little more than ten square miles with under just under 50,000 inhabitants. However, as historian Andrew Needham explores in the following essay from his award winning book *Power Lines: Phoenix and the Making of the Modern Southwest*, over the next thirty years Phoenix went from being an irrigated oasis to a Southwestern metropolis as its population grew by 900 percent to 439,170 people living on 290 square miles.

What accounted for the dramatic rise of this major metropolitan area in a desert climate? As Needham notes, Phoenix's postwar growth was both typical of many other American cities, and also a product of its unique physical environment and a social construct known as "The Valley of the Sun." Indeed, two powerful forces converged in the post-WWII era to transform Phoenix from being simply a city located at the center of the Salt River Valley, to a destination for those seeking "quality of life" with warm weather, open space, affordable housing, and individual opportunity. The creation of "The Valley of the Sun" was a political project born of New Deal and post-war government policies combined with efforts by local business and civic leaders to carefully craft an alternative urban lifestyle to traditional American cities in East and Midwest. The result, though, was a landscape of spatial inequality familiar to much of metropolitan America, wherein whites lived separate from blacks and Mexican Americans. **[See in particular Essay 8.4, Robert Self, "White Noose (2003)."]** Throughout the rest of *Power Lines*, Needham recounts the ecological transformation of the Colorado Plateau, in which the linkages between the physical environment, urbanization, and indigenous peoples became obscured, by examining the role of electrical power lines that ran between Phoenix and Navajo lands.

Andrew Needham is Associate Professor and Director of Graduate Studies in the Department of History at New York University. Dr. Needham specializes in recent U.S. history, with an emphasis in American Indian, environmental, urban, and suburban history, and history of the American West. His work *Power Lines* received the 2016 George Perkins Marsh Prize from the American Society for Environmental History, the 2015 Caughey Western History Prize, the Hal K. Rothman Prize, and the David J. Weber-Clements Prize, all from the Western History Association, and the 2015 Southwest Book Award from the Border Regional Library Association. His article, "Beyond the Metropolis: Metropolitan Growth and Regional Transformation in Postwar America," with Allen Dieterich-Ward from the *Journal of Urban History* (2009), won the Urban History Association Award for best article of 2009.

THE VALLEY OF THE SUN (2014)

Between 1940 and 1960, Phoenix changed from an irrigated oasis to a Southwestern metropolis. Hundreds of thousands of Americans moved to Phoenix, including almost 200,000 between 1955 and 1960 alone. The majority came from the East and Midwest, from the industrial cities and small towns of a region not yet known as the Rustbelt.[1] In twenty years, the city's population grew from 65,000 to 440,000. And the lands north of the Grand Canal changed from the agricultural heart-land of the Salt River Valley into a landscape of residential subdivisions containing 62,000 homes—58,000 more than in 1940. The names the city's boosters used to talk about Phoenix symbolized that transition. In the early twentieth century, visitors learned that Phoenix was located at the center of the Salt River Valley. By the postwar years, they found themselves in the Valley of the Sun.

Early in this era of mass migration, Raymond Carlson, editor of *Arizona Highways*, tried to explain its underlying dynamics. "Lots of folks, apparently, ... have decided that living in the sun is a lot more fun than living in places where the climate and other living conditions are less conducive to a full and happy life."[2] Carlson's magazine displayed the various aspects of this "full and happy life" in vivid color photographs and often purple prose. In Phoenix, new residents would find a modern city with all the comforts of contemporary life. Phoenix home buyers shopped in a market providing "more house per dollar ... than in any other section of the country."[3] Within the city, residents could enjoy golf, tennis, even horseback riding in the many parks. If Phoenix's leisured life became overbearing, undeveloped landscapes nearby allowed people to "sit quietly under a mesquite tree and watch the clouds cavort, or hum a tune or ponder the sweet and bitter mysteries of life or puzzle out the ways of mountains and mice and of meek and mighty men."[4] If residents had particularly "jangled nerves," the spectacular landscape of the Colorado Plateau, "where our scattered Indian tribes

live complacently, completely undisturbed by the frenzied civilization about them," was only a short drive away.[5] The Valley of the Sun, in short, was a place that presented its residents with a lifestyle that balanced suburban living, stripped of the long commutes, cold winters, and other problems that plagued Eastern cities, with easy escape to the Grand Canyon, "Navajoland," or numerous other natural spaces.

"The Valley of the Sun" was not only an idealized place. It was also a political project, the result of two of the most powerful forces in the postwar American political economy. The first was the ongoing legacy of New Deal policies that sought to fuel the national economy through debt-driven personal consumption. Part of the general postwar economic philosophy historians have labeled "growth liberalism," policies such as the National Housing Act, the Banking Act of 1935, and the G.I. Bill, offered federal loan guarantees to a select population of white Americans choosing suburban living. Manifesting the same metropolitan preferences that underlay the distribution of Boulder Dam's power, the authors of these policies viewed residents of the metropolitan periphery as the vital agents of postwar growth and offered credit at terms advantageous for both borrowers and lenders. The resulting "landscape of mass consumption," to use Lizabeth Cohen's term, was plainly evident in Phoenix, both in the huge numbers of homes built after World War II and in the increasing numbers of electrical appliances that filled them.

Local efforts to attract these consumers, and the potential capital they embodied, was the second force that created the Valley of the Sun. Migrants to Phoenix in the 1940 and 1950s were not fleeing the Rustbelt. Rather, they were enticed to Phoenix by a series of appeals related to the quality of life and cost of living available there. State officials and local businessmen alike presented Phoenix as different from other cities as a means to attract capital. [...] Much of this capital took the form of high-tech manufacturers and other elements of the Cold War military-industrial complex, which Phoenix's officials wooed with a range of political guarantees and economic enticements. In the economy of postwar America, however, white, middle-class Americans to whom the federal government guaranteed credit were also a form of capital. By attracting such people to their city, Phoenix's bankers, retailers, home builders, electric utility officials and other businessmen profited dually, first as their businesses became the conduits through which the federally guaranteed credit of growth liberalism flowed into the local economy and then as consumers gradually paid off their locally incurred debts. Their concentration in space represented a pool of capital that, by their presence, created more capital.

Place mattered as well in this political economy. Representations of Phoenix as a locus of clear skies, warm weather, open space, cheap homes, and individual opportunity attracted new residents seeking "quality of life." There were also material and political consequences, created by expectations about "quality of life" that disciplined local officials to maintain the opportunities for lifestyles that were particularly desirable, included among them residential segregation and the environmental amenities of clear skies, open space, and recreation that Phoenix's boosters emphasized. The result, by the 1960s, would be a very particular form of spatial inequality. By then, the center of Phoenix's landscape of mass consumption would exist in residential neighborhoods that were almost entirely white, isolated from the neighborhoods of black and Mexican American Phoenicians, and powered by distant power plants on Indian land. In the 1930s and 1940s, this spatial arrangement had not yet come to be. Instead, Phoenix remained a small city, reliant on commodity agriculture and marginalized within the new regional space created by Boulder Dam. The efforts that recast the Salt River Valley as the Valley of the Sun were local political efforts by a class of businessmen attempting to change these economic conditions and regional dynamics. To understand them, we need to start not at the metropolitan periphery, but downtown.[6] [...]

"The Valley of the Sun" represented more than a name change. It reflected a new vision of Phoenix as a place whose reputation for leisure would draw residents. Initially, Phoenix's businessmen targeted wealthy Americans who retained disposable income for travel and recreation in the midst of the Depression. The Phoenix-Arizona Club's 1938 publication *Life in the Valley of the Sun* featured photos of well-manicured resorts and the luxurious homes of winter residents such as Philip Wrigley and Henry Luce. As Snell recalled, "They were seeking people who could afford to come here and were not looking for jobs." The hope was, Snell explained, that resort visits by wealthy Americans would lead such visitors to establish "winter residence, then build businesses here."[7]

Following World War II, the Phoenix Chamber of Commerce spread the appeal of the Valley of the Sun more broadly. Beginning in 1949, the Chamber initiated both a national advertising campaign, underwritten by financing from the city's general fund, proclaiming that "It's Fun in the Valley of the Sun." It also began a long-running program in which the Chamber invited writers from "trade journals, national magazines, syndicated writers, and leading newspaper editors" to visit Phoenix on five- to six-day junkets, usually between December and April.[8] In 1960 the Chamber sent such invitations to *Life, Newsweek, U.S. News & World Report*, the *Saturday Evening Post, Time, Ladies' Home Journal, Better Homes and Gardens, Good Housekeeping, Saturday Review*, and seventy-nine additional newspapers.[9] The results could be seen in articles titled, "Fun in Sun City," "It's Fun to Live in Phoenix," "Big Boom in the Desert," and "What It's Like to Live in Arizona."[10] Articles in national magazines followed similar narrative patterns. Almost all commented on the bountiful recreational possibilities of the "Sunniest City in the U.S.A.," according to *Holiday magazine*. *Good Housekeeping* wrote that Phoenix was "perfect for whatever outdoor activity a family wants." Magazines targeted at men almost universally emphasized the possibility of "Golf! Year-Round!" as

Esquire excitedly announced. A separate *Holiday* article detailed the natural recreation located in close proximity to downtown: "City dwellers can escape to desert and mountain picnic areas of untouched natural beauty, 10 minutes from Phoenix. Rugged South Mountain Park is the nation's largest city park, and Papago one of the most picturesque."[11]

Climate did not only shape recreational possibilities in these profiles. It also shaped domestic life. Phoenix boosters coined a phrase, "outdoor living," to describe the ways in which Arizona's climate allowed a different everyday experience from that of the East Coast. "Back there [in Boston] a house was important because we had to stay inside so much. We resent it here when we have to stay inside," one transplant explained in *Better Homes and Gardens*. "We spend our money for more pleasurable things. We have a swimming pool, and our recreation is simpler, more oriented to the outdoors, and less expensive. We don't have to buy snow suits or pay those heating bills."[12] Other articles pointed to designs that made outdoor areas a virtual extension of the home. *Life* portrayed a family eating dinner on a terrace "built around a spiky yucca tree with a view extending past [a] 600-year-old giant cactus to Camelback Mountain," while *Architectural Record* examined the ways in which a home nearby had "three separate outdoor living areas," one for dining, a second for "enjoyment of the cool summer breezes," as well as a children's play area.[13] Finally, articles in women's magazines suggested that "outdoor living" was particularly beneficial to their audiences. Regular articles in *Redbook* and *Good Housekeeping* touted the fashions being worn in Arizona during the winter: "trim little jackets ... designed for the outdoor life in patio and at poolside," "a short cotton cocktail outfit laden with gold rickrack," "backs are out—in the open, beautifully bared by shadow brown maillot that merely loops the shoulder."[14] Not only did the climate allow women to wear lighter, more flattering clothes throughout the years, "outdoor living" was presumed to encourage women to stay active and thin.

One article in *Vogue* went so far as to say, "I never saw a fat person, except tourists, while I was there."[15]

The similar themes contained in the articles suggested the success of the Chamber's junkets in conveying the central message of the Valley of the Sun campaign. In the pages of national magazines, Phoenix came across as a place with a remarkable possibility not only for outdoor living, but self-invention through individual lifestyle choices. As the subject of "What It's Like to Live in Phoenix" told the readers of *Better Homes and Gardens*, "Back in the East, everything is defined for you. Here the whole place is growing, expanding, and there's no limit. ... If I do something, it's my triumph. If I fail, it's my failure. I'm a lot more of an *individual* in Arizona."[16]

No magazine exported the message of Phoenix's businessmen more consistently, however, than *Arizona Highways*. Founded in 1921, the magazine spent its first two decades instructing readers on the finer points of Arizona's development, including "must see" sites including the vast open-pit copper mines near Bisbee and the newly paved highway linking Prescott and Phoenix. The latter site reflected the magazine's dual emphasis on Arizona's development and the promotion of paved roads, best seen in its early motto, "Civilization Follows the Improved Highway." In 1937, however, *Arizona Highways'* focus began to change. That year, the state hired Raymond Carlson, a recent graduate of Stanford, to be the magazine's first non-engineer editor. Carlson quickly changed the magazine from a staid black-and-white journal whose articles featured passages such as "From the dim dawn of history on the great Babylonian plains...each age has embalmed its ideals, ambitions, its very spirit, in its bridges," to a lush photo journal in the style of *Life*, filled with two-page color spreads of cactus flowers, canyon sunsets, and Navajo and Hopi dancers, and featuring a new motto, "House Organ of Heaven." The magazine's circulation also increased dramatically, from fewer than 8,000 in the early 1930s to 250,000 in 1951, with more than 150,000 of those subscribers being "vicarious Arizonans" who lived out of state.[17]

Carlson quickly fell in with Phoenix's downtown businessmen, likely due to the downtown location of the magazine's office. Carlson lunched daily at the Arizona Club and bonded with Barry Goldwater in particular over their interests in photography and recounting Arizona's history. And by the middle of World War II, the promotional rhetoric of the Valley of the Sun had assumed a central place in the magazine. "You may think of January as a cold, dismal, gloomy month," a 1943 article titled "The Sun Is Our Fortune," explained, "but Phoenix will enjoy two hundred and thirty-nine hours of the sun's friendly presence." Another article told servicemen overseas, "You enjoy the pictures of fun in the Sun Country with this invitation in mind, 'This can be you when the war is won.'" Such rhetoric filled the magazine in the following decades in articles such as "Phoenix: City in the Sun," "You'll Like Living in Phoenix," "Phoenix, City on Wings" and "Dream Homes by the Dozens."[18] Carlson's interactions with Phoenix's businessmen extended to other areas as well. Goldwater, who had traveled since his childhood throughout northern Arizona, flew Carlson in his Cessna to various natural settings that could be featured in the magazine. Carlson reciprocated by publishing Goldwater's photography of northern Arizona and its Indian people. Moreover, he adopted Goldwater's sense that, in Peter Iverson's words, "The 'real' Arizona could not be found among the tall buildings lining Central Avenue in Phoenix" as the central visual message of the magazine. Between 1946 and 1955, photographs of the natural landscapes of northern Arizona and its Indian people and their material culture made up 85 percent of the magazine's covers. As Iverson writes, "Again and again, the magazine and thus its readers returned to the Arizona north of old Route 66 and the Santa Fe Railroad and from the Grand Canyon eastward to the New Mexico line."[19]

Arizona Highways represented those landscapes as providing perspective on the modern world. "There's room enough to get off by yourself," Carlson wrote of the canyons of the Little Colorado River. "And you and your little affairs become very little indeed when placed in such spacious and majestic surroundings." In portraying the yawning, empty canyons of the Little Colorado as, in the article's title, a "Happy Land," Carlson flipped the nineteenth-century notion of the sublime on its head. Rather than an awe-inspiring confrontation with nature's immense scale and elemental power, a hiking excursion on the Little Colorado would quiet dissonance caused by modern life. Rather than revelation, the goal was rehabilitation. Arizona's nature provided inner peace that could remain with individuals and fortify them upon their return to the duties of modern life. As Joyce Muench suggested in "Pilgrimage into Spring," "When the work at your desk...grows dull, you have only to listen to the call of Arizona's awakening. Close your eyes and see the breezes tousling the heads of flowers on the Desert.... Then open them again and start off on your work."[20]

Arizona's native peoples served a similar purpose of reminding modern Americans of a simpler life. A 1953 article about the Navajo, "Colorful People," explained that "Many of them have never seen a train or a plane, have never basked in the glow of Neon lights, have never been carried away by the high emotions inspired by the stridence of a juke box.... They manage to entertain themselves without movies, radio, or television." Without the constant distractions that characterized modernity, the article suggested, Navajos were free from anxieties that could even drive many people to illness. "They manage to be happy in their own little worlds, they find the ways of their fathers sufficient for full and complete lives, they accept their lot with a philosophical calm. They live a life of slower tempo, less hectic than ours, much freer from nervous tensions and ulcers."[21] Again and again, the magazine returned to such portraits of Navajos, and other Indians, living not only spatially, but temporally distant from the ills that plagued modern Americans. Navajo children cared for their sheep and respected their elders, adults worked hard and provided for their families, and Navajo life continued "completely undisturbed by frenzied civilization about them."[22]

Such portraits, of course, bore no resemblance to the actual experience of Navajos, who, at the time Carlson wrote, were struggling through the dire aftereffects of stock reduction. Indeed, one year before Carlson wrote that Navajos were "completely undisturbed by frenzied civilization," the Red Cross had airlifted 95,000 pounds of food, medicine, firewood, and forage to Navajos, an operation likened by one reporter to "a domestic Berlin airlift."[23] While photos of Navajo sheep herders filled the pages of *Arizona Highways*, Navajos relied on pastoralism less and less, drawing only 10 percent of their income from stock raising by the mid-1950s.[24]

Accurate representation of Navajos' lives, of course, was not Carlson's intent. Instead, "the Navajo" represented difference, in two senses. "The Navajo's" presence in the magazine served to highlight Phoenix's modernity, which [...] its businessmen sought to buttress by creating artistic institutions, funding the architecture of Frank Lloyd Wright, and most importantly, attracting high-tech industry. The presence of native culture on Phoenix's periphery showed the city as the state's modern center. At the same time, representations of Indians served to distinguish the Valley of the Sun from other locations where people might consider relocating. The presence of Indians could be added to the valley's other attractions to create a sense of endless possibilities for personal invention lacking in other areas. This sense of possibility shaped portraits of Phoenix in other magazines as well. As a former New York executive told *US News*, "I used to commute from Oyster Bay ... everyday— an hour and a half each way. Now I live on the desert just beyond town. ... I can go home at lunchtime and take a dip in my pool. After work or on weekends, I play tennis and golf. Sometimes I go prospecting for uranium in the Superstition Mountains with an Indian friend of mine. I just enjoy life about 10 times as much."[25] By encouraging such representations, *Arizona Highways* helped turn Phoenix's parochialism on its head. No longer was it a source of grievance, a reason why the Colorado River's water and energy flowed toward Los Angeles. Instead, it

was an attraction, allowing a life perfectly balanced between the modern and its escape.

The efforts to reshape Phoenix's image were widely successful. It is rare today to find a reference to the Salt River Valley even in Phoenix itself. The Valley of the Sun, by contrast, became ubiquitous, its name gracing commercial enterprises and community institutions alike. The name change and the efforts to create a sense of Phoenix's uniqueness, however, would be rather unimportant had they not occurred in concert with the federal policies remaking metropolitan America at the same time. In Phoenix, the transition from the Salt River Valley to the Valley of the Sun was not only a rhetorical change. It was also manifested in the transformation of property itself.

SUBDIVISION

Perhaps no institution in Phoenix benefited more from federal intervention in the economy than Valley National Bank. Policies initiated early in the New Deal that regulated private banks, provided capital, and underwrote a vast array of lending practices fueled the bank's rise to the largest in the intermountain states. These policies facilitated, in the words of David Freund, "a monetary and credit revolution" that "made it easier—in many cases risk free—for the private sector to lend and borrow."[26] Most prominently, the Federal Housing Authority (FHA), created by the National Housing Act of 1934, guaranteed mortgage loans for 80 percent of the value of approved residential property and for 20 percent on smaller home-improvement loans. Such extensive federal guarantees encouraged banks to loan money, since, as Kenneth Jackson wrote, "there was very little risk to the banker if a loan turned sour."[27] In guaranteeing mortgage loans, the FHA worked indirectly, subsidizing private banks, in order to, in terms used by FFIA officials, "unleash" and "unloosen" "sleeping capital."[28]

Valley Bank was well positioned to take advantage of the FHA's guarantees. Carl Bimson helped write legislation creating the FHA and testified before Congress in its support. After joining his brother at Valley Bank, Carl Bimson "made a crusade" of spreading word of the new policies, "organizing crews to ring doorbells and talk up loans" for home improvement or large appliance purchases guaranteed by the FHA. According to Bimson, in the program's first year, Valley Bank established 59 percent of such loans made in Arizona while the state's eight other banks made a mere 7 percent.[29] Even during the Depression years of the late 1930s, the bank made 198,000 federally guaranteed loans. Many of these were smaller Title I loans for home improvements and appliances. Those loans cascaded through the depressed local economy, employing contractors and bolstering sales at Goldwater's and other retail outlets selling large appliances.[30] As returning veterans flocked to Phoenix after World War II, many familiar with the city after training in one of Phoenix's four military bases, the bank's business in more substantial home-mortgage loans exploded. The annual dollar amount of FHA mortgages offered by Valley Bank rose from $11,335,407 in 1947 to $203,552,084 in 1970, representing between 16 percent and 25 percent of the bank's lending portfolio throughout that period. VA loans under the GI Bill represented another 8 percent to 14 percent. Federal mortgage underwriting, Carl Bimson later explained, provided a baseline of secure loans that allowed the bank to loan money to new commercial, real estate, and manufacturing enterprises.[31] [...]

"APARTHEID IS COMPLETE"

In 1930, Phoenix was a spatially small, relatively dense city, with 48,118 people living within its limits and that contained a little more than ten square miles, a density of 7.4 people per acre. The city's population was located primarily between Van Buren Street and the Salt River. The city's northern border lay at McDowell Boulevard, only three miles north of the river. By 1960, the city had grown dramatically, in both population and size. As agricultural land north of the Grand Canal became residential property, Phoenix's municipal government pursued an aggressive annexation policy, an attempt by city officials to maintain control over the fiscal benefits of metropolitan growth. Fearing the incorporation of suburbs that would garner the tax dollars created by the subdivision of property and cause the city's core to decay, Phoenix's municipal government aggressively promoted the benefits of annexation among the new developments. As Phoenix mayor Timothy Barrow later explained, "we annexed the suburbs." By 1960, the city covered 290 square miles, with its northern border lying more than twelve miles north of the Salt River. Annexation dramatically lowered the city's density. Even as Phoenix's population grew by over 900 percent in thirty years, reaching a population of 439,170 by 1960, its territory grew more than 2,800 percent, with density dropping to 2.3 people per acre.[32]

As in cities nationwide, New Deal housing policies made it virtually impossible for nonwhites to participate in the new, federally underwritten markets in residential property. Believing that integration represented a risk to stable property values, FHA officials had, at the agency's inception, instituted policies that prevented the agency from insuring mortgages in neighborhoods with any significant nonwhite populations while rejecting nonwhite applicants for homes in newly built subdivisions.[33] These policies shaped the practices of the real estate industry in general. Real estate agents pledged to maintain the racial character of neighborhoods as a condition of licensing. "That the entry of Non-Caucasian[s] into districts where distinctly Caucasian residents live tends to depress real estate values," wrote realtor Stanley McMichael in *Real Estate Subdivisions*, an industry textbook, "is agreed to by practically all real estate subdivides and students of city life and growth."[34] Such agreements held firm in Phoenix. As local civil rights activist Lincoln Ragsdale testified at a hearing of the U.S. Commission on Civil Rights held in Phoenix in 1962, out of 31,000 homes built by three builders in northeastern Phoenix, homes all "built, directly or indirectly, through FHA commitments," not a single home, "not one," Ragsdale testified, "has been sold to a Negro."[35]

As subdivisions sprawled northward, racial inequality in Phoenix assumed a new spatial scale. As was the case for minorities in cities across the West, the racial segregation and squalid living conditions facing Phoenix's relatively small minority population had been the rule since before World War II. Schools were segregated by law until 1953. Local theaters restricted African Americans, Mexican Americans, and Indians to their balconies, while public pools and parks on the Salt River informally forbade all nonwhites from swimming.[36] The city's black population lived in two small enclaves, one on the east side and the other on the north bank of the Salt River, while others lived south of the river, beyond the city's limits.[37] Similarly, Phoenix's Mexican Americans, composing roughly 10 percent of the population, lived close to the river, in houses with limited plumbing and minimal, if any, electricity. Indeed, a 1946 report by Maricopa County officials reported "Steinbeckesque Joad families living in dilapidated housing, row after row of open backyard toilets, which smelled to high heaven, and dust blanketed, littered streets and even dirtier alleys." Even larger numbers of Mexican migrant laborers lived in the 150 to 160 agricultural labor camps that lay beyond the city limits with accommodations that included abandoned stables, and flies everywhere "on the garbage, the excreta, the soiled mattresses...and on the children's dirt-encrusted faces," in one social worker's account.[38]

As the city's population and territory boomed after World War II, its minority populations continued to be contained in those small areas. The 1960 census showed that 90 percent of Phoenix's African American population lived in just 9 of the city's 108 census tracts. These tracts, all located south of Van Buren Street within the city's 1930 limits, also contained one-third of the city's residents with "Spanish surnames." John Camargo, who grew up just south of downtown Phoenix in the 1950s recalled, "There were just Hispanics and blacks. I don't remember any whites." The tracts contained the oldest housing stock in the city. Whereas 55 percent of the housing in Phoenix had been built between 1950 and 1960, only 24 percent of the houses in South Phoenix were new. While these predominantly nonwhite areas of Phoenix contained less than 10 percent of the city's total housing units, they were the location of 27 percent of Phoenix's deteriorating units, houses which had one or more defects requiring repair for the house to remain habitable, and 46 percent of its dilapidated dwellings, houses which did not, according to the census worker, provide safe and adequate shelter.[39] In 1966 a British magazine reported that "Phoenix ... finds itself saddled with square mile after square mile of some of the most run-down, dilapidated housing in urban America.... [W]hole blocks are served by one or two water taps." In a city where the "housing dollar" went further than in any other part of the country, fewer than half the dwellings in the census tracts that housed the majority of the city's black and Mexican American population were owner occupied. As poor wiring and limited electrical outlets formed one of the key standards by which census workers measured deteriorating or dilapidated dwellings, a minority of homes housing the city's nonwhite population could use more than two large appliances. Nonwhite populations were, in large part, excluded from electrical modernity both by selective credit policies that favored whites and by housing stock that foreclosed the possibility of "living better, electrically." In only one of those tracts, at any rate, did the median income exceed the lowest median income north of Van Buren. Visiting South Phoenix in the wake of Barry Goldwater's failed presidential bid, a reporter for the *New Republic* found a "squalid slum" that "looks like a cross between a Mississippi Black Belt Negro ghetto and a Mexican border town.... Streets are unpaved, sewers unconnected, and public utilities inadequate; many houses have outdoor toilets, and many houses are no better than outhouses."[40]

The new landscapes north of Van Buren developed between 1950 and 1960 formed a stark counterpoint to southern Phoenix. During the 1950s, over 67,000 homes had been built on that territory, 85 percent of Phoenix's new housing construction. Only 4 percent of the homes were deteriorating and 1 percent dilapidated. Most strikingly, this landscape was almost exclusively white. Out of the 305,178 people who lived in this newly residential area, 235 were listed as "Negros," representing .07 percent of the population. The majority of the African Americans in North Phoenix lived in the census tracts with the highest median incomes, suggesting that most worked as live-in domestics. The census counted 9,252 people with "Spanish surnames"—3 percent of the population—north of Van Buren, suggesting that Mexican Americans possessed significantly more residential mobility in metropolitan Phoenix than African Americans. A closer examination, however, shows the "Spanish surname" population most heavily clustered into two types of census tracts. First, they located in tracts immediately north of Van Buren, suggesting that while Mexican Americans may have had more mobility than African Americans, their mobility was limited to houses recently vacated by whites moving farther north. Second, they located in tracts that, on the census's tract map, show significant undeveloped space, suggesting populations of farm laborers on agricultural land annexed in advance of residential development. Still, a small population of people with "Spanish surnames" did manage to reside and presumably buy the some of the new homes built in north Phoenix. The two census tracts covering Maryvale's moderately priced homes, census tracts where all but 4 of the 3,886 homes were built between 1950 and 1960, showed 397 people with "Spanish surnames" and 3 "Negros," out of 16,421 total residents."[41]

It was not only the FHA that maintained the color line between North and South Phoenix. "If you were black or Hispanic," John Camargo remembered, "you couldn't go north of Van Buren.... You would drive through there and just would be risking a fight with white kids that were in that area, and even...older whites that, you know,

didn't like Blacks or Hispanics."[42] White violence also met African Americans who sought to integrate northern Phoenix. In the late 1940s, African Americans who purchased homes even south of Van Buren were met with petitions from white neighbors and found garbage dumped on their lawn and graffiti defacing their homes. Lincoln and Eleanor Ragsdale, who managed to purchase a home in the exclusive Encanto neighborhood of northern Phoenix by having a sympathetic friend serve as a buyer and transfer title, faced threats from neighbors, defacement of their property, and harassment from Phoenix's police force. Reflecting on the police's actions, Ragsdale stated, "I looked suspicious. And all you had to do to look suspicious is to be driving a Cadillac and be black."[43] Reverend Bernard Black remembered that Willie Mays lived on his street in South Phoenix into the late 1960s because the San Francisco Giant, in Phoenix for spring training, could not find a willing renter anywhere north of Van Buren. John Camargo, as well, emphasized that Phoenix's police played a major role in enforcing the city's racial borders. Venture north of Van Buren and the police would, he explained, "stop you and talk to you and ask you what you were doing' there.... We never reacted, you know, it was almost a fact of life."[44]

Appearing before the U.S. Commission on Civil Rights in 1962, Phoenix mayor Sam Mardian portrayed his city as a center of enlightened race relations within a nation increasingly divided by race. He pointed to the Phoenix school board's desegregation of local schools one year prior to *Brown* (though he neglected to mention the state supreme court ruling that forced the school board's hand). He explained that Phoenix's hospitals had been opened to all people "without enactment of laws" and related that restaurants served patrons "without regard to race or color." Mardian told the commission that "the voluntary nature of desegregation" in Phoenix, which he regarded as "much healthier than forced integration," resulted from the particular nature of the city's growth. "There are many newcomers from all over the country, and I think," Mardian testified, "they are all anxious to be friendly and to treat other people in a friendly manner so that they might reciprocate and treat *them* in a friendly manner." The intersection of unfamiliar people had created, in Mardian's telling, a type of exceptionalism, in which individualism had won out over group prejudice.[45]

Mexican Americans and African Americans testifying before the commission as well as the 1960 census told a different story. Northern Phoenix, with its 99 percent white population defended by both state policy and popular violence, and southern Phoenix, where John Camargo did not "remember any whites," replicated the patterns of growing metropolitan areas in the nation at large, where, as Thomas Sugrue writes, "whiteness and blackness assumed a spatial form."[46] The spatialization of race in Phoenix also created a new form of invisibility even more profound than in Detroit or Philadelphia. [...] changes in the city's charter that placed municipal elections on a city-wide basis produced political invisibility in the sprawling metropolis, as candidates had little reason to appeal to the relatively small and powerless populations living south of Van Buren. Indeed, the city's annexation policy excluded predominantly minority areas south of the Salt River until close to the 1960 census, when its annexation promised to push the city over a population of 400,000."[47]

Invisibility manifested itself in public space as well. As new commercial strips and enclosed malls like Park Central developed in northern Phoenix, the city's middle-class whites no longer shared the downtown shopping district with blacks and Latinos. As Rev. Brooks told the Civil Rights Commission "the white community leadership for the most part is unaware of the problems, because the opportunities for exchange, intellectual, social, or economic, just do not exist."[48] As Andrew Kopkind, the reporter for the *New Republic*, explained the city in 1964, "Apartheid is complete. The two cities look at each other across a golf course."[49]

Such patterns were repeated across the nation. As the federal government underwrote postwar metropolitan growth, the patterns of race and residence in Phoenix resembled those in Charlotte and Atlanta, and Detroit for that matter, with a prosperous white noose surrounding neighborhoods of racialized poverty. These stark patterns of residential inequality were not, primarily, a consequence of overt discrimination, though as John Carmago's interview indicates, violence lingered not far below the surface. Indeed, Barry Goldwater bragged of his NAACP membership and his actions to integrate his department store just as Sam Mardian pointed to the voluntary nature of desegregation of movie theaters, department stores, and restaurants. While other Phoenicians testifying before the U.S. Commission on Civil Rights stated that they rarely saw Blacks or Mexican Americans dining in those restaurants, they too admitted that discrimination was not the main problem facing Phoenix. Rather, it was the uneven distribution of resources between northern Phoenix, where both public and private capital flowed into new subdivisions, and the nonwhite areas of the city, which remained underserved, underdeveloped, and ignored by both federal and local officials who focused their efforts on exclusionary metropolitan development. These dynamics were a consequence of the ways in which federal policy imbued with value not only space, but individuals. Capitalizing, in a sense, individual whiteness, growth liberalism helped determine where public money would flow to attract new people, and where private money would flow to serve them.

NOTES

1. Census reports listed 166,638 people moving from the North or West, out of 197,343 people who had moved to Phoenix from outside the area. U.S. Census Bureau, *U.S. Census of Population and Housing: 1960*, Census tracts, Phoenix, Ariz. Table P-I. General Characteristics of the Population, by Census Tract, 1960, 13–25.
2. Raymond Carlson, "Frontier," *AH* (November 1948), 1.

3. "Dream Homes by the Dozens," *AH* (February 1954), 12–18.
4. Carlson, "Happy Land," AH (January 1948), 18.
5. "Roads Through the Indian Country," *AH* (June 1953), 12.
6. For another work that shows the role of local businessmen in reshaping core-periphery relations, see Gray Brechin, *Imperial San Francisco: Urban Power, Earthly Ruin* (Berkeley: University of California Press, 1999).
7. Frank Snell Oral History, VNB.
8. Phoenix Chamber of Commerce, Advertising Committee Minutes, 10/10/49, Box 10, Lewis and Roca and Phoenix Chamber of Commerce Collection, 1949–63, AHS-Tempe.
9. "Promotional Committee Reports," *Phoenix Action*, September 1960, 3.
10. "Fun in Sun City," *Holiday* (January 1958), 45–51; "It's Fun to Live in Phoenix," *Better Homes and Gardens* (February 1957); "Big Boom in the Desert," *US News and World Report*, October 11, 1957, 78; Prentiss Combs, "What It's Like to Live in Arizona," *Better Homes and Gardens*, February 1962, 90–98.
11. "Phoenix in the Valley of the Sun," *Holiday*, March 1953, 62.
12. Mrs. David Prouty, in Combs, "What It's Like to Move to Arizona."
13. "Sands of Desert Turn Gold," *Life*, March 12, 1956, 79; "Phoenix Architect Designs His Own Home," *Architectural Record*, Sept. 1951, 131.
14. "Arizona's Fashions," *Better Homes and Gardens*, March 1958, 65–73.
15. John Cowan, "Baptism by Sunset," *Vogue*, January 15, 1966, 128.
16. Combs, "What It's Like to Live in Arizona," 93.
17. Circulation figures from "Understatement in the Southwest," *Fortune* 38, July 1948, 114; "People Like Pictures," *Time* 58, September 24, 1951, 75; and "Frontpiece," *AH* 28, December 1952. "A Look Inside the Business of Arizona Highways," *AH* 39, July 1963, 2–5.
18. "Phoenix: City in the Sun," *AH*, February 1951; "You'll Like Living in Phoenix," *AH*, April 1957; "Phoenix, City on Wings," *AH*, January 1962.
19. Peter Iverson, *Barry Goldwater, Native Arizonan*, 42–43.
20. Joyce Rockwood Muench, "Pilgrimage into Spring," *AH*, February 1955, 28.
21. "Colorful People," 10.
22. "Roads Through the Indian Country," *AH* (June 1953), 12.
23. "Operation Snowbound Successful," *Los Angeles Times*, February 8, 1949, 12. Alison Bernstein, *American Indians and World War II: Toward a New Era in Indian Affairs* (Norman: University of Oklahoma Press, 1991), 157.
24. White, *Roots of Dependency*, 327.
25. "Big Boom in the Desert," *US News and World Report*, October 11, 1957, 78.
26. David Freund, "Marketing the Free Market: State Intervention and the Politics of Prosperity in Metropolitan America," in Sugrue and Kruse, *The New Suburban History*, 15.
27. Jackson, *Crabgrass Frontier*, 203–5.
28. As Freund has shown, such language was intentionally chosen to obscure the new role of the state in stabilizing the construction industry even as the FHA's lending practices fueled debt-driven economic growth in newly created residential spaces. Freund, "Marketing the Free Market," 26.
29. Carl Bimson Oral History, VNB.
30. Schweikert, "A Record of Revitalization," 125. Schweikert writes it is likely, though unproven, that Walter Bimson's former employer, Harris Trust of Chicago, provided Valley Bank with the capital that allowed the nearly insolvent bank to begin initiating federally insured loans during the Depression years.
31. Valley National Bank, *President's Annual Report to Stockholders*, 1947–70 (years 1953, 1957, 1958 missing), Box 75, VNB; Carl Bimson Oral History, VNB.
32. For Phoenix's annexation policies in the 1950s, see Carol Heim, "Border Wars: Tax Revenue, Annexation, and Urban Growth in Phoenix," University of Massachusetts Political Economy Research Institute, Working Paper Series, Number 112, July 2006, 8–9. Available at http://www.peri.umass.edu/fileadmin/pdf/working_papers/working_papers_101-150/WP112_revised.pdf; and John Wenum, *Annexation as a Technique for Metropolitan Growth: The Case of Phoenix, Arizona* (Tempe: Institute for Public Administration, Arizona State University, 1970).
33. See Amy E. Hillier, "Redlining and the Homeowners' Loan Corporation," *Journal of Urban History*, 29 (4) (2003), 394–420.
34. McMichael quoted in Clement Vose, *Caucasians Only: The Supreme Court, the NAACP, and the Restrictive Covenant Cases* (Berkeley: University of California Press, 1959), 219–20.
35. Lincoln Ragsdale, testimony, *Hearings before the United States Commission on Civil Rights*, Phoenix, Arizona, Feb. 3, 1962, 48.
36. Roy Yanez Oral History, PHP. Luckingham, *Phoenix*, 178.
37. For the geography of black Phoenix, see Matthew Whitaker, *Race Work: The Rise of Civil Rights in the Urban West* (Lincoln: University of Nebraska Press, 2007).

38. O'Neill, *Working the Navajo Way*, 95.
39. The 1960 census defined deteriorating housing as needing "more repair than would be provided in the course of regular maintenance. It has one or more defects of an intermediate nature that must be corrected if the unit is to continue to provide safe and adequate shelter," while dilapidated housing failed to "provide safe and adequate shelter. It has one or more critical defects, or has a combination of intermediate defects in sufficient number to require extensive repair or rebuilding, or is of inadequate original construction. Critical defects result from continued neglect or lack of repair or indicate serious damage to the structure." U.S. Census Bureau; U.S. Censuses of Population and Housing: 1960. Census Tracts. Final Report PHC(I)-II. U.S. Government Printing Office, Washington, D.C., 1962.
40. 1960 Census of Population and Housing; John Camargo Oral History, PHP; British magazine quote from Bolin et al, "The Geography of Despair: Environmental Racism and the Making of South Phoenix, Arizona, USA," *Human Ecology Review* 12 (2005), 164. Andrew Kopkind, "Modern Times in Phoenix: A City at the Mercy of Its Myths," *New Republic* (November 1965), 15.
41. 1960 U.S. Census of Population and Housing, Phoenix Census Tracts.
42. Camargo Oral History.
43. Ragsdale quotes and accounts of interracial efforts to integrate northern Phoenix in Mary Melcher, "Blacks and Whites Together: Interracial Leadership in the Phoenix Civil Rights Movement," *Journal of Arizona History* 32 (1992), 203.
44. Rev. Bernard Black Oral History; John Camargo Oral History.
45. Sam Mardian, testimony, *US Commission on Civil Rights*, Phoenix, 8.
46. Sugrue, *Origins of the Urban Crisis*, xvi.
47. Heim, "Border Wars."
48. Benjamin Brooks, testimony, *US Commission on Civil Rights*, Phoenix, 53.
49. Kopkind, "Modern Times in Phoenix," 15.

DOCUMENTS FOR PART VI

6.1 SPECIAL MESSAGE TO THE CONGRESS ON CONSERVATION AND RESTORATION OF NATURAL BEAUTY (1965)

Lyndon B. Johnson

Source: *Public Papers of the Presidents of the United States, Lyndon B. Johnson: Containing the Public Messages, Speeches, and Statements of the President, 1965*, Book I—January to May 31, 1965 (Washington, D.C.: United States Government Printing Office, 1966).

EDITORS' INTRODUCTION

The Great Society is the name given to President Lyndon B. Johnson's domestic agenda, which emphasized civil rights, fair housing, the rejuvenation of cities, and the War on Poverty. While the environmental goals and policies of the Johnson administration have received much less attention, they were no less visionary than his other plans. The February 8, 1965 message to Congress enumerates the nation's many environmental problems, including dwindling open space, unsightly highways, and air pollution. **[See Illustration VI.5.]** President Johnson employed language reminiscent of the nineteenth and early twentieth century reformers who sought cleaner and healthier cities. He also articulated the vision of wilderness conservation advocates, who feared that industrialization and urbanization would destroy the natural landscape. Johnson called for a more integrated approach to reconfiguration of urban space, designing suburbs, and preserving architecture. These ideas are akin to the tenants of New Urbanism. **[See Document 7.8.]**

SPECIAL MESSAGE TO THE CONGRESS ON CONSERVATION AND RESTORATION OF NATURAL BEAUTY (FEBRUARY 8, 1965)

To the Congress of the United States

For centuries Americans have drawn strength and inspiration from the beauty of our country. It would be a neglectful generation indeed, indifferent alike to the judgment of history and the command of principle, which failed to preserve and extend such a heritage for its descendants.

Yet the storm of modern change is threatening to blight and diminish in a few decades what has been cherished and protected for generations.

A growing population is swallowing up areas of natural beauty with its demands for living space, and is placing increased demand on our overburdened areas of recreation and pleasure.

The increasing tempo of urbanization and growth is already depriving many Americans of the right to live in decent surroundings. More of our people are crowding into cities and being cut off from nature. Cities themselves reach out into the countryside, destroying streams and trees and meadows as they go. A modern highway may wipe out the equivalent of a fifty acre park with every mile. And people move out from the city to get closer to nature only to find that nature has moved farther from them.

The modern technology, which has added much to our lives can also have a darker side. Its uncontrolled waste products are menacing the world we live in, our enjoyment and our health. The air we breathe, our water, our soil and wildlife, are being blighted by the poisons and chemicals which are the by-products of technology and industry. The skeletons of discarded cars litter the countryside. The same society which receives the rewards of technology, must, as a cooperating whole, take responsibility for control.

To deal with these new problems will require a new conservation. We must not only protect the countryside and save it from destruction, we must restore what has been destroyed and salvage the beauty and charm of our cities. Our conservation must be not just the classic conservation of protection and development, but a creative conservation of restoration and innovation. Its concern is not with nature alone, but with the total relation between man and the world around him. Its object is not just man's welfare but the dignity of man's spirit.

In this conservation the protection and enhancement of man's opportunity to be in contact with beauty must play a major role.

This means that beauty must not be just a holiday treat, but a part of our daily life. It means not just easy physical access, but equal social access for rich and poor, Negro and white, city dweller and farmer.

Beauty is not an easy thing to measure. It does not show up in the gross national product, in a weekly pay check, or in profit and loss statements. But these things are not ends in themselves. They are a road to satisfaction and pleasure and the good life. Beauty makes its own direct contribution to these final ends. Therefore it is one of the most important components of our true national income, not to be left out simply because statisticians cannot calculate its worth.

And some things we do know. Association with beauty can enlarge man's imagination and revive his spirit. Ugliness can de-mean the people who live among it. What a citizen sees every day is his America. If it is attractive it adds to the quality of his life. If it is ugly it can degrade his existence.

Beauty has other immediate values. It adds to safety whether removing direct dangers to health or making highways less monotonous and dangerous. We also know that those who live in blighted and squalid conditions are more susceptible to anxieties and mental disease.

Ugliness is costly. It can be expensive to clean a soot smeared building, or to build new areas of recreation when the old landscape could have been preserved far more cheaply.

Certainly no one would hazard a national definition of beauty. But we do know that nature is nearly always beautiful. We do, for the most part, know what is ugly. And we can introduce, into all our planning, our programs, our building and our growth, a conscious and active concern for the values of beauty. If we do this then we can be successful in preserving a beautiful America. [...]

The Cities

Thomas Jefferson wrote that communities "should be planned with an eye to the effect made upon the human spirit by being continually surrounded with a maximum of beauty."

We have often sadly neglected this advice in the modern American city. Yet this is where most of our people live. It is where the character of our young is formed. It is where American civilization will be increasingly concentrated in years to come.

Such a challenge will not be met with a few more parks or playgrounds. It requires attention to the architecture of building, the structure of our roads, preservation of historical buildings and monuments, careful planning of new suburbs. A concern for the enhancement of beauty must infuse every aspect of the growth and development of metropolitan areas. It must be a principal responsibility of local government, supported by active and concerned citizens.

Federal assistance can be a valuable stimulus and help to such local efforts.

I have recommended a community extension program which will bring the resources of the university to focus on problems of the community just as they have long been concerned with our rural areas. Among other things, this program will help provide training and technical assistance to aid in making our communities more attractive and vital. In addition, under the Housing

Act of 1964, grants will be made to States for training of local governmental employees needed for community development. I am recommending a 1965 supplemental appropriation to implement this program.

We now have two programs which can be of special help in creating areas of recreation and beauty for our metropolitan area population: the Open Space Land Program, and the Land and Water Conservation Fund.

I have already proposed full funding of the Land and Water Conservation Fund, and directed the Secretary of the Interior to give priority attention to serving the needs of our growing urban population.

The primary purpose of the Open Space Program has been to help acquire and assure open spaces in urban areas. I propose a series of new matching grants for improving the natural beauty of urban open space.

The Open Space Program should be adequately financed, and broadened by permitting grants to be made to help city governments acquire and clear areas to create small parks, squares, pedestrian malls and playgrounds.

In addition I will request authority in this program for a matching program to cities for landscaping, installation of outdoor lights and benches, creating attractive cityscapes along roads and in business areas, and for other beautification purposes.

Our city parks have not, in many cases, realized their full potential as sources of pleasure and play. I recommend on a matching basis a series of federal demonstration projects in city parks to use the best thought and action to show how the appearance of these parks can better serve the people of our towns and metropolitan areas.

All of these programs should be operated on the same matching formula to avoid unnecessary competition among programs and increase the possibility of cooperative effort. I will propose such a standard formula.

In a future message on the cities I will recommend other changes in our housing programs designed to strengthen the sense of community of which natural beauty is an important component.

In almost every part of the country citizens are rallying to save landmarks of beauty and history. The government must also do its share to assist these local efforts which have an important national purpose.

We will encourage and support the National Trust for Historic Preservation in the United States, chartered by Congress in 1949. I shall propose legislation to authorize supplementary grants to help local authorities acquire, develop and manage private properties for such purposes.

The Registry of National Historic Landmarks is a fine federal program with virtually no federal cost. I commend its work and the new wave of interest it has evoked in historical preservation. [...]

Highways

More than any country ours is an automobile society. For most Americans the automobile is a principal instrument of transportation, work, daily activity, recreation and pleasure. By making our roads highways to the enjoyment of nature and beauty we can greatly enrich the life of nearly all our people in city and countryside alike.

Our task is two-fold. First, to ensure that roads themselves are not destructive of nature and natural beauty. Second, to make our roads ways to recreation and pleasure.

I have asked the Secretary of Commerce to take a series of steps designed to meet this objective. This includes requiring landscaping on all federal interstate primary and urban highways, encouraging the construction of rest and recreation areas along highways, and the preservation of natural beauty adjacent to highway rights-of-way. [...]

The Recreation Advisory Council is now completing a study of the role which scenic roads and parkways should play in meeting our highway and recreation needs. After receiving the report, I will make appropriate recommendations.

The authority for the existing program of outdoor advertising control expires on June 30, 1965, and its provisions have not been effective in achieving the desired goal. Accordingly, I will recommend legislation to ensure effective control of billboards along our highways.

In addition, we need urgently to work towards the elimination or screening of unsightly, beauty-destroying junkyards and auto graveyards along our highways. To this end, I will also recommend necessary legislation to achieve effective control, including Federal assistance in appropriate cases where necessary.

I hope that, at all levels of government, our planners and builders will remember that highway beautification is more than a matter of planting trees or setting aside scenic areas. The roads themselves must reflect, in location and design, increased respect for the natural and social integrity and unity of the landscape and communities through which they pass. [...]

Pollution

One aspect of the advance of civilization is the evolution of responsibility for disposal of waste. Over many generations society gradually developed techniques for this purpose. State and local governments, landlords and private citizens have been held responsible for ensuring that sewage and garbage did not menace health or contaminate the environment.

In the last few decades entire new categories of waste have come to plague and menace the American scene. These are the technological wastes—the by-products of growth, industry, agriculture, and science. We cannot wait for slow evolution over generations to deal with them.

Pollution is growing at a rapid rate. Some pollutants are known to be harmful to health, while the effect of others is uncertain and unknown. In some cases we can control pollution with a larger effort. For other forms of pollution we still do not have effective means of control.

Pollution destroys beauty and menaces health. It cuts down on efficiency, reduces property values and raises taxes.

The longer we wait to act, the greater the dangers and the larger the problem.

Large-scale pollution of air and waterways is no respecter of political boundaries, and its effects extend far beyond those who cause it.

Air pollution is no longer confined to isolated places. This generation has altered the composition of the atmosphere on a global scale through radioactive materials and a steady increase in carbon dioxide from the burning of fossil fuels. Entire regional airsheds, crop plant environments, and river basins are heavy with noxious materials. Motor vehicles and home heating plants, municipal dumps and factories continually hurl pollutants into the air we breathe. Each day almost 50,000 tons of unpleasant, and sometimes poisonous, sulfur dioxide are added to the atmosphere, and our automobiles produce almost 300,000 tons of other pollutants.

In Donora, Pennsylvania in 1948, and New York City in 1953 serious illness and some deaths were produced by sharp increases in air pollution. In New Orleans, epidemic outbreaks of asthmatic attacks are associated with air pollutants. Three-fourths of the eight million people in the Los Angeles area are annoyed by severe eye irritation much of the year. And our health authorities are increasingly concerned with the damaging effects of the continual breathing of polluted air by all our people in every city in the country.

In addition to its health effects, air pollution creates filth and gloom and depreciates property values of entire neighborhoods. The White House itself is being dirtied with soot from polluted air.

Every major river system is now polluted. Waterways that were once sources of pleasure and beauty and recreation are forbidden to human contact and objectionable to sight and smell. Furthermore, this pollution is costly, requiring expensive treatment for drinking water and inhibiting the operation and growth of industry.

In spite of the efforts and many accomplishments of the past, water pollution is spreading. And new kinds of problems are being added to the old:

- Waterborne viruses, particularly hepatitis, are replacing typhoid fever as a significant health hazard.
- Mass deaths of fish have occurred in rivers over-burdened with wastes.
- Some of our rivers contain chemicals which, in concentrated form, produce abnormalities in animals.
- Last summer 2,600 square miles of Lake Erie—over a quarter of the entire Lake—were almost without oxygen and unable to support life because of algae and plant growths, fed by pollution from cities and farms.

In many older cities storm drains and sanitary sewers are interconnected. As a result, mixtures of storm water and sanitary waste overflow during rains and discharge directly into streams, bypassing treatment works and causing heavy pollution.

In addition to our air and water we must, each and every day, dispose of a half billion pounds of solid waste. These wastes—from discarded cans to discarded automobiles—litter our country, harbor vermin, and menace our health. Inefficient and improper methods of disposal increase pollution of our air and streams.

Almost all these wastes and pollutions are the result of activities carried on for the benefit of man. A prime national goal must be an environment that is pleasing to the senses and healthy to live in.

Our Government is already doing much in this field. We have made significant progress. But more must be done. [...]

White House Conference

I intend to call a White House Conference on Natural Beauty to meet in mid-May of this year. Its chairman will be Mr. Laurance Rockefeller.

It is my hope that this Conference will produce new ideas and approaches for enhancing the beauty of America. Its scope will not be restricted to federal action. It will look for ways to help and encourage state and local governments, institutions and private citizens, in their own efforts. It can serve as a focal point for the large campaign of public education which is needed to alert Americans to the danger to their natural heritage and to the need for action. [...]

Conclusion

In my thirty-three years of public life I have seen the American system move to conserve the natural and human resources of our land.

TVA transformed an entire region that was "depressed." The rural electrification cooperatives brought electricity to lighten the burdens of rural America. We have seen the forests replanted by the CCC's, and watched Gifford Pinchot's sustained yield concept take hold on forestlands.

It is true that we have often been careless with our natural bounty. At times we have paid a heavy price for this neglect. But once our people were aroused to the danger, we have acted to preserve our resources for the enrichment of our country and the enjoyment of future generations.

The beauty of our land is a natural resource. Its preservation is linked to the inner prosperity of the human spirit.

The tradition of our past is equal to today's threat to that beauty. Our land will be attractive tomorrow only if we organize for action and rebuild and reclaim the beauty we inherited. Our stewardship will be judged by the foresight with which we carry out these programs. We must rescue our cities and countryside from blight with the same purpose and vigor with which, in other areas, we moved to save the forests and the soil.

6.2 TOXIC WASTES AND RACE IN THE UNITED STATES (1987)

Commission for Racial Justice, United Church of Christ

Source: *Toxic Wastes and Race in the United States: A National Report on the Racial and Socio-Economic Characteristics of Communities with Hazardous Waste Sites* (New York: Public Data Access, Inc., 1987). Reprinted with permission of the United Church of Christ.

EDITORS' INTRODUCTION

"Environmental racism" is a term referring to the disproportionate placement of environmental risks in communities of color, and the exclusion of representatives from those communities in the environmental decision making process. The earliest articulation of the term came in the 1987 report from the United Church of Christ's Commission for Racial Justice, *Toxic Wastes and Race in the United States.* The "Major Findings" from the report highlights the fact that blacks, Hispanics, Asian/Pacific Islanders, and Native Americans were over-represented in populations living near uncontrolled waste sites. Environmental hazards, however, are not exclusive to minority communities. In fact, as the summary asserts, more than half of all Americans live in communities with uncontrolled toxic waste sites.

TOXIC WASTES AND RACE IN THE UNITED STATES (1987)

Major Findings

This report presents findings from two cross-sectional studies on demographic patterns associated with (1) commercial hazardous waste facilities and (2) uncontrolled toxic waste sites. The first was an analytical study which revealed a striking relationship between the location of commercial hazardous waste facilities and race. The second was a descriptive study which documented the widespread presence of uncontrolled toxic waste sites in racial and ethnic communities throughout the United States. Among the many findings that emerged from these studies, the following are most important:

Demographic Characteristics of Communities with Commercial Hazardous Waste Facilities

- Race proved to be the most significant among variables tested in association with the location of commercial hazardous waste facilities. This represented a consistent national pattern.

- Communities with the greatest number of commercial hazardous waste facilities had the highest composition of racial and ethnic residents. In communities with two or more facilities or one of the nation's five largest landfills, the average minority percentage of the population[1] was more than three times that of communities without facilities (38 percent vs. 12 percent).

- In communities with one commercial hazardous waste facility, the average minority percentage of the population was twice the average minority percentage of the population in communities without such facilities (24 percent vs. 12 percent).

- Although socio-economic status appeared to play an important role in the location of commercial hazardous waste facilities, race still proved to be more significant. This remained true after the study controlled for urbanization and regional differences. Incomes and home values were substantially lower when communities with commercial facilities were compared to communities in the surrounding counties without facilities.

- Three out of the five largest commercial hazardous waste landfills in the United States were located in predominantly Black[2] or Hispanic communities. These three landfills accounted for 40 percent of the total estimated commercial landfill capacity in the nation.

Demographic Characteristics of Communities with Uncontrolled Toxic Waste Sites

- Three out of every five Black and Hispanic Americans lived in communities with uncontrolled toxic waste sites.
- More than 15 million Blacks lived in communities with one or more uncontrolled toxic waste sites.
- More than 8 million Hispanics lived in communities with one or more uncontrolled toxic waste sites.
- Blacks were heavily over-represented in the populations of metropolitan areas with the largest number of uncontrolled toxic waste sites. These areas include:

Memphis, TN	(173 sites)
St. Louis, MO	(160 sites)
Houston, TX	(152 sites)
Cleveland, OH	(106 sites)
Chicago	(103 sites)
Atlanta, GA	(94 sites)

- Los Angeles, California had more Hispanics living in communities with uncontrolled toxic waste sites than any other metropolitan area in the United States.
- Approximately half of all Asian/Pacific Islanders and American Indians lived in communities with uncontrolled toxic waste sites.
- Overall, the presence of uncontrolled toxic waste sites was highly pervasive. More than half of the total population in the United States resided in communities with uncontrolled toxic waste sites.

NOTES

1. In this report, "minority percentage of the population" was used as a measure of "race."
2. In this report, the terminology used to describe various racial and ethnic populations was based on categories defined by the U.S. Bureau of the Census: Blacks, Hispanics, Asian/Pacific Islanders and American Indians.

6.3 THE FLINT WATER CRISIS: SYSTEMATIC RACISM THROUGH THE EYES OF FLINT

Michigan Civil Rights Commission

Source: Michigan Civil Rights Commission, *The Flint Water Crisis: Systematic Racism Through the Lens of Flint: Report of the Michigan Civil Rights Commission* (February 17, 2017), www.michigan.gov/documents/mdcr/VFlintCrisisRep-F-Edited3-13-17_554317_7.pdf.

EDITORS' INTRODUCTION

Since the summer of 2014, the people of Flint, Michigan have experienced one of the nation's most egregious examples of environmental injustice. The Flint drinking water became so discolored, turbid, and otherwise contaminated that the United States Environmental Protection Agency (EPA) issued warnings that it contained dangerously high levels of lead. Scientists at Virginia Polytechnic Institute and State University, in fact, have found levels of lead in the drinking water high enough to be classified by EPA standards as hazardous waste. The Flint Water Crisis, as it has become known, began routinely enough. City officials issued advisories directing residents to boil water before consumption due to the presence of fecal coliform bacteria in the water supply. As the months, and then years, passed, the situation worsened. A series of dramatic, and often contradictory and condescending statements highlighted the multifaceted origins and complex nature of urban environmental contamination.

After months of adding chlorine to the water supply to flush out any potential contamination, General Motors announced in October 2014 that its plant in Flint would stop using the city's water due to concerns that high levels of chlorine would corrode engine parts. In January 2015, the Flint officials warned residents that although the water was safe for the general population it cautioned the elderly and young children against water consumption. After a June 2015 EPA memo on high lead levels in Flint's water, the city's Mayor Dayne Walling drank tap water on television in an attempt to assure residents of the water's safety. By December 2015, the city declared a state of emergency. In early 2016, Michigan National Guard troops were called in to help distribute bottled water to city residents and President Barack Obama declared a federal disaster in Flint. In April 2018, Michigan abruptly ended free water bottle distribution despite skepticism by many in Flint that the water was still not safe to drink. The political fallout and public health concerns of contaminated drinking water in Flint are far from over.

But what caused the Flint Water Crisis? While there are many twists and turns, including indictments and charges of malfeasance, the following excerpt from a report of the Michigan Civil Rights Commission provides the larger view of how the situation is a product of systematic racism. Flint is a city of just under 100,000 residents, the majority of whom are African American. Beginning in the 1980s, the city experienced massive deindustrialization. General Motors, which employed almost 80,000 workers there in the 1970s, laid off tens of thousands of employees as it divested from the city. The city's economic condition faltered precipitating a series of fiscal emergencies. In 2011, Republican Michigan Governor Rick Synder appointed Michael Brown as the city's emergency manager, and Brown temporarily took control of the city. Under Michigan law, emergency managers have the right to reduce employee pay, outsource services, and modify contracts. It was in this context that the fateful decision was made to terminate the long-standing agreement to purchase water from Detroit and segue to a cheaper, long-term supply from Lake Huron. In the short-term, Flint relied on the Flint River. In the switch of water supply to the Flint River, the water crisis began.

THE FLINT WATER CRISIS: SYSTEMATIC RACISM THROUGH THE EYES OF FLINT

EMERGENCY MANAGEMENT AND SYSTEMIC RACISM AT PLAY

The current emergency manager (EM) law has both proponents and opponents. State government has traditionally developed many policies affecting state-local relations, from debt limit to auditing requirements, and including state takeover of municipalities in financial distress.

We focus our attention on determining if and how the EM law addresses the role of space and race in Michigan and how that serves to counter the production and

reproduction of spatial and structural racism as evidenced in communities like Flint.

If you live in Michigan, there is a 10% chance that you have lived under emergency management since 2009. But if you are a black Michigander, the odds are 50/50.[1]

Whether one supports or opposes the EM law is not the issue. What is clear is that its application in Michigan has had a racially disparate effect. The record reveals that communities of color have been starkly overrepresented in jurisdictions placed under emergency management. This does not mean that the law or the people administering it are racist in their decisions to appoint an emergency manager.

We believe fixing the emergency manager law is not the proper place to start. Before we look for better ways to fix the problems associated with the EM law, we must ask whether we have properly identified the problems.

If a local jurisdiction's problem is poor bookkeeping or bad money management, the EM law might be an effective tool. But poor bookkeeping does not explain the overrepresentation of people of color in decaying urban areas surrounded by greater wealth. The problems that created the fiscal emergency are generally broader than balancing the books, and if it is going to work, the solution must be as well.

Using the EM law to balance the books by slashing the budget not only fails to address most of the root causes of financial distress, it exacerbates existing gaps between urban and suburban communities, and erects additional barriers to narrowing the racial gap. In short, the EM law as applied far too often addresses the problems of already financially stricken governments in second class communities, segregated based on race, wealth and opportunity, by appointing an emergency manager whose toolbox is filled with short term solutions that are contrary to the long-term interests of the people living there. This Commission examined the relationship between the city of Flint and its suburbs and found the following:

1. Declining property values in Flint continue to erode the property tax revenues for Flint.
2. Strong historical racial division between Flint and its suburbs and a lack of cooperation to address problems they created together.
3. Eroding business and industrial base leading to declining jobs in Flint while growth or no decline in the suburbs.
4. Continual flight of whites from Flint to the suburbs.
5. Declining income tax base as a source of revenue for Flint.
6. A history of spatial race discrimination, the legacy of which contributed greatly to the city's decline and the decline's disparate effects on people of color.
7. An aging and oversized water system that has been left to those least able to pay the highest water bills in the country.

Each of these has played a role in creating Flint's financial emergencies, yet none are addressed by the current EM law. Given the foregoing, how can a community like Flint increase its revenue base? And how can the state through an EM assist a community, such as Flint, address its financial distress, on both a short-term and long-term basis? Because the current EM law does nothing to address the foregoing factors, it is a fatally flawed response to the challenges facing Flint.

As a state, and as a nation, we must face the role race played in creating the urban problems and economic disparities that confront us. The Flint Water Crisis was more than 75 years in the making. Some form of emergency management may be necessary from time to time, but we will not cure the disease if we only treat one symptom.

We heard testimony from witnesses that the structure of the current EM law is too narrow, and that balancing the books and leaving does nothing if expenses still exceed revenues.

That's the problem, that the state statute does not address the long-term stability and economic climate for the community. The emergency manager goal is to balance the books, and if you can try to get something else done, I guess you can try that. But that's not what you go there for. And then the state's idea is to get out as soon as possible.[2]

The state must make one of the duties of an emergency manager the restructuring of an economy in that city for economic stability and must support with the finances to do it.[3]

We agree.

Presently the biggest difference between a local government official and an emergency manager is that the emergency manager does not have the residents' interests as its first priority. Balancing the books alone is at least as much about the welfare of creditors and other outside interests as it is about the residents. Investing to build a better future is not part of an emergency manager's job, but it should be. A more comprehensive approach to addressing communities facing financial distress is required than is currently found in the EM law.

The Commission also notes that the current emergency manager law imposes a policy prescription that may even create insolvent cities or minimal cities resulting from the imposition of dramatic austerity measures. Examples of such measures include budget cuts and asset sales leaving a stripped down version of core functions like irregular police and fire protection or rudimentary sanitation and water supplies. These can render communities like Flint barely operable, unable to meet obligations to creditors or address the needs of its residents. The fear is that such measures could create what the Kerner Report described as the creation of two societies, separate and unequal, black and white. We must prevent this from occurring.

The Commission heard of instances when emergency managers came in and took over positions, corrected problems and created efficiencies that made a positive difference. However, they left without training or preparing the people who would take over these responsibilities, sometimes the very people who had them before. Thus, any positive progress that was made was lost with the departure of the EM.

> Eric Lupher likened this to the Bible parable that if you give a man a fish he eats for a day, but if you teach him to fish he eats for a lifetime. Cities that came out of emergency management only to "recycle," he said, did so "because the municipal employees that were there didn't learn to fish. ... They don't have the financial management tools, they don't have the inventory controls, they don't have the basic management skills to run a government."[4]

We agree. An important part of an emergency manager's task must be to ensure their success is sustainable by the staff in place when they leave.

We heard testimony about emergency managers succeeding by using powers granted to them that are unavailable to local elected officials. Former Benton Harbor Emergency Manager Joe Harris, for example, spoke of the ability to renegotiate union contracts.[5]

We believe this creates an appearance of bias which can and should be prevented. The current emergency manager law assumes that there is a need for BOTH special powers and an outside person. Why is it assumed that the existing political structure could not fix things if it had the special powers? Why is it assumed that an outsider could not fix things without special powers? It MAY be the case that both are necessary, but this should require two separate findings.

The Commission heard testimony indicating that some of the problems in Flint would best be addressed regionally, but that there was no mechanism in place or authority to do so.

Chris Kolb, who co-chaired the Governor's Flint Water Advisory Task Force, questioned:

> In a state, and in a region where we had excess water capacity, why did we think we needed more? And when we are making decisions on infrastructure that cost billions of dollars, we should be able to, in this state, make decisions that take that into account.[6]

He later answered his own question, saying: "There is no system in Michigan really for regionalism... That really for us was the problem."[7]

This Commission believes that Michigan's strong home rule cities can sometimes work against each other's interests, thereby creating challenges that may be best solved regionally. Viewing Flint in isolation without considering its relationships with the suburbs is shortsighted. A much broader approach is required to address problems that were created by regional policies or practices. Fostering regional cooperation to solve problems may, in fact, be the most appropriate reason for appointing an emergency manager. If an emergency manager is given powers beyond those of Flint's elected officials, they should also be given the ability to reach beyond Flint's borders if that is where the solution, and perhaps even the cause, can be found.

Most glaringly, we heard from numerous Flint residents that they are no longer heard when an emergency manager is in place.

> *We have been under siege for two years. And for well over a year we were screaming, and nobody listened.*[8]

I drove people to Lansing on a regular basis, way before it even came out in the media, we were crying about this water.[9]

The people of Michigan voted down the emergency manager law on Monday, the following Wednesday they had another one, that we couldn't vote down. Do we trust the Government? NO![10]

And all of these people out here, they stood outside and told City Hall, the water is bad, it's discolored, it's repulsive, it smells.[11]

This is never acceptable. Every resident has the right to be heard by the elected officials making decisions that affect residents' life and health. This becomes even more important when an emergency manager is appointed to oversee local governments in distress. A manager from outside the community does not share the community's interests, and may not even understand them or know what they are. It is therefore imperative that (s)he listens to them.

But this is not enough; the key is to ensure meaningful involvement by hearing from local residents. We believe that local residents should have meaningful input into the decisions that affect them.

Conclusion

We end where we started – with two key concepts: Implicit bias and systemic racism. Both teach us that race will affect the decisions we make unless we consciously address these shortcomings.

Housing, education, the environment, and emergency management are all connected, and any policy that affects one, affects the others. Drawing a clear policy line defining where one ends and the next begins is impossible.

The same is true of racism, racialization, and systemic racism. They overlap and it is usually impossible to define precisely which applies and caused a particular outcome to be racially disparate. The structure, norms, policies and practices cut across institutions, neighborhoods, and communities with cumulative and compound effects. This Commission believes that, particularly applied to government, getting too caught up in precisely defining which is at play is both distracting and counterproductive. When we know policy will bring about disparate outcomes based on the color of people's skin, it is our responsibility to address it. It is not enough to say the result is unintended.

The manifestation of the Flint Water Crisis may or may not have involved bad actors, race-based decisions, criminal neglect, government negligence, or simply a lack of empathy for "the other." That will be determined by others. But to mitigate against or even prevent crises like this one we must look deeper.

It is abundantly clear that race played a major role in developing the policies and causing the events that turned Flint into a decaying and largely abandoned urban center, a place where a crisis like this one was all but inevitable. We cannot predict what the next crisis will be, when it will occur, or in which decaying urban center it will happen. But we do know that unless we do something, it will occur, and it will disparately harm people of color.

So was the Flint Water Crisis a case of discrimination?

The answer depends in large part with how "discrimination" is defined. Discrimination in the legal sense is defined and limited by our civil rights laws. In this context the question is whether an action is legal or illegal. In a more generalized use, "discrimination" also includes acts that do not meet the technical legal requirements. In this larger context the question is closer to whether the action was fair or unfair. Such an answer tells us not just about who we exclude versus include, but about the very foundation and ethos of our society, our moral fabric, our identity.

Ultimately, the legal question of whether the Flint Water Crisis was the result of illegal discrimination is one for the courts to decide. We do not seek to interfere with those proceedings, and therefore will not answer the legal question directly.

We can say that those pursuing civil rights claims will face an uphill climb.

There is no legal redress available to children who grew up in Flint because their father or grandfather returned from fighting for others' freedom in World War II were denied the ability to purchase a home because the G.I. bill and Federal Housing Authority effectively excluded black neighborhoods. It is indisputable that African Americans were routinely discriminated against by conduct that was legal at the time. Even if it had been illegal, the time in which to file a discrimination case has long since passed. As such, although we find that the history of housing in Flint is replete with spatial racism, racially discriminatory loan and realty practices, racialized structure, structural and systemic racism, any claim not based on recent events does not rise to the level of a legal claim.

We leave open the door to the possibility that a complaint may be brought to us that will meet the necessary legal requirements and falls within our jurisdiction. We note that the strongest argument for such a case would likely be a disparate impact claim under federal housing law based upon the 2015 U.S. Supreme Court decision, *Texas Department of Housing & Community Affairs v. The Inclusive Communities Project, Inc.* However, it is our understanding that the Department of Housing and Urban Development (HUD), who would be the most appropriate agency to pursue such a case under this federal law theory, has to date also not found a sufficient basis for doing so in this instance.

Nothing in this report should be read to imply that we do or do not believe there is merit in any of the civil suits that have been or may be brought related to the Flint Water Crisis. We have not reviewed the cases in detail and have not considered the issues presented by claims on theories and laws other than the ones discussed here. However, we note that while some testimony suggested that various manufacturers were responsible for the pollution that made the Flint River unusable, the choice to switch away from the Flint River as a water source was made because the river lacked a sufficient quantity of water, not quality. Additionally, the Flint River water intake was upstream from the industrial polluters, and any quality issues have had more to do with farm fertilizer and road salt runoff than industrial pollution.

The Attorney General's Office has brought criminal charges related to the Flint Water Crisis, and indicates more may be coming. Those charged are innocent until proven guilty, but the charges indicate that the Attorney General believes that some of the people involved in the events surrounding this crisis acted with some degree of *mens rea* (criminal intent). We have not considered criminal liability in this report.

There is no single cause for a crisis like the one still occurring in Flint; it requires a perfect storm of causes. Pointing to a specific cause for this crisis does not diminish the fact that the legacy of past policies in areas like housing, employment, the tax base and regionalization are all interconnected to the present. Identifying one bad actor doesn't indicate there aren't others.

Nor does it matter that people of color are not the only victims. Race, racism, structural racialization and systemic racism were responsible for the policies and events that created white flight, which decreased property values in the city while increasing them in the suburbs, and trapped anyone who remained in Flint regardless of color.

We find even the argument over whether a disparate impact results from policies and practices based on socioeconomics or racial differences to be more semantic than substantive. We have seen how a history of racist or racialized policies and practices resulted in African Americans being deprived of building wealth and taking advantage of opportunities.

The contamination of Flint's water system is deplorable, but it is only a symptom of a much larger disease, one that poisons all our structures and systems. Racialized outcomes do not need to be intentional. The poison of systemic racism will produce and reproduce them unless we consciously address then through implementation of policies and practices that have a racial equity framework. This is true of our government and it is true of ourselves.

The conditions that allowed the Flint Water Crisis are rooted in a time when racial separation and discrimination were intentional and expressed, a time when racism was not only accepted, it was official government policy that continued as accepted practices, processes, norms and rituals even when such policies were no longer official. Systemically we continue to produce racially disparate harm and benefit.

The fact that the problem is systemic and may be unintentional is an explanation, not an excuse. We can either consciously do something about it, or intentionally ignore it. That the problem is systemic doesn't mean there is nobody to blame. We are all to blame.

We must recognize that being colorblind is not the solution, it is the problem. Implicit bias and systemic racism ensure that when we refuse to see color, we are actually allowing it to influence our decisions while reinforcing racialized outcomes. Perpetuating those results without attempting to remedy past harm, and without consciously ensuring we don't cause new harm, isn't colorblindness, it is racism.

NOTES

1. 9.7% of all Michiganders, 49.8% of African Americans. See e.g., Richard C. Sadler and Andrew R. Highsmith, "Rethinking Tiebout: The Contribution of Political Fragmentation and Racial/Economic Segregation to the Flint Water Crisis," *Environmental Justice* (2016) at 7.
2. Michael Stampfler, former Emergency manager for Pontiac with nearly 30 years of city management experience, hearing 3, session 3 at 1:11:24.
3. *Id.* At 1:13:08.
4. Hearing 3, session 3 at 1:16:14.
5. Hearing 3, session 3 at 49:00.
6. Hearing 3, session 2 at 1:18:40.
7. *Id.* at 1:19:20.
8. Valerie Soughall, Flint resident, hearing 1 at 1:15:48.
9. Sister Janice Mohammed, Flint resident, Hearing 1 at 1:39:11.
10. Paul Herring, Sr., Flint resident, hearing 1 at 1:41:30.
11. Carolyn Shannon, Flint resident, hearing 3, session 4 at 1:09:50.

BRIDGE OVER THE MONONGAHELA RIVER, PITTSBURG, PENN.

Illustration VI.1 "Bridge Over the Monongahela River, Pittsburgh, Penn." (1857). Source: *Ballou's Pictorial*, February 21, 1857. Courtesy of the Center for Historic American Visual Culture at the American Antiquarian Society.

Pittsburgh earned a reputation as the "smokey city" early in the nineteenth century. This view of the city's busy waterfront in 1857 illustrates how smoke from steamboats, factories, and other sources obscures the impressive 1,500-foot bridge connecting Pittsburgh to Birmingham across the Monongahela River.

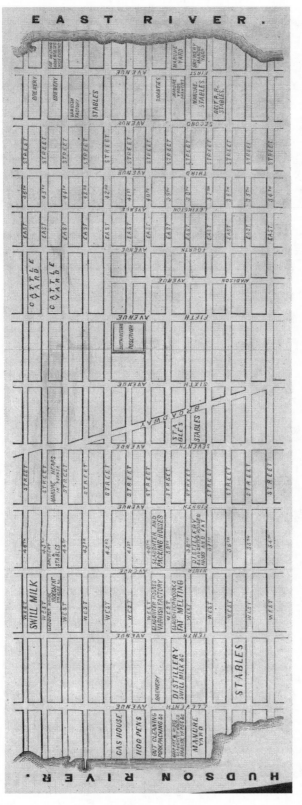

Illustration VI.2 Citizens' Association of New York, "Encroachment of Nuisances Upon Populous Up-Town Districts" (1864). Source: Citizens' Association of New York, *Report of the Council of Hygiene and Public Health of the Citizens' Association of New York Upon the Sanitary Conditions of the City* (New York: D. Appleton and Company, 1865). Courtesy of the Lionel Pincus and Princess Firyal Map Division, The New York Public Library, Astor, Lenox, and Tilden Foundations.

The mixed use of space characterized American cities before the rise of zoning and urban planning in the early twentieth century. This map identifies the location of "special nuisances," such as breweries, animal rendering plants, manure yards, and animal pens, in one of the most desirable residential areas of New York City during the middle of the nineteenth century. Contemporary public health reformers considered these nonresidential endeavors to be sources of disease and campaigned to have them relocated to less populated areas.

Illustration VI.3 "Demolished and Tilted by the Earthquake, Homes on Howard Street at 17ᵗʰ, 1906. (544–7961) Stereopticon view. Kelly and Chadwick." San Francisco Earthquake of 1906. Courtesy of the Center for Historic American Visual Culture at the American Antiquarian Society.

Illustration VI.4 "Smog, Salt Lake City, Utah, November 11, 1950." Courtesy of the United States Department of Health and Human Services, Center for Disease Control and Prevention/Barbara Jenkins, National Institute for Occupational Safety and Health.

PART VII

TRANSVERSING AND TRANSFORMING URBAN SPACE

Transportation and Planning

EDITORS' INTRODUCTION TO PART VII

Most courses in urban history and urban studies are not complete without the inclusion of materials related to transportation and physical mobility across and through the metropolis. Cities in the eighteenth century and earlier found physical growth circumscribed by the distance a person could easily transverse—a radius from the central city of about two miles. Our early, compact cities, normally crossed on foot, are referred to as "walking cities" by urbanists for this reason. Population pressures, the need for more extensive business sectors, and the economic ability of some (originally only the middle and upper classes) to live in the countryside and commute into the city for work led to the evolution of a modern transportation network, serving both residents of the city and commuters from the metropolitan region as a whole.

Urban history and urban studies, as taught and researched today, are as much about metropolitan and suburban growth as they are about central cities. Thus many urban academic programs are renaming themselves "metropolitan and community studies" programs or adopting similar monikers. By the 1990s, about half of the American population lived in areas that might be termed "suburbs." Suburban life did not change the fact that most Americans connected with "urban" culture on a daily basis, whether it be through commuting into the city for jobs and recreation, or through the multiple doorways of mass popular culture, streaming at us from the Internet, cable television, satellite radio, and the like. The subject of the modern suburb is somewhat outside of the scope of this reader, and already is ably handled in *The Suburb Reader* (New York: Routledge, 2016) by historians Andrew Weise and Becky Nicolaides. Yet some aspects of suburban growth must be touched on here. In the mid-nineteenth century, central cities grew increasingly differentiated from outlying hinterlands, while at the same time better transportation linked the widening city together. The wealthy and then the middle class took advantage of increased transportation options to relocate away from cities plagued with overcrowding, seemingly relentless noise, and growing levels of airborne and waterborne pollution.

The first city dwellers to realize the dream of residing beyond the central city were the wealthy, as depicted in Ernest W. Burgess' concentric zone model of 1920. [See Illustration I.2, **Ernest W. Burgess, Urban Areas (1925).**] Wealthy people could afford to keep their own horses and carriages, providing private means for them to move out from the city centers during the 1800s. Popular forms of mass transit allowed for the upper middle class, the middle class, and ultimately portions of the working class to afford daily commutes in some American cities. The earliest form of rudimentary travel within a metropolitan region (drawing on the model of the stagecoach, which offered privately owned service between cities with a set route and set stops) was the horse-drawn omnibus, a privately-owned vehicle open to all that could pay the fare which traveled a set route. Omnibuses were first used in New York City in 1827. Chicago featured omnibuses as a means to transport travelers between hotels and railroad stations in 1852. Modifications followed, including the introduction of rails, and the rail-reliant cars came to be known as horsecars or horse-drawn streetcars. Chicago opened its first horse-car line in 1859. Urban commuters also relied on trains headed for distant locations for local service, although this form of transportation was not designed for the local commuter. In 1873, San Francisco implemented the cable car, which became popular in many American cities. Even Chicago, which did not have San Francisco's daunting hills, relied on the cable car technology it acquired from San Francisco beginning in 1882, but the entire system had been converted to electric trolleys by 1906.

It was the electric trolley, whereby overhead wires transferred electricity to the vehicle, that transformed most American cities. This technological form caught on quickly in cities throughout the United States. Experiments had been ongoing on the trolley since the 1830s, but the power supply initially had proved inadequate and too unreliable for a city-wide system. Montgomery, Alabama put a rudimentary system in place in 1886, and one was built for the city of Richmond, Virginia by Frank J. Sprague in 1888. By the 1880s and 1890s, almost all cities of substantial size had a trolley system. The business of transportation systems was rife with corruption, for transportation made more money if lines were consolidated and politicians had to approve of licensing. Philadelphian Charles T. Yerkes, Chicago's own "robber baron," consolidated streetcar systems there by 1900 and had his business exploits fictionalized in Theodore Dreiser's works, *The Financier* (1912), *The Titan* (1914), and *The Stoic* (published posthumously in 1947). Trolleys ultimately became unprofitable and were dismantled in most cities due to the pressures of the automobile, intense regulation, and population relocation to the suburbs. [See **Transportation Revolution Photo Essay, Illustrations VII.1 to VII.7.**]

For some cities, urban congestion was so overwhelming that innovators sought a means to get mass transit off the city streets entirely. Trolleys added greatly to urban congestion, and having to cross the tracks proved to be a highly dangerous, yet disturbingly frequent, urban activity. So many were killed or maimed by trolleys that some wondered if trolley drivers were *trying* to injure pedestrians. By 1870, New York City had elevated its steam-powered railway system, eliminating the need for grade-crossings of at least one form of transportation. Unfortunately, elevating train systems blocked light to the street below, brought trains perilously close to second and third floor apartments, and occasionally contributed to stunning accidents (as was the case when an car derailed from the elevated tracks in New York City in 1919). Other cities realized the potential of placing mass transit underground. Boston implemented the first, albeit limited system in 1897, when the local streetcar franchise established a limited subway route under Tremont Street. New York City followed this lead in 1904, building an extensive system that transformed the city. No major subway projects followed until Chicago's work of the 1930s, as subways proved prohibitively expensive. Buses became popular in many cities in the 1950s, replacing streetcar systems in many cities. Chicago's red cars, operated by Chicago Surface Lines (CSL), carried almost 900 million riders per year, but were decimated by the implementation of a bus system in that city in the 1950s.[i]

The automobile radically transformed cities, in their reshaping of central areas (now filled by parking lots, parking spaces, parking meters, gas stations, and other car-related businesses), crowded the roads, and expanded the spaces made available to the individual driver. Commuting became a way of life for millions of Americans, and the house with the backyard became a reality for more former urbanites. By the 1920s, cars had become an essential component of the American lifestyle. Cars were so entrenched in the United States that many held on to their cars in the midst of the Great Depression. Americans considered cars a necessity, even as they re-evaluated the need for three square meals a day. By the time urban planners realized the full extent of the spatial changes the private car would bring to our cities and regions, the American reliance on the car was seemingly irreversible. By 1940, thirteen million Americans lived in places not served by public transportation.

Once we had made cars the standard form of transportation in the United States, Americans found its roads inadequate; the nation's roads were not efficient for travel within a city, travel between cities, or travel in the rural regions. Under the Eisenhower Administration, Congress authorized the Federal Highway Act of 1956 [see **Document 8.1**], which allowed for $27 billion dollars to be spent over what was initially to be a ten year effort to build 40,000 miles of interstate highway. Monies in part came from a "trust fund" of taxes pulled from the purchase of fuel, cars, trucks, and tires. But this unprecedented public works initiative cost far more in terms of time and money than first imagined. Upkeep on these roads would be a struggle passed down for generations. And the highways did not lessen traffic problems, but rather encouraged movement. Once built, it was possible for city dwellers to move away from dwellings near their jobs and to acquire the trappings suburban life. The interstate highway system was designed for projections on highway needs for 1972, but was not completed until the early 1990s. The highways also created physical and psychological scars within cities, tearing apart neighborhoods and disrupting surface traffic. One remedy came in the form of the Central Artery/Tunnel Project in Boston that placed portions of Interstate 93 underneath the city and its harbor. The so-called "Big Dig" cost in upwards of $14.6 billion.

In Part VII, five authors offer analyses of the changing city. Sam Bass Warner, Jr.'s "From Walking City to the Implementation of Street Railways," a portion of his work, *Streetcar Suburbs: The Process of Growth in Boston, 1870–1900* (Cambridge, MA: Harvard University Press, 1962), provides a classic reading of the way in which streetcars transformed Boston, leading to the creation of suburbs later formally annexed by the city. Warner's work opens a way into the discussions of physical and economic mobility that so preoccupied the emerging "new social historians" of the 1960s and 1970s and still shapes the field of social and urban history today. Marta Gutman's selection from her book, *A City for Children: Women, Architecture, and the Charitable Landscapes of Oakland, 1850–1950* (Chicago: University of Chicago Press, 2014), demonstrates how the vernacular architecture of the urban west was altered by power, gender, and race. Clifton Hood's "The Subway and the City," taken from his book, *722 Miles: The Building of the Subways and How They Transformed New York* (New York: Simon & Schuster, 1993), documents the opening of the New York City subway system—the most important local transportation system in the United States—and demonstrates how this system restructured this massive city. The excitement at the grand opening of the subway is palpable through the stories Hood relates. Robert Fogelson's "Wishful Thinking: Downtown and the Automotive Revolution," from his book, *Downtown: Its Rise and Fall, 1880–1930* (New Haven: Yale University Press, 2001), examines how urban leaders worked to provide better access to the downtown business district, and watched as its relevance seemed to slip away, despite their best efforts. In "Planning a Social Disaster," D. Bradford Hunt demonstrates how choices made by the Chicago Housing Authority left social and physical scars that still haunt the city in the present day.

NOTE

i   David M. Young, "Street Railways," in James R. Grossman, Ann Durkin Keating, and Janice L. Reiff, eds., *Encyclopedia of Chicago* (Chicago: University of Chicago Press, 2004), 791–792.

ESSAY 7.1

From Walking City to the Implementation of the Street Railways

Sam Bass Warner, Jr.

Source: Sam Bass Warner, Jr., *Streetcar Suburbs: The Process of Growth in Boston, 1870–1900* (Cambridge, MA: Harvard University Press, 1962).

EDITORS' INTRODUCTION

Despite its reputation for traditionalism and a conservative outlook, Boston, as portrayed by Sam Bass Warner, Jr., in his classic work *Streetcar Suburbs*, is a city of "ceaseless change." Warner notes that in the second half of the nineteenth century, the city experienced a dramatic evolution in which city leaders, home builders, transportation entrepreneurs, and enthusiastic new suburbanites transformed the city's physical form. Warner states, "In fifty years it changed from a merchant city of two hundred thousand inhabitants to an industrial metropolis of over a million. In 1850 Boston was a tightly packed seaport; by 1900 it sprawled over a ten-mile radius and contained thirty-one cities and towns."[i] Boston had a rapid metamorphosis from a "walking city" (a city of approximately two miles in radius easily accessible by foot) to a city reliant on transportation. The central city, which once housed people from all socio-economic backgrounds, lost its middle-class and upper-class population to the lures of suburban life. The central business district—the city area devoted to financial and business matters—grew up upon the increasingly expensive real estate of the central city. Thus the city and its related areas, or hinterlands, grew into a metropolis more and more divided by class. In an examination of the suburbs of Roxbury, West Roxbury, and Dorchester, all of which would come to be annexed by Boston in the late 1800s, Warner provides information on the origins of the suburb and the now well-known figure of the commuting worker.

Warner's work, originally published in 1962, is still assigned in college classrooms and underpins much of the work done on suburban growth and the impact of transportation on American cities. Warner demonstrates how sprawl preceded the advent of the automobile. His work relates with that of the Chicago School's Ernest W. Burgess, whose concentric zone model set the stage for much of the thinking about the evolution of urban physical space and differentiation by class within a city. **[See Illustration I.2, Ernest W. Burgess, Urban Areas.]** The upper class find themselves with access to the largest quantity of physical space, space they need only divide among a limited number of people. Suburbanites in effect create their own individual parks, and have many of the advantages of country life, including fresh air, physical beauty of landscape, and quiet. As the middle class grew and took advantage of their financial wherewithal to purchase suburban homes, the metropolitan lifestyles grew untenable, with very long, stress-inducing commutes, choked highways, and a loss of open land. As geographer John Corbett writes about the continued relevancy of

---

i Sam Bass Warner, Jr., *Streetcar Suburbs: The Process of Growth in Boston, 1870–1900* (Cambridge, MA: Harvard University Press, 1978), 1.

Warner's argument, "Decades later, we are still dealing with the forces of development that Warner first unlocked, and [are] as far as ever from finding a solution."[ii]

Sam Bass Warner, Jr., has served as Meyerhoff Professor of Environmental History at Brandeis University, William Edwards Huntington Professor of History at Boston University, and Visiting Professor at the Massachusetts Institute of Technology (MIT). In addition to *Streetcar Suburbs*, Warner has written and contributed to a number of books, including *Planning for a Nation of Cities* (Cambridge, MA: MIT Press, 1969), *The Private City: Philadelphia in Three Periods of Growth* (Philadelphia: University of Pennsylvania Press, 1987), *To Dwell is to Garden: A History of Boston's Community Gardens* (Boston, MA: Northeastern University Press, 1987), *The Urban Wilderness: A History of the American City* (Berkeley: University of California Press, 1995), and *American Urban Form: A Representative History* (with Andrew Whittemore) (Cambridge, MA: MIT Press, 2012).

FROM WALKING CITY TO THE IMPLEMENTATION OF THE STREET RAILWAYS (1962)

At any given time the arrangement of streets and buildings in a large city represents a temporary compromise among such diverse and often conflicting elements as aspirations for business and home life, the conditions of trade, the supply of labor, and the ability to remake what came before.

The physical plan of metropolitan Boston in 1850 rested upon a primitive technology of urban transport: Boston was a city of pedestrians. Its form reflected a compromise among convenience and privacy, the aspirations of homeownership, and the high price of land. The arrival of the street railway freed the elements of the compromise from their former discipline of pedestrian movement and bound them together again by its own new discipline. By 1900 the transformation of Boston had been completed. The patterns made by this new compromise are what today is recognized as the suburban form of the metropolitan city.

The Walking City

In 1850 the area of dense settlement hardly exceeded a two-mile radius from City Hall. It included only portions of the towns and cities of Boston, Brookline, Cambridge, Charlestown, Chelsea, Dorchester, Roxbury, and Somerville. Before the invention of the telephone in 1876 and the introduction of street railways in the 1850's, face-to-face communication and movement on foot were essential ingredients of city life.

One can only guess just how large metropolitan Boston would have grown had there been no invention of new communication devices. If the spread of the city had begun to exceed the distance a man might walk in about an hour, say a three-mile radius, the shops and offices of the metropolis would have fallen out of easy daily communication with each other. The result would have been the destruction of a single unified communication network and the development of semi-autonomous subcities which would have had to duplicate many of the services and facilities offered in other parts of the city. One of the principal contributions of nineteenth century transportation and communication technology was to preserve the centralized communication of the walking city on a vastly enlarged scale.

In 1850 carriages were a prominent sight on Boston's downtown streets. They moved only a small proportion of the city's population, however, because few people could afford to maintain a private horse and carriage. The omnibus and the steam railroad were likewise supplements to walking. The omnibus, an urban version of the stage coach, was first introduced in 1826. It

ii John Corbett, "Sam Bass Warner: Modeling the Streetcar Suburbs, 1962," Center for the Spatially Integrated Social Science (CSISS) Classics, accessed at http://www.csiss.org/classics/content/49.

moved slowly, held relatively few passengers, and cost a lot. The stream railroad, in operation since 1835, was also expensive and accomplished, during its first fifteen years, little to change the old pattern of the city. At best it was a limited method of mass transportation. The railroad was fast but its infrequent stops and its single terminal, often located at some distance from passengers' ultimate destinations, prevented it from offering the great variety of choices of entrance and exit that streetcar systems ultimately provided. Prior to the Civil War the principal contribution of the railroad lay in its joining of the port of Boston, with its wharves and warehouses, to the manufacturing and farming towns of New England. The result was to accelerate the industrialization of both the trading center and its hinterland. For residents of the Boston region the railroad simplified business transactions with outlying industrial cities like Lynn and Waltham. The railroad also enabled some men of wealth and leisure to settle permanently at their summer estates which lay in scattered clusters about the hills beyond Boston.[1]

Before 1850 Boston's geography had inhibited easy expansion. Marshes, rivers, and the ocean restricted the paths of pedestrian communication. Boston itself was a rough, hilly peninsula set on the end of a narrow strip of land that connected it to the mainland at Roxbury. In the general area where the wharves now stand, against the eastern and northern part of the peninsula, lay the deep-water harbor. The rest of the peninsula was surrounded by tidal basins and enormous marshes. So confined by the harbor, Boston land had always been expensive, and almost from the beginning of its settlement men cramped for space began damming and filling the marshes and flats, first for commercial, and later for residential, purposes. As the city prospered and housing standards rose, more extensive works became profitable. Hills were leveled and sea walls built. By the 1850's developers had reclaimed the area around Charles street, parts of the North End, and much of the South End, and had cut down a good deal of Beacon and other hills.

In the succeeding twenty years Boston's two most ambitious land filling schemes were executed: the South End and the Back Bay. The South End was almost completely taken up with houses by 1880; the Back Bay, by 1900. Only the rich and the prosperous segment of the middle class could afford most of the new houses in these sections even though the common design of narrow row houses, three and one-half to four and one-half stories high, required but small parcels of land.[2]

Under such circumstances speculators turned their attention to land just beyond the main peninsula. What they wanted was property that could be more easily developed and therefore sold at lower prices. The search for cheap land began long before central Boston was filled. In 1804 South Boston was opened as a housing speculation. Its progress remained slow, however, until the 1830's when the growth of Boston created a shortage of land sufficient to persuade people to move beyond the old peninsula and walk the added distance.[3] Similarly, Charlestown, parts of Cambridge, East Boston, and the nearby sections of Roxbury filled up rapidly in the period from 1830 to 1850 when Boston's industrial prosperity and expansion began to make headway.

These peripheral communities were not simple bedroom towns for commuters, not exact early models of the modern middle class residential suburb; rather they were mixed settlements of Boston commuters and local workers. All these communities lay at the edge of the harbor and possessed considerable industrial and mercantile potential. Charlestown and East and South Boston developed large shipbuilding and wharf facilities, while Cambridge and Roxbury became manufacturing centers.[4] Promoters of these areas, used to the tight scale of the walking city, saw no incompatibility between residences and factories; they wished to re-create the conditions of Boston.

Throughout the tiny metropolitan region of 1850, streets of the well-to-do lay hard by workers' barracks and tenements of the poor; many artisans kept shop and home in the same building or suite; and factories, wharves, and offices were but a few blocks from middle class homes. The wide physical separation between those who could afford new houses and those who could not awaited the expansion of the city that accompanied the introduction of the street railway.

Despite the peripheral towns' imitation of the central city some architectural differences marked the two areas. On the filled land of the main peninsula close copies of the brick London town row house predominated. In the peripheral areas, detached houses, continuations of eighteenth century American wooden construction, were the rule. These latter structures were often smaller and generally cheaper than their intown opposites. Today, after detached wooden styles have dominated residential fashions for over eighty years, the little wooden houses of South and East Boston appear to be significant alternatives to the brick row house. In the early nineteenth century, however, these houses were but a continuation of old habits. They were the products of a class of people who had yet to earn the wealth, had yet to learn the modes, of city life.

Compared to the enlarged lots, the picturesque houses, and the planted streets of the streetcar suburbs of the last third of the nineteenth century, the architecture of Boston in 1850 was strongly urban. The houses of the central city and the peripheral towns, set as they were on small narrow lots and generally placed against the street, created a town environment of dense settlement. Building in both areas was eminently suited to a city short of land, a city which depended on people's walking for its means of transportation, a city which depended upon face-to-face relationships as its means of communication.[5]

The Street Railways

The history of Boston's street railways in the nineteenth century is the story of fifty years of aggressive expansion. During both the early years of the horsecar and the later years of the electric, lines were rapidly lengthened and service frequently increased. This continuous expansion of surface transportation had a cumulative effect upon the city. The pace of suburbanization, at first slow, went forward with increasing acceleration, until by the 1890's it attained the proportions of a mass movement.

From 1852 until 1873 the horse railroads of Boston merely stretched out the existing city along already established paths. The outer boundary of dense settlement moved perhaps half a mile, so that at the time of the great Depression of 1873 it stood two and a half miles from Boston's City Hall. During the next fourteen years, from 1873 to 1887, horsecar service reached out about a mile and a half farther, bringing the outer edge of good transportation to four miles from City Hall. Lines of suburban settlement began to appear in what were formerly distant places. In the late 1880's and 1890's the electrification of street railways brought convenient transportation to at least the range of six miles from City Hall. The rate of building and settlement in this period became so rapid that the whole scale and plan of Greater Boston was entirely made over.

Boston's first street railway had but one car which began service between Harvard Square, Cambridge, and Union Square, Somerville, around 1852. The success of this experiment and the example of profitable lines in other American cities brought on a wave of entrepreneurial enthusiasm. To the local investment public, used to the relatively long periods necessary to realize profits on large-scale land speculations, the rapid construction of horse railroads seemed to promise a generous and immediate harvest. To real estate men the simple procedure of placing a coach on iron rails seemed a miraculous device for the promotion of out-of-town property.

The experience of the three towns of Roxbury, West Roxbury, and Dorchester was typical. The first line in this section of the metropolis commenced running in 1856. It followed the seventeenth century path which ran from downtown Boston along Washington street in the South End to Roxbury Crossing. In effect, the new service merely replaced the existing omnibus and supplemented the main traffic of pedestrians and carriages. In the short period from the first incorporation of 1852 to the Depression of 1873, seven companies were formed to serve the outlying towns of Roxbury, West Roxbury, and Dorchester. Only four ever operated. By 1873 only two companies, the Metropolitan Street Railway, and the Highland Street Railway, survived.

Some of Boston's street railways had been projected for routes with too light settlement and traffic, others were badly financed, and some were bogus companies put together to lure investors or to harass operating companies. The scramble for franchises, which were granted by the Boston Board of Aldermen, and for charters of incorporation, which were granted by the state legislature, further confused the ever shifting rivalries of the city's street railway companies.

These early difficulties of franchise and capitalization were soon superseded by the problems of the downtown. Boston's streets were just too narrow to carry all the needed cars. The downtown squeeze made necessary complicated lease arrangements for competitors' use of each other's tracks. The tempers of street railway employees were not always equal to this requirement of cooperation in a field of intense competition. All too often rival drivers raced for switches, stalled, and in general interfered with each other's progress. Nevertheless, despite early confusion, chicane, and false starts, by 1873 the main streets of the old city had become the new horsecar thoroughfares. During the years from 1852 to 1873 the periphery of dense settlement moved from 2 to 2.5 miles from City Hall.[6]

For the next fourteen years service in Greater Boston expanded steadily outward. Then, in 1887, Henry M. Whitney, a steamship operator and speculator in Brookline real estate, formed a syndicate out of his small West End Street Railway and began to purchase stock in the other five operating companies of Boston. After he had bought up large amounts of stock, especially in the biggest line, the Metropolitan, he offered by an exchange of stock and bonds to combine all the companies into one. Minority stockholders, probably helpless, and at any rate anticipating great profits from the rationalization of Boston service under one giant company, agreed to the merger. At the same time, the promise of rapid expansion of service and relief to downtown traffic jams persuaded the public and the legislature to allow the creation of the traction monopoly. Consolidation did in fact accelerate the rate of improvements in transportation.

Whitney continued two historic policies of street railway management. First, he was more interested in increasing the total number of fares on his system than in watching the relationship of distance, cost, and fare per ride. He, like his fellow streetcar managers the state over, was so convinced that the key to profit lay in the endless expansion of the numbers of passengers that, with little regard to costs, he constantly expanded the service area of the West End. As a result, by 1900 the outer limits of Boston's electric railways lay at least six miles from the downtown.

Second, Whitney, like all horsecar managers before him, was an ardent believer in the five-cent fare. Thus expansion of service took place without additional charge to the commuter. As crosstown lines were built, free-transfer points were added, so that the nickel fare was almost universal in 1900. During the 1870's and 1880's eight cents had been required for many transfer rides; two full fares had been required where riders moved to the cars of different companies.[7]

In his speeches before city clubs and regulatory agencies Whitney often pointed to these twin policies of rapid service expansion and the uniform five-cent fare as the proper basis for a public transportation system. He was an ardent champion of the suburban city. He frequently appealed to the popular belief that the rapid suburbanization of modern industrial cities was perhaps the most important single contribution of the street railway. Like his listeners, also, Whitney did not wish to control the form and direction of this suburban expansion, but rather to leave the development of suburbs to individual builders and homeowners. Though statistics of 1890 and 1900 showed that only one quarter of Boston's suburbanites owned their houses,[8] he, like his contemporaries, felt that the continued suburbanization of the city would bring a substantial increase in homeownership. He liked to use as a typical example of the coming benefits the rather untypical case of the workingman buying a lot of land in the suburbs upon which would be built his own home. Whitney's speeches were also full of comparisons to conditions in Europe and references to the old pre-streetcar sections of Boston where multi-family tenements and crowded old wooden houses were the rule.

Whitney made these appeals to what was then termed the "moral influence" of street railways both from personal conviction, and from the need to answer the numerous critics of his monopoly. He was continually before state and city agencies defending the profits and schedules of the West End Street Railway. Most important for the growth of the suburban city, criticism always took for its point of departure the same view of public transportation that Whitney's management undertook to carry out. For critics, the trouble with the West End Company was that its very vigorous performance was not vigorous enough: new service was not added fast enough, profits were too high, and fares not cheap enough.[9]

The demise of Whitney's West End Street Railway as an operating company was due not to the shortcomings of its suburban service, but to continued strife over downtown traffic conditions. The details of the decade of controversy over the control and pricing of tunnels and elevateds are not relevant to this history. In the end, in 1897, a group of rival capitalists formed the Boston Elevated Street Railway Company, and, under the supervision of the state-created Boston Transit Authority, leased the West End system in its entirety. With this new operating company the great subway and elevated projects were undertaken in a belated effort to solve downtown traffic problems. The Boston Elevated's suburban policy remained that of its predecessors: expand for more total passengers.

During the entire second half of the nineteenth century two things made possible this continuous expansion of service under all kinds of managements. The first was the declining costs of materials; the second was electrification. In 1888 the West End began experimenting with electric cars and in 1889 introduced its first trolley service. The electric car moved at least twice as fast as the horse drawn one and soon was perfected to carry three times the number of passengers. Of course offsetting these advantages, the new machines required a great deal more investment in heavy equipment than the horse and his carbarn.

In the center of the system, where traffic was heavy, the electric car was cheaper to operate per passenger mile than the horsecar. It seemed reasonable to run the electric car from the intown segment of a line out to the suburban terminal, especially since in the outer areas of less frequent stops the electric could really show its speed. In this way the electric-powered streetcar beguiled traction men who were careless about costs into spinning out the web of their service even beyond profitable limits.[10]

NOTES

1. At the time of writing Professor Charles J. Kennedy of the University of Nebraska was about to publish his history of the Boston and Maine Railroad. This book will contain a complete discussion of the early steam railroad and its associated commuting patterns. I am indebted to Professor Kennedy for a citation of *Hunt's Merchant Magazine* (December 25, 1851, p. 759), which published a one-day traffic count of Boston. This count showed three equally popular means of entering and leaving the city: walking, riding the railroad, and traveling by carriage or omnibus.

2. The common mid-century South End land plan located single-family row houses on the side streets and mixed these row houses with tenement and store combinations on the main traffic streets. Tremont and Washington streets and Columbus, Shawmut, and Harrison avenues offered some moderately priced small rental units before the wholesale conversion of the single-family houses. Walter Muir Whitehill, *Boston: A Topographical History*

(Cambridge, 1959), pp. 119–140; Suffolk Deeds, Liber 626, plan at end.

3. The original South Boston grid was broken in 1822 when narrow alleys were built behind the main streets. The alley lots were sold off for workers' housing. The resulting cramped land plan has provided a source of discomfort for 140 years. These alleys turn up in Harold K. Estabrook, *Some Slums in Boston* (Boston, 1898), pp. 21–23. Some alleys of houses have been replaced by federal housing projects; others still can be seen—for example, West 4th and 5th streets between E and F, and Silver and Gold streets. For the development of South Boston: Thomas C. Simonds, *History of South Boston* (Boston, 1857), pp. 72–104, 194–204, 300–313.

4. William H. Sumner, *A History of East Boston* (Boston, 1858), pp. 421–471; Suffolk Deeds, L. 401, end; Francis S. Drake, *The Town of Roxbury* (Roxbury, 1878), pp. 397–441; Woods and Kennedy, "The Zone of Emergence," chapters on Charlestown, South Boston, East Boston, Cambridgeport, East Cambridge and Roxbury.

5. Good examples of the popular varieties of pre-streetcar city housing may be seen in Boston proper at Porter street; and in the lower South End, the blocks from Castle street to Worcester Square between Harrison avenue and Tremont street. Examples of the cheaper styles of the peripheral towns: in East Boston at Saratoga, Princeton, Lexington, and Trenton streets, between Marion and Brooks; in South Boston on West 4th and 5th streets; in Roxbury from Madison to Vernon streets between Tremont and Washington street; in Charlestown from Chelsea street to the Bunker Hill Monument; in East Cambridge, 3rd to 5th streets between Cambridge and Charles street.

6. Prentiss Cummings, "Street Railways of Boston," *Professional and Industrial History of Suffolk County, Mass.* (Boston, 1894), III, 289–290; Richard Herndon, *Boston of Today* (Boston, 1892), pp. 310–311; *Boston Evening Transcript*, November 24, 1882, editorial, p. 4; Robert H. Whitten, *Public Administration in Massachusetts* (New York, 1898), pp. 112–126.

7. Roswell F. Phelps, *South End Factory Operatives, Employment and Residence* (Boston, 1903), pp. 18–19.

8. For further discussion of tenure, see Warner, "Residential Development," Appendix D.

9. The street railwayman's credo: Henry M. Whitney and Prentiss Cummings, *Additional Burdens upon the Street Railway Companies, etc.* (Boston, 1891); the critics: *Citizen's Association of Boston Explaining Its Position. Statement of the Executive Committee Regarding .... the Franchise Bill* (Boston, 1891).

10. The foregoing economic analysis of street railways is taken from Edward S. Mason, *The Street Railway in Massachusetts* (Cambridge, 1932), pp. 1–7, 71–113, 118–121.

ESSAY 7.2

The Landscape of Charity in California: First Imprints in San Francisco

Marta Gutman

Source: Marta Gutman, *A City for Children: Women, Architecture, and the Charitable Landscapes of Oakland, 1850–1950* (Chicago: University of Chicago Press, 2014).

EDITORS' INTRODUCTION

Marta Gutman's focus on vernacular architecture and the way in which power, gender, and race contributed to the outlines of the physical landscape in the western United States adds an important dimension to our understanding of the evolution of the American city. As historian Richard Wade has explained, the establishment of cities helped to drive the settlement of the American West, and enabled the achievement of Manifest Destiny. Gutman explores how white women repurposed urban spaces, many of them which had previously served as bastions of male urban life, to serve the needs of urban children. Former saloons became kindergarten classrooms. In limited instances, the white women's volunteer projects embraced the participation of children of color, and some of the earliest establishments serving the needs of urban children were integrated, allowing for the enrollment of white and black children. Latino children and Asian children were most often excluded from institutions serving white children.

Although the West had long been touted as an exceptional place, the region's urban history shared many characteristics with that of the rest of urban America. By the 1870s, Gutman reminds us, California Women gained the right to take part in civil society and public work by forming "respectable" voluntary associations. Thus the spaces they created for destitute children also gave them a public place in the city. The concerns of children seemed to be the realm of women, even when these concerns played out in the creation of kindergartens and playgrounds.

The women were most interested in ameliorating the hardships faced by economically disadvantaged families. Gutman explains that "During the Gold Rush, women in San Francisco realized that the physical world was more than a background for social practices. The materials facts of everyday life seized their imaginations and inspired them to act on the belief that they could, and should, amend their city to offer destitute children a better childhood."[i]

Marta Gutman is a professor of architecture and urban history at the City College of New York and a professor of art history at the Graduate Center/CUNY. She is a licensed architect.

---

i Marta Gutman, *A City for Children: Women, Architecture, and the Charitable Landscapes of Oakland, 1850–1950* (Chicago: University of Chicago Press), 33.

THE LANDSCAPE OF CHARITY IN CALIFORNIA: FIRST IMPRINTS IN SAN FRANCISO (2014)

When Elizabeth Betts walked out of the front door of her home, she entered the public realm of her Oakland neighborhood. She knew the spatial restrictions of separate spheres, the popular ideological construction that in the mid-nineteenth century presumed to link women to private, domestic spaces and men to the public realm. We know now that these rigid distinctions did not map easily or directly onto the physical city, and women challenged them historically when they crossed the public-private divide to organize, fund, and build charities for children.[1] Their decision was not unusual in northern California. In the early 1850s, Protestant and Catholic women started to ameliorate the physical city for children when they made the first imprints in the landscape of charity in San Francisco.

Having lived in San Francisco in the 1850s and extended her social circle in Sacramento in the 1860s, Watt knew some of the women who built the first charities for children after California entered the Union in 1850. In a period of aggressive westward expansion and rapid urbanization, her friends had applied habits of mind, learned in their former North American homes, as they opened orphanages for homeless boys and girls. In short order, women expanded the charitable landscape in the biggest, most important city in the American West to include not only orphanages and rescue homes for white, Protestant, and Catholic children, but also day nurseries and infant asylums for children of other religions, races, and ethnicities. By the 1870s, the scope of this network set a model for other institution builders in the region, including several in Oakland, where women also built a landscape of charity. With no state orphanages and very few other public institutions for children, middle- and upper-middle-class women shouldered the responsibility for social welfare for children in California for the balance of the century.[2]

Starting in the 1850s, women on the West Coast used this kind of institution building to win a foothold in urban public culture. During the second half of the nineteenth century, the gender order in California was as marked as any by the asymmetry of gender relations in the United States; women were relegated to second-class, segregated citizenship until the battle for suffrage was won in 1911. In this state, organizing to win the vote did coincide with and contribute to the remarkable flowering of women's public culture during the Progressive Era.[3] But even before the suffrage battle took off in the West, white women in California coalesced around other matters that brought them face-to-face with the effects of gender inequality. One of the most important issues was the feminization of urban poverty; and a principal corollary, the need to organize social welfare for children also motivated these reformers. The latter cause appealed to conservative, often very privileged Protestant women who ascribed to the ideology of domestic femininity, had little interest in suffrage, and did not support economic equality for women in the workplace. Even though not feminist in the strict political sense of the term, Protestant churchwomen, joined by Catholic nuns, grappled with charity for urban children as a pressing matter of public importance to the female sex. The female defense of children's well-being, because it contributed to maternalist politics, laid the groundwork for the welfare state and thus helped women reach and achieve citizenship.[4] In California as elsewhere in the West, this political work began locally, through churches, clubs, and charities, and demanded the construction of physical places as well as the organization of formal institutions.[5]

Women intervened in the chaotic years after the Gold Rush, when they were confronted with children living on the streets of San Francisco. In the face of market neglect and limited state interest, this crisis made palpable and vividly apparent the unmet social needs in the new, crude, and unhealthy city. The decision to intervene—white Protestant women organized an

Orphan Asylum Society in 1851, and others followed quickly—put into the limelight not only how rapidly homeless children became a problem for the urban elite, but also how women would cross the public-private divide to build for them. By the mid-1850s, impressive stone orphanages had been constructed for Protestant and Catholic children. South of the city, the San Francisco Board of Supervisors, in concert with the state legislature, set aside a large plot for a brick and stone "House of Refuge," renamed the Industrial School when it opened in 1859.[6]

These were the first architectural imprints, and thus the first nodes, in the charitable landscape for children: institutions owned and run by Protestant churchwomen, the Irish Catholic Sisters of Charity, and the city government. The large masonry buildings held architectural features in common, even if verbal rhetoric emphasized the contrary, given that Protestants and Catholics competed for the care of orphaned children. In California, public subsidies supported private charities for children at the same time as the gender division of labor supported the electorate's taste for low taxes and thus for inexpensive government. Private charities for children cost less to run than public ones, and they quickly outnumbered public (state-run) institutions.[7] Almost all the private charities were managed by women, if not owned by them outright.

From the outset, Protestant and Catholic women who promoted the ideology of domestic femininity used the constituent elements of civil society to win support from both sexes and alter the physical city for children. Protestant women called on models of organizing known to them, their mothers, and probably their grandmothers as they formed voluntary societies, publicized charities in newspapers and magazines, held public meetings, and called on social networks, including ties to prominent men in politics and business, to build institutions. The pursuit of reform causes had encouraged Protestant women to engage in activities like these, which had political character and had shaped civic behavior since the end of the eighteenth century.[8] The public voice of Catholic nuns was more limited, but

voluntary societies supported their charities; and Catholic women, like Protestant women, engaged with the market, law, and government as they bought, sold, and rented property, erected buildings, took advantage of public subsidies for childcare, and secured legal guardianship of children.[9] With these activities, women secured a foothold in the public sphere in San Francisco during the 1850s and in Oakland during the 1870s. This success becomes visible when the nature of urban public culture is assessed not only with written evidence, but also with artifacts.[10] Taken together, words and buildings offer first-rate clues about the significance of women's charity not only to women and children, but also to city building, urban politics, and public culture in the second half of the nineteenth century.

On the West Coast, organizing charities and building institutions went hand in hand with plans to expand the scope of services that needed spaces to house them.[11] Initially, women and men could afford to construct big, new freestanding institutions out of brick and stone—monumental markers of nationalist as well as philanthropic and gender ambition. In San Francisco the new charities were more startlingly visible in the urbanizing landscape than in the Northeast and Midwest, where charities for children were also built before and after the Civil War. In older cities, new institutions for children were added to existing landscapes of charity where almshouses, asylums, prisons, and so forth were clustered together and located in or relatively close to urban downtowns.[12] Make no mistake; it was hard to miss any of these buildings. However, the absence of state-run institutions made the landscape of charity a qualitatively different place in the new city rising from the sand dunes on the West Coast. Depending on the character of the architecture and the siting strategy (in town, at the edge of town, or distant from the urban center), the buildings could be seen for miles. For each building, the tangible presence was as important to the order and to the experience of the landscape of charity as other aspects of philanthropic service and building programs.

This characteristic stands out: the determination to carve out a special public realm for needy kids, an ambition with long roots in European culture. It began in the Renaissance when cities opened institutions for children in need of the care and assistance of the public. Municipalities sought to take care of foundlings and orphans in orphanages long before either families or schools gave attention to making special spaces for children.[13] Whether these spaces were repurposed or purpose-built, their effect was intended to be long-lasting, to endure—not only to shape childhood within each institutional home but also, through instruction and indenture, to direct children to specific futures in the adult world. By the mid-nineteenth century, children were sorted in institutions according to categories invented in England to describe adult poverty: dependent, delinquent, and disabled. One sociologist calls buildings like these "machines for the registration of human differences." Even if some sponsors hoped to deliver at least some aspects of the good childhood to boys and girls housed in philanthropic institutions, other convictions won out. Poor children were taken to be malleable enough to be savable, and unruly children, especially street children, were perceived to be a threat to the social order.[14]

The use of caregiving institutions to rationalize people and things was essential to the growth of an orderly, moral, and, above all, American society in the West. Not surprisingly, "American" was equated with white skin color in California, and claims to privilege based on it and other physical characteristics affected the lives of institutionalized children during this period of xenophobic nationalism. To begin with, public charities (reform schools) were racially integrated by force of circumstance, but private charities were not. Protestant and Catholic women largely took care of white children. However, the intent to order urban society on the basis of set categories (whether race, religion, sex, or age) was fraught with difficulty in the nineteenth century, especially in the multiethnic urbanizing West, where children and their needs defied easy, rigid classification.[15]

A Mixed Economy for Welfare in California

In the chaotic years that followed California's entry into the Union, its legislature adhered to a well-beaten path with respect to organizing charity. It embraced a mixed economy for social welfare, writing into law the expectation that private societies would work with government to deliver charity in the new state. The intertwined system of public and private responsibility was a familiar one in the United States; it developed in the Northeast, fed by the spread of a market economy, wage labor, and a taste for inexpensive government. In the climate of economic liberalism, the middle classes came to blame the poor for their poverty, extending the censure to immigrants, single mothers, and street children.[16] As evangelical Protestants spread the message of human perfectibility and benevolent associations petitioned city councils for financial support, modest cooperation between public authorities and private societies set in place a mixed economy for social welfare —one that kept taxes low, presumed to reward the worthy, and discharged elected officials from caretaking responsibilities.[17] In the middle of the nineteenth century, Californians were no different from other Americans in their faith in the efficacy of public-private partnerships; they were willing, very willing, to cede responsibility for poor relief to voluntary associations, including those run by women. This institutional framework, delivered from New England to points west, set in place a gendered culture of organization that benefited Catholic and Protestant charities as the two groups competed for the care of children.[18]

White men counted on white women to provide poor relief for less fortunate women and children, and the female sex obliged in California as elsewhere in the nation. The civic activism of pious Protestant women deferred to a conservative interpretation of gender norms early in the nineteenth century; the focus on children and the supposed "benign influence" of female benevolence did not unsex these activists. This stood in sharp contrast to allegations made about women who campaigned for the vote and the abolition of slavery.[19] In northern California, although women and men depended on one another to manage and fund philanthropic institutions, women deferred to the ideology of separate spheres, to the sense that there was a female dominion in philanthropy (focused on other women and children); they also expected charity to ameliorate rather than alter the structure of a capitalist economy. These conservative values, including the use of charity to articulate class interest and define racial advantage, held grave consequences for women of privilege and children in need on the West Coast. Benevolent women in San Francisco carried their conservatism into the public sphere, Mary Ryan has argued, by endorsing domestic seclusion and representing themselves as inspiring and pure in public ceremonies. This strategy affirmed rather than challenged female exclusion from the sphere of democratic participation.[20] However, organizing to meet collective needs, in addition to pressing for rights and civil liberties, may enhance democratic citizenship. It is in this sense that women planted the seeds of a democratizing political critique, as they built a network of caregiving institutions and suggested that child care ought to be a civic responsibility in modern society.[21]

The new American government declined to endorse that radical proposition. It adopted instead the worst aspects of the prevailing mixed economy of social welfare. Because it refused to organize an adequate machinery of government, the state legislature failed to redress the deleterious effects of laissez-faire capitalism on the citizens who were most in need of protection during westward expansion: poor women, children, and families; the sick and disabled; immigrants; Mexican workers; American Indians; and migrants of color. The legislature did make funds available to private charities, and it did set up state boards to supervise public schools, prisons, health, and labor.[22] Still, no group, public or private, won the authority to oversee charity and correction in California until early in the twentieth century.

Other urban states granted the privilege to regulate in the 1860s, but it was not possible to garner the will to do so in the West. Why? According to liberal analysts writing during the New Deal, entrenched interests and corruption occluded political imagination in California after statehood.[23]

Arriving for the most part from New England and the mid-Atlantic, the forty-niners and those who followed close on their heels destroyed the prevailing way of life in the small Mexican town of Yerba Buena and, with the aid of the US government during the Mexican-American War, challenged all prior claims to the territory of Alta California. After a military treaty delivered the fort, mission, and pueblo to the United States in 1848 and James Marshall found a chunk of gold at Sutter's Mill in Sacramento in the same year, newcomers flooded the city now called San Francisco. Arriving on sailing ships, these men would be known as Argonauts in deference to their arrogance, rough masculinity, and thirst for gold.[24]

Working fast to introduce a capitalist economy in a conquered land, city builders platted an extension close to the bay and at some distance from the dilapidated Spanish mission with the only (Catholic) church and the Presidio, the deteriorated Spanish fort. In the midst of meteoric growth—the settlement of eight hundred people in 1848 grew to thirty-six thousand by 1852 and fifty-six thousand by 1860—immigrants from France, Germany, Spain, and China claimed a piece of the urban territory as their own. The Irish, who came from Australia, New Zealand, and the Northeast, also formed ethnic enclaves, as did African Americans.[25] The first US census in California, recorded in 1852, reported a 9:8 ratio of foreign-to-native-born (one that exceeded that which existed in East Coast cities). Irish Catholics were the largest single ethnic group represented, followed by Germans (many of whom were Jewish) and Chinese. The financial elite in San Francisco included more Irish Catholics and Jews than elsewhere in the United States, and these wealthy leaders would be an important resource for each group when it started to build charities for children.[26]

Men and women immediately displayed an affinity for the practice of association by building churches and organizing voluntary societies. In the absence of a bona fide public system, men and women formed social networks that worked through and around government to address the need for welfare in San Francisco.[27] One historian has counted twenty-five organizations in the city with the words "benevolent or social" in their titles in 1852. Another found thirty houses of worship in 1856: two synagogues, and six Catholic and twenty-two Protestant churches.[28] Even though the bleak frontier town included manifestations of culture and civility, its rapid growth belied hopes that civil society would spring into life easily along the fecund Pacific Coast. "California had a fresh and vigorous start, with a clean bill of health," the attorney Frederick Billings told the Protestant Orphan Asylum Society in 1856 during its fifth annual meeting. "And she has fewer heir-looms of feebleness and infirmity, of dependence and disease, than the same number of people anywhere else in the world. Her troubles are those coming from and belonging to her own peculiar growth, and as that growth has been full of marvellous [sic] incidents and startling accidents and strange surprises, she has troubles that occur not to a State of slower and steadier development." Other observers seconded the point, linking "peculiar growth" to crime and vice, including that which occurred among children.[29]

Even if sentimentalized, these assessments of the urban scene alluded to the feminization of poverty. This problem was already known to Americans, as were the deleterious effects of economic liberalism on working-class and immigrant children.[30] These unfortunate circumstances led to a proliferation in the popular press of sentimental representations of women and children in need; the images capitalized on the sense of female dependence and the fragility of childhood to elicit feelings of sympathy, especially from other women.[31] These cultural constructions developed in concert with a national campaign to remove children from city streets, whether they were begging to support themselves or hawking goods to contribute to the family economy.

In New York City, the police launched the attack on street children a few years after the department was municipally organized. When the new chief of police, George W. Matsell, called the situation a "growing evil" in 1849, he meant "the constantly increasing number of vagrants, idle and vicious children of both sexes, who infest our public thoroughfares."[32] The Children's Aid Society, founded in 1853 by Charles Loring Brace, a young, charismatic, Protestant minister, took up the cause and used the new terms of "homeless child" and "street orphan" to describe children who may have been neither without a home or a parent. The society's sensational language and its ambitious programs made removing children from the evil of the streets fundamental to the reform of urban poverty.[33]

Sentiment aside, there was an urgent need to organize public assistance for urban children, especially in San Francisco where boys and girls were exposed on arrival to the hazards and privations of living in the West. The numbers were small (about one thousand school-age children lived in the city in 1851); and the newness and crudeness of the city exaggerated their vulnerability.[34] In the unfinished, unhealthy city, poor sanitation and rudimentary medical care exacerbated the ill effects of the boom and bust economy and explosive population growth on all residents, including children. The system of urban governance didn't help. Because elected officials wanted to encourage growth and preserve low taxes in the mid-nineteenth century, cities invested conservatively in public buildings and other amenities. The value of real estate determined the provision of infrastructure in a neighborhood because property taxes financed the construction of public works. As one historian has commented, the "market-based allocation rule might be considered 'fair.'" It was not "democratic."[35]

In San Francisco, a city known for its battles between vice and virtue, the fabled frontier spirit of cooperation fractured along familiar religious, racial, and ethnic lines in this period of aggressive westward expansion. Tolerant, pluralistic solutions were not imminent in reform landscapes for children on either coast during the 1850s, a period of chauvinistic racial nationalism.[36] At the beginning of this fractious decade, the Democratic Party, dominated by Irish Catholics, staked its claim in San Francisco politics; in conjunction with a celebrated murder, Protestants disparaged the Irish political machine as lawless and criminal. Periodically, the challenge to Irish hegemony erupted into civic violence, labeled "vigilante action" by native-born Protestant merchants and ministers.[37] Another telling example is that although California joined the union as a free state, it legitimatized second-class citizenship for blacks and denied it altogether to Chinese immigrants.-[38] At statehood, only white male citizens of United States and Mexico won the right to vote; after 1852, a black, mulatto, or Indian was prohibited from giving evidence in court against a white man; the rule applied to Chinese too.

This bigotry shaped a child's public world. Public schools were racially segregated; and private, including Catholic, schools did not receive public money after 1856 when an initial experiment in joint funding was abandoned. The former New Englanders who dominated the Board of Education and belonged to Protestant churches intended to build a school system like the one they had left behind. They supported the new state law that declared in 1852 that a school could not receive dispensation from the public purse unless it was "free from all denominational and sectarian bias, control, or influence whatsoever."[39] This directive, similar to public policy in the Northeast, did not interpret as sectarian the reading of the Protestant Bible in public schools.

The friction among Protestants arid Catholics invaded urban charity as each group laid claim to poor children. In keeping with the taste for sentiment, romantic stories of actual human deprivation set the tone for accounts describing the founding of each charity. Cholera proved a recurring fact and thus also a trope in discourse. A Protestant churchwoman reported that the plight of five children orphaned by the disease on the

journey west prompted the call to organize the Orphan Asylum Society in January 1851. "At the request of the Ladies of San Francisco public notice was given both from the pulpit and by the press as to the expediency of establishing an orphan Asylum on these western shores similar to the plans adopted by the eastern states."[40] Women met at the First Presbyterian Church to organize the charity and designated a "Board of Lady Managers" to run it. The board decided to open the orphanage in Happy Valley, south of Market Street and close to another Presbyterian church on Howard Street. William Howard, the Boston-born adventurer turned merchant, had donated the lot for the church and backed the orphan asylum. He provided a small cottage rent-free for a few months, and another backer did the same after the lease was up on Howard's property.[41]

Irish Catholic men answered in kind when they met in February 1851 to form the Roman Catholic Orphan Asylum and Free School Society. Intent to keep the care of Catholic children in church hands, the bishop egged them on, eager to win financial assistance from these men of affairs.

> Those who do not profess our religion have constructed asylums to which the Catholic orphans are admitted and invited; but oh! with what detriment to their faith, it is not necessary to inform you. But if we have not a Catholic institution to maintain our orphans, many of the Catholic children will have to take refuge in these asylums and receive a Protestant education![42]

Happy Valley was also the neighborhood of choice. Here, Bishop (later Archbishop) Alemany set up the second Catholic parish in the city, and after wealthy Catholic real estate brokers donated a prime building lot, he authorized the construction of the orphanage and a new church facing Market Street.[43] The Sisters of Charity arrived one year later to take charge of the charity, having been called to the city for this express purpose. Their first charge was a Catholic girl who had lost her mother to cholera on the trip west; her father died soon after. In the meantime, bouts of the disease devastated San

Francisco. Within two years the orphanage, a wood-frame building, was bursting at the seams, with sixty-five children in residence.[44]

The similarities between Catholic and Protestant institutions are as important to recognize as the differences.[45] As much as each group sought to protect indigent boys and girls from the other religion, instances of tolerance graced the landscape of charity in its early stages.[46] Nativists did not attack the Catholic orphanage; and businessmen of one faith supported charities of the other. Protestants and Catholics also depended on each other to care for white children. Neither group organized a private philanthropy for children of color—meaning African American, American Indian, and Asian children—although that would change. Mexican and other Hispanic children would find the doors of Catholic orphanages opened to them, at least in theory, in spite of widespread antipathy for *Californio* culture. As one Chilean journalist wrote, "The Yankee egoists persecute everywhere all that have the disgrace of being Spanish."[47]

The distaste infected building practice. Before the Mexican-American War, settlers from points east experimented with adobe construction.[48] This openness to local building culture persisted after California joined the Union, but not among Protestant and Catholic institution builders. They lost interest in the cultural syncretism that had produced the Monterey style, with buildings made from adobe and shaded with generous porches. Instead, they constructed a landscape of charity, with buildings made from stone, brick, and timber and decorated in a manner that expressed elite taste in Anglo-American culture.

Charity, Childhood, and Architecture

The joint effort of Protestants and Catholics to create a landscape of charity for children squared with new ideals of charity and childhood. Starting early in the nineteenth century, opposition to poor relief made it the custom to try to limit the distribution of charity to people in need, especially outdoors. The term "outdoor relief" and its corollary, "indoor relief," refer to the English practice of defining charity according to the physical setting where it was dispersed and the spirit of its delivery. Broadly speaking, indoor relief was aid given in institutions to people deemed worthy of its receipt; outdoor relief was charity received in homes and public spaces, usually without scrutiny of need.[49] "Working-class experience was a continuum; no clear line separated the respectable poor from paupers," one historian of social welfare reminds us.[50] Yet San Francisco and Oakland joined other cities in banning most forms of outdoor relief in the nineteenth century. Regardless of faith, unemployed men, orphaned children, and destitute women and children begging on streets, even unpaved ones, offended middle-class sensibilities; and street children were anathema to elites on either coast.[51]

Despite efforts to regulate the flow of poor relief in cities, market capitalism assured that charity would remain as much about "getting" a "gift" as it was about "giving" one.[52] Solicitations for relief made heterogeneous the charitable landscapes of American cities—a landscape made up of transitory sites and informal buildings as well as grand purpose-built institutions. Other historians have applied the term "charitable landscape" to alms-houses, asylums, prisons, and other public institutions that proliferated at the edges of cities in response to the crises of the early nineteenth century.[53] An excellent example is the node that the city of New York developed at Blackwell's Island. A new penitentiary opened there in 1832, followed by separate almshouses for men and women in 1848; a workhouse, an insane asylum and other institutions completed the complex by the early 1850s.[54] Here as elsewhere, the institution builders coupled monumental architecture put in out-of-the-way places with the newfound faith in human perfectibility. Using buildings to separate the worthy poor from paupers and criminals would facilitate personal reform, mitigate disease, and eradicate environmental influences that caused immorality and crime. Isolating institutions on large tracts of land at the edge of the urban settlement, a convention since the Middle Ages, offered the added benefit of low cost for property.[55] Regardless of motive, the spread of specialized facilities for the dependent, the disabled, and the delinquent and the application of these classifications to children helped to rationalize American cities by categorizing people and things. But the charitable landscape remained a dynamic, complicated space, much more than a static collection of formidable institutions for children surrounded by a geographically defined bubble of space.[56]

The sorting process accelerated in American institutions during the 1850s as agitation against the catchall character of almshouses intensified and cities faced the escalating costs of public charity. Special groups were removed ("siphoned") from the poorhouse to specialized institutions.[57] Children were targeted because they continued to live in almshouses even though orphanages, asylums for pauper children, and houses of refuge (reform schools) had been made expressly for them.[58] In California, county authorities sent impoverished children to the local almshouses—also known as county hospitals, county farms, county houses, and poor farms—until after the turn of the twentieth century. Boards of supervisors ran these sites, which all too often were set up in dilapidated buildings.[59] Nonetheless, it had become important at least to try to separate children from adults in institutions, as childhood came to be seen as a distinct, important phase in life, and as a child's upbringing was taken to be crucial in the shaping of adult behavior. Reformers had come to appreciate that a child's personality was plastic, that it could be molded and changed for the better or the worse. This recognition reinforced the conviction that poor children were vulnerable—susceptible to moral temptation and environmental degradation—and it encouraged the construction of more new, specialized institutions for them.[60]

In keeping with the federated system of government in the United States, the nature of public private partnerships varied from state to state. In general, private charities and churches ran orphanages (often receiving some public funding to defray daily expenses); state, county, and city governments divided responsibility for the rest.[61] Pieties were offered about the need to recreate home life in institutions, but boys and girls were subject to rigid routines and strict gender segregation, and were scrutinized according to these moralistic categories. In practice it proved easier for a private charity to sort a "dependent" from a "deficient" or "delinquent" child than for a public one to do so. Private societies could refuse to admit unruly or sick children, while public institutions had less discretion.

Whether applied in a private or a public facility, admissions policies also belied the singularity of purpose implied by the term "orphanage" or "orphan asylum." Doors were opened to half-orphans (with one living parent), abandoned children (with known parents who had left them at the orphanage), foundlings (left at the orphanage by unknown parents), and deserted children (found on city streets), as well as to bona fide orphans.[62] Since the Renaissance, architects had answered the need to shelter an abandoned baby from inclement weather and to render anonymous the person who delivered the child to the charity. The solutions ranged from arcades to porches or small revolving doors.[63] Exiting was also monitored closely. If not claimed by a parent, placed with a foster family, or indentured, the child was forced to leave the orphanage and start working for wages. The typical cutoff age was twelve (sometimes ten for boys) in the middle of the nineteenth century. One reason for this was cost. In California, the state didn't want to subsidize the care of older kids, who cost more to feed and clothe than younger ones. Another reason was the determination to put needy children to work, and yet another was fear of sexuality. Managers did not relish the challenge of supervising boys and girls as they approached puberty.

The nineteenth century is known for institution building, but the rapid diffusion of orphanages during that time is astonishing. There were six orphanages in the entire country in 1800 and almost one hundred in New York State alone by 1850. Nine out of ten institutionalized children were likely cared for in private establishments during the second half of the nineteenth century.[64] The proliferation held special meaning for the urban children who were asked to learn to live in these places. Occurring in tandem with the spread of public schools, the increase contributed to a highly regulated (in theory at least) public landscape for city children.[65] However, the rationalization of capitalist cities was a messy, drawn out, and contested process, and its effects on children and institutions were not always logical. This is shown by the faulty application of sorting mechanisms *inside* institutions. The imperfection of sorting mechanisms also points to contradictions rife in the ideology of separate spheres, whether for children or women. In the case of children, categories used to classify impoverished adults—delinquent, dependent, and disabled—were applied to boys and girls, even though adults were beginning to grasp that kids needed a different kind of care than men and women did. All of these issues and more would come to the fore in the charitable landscape that women built for children in California.

Delinquent or Dependent: Sorting Children in California

The new urban elite of San Francisco applied imperfect sorting mechanisms to the landscape of charity for children in the 1850s and 1860s. The familiarity with institutions in the East and the intent to import conventions, crucial to the construction of middle-class identity, ensured these results. Men took charge of delinquent children in nominally public buildings, isolated from the temptations and squalor of city life; women took charge of dependent boys and girls in nominally private ones, close to or in new downtowns; and Catholics and Protestants built separate institutions. This institution building was one way to connect to another place, a world, left behind. However, the speed with which the new buildings appeared is astonishing. In San Francisco the Industrial School, the Protestant Orphan Asylum, and the Roman Catholic Orphan Asylum offered prescient examples of specialization, inherent in modernization. Each institution, a monumental marker of morality and discipline, also benefited in some way from public subsidy and, to a lesser extent, Protestant and Catholic cooperation.[66]

The San Francisco Industrial School was the first institution to be purpose-built by the state for children in California. The state legislature authorized construction of the reform school in 1858 following public outcry over widespread juvenile crime and the incarceration of children in the San Francisco city jail. One advocate wrote, "We have amongst us an unusually large number of idle, vagrant, vicious, unprotected children in the city, who must in some manner be reclaimed, or they will grow quickly into confirmed thieves, drunkards, murderers and vagabonds; vice and crime mature as rapidly and attain as huge proportions under the festering influences that surrounded them here, as our vegetable wonders under the fertilizing effects of sunshine and rain."[67] Bob Durkin was one of the first children to be moved from the jail to the new school, and, astonishingly enough, the police photographed him on arrival.[68] Isaiah W. Lees, a patrolman who became chief of the police force, started photographing criminals in the early 1850s. According to a later admirer, Lees insisted that the pictorial record helped him execute his "duty": keeping a "watchful eye" on lawbreakers and furnishing his colleagues with "close descriptions" of offenders.[69] The photographs objectified even very young criminals, emphasizing their differences from other children. By the time Durkin arrived on the scene, Lees had abandoned daguerreotypes for the collodion wet plate process. The new method simplified picture taking and made it possible to mount inexpensive prints in portable leather-bound volumes.

This extensive collection of mug shots grew rapidly (more than forty thousand by 1901), and it came to be known as the Rogues' Gallery, touted by San Franciscans, at least, as the first in the United States. Durkin's mug shot, labeled no. 4, was posted on page two of the first book of the gallery.[70] Durkin moved into a grim institution on the outskirts of town. Explicitly based on

East Coast models, a geographical bubble of space surrounded this brand new node in the charitable landscape. The school sat in the middle of a one hundred-acre plot about five miles south of the city, on the road to San Jose. Known as the "House of Refuge" lot, the parcel offered commanding views (Mount Diablo could be seen in the distance) and contained plenty of arable land. The San Francisco Board of Supervisors, owner of the public institution, invested the organization of the reform school with some features of a private charity, to facilitate fundraising and management. After the all-male board of managers raised ten thousand dollars for the construction of the new school, the Board of Supervisors allocated an additional twenty thousand to build the place.[71]

The managers commissioned a grand design—one that would serve as an emblem of the moral authority of an expanding American nation. The hope was to organize the institution around a courtyard that would include a large building with apartments for the superintendent and his staff, topped by a bell tower and flanked with two dormitory wings for inmates. A separate service building with a dining room and hospital ward was proposed for the back of the lot. The managers instructed Reuben Clarke, the architect, to adopt for the principal structure the massing most often used for antebellum institutions in the United States: a central pavilion with pitched roof, flanked by two lower wings with hyphens (smaller projecting volumes) at each end. Built of brick, with a massive stone basement and exaggerated rustication, the severity of architectural style, referred to as "Roman," made clear the building's punitive purpose.

The special prison for children opened in 1859, surrounded by a twelve-foot high fence. Praise was lavished on the institution, although the cost of construction limited the scope of work. The central pavilion was built for staff, and even if it lacked the hoped-for bell tower, its generosity of amenity stood in sharp contrast to that in the one wing constructed for children. Although it was called the "dormitory wing," it included

a dining room, hospital ward, washrooms, bathrooms (in the end pavilion), and sleeping rooms (in the main segment, lit by six arched windows). These rooms may have been called dormitories, but the wing contained two banks of brick cells, three stories high. Each small cell, intended for a single inmate, 5' 6" by 7'6" in size, had a barred window and an iron grating in the door, as did the cells in the institution on which the design of the wing was based, the House of Refuge in New York State (1825).[72] To reach a toilet, an inmate had to leave his cell and go to one of four galleries that surrounded the cellblock.

The hope was that individual confinement in a cell would facilitate reform, but strict discipline (including hard manual labor for boys) and deteriorating physical conditions quickly obviated the optimistic aspiration in San Francisco.[73] "This is more like a prison than an 'Industrial School,'" a visitor commented in 1862. "Indeed they [the inmates] are made to feel by far too much that they are *juvenile prisoners*, rather than boys and girls who are placed there, by a generous public, for their physical, mental, and moral improvement." The absence of a gymnasium, workshop and a suitable playground were cited as evidence of poor treatment, as was the minimal time spent in school—two hours a day in the late afternoon and one hour after supper. With a workday that started at six-thirty in the morning and ended at three o'clock in the afternoon, with a short break for a midday meal, it's likely that the tired children did not absorb much in the classroom.[74]

In ways other than these, the Industrial School drove home the point that the state would do only so much for delinquent children. The social heterogeneity of the place, which replicated the ethnic mix of the city, was a result of public parsimony rather than of dedication to social inclusion in a democratic society. All sorts of kids were sent to the Industrial School: homeless children, orphans, children convicted of crimes, children of imprisoned parents, children who didn't get along with their parents, children rejected from orphanages, children of color (meaning African Americans, American

Indians, and Asians), boys and girls as young as three and as old as twenty-one.[75] Imagine the chatter inside this institution as children tried to speak to one another in languages that replicated the diversity of their city. Imagine the baffled look on the face of a German, Spanish, or Chinese boy as he tried to grasp a command offered in English. Imagine the swift punishment that followed his lack of comprehension.

Soon enough, the school was overflowing with children. In 1864 ninety kids lived in the forty-eight cells that made up the sole dormitory wing, and almost all were boys. By force of circumstance this concentration, almost two times the intended occupancy, defeated the intent to reform the delinquent child through isolation in one small room. One year later, the population jumped to 150 after the second dormitory wing was built.[76] Not surprisingly, there were repeat offenders, a fact made startlingly clear in the Rogues' Gallery. It included serial photographs of them, Bob Durkin being one, James (Nanny Goat) Burns another.[77]

The city responded first by sending some children to private orphanages, and then by dedicating the institution to boys.[78] Subject to abuse (one small girl was raped and murdered) and presumed to be a source of moral contagion, delinquent girls were sent to the Magdalen Asylum for wayward girls and unmarried pregnant women. Purposely isolated, the new asylum opened in 1864 and was partially subsidized by the state legislature after it was agreed that the Sisters of Mercy, the order charged with running the place, would assume responsibility for delinquent girls. Whether Protestant or Catholic, those girls were separated from other residents and housed in a special part of the facility, paid for by taxpayers.[79] The tactic, an "architecture of containment," resembled that taken in Ireland, where this order built similar institutions for wayward girls.[80]

Protestants and Catholics cooperated to create this new node in the charitable landscape—in this case, to shelter endangered daughters and fallen women, as well as to incarcerate street girls and prostitutes. In this instance, as Ruth Shackelford has shown, it seems certain that the Sisters of

Mercy were eager to extend their philanthropic work into the municipal terrain—and elected officials were willing to oblige, even though the order had been accused of impropriety in handling the funds of another private facility, a hospital supported with public money.[81] Although the presence of Irish Catholics on the board of managers of the Industrial School facilitated the exchange and a state board praised the charity, the benefits of mutuality should not be exaggerated. The Magdalen Asylum proved to be a grim place for girls, not so different from the reform school for boys. Repeated attempts at escape led to the installation of bars on the windows and the construction of cells in the basement and other floors. It was "a *dismal* and *terrible* thing called an asylum, where little girls who got into any kind of trouble were slammed in there like prisoners. They *were* prisoners," one woman recalled.[82]

With the Industrial School plagued by scandal and subject to investigation, the board of managers voted to disband in 1872. The school came under the direct control of the government, and the purpose narrowed from reform to one more thoroughly focused on punishment. Boys were no longer placed out in homes and jobs, and the construction of the House of Correction for adult male prisoners on the very same parcel seconded this shift in ethos.[83] By 1889 the deficiencies of the overcrowded school on the old House of Refuge lot became too egregious to ignore, and the state legislature decided to replace it with two new reform schools, the Whittier State School and the Preston School of Industry.[84] This may be hard to fathom, but the only other state-run facilities for children in the mid-1890s were a home for deaf and blind children and one for boys and girls suffering from mental illnesses.[85] Aside from county almshouses, four buildings constituted the public sites in the landscape of charity for children in California.

Churchwomen Build Charities for Children

With no state orphanages for children, private charities in California ran almost every institution for orphaned or otherwise needy children during the second half of the nine-teenth century. As Billings pointed out to the Orphan Asylum Society in 1856, "It is in the more variously active benevolence of individuals and associations that the fervent spirit and faithful labor of charity in Cali-fornia find their truest illustration."[86] The words of the San Francisco attorney direct our attention to the Protestant church-women who, with Catholic nuns, had by then amended the public sphere with three orphanages. The Protestant churchwomen's eagerness to build was prompted not only by class privilege, the gender ideology of domestic femininity, and a Christian sense of duty, but also by anxiety about their hold on propriety, which was key to the social standing of a middle-class woman in any nineteenth-century city. San Francisco was no exception; as Mary Ann Irwin has argued, its economic volatility, disease out-breaks, and periodic fires made clear to a woman the fragility of her class standing. All too easily she (or her orphaned daugh-ter) could find herself walking the streets of the rough frontier town.[87]

As a city made up of tents and shacks turned into one built of stone and brick, the lady managers of the Protestant Orphan Asylum decided to replace the rented cot-tage. The asylum's new stone building would be located not in Happy Valley but rather on Laguna Street, one block north-west of the intersection with Market Street and thus distant from the center of town and the raucous life along the waterfront [...].[88] The double lot at this location also happened to be owned by the city. The speed with which more than twenty-two thousand dol-lars was raised is clear evidence of the wealth flowing into the city as well as of the depth of concern about children. Elizabeth Waller and Anna Haight joined the Board of Lady Managers and called on their hus-bands, Judge Royal A. Waller and Super-visor Henry H. Haight (later a state governor), to expedite the new asylum's construction.[89]

Social networks and political contacts proved as important to women's success in San Francisco as they were to women's philanthropy in the East and would be in Oakland. The mayor smoothed the way for the purchase of the two city-owned lots for the excellent price of one hundred dollars; Supervisor Haight expedited the survey of two streets (subsequently named Waller and Haight), so that construction could proceed; a water company donated the stone, although the society paid to transport it .[90] Sited on the rise of a hill, topped by a bell tower and steep gable roofs and surrounded by empty lots, the four-story stone building could be seen for miles. It reminded San Franciscans that children's needs were a public matter, that women would organize to make sure they were met, and that Anglo-American culture had arrived in the West. Twenty-six children lived in the orphanage in 1853; the number more than doubled in three years as the charity took in orphaned and half-orphaned boys and girls.[91]

Like other antebellum charity workers, the organizers of this charity believed chil-dren's institutions should be modeled on the middle-class family and its home. Phys-ical interpretations of this mandate changed dramatically in the first half of the nine-teenth century. Orphanage managers started in the 1830s to reject the cellular sleeping spaces used in houses of refuge. The obvi-ous reason was their close resemblance to prison cells, even if they were called bed-rooms. Congregate sleeping rooms, associ-ated in nineteenth-century parlance with dormitories, came into favor because they recalled the setting of a middle-class home, where children shared sleeping spaces. Proper "shelter and sanctuary," coupled with training and rehabilitation, held great promise for molding the character of indi-gent children in the eyes of antebellum charity workers.[92]

An excellent illustration of these objectives may be found on a certificate of membership for an orphanage in Newburyport, Massachu-setts, from the 1830s [...]. The women who set up the female charitable asylum decided to embellish the certificate with an engraving and a poem. The text suggests the challenges faced in "teaching a young idea how to shoot," meaning to thrive and develop. Elizabeth Cox Akin, the engraver, used a popular technique, contrasting the "before" and "after" state of kids to underscore the benefits of institutional care. In line with romantic theories of childhood, Akin emphasized childlike innocence and vulnerability and the possibility of redemption from sin and temptation. In her engraving a modest young woman, the caretaker, encourages little girls in tattered rags, without shoes and hats, to leave a cave (their "natural" home) for an asylum (their "civil" home), which is lifted off the ground and equipped with a sturdy door. Having been thus protected, a girl would leave the institution respectably dressed and virtuous in demeanor. Departing probably at twelve years old meant that she would need to work before marriage. The usual job would be that of a servant, where long hours, poor pay, and unwanted attention from men in the household awaited her, even if she would be working for a lady manager of her former home. For that situation, the term "Janus-faced women" was applicable. The abolitionists Sarah and Angelina Grimké used the term to castigate the benevolent women of Charleston, South Carolina, who helped poor whites and free blacks during the day and abused slaves in the evening at home.[93]

As orphanages spread across the United States, critics began to question the efficacy of congregate care. Certainly, very large orphanages where one hundred or more children slept in enormous cavernous rooms were properly described as inhumane. As the reform attack escalated, the preference came to be for a ward that held no more than twenty-five children. Smaller congregate dormitories were used in the Protestant and Roman Catholic orphanages in San Francisco, and the same efficient, economical solution remained in use elsewhere through the end of the century, even for very young children. That was the case at the Chicago Nursery and Half-Orphan Asylum. A rare interior view of a congregate dormitory shows about twenty children gathered for bedtime prayers in 1899 [...]. Faith in the transformative effects of the environment is evident, with the trappings of domesticity (separate beds and clothes just for sleeping, the draped mantel, pictures on the wall) clearly present in this institutional setting. The matron, with her back turned modestly to the photographer, supervises children. Each child is assigned to a separate slot of space, is dressed in a white nightgown, and hair is shorn to prevent lice infestation. This routine, which repressed individuality in favor of conformity, and this material expression of the congregate ideal taught children to value order, piety, decorum, and cleanliness inside and outside the institution.

Respectable white Protestant women were hard to find in San Francisco in the early 1850s, where men outnumbered women by six to one. In this city bursting with single men, the scarcity of the female sex made all the more impressive their success in organizing the charity for children. "Beautiful as she is in all her ways, she [charity] is never so beautiful as when in the form of woman she takes by the hand the orphan child, wandering and lost in the confusion of the tumultuous city, and guides it to a home," Billings declared to the Orphan Asylum Society. "Woman, guarding and cherishing the orphan child! There is no sight in life more touching to the heart, no work of love more acceptable, I believe, to Heaven."[94]

The attorney gave voice to these sentiments at an exemplary site of the public sphere, the San Francisco Musical Hall, where the Orphan Asylum Society held its fifth annual meeting in 1856. In a city known for its newness, crudeness, and rough working-class masculinity, Billings adhered to middle-class conventions when he spoke for women in this public place. He urged men in the audience to recognize their manly duty and give "Charity a Living Presence" in California.[95] He alluded to the importance of the brand-new stone building, but did not enumerate these significant qualities: The first Protestant orphanage on the West Coast was a formidable work of architecture, owned in the clear by the women of the charity; in short, an impressive addition to urban public culture. Instead, he used sentimental metaphors—tumultuous city, lost child, safe home—and paid deference to the ideology of separate spheres—true womanhood, innocent childhood, bourgeois manliness—as he pressed hard for contributions. He reminded men in the audience that Christian duty obliged them to help children, as did their affection for childhood, motherhood, and a loving home. "The man never yet was born who was not blessed by the presence of children," he stated.[96]

The interlocking gender ideologies of domestic femininity and respectable masculinity were important themes in this speech, as was the sense that women and men were compelled to take care of children, using their unlike capacities for civic action. The phrases used in antebellum society to describe these qualities were "feminine influence" and "masculine power."[97] But as omniscient as these values were on the West Coast, they do not fully explain the place women claimed in this city as they built institutions for children. Billings made clear that the Protestant orphanage was already enmeshed in the state's mixed economy of social welfare—that it belonged to a charitable landscape, which was made up of private charities and a few public buildings. He also drove home the point that the government counted on men to support women's charity for children. "By the interest of the State—and the voice of the church, and the command of God, are we constrained to run with full hearts and full hands to the orphan's aid," he said, referring to his sex.[98]

By that time, the Orphan Asylum Society had received a modest, albeit short-lived, monthly subsidy from the San Francisco Board of Supervisors and a larger one from the state legislature. The new Poor Law of 1855 allocated a five-thousand-dollar lump sum grant to private charities taking care of homeless or orphaned children, regardless of religious affiliation.[99] In 1855, the only other beneficiary of either subsidy was the Roman Catholic orphanage in San Francisco. Between them, both woman-run charities took care of a large proportion of homeless children in the city. That amounted to about two hundred in 1855, more or less 10 percent of the number in enrolled in public schools.[100]

The Sisters of Charity had also faced the challenge of construction. The number of needy Catholic children kept increasing as Irish immigrants flocked to the city, and the church needed to replace the first orphanage with a bigger brick building in 1855 [...]. For the time being, the charity elected to stay in Happy Valley and erect an institution that mimicked the form of elite houses, with a Georgian form and a fence and front steps to separate it from the street. The cross, mounted atop the pediment on the centralized projecting entry, made clear that this was a Catholic institution while the site, facing Market Street and adjacent to St. Patrick's Church and the parish school, deftly illustrated the orphanage's connection to the new Irish (for the most part) Catholic community, rather than to what little remained of the Mexican one. After the US territorial conquest of 1848 the diocese had acquired the Mission Dolores and other ecclesiastical property, but in matters other than land acquisition it now showed little interest in forging strong ties with the older church.[101]

This decision to remain downtown made it possible for the Sisters of Charity to expand social services in a way that addressed the needs of the working class constituency.[102] More than 120 children lived in the San Francisco orphanage in 1857; the number would increase to 275. The Sisters of Charity also cared for the children of working mothers during the day. As the trustees explained,

> In our city there are many mothers who earn their support by their labor, at employment which oblige them to leave their homes. Many of these place their children under the charge of the Sisters in the morning, until their return from employment, and in this manner, through the Institution, are assisted to maintain their families.[103]

By the early 1860s, three more Catholic orphanages had been built in and around San Francisco: St. Vincent's Orphan Asylum, for boys (1856), and Mount St. Joseph's Infant Orphan Asylum, for babies of both sexes (1861), as well as the Magdalen Asylum. The Sisters of Charity opened St. Vincent's, but handed it over to the male-run Order of St. Dominic, since the sisters were prohibited by the rules of their order from caring for older boys. Irish Catholic immigrants quickly made up the bulwark of the working class in San Francisco; they and their children made up the city's largest ethnic minority after the Civil War. In this period, boys and girls of Irish parentage constituted a plurality in the city's institutions.[104]

The outreach to children and the interest in family preservation was typical of Catholic charity, as the church moved toward a national organization in the middle of the nineteenth century. The church was not a homogeneous institution; its policies were enacted in individual parishes and threaded with the class, gender, ethnic, racial, and generational divisions typical of immigrant society in American cities. Nonetheless and broadly speaking, focusing on child care helped the church reach across diverse urban constituencies as it protected children from "marauding" Protestant child savers.[105]

Building charities for children also helped defend the church from accusations of having failed to meet its obligation to care for children. Even so, nativists charged new institutions with not being "American" enough. In no small measure, the indictments zeroed in on the competing gender norms that shaped philanthropic practice as well as family life. During the 1850s and 1860s, nativists disputed the leadership role of nuns in Catholic orphanages in New York City, preferring the married women and mothers who usually ran Protestant charities. Protestants were interested in "saving" working-class Irish boys and girls from this un-American way of life, one historian argues, not only because the children were denied the benefits of a "good childhood" but also because they were white. Teaching Protestant values to future voters (and future mothers of voters) was vital to political stability in a racially segregated society.[106]

Irish Catholic women in San Francisco were as determined as they were in other cities to take care of orphans and otherwise needy Catholic children. Motivated by sentiment and faith, they wanted to control cultural reproduction through childhood, to save boys and girls from Protestant child

savers bent on refashioning immigrant culture, family life, and religious practice. Choices made in this city about location underscore the point. As soon as was possible, Protestant churchwomen moved the orphanage out of Happy Valley. The Sisters of Charity owned real estate in San Francisco in the 1850s (unlike the order in New York) and were keenly aware of the need for child care among working-class Irish Catholic women. Their Catholic orphanage was built downtown and remained there, next door to the parent church, for more than twenty years. Reluctantly, the Sisters agreed to move the orphanage to South San Francisco in 1872. The men who ran the diocese forced the relocation, to capitalize on the highly valued Market Street lot on which the original orphanage had stood, which they then sold to the developers of the Palace Hotel.[107]

It's important to understand that women who ran urban charities grasped the importance of location to the delivery of social services. Certainly, putting the Roman Catholic orphanage downtown made it easier for the Sisters of Charity to provide day care for working-class Irish Catholic families. But it would be a mistake to interpret this choice in San Francisco as a general rule for Catholic charities; architectural decisions did not characterize one religion or the other. As much as the Irish formed their ethnic identity in opposition to English culture, the spatial structure of Catholic charity for children was grounded in the discourse of Anglo-American philanthropic practice.[108] Catholics built charities at some remove from the city as well as close in; they tried to sort children in institutions using the same categories as Protestants; they built similar buildings and counted on women to run them without compensation. In San Francisco, similarities in institutional practice took on heightened meanings in light of the Irish Catholic experience of nativism and the ambiguous position of Irish immigrants in the regional social hierarchy. Although intense, the nativist attacks on Irish Catholics in San Francisco were not as severe as in Boston or New York, because the presence of Chinese immigrants, Mexicans, and American Indians helped to redirect nativist anger to other ethnic groups. This situation made it possible for the Irish to begin to share in the racial privileges of being white in a city where all residents were intensely aware of the advantages to be won, and lost, due to skin color.[109]

Children were on the front lines of this battle in California, just as they were elsewhere in the West. The willingness to negotiate nativism, if not the biological construction of race, left other marks on the local landscape of charity. A good example is the home built by the Ladies' Protection and Relief Society. The women of this charity, formed in 1853, helped white women and children without male protection to find work and housing; they also offered relief and in time expanded their mission to include providing shelter. The charity's managers rented space until they were able to buy a house; in 1863 it was replaced with a new home that was partially subsidized by the state legislature.[110] This new masonry building—a broad horizontal block with a central entry, projecting roof, and bell tower—was similar to the Catholic orphanage on Market Street and the main building of the Industrial School. Like the Protestant Orphan Asylum, the new institution sat on a large tract—an entire city block—at the edge of settlement [...]. The parcel was a gift—from a nativist who made similar donations to Catholic charities in spite of his membership in the Know Nothing Party, whose anti-Catholic stance is notorious in American history. Admission policies at the home run by the Ladies' Protection and Relief Society reflected the group's ambiguous link to nativism. The charity offered shelter and aid to white Protestant women, but opened the doors to boys and girls regardless of religion or race.[111] The admission of any child of color to an orphanage built by white women for white children was unusual in the West, to say the least, in the 1860s and 1870s.

More typically, Protestant and Catholic orphanages each competed to house children of the other, "wrong" religion. The religious interpretation of the open-door policy had manipulative, even coercive aspects when it came to religion, as women were determined to win converts to one or the other faith. However, identity was organized along more than religious lines in antebellum San Francisco, and other social formations were important in this multiethnic city where white people had a heightened consciousness of race privilege. The relative liberality of admissions spoke to the readiness of white women to share the project of using children and institutions to "civilize" the raucous West. New developments in public policy, which underscored the place of this work in the state's mixed economy of welfare, encouraged women to build.

Women Become Partners with the State

San Francisco's orphanages, whether affiliated with the Protestant or Catholic religion, benefited in exactly the same manner from the distinction between indoor and outdoor relief written into law in 1855. When the legislature agreed to aid children within institutions but not outside of them, it recognized the power of these historic categories in the structure of benevolence in the United States. However, the government used its discretion in setting parameters for dispensing relief to children. The 1855 law set in place a framework for institutionalization that was later called the "New York System"; this term meant that state subsidies would be used to care for orphaned children solely in *private* charities, regardless of faith.[112] The basic conditions remained in place in California until the twentieth century, although some provisions would be amended. As in-state residence requirements were stiffened, the subsidy would be extended to half-orphans and abandoned children, but refused to "Oriental" children. The new rules were one of many ways in which race prejudice left an ugly imprint on charity in the Golden State.

It is very difficult to extract from nineteenth-century records the exact figures needed to describe the precise demography of children's institutions. That said, and as New Deal researchers later pointed out, the

1890 US Census showed that California had a higher proportion of children in private institutions than was typical of the country as a whole. Because of the relatively generous state subsidy to private institutions, the number of people receiving public aid in private charities was larger proportionally than elsewhere in the country (exceeded only in New York State).[113] In large measure, children lived in woman-run institutions, because in the meantime women had continued to build. Following the first imprints erected in and around San Francisco, Protestant and Catholic orphanages were built in Los Angeles (1856), Grass Valley (1865), Sacramento (1867), and Oakland (1871); more orphanages opened in the San Francisco, including one for Jewish children (1872), an infant shelter (1874), and a nursery for homeless children (1878).[114] Protestant women also took a public stand against prostitution and determinism in the construction of race: the woman-run Methodist Episcopal Oriental Home (1870) and Presbyterian Chinese Mission Home (1872) offered shelter to Chinese prostitutes and their children. Although ethnocentric and self-righteous, the Protestant lady managers promoted women's moral authority and traversed sharply drawn racial and cultural boundaries to extend relief and rescue to Asian women and children.[115] Protesting this transgression of social boundaries, in 1877 the Workingman's Party rioted outside the Presbyterian mission home.[116]

Women also took the lead in organizing child care for women who worked outside the home (usually abandoned wives, widows, and single mothers). The solutions included the informal care offered in Catholic orphanages mentioned above. Women opened other charities for this express purpose: the Little Sisters' Infant Shelter (1871), a Protestant charity, and the day nursery that Elizabeth Armer started in 1872 for Catholic children. Armer, foster child of a wealthy Irish Catholic family, founded the Sisters of the Holy Family to run the day nursery and meet the need of Catholic families for daycare; the order would go on to build and operate day nurseries across the San Francisco Bay Area, including one in Oakland.[117]

The result was a charitable landscape that, because of its urbanity, diversity, and complexity, underscored an obvious and very important point: Since the nineteenth century new forms of charity have been imagined in cities because the need for these institutions has been a logical result of rapid urbanization. As R. J. Morris has written, "The nineteenth-century city became a vast laboratory, which tested the effectiveness of market mechanisms to the limit and the operation of other ways of producing and delivering goods and services.[118] Because cities are dense, big, and complex, their power structures needed to formulate responses to externalities— meaning in this context human services that could not be priced profitably, like social welfare. As cities grew, the need for these services, and thus the need for the power elite to intervene outside the market, only increased.[119] In California this situation put pressure on women to construct more buildings, to invent more material resources for children.

After 1870 the authorization of new subsidies for orphans in California strengthened the partnership of woman-run charities with the state government. In the 1869–70 session, the legislature changed the formula from a lump sum grant to one based on the actual head count in a charity; the per capita method remained in place for the rest of the century.[120] Why did the funding mechanism change? In the Progressive Era, a critic explained the decision as having been taken because requests for the lump sum subvention consumed too much time during the legislative session; the legislature found itself giving aid to the most demanding lobbyists rather than to the most worthy (likely a code word for woman-run) charities.[121] All that may have been true, but the change in state subsidy constituted a dramatic increase; it meant that a private facility with one hundred orphans in residence would receive $5,000 a year from the state government; previously, the orphanage would have qualified for this amount of money only once, rather than every year. In 1874 state aid was increased and extended to abandoned children. Inevitably this situation led to the proliferation of institutions for children and the elderly after the subvention was extended to include the "indigent aged."[122]

Looking back on the situation, New Deal reformers explained California's interest in expanding institutions for children as having resulted from the extreme skew in the state's sex ratio. The lack of women translated into an "acute need for a substitute for home life," especially among immigrants, because there were not enough women to take care of children, the elderly, the sick, and other people in need.[123] However, this explanation ignores the fact that the skew between the sexes began to equalize after the Civil War, and that the state government always counted on women to do the work in charities. The expectation was due not only to high-minded moralism, but also to the blunt facts of a political economy that was grounded in the gender asymmetry and hierarchy of American society. For the most part, a private charity, owned and managed by women, cost far less to operate than an institution owned and run by the state. Women worked for free as volunteers; they pressed men for money and scoured the city for in-kind donations of food, fuel, clothing, and other necessities. In other words, the regularization of state funding took account of the economic benefit to the people of California of female philanthropy for children.

The timing of the new law was fortuitous. In May 1869 Leland Stanford, president of the Pacific Railroad, picked up a silver sledgehammer in Promontory, Utah, and on his second try pounded in a gold stake that joined the parallel iron tracks stretching from coast to coast. On November 8, 1869, the first passenger train bound for the East Coast left Oakland on the Central Pacific; the first westbound transcontinental train pulled into town on the same day.[124] With the transcontinental telegraph line, completed in 1861, the transcontinental railroad linked city to nation and advanced dreams of westward expansion.[125] This new infrastructure tied California more securely to the national economy, with its booms and its busts, than before; it also delivered new people and more goods to the Pacific Coast and promised heightened industrial competition.

Women in Oakland took steps to organize the charitable landscape after the transcontinental railroad arrived in their city. Applying habits of mind used in San Francisco, habits that deferred to the preference for inexpensive government in the United States, white Protestant women defined public charity as a private responsibility. Their first step was to work with men to form the Oakland Benevolent Society, although within two short years a separate charity, the Ladies' Relief Society of Oakland, California, would be organized. Calling on their unlike capacities for civic action, these women altered the public sphere by taking charge of urban charity for children.

NOTES

1. For women's public culture, Linda K. Kerber, "Separate Spheres, Female Worlds, Woman's Place: The Rhetoric of Women's History," *Journal of American History* 75, no. 1 (1988): 17; Mary P. Ryan, *Women in Public: Between Banners and Ballots, 1825–1880* (Baltimore: Johns Hopkins University Press, 1990), 3–18; and for the gap between the city as imagined and as lived, Jessica Ellen Sewell, *Women and the Everyday City: Public Space in San Francisco, 1890–1916* (Minneapolis: University of Minnesota Press, 2011), xiii-xix.

2. For the state, Frances Cahn and Valeska Bary, *Welfare Activities of Federal, State, and Local Governments in California, 1850–1934* (Berkeley: University of California Press, 1936); William H. Slingerland, *Child Welfare Work in California: A Study of Agencies and Institutions* (New York: Department of Child Helping, Russell Sage Foundation, 1916); for Oakland, Joseph E. Baker, ed. *Past and Present of Alameda County, California*, 2 vols. (Chicago: S. J. Clarke Publishing Company, 1914), 1: 247–62; for San Francisco, M. W. Shinn, "Charities for Children," *Overland Monthly* 15, no. 1 (January 1890): 78–101.

3. For changing structure in the gender order, Mary P. Ryan, *Mysteries of Sex: Tracing Women and Men through American History* (Chapel Hill: University of North Carolina Press, 2006). For women

in California politics, Gayle Gullett, *Becoming Citizens: The Emergence and Development of the California Women's Movement, 1880–1911* (Urbana: University of Illinois Press, 2000); Sewell, *Women and the Everyday City*, 127–67.

4. The maternalist argument is made in Seth Koven and Sonya Michel, eds., *Mothers of a New World: Maternalist Politics and the Origins of Welfare States* (New York: Routledge, 1993); Theda Skocpol, *Protecting Soldiers and Mothers: The Political Origins of Social Policy in the United States* (Cambridge, MA: Harvard University Press, 1992); and debated in Linda Gordon, "Gender, State, and Society: A Debate with Theda Skocpol," *Contention* 2, no. 4 (1993): 139–56; Thed a Skocpol, "Soldiers, Workers, and Mothers: Gendered Identities in Early U. S. Social Policy," *Contention* 2, no. 3 (1993): 157–89.

5. Linda Gordon, *The Great Arizona Orphan Abduction* (Cambridge, MA: Harvard University Press, 1999), 159.

6. The great concern about homeless children is emphasized by Mary Ann Irwin, "'Going About Doing Good': The Politics of Benevolence, Welfare, and Gender in San Francisco, 1850–1880," *Pacific Historical Review* 68, no. 3 (August 1999): 394; Ruth Shackelford, "To Shield Them from Temptation: 'Child-saving' Institutions and the Children of the Underclass in San Francisco, 1850–1910" (PhD dissertation, Harvard University, 1991), 290. I am indebted to both historians and call on their research in the following discussion of architecture and urbanism. I agree with Irwin that the California case study demonstrates the limits of the "domestication of politics" argument in Paula Baker, "The Domestication of Politics: Women and American Political Society, 1780–1920," *American Historical Review* 89, no. 3 (June 1984): 620–47.

7. For comparative costs, see Irwin, "'Going About Doing Good,'" 387–91. For "free" female labor in Catholic charities, Dorothy M. Brown and Elizabeth McKeown, *The Poor Belong to Us: Catholic Charities and American Welfare* (Cambridge, MA: Harvard University Press, 1997), 23; Maureen Fitzgerald, *Habits of Compassion: Irish Catholic Nuns and the Origins of New York's Welfare System, 1830–1920* (Urbana: University of Illinois Press, 2006), 5ff; Mary J. Oates, *The Catholic Philanthropic Tradition in America* (Bloomington: Indiana University Press, 1995), 20–24.

8. For the concept, Jürgen Habermas, *The Structural Transformation of the Public Sphere: An Inquiry into a Category of Bourgeois Society*, trans. Thomas Burger with Frederick Lawrence (Cambridge, MA: MIT Press, 1989); Jürgen Habermas, "The Public Sphere: An Encyclopedia Article (1964)," *New German Critique*, no. 3 (Autumn 1974): 49–55. The feminist critiques are legion; I call on Bruce Dorsey, *Reforming Men and Women: Gender in the Antebellum City* (Ithaca, NY: Cornell University Press, 2002), 5, 29, 97–98; Nancy Fraser, "Rethinking the Public Sphere: A Contribution to the Critique of Actually Existing Democracy," in *Habermas and the Public Sphere*, ed. Craig Calhoun (Cambridge, MA: MIT Press, 1992), 109–42; Ryan, *Women in Public*, 10–11, 12–13, 130–37, 176.

9. The point is mentioned briefly in Edith Sparks, *Capital Intentions: Female Proprietors in San Francisco, 1850–1920* (Chapel Hill: University of North Carolina Press, 2006), 180–81. The California state constitution adopted a community property system, but married women did not win legal guardianship of children, even after the suffrage bill passed in 1911. See Hendrik Hartog, *Man and Wife in America: A History* (Cambridge, MA: Harvard University Press, 2000), 14; Alice Park, *California Women Under the Laws of 1912* (Palo Alto, CA, 1912).

10. The contribution of women through charity to urban public culture in San Francisco during the 1850s and 1860s is missed in Philip J. Ethington, *The Public City: The Political Construction of Urban Life in San Francisco, 1850–1900* (New York: Cambridge University Press, 1994). The criticism is echoed in Irwin, "'Going About Doing Good,'" 367. For a similar problem, see Dorsey, *Reforming Men and Women*, 89.

11. For similar points, see Francesca Guerra-Pearson, "Organizational Forms and Architectural Space: Building Meaning in Charitable Organizations in New York City, 1770–1920," *Nonprofit and Voluntary Sector Quarterly* 27, no. 4 (December 1998): 465.

12. For examples in the Northeast, see Lawrence J. Vale, *From the Puritans to the Projects: Public Housing and Public Neighbors* (Cambridge, MA: Harvard University Press, 2000); Rick Beard, ed. *On Being Homeless: Historical Perspectives* (New York: Museum of the City of New York, 1987); David J. Rothman, *The Discovery of the Asylum: Social Order and Disorder in the New Republic* (Boston: Little, Brown, 1971). The comparison also calls on US Bureau of the Census, *Report on Crime, Pauperism, and Benevolence in the United States at the*

Eleventh Census, 1890 (Washington: Government Printing Office, 1892); US Bureau of the Census, *Benevolent Institutions 1904* (Washington: Government Printing Office, 1905); US Bureau of the Census, *Benevolent Institutions 1910* (Washington: Government Printing Office, 1913).

13. For Italy, see Nicholas Terpstra, *Abandoned Children of the Italian Renaissance: Orphan Care in Florence and Bologna* (Baltimore: Johns Hopkins University Press, 2005); Nicholas Terpstra, *Lost Girls: Sex and Death Renaissance Florence* (Baltimore: Johns Hopkins University Press, 2012).

14. Nikolas Rose, *Governing the Soul: The Shaping of the Private Self*, 2nd ed. (New York: Free Association Books, 1999), 136 quote; Hugh Cunningham, *Children and Childhood in Western Society since 1500*, 2nd ed. (New York: Pearson Longman, 2005), 137–40; Eric C. Schneider, *In the Web of Class: Delinquents and Reformers in Boston, 1810s–1930s* (New York: New York University Press, 1992), 26–31.

15. For groups other than children, see Mary P. Ryan, *Civic Wars: Democracy and Public Life in the American City During the Nineteenth Century* (Berkeley: University of California Press, 1997), 78–84.

16. For effects on daily life, see Dorsey, *Reforming Men and Women*, 56–63.

17. For the term "mixed economy," Michael B. Katz, *In the Shadow of the Poorhouse: A Social History of Welfare in America*, rev. ed. (New York: Basic Books, 1996), 47.

18. Shinn, "Charities for Children," 78–79. For comment, Ryan, *Civic Wars*, 88; Irwin, "'Going About Doing Good,'" 370, 371; Shackelford, ."To Shield Them from Temptation," 290–92.

19. Dorsey, *Reforming Men and Women*, 165. See also Barbara Welter, "The Cult of True Womanhood: 1820–1860," *American Quarterly* 18, no. 2, part 1 (Summer 1966): 151–74; Kerber, "Separate Spheres, Female Worlds," 9–39; Lori D. Ginzberg, *Women and the Work of Benevolence: Morality, Politics, and Class in Nineteenth-Century United States* (New Haven: Yale University Press, 1990), 67–97.

20. Ryan, *Civic Wars*, 250–51.

21. This point draws on arguments made by Rose, *Governing the Soul;* Ethington, *Public City;* Linda Gordon, *Pitied But Not Entitled: Single Mothers and the History of Welfare* (Cambridge, MA: Harvard University Press, 1994). See also Joan C. Tronto, "Care as a Basis for Radical Political Judgments," *Hypathia: A Journal of Feminist Philosophy* 10, no. 2 (Spring 1995): 141–49.

22. Cahn and Bary, *Welfare Activities*, xiii-xiv.

23. In the 1880s, the commissioner of charities called for a state board of charities and correction to be set up in California, but it was not established until 1903. See Edmond T. Dooley, *Report of the State of California to the Fifteenth National Conference of Charities and Correction in Buffalo, July 7, 1888* (Boston: Geo. H. Ellis, 1888), 8–9, 10–11; W. Almont Gates, "State Boards of Charities and Corrections," paper read before the Third Annual Conference of Charities and Corrections, held in San Francisco, February 21–23, 1904.

24. Gunther Barth, *Instant Cities: Urbanization and the Rise of San Francisco and Denver* (New York: Oxford University Press, 1975), 94–100. For eradication of the Mexican way of life, Lisabeth Haas, *Conquests and Historical Identities in California, 1769–1936* (Berkeley: University of California Press, 1995); Tomás Almaguer, *Racial Fault Lines: The Origins of White Supremacy in California* (Berkeley: University of California Press, 1994); Miroslava Chávez-García, *Negotiating Conquest: Gender and Power in California, 1770s to 1880s* (Tucson: University of Arizona Press, 2004).

25. For population figures, Shackelford, "To Shield Them from Temptation," 287–88; for spectacular growth, William Issel and Robert Cherny, *San Francisco, 1865–1932: Politics, Power, and Urban Development* (Berkeley: University of California Press, 1986), 13–18; Roger Lotchin, *San Francisco 1846–1856: From Hamlet to City* (New York: Oxford University Press, 1974), 3–30; for ethnic enclaves, Bradford Luckingham, "Immigrant Life in Emergent San Francisco," *Journal of the West* 12, no. 4 (October 1973): 600–603.

26. Peter Decker, *Fortunes and Failures: White Collar Mobility in Nineteenth-Century San Francisco* (Cambridge, MA: Harvard University Press, 1978), 23–24, 32–34.

27. Ryan, *Civic Wars*, 99.

28. Respectively, Ryan, *Civic Wars*, 75; Lotchin, *San Francisco 1846–1856*, 323–24.

29. Frederick Billings, *An Address Delivered at the Fifth Anniversary of the Orphan Asylum Society of San Francisco* (San Francisco: San Francisco Orphan Asylum Society, 1856), 15; San Francisco Industrial School Dept., *First Annual Report of the Board of Managers of the Industrial School Department of the City and County of San Francisco* (San Francisco: Towne & Bacon, 1859), 11–12.

30. Katz, *Shadow of the Poorhouse*, 7; Sonya Michel, *Children's Interests/Mothers' Rights: The Shaping of America's Child Care Policy* (New Haven: Yale University Press, 1999),

16–20; Cunningham, *Children and Childhood*, 114–19.

31. Dorsey, *Reforming Men and Women*, 85–89, 188–93; Elizabeth B. Clark, "'The Sacred Rights of the Weak': Pain, Sympathy, and the Culture of Individual Rights in Antebellum America," *Journal of American History* 82, no. 2 (September 1995): 463–93.

32. As cited by Christine Stansell, "Women, Children, and the Uses of the Streets: Class and Gender Conflict in New York City, 1850–1860," *Feminist Studies* 8, no. 2 (Summer 1982): 322, 333n46.

33. Stansell, "Women, Children, and the Uses of the Streets," 322; Ralph da Costa Nunez and Ethan G. Sribnick, *The Poor among Us: A History of Family Poverty and Homelessness in New York City* (New York: White Tiger Press, 2013), 56.

34. Elliott West, *Growing Up in the Country: Childhood on the Far Western Frontier* (Albuquerque: University of New Mexico Press, 1989), 15; Shackelford, "To Shield Them from Temptation," 294–95.

35. Robin L. Einhorn, *Property Rules: Political Economy in Chicago, 1833–1872* (Chicago: University of Chicago Press, 1991), 14.

36. Dorsey, *Reforming Men and Women*, 196.

37. Issel and Cherny, *San Francisco, 1865–1932*, 19; Ryan, *Civic Wars*, 137, 139–51.

38. For an overview, Issel and Cherny, *San Francisco, 1865–1932*, 17–18.

39. The wording of the 1852 law is cited in Luckingham, "Immigrant Life in Emergent San Francisco," 613; see also John Swett, *History of the Public School System of California* (San Francisco: A. L. Bancroft and Co., 1876).

40. Nellie Stow, *The Story of the San Francisco Protestant Orphanage: A Tale of Seventy-three Years, 1851–1924* (San Francisco: 1924), 3, 4 quote; Irwin, "'Going About Doing Good,'" 374.

41. Anne B. Bloomfield, "A History of the California Historical Society's New Mission Street Neighborhood," *California History* 74, no. 4 (Winter 1995/1996): 374; Decker, *Fortunes and Failures*, 9–11, 108.

42. As cited in Luckingham, "Immigrant Life in Emergent San Francisco," 614.

43. R. A. Burchell, *The San Francisco Irish, 1848–1880* (Berkeley: University of California Press, 1980), 10.

44. Burchell, *San Francisco Irish*, 10–11; Shackelford, "To Shield Them from Temptation," 311–13; "Angels of the Barbary Coast," accessed July 11, 2011, *Catholic San Francisco Online Edition* (2010), http://catholic-sf.org/news_select.php?newsid=23&id=57639.

45. For this point, but without discussion of its relationship to architecture, see Dorsey, *Reforming Men and Women*, 202; Schneider, *In the Web of Class*, 111–19.

46. Lotchin, *San Francisco 1846–1856*, 324.

47. For the suggestion that Hispanic children resided in Irish Catholic institutions, see Cahn and Bary, *Welfare Activities*, 10–11. The comment of the Chilean journalist is cited in Luckingham, "Immigrant Life in Emergent San Francisco," 601; it was published in a Valparaiso newspaper.

48. Mark L. Brack, "Domestic Architecture in Hispanic California: The Monterey Style Reconsidered," in *Perspectives in Vernacular Architecture 4*, ed. Thomas Carter and Bernard L. Herman (Knoxville: University of Tennessee Press, 1991), 163–73.

49. For the English poor law, see J. R. Poynter, *Society and Pauperism: English Ideas on Poor Relief, 1795–1834* (London: Routledge and Kegan Paul, 1969); David Owen, *English Philanthropy, 1660–1960* (Cambridge, MA: Belknap Press of Harvard University Press, 1964). For adaptation of British practice to the United States, see Nunez and Sribnick, *The Poor among Us*, 7–17; Katz, *Shadow of the Poorhouse*, 13–26, 37–43.

50. Katz, *Shadow of the Poorhouse*, 10. Katz uses the concept to describe the crises that engulfed working-class life; it is also helpful in interpreting the charitable landscape. See also Amy Drew Stanley, "Beggars Can't Be Choosers: Compulsion and Contract in Postbellum America," *Journal of American History* 74, no. 4 (March 1992): 1272.

51. Gordon, *Great Arizona Orphan Abduction*, 10–11; Stansell, "Women, Children, and the Uses of the Streets," 309–36; Timothy J. Gilfoyle, "Street-Rats and Gutter-Snipes: Child Pickpockets and Street Culture in New York City, 1850–1900," *Journal of Social History* 37, no. 4 (Summer 2004): 853–82.

52. E. P. Thompson, "History and Anthropology," in *Making History: Writings on History and Culture*, ed. Dorothy Thompson (New York: New Press, 1994), 217.

53. The term is used in Monique Bourque et al., "The Development of the Charitable Landscape: The Construction of the Lancaster County Almshouse in Regional Context," *Journal of the Lancaster County Historical Society* 102–3 (Summer-Fall 2000): 114–34.

54. Nunez and Sribnick, *Poor among Us*, 67; Beard, *On Being Homeless*.

55. For example, see Carla Yanni, *The Architecture of Madness: Insane Asylums in the United States* (Minneapolis: University of Minnesota Press, 2007), 56–59; Lu Ann

De Cunzo, "On Reforming the 'Fallen' and Beyond: Transforming Continuity at the Magdalene Society of Philadelphia, 1845–1916," *International Journal of Historical Archaeology* 5, no. 1 (March 2001): 19–44; and Dell Upton, *Another City: Urban Life and Urban Spaces in the New American Republic* (New Haven: Yale University Press, 2008), 28.

56. Thomas A. Markus, *Buildings and Power: Freedom and Control in the Origin of Modern Building Types* (New York: Routledge, 1993), 101. See also Michel Foucault, "Space, Knowledge, and Power," in *The Foucault Reader*, ed. Paul Rabi now (New York: Pantheon Books, 1984), 239–41.

57. Katz, *Shadow of the Poorhouse*, 88.

58. Homer Folks, *The Care of Destitute, Neglected, and Delinquent Children* (New York: Macmillan Company, 1902), 72–81. See also Joan Underhill Hannon, "Poverty in the Antebellum Northeast: The View from New York State's Relief Rolls," *Journal of Economic History* 44, no. 4 (1984): 1014; Rothman, *Discovery of the Asylum*, 287–90; Michael B. Katz, *Poverty and Policy in American History* (New York: Academic Press, 1983), 72–89.

59. Cahn and Bary, *Welfare Activities*, 141–45. For the Alameda County Poor Farm (later hospital), see Margaret F. Sirch and Stuart A. Queen, "Report on Alameda County Hospital and Infirmary" (San Francisco: Typed report issued by the State Board of Charities and Corrections, 1917); M. W. Wood and J. P. Munro-Fraser, *History of Alameda County, California* (Oakland: M. W. Wood, Publisher, 1883), 212–13.

60. Schneider, *In the Web of Class*, 26; Rose, *Governing the Soul*, 156; Howard P. Chudacoff, *How Old Are You? Age Consciousness in American Culture* (Princeton, NJ: Princeton University Press, 1989), 17–18.

61. For the general point, Shackelford, "To Shield Them from Temptation," 34–35; for an excellent case study, Schneider, *In the Web of Class*.

62. Shackelford, "To Shield Them from Temptation," 35–36, 40–42, 336.

63. Jacques Donzelot, *The Policing of Families*, trans. Robert Hurley (New York: Pantheon Books, 1979), 26–28; Philip Gavit, *Charity and Children in Renaissance Florence: The Ospedale degli Innocenti, 1410–1536* (Ann Arbor: University of Michigan Press, 1991); Nicholas Terpstra, "The Qualita of Mercy: (Re)building Confraternal Charities in Renaissance Bologna," in *Confraternities and the Visual Arts in the Renaissance: Ritual, Spectacle, Image*, ed. Barbara Wisch and Diane Cole Ahl (Cambridge: Cambridge University Press, 2000), 122–24.

64. Folks, *Care of Destitute, Neglected, and Delinquent Children*, 52–55; and Robert Bremner, ed. *Children and Youth in America: A Documentary History, 1600–1865*, 3 vols. (Cambridge, MA: Harvard University Press, 1970), 2: 655.

65. Hugh Cunningham, "Childhood in One Country," Review of Steven Mintz, *Huck's Raft: A History of American Childhood*, H-Childhood, H-Net Reviews, February 2006 (accessed February 26, 2006), http://www.h-net.org/reviews/showrev.php?id=11410.

66. For comparison, Guerra-Pearson, "Organizational Forms and Architectural Space," 474; Kenneth Cmiel, *A Home of Another Kind: One Chicago Orphanage and the Tangle of Child Welfare* (Chicago: University of Chicago Press, 1995), 12.

67. San Francisco Industrial School Dept., *First Annual Report*, 14.

68. Starting in the 1890s and continuing through the 1930s, Jesse Brown Cook, a San Francisco policeman, collected images of crime, criminals, and various street scenes and pasted them into scrapbooks; volume 21 includes a photograph of Bob Durk in clipped from the "Rogue's Gallery." The boy is described as follows: "Bob Durkin alias Frank Russell alias John Reed No. 15252 was the first prisoner sent to the Industrial School in this city in the early days. Then on Feb 16th 1865 he was sent to San Quentin from Sacramento County for burglary. On June 21 1869 he was again sent over to S.Q. from El Dorado Co. for 3 years. July 25th 1874 he broke jail in this city amd [sic] was afterwards captured and sent to S.Q. for 2 years for breaking and injuring jail. Jan 29th 1877 was sent over to S.Q. from Butte County for 5 years Burglary. Fenruary [sic] 21st 1893 was sent again to S.Q. for 7 years from Kern County for Burglary. After coming out he was picked up at San Jose in 1897 and charged with Vagrancy and sent to jail there from whence he made his escape but was latter [sic] picked up and served out his time." See "Jesse Brown Cook Scrapbooks Documenting San Francisco History and Law Enforcement," vol. 21, BL/UCB.

69. Theodor Kytka, "The First Rogue Gallery in the World," *Camera Craft: A Photographic Monthly* 2, no. 5 (March 1901): 380. For access online, see http://archive.org/stream/cameracraft1219001901phot#

page/n495/mode/2up. My thanks to Dee Dee Kramer for this information.

70. Kytka, "First Rogue Gallery," 383. See also Sandra S. Phillips, Mark Haworth-Booth, and Carol Squiers, *Police Pictures: The Photograph as Evidence* (San Francisco: San Francisco Museum of Modern Art/Chronicle Books, 1997); Christian Parenti, *The Soft Cage: Surveillance in America from Slavery to the War on Terror* (New York: Basic Books, 2003), 39–40.

71. San Francisco Industrial School Dept., *First Annual Report*, 5, 6; Cahn and Bary, *Welfare Activities*, 46; J. M. Hutchings, "Sites Around San Francisco," *Scenes of Wonder and Curiosity in California*, 2nd ed. (San Francisco: J. M. Hutchings and Co., 1862), chap. 9, accessed June 11, 2013, at http://www.yosemite.ca.us/library/scenes_of_wonder_and_curiosity/san_francisco.html. The Board of Supervisors allocated one thousand dollars per month for operating costs.

72. San Francisco Industrial School Dept., *Specifications for the Industrial School Building of San Francisco* (San Francisco: Sterett & Butler, 185?); Hutchings, "Sites Around San Francisco." The characterization of this space as congregate dormitories is incorrect in Daniel Macallair, "The San Francisco Industrial School and the Origins of Juvenile Justice in California: A Glance at the Great Reformation," *UC Davis Journal of Juvenile Law & Policy* 7, no. 1 (2003): 1–60. For the national importance of the New York model, see Robert S. Pickett, *House of Refuge: Origins of Juvenile Reform in New York State, 1815–1857* (Syracuse, NY: Syracuse University Press, 1969); Rothman, *Discovery of the Asylum*, 209, 213, 215, 223–26, 230–34; David Schneider and Albert Deutsch, *The History of Public Welfare in New York State, 1867–1940*, 2 vols. (Chicago: University of Chicago Press, 1941), 2: 317–25; Robert M. Mennel, *Thorns and Thistles: Juvenile Delinquents in the United States, 1825–1940* (Hanover, NH: University Press of New England, 1973).

73. Shackelford, "To Shield Them from Temptation," 38. See also Dell Upton, "Another City: The Urban Cultural Landscape in the Early Republic," in *Everyday Life in the Early Republic*, ed. Catherine E. Hutchins (New York and Winterthur, DE: Norton and Winterthur Museum, 1994), 90.

74. Hutchings, "Sites around San Francisco." See also Burchell, *San Francisco Irish*, 30.

75. J. C. (Joseph C.) Morrill, *The Industrial School Investigation, with a Glance at the Great Reformation and Its Results* (San Francisco: 1872), 2–3.

76. Shackelford, "To Shield Them from Temptation," 351; Michael Hennessey, "The Ingleside Jail: A Narrated Timeline," chap. 4 in "The History of the San Francisco Sheriff Department," accessed June 11, 2013, http://sfsdhistory.com/The%20Ingleside%20Jail.htm. The California superintendent of public instruction documented the overcrowding in the first biennial report (1863–65) of the department.

77. See Durkin and Brown photos in the "Jesse Brown Cook Scrapbooks Documenting San Francisco History and Law Enforcement," vol. 21, BL/UCB.

78. Similar strategies were employed in mixed-sex institutions for delinquent children in the Northeast. Schneider, *In the Web of Class*, 41–45.

79. Burchell, *San Francisco Irish*, 93; Shackelford, "To Shield Them from Temptation," 317–18; Suellen Hoy, *Good Hearts: Catholic Sisters in Chicago's Past* (Urbana: University of Illinois Press, 2006), 20–21.

80. James M. Smith, *Ireland's Magdalen Laundries and the Nation's Architecture of Containment* (Notre Dame, IN: University of Notre Dame Press, 2007); Cynthia Imogen Hammond, *Architects, Angels, Activists, and the City of Bath, 1765–1965: Engaging with Women's Spatial Interventions in Buildings and Landscapes* (Burlington, VT: Ashgate Publishing Co., 2012), chap. 5.

81. Shackelford suggests the scandal was not about money, but success at converting Protestants to Catholicism. Shackelford, "To Shield Them from Temptation," 316, 359–60; Burchell, *San Francisco Irish*, 93.

82. The interview with Kathleen Norris (ROHO, BL/UCB) is cited by Shackelford, "To Shield Them from Temptation," 377, emphasis in original.

83. Burchell, *San Francisco Irish*, 29; Cahn and Bary, *Welfare Activities*, 48–50. The state opened two other facilities for children in the 1860s and 1870s: the State Reform School in Marysville (1861–68) and a "training school" (really a prison) on the ship *Jamestown* (1876–79).

84. After the San Francisco Industrial School closed, the building continued to be used for correctional purposes; it was turned into the city jail for women.

85. Cahn and Bary, *Welfare Activities*, 53–56, 114–15, 126, 143–44; Folks, *Care of Destitute, Neglected, and Delinquent Children*, 225; Arthur J. Pillsbury, *Institutional Life: Its Relations to the State and to the Wards of the State* (Sacramento: State Printing Office, 1906), 75–76, and for the Magdalen Asylum, Shackelford, "To Shield Them from Temptation," 380–81. The Deaf, Dumb, and Blind Asylum and the

California Home for the Training of Feeble-Minded Children were run by private societies, initially. Outside of San Francisco, delinquent children, eight years and older, were imprisoned in local jails until the state built the new reform schools and introduced a separate system of juvenile courts.

86. Billings, *Address*, 17.
87. Irwin, "'Going About Doing Good,'" 375–76. See also Dorsey, *Reforming Men and Women*, 88.
88. Shinn, "Charities for Children," 78; Bloomfield, "A History of the California Historical Society's New Mission Street Neighborhood," 374.
89. Stow, *Story of the San Francisco Protestant Orphanage*, 2–3; Mrs. W. A. Haight, *Some Reminiscences of My Connection with the Board of Management of the San Francisco Protestant Orphan Asylum for the Past Forty-Seven Years* (San Francisco: 1900), n.p.; Dolores Waldorf, "Gentleman from Vermont: Royal H. Waller," *California Historical Society Quarterly* 22, no. 2 (1943): 112.
90. Stow, *Story of the San Francisco Protestant Orphanage*, 4–5.
91. Irwin, "'Going About Doing Good,'" 380; Shackelford, "To Shield Them from Temptation," 319–21.
92. Rothman, *Discovery of the Asylum*, 210–12.
93. Maurie D. McInnis, *The Politics of Taste in Charleston* (Chapel Hill: University of North Carolina Press, 2005), 29, 337 n50 citing the testimony of Sarah Grimke as quoted in Barbara L. Bellows, *Benevolence among Slaveholders: Assisting the Poor in Charleston, 1670–1860* (Baton Rouge: Louisiana State University Press, 1993), 45–46.
94. Billings, *Address*, 17–18.
95. Billings, *Address*, 15. For duty and middle-class manhood, see Dorsey, *Reforming Men and Women*, 20–22, 102–6; Gail Bederman, *Manliness and Civilization: A Cultural History of Gender and Race in the United States, 1880–1917* (Chicago: University of Chicago Press, 1995), 10–15.
96. Billings, *Address*, 19 quote, 22.
97. Dorsey, *Reforming Men and Women*, 38, 83, 174.
98. Billings, *Address*, 22.
99. Cahn and Bary, *Welfare Activities*, 9–11, 13; Burchell, *San Francisco Irish*, 10–11.
100. The figures come from Lotchin, *San Francisco 1846–1856*, 334.
101. Burchell, *San Francisco Irish*, 88.
102. Oates, *Catholic Philanthropic Tradition*, 29–30.
103. The 1857 report of the trustees of the Roman Catholic Orphan Asylum is cited in Shackelford, "To Shield Them from Temptation," 313. See also Decker, *Fortunes and Failures*, 113.
104. Burchell, *San Francisco Irish*, 158–61; Shackelford, "To Shield Them from Temptation," 301–5. For comparison with New York and Chicago, see Fitzgerald, *Habits of Compassion;* Brown and McKeown, *Poor Belong to Us;* Hoy, *Good Hearts.*
105. Brown and McKeown, *Poor Belong to Us*, 3–4. For the move to a national church, Oates, *Catholic Philanthropic Tradition.*
106. Fitzgerald, *Habits of Compassion*, 84–98.
107. James Flamant, "Child-Saving Charities in This Big Town," *San Francisco Morning Call*, May 28, 1893, 18.
108. For comparison, Schneider, *In the Web of Class*, 119; Dorsey, *Reforming Men and Women*, 202.
109. Ronald H. Bayor and Timothy J. Meagher, "Conclusion," in *The New York Irish*, ed. Ronald H. Bayor and Timothy J. Meagher (Baltimore: Johns Hopkins University Press, 1996), 535.
110. Rowena Beans, *"Inasmuch …": The One Hundred Year History of the San Francisco Ladies' Protection and Relief Society* (San Francisco: The Society, 1953), 1–12, 13–31; San Francisco Ladies' Protection and Relief Society, *Fifteenth and Sixteenth Annual Reports of the Managers and Trustees of the San Francisco Ladies' Protection and Relief Society* (San Francisco: Edward Bosqui and Company, 1869), 10–16; Shinn, "Charities for Children," 79–80.
111. Shackelford, "To Shield Them from Temptation," 325, 327.
112. By the end of the nineteenth century, four systems of aid were used for dependent children: (1) the state school and placing out system, (2) the county children's home system, (3) the boarding-out and placing-out systems, and (4) the plan of supporting children in private institutions. Folks, *Care of Destitute, Neglected, and Delinquent Children*, chap. 5, 6, 7, 8.
113. US Bureau of the Census, *Eleventh Census of the United States* (Washington: Government Printing Office, 1890), 3: 321–22. The first federal census of benevolent institutions, published in 1892, occasioned widespread criticism of the cost of congregate orphanages, including that in California. See Cahn and Bary, *Welfare Activities*, 42–43, 144; Shinn, "Charities for Children," 85–86.
114. See Slingerland, *Child Welfare Work in California;* Shinn, "Charities for Children," 78–101.
115. Peggy Pascoe, "Gender Systems in Conflict: The Marriages of Mission-Educated

Chinese American Women, 1874–1939," *Journal of Social History* 22, no. 4 (Summer 1989): 631–52; Wendy Rouse Jorae, *The Children of Chinatown: Growing up Chinese American in San Francisco, 1850–1920* (Chapel Hill: University of North Carolina Press, 2009), 147–54.

116. Peggy Pascoe, *Relations of Rescue: The Search for Female Moral Authority in the American West, 1874–1939* (New York: Oxford University Press, 1990), 15–17; Ryan, *Civic Wars*, 294.

117. In the 1870s, the Sisters of Charity ran schools for working-class children and orphan asylums; the Sisters of Notre Dame and Sisters of the Presentation ran schools for middle-class and wealthy girls; the Sisters of Mercy ran hospitals and maternity homes. D. J. Kavanagh, *The Holy Family Sisters of San Francisco: A Sketch of Their First Fifty Years* (San Francisco: Gilmartin Company, 1922), 29, 129; Ellen Berg, "Citizens in the Republic of Childhood: Immigrants and the American Kindergarten" (PhD dissertation, University of California, Berkeley, 2004), 276–77.

118. As quoted in Marguerite Dupree, "The Provision of Social Services," in *The Cambridge Urban History of Britain, vol. 3, 1840–1950*, ed. Martin Daunton (Cambridge: Cambridge University Press, 2000), 353.

119. Jonathan Barry and Colin Jones, introduction to *Medicine and Charity before the Welfare State*, ed. Jonathan Barry and Colin Jones (New York: Routledge, 1991), 11.

120. In 1870, private orphan asylums received fifty dollars per year for a full orphan and twenty-five dollars for a half-orphan; there was no residence requirement. In 1873 and 1874 the grant was extended to abandoned children and increased the next year to one hundred dollars per orphan and seventy-five dollars per half-orphan. The aid remained at that level for the balance of the century. In 1888 counties as well as private and state-run institutions were permitted to receive state aid. The "indigent aged" received state aid, starting in 1883 and lasting until 1895, when the legislature terminated the assistance. Cahn and Bary, *Welfare Activities*, xvi, 1–2, 4, 11, 143–45, 365, table 1. For New York, Folks, *Care of Destitute, Neglected, and Delinquent Children*, 116–19. The Children's Law of 1875 formalized the per capita system in New York State. Nunez and Sribnick, *Poor among Us*, 98, 99.

121. W. S. Melick, "Some Points Regarding California's Aid to Dependent Children," in *Proceedings of the Third Annual California State Conference of Charities and Corrections, Held at San Francisco, February 21–23, 1904* (Ione, CA: State of California, 1904), 145.

122. Cahn and Bary, *Welfare Activities*, xvi, 137, 170–71.

123. Ibid., 144.

124. William Deverell, *Railroad Crossing: Californians and the Railroad, 1850–1910* (Berkeley: University of California Press, 1994), 23; US Census Office, "Oakland in 1880," in *Report on the Social Statistics of Cities; Part II: The Southern and the Western States*, ed. George E. Waring Jr. (Washington: Government Printing Office, 1887), 784.

125. Joshua D. Wolff, "'The Great Monopoly': Western Union and the American Telegraph, 1845–1893" (PhD dissertation, Columbia University, 2008); Robert Luther Thompson, *Wiring a Continent: The History of the Telegraph Industry in the United States, 1832–1866* (Princeton, NJ: Princeton University Press, 1947).

ESSAY 7.3

The Subway and the City

Clifton Hood

Source: Clifton Hood, *722 Miles: The Building of the Subways and How They Transformed New York* (New York: Simon & Schuster, 1993).

EDITORS' INTRODUCTION

New York City is a metropolis inexorably linked with the subway. Once the subway opened in 1904, the city was forever transformed. The subway inevitably affected the city's physical spaces. Subway stops defined real estate values, making some locations prime sites for retail, and some neighborhoods more enticing residential options for commuters. The subways became part of an elaborate transportation system whereby millions of people moved within and through the city's five boroughs (legally merged as a whole in 1898) and the greater New York metropolitan area. The subway became the setting where New Yorkers spent considerable time. Friendships were formed, love interests encountered, business deals secured, newspapers and books read, and entertainment produced by other riders on the subway. As Hood notes here, residents and tourists alike enjoyed the decorative tiles and other fine touches of the carefully designed subway stations, at least until the residents became blasé about the scenery after months of routine commuting. Subway riders balked at the initial installation of extensive advertisements within the stations, although that too became commonplace. In today's subways, advertisements have moved inside the trains themselves, and creative marketers think of seemingly endless ways to draw the attention of the commuter. As Clifton Hood notes, the subway, by knitting together once far-flung neighborhoods in unforeseen ways, "changed New York City almost beyond recognition."[i]

New York was not the first city in the United States to construct a subway, although New Yorkers rightly claim a special relationship with subway history for devising the fastest urban mass transit system in the world at the time. As Hood straightforwardly describes, "Although rapid transit engineering was quite sophisticated, there were just six other subways in the world by 1904, and the only other one in the Western Hemisphere was a short Boston line that had been in service for a mere seven years."[ii] Boston's subway, opened in 1897 and initially running just one and two-thirds miles under Tremont Street, was an off-shoot of the city's electric trolley franchise. As we have seen in Essay 7.1 by Sam Bass Warner Jr., Boston was a city defined by its above-ground commuter trains. **[See Essay 7.1, Sam Bass Warner, Jr., "From Walking City to the Implementation of Street Railways."]**

The excitement New Yorkers experienced at the dedication and grand opening of the subway on October 27, 1904, from Mayor George B. McClellan's refusal to give up the controls on the train filled with dignitaries, to the crowds of spectators waiting to see a glimpse of the subway cars on the viaduct between 122nd to 135th streets, testifies to the

---

i Clifton Hood, *722 Miles: The Building of the Subways and How They Transformed New York* (New York: Simon & Schuster, 1993), 111.
ii Hood, *722 Miles,* 92 and 98.

city's strong connection to its subway system. The Interborough Rapid Transit Company, or IRT, was one of three separate subway lines ultimately established in New York City. The IRT later merged with the BRT (Brooklyn Rapid Transit Company) to form the BMT (Brooklyn-Manhattan Transit Company) in 1923, and then Mayor Fiorello H. LaGuardia combined the BMT with the IND (Independent Subway System) to form one city-wide transit system in 1940.

Clifton Hood is the George E. Paulsen '49 Professor of American History and Government at Hobart and William Smith Colleges, where he teaches American history courses on cities, immigration, industrialization and the environment. He authored *722 Miles: The Building of the Subways and How They Transformed New York* (Baltimore, MD: Johns Hopkins University Press, 2004), *In Pursuit of Privilege: A History of New York City's Upper Class and the Making of a Metropolis* (New York: Columbia University Press, 2017), and essays for *The Journal of Urban History*, *The Journal of Social History*, and *Reviews in American History*. Hood was Senior Fulbright Lecturer at Seoul National University in 2001. Hood was interviewed for the 1997 PBS/American Experience series, *New York Underground*, as well as a number of other documentaries. **[See also Essay 4.5 Clifton Hood, "A Dynamic Businessman's Aristocracy: The 1890s (2017)."]**

THE SUBWAY AND THE CITY (1993)

October 27, 1904

Mayor George B. McClellan switched on the motor, turned the controller, and headed north from the city hall station for a tour of the new Interborough Rapid Transit subway. The underground railway had been dedicated earlier that day in October 1904 during a ceremony at city hall, and it would be opened to the general public four or five hours later; people were already waiting outside the stations for their first ride on the new subterranean wonder. For now, however, Mayor McClellan and a select group of the city's most distinguished leaders had it to themselves.[1]

Although Mayor McClellan was supposed to surrender the controls to a regular motorman once the excursion got under way, he was enjoying himself so much that he adamantly refused to step aside and insisted on running the train himself, despite the fact that, as he admitted with a boyish grin, he had never driven a railway car before.

McClellan's decision startled the two top Interborough executives on board the train, Vice-President E. M. Bryan and General Manager Frank M. Hedley. Although they naturally wanted to indulge a politician as powerful as the chief executive of New York City, Bryan and Hedley feared that McClellan might cause a serious accident which would turn the public against the IRT. Bryan and Hedley were concerned because the Interborough was so novel that city residents might not accept it. Although rapid transit engineering was quite sophisticated, there were just six other subways in the world by 1904, and the only other one in the Western Hemisphere was a short Boston line that had been in service for a mere seven years. Indeed, one wag had predicted years earlier that a New York subway was bound to flop because people would go below ground only once in their lifetimes—and that was after death.

Bryan and Hedley were particularly worried about the possibility of an accident because many prominent individuals were riding this special excursion train: President Nicholas Murray Butler of Columbia University and Chancellor Henry Mitchell McCracken of New York University; Archbishop John M. Farley of the Catholic Church and Bishop Coadjutor David H. Greer of the Episcopal Church; and bankers Jacob Schiff, Morris K. Jesup, and Henry Clews. These men represented elite groups that ruled New York City, and their participation in these opening day ceremonies underscored the importance of the subway. To these leaders the IRT belonged in the tradition of grand civic projects that made

New York the greatest metropolis in North America, such as the Erie Canal, the Croton Aqueduct water system, and the Brooklyn Bridge.[2]

But George B. McClellan was having the time of his life driving the train, and he did not share the IRT executives' anxieties. Mischievously ignoring the pained expressions on the faces of Bryan and Hedley, McClellan pressed the controller and sent the special train shooting through the tunnel. General Manager Hedley nervously glued himself to the emergency brake and kept blowing the whistle to alert track workers to the danger, while Vice-President Bryan stationed himself directly behind the mayor, ready to take charge in a crisis. At a point near Spring Street, Hedley tried to coax McClellan into ending his joyride by asking, "Aren't you tired of it? Don't you want the motorman to take it?" "No, sir!" McClellan replied firmly. "I'm running this train!"[3]

So he was. One mishap did occur when McClellan accidentally hit the emergency brake, bringing the four-car train to a violent stop that sent the silk-hatted, frock-coated dignitaries flying through the air. But McClellan confidently settled back at the controls after a few tense moments and, despite Hedley's panicked cries—"Slower here, slower! Easy!"—raised the train's speed even higher.[4] Up Elm Street (now Lafayette Street) and Fourth Avenue (now Park Avenue) to Grand Central Terminal, across Forty-second Street to Times Square on the West Side, and then up Broadway through the Upper West Side, the train roared on the straightaways and careened around the curves at over forty miles per hour. Afterward the "motorman mayor," as he was now called, attributed his success to his mastery of "automobiling."

Mayor George B. McClellan's escapade was hardly the only reason this trip was memorable, for the IRT subway ranked as the world's best rapid transit railway. A British transit expert who inspected the Interborough in 1904 concluded that it "must be considered one of the great engineering achievements of the age" and acknowledged that it was more advanced technologically than London's underground.[5] The IRT was not yet the largest subway in the world— London still held that distinction—but it was the longest ever completed at a single time, covering twenty-two route miles. Because the northern sections were still under construction, the special reached only as far uptown as 145th Street and Broadway on its run. [...]

The subway had been created not merely as a pedestrian municipal service but as a civic monument. The architects were Heins and La-Farge, who had designed America's largest church, the Cathedral of St. John the Divine, on New York's Morningside Heights, and made some of the subway stations works of art in themselves. For example, the flagship station at city hall was an underground chapel in the round that had beautiful Guastivino arches, leaded glass skylights, and chandeliers. Although the other stations were utilitarian boxes that could not compare to city hall's, they nonetheless had colorful tile mosaics, natural vault lighting, and oak ticket booths with bronze fittings that created an elegant impression. Their most popular feature was ceramic bas-relief name panels that depicted neighborhood themes: The Astor Place plaque had a beaver in honor of fur trader John Jacob Astor; Fulton Street showed Robert Fulton's pioneering steamboat, the *Clermont;* Columbus Circle had Christopher Columbus' flagship, the *Santa Maria;* and 116th Street (Broadway branch) displayed the Columbia University seal.

The Interborough was equally attractive above the surface. For instance, McKim, Mead & White had turned the facade of the IRT powerhouse—a colossal brick and terra-cotta structure on the Hudson River at Fifty-ninth Street where coal-burning furnaces generated electricity for the subway— into a classical temple that paid homage to modern industry. Still more impressive were the cast-iron and glass kiosks that covered the station entrances and exits. These ornate kiosks, which were patterned after similar structures on the Budapest metro, soon became an Interborough trademark, and for good reason. Cleverly designed to enhance rider comfort, the kiosks marked the entrances to the stations so that patrons could find the subways without getting lost on the street; they also shielded the passageways so that people were not drenched in rainstorms and segregated incoming from outgoing pedestrians so that traffic would flow more smoothly and riders going downstairs did not have to fight those going up.[6]

After the initial V.I.P. activities, the celebration took on a democratic air. In the words of a newspaperman who observed the festivities, New York City went "subway mad" over the IRT's inauguration. For the preceding few weeks, hundreds of New Yorkers had held "subway parties" to celebrate the big event. On October 27 courthouses, office buildings, shops, and private homes were decked out with flags and bunting just as on the Fourth of July; church bells, guns, sirens, and horns resounded all day long. Thousands of people began to gather around city hall early in the morning, waiting to see the dedication ceremony that would be held upstairs in the aldermanic chamber. Thousands more queued up at the kiosks, waiting for their first subway ride.[7]

The only place where the official train ran in full public view was on the viaduct over Manhattan Valley, from 122nd to 135th streets. A huge crowd of spectators went there for a look, blanketing rooftops, vacant lots, street corners, and fire escapes for blocks around. When the special emerged from the tunnel and started across the trestle, these onlookers began to cheer. The train slowed down and blew its whistle in response; sirens from local factories and from ships on the Hudson River let loose, too. The noise continued until the train reentered the tunnel and disappeared from sight.

The rest of the trip was uneventful, largely because Hedley and Bryan had finally persuaded Mayor McClellan to relinquish the controls. Very proud of himself, McClellan puffed away at a cigar and bantered with the other guests all the way back to city hall.

Finally, at 7:00 P.M., the IRT opened its doors to the public. Men and women who had been waiting all afternoon for this moment streamed down the stairways and onto the cars. A new era had begun in the history of New York City.[8]

More than 110,000 people swarmed through subway gates that evening and saw the stations and platforms for themselves. New Yorkers were so excited by their discovery of the IRT that they coined a phrase to describe the experience: "doing the subway."

The night took on a carnival atmosphere, like New Year's Eve. Many couples celebrated in style by putting on their best clothes, going out to dinner, and then taking their first subway ride together. Some people spent the entire evening on the trains, going back and forth from 145th Street to city hall for hours. Reveling in the sheer novelty of the underground, these riders wanted to soak up its unfamiliar sights and sensations for as long as possible. In a few instances high-spirited boys and girls took over part of a car and began singing songs, flirting, and fooling around. The sheer exuberance of opening night proved to be too much for others; although they bought their green IRT tickets and entered the stations like everyone else, these timid passengers were so overwhelmed by their new surroundings that they did not even attempt to board a train. All they could do was stand on the platform and gawk.

This popular hoopla climaxed three days later, on Sunday, October 30. Most New Yorkers still worked six days a week and had only Sundays to themselves. On this particular Sunday, almost one million people chose to go subway riding. The IRT was like a magnet, attracting groups from the outskirts of Brooklyn and Queens, two or three hours away. Unfortunately, the IRT could accommodate only 350,000 a day, and many people had to be turned away. The lines to enter the 145th Street station stretched for two blocks, and people grew so frustrated that police reserves had to be summoned to break up fights and restore order.[9]

That same week a public controversy erupted when the Interborough Rapid Transit Company suddenly began to install advertising placards in the stations. Although the Rapid Transit Commission had evidently always intended to permit advertising, it withheld this information from the public. Even the subway's architects, Heins and LaFarge, did not know about it. So when workers for the Interborough's advertising firm, Ward & Gow, began driving nails into the ornamental tile-work and covering the walls with large, tin-framed signs, New Yorkers reacted with surprise and anger. Many thought these unsightly billboards—for products such as Baker's Cocoa, Evans Ale ("Live the Simple Life"), Coke Dandruff Cure, and Hunyadi János ("A Positive Cure for Constipation")—detracted from the subway's stature as a noble civic monument. The *Real Estate Record and Builders Guide* blasted the placards as "an outrage" that "mar the appearance of an appropriate and admirable piece of interior decoration," while Rapid Transit Commissioner Charles Stewart Smith called them "cheap and nasty."[10] Both the Architectural League and the Municipal Art Society condemned the ads and demanded their removal. Aroused by this strong negative reaction, the municipal government filed a lawsuit against the Interborough to eliminate the ads. The Interborough expected to earn about $500,000 from this concession and vigorously defended its contractual rights; the company won the case several years later. The signs remained, an early indication that the subway was assuming a more pedestrian place in the life of the city.[11]

The initial thrill eventually wore off for the passengers, too, and a subway ride became nothing more than a daily habit. Elmer Rice, a twelve-year-old who had been badgering his parents to take him on the IRT, finally got his chance one Sunday afternoon late in November. Young Rice, his parents, his grandfather, and his uncle embarked on a family expedition through the subway. Years later Rice, by then an accomplished playwright, treasured this trip as a highlight of his boyhood. "So this was the subway!" he exclaimed, remembering how awed he had been by the beautiful tile mosaics and how he had pressed his face against the window glass and watched the station pillars flash by. But the excitement faded away when Rice began taking the subway to school every day. "At the end of six months," he admitted, "I had even stopped looking at the tiling."[12]

Long after most New Yorkers became bored with it, the IRT continued to fascinate out-of-towners. For years popular guidebooks put the subway high on their list of sights that travelers should see in New York. "The tourist," Rand McNally advised in 1905, "will be well repaid by a trip through the bore of this greatest of all underground railways," while the *Banner Guide & Excursion Book* strongly encouraged visitors to experience the subway's "surprising roominess and apparent rush and hustle and, especially, the fine finish and cheeriness of its stations."[13] As these guidebooks recognized, the IRT was an essential part of the metropolis. Along with the Brooklyn Bridge, the Statue of Liberty, the Flatiron Building, and Wall Street, the IRT embodied the wealth, power, and modernity that distinguished New York from all other cities.

For residents and tourists alike, the IRT represented a completely new kind of urban environment. Unlike the els and streetcars where the rest of the city was always in view, the underground railway enabled passengers to travel across New York without ever catching sight of the surface. For instance, riders could pass through the city hall subway station and never know what city hall, the Tweed courthouse, or the surrogate courthouse looked like. According to the *Utica Saturday Globe,* the subway had transformed New York into "the city of human prairie dogs." The paper noted that "just as the little burrowers of the West dart into their holes in the ground," so New Yorkers had developed a habit of disappearing beneath the surface and then reappearing somewhere else.[14]

A ride in the subway thus meant entering a separate and sometimes disorienting sphere, particularly in the long stretches between stations where the trains were shrouded in darkness. Isolated from their familiar surroundings and dependent on steel rails, track switches, electrical conduits, signals, and other mechanical devices, passengers thought of the subway as a realm of impersonal, complicated technology.[15]

Observers agreed that the IRT's most important technical attribute was its high speed. In fact, the Interborough was renowned for being the fastest urban mass transit railway in the world. The reason for this impressive performance was that it was the first rapid transit railway to have separate express and local service. Many other railways employed some kind of express service before 1904, but none could compare to the Interborough. For example, the Manhattan Railway Company's Ninth Avenue elevated route extended all the way from Cortlandt Street at the foot of the island to the Harlem River, but its expresses were confined to one part of this route, from Fourteenth Street to 116th Street, and to a single track. Consequently, Ninth Avenue expresses headed south during the morning rush hour and back uptown at night. In comparison, the Interborough's four tracks permitted permanent two-way express service, significantly improving the speed and range of its trains.[16] The Interborough expresses exceeded forty miles per hour, three times faster than the city's steam-powered els and six times faster than its streetcars.

NOTES

1. *New York Times,* October 28, 1904. *New York Evening Post,* October 27, 1904.
2. August Belmont to William Barclay Parsons, July 17, 1904, PL 79, BFP.
3. *New York Times,* October 28, 1904.
4. Ibid.
5. London County Council, *The Rapid Transit Subways of New York: A Report by Mr. J. Allen Baker, Chairman of the Highways Committee, of the Inspection made by him of the Rapid Transit Subways of New York* (London: Southwood, Smith & Company, 1904): 5.
6. Interborough Rapid Transit Company, *The New York Subway, Its Construction and Equipment* (New York: n. p., 1904): 15, 23–26.
7. *New York Times,* October 28, 1904. *New York Mail & Express,* October 28, 1904. *Brooklyn Eagle,* October 27, 1904. Elmer Rice, "Joy-Riding in the Subway," *New Yorker* 4 (December 29, 1928): 21–23.
8. *New York Times,* October 28, 1904. *New York Evening Post,* October 27, 1904. Although the capacity of the original subway was six hundred thousand, only part of the route was opened on October 27.
9. *New York Times,* October 30 and 31, 1904. *New York Commercial,* October 31, 1904. *New York Tribune,* October 29, 1904. Abraham Lincoln Merritt, "Ten Years of the Subway," in Electric Railroaders Association, *Interborough Bulletin* 77 (November 1987): 12. The capacity of 350,000 was for the portion of the subway that was opened on October 27, 1904, not the entire IRT.
10. *Real Estate Record and Builders Guide,* November 5, 1904: 949. *New York Times,* November 19, 1904.
11. *New York Times,* October 29 and November 2, 5, 11, 18, 19, and 29, 1904; June 17, 1990.
12. Rice, "Joy-Riding in the Subway," 22, 23.
13. *Rand McNally & Co.'s Handy Guide to New York City,* 18th ed. (Chicago: Rand McNally & Company, 1905): 23. *Banner Guide & Excursion Book* (New York: John D. Hall, 1904): 4.
14. *Utica Saturday Globe,* November 5, 1904.
15. *New York Commercial,* October 31, 1904. *New York Times,* October 29 and 31, and November 2, 1904.
16. The IRT express service was so innovative that the subway's planners did not foresee its significance and originally assumed that the locals would carry the greater part of the passenger load, hence their decision to restrict express operations to built-up areas south of Ninety-sixth Street. Original specifications had called for building only two local tracks above Ninety-sixth Street, but a third track for one-way express service was added after construction began, partly in response to the traffic increases caused by electrification of the elevateds. "Diary of William Barclay Parsons, Chief Engineer, Rapid Transit Commission, from the beginning of work, March 26, 1900, to his resignation as Chief Engineer, December 31, 1904," entry for January 28, 1901, Rare Book and Manuscript Library, Butler Library, Columbia University, New York, NY.

ESSAY 7.4

Wishful Thinking: Downtown and the Automotive Revolution

Robert Fogelson

Source: Robert Fogelson, *Downtown: Its Rise and Fall, 1880–1950* (New Haven: Yale University Press, 2001).

EDITORS' INTRODUCTION

In preceding essays by historians Sam Bass Warner, Jr., and Clifton Hood **[see Essays 7.1 and 7.3]**, downtown access is discussed as a matter of mass transportation. In Warner's classic text, transportation changes led to a movement away from the center city. Warner's wealthy and upper middle class Bostonians accessed the countryside by means of a newly constructed streetcar system; they had previously been living downtown. These new neighborhoods would later be considered suburbs. Hood demonstrates how the New York City subway system—so intriguing on an imaginative level—also made original contributions to the city's physicality, by transforming the far-flung city into coherent whole and irrevocably changing neighborhoods. But the transformative power of the streetcar and the subway was dwarfed by the influence of the car. By the 1920s, the automobile had radically altered urban concerns. At this time, Fogelson reveals, many Americans ceased using mass transportation. Some of these people, comfortably ensconced in the suburbs, were relying on the growth of new secondary business districts close to their homes. Others choose to access the central business district, yet got there by means other than mass transit. Since the dawn of the omnibus in the early nineteenth century, shared transit had often meant uncomfortable transportation; the omnibus was too cold in the winter, too warm in the summer, and continually overcrowded. And as if to add insult to injury, mass transportation oftentimes was unreliable and slow. In every American city other than New York, the "riding habit," or the reliance on public transportation, tended to dwindle, while the "driving habit," swiftly increased.

Urban business leaders and boosters promoting the use of downtown areas conceived of the problem as one of access, misunderstanding the variety of reasons people had stopped heading downtown. This contingent believed people wanted to get downtown, but were stymied. These urban leaders turned their focus to improving downtown accessibility. They considered the means by which to increase the flow of traffic in downtowns, the employment of traffic regulations, street widening, throughways for non-local traffic, and the implementation of the modern highway system. Proposals were made for garages at the edge of cities, served by train lines. Others suggested banning "pleasure" vehicles, but how could one ultimately gauge the intent of each driver? Some wondered if setting limits on building height could affect downtown overcrowding. Certainly designs for higher buildings led to much more populated central business districts. Others argued the opposite, noting that high urban concentrations led to a reduced need to crisscross the city on daily business; everything that one needed, especially if businesses were clustered by type, could be accessed on foot in a highly dense business district. Planning ideas grew increasingly creative, including dreams of multi-level roads. Versions of a multi-level road were constructed in many cities (this includes Wacker Drive in Chicago, proposed in Daniel Burnham's 1909 Plan of Chicago and in use by 1926 as the nation's first modern double-level boulevard, separating regular and commercial vehicles) but many of these ideas were too fanciful to warrant real consideration.[i] **[See Document 7.2, Walter D. Moody, *Wacker's Manual of the Plan of Chicago*.]** Ultimately, the road builders would find it impossible to adequately anticipate the need for roads and build enough of them. Once a city constructed a road, people used it, and then moved out to the often less expensive suburbs and commuted in to their downtown jobs. Far sooner than expected, gridlock returned.

In 1956, the United States Congress, with the support of President Dwight Eisenhower, passed the Federal Highway Act. With this act, Washington, D.C. unequivocally backed the automobile as the preferred type of transportation, and undercut the health of the nation's downtowns. The more than 41,000 miles of interstate highway created by the act, ostensibly as a means by which to get people more quickly and easily to the central cities, actually made many downtowns largely irrelevant to regional growth. **[See Document 7.1, "National Interstate and Defense Highways Act."]**

Robert Fogelson is a professor of history and urban studies and planning at the Massachusetts Institute of Technology (MIT). *Downtown: Its Rise and Fall, 1880–1950* was awarded the prize for the best book in urban history by the Urban History Association in 2002. Additionally, *Downtown* won the 2001 Lewis Mumford Prize for Best Book in American City and Regional History given by the Society for American City and Regional Planning. Fogelson is also the author of *Bourgeois Nightmares: Suburbia, 1870–1930* (New Haven: Yale University Press, 2005) and *The Great Rent Wars* (New Haven, CT: Yale University Press, 2013). *Bourgeois Nightmares* won Honorable Mention for the 2006 Peter C. Rollins Book Award sponsored by the Northeast Popular Culture/American Culture Association.

WISHFUL THINKING: DOWNTOWN AND THE AUTOMOTIVE REVOLUTION (2001)

In May 1941 the newly formed Downtown Committee, an organization of about thirty of downtown Baltimore's largest property owners, sent G. Harvey Porter, director of the committee's Downtown Study, on a trip to find out what other cities were doing about decentralization. Porter visited Oakland, Los Angeles, Kansas City, and St. Louis, "each of which," said the *Baltimore Sun*, "has taken more or less elaborate steps to combat the process." On his return he made several recommendations, most of which were later adopted by the committee. Porter's trip was enlightening. But it was also superfluous. On the basis of studies in other cities and reports by the Urban Land Institute, Porter and his associates had already made up their minds about how to curb (and, if possible, to reverse) decentralization. "The principal objective," Porter said shortly before leaving, "is to get persons in and out of the downtown area as quickly and easily as possible, by whatever means." Once downtown was made more accessible, business would pick up, values would rise, capital would flow in, and decentralization would slow down (or even stop).[1] Underlying this belief was the assumption that people were not going downtown because they were unable to—that, as a leading Los Angeles reformer (and sometime real estate speculator) pointed out when decentralization first appeared there two decades earlier, "They wanted to[,] but they couldn't."

---

i James R. Grossman, Ann Durking Keating, and Janice L. Reiff, *The Encyclopedia of Chicago* (Chicago: University of Chicago Press, 2004), 31–32. Additional portions were added to Wacker Drive in subsequent years. In one section, there is a third level of street.

The belief that accessibility was the key to the well-being of downtown had emerged in the second half of the nineteenth century and became part of the conventional wisdom in the first half of the twentieth. But between 1915 and 1925 the meaning of accessibility changed. Before then it had been synonymous with mass transit. For down through the 1910s most people used it to go downtown, the large majority traveling on streetcars (and, in a few cities, els and subways) and a small minority on ferries and commuter trains. The rest came by automobiles, trucks, taxis, bicycles, and horse-drawn vehicles (or on foot). None of these vehicles, not even the automobile, carried nearly as many people as the streetcar. According to early cordon counts, straphangers outnumbered motorists by close to five to one in San Francisco (1912), more than six to one in Denver (1914), and roughly four to one in Chicago (1921)—and almost twice again as much if the els and commuter trains are counted. That an effective system of mass transit was vital to the well-being of a highly compact and extremely concentrated business district was taken for granted before 1920, especially by the downtown businessmen and property owners. Witness their support for the attempts to build subways. Witness too their backing of the street railways in their efforts to drive the jitney out of business. A commercial motor vehicle that was faster than a streetcar and cheaper than a taxi, the jitney "stole" so many riders from the street railways that the railway companies saw them as a threat to their long-term solvency.[2]

Starting around 1920, however, many Americans stopped using mass transit to go downtown—some because they stopped going downtown, opting to patronize outlying business districts instead, and others because they stopped using mass transit. The growth of these business districts took Americans by surprise. So did the decline of the riding habit. According to the conventional wisdom about the relation between transit patronage and population growth, the riding habit should have gone way up in the 1920s, a decade during which big cities grew even bigger. But in every city except New York, where it went up about 15 percent, or around two-thirds as much as the population, the riding habit went down. Between 1920 and 1930 it fell 10 to 20 percent in Boston, Philadelphia, Chicago (the only cities other than New York with a rapid transit system), and San Francisco, whose riding habit was the highest in the country until 1927, when it dropped below New York's. Elsewhere the riding habit fell more sharply—20 to 30 percent in Pittsburgh and Milwaukee, 30 to 40 percent in Baltimore, Cincinnati, and St. Louis, and 40 to 50 percent in Buffalo, Cleveland, and Los Angeles. In general it fell even more sharply in small and medium-sized cities. During the 1930s, a terrible time for the transit industry, the riding habit dropped still further. By the end of the decade it was lower than it had been at any time since the turn of the century. As a result of gas rationing and other fallout from World War II, the transit industry regained some of its riders in the early and mid 1940s. But shortly after the war ended, it resumed its long and irreversible decline.[3]

Of the many Americans who stopped using mass transit but kept going downtown, most traveled by private automobiles (as opposed to taxis or other commercial vehicles). What might be called the driving habit soared in the late 1910s and 1920s, more than doubling in some cities, more than tripling in others. By 1930, 50,000 to 100,000 autos poured into downtown Boston, downtown Philadelphia, and downtown Detroit on a typical weekday. More than 100,000 poured into downtown Chicago, more than 250,000 into downtown Los Angeles. (Autos carried over three-fifths of the daytime population of downtown L.A. in 1931, up from under two-fifths in 1924, a period during which the number of people who went downtown by mass transit declined by nearly one-third.) The driving habit rose more slowly in the 1930s, partly because of the Great Depression and partly because of decentralization. Even so, by early 1941, a few months before Baltimore's Downtown Committee was organized, 30 to 40 percent of those who went downtown traveled by auto in Boston, Philadelphia, and Chicago, 40 to 50 percent in Pittsburgh, Detroit, and

San Francisco, and more than 50 percent in St. Louis and Los Angeles. Only in New York did less than 20 percent travel downtown by automobile. A larger proportion, from two-thirds to as high as nine-tenths, drove down-town in small and medium-sized cities. In only four cities other than New York did as many as one-half of downtown's daytime population still ride the streetcars, els, sub-ways, and motorbuses, which had replaced many of the streetcars in the 1920s and 1930s.[4]

To understand why a large and growing number of Americans opted to drive down-town after 1920, it is important to bear in mind that many of them had long been dis-satisfied with mass transit. The streetcars were extremely crowded, especially during rush hour, when it was very hard to find a place, much less a seat. They were uncom-fortable and unreliable, especially in inclem-ent weather. And once they reached the central business district, they moved "at a snail's pace," wrote the Los Angeles Times. The els and subways were faster and more reliable, but more crowded and less com-fortable. The service, bad before World War I, deteriorated afterward. In an effort to deal with the fiscal crisis triggered by the phenomenal wartime inflation, the railway companies kept antiquated equipment in service, deferred much-needed repairs and maintenance, and abandoned miles of unprofitable lines. They raised fares too. Exacerbating the industry's problems, driv-ing its revenues down and its expenses up, was the proliferation of private automo-biles, the number of which soared from 8,000 in 1900 to 500,000 in 1910, 8 mil-lion in 1920, and 23 million in 1930. By then, there was one automobile for every five people—and as many as one for every four in Detroit, the home of the auto indus-try, more than one for every three in Balti-more, and nearly one for every two in Los Angeles.[5] The bane of the transit industry, the automobile was a boon for many Americans, especially once the automakers began to build better and less expensive cars and the authorities began to construct more and better roads. Despite the traffic jams and parking problems, it was not long

before many decided that as a way of get-ting downtown the automobile was prefer-able to the streetcar and other forms of mass transit.

This decision had a number of momen-tous consequences, not least of which was that it changed the meaning of accessibility. By the late 1920s, about the time that many downtown business interests first became concerned about decentralization, accessibil-ity was no longer synonymous with mass transit. Instead, it was synonymous with private as well as public transit, with auto-mobiles as well as streetcars, with highways as well as railbeds. Thus when G. Harvey Porter said in 1941 that it was imperative to get people "in and out of the downtown area as quickly and easily as possible, by whatever means," he meant that the central business district had to be made more accessible to both electric railways and motor vehicles, and above all to private automobiles.[6] The change was reflected not only in what the downtown business inter-ests said, but also in what they did. Starting in the mid and late 1920s, they intensified their efforts to persuade the authorities to take whatever steps were necessary to enable motorists to drive "quickly and easily" to the central business district and to find a place to park when they arrived. During the 1930s and 1940s they also con-tinued their efforts to persuade the author-ities to build rapid transit systems, insisting that in view of the heavy traffic in and around the central business district rapid transit was the only viable form of mass transit. By virtue of these efforts, the down-town businessmen and property owners were drawn into several major controver-sies, the resolutions of which would have a great impact, not only on downtown, but on other parts of the metropolis as well. And the most momentous was over traffic congestion.

Traffic congestion had long been a ser-ious problem in American cities. As early as the 1870s New York's Real Estate Record and Builders' Guide wrote that the narrow downtown streets could no longer handle the growing traffic. "The universal cry down town is for 'more elbow room,'" it said. A product of the tremendous growth of commercial activity, the extreme concentration of the business district, and the growing separation of the business and residential sections, traffic congestion grew much worse in the 1880s and 1890s. And not just in New York. In downtown Boston, *American Architect and Building News* observed, the sidewalks were "jammed to suffocation" with pedestrians, while the streets, as narrow and crooked as any in the United States, were packed with streetcars, wagons, carts, and other horse-drawn vehicles. To make things worse, some of the streets were lined on one side by "a long string of [stationary] carriages" and on the other by "a similar string of miscellaneous vehicles, the horses attached to which munch their oats peacefully" while the traffic inches past them. Despite the electrification of the street railways and, in New York, Brooklyn, and Chicago, the construction of the elevated lines, the traffic problem was as serious as ever at the turn of the century. In 1903 *Scientific American* warned that "unless some heroic measures are taken, we are bound to witness within a few years in the busiest hours of the day a positive deadlock [in lower Manhattan]." In 1909, when only one of every two hundred Americans owned an automobile, the *Los Angeles Times* pointed out that traffic congestion downtown "has become so great that the police and the officials of the street railway companies are at their wits' end to find a solution."[7]

Some Americans believed that the automobile (and truck) would help solve the traffic problem by displacing slower and more cumbersome horse-drawn vehicles. One of them was Thomas Edison. If all of New York's horse-drawn vehicles "could be transformed into motor cars overnight," he remarked in 1908, it would "so relieve traffic [congestion] as to make Manhattan Island resemble 'The Deserted Village.'" Other Americans were less sanguine. By the late 1910s it was clear they were right. Motorcars did displace most horse-drawn vehicles, but as more people drove, they flooded the downtown streets, especially during rush hour. Visiting Los Angeles in 1919, a Cleveland doctor commented that at six in the evening it seems that "every automobile owner in the city suddenly decides to motor through the business section." With thousands of cars, trucks, streetcars, and the remaining horse-drawn vehicles fighting for space downtown, traffic often slowed down to a crawl—sometimes to a standstill. Traffic congestion in New York "is growing worse every day," the *Real Estate Record and Builders' Guide* said in 1917. It "[has] become well-nigh unbearable" in Atlanta, a special committee of the chamber of commerce reported three years later. In Chicago traffic congestion "is so great that matters have almost reached a deadlock," observed British city planner Raymond Unwin in 1923. In the business district of many American cities, he pointed out, it was no faster to drive than to walk.[8] The result was that by the early 1920s there was a widespread consensus that the traffic problem was in large part the product of the phenomenal proliferation of private automobiles.

Some engineers, city planners, public officials, and street railway executives held that the only way to solve the problem was to ban private automobiles (or at least "pleasure" vehicles) from the central business district. If a ban was imposed, its sponsors pointed out, motorists could drive downtown, park at the fringe, where garages and lots would be located, and take mass transit to the center. At the heart of this position was the belief that automobiles were a very inefficient means of urban transportation—that they took up more space than streetcars and carried fewer passengers. It was impossible to provide enough space downtown to accommodate the growing number of motor vehicles, a New York street railway executive declared in 1926. To open new streets and widen existing ones would only bring more motor vehicles into the business district, which would increase congestion and thereby encourage decentralization. Even if the city did not impose a ban on motorcars, said Boston mayor Malcolm E. Nichols in the mid 1920s, traffic congestion would force many motorists to use mass transit to get downtown. It was highly unlikely that private automobiles would continue to enjoy "unlimited access" to the central business district much longer, he predicted.[9]

But most Americans—most motorists, automakers, traffic experts, and above all most downtown businessmen and property owners—were opposed to a ban on private automobiles downtown. (A ban on "pleasure" vehicles only was impractical, argued one expert, for the simple reason that "no one but the motorist himself could tell whether the trip was for business or pleasure.") These Americans were well aware that the traffic problem was very serious and that the growing number of motorcars was largely responsible for it. By the mid and late 1920s they were also aware that traffic congestion was widely regarded as the main reason for the decentralization of business. But they were convinced, as the Building Owners and Managers Association of St. Louis put it in 1925, that "the so-called pleasure car is a business necessity." It made downtown more accessible, especially for well-to-do motorists, who were highly prized customers and tenants. The private automobile was "here to stay," most Americans assumed. And as the editors of *Engineering Magazine* put it, any attempt to limit its usefulness would be "altogether undesirable, ill-advised, and futile." "Some means simply will have to be found to make room for necessary auto traffic," said W. W. Emmart, a member of the Baltimore City Planning Commission, in 1925. Surely, most Americans believed, the authorities could do something less draconian to unclog "the arteries of the city" than impose a ban on private automobiles in the central business district.[10]

But what could they do? To find the answer, engineers, planners, and other experts made hundreds of studies of traffic congestion in the early twentieth century. Out of these studies, most of which were commissioned by down-town businessmen or, at their behest, by local officials, emerged a diagnosis, according to which traffic jams downtown were largely a product of four things other than the centralization of business and the proliferation of

private automobiles. One was that the streets were too few and too narrow—and, in many instances, poorly paved and badly designed. How, asked a New York City architect, could a street system that was developed when two- and three-story buildings were the rule possibly handle the traffic generated by sixteen- and twenty-story buildings? Another was that there were few traffic regulations—and few police officers to enforce them. And "without proper regulation[s]," a street railway executive warned, the motorcars will "congest new arteries as fast as they can be opened." Yet another was what experts viewed as nonessential traffic. Many motorists drive downtown not because they have "a desire to go there," a New Jersey engineer observed, but because they do not know "how to get through the city any other way." "They go through the Triangle," wrote a director of the Pittsburgh Chamber of Commerce, "because there is no other convenient way to [get from one part of the city to another]." The fourth was what planners termed "the promiscuous mixing of different types of traffic." By this they meant that all the surface traffic—rail and motor, commercial and pleasure, local and through—ran on the same streets, one type of vehicle blocking the other and the slowest holding down the speed of the fastest.[11]

From this diagnosis, it followed that the authorities could do several things to relieve traffic congestion short of imposing a ban on private automobiles. Perhaps most important, they could open new streets and widen existing ones. The streets should be widened, declared the Cleveland Building Owners and Managers Association, "wherever possible and as rapidly as finances will permit." Almost as important, the authorities could adopt and enforce tough traffic regulations to maintain a steady flow of vehicles. The authorities could also build crosstown highways (and inner and outer belts) to divert nonessential traffic from the business district. "What a rejuvenation down-town business organizations could experience through the removal of [the estimated] 40 to 50 percent of non-business-producing traffic and its replacement by an equal volume of business producing traffic!" proclaimed Pittsburgh's Better Traffic Committee. Last of all, the authorities could segregate the different types of traffic, forcing them to run along separate streets (or possibly on separate grades)—and perhaps even segregate vehicular and pedestrian traffic. Such a move, it was widely held, would not only relieve traffic congestion but also improve traffic safety—a subject of growing concern during the 1920s.[12]

Many Americans opposed these measures, some because they were skeptical of the diagnosis of the traffic problem and others because they were afraid that the solutions might be worse than the problem. Street opening and widening, they argued, was very disruptive, especially to abutting businesses. It was also very expensive. It was prohibitively so in the central business district—where the streets that had the heaviest traffic also had the most valuable real estate, a point that even some advocates of street improvements conceded. It was self-defeating too, opponents contended. No sooner was a street opened or widened than traffic increased and congestion worsened. In the face of such opposition, some proposals were shelved—among them a plan by New York mayor William J. Gaynor to relieve traffic congestion on Fifth Avenue by opening a new avenue that would run between Fifth and Sixth avenues from Washington Square to Fifty-ninth Street. But with the support of downtown businessmen, outlying real estate interests, motorists' associations, and auto manufacturers and distributors, many other schemes were carried out. At a cost of tens and even hundreds of millions of dollars, most of which came from bond issues, special assessments, and motor vehicle taxes, the authorities opened new streets in one city after another. Often laid out according to comprehensive plans prepared by Miller McClintock, Harland Bartholomew, and other experts, most of them were wide, direct, well designed, and well-paved roads that radiated from the central business district to the outlying residential sections. At the same time the authorities widened existing streets in city after city, sometimes by condemning the abutting property and sometimes by narrowing the adjacent sidewalks. By virtue of these measures, the street systems were able to handle far more motor vehicles in the late 1920s than in the early 1900s.[13]

The early attempts to regulate traffic ran into opposition too. It came from merchants who feared that one-way streets would render their stores less accessible and engineers who believed that traffic signals would slow down traffic. It also came from teamsters, taxi drivers, and ordinary motorists—many of whom, historian Clay McShane has written, regarded traffic regulations as "unwarranted intrusions on personal freedom." As a Baltimore reporter later observed, "It was not always easy to persuade citizens to break the habits of a lifetime and to prevent them from cutting corners, parking at random and driving both ways on a one-way street." But as traffic congestion and traffic safety grew worse, traffic experts, auto industry leaders, and downtown business interests forged a consensus that the authorities had to do something to regulate motor vehicles and their drivers. Beginning in the early twentieth century, they adopted a host of regulations, many of which were designed by William Phelps Eno, a well-to-do New Yorker who spent his life working for effective traffic control. All vehicles had to be registered, all drivers licensed. Drivers also had to stay to the right, signal before turning, abide by posted speed limits, and use lights after dark. To facilitate the flow of traffic, the authorities also created one-way streets, first in Philadelphia (1908) and then in Boston (1909), and installed stop signs, which first appeared in Detroit (1915), and traffic signals, at first manual semaphores with "go" and "stop" signs and later on electric lights with their familiar green, yellow, and red glow. To enforce these regulations, most cities formed a special traffic squad, a branch of the police department, and a special traffic court, which removed routine traffic violations from the criminal justice system.[14] Taken together, these measures revolutionized traffic control in America's cities in a short period and at little cost.

The authorities also took steps to divert nonessential traffic from the central business district. To enable motorists to go from one part of the city to another without going downtown first, they built a few crosstown highways, most of which were laid out according to the traditional gridiron plan. By the late 1920s some cities also began to build an outer-belt (or circumferential) highway system. To encourage motorists to drive around the central business district rather than through it, the authorities built a few inner belts, the best known of which was the quadrangle of streets—Roosevelt Road on the south, Michigan Avenue on the east, Canal Street on the west, and South Water Street on the north—that encircled the Chicago Loop. An integral feature of Daniel H. Burnham's famous plan for Chicago, this inner belt was strongly supported by the Chicago Plan Commission, on which the Loop's interests were well represented. Started in the early 1910s, it was completed in the late 1920s. But these crosstown highways and inner and outer belts made up only a small fraction of the major thoroughfares, most of which still converged on the central business district, funneling in tens of thousands of automobiles en route elsewhere.[15] Why were so few of them constructed before 1930? The answer is that the authorities could not build all the proposed bypasses and radial highways without raising property taxes to unacceptable levels. Given the choice, most downtown businessmen favored radial highways over bypasses. So did the many motorists who worked and shopped downtown. And though many planners and engineers thought bypasses were the most economical way to relieve traffic congestion, they also believed radial highways were necessary to make the central business district "directly accessible" to all the other parts.

The authorities took steps to segregate different types of traffic, too. They eliminated grade crossings, the points at which the railroads and highways intersected and the sites of many of the worst traffic jams and traffic accidents. In Atlanta, for example, they persuaded the voters to approve two bond issues, one in 1921 and

the other in 1926, to help pay for three north–south viaducts that carried motor vehicles over the railroad tracks that bisected the central business district. Other cities also built viaducts to separate motor traffic at busy intersections. Following the completion of the Bronx River Parkway in 1923, the authorities also created parkways in a handful of cities and suburbs. Most of them not only excluded cross traffic but also banned commercial vehicles. (After a highly promising start in the late nineteenth century, due in large part to the pioneering efforts of Frederick Law Olmsted, the parkway movement had fallen into disfavor in the early twentieth. And its revival in the late 1920s would be short-lived.) But these measures did little to segregate different types of vehicular traffic, much less to separate vehicular and pedestrian traffic. Most vehicles still ran on the same streets and on the same grade. These efforts were stymied by both financial and political constraints. Building separate street systems would have been prohibitively expensive, especially in or near the central business district. And banning private automobiles from commercial thoroughfares would have been very unpopular—and probably unenforceable. In a country that had already segregated land uses through zoning, and racial and economic groups through deed restrictions, the segregation of traffic may have seemed "inevitable," as the Cleveland Building Owners and Managers Association wrote in 1924.[16] If so, its time had not yet come.

By the late 1920s more automobiles were pouring into the central business district than ever, far more than would have been possible if the authorities had not opened new streets and widened existing ones. And as a result of the new regulations, traffic was more orderly than ever. American motorists are so well disciplined, observed a German visitor, that traffic "regulates itself to a large extent." In New York the policeman does not have "to wave his arms about like a windmill" to direct traffic; "A gesture of the hand and a tweet [of the whistle] are enough." But even though some motorists no longer went downtown to get from one part of the city to another and others no longer went downtown at all, traffic congestion was as bad as ever. "Despite every scheme of traffic control so far devised," midtown Manhattan still "ties itself up in a knot twice a day," wrote the *New Republic* in 1928. Broadway had traffic jams seventy-five years ago. "It has them still." Although Baltimore spent millions of dollars on street widening after the great fire of 1904, traffic conditions downtown were just as bad twenty years later, a special committee informed the mayor. Despite the efforts of Harland Bartholomew, chief planner for St. Louis, traffic downtown "moves slowly and irregularly," wrote the president of the St. Louis street railway system in 1926. "Conditions are bad in the middle of the day, and in the morning rush, but are well nigh intolerable in the evening rush." Conditions were very bad in downtown Los Angeles too, the city's traffic commission acknowledged in 1930, a decade after it had been formed by downtown business interests and civic and commercial groups to solve the city's traffic problem.[17]

Despite a good deal of evidence to the contrary, some Americans remained convinced that the cities could solve the traffic problem by building more and wider streets and imposing more and tougher regulations. But others were beginning to have second thoughts. As they saw it, the cities were caught in "a vicious circle." To relieve traffic congestion, the authorities opened and widened streets; but the new streets attracted more traffic, the additional traffic generated more congestion, and eventually every street system reached what a Minneapolis engineer called "a saturation point," a state of "almost but not quite intolerable congestion," to quote Frederick Law Olmsted, Jr., and two of his associates. Another planner, George A. Damon of Los Angeles, went even further. "Every possible cure [for the traffic problem] seems to be worse than the original disease," he wrote. From this pessimistic prognosis, Americans drew one of two very different conclusions. The first was that the traffic problem could be solved only if the cities reduced the number of motor vehicles that entered the central business district. Banning autos downtown would help. So

would imposing height limits, improving mass transit, and encouraging decentralization. The second conclusion, the one favored by most downtown businessmen and property owners, was that the problem could be solved only if the cities took what William J. Wilgus, a New York engineer, called "radical measures" to facilitate the flow of traffic —more expensive, more disruptive, and more far-reaching measures than any taken thus far.[18]

NOTES

1. *Baltimore Sun*, April 21, May 20/21, June 12/25, 1941. See also California Railroad Commission, *Application 1602: Reporter's Transcript* (1921), page 134, California Public Utilities Commission files, Sacramento.

2. San Francisco Department of City Planning, "Daily Trips in San Francisco" (1955), table 6; Roger W. Toll, "Traffic Investigation in Denver," *Electric Railway Journal*, August 21, 1915, page 311; R. F. Kelker, Jr., *Report and Recommendations on a Physical Plan for a Unified Transportation System for the City of Chicago* (1923), pages 39–40; Ross D. Eckert and George W. Hilton, "The Jitneys," *Journal of Law and Economics* (October 1972), pages 293–325.

3. John A. Beeler, "What Price Fares?" *Transit Journal*, June 1932, pages 263–266; American Transit Association, *Transit Fact Book: 1945*, pages 15–19; American Transit Association, *Transit Fact Book: 1951*, pages 7–8. By at any time since the turn of the century, I mean at any time other than the mid 1930s, the worst years of the Great Depression, when the riding habit was even lower.

4. Kelker, *Unified Transportation System*, page 40; Chicago Department of Streets and Electricity, Bureau of Street Traffic, "Cordon Count Data on the Central Business District" (1949), page 2; U.S. Works Progress Administration, *Traffic Survey Data on the City of St. Louis* (1937); Donald M. Baker, *A Rapid Transit System for Los Angeles California* (1933), page 37-e; Coverdale & Colpitts, *Report to the Los Angeles Metropolitan Transit Authority on a Monorail Rapid Transit Line for Los Angeles* (1954), page 62; *Automobile Facts*, January 1941, page 2.

5. Paul Barrett, *The Automobile and Urban Transit: The Formation of Public Policy in Chicago, 1900–1930* (Philadelphia, 1983), pages 104–120; *Los Angeles Times*, July

25, 1909; Robert M. Fogelson, *The Fragmented Metropolis: Los Angeles, 1850–1930* (Cambridge, 1967), chapter 7; Stanley Mallach, "The Origins of the Decline of Urban Mass Transportation in the United States," *Urbanism Past and Present*, Summer 1979, pages 1–15; U.S. Department of Commerce, *Historical Statistics of the United States: Colonial Times to 1970* (Washington, D.C., 1975), part 2, page 716; Baker, *Rapid Transit System for Los Angeles*, page 37-e; Clay McShane, *Down the Asphalt Path: The Automobile and the American City* (New York, 1994), pages 126–127.

6. *Baltimore Sun*, May 21, 1941. See also David Whitcomb, "Maintaining Values in Central Business Districts," *Proceedings of the Twenty-Second Annual Convention of the National Association of Building Owners and Managers: 1929*, page 95.

7. *[New York] Real Estate Record and Builders' Guide*, March 8, 1873, page 107, October 8, 1881, page 940; *American Architect and Building News*, July 27, 1878, pages 27–28, August 20, 1892, page 109; *Scientific American*, April 25, 1903, page 310; Clay McShane, "Urban Pathways: The Street and the Highway, 1900–1940," in Joel A. Tarr and Gabriel Dupuy, eds., *Technology and the Rise of the Networked City in Europe and America* (Philadelphia, 1988), page 68; *Los Angeles Times*, July 25, 1909.

8. McShane, *Down the Asphalt Path*, pages 122, 193–194; Mark S. Foster, *From Street-car to Superhighway: American City Planners and Urban Transportation, 1900–1940* (Philadelphia, 1981), pages 43–44; Amos Stote, "The Ideal American City," *McBride's Magazine*, April 1916, page 89; Scott Bottles, *Los Angeles and the Automobile: The Making of the Modern City* (Berkeley, 1987), pages 59–60; *[New York] Real Estate Record and Builders' Guide*. February 17, 1917, page 220; Howard L. Preston, *Automobile Age Atlanta: The Making of a Southern Metropolis, 1900–1935* (Athens, Georgia, 1979), pages 116–117; Raymond Unwin, "America Revisited—A City Planner's Impressions," *American City*, April 1923, page 334.

9. John A. Miller, Jr., "The Chariots That Rage in the Streets," *American City*, July 1928, pages 113–114; Stephen Child, "Restricted Traffic District Proposed," ibid., April 1927, pages 507–510; V. R. Stirling and Rensselaer H. Toll, "How to Eliminate Traffic from Downtown Sections," *National Municipal Review*, June 1929, pages 369–371; Robert H. Whitten, "Unchoking Our Congested Streets," *American City*, October 1920, pages 351–354; *Proceedings of the American Society of Civil Engineers*, September 1926, pages 1453–1454; *Boston City Record*, January 23, 1926, pages 100–101.

10. Miller, "The Chariots That Rage in the Streets," page 113; St. Louis Building Owners and Managers Association, *The St. Louis Traffic Problem* (St. Louis, 1925), pages 4, 16; Blaine A. Brownell, "A Symbol of Modernity: Attitudes Toward the Automobile in Southern Cities in the 1920s," *American Quarterly*, March 1972, pages 24–25; E. R. Kinsey and C. E. Smith, *Report on Rapid Transit for St. Louis* (St. Louis, 1926), page 147; *Engineering Magazine*, August 1906, page 738; *Baltimore Sun*, June 14, 1925; Stote, "The Ideal American City," page 89.

11. Julius F. Harder, "The City's Plan," *Municipal Affairs*, March 1898, page 34; *Proceedings of the American Society of Civil Engineers*, September 1926, pages 1459–1460; Louis G. Simmons, "The Solution of Big Cities Traffic Problems," *Illustrated World*, October 1917, page 267; *[Pittsburgh] Progress*, April 1922, page 2; Frederick Law Olmsted, Harland Bartholomew, and Charles Henry Cheney, *A Major Traffic Street Plan for Los Angeles* (Los Angeles, 1924), pages 12–14.

12. Cleveland Building Owners and Managers Association, *Cleveland's Traffic Problem* (Cleveland, 1924), pages 6–7; Harland Bartholomew, "Basic Factors in the Solution of Metropolitan Traffic Problems," *American City*, July 1925, pages 38–39; *Cassier's Magazine*, August 1907, pages 374–375; Morris Knowles, "City Planning as a Permanent Solution of the Traffic Problem," *Planning Problems of Town, City, and Region: Papers and Discussions at the International City and Regional Planning Conference: 1925*, page 60; "The Triangle's 'Thru' Traffic," *Better Traffic*, October 1931, page 6; Ernest P. Goodrich, "The Urban Auto Problem," *Proceedings of the Twelfth National Conference on City Planning: 1920*, page 84; Miller McClintock, *Street Traffic Control* (New York, 1926), pages 70–85.

13. Miller McClintock, *Report and Recommendations of the Metropolitan Street Traffic Survey* (Chicago, 1926), page 48; *[New York] Real Estate Record and Builders' Guide*, September 26, 1908, page 591, May 28, 1910, page 1137; *American Architect*, June 1, 1910, page 15; *Proceedings of the Engineers' Society of Western Pennsylvania*, November 1919, page 488; Sidney Clarke, "Special Report on Traffic Relief," in *Report of the Transportation Survey*

Commission of the City of St. Louis (1930), page 117; McShane, "Urban Pathways," page 77; McShane, *Down the Asphalt Path*, pages 213–216; Theodora Kimball Hubbard and Henry Vincent Hubbard, *Our Cities To-Day and Tomorrow* (Cambridge, 1929), chapter 12.

14. Raymond S. Tompkins, "Are We Solving the Traffic Problem?" *American Mercury*, February 1929, page 155; Cleveland Building Owners and Managers Association, *Cleveland's Traffic Problem*, page 6; Barrett, *The Automobile and Urban Transit*, pages 155–161; McShane, *Down the Asphalt Path*, chapter 9; McShane, "Urban Pathways," page 77; *Baltimore Sun*, May 15, 1932; J. Rowland Bibbins, "The Growing Transport Problem of the Masses," *National Municipal Review*, August 1920, pages 517–522. See also McClintock, *Street Traffic Control*, chapters 7–8, 11–12, 14.

15. John Ihlder, "The Automobile and Community Planning," *Annals of the American Academy of Political and Social Science*, November 1924, page 204; E. S. Taylor, "The Plan of Chicago in 1924," ibid., pages 225–229; Arthur A. Shurtleff, "The Circumferential Thoroughfares of the Metropolitan District of Boston," *City Planning*, April 1926, pages 76–84; Hubbard and Hubbard, *Our Cities*, pages 196, 204–205; "By-Pass Highways for Traffic Relief," *American City*, April 1928, page 89; Olmsted, Bartholomew, and Cheney, *A Major Traffic Street Plan for Los Angeles*, page 28.

16. Preston, *Automobile Age Atlanta*, pages 118–125; *American Architect*, May 28, 1919, pages 756–758; McShane, *Down the Asphalt Path*, pages 31–40, 220–223; McShane, "Urban Pathways," pages 71–74, 79–82.

17. Paul Barrett, "Public Policy and Private Choice: Mass Transit and the Automobile in Chicago Between the Wars," *Business History Review*, Winter 1975, pages 482–483; *Current Affairs in New England*, July 12, 1926, pages 3–4; "The Triangle's 'Thru' Traffic," page 1; Oscar Handlin, ed., *This Was America* (Cambridge, 1949), page 491; "Congested Traffic," *New Republic*, November 28, 1928, pages 29–31; *Report of the Committee on Traffic to His Honor Howard W. Jackson, Mayor of Baltimore, Maryland* (1923), page 5; Clarke, "Special Report on Traffic Relief," page 117; Bottles, *Los Angeles and the Automobile*, pages 101–102, 118–119.

18. "Traffic Problems and Suggested Remedies," *Public Works*, June 1924, pages 177–180; Carol Aronovici, "Down-Town Parking," *Community Builder*, December 1927, pages 28–34; Olmsted, Bartholomew, and Cheney, *A Major Traffic Street Plan for Los Angeles*, page 18; George A. Damon, "Relation of the Motor Bus to Other Methods of Transportation," *Planning Problems of Town, City, and Region: Papers and Discussions at the International City and Regional Planning Conference: 1925*, page 270.

ESSAY 7.5

Planning a Social Disaster

D. Bradford Hunt

Source: D. Bradford Hunt, *Blueprint for Disaster: The Unraveling of Chicago Public Housing* (Chicago: University of Chicago Press, 2009).

EDITORS' INTRODUCTION

During the Great Depression, American urban leaders bypassed their statehouses and began a direct relationship with the federal government. Well-intentioned progressive influences fueled a wide-range of federal-local partnerships aimed at improving life in the nation's largest cities. The New Deal proposed a corrective to capitalism rather than a replacement for the economic system. New Dealers introduced new ideas regarding government action within areas heretofore allowed to unfold at will. New Deal and post-war cities faced unprecedented challenges, including the question of how to adequately house large populations of working-class and lower-class urban dwellers. The Chicago Housing Authority, established in 1937, set out to provide housing solutions for its most vulnerable residents. Along the way, however, the CHA and its federal partners created social and physical scars that still haunt Chicagoans in the present day.

Chicago's housing shortage worsened during the 1940s. Following the Second World War, Chicagoans restored energy to the question of housing. Chicago's neighborhood layouts exacerbated white residents' long-standing antipathy toward integration. In part due to Chicago's relatively late birth as an American city, Chicago featured large white-only neighborhoods. In older American cities, "servant" housing grew up within walking distance of wealthier tracts. But Chicago's sprawling whites-only sections put pressure on the too-narrow ghettos. After attempts to overturn long-standing segregation, the CHA avoided building within the white neighborhoods. They avoided building along the seams dividing the white and black city, out of political concerns and the very real fear that such building would exacerbate racial conflict playing out daily in the streets. Yet the existing ghettos simply could not accommodate the thousands of new migrants choosing to call the city home. Thus Chicago's leaders, like CHA executive director Elizabeth Wood, struggled with not only *how* to build suitable housing, but *where*. As Arnold Hirsch explores in Part VIII, many large housing projects were built onto of the city's original black ghettoes. At times of change and with the large-scale investment of time, energy, and capital, cities have an opportunity to right previous wrongs. In constructing the second ghetto, urban leaders compounded earlier mistakes. Hunt proposes that Chicago Housing Authority leaders initially wanted to build racially integrated projects in areas near white neighborhoods, however, the dream did not become reality. Hunt demonstrates that policy decisions and the combination of federal and local decision-making coalesced to create enormous public housing complexes that cemented Chicago's racial segregation.

These efforts at better housing may have had no chance. Pre-war reformers had laid a blueprint for disaster, and the insufficiencies of later public policy, government malfeasance, a lack of a sound financial plan, and outright neglect did the rest. Project residents lacked the "collective efficacy" (a term introduced by sociologist Robert Sampson describing the ability to exert order) to conquer the conditions they had landed in. Project policies ensured that the ratio of children to adults in Chicago public housing was high, tipping the projects towards social disaster. Vandalism and crime mixed with concentrated poverty eroded community.

D. Bradford Hunt serves as the Vice President for Research and Academic Programs at The Newberry Library in Chicago. He has served as a professor and dean at Roosevelt University. *Blueprint for Disaster* won the Lewis Mumford Prize for best book in American planning history and honorable mention for the Kenneth T. Jackson prize for best book in American urban history.

PLANNING A SOCIAL DISASTER (2009)

During the protracted battle between the Chicago Housing Authority and Washington over designs in the 1950s, officials rarely offered precise rationales for their objections to high-rises as a form for housing families with children. Elizabeth Wood stated that low-rises were more "natural," while Catherine Bauer pointed to surveys of tenant desires. CHA administrators found it difficult to manage elevator buildings but offered no clear explanation why. "Experience," vaguely defined, indicated that high-rises were a bad idea, though knowledge was intuitive or anecdotal at best. But no one at the time questioned a planning choice that would lead to public housing's demise in Chicago and elsewhere. During the 1950s, the CHA programmed its high-rise projects to accommodate large families with many children; by the time the 1959 projects were planned, 80 percent of apartments had three, four, and even five bedrooms. This choice created an unprecedented ratio of youths to adults in public housing communities—with devastating implications.

Placing enormous numbers of children and relatively few adults in high-rise buildings resulted in widespread "social disorder," defined by Wesley Skogan as a breakdown in civil community and social control as evidenced by rampant vandalism, blatant vice, and "sundry problems relating to congregating bands of youth."[1] Sociologists, such as Skogan and Robert J. Sampson, theorized social disorder in the 1980s and 1990s, seeking to explain its prevalence in poor communities. They moved away from explanations centered on individual pathology and instead focused on the importance of "neighborhood effects" in controlling crime. They argued that safer communities resisted social disorder and enforced agreed-upon norms through collective efforts. Residents band together, informally policing shared space, especially from the potentially destructive impulses of youth, through social networks and local organizations, with formal police in support. Where the capacity of residents is weakened —by poverty changing populations, governmental neglect, and other factors—then communities struggle to restrain youths, resolve disputes, expel disruptive outsiders, and identify criminals. Sociologists labeled this capacity "collective efficacy," a measure of the ability of neighbors to work together and in cooperation with the police to maintain social order and limit crime. Sampson and his colleagues suggested that the variables most likely to influence collective efficacy, and hence social disorder and crime, involved community cohesion, concentrated poverty, residential turnover, and family disruption.[2]

Youth-adult ratios are an overlooked factor in collective efficacy and are essential to understanding the history of public housing's decline.[3] In project communities where youths far outnumbered adults, those seeking to enforce order faced a daunting, and perhaps insurmountable, demographic burden. Undoubtedly other structural variables like poverty influenced collective efficacy, but the timing of social disorder in public housing is material. Widespread social disorder emerged in Chicago's high-rise projects shortly after they opened in the 1950s and early 1960s, before poverty became entrenched, before jobs disappeared in black ghettos, before the CHA's finances collapsed, before deferred maintenance meant physical disorder, and before the drug scourge ravaged tenants. These structural forces later deepened problems in the 1970s, but social disorder was present in high-rises with large numbers of children right from the start. Design also mattered, as high-rise forms made collective efficacy more onerous. But many people live successfully in high-rise designs, including families with children; it is the relative number of children in high-rise buildings that counts. When coupled with high-rise building forms, public housing's youth-adult demographics undermined the collective efficacy of adults, caused extensive social disorder, overwhelmed community partners, and eventually sent the buildings themselves into a death spiral from which the CHA never recovered.

* * *

The unique magnitude of the CHA's youth demographics becomes astonishingly clear in youth-adult ratio comparisons.[4] During the twentieth century, the typical Chicago neighborhood, as defined by census tracts, averaged roughly one youth (defined as under age twenty-one) for every two adults; in 1960, the average youth-adult ratio for Chicago tracts was 0.53. Only a handful of tracts had more youths than adults (i.e. a youth-adult ratio greater than 1.0)—except those containing public housing. Most neighborhoods included not only families with children but also single men and women and childless couples of all ages, resulting in a predominance of adults. Even in the nation's postwar, baby-boom suburbs, such as Park Forest, Illinois, and Levittown, New York, youth-adult ratios never exceeded 1.0. Robert Hunter's 1901 survey of Chicago's worst tenement districts found desperate poverty and overcrowding, but youths were still outnumbered by adults. More contemporaneously, other high-rise, urban redevelopment projects with middle-class residents, such as Lake Meadows in Chicago or Stuyvesant Town in New York, had low average youth-adult ratios, as seen in Table 7.1.[5]

By contrast, Chicago's public housing projects inverted the ratios found in the rest of the city. The CHA's ratio grew from 1.42 youths per adult in 1951 to a peak of 2.39 in 1970, as more and more large, multi-bedroom apartments were completed. At the Robert Taylor Homes, a community with more residents than many Chicago suburbs, youths outnumbered adults nearly three to one (youth-adult ratio: 2.86). The youth-adult ratios in Chicago census tracts containing mostly public housing were 1.9

to 6.3 standard deviations away from the mean in 1960, showing the "off-the-charts" nature of the CHA's youth demographics.[6] In short, CHA planners produced communities with youth-adult ratios several magnitudes greater than any previously seen in the urban experience.

Changing family structure played some role in youth-adult ratios, especially after 1965, but such effects should not be overstated. CHA projects before the late 1960s housed predominantly two-parent and working-class families, not that far from city norms. An analysis of census data for 1960 shows that if public housing families were "average" in terms of both family size and rates of single-family households (compared to the Chicago metropolitan area), then the youth-adult ratio in CHA projects would have dropped slightly that year from 1.77 to roughly 1.5. Using 1970 census data, the corresponding drop is from 2.39 to roughly 1.6, as a rapid increase in the number of single-parent households in the late 1960s swelled the CHA's youth-adult ratio.[7]

But blaming families for having many children, or parents for separating, or even youth for exhibiting destructive behavior would miss the point. Policy choices, not the situation of individual families and youth, created a communitywide collective efficacy problem. The CHA's extraordinary youth-adult ratios were the result of intentional decisions to build projects specifically to accommodate large families. Although Elizabeth Wood and others wrestled with questions about the appropriateness of high-rises for families with children in the early 1950s, the implications of concentrations of youth for community life were simply not understood.

Progressive logic led public housing leaders across the country to choices that swelled the number of children in the projects. Reformers had long proclaimed with both sentiment and social science that public housing's main beneficiaries would be children saved from the evils of the slums. The CHA justified the exclusion of most childless families from its projects on the grounds that "the greatest possible social return from the public subsidies ...

Table 7.1 Ratios of youths to adults in various communities and jurisdictions, 1880–1975

	Year	Population	Ratio of youths (under 21) to adults
Large jurisdictions			
City of Chicago	1970	3,366,957	0.58
	1960	3,550,404	0.53
	1890	1,099,850	0.75
Chicago metropolitan area	1970	6,978,947	0.65
Chicago slum tenement districts	1901	45,634	0.97
New York's Lower East Side	1910	408,985	0.84
United States	1970	203,211,926	0.66
	1930	122,775,046	0.68
	1880	50,155,783	1.01
Suburbs			
Park Forest, IL	1960	29,993	0.97
Levittown, NY	1960	65,276	0.85
Urban renewal, moderate income high-rise housing			
Lake Meadows, Chicago	1960	5,022	0.35
Stuyvesant Town, New York City	1960	22,405	0.40
Public housing in Chicago			
Chicago Housing Authority, family public housing	1951	33,375	1.42
	1960	79,838	1.77
	1965	131,454	2.11
	1970	137,271	2.39
	1975	131,513	2.25
Cabrini-Green Homes	1965	17,750	2.09
ABLA	1965	13,600	1.67
Robert Taylor Homes	1965	27,000	2.86

would be realized from the better citizenship of children, rescued from the slums to grow to maturity in a decent environment." Elizabeth Wood proudly touted the CHA's "Children's Cities" in the 1940s: "The Authority has built its program around the children.... Already thousands of children have left the slums and had their first chance through Children's Cities at health, at normal family living, at happiness." The 1945 annual report noted with satisfaction that at Altgeld Gardens, "citizens under 19 made up 61 percent of the population.... [In] the rest of the city, those under 19 account for a mere 27 percent of the total population!"[8]

Market-failure concerns were also behind the effort to house families with many children. Such families struggled to find apartments of sufficient size at affordable rents,

and even those who could afford such spaces were often rejected by landlords as undesirable. Public housing waiting lists across the country testified to the extent of the problem. From the first days of the USHA, reports surfaced that projects did not have enough three- and four-bedroom apartments to accommodate the numerous large families who applied. In 1944, top-level administrators and public housing supporters encouraged a policy shift to build more multi-bedroom apartments, and PHA head John Egan told Congress in 1949, "I think we should ... put emphasis on the serving of families with a substantial number of children, rather than smaller families which need only one bedroom."[9] Egan later warned local housing authorities not to "attempt to make up the entire deficiency [in large apartments] in the first project ... since this may produce a project devoted to unusually large families." But the PHA's voluminous regulations never set limits on the proportion of multi-bedroom apartments in a project. Federal planning documents include virtually no discussion of the implications of the change in policy toward favoring large families, and no studies followed up on the social impact of the change.[10] Nor did the CHA consider the potential problems of high youth-adult ratios. Led by its market-failure logic and with astonishing little forethought, public housing drifted into building communities comprising enormous numbers of children.

Early CHA projects, while tenanted largely by families with children, had small apartments, with only one or two bedrooms, producing youth-adult ratios near 1.0. Cost obsessions contributed to these small apartments, but CHA planners also imitated community norms in working-class neighborhoods. In the late 1940s and early 1950s, planners steadily increased the number of multi-bedroom apartments in projects, though not without restraint. In early elevator buildings, for example, they resisted high proportions of multi-bedroom apartments, reflecting Elizabeth Wood's intuitive understanding by the 1950s that the low-rise was the best form for families with children. Of the 9,000 units in elevator buildings designed during Wood's tenure, 29 percent had three bedrooms and only 3 percent had four or more bedrooms.[11] Federal officials pushed the CHA to find ways to add more large apartments. In mid-1954, during the planning of Stateway Gardens, the PHA regional office charged the CHA with "ignoring the very urgent needs ... of large families" and contended that 40 four-bedroom, row-house units (a form they acknowledged to be better for children) could be shoehorned into Stateway within acceptable cost limits if another high-rise building were added to the plan as well. But the CHA rejected the idea of increasing overall density at the project just to secure a handful of large units.[12] Even so, federal high-rise projects planned in the Wood years had youth-adult ratios ranging from 1.5 to 2.0, or three to four times the city norm.

Wood's successors went even farther. They built projects that were top heavy with large apartments: of 10,500 units (nearly all in high-rises) designed between 1954 and 1964, over 39 percent had three bedrooms, and another 33 percent had four or more. Again, waiting lists pushed the CHA in this direction. A monthly report in 1955 noted that "the supply of large [public housing] dwellings has lagged far behind the demand.... A study of applications from eligible families on CHA waiting lists indicates that families requiring three-bedroom apartments usually wait a minimum of two or three years.... Many families with seven or more persons have been on CHA lists for five years or more."[13] Where the private market could not provide, the CHA intervened.

While applicants begged for large apartments, the CHA by the mid-1950s was challenged to find tenants for its existing one- and two-bedroom units. In one three-month period in 1957, the CHA reported that 1,400 families rejected offers of two-bed room units at various projects (though the CHA specified neither the race of the applicants nor which projects they were rejecting). These trends showed a surprisingly weak demand among small families for the CHA's housing product, as applicants preferred to remain on waiting lists and in private housing until an apartment in the most desirable projects (usually low-rise) became available. Even with subsidized rents and continued housing discrimination, smaller African American families had become more selective by the late 1950s about whether to accept a CHA unit, once akin to a winning lottery ticket. Meanwhile, large apartments were desperately sought after, making the choice to build a greater proportion of multi-bedroom apartments an obvious one for the CHA.[14] No analyses, either in Chicago or Washington, wrestled with the ramifications of this choice. Despite two decades of research on topics of space, design, site planning, population density, and construction cost, public housing planners never considered the youth density of their projects a concern. No one asked, in essence, "Are we are housing too many children here?"

Other cities also built high-rises with many large apartments, though Chicago stood out. Even before Chicago built its 1959 projects, St. Louis planned Pruitt-Igoe to handle large families, and in 1968 the project had a youth-adult ratio of 2.63, similar to Chicago levels. After experiencing massive social disorder, St. Louis demolished the project in 1973. Available data on average number of minors per unit—a reasonable proxy for youth-adult ratios—shows that Chicago in 1968 had the fourth-highest average among a selection of twenty-three large housing authorities (exceeded only by authorities without high-rises); Chicago had 3.1 minors per unit, while New York had only 1.8, a sizeable difference.[15]

* * *

Architects, community planners, and sociologists in the 1940s and 1950s had limited understanding of how adults informally police social space. While juvenile delinquency was frequently studied by urban reformers and sociologists, a street-level view of how neighborhoods contain the impulses of youth was not offered until social critic Jane Jacobs wrote *The Death and Life of Great American Cities* in 1961. Jacobs is best known for attacking modernist planning ideas and defending the organic messiness of the nineteenth-century streetscape. Instead of seeing the typical city street as dangerous and wasteful, as reformers and superblock advocates did, Jacobs celebrated street-level social interaction as an essential mechanism for community control and cohesion. A recurring theme in her book is the importance of neighborhood policing—not by uniformed officers, but by resident adults. Social order and viable neighborhoods require "natural proprietors," such as shopkeepers, homeowners, and long-time residents, to be "eyes on the street," demanding that children and outsiders adhere to community values. Jacobs was among the first to explain collective efficacy, well before sociologists invented the term.

In a telling and neglected passage, Jacobs maintains that "planners do not seem to realize how high a ratio of adults is needed to rear children at incidental play ... only people rear children and assimilate them into civilized society." Jacobs's use of the words "ratios" and "people" is significant: the daily interactions between children and adults who are nonparents are an important force in creating the boundaries of expected social behavior: "In real life, only from the ordinary adults of the city sidewalks do children learn—if they learn it at all—the first fundamental of successful city life: People must take a modicum of public responsibility for each other even if they have no ties to each other. This is a lesson nobody learns by being told. It is learned from the experience of having *other people without ties of kinship or close friendship or formal responsibility to you* take a modicum of public responsibility for you."[16]

Early CHA residents referred to this dynamic in concrete terms. "If somebody else's mom saw you doing something," recalled former Ida B. Wells resident Bertrand Ellis, "she just picked up the phone, and when you got home, you had to answer to that. And that was very important; it was a community raising children." When Ellis left Ida B. Wells in 1952, the low-rise project had a youth-adult ratio of 1.24—higher than any non—public housing neighborhood yet still low by CHA standards. But in larger projects full of children, this informal policing by neighbors broke down. Jerry Butler, later a Cook County commissioner, described his brand-new, twenty-two-story tower at Cabrini Extension (youth-adult ratio: 1.83) as "a very large building ... I didn't know anybody that even lived on my floor. I might know the kids—you know, what they looked like—but I didn't know their names. There were lots of kids.... It wasn't like the Cabrini Homes [row houses] where you walk out in the street, and the guy next door is sitting in the front yard and says, 'Hey, how yadoin'? It wasn't that. No, you can't develop a feeling of community in a tall building."[17] The scale of Butler's high-rise project and the large number of children created more anonymity than community.

At the same time that Jane Jacobs was writing about social control, Elizabeth Wood was also engaged in the topic. After her dismissal in 1954 from the CHA, she was hired as a consultant by the Citizens' Housing and Planning Council of New York. In a 1961 study entitled *Housing Design: A Social Theory*, one of a series of reports she wrote for the council, Wood wrestled with how to design public housing projects in New York City that could create a strong sense of community. She encouraged planners to design buildings that "richly fulfill people's needs and desires" and that allow residents to "create their own social controls and do their own self-policing." Wood understood the social problems of public housing emerging in the 1950s—what she called the "loitering" of teenagers, the "hostile and indifferent" tenants, and the "absence of commercial recreation." Design should counter these trends by fostering greater social interaction. If high-rises had to be built, as she assumed was unavoidable in New York City, then she suggested wide outdoor galleries (as at the CHA's Loomis Courts), lobbies with glass walls to encourage community policing, and greater recreation space. "Design," she wrote, echoing Jacobs, should include "the planned presence of people" and "should help the aggregation of strangers become less strange." But beneath this discussion loomed the core question of how to achieve a stable social environment in public housing that residents could informally police and easily control. As Wood admitted, public housing design was well studied, but "completely lacking is a study of design based on a theory of what kind of social structure is desirable in a project and how to design to get it."[18]

Not until the early 1970s did architects begin to evaluate how design influences social control and collective efficacy. In 1972, Oscar Newman published *Defensible Space*, an influential study on how design choices affect the ability of community residents to "defend" their homes and their shared public space. While Newman acknowledged debts to both Jane Jacobs and Elizabeth Wood, his work was more empirical than their qualitative approach, involving analysis of reams of crime reports from the New York City Housing Authority to determine exactly where incidents occurred and whether architectural choices made crime easier or harder. In a seminal comparison, Newman examined two neighboring public housing projects, one consisting mainly of fourteen-story high-rise slabs and the other a combination of three- and six-story walk-ups and mid-rises. Economic and social characteristics were similar in the two projects, but perceptions of safety differed dramatically. The "indefensible" high-rise project had open lobbies, long internal corridors, and emergency stairwells, which made it all but impossible for tenants and even security guards, when present, to monitor who entered and left buildings. Each high-rise building was shared by at least 112 families, so recognizing neighbors was difficult. By contrast, the walk-up project had entryways that served only 9 to 13 families, and site planning had created other zones of exterior space that tenants could control. Crime and vandalism were serious problems at both projects, but the walk-up design had comparatively less crime, less vandalism, and higher morale. In Newman's terms, the walk-up project exhibited far better "defensible space" than the high-rise one. The height of the project in Newman's view was less important than the ability of tenants to police their own space and monitor comings and goings outside their doors.

Newman's work shifted attention to public space, but like other analysts, he did not thoroughly investigate the possibility that youth-adult ratios might play a role in the ability of a community to defend itself. Buried in the regression tables at the back of *Defensible Space* are data that suggest average family size (an imperfect proxy for youth-adult ratios) is more closely correlated with higher crime rates in public housing than the physical design that received most of Newman's attention.[19] Criminologists since the 1940s have suggested that youth and poverty are strong correlates with criminal activity, but Newman shied away from drawing conclusions from his social data and instead clung to the idea that design mattered most.[20] The social characteristics of public housing were a given, but design could be altered to create more ordered space and reduce crime.

* * *

When enormous densities of youth resided in the "indefensible space" of Chicago's high-rise public housing, the result was social disorder on a staggering scale. Vandalism in the CHA's large high-rise projects was endemic within months of occupancy, directly affecting tenant quality of life. While quantifying vandalism is difficult, tenant complaints and managers' reports are filled with evidence that youths had the upper hand in the new projects. Within a year of the opening of Cabrini Extension, destruction of tenant mailboxes made mail delivery insecure, damaged laundry machines compelled tenants to wash clothes in their apartments, and profanity-laced graffiti in stairwells demoralized residents. Light-bulb breakage kept buildings fearfully in the dark; in 1958, the CHA reported replacing 18,000 light bulbs *a month* system wide, mostly as a result of theft and because boys ran through hallways smashing fixtures with base-ball bats. Within three years of the opening of the Harold Ickes Homes, every wooden front door had to be replaced with steel; because of excessive damage, glass in many public areas was removed. as well. At Stateway Gardens, thieves systematically stripped several hundred pounds of brass from CHA fire equipment and, at one building in 1961, turned the hoses on, flooding nine floors. After one year of operation at the Robert Taylor Homes, manager Robert H. Murphy conceded that "we have had problems—some very serious problems—with children playing on and abusing elevators" and that "unsupervised" youth "are continually breaking light bulbs, scribbling and drawing obscene pictures on stairwell walls, throwing toys and other objects over gallery railings, using the stairwells for toilet purposes, climbing trees and pulling flowers, [and] throwing rocks at passing trains."[21] In these new projects with high youth-adult ratios, constant disruptive vandalism marred project life.

Elevators were the Achilles' heel of public housing. With only two elevators serving most high-rise buildings, the loss of one caused irritation, but the loss of both— a frequent occurrence according to tenant complaints—created immediate and obvious hardship on residents on upper floors. Breakdowns were most often caused by youths, who routinely pried open doors, damaged electrical controls, or climbed on top of elevator cabs. At Grace Abbott Homes, a collection of seventeen-story buildings opened in 1955, managers complained of making elevator repair calls "almost daily" by 1957. Elevators became instruments of death for children as well. In 1956 at the new Henry Horner Homes, a nine-year-old boy died when an elevator crushed him during a game of "elevator tag." The *Sun-Times* reported that the game was played by "as many as 50 children at a time," a figure that, even if exaggerated, suggests the extent to which youths swarmed over the key mechanical system in high-rises. Other stories are equally tragic. In 1963, an elevator breakdown was blamed for the death of three children when firefighters had to walk up fourteen stories to reach a burning apartment at the new Robert Taylor Homes. During the 1970s, the only decade for which records survive, the CHA recorded 417 injuries and 15 deaths related to elevators. In 1980, the CHA's chief of maintenance lamented, "With so many kids, the elevators are just $80,000 playtoys."[22]

Press accounts blamed much of the destruction on youth "gangs." In 1958, a *Chicago American* reporter toured Dearborn Homes (completed in 1950) and charged "'teen-age gangs' who roam the CHA projects at night" with vandalism resulting in "torn window screens, mutilated storm doors, yards littered with garbage, ... walls, doors, and casings marked by knife slashes and crayon marks; holes gouged in plaster; obscenities scrawled on the stairway walls." *Chicago Sun-Times* reporter Ruth Moore, an astute observer who covered the CHA from 1956 to 1970, surveyed the CHA's Grace Abbott Homes two years after it opened and recognized a link between design, social disorder, and vandalism, though she missed the projects' high youth densities. "A project like Abbott is a magnet for teen-age gangs in the vicinity," she wrote in 1957. "The spacious grounds and the public lobbies are natural hangouts, and the neighborhood toughs converge. When the lights in the stairwells are smashed, as they are night after night, the dark makes a fine place to hide or meet a girl." Echoing Moore's reports from the late 1950s, the *Chicago Daily News* ran a five-part series in 1965 calling the CHA's Robert Taylor Homes "a human ant heap" and a "jungle" where "teenage terror and adult chaos" reign.[23] Media reports were, at best, only partial glimpses into project life, and they lumped any congregation of youth under the label of "gang activity." Organized gangs with criminal bents, such as Chicago's Vice Lords and the Cobras, did infiltrate Chicago's projects in the 1960s, and undoubtedly they found high youth densities conducive to gang organizing. But the press left the impression that widespread chaos was linked only to the presence of organized gangs or, more subtly and unfairly, to white notions of African American urban culture.[24]

Vandalism and criminal activity, of course, had complex causes. African American social critics pointed to the pernicious effects of segregation and the dispiriting aesthetics of public housing as the source of problems. James Baldwin in 1962 called public housing "hideous" and "colorless, bleak, high, and revolting ... cheerless as a prison." Writing about projects in New York City, he argued, "The projects in Harlem are hated. They are hated almost as much as policemen, and this is saying a great deal ... both reveal, unbearably, the real attitude of the white world, no matter how many liberal speeches are made, no matter how many lofty editorials are written, no matter how many civil rights commissions are set up." This hatred led to "the most violent bitterness of sprit" directed at their physical surroundings. "Scarcely had they moved in," Baldwin wrote of tenants in an urban renewal development in Harlem, "before they began smashing windows, defacing walls, urinating in the elevators, and fornicating in the playgrounds." African Americans understood segregation and lashed out at it. "The people of Harlem know they are living there because white people do not think they are good enough to live anywhere else," he concluded. Years later, Baldwin admitted that

residents of Harlem's projects were "much embittered by this description," but he wrote that those who deny the "common pain, demoralization, and danger" of segregation are "self-deluded."[25]

Baldwin's work resonated with Robert Murphy, who used it to explain the disorder at the Robert Taylor Homes. After an article appeared in the *New Republic* sourcing Murphy in reporting that rapes occurred in elevators, that stairwells were used as "convenient abodes for all kinds of mischief" and "serve as toilets for small children," Murphy was asked by his superiors to respond. "I'm afraid there are some people living at Taylor Homes today who do harbor deep-felt resentments, hostilities and bitterness, and are overly distrustful of management and the Housing Authority. And I don't doubt that some project youngsters vent their hostilities and resentments by destroying CHA property."[26] Similarly, sociologist Lee Rainwater studied St. Louis's chaotic Pruitt-Igoe project in the late 1960s and formulated a theory regarding the destructive behaviors he saw. The nation's racial caste system, he argued, denied opportunity based on race to which African Americans adapted with "social and personal responses," including aggression, which "results in suffering directly inflicted by Negroes on themselves and others." He summarized: "In short, whites, by their greater power have created situations in which Negroes do the dirty work of caste victimization for them."[27]

Murphy's experiences, Baldwin's anger, and Rainwater's theory all help explain why youths lashed out against their homes in response to their victimization. But vandalism is also a crime of opportunity, and public housing's youth-adult ratios were involved. If segregation and discrimination amplified vandalism and violence in the black community, then public housing's demographics made restraining destructive acts that much more difficult. Residents, security guards, and formal police authorities were handicapped by the odds facing them as they struggled to contain the impulses of youth.

* * *

From the early days of public housing, managers sought to channel youthful energy into nondestructive pursuits. But over time, growing youth-adult ratios, disagreements over the proper role of housing authorities in providing social resources, and limited staff capacity at the CHA and social service agencies hampered such efforts. In the end, the CHA and other city agencies were simply unprepared for the onslaught of youths in public housing communities.

During its experiment in the mid-1930s, the PWA allowed local housing authorities to spend rental income for direct provision of nursery schools, health clinics, summer recreation, and adult literacy. But USHA administrators changed this approach, arguing that public housing should not be isolated from existing community social services. Instead, projects were expected to include community space that would then be leased to local agencies with specialized expertise, such as the YMCA or a settlement house. At the CHA's early projects, Elizabeth Wood achieved considerable success in recruiting private agencies and public entities such as the Chicago Park District to serve public housing residents. Ida B. Wells included a city-run health clinic, and settlement houses were active at both Cabrini and Brooks Homes.[28]

But maintaining relationships with such agencies and ensuring they provided sufficient programs for youth met obstacles large and small. For example, the Chicago Park District built a small indoor field house to serve residents of Ida B. Wells, but by the early 1950s it had deteriorated under heavy usage. The park district proposed building a new, larger field house to meet recreational needs not only for Wells, but for the Wells Extension, scheduled to open in 1955. For its part, the CHA also planned to build a small community center at Wells Extension, which would be leased to the park district and other agencies for youth programs. But the park district dropped its plans for the new field house and elected to cram its programming into the CHA's small community center, a completely inadequate space for indoor recreation. At the same time it closed the old field house;

neighborhood youths, enraged at the turn of events, vandalized the old building. As a result, Wells both grew in size and shrunk its indoor facilities. Similarly, outdoor programs for youths fell short. A review by federal officials in 1958 found that summer programs at the CHA were "lacking in quality and in the number of leaders necessary for the proper conduct of a program of activities." But rather than propose the direct provision of a CHA summer program, Washington told the authority to "work more closely" with the park officials who had already slighted them.[29]

At low-rise projects with fewer youths, strong management overcame the anarchic tendencies of youth. The Jane Addams Homes had a relatively low youth-adult ratio by CHA standards (1.0 youths per adult, still double the city norm), but in the early 1950s Addams teenagers battled over project space. Managers believed two Italian-American youth gangs within the project were relentlessly destroying the buildings and demoralizing tenants, management, and social service agencies. "Vandalism was the catchword that explained everything," observed Mary Bolton Wirth, a CHA community and tenant relations staff member.[30] Wirth counted over four hundred broken windows in the 1,000-unit project shortly after she arrived in 1952, with windows broken as fast as maintenance crews could replace them. Community rooms used by the Boys Club, a Jewish school, and the Near West Side Community Council were repeatedly wrecked. Wirth undertook extensive efforts to control the projects' youths with both sticks and carrots. She recruited gang leadership into various youth organizations and pressed management to threaten eviction of those families who did not cooperate. Her efforts had some success, at least through the late 1950s: the broken-window problem at Addams diminished and morale improved.[31]

Wirth, the widow of University of Chicago sociologist Louis Wirth, who himself had been a strong supporter of public housing, was promptly promoted to head of tenant and community relations. She began a long battle to keep park programs running and to find settlement houses willing to take on the CHA's large new projects."[32] At her suggestion, the CHA doubled the community relations staff and partnered with over forty organizations to provide services ranging from recreation to mental health care for residents. Community space, underestimated by project planners, was expanded by converting 171 apartments for agency uses.[33] In 1961, executive director Alvin Rose proposed using the CHA's plentiful reserve funds for expanded social programs for teenagers, but the board rejected the idea on the grounds that Washington would not approve such a move.[34] A year later, he recommended using surplus CHA development funds to construct an indoor swimming pool at the Henry Horner Homes, an idea allowed under PHA rules, but only board member Charles Swibel backed the proposal. The rest of the board wanted the Chicago Park District to construct pools, which they belatedly did at several projects in the late 1960s, supplemented in part by CHA funds. Most of the pools, however, were far too small, were immediately swamped by youths, and were never properly maintained.[35]

Rose also threw his energy into a crusade to expand scouting programs as a way to deal with the crushing numbers of youths in public housing. He proposed using a piece of land at the Robert Taylor Homes for a Boy Scout "headquarters or capital" in the form of a log cabin built by the boys themselves. (The Girl Scouts were left out.) Rose passionately detailed the possibilities at a CHA board meeting, suggesting overnight camping, cookouts, and hikes from the site "to all points of the city." He hoped "to change the bad image surrounding" Robert Taylor so that the project "referred to as a jungle" could become "the Boy Scout Capital of the World." But the board opposed the plan, as it had done with Rose's other scouting initiatives over the previous four years, and then the debate turned personal. The minutes record that Theophilus Mann, the only African American commissioner, told Rose to "stay out of Boy Scouting, the Board of Education, and the Chicago Park

District and run the CHA the way it should be run"—condemning the entire scope of Rose's community-building efforts. Rose jumped up and stated furiously, "I refuse!"-[36] On a final vote, the board rejected Rose's proposal and, critically, expressed their lack of confidence in his ability to lead day-to-day operations. But rather than fire him, Swibel—now chairman—allowed Rose to remain as executive director for three more years (until he had turned sixty-five and could retire), though in the final year, the two men never spoke face-to-face.[37] Of all the issues debated by the board in the 1960s, none generated more fervor than Rose's quixotic scouting crusade.

Indeed, many residents responded to Rose's campaign and formed scout troops, often against great odds. A 1964 news story profiled the heroics of CHA janitor and scout master Clarence Phillips, who had successfully organized 25 percent of the boys in one Stateway Gardens building— 132 boys in all—including "former Cobras and Vice Lords Juniors." The effort won him few accolades, however. Gang members warned Phillips to quit his activities and then smashed his car windows and slashed his tires. Several scouts had their uniforms torn off while selling candy door-to-door to raise money to attend a summer camp. But Phillips still told a reporter, "I could start five more troops down here if I could find some brave parents."[38]

While numerous groups made serious efforts to address the situation, the CHA and the city were unprepared to provide the resources needed for environments with so many youths and so few adults. In 1962, during final construction of the 1959 projects, the CHA's management department (in charge of running the future developments) asked its colleagues in the development department (in charge of design and construction) to provide more play areas for children, even to the extent of exceeding federal limitations. At existing projects the management department had already paved over large areas of grass in an effort to accommodate the overflow from small playgrounds by children "seeking legitimate pursuit of their recreation."[39] Despite clear knowledge of the need for playgrounds, the CHA and federal officials failed to include adequate space in the 1959 projects; inevitably, children overran the equipment provided. A year after the projects were fully occupied, the CHA wrote to the PHA seeking funds for more playgrounds. "Children line up seven and eight deep just waiting to use a piece of play equipment" at the Robert Taylor Homes, the CHA complained, and "upwards of 2,000 children may be cramped into one or two relatively small play areas."[40] Without sufficient recreational space at the massive project, children turned stairwells and elevators into playgrounds—with the inevitable consequences for social disorder.

Nor did other social service agencies or city organizations have the capacity to serve the 90,000 young people concentrated in CHA projects, and Herculean efforts made little headway. Firman House, a settlement organization serving the Robert Taylor Homes, used a federal War on Poverty grant in 1965 to launch an ambitious preschool program for 425 children, but at least 3,000 children at the project were eligible.[41] Similarly, 46 separate tutoring projects organized 800 volunteers to work with 2,000 school-age students at CHA projects in 1965. This major educational accomplishment, however, reached only 3 percent of the CHA's school-age population, numbering some 70,000.[42] The Chicago Public Library opened branches using converted apartments at Ickes Homes, Robert Taylor, and Rockwell Gardens in late 1968. Each library was besieged by children clamoring to use its limited facilities.[43]

In contrast, the Chicago School Board neglected its obligations to public housing residents, often willfully.[44] In early 1960, the CHA informed the school board to expect 10,583 new elementary school children in the Robert Taylor Homes area by 1963. School superintendent Benjamin Willis planned three new schools but failed to acknowledge that the proposed facilities would accommodate only 7,765 students, even assuming 35 children per room. Frustrated CHA staff members tipped off Noel Naisbitt, an Urban League researcher and citywide PTA member, who confronted the school board about the obvious discrepancies in its numbers. She

exposed how Willis had plainly underestimated space needs while at the same time refusing to integrate nearby half-empty classrooms. Chicago School Board staff responded that the CHA had overestimated the number of students, that 40 students could be placed in each classroom, and that trailers—dubbed "Willis Wagons" by opponents—could be set up in any event. Naisbitt appealed to federal officials, noting that the CHA "is under a great deal of pressure from (School Board head) Dr. Willis to layoff, not to fuss about this situation." Willis then proposed to convert ground-floor apartments into classrooms (ready-made Willis Wagons), a plan that CHA commissioner Mann decried as "dynamite."[45] But with few immediate options and with no interest in a public confrontation that might embarrass the mayor over the explosive issue of school integration, in 1962 the CHA leased to the school board a total of seventy-eight apartments for use as classrooms at the Robert Taylor Homes, Washington Park Homes, and Lake Michigan Homes, three 1959 projects. Despite their supposed "temporary" nature, and despite numerous protests and even boycotts from public housing tenants, the leases were renewed annually until 1972.[46]

NOTES

1. Wesley Skogan, *Disorder and Decline: Crime and the Spiral of Decay in American Neighborhoods* (New York: Free Press, 1990), 2.
2. The sociological literature on social disorder has a long pedigree going back to the Chicago School of Sociology in the 1920s. Influential books include Clifford R. Shaw and Henry D. McKay, *Juvenile Delinquency and Urban Areas* (Chicago: University of Chicago Press, 1942); Gerald Suttles, *The Social Construction of Communities* (Chicago: University of Chicago Press, 1972); Ruth Kornhauser, *Social Sources of Delinquency* (Chicago: University of Chicago Press, 1978). I am most influenced in this chapter by the work of Robert Sampson and his colleagues. See especially Robert J. Sampson, Jeffrey D. Morenoff, and Thomas Gannon-Rowley, "Assessing 'Neighborhood Effects': Social Processes and New Directions for Research." *Annual Review of Sociology* 28 (2002): 443–78;

Robert J. Sampson and Byron W. Groves, "Community Structure and Crime: Testing Social-Disorganization Theory," *American Journal of Sociology* 94, no. 4 (1989): 774–802; Robert J. Sampson, Jeffrey D. Morenoff, and Felton Earls, "Beyond Social Capital: Spatial Dynamics of Collective Efficacy for Children," *American Sociological Review* 64, no. 5 (1999): 633–60; Robert J. Sampson and Stephen W. Raudenbush, "Systematic Social Observation of Public Spaces: A New Look at Disorder in Urban Neighborhoods," *American Journal of Sociology* 105, no. 3 (1999): 603–51.

3. The direct connection between youth density and public housing's demise is nearly absent from the literature on planning or public housing. The earliest mention can be found in Anthony F. C. Wallace, *Housing and Social Structure: A Preliminary Survey* (Philadelphia: Philadelphia Housing Association, 1952), 89. Wallace noted the managerial problems faced in the high-rise Jacob Riis houses with their "very high proportion of small children." But no serious comparative work on youth densities or its effect on public housing management has been completed. One study of "problem families" in Boston makes a hesitant link between child density and negative "project reputation," finding Boston's managers connected high concentrations of children with "problem areas" in their projects. See Richard S. Scobie, *Problem Tenants in Public Housing: Who, Where, and Why Are They?* (New York: Praeger Publishers, 1975), 63. A planning treatise from 1986 encourages housing developers to be careful about youth densities: "Ratios of adults to children of less than 3 to 1 [i.e. youth density greater than 0.30] and densities of more than 30 children to the acre are 'warning devices.' They signal the need for careful planning, special provision for child recreation, and more-than-adequate maintenance." See Clare Cooper Marcus and Wendy Sarkissian, *Housing As If People Mattered* (Berkeley and Los Angeles: University of California, 1986), 280–81. Marcus and Sarkissian cite a handful of British reports from the late 1970s. Extensive research in the late 1960s and 1970s asked how children adapted to high-rise buildings and public project grounds, especially in Great Britain and Canada. See also Clare Cooper Marcus and Robin C. Moore, "Children and Their Environments: A Review of Research" *Journal of Architectural Education* (April 1976), 22–25; E. W. Cooney, "High Flats in Local Authority Housing in England and Wales since 1945," in *Multi-Storey Living, the British*

Working Class Experience, edited by Anthony Sutcliffe (London: Croom Helm, 1974), 161; Vancouver City Planning Department, *Housing Families at High Densities*, 1978, 11, 17, 26; Joan Maizel, *Two to Five in High Flats: An Enquiry into Play Provision for Children Aged Two to Five Years Living in High Flats* (London: Housing Centre Trust, 1961); Pearl Jephcott, *Homes in High Flats* (Edinburgh: Oliver and Boyd, 1971), 65–67. Mark Baldassare, in *Residential Crowding in Urban America* (Berkeley and Los Angeles: University of California Press, 1979), an important work on residential densities, only examines "persons per residential acre" but never addresses youth-adult ratios.

4. Youth-adult ratios are defined as the number of people under age twenty-one divided by the number of people age twenty-one and over. Demographers often use percentage of minors to describe age composition, and this is a valid measure, but using youth-adult ratios highlights the relative numbers of each more clearly. Like a student-teacher ratio for measuring classroom conditions, the youth-adult ratio is one measure of the capacity of adults to manage the youths in their environment.

5. Sources for table 1: U.S. Bureau of the Census, *U.S. Census of Population: 1970*, vol. 1 (Washington, DC, 1973), pt. 1, sec. 1, table 52, 1–269, also pt. 15, Illinois —sec. 1, table 24, 111–13, and table 28, 15–183; *Sixteenth Census of the United States: 1940*, vol. 2, *Population* (Washington, 1943), pt. 1, table 7, 22, and pt. 2, Florida-Iowa, table A-35, 639; *Report on Population of the United States at the Tenth Census* (Washington, 1883), table 20, 548; *Report on Population of the United States at the Eleventh Census: 1890* (Washington, 1897), pt. 2, table 8, 117; Robert Hunter, *Tenement Conditions in Chicago* (Chicago: City Homes Association, 1901), 195–96; *Census of Population: 1960*, vol. 1 (Washington, 1963), pt. 34, New York, table 20; *U.S. Census of Population and Housing: 1960* (Washington, 1962), Census Tracts, Final Report PHC (1)-104, pt. 1, table P-2, 371, and Final Report PHC(1)-26, table P-1, 58; Chicago Housing Authority, *Annual Statistical Report*, 1951, 1960, 1965, 1970, and 1975.

6. The standard deviation calculation uses youth-adult ratios for census tracts in the city of Chicago for 1960 and a definition of youth as eighteen or under, because of limitations in census data at the tract level. Twelve census tracts that year consisted of 90 percent or more public housing. See

U.S. Census of Population and Housing: 1960, Final Report PHC(1)-26, Census Tracts for Chicago, IL, Standard Metropolitan Statistical Area, table P-1.

7. U.S. Bureau of the Census, *Census of Population: 1970*, vol. 1, *Characteristics of the Population* (Washington, DC, 1973), pt. 1, Illinois, table 155.

8. CHA, *What Is a Low Income Family?* November 1947, 17; CHA, *Annual Report*, 1945; CHA, *Facts about Public Housing in Chicago*, June 1947, 28; CHA, *Annual Statistical Report*, 1952, chart 7; CHA, *Children's Cities*, pamphlet, 1945, HWLC-MRC; CHA operating manual, 1940, HWLC-MRC.

9. "Meeting for discussion of desirable legislation," July 13 and 14, 1944, box 1, Vinton Papers; CHA, *Facts about Public Housing in Chicago*, 10; CHA, *Monthly Report*, November 1948; John Taylor Egan, "Supplemental Statement on Costs of Public Housing and Appropriate Cost Limits," testimony before the Senate Committee on Banking and Commerce, February 7, 1949, and "Address by John T. Egan, NAHO Conference, October 16–19, 1950," both in box 10, "Miscellaneous Records of the Liaison Division," RG 196; Abrams, *The Future of Housing*, 272.

10. Major federal planning documents include: USHA, *Planning the Site: Design of Low-Rent Housing Projects*, Bulletin no. 11, May 1939; FPHA, *Minimum Physical Standards and Criteria for Planning and Design of FPHA-Aided Public Housing Projects*, 1945; FPHA, *The Livability Problems of 1,000 Families*, 1945; PHA, *Low-Rent Public Housing*. Only one document makes brief mention of the problems of youth, quoting without explanation an unnamed housing official from Ohio: "Multi-story buildings containing dwelling units housing a number of children are, we find, extremely unsatisfactory." See FPHA, *Public Housing Design: A Review of Experience in Low-Rent Housing*, 1946, 88.

11. CHA, *Annual Statistical Report*, 1951–60.

12. Theodore A. Veenstra to Stanley W. Hahn, June 23, 1954, CHA Development files, IL 2–22.

13. CHA, *Annual Statistical Report*, 1951–67; CHA, *Monthly Report*, April 1955; CHA to Richard J. Daley, July 19, 1957, in "Mayor's file," CHA Subject files; CHA, *Official Minutes*, December 6, 1957, CHA files; *Chicago Tribune*, November 28, 1957, January 10 and 14, 1958.

14. Elizabeth Wood to the commissioners, "The Tenant Selection Process," December 22, 1952, CHA Gautreaux files; *Chicago*

Tribune, January 14, 1958. Pruitt-Igoe also had difficulty renting smaller apartments. See Rainwater, *Behind Ghetto Walls*, 13.

15. William Moore, *The Vertical Ghetto*, xv; Frank de Leeuw, *Operating Costs in Public Housing: A Financial Crisis* (Washington: Urban Institute, 1968), 24.

16. Jane Jacobs, *The Death and Life of Great American Cities* (New York: Vintage Books, 1992), 35, 50, 82 (emphasis in the original).

17. Fuerst, *When Public Housing Was Paradise*, 48, 79,114, 127, 131, 174.

18. Elizabeth Wood, *Housing Design: A Social Theory* (New York: Citizens' Housing and Planning Council, 1961).

19. See Newman, *Defensible Space*, 234–37, especially tables A-6 and A-7.

20. Criminologists have attributed some of the drop in overall crime in the 1990s to the decline in the youth population following the baby-boom "echo." See Robert Agnew, "An Integrated Theory of the Adolescent Peak in Offending," *Youth and Society* 34, no. 3 (March 2003): 263–300; Alfred Blumstein and Joel Wallman, *The Crime Drop in America* (New York: Cambridge University Press, 2000); Sampson and Rauderbusch, "Systematic Social Observation of Public Spaces."

21. Alvin Rose to William Bergeron, January 6, 1959, CHA Development files, IL 2–30; CHA, *Official Minutes*, January 25, 1961; *Chicago Sun-Times*, April 5, 1959; *Chicago Daily News*, March 8, 1958; Robert H. Murphy, "City within a City: Robert R. Taylor Homes," *FREE: A Roosevelt University Magazine* 2, no. 1 (spring 1963): 6–13, CHM; Wolf Von Eckardt, "The Black Neck in the White Noose," *New Republic*, October 19, 1963, 14–18; Robert H. Murphy to Harry J. Schneider, "Taylor (37): Comments on Magazine Article," October 28, 1963, manager's folder, Robert Taylor Homes, CHA Subject files. For descriptions of youth-inspired social disorder in other cities, see Rainwater, *Behind Ghetto Walls*, 66.

22. See reports in the *Chicago Daily News*, April 25, 1959; *Chicago Sun-Times*, September 4, 1957, March 12, 1956, February 4, 1959, and August 25, 1967; and *Chicago Tribune*, June 27, 1980. Also the CHA records: Robert Murphy, internal memo, September 16, 1963, manager's folder, Robert Taylor Homes, CHA Subject files; Jack Doppelt to file, "Interviews with Virgil Cross, CHA Chief of Central Maintenance," July 31, 1980, box 134, BGA Papers.

23. *Chicago American*, April 5, 1958; *Chicago Sun-Times*, September 4, 1957; *Chicago*

Defender, September 2, 1960; *Chicago Daily News*, April 12–17, 1965; see also *Chicago Daily Defender*, editorial, October 19, 1966. For earlier examples of similar concerns with the large number of youths, see *Chicago Sun-Times*, September 4, 1957, May 7, 1958, and April 4, 1959.

24. Sociologists studying gang behavior have explained that the term "gang" covers a wide range of organization and activity. Some of the city's more violent and organized gangs did stake out turf at projects soon after they were opened. On the first identification of the Vice Lords and Cobras in public housing, see CHA, *Official Minutes*, February 28, 1962. For the complex identities of gang members within a community, see Mary Pattillo-McCoy, *Picket Fences: Privilege and Peril among the Black Middle Class* (Chicago: University of Chicago Press, 1999). On gangs in the 1990s in public housing, see the work of Sudhir Venkatesh, including *American Project* (Cambridge: Harvard University Press, 2000).

25. James Baldwin, *The Price of the Ticket: Collected Nonfiction, 1948–1985* (New York: Macmillan, 1985), 209–10.

26. Murphy to Schneider, "Taylor (37): Comments on Magazine Article."

27. Rainwater, *Behind Ghetto Walls*, 4, 66.

28. USHA, *Community Activities in Public Housing*, May 1941; CHA, *Annual Report*, 1945.

29. PHA, Chicago Regional Office, *Management Review, Chicago Housing Authority*, January 1958, HWLC-MRC, 31–32.

30. Mary Bolton Wirth studied with Edith Abbott at the University of Chicago in the 1920s and then supervised WPA social workers during the 1930s. After the death of her husband, she went to work for the CHA in 1952 as a community and tenant relations aide at the Jane Addams Homes. Her papers, housed at the University of Chicago, are a rich source on public housing management in the city.

31. Mary Bolton Wirth, "Reminiscences of My Assignment As an 'Aide'—1953–1954," "Report on Activities at the Jane Addams Homes," and Wirth to Albert Rosenberg, May 15, 1953, all in folder 1, box 1, Mary Wirth Papers. See also "Mary Bolt on Wirth," in *Women Making Chicago*, edited by Rima Schultz (Bloomington: Indiana University Press, 1995), 998–91.

32. Mary Bolton Wirth, "Meeting with Recreation Agencies of Near West Side" April 23, 1953; Mary Bolton Wirth to Albert Rosenberg, May 15, 1953; Wirth, "Memorandum of Record," August 17, 1954, folder 1, box 1, Mary Wirth Papers. Also,

Albert Rosenberg, "The Community and Tenant Relations Program of the Chicago Housing Authority," May 25, 1953; Wirth, "Memorandum of Record: Re: Meeting on March 19, 1957 with the Chicago Park District," March 27, 1957, folder 2, box 1; Mary Bolton Wirth, "Recreation and Group Work at CHA Projects," June 28, 1958.

33. CHA Press Release, February 10, 1959, CHA clipping folio, CHA Public Affairs files; *Chicago Sun-Times*, June 1, 1958; *Chicago Daily News*, October 16, 1958; CHA, *Official Minutes*, June 8, 1960, and March 25, 1965; Chicago Metropolitan Welfare Council, *Proposed Co-operative Survey and Planning Project on Social Welfare and Health Services in Public Housing*, appendix, March 1967, folder "Management—General," CHA Legal files. On Rose, see Edward Banfield, *Political Influence: A New Theory of Urban Politics* (New York: Free Press, 1961), 65–66.

34. Alvin Rose, "A Public Houser Speaks," *Public Welfare*, 20, no. 2 (1962): 91–92, 137; CHA Press Release, February 10, 1959, CHA clipping folio, CHA Public Affairs files; *Chicago Daily News*, October 16, 1958; *Chicago Sun-Times*, June 14, 1960, and August 10, 1961; CHA, *Official Minutes*, June 8, 1960.

35. CHA, *Official Minutes*, May 25 (Kay Kula to Theophilus Mann, May 23) and June 13, 1962; March 9, 1967; March 28, 1968. Also Better Government Association, "Memo to Hoge, re: CHA," no date [1975?], folder "background," box 66, BGA Papers.

36. CHA, *Official Minutes*, July 22, 1965. On Rose and the National Scouts, see CHA, *Official Minutes*, August 12, 1965.

37. Chicago *Sun-Times*, November 10, 1967.

38. Undated, unnotated clip from unknown newspaper, folder "Authorities—Miscellaneous," CHA Subject files, likely from late 1964.

39. CHA director of development J. W. Hasskarl to William Bergeron, February 15, 1962, CHA Development files, IL 2–37.

40. Harry J. Schneider to Bergeron, August 25, 1964, CHA Development files, IL 2–37.

41. Gus Master to Bergeron, July 29, 1969, and Alvin Rose to Bergeron, November 4, 1964, CHA Development files, IL 2–37. In 1962, the CHA estimated that 6,700 Taylor residents would be prekindergarten age (Rose to Bergeron, February 8, 1962, CHA Development files, IL 2–37).

42. Claude P. Miller, chief of community and tenant relations, to Harry J. Schneider, January 21, 1966, folder "Management—General," CHA Legal files.

43. *Chicago Tribune*, October 24, 1968; Master to Bergeron, July 29, 1969, CHA Development files, IL 2–37.

44. In 1944, the all-black Altgeld Gardens project opened on the far South Side without sufficient school space, and the CHA had little choice but to offer thirty-six apartments to the school board for use as classrooms. A new school finally opened in 1947, but only after federal officials intervened by threatening to block renewal of the temporary solution. See CHA, *Official Minutes*, June 10, 1947.

45. Noel Naisbitt, telephone interview by the author, March 28, 2000, notes in author's possession; Noel Naisbitt to William Bergeron, January 21, 1962, CHA Development files, IL 2–37; CHA, *Official Minutes*, January 24, 1962.

46. CHA, *Official Minutes*, April 11, 1962, May 11, 1967, June 8, 1972; *Chicago Defender*, October 21 and 22 and November 10, 1964. For more on the challenge by African Americans to the school board's leadership, see Arvarh E. Strickland, *A History of the Chicago Urban League* (Champaign: University of Illinois Press, 1966), 235–41; Christopher Reed, *The Chicago NAACP and the Rise of Black Professional Leadership, 1910–1966* (Bloomington: Indiana University Press, 1997), 168.

DOCUMENTS FOR PART VII

7.1 NATIONAL INTERSTATE AND DEFENSE HIGHWAYS ACT (1956)

Source: National Interstate and Defense Highways Act (PL 627, 29 June 1956), 70 *United States Statutes At Large.*

EDITORS' INTRODUCTION

By the late 1930s, federal government officials were taking increased interest in building a national system of interstate highways. Mobility remained a particular concern of cities, where commerce slowed with snarled traffic. Worries abounded about city evacuation in the event of war, and the outbreak of the Second World War and the dawn of the nuclear age exacerbated this anxiety. Rural areas also supported an improved transportation infrastructure, in part because the roads gave them better access to urban markets and amenities. In 1956, Congress passed the National Interstate and Defense Highways Act, commonly known as the Federal Highway Act of 1956. President Dwight D. Eisenhower, who had spent a lifetime in the military, championed the cause of the interstate system, which was renamed the Dwight D. Eisenhower System of Interstate and Defense Highways in 1990. The system construction, first estimated to cost $27 billion dollars and to be completed in about ten years, cost far more than first planned and extended for decades. Although nominally completed during the 1990s, some aspects of the proposed system have yet to be built. The Interstate Highway System is considered the largest public works program in the world. The highways changed cities in vital ways, but did not put an end to traffic problems. The system as initially designed (there were later adjustments) was meant to serve the estimated population of the 1970s.

NATIONAL INTERSTATE AND
DEFENSE HIGHWAYS ACT (1956)

AN ACT

To amend and supplement the Federal-Aid Road Act approved July 11, 1916, to authorize appropriations for continuing the construction of highways; to amend the Internal Revenue Code of 1954 to provide additional revenue from the taxes on motor fuel, tires, and trucks and buses; and for other purposes.

Be it enacted by the Senate and House of Representatives of the United States of America in Congress assembled,

TITLE I—FEDERAL-AID HIGHWAY ACT OF 1956
SEC. 101. SHORT TITLE FOR TITLE I.
This title may be cited as the "Federal-Aid Highway Act of 1956".
SEC. 102. FEDERAL-AID HIGHWAYS.

(a) (1) AUTHORIZATION OF APPROPRIATIONS.—For the purpose of carrying out the provisions of the Federal-Aid Road Act approved July 11, 1916 (39 Stat. 355), and all Acts amendatory thereof and supplementary thereto, there is hereby authorized to be appropriated for the fiscal year ending June 30, 1957, $125,000,000 in addition to any sums heretofore authorized for such fiscal year; the sum of $850,000,000 for the fiscal year ending June 30, 1958; and the sum

(*Continued*)

(Cont.)

of $875,000,000 for the fiscal year ending June 30, 1959. The sums herein authorized for each fiscal year shall be available for expenditure as follows:

(A) 45 per centum for projects on the Federal-aid primary high- way system.
(B) 30 per centum for projects on the Federal-aid secondary high- way system.
(C) 25 per centum for projects on extensions of these systems within urban areas.

(2) APPORTIONMENTS.—The sums authorized by this section shall be apportioned among the several States in the manner now provided by law and in accordance with the formulas set forth in section 4 of the Federal-Aid Highway Act of 1944; approved December 20, 1944 (58 Stat. 838): Provided, That the additional amount herein authorized for the fiscal year ending June 30, 1957, shall be apportioned immediately upon enactment of this Act.

(b) AVAILABILITY FOR EXPENDITURE.—Any sums apportioned to any State under this section shall be available for expenditure in that State for two years after the close of the fiscal year for which such sums are authorized, and any amounts so apportioned remaining unexpended at the end of such period shall lapse: Provided, That such funds shall be deemed to have been expended if a sum equal to the total of the sums herein and heretofore apportioned to the State is covered by formal agreements with the Secretary of Commerce for construction, reconstruction, or improvement of specific projects as provided in this title and prior Acts: Provided further, That in the case of those sums heretofore, herein, or hereafter apportioned to any State for projects on the Federal-aid secondary highway system, the Secretary of Commerce may, upon the request of any State, discharge his responsibility relative to the plans, specifications, estimates, surveys, contract awards, design, inspection, and construction of such secondary road projects by his receiving and approving a certified statement by the State highway department setting forth that the plans, design, and construction for such projects are in accord with the standards and procedures of such State applicable.
[…]

SEC. 108. NATIONAL SYSTEM OF INTERSTATE AND DEFENSE HIGHWAYS.

(a) INTERSTATE SYSTEM.—It is hereby declared to be essential to the national interest to provide for the early completion of the "National System of Interstate Highways", as authorized and designated in accordance with section 7 of the Federal-Aid Highway Act of 1944 (58 Stat. 838). It is the intent of the Congress that the Interstate System be completed as nearly as practicable over a thirteen-year period and that the entire System in all the States be brought to simultaneous completion. Because of its primary importance to the national defense, the name of such system is hereby changed to the "National System of Interstate and Defense Highways". Such National System of Interstate and Defense Highways is hereinafter in this Act referred to as the "Interstate System".

(b) AUTHORIZATION OF APPROPRIATIONS.—For the purpose of expediting the construction, reconstruction, or improvement, inclusive of necessary bridges and tunnels, of the interstate System, including extensions thereof through urban areas, designated in accordance with the provisions of section 7 of the Federal-Aid Highway Act of 1944 (58 Stat. 838), there is hereby authorized to be appropriated the additional sum of $1,000,000,000 for, the fiscal year ending June 30, 1957, which sum shall be in addition to the authorization heretofore made for that year, the additional sum of $1,700,000,000 for the fiscal year ending June 30, 1958, the additional sum of $2,000,000,000 for the fiscal year ending June 30, 1959, the additional sum of $2,200,000,000 for the fiscal year ending June 30, 1960, the additional sum of $2,200,000,000 for the fiscal year ending June 30, 1961, the additional sum of $2,200,000,000 for the fiscal year ending June 30, 1962, the additional sum of $2,200,000,000 for the fiscal year ending June 30, 1963, the additional sum of $2,200,000,000 for the fiscal year ending June 30, 1964, the additional sum of $2,200,000,000 for the fiscal year ending June 30, 1965, the additional sum of $2,200,000,000 for the fiscal year ending June 30, 1966, the additional sum of $2,200,000,000 for the fiscal year ending June 30, 1967, the additional sum of $1,500,000,000 for the fiscal year ending June 30, 1968, and the additional sum of $1,025,000,000 for the fiscal year ending .June 30, 1969…

7.2 WACKER'S MANUAL OF THE PLAN OF CHICAGO (1913)

Walter D. Moody

Source: Walter D. Moody, *Wacker's Manual of the Plan of Chicago* (Chicago: Chicago Plan Commission, 1913). Original accessed at the Newberry Library, Chicago, Illinois.

EDITORS' INTRODUCTION

Walter D. Moody (1874–1920) served as Managing Director of the Chicago Plan Commission. The commission was confident that Chicago was "destined to become the center of the modern world, if the opportunities in her reach are intelligently realized, and if the city can receive a sufficient supply of trained and enlightened citizens."[i] Daniel Hudson Burnham, the mastermind behind the breathtaking and influential architecture of the Columbian World's Fair held in Chicago in 1893, brought his ideas for civic improvement to the Commercial Club of Chicago and the Merchants Club, and secured their solid support. Burnham, an architect, city planner, and the formal plan's chief author, wanted to build a series of parks, wide open avenues, and new cultural and government buildings in Chicago. The resulting *Plan of Chicago*, published with accompanying drawings by the Commercial Club in 1909, inspired cities all over the United States to invest in physical changes; this movement became known as the "City Beautiful" movement. Here, we learn about the plan in a book designed for Chicago schools. Moody wanted school children to play an active role in bringing the ideas of the plan to fruition. Fresh air and easy access to outdoor recreation promised to offer relief for the perceived anxieties of urban life. A physically improved city also aids business by speeding-up the movement of people, ideas, and capital and encourages a higher number of tourists to visit the city.

WACKER'S MANUAL OF THE PLAN OF CHICAGO (1913)

The Plan of Chicago; Its Purpose and Meaning

The Plan of Chicago, as it has been worked out, is a plan to direct the future growth of Chicago in a systematic and orderly way. Its purpose is to make Chicago a real, centralized city instead of a group of overcrowded, overgrown villages. It will hold her position among the great cities of the world, that Chicago is to be given opportunities for indefinite growth in wealth and commerce, and that Chicago is to become the most convenient, healthful and attractive city on earth. History shows that this work will give

to us, the owners and builders of Chicago, world-wide fame that will be everlasting.

We have seen that in the history of the cities of the past their building according to a definite plan has to do chiefly with two elements, namely, congestion, which means the crowding of large numbers of people into small areas; and traffic, which means the movement of merchandise and people from one part of the city to another. We modern people, owing to the advance of science during our times, recognizes [sic] another element as of great importance, namely, the creation and preservation of conditions promoting public health. We know that if a city is to continue strong and progressive, or even if it is to continue to exist at all, its people must be healthy and its children robust.

---

i Walter D. Moody, *Wacker's Manual of the Plan of Chicago* (Chicago: Chicago Plan Commission, 1913), no page. See also Carl Smith, *The Plan of Chicago: Daniel Burnham and the Remaking of the American City* (Chicago: University of Chicago Press, 2006).

Above everything else, then, the Plan of Chicago is concerned with our vital problems of congestion, traffic and public health. The plan will do away with congestion in the city and its streets, and so promote the health and happiness of all. It will make traffic easy and convenient, and so make it easier and cheaper to carry on business, thus increasing the wealth of the city and its people faster than will be possible otherwise. The plan will give Chicago more and larger parks and playgrounds, and better and wider streets, and thus make the whole people more healthy and better able to carry on the work of commerce and civilization of our great city.

All over the world today cities are growing as they never did before. Steam and electric transportation have made it easy to transport food for multitudes. Modern manufacturing methods draw large numbers of men together in cities to cheaply produce clothing, machinery and the varied supplies men need in their daily lives throughout the world. No country in the world, however, has given rise so rapidly to large cities as the United States, where it was shown by the census of 1910 that forty out or every one hundred people now reside in cities, and, of these, twelve reside in the three cities of New York, Philadelphia and Chicago.

Wise men who have made a study for years of city growth tell us that this moving of mankind toward the cities is only starting, and that it is sure to continue, probably with a stronger and stronger tide, for many years to come. At the same time other men of science, devoting their lives to a study of the effect of city life upon humanity, declare to us that the physical condition of people in the cities, as compared with the people of the open country, is deteriorating. City life, they say, saps the energy of men, and makes them less efficient in the work of life. The remedy for this, they tell us, lies in providing increased means of open-air recreation, better sanitation in city houses, and more light and air in city streets. The Plan of Chicago provides for complying with this imperative demand. To preserve ourselves and our city by meeting this call for better health conditions is an aim of the Plan of Chicago.

Another appeal for the adoption of the Plan of Chicago is that made to the business instinct of our people. To carry it out means to attract to our city millions of dollars now being spent every year in other cities. When we have created a great attractive city here people will be drawn to it from all over our country, as today people are attracted to Paris. They will visit Chicago with their families and friends and remain indefinitely to enjoy the delights of the city, with vast resultant benefit to all our citizens.

In drawing the Plan of Chicago, the architects constantly kept in mind the needs of the future city in the three great elements of congestion, traffic and public health. They took the city as it has grown up and applied to it the needs of the future in transportation in recreation and in hygiene.

Because we are a commercial people, and live in a great commercial city, first thought was given to transportation. The architects' first care, therefore was to create a proper system of handling the business of Chicago in its streets, and upon its street railways, its steam railroads and its water courses. The greatest part of the plan, then, refers to improving the existing streets, to cutting new ones where necessary, to arranging the city's railway and water terminals most effectively, and to the quick and cheap handling of all the business of Chicago.

This plan of transportation completed, the architects set about a plan of making Chicago more attractive, of providing parks for the people in places where they should be provided, of giving the people recreation grounds both within the city and in the outer district nearby, of improving and beautifying the lake front of the city, and so arranging all things that the future people of Chicago may be strong and healthy, and so ambitious to extend the fame and the commerce of their city.

Finally, in their planning, the architects recognized the need of giving the people of Chicago a way to express in solid form their progressive spirit. The people of Chicago have always been proud of their city, of its importance and its power. The architects strove, therefore to provide a means whereby the civic pride and glory of Chicago could be shown to the world in imposing buildings of architectural grandeur. Thus they provided a civic center upon a vast scale, to be improved with towering buildings serving as the seat of the city government, uniting and giving life to the whole plan of the metropolis, and standing as a notice to the world of the tremendous might and power of a city loved and revered by its millions of devoted and patriotic citizens.

7.3 A SELECTION FROM THE HOUSING ACT OF 1949

Source: Housing Act of 1949 (PL 171, 15 July 1949), 68 *United States Statutes At Large*.

EDITORS' INTRODUCTION

In 1949, Congress passed the Housing Act of 1949, one of the most important laws in the federal government's toolbox for promoting change in urban areas. This act, part of President Harry Truman's Fair Deal, established the idea of urban renewal—that areas considered under-utilized could be razed and set to another purpose. In addition to urban renewal, the Housing Act of 1949 called for the Federal Housing Authority to back mortgages, build more public housing, and extend FHA loan guarantees to rural dwellers.

The Housing Act of 1949 used the terms "blight" and "slums" in reference to places where poor people resided in substandard housing. Much of the housing for the impoverished in urban areas was highly inadequate. As these terms had loose definitions, however, there were instances in which government officials employed them in reference to physically appealing neighborhoods out of political expediency. The question of slums is further confused because of the highly-segregated nature of American cities. High segregation meant that minority group members of all classes tended to reside in a single neighborhood; if such a neighborhood was completely torn down, the homes of doctors, politicians, and other leaders of the community were raised along with the homes of the financially insecure. As this portion of the law states, the federal government encouraged partnerships with private entities, like business, whenever possible. The Housing Act of 1949 and other related housing acts came to be equated with "Negro removal," as so many of the actions targeted African American neighborhoods. In 2005, the U.S. Supreme Court dealt with the Takings Clause of the Fifth Amendment in the case of *Kelo v. City of New London* (Connecticut) and upheld the controversial practice of eminent domain (citing public good) and the use of this property for a private purpose (like building a shopping center). By a vote of 5–4, the court maintained eminent domain yet signaled a growing discomfort with the practice.

AN ACT

To establish a national housing objective and the policy to be followed in the attainment thereof, to provide Federal aid to assist slum-clearance projects and low-rent, public housing projects initiated by local agencies, to provide for financial assistance by the Secretary of Agriculture for farm housing, and for other purposes.

Be it enacted by the Senate and House of Representatives of the United States of America in Congress assembled, That this Act may be cited as the "Housing Act of 1949."

DECLARATION OF NATIONAL HOUSING POLICY

SEC. 2. The Congress hereby declares that the general welfare and security of the Nation and the health and living standards of its people require housing production and related community development sufficient to remedy the serious housing shortage, the elimination of substandard and other inadequate housing through the clearance of slums and blighted areas, and the realization as soon as feasible of the goal of a decent home and a suitable living environment for every American family, thus contributing to the development and redevelopment of communities and to the advancement of the growth, wealth, and security of the Nation. The Congress further declares that such production is necessary to enable the housing industry to make its full contribution toward an economy of maximum employment, production, and purchasing power. The policy to be followed in attaining the national housing objective hereby established shall be: (1) private enterprise shall be encouraged to serve as large a part of the total need as it can; (2) governmental assistance shall be utilized where feasible to enable private enterprise to serve more of the total need; (3) appropriate local public bodies shall be encouraged and assisted to undertake positive programs of encouraging and assisting the development of well-planned, integrated residential neighborhoods, the development and redevelopment of communities, and the production, at lower costs, of housing of sound standards of design, construction, livability, and size for adequate family life; (4) governmental assistance to eliminate substandard and other inadequate housing through the clearance of slums and blighted areas, to facilitate community development and redevelopment, and to provide adequate housing for urban and rural nonfarm families with incomes so low that they are not being decently housed in new or existing housing shall be extended to those localities which estimate their own needs and demonstrate that these needs are not being met through reliance solely upon private enterprise, and without such aid; and (5) governmental assistance for decent, safe, and sanitary farm dwellings and related facilities shall be extended where the farm owner demonstrates that he lacks sufficient resources to provide such housing on his own account and is unable to secure necessary credit for such housing from other sources on terms and conditions which he could reasonably be expected to fulfill. The Housing and Home Finance Agency and its constituent agencies, and any other departments or agencies of the Federal Government having powers, functions, or duties with respect to housing, shall exercise their powers, functions, and duties under this or any other law, consistently with the national housing policy declared by this Act and in such manner as will facilitate sustained progress in attaining the national housing objective hereby established, and in such manner as will encourage and assist (1) the production of housing of sound standards of design, construction, livability, and size for adequate family life; (2) the reduction of the costs of housing without sacrifice of such sound standards; (3) the use of new designs, materials, techniques, and methods in residential construction, the use of standardized dimensions and methods of assembly of home-building materials and equipment, and the increase of efficiency in residential construction and maintenance; (4) the development of well-planned, integrated, residential neighborhoods and the development and redevelopment of communities; and (5) the stabilization of the housing industry at a high annual volume of residential construction.

7.4 SOUTHDALE MALL, EDINA, MINNESOTA (2006)

Toni Randolph

Source: MPR News, October 2006. Accessed at www.mprnews.org/story/2006/10/04/south dale. Reprinted with Permission of Minnesota Public Radio.

EDITORS' INTRODUCTION

Opened in 1956 to great enthusiasm, Victor Gruen's design for an enclosed shopping mall in Edina, Minnesota provided the model for malls that came to anchor suburban communities across the United States in the second half of the twentieth century. Gruen, who was born in Vienna, created an enclosed streetscape encapsulated by a blank outward facing shell and surrounded by vast parking lots. The Sidewalk Café in Southdale even featured unnecessary umbrellas, recreating the experience of eating outside. The mall cost $20 million to construct, and its investors employed 800 workers to complete the project. The 500 acre space initially covered three floors.

Gruen was anti-car, and he envisioned malls like Southdale as set within a larger community center. Yet this dream did not come to pass at the time, and the malls were completely reliant of automobiles and bus lines for their shoppers. Frank Lloyd Wright was quick to criticize Gruen's ersatz downtown.

For those who grew up in or near Edina, Southdale created many memories. Although it was a palace of consumerism, Southdale was the site in which many families spent their free time.

SOUTHDALE MALL, EDINA, MINNESOTA (2006)

When Southdale Center opened Oct. 8, 1956, it was a such a big event that *The New York Times* was among the national news organizations covering the story.

Malls are commonplace now, but in 1956, Southdale was a novelty. Seventy-five-thousand people turned out on opening day to see what would become the model for the modern mall. Southdale featured two department stores – Dayton's and Donaldson's – and about 70 other shops in between. And you could get to all of them without stepping outside.

Two months after the mall opened, Ron Roase's father opened his shoe repair shop in the lower level. Roase says his father already had a shop a mile away, but worried it wouldn't survive.

"He said, 'If I don't go in there, somebody else will and then we'll just get drained out.' He said, 'So I think I want to do it,'" Roase said.

Ralph's Shoe Repair is the only nameplate that remains from Southdale's first year.

Today, Southdale is similar to most other malls, filled with chain clothing stores. Roase says in the early days there was a broader range of offerings.

"We had bakeries, we had a drug store. There were delis; there was a meat market. We also had a flower shop. The bank was here," he said.

Those stores are long gone now. But the mall still stands. And so does the mark it made.

"I would argue that it's the most important mall ever built," said St. Olaf College history professor Jim Farrell, who wrote a book on malls, "One Nation Under Goods." He said Southdale was the prototype for the modern mall.

"Every mall after Southdale in 1956 is just basically a variation on a theme of Southdale because there were lots of problems with malls that Southdale solved and everyone just picked up those kinds of innovations," he said. Those problems, Farrell said, included the weather. Before Southdale, existing shopping centers required people to go outdoors to move between stores.

Surveys at the time showed only one in three days in Minnesota were the sort of days that people wanted to walk outside while shopping.

Farrell says Southdale was also the first introverted mall; that is, one where all of the shops face the inside. That made it easier to navigate.

Famed architect Victor Gruen designed Southdale as a two-story mall. And Farrell said Gruen figured out how to entice people to go to both floors.

"Until Southdale ... people just didn't like to go up and down stairs in a mall. Some of them actually failed because they were two stories," Farrell said. "Gruen designed Southdale so that there was parking at both levels and then escalators in the middle and a lot of vertical sight lines in the central court."

Farrell says that got people to first look up, and then move up to the second floor.

But 50 years later, Southdale faces challenges. The space abandoned by Mervyns nearly two years ago remains empty.

University of St. Thomas retail expert Dave Brennan says Southdale needs to adjust to new competitors, including so-called "lifestyle centers" which feature fancy stores catering to fancy customers.

"Those centers are siphoning off some of the sales potential that was normally captured by some of the regional centers like South-dale," Brennan said.

Southdale is the property of Maryland-based Mills Corp., which planned to revamp the shopping center. But those plans stalled when Mills announced it had serious finan-cial problems and is the subject of an investi-gation by securities regulators.

There's now speculation the mall could go on the sale block for the fourth time in nearly a decade. Mills wouldn't comment.

But analyst Rich Moore with RBC Capital Markets says, even so, the mall's econom-ics remain strong and it has a lot of life left.

"The sad part for Southdale is that some-thing that should be happening, some changes that should be occurring may happen more slowly. But in the long run those changes will still happen," Moore said. "Whatever redevelopment or expansion or new tenants should go in there will eventually go in there on the merits of Southdale, not so much on the merits Mills or Simon or who-ever else might own them."

At 50, the first mall may be middle-aged – or even old, by mall standards – but Moore says Southdale is hardly in its dotage.

7.5 THE USE OF SIDEWALKS: ASSIMILATING CHILDREN

Jane Jacobs

Source: Jane Jacobs, *The Death and Life of Great American Cities* (New York: Random House, 1961).

EDITORS' INTRODUCTION

People who do not live in the city often confuse the energy of the streets with disorder. In this selection, the late Jane Jacobs (1916–2006) tackles one of the most enduring, yet woefully inaccurate of all urban legends; namely, that the streets corrupt and endanger the lives of children who play in them. She uses as her foil the long-standing association between open spaces, especially urban parks, and moral order. Few urban theorists have achieved the stature of Jane Jacobs. Although she received no formal training as a planner, *The Death and Life of Great American Cities* is arguably the most influential book ever writ-ten on the subject. Many of Jacobs' points and her overall common sense approach to planning and appreciation for city life is echoed today in the principles of New Urbanism. **[See Document 7.6, "Charter of the New Urbanism."]** Jacobs was also a noted com-munity activist in her adopted cities of New York and Toronto. In addition to *The Death and Life of Great American Cities*, Jacobs was the author of several other books on urban and economic affairs.

THE USES OF SIDEWALKS: ASSIMILATING CHILDREN (1961)

Among the superstitions of planning and housing is a fantasy about the transform-ation of children. It goes like this: A popu-lation of children is condemned to play on

the city streets. These pale and rickety children, in their sinister moral environ-ment, are telling each other canards about sex, sniggering evilly and learning new forms of corruption as efficiently as if they were in reform school. This situation is called "the moral and physical toll taken of our youth by the streets," sometimes it is called simply "the gutter."

If only these deprived children can be gotten off the streets into parks and playgrounds with equipment on which to exercise, space in which to run, grass to lift their souls! Clean and happy places, filled with the laughter of children responding to a whole-some environment. So much for the fantasy.

Let us consider a story from real life, as discovered by Charles Guggenheim, a documentary-film maker in St. Louis. Guggenheim was working on a film depicting the activities of a St. Louis children's day-care center. He noticed that at the end of the afternoon roughly half the children left with the greatest reluctance.

Guggenheim became sufficiently curious to investigate. Without exception, the children who left unwillingly came from a nearby housing project. And without exception again, those who left willingly came from the old "slum" streets nearby. The mystery, Guggenheim found, was simplicity itself. The children returning to the project, with its generous playgrounds and lawns, ran a gauntlet of bullies who made them turn out their pockets or submit to a beating, sometimes both. These small children could not get home each day without enduring an ordeal that they dreaded. The children going back to the old streets were safe from extortion, Guggenheim found. They had many streets to select from, and they astutely chose the safest. "If anybody picked on them, there was always a store-keeper they could run to or somebody to come to their aid," says Guggenheim. "They also had any number of ways of escaping along different routes if anybody was laying for them. These little kids felt safe and cocky and they enjoyed their trip home too." Guggenheim made the related observation of how boring the project's landscaped grounds and playgrounds were, how deserted they seemed, and in contrast how rich in interest, variety and material for both the camera and the imagination were the older streets nearby. [...]

"Street gangs" do their "street fighting" predominately in parks and playgrounds. When the *New York Times* in September 1959 summed up the worst adolescent gang outbreaks of the past decade in the city, each and every one was designated as having occurred in a park. Moreover, more and more frequently, not only in New York but in other cities too, children engaged in such horrors turn out to be from super-block projects, where their everyday play has successfully been removed from the streets (the streets themselves have largely been removed). The highest delinquency belt in New York's Lower East Side, is precisely the parklike belt of public housing projects. The two most formidable gangs in Brooklyn are rooted in two of the oldest projects. Ralph Whelan, director of the New York City Youth Board, reports, according to the *New York Times*, an "invariable rise in delinquency rates" wherever a new housing project is built. The worst girls' gang in Philadelphia has grown up on the grounds of that city's second-oldest housing project, and the highest delinquency belt of that city corresponds with its major belt of projects. In St. Louis the project where Guggenheim found the extortion going on is considered relatively safe compared with the city's largest project, fifty-seven acres of mostly grass, dotted with playgrounds and devoid of city streets, a prime breeding ground of delinquency in that city. Such projects are examples, among other things, of an intent to take children off the streets. They are designed as they are partly for just this purpose.

The disappointing results are hardly strange. The same rules of city safety and city public life that apply to adults apply to children too, except that children are even more vulnerable to danger and barbarism than adults.

In real life, what significant change *does* occur if children are transferred from a lively city street to the usual park or to the usual public or project playground?

In most cases (not all, fortunately), the most significant change is this: The children have moved from under the eyes of a high numerical ratio of adults, into a place where the ratio of adults is low or even nil. To think this represents an improvement in city child rearing is pure daydreaming.

City children themselves know this; they have known it for generations. "When we wanted to do anything antisocial, we always made for Lindy Park because none of the grownups would see us there," says Jesse Reichek, an artist who grew up in Brooklyn. "Mostly we played on the streets where we couldn't get away with anything much."

Life is the same today. My son, reporting how he escaped four boys who set upon him, says, "I was scared they would catch me when I had to pass the playground. If they caught me *there* I'd be sunk!"

A few days after the murder of two sixteen-year-old boys in a playground on the midtown West Side of Manhattan, I paid a morbid visit to the area. The nearby streets were evidently back to normal. Hundreds of children, directly under the eyes of innumerable adults using the sidewalks themselves and looking from windows, were engaged in a vast variety of sidewalk games and whooping pursuits. The sidewalks were dirty, they were too narrow for the demands put upon them, and they needed shade from the sun. But here was no scene of arson, mayhem or the flourishing of dangerous weapons. In the playground where the nighttime murder had occurred, things were apparently back to normal too. Three small boys were setting a fire under a wooden bench. Another was having his head beaten against the concrete. The custodian was absorbed in solemnly and slowly hauling down the American flag.

On my return home, as I passed the relatively genteel playground near where I live, I noted that its only inhabitants in the late afternoon, with the mothers and the custodian gone, were two small boys threatening to bash a little girl with their skates, and an alcoholic who had roused himself to shake his head and mumble that they shouldn't do that. Farther down the street, on a block with many Puerto Rican immigrants, was another scene of contrast. Twenty-eight children of all ages were playing on the sidewalk without mayhem, arson, or any event more serious than a squabble over a bag of candy. They were under the casual surveillance of adults primarily visiting in public with each other. The surveillance was only seemingly casual, as was proved when the candy squabble broke out and peace and justice were re-established. The identities of the adults kept changing because different ones kept putting their heads out the windows, and different ones kept coming in and going out on errands, or passing by and lingering a little. But the numbers of adults stayed fairly constant—between eight and eleven—during the hour I watched. Arriving home, I noticed that at our end of our block, in front of the tenement, the tailor's, our house, the laundry, the pizza place and the fruit man's, twelve children were playing on the sidewalk in sight of fourteen adults.

To be sure, all city sidewalks are not under surveillance in this fashion, and this is one of the troubles of the city that planning ought properly to help correct. Underused sidewalks are not under suitable surveillance for child rearing. Nor are sidewalks apt to be safe, even with eyes upon them, if they are bordered by a population which is constantly and rapidly turning over in residence—another urgent planning problem. But the playgrounds and parks near such streets are even less wholesome.

Nor are all playgrounds and parks unsafe or under poor surveillance. But those that are wholesome are typically in neighborhoods where streets are lively and safe and where a strong tone of civilized public sidewalk life prevails. Whatever differentials exist in safety and wholesomeness between playgrounds and sidewalks in any given area are invariably, so far as I can find, in the favor of the much maligned streets.

7.6 CHARTER OF THE NEW URBANISM (1996)

Congress for the New Urbanism

Source: Congress for the New Urbanism, www.cnu.org/charter. Copyright 1996, Congress for the New Urbanism.

EDITORS' INTRODUCTION

New Urbanism arose in the early 1990s through the efforts of a small group of architects who drafted a set of principles emphasizing diversity, pluralism, and environmentally friendly design in local and regional planning. These architects formally incorporated as the nonprofit group Congress for the New Urbanism (CNU) and held their first meeting in 1993. At their fourth annual gathering in 1996, the organization ratified the Charter of the New Urbanism with twenty-seven principles to guide public policymakers, planners, architects, and others committed to reducing automobile sprawl and the inefficient use of space by building more viable and sustainable communities.

CHARTER FOR THE NEW URBANISM (1996)

The Congress for the New Urbanism views disinvestment in central cities, the spread of placeless sprawl, increasing separation by race and income, environmental deterioration, loss of agricultural lands and wilderness, and the erosion of society's built heritage as one interrelated community-building challenge.

We stand for the restoration of existing urban centers and towns within coherent metropolitan regions, the reconfiguration of sprawling suburbs into communities of real neighborhoods and diverse districts, the conservation of natural environments, and the preservation of our built legacy.

We recognize that physical solutions by themselves will not solve social and economic problems, but neither can economic vitality, community stability, and environmental health be sustained without a coherent and supportive physical framework.

We advocate the restructuring of public policy and development practices to support the following principles: neighborhoods should be diverse in use and population; communities should be designed for the pedestrian and transit as well as the car; cities and towns should be shaped by physically defined and universally accessible public spaces and community institutions; urban places should be framed by architecture and landscape design that celebrate local history, climate, ecology, and building practice.

We represent a broad-based citizenry, composed of public and private sector leaders, community activists, and multidisciplinary professionals. We are committed to reestablishing the relationship between the art of building and the making of community, through citizen-based participatory planning and design.

We dedicate ourselves to reclaiming our homes, blocks, streets, parks, neighborhoods, districts, towns, cities, regions, and environment.

We assert the following principles to guide public policy, development practice, urban planning, and design:

The Region: Metropolis, City, and Town

1. Metropolitan regions are finite places with geographic boundaries derived from topography, watersheds, coastlines, farmlands, regional parks, and river basins. The metropolis is made of multiple centers that are cities, towns, and villages, each with its own identifiable center and edges.

2. The metropolitan region is a fundamental economic unit of the contemporary world. Governmental cooperation, public policy, physical planning, and economic strategies must reflect this new reality.

3. The metropolis has a necessary and fragile relationship to its agrarian hinterland and natural landscapes. The relationship is environmental, economic, and cultural. Farmland and nature are as important to the metropolis as the garden is to the house.

4. Development patterns should not blur or eradicate the edges of the metropolis. Infill development within existing urban areas conserves environmental resources, economic investment, and social fabric, while reclaiming marginal and abandoned areas. Metropolitan regions should develop strategies to encourage such infill development over peripheral expansion.

5. Where appropriate, new development contiguous to urban boundaries should be organized as neighborhoods and districts, and be integrated with the existing urban pattern. Noncontiguous development should be organized as towns and villages with their own urban edges, and planned for a jobs/housing balance, not as bedroom suburbs.

6. The development and redevelopment of towns and cities should respect historical patterns, precedents, and boundaries.

7. Cities and towns should bring into proximity a broad spectrum of public and private uses to support a regional economy that benefits people of all incomes. Affordable housing should be distributed throughout the region to match job opportunities and to avoid concentrations of poverty.

8. The physical organization of the region should be supported by a framework of transportation alternatives. Transit, pedestrian, and bicycle systems should maximize access and mobility throughout the region while reducing dependence upon the automobile.

9. Revenues and resources can be shared more cooperatively among the municipalities and centers within regions to avoid destructive competition for tax base and to promote rational coordination of transportation, recreation, public services, housing, and community institutions.

The Neighborhood, the District, and the Corridor

1. The neighborhood, the district, and the corridor are the essential elements of development and redevelopment in the metropolis. They form identifiable areas that encourage citizens to take responsibility for their maintenance and evolution.

2. Neighborhoods should be compact, pedestrian-friendly, and mixed-use. Districts generally emphasize a special single use, and should follow the principles of neighborhood design when possible. Corridors are regional connectors of neighborhoods and districts; they range from boulevards and rail lines to rivers and parkways.

3. Many activities of daily living should occur within walking distance, allowing independence to those who do not drive, especially the elderly and the young. Interconnected networks of streets should be designed to encourage walking, reduce the number and length of automobile trips, and conserve energy.

4. Within neighborhoods, a broad range of housing types and price levels can bring people of diverse ages, races, and incomes into daily interaction, strengthening the personal and civic bonds essential to an authentic community.

5. Transit corridors, when properly planned and coordinated, can help organize metropolitan structure and revitalize urban centers. In contrast, highway corridors should not displace investment from existing centers.

6. Appropriate building densities and land uses should be within walking distance of transit stops, permitting public transit to become a viable alternative to the automobile.

7. Concentrations of civic, institutional, and commercial activity should be

embedded in neighborhoods and districts, not isolated in remote, single-use complexes. Schools should be sized and located to enable children to walk or bicycle to them.

8. The economic health and harmonious evolution of neighborhoods, districts, and corridors can be improved through graphic urban design codes that serve as predictable guides for change.

9. A range of parks, from tot-lots and village greens to ballfields and community gardens, should be distributed within neighborhoods. Conservation areas and open lands should be used to define and connect different neighborhoods and districts.

The Block, the Street, and the Building

1. A primary task of all urban architecture and landscape design is the physical definition of streets and public spaces as places of shared use.

2. Individual architectural projects should be seamlessly linked to their surroundings. This issue transcends style.

3. The revitalization of urban places depends on safety and security. The design of streets and buildings should reinforce safe environments, but not at the expense of accessibility and openness.

4. In the contemporary metropolis, development must adequately accommodate automobiles. It should do so in ways that respect the pedestrian and the form of public space.

5. Streets and squares should be safe, comfortable, and interesting to the pedestrian. Properly configured, they encourage walking and enable neighbors to know each other and protect their communities.

6. Architecture and landscape design should grow from local climate, topography, history, and building practice.

7. Civic buildings and public gathering places require important sites to reinforce community identity and the culture of democracy. They deserve distinctive form, because their role is different from that of other buildings and places that constitute the fabric of the city.

8. All buildings should provide their inhabitants with a clear sense of location, weather and time. Natural methods of heating and cooling can be more resource-efficient than mechanical systems.

9. Preservation and renewal of historic buildings, districts, and landscapes affirm the continuity and evolution of urban society.

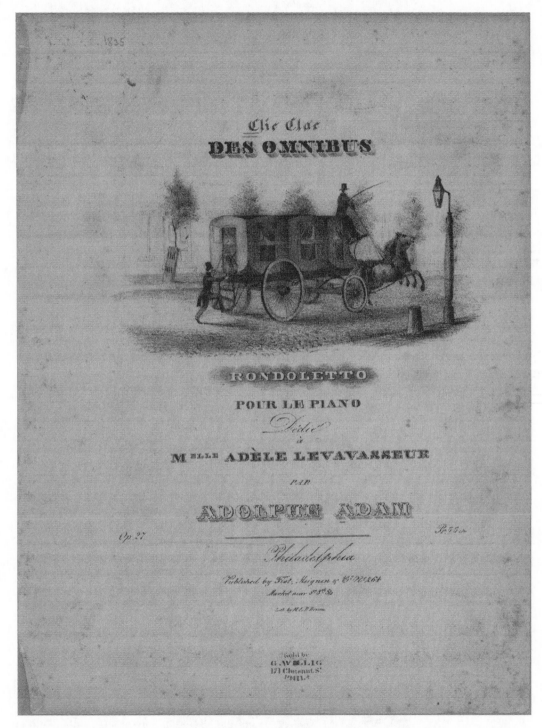

Illustration VII.1 "Clic-Clac Des Omnibus." Street Scene on Sheet Music, 1835. Courtesy of the Center for Historic American Visual Culture at the American Antiquarian Society.

Illustration VII.2 "Whitehall, South, and Staten Island Ferries and Revenue Barge Office, New York." c. 1850s–1860s. Courtesy of the Center for Historic American Visual Culture at the American Antiquarian Society.

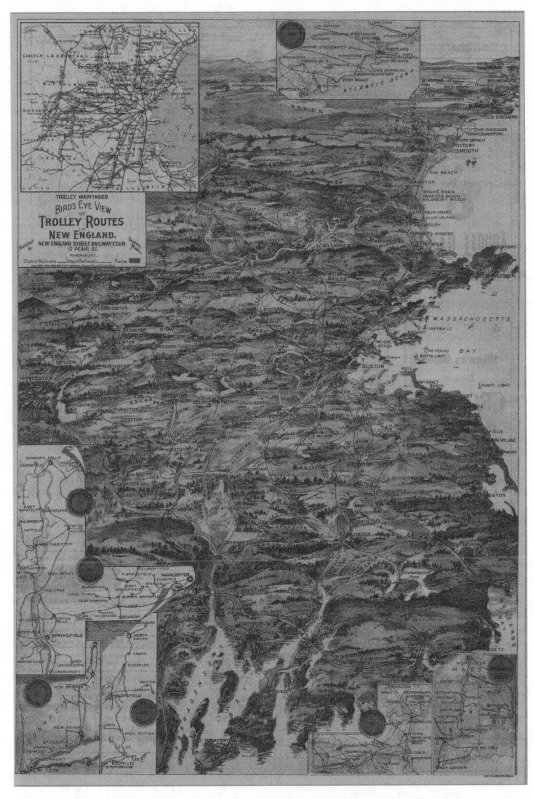

Illustration VII.3 Trolley Wayfinder, "Bird's Eye View of Trolley Routes in New England," New England Street Railway Club, 1907. Courtesy of the Center for Historic American Visual Culture at the American Antiquarian Society.

Illustration VII.4 Horsecar, New York City, 1908. Library of Congress, Prints and Photographs Division.

Illustration VII.5 Norfolk, Virginia, Granby Street, c. 1915. Library of Congress, Prints and Photographs Division.

Illustration VII.6 Cable Car, Hyde Street Hill, San Francisco, c. 1970s. Library of Congress, Prints and Photographs Division.

Creeping Sickness

A MODERN MUNICIPAL MALADY DEMANDING BOTH PREVENTION AND CURE

Illustration VII.7 Creeping Sickness. *American City*. April 1929.

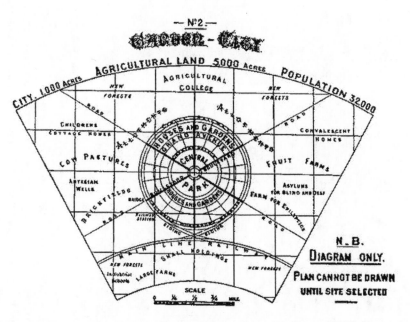

Illustration VII.8 Ebenezer Howard, Garden-City Diagram, *Garden Cities of To-Morrow* (1902). Source: London: Swan Sonnenschein & Company, 1902.

English-born Ebenezer Howard (1850–1928) created a powerful legacy with his idea of mixing open pastoral spaces with urban living in his plan for what he termed "garden cities." Howard, deeply influenced by the ideas of Edward Bellamy's 1888 novel *Looking Backward*, penned his visionary ideas for a new city with *Garden Cities of To-Morrow*, originally published as *To-morrow: A Peaceful Path to Real Reform* (1898), and founded the Garden Cities Association in 1899. Howard's publication brought his ideas to the general public and two garden cities, Letchworth Garden City and Welwyn Garden City, were built in the United Kingdom during his lifetime. Other communities and measures that drew upon his ideas are Radburn, New Jersey, the 1930s greenbelt towns in the United States, England's New Town's Act of 1946, and the open land movements in modern America. Critics of these planned communities point out that they draw people and resources away from nearby traditional urban centers. Although designed to be self-contained urban villages, they often become bedroom communities of major metropolitan areas and serve to intensify urban sprawl. New Urbanists, who tout projects within existing cities (often referred to as "infill projects"), are in fact similarly criticized for the high number of New Urbanist developments built on remote "greenfields."

Illustration VII.9 "A Perspective View of Part of the Model Town of Radburn, New Jersey." Source: *Neighborhood and Community Planning, Regional Plan of New York and Its Environs, Volume VII* (New York, Regional Plan of New York and Its Environs, 1929).

Radburn, New Jersey was one of several model communities built in the New York metropolitan region in the early twentieth century. Conceived along the lines of "Garden City" principles in the 1920s by associates of the New York based City Housing Corporation, Radburn was designed to be the archetype industrial town that served the needs of the motor age. The founders of Radburn sought to create a new type of city by purchasing an open area of land, attracting manufactures to the site, and erecting spacious and healthy homes for workers. Given the high cost of land near New York City—Radburn is just thirteen miles from Columbus Square in Manhattan and much closer to Paterson and Passaic, New Jersey—the concept of an open belt of land surrounding the original Garden City was abandoned and instead, as indicated in this perspective illustration, a series of smaller parks and playgrounds were mixed in with through streets and short dead-end streets that resembled cul-de-sacs.

Illustration VII.10 Celebration, Florida, 2008. Source: Photograph by Lisa Krissoff Boehm.

Illustration VII.11 The New York Highline, 2017. Source: Photograph by Lisa Krissoff Boehm.

PART VIII

URBAN MIGRATIONS, RACE, AND SOCIAL MOBILITY

EDITORS' INTRODUCTION TO PART VIII

There are four general ways in which a city can increase in population: (1) natural increase through higher numbers of births than deaths; (2) migration of people from the country-side, towns, and other cities into the city in question; (3) immigration from foreign nations; and (4) annexation of surrounding territories. Biological increase is well understood, and the annexation of population through political restructuring and the redrawing of maps, while an interesting aspect of urban history, does not of course bring any new people into the region. Immigration, a process vital to the understanding of cities and an integral part of the American mythology, was discussed in earlier parts of this reader. Migration, the study of the flow of people from within the national borders into a city, has extensively transformed cities, yet is under-acknowledged.

Migration proves to be a confusing term, because scholars apply it in a variety of ways. Defining migration as a movement of people within national borders keeps the term straightforward enough to be meaningful. Yet others have used the term migration to refer to the act of emigration (leaving one's country of origin) or immigration (entering into a new country), complicating the word's usage. In urban studies and urban history, migration most often refers to intra-national movements, unless the context is clear. Referring to migration as regional migration might help clarify its meaning. Scholars recognize the major migration or migrations of African Americans out of the South and to the West and North during the twentieth century. The movement of blacks began right after Emancipation, but gathered momentum around the time the First World War broke out in Europe. Historians differ on where to put the emphasis: some highlight the importance of migration within the South[i]; others focus on the movement westward; and others look at the people moving north. Those relocating from rural locations in the South often lived temporarily in a southern city before heading on to other regions. Some scholars note that some of those moving north settled in rural areas or small cities. But the millions moving into major cities played a highly influential role in redefining American culture and transforming the political landscape of the century. The migration north is often, but not always, divided into two major movements divided by the Great Depression, a period in which migration slowed. As with any social movement, the dates of the migration are approximate. Scholars date the First Great Migration, the movement of close to 1.5 million from the South to the North, as approximately 1914–1930, with some using 1916 as a starting date. The Second Great Migration, a movement of approximately 5 million people, is normally defined as occurring between 1940–1960 or 1940–1970.

This part opens with a piece taken from Arnold R. Hirsch's blockbuster work, *Making the Second Ghetto: Race and Housing in Chicago* (Chicago: University of Chicago Press,

1998; first published in 1983 by Columbia University Press). Hirsch offers a multi-faceted study of the Second Great Migration, when hundreds of thousands of African Americans came to Chicago. Once in Chicago, blacks were forced by convention and law into tightly restricted neighborhoods on the South Side and, ultimately, on the West Side of the city. Even with expanded boundaries, the black belt could not adequately accommodate all the migrants, who made their homes in highly inadequate spaces. Many lived in one room kitchenette apartments with extended family members; the very desperate carved out spaces in tenement basements and subdivided the rooms with highly flammable materials like cardboard. Because of the city's decision to keep housing segregated, even in the face of increased numbers of African Americans, Chicago created a new ghetto on top of its old one, a place that became associated with rampant poverty, political corruption, and crime. The influence of Hirsch's arguments cannot be overstated; all those studying race in modern urban America have been influenced by this important work.

When scholars study watershed historical movements, they often do not pause to consider the movement as a gendered experience. With the growing strength of the sub-field of women's history, the time has come to examine migration from the perspective of women. As migration within the United States and immigration to the United States have so often been fueled by employment opportunities, men's concerns have figured centrally in studies of the movements. This is beginning to change. Following in the steps of immigrant historians Hasia Diner, Elizabeth Ewing, and Donna Gabbacia, Suellen Hoy makes a persuasive argument in her work, *Good Hearts: Catholic Sisters in Chicago's Past* (Urbana: University of Illinois Press, 2006), of the significance of Irish nuns to the story of Irish immigration to the United States. In a similar fashion, urban historian Lisa Krissoff Boehm reconceptualizes African American migration by placing women front and center in the story. Krissoff Boehm's book, *Making a Way out of No Way: African American Women and the Second Great Migration* (Jackson: University Press of Mississippi, 2009), demonstrates the power of oral histories in broadening historical understanding. Archival resources on the Second Great Migration (1940–1970) are slim, especially in terms of women migrants. Luckily, Krissoff Boehm had the opportunity to collect oral histories with the migrants themselves, and add their voices to the historical record. The oral histories collected for this study are archived at the Schlesinger Library for the History of Women in America at Harvard University and the Grand Rapids Public Library.

Concurrent with the movement of millions of African Americans to the North, but less often documented in historical literature, was the migration of southern whites. This migration often surpassed—in terms of numbers—the migration of southern blacks. Yet the southern whites are more difficult to track, and proved more willing to relocate back to the South. Southern migrants faced ridicule in their new homes based on cultural stereotypes, yet they had an easier time than blacks at assimilating after a few generations. Southern whites bequeathed their own cultural legacy to their new region, for instance in the flowering of a new, commercially-appealing popular music with rural roots. In Chad Berry's influential *Northern Migrants and Southern Exiles* (Urbana: University of Illinois, 2000), we again see oral history put to good use for shedding light on a modern historical phenomenon. We also see how urban history and labor history are difficult to disentangle. Berry's work provides us with a new framework of understanding of the social history of midwestern cities in the mid- and late-twentieth century.

Migration complicated the racial interactions in major American cities. In the twentieth century, it has become important to study urban California. The transcontinental railroad, migration, and immigration changed the nature of the state. By 1920 it had almost 3.5 million inhabitants. California continued to contain a high percentage of the American population throughout the twentieth century, and due in part to the film industry, set cultural trends followed by the rest of the country. Robert O. Self's important work, *American Babylon: Race and the Struggle for Postwar Oakland* (Princeton, NJ: Princeton

University Press, 2003), provides a model for excellent urban history in the manner of Arnold R. Hirsch. Digging into the power structures and urban geography, we can see how the promising "urban garden" of Oakland could not live up to the hopes imbedded within the postwar liberalism of its founders. This liberalism loses proponents as the twentieth century ages. Perhaps paradoxically, the Black Power movement grew up in Oakland, as did a white conservatism that eschews taxation. Moving southward within California, Emily E. Straus examines the way in which the changing racial profile of Compton, California effected the role the public school played in the community. Using the story of Compton, we can better understand how differing rates of taxation exacerbates class distinctions, because the uneven quality of area schools and other services creates lingering effects on the pooulation.

All major cities, not just those of the North and West, proved popular destinations for migrants. Southern cities were increasingly popular places to relocate in the second half of the twentieth century. The inflow of migrants was joined by new immigrants to urban areas, particularly after the legal changes of 1965, which eased immigration restrictions. Asian and Asian Indian immigrants came in increased numbers to American cities, along with additional settlers from such places as the Middle East, Eastern Europe, and Central and South America. Debates about bi-lingual education and assimilation raged as they had in the early twentieth century.

The first document in this part reflects the tensions stemming from the growing social diversity of cities in the twentieth century. During the Second World War, white servicemen in California targeted and attacked Hispanic youth who wore eye-catching zoot suits. Migrants and immigrants bravely moved to unknown locations seeking better economic and social opportunities. Alverrine Parker details the reasons she fled the South in her oral history, featured here. In Sloan Wilson's blockbuster novel, *The Man in the Gray Flannel Suit*, we see an East Coast version of the middle class white neighborhoods that form the white noose detailed by Robert O. Self. And in Harriette Arnow's bestselling novel, *The Dollmaker* (1954), Gertie Nevels leaves Kentucky for the industrial city of Detroit, but finds the new setting impersonal and unappealing.

NOTE

i. See Bernadette Pruitt, "For the Advancement of the Race: African-American Migration to Houston, 1914–1941," *Journal of Urban History* vol. 31, no 4 (May 2005): 435–78.

ESSAY 8.1

The Second Ghetto and the Dynamics of Neighborhood

Arnold R. Hirsch

Source: Arnold R. Hirsch, *Making the Second Ghetto: Race and Housing in Chicago, 1940–1960* (Chicago: University of Chicago Press, 1998; first published in 1983 by Columbia University Press).

EDITORS' INTRODUCTION

Chicago was a major destination for the First and Second Great Migrations, the historic flow of African Americans from the South to the urban North launched by the pull of industrial work during the world wars. The First Great Migration (approximately 1914–1930) is generally thought to have numbered about 1.5 million, and the Second (approximately 1940–1970), approximately 5 million people. Yet these numbers are difficult to gauge, as some migrants came in and out of the city repeatedly and many migrants left little historical evidence in their wake. African Americans also migrated before and after these major waves. While it is important to understand this movement as transformative in a variety of ways (including economically, politically, socially, and culturally) to major cities, some migrants also settled in small towns and rural areas. By 1920, at least 110,000 blacks had settled in Chicago. The U.S. Census concluded there were 812,637 African Americans in Chicago in 1960, making up over 22 percent of the population.[i] As we will see later in this part, the black migration occurred contemporaneously with a sizable white migration, a movement that most likely exceeded the black migration. **[See Essay 8.3, Chad Berry, "The Great White Migration, 1945–1960."]** Historian James N. Gregory writes that "More than 28 million southerners left their home region during the course of the twentieth century."[ii] Although black women were largely restricted from war work—even during these times of national crisis—the world wars provided black men with an unprecedented opportunity to find industrial employment, albeit often in the most dangerous and distasteful aspects of industry. This expanded opportunity ultimately helped to bring many African American migrants into the middle class. But others found themselves stuck in newly reinforced ghettoes in northern cities. As Hirsch emphasizes, black settlers of longer duration had already lived in Chicago ghettoes; Hirsch chronicles the establishment of Chicago's startlingly narrow (three miles long by only a quarter mile wide) ghetto between 1890 and 1930. The ghetto, rather than being dismantled, was *reinforced* during the dawn of the Second Great Migration. Although the black population of Chicago grew, and the boundaries of the black belt expanded due to the pressures of this growing population, black isolation intensified, with the majority of African Americans living in almost completely black neighborhoods.

i Arnold Hirsch, *Making the Second Ghetto: Race and Housing in Chicago, 1940–1960* (Chicago: University of Chicago Press, 1998), 3 and 17.

ii James N. Gregory, *The Southern Diaspora: How the Great Migrations of Black and White Southerners Transformed America* (Chapel Hill: University of North Carolina Press), 19.

Chicago's highly segregated neighborhoods were not created by accident. Public policy dictated that blacks could not buy or rent homes in most Chicago neighborhoods, and where any doubt remained, the organizational practices of realtors' professional associations and pressures by institutions assured that neighborhoods would not be integrated. Public housing projects adhered to the "neighborhood composition rule" promulgated by Chicagoan Harold Ickes, head of the housing division of the New Deal creation, the Public Works Administration. Only with the Supreme Court decision *Shelley v. Kraemer* of 1948, which upended the use of restrictive covenants, and the Fair Housing Act of 1968, would the well-fortified palisades of segregation begin to crack. Hirsch explains, "The ghetto was to be reinforced with taxpayers' dollars and shored up with the power of the state."[iii]

As Hirsch explores, the renewed efforts at segregation in response to the increased flow of African Americans to the North during the Second World War ultimately created an untenable situation in Chicago, leading to the establishment of a city within a city, with redundant businesses and services and an increasingly powerful black political leadership. The area became associated with intense poverty, and the highly controversial term, "underclass," assigned to families who seemed mired in poverty generation after generation. Contemporaneous observers began to assign some of the causation for this deep poverty to the culture of the southern migrants, although recent studies like the quantitative work of sociologist Stewart Tolnay now offers evidence to refute these accusations.[iv] We can clearly see, however, how the pressures of a large flow of migrants into a highly restricted space encouraged devastating housing conditions within the black belt and great tension with the bordering white neighborhoods, which often ignited violence.

Hirsch's work follows on an earlier generation of historiographical works on the ghettoization of American blacks in northern cities, such as the influential work of Allen H. Spear.[v] Hirsch's work intrigued urban scholars for its analysis of public policy's role in creating what Hirsch terms a "Frankenstein's monster," a highly regrettable artifact of incorrect assumptions and a host of prejudices. Postwar urban development, in an attempt at "urban renewal," created deep segregation, generations of poverty, and nearly impenetrable physical divides within the city.[vi]

Arnold R. Hirsch was the Ethel and Herman L. Midlo Professor for New Orleans Studies and University Research Professor in the department of history at the University of New Orleans. Hirsch wrote articles on a variety of urban topics and served as the co-editor and contributor to *Creole New Orleans: Race and Americanization* (Baton Rouge: Louisiana State University Press, 1992) and *Urban Policy in Twentieth-Century America* (New Brunswick, NJ: Rutgers University Press, 1993).

THE SECOND GHETTO AND THE DYNAMICS OF NEIGHBORHOOD (1983, 1999)

I have walked the South Side Streets
(Thirty-first to Sixty-ninth) from State to

Cottage Grove in the last 35 days searching for a flat.

Anonymous to the *Chicago Defender*,
November 28, 1942

---

iii Hirsch, *Making of the Second Ghetto*, 9–10. **[See Essay 9.1, Thomas J. Sugrue, "Class, Status, and Residence: the Changing Geography of Black Detroit."]**

iv Stewart E. Tolnay, "The Great Migration and Changes in the Northern Black Family, 1940–1990," *Social Forces* 75 (June 1997): 1213–1238.

v See Allen H. Spear, *Black Chicago: The Making of a Negro Ghetto, 1890–1920* (Chicago: University of Chicago Press, 1967) and St. Clair Drake, Horace Roscoe Cayton and Richard Wright, *Black Metropolis: A Study of Negro Life in a Northern City* (New York: Harcourt, Brace, and Company, 1945).

vi For an extended analysis of the impact of Hirsch's work, see a group of essays in the *Journal of Urban History* (March 2003).

Something is happening to lives and spirits that will never show up in the great housing shortage of the late '40s. Something is happening to the children which might not show up in our social records until 1970.

Chicago Sun-Times, undated clipping,
Chicago Urban League Papers,
Manuscript Collection,
The Library, University of
Illinois at Chicago

The race riot that devastated Chicago following the drowning of Eugene Williams on Sunday, July 27, 1919, was notable for its numerous brutal confrontations between white and black civilians. White hoodlums sped through the narrow sliver of land that was the Black Belt, firing their weapons as they rode, wreaking havoc and killing at least one person.[1] Nor was that all. Aside from the many assaults and casualties taken in the Stock Yards district immediately west of the Black Belt, serious clashes occurred in the Loop and around the Angelus building, a rooming house that remained the abode of white workers in the predominantly black area around Wabash Avenue and 35th Street. Blacks retaliated by attacking whites unfortunate enough to be caught on their "turf."[2] By the time the riot ended, 38 persons – 23 blacks and 15 whites – lay dead and 537 were injured.[3]

In early April 1968, following the assassination of Dr. Martin Luther King, Jr., Chicago was again the scene of serious violence. Although labeled a "race riot," the events of 1968 differed sharply from those of 1919. Instead of an interracial war carried on by black and white citizens, the "King riot," largely an expression of outrage by the city's black community, was characterized by the destruction of property. The deaths that did occur during the riots (there were nine) resulted primarily from confrontations between black civilians and the police or National Guard.[4]

There were other significant differences as well. The worst rioting in 1968 occurred on the West Side. Merely a minor black enclave in 1919, by the time of Dr. King's assassination Chicago's West Side housed more than twice the number of blacks resident in the entire city during the earlier riot. A vast ghetto of relatively recent origin, the West Side thus established itself as a scene of racial tension to rival the older, and larger, South Side Black Belt. Moreover, the Loop, where blacks were viciously hunted in 1919, was now subjected to roving groups of black youths who had walked out of nearby inner-city high schools. This time, however, harassment of pedestrians and petty vandalism replaced the deadly violence of the earlier era. Confrontations such as the one around the Angelus building were impossible in the more rigidly segregated city of the 1960s, and white injuries, reportedly few in number, generally occurred as motorists were unluckily trapped in riot areas. There were no armed forays into "enemy" territory. In sum, clashes between black and white Chicagoans (other than the police) were infrequent, fortuitous, and not lethal. The prevailing image of the 1968 disorder was evoked not by mass murder but by the flames that enveloped stores along a 2-mile stretch of Madison Street and those that engulfed similar structures along Western, Kedzie, and Pulaski avenues.[5]

The close relationship between the growth of the modern black metropolis and the changing pattern of racial disorder is clear. After an era of tremendous ghetto expansion and increasing racial isolation, "communal" riots on the scale of those that shook the nation in 1919 became impossible. The thought of white mobs attacking the black ghettos of the 1960s boggles the imagination. Additionally, the large concentration of blacks in the inner city rendered exceedingly unlikely the stalking and killing of individual blacks on downtown streets. The burning and looting of primarily white-owned property in massive black ghettos was the most visible manifestation of racial tension permitted in the modern city. Able to quarantine black neighborhoods, police were much less able to control actions taken within them. The eruption of the "commodity" riots of the 1960s heralded the existence, in Chicago at least, of that city's "second ghetto."[6]

The reasons for making a distinction between the "first ghetto" of the World War I era and the "second ghetto" of the post-World War II period are quantitative, temporal, and qualitative. As Morris Janowitz noted in his analysis of racial disorders in the twentieth century, the "commodity" riots of the 1960s took place in black communities that had grown enormously in both size and population.[7] Ten times as many blacks lived in Chicago in 1966 as in 1920. Representing but 4% of the city's population in the latter year, blacks accounted for nearly 30% of all Chicagoans by the mid-1960s. The evolution of the West Side black colony, from enclave to ghetto, was a post-World War II development. And the South Side Black Belt's expansion between 1945 and 1960 was so pronounced that its major business artery shifted a full 2 miles to the south, from 47th Street to 63rd.[8]

There is a chronological justification for referring to Chicago's "second ghetto" as well. The period of rapid growth following World War II was the second such period in the city's history. The first, coinciding with the Great Migration of southern blacks, encompassed the years between 1890 and 1930. Before 1900, the earliest identifiable black colony existed west of State Street and south of Harrison; an 1874 fire destroyed much of this section and resulted in the settlement's reestablishment between 22nd and 31st streets. By the turn of the century, this nucleus had merged with other colonies to form the South Side Black Belt. Where, according to Thomas Philpott's meticulously researched *The Slum and the Ghetto,* "no large, solidly Negro concentration existed" in Chicago until the 1890s, by 1900 the black population suffered an "extraordinary" degree of segregation and their residential confinement was "nearly complete." Almost 3 miles long, but barely a quarter mile wide, Chicago's South Side ghetto – neatly circumscribed on all sides by railroad tracks – had come into being.[9]

By 1920 the Black Belt extended roughly to 55th Street, between Wentworth and Cottage Grove avenues. Approximately 85% of the city's nearly 110,000 blacks lived in this area. A second colony existed on the West Side between Austin, Washington Boulevard, California Avenue, and Morgan Street. More than 8,000 blacks, including some "scattered residents as far south as Twelfth Street," lived here. Other minor black enclaves included the area around Ogden Park in Englewood, Morgan Park on the far South Side, separate settlements in Woodlawn and Hyde Park, and a growing community on the near North Side. Between 1910 and 1920 three additional colonies appeared in Lilydale (around 91st and State streets), near the South Chicago steel mills, and immediately east of Oakwood Cemetery between 67th and 71st streets.[10]

Ten years later it was possible to speak of an almost "solidly" black area from 22nd to 63rd streets, between Wentworth and Cottage Grove. Whole neighborhoods were now black where, according to Philpott, "only some buildings and some streets and blocks had been black earlier." By 1930 even such gross measuring devices as census tracts documented a rigidly segregated ghetto. In 1920 there were no tracts that were even 90% black; the next census revealed that two-thirds of all black Chicagoans lived in such areas and 19% lived in "exclusively" (97.5% or more) black tracts. The West Side colony grew as well. Although it expanded only two blocks southward to Madison Street, it went from only 45% black to nearly all black in the same period; and a new colony appeared in an area previously occupied by Jews near Maxwell Street. By the time of the Depression, Black Chicago encompassed five times the territory it had occupied in 1900. Its borders were sharp and clear, it had reached maturity, and all future growth would spring from this base.[11]

The Depression, however, marked a relaxation in the pace of racial transition, in the growth of Chicago's Black Belt. Black migration to the Windy City decreased dramatically, thus relieving the pressure placed on increasingly crowded Black Belt borders. The period of the 1930s, consequently, was an era of territorial consolidation for Chicago's blacks. Over three-quarters of them lived in areas that were more than 90% black by 1940, and almost half lived in areas that were more than 98% black. On the eve of World War II, Chicago's black population was, according to sociologist David Wallace, "very close to being as concentrated as it could get."[12]

This meant that the 1930s and early 1940s produced only slight territorial additions to the Black Belt (such as the opening of the Washington Park Subdivision). Such stability provoked few black–white clashes, and a similar calm prevailed in the border areas surrounding the other enclaves. The colony in Englewood saw whites replace the few scattered blacks on its periphery, whereas its core around Ogden Park became increasingly black. The Morgan Park community grew in both numbers and area, but its population became virtually all black, and its expansion was accomplished through new construction on vacant land rather than the "invasion" of white territory. The Lilydale enclave followed the same pattern. The South Chicago and Oakwood settlements likewise grew in numbers but actually decreased in size as they became more solidly black.[13] By 1940, St. Clair Drake and Horace R. Cayton were able to assert that the Black Belt "had virtually ceased to expand."[14]

The two decades between 1940 and 1960, and especially the fifteen years following the conclusion of World War II witnessed the renewal of massive black migration to Chicago and the overflowing of black population from established areas of residence grown too small, too old, and too decayed to hold old settlers and newcomers alike. It was during the 1940s and 1950s that the Black Belt's boundaries, drawn during the Great Migration, were shattered. To the east, the Cottage Grove Avenue barrier – which had been buttressed by the activity of local improvement associations after the 1919 riot – fell as blacks entered the communities of Oakland, Kenwood, Hyde Park, and Woodlawn in large numbers. To the south and southwest, Park Manor and Englewood also witnessed the crumbling of what were, by 1945, traditional borders. On the West Side, the

exodus of Jews from North Lawndale created a vacuum that was quickly filled by a housing-starved black population. The first new black settlement since the 1920s, the North Lawndale colony was the largest of several new black communities created in the post-World War II period.[15]

Every statistical measure confirmed that racial barriers that had been "successfully defended for a generation," in Allan Spear's words, were being overrun after World War II. The number of technically "mixed" census tracts increased from 135 to 204 between 1940 and 1950. The proportion of "non-Negroes" living in exclusively "non-Negro" tracts declined from 91.2% in 1940 to 84.1% in 1950, reversing a twenty-year trend. Moreover, of the city's 935 census tracts, only 160 were without a single nonwhite resident in 1950; there were 350 such tracts just ten years earlier. Such startling figures prompted the Chicago Commission on Human Relations to hail them as signifying a reversal of the city's march toward complete segregation. Their conclusion, however, was hastily drawn.[16]

The census figures for 1950 revealed not a city undergoing desegregation but one in the process of redefining racial borders after a period of relative stability. Black isolation was, in fact, increasing even as the Black Belt grew. Nearly 53% of the city's blacks lived in exclusively black census tracts in 1950 compared with only 49.7% in 1940; more people moved into the Black Belt than were permitted to leave it. As overcrowded areas became more overcrowded, the pressure of sheer numbers forced some blacks into previously all-white areas. Thus, whereas blacks were becoming more isolated from the white population generally, a large number of whites found themselves living in technically "mixed" areas. Segregation was not ending. It had merely become time to work out a new geographical accommodation between the races.[17]

If, however, the territorial arrangement forged by the end of the 1920s needed revision, the postwar era provided, theoretically at least, an opportunity for dismantling, instead of expanding, the ghetto. That such a possibility existed has been obscured by the dreadful air of inevitability that permeated the ghetto studies produced in the 1960s and that sped analysis from the Stock Yards to Watts.[18] Such telescopic vision blurred what occurred in between, placed an unfair measure of responsibility on those living in the World War I period for what later transpired, and provided absolution through neglect for those who came later. Indeed, the real tragedy surrounding the emergence of the modern ghetto is not that it has been inherited but that it has been periodically renewed and strengthened. Fresh decisions, not the mere acquiescence to old ones, reinforced and shaped the contemporary black metropolis.

Certainly close observers of the housing situation in the years following World War II saw nothing inevitable about the continued expansion of preexisting ghetto areas. Robert C. Weaver, a member of the Mayor's Committee on Race Relations and later the first secretary of the Department of Housing and Urban Development, emphasized the malleability of the future in *The Negro Ghetto,* the most significant contemporary survey of the problem. Viewing the increased involvement of government on all levels in urban affairs, he expressed with some trepidation the notion that postwar redevelopment could be either a "threat or an opportunity." "Provision of more space for minorities is the most immediate need," Weaver wrote, "and it will be accelerated by a sound national housing program which insists upon widespread participation by all elements in the population." "But it is extremely important," he warned, "that we avoid the creation of additional ghettos."[19] Weaver's sense of uncertainty and opportunity were genuine. The 1960s fires, which illuminated the past as well as the present (and thus facilitated the use of hindsight), should not be permitted to obscure the fact that paths other than the one eventually taken were available. Moreover, by stressing the role to be played by government intervention in urban affairs, Weaver pinpointed the qualitative distinction that separated the second ghetto from the first.

The most distinguishing feature of post-World War II ghetto expansion is that it was carried out with government sanction and support. As black migration northward increased in the first quarter of the twentieth century and racial lines began to harden, it was apparent that white hostility was of paramount importance in shaping the pattern of black settlement. Sometimes violent, sometimes through the peaceful cooperation of local real estate boards, white animosity succeeded, informally and privately, in restricting black areas of residence.[20] Direct government support for segregation, before the New Deal, consisted primarily of the judicial enforcement of privately drawn restrictive covenants.

After World War II, however, government urban redevelopment and renewal policies, as well as a massive public housing program, had a direct and enormous impact on the evolution of the ghetto. In Chicago such programs reshaped, enlarged, and transformed the South Side Black Belt. Decaying neighborhoods were torn down, their inhabitants were shunted off to other quarters, and the land upon which they stood was used for middle-class housing and institutional expansion. High-rise public housing projects, created, in large part, to rehouse fugitives from "renewed" areas, literally lined State Street for miles as a new, vertical ghetto supplemented the old. To the east, Hyde Park became first a new area of black settlement and later, after implementation of an urban renewal program designed specifically to meet the challenge of racial succession, an obstacle around which most blacks had to move en route to accommodations farther south. The peculiar characteristics of Chicago's racial geography – the Black Belt's concrete northern end, the white thorn in its flank, and its newly occupied southern and western provinces – were all, in some measure, acquired through government action after World War II.

Increased government concern with housing was apparent, of course, before the postwar period. Beginning in the 1930s, and continuing thereafter, the operation of national agencies such as the Home Owners Loan Corporation (HOLC) and the Federal Housing Administration (FHA) reflected prevailing segregationist attitudes. Indirectly at least, they furthered the racial segmentation of metropolitan America and inner-city decay by supporting the flight of the white, middle-class population to the suburbs (which, despite government support, remained closed to blacks). A contemporary survey revealed, for example, that of 374 FHA-guaranteed mortgages in metropolitan Chicago, only 3 were in the central city.[21] More direct and immediate, however, were the federal government's attempts to clear slums and provide public housing to the urban poor. Although these programs were limited in scope and halting in practice, they pointed the way to the future. The ghetto was to be reinforced with tax-payers' dollars and shored up with the power of the state.

The first signs that this was happening in Chicago came with the construction of the Ida B. Wells housing project in the late 1930s. Covering 47 acres and costing nearly $9 million, the Ida B. Wells Homes provided shelter for 1,662 black families. Like similar projects in Cleveland, this black development was located in the ghetto, between 37th and 39th streets, South Parkway (now Martin Luther King Drive), and Cottage Grove. Opposition to the project came only from realtors and others outside the black community. Never once raising the issue of segregation, the Chicago *Defender* claimed that nearly "all of our political leaders, our ministers, social workers and civic organizations have united their resources to combat the opposition." The completion of the project, the black press asserted, was a "brilliant climax to Mayor Kelly's fight to see to it that the people of Chicago are properly housed." The reasons for such enthusiasm were apparent. Conditions within the Black Belt were so appalling that decent housing, wherever it was located, was desperately desired by the community, leaders and masses alike. The huge Wells development was a gift horse (albeit a Trojan one) not to be scrupulously examined. And, in some ways, the project did represent a gain for "the race." Black contractors, technicians, engineers, draftsmen, architects, and skilled and unskilled laborers were all employed in the construction process. Nonwhite plumbers, lathers, steam fitters, and structural-steel workers were granted temporary union cards so that they, too, could labor at the Wells Homes. Such "firsts," the promise of decent, safe, and sanitary dwellings, and the prospect that slum areas would be redeemed were more than enough to assure the undivided support of Black Chicago.[22]

This pattern of federal action, which became firmly established with the wartime emergency, soon generated bitter denunciations, however. As early as 1943 black Chicagoans were calling for the dismissal of the National Housing Agency's John Blandford for his "deference to the principle of residential segregation." There was truth to the charge. Federal respect for restrictive covenants and the delegation of site selection responsibilities to local interests vitiated all efforts to house black war workers. By 1944, despite the documented presence of 500 "emergency" cases and 10,000 other eligible in-migrants, the NHA had contributed but 93 units to the black housing supply. Blandford, the *Defender* charged, lacked even the "backbone of a jellyfish."[23]

Proposed solutions to the problem emphasized this growing black concern and awareness of the potential impact of government action. One possibility was temporary housing; yet the mere mention of such quarters sparked stinging rebuttals from blacks who suspected the units would be placed in their areas and who, like Chicago Housing Authority (CHA) chairman Robert R. Taylor and onetime alderman Earl Dickerson, rejected "any palliative that preserved [the] ghetto." Well-meaning whites hesitated before suggesting these emergency measures in 1944, knowing that their counsel "place[d] us under suspicion by Negroes, because they place segregation above all other problems." Similarly, proposals to rebuild the ghetto with high-rise apartment buildings "so that the same area can take care of a greater number of people" led Robert Weaver to denounce them as "inconsistent" with the American creed. Moreover, Weaver felt, once the "existing Negro population became accommodated" to such an arrangement, "bars to its future expansion would become more inflexible than they are now."[24] However, the Depression-era and wartime government building programs were not particularly large, and their significance lay elsewhere. By the end of the war the Chicago Housing Authority operated 7,644 permanent low-income housing units, including the nearly 4,000 that segregated blacks in the Ida B. Wells, Robert H. Brooks, and Altgeld Gardens projects. But this was merely a fraction of the nearly 40,000 such units in existence by 1976 (contained in 1,273 separate buildings and housing roughly 5% of the city's population).[25] The significance of these early government efforts lay in their demonstration of the difficulty in breaking established racial patterns. The building of ghettos was a cumulative process. The existence of the first ghetto made the rise of the second much easier, if it did not, in fact, produce overwhelming forces assuring its appearance. Ultimately, the dismantling of the ghetto in postwar Chicago under the hammerblows of a massive, nondiscriminatory government building program proved an insurmountable challenge. Local and federal authorities sustained, rather than attacked, the status quo.

At times the ties between the first and second ghettos were close and direct. Charles S. Duke, an architect and consulting engineer on the Wells Homes, as well as one of the select black group that had originally sponsored the project, was also the author of *The Housing Situation and the Colored People of Chicago, with Suggested Remedies and Brief References to Housing Projects Generally*. Published in April 1919, shortly before the riot of that year, Duke's treatise condemned "all attempts at racial segregation" but called for new construction and "decent living conditions" within existing black communities as a means of relieving both their distress and the pressure they placed on adjacent white neighborhoods. Duke was concerned not only with housing but also with the economic benefits such activity would bring to black realtors and businessmen; it was an attempt – in the context of the racial hatreds of that era – to deal constructively with the fact of segregation and real black needs. His approach was emulated by the governor's riot commission,

which investigated the ensuing holocaust. The commission's report, *The Negro in Chicago*, denounced *forcible* segregation while proposing, in Thomas Philpott's words, a "dual solution" to the city's racial and housing difficulties; it recommended "not open housing but better *Negro* housing" as the solution to racial tension. For a decade after the riot, reformers, philanthropists, and entrepreneurs tried to provide more and decent housing for blacks and working-class whites while observing both the color line and the bottom line. The construction of the Garden Homes, the Marshall Field Garden Apartments, and the Michigan Boulevard Garden Apartments (Rosenwald Gardens), however, was testimony only to their good intentions, the strength of the "business creed," and their futility – except for their success in leaving the prevailing pattern of segregation intact. If the private sector's "dual solutions" proved abortive in the twenties, though, they were substantially resurrected and brought to fruition in the modern era through the exercise of public power. One need only look, in 1980, at the unbroken wall of high-rise public housing along State Street, stretching all the way from Cermak Road (22nd Street) to 55th, to realize that the riot commission's recommendations were followed in spirit, if not in detail, more than a generation after they were made.[26]

Similarly, forces at work on the national level stretched back to the age of Progressive reform. Former settlement house resident, NAACP leader, and Chicagoan Harold Ickes headed the housing division of the Public Works Administration (PWA). Perhaps wishing to make the novel federal presence in urban America as unobtrusive as possible, it was Ickes who promulgated the "neighborhood composition rule," which prevented government projects from altering the racial composition of their host neighborhoods. Progressive willingness to work within the constraints of the color line, so evident at the beginning of the century, thus left its mark on the early federal programs as well. Not only were the "black" projects located in ghetto areas, but Chicago's Lathrop and Trumbull Park Homes, located in white areas, excluded blacks; and the Jane Addams Homes, which adhered to a racial quota in keeping with previous black presence on the site, was alone in its mixed clientele in the prewar era.[27] Federal policy later changed, of course, but these precedents were difficult to overcome and they became sources of controversy in the postwar period.

Other links between the first and second ghettos were less visible but equally important. The emergence of Chicago's "black metropolis" gave rise to institutional, economic, and political forces that had their roots, and therefore a stake, in the ghetto. The white hostility that isolated blacks spatially necessitated the creation of an "institutional ghetto," a city within a city, to serve them. It also produced a leadership class eager, or at least willing (as suggested by Duke's approach to housing), to pursue separate development rather than total assimilation – which is to say it created interests that could only view the ghetto's destruction with grave misgivings.[28]

In the late 1940s and 1950s, given the growing significance of government action, the conservative nature of black politics and politicians was of particular importance. Throughout the period, Chicago's black leadership was fragmented by the issues of redevelopment and renewal, and those who joined the opposition received little help in the political arena from William L. Dawson's black "sub-machine." Constrained by their accommodation to Chicago's brand of ethnic and machine-style politics, and their subordination to the dominant, white-controlled Cook County Democratic Organization, the professional black politicians lacked the desire or ability to fight those forces shaping the postwar ghetto. They would, according to political scientist Milton Rakove, "rather gild the ghetto than break it up." Such action, Rakove asserted, "insure[d] their tenures of office, indebt[ed] their constituencies to them, and enable[d] them to advance themselves within the Democratic machine in the city." The ghetto was a self-sustaining organism, which, politically at least, could not effectively challenge the forces that preserved and enlarged it.[29]

It was the sheer presence of the first ghetto and the white reaction to it, though, that did the most to produce the second. In creating it, white Chicago conceived a "Frankenstein's monster," which threatened to "run amok" after World War II. The establishment of racial borders, their traditional acceptance, and the conditions spawned by unyielding segregation created an entity that whites feared and loathed. Those who made it were soon threatened by it, and, desperately, they both employed old techniques and devised new ones in the attempt to control it. Others elected to flee to the suburbs, thus compounding the difficulties of those left behind. In any event, the very process of racial succession, dormant for nearly a generation, inspired both the dread and the action that called forth the second ghetto.

NOTES

1. Chicago Commission on Race Relations (hereafter cited as CCRR), *The Negro in Chicago* (Chicago: University of Chicago Press, 1922), pp. 6, 18–19; William M. Tuttle, Jr., *Race Riot: Chicago in the Red Summer of 1919* (New York: Atheneum, 1970), pp. 33–4, 40.
2. CCRR, *The Negro in Chicago*, pp. 6–7, 19–20, 31–2, 655–67; Tuttle, *Race Riot*, pp. 41, 46.
3. Of the injured, 342 were black and 195 were white. See Tuttle, *Race Riot*, p. 64.
4. *Report of the Riot Study Committee to the Honorable Richard J. Daley* (Chicago: City of Chicago, 1968), passim.
5. Ibid., pp. 5–20, 27, 36–8, 66.
6. Morris Janowitz, "Patterns of Collective Racial Violence," in Hugh Davis Graham and Ted Robert Gurr, eds., *Violence in America: Historical and Comparative Perspectives* (New York: New American Library, 1969), pp. 412–44; August Meier and Elliott Rudwick, "Black Violence in the 20th Century: A Study in Rhetoric and Retaliation," in ibid., pp. 399–412.
7. Janowitz, "Patterns of Collective Racial Violence," pp. 424–5.
8. Allan H. Spear, *Black Chicago: The Making of a Negro Ghetto, 1890–1920* (Chicago: University of Chicago Press, 1967), pp. 223–4; St. Clair Drake and Horace R. Cayton, *Black Metropolis: A Study of Negro Life in a Northern City*, 2 vols. (New York: Harcourt, Brace, 1945;

reprint ed., New York: Harper & Row, Harper Torchbooks, 1962), 2:xvi.

9. David A. Wallace, "Residential Concentration of Negroes in Chicago" (Ph.D. dissertation, Harvard University, 1953), p. 64; Thomas L. Philpott, *The Slum and the Ghetto: Neighborhood Deterioration and Middle-Class Reform, Chicago, 1880–1930* (New York: Oxford University Press, 1978), pp. 119, 121, 130, 146.

10. Spear, *Black Chicago,* pp. 142, 146; CCRR, *The Negro in Chicago,* pp. 106–8; Otis Duncan and Beverly Duncan, *The Negro Population of Chicago* (Chicago: University of Chicago Press, 1957), p. 92; Wallace, "Residential Concentration of Negroes," p. 69, claims no new communities came into being between 1910 and 1920.

11. Duncan and Duncan, *The Negro Population,* pp. 95–6; Wallace, "Residential Concentration of Negroes," p. 111; Philpott, *The Slum and the Ghetto,* p. 121.

12. Duncan and Duncan, *The Negro Population,* pp. 95–7.

13. Drake and Cayton, *Black Metropolis,* 1:184–7; Frederick Burgess Lindstrom, "The Negro Invasion of the Washington Park Subdivision" (M.A. thesis, University of Chicago, 1941); Wallace, "Residential Concentration of Negroes," pp. 79–80.

14. Drake and Cayton, *Black Metropolis,* 1:174.

15. Wallace, "Residential Concentration of Negroes," pp. 85, 88, 148, 149n.

16. Spear, *Black Chicago,* pp. 223–4; Wallace, "Residential Concentration of Negroes," p. 113; Duncan and Duncan, *The Negro Population,* pp. 96–7; Chicago Commission on Human Relations (hereafter cited as CHR), *Fourth Chicago Conference on Civic Unity: Abridged Report of Proceedings* (Chicago: CHR, 1952), p. 7.

17. Duncan and Duncan, *The Negro Population,* pp. 95–6.

18. The previously mentioned works of Spear and Philpott, which were both written in the aftermath of the 1960s riots, have clear implications for contemporary race relations but halt their analysis at 1930 – or earlier. The same is true for Gilbert Osofsky, "The Enduring Ghetto," *Journal of American History* 55 (September 1968): 243–55, and idem, *Harlem: The Making of a Ghetto; Negro New York, 1890–1930* (New York: Harper & Row, 1966); David M. Katzman, *Before the Ghetto: Black Detroit in the Nineteenth Century* (Urbana: University of Illinois Press, 1973); and Kenneth L. Kusmer, *A Ghetto Takes Shape: Black Cleveland, 1870–1930* (Urbana: University of Illinois Press, 1976).

19. Robert C. Weaver, *The Negro Ghetto* (New York: Harper & Row, 1948), pp. 275, 324, 369.

20. For the impact of white hostility on black residential patterns in Chicago, see Spear, *Black Chicago,* pp. 6–8, 20–3, 26, 201, 208–13, 219–21; Tuttle, *Race Riot,* pp. 157–83; CCRR, *The Negro in Chicago,* pp. 113–35; Drake and Cayton, *Black Metropolis,* 1:213–74; Philpott, *The Slum and the Ghetto,* pp. 146–200; Kusmer similarly emphasizes white hostility in restricting the choices of black Clevelanders; see his *A Ghetto Takes Shape,* pp. 46–7, 165, 167–70; see also Katzman, *Before the Ghetto,* pp. 69–80, and Osofsky, *Harlem,* pp. 46–52, 81. It also should be noted that Spear and Wallace feel that the blacks' weak economic position was relatively unimportant as a cause for their segregation. See Spear, *Black Chicago,* p. 26, and Wallace, "Residential Concentration of Negroes," p. 195.

21. Kenneth T. Jackson, "Race, Ethnicity, and Real Estate Appraisal: The Home Owners Loan Corporation and the Federal Housing Administration," *Journal of Urban History* 6 (August 1980): 419–52; Mark I. Gelfand, *A Nation of Cities: The Federal Government and Urban America, 1933–1965* (New York: Oxford University Press, 1975), p. 123.

22. *Chicago Defender,* October 26, 1940, has a special section devoted to the Ida B. Wells Homes. For the Cleveland experience, see Christopher G. Wye, "The New Deal and the Negro Community: Toward a Broader Conceptualization," *Journal of American History* 59 (December 1972): 621–39.

23. *Chicago Defender,* June 12, 1943; Horace R. Cayton and Harry J. Walker, Memorandum to Mr. Blandford and Mr. Divers, National Housing Agency, January 14, 1944; Metropolitan Housing [and Planning] Council (MHPC), Minutes of the Executive Committee Meeting, November 21, 1944, both in the Metropolitan Housing and Planning Council Papers (hereafter cited as MHPC Papers), Manuscript Collection, The Library, University of Illinois at Chicago (UIC). The Metropolitan Housing Council changed its name to the Metropolitan Housing and Planning Council in 1949. To avoid confusion, the amended name will be used throughout this study.

24. *Chicago Bee,* May 14, 1944; Eugene O. Shands to John Blandford, n.d.; Metropolitan Housing [and Planning] Council, Minutes of the Executive Committee Meeting, November 21, 1944; Metropolitan Housing [and Planning] Council, Minutes of the

Regular Meeting of the Board of Governors, April 4, November 1, 1944; Ferd Kramer to Robert Taylor, May 19, June 2, 1944; Ferd Kramer to Louis Wirth, May 31, 1944; Robert R. Taylor to Ferd Kramer, May 24, 1944, all in the MHPC Papers.

25. Devereux Bowly, Jr., *The Poorhouse: Subsidized Housing in Chicago, 1895–1976* (Carbondale: Southern Illinois University Press, 1978), pp. 17–54, 221.

26. Philpott, *The Slum and the Ghetto*, pp. 209–27; 244–69; *Chicago Defender*, October 26, 1940.

27. For the willingness of Chicago Progressives to observe the color line, see Philpott, *The Slum and the Ghetto*, pp. 271–347.

28. Spear, *Black Chicago*, pp. 71–89; 91–126; 181–200.

29. Ibid., pp. 111–26; Milton Rakove, *Don't Make No Waves – Don't Back No Losers: An Insider's Analysis of the Daley Machine* (Bloomington: Indiana University Press, 1975), pp. 256–81; James Q. Wilson, *Negro Politics: The Search for Leadership* (New York: Free Press, 1960); Harold F. Gosnell, *Negro Politicians: The Rise of Negro Politics in Chicago* (Chicago: University of Chicago Press, 1935; reprint ed., 1967); Ira Katznelson, *Black Men, White Cities* (New York: Oxford University Press, 1973); Charles Branham, "Black Chicago: Accommodationist Politics Before the Great Migration," in Melvin G. Holli and Peter d'A. Jones, eds., *The Ethnic Frontier: Essays in the History of Group Survival in Chicago and the Midwest* (Grand Rapids, Mich.: Eerdmans, 1977), pp. 211–62.

ESSAY 8.2

Making a Way out of No Way: African American Women and the Second Great Migration

Lisa Krissoff Boehm

Source: Lisa Krissoff Boehm, *Making a Way out of No Way: African American Women and the Second Great Migration* (Jackson: University Press of Mississippi, 2009).

EDITORS' INTRODUCTION

This essay asks us to reconsider the history of the Second Great Migration by rethinking periodization and questions of gender. The First (1914–1930) and Second (1940–1970) Great Migrations brought approximately 6.5 million African Americans from the South to northern cities.[i] The migrations are often explained as the time in which African Americans gained access to industrial work, and thus at long last secured the types of salaries necessary to gain a foothold in the middle class. Yet the story is rarely told from the *female* migrant's perspective. While men migrated for a chance at securing industrial work, African American women were largely excluded from jobs at the major war factories, especially in the early years of the Second World War. The much lauded "Rosie the Riveter" figure was usually white. Thus the advent of war industry had less effect on the work lives of African American women than other workers of the time period. The women did not simply follow men northward; regional migration constituted a monumental life change, requiring considerable planning and decision-making. Women numerically predominated among the migrants, and, while many moved due to the wishes of their husbands or male relatives, in other cases it was women themselves who led the migration to northern cities.[ii]

We see here an extensive use of oral histories that reveals a once obscured historical story. The voices of African American women migrants show up only intermittently in the historical record, and most often then in the context of strife, such as in court records. Oral history projects of African Americans, like oral history projects in general, began recording the voices of prominent citizens, overlooking lesser-known, more representative, individuals. Boehm demonstrates how powerful oral histories can be when used as historical evidence.[iii] She presents the voices of migrants in extended edited transcripts throughout her book, allowing the migrants to tell their own stories. In this essay, we encounter the edited transcript of migrant Ella Sims, a migrant from Mississippi who came to Michigan in 1946 and joined the cleaning staff of the C & O Railroad.

---

i The periodization of these two migrations are approximate, and a variety of dates are employed by scholars. This reflects the complexity of social movements in general. African Americans have experienced a great deal of mobility since the end of the Civil War. Some moved within the South, while others sought residence in the North, or even relocated to Africa.

ii Leslie Brown, "Sisters and Mothers Called to the City: African American Women and an Even Greater Migration," in Catherine Higgs, Barbara A. Moss, and Earline Rae Ferguson, eds., *Stepping Forward: Black Women in Africa and the Americas* (Athens: Ohio University Press, 2002).

iii See "Oral History Evaluation Guidelines," at http://www.oralhistory.org/network/mw/index.php/Evaluation_Guide. Also available as a pamphlet from the Oral History Association.

Although pockets of misunderstanding remain in academic circles, oral historians have proven that oral histories are no less reliable than other historical sources and indeed offer unique windows onto the past. Oral histories greatly expand our understanding of urban history. Indeed, the vagaries of personal memory, instead of presenting roadblocks to research, can provide compelling openings for exploration. Analyzing what is said, how it is said, and what goes unsaid, provides invaluable insight into the past. Such techniques are becoming known as the "history of memory."[iv] **[See Document 8.3, Alverrine Parker, "Memories of the Second Great Migration (2002)."]**

Lisa Krissoff Boehm, co-editor of this volume, is Dean of the College of Graduate Studies and Professor of History at Bridgewater State University. In addition to *Making a Way out of No Way*, she is the author of *Popular Culture and the Enduring Myth of Chicago, 1871–1968* (New York: Routledge, 2004), co-author (with Steven H. Corey) of *America's Urban History* (New York: Routledge, 2015) and co-editor of the two editions of *The American Urban Reader: History and Theory* (New York: Routledge, 2011 and 2020). She has been awarded oral history fellowships from the Baylor University Institute for Oral History and the Schlesinger Library, Radcliffe Institute of Advanced Study, at Harvard University. Krissoff Boehm has created oral history collections that are archived at the Schlesinger Library, the Grand Rapids Public Library, Emmanuel College, Manhattanville College, and Bridgewater State University. She held an appointment as Visiting Scholar at the Women's Studies Research Center at Brandeis University for several years. Krissoff Boehm served as the guest editor of the January 2010 volume of the *Journal of Urban History* dedicated to the teaching of urban history. Krissoff Boehm and Corey are at work on a new book on gender in the American city.

MAKING A WAY OUT OF NO WAY: AFRICAN AMERICAN WOMEN AND THE SECOND GREAT MIGRATION (2009)

This essay showcases and analyzes recently collected oral histories with forty African American women, most of whom were born in the southern United States in the first part of the twentieth century and then migrated to northern cities in the movement known as the Second Great Migration, 1940–1970. The Second Great Migration brought approximately five million black migrants to northern and western cities, leaving these cities, and the migrants themselves, forever transformed. The essay presents an analysis of the life stories of women migrants, with a focus on their reasons for moving and their thoughts on how work shaped their lives. Although the First and Second Great Migrations have been the subject of a number of wonderful books, the woman migrant herself has rarely been placed in the foreground within these works. Analysis of the oral histories demonstrates how black women forged purposeful lives for themselves despite multifaceted pressures. As migrant Inez Smith said in characterizing her own mother, a talented businesswoman who supported her daughters by the efforts of her hard work, the women featured here "made a way out of no way."

Social historians seek to understand trends in American culture and lived experience. Yet it is difficult for scholars to truly comprehend a trend if the supporting documents have not yet made their way to the archives. Documentation regarding the Second Great Migration has not yet been assiduously collected. Oral histories with black women who were not famous are

---

iv For more on the history of memory, see Jacques LeGoff, *History and Memory*, translated by Steven Randall and Elizabeth Claman (New York: Columbia University Press, 1992), John Bodnar, *Remaking America: Public Memory, Commemoration, and Patriotism in the Twentieth Century* (Princeton: Princeton University Press, 1993), Barbara Misztal, "Memory and Democracy, *American Behavioral Scientist* 28 (June 2005): 1320–1338, *Theories of Social Remembering* (Philadelphia: Open University Press, 2003), James Fentress and Chris Wickham, *Social Memory: New Perspectives on the Past* (Cambridge: Blackwell, 1992).

found in only a limited number of library collections. Thus, to better understand the way in which African American women viewed the migration, I went and asked them, tape recorder or digital recorder in hand. Many black migrants were born in rural parts of the South, while others began their lives in cities. Some transitioned from rural settings to southern cities before making the trek to the North. The North figured centrally in their dreams and hopes, yet the region rarely lived up to expectations.

To understand this migration, a movement in which women predominated, we are well served to consider individual stories. Examination of personal narratives proves particularly weighty when the narrators represent a people and a gender whose documents are underrepresented in the archives. Although millions made the choice to migrate, each individual migrant made the decision to uproot on her own, weighing carefully what she knew of American social structures, pay scales, living conditions, and family concerns. Due to the limits society placed on African American women, the majority of the respondents in this study worked as domestic laborers during at least a portion of their work lives. A great many African American women undertook domestic work, and many used the work as a bridge to other fields or as an expedient measure between more desirable careers.

The Migration

Ella Sims

Grand Rapids, Michigan

Ella Sims and I met in her lovely, second-floor apartment in Grand Rapids, Michigan, on a warm summer day. It was Sims's leadership roles at the local Office of Economic Opportunity in the 1960s and in later years as an employee and trustee of Aquinas College, a local Catholic institution, that had garnered her great respect in the city.

Sims explored her motivations for moving to Michigan. Like many migrants, she came north on a vacation and stayed.

She came to Grand Rapids for a short-term visit to her female cousin and was offered a job. Blue-collar jobs were relatively easy to locate and obtain.

Well, I was born in the South. My parents were sharecroppers—we grew cotton and corn. One of three girls, and I'm the middle girl. My daddy was a Baptist preacher. We moved a heck of a lot. Because they always say the preacher's always moving, and I think that was the truth. But I guess we had a normal childhood. We used to go and sing while my daddy preached.

When I went over to Arkansas and went to high school,[1] I married right out of high school in my senior year, when I was seventeen. I met him right there in high school; he was just a grade ahead of me, and I guess that's how come it was so easy to talk me into getting married.

I was married for three years before I got pregnant. I had a baby boy. And my baby lived to be ten months old and died very suddenly one night. Soon after that I got pregnant again. So then my second son was born. And he was born the twenty-eighth day of September, and on Thanksgiving morning my husband woke up sick. So the baby was about two months old. And my husband was just sick five days, and he died.

When we went to bed that night, I woke up the next morning with him calling me, and he said, "Oh, I'm as sick as I could be." Now this is what's strange—from the moment when he said that until he died, he never had another pain. He was just very sick. Something had burst in his ear. We had a very hard time getting a doctor on Thanksgiving, and so I finally got a doctor out to the house, and he didn't tell me much, just to give him some pills. And so then our doctor, who was gone Thanksgiving, was back in town. My husband's uncle went to his house. You know, a little small town, everybody knows everybody.

I knew there was something very serious by the way the doctor put his tube in my husband's ear, and he wasn't saying anything. The doctor said these words to me, he said, "We're going to see if we can save his life. We're going to take him to the hospital right now, and we are going to start giving him this new drug [penicillin]." Now, after he died, the doctor put on the death certificate "abscess in the brain." And with my children, if somebody says they have an earache, I am scared to death.

I remember saying over and over, "I'm twenty-two years old and my life is over." By March, I was in such terrible shape. My doctor asked me if I had any relatives anywhere so I could just take a vacation. And that's how I came to Michigan. Incidentally, my cousins that had moved to Grand Rapids, Michigan, was the same cousins that I went to live with to go to high school in Arkansas.

I came for vacation. My cousin said, "Oh, why don't you stay for the summer?" I said, "Well, I think I will." She said, "I bet you could get hired at the Pantlind Hotel." And so, I got hired at the Pantlind Hotel. Back then, even if you went to General Motors, you could get hired the same day. I came here in March of 1946. My husband died December 1945. My baby was born September 1945.

And so, when I started working, I had to have a babysitter. A neighbor, she sat keeping the baby for me. And so one day she said to me, she was asking me if everything was okay, and I said, "Well, I don't know." I wasn't getting the check from Social Security then. She said, "They are hiring at the railroad." And she told me how to get out there on the bus. And I went out there and got hired! They hired me on the second-shift job, and they wanted me to come to work that night. And she still kept the baby, because she just stayed two doors from my cousin's. So I could pick the baby up—I didn't get off until eleven at night. I must've maybe worked out there for a year before I got on days. But she was a good friend and she kept the baby. After that I got an apartment away from my cousin, and I also met my future husband. I'd been there a year when I met him.[2]

Existing archival collections feature few stories of the Second Great Migration, and only rarely has the movement been considered from the female viewpoint in oral histories. Of the resources that exist, few could rival the specificity and wrenching emotion of Sims's memories. An examination of the broad array of reasons for African American women's migration expands our understanding of this key American movement. Sims's tale of her difficult southern life, including the frightening details of her first husband's illness, makes her need for a Michigan vacation clear. Her recollection of an almost accidental decision to remain in Grand Rapids bears noticing; so often major life moments "fall into place" as this regional shift does for Sims. Darlene Clark Hine, in her article "Black Migration to the Urban Midwest: The Gender Dimension, 1915–1945," argues that historians must focus much more effort on analyzing the story of the female migrant. She writes:

> we need micro-studies into individual life, of neighborhoods, families, churches, and fraternal lodges in various cities. Examination of these themes makes imperative an even deeper penetration into the internal world of Afro-Americans. Perhaps, even more dauntingly, to answer fully these questions requires that the black woman's voice and experience be researched and interpreted with the same intensity and seriousness accorded that of the black man.

Information derived from statistical and demographic data on black midwestern migration and urbanization must be combined with the knowledge drawn from the small, but growing, numbers of oral histories, autobiographies, and biographies of twentieth century migrating women … Actually these sources, properly "squeezed and teased," promise to light up that inner world so long shrouded behind a veil of neglect, silence, and stereotype, and will quite likely force a rethinking and rewriting of all of black urban history.[3]

This study adds a somewhat overlooked element to the history of African American migration: analysis of women's personal reasons for the migration. Certain societal structures, including the economics of southern society, political disfranchisement, the raging, daily insults of a discrimination defended by law, and the threat and reality of violence—a violence for which few whites were ever punished—pushed families from their homes. Simultaneously, the pace of the northern industrial world and the culture of the northern cities pulled individuals to the bus depots, train stations, and highways. However influential such factors were for southern African Americans, every migration began with a very private and personal discussion. Although everyone follows trends, we do not choose to comprehend the great changes in our lives as defined by the grand structures or systems in place in society, but as our very own, very private history. Only the individual truly understands the interplay of factors contributing to the watershed moments in his or her life; oral history proves to be an excellent way of documenting what individuals know about these factors.

Historian Peter Gottlieb argues that frequent movement within the South became a critical means by which African American families negotiated the almost nonnegotiable economic structures there. Blacks had long considered changes in physical location as a reasonable, feasible means by which to better their lives. Migration out of the region followed a long-lived practice of moving within the region. Since the dawn of Reconstruction, African Americans had relocated. Gottlieb focuses on the First Great Migration, which began about the time World War I broke out in Europe. He writes, "Long experience in moving to jobs within their native regions gave southern blacks added traction as they began moving toward new job openings during the war."[4] For Gottlieb, the move north came as a result of a combination of the inequities of the South and the migrants' culture, which at times encouraged migration as a response to difficulties. Just generations ago, any movement whatsoever had been solely at the discretion of the slave owner. For black sharecroppers, moving to another farm brought the hope of a fairer share of the crop yield, a better accounting in the books kept at the plantation commissary, or more humane treatment by area whites. Migration to southern cities brought access to a broader array of jobs and the delights of urban life. And migration northward brought even wider job opportunities, access to the glittering entertainment venues of the cities, and the whispered promise, often unrealized, of a more just society. Unfortunately, the North had its own system of legalized and de facto discrimination and segregation. Recent scholarship has taken to calling this formalized system "northern Jim Crow."[5]

Family ties figured strongly in the moves. Some migrants moved primarily because of the decisions of male family members. In traditionally oriented families, male heads of households often had the most weight in decision making. Yet some husbands did follow their wives to the North. Although almost all the women of this study were part of tight-knit family units, the women consciously structured their economic choices and weighed their options regarding physical location—these women did not "end up" living in the North, but deftly negotiated the narrow labor market open to them as well as their migratory path. Few of the study's respondents claimed to be the very first family member to make the move, however. Almost all followed siblings, cousins, husbands, or other relatives to their intermediate and final destinations. This "chain migration" brought the approximate six and a half million migrants north and west during the First and Second Great Migrations.

As shown in Ella Sims' history, some of the women came north without male guidance, following a female family member to the northern city. With historical hindsight, this appears to be quite revolutionary behavior. Fitting the definition of "women adrift," the term put forth by historian Joanne Meyerowitz to describe unchaperoned women in the city, the women made history by traveling unfettered by male bonds, but they did not envision their moves as atypical. Meyerowitz's term uses historical language to describe the women's lack of male supervision; she does not imply that these women were literally lost or adrift, and the oral testimony demonstrates that the migrants felt fairly secure traveling and relocating without men. Acting on their own seemed a reasonable solution and, in most instances, perfectly within the bounds of propriety for the era. Sims, for example, surely would have preferred to remain within a household with a male head, but her husband had died. The female-oriented chain migration resembles a female pattern for women immigrants, particularly the women of Ireland.[6]

Florence Allison, born in Livingston, Alabama, in 1926, represents those migrants who moved primarily due to the wishes of their husbands. Her husband, a marine who later worked at the Chrysler assembly plant in Detroit, led the way in this particular choice. Allison explained, "After being in the army he didn't want to be back in the country anymore so he decided to move."[7] Annie Benning, born in Georgia in 1911, came to River Rouge, Michigan, so her husband could work in the auto industry. Her husband's brother had already arrived. Benning remembered, "Well, he had a brother that lived here and his brother wanted him to come here and to work with him in the steel mill but he didn't like working in no mill. He come here and got him a job as a mechanic and that's where he stayed until he passed." Mr. Benning made a comfortable living in a garage of a car dealership. Benning continued, "He couldn't get no job working down there [in the South] and he wanted to come where he could make it. It didn't make no difference to me and he come to find him a job. I stayed home about three months and then I come to Michigan." Benning's husband also disliked the way black men were treated in the South. She said, "He did [face discrimination] when he was in the southern states, so that's when he come here, but he didn't have no trouble here." The Bennings proved typical in that the husband got settled in his position and established a living space for the couple before the wife made the move. Such systems also were typical of many immigrant groups coming to America in the early twentieth century. Like many African American men, Annie Benning's husband located a job quickly. Benning characterized her view of Detroit by saying, "It was real nice and you could get jobs. No job was too hard to find here."[8]

The majority of the respondents reported that their husbands had initiated the migration. The women did not express displeasure at the move, but in their patriarchal homes, the husband's plans dominated. Such male leadership is not unusual, even today. Because men still tend to earn higher salaries than their spouses, it proves reasonable for families to favor finding the most lucrative position possible for male workers. It remains highly unusual for families to relocate regionally for a female's job.

In the world of blues music, the oft-repeated tale told by migrant and blues vocalist Koko Taylor represents the sharp distinction between southern and northern pay rates, and the number of hopes and dreams bound up in the decision to migrate. Taylor, interviewed in 1993, recounted her future husband's announcement that he was heading to Chicago in 1953. Taylor refused to be left behind. Robert "Pops" Taylor landed a position at the Wilson Packing Company, a real achievement. Koko found work as a housekeeper for a Wilmette family, where she would earn $5.00 for an eight-hour day. In Tennessee, Taylor had had to care for white families for $1.50 a day, and sometimes just $3.00 a week. The couple was thrilled with their new city, yet they had arrived with very little in their pockets. Taylor said, "We rode from Memphis to Chicago with 35 cents in our pockets and a box of Ritz crackers."[9]

Faith Richmond boarded a train in North Carolina to go and live with her husband's family. Yet her family of origin warned her about the difficulty of living with in-laws. Richmond related, "He brought me up to Boston and [I] had to live with his family. I remember my aunt saying, if you must live with your in-laws, try very hard to get along."[10] Lillian Clark followed her husband to Detroit soon after he secured a job at Uniroyal. Her husband had followed his brother-in-law to Michigan. Clark's husband's joy at arriving in the Midwest has become a favorite family anecdote. Clark related, "When he got off the train, he was so excited he left the bags on the train."[11] Minnie Chatman depicted her migration story as a rather passive part of her life; in keeping with her husband's leadership position in the household, he made most of the decisions for the couple. His position at U.S. Rubber, far better than he could hope for in Mississippi, launched the family's migration. Chatman recalled, "He came first and he was working and then I stayed and later he sent for me." Chatman's husband had no desire to live in the South again. Chatman said, "He was looking around to see if we could find a place because he say we never going back there and he didn't go back there." Chatman remained in Michigan although her husband passed away about a decade after she arrived.[12]

Mattie Bell Fritz moved to the North immediately after she married, motivated by her husband's wishes. Fritz, born in Montgomery, Alabama, in 1927, married Andrew Fritz shortly before he headed off to the army. Fritz admits, "I got married on a Sunday and left [the South] on a Monday. He [Andrew Fritz] is originally from Pittsburgh, but his family was in Alabama so they moved back and then he moved here [Detroit] and he went into the army from here." Her father balked at the sudden wedding and move. At just eighteen and a recent high school graduate, Mattie Bell married in the recreation center near her home. She recalled, "I told my dad, he say, 'But baby, why do you want to get married so early?' I said, 'He swept me off my feet.'" Mattie Bell settled in near her husband's cousins in Ecorse, Michigan, outside of Detroit, and visited the cousins often. She entered into her husband's tight-knit family.[13]

Liddie Williams came to Chicago from Mississippi in 1954; she was just seventeen years old. Newly married, Williams accompanied her mother-in-law to the big city; Williams's husband had already relocated. Perhaps because of her young age at the time, she found the migration difficult. She said, "It was pretty hard. My mother was in the South. A couple of years later, she came here." Williams also revealed that her stepfather's behavior contributed to her desire to move north. She intimated, "I had kind of [a] mean stepfather, that's why I

wanted to leave, but I hated to leave my mother." Many years earlier, Williams's parents' divorce had come as a direct result of her father's move to Chicago. She explained, "Her and my father, the reason they separated, it wasn't that they didn't get along, he wanted to come to Chicago and she wouldn't come with him. So they separated." Williams's story demonstrates that a wife's relocation was not a foregone conclusion; all married women did not dutifully follow their spouses. The married women also weighed the consequences, and determined if the migration fit their own needs as well as their husband's.

Of the migrants who admitted to misgivings, homesickness for family members played a significant role.[14] Rosa Young, who followed her father to Michigan from Mississippi in 1944 (she was about seventeen), recalled sadness over leaving her small town. Young's father came to Grand Rapids to attend his son's wedding, and found work in a railroad yard during his vacation. Young mused, "I was glad, I guess I was glad to come, but I hated to leave my home, you know, my homeland, Holly Springs, because that was really tough for me, you know."[15]

Esther Woods presented the decision to migrate as her own, but also cited her brother's need for help with his nieces and nephews, who lived with him in Grand Rapids. Woods's sister had entered the state hospital, leaving the children without a parent to care for them. One of the nieces ended up living with Woods for much of her childhood. Woods admitted, "And I came here—frankly that's why I came here—to help him with those kids." Yet this pressing need only provided the catalyst for the move. Woods believed the migration to be her only reasonable option for a solid economic future. Note that her language points to a return to the South constituting more than a visit; her relocation did not occur all at once. "I wouldn't have stayed there," she said bluntly, "because there was nothing there to do. I worked in York, Alabama, which was about eight miles from my home, before I ever left there *the first time*. But it is a small town—wasn't very much work there for me any longer, so I figured it was time for me to move on for something better." Members of Woods's family migrated to many cities, including Los Angeles, Toledo, Detroit, and New York City. Her personal inclination to move was in keeping with the decisions made by the rest of her family, yet she came to her decision over a matter of years and with considerable personal reflection.[16]

It is important to highlight the significant minority of the respondents who followed other women to northern cities. Annie Evelyn Collins of Detroit migrated due to female ties. Like Sims and other migrants, Collins meant to come to Michigan for a visit, yet she stayed permanently. She joked a little about the casual beginning of this major life change. Economics greatly influenced her decision. Collins sought to keep a female relative company. Collins's mother proffered important advice. In the passage below, Collins worked through a degree of incredulity at the way in which small choices end up affecting people's lives in major ways. Her words attest to a degree of ambivalence about the migration. She clearly had not worked through her ideas on the migration fully, and perhaps had not been asked about it for some time. Collins explained at length:

> My sister was here and my mother [felt] that she shouldn't be by herself. She had two sisters in Kentucky and one sister in Cincinnati and she [her mother] told me to come to Detroit so this sister wouldn't be here by herself. I come to stay two weeks and then have fifty years. Ain't that terrible. Now, ain't that terrible. Come to spend two weeks and then get fifty-three years. Fifty-three years, now that's terrible, ain't it. No, that's good, I like living here.
>
> Well, coming here you had better ways of living and making money. The houses was different and the money was different and it was different than the South, even though it wasn't all bad living in the South. There is more money in Michigan, you know. I didn't work that much, but I had more chance to work.[17]

Mary Smith also relied on a network of female relatives to help her decide where to live. Smith, born in 1938 in Sylvester (Worth County), Georgia, moved to find better-paying work. Her quest led her on a circuitous journey—to New York City, back to Georgia, back to New York, on to Miami, Florida, back to Georgia, and finally to Boston. Childbearing also played a part in helping Smith choose her location, because she returned to Georgia to give birth to her babies in a familiar location. The children all stayed with her mother in Georgia for most of their lives. An aunt and a sister had found work in Miami before she arrived. Smith said of her job hunt, "The jobs were very easy to find. All you do is get the paper and you call, and you go for an interview, and most of the time, you know, they hire you." Smith lived in a female-centered world. Although she mentioned off-handedly that she had married, she raised all of her three children with only her mother's assistance, and seemed to provide the sole economic support for her family. Smith made her way to Boston, where she ran a day care center out of her three-decker home. The three decker, a common housing type in New England, consists of three separate apartments, arranged one per floor. Smith owned the building, and she resided on the top floor, where she also located the day care. Smith came to Boston at her sister's urging. Smith said straightforwardly, "She sent for me and I came here."[18]

Work also led Rebecca Strom from Alabama to Boston. Strom, born in 1944, stood out as the only respondent not to mention another relative blazing the trail north ahead of her. She did not remember how she heard of the option of working in Boston, guessing only that someone she knew had probably made the trip. Strom also remained one of the few respondents, joining Mary Smith, Anniese Moten, and a handful of others, who labored as a live-in domestic. Most domestics had abandoned live-in work for day work by this time. The fight for the right to live out had been undertaken by an earlier generation of domestic workers, such as the Washington, D.C., workers chronicled by historian

Elizabeth Clark-Lewis.[19] As with any social practice, however, change came incrementally. Not all employers allowed workers this advantage, and some women did not desire this option. For a very young woman like Strom, rent for an apartment would have proved prohibitive at this stage of her career. Strom stated, "Well, see there was not a lot of work there [in Alabama], and we heard about working for families that would pay for you to come here. So, you would work for them to pay them back, and then you would have your regular money." The systematized approach to migration mentioned here allowed Strom to move without even having to come up with travel fare. Working to pay off travel costs echoes the technique employed by many immigrants from abroad, who had employers advance the cost of their ship fare. Strom's reference to "we" in the above excerpt indicates her understanding of the great flow of migrants she joined by heading to the North. Strom remembered, "They met you at the bus station and you went to their home. That was our home till I met some other people who told me about Freedom House on Crawford Street, and how you got a regular job outside of living in with a family." (Freedom House, a social service agency run by social workers Otto and Muriel Snowden, drew together the white and black residents of its Dorchester neighborhood in Boston.)[20] All of Strom's siblings left Alabama, leaving her parents behind. Strom felt that she would have eventually located work or entered college if she had remained in her home state. Boston brought her alternative work and an alternative future, but relocation to the city was not the only option open to her. By the time she left, in the last decade of the Second Great Migration, the South was, according to her, a region with some economic opportunities. Like Mary Smith, Strom made a living at the time of the interview by operating a home day care.[21]

Migrants could move back and forth between regions, taking jobs in the North for a time, yet returning to family and friends in the South for several years or more. African American migrants undertook this form of "shuttle migration" to a lesser extent than the white, southern migrants detailed in Chad Berry's excellent study, *Southern Migrants, Northern Exiles*. Most African American migrants did not carry quite the case of "divided heart" that the white migrants did. White migrants considered the South home, but needed the heavier pay packets to be found in northern industry. African American migrants' searing memories of southern Jim Crow restrictions somewhat tempered any warm feelings for their home states. Despite some of the pleasant childhood memories held by the migrants, many believed strongly that the North offered them the possibility of a more just society along with the higher pay.[22]

Yet, the study respondents did report some cases of shuttle migration that mirrored that of the white southern migrants. Not only did Avezinner Dean move between a number of cities and towns around the United States, but her relocation was motivated by her desire to further her education and career. Dean, a domestic worker turned hair stylist born in Mississippi in 1928, moved frequently between South and North. She characterized the moves as fitting her own needs, rather than complying with the wishes of a male family member. Dean related her convoluted path: "I worked in Alabama and had a [beauty] shop. I lived in Alabama and moved to Inkster [Michigan]. I moved back to Alabama and stayed seven years. My big girl was born in Alabama. I went to Nashville and got another diploma. I wanted to bob hair and I didn't know how. Then I moved back to Michigan and married my sweetheart in 1955. I have been here ever since."[23]

Beatrice Jackson moved to Michigan to join her family, and, unusually, her fiancé followed her to their new home. Jackson traveled to Michigan to live near her brother and his family. Years before, she had joined her sister in Tulsa. The sister needed her help because her husband had entered a sanitarium; during Jackson's years in Tulsa, she worked as a domestic and earned a college degree in elementary teaching, which she never utilized directly in her employment. Jackson did not think highly of the Motor City. "The summer of 1941," Jackson said in her low, tired voice, "I went to Detroit and my husband-to-be followed me. My brother was in Detroit. He didn't have a job at that time. His wife didn't have a job. They had two kids—I was disgusted with Detroit."[24]

Jerliene "Creamy" McKinney followed a female family member northward, and also drew her boyfriend along with her. McKinney, born in Alabama in 1940, followed her sister to New York City. Anticipating her move, McKinney's boyfriend (and later husband), Theodosis, moved to the Bronx. McKinney detailed, "My sister moved from Florida to New York because she used to do jobs of living in with peoples, doing housekeeping and stuff like that. So she moved from Florida to New York, and when I got old enough, I kept asking my mom, 'Can I come to stay with her for a while?' So, when I got older, my mom let me come up to New York to stay with her." After about four years, Creamy and Theodosis married, and had four children in New York. "Then the peoples that she was living there with moved here [to Massachusetts]," McKinney explained, "and they wanted my husband and her husband to come to live with them here." Both husbands found jobs at Boston's airport, while Creamy and her sister worked for the family. Eventually McKinney moved her family to Worcester, Massachusetts, and her sister followed.[25]

The interviewees who shared their memories for this study add considerably to our understanding of the Second Great Migration. Although many did move north at the behest of their husbands or other male relatives, their stories reveal important facts about the men's roles as family leaders and the women's views of themselves. In the twenty-first century, it remains highly unusual for women to initiate cross-country migrations for their families. In the mid-twentieth century, it would have been atypical for families to travel hundreds of miles solely to pursue better-paying work for the females of the family. Black women of this generation made more money in the North than the South, but they largely remained in domestic positions until the last decades of the twentieth century.

Stories like that of Creamy McKinney and Beatrice Jackson, however, document that some men did follow their girlfriends and wives northward. McKinney and Jackson, both exceedingly motivated, knew the region would improve their economic security. Their male counterparts refused to be left behind. Other women, including Mary Smith and Rebecca Strom, came north without any male companion at all. Smith would remain the sole breadwinner for her family, and Strom would meet her husband only after settling permanently in Boston. Some women, like Liddie Williams's mother, divorced their husbands rather than follow them to the North.

Viewing the Great Migration through a feminine lens upsets our previous understanding of what was arguably the most historically important movement of people in the United States before the present era. Although millions relocated, the decision to do so stemmed from highly personal life choices. Each family struggled, sometimes for decades, over where to best make a life. And for many families, the decision to head north was never truly conceived of as permanent. In the late twentieth and early twenty-first centuries, hundreds of thousands of African Americans have been migrating to the South. Many are the children and grandchildren of migrants. Migrants themselves have returned to their region of origin. In this period, African American college graduates are more likely to settle in the South than the North after graduation. The vast majority of the new migrants settle in the southern suburbs.[26] The South draws new residents of all races with its job opportunities and sunny weather. Interestingly, many of the African Americans flowing south to follow their dreams envision the move as a "return" rather than a simple migration. The South still figures as an actual or metaphorical homeland for a significant number of African American families.

NOTES

1. Ella Sims's father sent his children to board with relatives in Helena, Arkansas, to attend school, there being no high school for black children in their Mississippi town.

2. Ella Sims, interview with Lisa Krissoff Boehm, Grand Rapids, Michigan, July 2, 2002.

3. Darlene Clark Hine, "Black Migration to the Urban Midwest: The Gender Dimension, 1915–1945," in Joe William Trotter, Jr., ed., *The Great Migration in Historical Perspective: New Dimensions of Race, Class, and Gender* (Bloomington: Indiana University Press, 1991), 129.

4. Peter Gottlieb, "Rethinking the Great Migration: A Perspective from Pittsburgh," in Joe William Trotter, Jr., ed., *The Great Migration in Historical Perspective*, 71.

5. See Davison M. Douglas, *Jim Crow Moves North: The Battle over Northern School Segregation, 1865–1954* (New York: Cambridge University Press, 2005).

6. Suellen Hoy, *Good Hearts: Catholic Sisters in Chicago's Past* (Urbana: University of Illinois Press, 2006), 12, 20, 30–31.

7. Florence Allison, interview with Elizabeth Cote, Detroit, Michigan, July 31, 2002.

8. Annie Benning, interview with Lisa Krissoff Boehm and Elizabeth Cote, Detroit, Michigan, June 26, 2002.

9. Katherine Aldin, "Koko Taylor: Down in the Bottom of that Chitlin' Bucket," *Living Blues* (July/August 1993), 13.

10. Faith Richmond (pseudonym), interview with Lisa Krissoff Boehm and Patricia Burke, Boston, Massachusetts, October 3, 2002.

11. Lillian Clark, interview with Lisa Krissoff Boehm and Elizabeth Cote, Southfield, Michigan, January 2, 2003.

12. Minnie Chatman, interview with Lisa Krissoff Boehm and Elizabeth Cote, Detroit, Michigan, October 19, 2001.

13. Mattie Bell Fritz, interview with Lisa Krissoff Boehm and Elizabeth Cote, Detroit, Michigan, August 4, 2001.

14. Liddie Williams, interview with Lisa Krissoff Boehm, Chicago, Illinois, November 16, 2001.

15. Rosetta "Rosa" Lewis Young, interview with Lisa Krissoff Boehm, Grand Rapids, Michigan, January 4, 2003.

16. Esther Woods, interview with Lisa Krissoff Boehm, Grand Rapids, Michigan, June 10, 2000. Statistics for York, Alabama, in 2005 found median household income in this town of less than three thousand people to be close to nineteen thousand dollars. The town was 78.3 percent African American. See www.citydata.com.

17. Annie Evelyn Collins, interview with Elizabeth Cote, Detroit, Michigan, January 11, 2003.

18. Mary Smith, interview with Lisa Krissoff Boehm, Audrey Kemp, and Patricia Burke, Boston, Massachusetts, October 12, 2002.

19. Elizabeth Clark-Lewis, *Living In, Living Out: African American Domestics and the Great Migration* (New York: Kodansha American, 1994), 124–146.

20. For more on Freedom House, see www.freedom-house.com.

21. Rebecca Strom, interview with Lisa Krissoff Boehm, Audrey Kemp, and Patricia Burke, November 12, 2002.

22. Chad Berry, *Southern Migrants, Northern Exiles* (Urbana: University of Illinois Press, 2000), 21.

23. Avezinner Dean, interview with Lisa Krissoff Boehm and Elizabeth Cote, Detroit, Michigan, June 25, 2002.

24. Beatrice Jackson, interview with Lisa Krissoff Boehm and Elizabeth Cote, June 23, 2002.

25. Jerliene "Creamy" McKinney, interview with Lisa Krissoff Boehm, Worcester, Massachusetts, January 9, 2003.

26. Roderick J. Harrison, "The Great Migration South," *New Crisis* (July/August 2001): 20; William H. Frey, *The New Great Migration: Black Americans' Return to the South, 1965–2000,* Center on Urban and Metropolitan Policy, Brookings Institution, May 2004.

ESSAY 8.3

The Great White Migration, 1945–1960

Chad Berry

Source: Chad Berry, *Southern Migrants, Northern Exiles*
(Urbana: University of Illinois Press, 2000).

EDITORS' INTRODUCTION

In his book, historian Chad Berry offers an extended study of the white migration from the South of the United States to the North. Heretofore, this massive migration of white southerners, which reached its peak in the 1950s, had been largely overlooked. Declining opportunities for small farmers and the precarious position of coal mining sent many upland southerners towards northern cities. As historian James N. Gregory demonstrates in his important book, *The Southern Diaspora: How the Great Migrations of Black and White Southerners Transformed America* (Chapel Hill: University of North Carolina Press, 2005), we cannot truly understand the history of the twentieth century without a careful accounting for these massive movements of people. More than 28 million people from the South left their homes during the twentieth century. The numbers of whites flowing out of the South each decade dwarfed the numbers of black migrants, although the black migrants were more evident to the long-term residents of the receiving cities. Still, searing anti-southern attitudes were directed towards the white newcomers, who were branded with the term "hillbillies" (although, as Berry warns us, not all were from Appalachia).[i] **[See Document 8.4, Harriette Arnow, "*The Dollmaker* (1954)."]** The newcomers faced hiring discrimination and found themselves relegated to certain neighborhoods. So many southerners transplanted themselves in the West and North that these regions were transformed culturally. Berry's edited collection, *The Hay Loft Gang: The Story of the National Barn Dance* (Urbana: University of Illinois Press, 2008), tells the story of how the largest city in the Midwest, Chicago, served as an early home of country music, with its nationally broadcast National Barn Dance. The National Barn Dance even preceded Nashville's Grand Ole Opry, for which the midwestern program served as a model.[ii]

Certainly white southerners had a different connection with their homeland than black southerners. Berry argues that the migrants had "divided hearts," for they missed the land of their childhood and came almost entirely for economic reasons. They relocated out of dire need, however, and thus Berry terms them exiles. Yet he also finds evidence of "shuttle migration," frequent movements between the South and North, with some families migrating back home each year between April and October for the planting season. African Americans had a host of reasons for leaving the South, including the restrictions of Jim Crow, rampant violence, mechanization of farming, and disenfranchisement. As Lisa Krissoff Boehm has shown in *Making a Way out of No Way: African American Women and the Second Great Migration* (Jackson: University Press of Mississippi, 2009) **[see Essay 8.2]**,

---

i   Chad Berry, *Southern Migrants, Northern Exiles* (Urbana: University of Illinois Press, 2000), 104 and 110.

ii James N. Gregory, *The Southern Diaspora: How the Great Migrations of Black and White Southerners Transformed America* (Chapel Hill: University of North Carolina Press), 15 and 19.

black women's oral histories revealed a closer connection with their southern homes than is usually understood and were at times also shuttle migrants. The fact that white and black southern migration occurred simultaneously had some negative repercussions for black migrants, who found southern racial prejudice, as well as the northern variety, in cities like Detroit.

White southern migration also has connections with the movements of Hispanic and Caribbean peoples, for, like Mexican immigrant farm workers, southern whites segued from harvesting crops in locations like southeastern Michigan to becoming permanent residents. Some of these migrants went on to work for corporations in the area—such as the ones Berry documents at the Whirlpool plant in Benton Harbor, Michigan—and settled permanently. Likewise, seasonal Mexican workers, formerly just passing through, came to make their homes in small cities like Holland, Michigan, taking on industrial jobs in the Heinz pickle factory and the Haworth office furniture plant, and forever changing the demographics of this once predominantly Dutch settlement. Berry concludes that the new group of southern, white industrial workers was much more open to union activism than has previously been assumed.[iii]

Relying on sixty oral histories and extensive archival research, Berry provides a compelling new way to view the southern migration. His book puts the start of significant migration at the beginning of the twentieth century, quite a bit earlier than other scholars. The work also confronts stereotypes regarding southerners. Berry considers anew the success rate of southern white transplants, who were considered ill-fit for northern urban life. He demonstrates that the southerners adapted to their new homes far more successfully than anti-southern, contemporaneous observers reported.

Chad Berry is Academic Vice President and Dean of the Faculty at Berea College. He served for five years as Director of the Loyal Jones Appalachian Center at Berea, and had also served as Director of the Center for Excellence in Learning through Service. Berry is the author of *Southern Migrants, Northern Exiles* (Urbana: University of Illinois Press, 2000), and the editor of and contributor to *The Hay Loft Gang: The Story of the National Barn Dance* (Urbana: University of Illinois Press, 2008). He is co-editor of *Looking and Learning: Visual Literacy across the Disciplines* (San Francisco, CA: Jossey-Bass, 2015) and *Studying Appalachian Studies: Making the Path by Walking* (Urbana: University of Illinois Press, 2015). Before coming to Berea, Berry taught for eleven years at Maryville College. Berry is at work on a project examining the development of Appalachian Studies after the Second World War.

THE GREAT WHITE MIGRATION, 1945–1960 (2000)

IN THE LATE 1940s, Knott County, Kentucky, had a peculiar problem. The county, with plenty of youngsters around, was having a hard time finding teachers to staff its schools. Simeon Fields was only seventeen years old when he "took one of these schools on the emergency basis." As Fields explained, "There were about six schools in the county that were not able to get on their way because they had no teachers.

These were the days when young seventeen- and eighteen-year-old boys were finishing high school and buying a coal truck, and some were going to Detroit and Cleveland and Cincinnati—the great out migration was in full swing, 1947, '8, and '9."[1]

By the mid-1950s, nearly three thousand people born in Cocke County, Tennessee, deep in the Smoky Mountains, had settled in Cleveland, Ohio. Jack Shepherd, who edited the county's *Plain Talk-Tribune*, published in Newport, Tennessee, said that he had more than four hundred subscribers

---

iii Berry, *Southern Migrants, Northern Exiles,* 108.

who were living in Cleveland who "pass the paper around for other Cocke families up there." One Lorain Avenue furniture store in Cleveland ran advertisements in the Tennessee paper simply to reach migrants in Ohio. "Cleveland," said Cocke County Judge Benton Giles, "gets more people from Cocke County than any other city, but Detroit runs a close second." Alluding to the divided heart of the exiles, he declared, "They'd all rather stay here if they had jobs. I have a nephew who is happier here making half the money he made in Cleveland. They don't like living in a big city." Between 1940 and 1960, the 201 counties of the Tennessee Valley region lost more than 1.3 million people to migration. Out-migration had become such a problem in the state by the mid-1950s that Tennessee proclaimed the annual loss of ten thousand young people its number-one social problem.[2]

These are but two examples of the great white migration that resumed with unprecedented force after World War II. As the northern economy was booming, pockets of the southern economy, particularly mining, were as depressed as ever, and out-migration began again, reaching a peak during the 1950s. In the urban Midwest, industry was beckoning southerners northward, and southerners were arriving by the bus load. The Brooks Bus Line, for example—only one of a number of small bus lines that serviced people moving between the North and South—made daily round-trips between Detroit and Paducah, Mayfield, and Fulton, in western Kentucky. Since for many years throughout the South, particularly in depressed regions, what occurred outside determined whether, in the sociologist James S. Brown's words, "there will be a great or a greater movement out," southern whites responded to the calls in droves. In the late 1940s, Brown had studied the Beech Creek community in Clay County, Kentucky, for his doctoral dissertation. In 1961, Brown returned to Beech Creek, which had become something of the Middletown of southern Appalachia, to reinterview residents and was stunned by the extent of migration: more than half had relocated outside Appalachia, and of these,

almost two-thirds had moved to southern Ohio and the rest elsewhere in Ohio and Indiana. "You are just thunderstruck," he said, "by how many people have left that part of the country. There are many more people ... that I knew 15 years ago on Beech Creek in Clay County now in South Lebanon, Ohio, than there are on Beech Creek itself today." When he asked Beech Creek members whether they would want their children to stay in the community or move away, the answer was "*outside* for more *opportunity*."[3]

The period of upland southern out-migration between 1945 and 1960—one of the largest internal migrations in the history of the United States—has four important characteristics. First, although the migration has been portrayed as a hegira from the hills, in reality people from throughout the Upland South left the region for the Midwest between 1945 and 1960. It is incorrect, in short, to speak of this migration as exclusively "Appalachian." Second, census data show the extraordinary numbers involved in what previous scholars have called the "invisible minority" of migrants in the Midwest. Considering such stunning numbers, one wonders how such a horde of people could remain invisible. Third, kinship determinism often characterized this migration. People from the Appalachian Mountains, for example, have long been (mis) understood as being too cemented to kindred relationships to search out a better place to live. Those who migrated disproved this view often by making sure that kin came along with them. Finally, even during this period, upland southerners were beginning to find economic success, again debunking the idea that those who did leave the South remained mired in poverty in the Midwest.

Cheap Labor to Sustain the Boom

Economically, of course, one of the most important results of massive southern white out-migration was that the biggest economic boom in U.S. history was sustained, in part, by the sweat, muscles, and backs of southern migrants, many of them young, thus ensuring years of labor for their employers. The boom in the economy and the subsequent need for cheap labor were the primary reasons the "migrant problem" ceased after World War II. Indeed, a personnel manager for the Randall Company in Cincinnati, which employed about eight hundred people, more than half of whom were migrants, said that "they're proving they can be adaptable and can be a worthwhile addition to the community and to labor." "Industry," he summed, is "better off with them." Journalists in several cities began writing series on southern migration that actually attempted to revise commonly held stereotypes about southerners. By the 1960s, for example, a survey of hourly workers in Columbus, Ohio, discovered that a third were from "Appalachia" and that almost half of these workers had been at their current jobs for more than six years; two-thirds of those from the South had lived in Columbus longer than ten years. Others estimated that for Ohio as a whole, one in three workers had been born in southern Appalachian counties.[4]

The demand for workers in the Midwest strengthened the migration between the North and the South. When times were good, the flow of people went northward, and when times were bad, the flow often reversed, as it had in the Great Depression; the needle that indicated northerly or southerly flows of people was very sensitive. Take, for example, Harlan County, Kentucky, and Detroit. In the 1950s, the county was losing as many as one thousand people annually; the majority, it seemed, were headed to Detroit, since a bus line ran daily departures for Detroit. In the recession of 1957–58, however, the northward flow of people reversed, as laid-off autoworking southerners assumed they could make a better living in the South. Requests for surplus food, for example, in Black Mountain, near Harlan, soared by 30 percent the month after auto industry layoffs in 1957. A report in Chicago, too, noted:

> Former coal miners and farmers from the South are the most visible evidence of shuttle migration: when jobs are available in

Chicago, the streets of the Uptown area are lined with cars bearing licenses from Kentucky, Tennessee, West Virginia, Alabama, etc. Conversely, when jobs are very limited, the roads in these home states are filled with cars carrying Illinois, Indiana, and Michigan licenses. Nothing has yet improved the job situation at home, so the southern whites continue to move restlessly from town to town and home again.[5]

In 1950, a West Virginian traveled to Chicago to find work, thinking he would return once he saved up some money or if conditions back home improved. When things in West Virginia began to look promising, he quickly returned. His sojourning continued for ten years, until September 1960, when he moved his family permanently to Chicago, realizing that things would never again look promising in West Virginia. While many southerners made return trips to avoid harsh winters, especially during winter slowdowns, others from rural areas returned in April to plant a crop and then came north in October once the harvest was in. In Chicago's Uptown in the 1950s, for example, school attendance among migrant children was highest in November and lowest in April.[6]

Hundreds of white migrants flocked to both agricultural and industrial areas to fuel the economy. Southwestern Michigan, south-central and east-central Indiana, and western Ohio continued to see large numbers of white farm migrants, though by the 1950s farm owners began looking farther south to Texas and Mexico for their labor needs, particularly in Ohio, where Kentuckians who struck the Scioto Marsh's onion fields in the 1930s had left a pungent memory among landowners. Many migrants who began as agricultural workers, of course, moved into factory work.[7]

Take, for example, the case of Adolph Lacy, who grew up in Cleburne County, in north-central Arkansas, the child of farmers. In 1942, Adolph, his three siblings, his parents, Clarence Lackey, Gyle Lacy, and Luther Vance and his wife piled in a pickup truck "like a bunch of cattle" and traveled to Milburg, Michigan, in Berrien County, to harvest fruit. The families returned to

Arkansas after the harvest and used the money earned to send their children to school. "Michigan farmers loved to hire southern people," Adolph explained, "because they would work." Each of his family members was paid fifteen cents an hour. Just after World War II, he said, large numbers of Arkansans migrated northward because all there was to do in Arkansas was farm or work in timber, and by the end of the war most of the timber had been cut. In Berrien County, they worked for Wesley Miller picking cherries, apples, strawberries, and peaches and planting tomatoes. They were housed in little "huts," chicken coops and cow pens were common homes for the migrants. Initially, migrants were happy to harvest fruit, but the Whirlpool Corporation's giant plant in nearby Benton Harbor became the employment dream of many migrant pickers. Whirlpool, Adolph said, would "rather hire a southerner than their own. The only problem they had is most of the time they'd get a little money in their pocket and they'd want to go back south."[8] On August 21, 1949, Adolph, now married with two children, left Cleburne County for Benton Harbor with a friend. "This is the God's truth: When I left Arkansas," he said, "I had thirty-seven dollars and a half in my pocket. I had two pairs of blue overalls, two blue denim shirts, and my underwear—the wife had made them out of V.C. fertilizer sacks. It had the V.C. still on the hip back there." It took them two days to get to Michigan. Once they arrived, Adolph and his friend stayed in a chicken house near his parents, who had been there since the early summer picking fruit. By the end of the first week, he had a job working the night shift at Kaywood Corporation in Benton Harbor making venetian blinds for $1.04 an hour. It was Adolph's first factory job. During the day, he picked fruit for 75 cents an hour. Even with his parents nearby, he said, "I got so homesick I thought I couldn't stay there. But I didn't have no other choice." In October, his wife, Jemae, arrived with their children. She had come with her brother, who was moving to Mishawaka, Indiana, about forty miles south, to do carpentry work. She also longed for home, but not nearly as badly as Adolph. They were living in a furnished three-room

apartment in adjacent St. Joseph for seven dollars a week and were able to laugh about their northern "home" when interviewed. In January, Adolph was laid off, but he found a job in St. Joseph at Leeco Platers. After four consecutive days of nosebleeds, he quit and found a job at Auto Specialists, pouring crankshafts for $1.25 an hour. "Of course, they had piece work there," he said:

> They were pouring crankshafts then. They'd make four at a time. And them guys there on them core machines, it was piece work. And I asked somebody about them coremakers if they made any money. They said, Yeah. They was making a hundred bucks a week. And I said, "Boy, that's for me!" And the foreman happened to hear me, and that's all he wanted to hear, you know. The next day I went in and he said, "How would you like to have one of them machines over there?" And I said, "Man, you're looking at the guy that would like to have one of them." And I went to work on that thing and I'll tell you what: I'm no core-maker. I'd work myself to death. I'd get up in the morning and my hand—I had a pound-and-a-half hammer; you had to beat that machine to pack that thing. She'd have to soak my hand in hot salt water to get it back where I could use it the next day. And I think the most I ever made was fifty-eight dollars a week.

Frustrated, Adolph went to Whirlpool in Benton Harbor to complete an application, and on April 8, 1950, he went to work, much more comfortable around the many southern transplants working there. "It was full of them," he said, most of whom had gone first to pick fruit and ended up in a factory job.[9]

Elements of associational life often eased the adjustments of the exiles. One of the strongest examples was union activity. As more southerners migrated, they filled the ranks of union rolls, duping industrialists, many of whom looked favorably upon southern whites because they were thought to be "independent" enough to resist unionization. Few migrants became labor radicals; most seem to have been typical postwar bread-and-butter unionists, eager primarily to gain higher wages and more benefits. Southern migrants were not only active rank and filers but also leaders, again not so much because they were radicals but because they were willing to answer the call of fellow workers. Earl Cox was active at TRW, Daymon Morgan in the UAW at Chrysler, Joe Clardy was a union steward at Studebaker, as was Adolph Lacy at Whirlpool, while Grady Roberson, who began work at Dodge Brothers in Mishawaka in 1959 as a lathe operator, soon became the shopwide set-up man. Eventually, he was elected president of the Steelworkers' local there, though he emphasized modestly that it was others in the plant who forced him into becoming a steward and then ultimately voted him president. John Weatherford also worked at Dodge during the Korean War but says he was never greatly involved with the union because of the "family" atmosphere at Dodge—a feeling of separation between management and labor did not exist, according to him. In 1952, he went to Bendix, and six years later was asked to run for steward. Although also nominated without wanting the job, he won and remained in the position for eleven years, at which time he was "talked into" running for the bargaining committee. Since that time, he has served the UAW as committee member, vice-president, and most recently as president. Clardy, Roberson, and Weatherford pointed out that it was others in the plant (including natives and ethnics) who pushed them into union leadership, mostly because of their social qualities, not their militancy. Roberson and Weatherford, for example, said they socialized with everyone after arriving in the North. Weatherford maintained that his base was much larger than southern whites; native whites, Poles, Hungarians, and African Americans often voted for him more often than southerners did.[10]

My research reveals little of the coolness toward unions that previous scholars have ascribed to migrants. Roscoe Giffin and William W. Philliber, for example, maintain that southern newcomers were not active in unions because of their independence. The sociologist Harry Schwarzweller writes that "Appalachian people just aren't good joiners," feeling "uncomfortable in formal gatherings, and their participation in union activities is in most cases minimal. A

general behavioral apathy prevails." He continues:

> Participation in union meetings and activities outside of the immediate job situation are seen as interfering with home life and most migrants are unwilling to allow this to happen. They accept union membership in much the same way as they accept other, more discomfiting aspects of factory work life, and they obey union dictums in much the same way that they obey shop regulations or the orders of a foreman. Further involvement demands a social commitment over and above that for which the familistically-oriented mountaineer is prepared.

Not every migrant became an avid unionist (some may have seen themselves as only temporary sojourners, not permanent employees), but many did, even among the agricultural workers. Although many mountaineers and western Kentuckians came to northern urban areas believing John L. Lewis stood on the right side of God, some southerners, particularly from undeveloped areas outside the Appalachian South, undoubtedly came north with little if any understanding of labor unions. Many, however, were soon converted, as Grady Roberson pointed out: "Well, after you get into a place and you get to working and you understand the jobs and know that the company's really making a lot of money and you're not getting much, you're going to go fighting for more money; that's just all there is to it." Frank Plemons agreed: "Of course, down South, even today there's a lot of places down there that's nonunion. These companies today, they don't want no unions. But I can see what the union's done for the people, you know, over the years. I mean, the things that the company give me, there's no way they'd give it to me if they didn't have to. The company is just common sense." "The company," he concluded, "don't give you nothing if they don't have to, I don't think."[11]

The Upland Southern Hegira

The coalfields continued to transform southerners into exiles following World War II. Although coal mining enjoyed prosperity during World War II, by the 1950s coal mining operations, using their profits from the war, were scrambling to buy automated equipment, and thousands of miners, whose existence had always been precarious, were expelled from the mines. Company stores closed, movie theaters shut their doors, and train and bus services stopped. Ironically, many ex-miners were going to such places as Columbus, Ohio, and getting jobs with the Joy Company, which manufactured much of the equipment that was replacing miners. "It was kind of like watching the place die around me," the novelist Denise Giardina recalled of her youth in West Virginia's coalfields. "The older I got the more things left," including people. "Mostly I remember people leaving and not coming back, or they might have come back to another place where they had relatives. It seemed like everybody left at the same time," she said. "People did try to stay around—sometimes they moved to another coal camp like we did for a while. Sometimes they moved to the next county or something, but probably just as many left for good." When the mine that employed her father closed, the family moved to a nearby coal camp when she was twelve; a year later they moved to Charleston, West Virginia.[12]

The statistics speak for themselves. Between 1950 and 1955, for example, the number of miners in Kentucky fell by almost one-half, hemorrhaging 22,000 people. In McDowell County, West Virginia, 30,000 miners were employed in 1945; ten years later less than half that number were still mining coal. Farther south, Campbell County, Tennessee, was suffering a similar fate. In 1946, 6,000 people were employed in the mines; by 1955, the figure had dropped to 4,000 and by 1958, said C.J. Daniels, editor of the *LaFollette Press*, "I doubt if there are a thousand miners working today." Some of the mines, he explained, were played out, "but the chief reason for the great decline in the industry is automation in the mines." Many of the people were leaving Tennessee for Cleveland and Dayton. Frank Bradburn, pastor of the local Baptist church, said 47 of his 200-member congregation left for northern jobs in 1957 alone. A Bluefield, West Virginia, bus line was

selling a hundred tickets each week for Cleveland. Between 1950 and 1960, over half a million people left West Virginia; more than 67,000 people left the state for Cleveland alone between 1955 and 1960. Estimates on the number of ex-miners and other southern whites in Cleveland ranged between 35,000 and 50,000—as many as one in every eighteen people—clustered mainly on the west side.[13]

The zenith years of upland southern white migration to the Midwest were dawning. In the southern Appalachian region alone, 704,000 people left between 1940 and 1950 compared with a paltry 81,000 between 1935 and 1940. Between 1950 and 1957, another 784,000 fled; between 1940 and 1970, a total of 3.2 million mountaineers bolted. Although the southern Appalachian birthrate had actually begun to fall, out-migration was significant enough to produce losses through interstate migration for each southern state.[14]

Kentucky, always one of the big suppliers of migrants northward, lost almost 400,000 people through migration during the 1940s; during the 1950s, thirteen out of every one hundred people—from western areas and eastern areas—were leaving the state. The high birthrate and limited opportunity left many Kentuckians with little choice but to leave. Harlan County alone lost more than 23,000 people between 1940 and 1950, almost a third of its population, and Leslie County, long having the dubious distinction of the nation's highest birthrate, lost almost a third of its population the following decade. Seven other eastern Kentucky counties (Breathitt, Elliott, Jackson, Magoffin, Owsley, Rockcastle, and Wolfe) between 1940 and 1950 lost 40 or more percent of their populations to migration. While demographers seemed to focus on eastern counties, western and central counties were also losing people to migration: nine western and south-central counties lost more than 30 percent of their 1940 population figures, proving that migration was a *southern,* not exclusively an *Appalachian,* phenomenon— not a hegira from the hills but rather from the Upland South. Data indicate that more western than eastern Kentuckians were leaving the state.[15]

But it was the southern Appalachian person who was getting all of the attention in the media, beginning in the late 1950s. Census data, however, reveal that almost twice the number of people left western Tennessee than eastern Tennessee between 1955 and 1960, most of whom were bound for Chicago. More western Kentuckians migrated to Indiana than eastern Kentuckians during the same period, although twice as many Tennesseans bound for Indiana left middle and eastern areas than western areas. Of white migrants from Kentucky to Illinois, a little more than half of whom were bound for Chicago, more than twice the number came from western counties than from eastern ones, although slightly more eastern Kentuckians and Tennesseans went to Detroit than did their western counterparts. In spite of these data, Lewis Killian writes that "the stereotype of the hillbilly definitely includes the notion that he is a mountaineer, a white southerner whose caricature is to be seen in Snuffy Smith of the comic strip."[16]

NOTES

1. Fields interview, 2.
2. Shepherd and Giles quoted in "Cocke County Boasts Scenery and Moonshine," mimeographed clipping (from *Harlan Daily Enterprise)*, Urban Migrant Project, folder 3, box 278, Records of the Council of the Southern Mountains (hereafter CSM Collection), Southern Appalachian Archives, Hutchins Library, Berea College, Berea, Ky.; Tennessee Valley Authority, *Tennessee Valley Region,* n.p.; Norma Lee Browning, "Poverty Spurs Hill Folk on Road to North," *Chicago Daily Tribune,* May 11, 1957. For more on Cleveland's migrants, see Julian Krawcheck, "Smile When You Say 'Hillbilly!'" *Cleveland Press,* Jan. 29–Feb. 4, 1958.
3. James S. Brown, "Migration within, to, and from the Southern Appalachians, 1935–1939," 18, 20, Urban Migrant Project, folder 3, box 278, CSM Collection. For the original study, see Brown, "Social Organization of an Isolated Kentucky Mountain Neighborhood."
4. William Collins, "Your Neighbor!" clipping (from *Cincinnati Enquirer),* Migrants II folder, CSM Collection (quote); Roscoe Giffin, "Newcomers from the Southern Mountains," 3, Southern Appalachia—General, folder 8, box 3, Roscoe Giffin Collection, Southern Appalachian Archives; "Appalachian Workers in Columbus Surveyed," 37. For journalistic revisionism, see the series by Krawcheck, "Smile When You Say 'Hillbilly.'" There were exceptions, of course, particularly in Chicago, such as Norma Lee Browning's series on "Otter Hollow, Appalachia, U.S. A.," the first of which was printed in the *Chicago Daily Tribune* on May 5, 1957. The complete collection of articles is in Newspaper Clippings, folder 15, box 293, CSM Collection. See also one of the most notorious articles: Votaw, "Hillbillies Invade Chicago," 64–67. Not surprisingly, when the economic boom slowed in the 1960s, voices once again began to clamor about the migrant problem.
5. Drake, "Recession Is Far from Over in the Southern Mountains," 36–37; Chicago Commission on Human Relations, *1960 Annual Report of the Migration Services Department,* 3, 6 (quotation), Urban Migrant Project, folder 2, box 283, CSM Collection.
6. Lake View Newcomer Committee, *Summary of Visits to Southern White Families,* 4; Killian, *White Southerners,* 106.
7. Mary Ellen Wolfe, "Migrants Loyal, Easily Adjust to Jobs," *Dayton Journal Herald,* Feb. 26, 1960; Hundley, "Mountain Man in Northern Industry," 34–38.
8. Lacy interview.
9. Ibid.
10. Roberson interview; Weatherford interview.
11. Giffin, "Appalachian Newcomers to Cincinnati," 79–84; Philliber, *Appalachian Migrants in Urban America,* 89; Schwarzweller, "Occupational Patterns of Appalachian Migrants," 136; Roberson interview; Plemons and Collins interview, 22. James Gregory found "little reluctance" and "considerable enthusiasm for workplace organization" among "Okies" in California. See Gregory, *American Exodus,* 163.
12. Stroud interview; Giardina interview.
13. Daniels quoted in Browning, "Poverty Spurs Hill Folk on Road to North"; "Industry Comes, but Workers Quit Tennessee," clipping, Urban Migrant Project, folder 3, box 278, CSM Collection, "'Bloody Harlan' Hit Hard by Strike," clipping, Urban Migrant Project, folder 3, box 278, CSM Collection; Krawcheck, "Smile When You Say 'Hillbilly' "; Julian Krawcheck, "Coal Industry Decline Sends Southerners Here," *Cleveland Press,* July 20, 1959; Schweiker, "Some Facts and a Theory of Migration." Many ex-miners, of course, also traveled to Chicago. See

Chicago Fact Book Consortium, *Local Community Fact Book*, 6.

14. Brown, "Migration within, to, and from the Southern Appalachians," 10. Southern-born people constituted ever increasing percentages in midwestern states, including 12 percent of Ohio's total population, 11 percent of Indiana's, 10 percent of Michigan's, and 9 percent of Illinois's. See U.S. Bureau of the Census, *U.S. Census of Population: 1950*, vol. 4, *Special Reports*, part 4, chap. A, State of Birth, tables 4, 8, 9, and 14. See also U.S. Bureau of the Census, "Estimates of the Population of States and Selected Outlying Areas of the United States, July 1, 1957 and 1956."

15. James S. Brown and Paul D. Richardson, "Changes in Kentucky's Population by Counties: Natural Increase and Net Migration," 1–4, manuscript, Southern Appalachian Studies—Roscoe Giffin, folder 7, box 3, Faculty and Staff Collection, Berea College Archives; "Exodus from the Hills," *Hazard (Ky.) Herald*, Feb. 28, 1963; Jim Hampton, "Exodus," *Louisville Courier-Journal*, June 16, 1962; "Area Still Gets Steady Stream from South," *Dayton Journal Herald*, July 22, 1961; Mary Ellen Wolfe, "Daytonians Accept South's Migrants," *Dayton Journal Herald*, Feb. 22, 1960. For exact out-migration numbers, contact author.

16. U.S. Bureau of the Census, *U.S. Census of Population: 1960, Subject Reports, Mobility for State Economic Areas*, Final Report PC (2)-2B, tables 33–36; Donald Janson, "30,000 Hill People Now Cluster in Chicago," *New York Times*, Aug. 31, 1963; Killian, *White Southerners*, 103.

ESSAY 8.4

White Noose

Robert O. Self

Source: Robert O. Self, *American Babylon: Race and the Struggle for Postwar Oakland* (Princeton: Princeton University Press, 2005).

EDITORS' INTRODUCTION

Robert O. Self deftly employs the framework of property to provide us with a nuanced understanding of the Bay Area, a pivotal battleground in the long civil rights movement of the twentieth century and a center of growing white activism, which, according to the author, cannot be solely seen as a backlash movement. The whites, disingenuously to some degree (or perhaps much more), described their own efforts with the rhetoric of individual rights. As a state, California faced the challenges of great growth, struggling with open access to public housing and the costs of other social programs for its poorer residents. Groups like the California Real Estate Association (CREA) argued that the free ownership of private property allowed for the greatest social good, and that the housing market should be unregulated. Self writes that the homeowner populism of the time "precipitated a series of suburban counterrevolutions in these two decades that lay the groundwork for the so-called tax revolt of 1978. The price of California's extraordinary growth had to be met, but not, if suburban homeowners had their way, by them."[i] The largely white suburbs came to form a physical and metaphorical noose around Oakland, strangling the city in terms of housing needs and economic viability. Those taking part in the white flight to the suburbs refused to pay higher taxes for the social and economic support of the city and the less affluent residents there. They refused to acknowledge their own tax benefits, coming from such governmental agencies as the Veteran's Administration and the Federal Housing Administration, which offered loan guarantees to white home buyers to a much higher degree than home buyers of color. Once families had purchased housing, of course, the interest on the mortgage payments became tax deductible. Additionally, continued racist controls of housing access helped suburban properties gain market value at a rate unmatched in Oakland itself.

The region's initial promise of serving as a postwar industrial garden—a region replete with jobs, fine housing options, and a pleasing metropolitan setting—would not unfold as many had hoped. At the two extremes, the dream ended in the radical politics of the separatist Black Panther Party, born in the area, and the individualistic, anti-tax conservative politics of the white homeowners. **[See Document 9.3.]** The latter view quickly became common throughout the nation, and ushered in the Reagan Revolution of the 1980s. Although American cities had long featured suburbs, the city-suburb dualism came of age in these decades, defining the period's politics and lived reality.

Robert O. Self is Mary Ann Lippitt Professor of American History and Department Chair of History at Brown University. *American Babylon* was awarded four major prizes: The

---

i Robert O. Self, *American Babylon: Race and the Struggle for Postwar Oakland* (Princeton: Princeton University Press, 2003), 259.

James A. Rawley Prize, Best Book on U.S. Race Relations (2005) from the Organization of American Historians; the Best Book in Urban Affairs from the Urban Affairs Association (2005); the Ralph J. Bunche Award, Best Book on Ethnic Pluralism (2004) from the American Political Science Association; and the Best Book in North American Urban History (2004) from the Urban History Association. In 2012, Self published *All in the Family: The Realignment of American Democracy since the 1960s* (New York: Hill and Wang). Self is at work on a new book on the history of the nuclear family and the resulting economic order.

WHITE NOOSE (2005)

THE SUBURBAN "white noose" surrounding the urban black community stood metaphorically for metropolitan inequality and segregation. Unwelcome in the South County (Southern Alameda County) suburbs, African Americans in Oakland were denied access to the region's fastest growing employment and housing markets. Suburban Alameda County, from San Leandro through Fremont (and across the Santa Clara County line into Milpitas) *was* closed to black homebuyers in most important respects through the middle 1970s. But the denial of access was only one story. It must be joined to others. Suburban homeowners shaped regional distributions of opportunity and resources in more ways than just policing racial boundaries. Indeed, by the 1970s white East Bay homeowners were more interested in reducing taxes than in managing race. But unequal metropolitan development meant that fighting taxes represented the reproduction of racial disadvantage by other means — and therefore the reproduction of race by other means. In the 1960s and 1970s the suburban politics of property were an extension, under changing economic conditions, of the processes that underlay city building in the 1940s and 1950s. Even as they remained major beneficiaries of public subsidy, South County suburban homeowners nonetheless claimed that they were under siege and victimized. In their view, the industrial garden had begun to show signs of wilting, the suburban dream signs of malaise. Keeping it alive and flourishing remained their overriding objective.[1]

The pace and reach of postwar suburbanization had transformed California in a single generation. Between 1950 and 1970 the state's population doubled, from just over ten million to just under twenty. Men and women from every state, Mexico, and, after 1965, Southeast Asia poured into California in these two decades, dwarfing even the enormous World War II migration. To accommodate them, three and a half million new housing units were built — double the number that existed in 1950 — in a twenty-year construction bonanza of enormous scope. The new population was overwhelmingly young. As the median age in the state dropped from thirty-two to twenty-seven, the percentage of people over sixty-five years of age fell from 8 to 3, and the percentage of school-age children shot up from 17 to 25. In all, the number of California school-age children quadrupled in two decades. Population growth and development fed a real estate boom in which the median home price jumped by 50 percent — and it would increase even more dramatically during the 1970s. In the space of twenty years, California had become the nation's economic engine and population magnet.[2]

In the late 1960s the East Bay suburban corridor, from Oakland to San Jose, looked like much of postwar California. Two decades of industrial-garden city building had made the "Metropolitan Oakland Area" one of Northern California's leading poles of growth. A forty-mile river of concrete, the Nimitz Interstate Highway, spanned its length and stitched together the landscape in linear regularity. South of Oakland, Nimitz exits led first to San Leandro and its booming industrial districts. Fifteen thousand blue-collar workers labored here, at Caterpillar Tractor, International Harvester, National Can, Frieden Calculators, Simmons Mattresses, the Latchford Glass Company, and dozens upon dozens of small, ten- and fifteen-employee machine shops and light assembly plants. They drove to work on the Nimitz and parked on vast asphalt acreages. Others arrived on surface streets through San Leandro neighborhoods, patchworks of ranch homes and stucco bungalows that looked much like Oakland's. Outside the city limits lay San Lorenzo, one of the largest subdivisions in Northern California, five thousand wartime ranch homes on unincorporated county land with a population of seventeen thousand. Filled with World War II veterans turned machinists, welders, teachers, civil servants, clerks, and salespeople, San Lorenzo's government was its homeowners association, its downtown the Bayfair Mall in San Leandro. Here, and in neighboring Castro Valley, racial segregation was a given, and homes appreciated ahead of inflation every year.

Further south, exit ramps led east into Hayward, by the late 1960s a city more than double its prewar physical size. Ethnic Mexican *colonias*, once on marginal land, had been incorporated through annexation, as had acres of Anglo tract homes. Near Hayward's prewar downtown, the giant Hunt Foods canneries hummed with seasonal activity and four thousand workers. Hunt's large ethnic Mexican workforce lived in *barrios* in Hayward, Union City, Milpitas, Alviso, and even on San Jose's East side. Surrounding downtown and the canneries were new subdivisions with names like Fairway Greens and Holiday Estates, and new shopping malls indistinguishable at a distance from factories and warehouses with their low-slung, horizontal design and gargantuan parking lots. In Hayward, Okie and Arkie migrants and their descendants lived in close proximity to Mexican migrants and their families, with multiple subdivisions of white-collar WASPs in between, in a city that symbolized the sudden and often jarring confluence of an agricultural past and a suburban future. Hayward was the most eclectic South County suburb, a mish-mash of working-class and ethnic cultures stirred together with an ascendant managerial and commercial Anglo middle class.

Leaving Hayward, the Nimitz passed quickly through Union City and then into the largest municipality in Northern California, Fremont. In the 1960s Fremont's population more than doubled, from forty-three thousand to just over a hundred thousand — within corporate limits larger than either San Francisco or Oakland. Horizontal, diffuse, uncentered, Fremont lived up to America's suburban clichés. On the far south side of town, Nimitz traffic buzzed along within a hundred yards of the sprawling General Motors plant, set in near-perfect industrial garden coincidence against the vacant, verdant hillside. Back in the city proper, wide boulevards criss-crossed one another in a broad latticework that linked each new subdivision to the next. Nearly devoid of any pre-World War II structure, Fremont boasted the newest housing stock in the country, cul-de-sac after cul-de-sac of ranch-style homes set back behind front lawns and rows of freshly planted maple trees. By far the greenest South County suburb, Fremont's parks, lake, nearby hills, huge blocks of undeveloped land, and plentiful crabgrass on both public and private property, along with the ubiquitous sunshine common in the southern part of the Bay Area, gave the city literally the feel of a garden. Past Fremont lay the autoworker suburb of Milpitas and San Jose's sprawling Eastside, the center of Mexican and Chicano life in Northern California.

The Nimitz provided one possible viewing frame of this emerging landscape. By the 1970s, BART offered another. With its multiple stops along the length of the East Bay, BART took managers to work in Oakland from Fremont, but also auto-workers to Fremont assembly lines from Oakland. Nurses at Kaiser Hospital in Oakland or San Francisco traveled from their homes in Hayward. Seasonal cannery workers in Hayward commuted from their homes near the Fruitvale stop in Oakland. Workers passed back and forth across one another's paths in a complex set of daily migrations that did not always correspond to the organization man model — commuting to central city jobs from bedroom suburbs. Two long bridges across San Francisco Bay in South County, intersecting with the Nimitz at Hayward and Fremont, respectively, multiplied the commuting combinations. They made it possible for aerospace engineers at Lockheed in Sunnyvale or electrical engineers at the Stanford Industrial Park to live in Fremont, which many did. The bridges also carried ethnic Mexicans from the barrio in Redwood City south of San Francisco to work in Hayward or Union City or, by the 1970s, at General Motors in Fremont and Ford in Milpitas. Black autoworkers Jim Crowed out of Fremont and Milpitas in the 1960s lived in East Palo Alto, at the foot of the Dumbarton Bridge. Shopping malls and factories on the fringe, multicity commutes, and vast subdivisions spread life, labor, and leisure horizontally across the spaces of the flatlands.

The most powerful frame in which to understand South County, however, remains property. Underneath the commuting, subdivisions, and development lay a history of property markets and the politics that shaped them. The expectations of racial segregation and low taxes produced in suburban South County after World War II could not be contained by the boosters and public officials who helped to construct them. They would take on a life of their own. Homeowners in the 1960s and 1970s remained focused on how property would be developed and taxed, how space would be mobilized for social and political ends. That concern, animated by the homeowner populism that was a foundation of suburban city building in the 1950s, precipitated a series of suburban counterrevolutions in these two decades that lay the groundwork for the so-called tax revolt of 1978. The price of California's extraordinary growth had to be met, but not, if suburban home-owners had their way, by them. On three key issues — racial segregation, affordable housing, and taxes — suburbanites in the East Bay joined with their counterparts statewide in a political retrenchment with far-reaching consequences. Suburban home-owners in Alameda County presented themselves as protecting their economic future and preserving the promises of the industrial garden, but their actions, embedded in already skewed metropolitan structures of opportunity, continued to shift a disproportionate share of the costs of postwar capitalism to Oakland. Furthermore, they participated in the creation of a narrative of victimization, which appealed to increasing numbers of

homeowners over these decades, that may have reflected genuine feeling but belied the enormous privileges they enjoyed. The suburban break with liberalism, so evident in the East Bay by the late 1960s, changed California politics within a decade and national politics within another.[3]

The Suburbs in Black and White

In November 1964 tens of thousands of southern Alameda County suburbanites drove to the polls. They voted in overwhelming numbers for the figurehead of mid-1960s liberalism, President Lyndon B. Johnson, while casting ballots in equal proportion against one of California liberalism's signature achievements, fair housing. Two million Californians statewide joined in this performance, making a contradictory case to the nation about where the state stood on race and equality. But the results likely did not appear contradictory to residents of South County, because they had come to understand the limits of liberalism and the American welfare state through the lens of property. Property and homeownership organized a set of primary concerns and issues for suburban voters. It also structured the mechanics of political participation — who was heard and which groups defined the debate. Homeownership dominated the framing of social and political questions. But homeowners were not alone in setting forth these parameters. Leaders of the real estate industry — at every level, from local to national — kept watch on the California housing market, one of the most dynamic and profitable in the nation, carefully and deliberately. That industry's investment in residential racial segregation had ebbed little by the early 1960s. In 1964 no threat to property markets seemed greater to either homeowners or the real estate industry than the Rumford Fair Housing Act, passed in 1963 after a decade of work by Byron Rumford, the East Bay Democratic Club, and the statewide liberal coalition.[4]

The California Real Estate Association (CREA) brought Proposition 14, repeal of the Rumford Act, before voters in 1964.

Part of the CREA's broad antiliberal agenda, Proposition 14 made California "a battle-ground for a national showdown on housing legislation," in Byron Rumford's phrase. One of the most important social movement organizations in the postwar United States, the CREA organized people on the presumption that property, as space that produces capital, is the highest social good and should remain the least regulated, most "free," arena of human activity. The CREA campaign in 1964 emphasized the sanctity of private property and its centrality to Americanism. "I want to talk about the preservation of this *real* American," a CREA representative explained in 1964, "an individual who, at least up until now, has been endowed with personal freedom as to choice." Co-opting the rights language of the national black liberation movement, the CREA and its political supporters aggressively shaped public discussion of fair housing. "If we believe in the American democratic system," a Republican state senator explained, "we must acknowledge that it is the right of the people to tell the government what to do." He concluded his defense of Proposition 14 by warning that "[w]hen the government tells the people what to do and think, we have a dictatorship." In place of the "traditional right" of property ownership, the president of the National Association of Real Estate Boards asserted, the Rumford Act supposedly established "a new so-called right for individuals of a minority group."[5]

This individual rights language represented a profound dissembling on the part of real estate interests. Industry leaders had long shaped segregation with institutional bulwarks and market manipulation. Through its buying and selling policies, the CREA controlled local real estate boards and set standards for segregation in hundreds of local communities statewide. The Southern Alameda County Board of Realtors, a CREA member, determined, for example, which homes in the East Bay would be advertised as "white only." Prior to 1948 the CREA used racial covenants to prevent the sale of homes to "non-Caucasians," and after 1948 it endorsed "corporation contract agreements" like those used in the East Bay by M. C. Friel to keep communities white. The CREA also maintained a powerful presence in the state legislature in Sacramento, where it influenced property tax legislation, state building codes, and a host of other property-related matters. Indeed, the CREA remained a more consistent reservoir of conservative politics in 1960s' California than the Republican Party and stood as the principal force in the state opposing liberal or social democratic claims on private property. On the eve of the 1964 election, the CREA had 2,600 member realtors in Alameda County and a statewide grassroots network of realtors, realty boards, and business connections that rivaled any political party. A late-1960s report by the California Committee for Fair Practices estimated that "the California Real Estate Association is, among profit-making trade groups, without parallel in power and prestige."[6]

Proposition 14 passed in southern Alameda County by an overwhelming margin. In an election in which Lyndon Johnson won the county by a margin of two to one, and voters returned Democrats to seats in the state legislature and U.S. Congress, Proposition 14 received a stunning endorsement. San Leandro, for instance, voted to repeal the Rumford Act 80 percent to 20 percent while endorsing Johnson over Goldwater nearly two to one. In Hayward, three-fourths of the voters favored repeal, with two to one margins for Johnson as well. Only in Union City, where the Mexican American community remained a near majority, and in Milpitas (in Santa Clara County), where Ben Gross and the UAW campaigned relentlessly against Proposition 14, was the vote against fair housing reasonably close; however the proposition still won in both cities. The San Leandro-Oakland municipal border offered the most striking instance of Proposition 14's intersection with local racial segregation. In San Leandro precincts along the Oakland city line, Proposition 14 passed with slightly more than 80 percent of the vote — in three precincts it was as high as 85 percent. In parallel precincts directly across the city line, African American neighborhoods in

East Oakland voted *against* Proposition 14 by more than 92 percent — in one precinct the vote to defeat the referendum was 204 to 3. Such patterns, and the remarkable totals for Alameda County as a whole, belied the CREA's insistence that Proposition 14 was a race-neutral issue of "freedom." South County voters endorsed the CREA discourse of property rights as a rhetorical standing for resistance to desegregation. Byron Rumford lamented that "the whole proposition was built on fear and discrimination and racism," such that even "those who expressed themselves as liberals" believed they needed Proposition 14 "in order to protect their homes." Nationally, Proposition 14's victory was widely regarded as a severe blow to the civil rights movement, what "No on 14" advocate Edward McHugh called "the severest setback to the forces of fair housing since the current phase of the civil rights struggle began."[7]

Homeowners, however, were not Proposition 14's only constituents, nor was the measure a transparent expression of homeowner political objectives. In Alameda County, as in all developing localities in California and nationwide, dense home finance and construction networks linked a variety of individuals and institutions to the process of community building. Land speculators and developers, as well as the banks that lent them money, were in this group. Real estate brokers and home mortgage brokers, as well as the banks that lent them money, were in it too. The process of home building, from the subdivision planning stage to the handshake over the final sale, involved attorneys, title companies, professional planners, and a host of other subsidiary planning and finance institutions. These multiple constituencies symbolized the range of both personal and structural investments in segregation. At the same time, the uproar over the Rumford Act was ignited and fueled by the CREA and the National Association of Real Estate Boards, not by a spontaneous homeowner revolt. Both the CREA and the NAREB had been fighting fair housing in the California Assembly and promoting segregated communities for decades. When the Rumford Act passed in a close vote

in 1963, CREA representatives, not homeowners' organizations, were on hand in Sacramento to declare their intention to repeal it. Proposition 14 *engendered* a grassroots response, with hundreds of thousands of homeowners enthusiastically championing the campaign. But the campaign itself was organized and directed by the CREA and its affiliates.[8]

Indeed, if there was a grassroots dimension to the 1964 campaign, it came from Proposition 14's opponents. The measure passed in South County despite enormous public efforts to defeat it. "The 'No on 14' campaign," according to one postelection assessment "was strongly endorsed, relatively well financed, and backed by a hardworking army of volunteers." Outside of San Leandro, which remained the most segregationist city in the county, virtually every major public official — from state legislators to mayors and city council members — opposed the measure. "In the interests of justice and common decency, it should be defeated," declared the Tri-Cities Committee Against Proposition 14, a group that included the mayor and city council of Fremont, South County's congressional and assembly representatives, and Union City's major public figures. Another prominent member added that the referendum "would create a new kind of right — alien to our state and not found in any other state, including Mississippi ... the absolute right to discriminate." Governor Brown called it "the segregation initiative" and referred to it as "legalized bigotry." Californians Against Proposition 14, the umbrella organization for the anti-14 forces, drew on the same grassroots networks of churches, labor unions, and civil rights organizations that had come together to defeat the right-to-work measure in 1958. Proposition 14 "would erect a Jim Crow Wall around the ghettoes of California," opponents of the measure emphasized. In press releases, public debates, radio announcements, and innumerable public meetings and information sessions, Alameda County's political, religious, and business leaders vigorously opposed Proposition 14. Only realtors and homeowners associations were absent from the No on 14 coalition. But they, operating through institutional networks cultivated over two decades of city building, proved far more able to convince and mobilize voters than the county's political leadership.[9]

The CREA framed Proposition 14 as a decision between "freedom of choice" and "forced housing" and asked California homeowners to choose segregation under a different name. Naming was especially important in the election. Opponents of the Rumford Act rehearsed in California a well-worn rhetorical strategy that would become increasingly popular in national conservative circles in the late 1960s and early 1970s: employing a putatively race-neutral civil rights language. The Rumford Act's detractors discussed race only to place liberal supporters of fair housing on the defensive and accuse them of "naiveté." Encouraged by the CREA, those aligned against Rumford used a discourse of property rights to argue that the law "forced" property owners to rent or sell to a specific group, namely, African Americans. Further, the CREA claimed in public that they had no influence over housing markets and could not control the racial preferences of property owners or renters. "When one of the so-called minority groups moves in, the majority group moves out," Oscar Brinkman, a lobbyist for the National Apartment Owners Association and its California affiliates, told the House Judiciary Committee in 1963, "and the end result will be financially calamitous to an owner who had no racial prejudice of his own." While such claims may have contained an element of truth, given the segregationist prejudice of most whites, their larger duplicity was evident. After decades of lobbying both state and federal governments against fair housing, and decades of promoting segregation in local communities, representatives of the real estate industry then claimed that they were merely looking out for the "rights" of their constituents and were innocent of any complicity in discrimination. This purposeful deception underscored the lengths to which industry representatives would go to preserve their control over one of the most lucrative real estate markets in the nation.[10]

That control had three principal dimensions. First, since well before the New Deal, NAREB and the CREA had segregated property markets using racial covenants. This allowed the industry both to manipulate the racial prejudice of home buyers and to create predictable markets. The real estate industry wanted reliable control over any market fluctuations created by white prejudice. This emerged as an even more pressing issue within New Deal housing policy. Under Home Owners Loan Corporation (HOLC), FHA, and VA guidelines, the most profitable real estate strategy was to treat black and white housing markets as entirely distinct entities. There was a second, related dimension. Open housing threatened real estate industry control because it raised the possibility of chaotic market fluctuations. Rapid white turnover and property devaluation, wholesale white abandonment of rental properties, or the refusal of developers to build or banks to finance mixed-race developments, to name a few select fears, introduced market factors that undermined steady, predictable, upwardly trending property valuations — the real estate industry's chief concern. Finally, there was a third dimension to industry control. African American residential mobility was always understood in negative terms, because it forced ever wider readjustments of property values in white neighborhoods. Among other factors, white home values were affected by their proximity to African American neighborhoods. Containment is not too strong a word for the industry's desire to minimize these readjustments. In all, the real estate industry came to see the promotion, preservation, and manipulation of racial segregation as central — rather than incidental or residual — components of their profit-generating strategies.[11]

To dramatize the industry's promotion of segregation in suburban Alameda County, in the summer of 1963, a year before Proposition 14, African American leaders from Oakland had appealed to suburban Alameda County in an effort to dramatize suburban segregation and lay the groundwork for application of the Rumford Act. They delivered prescient warnings of impending social distress in Oakland and pleas for justice in the language of liberalism and progressive Americanism. In a major speech before the Southern Alameda County Bar Association, Don McCullum explained that the condition of impoverished black Oaklanders was made worse by the "rigid housing discrimination in Southern Alameda County — beginning at the San Leandro city limits." "This is not good — not good for America, not good for yourselves individually or for your children," he continued. He related his own frustration at being turned down by South County housing developments in a three-year search for a new home. "The minority people cannot break out of the city because of the irresponsibility of the suburban areas," he told the audience of journalists. Clinton White, an Oakland attorney and NAACP official, also toured South County communities urging residents to accept integration. "Fairness in jobs, housing, and education can give Fremont a 'welcome wagon' appearance," White told the Fremont Council of Social Planning in the summer of 1963. That same summer, Berkeley and Oakland CORE chapters staged "Operation Windowshop" in East Bay suburbs, demonstrations in which black home buyers strolled through all-white neighborhoods where homes were listed for sale. In these and other instances, beginning in 1963 and continuing well into the 1970s, South County communities were under constant pressure from Oakland's black leaders to open housing to African American buyers and, in a more general sense, to improve their relationship with African American Oakland.[12]

Black leaders from Oakland could reprimand and cajole suburban residents and appeal to what McCullum called the "responsible white community," but moral rhetoric was virtually their only leverage. McCullum could insist that the notion of property rights articulated by the CREA preserved segregation and trampled on the rights of African Americans, but he and the community he represented were positioned at great remove from the levers of municipal power in places like San Leandro and Fremont. Here was the national civil rights dilemma writ small. The geographic

concentration of the African American political community and the structure of American political authority — around municipal, state, and federal, but not regional, poles — made addressing regional problems extraordinarily difficult. State laws like the Rumford Act and federal civil rights legislation represented the best hope that these political boundaries could be superceded. In places like Oakland, there was a constituency for civil rights legislation, especially for the federal Civil Rights Act of 1964, every bit as large, vocal, and determined as in Birmingham and Selma, a constituency that hoped to turn moral suasion into political leverage. But their adversary was not "massive resistance," the South's campaign against desegregation. It was sunbelt metropolitanization and its structure of property markets, homeowner politics, and segregated municipal enclaves.[13]

Resistance to open housing in southern Alameda County rested simultaneously on both willful action and a rhetoric of innocence. Willful acts included Proposition 14, homeowners association agreements, and, prior to the 1960s, all of the architecture of suburban apartheid. These cleared the way for inaction, including homeowners' protestations in 1963 and afterward that no "civil rights problems" existed in South County suburbs. In San Leandro, for instance, when Democratic Mayor Jack Maltester proposed a Committee on Human Rights and Responsibilities in the civil rights heat of 1963, he was stonewalled by the city council. The council, controlled by the city's homeowners associations, three separate times refused to create such a committee, the last two after direct appeals from Don McCullum. "I feel that the great majority of the residents of San Leandro feel that we have no problem that requires the establishment of any committee on human rights," a typical letter to the editor read. Indeed, when David Creque, a San Leandro resident, spoke in support of establishing the civil rights commission, the homeowners association of which he was president quickly dismissed him, claiming that his statements "do not necessarily reflect the views of the board of directors." Homeowners contended that the absence of African Americans meant the absence of a "civil rights problem," much as an earlier generation of whites had denied complicity in a "Negro problem." Such willful inaction and its rhetoric of innocence underscored the physical and social remove that were the privileges of San Leandro's whiteness as well as the power of segregation to perpetuate racism and false consciousness among whites. Combinations of action and inaction sustained suburban segregation in the East Bay for two postwar generations.[14]

Homeowners were not innocent. In conjunction with their real estate industry patrons, they participated in the construction of a new white racial ideology with sweeping implications. Across the middle of the twentieth century, classic forms of white supremacy in the United States slowly gave way in public forums to a right-based language of individualism and freedom. The discourse was not itself new. It had been used for at least two centuries to buttress private property claims, including those of former slaveholders in the postbellum South and those of homeowners who placed racial covenants on their property in cities like Chicago, Detroit, and San Francisco in the first half of the twentieth century. But the aggressive assertion of this rights language as the dominant discourse through which white racial privilege was articulated was new. The Proposition 14 campaign in California played an important role in this larger, mid-twentieth-century development. On the eve of the 1964 election, California Assemblyman Robert Stevens gave voice to this language in a television debate. Claiming that prejudice and discrimination were "not the issue before us," Stevens likened the Rumford Act to the "witch hunts" of early colonial times, insisted that it denied "freedom of choice," and asserted the primacy of "the right to acquire and protect property." Labeling white resistance to open housing in the 1960s a "backlash," as many historians and other commentators have done, distracts attention from the central fact of that resistance: it took the form of rights-based counterclaims. These claims were intended to inoculate segregation and white privilege against charges of racism

through appeals to hallowed American rights traditions. Homeowners in California in 1964 helped to advance this project, one that would increasingly come to shape how racial equality was debated and contested in the national political culture.[15]

The California Supreme Court declared Proposition 14 unconstitutional in 1966, but desegregation advocates had lost three years fighting the CREA. Finally enforceable, the Rumford Act eventually became a critical tool for equal rights in California. But lost time, coupled with the long legacy of housing discrimination, meant that change came slowly. In 1971 a national report brought South County's history of racial exclusion to the surface. That year, the National Committee against Discrimination in Housing (NCDH) published the results of a study warning that "developing Bay Area suburbs will be racist enclaves in the image of San Leandro if the segregated housing development and marketing policies are not reversed." Focusing on San Leandro, the NCDH report blamed federal housing policy, homeowners associations, the city government, and the county real estate board for racial restriction, the familiar cast of characters in what NCDH Chief Executive Ed Rutledge called "typical of the situation across the nation." "The Veterans Administration guaranteed more than $1.6 million in home loans" in San Leandro, the report observed; "while the Federal Housing Administration insured more than $1.7 million in home mortgages." All went to white buyers. Those loan guarantees became, in the hands of real estate brokers and homeowners associations, bulwarks against desegregation, subsidized apartheid. In the 1970 census more than three quarters of Oakland census tracts along the San Leandro city line had a black majority. San Leandro itself was less than one-tenth of 1 percent African American. Here was a racial gradient as steep as any in the nation, preserved deep into the 1970s by both custom and structure.[16]

Segregation in suburban housing markets raised concrete economic questions about how resources were distributed in the divided metropolis. "Ironically," sociologist

Wilson Record wrote in a 1963 study, "San Leandro may get [industrial] plants which, if located in Oakland, would provide the tax base upon which Oakland needs to draw in order to service the Negroes excluded by San Leandro." A major study of California housing in the early 1960s predicted that segregation would ultimately force older cities like Oakland "to look largely for their revenues to poorer groups of taxpayers who will require higher outlays for social services." Advocates of racial just-ice made their case against suburban segre-gation in these concrete economic terms. Trapped in declining cities, they argued, poor African Americans required a greater share of public resources but received a lesser. "Our cities are already virtually bankrupt," Whit-ney Young, executive director of the Urban League, wrote in his 1969 *Beyond Racism*, citing "the mushrooming demand for costly social services required by the impoverished slums" as the principal reason. Of all the consequences of unequal metropolitan development, the redistribution of the tax base was ultimately one of the most severe and consequential. Even as housing and employment barriers lifted in degrees after the 1960s and metropolitan boundaries became more porous for African Americans, property markets changed slowly. Property value differentials hardened across space, and gaps between the urban and suburban per capita revenue from municipal property taxes widened, creating vast inequalities that func-tioned to reproduce racial disadvantage — especially in key property tax-supported urban services like education and health and welfare.[17]

Exclusion and containment kept African Americans from making substantial inroads in South County housing markets through the 1960s. Black workers enjoyed slightly more success in obtaining employment in the suburban East Bay, but these gains were limited to the General Motors and Ford plants in Fremont and Milpitas and the U.S. Naval Air Station in Alameda. In the late 1960s the GM plant was thought to employ between 1,500 and 2,000 black workers out of a fluctuating total employment of between 5,000 and 6,000. The Ford plant

employed a similar figure. Both hired large numbers of Mexican Americans as well, increasingly so during the 1970s. The Naval Air Station employed between 1,600 and 1,800 black workers out of a total work force of about 8,000. Outside of the auto-mobile factories and the Naval Air Station, however, black workers could be found in only a few corners of the suburban East Bay labor market. A Federal Civil Rights Commis-sion study of San Leandro in 1967 revealed that only 5 percent of employees in the city's industries were black. A similar study for Fre-mont, Union City, and Newark found 6 per-cent. Both studies, however, were limited by their reliance on companies required to file reports with the Equal Employment Oppor-tunity Commission. Companies outside of the EEOC's purview may well have employed even fewer African American workers.[18]

Employment discrimination against black workers in the East Bay was capricious and demoralizing. In blue collar fields, East Bay suburban communities were dominated by a few medium-sized employers — like GM and Ford, but also Trailmobile, Caterpillar Tractor, Pacific States Steel, Peterbuilt, and International Harvester — and an enormous number of smaller companies, plants, and establishments that employed less than one hundred workers. For black job seekers, the mixed-industrial landscape envisioned by both the MOAP and suburban city-builders could be almost impossible to navigate. Local offices of the California State Employment Service, for instance, filled jobs in Fremont, Union City, and other South County cities with local residents first. Only then were unfilled jobs forwarded to offices in Oakland. For those who could not afford an automobile, suburban work was espe-cially difficult to secure, because the tasks of finding an opening and appearing for an interview required transportation. After finding a job announcement and driving (or taking BART or a bus) into a suburban city, an African American applicant still might be told that the position had been filled. Race entered the decisions of man-agers, employment agencies, owners, and others in control of hiring in unpredictable ways. Furthermore, Bay Area employment in the manufacturing, transportation, and wholesale trade sectors was highly unionized, over 90 percent in many industries. In general, African Americans fared best in those sectors of the suburban labor market where they had gained a foothold in plants previously located in black population centers — Ford in Richmond and GM in Oakland, for instance — and in federal military installations.[19]

Between 1963 and 1970, after a decade of attempts to reclaim and revitalize Oakland's neighborhoods, African Americans there looked outward. They turned toward the East Bay suburbs, the lengthy residential and industrial landscape stretching from San Leandro to Milpitas, McCullum's white noose. "The flight to the suburbs is the highest form of social irresponsibility," McCullum charged in 1969, in his most stinging indictment of suburbanization. The metaphor of white strangulation of the black city was powerful precisely because it reduced the complexity of metropolitan patterns of residence and industry to an essential trope of American race and cast the metropolis in black and white. In instances like Proposition 14, the noose seemed very much in evidence. But the trope itself raised questions about how best to address regional racial inequality. Was it a product of overt racism, market economics, or both? Would appeals to suburban whites make a difference? How could African Americans develop a regional program to change the distribution of resources while remaining politically isolated in Oakland? Searching for the answers would occupy Oaklanders for a generation.

With remarkable speed in the mid-1960s, the city-suburb dualism replaced the bigoted southern sheriff, the lynch mob, and the lunch counter as the archetypal national symbol of American racial inequality. Oakland experienced this shift in metaphor and language with the nation. Beginning as early as the 1950s, northern civil rights, nationalist, and grassroots radical leaders alike had adopted variations on the city-suburb contrast in their speeches, writings, and interviews. The center of these efforts was initially battles over open housing in

the industrial Northeast and upper Midwest, where indices of segregation were higher than anywhere in the nation. Confined largely to local political arenas in the 1950s, by the mid-1960s these voices found a national stage with two dramatic episodes in California. The first was Proposition 14. The second came the following summer, with rebellions in Watts in Southern California. Though African Americans across the nation had been pointing to the destructive effects of white suburbanization and the hardening of segregation in "second ghettoes" since World War II, the national press was slow to take the issue seriously. Indeed, as late as 1960 the *Saturday Evening Post* was writing of the "great human tides, made up of middle-income Americans ... flowing out of the cities. Into the cities, to take their place, dark tides were running." Such rhetoric not only buttressed segregationist thinking ("dark tides running"), it also reinforced the widespread white interpretation of black migration as a cause of urban decline. Not until Proposition 14 and the eruption of violence between 1964 and 1968 did either the national press or the federal government begin to discuss with some seriousness the postwar trend toward metropolitan segregation.[20]

Between 1961 and 1968 official white circles slowly took notice of this segregation in ways that black leaders had been urging for decades. In 1961, reports of the U.S. Commission on Civil Rights used the term "white noose" to describe suburbanization, introducing that term into white policy arenas for the first time. Four years later, when the McCone Commission report on Watts in 1965 blamed African Americans for instigating the violence and made no mention of the Proposition 14 election from the previous fall, African Americans in California and elsewhere scathingly criticized the commission. A near total "whitewash," in the words of one local black critic, the report was also criticized by white federal officials. The U.S. Commission on Civil Rights called it "elementary, superficial, unoriginal and unimaginable." Though weak-kneed and retrograde, the McCone report had the effect of generating a national discussion among both whites and blacks over the segregated metropolis. In 1968 the report of the Kerner Commission (National Advisory Commission on Civil Disorders), the federal government's official interpretation of the urban violence of 1967, appeared. The commission's indictment of white America — "[w]hite institutions created it [ghetto], white institutions maintain it, and white institutions condone it" — represented what African American leaders in major cities had been saying for decades, but it took Proposition 14, four summers of violence, the glare of national publicity, and multiple government reports to reorient white discussion of civil rights to a metropolitan (and northern/western) context.[21]

For white East Bay suburban homeowners, Proposition 14 represented the early phases of a long engagement with the changing nature of California. That engagement only occasionally took explicit racial form, though race was nonetheless embedded in every stage. The rhetoric of Americanism and "free" property encouraged by the CREA thinly veiled a resistance to desegregation. More typically, homeowners joined causes that kept racial assumptions and prejudices at a greater remove even as their politics reverberated with profound racialized consequences. Ensuring ever rising property values while keeping other housing costs, especially taxes, as low as possible in the midst of the state's convulsive growth remained homeowners' dominant political objective. In the name of that objective, they collectively resisted the broad structural changes necessary to desegregate the housing market, and they fought other claims on the financial resources of their segregated communities.

NOTES

1. As a description of suburbanization, "white noose" gained popular attention in 1961, when it appeared in *Volume 4: Housing, 1961 United States Commission on Civil Rights Reports* (Washington, DC, 1961). By the late 1960s it was in common usage across the country.
2. U.S. Department of Commerce, *Census of Population: 1950, Characteristics of the Population, California* (Washington, DC,

1951); *1970 Census of the Population, Characteristics of the Population, California* (Washington, DC, 1973).
3. For distinct, but similar, political stories in Southern California, see Nicolaides, *My Blue Heaven*; McGirr, *Suburban Warriors*.
4. See newspaper clippings and other material in "Fair Housing — 1963" and "Fair Housing Bill" folders, Box 1, Rumford Papers. See also Casstevens, *Politics, Housing, and Race Relations*; Denton, *Apartheid American Style*.
5. *California Real Estate Magazine*, May, June, July, August, and December 1964; *NYT*, 10 May 1964; *CV*, 17 May and 9 August 1963; state senator quoted in *California Real Estate Magazine*, February 1964, 5; Rumford quoted in Regional Oral History Office, *William Byron Rumford: Legislator for Fair Employment, Fair Housing, and Public Health* (Berkeley, 1973), 120, 124.
6. *California Real Estate Magazine*, May, June, July, August, and December 1964; *NYT*, 10 May 1964; *CV*, 17 May and 9 August 1963; California Committee for Fair Practices, "Public Education and the CREA — Control by the Subsidized," manuscript, Box 2 Rumford Papers; Clare Short, "What Are the Obligations of the Housing Industry to Resolve Such Conflicts as Exist in This Area?" speech manuscript, University of California, Berkeley Library; Raymond Wolfinger and Fred Greenstein, "The Repeal of Fair Housing in California: An Analysis of Referendum Voting," *American Political Science Review* 62 (September 1968): 753–69.
7. *William Byron Rumford* [??274] of All Votes Cast, General Election, November 3, 1964" (Sacramento, 1964); Wolfinger and Greenstein, "The Repeal of Fair Housing in California."
8. *Ramparts*, April 1966, 7; Denton, *Apartheid American Style*; "Remarks on the Rumford Act and the Housing initiative," by State Senator Albert S. Rodda, and "California's New Fair Housing Law," by Carmen H. Warschaw, Box 7, Rumford Paper s.
9. *Ramparts*, April 1966, 7; *FNR*, 23 July, 10 September, 26 October 1964; Alameda County Committee Against Proposition 14, *News*, Central Labor Council of Alameda County Collection, Box 88, Folder 7, CLCAC/LARC; *California Real Estate Magazine*, April 1964, 5; "Proposition 14 — Campaign Flyers," Box 7, Rumford Papers.
10. Denton, *Apartheid American Style*, 30, 32–37.
11. For evidence of these practices and the real estate industry's investment in control of racial segregation in California, see ibid. For the nation as a whole, see Massey and

Denton, *American Apartheid*; Bruce D. Haynes, *Red Lines, Black Spaces: The Politics of Race and Space in a Black Middle Class Suburb* (New Haven, 2001). See also any volume of the *Hearings Before the National Commission on Urban Problems* (Washington, DC, 1968), where these issues received an open hearing in cities across the country.

12. *SLMN*, 27 March, 26 July, 8 August 1963; *FNR*, 25 June, 26 August, 5 and 6 September 1963.

13. I owe these last observations to Martha Biondi and Matthew Lassiter.

14. *SLMN*, 9, 23, 24, 26, and 27 July, 1, 17, 29, and 31 August, 17 September, 21 November 1963; 10 January, 1 May 1964.

15. Transcript of a debate on Proposition 14 and the Rumford Act, 19 September 1964, KNXT TV, Box 2, Rumford Papers.

16. *SLMN*, 14 and 15 May 1971; *FNR*, 1 September 1971.

17. *OT*, 5 January 1969; Wilson Record, "Minority Groups and Intergroup Relations in the San Francisco Bay Area," 1963, 22–23, IGS; "Draft Report to the Governor's Advisory Committee on Housing Problems," ms., 1962, Box 7, Catherine Bauer Wurster Collection, Bancroft Library, 4; Young, *Beyond Racism*, 6.

18. *Hearings Before the U.S. Commission on Civil Rights*, 587, 687, 1036; *FNR*, 25 June, 5 and 6 September 1963.

19. Oakland Chamber of Commerce, Research Department, "Fifty Largest Private Employers in Alameda County," April 1970; Bay Area Council, "A Guide to Industrial Locations in the San Francisco Bay Area," 1964. For a discussion of the relative weight historians should place on union versus employer discrimination in labor markets, see the set of essays in *International Review of Social History* 41 (1996): 351–406.

20. Harold H. Martin, "Our Urban Revolution, Part I: Are We Building a City 600 Miles Long?" *Saturday Evening Post* 232 (January 2, 1960): 15.

21. Gerald Horne, *Fire This Time: The Watts Uprising and the 1960s* (New York, 1995).

ESSAY 8.5

Separate but Unequal

Emily E. Straus

Source: Emily E. Straus, *Death of a Suburban Dream: Race and Schools in Compton, California* (Philadelphia: University of Pennsylvania Press, 2014).

EDITORS' INTRODUCTION

In this essay and her book project, Straus explores the history of the public school in Compton, California, and the role the public school played in shaping local conditions within the community. As Straus herself explains, her work is about "race, place, and education."[i]

Compton transitioned from a working class white suburb to a struggling black and Latino community. Importantly, Straus reminds us, as do other authors in this collection, that in America our racial dialogue is not a binary, black and white (pun intended), discussion. Not only is the discussion not binary in terms of race, but it is also not binary in terms of suburb v. city. Although leading high schools once thrived in cities, in the twentieth century many Americans sought out quality public schools in suburbs.

Born as a suburb, Compton appeared to hold promise as an escape from the fractured city, and white families settled down in the new housing built there. But as time went on Compton grew more complex. Once seen as suburban, and representative of the American dream of the single-family home and a chance for a bright future, Compton transformed into a suburb with urban aspects, and became synonymous with crime and a lack of opportunity.

Straus demonstrates that the public school, caught in the web of problems plaguing inner ring suburbs in the second half of the twentieth century, could not solve community problems alone. While well-funded public schools are essential to the promotion of democracy and economic opportunity for all Americans, schools cannot operate in a vacuum and make up for all the hurdles placed in the way of success. Improvement in a single school may be of great importance to one locality, yet it does nothing to change the structure of public education in the nation.

In urban history courses, discussions often turn to the funding structure of our public schools. Because schools are financed in large part by local taxes, and the wealthy can add to their schools' coffers via fund-raising, public schools are not equal. Compare the dollars spent per pupil in public schools you are familiar with, or compare and contrast spending in wealthier and poorer communities. Available funding directly influences learning. With more availability of funding per student, school districts can lower student teacher ratios, increase classroom supplies, support school libraries, recruit more experienced teachers, expand opportunities like music and art that are demonstrated to encourage learning across disciplines, and design meaningful field trips and after-school opportunities.

---

i Emily E Straus, *Death of A Suburban Dream: Race and Schools in Compton, California* (Philadelphia: University of Pennsylvania Press, 2014), 4.

Emily E. Straus is an independent scholar of race, class, and urban settings. Formerly Straus served as Associate Professor of History at SUNY-Fredonia. Straus earned her doctorate at Brandeis University. She held a Postdoctoral Fellowship at the Kinder Institute for Urban Research at Rice University. She has published articles in the *History of Education Quarterly* and *New York History*.

SEPARATE AND UNEQUAL (2014)

While picketing the freshly built Compton Crest development, a black GI and his friend a white GI, both just two weeks back from Korea, argued with the white residents. "We're fighting for you—we're facing bullets for you—why can't we live here?"[1] Irate white homeowners told the *California Eagle*, a black newspaper, "We fought all the way from Normandy to the Battle of the Bulge! We have a right to these homes. When we bought 'em—there were big signs all through this Compton tract, 'Highly Restricted!'—that's the way we bought and that's the way it's going to stay!"[2] Though the advertisements for the 535-home tract called out to veterans, the developers never intended to include all of them. Compton Crest, like the rest of the town in 1950, was explicitly meant for whites.[3] Like blacks across the country, African Americans in the Los Angeles area did not accept Compton's racial lines, and, along with some white allies, actively challenged the development's restrictions. In the debates that arose over integrating Compton Crest, both proponents and opponents used their status as veterans to justify their position on residential segregation. Integration was coming to Compton, but not easily.

As they began to reap the benefits of full citizenship after serving their country in wartime, African Americans sought their own suburban dream, and it was no coincidence that they settled in Compton. Like their white predecessors, they desired home-ownership, quality schools, and safe streets. Having been segregated into a few over-crowded Los Angeles neighborhoods with the worst housing stock, blacks pushed against decades-long practices of racial discrimination and pursued the promise of the suburbs.[4] While Compton was not an upper-middle-class area, it offered relatively affordable houses and was, both culturally and physically, a step out of the ghetto and toward that middle-class dream.

Though Compton was an improvement from their previous neighborhoods, the full promise of the suburban good life eluded many of the town's black residents. First, African American migration to Compton caused anxiety among some of the white residents, who linked their physical location to their class identity. Yet, while whites resisted, this is not a merely a story of blacks moving in and whites moving out, because not all whites could afford to leave Compton. As a result, this inner-ring su burb became contested ground. Comptonites fought vigorously over where people lived, who got jobs, and what schools children attended. At first whites' racial discrimination kept Compton's black population segregated on the west side of town. This restriction took its toll as it fostered racial prejudices in the school districts, which played out in the classrooms and school-yards. Community leaders drew school boundaries to reinforce racial lines and the boundaries helped create social divisions. The stratification affected Comptonites' daily lives as schools helped define the physical, cultural, and discursive divisions of the town. The segregation also proved costly for the already financially strapped suburb.

Compton's financial and social status became further threatened as white flight to other suburbs increased. Compton became a more racialized space, carrying all the assumptions that came along with being a minority town. As Compton got blacker, it lost its already precarious toehold on economic stability. Compton's whites took their businesses with them as they left, and new businesses failed to invest in Compton. The black Compton suburbs were not the white Compton suburbs.

Testing the Barrier

Changes in the Los Angeles social geography as well as the 1948 *Shelley v. Kraemer* and the 1953 *Barrows v. Jackson* Supreme Court decisions to eliminate racial covenants directly affected Compton.[5] Many black families earned double incomes, allowing them realistically to set their sights on moving for "an opportunity, a step up."[6] Compton became this step. From 1947 through 1953, Compton annexed a little over two-and-a-half square miles, aiming to increase its tax base through residential and industrial growth.[7] Much of this land was on the town's western edge, adjacent to black communities. Tract developers took advantage of the unrestricted land and built houses that they sold to African Americans.[8] As a result, Compton began to shift away from a virtually all-white citizenry, with a small Latino population, to include a growing population of middle-class African Americans, many from the increasingly impoverished area of Watts. African Americans comprised 17 percent of Compton's community in 1955, and 40 percent just five years later. The town experienced the most profound racial change of any municipality in Los Angeles County during the 1950s precisely because as a working-class area it was within the means of some blacks.

Along with the town's affordability, African Americans were attracted by the suburban promises of a better educational environment for their children and a higher-class status for their families. Even though Compton schools were overcrowded and underfunded, they seemed like an improvement (or at least an equivalent) to what migrating blacks had in their former neighborhoods. Los Angeles city schools were racially gerrymandered and willfully neglected by the local government.[9] Compton's districts were smaller and parents ostensibly could have more of a say in their children's education.

Lifelong Compton resident (and future Compton mayor) Omar Bradley reflected that "living in Compton in the fifties and sixties signaled a successful step toward economic prosperity." He explained that "most blacks who lived there were working-class folk who'd begun their California saga in Watts or Willowbrook," and once they developed "greater economic resources," they moved to the "green and well-manicured" neighborhoods of Compton.[10] According to Bradley, unlike Watts and Willowbrook, Compton became home to an upper class of African Americans who "inspired poorer black families to do better."[11] Another black resident remembered, "for once, the Negro did not move into slums; for once he came into good housing."[12] Compton did not mean that one had fully attained middle-class status, but it was a definite step toward it.

Individual family stories support this notion that the town offered blacks the chance to pursue the suburban American dream. Maxcy and Blondell Filer left Arkansas for California (by way of Indiana) to find a place where they could buy a house with "grass in our front yard."[13] When they moved, in 1953, Compton was one of the few suburbs in the county where blacks settled. Linda Allen's family moved to Compton that same year. When they first settled in Compton there were only three other black families on Caswell Street. Linda attended the local elementary school, Charles Bursch, where most of her classmates and teachers were white.[14]

Fred Cressel was born in Ashdown, Arkansas, a small town near the Texas border. In 1955, at seventeen, Fred visited family in Compton, a vacation that convinced him to stay in California. Once settled, he found a job as a welder (he had already completed trade school) and attended academic classes at night, finishing high school in California. As a welder, Fred worked at Douglas Aircraft, becoming "the first black person hired off the street" for that position. Douglas employed him for fourteen years, during which time he learned how to work with all the "exotic" metals, even becoming one of thirteen specialists who made "all the boosters that go to the moon."[15]

Sylvester Gibbs's experience also demonstrated the early stages of Compton's racial change. In 1952, he bought his first house, and it was in Compton. When he first moved to Southern California he resided in Wilmington, in what they called "the Army barracks" because "veterans had the first privilege for those." As he looked to buy a home in the suburbs, he realized his options were limited. He recalled: "when you looked out in Lakewood, they'd say we only sell to whites. So I moved into Compton in a place that was a corn fields and they built tract homes so mostly blacks moved in and a couple of Mexicans and a few whites."[16]

Lorraine Cervantes's family exemplified this interracial mix. Lorraine's mother was of Mexican descent while her biological father's family came from England. The first few children in the family came from this pairing. After that relationship dissolved, Lorraine's mother began seeing the man Lorraine would come to consider her father, even taking his name as her own. He was African American and he and Lorraine's mother had six children together. At home Lorraine and her family spoke both Spanish and English.

In December 1952, Lorraine moved with her parents and siblings to the Compton area from East Los Angeles, a majority Mexican American area. She was in the middle of sixth grade when her mother and her stepfather bought their first home. Having only rented previously, they jumped at the opportunity to move their large family to 124th Street, between Willowbrook and Wilmington Avenues, in the unincorporated county area of Willowbrook, which Lorraine recalled as being a relatively integrated neighborhood: "White, black, Mexican and Japanese. And there was one Filipino, who was married to a Mexican. A Filipino woman married to a Mexican guy." As a result, the schools were moderately integrated though the teachers remained mostly white. By the time Lorraine reached high school in 1955, her neighborhood school, Centennial High, was "just blacks and Mexicans," however. White families had moved on.[17]

Guarding Homes

Not all Compton's white residents could afford to, or wanted to, leave. Compton was their home, and they wished to protect the space they called their own. The town's relatively affordable housing stock made it a place where people could buy a house. Through homeownership, the residents gained independence and status for their families. And those who stayed often defended their social standing. This experience was not unique to Compton. Historian Thomas Sugrue explains: "rapidly changing neighborhoods in northern cities, particularly those whose white residents could not afford to pick up and move easily, became bloody battlegrounds."[18] Compton shows that this was not just an urban phenomenon but also happened in inner-ring suburbs.

The town's newcomers worried many of Compton's white residents. White resident Pam Grimm first became aware of her family's racial prejudice after she attended a week at a local day camp. During that week she "palled up with a little black girl," and when Pam got home she wanted to call the girl to make a play date. In response her parents called a "family meeting" with her uncle and grandmother to figure out what they were going to do with her. In Grimm's words: "They were scared because they didn't even know her. She was a nice girl ... they were in alarm, really in alarm." The family forbade Grimm from playing with the black girl.[19]

Some white Comptonites' behavior made Grimm's family look civil by comparison. Despite the claims by town leaders like city manager Harry Scott that Compton was "one of the friendliest cities in a state that is noted for its hospitality to the newcomer," white Compton residents' actions told a different story. Whites employed a variety of tactics—from real estate restrictions, to school zoning plans, to violence—to prevent African Americans from becoming their neighbors or their children's schoolmates.[20] Their targets included both blacks who wished to move to Compton and whites who aided them in the process. In February 1953, several white property owners were beaten and threatened for listing their properties with South Los Angeles Realty Investment Company, a real estate company that sold to both whites and blacks. The *California Eagle*, Los Angeles's black newspaper, called it "a reign of terror," and cited observers on the scene that "certain sections of Compton resembled an armed camp as home owners in the area, goaded on by the Compton Chamber of Commerce, the *Compton Daily Press* and the Ku Klux Klan elements in the district, seemed determined to keep their neighborhood lilly-white [sic] by force and violence."[21] Also citing unnamed members of the community, the *Eagle* noted that white residents had been organizing for some time, holding meetings in homes as well as in the Long-fellow School about how to circumvent the outlawing of racial covenants.[22] The use of the home and the school lent both physical space and rhetorical weight to the protests. Both represented the heart of the community, what residents wanted to defend.

Whites' defense of community continued. In March a group of home-owners dug up a law against peddlers, using it as a basis for arresting two black real estate brokers and three of their salespeople. Despite being on the books for years, the ordinance had never been used against white real estate agents.[23] In response to these actions the *Eagle* ran an editorial declaring "we've got news for Compton." The news: "Compton must face the fact that the Constitution, with its guarantee of equality for all citizens, covers that city, too."[24] The arrests signaled trouble for all real estate agents, not just black agents, and as a result, the fight against the use of the Compton ordinance went beyond the black community. In response to the arrests, locals working in real estate formed the Brokers Protective Committee to defend the rights of licensed property brokers and salespeople to solicit listings.[25] The defendants were acquitted.[26]

Still, whites' hostile behavior continued. In April 1953, unidentified "vandals" left a "vile note" for the Whittaker family who moved to Reeve Street, which was part of the "'forbidden' area south of Olive Street."[27] In May 1953, black homeowners in Compton had to guard their homes as white residents picketed another house on Reeve Street, where a black family had recently moved.[28] According to the *Eagle*,

Reeve was a "quiet, nice street of new two and three bedroom homes" inhabited by working-class whites who labored in Los Angeles area shipyards, defense plants, and factories.[29] Comptonites may have tolerated integration in their workplaces, but they actively resisted having it in their neighborhoods and their schools. In fact, the president of the Compton Crest Improvement Association, Joe Williams, was a member of the United Auto Workers, an integrated union that "unconditionally condemned" and ultimately censured him for his actions in picketing the homes of African Americans.[30] Despite the union's pressure, Williams continued. He and other Compton residents would not accept at home and in school what they would allow on the job. Their dislike translated into a constant threat of violence for their new neighbors.

Williams's behavior exemplified the types of conflicts that were occurring across the nation. Whites created homeowners' associations to secure their neighborhood from integration and protect their status as middle-class Americans.[31] At the very same time the battles raged in Compton, the U.S. Supreme Court was still resolving aspects of the case against racial covenants.[32] But, as the clashes on Reeve Street displayed, these encounters had high stakes. While for African Americans moving to the suburbs meant asserting a new class status, for many whites, like the parents of Pam Grimm, having black neighbors meant losing theirs.

The women of Compton, both black and white, actively defended their social standing, their homes, and their families. When Luquella Jackson, the mother in the black family that moved to Reeve Street, put her eleven-year-old daughter Jacqueline to sleep she did so with "a .45 Colt in her cotton dress pocket."[33] And, when a group of white "banner-carrying housewives" marched up and down in front of her home with signs that read such things as "protect our children's homes," Jackson kept her own children inside the house "with a shotgun within easy reach."[34] Promises of peace and security defined the suburban lure and, ironically, that ideal was worth fighting for.

The stories of Compton Crest's integration never made it into the local Compton newspaper or the *Los Angeles Times*. Perhaps the papers' editors did not consider the threats to African Americans newsworthy because such efforts to intimidate were so common, or perhaps it was because they thought their readers would not find the story compelling. The stories did run quite prominently, however, in the *California Eagle*, whose editors clearly saw the battles in Compton Crest as momentous. In spring 1953, the *Eagle* ran a series on Compton's housing battles, with each issue featuring a banner headline as well as numerous pictures and articles. It also published a series of editorials, even calling out the leading Compton newspaper as "leading the agitation for this racial residential segregation."[35]

Yet the *Eagle* hesitated to blame local white residents' racism entirely. The newspaper's writers and editors defined Compton's situation was "an involved one" and they chronicled the nuances of the story. The paper identified Compton as the site where African Americans sought homes and a community where residents "nursed on the myth" that black homeownership destroyed property values. Compton was both a place where a property owners' association "concocted a fantastic scheme of secret mortgages to penalize neighbors who sell to Negroes" and a place where residents made a "sincere, conscientious attempt ... to put out the fires of racial prejudice before they flare[d] into violence." The molding of Compton's story, however, went beyond its own borders; banks and financial institutions acted "hand in glove with attempts to restrict credit and limit Negro occupancy of homes in Compton."[36] Redlining shaped Compton like it did in many other American cities and suburbs.

Ultimately, according to the *Eagle*, the problem of Compton was "the story of men and women, white and Negro, who [were] caught up in a population trend and who [were] bewildered by what [was] happening."[37] Throughout the town "general fear and panic prevailed [because] everyone thought Compton would become a shantytown overnight," according to a merchant group.[38] White residents fretted that the very presence of African Americans would turn their neighborhoods into ghettos and they did not have to look too far for an example: the nearly all-black neighborhood of Watts stood as a nearby and constant reminder. Once an ethnically and racially integrated space, South Central Los Angeles became increasingly black. During the 1950s, this area, once two separate communities of Watts and South Central, housed approximately 94 percent of the city's black population.[39] As such, the area, in the words of historian Eric Avila, "became synonymous with the black ghetto."[40] For whites, this new conceptualization defined not only Watts but also their own white spaces. They viewed suburbs, like Compton, in opposition to the metropolis. Consequently, many whites rushed to sell their homes at the first sight of a black family moving in down the street.[41] White and black real estate brokers fueled the fire by engaging in the practice of blockbusting, inducing homeowners to sell their property in a panic at prices below market value, usually by exploiting racial prejudices.

Some white, local realtors sought to protect their community from black newcomers. African American Douglas Dollarhide recalled that when he and his family wanted to move to Compton in 1956, he needed a lawyer to help him find a home because a local real estate agent refused to sell him one. Once they bought the house and moved to Compton, the violent prejudice heightened, as, he explained, white Compton residents "would paint swastika stickers on my door."[42] This type of behavior sprung up around the country. "Cross burnings, arson, window breakings, and mobs," as historian Thomas Sugrue has shown, "greeted black newcomers to white neighborhoods in nearly every major northern city between the 1920s and the 1960s."[43] Compton was no different. In June 1953, Mr. and Mrs. Herman White and their two-and-a-half-year-old daughter Francia moved to South Dwight Street in Compton. South Dwight was covered by the Longfellows Homeowners Association, a group of approximately two hundred families dedicated to keeping their neighborhood racially exclusive. A week after they moved in a cross was burned in front of their house. Two days later a rock smashed through one of the home's front windows. Wrapped around the rock was a note saying "You're not wanted" and signed "KKK."[44] That Saturday night "threatening crowds," including a band of "white teenage hoodlums," milled in front of and circled the block around the South Dwight home until three in the morning.[45] In response the *Eagle* ran an editorial cartoon asserting that the "decent citizens" of Los Angeles would beat back "race hate."[46]

The *California Eagle* continued to spotlight incidents in Compton. It reported on both the actions of the attackers and the inaction of the Compton police. On June 25 the *Eagle* asked "Why No Action, Compton Police?"[47] The next week the *Eagle* reported that "while police looked the other way, Compton vandals struck again in two sneak attacks."[48] In one case someone inserted a hose into a mail slot of a house at 502 Aprilla Street when the residents were away. The water flooded the hardwood floors. Whites owned this home and had listed their property with a black real estate broker. In a separate incident at a home owned by a black family, 2504 West Cypress Street, a brick crashed through a kitchen window. At the same home two days later white teenagers threw garbage on and tossed insults toward a ten- and an eleven-year-old playing in the yard. In each case, the residents called the Compton police, who did nothing, claiming the wave of attacks was just the "work of youngsters and pranksters."[49] The *Eagle* perceived the inaction of police as purposely allowing for impunity of whites.

Fear and violence also erupted in Compton's schoolyards. In January 1953, white and black youths fought at the gate of Enterprise Junior High. White youths were stabbed and the police took seventeen black Comptonites into custody, ten of whom were later found guilty of the assaults. Black parents protested the sentencing of four black students to "indeterminate terms in lumber camps," asserting that the black teenagers were singled out unjustly and were being used as an example while the whites involved were allowed to go free.[50] While the court eventually suspended the sentences, those charged still protested the unequal treatment.[51] According to police records and school officials, the white teenagers did not provoke the fight. Rather, the fight occurred when three carloads of black students randomly stopped and beat up the white students. Writers at the *California Eagle* remained skeptical about the purposelessness of the fight, however, and contended it reflected the larger tensions between whites and blacks in Compton.[52] For the white media, racial tension remained unworthy of reporting: the local Compton paper and the *Los Angeles Times* continued their silence. In the next decade, however, racial tensions would become more difficult to ignore.

A few months after the incidents on Reeve and South Dwight Streets and outside Enterprise Junior High, the United States Supreme Court in *Barrows v. Jackson* rejected the use of racial covenants by realtors in Los Angeles. The *Barrows* ruling meant that blacks could move into all-white neighborhoods and towns.[53] The decision had a profound impact on areas close to Watts. Between 1952 and 1955, the nonwhite population of Compton nearly doubled, from 11.6 to 37.6 percent of the town's population. White Comptonites' weak hold on their neighborhoods grew more tenuous, but, despite what the law said, many tried to strengthen their control over Compton.[54]

Behind these numbers lay the fact that, even with the threat of violence, Compton still provided one of the few opportunities for African Americans to move out of the awful living conditions in Los Angeles's historically black neighborhoods. African American migrant Mary Cuthbertson recalled that her husband felt proud of his home in Compton. In her words: "It was a very old house, but being the first house he owned in his lifetime, it just meant a lot to him to *own your own house.*"[55]

Though Compton was a rung above, it still did not completely fulfill the promise of suburbia. When just a boy, for example, Omar Bradley lived with his parents and six siblings in a three-bedroom house in Compton. The bedroom he slept in with his brothers barely accommodated five beds. Even though his family lived in extremely tight quarters, they still saw it as a step up from the "Sardine Days" of their prior living arrangement. The highlight of the Compton house was its "spacious back yard full of thick green grass surrounded by a tall pink brick fence." It was a place the Bradley family could call its own. Bradley recalled: "It was our private playground, a place where we'd turn into Army men or cowboys and Indians. My brother and sisters taught me how to crawl and walk there."[56]

"An Us/Them Thing in Our Town"

Increased population numbers did not translate into integrated schools. Racism manifested in the purposeful racial segregation in the schools. White politicians and school officials strategically zoned the schools and located new school facilities to ensure racial segregation. Originally, Compton High served the entire district. But as the general population grew in the town, and as the school became more integrated, the district opened Centennial High in 1953 to serve Compton's growing black community on the west side. Centennial would serve black students and Compton High would serve whites. Soon this new facility was not enough to keep Compton High segregated, however. As the black population crept toward the town's east side, Compton High was once again integrated. In response, the district opened Dominguez High in 1957 on the east side to serve the white community. Despite its low tax capacity, the town continued to build new facilities.

Segregation affected the students. Grimm remembered: "there was a lot of prejudice among the kids I grew up with. When Compton High came over for our baseball games ... their drill team was great. It was cool. I mean, they really had the moves and, you know, they were really jazzy. But I remember everybody laughing at them and calling them 'jungle bunnies' and all of that." She continued: "It was an us/them thing in our town, and I don't know how they felt."[57]

White resident Shirley Holmes Knopf recalled that her elementary school was nearly "a hundred percent white," with maybe a couple of black students. By the time she went to Compton High in 1956, she had a few black and Latino classmates. In fall 1958, Knopf's senior year, Compton High had its first black homecoming queen, Nadine "Naddie" Smith. Smith was one of five candidates, competing against three whites and one Latina. The three white candidates split much of the white vote, allowing Smith, the most unlikely candidate, to seize the title, and the Latina candidate to be the runner-up. This is not to say that only African Americans voted for Smith, because, as white resident Shirley Knopf recalled, "Naddie was one of the top people. She was in [the select and exclusive service club] the Chimettes and everything else."[58] The local branch of the NAACP saw the election as worth reporting back to the organization's West Coast field secretary.[59]

Despite Smith's reputation, Knopf remembered her winning as "just a shock to everyone."[60] The evening Smith received her crown at a Compton-Lynwood football game, a white youth reportedly hurled derogatory remarks about her race and "a group of boys of her race allegedly tried to mop up the street near Compton High stadium with him," according to the *Los Angeles Sentinel*.[61] Ron Finger, who was a senior at Compton High that year, remembered that on the day after Smith was elected queen, "on Compton stadium in bright red painting was 'We don't want your nigger queen.'"[62] While Smith's election may have indicated that attitudes were changing slowly among the younger generation (or it may have indicated that the white vote was indeed split), the reaction to her election showed that racism endured in Compton.

The practice of racial segregation occurred in school districts across Los Angeles County and California. Residency determined school zones and neighborhoods were largely segregated. The Los Angeles city board of education purposely placed both schools and students based on race. Even in racially mixed areas, the school district maintained white schools even if it meant students' traveling. This policy, along with residential segregation, ensured racially segregated schools across the district. Furthermore, the conditions of the schools reflected their racial composition. Not surprisingly, the school district was less likely to maintain a school that was predominantly black or Latino.[63]

Other Los Angeles County school districts also maintained segregated schools. Pasadena school district sustained such practices. Although most of the district's residents were affluent middle- and upperclass whites, Pasadena had always had a small black population who worked in the town's resort hotels or as domestics in the town's mansions. During World War II, Pasadena's black population grew alongside Southern California's defense-related economy.[64] As in Compton, white residents of Pasadena resisted the integration of their schools by enforcing racial segregation. As a result, blacks and Latinos lived in the densely populated northwest section of Pasadena.

The racial segregation also reflected class differences; Pasadena's black residents were significantly less affluent than white residents. Whites who recently moved up into the middle class populated the sections bordering the minority-populated northwest, while upper- and upper-middle class whites lived in older sections of Pasadena.[65] The wealthier residents could afford to send their children to private school or to move to other, more segregated, towns if integration encroached on their children's schools. Unlike their richer neighbors, Pasadena's newly minted middle-class whites could not afford either option, however, and as such carefully protected the racial composition of their children's schools, in turn protecting their own tenuous class status.

Racial and class prejudices played into the Pasadena school board's desire to segregate schools. In addition to residential patterns, the board wielded another weapon of segregation; since the 1930s, the Pasadena school district allowed parents to request transfers within the district.[66] White parents used this policy as a ticket to an all-white school. The district maintained such overtly separate schools that the NAACP had even considered including Pasadena as one of the cases that would eventually comprise *Brown v. Board of Education*, whose 1954 Supreme Court decision would declare it illegal to segregate public school students by race.[67]

While the NAACP did not ultimately involve the west coast suburb in the landmark case, it did, along with black churches, support black residents' continuous protests against school segregation.[68] The NAACP vigorously organized, holding mass meetings and threatening a lawsuit when the school board proposed building new classrooms at the overcrowded all-white Arroyo Seco School, while classrooms stood empty at the neighborhood Garfield School. The overcrowding occurred largely due to the school board's approved transfer of white children out of the Garfield School where the pupils were predominantly black, Latino, and Japanese.[69] In response, the school board redrew neighborhood boundaries and put an official end to intradistrict transfers. Racial segregation continued, however, as parents used means such as fake addresses to get their children into the schools they desired.[70]

Parents' resistance to integration before and after *Brown* was a national phenomenon. *Brown*'s most notorious test came in 1958 in Little Rock, Arkansas, where Governor Orval Faubus ordered the Arkansas National Guard to prevent black students' entrance into the city's Central High School. Eyes focused on Little Rock as television cameras caught white Arkansans' violent reactions. While extreme, their response to integration was not unique, and could be seen in districts across the country, including some in California, like Pasadena and Compton.

Eventually a lawsuit challenged Pasadena's school assignment policies. In this 1963 suit, *Jackson v. Pasadena City School District*, the California Supreme Court applied *Brown* and found that Pasadena intentionally segregated its schools. The court required the district "to alleviate racial imbalance in schools regardless of its cause."[71] By framing its decision in such a way, the court mandated that Pasadena eradicate both the de jure gerrymandering and the de facto segregation that came through housing patterns built on discrimination. By this time, the California State Board of Education was moving toward a similar doctrine, and after the *Jackson* decision the board asked the state attorney general whether it could begin to identify students by race to balance school attendance. The attorney general ruled that districts could consider race and ethnicity in formulating desegregation plans, a decision that opened the door for a statewide racial census.[72]

Like school districts across the country, Pasadena found ways to abide by the court's decision while circumventing its intent. In order to comply, the school district adopted a voluntary, open enrollment plan, allowing blacks to leave segregated schools on a space-available basis.[73] The plan only included certain "white" schools, leaving others completely segregated. Like many of its southern counterparts, the majority conservative Pasadena school board implemented a purposely ineffective desegregation plan, successfully forestalling any immediate outside intervention. Its ineffective plan would lead, however, to later court battles.

As in Pasadena and other districts across California, Compton's schools were separate and unequal. In August 1958, a letter declared Centennial graduates unqualified to attend major colleges in California and asked that the board change the curriculum and academic standing of the school.[74] One week later, a group of voters from the Centennial area, a predominantly black neighborhood, sent a different letter to the board of the Compton Union High School District, protesting the school's lack of facilities—specifically an auditorium, swimming pool, football stadium, baseball facilities, or gymnasium—and complaining of the low grade averages of Centennial graduates. Two weeks after that, Centennial's principal, Benjamin Jamison, reported to the board of trustees that he had written to each 1958 graduate to impress on them the importance of attending college for the sake of the school. In this analysis, the students' personal decisions and achievements not only reflected on themselves but also served as a marker for the success of the school. At the same meeting, he also informed the board he intended to review the grading procedure of the school and "that the

students and teachers alike would be imbued with the fact that the school is an educational and not a social institution."[75] While suburbia was supposed to offer strong educational opportunities, some of Compton's schools were not fulfilling this dream for black residents.

Population growth did necessitate that the districts build some new schools, and district officials planned them to be segregated. In 1958 Compton Union opened another junior high school to serve the black community. Ironically the district chose to name the school after civil rights leader Ralph J. Bunche. Enterprise had named an elementary school a few years back for Bunche, but this did not dissuade the high school district from doing the same. Bunche himself attended the school's opening, giving the dedication speech. In his remarks he did not explicitly mention the fact that the school would mostly serve black students but a tacit acknowledgment came as he reflected on the possible benefits of a school bearing his name. He noted that he was "mindful, of course, of the helpful effect on race relations in the country resulting from any meritorious recognition accorded an individual Negro." He continued: "It is also true, that such recognitions serve as sources of hope and inspiration to young Negroes and encourage them to aspire and strive and improve despite the discouragements and frustrations of racial handicap."[76] While the law books did not condone the segregation policy, it was an open secret, so much so that even the students were aware of the planned segregation. "We all talked, each new school year, 'oh, they moved the [school] boundaries again,'" recalled Grimm.[77] While population growth made the new facilities necessary, their placement highlighted the white establishment's desire to thwart integration and maintain the segregated status quo.

The segregation of black and white residents in schools and neighborhoods helped further racial tensions. During Grimm's senior year at the traditionally all-white Dominguez High, she served on the student government. One day the cabinet held a special meeting because the school was "getting our first black boy." The cabinet was charged with watching out for the student. While, according to Grimm, there was "no scene," they were all very "conscious" that there very well could have been.[78] Compton's whites had shown a strong resistance to integration and Dominguez High remained one of the last strongholds.

At times the tension manifested in both subtle and overt ways. One example of the friction was that black children stayed away from youth dances because it was "commonly held that Negro youths would not be welcomed as members of either of the dance clubs. The absence of membership from Centennial High School (whose enrollment [was] entirely Negro) would support this impression."[79] Though not overtly barred, black children were simply not integrated into the fabric of the greater Compton community. Some whites' actions were harsher. Bradley recalled that whites made it clear that they did not want blacks in their side of town at night, even if it meant giving up some business. He recollected: "blacks were encouraged by the all-white Compton Police Department to 'get out of the east side before sunset.' If the white cops didn't get the ugly message across, the storeowners, employees, and a Compton-born-and-bred street gang known as the Spook Hunters sure as hell did."[80]

Blacks and whites were separate in both housing and schooling, the very idea that would later be expressed by the 1968 Kerner Commission, which in the wake of a series of riots concluded: "Our nation is moving toward two societies, one black, one white—separate and unequal."[81] But, Comptonites' experiences complicate that narrative in two ways. First, the Kerner Report diagnosed this divide as white suburban affluence versus black urban poverty.[82] Compton was a suburb that was neither all white, nor affluent. Second, Compton experienced the divide within its own borders.

Living in the same town, whites and blacks fought over resources. School districts' hiring practices exemplified this. Schools were the largest employer in Compton, and white residents held tightly to their control of the hiring process. As black resident Maxcy Filer recalls, "We didn't have one black teacher when I came here, or one black administrator. We didn't even have a custodian in the schools when I moved here, nor the city."[83] The high school district had hired its first black employee in 1950, but even into the 1960s the hiring policies for ethnic groups came under scrutiny. At a June 1963 board of trustees meeting, Compton Union superintendent Rae Cargille asserted that "assignment policies of the Compton Union High School District could be open to criticism from the fact that there are no full time Negro teachers assigned to Roosevelt, Whaley and Dominguez Schools," three schools in Compton's predominantly white east side.[84]

At the same meeting in which he conceded a viable critique of district assignment practices, Cargille also explained away one of Compton's black community's main complaints, which centered on the districts' promotional policy regarding ethnic groups. Cargille stood by the district policy, saying that "if logic is applied rather than emotion our policy concerning administrative openings in the district is sound." It took an average of nine years before administrators received their first administrative assignment in Compton Union and an additional eight years before receiving principalships, and, Cargille reasoned, because the district had only employed African Americans for thirteen years, they could not have at that time reached the top positions of power.[85] According to this logic, all job candidates regardless of color began the job ladder on an even rung and moved up equally based solely on competency and seniority; the lack of African Americans in certain positions was due to standard operating procedures, rather than to any systemic discrimination. The reality of Compton's community contradicted this theory as whites continued to deny African Americans access to jobs.

For the black community, the barriers to job opportunities "fostered a feeling of frustration and lack of confidence in decisions reached by these municipal and civic bodies," according to a report by the Welfare Planning Council.[86] One member of the Compton Community Center board explained: "The innumerable and subtle barriers to full participation in community life for the Negro in Compton might well make him feel completely hopeless."[87] All members of the board agreed that "the iniquitous effects [were] wide-spread, particularly in the feeling of being unwelcome, and in the form of increased school drop-out, crime, and delinquency."[88] The educators and administrators did not improve the situation, tending either to talk around issues of race and class or to aggravate anxieties.

African Americans created communities that would aid them in fighting these problems. According to Bradley "the unity was apparent in our neighborhoods." He explained that the "cohesion was borne of two inalterable conditions," living in crowded neighborhoods and attending the same schools. "Everybody knew everybody's business," he continued, and as a result, if you did something wrong, you were easily "snitched out" when the "elders got together at church, PTA, or the grocery store.[89] Kelvin Filer had a similar experience. In his immediate vicinity lived ten children all around his age, and "we all grew up together, this is from elementary school on, so we all hung out together. We were all friends. Our parents all knew each other so you really had the community feeling, particularly with the parents. I mean, there was nothing ... if I did something wrong, there was no problem with Mrs. Simmons snatching me, Mrs. Kelly snatching me and you know, 'I'm going to tell your dad.' That was the same thing, they were all with my parents. They had the same areas of responsibility and they had the same expectations in terms of how they wanted to be treated so we were all real close. And to this day, really, still are close. So that was the neighborhood feeling. We all played together. We all played Little League, football. We went to the same church."[90] Pamela Samuels-Young also recalled growing up in a supportive environment, which she defined as "church, school, and parents." Her mother was one of the founding members of the Community

Baptist Church in Compton, which became a center point for Samuels-Young, just as the church had done for African Americans across the country. From there, and from school, she built her social circle.[91]

Building from this community, Maxcy Filer, along with some other residents, organized the Compton chapter of the NAACP and local teenagers established a youth branch. The chapter initiated local actions as well as supporting the organization's actions on the regional, state, and national level. In 1958, the Compton branch urged its members to participate in a voter registration drive as well as a boycott of Budweiser beer, a campaign initiated by the Los Angeles branch and endorsed by the regional and national offices. The local chapter also sought to establish fair employment practices in Compton and supported both financially and ideologically the establishment of a statewide commission to enforce such practices.[92]

While recognizing its role in regional and national struggles, and at times taking a page from their playbook, the branch also publicized its own "home grown problems." In the March 1958 newsletter the local NAACP reminded its readers: "We don't have to go to the South to cure the evils of prejudice and discrimination. The defeat of the civil rights ordinance in our own Compton City Council, the subsequent rebuff by the Compton Chamber of Commerce in refusing to discuss FEP [Fair Employment Practices] with our Labor and Legislation Committee, the reports of inadequate education of our young people, the lack of employment opportunities in Compton."[93] Mirroring the actions of southern chapters, the members of the Compton branch picketed city hall, the school district, and private businesses such as Sears and Woolworths, in order to protest their discriminatory hiring practices and pressure them to hire African Americans.[94] In 1958, the Compton group fought for fair employment at the town's branch of Bank of America as well as the local Sears store. The branch's newsletter urged black women with office experience or training to apply at the two businesses because "the managers of both these institutions have indicated their hiring policy was one of nondiscrimination and at the same time have said that they have had few Negro applicants for such positions." The newsletter went on to note that "opportunities in most Compton businesses are limited," and the NAACP's goal was "equal opportunity to work where we live."[95] Similar tactics were used across the Los Angeles region to combat segregation in schooling, housing, and hiring, with varying degrees of success.[96]

The Compton branch's campaign against Bank of America illustrates African Americans' ability to organize and sustain protests against Compton's white power structure. In addition to urging black women to apply for jobs, NAACP members distributed fliers urging folks to speak with the bank manager either by phone or in person, requesting that he discontinue the discriminatory practices. They also asked patrons to withdraw their funds from the bank until it hired black employees. According to the flier, the bank manager used such excuses for the practices as, "'if I hire a Negro, my white employees will quit'; 'when Compton becomes predominantly Negroid, I will consider it'; [and] 'I have lived in Compton twenty three years and I am not going to be pressured by the NAACP to do anything.'"[97] His resistance worked for awhile, but as Filer recalled "after about a year or so picketing, the manager came out and said, 'Maxcy, you could put your picket sign down now, we have a black working in Bank of America.' ... And, I said, 'Where, where, where?' And, he said, 'There she is.' Well, she was fair skinned, blond hair, blue eyes, but they called her black and she was."[98] Despite the manager's obvious attempts to placate the black activists by manipulating understandings of race, the group considered the battle against Bank of America a victory.

The local chapter of the NAACP also monitored employment gains. In March 1958 the Los Angeles County Sheriff's Department was changing hands and the local chapter commended the outgoing sheriff on his fair employment practices. The chapter, however, feared that the sheriff-elect would return to "the old trend of hiring negroes last and firing them first."[99] The local chapter also monitored the school districts. In 1959, the leaders of the Compton NAACP joined with parents and other civic groups to protest the firing of Vivian Thomas, the librarian at Centennial High School. School principal Benjamin Jamison recommended her contract not be renewed on the grounds of incompetency. In doing so Jamison sparked a heated controversy and charges that his own actions were unethical and unprofessional, which eventually led to the board removing him from his principalship.[100] With these and other campaigns, Compton's local branch of the NAACP grew quickly, reporting approximately five hundred members in October 1959.[101]

As it grew in number and action, Compton's NAACP received threats. In October 1960, in response to the group's picket lines in front of the town's Woolworth stores, the NAACP local office had swastikas painted on its windows and received menacing letters.[102] A month later someone threw a brick through the office window with a note attached, stating "Get the hell out of town."[103]

Tensions became so palpable that in June 1961 Compton established the Council on Human Relations to create a "wholesome community atmosphere."[104] While the establishment of the committee showed some movement toward addressing the town's problems, it was not a cure-all.[105] Only a few months later two "hoodlums" fired thirteen shots into the glass window of the Compton NAACP's office.[106] Violence between black and white students also erupted on some of Compton's school campuses. In February 1962 three African American Compton High students clashed with four white Dominguez High students after an interschool basketball game. A white student ended up hospitalized with a fractured skull. The booster club at the predominantly white Dominguez High discussed canceling, or at least moving to the daytime, all future basketball games against the predominantly black Compton High.[107]

The local newspaper, the *Compton Herald American*, already notorious for its racist commentary on blacks as well as stirring up tension between black and white Compton residents, called the attacks "brutal and savage." The paper, using charged language, described the African Americans as part of a "gang."[108] The newspaper's polemic framing of the incident may have led to its continued interest in the story. It reported that in the wake of the skirmish, three black students were arrested, with fourteen more soon to follow. The fissures between Compton's black and white residents grew deeper, and their segregated schools embodied their disunion.

The Consequences of White Flight

The spread of Latinos also affected Compton's social fabric. Latinos were always a portion of Compton's population but by 1957 they lived throughout the town.[109] This dispersal meant that Latinos attended several of Compton's schools, but the majority remained within the Willowbrook and northern Compton schools.[110]

As blacks and Latinos moved into an established white neighborhood, whites moved out. In the period between 1955 and 1960, the white population of Compton decreased by 19 percent, while the nonwhite population increased by 165 percent.[111] The flight of Compton's whites was part of a movement occurring nationally. For example, between 1950 and 1960, 700,000 whites moved to Philadelphia's suburbs, while the city lost 225,000 whites and gained 153,000 blacks.[112] During the 1960s roughly 60,000 whites fled Atlanta, and during the 1970s another 100,000 would follow.[113]

While similar to the big cities' stories, Compton deviated from the norm. Unlike traditional white flight, from city to suburb, Compton's whites fled first from one part of Compton to another, and then from one suburb to the next. In 1961, white resident Ron Finger's parents also moved out of Compton because "the neighborhood by then had pretty much become black." For his parents and their white neighbors, "it was kind of like the first [African American] family that moved in was okay. The second

family moving in, then it was like 'there goes the neighborhood,' and so people started selling their houses." By the time his parents left, there were only a few white families left on the block.[114]

White Comptonites also worked to keep neighborhoods segregated, with whites on the town's east side and African Americans on its west. A 1962 study by the Welfare Planning Council found "'two Comptons'—essentially white and non-white, segregated rigidly," with the commercial Alameda Boulevard as the line of demarcation between two residential areas.[115] As in other cities during these years, this segregation was not coincidental: white developers and residents played active, and important, roles in creating and maintaining the two Comptons.[116] While the new developments were open to anyone who could afford to buy, mostly blacks and Latinos moved in.

The suburban space of Compton no longer provided the desired social markers. In 1962, Katherine Nelson, an African American nurse, moved with her family to the town's west side. She recalled, "[the neighborhood] was all white. I think we were the first African American family to move there. And, my husband said, the next morning when he woke up, we woke up, that there were signs in everybody's yard that said 'House for Sale.'"[117] White Comptonites' responses were both overt and swift, as they relocated to nearby suburbs that, unlike Compton, had remained overwhelming white.

Pam Grimm's was another such family that fled to outer-ring suburbs. She heard her mother's racism "every night at the dinner table," as she and her father discussed the influx of African Americans into Compton. She recalled: "When we were at the dinner table every night, 'we have to get out.' It's called white flight. Everybody talked about it." The fear wasn't limited to talk. Grimm explained that her cousins "had this brand new house, maybe four, five years old and they didn't like black people and they were moving in. And the next time I went over [to their house,] there was a 'for sale' sign in almost every yard in the block." When African Americans moved closer to her own neighborhood, Grimm's parents moved their family to the nearby, almost exclusively white suburb of Lakewood.[118]

Just north of Long Beach, and east of Compton, Lakewood was a planned community formed by developers, who mapped out a town with single-family homes on individual lots and used principles of mass production in forming the new community. Like its east coast cousin Levittown, Lakewood was built in a deliberate and efficient multistep process. Plans for the development began in 1950, and by 1952 ten thousand homes already stood.[119] In describing Lakewood's houses, scholar Alida Brill observed, "despite the promotional rhetoric to the contrary about exterior trim styles and different floor plans, to the untrained eye they looked identical."[120] These identical rows of homes sat on a grid system of streets, which typified the efficiency model of the community.

The town's population mirrored the homogeneity of its houses. Lakewood became the fashionable locale, not simply because of its new homes, but also, and perhaps more important, because it was a white district in a metropolitan region that was becoming increasingly integrated. Lakewood's realtors touted the town as the county's new white enclave and denied African Americans home applications, steering them instead to Los Angeles' South Central district.[121] As blacks moved into inner ring suburbs like Compton, whites fled farther out. Civil rights attorney Loren Miller noted in 1955 that Lakewood was "a bean field ten years ago, a thriving metropolis today—lily white, made white, kept white by builders with the active consent of the FHA."[122] According to the 1960 census, of Lakewood's 67,126 residents, only 75 were classified as nonwhite.[123]

Lakewood soon became its own town. In order to stave off annexation by Long Beach (and to avoid that city's tax rate and retain its own retail taxes and home values), the development company and local residents fashioned the "Lakewood Plan," in which Los Angeles County contracted services such as fire and police to Lakewood,

which thus did not have to develop and pay for its own. Lakewood residents paid for these services at a low rate, which as scholar Mike Davis points out, was "indirectly subsidized by all county taxpayers."[124] Under this plan, residents could control local decisions, such as zoning, while avoiding public expenditures required by providing public services. Outsourcing services represented a major difference between Lakewood and the older suburbs like Compton, which shouldered the burden of the vast majority of its municipal services.

Incorporated in 1954, Lakewood became the model for other towns that wanted to keep down their tax rates. The Lakewood Plan inspired a wave of municipal incorporations across Los Angeles County.[125] By 1961, all cities and towns contracted some of their services from the county. Not surprisingly, the county provided the fewest services to Los Angeles and Long Beach, only assessment and collection of taxes for the former and the final map check of subdivisions for the latter, as well as election services for both. The county supplied Compton with six services and Lakewood with thirty-four.[126] Lakewood with its lower tax rates became an attractive alternative to the heavy tax burdens of the original suburbs.[127]

Lakewood, and other surrounding suburbs, affected Compton's economy by providing other retail and manufacturing centers. In the postwar years, Compton had grown in population and geographic size, but its new construction centered solely on residential housing and school plants. No new manufacturing plants were erected in Compton during this period and industry settled in neighboring towns.[128] The anemic industrial base lessened the potential income from property taxes and, as a result, the town relied disproportionately on monies from its sales tax. Unfortunately for the town's coffers, Compton's retail sector also struggled to bring in funds. In the early 1950s, the stores in Compton's central business district served people from both inside and outside the town. When agricultural towns around Compton became less rural, they developed their own shopping areas and relied less on Compton's. Furthermore, developers created new retail centers in other Los Angeles County areas, such as Lakewood and Torrance. The Lakewood Center, the largest shopping center in the country at that time, embodied many of the postwar changes. In fact, when the developers built Lakewood, they first constructed the shopping center and then built the houses around it.[129] The 100-store outdoor mall stood in the middle of a vast parking lot, which unlike traditional downtown areas, like the one in Compton, accommodated the rising car culture of the 1950s.[130] These areas contributed directly to the decline of business activity in Compton. Peaking in 1958, Compton's retail sales, along with their taxable portion, plunged at the end of the 1950s, further depressing the tax base.[131] In terms of financing the schools, all the component elementary school districts were mainly residential and therefore had a small tax capacity.[132]

The demographic shifts also had economic implications for Compton. As Davis shows, new suburbs under the Lakewood plan "gave suburban home-owners a subsidized 'exit option' as well as a powerful new motive for organizing around the 'protection of their home values and lifestyles."[133] Scholar Michan Connor concurs: "Lakewood's settlers had made significant capital and social investment in their homes, and quite sensibly viewed the politics of incorporation as a means of protecting those investments."[134] Lakewood was a good deal —it had new homes, a retail tax base, a low property tax rate, and firm racial lines, which promised to keep housing values high. The contracting of services in Lakewood and other municipalities like it allowed residents to reject metropolitan political and residential integration.[135]

These new developments and incorporations helped widen Los Angeles County's racial and income divides. These effects could be seen clearly in Compton. In 1949, when the town was predominantly white, the residents were for the most part middle and working class, with 83 percent in the middle brackets, just over 15 percent below the poverty line and almost 2 percent in the high wage bracket.[136] As the proportion of blacks and Latinos increased, the town's income level decreased, because discrimination in educational and employment opportunities often relegated nonwhites to lower-paying jobs.

Racial segregation in Southern California became even more acute, spreading from the center of Los Angeles to its outskirts, like the San Fernando Valley, as well as to other areas, not the least of which was Los Angeles County's neighbor, Orange County. Both the San Fernando Valley and Orange County exploded in population and money during and after World War II, and their rise affected Los Angeles's older suburbs like Compton. The new suburbs' expansion added to the racial segregation and economic stratification in Southern California as a whole. The aerospace industries had been suburbanizing for years, and in the early 1950s, they moved even farther from the central city and its surrounding communities to the more far-flung Valley. Between 1950 and 1960 the Valley's population more than doubled as companies worked with housing developers to sponsor planned communities for their workers, leading to further suburbanization of its workforce.[137] Developers and realtors systematically excluded blacks even after this type of practice was ruled unconstitutional.[138] Because residency determined school zones, schools remained racially segregated, and during this period more than a hundred new public school sites were built in the Valley.[139] In 1960, fifteen of the sixteen towns in the Valley had a black population of less than 1 percent.[140] Moving to the Valley ensured racially segregated neighborhoods and schools.

A similar pattern occurred in Orange County, where defense money brought job opportunities and a flood of new residents. In 1950, Orange County housed 216,224 residents and by 1970, nearly 1.5 million people called it home.[141] African Americans comprised less than 0.5 percent of the county's 1960 population of 703,935.[142] When white residents in older suburbs like Compton failed at keeping their areas racially segregated, they had options as to where to move.

In March 1959, recognizing the intertwined fates of towns, Edmund "Pat" Brown, governor of California, commissioned a study for recommendations on problems in the state's metropolitan areas. The study identified the crux of the issue as "whether California can maintain a suitable working and living environment for future urban growth."[143] The report analyzed the metropoles, recommended action programs, and identified areas for further research. Many of the issues, such as the concepts of local government and home rule, had been plaguing Compton for years. Many of the identified problems such as the economic and social structure of the metropolis were reasons people left Compton.

Living with Economic Disparities

Wage disparities across ethnic lines held true even after California's 1959 creation of the Fair Employment Practices Commission (FEPC).[144] In 1960, the median family income in Compton was $6,256, with 22 percent of the families having incomes under $4,000; 52 percent of employed male residents were in the craftsman, foreman, operatives and kindred workers category. Professional and related categories accounted for 14 percent of the employed males. With 12 percent of Compton's population, the west side, which was majority African American, had about 20 percent of the unemployed persons in the labor force. Less than half as many neighborhood residents were working in technical, professional, and proprietor type jobs; most people were semiskilled or unskilled.[145] Moreover, Compton's proportion of youth rose, lowering the number of wage-earners (and their tax dollars) while simultaneously necessitating greater city spending for their education. The Willowbrook School District also had a large number of youths. In 1960, there were proportionately more children twelve and under in the Willowbrook School District than in Los Angeles County as a whole.[146]

Compton struggled with raising the essential money for financing all its municipal services. Dividends from sales, use, and property taxes comprised most of the town's funds. Compton's bonded debt meant that the town could not dedicate enough of its tax revenues to schools, police, and other municipal responsibilities.[147] Compton's tax problems did not end with its bonded debt, however. The suburb lacked a base because its citizens valued living in a bedroom community. Town leaders' annexation policies reflected this desire as they emphasized annexing residential rather than industrial areas. Large industries that could normally support such an area located outside the municipality. Only small firms settled in the suburb and they did not generate generous tax revenues.[148]

Even the land zoned for industry was used for other purposes and little vacant land existed for industrial development. In 1964, there were about 2.3 acres of land per thousand population used for commercial purposes in the city of Compton, compared with 3.5 acres per thousand in all Los Angeles County. Compton had less commercial development for its population than surrounding communities or the county as a whole.[149] This meant that for the most part Compton residents worked outside the town. Between 1950 and 1960 the Compton labor market doubled its number of employees, but increased its employment opportunities by only 50 percent.[150]

Recognizing the detrimental effects of a weak tax base, Compton boosters hoped to attract more industry and produced a booklet in 1959 entitled "Compton: Industrial Heart of the California Southland." The brochure promised that land in Compton would become available for development but, while it showcased the town's machine shops, manufacturing plants, and retail stores, the pamphlet also confessed that Compton lacked any "industrial 'giants.'"[151] While aiming to remedy this, the authors also made sure to quell the fears of any potential homebuyer who might have doubted whether a town with industry could also provide a suburban existence. The authors claimed the contrary: "Industry has accepted a responsibility to the community as a whole. Not only do the more recently constructed Compton plants refrain from defacing a landscape: they beautify it."[152] They also highlighted Compton's suburban amenities, such as a summer recreation program that included children's baseball leagues, which in 1958 had over 1,200 players who participated in over 700 games.[153] Though not the authors' focus, these types of activities and facilities remained central to Compton. Despite boosters' efforts to court businesses and their claim of Compton as the "hub city," Compton remained a residential suburb, and its residents went elsewhere for work.

Due to their financial shortcomings, the component elementary districts and the high school district took on more debt. Some of the monies came as direct loans, and when the loans came due, the voters approved bond issues to pay back some of these debts. Furthermore, the districts issued more bonds to pay for construction of new schools and additions to existing ones.[154] Compton area schools continued to spend less on their pupils and have bigger class sizes than other Los Angeles County schools.[155] Due to financial restraints, Compton students lost out. While much had changed in Compton since the 1930s, the financial problems that challenged the community persisted and deepened.

Faced with tight funds and threatened by newcomers, Compton's white leaders continued to discriminate against blacks by controlling access to both education and jobs. African Americans pushed against these limits. In November 1964, Ted Nelson, a representative of the Parent Teacher Action Group, NAACP, and Congress of Racial Equality (CORE), submitted a letter to the Compton Union board of trustees beseeching the district to make seven major changes "to insure an equal educational opportunity for all our children and fair and equitable working conditions for all district employees, certified and classified." In terms of improving the educational component of the schools, the groups implored district officials to implement "an enriched educational program, compensatory education, and a crash program to discourage drop outs in the ghetto." They also appealed for smaller classes and "adoption of textbooks that represent the multiracial and multicultural conditions of our society." Regarding racial

divisions in the schools, Nelson and the groups demanded immediate integration and "a stop to boundary changes that perpetuate school segregation." Concerning employment, they asked for a written statement of district policy of hiring, promotions, and transfers as well as an issuance of "a directive for placement of all teachers regardless of race or creed in all schools."[156] Met with an entrenched white power structure, African Americans sought to change the community and its schools.

A Change Is Coming

Some political change did come to Compton. In 1963, U.S. Representative Clyde Doyle died, opening his seat for a special election. City council member Delwin "Del" Clawson was elected to Congress, vacating his council position. In its own special election, Compton elected Douglas Dollarhide its first black council member by a mere 73 votes.[157] Dollarhide ran on the platform of encouraging more businesses to locate in Compton and more representation for blacks on boards and commissions of the town government. He called for closer scrutiny of the oral portions of the civil service examinations, as they were used to discriminate against blacks.[158]

African Americans soon gained political power in Compton as a whole. In July 1963, Jesse Robinson became the first African American to sit on Compton Union's school board when he was appointed to fill a vacancy left by the death of Ramon Gonzales.[159] The next month Ross Miller was appointed to the town's Parks and Recreation Commission and Foster Ricardo Sr. was appointed to the Compton City Planning Commission.[160] Some positions came through elections as well. Two years later, Compton voters elected Doris Davis as city clerk. Davis, an African American, defeated incumbent Clyde Harland and another white candidate. Compton's black residents had won victories, increasing their political power. These triumphs were harbingers of changes yet to come.

Nevertheless, these elections did not mean Compton had rid itself of discrimination. They indicated that blacks were growing in numerical strength, not that white voters had fundamentally changed. The same year Ross Miller was appointed to the town's commission, he and his wife also moved to the town's predominantly white east side. A day after taking possession of their new house, the Millers found part of their lawn burning in the shape of a cross. Ironically Miller was at a Human Relations Committee meeting at the time of the incident.[161] In another example, shortly after his election, newly selected U.S. Representative Del Clawson, who served Compton as well as other white working-class suburbs, conducted a district-wide survey by sending one hundred thousand surveys to registered voters in his district, twenty-five thousand of which were returned. According to Clawson, the survey responses indicated that "racial prejudice is far deeper than we had anticipated."[162] Respondents, for the most part, rejected the idea that the government had the right to prohibit discrimination, whether in integration of public schools, hiring for job opportunities, or selling homes. Clawson followed his constituents' lead and vowed to vote against any civil rights bill, a promise he followed through on when in February 1964 he became one of five representatives from California who voted against the federal civil rights bill.[163]

The California state government, however, sought to tackle certain manifestations of racial discrimination. In 1959, the state legislature created the FEPC to enforce equal employment opportunities and enacted the Unruh Civil Rights Act, which required equal access to any business. The California Supreme Court decided in a series of cases that the law included real estate brokers and housing developers, forbidding them to discriminate.[164] The court drew a line at the private home owner, saying real estate brokers and developers were not responsible for a homeowner's discrimination. As a result, fair housing advocates looked to establish new legislation that did prohibit such bias.[165] Assemblyman William Byron Rumford led the charge in the legislature, and in June 1963 the California legislature passed a law bearing his name, the Rumford Fair Housing Act,

which prohibited racial discrimination in private housing financed by any public source and any housing with five or more units. Though the legislation did not cover all the state's housing, it covered a large percentage and empowered the FEPC to investigate and adjudicate discrimination complaints.[166] California joined fourteen other states that passed some version of open housing legislation enforceable by an administrative body.

Immediately after the bill's passing, the real estate industry spearheaded a movement to overturn it. In response to the law, they placed an initiative, which became known as Proposition 14, on the November 1964 ballot. If passed, this statewide initiative would amend the state constitution to repeal the Rumford Act and prevent enactment of any similar fair housing measures on the state or local level.[167] The Compton Council on Human Relations vigorously supported the Rumford Act and worked to save it, as did other groups across the state.[168]

Proposition 14 was a bellwether, as it became "a virtual referendum on civil rights." In framing the language of the proposition its authors avoided racial language, yet its proponents justified their campaign as opposing special privileges for minorities.[169] Instead, they employed the language of rights—such as the right to private property—as the language of their campaign to overturn the Rumford Act, framing it as a decision between "freedom of choice" and "forced housing."[170] Using this logic, white residents became the victims of discrimination.

The debate over the initiative gave California residents a means to discuss federal civil rights legislation, as the election came on the heels of the passage of the Civil Rights Act of 1964. After President John F. Kennedy's assassination in November 1963, his successor Lyndon Baines Johnson called for enactment of the civil rights bill as a memorial for Kennedy. Johnson signed the bill into law in July 1964. The passage of the Civil Rights Act all but ensured that California's Proposition 14 would be found unconstitutional, yet California voters wanted their opinions heard.[171]

And heard they were. Proposition 14 passed with 65.4 percent of California voters in favor and 34.6 percent opposed. In Los Angeles County, 67 percent voted for repeal, while, paradoxically, Johnson received 58 percent of the county's vote.[172] This vote was consistent with what had been happening in Compton for years, as white Compton residents had sought to prevent African Americans from moving into their town and their school districts. For over two decades prior to the passage of Proposition 14, white Comptonites protected their middle-class suburban dream by enforcing racial covenants, refusing to unify their school districts, and, when all else failed, moving out of their homes and neighborhoods. All these efforts compounded existing financial, organizational, and political strains on Compton and its school districts. They also created enormous tensions between blacks and whites in Compton.

The vote on Proposition 14 indicated that something was different in Compton, however. The city council had unanimously opposed the proposition on the basis it would amend the state constitution to legalize discrimination.[173] More people in the town voted against its passage. The vote—10,888 for and 15,259 against—reflected a political shift that had already begun to occur, even though Compton was only 40 percent African American at the time.[174] The white population, however, still included Latinos. While a demographic and political shift had happened in Compton that change served as a model of what could happen in other places and for many California voters that possibility was scary.

These tensions were not unique to Compton as racial and economic segregation seemed ever more entrenched with the passage of Proposition 14, which stoked the alienation of African Americans in South Los Angeles. Already feeling pressure from the stark economic realities of chronic underemployment and unemployment, many African Americans felt discouraged by its passage. For many blacks, California, and Los Angeles in particular, represented the promise of a better life. The national Urban League had rated sixty-eight American cities and found that Los Angeles offered African Americans the most opportunities.[175] Though better

than other cities, Los Angeles, particularly the Watts section, where the vast majority of black Angelenos lived, was no paradise. Residents faced overcrowded neighborhoods, filthy streets, and troubled schools. As journalist Ethan Rarick writes, the people of Watts cared little about how they compared to other cities because "they were Californians; they wanted the California life."[176] California had represented employment and housing opportunities, but the passage of Proposition 14 crushed many of these interrelated dreams as it limited fair housing and exposed racial fissures.[177] Though the California Supreme Court would later overturn Proposition 14 and the United States Supreme Court would uphold that decision, the passage of the proposition remained an indelible mark. Within a few months, this alienation would ignite Los Angeles and bring the struggles of black communities into the glare of the national spotlight.

The growth and shifts in demographics reconfigured control over political power in Compton. As African Americans moved in, many white Compton residents resisted the demographic changes in their neighborhoods, sometimes violently, but more often simply by leaving. The white exodus left black Comptonites with a series of problems—high taxes, low revenues, poorly structured school districts, and overcrowded schools. These problems, along with Compton's growing status as a black town, left the residents with a troubled legacy. As infrastructure costs skyrocketed, whites fled to outer suburbs, and the inner ring suburbs experienced the stresses and decay of the central city.

In the decade from the mid-1950s to the mid-1960s, Compton was essentially an intermediary suburb, one that was home to working-class whites and blacks aspiring to the same ideals of the suburban dream that dominated the popular culture and discourse. Both sought to live in a nice town with nice schools. But Compton's spatial boundaries of the suburban city made it difficult to achieve and maintain these suburban dreams for whites. Compton was a working-class suburb, and as such could not avoid integration. The invalidation of racial covenants and the modest housing prices made it almost impossible to prevent racial transition as residents from the neighboring minority neighborhoods of the Los Angeles moved into the once vastly white town. In this middle ground between the central city and the elite suburbs, African Americans and whites took a step toward the middle-class suburban dream and each group fought ferociously to protect their access to that dream.

NOTES

1. As cited in Bob Ellis, "The Story of Reeve Street in Compton," *CE*, May 14, 1953, 8.
2. As cited in Bob Ellis, "Frightened Family Hides After Sale of Home to Negro," *CE*, May 21, 1953, 8.
3. "Compton Tract Will Be Open," *LAT*, July 23, 1950, F1; Ellis, "The Story of Reeve Street in Compton," 1. For the advertisements, see, for example, Classified Ad, No Title, *LAT*, July 14, 1950, B11; Classified Ad, No Title, *LAT*, July 19, 1950, B14.
4. Camarillo, "Black and Brown in Compton"; Josh Sides, *L.A. City Limits: African American Los Angeles from the Great Depression to the Present* (Berkeley: University of California Press, 2003), 125–29; Josh Sides, "Straight into Compton: American Dreams, Urban Nightmares, and the Metamorphosis of a Black Suburb," *American Quarterly* 56 (September 2004): 583–605.
5. *Barrows v. Jackson* 17 346 U.S. 249 (1953); *Shelley v. Kraemer* 334 U.S. 1 (1948). Change was not immediate. It was not until two years after the Shelley decision that the Federal Housing Administration stopped issuing mortgages to real estate that had covenants. Even then real estate agents found ways of discriminating. See Kenneth T. Jackson, *Crabgrass Frontier: the Suburbanization of the United States* (New York: Oxford University Press, 1985), 208. For Los Angeles in particular, see Susan Anderson, "A City Called Heaven: Black Enchantment and Despair in Los Angeles," in *The City: Los Angeles and Urban Theory at the End of the Twentieth Century*, ed. Allen J. Scott and Edward W. Soja (Berkeley: University of California Press, 1998), 344–46.
6. Otis Skinner, interview with author, October 19, 2004, Compton, California, interview in possession of author. Sides, "Straight into Compton," 585–86; Camarillo, "Black and Brown in Compton," 363–65. For a more general discussion on race and housing in all Los Angeles during the postwar, see Sides, *L.A. City Limits*, 95–130.
7. Winston W. Crouch and Beatrice Binerman, *Southern California Metropolis: A Study in Development of Government for a Metropolitan Area* (Berkeley: University of California Press, 1964), 231.
8. Sides, *L.A. City Limits*, 126.
9. Ibid., 159.
10. Omar Bradley, *The King of Compton! The Assassination of a Dream* (Los Angeles: Milligan Books, 2007), 16; David Franklin, "Compton: A Community in Transition" (Los Angeles: Welfare Planning Council, 1962), 1–3. For an overview of African American suburbs, see Wiese, *Places of Their Own*.
11. Bradley, *The King of Compton!*, 17.
12. As cited in Sides, *L.A. City Limits*, 126.
13. Maxcy Filer, interview with author, June 23, 2005, Compton, California, interview in possession of author.
14. Linda Allen, interview with author, October 18, 2004, Compton California, interview in possession of author.
15. Fred Cressel, interview with author, October 19, 2004, Compton, California, interview in possession of author.
16. Interview with Sylvester Gibbs, conducted by Josh Sides, June 2, 1998, transcripts donated to SCLSSR.
17. Lorraine Cervantes, interview with author, October 20, 2004, Compton, California, interview in possession of author.
18. Thomas J. Sugrue, *Sweet Land of Liberty: The Forgotten Struggle for Civil Rights in the North* (New York: Random House, 2009), 204.
19. Grimm, interview with author.
20. "Compton: Industrial Heart of the California Southland," 10, Local History Collection, box 3, History Business Directories folder, CSUDH.
21. Wendell Green, "Vigilantes Brutally Beat Man over Sale to Negroes," *CE*, February 19, 1953, 1.
22. Ibid., 2.
23. Grace E. Simons, "Brokers Arrested," *CE*, March 5, 1953, 1.
24. "Compton and the Constitution," *CE*, March 5, 1953, 4.
25. "Brokers Lay Plans for Compton Battle," *CE*, April 16, 1953, 3.
26. "Compton Acquits All 5 Realty Board Brokers," *CE*, May 7, 1953, 1.
27. "Compton Vandals Stage Sneak Attack," *CE*, April 16, 1953, 1.
28. "Guard Homes as Pickets March," *CE*, May 14, 1953, 1.

29. Ellis, "The Story of Reeve Street in Compton," 1.
30. "Auto Worker Condemned for Aiding Pickets," *CE*, May 21, 1953, 1; "UAW Censures Member for Compton Action," *CE* July 23, 1953, 1.
31. For discussion of homeowners' associations as the arbiters of the middle class in Los Angeles, see Mike Davis, *City of Quartz: Excavating the Future in Los Angeles* (New York: Verso, 1990), 160–64. For discussion of white homeowners 'protection of their neighborhoods as protection of their class status, see Becky M. Nicolaides, *My Blue Heaven: Life and Politics in the Working-Class Suburbs of Los Angeles, 1920–1965* (Chicago: University of Chicago, Press, 2002); Thomas J. Sugrue, *Origins of the Urban Crisis: Race and Inequality in Postwar Detroit* (Princeton, N.J.: Princeton University Press, 1996).
32. "Plans Laid to Fight Against Compton Bias," *CE*, April 9, 1953, 2.
33. Ellis, "The Story of Reeve Street in Compton," 8.
34. "Compton Housing Row Flares," *CE*, May 14, 1953, 1.
35. "Invitation to Disaster," *CE*, April 23, 1953, 4.
36. All quotations in paragraph from "Full Compton Story Told in Eagle Series," *CE*, May 14, 1953, 8.
37. Ibid.
38. As cited in Franklin, "Compton," 83.
39. Eric Avila, *Popular Culture in the Age of White Flight* (Berkeley: University of California Press, 2004), 49; Sides, *L.A. City Limits*, 97.
40. Avila, *Popular Culture in the Age of White Flight*, 50.
41. Sides, *L.A. City Limits*, 127.
42. Gisele Hudson, "Compton Boosters Claim Affordable Homes, City Location Are Big Assets," March 1990, Compton Unified School District Folder, Compton File CPL.
43. Sugrue, *Sweet Land of Liberty*, 205.
44. "Compton Home Attacked," *CE*, June 25, 1953, 2.
45. Ibid.
46. *CE*, June 25, 1953.
47. "Why No Action, Compton Police?" *CE*, June 25, 1953, 2.
48. Grace E. Simons, "Compton Vandals in Sneak Attacks," *CE*, July 2, 1953, 1.
49. "Curb These Hudlums Now," *CE*, July 9, 1953, 4; Simons, "Compton Vandals in Sneak Attacks," 1–2.
50. Grace E. Simons, "Teenagers Sentenced," *CE*, February 26, 1953, 1.
51. "Compton Lads Get Suspended Terms," *CE*, March 5, 1953, 1.
52. Ellis, "Frightened Family Hides After Sale of Home to Negro," 1, 8.
53. *Barrows v. Jackson*; Patricia Rea Adler, "Watts, from Suburb to Black Ghetto" (PhD diss., University of Southern California, 1976), 301; Sides, *L.A. City Limits*, 121.
54. Bureau of the Census, U.S. Department of Commerce, "Special Census of Compton, California, April 30, 1952" (Washington, D.C.: Government Printing Office, 1952); Bureau of the Census, U.S. Department of Commerce, "Special Census of Compton, California, March 7, 1955" (Washington, D.C.: Government Printing Office, 1955). White residents' desire to resist the *Shelley* and *Barrows* decisions was not unique to Compton and existed in other Los Angeles suburbs. See, for example, Nicolaides, *My Blue Heaven*, 211.
55. Interview with Mary Cutherbertson, conducted by Josh Sides, June 20, 1998, transcripts donated to SCLSSR. Emphasis is in the original transcript.
56. Bradley, *The King of Compton!*, 4.
57. Grimm, interview with author.
58. Knopf, interview with author.
59. Letter to Everett P. Brandon, Field Secretary, NAACP, from Vannoy Thomspon, folder 37, Compton Ca, Undated 1955–1981, box 78, NAACP.
60. Knopf, interview with author.
61. Brad Pye, Jr., "Compton 'Queen' Causes Row," *LAS*, October 30, 1958, A1.
62. Finger, interview with author.
63. Sides, *L.A. City Limits*, 159. These problems of segregation and unequal education opportunities and facilities became the basis for the 1963 lawsuit *Crawford v. Board of Education of the City of Los Angeles*. The suit concerned Watts Jordan High school and nearby South Gate High. Separated by only a mile, their racial compositions were polar opposites. Jordan was 99 percent black while South Gate was 97 percent white. It took the judge seven years to rule on the case, but when he did in 1970, he ordered the school district to desegregate its nearly 700,000 students. Schneider, "Escape from Los Angeles," 999.
64. Charles Wollenberg, *All Deliberate Speed: Segregation and Exclusion in California Schools, 1855–1975* (Berkeley: University of California Press, 1976), 139.
65. Julie Salley Gray, "'To Fight the Good Fight': The Battle over Control of the Pasadena City Schools, 1969–1979," *Essays in History* 37 (1995).
66. Ann Scheid Lund, *Historic Pasadena: An Illustrated History* (San Antonio: Lammert Publications, 1999), 90.

67. Michael E. James, *The Conspiracy of the Good: Civil Rights and the Struggle for Community in Two American Cities, 1875–2000* (New York: Peter Lang, 2005), 275. *Brown* was not the only event to push the federal government into the arena of public education. When the Soviet Union launched Sputnik, the first satellite to orbit the earth, in October 1957, Americans panicked that they had lost their edge in the Cold War. Americans examined their own country in relation to the Soviet's success and concluded that American children needed to learn more mathematics and science to be competitive in the Cold War world. The federal government followed this lead, passing the National Defense Education Act the next year. The act granted over $1 billion in aid to public schools originally for a four year period beginning with the 1958–59 school year. This was the first comprehensive education legislation on the federal level. Along with this federal aid came a push for curricula revision, which came to fruition in the late 1950s and 1960s. Disciplinary scholars in the sciences and in mathematics developed new courses for K-12 students. Changes in history and social science course curricula soon followed. Yet, the renovations resulted in mixed outcomes because the authors lacked knowledge of the ins-and-outs of schooling and the teachers who implemented the new curriculum often lacked the nuanced knowledge of the discipline. Wayne J. Urban and Jennings L. Wagoner, Jr., *American Education: A History*, 3rd ed. (Boston: McGraw Hill, 2004), 296–97.
68. Gray, "'To Fight the Good Fight.'"
69. Grace E. Simons, "Pasadena Board Okehs Jim Crow School," *CE*, September 17, 1953, 1; "Push Fight Against Pasadena Schools," *CE*, November 19, 1953, 1.
70. Lund, *Historic Pasadena*, 90.
71. *Jay R. Jackson Jr. v. Pasadena City School District et al.*, 59 California 2d 876.
72. Wollenberg, *All Deliberate Speed*, 143.
73. James, *The Conspiracy of the Good*, 280.
74. "Minutes of Regular Meeting, Compton Union High School District Board of Trustees, August 5, 1958," Ed-P.S.R.- 81–94, box 3, CU.S.D Board Minute Files, CSA.
75. "Minutes of Regular Meeting, Compton Union High School District Board of Trustees, August 26, 1958," Ed-P.S.R.- 81–94, box 3, CU.S.D Board Minute Files, CSA.
76. "Dedication of Bunche Junior High school, Compton Union High School

District, Speech 1958 April 10," Collection 2051, box 372, UCLA.
77. Ibid.
78. Grimm, interview with author.
79. Franklin, "Compton," 68–69.
80. Bradley, *The King of Compton!*, 18–19.
81. National Advisory Commission of Civil Disorders, *Report of the National Advisory Commission on Civil Disorders*, 2 vols. (Washington, D.C.: Government Printing Office, 1968).
82. Lassiter and Niedt, "Suburban Diversity in Postwar America," 4.
83. M. Filer, interview with author.
84. "Minutes of Regular Meeting, Compton Union High School District Board of Trustees, June 25, 1963," Ed-P.S.R.- 81–94, box 3, CU.S.D Board Minute Files, CSA.
85. Ibid.
86. Franklin, "Compton," 71.
87. As cited in ibid., 70.
88. Ibid., 70.
89. Bradley, *The King of Compton!* 20–21.
90. Kelvin Filer, interview with author, June 23, 2005, Compton, California, interview in possession of author.
91. Pamela Samuels-Young, interview with author, June 20, 2005, Compton, California, interview in possession of author.
92. *The Challenge*, Compton NAACP newsletter, March 1958, folder 39, Compton Ca, newsletters 1958, 1970–1972, box 78, NAACP; Letter to Hadessah Snider, from Tarea Hall Pittman, folder 37, Compton Ca, Undated 1955–1981, box 78, NAACP.
93. *The Challenge*, March 1958, ellipses in original.
94. M. Filer, interview with author.
95. *The Challenge*, February 1958.
96. Sides, *L.A. City Limits*, 165–67.
97. NAACP Flier, undated, folder 37, Compton CA, Undated 1955–1981, box 78, NAACP.
98. M. Filer, interview with author; "Compton NAACP Claims Bias in Bank Hiring," *LAS*, July 10, 1958, A2; "Compton NAACP Vows to Picket Bank Until Negroes Hired," *LAS*, September 4, 1958, A2; "Compton NAACP's Bank Picket Enters 3rd Month," *LAS*, October 30, 1958, A3.
99. *The Challenge*, March 1958, folder 39, Compton Ca, newsletters 1958, 1970–1972, box 78, NAACP.
100. Brad Pye, Jr., "Will Centennial High Become Another Little Rock?" *LAS*, April 16, 1959, C1; Brad Pye, Jr., "Librarian Case Held 'Explosive'" *LAS*, April 30, 1959, A1; Brad Pye, Jr.,

"Centennial Librarian Stays" *LAS*, May 14, 1959, A1, A2.

101. Letter to unnamed Field Secretary of the NAACP, from Odessa Ausbrooks, folder 37, Compton Ca, Undated 1955–1981, box 78, NAACP.

102. "Compton NAACP Told 'Get Hell Out of Town,'" *LAS*, October 13, 1960, A1.

103. "Bigots Hit NAACP Office in Compton," *LAS*, November 10, 1960, A4.

104. Franklin, "Compton," 51–52, 83; "Human Relations Council Begins Membership Drive," *LAS*, June 27, 1963, B3.

105. For the debate over the establishment of the Human Relations Committee, see "City Council Minutes, February 18, 1964" and "City Council Minutes, September 1, 1964," CCH. For the resolution, see "City Council Minutes, September 14, 1965," CCH.

106. "NAACP Offices Hit by 13 Shots," *LAS*, December 14, 1961, A1.

107. Ibid., 1, 2; "Teen Violence Plagues Police at High School," *CHA*, February 9, 1962, 1, 2. These were not the first set of brawls. Similar incidents had occurred in 1959 and 1960. See "Police Quell Post-Game Teen Brawl," *LAS*, October 8, 1959, A1; Clarice Gray, "PTA Council Probes Rioters," *LAS*, October 13, 1960, B12.

108. "Fourteen More Arrested in High School Violence," *CHA*, February 15, 1962, 1.

109. Alberto M. Camarillo, "Chicano Urban History: A Study of Compton's Barrio, 1936–1970," *Aztlan* 2 (1971): 81.

110. Ibid., 90.

111. Franklin, "Compton," 25.

112. Sugrue, *Sweet Land of Liberty*, 205.

113. Kevin M. Kruse, *White Flight: Atlanta and the Making of Modern Conservatism* (Princeton, N.J.: Princeton University Press, 2005), 5.

114. Finger, interview with author.

115. Franklin, "Compton," 28.

116. Interview with Sylvester Gibbs, conducted by Josh Sides, June 2, 1998, transcripts donated to the SCLSSR.

117. Katherine P. Nelson, interview with author, October 21, 2004, Compton, California, interview in possession of author.

118. Grimm, interview with author.

119. Gary Miller, *Cities by Contract: The Politics of Municipal Incorporation* (Cambridge, Mass: MIT Press, 1981), 17.

120. Alida Brill, "Lakewood, California: 'Tomorrowland' at 40," in *Rethinking Los Angeles*, ed. Michael J. Dear et al. (Thousand Oaks, Calif.: Sage, 1996), 99.

121. Avila, *Popular Culture in the Age of White Flight*, 42–43.

122. As cited in Daniel HoSang, *Racial Propositions: Ballot Initiatives and the Making of Postwar California* (Berkeley: University of California Press, 2010), 58.

123. 1960 Census.

124. Davis, *City of Quartz*, 165; Miller, *Cities by Contract*, 20; Michan Andrew Connor, "'Public Benefits from Public Choice': Producing Decentralization in Los Angeles, 1954–1973," *Journal of Urban History* 39 (2013): 79–100.

125. Connor, "Public Benefits," 80.

126. Crouch and Binerman, *Southern California Metropolis*, 220–21.

127. Miller, *Cities by Contract*, 177.

128. Michael K. Brown, John O'Donnell, Averill Strasser, and Walter Szczepanek, "Social and Economic Problems of the City of Compton," in *Report on the Compton-UCLA Urban Research and Development Project, September 1968 to June 1969*, ed. Deena R. Sosson (Los Angeles: Institute of Government and Public Affairs, 1970), b-3.

129. Miller, *Cities by Contract*, 17.

130. Avila, *Popular Culture in the Age of White Flight*, 46.

131. Brown, O'Donnell, Strasser, and Szczepanek, "Social and Economic Problems of the City of Compton," b-3; Ahmed Mohammed Widaatalla, "Effect of Racial Change on the Tax Base of the City of Compton" (Ph.D. dissertation, University of California, Los Angeles, 1970), 158, 122, 126, 11–12.

132. Regional Planning Commission, "Willowbrook School District Study, Phase No. 1," 15.

133. Davis, *City of Quartz*, 169.

134. Michan Connor, "Creating Cities and Citizens: Municipal Boundaries, Place Entrepreneurs, and the Production of Race in Los Angeles County, 1926–1978" (Ph.D. dissertation, University of Southern California, 2008), 301.

135. Connor, "Public Benefits," 81.

136. Widaatalla, "Effect of Racial Change on the Tax Base of the City of Compton," 98.

137. HoSang, *Racial Propositions*, 58.

138. Sides, *L.A. City Limits*, 86–87.

139. Connor, "Creating Cities and Citizens," 202.

140. HoSang, *Racial Propositions*, 58.

141. Avila, *Popular Culture in the Age of White Flight*, 47.

142. Ibid.

143. Ernest A. Engelbert, ed., *Metropolitan California* (Sacramento: Governor's Commission on Metropolitan Area Problems), 3.

144. For discussion on the passage of California's Fair Employment Practices Commission, see Ethan Rarick, *California Rising: The Life and Times of Pat Brown* (Berkeley: University of California Press, 2005): 123–34; Mark Brilliant, *The Color of America Has Changed: How Racial Diversity Shaped Civil Rights Reform in California, 1941–1978* (New York: Oxford University Press, 2010), 159–61.

145. Compton City Manager, "Planning Grant Application: Model Neighborhood Demonstration Program" (Compton, 1967): Part 1A, 2; Part 1B, 1.

146. Ibid., 112–14; Regional Planning Commission, "Willowbrook School District Study, Phase No. 1," 9.

147. In discussing San Leandro, a northern California East Bay suburb, Robert Self showed the benefits of a town not holding any bonded debt. See Robert O. Self, *American Babylon: Race and the Struggle for Postwar Oakland* (Princeton, N.J.: Princeton University Press, 2003), 108.

148. Morrisett and Sexson, "A Report of a Survey," 193.

149. Tai Jun Cho, "Commercial Structures in Three Ethnically Different Areas: Compton, East Los Angeles, and Riverside" (Ph.D. dissertation, University of California, Riverside, 1975), 128.

150. Brown "Social and Economic Problems of the City of Compton," b-5.

151. "Compton: Industrial Heart of the California Southland," 44, Local History Collection, box 3, History Business Directories folder, CSUDH.

152. Ibid., 43.

153. Ibid., 75.

154. For example, see "Willowbrook School Bonds Approved," *LAT*, January 30, 1957, 7; "Compton Plans to Build Schools," *LAT*, March 8, 1959, SC3; "Minutes of Regular Meeting, Compton City School District Board of Trustees, October 22, 1962," Ed–P.S.R. 85–87, box 1, CU.S.D Board Minute Files, CSA. Not all their attempts to pass bonds succeeded, though. For an example of a failed attempt, see "Minutes of Regular Meeting, Compton Union High School District Board of Trustees, April 23, 1963," Ed–P.S.R. 81–94, box 5, CU.S.D Board Minute Files, CSA.

155. "Minutes of Regular Meeting, Compton Union High School District Board of Trustees, October 22, 1963," Ed-P.S.R. 81–94, box 5, CU.S.D Board Minute Files, CSA; "Minutes of Regular Meeting, Compton Union High School District Board of Trustees, October 27, 1964," Ed-P.S.R. 81–94, box 6, CU.S.D Board Minute Files, CSA.

156. "Minutes of Regular Meeting, Compton Union High School District Board of Trustees, January 26, 1965," Ed-P.S.R. 81–94, box 6, CU.S.D Board Minute Files, CSA.

157. "Dollarhide Wins Council Seat: Victory Sets a Precedent," *LAS*, June 6, 1963, A1.

158. "Dollarhide Stuns Compton, Winds in City Council Race," *LAS*, May 9, 1963, A2.

159. A.S. "Doc" Young, "Appoint Negro to Compton School Board," *LAS*, July 18, 1963, B1.

160. "Name Negro to Compton City Planning Commission," *LAS*, August 29, 1963, C3.

161. "Burning Cross on Lawn Greets Doctor on All-White Block," *LAS*, November 21, 1963, A1, A4.

162. "Clawson Survey Finds 'Deep Racial Prejudice,'" *LAT*, October 12, 1963, 12. Clawson's district encompassed the suburbs of South Gate, Huntington Park, Bell Maywood, Vernon, Bell Gardens, Cudahy, Lynwood, Compton, Paramount, Bellflower, and Downey.

163. "Clawson Votes Against Rights Bill," *LAS*, February 13, 1964, B1.

164. *Burks v. Poppy Construction Company*, 20 Cal. Rptr. 618 (1962); *Lee v. O'Hara*, 20 Cal. Rptr. 617 (1962); *Vargas v. Hampson*, 20 Cal. Rptr. 618 (1962).

165. HoSang, *Racial Propositions*, 61–62.

166. For discussion on the passage of the Rumford Act, see Rarick, *California Rising*, 261–67; Brilliant, *The Color of America Has Changed*, 176–92; HoSang, *Racial Propositions*, 53–90.

167. Thomas W. Casstevens, *Politics, Housing and Race Relations: California's Rumford Act and Proposition 14* (Berkeley, Calif.: Institute of Governmental Studies, 1967), Raymond Wolfinger and Fred Greenstein, "The Repeal of Fair Housing in California: An Analysis of Referendum Voting," *American Political Science Review* 62 (September 1968): 753; Nicolaides, *My Blue Heaven*, 308; Rarick, *California Rising*, 273–75, 288–89.

168. "Rumford Housing Act Discussed at Human Relations Council Meeting," *LAS*, October 31, 1963, C3; "Negroes Unite to Save Fair Housing Bill," *LAS*, December 5, 1963, B1; "No Vote on 14 Group Open in Compton Sat," *LAS*, July 16, 1964, D1.

169. Nicolaides, *My Blue Heaven*, 308.

170. As cited in Self, *American Babylon*, 264. For discussion of the movement in support of Proposition 14 using rights-based language, see Self, *American Babylon*, 260–68; Brilliant, *The Color of America Has Changed*, 194.

171. *Understanding the Riots: Los Angeles Before and After the Rodney King Case* (Los Angeles: *Los Angeles Times*, 1992), 21.

172. David O. Sears, "Black-White Conflict: A Model for the Future of Ethnic Politics in Los Angeles?" in *New York and Los Angeles: Politics, Society, and Culture, a Comparative View*, ed. David Halle (Chicago: University of Chicago Press, 2003), 369.

173. "Compton City Council Nixes Proposition 14," *LAS*, August 13, 1964, D2.

174. Frank M. Jordan, California Secretary of State, *Supplement to Statement of Vote, November 3, 1964* (Sacramento: California Secretary of State, 1964), 68; 1960 Census.

175. Governor's Commission on the Los Angeles Riots, *Violence in the City—An End or a Beginning? A Report* (Los Angeles, 1965), 3.

176. Rarick, *California Rising*, 320.

177. Kevin Starr discusses in depth the "California Dream" in his book series Americans and the California Dream (New York: Oxford University Press) For the rise and fall of the "California Dream," also see Peter Schrag, *Paradise Lost: California's Experience, America's Future* (Berkeley: University of California Press, 1998), 27–62.

DOCUMENTS FOR PART VIII

8.1 ZOOT SUIT RIOTS (1943)

Source: Memo from Commander Clarence Fogg to District Patrol Officer, Downtown Los Angeles, June 8, 1943. United States Navy, Eleventh Naval District, San Diego, California.

EDITORS' INTRODUCTION

During the early 1940s, a new style of clothing called the zoot suit took hold in cities across the country. Baggy pegged pants, a knee-length jacket with wide lapels and padded shoulders, and a wide brimmed, low-crowned hat typified the zoot suit look. Despite wartime restrictions imposed in April 1942 on excessive material in clothing—such as cuffs, pleats, and long coats—zoot suits remained in style with urban youth, especially African Americans in Harlem (New York City) and Chicanos in Los Angeles.

During the spring of 1943, a series of altercations broke out between Chicanos wearing zoot suits and white servicemen stationed at military bases in Southern California. Racial tensions ran high in the area following a murder trial a year earlier, referred to as the Sleepy Lagoon case, in which seventeen Chicano youths were convicted of murdering a man. Newspaper accounts sensationalized the trail, playing on anti-Mexican stereotypes and fanning racial fears.

Riots broke out when white servicemen and civilians attacked Chicanos to remove their zoot suits and cut off their long hair. Chicanos fought back and full-scale rioting erupted, as roving bands of sailors and soldiers (which often numbered into the hundreds) hunted down their victims. The rioting eventually stopped in June 1943, when the U.S. military authorities suspended all leave and ordered personnel to return to base. The following document is a copy of one such order from Naval Commander Clarence Fogg to the Senior Patrol Officer in Downtown Los Angeles.

ZOOT SUIT RIOTS (1943)

The following message for information to the District Patrol Officer.

Dictated by Senior Patrol Officer downtown Los Angeles.

0045, June 8, 1943

Quote:

Continued disorder.

Hundreds of service men prowling downtown Los Angeles mostly on foot—disorderly—apparently on prowl for Mexicans.

Have by joint agreement with Army Provost Marshall declared following Los Angeles city territory out of bounds to all Navy-Marines, Coast Guard, and Army personnel. — Main Street east to Los Angeles city limits.

All shore patrol are concentrated in the downtown area.

Disorderly personnel are being arrested by shore patrol.

Expect adverse publicity in morning newspaper.

Los Angeles Police have called in all off-duty men and auxiliary police to handle situation.

Naval Reserve Armory did not grant liberty. Men involved are from Marine activities, San Diego and El Toro, Navy activity composed of Roosevelt Base, Port Hueneme, and Destroyer Base, San Diego.

Situation under control at present except for widely separated incidents.

Groups vary in size from 10 to 150 men and scatter immediately when shore patrol approach. Men found carrying hammock clues, belts, knives, and tire irons when searched by patrol after arrest.

Army personnel are predominate [sic] tonight at ration [sic] of 4 or 5 to 1.

Senior Patrol Office will call District Patrol Officer at about 1000 today, June 8, 1943, if there is anything additional to report.

Given by R. O. Smith, C.M.M. Commander Fogg

8.2 THE MAN IN THE GRAY FLANNEL SUIT (1955)

Sloan Wilson

Source: Sloan Wilson, *The Man in the Gray Flannel Suit* (New York: Simon and Schuster, 1955).

EDITORS' INTRODUCTION

Sloan Wilson published this bestselling novel, largely believed to be autobiographical, in 1955. The novel provided its readers with a recognizable portrait of the 1950s suburban lifestyle. The phrase "the man in the gray flannel suit" became a common expression in American popular culture and vernacular language. The phrase denoted a middle class or upper middle class man who was forever tied to his job and financial obligations. In the novel, the main character, Tom Rath, was a graduate of Harvard University and a Second World War veteran. Sloan Wilson shared these characteristics with Rath. Rath's life, including his grinding work-day, his daily train commute, his tense relationship with his unfulfilled wife, and his growing financial responsibilities for his three children, was one shared by many Americans. Novelist Sloan Wilson, who published fifteen books, as well as articles and essays, had worked as a reporter for *Time* and as a professor of English at the University of Buffalo. *The Man in the Gray Flannel Suit* was made into a 1956 film starring Gregory Peck and Jennifer Jones. *The Man in the Gray Flannel* suit provided fodder for the popular television program *Mad Men* (2007–2015), and the title phrase was even employed within the script to describe the program's main character, Don Draper, as played by actor Jon Hamm.

THE MAN IN THE GRAY FLANNEL SUIT (1955)

By the time they had lived seven years in the little house on Greentree Avenue in Westport, Connecticut, they both detested it. There were many reasons, none of them logical, but all of them compelling. For one thing, the house had a kind of evil genius for displaying proof of their weaknesses and wiping out all traces of their strengths. The ragged lawn and weed-filled garden proclaimed to passers-by and the neighbors that Thomas R. Rath and his family disliked "working around the place" and couldn't afford to pay someone else to do it. The interior of the house was even more vengeful. In the living room there was a big dent in the plaster near the floor, with a huge crack curving up from it in the shape of a question mark. That wall was damaged in the fall of 1952, when, after struggling for months to pay up the back bills, Tom came home one night to find that Betsey had brought a cut-glass vase for forty dollars. Such an extravagant gesture was utterly unlike her, at least since the war. Betsey was a conscientious household manager, and usually when she did something Tom didn't like, they talked the matter over with careful reasonableness. But on that particular night, Tom was tired and worried because he himself had just spent seventy dollars on a new suit he felt he needed to dress properly for his business, and at the climax of a heated argument, he picked up the vase and heave it against the wall. The heavy glass shattered, the plaster cracked, and two of the laths behind it broke. The next morning, Tom and Betsey worked together on their knees to patch the plaster, and they repainted the whole wall, but when the paint dried, the big dent near the floor with the crack curving up from it almost to the ceiling in the shape of a question mark was still clearly visible. The fact that the crack was in the shape of a question mark did not seem symbolic to Tom and Betsey, nor even amusing—it was just annoying. Its peculiar shape caused people to stare at it abstractedly, and once at a cocktail party one of the guests who had had a little too much to drink said, "Say, that's funny. Did you ever notice that big question mark on your wall?"

"It's only a crack," Tom replied.

"But why should it be in the form of a question mark?"

"It's just coincidence."

"That's funny," the guest said.

Tom and Betsey assured each other that someday they would have the whole wall replastered, but they never did. The crack remained as a perpetual reminder of Betsey's moment of extravagance, Tom's moment of violence, and their inability either to fix walls properly or to pay to have them fixed. It seemed ironic to Tom that the house should preserve a souvenir of such things, while allowing evenings of pleasure and kindness to slip by without a trace.

The crack in the living room was not the only reminder of the worst. An ink stain with hand marks on the wallpaper in Janey's room commemorated one of the few times Janey had ever willfully destroyed property, and the only time Betsy ever lost her temper with her and struck her. Janey was five, and the middle one of the three Rath children. She did everything hard: she screamed when she cried, and when she was happy her small face seemed to hold for an instant all the joy in the world. Upon deciding that she wanted to play with ink, she carefully poured ink over both her hands and made neat imprints on the wallpaper, from the floor to as high as she could reach. Betsy was so angry that she slapped both her hands, and Janey, feeling she had simply been interrupted in the midst of an artistic endeavor, lay on the bed for an hour sobbing and rubbing her hands in her eyes until her whole face as covered with ink. Feeling like a murderess,

Betsey tried to comfort her, but even holding and rocking her didn't seem to help, and Betsy was shocked to find that the child was shuddering. When Tom came home that night he found mother and daughter asleep on the bed together, tightly locked in each other's arms. Both their faces were covered with ink. All this the wall remembered and recorded.

A thousand petty shabbinesses bore witness to the negligence of the Raths. The front door had been scratched by a dog which had been run over the year before. The hot-water faucet in the bathroom dripped. Almost all the furniture needed to be refinished, reupholstered, or cleaned. And besides that, the house was too small, ugly, and almost precisely like the houses on all sides of it.

The Raths had bought the house in 1946, shortly after Tom had got out of the army and, at the suggestion of his grandmother, become an assistant to the director of the Schanenehauser Foundation, an organization which an elderly millionaire had established to help finance scientific research and the arts. They had told each other that they probably would be in the house only one or two years before they could afford something better. It took them five years to realize that the expense of raising three children was likely to increase at least as fast as Tom's salary at a charitable foundation. If Tom and Betsy had been entirely reasonable, this might have caused them to start painting the place like crazy, but it had the reverse effect. Without talking about it much, they both began to thing of the house as a trap, and they no more enjoyed refurbishing it than a prisoner would delight in shining up the bars of his cell. Both of them were aware that their feelings about the house were not admirable.

"I don't know what's the matter with us," Betsey said one night. "Your job is plenty good enough. We've got three nice kids, and lots of people would be glad to have a house like this. We shouldn't be so *discontented* all the time."

"Of course we shouldn't!" Tom said.

Their words sounded hollow. It was curious to believe that that house with the crack in the form of a question mark on the wall and the ink stains on the wallpaper was probably the end of their personal road. It was impossible to believe. Somehow something would have to happen.

Tom thought about his house on that day early in June 1953, when a friend of his named Bill Hawthorne mentioned the possibility of a job at the United Broadcasting Corporation. Tom was having lunch with a group of acquaintances in The Golden Horseshoe, a small restaurant and bar near Rockefeller Center.

"I hear we've got a new spot opening up in our public-relations department," Bill, who wrote promotion for United Broadcasting, said. "I think any of you would be crazy not to take it, mind you, but if you're interested, there it is ..."

Tom unfolded his long legs under the table and shifted his big body on his chair restlessly. "How much would it pay?" he asked casually.

"I don't know," Bill said. "Anywhere from eight to twelve thousand, I'd guess, according to how good a hold-up man you are. If you try for it, ask fifteen. I'd like to see somebody stick the bastards good."

It was fashionable that summer to be cynical about one's employers, and the promotion men were the most cynical of all.

"You can have it," Cliff Otis, a young copy writer for a large advertising agency, said. "I wouldn't want to get into a rat race like that."

Tom glanced into his glass and said nothing. Maybe I could get ten thousand a year, he thought. If I could do that, Betsey and I might be able to buy a better house.

8.3 MEMORIES OF THE SECOND GREAT MIGRATION

Alverrine Parker

Interviewed by Lisa Krissoff Boehm, Grand Rapids, Michigan, December 28, 2002.
Source: Lisa Krissoff Boehm, *Making a Way out of No Way: African American Women and the Second Great Migration* (Jackson: University Press of Mississippi, 2009), 79–81.

EDITORS' INTRODUCTION

Alverrine Smith Parker's oral history illuminates the Second Great Migration, the movement of African Americans from the South to the North between 1940 and 1970. Parker was born in 1936. She lived in Columbus, Mississippi. Her mother worked at a bakery; her father labored as a bellhop at the Gilmore Hotel and also cleaned the Merchant's and Farmer's Bank. Her parents had eight children. Parker also lived in Muskegon Heights, Michigan, in Los Angeles, and in Grand Rapids, Michigan. She first moved north about 1944–1945, when her father went to Michigan to work in a foundry. She returned to Mississippi to live with her grandmother during her formative childhood years. As a child in the South, Parker worked as a babysitter and house cleaner. In Michigan and California, she engaged in factory work and nursing home positions. Later she drove buses for Grand Rapids public schools. Parker married in 1960 and had two children. The Jim Crow system left her with unforgettable incidents that changed her outlook forever. In her interview, Parker stressed that the United States was far from achieving racial justice.

ALVERRINE PARKER, MEMORIES OF THE SECOND GREAT MIGRATION, INTERVIEWED BY LISA KRISSOFF BOEHM, GRAND, RAPIDS, MICHIGAN, DECEMBER 28, 2002.

I'm Alverrine Parker. I spell my name with two r's. I don't know why, but my dad wanted to make it difficult. I was born in Columbus, Mississippi, March 14, 1936. My father had two jobs—he worked as a bellhop at the Gilmore Hotel, and then he did cleaning at a bank. Merchant's and Farmer's Bank. My mother did work at one time at a bakery at night to help out with money.

My dad moved to Muskegon Heights, Michigan to escape prejudice and to try to find a better living for his family. He must've had friends, because they went to work at Lakey Foundry. He didn't really know it was hard, dirty work. My younger sister was born in 1944. And he come back after she was born and had to go back to Michigan, but he came back to Mississippi. And we must've come to Michigan, probably around 1945.

It was hard for me to understand how people judge people because of their color. And it's still hard for me to understand that. Because your blood is red and mine is red, and if something would happen with you, my blood wouldn't turn you black, and yours wouldn't turn me white. So it's God's plan that all people are people, you know, and not to be judged and put down in slavery and all that because of the color of their skin. Something that they could not help. Nobody can control the way they come into the world.

So, it was hard for me to understand that black people had to say yes-sir, no-sir and ride on the back of the buses and all like that. I never could understand that. So, my grandmother protected us a lot. We did a lot of walking, to avoid a lot of things. My grandfather must've died when I was around ten or eleven, and I went to school in Muskegon through the sixth grade. And my grandmother wanted us to come back and live, so I went back. I am the only one that graduated school in the South, so I'm happy that I did now. I graduated R.E. Hunt High in Columbus, Mississippi in 1955.

I worked; I did little jobs for some of the neighbors. We lived in an area where blacks owned everything. They were owners of little restaurants, cafes, barber shops and shoe shops, all that. So I did some babysitting and I worked to be able to support myself. I lived with my grandmother. Babysitting and cleaning and stuff [for white people], you learn a lot.

One white family that I worked for, he was the principal of a school. He was glad that I was graduating because he said he knew then it was going to be terrible when the schools integrated.

I didn't understand why we always had to be taking care of white people. And they never did anything, you know, you were always yes-ma'am, no-ma'am and taking care of them.

I graduated in the top ten from high school. I could make a skirt then in about thirty minutes. With two yards of material, you had a real nice, little pleated skirt. Black teachers taught a lot, because they know what we had to go through. So we learned how to make our clothes. In fact, I made curtains for my grandmother's window. You learn to do a lot. So that's what we did. We learned to sew, and most of my friends, we had jobs after school. Professor Hunt is the man that they named the school after, right across the street from us on Ninth Avenue, in Columbus. There were mostly teachers in that block. Everyone helped everybody. Kids had to obey all older people. But I didn't like how they called our grandparents auntie and uncle [when we called whites ma'am and sir.]

In the South, you knew exactly where you stood. I could never understand it. We all come here the same way, and we go the same way. See, that's what I can't understand, the prejudice about color and work. See, they try to make black people feel like they're not capable of doing it, and it's not true.

See, that's another thing too, the white man was after the black woman. Because my grandmother used to tell me that they had to send her to Alabama and leave her four children. A couple of white men was after her in Mississippi there. See, they had children by black women, and they didn't treat them fair.

I used to walk downtown to pay her light bill for my grandmother, and there were two white boys that pushed me off the sidewalk and down onto the ground. I was supposed to get off the sidewalk. And they just pushed me down. But I looked and saw a great big lock, a rusty lock in the grass. And I took one and banged one of them so hard, trying to get them off of me. Blood came from them. They ran. But when I got home, my little starched and ironed dress dirty, my grandmother was wondering. I had to leave home that night; she sent me back to Michigan. She was afraid they would come and try to hurt me. Because I think, after that, Emmett Till was killed down there in Mississippi.

Now these were two healthy big boys that she felt would've hurt me. You have a lot of experiences where black people have to fly away by night. I remember she put me on a Greyhound Bus. It was during my cycle. And I remember her taking her table-cloth off her table. She tore a piece out of it, and she made a strip for me to sit on, because you couldn't go to the bathrooms and stuff like that to change. That vinyl cloth kept me from soiling my clothes. The further North you came, you could change, you know. We had to sit in the back of the bus. That still rings—I'm sixty-six years old, and that still rings in my mind.[1]

NOTE

1. Alverrine Parker, interview with Lisa Krissoff Boehm, Grand Rapids, Michigan, December 28, 2002.

8.4 *THE DOLLMAKER* (1954)

Harriette Arnow

Source: Harriette Arnow, *The Dollmaker* (New York: Avon Books, 1954).

EDITORS' INTRODUCTION

Harriette Arnow's best-selling and critically acclaimed novel, *The Dollmaker*, offers insight into the emotional effects of migration and immortalizes the important, but often overlooked, massive migration of white southerners to northern farms and cities. Arnow focuses on the white southern migration accompanying American entrance into the Second World War. Chad Berry brought out the importance of white southern migration in his essay, "The Great White Migration, 1945–1960," included in this part. **[See Essay 8.3.]** Arnow, born in Kentucky in 1908, attended Berea College and graduated from the University of Louisville. Arnow's writing blossomed while she lived in Cincinnati, and she and her husband, news-paperman Harold B. Arnow, eventually settled on a farm in Ann Arbor, Michigan. In this section, the novel's main character Gertie Nevels and her children Reuben, Amos, Clytie, Cassie, and Enoch travel from Kentucky to Detroit, to reunite with Gertie's husband Clovis who labors in a war factory. They leave the train, only to hear comments of "hillbilly" around them, and take a cab through the surprising urban sights to their new lodgings.

THE DOLLMAKER (1954)

The children fell silent as the driver, after much slow turning and slow driving through the narrow, crowded streets, came at last to a straight wide street, half buried in the ground, bounded by gray cement walls and crowded with cars and monstrous truck-like contraptions such as none of them had ever seen. Here there were no lights to stop them, and they went so fast that Gertie could only sit, shivering, staring straight ahead, or blinking and crouching over Cassie when they shot under bridges carrying more cars, buses, and even trains. The wind pried at the doors and the windows, finding every crack; and as there seemed to be no heat in the cab all of them were as cold, almost, as when they had waited on the sidewalk.

The unbroken rush past the gray walls and under the bridges ended at last. There followed more turnings down narrow streets, strange streets that, though crowded, seemed set at times in empty fields until one saw a slowly moving switch engine or a mountainous pile of coal blown free of snow. The smoke thickened, and through it came sounds such as they had never heard; sometimes a broken clanking, sometimes a roar, sometimes no more than a murmuring, and once a mighty thudding that seemed more like a trembling of the earth than sound. "Boy, I'd hate to live by one of them big press plants," the driver said, then asked of them all, "Don'tchas know where youses at? Right in u middle a some of Detroit's pride and glory—war plants."

Enoch kept twisting around to see, but there was little to be seen save blurred shapes through the snow and smoke. The railroad tracks multiplied, and twice jangling bells and red lights swinging in the wind held them still while long freight trains went by with more smoke rolling down and blotting out the world. It seemed suddenly to Gertie as if all the things she had seen—the blurred buildings, the smokestacks, the monstrous pipes wandering high above her, even the trucks, and the trains—as if all these were alive and breathing smoke and steam as in other places under a sky with sun or stars the breath of warm and living people made white clouds in the cold. Here there seemed to be no people, even the cars with their rolled-up windows, frosted over like those of the cab, seemed empty of people, driving themselves through a world not meant for people.

They drove for a long while through the sounds, the smoke and steam, past great buildings which, though filled with noise, seemed empty of life. They were stopped again on the edge of what looked to be an endless field of railroad tracks, to wait while a long train of flat cars went by. Each car carried one monstrous low-slung, heavy-bodied tank, the tank gray green, wearing a star, and holding, like the black feelers of some giant insect reaching for the sky, two guns. Gertie, hoping for something better to see, scratched another hole in the window frost. She was just turning away in disappointment when the whirling snow, the piles of coal, the waiting cars, the dark tanks moving, all seemed to glow with a faint reddish light. The redness trembled like light from a flame, as if somewhere far away a piece of hell had come up from underground.

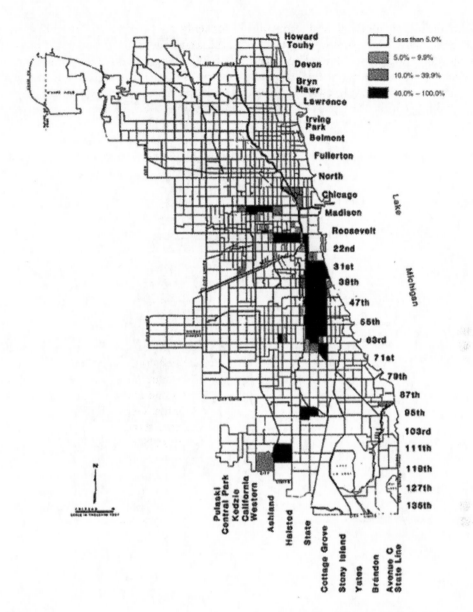

Illustration VIII.1 "Map 1. Percentage of black population, in census tracts, city of Chicago, 1940. Source: Arnold R. Hirsch, *Making the Second Ghetto: Race and Housing in Chicago, 1940–1960* (Chicago: University of Chicago Press, 1998; first published in 1983 by Columbia University Press).

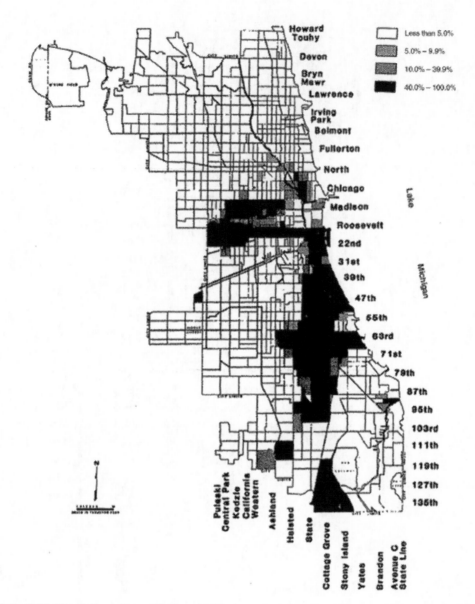

Illustration VIII.2 "Map 3. Percentage of black population, in census tracts, city of Chicago, 1960. Source: Arnold R. Hirsch, *Making the Second Ghetto: Race and Housing in Chicago, 1940–1960* (Chicago: University of Chicago Press, 1998; first published in 1983 by Columbia University Press).

PART IX

RACE AND BORDERLANDS IN THE POST-WAR METROPOLIS

EDITORS' INTRODUCTION TO PART IX

In the epilogue to his important American history survey, *America Becomes Urban: The Development of U.S. Cities & Towns, 1780–1980*, the late Eric H. Monkkonen cautions against the reduction of urban history to a set of problems. This warning is well-taken. Urban history contains stories of sexual scandal, political imbroglios, mobsters and gangsters, weather-related disasters, devastating fires, clashes between rich and poor, interracial violence, inadequate housing, dire poverty, families in crisis, and the like. Monkkonen concludes however, that "American cities are far more successful than we sometimes realize." American cities are the sites of considerable progress—technological, social, economic, political, and otherwise. Cities are simply large settlements of people, centers for human experiment, failure, and sometimes, success. Monkkonen posits that by studying the cities:

> We learn that our cities are highly flexible, that they have never experienced stasis, that diffuse sprawl and blurred boundaries are their heritages, that a hustling support of private enterprise is a long tradition, and that numerous multiple and small governments have been with us from the start. We also learn that American taxpayers have always been stingy as we tried to pass on the costs of services to the future through growth, but that we have historically been willing to create the service providing city and to indebt ourselves for infrastructural expansion, which in turn has promoted technological change. It is a complex legacy, one without easily identified heroes and villains. But the promise is there of an adaptive and potentially humane future.[i]

It is easy to only see the troubling aspects of the post-war metropolis. The promise of the post-Second World War economic recovery never translated into concrete, long-term improvements for urban civic life. Scholars have highlighted the weighty issues facing the post-war city as a corrective to the rampant myth-making about the period, much heralded as the heyday of the "greatest generation," who, after coming home from fighting in the Second World War, settled into pretty, multi-colored homes in the suburbs, raised their baby-boomer children, and held weekend barbeques. In the main, national and civic leaders of the period perpetuated racism in the housing market despite strong legal challenges and unsuccessfully turned to consumerism to solve American problems.

The part opens with an essay by Thomas J. Sugrue, whose case study of Detroit leaves us astounded by the exclusionary practices of the housing market. Sugrue builds on Arnold R. Hirsch's "second ghetto thesis" to explain how segregation continued into the late twentieth century.

Optimism abounded in post-war, white/non-Hispanic America, but what largely resulted was a retreat from civic involvement and a failure to create the racially integrated neighborhoods necessary for a stronger nation. Urban renewal, launched in 1949 with the Housing Act of that year, promised a revitalized effort to improve our cities but led to the warehousing of the poor in high-rise public housing that later came to be torn down in most cities. The lessons learned in the Great Depression regarding care for the poor and the elderly largely fell from the public consciousness as good times returned for the white majority. Suburbanites started refusing to pay the bill for increased social services in the 1950s, a trend that only grew as the century went on. The majority of Californians voted for President Lyndon Baines Johnson in 1964, but voted against fair housing, one of Johnson's major issues. The contradictions of the post-war years are difficult to grasp. Jon C. Teaford surmises that the period is best understood not as a time of triumph or of strife, but of a difficult road to an unrealized renaissance. Some of the best American minds tried to alleviate the problems of the city, but the battle was surely not won outright. Teaford writes, "Along that road there were enough pitfalls to warrant serious consideration whether the journey was worth the effort and whether the billions of dollars spent on physical and social renewal were wasted. To the perceptive observer the road was lined with ample monuments both to the possibilities and limitations of recent public policy."[ii]

NBD Connolly takes us to Miami, Florida, a city of great importance in modern American history. His examination of land use allows readers to untangle the onerous weight of Jim Crow practices and see how land ownership has a real effect on democracy. In many American cities, including Miami, ownership of land and buildings connoted power. Naively, we had thought that real estate markets would operate fairly without regular intervention. But the power to be drawn from real estate was too high, too tempting, and the market would not move us towards building integrated communities unless they were properly regulated.

Monica Perales also demonstrates how urban Americans struggled with disparities within communities in her examination of the Smeltertown area of El Paso, Texas. The ethnic Mexican residents she studied did not even have formal rental agreements for their housing, clustered in the shadow of the copper smelter where they labored. Despite the odds against them, the workers and their families devised community and identity, even in the face of environmental challenges. Perales' insightful work allows us to think about a variety of borders within our nation's cities, both figurative and literal.

A.K. Sandoval-Strausz uses Oak Cliff, a neighborhood in Dallas, Texas, as an example of an American place with strong transnational connections—connections it has been relying on to "repopulate and revive." Sandoval-Strausz, like Monkonnen, applies a positive lens to modern U.S. cities. *Nuevo* Oak Cliff residents applied behaviors learned in Mexico and Latin America more broadly in their daily life, and in doing so added new life and energy to what had been seen as a dying city. Sandoval-Strausz boldly contends that it is time we moved beyond the context of the second ghetto thesis to study the new energy in our cities.[iii]

The documents in this part expand on the theme of social and economic tensions of post-war America, specifically conflicts that arose from the quest for fair and decent housing, good public schools, and civil and economic rights. **Document 9.1** on the Watts Riots of 1965 demonstrates how quickly a Los Angeles neighborhood ignited when black motorist Marquette Frye was arrested by white police officers. American Indians displaced from reservations by the unfulfilled promised of urban jobs sought justice throughout the 1960s as seen in **Document 9.2**. The actions of the Oakland Black Panther Party for Self-Defense riveted the nation in the late 1960s; they set out their platform for equity, the Ten Point Plan, in 1966, as given in **Document 9.3**. And in **Document 9.4** President George H. W. Bush addresses the nation regarding the eruption of violence in Los Angeles and other American cities following the acquittal of four Los Angeles police officers involved and captured on a viral video of the beating of African American Rodney King.

In a movement that began in the late nineteenth century and gained momentum in the 1950s, white families fled cities and moved to the suburbs to escape perceived urban disorder. After decades, this suburban lifestyle became so firmly entrenched that suburbanites grew estranged from the urban center. Some balked at paying taxes, especially those that might fund social services and other programs to benefit city residents. Many urban residents who were white and/or middle- to upper-class, abandoned urban public education, once a linchpin of upward mobility, and sent their children to private and parochial schools. At the same time, Latinos settled in cities that had been declining in population, and utilized transnational connections to sustain American cities. These urban residents improved the population figures of the urban centers, and utilized public spaces in new ways.

NOTES

i. Eric H. Monkkonen, *America Becomes Urban: The Development of U.S. Cities & Towns, 1780–1980* (Berkeley: University of California Press, 1988), 238 and 243–244.

ii. John C. Teaford, *The Rough Road to Renaissance: Urban Revitalization in America, 1940–1985* (Baltimore, MD: Johns Hopkins, 1990), 9.

iii. A. K. Sandoval-Strausz, "Latino Landscapes: Postwar Cities and the Transnational Origins of a New Urban America," *Journal of American History* (December 2014): 805 and 812.

ESSAY 9.1

Class, Status, and Residence: The Changing Geography of Black Detroit

Thomas J. Sugrue

Source: Thomas J. Sugrue, *The Origins of the Urban Crisis: Race and Inequality in Postwar Detroit* (Princeton: Princeton University Press, 1996).

EDITORS' INTRODUCTION

With its riot of 1943, Detroit rocketed to the forefront of national public consciousness. Known as the "Arsenal of Democracy" for its substantial role in providing industrial goods to the war effort, racial tensions ran extremely high in this midwestern metropolis. Detroit's symbolic power heightened even further with the city's riots in 1967. Detroit's symbolic resonance gained strength in the early twenty-first century. As the American auto industry, centered in Detroit, faltered, the city remained in the national news. Just uttering the city's name "Detroit" quickly summoned a variety of themes, including white flight, deindustrialization, and the financial ramifications of global competition. Pundits and scholars continue to debate the extent to which this largely one-industry city is a bellwether of the rise and fall of American industrial cities.

Detroit, in the early post-war years, was primarily a black and white city, with few Hispanic or Asian residents. In Detroit, racial politics and the harsh effects of high levels of "white flight" play out in dramatic ways. The city certainly provides a window onto the great inequities of American life, inequities whose ramifications are only just being grasped by middle class Americans many decades later. The post-war years were much heralded as a time of prosperity for millions of white Americans, but as Michael Harrington's 1962 book, *The Other America*, points out, the seeds of disquiet were planted in the 1950s. The industrial belt of the United States, stretching from the Middle Atlantic States on through the Middle West, began to atrophy during the 1950s. Industry moved southward or moved overseas. It was once said of Detroit, "When Detroit sneezes, other cities catch pneumonia." Detroit, linked to one of the most important national industries, seemed a stable place to be. By the early twentieth-first century, the saying no longer applied. Michigan led the nation's unemployment ratings and felt the impact of the economic downturn deep to its core.

Sugrue brings much-needed historical perspective to the history of the multi-generational poor, oftentimes referred to as the underclass (but not without substantial debate). Those, like Daniel Patrick Moynihan and E. Franklin Frazier, who have connected the existence of the underclass with what they perceive to be problems within the black family, have been successfully refuted. **[See Document 5.4, Daniel Patrick Moynihan, "The Negro Family and the Case for National Action" (1965).]** Those scholars, such as William Julius Wilson and Douglas Massey, who attribute the existence of generational poverty to structural issues within American society, have received more positive attention.[i] Sugrue steps into this

---

i. See E. Franklin Frazier, *The Negro Family in the United States* (Chicago: University of Chicago Press, 1939), Lee Rainwater and William L. Yancey, eds., *The Moynihan Report and the Politics of Controversy* (Cambridge, MA:

treacherous intellectual ground confidently. As he points out, we can benefit by adding political analysis to this discussion. Sugrue writes, "This book is a guide to the contested terrain of the postwar city, an examination of the unresolved dilemmas of housing, segregation, industrial relations, racial discrimination, and deindustrialization. I argue that the coincidence and mutual reinforcement of race, economics, and politics in a particular historical moment, the period from the 1940s to the 1960s, set the stage for the fiscal, social, and economic crises that confront urban America today."[ii]

Sugrue's work draws on the findings of Arnold R. Hirsch's "second ghetto" thesis and brings our understanding of the segregated city further forward in time. **[See Essay 8.1, Arnold R. Hirsch, "The Second Ghetto and the Dynamics of Neighborhood."]** Like Hirsch, Sugrue concluded that the segregated city was not inevitable, but carefully created through public policy. Analyzing Sugrue's maps of the expanding black neighborhoods of Detroit echoes the expansion of Chicago's black belt as seen in the maps following the Hirsch essay. In this essay, Sugrue opens with the landmark *Sipes v. McGhee* case, which challenged the legality of the restrictive covenants that allowed for segregated neighborhoods. The case joined with three other similar court battles to constitute the U.S. Supreme Court case, *Shelley v. Kraemer* (1948), which at long last invalidated restrictive covenants with racial restrictions.

Thomas J. Sugrue is Professor of Social and Cultural Analysis and History at New York University. Previously he served as the Edmund J. and Louise W. Kahn Professor of History and Sociology and the David Boies Professor of History and Sociology at the University of Pennsylvania. He is also the author or editor of the books *The Origins of the Urban Crisis: Race and Inequality in Postwar Detroit* (Princeton, NJ: Princeton University Press, 1996), *W.E.B. DuBois, Race, and the City: The Philadelphia Negro and its Legacy* (co-edited with Michael B. Katz) (Philadelphia: University of Pennsylvania Press, 1998), *The New Suburban History* (co-edited with Kevin Kruse) (Chicago: University of Chicago Press, 2006), *Sweet Land of Liberty: The Forgotten Struggle for Civil Rights in the North* (New York: Random House, 2008), *Not Even Past: Barack Obama and the Burden of Race* (Princeton, NJ: Princeton University Press, 2010), and, with Glenda Gilmore, *These United States: A Nation in the Making, 1890 to the Present* (New York: W. W. Norton, 2015). In 2017 he co-edited, with Domenic Vitiello, *Immigration and Metropolitan Revitalization in the United States* (Philadelphia: University of Pennsylvania Press). *The Origins of the Urban Crisis* garnered several awards, including the Bancroft Prize in American History (1998), the Philip Taft Prize in Labor History (1997), the Social Science History Association's President's Book Award (1996), the Best Book in North American Urban History Award, Urban History Association, of 1997, and one of Choice's Outstanding Academic Books for 1997.

CLASS, STATUS, AND RESIDENCE: THE CHANGING GEOGRAPHY OF BLACK DETROIT (1996)

The family who moves in next door to you or down the block, whether white or colored, is not the advance guard of an invasion. They are just folks following the old American custom of bettering their living conditions by seeking a finer place to live.

—Maceo Crutcher, president of the Detroit Realtist Association, and Walker E. Smith, Chairman of the Committee on Race Relations, the Detroit Realtist Association (1948)

MIT Press, 1967), William Julius Wilson, *The Truly Disadvantaged: The Inner City, the Underclass, and Public Policy* (Chicago: University of Chicago Press, 1987), and Douglas Massey and Nancy Denton, *American Apartheid: Segregation and the Making of the Underclass* (Cambridge, MA: Harvard University Press, 1994).

ii. Thomas J. Sugrue, *The Origins of the Urban Crisis: Race and Inequality in Postwar Detroit* (Princeton: Princeton University Press, 1996), 4–5.

The scene was tense with drama. The place was the Wayne County Circuit Court in May 1945. The case was a civil suit against a middle-class black couple who had bought a house in an all-white West Side neighborhood. The defendants, Minnie and Orsel McGhee, were upwardly mobile, better off than most Detroit blacks at the end of World War II. She was one of Detroit's two hundred black school teachers, he was a relatively well-paid automobile worker. The plaintiffs were Benjamin and Anna Sipes and other members of the Northwest Civic Association. With the assistance of the NAACP and two leading black lawyers, Willis Graves and Francis Dent, Minnie and Orsel McGhee used the defense to challenge racially restrictive covenants, agreements that covered virtually all Detroit neighborhoods outside the center city. Their immodest goal was "to wipe out Detroit's ghetto walls."[1]

When the McGhees bought a house on Seebaldt Street, in a white neighborhood just beyond the black enclave near Grand Boulevard and Tireman Avenue, Benjamin Sipes, their next-door neighbor, along with a delegation from the all-white Northwest Civic Association, sent the McGhees a letter asking them "to kindly vacate the property." When the McGhees refused, Sipes and the Northwest Civic Association filed suit to prevent them from moving in, on the grounds that the entire neighborhood was covered by a covenant that specified that houses could not be "sold nor leased to, nor occupied by any person other than one of the Caucasian race." Sipes testified that Orsel McGhee "appears to have colored features," and that Minnie McGhee "appears to be the mulatto type." Attorneys Dent and Graves tried to challenge Sipes's testimony, to no avail, on the grounds that "there is no simple way to determine whether a man is a member of the Mongoloid, Caucasoid, or Negroid race." The Wayne County Circuit Court held that the McGhees were indeed "colored" and that the covenant was valid.

That was only the beginning of the McGhees' legal assault on Detroit's ghetto walls. With the assistance of the NAACP Legal Department, they appealed to the Michigan State Supreme Court, this time deploying a more powerful legal weapon. They argued that the covenants violated state antidiscrimination laws and were unconstitutional under the Fourteenth Amendment. Again, their arguments fell on deaf ears. Michigan's conservative senior jurists denied their appeal and wrote an opinion reaffirming the validity of restrictive covenants. Still confident of the merits of their case, the McGhees' lawyers appealed to the United States Supreme Court.

Sipes was one of dozens of restrictive covenant cases that the NAACP and other civil rights groups argued before the courts in the 1940s (including several others in Detroit), with the hopes of undermining residential Jim Crow throughout the United States. Judges around the country had regularly upheld such covenants as necessary and proper to protect the rights of property owners. In addition, the Home Owners' Loan Corporation and Federal Housing Administration used racial restrictions to determine the actuarial soundness of a neighborhood. FHA underwriting manuals, in fact, encouraged developers to put racial restrictions on their properties to protect the "character" of a neighborhood and to maintain high housing values.[2]

In 1948, the U.S. Supreme Court heard arguments on *Sipes* along with three other covenant cases, including *Shelley* v. *Kraemer,* a similar case from Saint Louis after which the court's decision would be named. A team of lawyers, led by the NAACP's talented Thurgood Marshall, argued against racially restrictive covenants using both sociological evidence about the impact of covenants on black housing opportunities, and constitutional arguments about the illegality of state action that sanctioned racial discrimination. Persuaded by the NAACP's effective combination of constitutional and sociological arguments, the Vinson court unanimously ruled that restrictive covenants, including that at issue in *Sipes,* could not be enforced by the state. Detroit blacks were elated at the decision. "We Can Live Anywhere!" ran a banner headline in the *Courier.* "This far reaching decision means that a mortal blow has been struck at racial restrictions in homes, artificially created ghettoes, ... and countless other jim-crow manifestations made possible because of heretofore enforced segregation in home ownership." The attack on restrictive covenants raised blacks' hopes that their housing woes would soon be over. And it inspired blacks in Detroit to move forth more boldly, looking for housing in the predominantly white neighborhoods beyond the city's racial frontier.[3]

In the era of *Sipes* v. *McGhee*, civil rights activists were optimistic that Detroit would soon be a racially integrated city. The wartime rhetoric of pluralism, tolerance, and antiracism, forged in response to Nazi atrocities, promised a future free of racial conflict. Even though the failure of public housing was a portent of resistance to racial change, the creation of a "second ghetto" in Detroit hardly seemed inevitable to observers of the postwar city. Liberals pointed to statistics showing mixed racial composition in certain neighborhoods as the herald of an era of equality. And civil rights groups clung to the hope that a combination of litigation, legislation, and moral suasion would break down the barriers of race that had kept blacks confined to the inner city. Just five years after the *Shelley* decision, Charles Wartman, editor of the *Michigan Chronicle,* Detroit's most important black weekly, believed that "private housing has become the means of bringing the Negro housing problem nearer solution, with every indication that ultimately it will solve the whole problem of the ghetto."[4]

Motivated by a hopeful vision of an interracial metropolis, civil rights organizations and city officials took an active role in challenging Detroit's racial boundaries. At the same time that African Americans battled to gain access to equal opportunities in the workplace, civil rights organizations directed their energies toward the private housing market. Their beneficiaries were growing numbers of black "pioneers" like the McGhees. Many were members of the city's African American elite.

Beginning in the late 1940s, black Detroit began to expand outward from the prewar concentrations on Detroit's East Side and the outlying enclaves (Map 7.1). Detroit blacks moved beyond the inner city to the east, and especially to the northwest. Between 1940 and 1950, the number of census tracts in Detroit with more than five hundred blacks increased from 56 to 73; between 1950 and 1960, the number increased to 166. The impact of the movement out of the traditional ghetto was mixed. Between 1948 and 1960, black housing conditions in Detroit improved significantly. The number of blacks in substandard buildings (dilapidated buildings or those that lacked running water or indoor toilets) plummeted between 1950 and 1960 from 29.3 percent to only 10.3 percent, and the number of overcrowded residences fell from 25.3 percent to 17.5 percent. The reason for the decline was simple: blacks moved out of the oldest, most run-down sections of the city into newer neighborhoods, including some that contained some of Detroit's finest housing stock, that had been all-white through World War II.[5]

Even though black housing conditions improved, patterns of residential segregation remained intact. Virtually all of Detroit's blacks—regardless of class and education, occupation, age, or place of birth—shared the experience of discrimination in the city's housing market. Only a handful of blacks ever lived for any significant period of time within predominantly white sections of the city, unless they were living-in servants. But to describe the experience of blacks after World War II as a single process of "ghettoization" is to simplify a complex reality. Within the constraints of the limited housing market, Detroit's blacks created distinct sub-communities. The universality of the experience of segregation should not obscure other aspects of the residential life of black Detroiters. An unintended consequence of the opening of Detroit's housing market was a hardening of class divisions within black Detroit. As white movement increased the housing options available to black city dwellers, blacks began the process of sifting and subdividing, replicating within Detroit's center city the divisions of class that characterized the twentieth-century metropolis as a whole.[6]

In the rapidly changing economic climate of postwar Detroit, blacks had two increasingly divergent residential patterns. Those who were able to obtain relatively secure, high-paying jobs were able to purchase their own homes. Increasingly, they put pressure on the racial boundaries that confined them to the center city. But those who were trapped in poor-paying jobs and thrown out of work by deindustrialization remained confined in the decaying inner city neighborhoods that had long housed the bulk of Detroit's black population.

Pushing at the Boundaries: Black Pioneers

As one observer noted in 1946, "it is physically impossible to keep the Negro population imprisoned in its present warren."[7] Families with resources found the housing shortage especially frustrating, because their expectations far exceeded the reality of housing in the city. As sociologists Alfred McClung Lee and Norman D. Humphrey observed: "Take an already crowded situation, add half again as many people, give them a great purchasing power, and still attempt to confine them within ... the old area, and the pressures developed within the increasingly inadequate 'container' will burst the walls."[8] Adequate housing for African Americans remained one of the great unfulfilled promises of postwar Detroit.

First to push at the city's racial boundaries was the rapidly growing black bourgeoisie. Since the early twentieth century, black entrepreneurs in Detroit had carved out an important niche in the city's economy by providing services to a clientele that white businessmen largely ignored. Because of systematic discrimination in public facilities, blacks created a separate system of "race" businesses—black-owned private hospitals, hotels, restaurants, and funeral homes. Hotelier A. G. Wright made his fortune through his ownership of Detroit's Hotel Gotham, known for providing luxurious accommodations to black travelers who were closed out of Detroit's white-owned hotels. Democratic political leader and U.S. Representative Charles Diggs had followed the typical trajectory of Detroit's black

bourgeoisie, starting his career in his family's enormous "House of Diggs" Funeral Home. In addition, many African Americans in the city moved into the black elite through the traditional route of the ministry or education, and a growing number of women joined the ranks of the professions, primarily teaching and social work, after World War II.[9]

As the city's black population grew in the 1940s and 1950s, Detroit's black bourgeoisie kept pace. In 1953, Detroit boasted the largest number of independently owned black businesses of any city in the United States. Most black business leaders continued to find opportunities in traditional "race" businesses, which grew to meet the needs of the city's expanding African American population. As blacks joined the postwar consumer culture with the same fervor, if not the same resources, as whites, a number of black entrepreneurs began to cross over into sectors of the economy that had been white-dominated. Like white Americans, if they could afford it, blacks purchased radios, televisions, cars, and new electric appliances. Some of Detroit's wealthiest African Americans made their fortunes by bringing the fruits of postwar prosperity to well-paid black auto workers and their families. One, Edward Davis, opened the nation's first black-owned car dealership in Detroit on the brink of World War II and profited handsomely from the postwar boom. Another, Sidney Barthwell, followed the trend of franchising and consolidation that reshaped the postwar retail industry. He owned a ten-store chain of pharmacies in black neighborhoods, catering to a rapidly growing base of customers that white-owned firms ignored. Black-owned savings and loan associations and insurance companies filled the niche left by bankers and actuaries who relentlessly redlined African American neighborhoods. Real estate brokers and developers like Pete W. Cassey, Jr., James Del Rio, and Samuel Gibbons profited from the growing demand of Detroit blacks for single-family homes. Detroit was also home to two of the nation's largest black-owned financial institutions: the Great Lakes Mutual Life Insurance Company and the Home Federal Savings and Loan Association. And cultural entrepreneurs also fueled a creative expansion of the consumer market in radio and music, starting the city's first black radio station, and marketing (to an increasingly interracial audience) the Detroit sounds of blues, jazz, and Motown.[10]

Detroit's black elite sought the status and security of residence in districts outside of the traditional inner-city neighborhoods that had confined blacks through World War II. They looked for houses of the size and grandeur appropriate to their economic and social status. Paradise Valley, reported the elite, boosterish *Color* magazine, "can no longer hold the ambitious Negro. He wants to get out of this mecca for card sharks, numbers players, cult leaders, 'prophets,' and shady entertainment." By the late 1940s, Detroit's well-to-do blacks had the desire and the means to flee the overcrowded and decrepit inner city.[11]

Detroit's high-status blacks were not alone in their aspirations to escape the inner city. Also seeking to escape Detroit's "rat belt" were black city employees and automobile and defense workers, especially those who were able to obtain seniority in relatively high-paying factory jobs. Chrysler worker James Boggs recalled that "everybody saved some money during the war. That's how they bought all those houses when the war was over, because people had four years there when they just worked and there wasn't nothing to buy." For the first time, as a city race relations official reported in 1946, black workers had "sufficient funds …. to free themselves from the tragic overcrowding" in inner-city Detroit.[12] Working-class blacks looked in white neighborhoods on the periphery of black enclaves, whose streets, lined with modest frame and brick houses, had fulfilled the aspirations of a generation of blue-collar homeowners. In addition, by the early 1950s, they hoped to benefit from the new housing opportunities in outlying Detroit neighborhoods and suburbs. Thousands of new houses were constructed on vacant land in northeast and northwest Detroit, and in the booming suburbs to the north and west of the city. Once the Detroit housing market became fluid, the pent-up black demand for housing spilled over racial boundaries. As the housing market opened, black "pioneers" with more modest incomes began moving into neighborhoods on the periphery of black Detroit. By the late 1940s, several neighborhoods, most on the city's near Northwest Side, attracted upwardly mobile blacks fleeing the inner city. Many who moved into the older neighborhoods being abandoned by whites did not view their new homes as permanent residences, but instead treated their purchases or rentals as "a temporary route to the 'best' neighborhoods." Movement to older, formerly white areas gave black strivers a boost in status, while allowing them to build up equity or savings to fund the purchase of a better home in the future.[13] They hoped that eventually they would have the opportunity to live anywhere in the city, and that, like whites, they would enjoy unrestricted residential mobility.

The Open Housing Movement

The aspirations of Detroit's black elite and steadily employed working-class blacks coincided with the rapidly growing integrationist movement. Civil rights activists believed that blacks should have equal access to the housing market, but more than that, they should live side by side with whites to create a racially harmonious city. Only daily contact between the races would solve the nation's pressing dilemma of racial prejudice and inequality. Beginning modestly in the late 1940s, and expanding dramatically in the 1950s, a coalition of civil rights groups, religious organizations, and African American leaders directed their energies toward desegregating the city's housing market. They found a powerful ally in the Detroit Mayor's Interracial Committee (MIC), which had been founded after the race riot of 1943 to monitor racial tension in the city and advocate civil rights reform. Dominated by liberal whites and blacks who had close ties with civil rights organizations, the MIC consistently opposed segregation in public housing and other facilities, worked to abolish restrictive covenants, and investigated incidents of racial conflict in the city. The MIC, despite its name, was a largely independent city agency whose members were protected by civil service laws. Under [mayors] Jeffries and Cobo, it became a refuge for a small, dedicated band of integrationists, who maintained close ties with civil rights groups throughout the country. In the late 1940s, the MIC spearheaded a joint campaign with civil rights and religious groups around the city to open the housing market to blacks.[14]

Inspired by the victory in *Shelley* v. *Kraemer,* open housing advocates hoped that with concerted action, they could abolish residential segregation once and for all. At first their attempts were primarily educational. The Coordinating Council on Human Relations (CCHR), founded in 1948, brought together the MIC and dozens of religious and civil rights organizations to persuade whites that they should support racial integration for moral and economically rational reasons. Throughout the 1950s, the CCHR held meetings with white church groups, parent-teacher associations, and community organizations. The primary goal was to convince whites to "act with intelligence and courage" when blacks moved in. Open housing activists attempted to persuade skeptical white homeowners that "racial change was inevitable," and that it was in their self-interest to "work for a sound, stable, liveable community." The CCHR's primary task was to challenge the conventional wisdom that "the movement of Negroes into your community will inevitably cause depreciation of value." If whites acted rationally rather than panicking and fleeing, their property values would remain stable or rise.[15]

To further their goal, civil rights organizations published pamphlets, brochures, and booklets extolling the virtues of integrated housing. They wrote articles and letters for local newspapers on the dangers of racial division and the benefits of racial integration, and published materials attempting to assuage homeowners' fears of property depreciation and crime following black movement into their neighborhoods. They looked to other cities for models of successful racial change. Open housing groups in Philadelphia, Cleveland, and Chicago shared materials with their Detroit counterparts. Detroit open housing advocates also assiduously cultivated contacts with national newspapers and magazines and worked with authors to develop stories on successful racial integration. A typical story, authored by NAACP head Walter White in *Saturday Evening Post* in the summer of 1953 and reprinted by civil rights groups around the country, added an interracial twist to typical 1950s depictions of family life. Included as an example of how "Detroit is now setting an example" of integration were photographs of black and white children playing together, and black and white housewives amiably chatting on their lawns.[16]

Religious leaders also joined together in an ecumenical call for racial harmony, even if many of their rank-and-file clergy members and coreligionists did not support them. In 1957, Edward Cardinal Mooney, the Roman Catholic Archbishop of Detroit, Reverend G. Merrill Lenox of the Detroit Council of Churches, and Rabbi Morris Adler of the Jewish Community Council issued a joint call for integration. To "deny the right of homeownership" to blacks, they argued, "is contrary to our American Constitution and an affront to the righteousness of God." In a typical exchange with a correspondent who denounced racial integration as "the hysterical championing of the primitive black minority," the Reverend Lenox challenged her to avoid the "course that is comfortable and in line with our accustomed thinking," and to act "in agreement with the will of God." But because most Protestant churches were congregationally controlled, many of their members paid little heed to the exhortations of the Detroit Council of Churches, particularly those that challenged conventional racial wisdom. As a result, Presbyterian, Congregationalist, Baptist, and Reformed churches tended to move quickly from racially changing neighborhoods.[17]

The Catholic response was somewhat different. Unlike Protestants, the vast majority of Catholics lived in territorial parishes, whose boundaries were strictly defined and whose churches were permanent fixtures on the cityscape. Local priests and their parishioners had long resisted black encroachment onto parish turf. Yet in the 1950s, a growing number of Catholic bishops and clergy, and a vocal minority of laypeople, began to speak out on civil rights issues. In 1957,

Cardinal Mooney met with the pastors of St. Brigid and St. Cecilia parishes to work out a strategy to dampen white parishioners' resistance to blacks moving into their area. Liberal Catholic clerics like University of Detroit Professor John Coogan, S. J. joined in calls for racial equality. Taking a stand alongside Coogan were members of the small but vocal Catholic Interracial Council, and in the late 1950s, the Archdiocesan Council for Catholic Women. And in 1960, then-conservative Archbishop John Dearden (Mooney's successor) heeded the voices of racial liberalism in the Church and established a Commission on Human Relations. The hierarchy's growing racial tolerance brought it into conflict with parishioners who lived in racially changing neighborhoods and with pastors who often shared racial prejudices and looked with chagrin on white flight from their parishes. Angry Catholics barraged Father Coogan, a longstanding member of the Commission on Community Relations, with hate mail. And parishioners often greeted Catholic interracial activists with suspicion and hostility.[18]

Motivated by the burgeoning national civil rights movement, open housing groups moved beyond moral suasion to political action. In the mid-1950s, DUL officials lobbied the Federal Housing Administration and Home Owners' Loan Corporation to allow blacks to purchase foreclosed houses in white neighborhoods. United Automobile Workers officials also supported behind-the-scenes efforts to open the housing market to blacks (although they worked quietly, so as to avoid rankling the white rank and file who had so vocally repudiated the union on public housing issues in the 1940s). And by the late 1950s, civil rights groups began targeting the racially exclusionary practices of real estate brokers. Civil rights groups allied with liberal Democrats in the state legislature to extend the principles of the FEPC to the real estate market. In 1958 and 1959, Michigan's Senate and House of Representatives debated bills that would have fined real estate brokers who failed to sell or rent to anyone because of race. The bills did not pass, but increasing pressure from civil rights groups kept the issue on the table for the next decade.[19]

The challenge to real estate discrimination in Detroit burst onto the national scene in 1960, in the wake of revelations that realtors in suburban Grosse Pointe used a "point system" that ranked perspective home buyers by race, nationality, occupation, and "degree of swarthiness." Blacks and Asians were excluded from Grosse Pointe altogether, and Poles, Southern Europeans, and Jews needed higher rankings than families of northwestern European descent to be approved to move into the community. Private detectives, paid with money from assessments on property owners and real estate brokers, investigated the backgrounds of potential residents, excluding them for such offensive practices as using outdoor clotheslines or painting their houses in gaudy colors. Even though the "point system" affected a relatively small segment of the metropolitan area's housing market, it brought the issue of discriminatory real estate practices to the center of political debate. In the wake of public hearings on Grosse Pointe, the state corporation and securities commissioner issued a regulation that would prevent the issuance of licenses to real estate brokers who discriminated on the basis of race, religion, or national origin.[20]

More importantly, the Grosse Pointe revelations led to a dramatic expansion of open housing activity in Detroit. In 1962, Catholic, Protestant, and Jewish leaders formed the Open Occupancy Conference (later renamed the Religion and Race Conference) to promote housing integration, particularly in suburban communities. The Conference had as its primary goal "to assist middle-class blacks to move into the larger community." As Leonard Gordon, one of the Conference's organizers, noted, "the inner city areas per se were not a programmatic focus." Like earlier open occupancy efforts, the Conference targeted the "small part of the Negro community that could afford outer-city and suburban housing." To that end, conference organizers embarked on a "challenge to conscience" campaign "to teach whites their moral duty" to support integration. A related open housing group, the Greater Detroit Committee for Fair Housing Practices, also appealed to religious sentiments. Greater Detroit Committee organizers handed out fair housing "Covenant Cards" in white churches, that churchgoers could sign and carry as proof of their commitment to housing integration. Committee members also assisted blacks trying to move to white areas and escorted blacks to real estate offices in Detroit's suburbs. Beginning in 1964 and 1965, open housing advocates began using testers—paired black and white home buyers who met separately with real estate brokers—to document discriminatory sales practices. Their efforts ensured that open housing remained a central issue in discussions of race, politics, and civil rights in Detroit throughout the 1960s.[21]

NOTES

1. Materials on *Sipes v. McGhee* can be found in NAACP, Group II, Boxes B135–137. Quotes from *Benjamin J. Sipes and Anna C. Sipes, James A. Coon, and Addie A. Coon, et al. v. Orsel McGhee and Minnie S. McGhee*, January 7, 1947. On other restrictive covenant cases, see Gloster Current to Shirley Adelson, July 12, 1946, ibid., Box B135, Folder: Sipes v. McGhee, 1946; Memorandum to Mr [Thurgood] Marshall from Marian Wynn Perry, May 1, 1946, ibid., Box B74, Folder: Legal, Detroit, Mich., General 1946, 1947; *Michigan Chronicle*, October 26, 1946; John C. Dancy, *Sand Against the Wind: The Memoirs of John C. Dancy* (Detroit: Wayne State University Press, 1966), 215–16; Marshall Field Stevenson, "Points of Departure, Acts of Resolve: Black-Jewish Relations in Detroit, 1937–1962," (Ph.D. diss., University of Michigan, 1988), 346–49; Clement Vose, *Caucasians Only: The Supreme Court, the NAACP, and Restrictive Covenant Cases* (Berkeley: University of California Press, 1959), 125–27.
2. See especially ibid.; also Charles Abrams, *Forbidden Neighbors: A Study of Prejudice in Housing* (New York: Harper, 1955).
3. *Shelley v. Kraemer*, 334 U.S. 1 (1948); *Pittsburgh Courier* (Detroit edition), May 8, 1948; for similar articles, see *Michigan Chronicle*, May 8, 1948; for an overview of the NAACP's strategy, see Mark V. Tushnet, *Making Civil Rights Law: Thurgood Marshall and the Supreme Court, 1936–*
1961 (New York: Oxford University Press, 1994), 81–98.
4. On wartime racial liberalism, see Philip Gleason, "Americans All: World War II and the Shaping of American Identity," *Review of Politics* 43 (1981): 483–518; and Gary Gerstle, "The Working Class Goes to War," *Mid-America: An Historical Review* 75 (October 1993): 303–22. Civil rights organizations and observers of race relations in the city retained a remarkable confidence in the possibility of integration. See George Schermer, "The Transitional Housing Area" (A Statement Prepared for the Housing Workshop Session of the 1952 NAIRO Conference, Washington, D.C.), November 10, 1952, DUL, Box 38, Folder A2–8; *Michigan Chronicle*, February 28, 1953; this and other interesting articles on black Detroit in the 1950s are reprinted in Charles J. Wartman, *Detroit—Ten Years After* (Detroit: Michigan Chronicle, 1953). As late as 1964, the *Detroit News* ran an article, "Housing Bias Crumbling in Detroit, Expert Finds," which cited city race relations official Richard Marks criticizing the cynicism of those who argued that "integration is the period between the arrival of the first Negro and the departure of the last white" (*Detroit News*, March 22, 1964).
5. Bernard J. Frieden, *The Future of Old Neighborhoods: Rebuilding for a Changing Population* (Cambridge: MIT Press, 1964), 24, 26, Tables 2.4 and 2.5.
6. For a general discussion of the social geography of cities, see Thomas J. Sugrue, "The Structures of Urban Poverty: The Reorganization of Space and Work in Three Periods of American History," in *The "Underclass" Debate: Views from History*, ed. Michael B. Katz (Princeton, N.J.: Princeton University Press, 1993), 85–117.
7. Henry Lee Moon, "Danger in Detroit," *Crisis* 53 (January 1946) 28.
8. Alfred McClung Lee and Norman D. Humphrey, *Race Riot* (New York: Dryden Press, 1943), 93.
9. For a thorough discussion of Detroit's black-owned businesses, see Richard W. Thomas, *Life for Us Is What We Make It: Building Black Community in Detroit* (Bloomington: Indiana University Press, 1992), 201–23. On the growing number of black women professionals (most of whom were schoolteachers), see Appendix B, Table B. 2.
10. *Detroit Free Press*, March 3, 1953, June 20, 1957; "Detroit's Top 100 Negro Leaders: Aces Who Help Build World's Motor City," *Color*, August 1948, 24–25; "Detroit's Top 100 Negro Leaders, Second

Installment," ibid., October 1948, 38–39. Ed Davis, *One Man's Way* (Detroit: Edward Davis Associates, 1979); "Why Detroit is the Money City for Negroes," *Color*, December 1955, 16–21 (thanks to Eric Arnesen for this reference). On the rise of Motown, see Suzanne Smith, "Dancing in the Street: Motown and the Cultural Politics of Detroit" (Ph.D. diss., Yale University, 1996). The proportion of black men who were professionals, managers, proprietors, and officials did not rise until the 1960s, but it grew in absolute numbers as Detroit's black population rose. The number of black women managers, proprietors, and officials remained very small. See Appendix B, Tables B.1 and B.2.

11. "Why Detroit is the Money City," 16.

12. City of Detroit Interracial Committee, "Demonstrations Protesting Negro Occupancy of Houses (Area Bounded by Buchanan Street, Grand River Avenue, Brooklyn Avenue, Michigan Avenue, and Maybury Grand), September 1, 1945 to September 1, 1946," 2, 4, in CCR, Part I, Series 1, Box 3.

13. Mayor's Committee—Community Action for Detroit Youth Report, "A General Introduction to the Target Area," n.d.[c. 1963], DNAACP, Part I, Box 23.

14. For an overview of the MIC's history, see Tyrone Tillery, *The Conscience of a City: A Commemorative History of the Detroit Human Rights Commission and Department, 1943–1983* (Detroit: Detroit Human Rights Department, 1983). Cincinnati (and a number of other cities) had similar organizations. See Robert A. Burnham, "The Mayor's Friendly Relations Committee: Cultural Pluralism and the Struggle for Black Advancement," in *Race and the City: Work, Community, and Protest in Cincinnati, 1820–1970*, ed. Henry Louis Taylor, Jr. (Urbana: University of Illinois Press, 1993), 258–79. The notion that integration was a solution to America's racial "dilemma" was most forcefully articulated by Gunnar Myrdal, *American Dilemma* (New York: Harper, 1944).

15. Schermer, "The Transitional Housing Area," 5–6.

16. Walter White, "How Detroit Fights Race Hatred," *Saturday Evening Post*, July 18, 1953, 26–27; "Buyer Beware," *Time*, April 16, 1956, 24; "Prejudice is Not Sectional," *Christian Century*, April 18, 1956, 477; "A Northern City Sitting on the Lid of Racial Trouble," *U.S. News and World Report*, May 11, 1956, 34–40; "New Carpetbaggers," *The New Republic*, July 30, 1956, 6; "Detroit Collision," *Ebony*, August 1961, 77–80; *New York Times*, April 22, 1962 (reprinted in "The Bagley Community: A Good Place to Live in Near-Northwest Detroit," copy in DUL, Box 53, Folder A17–2). On the open housing movement in Chicago, see James R. Ralph, Jr., *Northern Protest: Martin Luther King, Jr., Chicago, and the Civil Rights Movement* (Cambridge, Mass.: Harvard University Press, 1993).

17. In southwest Detroit, for example, a Methodist Church fled from a racially changing neighborhood, while members of the Catholic parish held fast. See Mayor's Interracial Committee, Minutes, April 17, 1950, CCR, Part III, Box 25, Folder 25–114; "Joint Statement," March 8, 1957, MDCC, Part I, Box 8, Folder: Press Releases—Civil Rights, 1952–64; G. Merill Lenox to Dorothy L. Tyler, April 19, 1956, ibid., Box 9, Folder: Civil Rights Activity Feedback; *Michigan Chronicle*, March 14, 1953; *Detroit Free Press*, June 24, 1957. On Jewish civil rights efforts, see Sidney Bolkosky, *Harmony and Dissonance: Voices of Jewish Identity in Detroit, 1914–1967* (Detroit: Wayne State University Press, 1991), 368–71.

18. "Activities Report, February 1–March 1, 1957, Cherrylawn Case," DUL, Box 38, Folder: A2–23; Detroit Urban League Board of Directors, Annual Meeting Minutes, February 28, 1957, CCR, Part III, Box 11, Folder 11–19; Interview with Mel Ravitz, in *Untold Tales, Unsung Heroes: An Oral History of Detroit's African American Community, 1918–1967*, ed. Elaine Latzmann Moon (Detroit: Wayne State University Press, 1994), 334–35; Gerhard Lenski, *The Religious Factor: A Sociological Study of Religion's Impact on Politics, Economics, and Family Life* (Garden City, N.Y.: Doubleday, 1961), 65, 148, 190. Lenski's study was primarily based on Detroit research. See also John T. McGreevy, "American Catholics and the African-American Migration" (Ph.D. diss., Stanford University, 1992), 61, 159–62; Leslie Woodcock Tentler, *Seasons of Grace: A History of the Catholic Archdiocese of Detroit* (Detroit: Wayne State University Press, 1990), 308–9. [...]

19. William H. Boone, "Major Unmet Goals that Suggest Continuing Attention," March 9, 1956, DUL, Box 38, Folder A2–16; Draft of Letter from UAW Legal Department to Thomas Kavanagh, Michigan Attorney General, July 18, 1956, ibid., Folder A2–17, "Election Warning" [1958], CCR, Part III, Box 13, Folder 13–28; *DREB News*, April 24, 1959, copy ibid., Box 14, Folder 14–5; "Your Co-operation Asked" [1959], flyer attached to letter from Robert Hutton to Merrill Lenox, March 31, 1959; Merrill Lenox to Robert Hutton, April 8, 1959,

MDCC, Part I, Box 10, Folder: Housing-Detroit Real Estate Board; Detroit Branch NAACP, Board of Directors Meeting, September 14, 1959, NAACP, Group III, Box C65, Folder: Detroit, Michigan, Sept.–Dec. 1959.

20. *Detroit Free Press*, April 21, 1960, June 22, 1960; *New York Times*, June 5, 1960; *Detroit News*, August 5, 1960, October 19, 1960, November 28, 1960; "Memorandum in Opposition to Proposal 1007," December 6, 1961, in DNAACP, Part I, Box 14; Kathy Cosseboom, *Grosse Pointe, Michigan: Race Against Race* (East Lansing: Michigan State University Press, 1972).

21. Detroit Urban League, Department of Housing, Second Quarterly Report, April–June 1964, in DUL, Box 53, Folder A27–2; Eloise Whitten, "Open Occupancy: A Challenge," ibid., Folder A17–7; *Detroit News*, January 3, 1963, July 28, 1963, September 19, 1963; Citizens for a United Detroit, "Why We Oppose the Proposed Home Onwer's Ordinance," MDCC, Part I, Box 10, Folder: Housing—Home Owners' Ordinance, Citizens for a United Detroit; Leonard Gordon, "Attempts to Bridge the Racial Gap: The Religious Establishment," in *City in Racial Crisis: The Case of Detroit Pre- and Post- the 1967 Riot* (n.p.: William C. Brown Publishers, 1971), 18–24, quotes 23–24; see also Mayor Jerome Cavanagh, Richard Marks, and Charles Butler, "Messages to the Open Occupancy Conference," ibid., 29–33; materials on "Operation Open Door," March 1965, RK, Box 5, Folder 5–24. For resistance to open housing efforts in the wealthy suburb of Birmingham, see *Brightmoor Journal*, March 17, 1966.

ESSAY 9.2

Bargaining and Hoping

N.D.B. Connolly

Source: N.D.B. Connolly, *A World More Concrete: Real Estate and The Remaking of Jim Crow South Florida* (Chicago: University of Chicago, 2014), 166–198.

EDITORS' INTRODUCTION

At its core, urban history is about people living within urban spaces over time. Some particular urban histories take on explanatory power that extends beyond the specificity of location and period. N.B.D. Connolly examines the rise of Miami, Florida and posits that examining land use within this south Florida city allows us to better comprehend the Jim Crow system and the myriad and tangled links between land ownership and democracy within the United States. Miami's history in this regard is not exceptional. Rather, Connolly admits, he is offering a "regrettably commonplace and *un*exceptional story about how people sought and used power over the land to make and unmake wealth, neighborhoods, and individual and collective identities."[i] Connolly's story occurred in Miami, but the tale contains recognizable characters and plots. Access to land ownership, housing prices, and the fairness of landlords—all these matters raise essential questions of democracy.

Until 1947 and the Supreme Court Case, *Shelley v. Kraemer*, restrictive covenants could legally be enacted to segregate neighborhoods by race, religion, or other attributes. Post-Shelley, the Fair Housing Act of 1965 would seem to solidify the concept that exclusion is not an American ideal. Despite laws that tout togetherness, great physical gulfs still exist in urban America. Most Americans simply do not live in racially, culturally, or economically diverse neighborhoods. Some of this can be attributed to historically developed patterns. Past discrimination continues to shape our real estate options. And new, legal restrictions remain, such as communities that mandate a minimum lot size of two acres per home and communities that do not allow public housing or affordable units to be constructed within their borders.

Have we expected the market to enable fairness? Connolly writes, "Home prices, as in the 1930s, are still set on the basis of class exclusion and largely in relation to the location of black ghettoes. Yet somehow, in the absence of strong fair housing enforcement, Americans expect the real estate market to help the United States finally realize racial integration." Connolly's examination of Miami leads readers to conclude that the real estate market is not likely to regulate itself.

N.B.D. Connolly is the Herbert Baxter Adams Associate Professor of History at Johns Hopkins University. *A World More Concrete* received the 2014 Kenneth T. Jackson Book Award from the Urban History Association, the 2015 Liberty Legacy Foundation Book Award from the Organization of American Historians, and the 2016 Bennett H. Wall Book Award from the Southern Historical Association.

---

i N.B.D. Connolly, *A World More Concrete: Real Estate and the Remaking of Jim Crow South Florida* (Chicago: University of Chicago Press, 2014), 278.

BARGAINING AND HOPING (2014)

This essay examines the integral role colored communities and black property culture played in the development of American liberalism in the immediate postwar period by exploring the overlapping political visions of white and black landlords. In particular, it explores how Jim Crow's rental owners and property managers made use of the hard power of the state and the soft power that came from building community in the colored neighborhoods of the late 1940s and the early 1950s. White rental entrepreneurs drew great social and political power from their investment in black communities. But such power was only possible because of the racial structure of rental capitalism and the role played by landlords and property managers. In particular, real estate entrepreneurs who had their livelihoods rooted in Jim Crow's ghetto served as powerful intermediaries between apartheid's white and colored worlds. Through savvy practices of racial uplift and paternalism, Luther Brooks, Ira Davis, and countless other capitalists effectively tied black people into the Jim Crow state. How well real estate interests managed the slums determined, in effect, the degree to which urban land reform and Negroes' visions of racial uplift would remain beholden to the authority of property owners.

Theodore Gibson, Elizabeth Virrick, and the Coconut Grove Committee for Slum Clearance were largely stymied in their first efforts at housing reform, thanks, in no small part, to Luther Brooks and other well-connected real estate interests in South Florida. Yet, the slum committee's activism, like that of concurrent movements elsewhere in the United States, helped change some important features of rental capitalism in Greater Miami's Negro neighborhoods. Chiefly, the actual building material that made up Jim Crow's ghetto underwent a slow, but important transformation under the pressures of interracial housing reform. Miami's nascent urban reform movement, combined with new and threatening provisions of the Housing Act of 1949, prompted landlords to utilize the federal loan programs of the Federal Housing Administration. Their goal was to replace sloppily maintained wood construction with concrete housing, and, in the process, to keep both black militancy and federal "intrusion" at bay. In one of the most dramatic and overlooked transformations of American housing, the move from wood tenements to concrete apartments would serve as an integral feature of landlords' take on postwar liberalism. And by apparently proving that Miami did not need public housing, the move to make Miami's housing more concrete would provide a potent expression of the kinds of "free market" alternatives that effectively allowed real estate interests to set the liberal state against itself.

Valuing Colored Town

As the slum clearance debates of the late 1940s raged on, Luther Brooks was becoming a rich man. His company, Bonded Collection Agency, had grown into the undisputed juggernaut in the business of managing colored living accommodations. The key to Brooks's business model, particularly as South Florida's colored population continued to grow, lay in his insistence on building and managing, but never actually owning, Negro-inhabited dwellings. Brooks offered what one might call "full-service" management packages, or a kind of Negro rental franchise, perfect for white absentee landlords from Miami Beach or elsewhere seeking minimal entanglements and maximum profits. Brooks, indeed, made slum housing a "clean" investment for white landlords, as Miami's black ghetto fueled prosperity in faraway corners of the country. Vacationing whites from Illinois or New Jersey could pick up several units with the ease one would now experience acquiring a time-share. Once tourists returned home, deeds in hand, weekly checks would simply arrive in their mailboxes. Based on Brooks's own statements in the press, 60 percent of his white clients had never even seen the rental property they owned[1] Bonded Collection paid the mortgage, taxes, and insurance on a landlord's investment property. It also made repairs, handled tenant complaints, and collected the rent. In return, the property owner, who in more than a few instances bought a house or apartment building built by Bonded, agreed to give Brooks's company between 8 and 9 percent of the total rent collected from tenants each month. This was a favorable rate, to be sure; properties managed under Bonded generally secured the highest available profit margins in the Negro housing game.[2]

It is hard to overstate the profitability of slum housing in the Jim Crow era. In our present-day economy, rental properties considered profitable yield between 4 and 6 percent net annual return. Slumlords in Baltimore, Maryland, according to the geographer David Harvey, enjoyed remarkable returns hovering between 10 and 15 percent annually during the recession years of the 1970s.[3] By comparison, the owners of Negro rentals in Greater Miami, according to Bonded's own bookkeeper, enjoyed an astounding *27 percent* return on their investment every year.[4]

Making money on the front end through construction and on the back end from property management, Brooks gained handsome profits. Of the nine collection agencies managing rental properties in the Central Negro District, Bonded was by far the most successful. By the mid-1950s, Brooks had made enough money to buy several thirty- to forty-foot Chris-Craft deep-sea fishing boats and homes in the Florida Keys, the exclusive suburbs of Miami Springs and Bay Point, and the sleepy town of Sopchoppy in the Florida Panhandle.[5] The 1950s would also see Bonded Collection Agency boast ten satellite offices, and over fourteen thousand units under its management. In 1959 dollars, the company secured more than $640,000 in annual revenue.[6] At the company's height, Bonded managed the tenants for six of the city's fifteen largest property owners. And, at midcentury, nearly half of all the black people who rented apartments in Dade County lived in a unit managed by Bonded Collection Agency. The company was, by Brooks's own account at least, "the largest private housing rental and management agency in the South."[7]

When asked in 1975, after nearly forty years in property management, how he would fix what was, at that time, Miami's still deplorable slum problem, Luther Brooks remarked, somewhat glibly, "Somebody as smart as me has to give it a lot of study."[8] As smart as Brooks clearly was, his success depended chiefly on layer upon layer of racial apartheid. White vigilantism held the color line in some corners of South Florida; discrimination from white lenders held it in others. In Miami proper, as occurred in cities as varied as Birmingham, Alabama, and Detroit, Michigan, planning officials and city commissioners used a variety of zoning techniques to maintain the city's myriad color lines.[9] One especially effective tactic was to use "industrial" zoning designations to keep white and black families separate. Whites lived on "residential" land, Negroes mostly on "industrial." Where city officials *had* allowed for "residential" designations in black communities, developers routinely secured variances, or exemptions to zoning law, which allowed more cagey entrepreneurs, such as John Bouvier and Malcolm Wiseheart, to build duplexes on plots zoned for single-family housing, or to open liquor stores or bars mere steps from family homes and churches.[10] Combined with the Home Owners Loan Corporation's system of neighborhood grading, the patchwork zoning designations of colored neighborhoods made most black property patently ineligible for federally insured mortgages. Moreover, Jim Crow's web of residential color lines made Miami's Central Negro District an especially fertile hotbed of substandard housing and white profiteering, both of which buoyed Bonded's bottom line.

In 1947, wooden shotgun shacks still made up nearly 80 percent of all the homes in Colored Town. Other kinds of wood construction continued to house black folk throughout Dade, Broward, and Monroe Counties. Colored Town's "Good Bread Alley" was a notoriously packed section of the neighborhood, with 178 different one-story apartments, a theater house, a church, and several stores all on a single block. When testifying before the US Congress about the need for real estate reform, Edward Graham, the popular pastor of Mt. Zion Baptist Church, specifically highlighted Good Bread Alley's density as evidence of the cramped and dire housing situation in Colored Town.[11]

Lots in black communities tended to be small, allowing as many investors as possible to get a piece of colored housing. Individual landlords also crammed as many buildings as they could fit onto a single lot in order to maximize their return on investment. Lots south of NW Fourteenth Street, which included Good Bread Alley, remained built up almost exclusively with rental units. In keeping with the notion that greater density equaled greater profits, these tightly packed blocks were valued higher than the lots north of NW Fourteenth Street. Those particular lots, with their mix of large single-family homes, rental units, and commercial property, further evidenced the city's ad hoc approach to zoning in black neighborhoods.

One paradox of colored housing in the postwar United States was that, while often in bad physical shape, black homes were usually on what city planners and commercial real estate developers were increasingly imagining to be some of the most valuable land in American cities. The country's old colored towns—vividly rendered in dance, as was Detroit's "Black Bottom," or at times entirely fictionalized, as in Ann Petry's *The Narrows*—served, for years, as very real "servants quarters" for Negroes servicing white privilege prior to and immediately following World War II. In the expanding cities of the 1940s and 1950s, neighborhoods bursting with black workers seemed less like an asset than a hindrance. They ran up against blossoming down-town business districts featuring "whites only" hotels, department stores, and universities.[12] As a second paradox, unique to the urban South, the residents of Dixie's colored enclaves were, by the sweat of their brows, supposed to man the material emergence of the modern New South city. They also represented, through their very bodies, the kinds of colored servility most whites deemed a southern tradition or, in Greater Miami's case, an added perk of Caribbean vacationing. A central tension of the postwar period, thus, was that colored neighborhoods were both racially necessary and, increasingly for many, economically expendable.

Planners viewed Colored Town as having some of the most valuable land in Florida.

The Central Negro District lay less than one mile west of the hotels of center city. It was also three and a half miles from the hotels of Miami Beach, six miles east of the Hialeah racetrack, and six miles northwest of the exclusive white city of Coral Gables. Few areas enjoyed such spatial proximity to South Florida's most lucrative locations. "Miami's life pulsates from this heart," Miami's City Planning Board explained, using an anatomical metaphor typical of the day. Hoping to encourage the total slum clearance of Good Bread Alley in 1941, planners remarked, "A healthy heart with adequate arteries is greatly needed to provide for Miami's unhampered sturdy growth."[13] City officials hoped to replace Good Bread Alley with a new train terminal in 1941, but the outbreak of war and several lawsuits from black and white landlords thwarted the effort.

In Coconut Grove, close proximity between black tenants and white homeowners helped give birth to the Coconut Grove Committee for Slum Clearance. Yet that same proximity between colored property owners and the assets of white landlords made slum clearance and other government redevelopment programs a bitter pill. In part the result of Brooks's business acumen, white landlords owned over 70 percent of the housing in Colored Town during the 1940s and 1950s. By comparison, Caribbean and American blacks owned some seventeen hundred rental units, or roughly 20 percent, of the apartments in Colored Town. The remaining portion of the neighborhood's residents consisted of black homeowners. Landlords' defense of their own property interests over several decades protected the black homeowners crammed among the tenements, and white businessmen like Luther Brooks made sure to let them know it.[14]

Of Power and Paternalism

One of the most important characters in the story of the Negro in Miami is a white man.
—*Miami News*, 2 March 1962

In a real estate industry increasingly defined by mathematical models of property assessment and expert city planning in downtown offices, Luther Brooks understood the power of street-level politics and the cultural value of collective "colored" ownership. From Bonded's main office, he operated a radio show on Negro affairs. Called *The People Speak*, the interracial program addressed problems such as black voter registration, domestic cleanliness, and race relations. Other radio programs put black rental owners in touch with those lenders who would grant Negroes loans for building or renovations. Much of the show's content actually flowed from the activities of the Greater Miami Colored Research and Improvement Association. This was an advocacy group that Brooks, as president, founded in 1950 and staffed with black and white notables, including Lawson Thomas, Ira Davis, and politicians sympathetic to Brooks's political positions. Through this association, Brooks compiled important allies and favorable public relations in black Miami; the group gave, in essence, an organizational name to the philanthropic and political efforts of the city's black and white landlords. The association, for instance, made a one thousand dollar donation to a local colored nursery and made regular contributions to colored social clubs and church auxiliaries. Brooks, as the group's public face, even sent promising Negro students from Booker T. Washington High School to college and, eventually, medical and professional school. From the late 1940s through the late 1960s, Brooks could be seen helping out with something as small-scale as sponsoring a local colored boys' softball team or making more substantial commitments, such as his long-term role as benefactor and board member of William Sawyer's Christian Hospital, the only hospital serving Negroes in all of South Florida.[15] "Leading citizens of the Negro," wrote one black editorialist in the *Miami Herald*, "hold a very high regard for Brooks, as well as the many fine community contributions and services that he has rendered."[16] Of his apparent generosity in Miami's black neighborhoods, Brooks explained, "I get my money from Negroes. I owe it to them to help them."[17]

In economic terms, Brooks also kept money, goods, and services churning through Colored Town. He made a point, for instance, of hiring only Negro maintenance men, and, in 1951, he had a total of forty such men in his employ. Bonded sent these men to repair jobs about town in a fleet of thirty-four brand-new cars, each tied to Brooks's main Third Avenue office by radio dispatch. And he always made sure to buy a brand-new fleet of cars and trucks every year from local colored salesmen. Through the wages he paid his workers, Brooks injected more than thirty-eight hundred dollars a week into the local economy. As with his apparent philanthropy, Brooks made sure to publicize all these efforts through various annual reports on the state of Negro housing. And these publications, like his other company advertisements, all ran through the press of the Reeves family's *Miami Times*, providing further evidence of his support for black business.[18] Brooks's associates, who included US congressman George Smathers, helped bring black college football to Miami in 1947. Yet again, even small things, like gifting Christmas dinners to black tenants, came as the result of Brooks's careful management of the relationship between white capitalists and black tenants.[19]

Much of the point of this largess was to turn popularity into political power. Brooks understood the power of the black vote, both in its presence and, as in the rural Black Belt communities of his youth, in its absence. A string of voting reforms, including Florida's banning of the all-white primary in 1933 and the abolition of the poll tax in 1938, had emboldened Florida's urban Negroes to pursue voting power earlier than blacks had in other corners of the South. In 1939, Sam Solomon, a thirty-four-year-old Negro mortician from Albany, Georgia, seized the chance to put his name on the ballot for city commissioner. His defiance of Jim Crow custom inspired nearly two thousand blacks to register to vote for the first time.[20] Solomon and other black Miamians suffered the expected death threats in the lead-up to the election. Members of the Ku Klux Klan marched through the heart of Colored Town at midnight, hanging a black voter in effigy and planting burning crosses on street corners. But when white-hooded protesters reached the corner of Third Avenue and Twelfth Street, a mob of irate black residents snatched the burning cross from the Klansmen and trampled it underfoot, shouting defiant threats. Though Solomon lost the election, Langston Hughes immortalized the moment in his poem "The Ballad of Sam Solomon."[21] In short order, Luther Brooks hired the now-famous Solomon as Bonded Collection Agency's public relations director.[22]

Between 1939 and 1957, Brooks fought to keep eminent domain weak or to oppose the restructuring of local government to expand the regulatory powers of municipal or county government. And in each effort, Negroes voted heavily with landlords, sometimes by margins of two to one. In a 1953 push to strengthen Miami's powers of land expropriation, for instance, Miami's black voters opposed the measure 67 percent to 33 percent, even though the primary argument in favor of stronger land expropriation pointed to improved slum clearance.[23] Similar voting habits marked elections in the early 1940s and again in the late 1950s.[24] With carefully chosen words, Brooks warned black voters in 1951 to pay attention to "how elections are controlled in slave countries. ... It can happen here." "Always vote against public housing," he admonished, because "tenants who rent, and all homeowners pay a part of the rent of each dweller in public housing."[25] It's difficult to know the degree to which such arguments resonated with black Miamians, and black renters in particular, on a person-by-person basis. In a 2006 interview, however, one black Miamian plainly expressed the trend of black people voting against expanded land powers for the local state: "We just didn't trust what those white folks were doing."[26] Clearly, some white folk were more trusted than others. In his political fortunes, Luther Brooks was not just the beneficiary of segregationist policies and practices. He was the beneficiary of America's racial history.

Welfare for Landlords

Since the 1930s, mortgage insurance, as part of the New Deal state, served as Jim Crow's social insurance. And in that vein, the Federal Housing Administration was likely the most effective vehicle for racial segregation in American history. Still, housing officials within and affiliated with the administration did not enforce discriminatory housing policy uniformly across the country because actual social needs for preserving apartheid's racial peace played out differently on the ground from one context to the next. In the early 1940s, the race relations director for the Chicago FHA assisted black people in their efforts to undo restrictive covenants.[27] Similarly, the FHA made adjustments to and improved equal protections in various programs in response to constant pressure from civil rights organizations, white developers, and highly educated black bureaucrats within the federal government. In Los Angeles, California, the need to keep minorities confined forced the local FHA to expand the availability of mortgage insurance to Japanese and Chinese Americans.[28] The FHA, in brief, was hardly a monolith. It had a lot of moving institutional parts and myriad programs. Furthermore, its agenda changed as the legal and political environment changed, locally and in Washington. That the FHA's segregationist impulses lasted as long as they did—from the 1930s into the 1970s—does not evidence the existence of a single agency of single mind. It speaks, rather, to the suppleness of apartheid and to the pervasiveness of Jim Crow rationale across several different populations, debates, and historical contexts.

In Miami, one critical feature of the FHA, and indeed one that has gone widely overlooked as a national practice, was the way landlords and rental developers used FHA mortgage insurance to maintain both the profitability of Jim Crow and the integrity of black real estate in the face of purportedly racist applications of eminent domain. As part of a nationwide effort to keep out public housing and slum clearance after the passage of the Housing Act of 1949, landlords changed the face, though not the complexion, of Jim Crow's ghetto.[29]

Almost immediately following the passage of the 1934 Housing Act, real estate developers around the country began seeking federal mortgage insurance for building tenements. Initially, FHA officials in Washington and regional offices mostly rejected such requests, and, for the agency's first three years, it insured mortgages on a total of only twenty-one rental properties nationwide. In the eyes of the FHA's early administrators, rentals carried too many risks, including high maintenance costs, delinquent tenants, and the possible burden of rent control from state to state. Rentals, it seemed, promised very little in the way of short- and medium-term profits. Most landlords, moreover, were unwilling to meet the FHA's building requirements lest they cut into their rate of return. Shotgun shacks made plenty of money on their own without the burden of the FHA's building requirements.

During the 1930s, as part of America's first attempt at federal housing and slum clearance, Miami's developers joined a swelling chorus of rental capitalists around the country. They argued that rental housing in general and black housing in particular could fetch high returns, thereby serving as a safe investment of FHA-backed loans. In 1936, Miami's George Merrick, the founder of the University of Miami and its restricted surrounding community, Coral Gables, boasted, "Personally I have handled several Negro towns and know there is money in it!" Merrick, like Carl Fisher and many fellow speculators, had been all but wiped out by the 1926 hurricane and the ensuing market downturn. But investing in Negro rental property helped him get back on his feet. The money Merrick made from black housing kept his experiment at Coral Gables alive. It was thus with great conviction that he explained how no monopoly provided higher profits than control of Negro housing in "just one State of the Southeast." Merrick promised real estate boards "Woolworth-Ford-type volume[s of] money." All the government needed to do was provide "unit loan facility on [a] sound long time basis." With a little loan insurance from the Federal Housing Administration, Merrick argued, any entrepreneur or real estate board would come to appreciate the "millions that are available in this [Negro housing industry]."[30]

Several factors finally brought the FHA squarely into the rental business. The first was the threat of competition from another government agency. The United States Housing Authority (USHA), which Senate Democrats had included in the Housing Act of 1937, emerged with the power to develop local housing authorities across the country and, through them, more public housing projects. By offering government housing options and increasing the oversight of landlords more generally, the USHA threatened to drive down rents and, landlords claimed, slow down the country's economic recovery.[31] This prompted the second factor: coordinated attacks on public housing from landlord lobbying groups. Members of the National Association of Real Estate Boards and its local affiliates peppered Washington with complaints that, among other things, public housing cost too much, did not actually help the poor, smacked of socialism, and did not clear slums.[32] Pressure from them, combined with America's entry into the Korean War, prompted President Harry Truman and members of Congress to scale back greatly the country's public housing program.[33] Developers in localities around the country, as a third factor, began working with black civic elites to push the massive rezoning of black communities, so that America's old colored towns could finally be eligible for some form of FHA loans.

As it concerned South Florida, the effort to rezone black communities brought together black and white housing reformers, but it also galvanized yet another instance of opposition from both colored property owners, tenants, and their landlords. Bearing news from members of the Miami Chamber of Commerce and the city planning office, several black neighborhood leaders, including Lawson Thomas and Ira Davis, held a town hall meeting in Colored Town to explain the city's plan to rezone nearly 150 acres of the neighborhood for the purposes of new single-family homes and concrete apartment buildings.[34] The plan was to facilitate the demolition of the worst housing in Colored Town and to open more of the neighborhood to "better-class homes" for the Negro professional class.[35] Part of the plan included the displacement of over 190 colored families from Colored Town's Good Bread Alley.[36] At the meeting, black tenants vocally opposed forcible eviction. Several black landlords promised to sue. Ultimately the matter was left to Good Bread's primarily white owners, and most of them had no interest in upgrading their wood housing in pursuit of government-backed loans. What the 1949 rezoning *did* do was open up the prospect for new concrete development in areas surrounding Good Bread Alley.

Coming of the "Concrete Monsters"

At the start of the postwar period, Greater Miami received relatively little federal mortgage insurance for Negro rentals. In 1946, the city had only sixty-two units of black rental housing backed by the Federal Housing Administration. By comparison, FHA-backed apartments numbered in excess of twelve hundred in Jacksonville, two thousand in Chicago, and four thousand in Washington, DC. In response to black people's postwar housing needs, a paltry six hundred new apartments went up in Miami's Central Negro District in 1947, mostly of the cheaper, shotgun variety.[37] As the *Pittsburgh Courier's* Miami correspondent, John Diaz, reported, "Negroes in Miami ... are worse off now than they were ten years ago."[38] Then, just a year later, in 1948, Miami's FHA commitment to black rentals increased tenfold. That number then tripled again the following year to reach a total of over nineteen hundred apartments. This was, by far, the most rapid expansion of FHA rental underwriting anywhere in the United States, and it sparked a proliferation of privately owned black rental housing in Miami matched by only the largest American cities.[39]

Noting the sudden increase, the FHA's southeast US zone commissioner, Herbert Redman, encouraged mortgage-insured lenders to give further priority to those rental developers targeting the Negroes of Miami's Colored Town. The aim was to outpace local public housing authorities. Continued FHA help would allow, in Redman's words, "substantial housing [to be] provided profitably by private capital for a number of tenants in the area."[40] That same year, 1949, Miami's landlords received nearly ten million dollars in federal mortgage insurance to complete construction of almost two thousand new black-occupied tenements. This doubled, yet again, the number of FHA-backed apartment units for Negroes.[41] During all this, by every measure of property appraisal, Colored Town never stopped being a "D" neighborhood.

Miami's transformation was but the tip of the spear in a remarkable movement that landlords and real estate developers around the country advanced in response to the lifting of rent control and in opposition to local public housing and slum clearance campaigns. In 1950, an astounding 99 percent of the 159,000 new rental units purchased in the United States received mortgage insurance from the Federal Housing Administration. The following year, that proportion fell to a still substantial 89 percent.[42] Between 1935 and 1953, fully half of all multifamily dwellings built in the United States were backed by federal mortgage insurance, and 54 percent of those units were built between 1949 and 1951, immediately following the Housing Act of 1949.[43] Electing to conform, finally, to FHA building guidelines, developers in Miami built concrete housing in Colored Town and dramatically expanded the reach of black-occupied rental property across South Florida.

What most developers built would later be called "Concrete Monsters." By the standards of rental units in much of the urban North, "Concrete Monsters" were small, two- to three-level apartment buildings [...]. Miami's new concrete tenements were often short on green space, offered no off-street parking, and, because of high rents, were still quite crowded. The ceilings were low, shade trees were rare, and interiors were cheaply outfitted.[44] Perhaps most important to both housing reformers and landlords, rent collection practices in these apartment buildings went entirely unregulated.

Many of the same abuses that defined tenant life in shotgun shacks continued under concrete roofs. Repair crews could be unresponsive, and as early as 5:30 in the morning the rent man could come rapping on your door. Most of Bonded Collection's maintenance men were black, but all of the company's rent collectors, at this time, were white men. Their occasional brashness and their not uncommon use of racial epithets, particularly in the wee hours, could feel like a particularly cruel form of mistreatment. Still, at a basic architectural level, Miami's new "Concrete Monsters" seemed to mark the (delayed) closing of the frontier age in Miami's colored communities. The buildings were certainly more resistant to fire and storm damage than wood-frame housing.

Symbolically, they also marked an invitation for black Miami to join the wider, more modern tropics. [...] "Any person who has been away from this tropical playground 10 or more years would never recognize it today—for a miracle has been wrought in Miami[:] ... absolutely new, streamlined housing with an architectural design which has turned a once-blighted slum area into a tropical delight to the eye."[45] "Let us be proud of our modern buildings," wrote one columnist for the *Miami Times* in 1955. The paper pointed out the better behavior of tenants from "other parts of the city" (i.e., white Miami), and the *Times* asked renters to "PLEASE ASSIST ... [those] who are interested in the welfare of the tenants" by tending to trash, minding where one hung one's laundry, and keeping "the children [from] running on everyone else's front porches." Noting all the new concrete construction, Miami's largest black newspaper encouraged renters to trust their property manager and reminded its readers, "The landlord has a heart, too."[46] Attempting to prove the point, Brooks made sure to paint ribbons of two-tone colors, pastels, and heavy tropical hues around the buildings he managed—the colors of Art Deco Miami Beach brought to Colored Town.[47] Photographs of Brooks's projects accompanied articles in both the *Courier* and the *Miami Times*.

For those who lived outside the Central Negro District, the arrival of concrete tenements seemed to wall in colored people's suburban dreams. Black Liberty City residents noted the "rapid construction" of three-level buildings in the neighborhood. Trees were cleared; open fields were fenced off, dug out, and built up. Miami's white residents noticed the expansion as well. The Dade County Commission and Miami City Commission remained too tied up in procedural wrangling to monitor the size and layout of the new projects. Developers, instead, showed their talent for segregationist self-regulation. They tended to build only on clearly demarcated "colored" or "white" sites, or to erect the requisite concrete walls around projects built in racial "border" zones.

In 1940, some 60 percent of Dade's black housing was in Colored Town. By 1950, that percentage dropped to 40 percent. However, because concrete apartments could literally stack black folk on top of one another, the overall number of black-occupied dwellings in Miami's downtown neighborhood actually doubled. Black Miami was growing just that fast. Opalocka and Brownsville, areas that had barely any black inhabitants during the 1930s, saw, by 1950, the arrival over some thirty-five hundred units of black housing, much of it in new concrete rental properties. One "Concrete Monster" at a time, real estate speculators scattered Greater Miami's colored population to areas far outside the old Central Negro District.[48]

Landlords and Liberalism

The FHA's massive underwriting of black rental housing, though a national phenomenon, served as Jim Crow's social insurance against black unrest in southern cities such as Miami. [...] The FHA's new engagement with black rental housing served as a critical piece of the equalization movement sweeping across the South. For tenants, it took black housing and made it look more like what whites had long enjoyed. For Ira Davis and other black leaders, broadening the availability of FHA loans for Negro rental housing represented a step toward expanding colored people's access to FHA funds more broadly, also a benefit largely reserved for whites.

Striking the Right Tone

"Free market" arguments helped landlords profit openly from racial segregation while concealing the government's role in breathing new life into Jim Crow's ghetto.[49] The Miami Chamber of Commerce, in 1950, developed a special subcommittee, calling it the Committee against Socialized Housing, or CASH. Alongside other groups, such as the Property Owners Development Association and the Free Enterprise Association, CASH was one of several landlord lobbying groups in Florida to recruit state politicians, engineers, and attorneys in an effort to keep government mortgage insurance coming in and government land expropriation and public housing out. As evidence of their success, the state of Florida received over seventy-six million dollars in monies earmarked for welfare between January of 1949 and June of 1951. Not a dime of it went toward filling the nonmilitary public housing vacuum. In fact, thanks to white homeowner intransigence about the location of public housing sites, and landlord lobbying at both the state and municipal levels, no government housing would be built at all in Dade County between 1940 and 1954.[50] This was roughly the same period during which landlords received ten million dollars in mortgage commitments from the FHA.

The Cold War arguments that developed in the battle between the Coconut Grove Committee for Slum Clearance and Greater Miami's developer community continued to govern the political debate over the state's role in the housing market. Rental lobbyists, still crying "socialism," argued that, rather than subject businesspeople to undue government competition or regulation, landlords should have the freedom to self-regulate. In 1950, Miami's mayor, William Wolfarth, granted rental owners the necessary latitude by passing weak, almost token, slum clearance oversight, with no federal funding.[51] The measure did little to quell activists in Coconut Grove and other observers, who continued to advocate for federal slum clearance and public housing. One columnist at the *Miami Herald*, a paper sympathetic to slum clearance advocates, noted that "the socialism epithet was not raised when Federal money went into our International Airport." Neither was it raised when "Federal money financed the Orange Bowl, [or when] Federal guaranteed mortgages touched off the building boom here."[52] At issue, it seemed, was the *kind* of liberalism South Floridians should accept.

So it was on the race question as well. In spite of the federal government's impressive record on maintaining racial segregation, the US Supreme Court, in 1948, ruled that racially restrictive covenants were unconstitutional (*Shelley v. Kraemer*). This, combined with the apparent liberalization of the FHA's position on single-family homes in 1950, seemed to uncork the triple threat of integration, miscegenation, and white downward mobility. "Obviously," wrote CASH representatives, "recent supreme court rulings [mean] … the federal government cannot permit race segregation in its own public housing projects. … We wonder what effect these things are going to have on property values." But it was other and more traditional racist "values" that CASH would employ in its race-mongering publicity campaign. Citing a 1948 congressional investigation of public housing in San Diego and Los Angeles, CASH exposed the discovery of a "Negro Communist leader living in the project with a White woman employee of the [housing] project." "Are the Communists for Public Housing?" asked the members of Miami's most powerful real estate lobby. "You Bet They Are!"[53]

By the same turn, black landlords were critical to the arguments, advanced by Luther Brooks and others, that private enterprise was the best remedy for apartheid's hardships. William Sawyer was sixty-three years old when, in 1949, he bought the three-acre stretch of Brownsville land that would serve as the site for his Alberta Heights project. The six-building concrete development, which he named after his wife of forty years, was among the first financed by an FHA-backed mortgage. The same was true of John Culmer's Francina Apartments, which had twenty units and was located in the Central Negro District.[54] Culmer, who had been quite effective at using the government's slum clearance power to rein in the abuses of black landlords in the 1930s, was also very critical of the administration's discriminatory practices toward colored people. He often cited FHA racism as evidence of black people's need to look for help beyond the state.[55] Yet he, like white developers, clearly did not oppose state programs in the abstract. Continuing black traditions of *spatial* uplift, both Culmer and Sawyer used the FHA's favorable loan terms to outfit their apartments with modern accents and amenities, including aluminum blinds, gas refrigerators, stoves, and water heaters.[56] Citing "well-appointed" units and "the latest conveniences," local FHA officials, white property rights advocates, and the local black press celebrated these and other new black FHA developments as evidence of racial progress secured by the "free market."[57]

Though he came of age as a white man in the Depression-era South, Luther Brooks was never recorded engaging in overtly racist rhetoric. He instead used the weight of his wealth and reputation as a businessman to drive his corner of a landlord movement, protecting his clients' interests in various ways. "What he did was behind the scenes. He was a silent lobbyist," remembered his son-in-law and business partner, George Harth.[58] Congressmen, US senators, and even a few Florida governors found themselves guests on one of Brooks's Caribbean fishing excursions.[59] A day of deep-sea angling—and, with luck, a marlin strike—would sometimes be all it took to remove a few troublesome lines from proposed legislation. Brooks openly paid the way for city commissioners to take trips out of town.[60] And later, he even got his son-in-law placed on the Miami City Planning Board, again, just for a little insurance.[61]

But the debate over postwar housing was hardly an intellectual one, or even one strictly about political favors. It was about the location and profitability of black housing, and it drew from the basest politics driving American apartheid. Newspapers reported that CASH, in addition to spending perhaps as much as one hundred thousand dollars in its campaign against "socialism," "spread vicious rumors" and resorted to "intimidation of the Negro population."[62] Luther Brooks denied being a member of CASH.[63] Still, rumors surfaced that maintenance men in properties managed by Bonded Collection Agency were turning off the electrical service to the apartments of any black tenants known to vote for federal slum clearance or public housing. In search of white voters in the 1950 referendum against federal slum clearance, Miami's real estate developers touted their support of segregation as a public service. CASH asked those white citizens pondering slum clearance to consider, "Where will the displaced colored families go?" It then pointed out, "More than 3,500 home units, exclusively for colored, are now under construction by Free Enterprise."[64]

Miami's real estate interests knew they were playing with potentially incendiary materials. Even as developers used race baiting to limit government involvement, they were actively expanding black housing right up against white enclaves. In 1951, any claims about the free market's progressive gifts seemed undone by the age-old problem of Jim Crow's violence.

Conclusion

As black Miami's old wooden homes and slums became more concrete, so did the wall between South Florida's colored folk and the tree-lined streets of Coral Gables, the swaying palms of Miami Beach. The FHA, in the hands of landlords, would continue to facilitate the profitability of racial segregation. So, too, would public housing, resurgent in 1953 as the answer to both slum conditions and racial violence. [...] White housing officials and landlords maintained their faith in residential segregation as a social balm and a source of profit. Black folk's knowledge of that faith [...] haunted black people's collective narratives about serial displacement. [...]

Because of the reality of white violence, the belief in property as power remained critical to black visions of civil rights. But Jim Crow's property politics also gave white capitalists and homeowners the opportunity to preserve one of the most destructive and foundational myths of racial segregation—namely, that apartheid and the free market, at their best, were mutually beneficial, so long as everyone had the chance to own and improve their assets. As landlords continued to fend off slum clearance and public housing, their particular version of liberalism in the late 1940s and 1950s seemed to offer proof positive that American capitalism, with a little insurance, could meet "the Negro's" needs.

Among the many instruments of racial segregation in postwar Miami, FHA mortgage insurance became critical to how landlords governed within Jim Crow's political culture. The administration, as an advocate for "free enterprise," allowed rental developers and their lobbyists to cast themselves as friends of black homeowners threatened by urban redevelopment, public housing projects, and other uses of eminent domain. FHA programs also enabled landlords to generate support among white voters in opposition to "socialistic" government housing and slum clearance programs, which, real estate lobbyists argued, threatened to encourage "race mixing" and drive down white property values. The FHA, in short, became critical to arguments about the *social* benefits of "free enterprise." It helped harden the notion that "the market" could somehow bring about racial justice without compromising white pursuits of private property.

"Our economy promises all equal access to consumer goods in a free market." So said Robert Weaver, a black economist and federal official, to a roomful of Urban League activists in 1948. "But for minorities," he added, "the housing market has not been and is not free. We must take steps to make it so."[65] The free market, from Weaver's perspective, was liberalism's promise. And colored people's broad commitments to private property as a source of power inspired the kind of liberalism that would propel black activism in the 1950s and 1960s, even as many black people fell victim to more—and more dramatic—incidents of state-sponsored displacement.

NOTES

1. "'General' Brooks Collects Rents," *MN*, 2 March 1962.
2. "Depreciated Shacks Bringing Top Profits," *MH*, 6 November 1959. Beyond the 8 to 9 percent for Brooks, the landlord was responsible for paying all fees and expenses, including labor and materials used by Bonded Rental's twenty-four-man maintenance department; "Slumlords' Agent: A Matter of Profit," *MN*, 15 October 1974.
3. Harvey argues that if landlord returns dropped below 10 percent, owners would most often abandon their investment. See David Harvey, *The Urbanization of Capital: Studies in the History and Theory of Capitalist Urbanization* (Baltimore: Johns Hopkins University Press, 1985), esp. chap. 3.
4. Margie and George Harth, interviewed by N. D. B. Connolly, 9 March 2010. In 1962, Elizabeth Virrick corroborated this astounding figure, telling a reporter from the *Miami News*, "Most of the owners of Negro housing get their investment back in three years." Perhaps as further evidence of its veracity, Brooks for years evaded the question of his landlords' profit margins, until 1974, when a host of political and demographic factors lowered it to 10 percent; "'General' Brooks Collects Rents"; and "Slumlords' Agent."
5. Leonard Barfield, interviewed by N. D. B. Connolly, 23 February 2010, notes in author's possession.
6. "Luther Brooks, 80, Expowerbroker," *MH*, 31 December 1988. Limited financial records and client information for Bonded Collection Agency are also available at the Black Archives History and Research Foundation of South Florida Inc., Miami.
7. "Biggest Property Owners? Here's List of the Top 15," *MH*, 6 November 1959; "Slumlords' Agent"; "Luther Brooks, 80"; and Bonded Rental Agency advertisement (ca. 1969), "Newspaper Clippings on Housing, 1966–1970," Bonded Rental Agency Inc. Collection, BA.
8. "Miami Condemned: Update '75" (station WCKT, Miami, 1975), University of Georgia Peabody Collection, accessed 28 May 2013, http://dlg.galileo.usg.edu/peabody/id:1975_75025_nwt_1.
9. Charles E. Connerly, *"The Most Segregated City in America": City Planning and Civil Rights in Birmingham, 1920–1980* (Charlottesville: University of Virginia Press, 2005), 2–3; and David M. P. Freund, *Colored Property: State Policy and White Racial Politics in Suburban America* (Chicago: University of Chicago Press, 2007).
10. Robert C. Weaver, *Dilemmas of Urban America* (Cambridge, MA: Harvard University

Press, 1967), 19; Raymond Vernon, "The Changing Economic Function of the Central City," in *Urban Renewal*, ed. John Q. Wilson (Cambridge, MA, and London: Massachusetts Institute of Technology Press, 1966), 16; and M. Athalie Range, interviewed by Stephanie Wanza, 28 August 1997, 9–10, Tell the Story Collection, BA.

11. Edward Graham in Joint Committee on Housing, *Study and Investigation of Housing: Hearings before the Joint Committee on Housing*, 80th Cong., 1st sess., 27 October 1947, 1019–20.

12. Thomas W. Hanchett, *Sorting Out the New South City: Race, Class, and Urban Development in Charlotte, 1875–1975* (Chapel Hill: University of North Carolina Press, 1998), esp. chap. 5, "Creating Black Neighborhoods"; and LaDale Winling, "Building the Ivory Tower: Campus Planning, University Development, and the Politics of Urban Space" (PhD diss., University of Michigan, 2010), 93–95.

13. City Planning Board of Miami, "Railway Terminal 14th Street Plan" (26 December 1941), 1; City Planning Board of Miami, *Miami's Railway Terminal Problem* (6 January 1941), 8; and City Planning Board of Miami, *Report of City Planning Board of Miami Relative to New Railway Terminal* (1940), 55.

14. US Census Bureau, *Housing: Supplement to the First Series Housing Bulletin for Florida: Miami: Block Statistics* (Washington, DC: Government Printing Office, 1942), 21–22; Metropolitan Dade County Planning Department Comprehensive Plan Division, *Urban Growth in Dade County Florida: Planning Staff Report No. 2* (Metropolitan Dade County, March 1960), 5, WTVJ Collection, "Metro Land Use Plan" folder, box 50, HASF; Charles D. Thompson, "The Growth of Colored Miami," *Crisis* 49, no. 3 (March 1942): 83; and Planning Board of the City of Miami, Slum Clearance Committee and Dade County Health Department, *Dwelling Conditions in the Two Principal Blighted Areas* (1950), 41.

15. "Miracle Changes Face of Miami," *PC*, 30 November 1957; and Bonded Collection Agency, "A Pictorial Review of Miami's 'Parade of Progress': What Is Being Done by Private Enterprise in Miami's Slum Clearance Program," 6, 14, 21, Bonded Rental Agency Inc. Collection, BA.

16. "Voice of the People: Slum Conditions Not One-Man Blot," *MH*, 29 April 1958.

17. "Miracle Changes Face of Miami."

18. Bonded Collection Agency, "Pictorial Review of Miami's 'Parade of Progress,'" 11–12, 21.

19. "Merry Christmas," a notice from Abe Schonfeld Properties and Bonded Collection Agency to Schonfeld's tenants, December 1956, Bonded Rental Agency Inc. Collection, "Newspaper Clippings on Housing, 1960 and Back to 1952," BA.

20. Office of the County Manager, "Profile of the Black Population in Metropolitan Dade County" (January 1979), 56; "Solomon Faced Death; Earned Undying Fame," *PC*, 22 June 1940; and "Over 500 Negro Arrests in Albany," *PC*, 23 December 19 61.

21. "Miracle Changes Face of Miami"; and Langston Hughes, "Ballad of Sam Solomon," published in "Poet's Corner," *New York Amsterdam Star-News*, 12 July 1941.

22. "Solomon Pioneered Miami Vote Surge," *PC*, 30 November 1957.

23. "Here's How No's Beat Merger," Bonded Rental Agency Inc. Collection, "Newspaper Clippings on Housing, 1960 and Back to 1952," BA.

24. "Rent Collector Pounding Pavements," *MH*, 22 November 1957.

25. *Negro Housing in Greater Miami and Dade County: A Pictorial Presentation* (ca. 1951), UM, 45.

26. Enid Curtis Pinkney, interviewed by N. D. B. Connolly, 26 September 2006, notes and recording in author's possession.

27. St. Clair Drake and Horace Cayton, *Black Metropolis: A Study of Negro Life in a Northern City* (1945; repr., Chicago: University of Chicago Press, 1993), 212.

28. Charlotte Brooks, *Alien Neighbors, Foreign Friends: Asian Americans, Housing, and the Transformation of Urban California* (Chicago: University of Chicago Press, 2009), 117–18.

29. "Slum Area Rent Boosts in Miami Draw Ire, Favor," *WAA*, 16 August 1949. For the most influential discussion of FHA discrimination among historians, see Kenneth Jackson, *Crabgrass Frontier: The Suburbanization of the United States* (Oxford: Oxford University Press, 1985); Arnold R. Hirsch, *Making the Second Ghetto: Race and Housing in Chicago, 1940–1960* (Chicago: University of Chicago Press, 1998); and Freund, *Colored Property*.

30. George Merrick, "Real Estate Development Past and Future," transcript of address to the Southeastern Convention of Realty Boards, 29 November 1937, RG 196, box 298, NARA, cited in John A. Stuart, "Liberty Square: Florida's First Public Housing Project," in *The New Deal in South Florida: Design, Policy, and Community Building, 1933–1940*, ed. John A. Stuart and John F. Stack (Gainesville: University Press of Florida, 2008), 212.

31. D. Bradford Hunt, *Blueprint for Disaster: The Unraveling of Chicago Public Housing*

(Chicago: University of Chicago Press, 2009), 25.

32. House Select Committee on Lobbying Activities, *Housing Lobby: Part 2 of Hearings before the Joint Committee on Lobbying Activities*, 81st Cong., 2nd sess., 19, 20, 21, 25, 26, 27, 28 April 1950; 3, 5, and 17 May 1950, 365–68.

33. Don Parson, "The Decline of Public Housing and the Politics of the Red Scare: The Significance of the Los Angeles Public Housing War," *Journal of Urban History* 33, no. 3 (March 2007): 400–417, esp. 406; and Alexander von Hoffman, "A Study in Contradictions: The Origins and Legacy of the Housing Act of 1949," *Housing Policy Debate* 11, no. 2 (2000): 299–326, esp. 311.

34. "Property Owners Protest New Zoning," *MT*, 21 May 1949.

35. Miami Chamber of Commerce, Meeting Minutes of the Inter-racial Committee, 26 January 1945, *Committee Meetings Minutes, vol. 2 (1941–1946)*, Greater Miami Chamber of Commerce collection, HASF.

36. "Property Owners Protest New Zoning."

37. "Miami Plans Negro Jury Panel, More Race Police and End of Slums," *CD*, 10 July 1948.

38. "Race Being Squeezed Out of Miami Area," *PC*, 30 August 1947.

39. "Estimates of Mortgage Insurance Commitments on Negro Housing," 1946, 1948, 1949, RG 207, Race Relations Program 1946–48 Collection, "Housing Programs—FHA" folder, box 747, NARA.

40. Interoffice memo from Herbert C. Redman, zone commissioner, Federal Housing Administration, to A. L. Thompson, racial relations advisor, Housing and Home Finance Agency, 1 November 1949, 4, RG 207, Housing and Home Finance Agency Racial Relations Collection, "Miami, Florida Race Relations" folder, box 750, NARA.

41. HOLC Security Map Appendix, table 11, Records of the Federal Home Loan Bank Board, Home Owners Loan Corporation, Records Relating to the City Survey File, 1935–40, entry 39, "Florida Miami" folder, box 81, NARA; and intraoffice memo from Frank S. Horne, 3 April 1953, RG 207, Housing and Home Finance Agency Racial Relations Collection, "Miami, Florida Racial Relations" folder, box 750, NARA.

42. Leo Grebler, David M. Blank, and Louis Winnick, *Capital Formation in Residential Real Estate: Trends and Prospects* (Princeton, NJ: Princeton University Press, 1956), 146.

43. Ibid., 147.

44. "'Concrete Slums' Beat Zoning Deadline," *MT*, 18 May 1957.

45. "Miracle Changes Face of Miami."

46. "Is Your Rent Too High?," *MT*, 28 May 1955.

47. Barfield interview.

48. Between 1940 and 1950, the number of Negro-occupied dwellings in Dade County almost doubled, from nearly 11,300 to about 22,300; "Dade Negro Housing Has Nearly Doubled in Past Ten Years," *MH*, 6 May 1951.

49. David M. P. Freund, "Marketing the Free Market: State Intervention and the Politics of Prosperity in Metropolitan America," in *The New Suburban History*, ed. Kevin M. Kruse and Thomas J. Sugrue, 11–32 (Chicago: University of Chicago Press, 2006).

50. "Public Housing in Dade County: Statement of Non-federal Contribution," RG 207, General Records of the Department of Housing and Urban Development; Model Cities Reports, 1966–73, "Florida; FL 4 (part)—FL 5; Vol. 2, Part 1" folder, box 49, NARA.

51. Mohl, "Elizabeth Virrick and the 'Concrete Monsters,'" 19; and "Slum Clearance vs. Rehousing," *MN*, 8 April 1950.

52. *Miami Herald*, quoted in "Tale of Two Cities," *SPT*, 1 July 1950.

53. "Both Sides Give Their Arguments on Proposed Low-Cost Housing Project for Miami," *MN*, 25 June 1950.

54. *Negro Housing in Greater Miami and Dade County*, 31.

55. Clarence Taylor, *Black Religious Intellectuals: The Fight for Equality from Jim Crow to the 21st Century* (New York: Routledge, 2002), 91.

56. "Florida Physician Builds 80-Unit Housing Project," *ADW*, 12 January 1950; and "Project in Florida May Solve Problem of Minority Housing," *PC*, 21 January 1950.

57. *Negro Housing in Greater Miami and Dade County*, 12.

58. Harth and Harth interview.

59. Barfield interview.

60. "When DuBreuil Took Trip Paid by Brooks," *MN*, 24 July 1961.

61. "How Harth Got Job," *MH*, 7 April 1958.

62. "Slum Group Would Testify before House Lobby Probers," *MN*, 21 April 1950; and "Tale of Two Cities."

63. "In the Bag," *MN*, 14 April 1950.

64. "Government Housing Is Not Slum Clearance," *MN*, 15 April 1950.

65. "Statement of Robert Weaver," ca. 1948, 6, "Restrictive Covenant, May 1948–May 1953, Jan. 1960" folder, National Urban League Papers, Part III, box 76, LOC.

ESSAY 9.3

Making a Border City

Monica Perales

Source: Monica Perales, *Smeltertown: Making and Remembering a Southwest Border Community* (Chapel Hill: University of North Carolina Press, 2010).

EDITORS' INTRODUCTION

Perales's study of what was known as Smeltertown, or as referred to by its Spanish speaking residents, La Esmelda, utilized oral history, photographs, newspaper coverage, and personal archives to provide us with a case study of a Mexican-American neighborhood in El Paso, Texas. Perales demonstrates that American border cities have a complex and intriguing history. Even in the face of great prejudice and economic disparity, Mexican Americans shaped their communities and constructed connection and meaning within cities.

Smeltertown is a company-town, its workers living on company land. The American Smelting and Refining Company (ASARCO) refined copper and lead in El Paso. More informally organized than many other well-known company towns (Pullman, Illinois), the Spanish-speaking residents for the most part squatted on land owned by the company and constructed shelters that they improved over time.

Like many working-class areas clustered near industrial facilities, Smeltertown faced environmental contamination. Unfortunately lead from the smelters became a public health risk, especially for the children growing up there. Lead poses a high risk due to its permanence—children effected by lead will suffer a variety of health effects, including decreased mental acuity. **[For more on the urban environment, see Part VI.]**

Smeltertown sat literally on the border between the United States and Mexico, and also on a variety of figurative borders—between employee and employer, between the working class and the manager class, between Spanish-speakers and non-Spanish speakers, and others. Ultimately the residents of Smeltertown, including Perales' own ancestors, skillfully merged Anglo ideas with Mexican ones to speak out about their own rights and community. **[See Essay 9.4 for A.K. Sandoval-Strausz's discussion of transnationalism in "Latino Landscapes."]** Perales' work is also intriguing because she is writing about a community that no longer exists. The smelter is closed and the Mexican-American community that rose on the banks of the Rio Grande has been abandoned, except for some graves left behind to remind us of the former community.

Monica Perales is Associate Professor of History at the University of Houston, where she also serves as Associate Director of the Center for Public History. She has held a variety of fellowships, including the Summerlee Fellowship in Texas History at the William P. Clements Center for Southwest Studies at Southern Methodist University. Perales is a member of the Board of Directors of Humanities Texas, a state affiliate of the National Endowment of Humanities, and has served on the boards of the Urban History Association and the Labor and Working Class History Association. *Smeltertown* won the 2011 Kenneth Jackson Award from the Urban History Association.

MAKING A BORDER CITY (2010)

The story of Smeltertown is a story about the U.S.–Mexican border, but it does not begin on the banks of the Rio Grande. It begins deep in the ground, in the mineral-rich mines of Santa Rita, New Mexico, the Santa Barbara and Ahumada mines of Chihuahua, and the numerous independently operated mining properties throughout the U.S. Southwest and northern Mexico. It was there that thousands of tons of copper and lead-silver concentrates began their journey to El Paso on the intricately interlaced tracks that wove their way to this West Texas town. Small rail lines connected the mines to the major railways—the Mexican National Railroad, the Santa Fe, and the Southern Pacific—and all converged in El Paso and the unloading yards of the El Paso Smelting Works. Capable of handling 350,000 tons of lead charge and 500,000 tons of copper charge annually by 1914, the smelter had made El Paso the premier center for copper and lead processing in the region, virtually unparalleled in its importance. Unloaded by an army of Mexican contract workers, the ores began their odyssey from railroad cars and gondolas into the mouth of the massive plant. After hand sampling, the lead ores went through a complicated process of crushing and roasting before being blasted in one of the plant's eight lead furnaces and then poured into small pots. Skimmed of its impurities, the molten end product was cast into bars. Copper extracted from the lead ores, as well as copper concentrates, followed a separate path, each load making its way through one of the smelter's eight Wedge roasters, three reverberatories, and three converters. Forgoing mechanized cranes, the company employed a crew of Mexican workers to load locomotives to haul copper slag, matte, and bullion out of the converters. Giant ladles poured the molten copper into cast-iron cylinder molds. With the excursion through the smelter complete, another team of Mexican workers loaded the lead bars and copper anodes back onto railroad cars headed for their final destinations: the ASARCO-owned Perth Amboy, New Jersey, refinery for the lead and the Baltimore refinery for copper, where they would be processed into finished products. The migration process resumed, this time moving east and north on the same tracks out from El Paso.[1]

Ore was not the only product that made the journey to El Paso on the rails in those days. With revolution brewing south of the border, the grandparents of Manuela Vásquez Domínguez began to look at the tracks as a possible way to escape economic hardship and secure their personal safety. Sabino Vásquez's family, like countless other Mexican families across the country-side, had been deeply affected by the devastating poverty that wracked the country. The economic policies enacted by Mexican dictator Porfirio Díaz simultaneously encouraged the corporatization and proliferation of mines and smelters owned and operated by American-based companies like ASARCO and discouraged small-scale farming, leaving many families in dire straits. With few options available, Manuela's grandparents and several of their children began their own journey that would lead them north. Initially, they migrated from hacienda to hacienda as a means of scraping together enough resources to support their growing family. The oldest daughter had already made the trip to El Paso, settling in the bustling district of Smeltertown, where her husband worked at the Southwestern Portland Cement Company. Opened in 1907, the cement plant was booming in the early decades of the twentieth century; as the only cement plant in the area, it provided building materials for the growing city as well as the entire region.[2] Producing as many as 1,500 barrels of cement per day required hundreds of laborers; add those jobs to the ones at the smelter, the nearby limestone quarry, and brick plant, and economic stability seemed all but assured in El Paso. Personal issues factored in too. Vásquez's daughter urged her parents to join her there so they might be reunited. "She would say, 'Come, so that we might die together,'" Domínguez explained. One day they finally decided to make the trip north. Vásquez helped his family board the flatbed railroad car pulling out of the station at San Luis Potosí, but the train began to move before he could get on. Determined, he followed the tracks on foot, eventually catching up with his family. And thus they slowly embarked on their trek toward El Paso. The rail lines, built largely by American investors to extract mineral wealth from Mexico, became the channels by which its other valuable resource—laboring hands—also moved up the line.[3]

These migration stories powerfully illustrate how the global forces of capitalist development and human migration, facilitated by the expansion of the railroad, became deeply intertwined in the late nineteenth century, and how the destinies of a region, city, and individuals converged in the border city of El Paso. This essay illustrates how copper and capital transformed El Paso into an international center for railroad, mining, and smelting activities by the turn of the twentieth century. For centuries, El Paso had served as a center of trade and transportation, first for the native populations that inhabited the region and later as a point on the heavily traveled Camino Real. In the years following the Civil War, the United States engaged in an aggressive campaign to extend its dominance to the territories of the Southwest and Mexico. As American financiers and industrialists established the broad architecture of an economic imperial project in Mexico and Latin America more generally, El Paso emerged as a critical player in these efforts.[4] With lines that connected east and west as well as north and south, El Paso became the nerve center of the flow of capital—in the form of money, resources, and labor—throughout the region. The city's political and economic elite, recognizing the benefits of making El Paso into an industrial and commercial city, energetically worked to cultivate its image as a center for industry and tourism. They took full advantage of the perfect storm of conditions that existed in the border city: a convenient and strategic location as the geographic passageway to the north; a long-standing history of travel, trade, and commerce on the Spanish, Mexican, and, eventually, American frontier; thirty years of Porfirian-era policies courting American investment in Mexico; and most important, the proximity of Mexico, with its vast mineral resources and its seemingly limitless supply of cheap labor a short distance from

the center of town. Seizing on its advantageous position on the eve of one of the largest waves of migration from Mexico, city leaders, boosters, and business giants placed El Paso squarely on the national and international map. In terms of financial power and significance, the El Paso they made remained one of the most prominent industrial southwestern cities for more than half a century.

Once the economic infrastructure had been laid, El Paso's business and political leaders also determined the roles that people would play within it. At the same time that they encouraged economic development in the making of their modern city, they also had to confront the realities of being a border city. Although the abundance of Mexican labor and the accessibility to Mexican resources and markets were clear advantages to the city's growth strategy, it did not necessarily mean that El Paso was, or should ever be, a Mexican city. Anglo leaders remained ambivalent about Mexicans' place in their city. On the one hand, some praised the cultural diversity and expressed a desire to maintain certain customs that spoke to the region's rich history. But more often, Mexican residents found themselves on the literal and figurative wrong side of the very tracks that had brought many of them to El Paso. While the line between Anglos and wealthy Mexican exiles was less absolute, for the vast majority of working-class Mexicans, daily life was marked by residential, economic, and social segregation.

This essay also traces how El Paso's political and business powerbrokers not only shaped the political economy of the city, but sought to establish a social and racial hierarchy within its boundaries as well. Despite El Paso's origins and long-standing connections to Mexico, from the 1880s to the 1920 its leaders crafted their idea of a modern American border city: the gateway to old Mexico yet markedly different from anything in its sister republic. In El Paso, Mexicans fit into a distinctly subordinate social position, its boundaries reinforced by daily practice and law. In the end, this context would determine how residents of Smeltertown came to see themselves: essential to the city's growing economy and to one of the most important companies in town, but occupying the lower rungs of the social pecking order. Over the course of nearly a century, Esmeltianos struggled to define their place in the border city whose economic, social, and racial contours were coming into clear relief at the dawn of the new century.

From Supply Outpost to Railroad Hub and Manufacturing Center

Historically, El Paso had always served as an important transportation and commercial center-a place of movement and migrations of people and products. The region that would become modern-day El Paso and Ciudad Juárez sat at the natural conduit between two rugged mountain ranges that cut across a vast swath of desert landscape. The area was home to diverse native populations who began to blaze the trails later generations would use for trade, exchanging surplus crops with communities as far away as Casas Grandes Chihuahua.[5] Following the conquest of the Mexican interior, Spanish explorers and missionaries set about to claim their vast empire. Through a combination of violence produced through military force, missionary efforts, and cultural adaptation and coercion, Spain secured its foothold in the Southwest.[6]

It was the arrival of the railroad that dramatically changed the city. Prior to the Civil War, much of the railroad track in Texas was in the east, serving the large cotton-producing areas of East Texas. Although two Texas railroads were chartered to build lines through El Paso in the 1850s, it was not until the Southern Pacific Railroad pushed to be the first southern trans-continental rail that El Paso appeared on the radar. With the coming of the Santa Fe Railroad in April 1881, almost overnight El Paso was transformed from a "little adobe village" into a "flourishing frontier community."[7] The Southern Pacific and Santa Fe railroads both constructed terminals in El Paso. The Southern Pacific also built a fifteen-stall roundhouse, car shop, passenger station, and freight depot to the tune of $150,000. The Santa Fe erected a $100,000 facility. Although El Paso greatly benefited from the passenger service offered by the expanding lines, the primary goal was to increase commercial transportation and activities. Not only would the rail lines bring the so-called blessings of civilization to this budding border community, but they would also provide the means to ship local products to outside markets. The modern transportation lines introduced by the railroads reinforced old connections and traversed the same routes previously traveled on foot and by mule train.

Thanks in large measure to the railroads, the population of El Paso grew by leaps and bounds; in the decade after the first train arrived, the population exploded fourteenfold (from 736 in 1880 to more than 10,300 in 1890) as did the city's wealth.[8] In just three short years, El Paso had become one of the premier railroad centers in North America. At the turn of the twenty century, El Paso had seven connecting railroads: the Atchison, Topeka, and Santa Fe; the Southern Pacific; the Texas and Pacific; the Galveston, Harrisburg, and San Antonio; the Mexican Central; the Rio Grande, Sierra Madre, and Pacific; and the El Paso and Northwestern.[9] In 1919, the Chamber of Commerce declared that more than two thousand freight cars coursed through El Paso rail yards each day, carrying 800 million tons of goods annually; that the city held the distinction of being a terminus for five major rail lines from points east, north, and west, and two from the south; and that as many as forty passenger trains made their way through El Paso daily.[10] "What a few years earlier had been a small, sleepy, and extremely isolated adobe village," one historian wrote, "was now a fast-growing small city with rapid and dependable freight and passenger transportation to every major population center on the continent."[11]

El Paso's emergence as a major rail center was not an accident, nor did it occur in isolation. At the same time that the United States sought economic domination across the western territories, it also directed its attention toward Mexico. El Paso sat at the center of this crossroads. Railroad investment and construction in Mexico represented the realization of the dreams of some of the most powerful American financiers, industrialists, and politicians to establish a transcontinental and transborder railway infrastructure connecting U.S. economic interests and Mexican resources through border cities like El Paso. From the close of the Civil War, American financiers clamored for concessions and land grants to begin railroad projects in Mexico. In Porfirio Díaz—who viewed modern transportation and communication lines as vital to Mexico's ultimate growth and success—American investors found a willing partner. Under his regime, U.S.-financed railroad lines spread like wild-fire. Before Díaz assumed power, Mexico possessed less than 700 kilometers of track. By the start of the revolution in 1910, it totaled more than 24,000 kilometers, much of it heading to U.S. border cities.[12] In late 1881 Boston financiers arranged with the Mexican government to begin construction on the Mexican Central Railroad lines from Paso del Norte to Mexico City, and by World War I the Mexican Central's terminal point was in El Paso.[13] As historian John M. Hart explains, "the railroads were the fundamental element in American power and influence," enabling American capitalists to entrench themselves in nearly every aspect of the Mexican economy.[14]

El Paso's business elite strategically highlighted the city's best features to ensure its development as a crucial center for transportation, business, and tourism. The Chamber of Commerce lobbied to reduce freight rates on its rail lines to make El Paso competitive with St. Louis and other railroad centers for companies wishing to ship goods both within the United States and to Mexico. It also offered rebates to merchants who purchased at least $1,500 worth of goods manufactured in the city and more generally pursued antilabor policies to prevent unions from hampering production and profitability.[15] As important as these inducements was the chamber's campaign of words heralding the border city's potential. Its trade territory encompassed "a greater area than that comprised in the New England States, New York and Pennsylvania added for good measure."[16] Its ideal climate, most notably its "high percentage of sunshiny days, a low average

rainfall, [and] a consequential slight humidity," allowed El Paso to market itself as a haven from rough northern winters and ailments like rheumatism, tuberculosis, and nervous disorders aggravated by cold climes.[17] The chamber also primed the city for tourism and conventions. El Paso offered "the wearied transcontinental tourist, a veritable Nile-like oasis in a wide stretch of barren country," as well as access to one of only two eighteen-hole golf courses between San Antonio and the Pacific, and, in the words of one newcomer, "so many good hotels, I would dare not state the number."[18] In sum, El Paso was not only "the largest and most important city between Denver, Colorado, and the City of Mexico, or between San Antonio, Texas and Los Angeles, California." It was a "dominant metropolis" of a region whose territory encompassed an area the size of the entire country east of the Mississippi River.[19] In the minds of its most vocal boosters, the old eastern manufacturing cities were relics of the past. El Paso represented a new future on the horizon.

Although access to natural resources, railroad connections, and balmy weather made it a logical choice for transportation and tourism, it was El Paso's prominence as the largest city on the 2,000-mile border with Mexico that provided the biggest advantage from a marketing perspective. As such, El Paso was uniquely positioned to be the "Gateway to Mexico," providing not only an entrepôt for manufactured products but also accessibility to raw materials and labor. For boosters, the city's proximity and historical relationship with Mexico reinforced this view. The July 1920 issue of the *Greater El Paso* proclaimed that El Paso "is thoroughly familiar with the requirements of this foreign commerce, speaks the language of the neighboring republic, knows the Mexicans by their first names, has the stocks at the right prices, and, being the natural gateway to Mexico, is in a predominating position to expedite delivery."[20] The proof was in the receipts. El Paso's warehouses were filled with merchandise and machinery awaiting transport to and from Mexico and by 1918 the city's customhouse imports and exports totaled in the millions of dollars.[21] Products manufactured in El Paso firms not only supplied the local area and the U.S. Southwest, but also reached deep into Mexico, to "the farms, ranches, plantations and mines of the Mexican states of Sonora, Sinaloa, Nayarit, Chihuahua, Durango, Coahuila and Zacatecas."[22] Working closely with the Ciudad Juárez Chamber of Commerce, El Paso business leaders cultivated international cooperation by highlighting the economic vitality of the border region and courted Mexican consumers by supporting Spanish language advertising of American goods.[23] By the 1920s, as the disruption and violence caused by the Mexican Revolution gave way to economic reconstruction, El Paso business and banking interests continued to aggressively assert their mastery to shape and revitalize the Mexican economy. Mexico needed the power of U.S. capital, they reasoned, but America needed Mexico's resources. As a result, American businesses continued to view Mexico in terms of the potential profits it could offer. It was in this spirit that the former Mexican consul in Kansas City, Jack Danciger, encouraged American entrepreneurs to "go to Mexico, old boy, grow up with Mexicans."[24] These activities would no doubt continue to benefit El Paso's economy, as well as reflect a concerted effort on the part of the business elite to raise the profile of the city as an international banking, commercial, trade, and shipping powerhouse.

Though the potential for international commerce was certainly a major attraction for manufacturers, access to inexpensive Mexican labor was perhaps the most enticing of all. Laws intended to stem the tide of immigration had employers scrambling to secure continued access to cheap immigrant labor. The exclusion of Chinese immigrant workers in 1882 and the Gentleman's Agreement with Japan in 1907 effectively cut off access to Asian immigrant labor. The head tax and literacy test provisions of the 1917 Immigration Act, as well as the progressively restrictive racialized population quotas established by the 1921 Emergency Immigration Act and the 1924 Johnson-Reed Act, posed additional challenges, particularly to firms up North and back East that relied on steady immigration from Europe. Thus El Paso's seemingly unlimited supply of Mexican laborers appealed especially to manufacturers hoping to keep their financial bottom line in check. In sheer volume, the number of workers of Mexican origin in El Paso—native and foreign born—was a tremendous perk. "Because it is the only city of size on the Mexican border and also because by composition it is nearly half a Mexican city," Chamber of Commerce officer Frank H. Knapp noted, "it has always been a reservoir for Mexican labor." Knapp further emphasized the great advantages of hiring Mexicans because of their perceived adaptability, docility, and willingness to work. He pointed out that historically Mexicans had been employed throughout the Southwest to great effect and were eminently suited to factory work given that "by nature the Mexican laborer prefers a community environment." Moreover, Mexican workers had the advantage of being "employed at a wage scale that makes the labor charge for work done only a fraction of that demanded in the East and North." Addressing manufacturers concerned about union mobilization, Knapp contended that, "contrary to the general impression prevalent in the North, the Mexican workman is loyal and steady, at least in the United States. Labor trouble among Mexican laborers has never occurred in El Paso."[25] Although this last point completely ignored the long history of labor mobilization throughout the West in which Mexicans played an integral role, not to mention the highly publicized (if ultimately unsuccessful) strikes by Mexican smelter workers and Mexican and Mexican American laundresses in El Paso in those years, Knapp spoke the words that businesses wanted to hear.[26] If Knapp was correct, and a Texas cotton mill using Mexican labor could save as much as $200,000 annually in labor costs over an identical mill operating in Rhode Island, then the choice was clear. El Paso, with its army of willing Mexican workers, made simple business sense.

Making the "Copper Capital of the Southwest"

On first glance, El Paso did not seem to be the most obvious place in which to develop a leading smelter center in the Southwest, especially considering its distance from the mines located deep in the Chihuahua and Sonora deserts. However, with the creation of a vast transborder railroad network, the marketing of the city as a site of industry and manufacturing, and its position as the gateway to Mexico's rich mineral deposits, El Paso soon emerged as the *only* logical choice. In response to the global demands for copper and lead—in such varied forms as pipe and wiring for commercial and household use and military arms and ammunition at the dawn of World War I-commercial mining in the West expanded at near-breakneck speed. Boosters like Charles Longuemare, publisher of the newspaper Bullion in nearby Socorro, New Mexico, were among the strongest advocates of cultivating the mining and smelting industry in El Paso. In an article published in the *El Paso Times* in December 1888, Longuemare predicted that, "while the smelting interests of this city have assumed great magnitude, they are but a shadow of what they will be in the course of time."[27] For him, the city's future lay in ore production; with mining and smelting as its main focus, El Paso was poised to compete with, if not surpass, the great copper giants in Colorado.

The smelting industry quickly took root. "El Paso has been singularly blessed with the mining industry and put right in the midst of the richest mining territory," explained El Paso historian Cleofas Calleros. By the closing years of the nineteenth century, "almost every adult in El Paso was a mining man, actively engaged and very interested in promoting a smelter, or prospecting, or studying a 'retodero' or looking for the famous 'Padre Mine' which has been legend around these parts since time immemorial."[28] One of those men was Robert Safford Towne. Towne was among the many American businessmen of the day who sought his fortune in mining, focusing much of his attention on the abundant reserves of northern Mexico. In 1887 Towne, a mining developer and president of the Mexican Ore Company, collaborated with the Argentine, Kansas-based Kansas City Consolidated Smelting and Refining Company to build a smelter on the far northwestern outskirts of El Paso to process silver-

lead ore from his Santa Eulalia and Sierra Mojada mines.[29] Towne established a lead grading and sampling facility in El Paso in 1883, but then transported the lead to Socorro, New Mexico, for smelting. Recognizing the financial benefits of smelting the ore in El Paso, Towne interested Kansas City Consolidated in building a smelter closer to El Paso's rail connections. His lead smelter, complete with four lead blast furnaces and four hand roasters, opened in 1887 and was an immediate success.[30] Operating as a custom smelter, Towne's plant contracted with independent mines to process their ores for a fee, thereby securing a reliable source of incoming ores to keep the plant churning at a steady pace. In its first year of operation, the smelter produced 12,000 tons of lead bullion; as one historian wrote "It represented the only really important custom smelting works in the South-west. It remained so for over thirty years."[31] Indeed, if the railroads "formed the spokes for the mining hub that was El Paso ... the smelter served as the bearings upon which that hub rotated."[32]

Towne sold the smelter to Kansas City Consolidated in 1887. In 1899, the El Paso Smelting Works (as it was known locally) became incorporated as part of the American Smelting and Refining Company, a move that assured the smelter's, and the city's, international prominence for nearly one hundred years.[33] A product of the Gilded Age business pattern of consolidation, ASARCO was a classic trust, formed by eighteen of the biggest smelting operations in the country. Like other powerful corporations of its time, ASARCO's goal was to control its industry, choking out competition in the process. Unfortunately for its shareholders, by the early 1900s ASARCO found itself in serious financial straits. Salvation for the ailing trust came in the form of the Guggenheim family, quickly becoming one of the most important players in the business world. A Swiss immigrant of German Jewish heritage, Meyer Guggenheim and his family arrived in Philadelphia in 1847. After establishing a respectable fortune in lace manufacturing and importing, railroads, and mining ventures, Guggenheim turned his interest to smelting. By

1890, Meyer Guggenheim Sons was already the largest and most successful silver and lead smelting company in the United States, owning several properties in Colorado. Although they had initially resisted inclusion in ASARCO, by 1901 the Guggenheims were amenable to a merger. After months of negotiations, they agreed to commit their highly successful smelter operations, refineries, and up to $18 million in cash and equipment to infuse much-needed cash into the debt-ridden company. In return, they received, among other concessions, $45.2 million in common and preferred ASARCO stock, making the family the single largest shareholder.[34] After the deal was sealed, Meyer Guggenheim's five sons joined the company's board of directors, and Meyer took his place as the "patriarch of the copper industry" and head of one of the largest mining and smelting firms in the world.[35]

The growth of the Guggenheims' empire was not bound by the Rio Grande. As in the case of the bankers and railroad financiers before them, highly capitalized mining ventures looked toward Mexico's vast mineral wealth as the next step in their quest for market dominance. Díaz actively courted American mining companies with generous incentives including subsoil rights and seemingly unlimited access to Mexico's resources. The Guggenheims benefited handsomely from the arrangement. Even before their merger with ASARCO, Daniel Guggenheim met with Díaz, who granted Meyer Guggenheim Sons wide latitude in mining exploration, as well as permission to build and operate three smelters at locations of their choice.[36] The family also received other perks in the form of rights to federal land, speculation rights, and tax and import duty exemptions. By 1898, Meyer Guggenheim Sons was the largest metals-producing corporation operating in Mexico, with smelters in Monterrey and Aguascalientes and earnings of $1 million.[37] By the start of the Mexican Revolution, ASARCO owned and controlled claims in the states of Chihuahua, Durango, San Luis Potosí, Zacatecas, Coahuila, and Michoacán, in addition to major custom smelters in Monterrey, Chihuahua, and Aguascalientes. In

addition, small railroads linking the mines and smelters came under ASARCO ownership, creating an intricate web of interrelated interests that blanketed the Mexican landscape. ASARCO also consolidated the management of its Mexican properties under a Mexican Mining Department, devoting tremendous financial and manpower resources including an army of leading engineering, accounting, management, and legal experts.[38] Combining their vast holdings throughout the North American West and northern Central Mexico, the Guggenheims laid the foundations of their transborder empire. Soon ASARCO emerged as the largest privately owned business in Mexico, planting roots in Mexico that ran deeper than the veins of ore coursing beneath its soil. With total assets valued at more than $185 million by 1911 and properties throughout the United States and Mexico, ASARCO had, in the words of one historian, "risen to the premier position in its field, with a prestige undisputed."[39] In two decades' time, ASARCO consisted of thirty affiliated companies operating under individual local management but all directed by corporate headquarters in New York. When one historian claimed that "the sun never sets upon [ASARCO's] activities," he was not exaggerating.[40]

For ASARCO officials, El Paso was no isolated outpost or afterthought; it was the center of their multimillion-dollar international operations and a critical point of production in a multinational network of mines, smelters, refineries, railroads, and shipping lines that spanned the North and South American continents. The El Paso smelter operated as two smelters under one roof, with separate lead and copper operations each producing tens of thousands of tons of ore per month. El Paso also became the headquarters of the metals giant's Southwestern Smelting Department (which included the local plant and the one located in Hayden, Arizona). The management offices of the Mexican Mining Department, one of the company's most important divisions given its transnational focus, were also located in the borders areas. With more than fifty employees, the El Paso offices purchased more than $2 million in supplies to support ASARCO's Mexican mining ventures, which "taken as a whole, are by far the largest mining operations in that country, and one of the largest in the entire world."[41]

Coming to El Paso

El Paso's geographic location at the center of a transnational network of capitalism helped to make it the busiest port of entry on the southern border. The city's growth coincided with, and to a large degree contributed to, one of the largest human migrations of the twentieth century. Scholars estimate that between 1900 and 1930, as many as 1.5 million Mexicans entered the United States. Railroad and mining networks like those headquartered in El Paso were not just apparatuses for the physical transport of Mexican labor. In fact, they were a part of the carefully constructed machinery forged by American capitalist development and business interests that drew Mexicans northward, making them crucial pieces that kept the machinery in motion.

The same government and economic policies that allowed American corporations to gain a foothold in Mexico wreaked havoc for the millions of poor Mexicans living throughout the countryside. Liberal land policies dating back to the 1850s favored the consolidation of agricultural lands into haciendas to produce crops for export, leaving poor campesinos landless, mired in poverty, and forced into itinerant labor or sharecropping. Conditions only worsened by the end of the century. Many of the displaced began migrating to the American-owned mines and railroads, which paid comparatively better wages, but which had also done their own part to destabilize the economic situation for campesinos by raising land prices. This transition was brutal and disruptive for the people who experienced it in their daily lives. These sweeping changes had tangible personal meaning for people like Sabino Vásquez. Unable to support his family, he was forced to seek temporary migratory work from the large hacendados until finally deciding to leave Mexico and take his family north. "They were very poor, see," his granddaughter Manuela remembered many years later. "They helped harvest the crops of the landowners."[42] The revolution that erupted in 1910 only compounded already desperate conditions. Simultaneously, southwestern growers, manufacturers, and industries looked to Mexico to provide much-needed labor to meet the increased demand in agriculture as well as copper and lead production for sale to European countries at the outset of World War I. The pattern of circular migration emerging between the Mexican countryside and Mexican towns logically expanded across the border and into U.S. cities like El Paso. The presence of a highly organized, intricate infrastructure that entwined two nations and their economic destinies had all but guaranteed it. People made the choice to head north, but their available options were fundamentally shaped by the calculated and organized efforts of American capitalists to exploit Mexico's most valuable resources for their own economic benefit.

In the late nineteenth and early twentieth centuries, Mexicans immigrated to the United States with relative ease—in large measure due to the existence of such transborder economic flows. The primary concern of the Bureau of Immigration in these years was European immigration by way of Ellis Island. The small force of mounted inspectors that would become the U.S. Border Patrol focused more on preventing the entry of excluded Chinese immigrants through the southern border. U.S. immigration law prohibited contract labor and barred the entry of those likely to become a public charge, policing movement through the nation's ports of entry. State officials scrutinized poor women and children with a close eye in an attempt to enforce sexual and moral order, while they were more likely to view men as potential laborers.[43] Even with such restrictions, the movement continued to flow across the international boundary, and inspectors often looked the other way as Mexicans crossed into the United States. As a result of the interrelated factors of labor demands, economic necessity, and revolution, the numbers of Mexicans entering El Paso exploded. During one week alone in May 1902, the Bureau of Immigration reported that as many as 500 Mexicans entered El Paso, and an average of 250 more applied for entry each day. With the start of the revolution, the numbers skyrocketed. Depending on conditions, immigration officials reported between 1,000 and 2,000 entrants per month, and in one week in 1916 more than 4,800 Mexicans passed through El Paso's border checkpoint.[44]

The passage of the 1917 Immigration Act, on its face, would seem to have tightened immigration of Mexicans coming through El Paso. Although it still placed no numerical quota on Mexicans entering the United States, its head tax and literacy test provisions threatened to curb the flow of much-desired Mexican laborers. However, the act allowed for the importation of unskilled agricultural, railroad, and mine workers, and provided an exemption for the admission of foreign skilled workers in industries where no native-born equivalent could be secured.[45] Railroad and mining companies were quick to take advantage of this exemption."[46] It also tried to stretch the law to include laborers not only in mines, but also in smelters, arguing that smelting was a necessary immediate step between mining and the creating finished metal products, and was thus of critical importance to meet the wartime demand. Immigration officials reported that more than twenty thousand laborers admitted in the 1919 fiscal year fell under the guidelines of these exemptions.[47] Of course, laborers arriving under these conditions were not the only immigrants crossing during this period. Recognizing the economic reality of the region, inspectors allowed the movement of Mexicans to work in agriculture or one of the other industries of the Southwest, effectively defining immigration policy on the ground to meet local circumstances.[48] Local employers, politicians, and lobbyists like the El Paso Chamber of Commerce's Washington, D.C., representative, J. A. Happer, pressured Congress for, and secured, the extension of Mexican exemptions even after the war ended, thereby ensuring their continued access to immigrant labor from south of the border.[49]

The loose application of immigration restrictions notwithstanding, Mexicans found it harder to cross the border by the 1920s. Outbreaks of typhus in Mexico's interior and fears of contagion from El Paso's Mexican barrios led to the institution of invasive and humiliating inspection and delousing procedures at the city's border checkpoint, even as these methods were eliminated elsewhere. In addition, the 1924 National Origins Act tightened control on the land borders, and in the 1920s Mexicans coming into the United States faced more formalized requirements and inspections as well as more vigorously utilized deportation procedures. The implementation and application of such practices set "the U.S.-Mexico border as a cultural and racial boundary, as a creator of illegal immigration," thereby "creating a barrier where, in a practical sense, none had existed before."[50] Although they faced greater a challenges, Mexicans continued to make their way to the border city and reshaped the face of El Paso.

The large numbers of Mexican workers arriving in the border city made El Paso the most important labor recruiting center in the Southwest. Though laws banning contract labor were on the books, enterprising individuals, companies, and even state agencies became involved in the business of securing Mexican workers and placing them into jobs in American firms not just in El Paso but throughout the United States. From 1905 to 1920, several privately run recruiting agencies operated in El Paso. For example, Román Gómez González used his community ties in the Mexican neighborhood near the border called Chihuahuita to organize one of the most successful of these businesses, placing as many as six thousand laborers in jobs with railroads and growers in 1909 alone.[51] Several companies established their own systems for hiring workers. As early as 1894, the Southern Pacific opened a recruitment office in El Paso to secure workers for its line, and soon several other railroads and agricultural interests set up operations. Not all of this recruiting activity went unnoticed. Robert Towne found himself in trouble with the law in 1888 for illegally contracting for and transporting forty workers from the Mexican town of Santa Rosalía to work at his recently opened smelter. The arrival of more than one hundred skilled railroad workers in El Paso from Aguascalientes between June 1 and July

18, 1918, also raised the suspicions of immigration officials.[52] By 1918, in response to complaints from the Mexican government, the Texas Bureau of Labor Statistics and the U.S. Department of Labor had opened employment agencies in El Paso in an attempt to regulate labor recruitment practices and prevent abuses.[53] Although the sheer volume of workers entering El Paso made for a highly competitive market in which agencies needed workers more than workers needed agencies, the presence of these firms reveals how labor and immigration were deeply connected in this border city.

Although the global forces of capitalist development and war created the conditions that set migration in motion, at its heart were people who made choices based on their knowledge of the region's mining and railroad connections and personal relationships. Parents, siblings, and extended families all aided in the migration process, passing along news about job possibilities and providing material and emotional support for new arrivals.[54] It was through the help of his compadre, Pablo Saenz, who already lived in El Paso, that José Luján Meléndez was able to bring his wife and five children to Smeltertown. These kinship networks and migration practices contributed to large clusters of families in El Paso's barrios. Melchor Santana Sr. laughingly recalled: "One time I heard an Anglo say 'If you find one Martínez in this house [in Smeltertown], you'll find three generations of Martínez[es] around there because they all stick together!'"[55] Ramón Salas's father heard about steady work available at ASARCO and came to El Paso before sending for his wife and family in Durango in February 1923.[56] Carmen Escandón's mother

moved her and her brother Antonio to Smeltertown from Aguascalientes after their father died. Escandón's grandmother, aunt, and uncle already lived in Smeltertown, and the presence of family plus the availability of work at the smelter for Antonio made the move a practical choice.[57] The fact that nearly one-third of the Mexicans working at and settling around the smelter in 1920 were born in Texas and many others hailed from southwestern states that were part of the copper and railroad network reveals not only the power of such labor circuits over people's lives, but also the creation of families and relationships along the lines.

The stories of Sabina Alva and her daughter Enriqueta Beard underscore how these labor and familial networks shaped the lives of individuals. Sabina, whose father was a road master for the Southern Pacific Railroad in Camargo, Chihuahua, Mexico, was born in Smeltertown in 1905, when her mother came to stay with an aunt who lived there. About a month later, Sabina's mother rejoined her husband in Casas Grandes, Chihuahua. Within a short time, however, Sabina's father decided to look for a job at the smelter in El Paso. Given his experience with Southern Pacific, he was quickly employed at ASARCO and relocated the family to Smeltertown permanently.[58] Eventually Sabina married José Alva, and the labor networks that brought her own family to El Paso soon carried her new family farther north. Unable to find work in El Paso following a layoff at the smelter, the Alvas embarked on the migrant circuit; José's smelter skills proved invaluable in getting a job with the railroad. Their daughter, Enriqueta, was born in a railroad car in DePew, Illinois, in 1924. According to Enriqueta, her mother simply

Table 9.1 Smeltertown Population Totals, 1900–1930

Year	Total Polulation	Spanish-Surnamed Population	Percentage Spanish-Surnamed
1900	2,721	NA	NA
1910	2,903	NA	NA
1920	3,119	2,974	95.35
1930	2,876	2,779	96.62

Source: U.S. Bureau of the Census, Manuscript Census, *Twelfth, Thirteenth, Fourteenth, and Fifteenth Census of the United States*, microcopies 623–26 (Washington, D.C.: National Archives and Records Administration).

could not adjust to the snow and missed her own mother too much. So Sabina returned to Smeltertown with nine-month-old Enriqueta while her husband finished out his employment in the Midwest. By the time he returned two years later, he again found a job at ASARCO.[59] As these cases illustrate, ASARCO had crafted world to meet its own business ends, but it also intimately connected people from Montana to Chihuahua to Illinois and back to El Paso. These workers it were all a part of the whole, and their lives converged in El Paso.

El Paso: The Modern American Border City

In his March 1921 article for the *Greater El Paso and Southwestern Commerce*, Dallas reporter John Sneed remarked on the great strides the city of El Paso had made in developing and broadening its economic activities. But more to the point, he praised the diligent efforts, hard work, and inexhaustible drive the business community had put in to making the former frontier village into a prominent southwestern city. "For the city that sprang magically from an environment of arid desert and volcanic rock is their handiwork," he wrote, "and they have a right to be proud of her." Although El Paso's rise was certainly attributable to the "natural course of events," city leaders bore a lion's share of the credit. "They were possessed of supreme confidence, child-like faith in their future, also untiring energy, co-operation, pluck and liberality"— that thing called "the El Paso spirit," he explained. But more important, "They watched and tended the little town of twenty years ago as diligently as a horticulturist watches and nurtures a tender plant and they fashioned her development. The result is shown today."[60]

To the casual observer, the cities of the American West seem to have simply appeared out of nowhere, a result of the natural course of events, the inevitable move of progress and modernity ever westward. In reality, as Sneed's observations on El Paso reveal, cities are carefully made and remade to suit the needs of their inhabitants. In the closing years of the nineteenth century, politicians, industrial entrepreneurs, and civic boosters tirelessly engaged in the making of the modern American border city of El Paso. By the early twentieth century, they had created one of the most efficiently operating machines in the borderlands. El Paso emerged as a railroad and mining hub not through the "natural course" of events, but rather as the deliberately crafted center of industry that leaders envisioned. And it was not just the industrial city that had to be made. The social relations that structured power, influence, and prestige also had to be created. City framers knew they needed Mexico and Mexicans to ensure the success of their city, but decided on how, where, and to what extent their presence would matter. Within the city limits, Mexicans would continue to be vital fuel for El Paso's industries.

Despite the best efforts of the elite to craft their ideal American city where Mexicans would be indispensable but invisible, the Mexicans of El Paso were not just cogs in the machine. They also made their own connections to this place and to the machinery of which they were an essential part. Integrated fully into the regional networks of capital, Mexicans made their own choices and came to see themselves as vital parts of the apparatus that kept the border city moving. Some merely passed through the city, some stayed briefly, but many others chose to remain in El Paso. The people in one tiny corner on the outskirts of town—under the shadow of the giant brick smokestacks, the black steel railroad trestles, and the deafening hum of the blast furnaces— planted their roots firmly into the city's industrial future. In Smeltertown, they would fashion their own image of a border city, and for the next hundred years they would play a critical role in the making of a modern El Paso.

NOTES

1. Richard H. Vail, "El Paso Smelting Works —I," *Engineering and Mining Journal 98 no. II* (September 12, 1914): 465–68, and "El Paso Smelting Works—II" *Engieneering and Mining Journal 98*, no. 12 (September 19, 1914): 515–18.
2. Capt. E. H. Simons, "Cement Plant Made Cement for Dam," SP.
3. Manuela Vásquez Domínguez, interview by author (Spanish), May 29, 2002; tape recording, El Paso.

4. On the impact of U.S. investment in Mexico, see John Mason Hart, *Empire and Revistaolution: The Americans in Mexico since the Civil War* (Berkeley: University of California, Press, 2002), and Gilbert G. González, *Culture of Empire: American Writers, Mexico and Mexican Immigrants, 1880–1930* (Austin: University of Texas Press, 2003).

5. W. H. Timmons, *El Paso: A Borderlands History* (El Paso: Texas Western Press, 1990), 1–3.

6. Antonia Castañeda, "Sexual Violence in the Politics and Policies of Conquest Amerindian Women and the Conquest of Alta California," in *Building with Our Hands: New Directions in Chicana Studies*, ed. Adela de la Torre and Beatríz Pesquera hay (Berkeley: University of California Press, 1993), 15–33; Ramón Gutiérrez *When Jesus Came, the Corn Mothers Went Away: Marriage, Sexuality, and Power in New Mexico 1500–1846* (Stanford, Calif.: Stanford University Press, 1991); Lisbeth Haas *Conquests and Historical Identities in California, 1769–1936* (Berkeley: University of California Press, 1996).

7. Ibid., xix.

8. U.S. Bureau of the Census, *Fifteenth Census of the United States*, 1930 *Abstract of the Census, Population*, Table 14: "Population of Cities Having, in 1930, 100,000 Inhabitants or More" (Washington, D.C.: GPO, 1933), 24.

9. James M. Day, "El Paso: Mining Hub for Northern Mexico, 1880–1920," *Password* 24, no. 1 (Spring 1979): 24.

10. "Making the Rounds with El Paso—El Paso Trade Territory," *GEP* I, no. 1 (November 1919): 17.

11. Edward A. Leonard, *Rails at the Pass of the North*, Monograph 63 (El Paso: Texas Western Press, 1981), 36.

12. Hart, *Empire and Revolution*, 33–34, 128; George J. Sánchez, *Becoming Mexican American: Ethnicity, Culture, and Identity in Chicano Los Angeles, 1900–1945* (New York: Oxford University Press, 1993), 21–22.

13. Leonard, *Rails at the Pass*, 30, 41.

14. Hart, *Empire and Revolution*, 122–23.

15. "El Paso: What It Is; Why It Is the Chief Gateway to Mexico," *GEPSC* 2, no. 3 (April 1921): 18; "El Paso Bids for Business of the Southwest," *GEP* I, no. 1 (November 1919): 20; "Review of Industrial Activities in El Paso during the Year 1919, and Report on the Meeting of Southwestern Open Shop Association," *GEP* 1, no. 4 (March 1920): 85.

16. "Making the Rounds with El Paso," 17.

17. John Sneed, "Frontier Village Now Big City: El Paso People Love Their Town," GEPSC 2, no. 1 (March 1921): 5; Dr. Hugh Crouse, "With Every Natural Resource Plus Climate El Paso Becomes Not Only Great Tourist Point, but Stands Out in the Nation as a Health Resort," GEP I, no. 4 (March 1920): N.p.

18. Crouse, "With Every Natural Resource Plus Climate"; Sneed, "Frontier Village Now Big City"; "Here's What a New El Pasoan Says We Are; Let's Get Busy," *Chamber of Commerce News* 1, no. 9 (January 1923), MS 557, El Paso Chamber of Commerce, Southwest Collection, EPPL.

19. "El Paso: What It Is," 18.

20. "El Paso Welcomes Mexico's Trade," GEP 1, no. 7 (July 1920): 11.

21. "El Paso: What It Is," 19; "Making the Rounds with El Paso," 17.

22. "El Paso: What It Is," 19

23. Silvestre Terrazas, "Reaching the Mexican Consumer by Advertisements That Take into Account Latin Psychology and Mexican Trade Customs" (text of speech), GEP 1, no. 5 (April-May 1920): 8. On at least one occasion, the monthly publication of the El Paso Chamber of Commerce, GEPSC, ran stories in Spanish and English singing the praises of the city. "El Paso: What It Is," 18–19.

24. Jack Danciger, "Go to Mexico, Old Boy, Grow Up with the Mexicans," GEP. 1, no. 7 (July 1920):8.

25. Frank H. Knapp, "El Paso, Growing Factory Center, Has Requisites for Success, GEPSC 2, no. 5 (November 1921): 4.

26. Mexican smelter worker strikes in 1913 are addressed in Chapter 3. On the 1919, El Paso Laundry Workers' Strike, see Mario T. García, "The Chicana in American History: The Mexican Women of El Paso, 1880–1920: A Case Study," *Pacific Historical Review* 49, no. 2 (May 1980): 315–37.

27. Charles Longuemare, "Treasures of Metal," EPT, December 27, 1888.

28. Cleofas Calleros, "El Paso—Then and Now: City's Earlyday Smelters Played Vital Role in Area's Colorful History," EPT, ca. February 1956, "Smelting Industry EPVF.

29. Mary Antoine Lee, "A Historical Survey of the American Smelting and Refining pany" (M.A. thesis, UTEP, 1950), 3–16; "Article on El Paso Smelter Prompts Interesting Reminiscences," *Engineering and Mining Journal*, January 5, 1929, 18, Dudley Collection, folder no. 59, "Mining File, Smelters, American Smelting and Refining," EPPL; Horace D. Marucci, "The American Smelting and Refining Company in Mexico" (Ph.D. diss., Rutgers University, 1995), 45–46.

30. Date cited in Mary Antoine Lee, "A Historical Survey." There are conflicting dates on the opening of the smelter—ranging from 1885 ("AS&R," EPH, October 14, 1930, "Smelting Industry," EPVF) to September 1887 ("Big Smelter Largest of Its Kind," EPT, April 25, 1954, "Smelting Industry," EPVF). James M. Day ("El Paso: Mining Hub") places the date as August 29, 1887.

31. Marucci, "American Smelting and Refining Company," 46; "El Paso: Mining Hub," 23 (quotation)

32. Day, "El Paso: Mining Hub," 24.

33. Chris P. Fox, "El Paso Smelter Anniversary," *Password* 22, no. 4 (Winter 1977): 186.

34. Irwin Unger and Debi Unger, *The Guggenheims: A Family History* (New York: Harper Collins Press, 2005), 69–80.

35. "El Paso Smelting Firm Founded on Man's Ambition to Make Sons Rich," EPHP, September 2, 1936, "Smelting Industry," EPVF.

36. Marucci, "American Smelting and Refining Company," 75.

37. Ibid., 99.

38. Julie Puentes, "Villa, the Mining Industry, and the American Smelting and Refining Company," History Seminar Paper, 1971, Special Collections Department, UTEP Library, El Paso.

39. ASARCO, "Thirteenth Annual Report of the American Smelting and Refining Company, December 31, 1911," Jackson Business Library, Stanford University, Stanford, Calif.; Isaac F. Marcosson, *Metal Magic: The Story of the American Smelting and Refining Company* (New York: Farrar, Straus, 1949), 21 (quotation).

40. Marcosson, *Metal Magic*, 21.

41. "Smelter Here Is the Largest Customs Plant in the World," EPP, October 24, 1929, and "AS&R 30 Affiliated Companies Operate in U.S., Mexico," EPH, October 14, 1930, both in "Smelting Industry," EPVF.

42. On the haciendas and poor Mexican campesinos, see Hart, *Empire and Revolution*, 17–22; George J. Sánchez, *Becoming Mexican American*, 20–24; and Manuela Vásquez Domínguez, in terview.

43. Yolanda Chávez Leyva, "Cruzando la Linea: Engendering the History of Border Mexican Children during the Early Twentieth Century," in *Memories and Migrations Mapping Boricua and Chicana Histories*, ed. Vicki L. Ruiz and John R. Chávez (Urbana:University of Illinois Press, 2008), 71–92; Eithne Luibhéid, *Entry Denied: Controlling Sexuality at the Border* (Minneapolis: University of Minnesota Press, 2002).

44. Mario T. García, *Desert Immigrants: The Mexicans of El Paso, 1880–1920* (New Haven, Conn.: Yale University Press, 1982), 38–44.

45. "Circular and Instructions Replacing Department Letters 5/23 and 26–1917, April 1918, reel 7, frame 0003, INS; Commissioner General of Immigration to Mr. E. J. Fangall, Vice President and General Manager, Fullers Earth Co., Cleveland, November 14, 1917, reel 7, frame 0378, INS.

46. [Illegible name] to W. B. Wilson, Secretary of Labor, July 29, 1918, reel 7, frame 0740, INS.

47. U.S. Department of Labor, Bureau of Immigration, "Annual Report of the Supervising Inspector, District 23 Comprising Texas (Except District 9) Headquartered in El Paso," 1919, 707.

48. On the construction of immigration law and the specific lived experiences of the borderlands, see Mae M. Ngai, *Impossible Subjects: Illegal Aliens and the Making of Modern America* (Princeton, N.J.: Princeton University Press, 2004); S. Deborah Kang, "The Legal Construction of the Borderlands: The INS, Immigration Law, and Immigrant Rights on the U.S.-Mexico Border, 1917–1954" (Ph.D. diss., University of California at Berkeley, 2005); George J. Sánchez, *Becoming Mexican American*, 50–51.

49. J. A. Happer, "Washington Department: Immigration," GEP I, no. 4 (March 1920): 57. For the debate on the extension of exemptions for Mexican labor, see House Committee on Immigration and Naturalization, *Hearings on the Temporary Admission of Illiterate Mexican Laborers*, 66th Cong., 2nd sess., January 30, February 2, 1920 (Washington, D.C.: GPO, 1920), 26–28.

50. Ngai, *Impossible Subjects*, 67.

51. Gunther Peck, *Reinventing Free Labor: Padrones and Immigrant Workers in the North American West, 1880–1930* (Cambridge: Cambridge University Press, 2000), 42.

52. García, *Desert Immigrants*, 52. On the Aguascalientes workers, see INS, reel 7, frames 0718–19, 0721–25.

53. García, *Desert Immigrants*, 51–62.

54. Richard Griswold del Castillo, *La Familia: Chicano Families in the Urban Southwest, 1848 to the Present* (Notre Dame, Ind.: University of Notre Dame Press, 1984), 40. See also Albert Camarillo, *Chicanos in a Changing Society: From Mexican Pueblos to American Barrios in Santa Barbara and Southern California, 1848–1930* (Cambridge: Harvard University Press, 1979), 12–13.

55. Melchor Santana Sr., interview by author, March 25, 1995, tape recording, El Paso.

56. Ramón Salas, interview by author, August 18, 1995, tape recording, El Paso.

57. Carmen Escandón, interview by author (Spanish), May 7, 2002, tape recording, El Paso.

58. Sabina Alva, interview by author (Spanish), March II, 1995, tape recording, El Paso.

59. Enriqueta and Alberto Beard, interview by author (Spanish), July 20, 2000, tape recording, El Paso.

60. Sneed, "Frontier Village Now Big City," 5.

ESSAY 9.4

Latino Landscapes: Postwar Cities and the Transnational Origins of a New Urban America

A.K. Sandoval-Strausz

Source: A.K. Sandoval Strausz, "Latino Landscapes: Postwar Cities and the Transnational Origins of a New Urban America," *The Journal of American History* (December 2014): 804–826.

EDITORS' INTRODUCTION

Urban historians whose scholarship focuses on cities within the United States have long adopted a nation-oriented viewpoint. We have, as is argued in many essays in this part, taken the stance that urban history is a good way to study national history. However, of late, the discipline of history as a whole has benefited from embracing a more global outlook. Urban historians, surprisingly, were a bit late to the game of applying a global outlook to their work. Because cities—especially big cities—are an important part of the global exchange of capital, knowledge, and cultural trends, it clearly makes sense to consider them within a transnational framework. Border cities easily lend themselves to global examination. Cities with large immigrant populations are of course subject to the effect of international trends.

Sandoval-Strausz' article also importantly demonstrates that we must move on from the frame of the "urban crisis." It is true that deindustrialization and ghettoization of groups of urban dwellers destabilized the economies and cultural lives of almost all American cities. The cities in the Rust Belt of the Northeast, Middle Atlantic, and Midwest were particularly hit by the scourge of deindustrialization in the late twentieth century. However, new energy is gathering in many American cities. We need to view the developments of the modern American city with open eyes. **[See Essay 9.1, Thomas J. Sugrue, "Class, Status, and Residence: The Changing Geography of Black Detroit (1996)."]**

In this part we have focused on how the First and Second Great Migration altered the history of the American city, and of the nation itself. All told, approximately six and a half million African Americans moved from the South to the North between 1914–1970. This movement effected American politics, economics, and culture. The Latino migration we are currently witnessing is even larger than the African American migrations. **[See Essay 8.2, Lisa Krissoff Boehm, "Making a Way out of No Way: African American Women and the Second Great Migration" (2009).]** Sandoval-Strausz informs us that 25 million Latinos have migrated or immigrated to American cities. Latinos had unique ways of interacting with and shaping urban spaces. These cultural ways of interacting with cities were born in Latin American communities and transplanted in the United States. Latino Americans held positive attitudes about cities; unlike many non-Hispanic Americans who had been raised on anti-urban sentiments, Latinos embraced and promoted the energy and possibility of the city. Latin American nations had grown due to the power of cities, and cities could positively power the economic and cultural growth of United States as well. Latinos embraced the urban way of life, walking around the city rather than driving, and making the most of city parks. By employing the case study of Oak Cliff, Texas, a community outside of Dallas,

Sandoval-Strausz demonstrates how effective a transnational lens can be for urban history. He takes us beyond the urban crisis to what is beginning to look like an urban renaissance. Oak Cliff transformed from a white community, to an African American community, to a Latino center. By the 1990s, more than 86,000 Latinos lived in Oak Cliff, 51 percent of them foreign-born.

A.K. Sandoval-Strausz directs the Latinx Studies program at Pennsylvania State University, where he is Professor of History. He is the author of *Hotel: An American History* (New Haven, CT: Yale University Press, 2007), which won the Pacific Coast Branch of the American Historical Association's book prize, and was also named one of the best books of 2007 by *Library Journal*. He is the co-editor of *Making Cities Global: The Transnational Turn in Urban History* (Philadelphia: University of Pennsylvania Press, 2018). Sandoval-Strausz received an NEH Public Scholar grant in support of his new book on Latinos and U.S. cities.

LATINO LANDSCAPES: POSTWAR CITIES AND THE TRANSNATIONAL ORIGINS OF A NEW URBAN AMERICA (2014)

The time has come for the next urban history: one that analyzes U.S. cities in their transnational contexts, particularly as they relate to the Americas. Oak Cliff will serve as an example of how this perspective can revise prevailing narratives about cities in the postwar era. I analyze how U.S.-born, immigrant, and migrant Latinos were able to repopulate and revive the area, and how they integrated it into a pan-American urban system in which faraway municipalities became tightly bound to one another. While my focus is on a single neighborhood to provide needed analytical detail, analogous processes of Latinization have taken hold in numerous city districts, including Pilsen–Little Village in Chicago; the North Corona section of Queens, New York; the Mitchell Street area in Milwaukee; Barry Square in Hartford, Connecticut; vast stretches of Central, East, and South Los Angeles; and practically all of Miami. Taken together they represent a transnational transformation of American cities that calls for a new phase in urban history.

The historiography of cities in the postwar United States is superb, but it has reached a chronological and conceptual impasse. We have a broad and sophisticated understanding of the decline of cities and the rise of suburbia thanks to two generations of scholarship, from the foundational works of Kenneth Jackson and Arnold Hirsch in the 1980s to outstanding books published since the mid-

1990s. By analyzing dramatic changes in the way Americans structured their built environments and occupied the national landscape, historians have revealed major transformations in the everyday lives and political choices of tens of millions of people.[1]

But these histories explain an urban America that is no longer the one we see around us. This scholarship developed in an era of urban crisis when attention was focused on white flight, neighborhood abandonment, rising crime, and severe fiscal deterioration. The period was bounded by the Watts riots of 1965 and the Los Angeles riots of 1992, and emblematized by the municipal near-bankruptcies of the 1970s and the crack cocaine and crime epidemic of the years 1985–1991. Due to the early 1990s recession and the time lag in gathering and publishing demographic, economic, and criminological data, the crisis narrative persisted into the mid-1990s, when some of the most recent mono-graphs were conceptualized. It made sense for scholars confronted with urban pathologies to explain their historical origins. By the late 1990s, however, many of the nation's cities had found paths to recovery (though by no means all of them, and not by every measure, and never without new difficulties). To take just one index of urban well-being, in his hugely influential book *Crabgrass Frontier* (1985), Kenneth Jackson noted that of the twenty-five most populous cities in 1950, eighteen had lost residents by 1980; but if we refer to that same measure today, we find that of the twenty-five biggest cities in 1980, seventeen *gained* residents over the subsequent thirty years. The single largest factor in this reversal has been a rapid increase in the population of Latinos, whose numbers have reached 50 million—one out of every six people in the United States.[2]

These momentous demographic shifts have yet to be incorporated into the paradigms of urban history, in part because the field is still bounded by the nation-state. The postwar historiography remained overwhelmingly domestic until very recently, even as other areas of U.S. history were challenged, and in some cases transformed, by the transnational turn in historical writing. Moreover, in related fields such as urban sociology, geography, and anthropology, much influential research has analyzed cities according to their role in globalization. After forty years in which some of the most important demographic and economic forces acting on cities have operated across borders, urban historians need to reconsider basic assumptions and explanatory frameworks in the field. It stands to reason that this project should begin with the nation's largest transnational population.[3]

This historical reinterpretation puts Latinos at the center of one of the most interesting and important debates in the profession. In "Nuestra América," her 2006 presidential address to the Organization of American Historians, Vicki Ruiz emphasized the need for "a fuller recounting" of the Latino past "encompassing both transhemispheric and community perspectives" because, as she put it—echoing José Martí—"Nuestra América *es* historia americana. Our America *is* American history." This need continues to be a central concern for scholars of Latino history, as attested by the participants in the 2010 "interchange" in the *Journal of American History*. Some of them focused on redefining the geographic boundaries of U.S. history. Adrian Burgos stressed the benefits of "thinking about U.S. history in a transhemispheric frame" in a way that "decenters the United States"; Matt Garcia advocated an "approach [that] would encompass the transnational flows of goods, labor, and culture among Canada, the United States, the Caribbean, and Mexico" to create "a more inclusive conception of what we now call 'American history.'" Another important consideration was the possibility of recasting the

national story. As María Montoya asked, "How does Latina/o history help us tell a richer (and more accurate) story about the founding, making, and telling of U.S. history?" Toward the end of the exchange, Garcia summed up the participants' shared "recognition that Latino history has the power to transform the narrative of 'American history'" in areas such as "labor history, history of the West, economic history, etc."[4]

Latino history is the key to rethinking urban history because Latinos have been central to stabilizing numerous U.S. cities that would otherwise have suffered drastic demographic loss. Over several decades, as Mike Davis has noted, Latinos have become the second most urbanized demographic group in the nation (after Asian Americans, whose history is also essential to reinterpreting postwar urbanism), and any attempt to understand the trajectory of the nation's cities must reckon with the arrival since 1950 of millions of people from elsewhere in the hemisphere. While it would be an oversimplification to say that Latinos saved the nation's cities, it is difficult to imagine how urban America could have sustained itself without this influx of new city dwellers. To foreground my claims with a single numerical comparison: the great migrations of African Americans that so profoundly influenced U.S. cities and the national culture totaled about 5 million people; the migration and immigration of Latinos to the nation's cities has involved approximately 25 million people; and these are just a small subset of the 250 million new urbanites in Latin America in the half century after 1950.[5]

The impact of Latinos on postwar U.S. cities involves far more than numbers, however. Equally important were the culturally specific ways they occupied and produced urban space: their everyday behaviors, residential practices, ownership and patronage of small businesses, and commitment to public presence. We should focus on how Latinos adapted their spatial preferences to the United States: the way they brought distinctive forms of urbanism from culture hearths in Mexico, the Caribbean, and Central and South America. Furthermore, we must recognize this process as a mutually constitutive one that also reshaped landscapes in Latin America. This dynamic became increasingly important because Latinos in effect incorporated U.S. cities into the broader operation of Latin American urban development. In fact, this interdependence grew so markedly—with the timing, volume, geography, and class composition of migrant arrivals and departures determined largely by patterns of urbanization in Latin America—that we need to reinterpret the postwar period in terms of the formation of a hemispheric urban system. While historians have written extensively on postwar deurbanization and suburban growth, a great deal remains to be said about the significant countertrend of Latino urbanization. Indeed, we might even see the existing U.S. historiography as the chronicle of an Anglo exception to the much larger trend of Hispanic urbanization throughout the Americas; and we could further broaden the context to include the post-1950 urbanization of Asia and Africa.

Old Oak Cliff

Oak Cliff lies across the Trinity River from downtown Dallas [...], about three miles southwest of Dealey Plaza. Once a small agricultural community, Oak Cliff was bought up by developers who incorporated it as a town in 1890; when the area attracted fewer residents than hoped, voters approved its annexation to Dallas in 1903. By 1930 the neighborhood consisted of a few thousand mostly single-family homes centered on a small shopping district.[6]

It was federal spending that led to rapid growth in Oak Cliff. In 1941 the War Department ordered the construction of the Naval Weapons Industrial Reserve Plant, an 85-building, 153-acre manufacturing site just eight miles west of the neighborhood. The plant operated throughout World War II and continued for four decades of the Cold War, producing aircrafts, missiles, and other armaments, and providing jobs for tens of thousands of local people. In 1957 the *Dallas Times Herald* reported that the area's population had grown by more than

75 percent between 1940 and 1950, and the *Dallas Morning News* estimated that fifty families were moving in each month. The effect on the urban landscape was remarkable. Aerial photographs from 1942 display only seven or eight blocks of large retail buildings along Jefferson Boulevard and show that a walk of less than ten blocks off this main street would put a person in an undeveloped grassland. Photographs of the same area from 1950 reveal more than twice as many large-scale commercial properties and show numerous roads, house lots, and residences being built on previously open fields.[7]

Population growth in Oak Cliff provided a strong base of consumers and proprietors for the Jefferson Boulevard commercial district, which boomed around midcentury. Photographs from the period show a streetscape crowded with pedestrians, lined with automobiles, and served by a streetcar. Well-maintained storefronts sported elaborate signage, and shops displayed an abundance of consumer goods. [...] City directories likewise attest to a broadly subscribed prosperity. Jefferson Boulevard was served by a number of leading national retailers, including Sears, J.C. Penney, Woolworth, and Kress, but the real backbone of local commerce was the many independent small businesses that clustered along the street. In 1950, for example, the boulevard was home to twenty-four restaurants, nineteen beauty parlors and barbershops, sixteen laundries and cleaners, fourteen furniture stores, thirteen physicians, thirteen dentists, twelve used car dealers, twelve shoe stores, eleven account ants, nine drug stores, and eight lawyers. Occupancy rates of properties on Jefferson also revealed neighborhood prosperity. The 1950 city directory recorded only 27 vacancies out of 744 available storefronts and dwellings along the boulevard. The 1960 city directory showed an increase to 78 vacancies, but this was still a moderate rate given the 1960–1961 recession. Indeed, the neighborhood's prospects were so strong in the early 1960s that the Oak Cliff Bank & Trust decided to erect an expensive fifteen-story modernist headquarters with a glass-and-steel facade that stood out dramatically from the almost entirely low-rise masonry buildings on and around Jefferson.[8]

Oak Cliff had, however, been built on a foundation of racial segregation. The 1940 census recorded that every one of the neighborhood's eleven census tracts was over 95 percent white, and in 1960 all but two of its twenty tracts were over 95 percent white and non-Hispanic. Meanwhile, an adjacent black neighborhood ended abruptly at central Oak Cliff's eastern edge: Ewing Avenue marked the approximate limit of African American settlement, with thousands of black families to the east and very few to the west. These boundaries had been created and maintained by every available means. In the 1910s and 1920s, city officials endorsed restrictive covenants and enacted racial zoning ordinances, and private citizens repeatedly used intimidation and violence to perpetuate residential segregation. These divisions were reinforced in concrete in the 1950s with the construction of Interstates 30 and 35, which cordoned off populations of color to the north and east.[9]

The decline of Oak Cliff was primarily a story of race, though not exclusively or straightforwardly so. The neighborhood suffered significant economic damage early on: in 1955 the city canceled streetcar service from downtown Dallas, reducing foot traffic along Jefferson Boulevard, and in 1956 a local "dry" vote closed Oak Cliff's drinking establishments and limited the profitability of many other businesses. Regarding race relations, the city achieved peaceful integration in many areas. The "Dallas way" involved the kind of incremental (often token) desegregation seen elsewhere in the upper and outer South, where municipal leaders were keen to avoid the kind of racial violence that could jeopardize efforts to attract outside investment and federal spending. In 1953 the mayor promised to desegregate the state fair, though full implementation required eight more years of protests. In 1956, to avoid a proposed Montgomery-style boycott, city officials agreed to establish equal seating on city buses. And in 1961, after several months of sit ins, Dallas restaurants were persuaded to serve black customers, and hotels and other public accommodations soon followed.[10]

But the city fathers proved less capable of managing the desegregation of neighborhoods and schools. Decades of white enforcement of the color line had created a severe shortage of decent housing for African American families. When middle-class black people tried to escape the city's increasingly crowded and run-down ghettoes, whites responded violently. Between 1939 and 1941 a new black high school in South Dallas drew bomb threats and rock-throwing mobs, and even resulted in the use of dynamite to destroy black peoples' homes. In 1950 and 1951 a few black families who moved into the Exline Park neighborhood faced another wave of harassment, vandalism, and house bombings. And when African Americans began to buy homes in eastern Oak Cliff in the late 1950s and early 1960s, white residents engaged in intimidation tactics such as assembling a hostile crowd in one black homeowner's front yard and preparing to burn a cross on another black family's lawn. Tellingly, the Oak Cliff police substation began training local officers in riot-control procedures.[11]

In the past, the city's white leadership had managed such situations by privately buying out African American families, financing segregated housing developments for middle-class blacks, and securing indictments (though never convictions) of alleged bombers. When it became clear, however, that such half measures could no longer preserve residential segregation, whites began to leave city neighborhoods for racially homogeneous districts in North Dallas and the suburbs. The largest wave of departures came later, though. In 1971, in response to the refusal of Dallas officials to enact meaningful school desegregation, a federal court ordered the implementation of an integration plan that included busing. In 1986 Jim Schutze, an astute observer of race relations in Dallas, concisely described the response: "The whites yanked their kids, took off for the educational hills, and they haven't come back yet."[12]

The Making of Nuevo Oak Cliff

The Latinization of Oak Cliff was the most prominent example of the broad transformations that swelled the previously small

Hispanic population of Dallas until it surpassed that of both white Anglos and African Americans to become the largest demographic in the city. This process, while initially determined by local decisions, became increasingly driven by factors originating beyond the nation's borders. Correspondingly, the Mexican Americans who were first involved were soon joined by Latino migrants who made the neighborhood into a major locus of economic, social, and cultural interaction between the United States and Latin America.[13]

Before the transformation of Oak Cliff, Hispanic settlement in Dallas was centered in Little Mexico, the area just west of downtown where people from across the border gathered beginning around 1910 and for more than fifty years thereafter. There were other ethnically Mexican neighborhoods in Dallas, but it was Little Mexico that people understood as the heart of the community—the place they referred to as simply "el barrio." It contained the most important institutions, including Our Lady of Guadalupe Church, the main Spanish-speaking commercial district, St. Ann's School, Crozier Tech High School, and especially Pike Park. Little Mexico was home to the great majority of what was nonetheless a small Spanish-surnamed population, one that as late as 1960 totaled 29,464 people, only 4.3 percent of all Dallasites.[14]

The Latino presence in Oak Cliff began in the late 1940s with Mexican Americans coming in from el barrio across the Trinity River. Anita Martínez, who was born in Little Mexico in 1925, recalled that after World War II all four of her sisters moved to Oak Cliff. The neighborhood also proved attractive to the owners of El Fénix restaurant—a Little Mexico landmark and the oldest and most recognizable Mexican American business in Dallas; they opened their second location in Oak Cliff in 1948. These and other early arrivals initially made up a very small population: of the 83,000 people the 1960 census counted in Oak Cliff, only about 1,500 had Spanish surnames, and of these Latinos only 130 were foreign-born.[15]

The transition of Latinos to Oak Cliff hastened dramatically in the late 1950s and 1960s, when Dallas's entirely white and Anglo leadership ran three highway projects through Little Mexico, displacing or disrupting much of el barrio. For Dallas Mexican Americans it is clear what happened. As Ronnie Villareal recalls, "they cut right through the heart of the barrio with the Dallas North Tollway. When you cut right through the heart of it, what are you going to do?" He adds: "We were young at that time. ... We didn't participate in politics, you know, and they just went through. ... People were, they were good people." At this point his wife, Leonor, breaks in: "No se sabían defender. Eramos tan inocentes y tan buenos." (They did not know how to defend themselves. We were so innocent and so good.) Jesse Tafalla agrees: "Back then we didn't have any recourse ... we didn't get our first elected officials until the 1970s. ... We had no representation, we didn't understand the politics. They just kept us in the barrio." The gradual dismantling of Little Mexico forced thousands of people to find new places to settle; one result was that during the 1960s Oak Cliff's Spanish-heritage population rose more than sixfold to over 9,500 while remaining overwhelmingly American-born.[16]

The era of Latino transnationalism in Oak Cliff, which began around 1970, owed to changing economic conditions in Mexico and to private and public decision making in both countries. The late 1960s crisis in Mexican agriculture caused great hardship in rural areas, setting off an intensified exodus from the countryside. Employers in the United States continued their search for low-wage labor, and the two nations' long history of migration positioned Mexico as the likeliest source of workers. The Immigration and Nationality Act of 1965 (also known as the Hart-Celler Act), often understood as a source of increased immigration, actually had a contradictory effect on newcomers. As Mae Ngai has demonstrated, the act imposed the first-ever quota on immigration from Latin America while also making nonquota familial admissions easier. In the short term the law criminalized older patterns of migration; in the longer term it quickened the pace of documented arrivals from the region.[17]

In the early years of immigration to Oak Cliff, most new arrivals came from small communities in central Mexico. Tereso Ortiz left the town of Ocampo in the state of Guanajuato in 1971 at the age of twenty-one. With only a fourth-grade education, he initially worked as a dishwasher and vegetable packer, then as a store manager and eventually as a construction supervisor. Ortiz also became one of the foremost community leaders in Dallas as the director of Casa Guanajuato, an immigrant service organization headquartered in Oak Cliff. Recalling the early years among his Mexican compatriots, he says: "We came from rural areas, little villages, ninety or ninety-five percent of us, I would say. Very few people came from offices where they used computers, or in those years, typewriters ... we basically came from the countryside." The same was true of immigrants throughout the city well into the 1980s. *The Other Side of the Border* (1987), a Dallas Public Television program that examined the origins of Mexican immigrants to the city, documented the rudimentary conditions of rural Mexico using footage of unpaved roads, small adobe dwellings with dirt floors and no running water, and outdoor food markets lacking refrigeration. While these conditions were not representative of Mexico generally, they were not entirely atypical of a country where, as late as 1980, almost half the population lived in localities of fewer than 15,000 people.[18]

These rural Mexicans were joined beginning in the 1980s by migrants from urban areas throughout Latin America, where changes in economic policy, escalating civil conflicts, and financial crises set new groups of people into motion. Claudia Torrescano, a journalist with Univisión in Dallas, was both a participant and an observer in this process. She came from Mexico City in 1989 soon after finishing college, drawn to Dallas by increasing opportunities for bilingual professionals in the business and communications sectors. "Before it was everything rural," she recalls, but Mexico's professional classes increasingly emigrated "because they just cannot find jobs in the cities in Mexico." Torrescano is seconded by Yolette García, who covered Dallas for twenty years as a journalist at the public television affiliate KERA. Agreeing that later Latin American immigrants were "not only the poor" but "middle-class and upper-middle-class people as well," García points to a "brain drain" of educated urbanites pursuing economic opportunities in the United States. Some of these newcomers were refugees from intensifying civil wars in Central America, where U.S. intervention had helped destabilize the region; Dallas became a major destination for Salvadorans, in particular.[19]

These transnational factors caused a marked upsurge in the number of Latinos in Oak Cliff, with Latin American newcomers surpassing U.S.-born Hispanics as the predominant presence. In the 1970s the Latino population rose to over 27,000, of whom slightly under 30 percent were immigrants. These trends then accelerated: in the 1980s Latino numbers swelled to almost 53,000; and by the close of the 1990s they totaled over 86,000, with the foreign-born accounting for over 51 percent, a figure that understates the influence of the immigrants because thousands of Latinos whom the census enumerated as citizens were the immigrants' U.S.-born children.[20]

These new arrivals were essential to Oak Cliff's viability because they eventually reversed the area's long-term demographic crisis. The neighborhood's growth had stalled after midcentury, a particularly worrisome development because Dallas as a whole nearly doubled its population between 1950 and 1970 and continued to grow in every subsequent decade. Oak Cliff was losing its hold in particular on the white Anglo residents who had made up virtually all of the area's population. The trend began slowly, in the 1950s and 1960s, with the loss of over 11,000 Anglo residents, or 13 percent of the neighborhood. Departures hastened in the 1970s, and by 2000 Oak Cliff had lost 80 percent of its peak population of non-Hispanic whites.[21]

Yet the neighborhood's demographic history is more complex than can be summed up by conventional notions of white flight or racial succession. Over fifty years, Oak Cliff changed from an almost exclusively white Anglo neighborhood into a majority Latino neighborhood with substantial minorities of whites and blacks. Notably, when the area's population was near its postwar low around 1980, its residents were still mostly (55 percent) white Anglos. Black people had only started moving into the area at the same time as the first immigrant Latinos: while African Americans had accounted for only 0.5 percent of the population of Oak Cliff as late as 1970, their numbers grew substantially thereafter, and by 1990 they composed almost 12 percent of the neighborhood. And although most whites had indeed left, a loyal core of long-time residents remained and were joined by other whites who chose to move in. Meanwhile, the proportion of Latino residents rose from under 2 percent in 1960, gaining in every decade until, by 2000, they made up fully 76 percent of this new *barrio*. The aggregate effect of these shifts was striking. After more than three decades of stagnating or shrinking population, sometime after 1980 the neighborhood began to grow quickly. Its population increased by 10 percent in the 1980s and 22 percent in the 1990s, outmatching even the rapid pace of growth in Dallas as a whole. By 2000, it boasted over 113,000 residents, 30 percent more than at its previous peak in 1950.[22]

The Latino-led revitalization of Oak Cliff was by no means achieved solely through the force of numbers, however. Just as important were the distinctive urbanistic practices of new residents—the way they socialized, walked, shopped, and dwelled. Their everyday customs were adaptations of long-standing urban behaviors common in Mexico and elsewhere in Latin America.

While the claim of a distinctively Latin American urbanism may strike some readers as essentialist, there are good reasons to believe that the Spanish American approach to cities has for centuries been very different from the Anglo American one. In Latin America a particularly urban orientation was built into the region's landscape at least as far back as 1573, when the *Recopilación de leyes de las Indias* (Laws of the Indies) codified rules for constructing colonial settlements, mandating numerous details of city form and rewarding town founders with heritable titles of nobility. The region's leading intellectuals likewise counterposed the culture and sociability of the city against the isolation and backwardness of rural life, a trope most clearly expressed in Domingo Faustino Sarmiento's extraordinarily influential *Facundo: Civilizacióny barbarie* (Facundo: Civilization and barbarism) (1845) and recapitulated many times thereafter. This valorization of city life contrasted sharply with the persistent antiurbanism of English and Anglo-American culture, from the eighteenth-century rural idealization of Daniel Defoe and Thomas Jefferson to the twentieth-century suspicion of urbanism shared by Ebenezer Howard and Frank Lloyd Wright. It is worth noting that Kenneth Jackson and Robert Fishman cite Anglo-American antiurbanism as a key determinant of suburbanization. Moreover, throughout much of the twentieth century, many governments in Latin America explicitly and unequivocally used the power of the state to encourage urban growth, as with Mexico's policy of centralizing industry while burdening agriculture, or the Dominican Republic's decision to simultaneously clear rural areas and subsidize city building. Here, too, is an instructive contrast with the United States, where the federal government provided massive subsidies for suburbanization in the form of mortgage aid, highway construction, tax deductions, and other national policies. In sum, Latin America's tendency toward urban megalocephaly—with residents of the largest city in a given country regularly accounting for 20 to 35 percent of the entire national population—is neither coincidence nor the result of impersonal globalizing forces. Rather it is a product of deeply rooted cultural preferences and deliberate political decisions.[23]

This urban tradition had already been exemplified in Dallas's Little Mexico, where the city's ethnic Mexicans had imbued *el barrio* with a strong Hispanic place identity. Nowhere was this clearer than in Pike Park, which residents refashioned into the plaza for the entire city. [...] As Daniel Arreola and Chris Wilson have shown, *plazas* have long been vital aspects of Hispanic urbanism as the places where people have manifested themselves as solidary communities through fiestas and everyday sociability. Dallas Mexican Americans used Pike Park in exactly this way. Anita Martínez remembers that the Pike Park "pool was right in the center ... so the boys would go one way, and the girls would go the other way, and we'd pass little notes to one another," a description that precisely matches the *paseo*, a historically popular Spanish and Mexican courtship activity in which men and women promenaded around the *plaza* in opposite directions. Jesse Tafalla, who lived in the city's El Pozo *barrio* in the 1950s, similarly recalled the park as the most important destination for young people out socializing. Decades later, people spoke of Pike Park in the same terms. At a public hearing in 1975 Mexican American participants called the park "a form of downtown ... a center for our people," asserted that "people all over come to Pike to see what's happening among us Mexican Americans," and affirmed that "if a person is new in town and wants to get to know people he soon comes to Pike." In 1975, in response to Mexican Americans' requests for "a more Mexican kind of park," the Dallas Planning Department partnered with more than two dozen Hispanic civic organizations in a major renovation that refurbished Pike Park's community clubhouse in a Mexican architectural style, replaced the pool with an actual *plaza*, and installed a *kiosco*, a type of open pavilion or bandstand that has for 150 years been one of the characteristic landscape elements of the Mexican *plaza*. These efforts to create a distinctively Hispanic urbanism were unmistakable gestures of cultural ownership.[24]

As Mexican Americans settled in Oak Cliff and Latin American immigrants came to the neighborhood, they re-created a new Latino urbanism. The most basic element of this transformation involved an affinity for walking. Compared with most Dallasites, Latino immigrants were avid pedestrians. As Tereso Ortiz put it recently, one of the reasons he and his compatriots were attracted to Oak Cliff in the 1970s was its scale and compactness, which made it accessible on foot. "You could play in the street, in the parks," he noted, "not like North Dallas, where you never got out of your car." A similar note is sounded by Rosario Gaytán, an American-born Oak Cliff bank officer who came to the neighborhood in 1974. Contrasting the customs of newer Latino residents with what she saw decades ago, she observes: "Walking, I mean, it's a culture thing to me. Around here, everybody, they'll walk to the bank, they'll walk down the street. And growing up, Anglos didn't." These recollections are substantiated by census data. In 1990, when Oak Cliff was 57 percent Latino, in every tract in the neighborhood Hispanic households owned substantially fewer automobiles per person than did white Anglo households. The tract-by-tract disparity ranged from a low of Anglos having almost half again as many cars available to a high of almost two and a half times as many. Such differences should be unsurprising given the history of the automobile in the Americas. Mexicans who settled in Oak Cliff had grown up in a nation where private car ownership was relatively uncommon until the 1970s. Moreover, most of these immigrants had come from rural areas, where automobiles were least common. For example, in the village of Tzintzuntzan, Michoacán, none of the 246 inhabitants owned a car or truck in 1945, only one of 320 (0.3 percent) did in 1960, and just eleven of 360 (3.1 percent) did in 1970. Considering that historians grant the automobile a virtually unparalleled degree of influence on the decline of center cities and the rise of suburbia in the United States, the propensity of immigrant Latinos to move about on foot should be accorded tremendous significance in the morphology of late twentieth-century cities.[25]

A related element of Oak Cliff's Latino urbanism involved changes in the ownership, scale, and location of businesses. A leading symptom of the U.S. urban crisis was the gradual relocation of retailing from city centers to suburban malls, which severely damaged neighborhood viability and municipal tax bases. In Oak Cliff this trend was countervailed by Latinos, who served as both customers and proprietors of local shops. Nick Cordova, the Anglo owner of Charco Broiler restaurant, recounts how his family's decades-old business on Jefferson Boulevard nearly had to close in the early 1990s. "I think the Hispanic crowd is what saved us," he explains. "There's people in this area, Hispanics mainly, who walk. They walk up to the dollar store, they walk up to Famsa to buy furniture, but then they gotta walk by us, and they're gonna get a steak or a burger or chicken or whatever ... I mean, it's just a difference—not everybody's driving everywhere like your Americans are used to." The same dynamic benefitted many other Anglo-owned businesses: for example, the Oak Cliff Bank & Trust tower became home to a Bank of America branch that began to offer services in Spanish in the 1980s and prospered by catering to a mostly Latino clientele.[26]

As older neighborhood businesses closed, a wide variety of operations owned by American-born, and especially immigrant, Latinos sprang up in their place. City directories reveal that Spanish-surnamed proprietors operated only a single business on Jefferson Boulevard in 1970 and a mere handful in 1980; but they accounted for dozens of stores in 1990 and by 2000 represented the overwhelming majority of shopkeepers. A few of these grew into large-scale concerns, most notably Gloria's Restaurant, which was opened in 1985 by Gloria Rubio, who was then an undocumented immigrant from El Salvador who came to the United States in 1983 after fleeing her homeland's civil war. From operating a single Oak Cliff location that catered to other Salvadoran expatriates, Rubio expanded her business to twelve locations eventually serving a more Anglo than Latino clientele. Much more common, of course, were smaller businesses of the kind familiar in Latino neighborhoods: *bodegas* (small groceries), *panaderías* (bakeries), *taquerías* (taco shops) and other restaurants,

insurance agencies, *botánicas* (shops selling alternative medicines and religious items), jewelers, travel agencies, *quinceañera* (sweet fifteen party) and bridal shops, and international money transfer agencies. Establishments such as these became mainstays of Oak Cliff retailing.[27]

This rapid growth in Latino small businesses took place in a climate of shrinking opportunities for English-speaking local entrepreneurs. Beginning in the 1980s, transformations in information technology, pricing practices, and organizational theory increasingly favored large-scale corporate retailers over family-run stores and other small proprietorships. Latino businesses remained viable in Oak Cliff due to the culture of the areas immigrant population. Foreign-born Latinos were accustomed to operating and patronizing neighborhood businesses because before the 1990s, retailing in Latin America was far less consolidated than in the United States, and microentrepreneurship became a common economic strategy across the region in the 1980s. This corresponded well with the early twentieth-century commercial streetscapes of Jefferson Boulevard and Davis Street, where small storefronts once run by independent Anglo shopkeepers were now occupied by Hispanic proprietors. And because they could cater to a Spanish-speaking clientele in their native language, these businesspeople retained their customers while Anglophone mom-and-pop operations were being driven out of business by big-box stores.[28]

The neighborhood's commercial expansion proceeded in tandem with residential growth. The Latinos who moved into Oak Cliff saved it from the kind of mass abandonment that elsewhere in America emptied out block after block and turned so much housing stock into derelict or burned-out husks. The multigenerational and multifamily living arrangements common among local immigrants generated marked increases in the neighborhood's population density. While this often indicated overcrowding, density has also been used as a rough proxy for viable urbanism in the United States. From 1950 to 1980 the population density of Oak Cliff hovered around 5,600 to 5,800 people per square mile before immigration drove that number much higher: 6,173 in 1990 and 7,558 in 2000. This dense settlement pattern was specific to Latin Americans across the Dallas region: census plots of foreign-born Mexicans and Central Americans in 1990 correspond very closely to the most densely populated census tracts in the metropolitan area—and notably, there was no such strong correlation with census plots of immigrants from Europe, Asia, or Africa.[29]

Moreover, by the late 2000s, Oak Cliff's nearly 100,000 new Latino residents collectively devoted millions of hours of labor and billions of dollars to the upkeep of houses and grounds; and because so many of them were employed in construction, landscaping, and housekeeping, they brought specialized knowledge of materials and techniques to the task. The aggregate effect of these efforts was remarkable. In the 1960s and 1970s the median value of owner-occupied property had fallen in, respectively, seventeen and sixteen of Oak Cliff's twenty census tracts—this at a time when property values in Dallas as a whole were rising. But beginning in the 1980s these values in Oak Cliff increased in every single tract, climbing far faster than in the city as a whole. Median gross rents in the neighborhood had remained fairly stable in the 1960s but had fallen in sixteen out of the twenty tracts during the 1970s; starting in the 1980s they rose in all tracts but one, far outstripping the citywide rate of increase.[30]

Just as importantly, Oak Cliff's newest residents occupied their dwellings in culturally particular ways conducive to neighborhood improvement. The Dallas Morning News columnist Tod Robberson has noted that the most visible change in the built environment was the appearance of fences around many front yards. Front-property enclosure was the most common feature of what geographers and urbanists first identified in the 1980s as a Mexican American residential form that combined the freestanding Anglo dwelling with the Mexican courtyard house. This hybrid homescape extended the social space out of the house, onto the porch, and into the front yard to a chain link or wrought iron fence at the property line. In contrast with the archetypal Anglo front yard—well kept but empty of people—this Latino domestic space saw constant use, with family and friends sitting on porches or stairs, supervising small children who could play safely inside the fence line. (This use of la yarda, as many Spanish speakers called it, also had implications for street life and safety, as we shall see shortly.) In 1991 the urbanist and planner James Rojas interpreted this homescape as a deliberate departure from the bourgeois household's emphasis on indoor areas and backyards, which he saw as increasingly privatized spaces that implicitly turned away from neighbors and the street. It is thus not surprising that the rising number of immigrants in Oak Cliff was accompanied by conflicts over the proper use of public space. Anglo overreactions to peaceable streetside gatherings were so frequent that in 1993 a Latino commentator for the Dallas Morning News repeated a popular joke that "the definition of a 'gang' by law enforcement officials is any gathering of five or more Hispanics."[31]

The Latino landscapes of Oak Cliff were not simply the result of cultural diffusion from Latin America—they also developed in constant interaction with the newest residents towns and cities of origin, with decision making in each location increasingly predicated on the other. Some of the best evidence of the way immigrants integrated their Dallas neighborhood into a transnational urban system lies in the reciprocal changes in their home communities. This can be seen most clearly through the methodology of the architecture scholar Sarah Lynn López, whose fieldwork in Jalisco, Mexico, led to her concept of "remittance space"—the various built environments created by migrants as they move between Mexico and the United States. My own research indicates that in Oak Cliff this process began with migrants who devoted income they earned in Dallas to reshaping the landscape in their hometowns. César Valenciano Vázquez, the president of the local Casa Durango (a service organization run by and for people from the state of Durango), recalls that "as soon as we established ourselves in Dallas and managed to get steady jobs ... we set about finding ways to build or renovate our homes in Mexico." Community projects soon followed: "We started inviting friends, neighbors, and relatives," and in this way the city's *duranguenses* "organized migrant clubs and neighborhood associations ... and started pooling our money to pave the streets of our towns, fix up the schools, provide electricity, and paint our churches."[32]

Grassroots efforts such as these attracted the attention of government officials, who responded by fostering new forms of cooperation with migrants. In Mexico in 1992, the state governor of Zacatecas, Mexico, established Dos por Uno (Two for One), a program under which the state provided double matching funds for hometown infrastructure and development projects. Dallas's Zacatecans joined the program in 1997 by establishing the U.S. nonprofit organization Federación de Clubes Zacatecanos del Norte de Texas (FCZNT) (Federation of Zacatecan Clubs of North Texas). Its first president was Manuel Rodela, who came to the United States from Zacatecas in 1971 at the age of twenty-nine and settled in Oak Cliff in 1985. Rodela maintains an archive of correspondence, official paperwork, photographs, newspaper clippings, posters, and reports that document the organization's more than fifteen years of coordinating its many constituent clubs. These usually hometown-based clubs had financed projects in the years before Dos por Uno—an era with no matching funds that some migrants jokingly refer to as "Cero por Uno"—but with the support of state and municipal authorities they multiplied their initiatives, which included a medical clinic, a church, and a rodeo ring.[33]

The Mexican government adopted Dos por Uno at the national level in 2002 as Tres por Uno (Three for One), a program in which federal, state, and municipal governments each matched migrants' spending on local projects. This additional funding further intensified the Zacatecans' efforts. The FCZNT's archive contains numerous examples of the Mexican government's official forms certifying each new club that joined the organization to qualify for matching funds, and its collection of photographs documents a wide variety of activities in the following years. Hundreds of images show FCZNT officers attending national conferences that brought together Zacatecan clubs and federations from across the United States; official visits to Dallas by Mexican state and federal delegations; and the fund raising for, the sculpting of, and the transportation from Zacatecas to Dallas of the *Monumento al Migrante Caído* (Monument to the Fallen Migrant), a memorial to those who lost their lives going from Mexico to the United States. These photographs also depict many trips home to Zacatecas to unveil Tres por Uno projects: in one, Rodela stands in front of a poster announcing the 2005 construction of new classrooms in the tiny town of El Fuerte; in another, FCZNT members cut the ribbon and open the main valve of a new water well they financed in the *municipio* (roughly equivalent to a U.S. county) of Tepechitlán. But perhaps the clearest evidence of what these projects meant to the *zacatecanos* comes from the *anuarios*, the federation's yearly publications. [...] In addition to letters of greeting from state officials and advertisements for Zacatecan-owned local businesses, the *anuarios* contain numerous announcements of the projects completed that year by Dallas clubs. These public notices demonstrate the migrants' pride in their contributions to improving infrastructure and institutions in the small towns and cities of Zacatecas.[34]

Dallas-based migrants from many other Mexican states and towns also registered clubs and federations and began undertaking projects as part of Tres por Uno. The records of the Secretaría de Desarrollo Social (Secretariat of Social Development), the federal agency responsible for coordinating these initiatives, display the tremendous variety of projects initiated from Dallas: these included the construction, extension, or renovation of roads, housing, drainage systems, electrical grids, street paving, potable water pipes, lecture halls, community centers, streetlights, schoolyards, shelters, chapels, athletic fields, public resorts, a town cemetery, and a water park. By decade's end, Dallas's Mexican migrants were starting dozens of projects every year, setting into motion tens of millions of pesos in construction funding annually. Moreover, their compatriots in other U.S. cities were doing the same. Within two years of the introduction of Tres por Uno, the Secretaría de Desarrollo Social had registered projects by migrant clubs in dozens of cities ranging in size from Watsonville, California, to Racine, Wisconsin, to Portland, Oregon, to Los Angeles and New York City. In its first ten years, the program grew from twenty clubs and just over 100,000 pesos to 795 clubs and more than 546 million pesos in annual spending. Between 2002 and 2012, 12 billion pesos were invested in Mexico through Tres por Uno.[35]

Meanwhile, other governments across Latin America established closer cooperation with their citizens abroad and instituted their own migrant building programs. Dallas's Salvadorans, the second largest group of Latino migrants in the city, formed the Asociación Salvadoreña Americana (Salvadoran American Association) in 1991 and began to sponsor public projects in their hometowns. The association started channeling remittances through the government as part of relief efforts after the 1998 hurricane and the 2001 earthquakes, and in 2004 the government of El Salvador established Unidos por la Solidaridad (United for Solidarity), a program modeled upon Tres por Uno. Similar programs were launched by Colombia, Ecuador, and Guatemala; Honduras and Nicaragua have also made initial efforts in this direction. In the broadest sense, then, transnational migrants initiated a sustained exchange of people, money, and construction that officially linked communities and reshaped built environments throughout the hemisphere.[36]

This emergent transnational urban system was also crucially shaped by government action in the United States. The Immigration Reform and Control Act (IRCA) of 1986, which immigrant Latinos call la amnistía (the amnesty), offered permanent-resident status to those who had entered or remained in the country illegally before 1982 and maintained continuous residence; this amnesty provision ultimately allowed 3 million people to regularize their status. In Oak Cliff the IRCA was a transformative event because it allowed immigrants to invest in their neighborhood in a way they could not when they were undocumented. "The key was when they passed the amnesty for so many people," Gloria Rubio remembers, "and the people who were here, we started investing, started buying homes, started opening second businesses, third businesses, and so all those people, just like us, that's what they did, and that's what made Oak Cliff improve." Similarly, Alberto López, for over twenty years the owner of a large jewelry store on Jefferson Boulevard, observes that while business dropped off right after the IRCA because many newly regularized residents went home to Mexico for extended visits, spending recovered when they returned to Oak Cliff and began to buy houses, cars, and other goods; he also emphasizes the importance of Mexican investment capital in his and other businesses.[37]

The precise role of the IRCA is important to a debate more than a decade old: in the *Journal of American History*'s 1999 special issue on transnationalism, Jorge Durand, Douglas Massey, and Emilio Parrado asserted that "IRCA inaugurated a new era of Mexico—United States migration" because "it was instrumental in transforming a predominantly rural, male, and temporary flow of migrant workers into a feminized, urbanized, and permanent population of settled immigrants." According to this argument, while la amnistía allowed many immigrants to stay permanently, millions who were not eligible were trapped inside the country by increased border enforcement. The evidence from Oak Cliff additionally foregrounds the new legal residents created by the IRCA: people whose regularized status allowed them to establish or expand transnational travel, business, informational, and family linkages. The creation of a cross-border transit network between Dallas and Mexico provides one example. As late as the mid-1980s, the city's Mexican immigrants still relied upon an unlicensed fleet of large vans called camionetas to carry them to and from their homeland. After the IRCA, however, Latino entrepreneurs built larger, more durable, and more professional transport businesses. Seven firms still in business in 2007 were established between 1986 and 1989, another thirteen in the 1990s, and fourteen more after 2000. These newer companies—of which "none had officially existed before the 1986 IRCA legislation"—added full-size motor coaches and computerized ticketing, and eventually offered passengers continuous carriage without the need to transfer to Mexican-registered buses. They provided direct service to scores of cities, and even small *municipios* such as Ocampo had Dallas-based bus lines. Oak Cliff emerged as the most important travel hub, boasting "the greatest number and highest concentration of Hispanic transportation firms" in the metropolitan area. Indeed, travel between parts of Mexico and Dallas even spawned a transnational television program. *Me voy pa'l Norte* (I'm off to the North), a weekly show about small communities in Guanajuato state and the lives of migrant *guanajuatenses* there and in the United States, was produced in Guanajuato and broadcast there and in Dallas.[38]

Looking at *nuevo* Oak Cliff more broadly, we can see how its new residents initiated a large-scale process of urban reinvestment: Latinos not only devoted a great deal of economic capital to their homes and businesses but they also built up social capital in the neighborhood. In her enormously influential book *The Death and Life of Great American Cities* (1961), Jane Jacobs wrote at length of the importance of "eyes upon the street"— casual surveillance by people sitting on stoops, looking out of windows, and minding stores—in keeping order in urban neighborhoods. In Oak Cliff the Latinos who socialized in front of their homes and ran storefront and sidewalk businesses accomplished precisely that kind of neighborhood monitoring. Their participation in local clubs and transnational hometown associations further fostered street presence and civic engagement. There is good reason to believe that these practices made the neighborhood safer. The National Neighborhood Crime Study's multicity dataset for the 1999–2001 period reveals that even though virtually every Oak Cliff tract was more socioeconomically disadvantaged than the median Dallas tract, the neighborhood's murder rate was statistically significantly lower than in similar areas. The fast-growing immigrant population may also have been a factor in the broad-based decline in crime throughout Dallas, where the

number of homicides per year peaked at more than 500 in 1991 before falling almost every year thereafter to 133 in 2011, the safest year since 1967. Sociologists increasingly agree on the causal link between immigrant Latino population growth and a decrease in crime. The Harvard University criminologist Robert J. Sampson has demonstrated that immigrants are less likely to break the law than native-born Americans and that concentrations of Hispanic immigrants in a neighborhood consistently reduce rates of violent crime; other studies echo these findings. Indeed, researchers have identified a "Latino paradox" in which Hispanics "do better on a wide range of social indicators ... than one would expect given their socioeconomic disadvantages."[39]

These conclusions raise questions about whether the classic literature on urban space and social capital is contradicted by neighborhood life among transnational Latinos. For more than thirty-five years, scholars have decried the loss of community, the rise of privatized sociability, and the decline of civic participation in the postwar United States. From Richard Sennett's influential *The Fall of Public Man* (1974) to Robert Putnam's *Bowling Alone* (2000), a rising chorus of alarm has been raised about the state of the public realm. This narrative may accurately describe changes among non-Hispanics, but it does not fit places such as Oak Cliff, where immigrants have made constant use of public space and maintained exceptionally strong associational connections locally and with their home communities. [...] Because the experiences of this fastest-growing group of new Americans so sharply diverge from existing accounts, we will need to reconsider our assumptions about civil society in the United States.[40]

NOTES

1. Kenneth T. Jackson. *Crabgrass Frontier: The Suburbanization of the United States* (New York, 1985); Arnold R. Hirsch, *Making the Second Ghetto: Race and Housing in Chicago, 1940–1960* (New York, 1983); Sugrue, *Origins of the Urban Crisis*; Becky M. Nicolaides, *My Blue Heaven: Life and Politics in the Working-Class Suburbs of Los Angeles, 1920–*

1965 (Chicago, 2002); Robert O. Self, *American Babylon: Race and the Struggle for Postwar Oakland* (Princeton, 2003); Eric Avila, *Popular Culture in the Age of White Flight: Fear and Fantasy in Suburban Los Angeles* (Berkeley, 2004); Alison Isenberg, *Downtown America: A History of the Place and the People Who Made It* (Chicago, 2005); Kevin M. Kruse, *White Flight: Atlanta and the Making of Modern Conservatism* (Princenton, 2005); Matthew D. Lassiter, *The Silent Majority: Suburban Politics in the Sunbelt South*(Princeton, 2007).

2. On the riots, near-bankruptcies, and crack and crime epidemics, see Jon C. Teaford, "The Debacle," in *The Metropolitan Revolution: The Rise of Post-urban America*, by Jon C. Teaford (New York, 2006), 125–64. Jackson, *Crabgrass Frontier*, 4; U.S. Census Bureau, *Statistical Abstract of the United States: 2003; No. HS-7. Population of the Largest 75 Cities: 1960–2000* (Washington, 2003). U.S. Census Bureau, *United States Summary: 2010; Population and Housing Unit Counts—2010 Census of Population and Housing, CPH-2-1* (Washington, 2012), table 37. U.S. Census Bureau, *United States: 2010; Summary Population and Housing Characteristics—2010 Census of Population and Housing, CPH-1-1* (Washington, 2013), table 2. I use the term *Latino* because this article involves communities consisting of U.S.-born citizens of Hispanic heritage; documented, undocumented, and naturalized U.S. residents from Mexico and other nations in Latin America; and the often-mixed-status households in which they live. On the conceptual complexity of the term *Latino*, see Suzanne Oboler, *Ethnic Labels, Latino Lives: Identity and the Politics of (Re)Presentation in the United States* (Minneapolis, 1995); Arlene Dávila, *Latinos, Inc.: The Marketing and Making of a People* (Berkeley, 2001); and Cristina Beltrán, *The Trouble with Unity: Latino Politics and the Creation of Identity* (Oxford, 2010).

3. Transnational urban histories include Jesse Hoffnung-Garskof, *A Tale of Two Cities: Santo Domingo and New York after 1950* (Princeton, 2008); Lorrin Thomas, *Puerto Rican Citizen: History and Political Identity in Twentieth-Century New York City* (Chicago, 2010); Christopher Klemek, *The Transatlantic Collapse of Urban Renewal: Postwar Urbanism from New York to Berlin* (Chicago, 2011); Geraldo L. Cadava, *Standing on Common Ground: The Making of a Sunbelt Borderland* (Cambridge, Mass., 2013); Joshua B. Guild, *In the Shadows of the Metropolis: Cultural Politics and Black Communities in Postwar New York and London* (New York,

forthcoming); and Nancy Haekyung Kwa Homeownership for All: American Powe and the Politics of Housing Aid Post-194 (Chicago, forthcoming). Transformative transnational histories include Daniel T. Rodgers, *Atlantic Crossings: Social Politics in a Progressive Age* (Cambridge, Mass., 1998); "Rethinking History and the Nation-State: Mexico and the United States as a Case Study; A Special Issue," *Journal of American History*, 86 (Sept. 1999); "The Nation and Beyond: Transnational Perspectives on United States History; A Special Issue," *ibid.* (Dec. 1999); Jefferson Cowie, *Capital Moves: RCA's Seventy-Year Quest for Cheap Labor* (Ithaca, 1999); Organization of American Historians/New York University Project on Inter-nationalizing the Study of American History, Thomas Bender, director, *The La Pietra Report: A Report to the Profession*, 2000, http://www.oah.org/about/reports/reports-statements/the-lapietra-report-a-report-to-the-profession/; Mary L. Dudziak, *Cold War Civil Rights: Race and the Image of American Democracy* (Princeton, 2000); Leon Fink, *The Maya of Morganton: Work and Community in the Nuevo New South* (Chapel Hill, 2003); Thomas Bender, *A Nation among Nations: America's Place in World History* (New York, 2006); and C. A. Bayly et al., "AHR Conversation: On Transnational History," *American Historical Review*, 111 (Dec. 2006), 1441–64. The globalization literature in these fields includes David Harvey, *The Urbanization of Capital* (Oxford, 1985); Saskia Sassen, *Cities in a World Economy* (Los Angeles, 2012); Michael Peter Smith and Luis Eduardo Guarnizo, eds., *Transnationalism from Below* (New Brunswick, 1998); Roger Waldinger, ed., *Strangers at the Gates: New Immigrants in Urban America* (Los Angeles, 2001); and Robert Courtney Smith, *Mexican New York: Transnational Lives of New Immigrants* (Berkeley, 2006). Saskia Sassen's *Cities in a World Economy* has been through four editions since 1994. I use the term *transnational* to describe people and processes that operate between nation-states, are not easily categorized by nationality, and create spaces geographically distinct yet mutually and simultaneously constitutive. *Binational* is insufficient because these communities and patterns of influence involve exchanges among multiple nations and national groups. *Cosmopolitan(ism)* connotes very different scholarly questions involving nationhood, loyalty, belonging, and otherness. See, for example, Martha C. Nussbaum et al., *For Love of Country: Debating the Limits of Patriotism*, ed. Joshua Cohen (Boston, 1996); and Carol A. Breckenridge et al., eds., *Cosmopolitanism* (Durham, N.C., 2002).

...z, "Nuestra América: Latino ...S. History," *Journal of Ameri-ry*, 93 (Dec. 2006), 672; Adrian ...Jr. et al., "Latino History: An Inter-...ge on Present Realities and Future Pro-...ects," *ibid.*, 97 (Sept. 2010), 431, 440, 449, 457. Works in the field that have revised long-held historical narratives include David Montejano, *Anglos and Mexicans in the Making of Texas, 1836–1986* (Austin, 1987); Ramón A. Gutiérrez, *When Jesus Came, the Corn Mothers Went Away: Marriage, Sexuality, and Power in New Mexico, 1500–1846* (Palo Alto, 1991); David J. Weber, *The Spanish Frontier in North America* (New Haven, 1992); David G. Gutiérrez, *Walls and Mirrors: Mexican Americans, Mexican Immigrants, and the Politics of Ethnicity* (Berkeley, 1995); Neil Foley, *The White Scourge: Mexicans, Blacks, and Poor Whites in Texas Cotton Culture* (Berkeley, 1997); and María E. Montoya, *Translating Property: The Maxwell Land Grant and the Contest over Land in the American West, 1840–1900* (Berkeley, 2002).

5. Mike Davis, *Magical Urbanism: Latinos Reinvent the U.S. Big City* (London, 2000), 7; Alejandro Portes and Rubén G. Rumbaut, *Immigrant America: A Portrait* (Berkeley, 2006), 37–66; David R. Colburn and Jeffrey S. Adler, *African-American Mayors: Race, Politics, and the American City* (Urbana, 2001), 4; Miguel Villa and Jorge Rodríguez, "Demographic Trends in Latin America's Metropolises, 1950–1990," in *The Mega-City in Latin America*, ed. Alan Gilbert (New York, 1996), 25–52.

6. Billk Minutaglio and Holly Williams, *The Hidden City: Oak Cliff, Texas* (Dallas, 1990), 46.

7. "NWIRP Dallas: A World War II and Cold War Aircraft and Missile Manufacturing Plant," n.d., National Park Service Form 10-900-a, National Register of Historic Places Continuation Sheet (in A. K. Sandoval-Strausz's possession); "Dallas Builder Cites Growth of Oak Cliff," *Dallas Times Herald*, March 23, 1957, p. 1B; "Oak Cliff Getting New Families Each Month," *Dallas Morning News*, April 4, 1957, pt. 1, p. 18; "CXA-4-84," Jan. 28, 1942, photograph, 1942 Section G8a, Aerial Photograph Collection (J. Erik Jonsson Central Library, Dallas, Tex.); "DJU-4G-7," Dec. 11, 1 950, photograph, 1950 Section G8, *ibid.*

8. See the scores of newspaper clippings in Oak Cliff folders, Vertical Files, Texas/Dallas History and Archives Division (Jonsson Central Library). Alan C. Elliott, Patricia K. Summey, and Gayla Brooks Kokel, *Images of America: Oak Cliff* (Charleston,

2009); *Cole Directory for Dallas and Vicinity* (Lincoln, 1950), 1102; *Cole Directory for Dallas and Vicinity* (Lincoln, 1961), 269; "Towering over the Cliff Skyline," *Dallas Times Herald*, Aug. 16, 1964, p. 8.

9. U.S. Census Bureau, *Sixteenth Census of the United States: 1940. Population and Housing. Statistics for Census Tracts. Dallas, Texas and Adjacent Area* (Washington, 1942), table 1; U.S. Census Bureau, *U.S. Censuses of Population and Housing: 1960. Census Tracts. Final Report PHC(1)-34, Dallas, Tex. Standard Metropolitan Statistical Area* (Washington, 1962), table P-1. All statistics for Oak Cliff are based on census tracts 20, 42, 44–48, 50–53, 62–65.02, 67–69, and 199 (tract 199 was previously designated as D-7). The racial boundary is revealed by the sharp demographic contrast with tracts 34, 41, 49, and 89. Robert B. Fairbanks, *For the City as a Whole: Planning, Politics, and the Public Interest in Dallas, Texas, 1900–1965* (Columbus, 1998), 29–30, 150–52, 191.

10. "Trolleys to Give Way to Buses in January," *Dallas Morning News*, Sept. 15, 1955, sec. 1, p. 20; "Oak Cliff Rejects Beer," *ibid.*, Dec. 16, 1956, p. 1; Brian D. Behnken, "'The Dallas Way': Protest, Response, and the Civil Rights Experience in Big D and Beyond," *Southwestern Historical Quarterly*, 111 (July 2007), 6–15; W. Marvin Dulaney, "Whatever Happened to the Civil Rights Movement in Dallas, Texas?," in *Essays on the American Civil Rights Movement*, ed. John Dittmer, George C. Wright, and W. Marvin Dulaney (College Station, 1993), 78–81.

11. Dulaney, "Whatever Happened to the Civil Rights Movement in Dallas, Texas?," 75–76; Jim Schutze, *The Accommodation: The Politics of Race in an American City* (Seacaucus, 1986), 12–19, 110–15. On white neighborhood violence, see Arnold R. Hirsch, "Massive Resistance in the Urban North: Trumbull Park, Chicago, 1953–1966," *Journal of American History*, 82 (Sept. 1995), 522–50; Thomas J. Sugrue, "Crabgrass-Roots Politics: Race, Rights, and the Reaction against Liberalism in the Urban North, 1940–1964," *ibid.*, 551–78; and Kruse, *White Flight*, 42–77.

12. Brian D. Behnken, *Fighting Their Own Battles: Mexican Americans, African Americans, and the Struggle for Civil Rights in Texas* (Chapel Hill, 2011), 207–13; Schutze, *Accommodation*, 156–63.

13. Census Bureau, *United States: 2010; Summary Population and Housing Characteristics*, table 10.

14. Census Bureau, *Censuses of Population and Housing: 1960*, table P-1. On another Dallas barrio, see Shirley Achor, *Mexican*

Americans in a Dallas Barrio (Tucson, 1978).

15. Anita Martínez interview by A. K. Sandoval-Strausz, July 23, 2010, digital audio file (in Sandoval-Strausz's possession); *Census Bureau, Censuses of Population and Housing: 1960*, table P-1.

16. Leonor Villareal and Ronnie Villareal interview by Sandoval-Strausz, July 18, 2010, digital audio file (in Sandoval-Strausz's possession); Jesse Tafalla interview by Sandoval-Strausz, July 22, 2010, digital audio file, ibid.; U.S. Census Bureau, *Census of Population and Housing: 1970. Census Tracts, Final Report PHC(1)-52, Dallas, Texas SMSA* (Washington, 1972), table P-2.

17. Leslie Bethell, ed., *Mexico since Independence* (New York, 1991), 323–32; Villa and Rodríguez, "Demographic Trends in Latin America's Metropolises," in *Mega-City in Latin America*, ed. Gilbert, 33; Mae M. Ngai, *Impossible Subjects: Illegal Aliens and the Making of Modern America* (Princeton, 2004), 227–64.

18. Tereso Ortiz interview by Sandoval-Strausz, July 12, 2010, digital audio file (in Sandoval-Strausz's possession). I have translated into English the quotation from this Spanish-language interview. *The Other Side of the Border*, dir. Ginny Martin (KERA Dallas/Ft. Worth, 1987) (videotape, PBS Video); Instituto Nacional de Estadísticay Geografía, *Estadísticas históricas de México* (Historical statistics of Mexico) (Mexico City, 1995), vol. 1, table 22.9. See also Manuel Garcíay Griego and Roberto R. Calderón, *Más allá del Río Bravo: Breve historia Mexicana del norte de Texas* (Beyond the Rio Bravo: A brief Mexican history of north Texas) (Mexico City, 2013).

19. Claudia Torrescano interview by Sandoval-Strausz, April 20, 2010, notes (in Sandoval-Strausz's possession); Yolette García interview by Sandoval-Strausz, July 19, 2010, notes, *ibid.* For corroboration, see Gustavo Verduzco Igartúa, "La migración urbana a Estados Unidos: Un caso del occidente de México" (Urban migration to the United States: A case from western Mexico), *Estudios Sociológos*, 8 (Jan.–April 1990), 117–39; Wayne A. Cornelius, "From Sojourners to Settlers: The Changing Profile of Mexican Immigration to the United States," in *U.S.–Mexico Relations: Labor Market Interdependence*, ed. J. A. Bustamante, Clark W. Reynolds, and Raúl A. Hinojosa Ojeda (Stanford, 1992), 155–95.

20. U.S. Census Bureau, *1980 Census of Population and Housing. Census Tracts. Dallas—Fort Worth, Tex. Standard Metropolitan Statistical Area, phc 80-2-131* (Washington,

1983), tables P-7, P-20; U.S. Census Bureau, *1990 Census of Population and Housing. Population and Housing Characteristics for Census Tracts and Block Numbering Areas. Dallas—Fort Worth, TX CMSA. CPH-3-125A* (Washington, 1993), table 8; "Census 2000 Summary File 1 (sf 1), QT-3: Race and Hispanic or Latino," table created from data at U.S. Census Bureau, *American Fact Finder*, http://factfinder2.census.gov (table in Sandoval-Strausz's possession); "Census 2000 Summary File 3 (sf 3), DP-2: Profile of Selected Social Characteristics," table created from data at Census Bureau, *American Fact Finder*, http://factfinder2.census.gov, ibid.

21. U.S. Bureau of the Census, *Census of Population, Volume III: Census Tracts Statistics, Part I, Akron-Dayton* (Washington, 1953), table 1; Census Bureau, *U.S. Censuses of Population and Housing: 1960*, table P-1; Census Bureau, *Census of Population and Housing: 1970*, table P-1, P-2; U.S. Census Bureau, *1980 Census of Population and Housing*, table P-7; Census Bureau, *1990 Census of Population and Housing*, table 8; "Census 2000 Summary File 1 (SF 1), QT-3."

22. Amanda I. Seligman, *Block by Block: Neighborhoods and Public Policy on Chicago's West Side* (Chicago, 2005); Census Bureau, *Censuses of Population and Housing: 1960*, table P-1; Census Bureau, *Census of Population and Housing: 1970*, tables P-1, P-2; Census Bureau, *1980 Census of Population and Housing*, table P-7; Census Bureau, *1990 Census of Population and Housing*, table 8; "Census 2000 Summary File 1 (SF 1), QT-3."

23. James R. Scobie, *Argentina: A City and a Nation* (New York, 1964); Jorge Hardoy and Richard Schaedel, *Las ciudades de América Latinay sus áreas de influencia a través de la historia* (Latin American cities and their areas of influence across history) (Buenos Aires, 1975); Jorge Hardoy, *Urbanization in Latin America: Approaches and Issues* (Garden City, 1975); Richard M. Morse and Jorge E. Hardoy, *Repensando la ciudad de América Latina* (Rethinking the Latin American city) (Buenos Aires, 1988); Philip II, *Ordenanzas hechas para los decubrimientos, nuevas poblaciones y pacificaciones. Bosque de Segovia, 13 de julio, 1573* (Ordinances for discovering new settlements, and pacifications, Bosque de Segovia, July 13, 1573), esp. ordinances 33, 37, 39, 89–92, 99–107, 110–35, sourced and partially translated in Zelia Nuttall, "Royal Ordinances Concerning the Laying Out of New Towns," *Hispanic American Historical Review*, 4 (Nov. 1921), https://archive.org/

stream/jstor-2505686/2505686#page/n11/mode/2up, pp. 743–53; Domingo Faustino Sarmiento, *Facundo: Civilzación y barbarie* (Civilization and barbarism) (Santiago, 1845); José Luis Romero, *Latinoamerica: Las ciudades y las ideas* (Latin America: Cities and ideas) (Buenos Aires, 1976); Ángel Rama, *La ciudad letrada* (The lettered city) (Hanover, 1984); Morton White and Lucia White, *The Intellectual versus the City: From Thomas Jefferson to Frank Lloyd Wright* (Cambridge, Mass., 1962); Jackson, *Crabgrass Frontier*; Robert Fishman, *Bourgeois Utopias: The Rise and Fall of Suburbia* (New York, 1987); Gilbert, *Mega-City in Latin America*, 1–21, 173–83; Hoffnung-Garskof, *Tale of Two Cities*, 36–38; Thomas W. Hanchett, "The Other 'Subsidized Housing': Federal Aid to Suburbanization," *Journal of Housing and Community Development*, 58 (Jan.—Feb. 2001), 18–29.

24. Daniel D. Arreola, *Tejano South Texas: A Mexican American Cultural Province* (Austin, 2002), esp. 78–80, 117–19; Chris Wilson and Stefanos Polyzoides, eds., *The Plazas of New Mexico* (San Antonio, 2011); Martínez interview; Tafalla interview; Dallas Department of Planning, *El Barrio Study Phase 1: City of Dallas* (Dallas, 1978), 32, 54, 56; Texas Historical Commission, official Texas historical marker report for Pike Park, July 1981 (in Sandoval-Strausz's possession).

25. Ortiz interview; Rosario Gaytán interview by Sandoval-Strauz, July 22, 2010, digital audio file (in Sandoval-Strausz's possession). See also Achor, *Mexican Americans in a Dallas Barrio*, 71; tables 42 and 44 divided by tables 6 and 7 for the Oak Cliff census tracts (20, 42, 44–48, 50–53, 62–65.02, 67–69, 99), in *1990 Census of Population and Housing*, by Census Bureau; Joyce Dargay Dermont Gately, and Martin Sommer, "Vehicle Ownership and Income Growth, Worldwide, 1960–2030," *Energy Journals*, 28 (2007), 146, 147; Robert Kemper, *Migration and Adaptation: Tzintzuntzán Peasants in Mexico City* (Beverly Hills, 1977), 25; Jackson, *Crabgrass Frontier*; Fishman, *Bourgeois Utopias*; Clay McShane, *Down the Asphalt Path: The Automobile and the American City* (New York, 1995); Owen Gutfreund, *Twentieth-Century Sprawl: Highways and the Reshaping of the American Landscape* (New York, 2004); and Michael Mendez, "Latino New Urbanism: Building on Cultural Preferences," *Opolis*, 1 (no. 1, 2005), 33–48.

26. Lizabeth Cohen, "From Town Center to Shopping Center: The Reconfiguration of Community Marketplaces in Postwar America," *American Historical Review*, 101 (Oct. 1996), 1050–81; Richard Longstreth, *City Center to Regional Mall: Architecture, the Automobile, and Retailing in Los Angeles, 1920–1950* (Cambridge, Mass., 1998); Nick Cordova interview by Sandoval-Strausz, July 19, 2010, digital audio file (in Sandoval-Strausz's possession).

27. *Cole's Directory, Cross-Reference Directory Greater Dallas, 1970 Issue* (Dallas, 1970), 335–36; *Cole's Cross Reference Directory, Greater Dallas, 1980 Issue* (Dallas, 1980), 426–27; *Cole's Cross Reference Directory, Dallas and Suburbs, 1990–91 Issue* (Dallas, 1990), 474–75; *Cole Cross Reference Directory, Greater Dallas and Vicinity, 2000 Issue* (Dallas, 2000), 479–80; Gloria Rubio interview by Sandoval-Strausz, July 19, 2010, digital audio file (in Sandoval-Strausz's possession).

28. Nelson Lichtenstein, *The Retail Revolution: How Wal-Mart Created a Brave New World of Business* (New York, 2009), esp. 46–69; Alejandro Portes and Kelly Hoffman, "Latin American Class Structures: Their Composition and Change during the Neoliberal Era," *Latin American Research Review*, 38 (Feb. 2003), 59–62.

29. See, for example, Robert Bruegmann, *Sprawl: A Compact History* (Chicago, 2005); U.S. Census data for Oak Cliff tracts 20, 42, 44–48, 50–53, 62–65.02, 67–69, and 199 compiled using, "U.S. Demographic Maps, 1790–2010," *Social Explorer*, http://www.socialexplorer.com/pub/maps/home.aspx.

30. "U.S. Demographic Maps, 1790–2010." Census Bureau, *Censuses of Population and Housing: 1960*, table H-2; Census Bureau, *Census of Population and Housing: 1970*, tables H-1, H-2; Census Bureau, *1980 Census of Population and Housing*, tables H-1, H-8; Census Bureau, *1990 Census of Population and Housing*, tables 9, 33. All figures adjusted for inflation using the value calculator at http://measuringworth.com/uscompare/.

31. Tod Robberson interview by Sandoval-Strausz, Jan. 15, 2010, notes (in Sandoval-Strausz's possession); Daniel D. Arreola, "Mexican American Housescapes," *Geographical Review*, 78 (July 1988), 299–315; James Rojas, "The Enacted Environment: The Creation of 'Place' by Mexicans and Mexican Americans in Los Angeles" (Master's thesis, Massachusetts Institute of Technology, 1991), esp. 89–92; Michael Anthony Mendez, "Latino Lifestyle and the New Urbanism: Synergy against Sprawl" (Master's thesis, Massachusetts Institute of Technology, 2003). See also Victor M. Valle and

Rodolfo D. Torres, *Latino Metropolis* (Minneapolis, 2000); Daniel D. Arreola, ed., *Hispanic Spaces, Latino Places: Community and Cultural Diversity in Contemporary America* (Austin, 2004); David R. Diaz, *Barrio Urbanism: Chicanos, Planning, and American Cities* (New York, 2005); and Edward T. Rincón, "Police Invasion of Oak Cliff Dampens Hispanic Fete," *Dallas Morning News*, Oct. 21, 1993, p. 23A.

32. Sarah Lynn López, "The Remittance Landscape: Space, Architecture, and Society in Emigrant Mexico" (Ph.D. diss., University of California, Berkeley, 2011); César Valenciano Vázquez to Sandoval-Strausz, e-mail, Dec. 1, 2012 (in Sandoval-Strausz's possession). See also Natasha Iskander, *Creative State: Forty Years of Migration and Development Policy in Morocco and Mexico* (Ithaca, 2010).

33. Michael Peter Smith and Matt Baker, *Citizenship across Borders: The Political Transnationalism of El Migrante* (Ithaca, 2008), 31–41; Manuel Rodela interview by Sandoval-Strausz, March 6, 2013, digital audio file (in Sandoval-Strausz's possession); Federación de Clubes Zacatecanos del Norte de Texas, *Zacatecas, patrimonio cultural de la humanidad* (Zacatecas, world cultural heritage) (Dallas, 2002), 10, 11, 22 (in Manuel Rodela's possession).

34. Smith and Baker, *Citizenship across Borders*, 31–41; Federación de Clubes Zacatecanos del Norte de Texas archive photo collection (in Rodela's possession); Federación de Clubes Zacatecanos del Norte de Texas, *Zacatecas, X Aniversario* (Zacatecas, tenth anniversary) (Dallas, 2007); Federación de Clubes Zacatecanos del Norte de Texas, *Zacatecas, XII Aniversario* (Zacatecas, twelfth anniversary) (Dallas, 2009); Federación de Clubes Zacatecanos del Norte de Texas, *Zacatecas, XV Aniversario* (Zacatecas, fifteenth anniversary) (Dallas, 2012).

35. Secretaría de Desarrollo Social (Department of Social Development) spreadsheets from 2004, 2009, 2010, and 2011 from Roberto Joaquin Galíndez, Secretaría de Desarrollo Social Eastern Zone representative, e-mails to Sandoval-Strausz, Nov. 26, Dec. 10, 2012, Jan. 9, 2013 (in Sandoval-Strausz's possession); Secretaría de Desarrollo Social, *Logros Programa 3x1 para Migrantes* (Achievements of the 3x1 Program for Migrants) (Mexico City, 2012), 3 (in Sandoval-Strausz's possession). The peso-dollar exchange rate in this period varied from about 9:1 to 13:1. See Board of Governors of the Federal Reserve System, "Foreign Exchange Rates – H.10: Historical Rates for the Mexican Peso," http://www.federalreserve.gov/releases/h10/hist/dat00_mx.htm.

36. Nicolás Argueta, former Asociación Salvadoreña Americana (Salvadoran American Association) president, to Sandoval-Strausz, e-mail, March 13, 2013 (in Sandoval-Strausz's possession); Secretaría de Desarrollo Social, *Memoria del Programa 3x1 para Migrantes, 2007–2012* (Report on the 3x1 Program for Migrants) (Mexico City, 2012), sec. A2 *ibid.*; Carolina Stefoni, "Migración, remesas, y desarrollo: Estado del arte de la discusión y perspectivas" (Migration, remittances, and development: State of the art of the discussion and perspectives), *Polis*, 30 (2011), 5; Manuel Orozco, "Migration and Development in Central America: Perceptions, Policies, and Further Opportunities," Nov. 2013, *Inter-American Dialogue*, http://www.thedialogue.org/uploads/IAD9337MigrationEnglish_v6.pdf, pp. 22–25.

37. On the Immigration Reform and Control Act, see Wayne A. Cornelius, "Impacts of the 1986 US Immigration Law on Emigration from Rural Mexican Sending Communities," *Population and Development Review*, 15 (Dec. 1989), 689–709; and Helene Hayes, *Immigration Policy and the Undocumented: Ambivalent Laws, Furtive Lives* (Westport, 2001). Portes and Rumbaut, *Immigrant America*, 142. Rubio interview. I have translated into English the quotation from this Spanish-language interview. Alberto López interview by Sandoval-Strausz, July 20, 2010, digital audio file (in Sandoval-Strausz's possession).

38. Jorge Durand, Douglas S. Massey, and Emilio A. Parrado, "The New Era of Mexican Migration to the United States," *Journal of American History*, 86 (Sept. 1999), 535, 527. See also Douglas S. Massey, "Understanding America's Immigration 'Crisis,'" *Proceedings of the American Philosophical Society*, 151 (Sept. 2007), 309–27. Robert V. Kemper et al., "From Undocumented Camionetas (Mini-Vans) to Federally Regulated Motor Carriers: Hispanic Transportation in Dallas, Texas, and Beyond," *Urban Anthropology*, 36 (Winter 2007), 382–84, 405, 409–10; Smith and Baker, *Citizenship across Borders*, 61. On *Me voy pa'l Norte*, see *ibid.*; and Mary Sutter, "Mexicanal Added to DTV," *Variety*, July 27, 2005, http://variety.com/2005/digital/news/mexicanal-added-to-dtv-1117926644/.

39. Jane Jacobs, *The Death and Life of Great American Cities* (New York, 1961), 35–36, 53–56, 77–78; Ruth D. Peterson and Lauren J. Krivo, "The National Neighborhood Crime Study (NNCS), 2000," available at *Inter-University Consortium for Political and Social Research*, University of Michigan, http://thedata.harvard.edu/dvn/

dv/icpsr/faces/study/StudyPage.xhtml?study Id=45870&tab=catalog; Public Safety Committee, *Dallas Police Homicide Report*, Jan. 9, 2012, http://dallascityhall.com/committee_briefings/briefings0112/PS_DallasPoliceHomicide Report_010912.pdf; Robert J. Sampson, "Rethinking Crime and Immigration," *Contexts*, 7 (Winter 2008), 28–33, esp. 29; John Hagan and Alberto Palloni, "Sociological Criminology and the Mythology of Hispanic Immigration and Crime," *Social Problems*, 46 (Nov. 1999), 617–32; Tim Wadsworth, "Is Immigration Responsible for the Crime Drop? An Assessment of the Influence of Immigration on Changes in Violent Crime between 1990 and 2000," *Social Science Quarterly*, 91 (June 2010), 531–53. On the National Neighborhood Crime Study, see Christopher J. Lyons, María B. Vélez, and Wayne A. Santoro, "Neighborhood Immigration, Violence, and City-Level Immigrant Political Opportunities," *American Sociological Review*, 78 (Aug. 2013), 604–32.

40. Richard Sennett, *The Fall of Public Man* (New York, 1974); Robert D. Putnam, *Bowling Alone: The Collapse and Revival of American Community* (New York, 2000); Fink, *Maya of Morganton*, 4, 145.

DOCUMENTS FOR PART IX

9.1 WATTS RIOTS (1965)

Source: *Report of the National Advisory Commission on Civil Disorders.* Washington, D.C.: U.S. Government Printing Office, 1968.

EDITORS' INTRODUCTION

The National Advisory Commission on Civil Disorders was informally referred to as the Kerner Commission, named after its chairman, former Illinois governor Otto Kerner. The Kerner Commission concluded in this report that the United States was "moving toward two societies, one black, one white—separate and unequal."[i] The eleven-member committee had been formed in July 1967 to study the series of riots that had swept the United States in the twentieth century. The tension seemed to be building in the 1960s, and President Lyndon B. Johnson expressed great concern. In April 1968, just a month after the issuance of the Kerner Commission report, Martin Luther King was assassinated, and cities across the nation again erupted in violence. In this section of the report, the committee tells the story of the Watts Riot of 1965. Watts, by this point a low-income, largely African American section of Los Angeles, broke out in riots following the arrest of a young African American man, Marquette Frye, and his brother Ronald Frye. The story of Watts had first officially documented in the McCone Report, published in December 1965 and named after the riot investigation committee chairman, John McCone. Thirty-three years later, the National Advisory Commission on Civil Disorders issued a follow-up to the Kerner Commission report. The 1998 addendum demonstrated that many American cities still faced racial strife, but African Americans and other minority groups had also resettled in the suburbs in significant numbers.

WATTS RIOTS (1965)

As late as the second week of August, there had been few disturbances outside the South. But, on the evening of August 11, as Los Angeles sweltered in a heat wave, a highway patrolman halted a young Negro driver for speeding. The young man appeared intoxicated, and the patrolman arrested him. As a crowd gathered, law enforcement officers were called to the scene. A highway patrolman mistakenly struck a bystander with his billy club. A young Negro woman, who was erroneously accused of spitting on the police, was dragged into the middle of the street.

When the police departed, members of the crowd began hurling rocks at passing cars, beating white motorists, and overturning cars and setting them on fire. The police reacted hesitantly. Actions they did take further inflamed the people on the streets.

The following day the area was calm. Community leaders attempting to mediate between Negro residents and the police received little cooperation from municipal authorities. That evening the previous nights' pattern of violence was repeated.

Not until almost 30 hours after the initial flareup did window smashing, looting, and arson begin. Yet the police utilized only a small part of their forces.

---

i *Report of the National Advisory Commission on Civil Disorders* (Washington, D.C.: U.S. Government Printing Office, 1968), 1.

Few police were on hand the next morning when huge crowds gathered in the business district of Watts, two miles from the location of the original disturbance, and began looting. In the absence of police response, the looting became bolder and spread into other areas. Hundreds of women and children from five housing projects clustered in or near Watts took part. Around noon, extensive firebombing began. Few white persons were attacked; the principal intent of the rioters now seemed to be to destroy property owned by whites, in order to drive white "exploiters" out of the ghetto.

The chief of police asked for National Guard help, but the arrival of military units was delayed for several hours. When the Guardsmen arrived, they, together with police, made heavy use of firearms. Reports of "sniper fire" increased. Several persons were killed by mistake. Many more were injured.

Thirty-six hours after the first Guard units arrived, the main force of the riot had been blunted. Almost 4,000 persons were arrested. Thirty-four were killed and hundreds injured. Approximately $35 million in damage had been inflicted.

The Los Angeles riot, the worst in the United States since the Detroit riot of 1943, shocked all who had been confident that race relations were improving in the North, and evoked a new mood in the ghettos around the country.

9.2 URBAN INDIANS (1964–1969)

Adam Fortunate Eagle

Source: Adam Fortunate Eagle, *Alcatraz! Alcatraz!* (California: Heyday Books, 1992). Reprinted with permission of Adam Fortunate Eagle.

EDITORS' INTRODUCTION

Adam Fortunate Eagle was born Adam Nordwall. A member of the Red Lake Minnesota Chippewa, Eagle played an instrumental role in the occupation of Alcatraz Island, located in San Francisco Bay, between 1969–1971, bringing considerable publicity to the cause of Native American rights. He contributed to the writing of the group's manifesto, "The Alcatraz Proclamation to the Great White Father and his People." The 1969 Alcatraz takeover actually began in 1964, when a group of Sioux sailed to Alcatraz and claimed its land under the auspices of Sioux Treaty of 1868. So much land had been taken from native peoples, and the Alcatraz occupation was an attempt to take some back again or at least garner media attention. The Alcatraz proclamation offered $24 in glass beads and red cloth for the land, at that time not in use by the federal government, and urged the creation of the Bureau of Caucasian Affairs, for the care of any white people on the island. In addition to *Alcatraz! Alcatraz!*, Eagle is the author of *Heart of the Rock: The Indian Invasion of Alcatraz* (Norman: University of Oklahoma Press, 2002) and a memoir, *Pipestone: A Boy's Life in an Indian Boarding School* (Norman: University of Oklahoma Press, 2011). He narrated the film *Sitting Bull: A Stone in My Heart*, directed by John Ferry, in 2007, and is the subject of a film by Ferry and Lillimar Pictures, *Contrary Warrior: The Life and Times of Adam Fortunate Eagle*, released in 2009.

URBAN INDIANS (1964–1969)

I remember that as we were heading back to the mainland that March day in 1964, one of the non-Indians asked another non-Indian, "What are a bunch of Sioux Indians doing here in the Bay Area? Why aren't they back in the Midwest, or wherever they're from?"

I am sure he wasn't the only one wondering why we Indians would be so concerned about a little rock in the middle of San Francisco Bay when we supposedly had vast reservations to live on and the government was reportedly paying us to do nothing. Why would we leave such a paradise and move to the big city where we might even have to work?

If you visit a reservation today you will probably see poverty, alcoholism, and desperation. These problems persist despite improvement due to recent Indian activism, such as the Alcatraz occupation. In 1964, the reservations were much worse. Corruption in the Bureau of Indian Affairs (BIA) and the tribal governments often allowed greedy speculators to purchase tribal resources such as land and mineral deposits; Indians remained poor and their reservations remained undeveloped.

In 1968, a Senate subcommittee stated that "50,000 Indian families live in unsanitary, dilapidated dwellings, many in huts, shanties, even abandoned automobiles." The report went on to state that the average annual Indian income was $1500, 25% of the national average; the unemployment rate among Indians was 40%, more than ten times the national average; the average age of death for American Indians was 44 years and for all other Americans 65 years; infant mortality was twice the national average; and thousands of Indians had migrated or been relocated into cities only to find themselves untrained for jobs and unprepared for urban life. Many returned to their reservations more disillusioned and defeated than when they left. And this report appeared after several years of "Great Society" programs, none of which seemed to be directed towards helping the Indians. For many, reservation life was one of hopeless poverty and ongoing misery.

Many people think that these conditions were due to laziness, a sort of welfare mentality. They don't realize the conditions were a deliberate creation of the U.S. Government, the result of decades of manipulation, contempt, and control.

The government and the speculators knew that the tribes held vast amounts of natural resources. In 1952 the government prepared an 1800-page report on Indian conditions. Indians called it the "Doomsday Book." The report discussed the complicated task of eliminating the reservation system and concluded that the expense and difficulty were justified by the prospect of gaining control of the natural resources held by the tribes. In addition to timber and water, it was estimated that the 23 Western tribes controlled 33 percent of the country's low-sulfur coal, 80 percent of the nation's uranium reserves, and between 3 and 10 percent of the gas and petroleum reserves. I have never seen the monetary value of these tribal holdings quoted in any report, but the amount would have to be very large.

Considering all these natural resources, one would think that the BIA would have trained Indians to develop these resources to create jobs and wealth for all the Indians on the reservation. Self-sufficiency would have been the humane solution, but it might have interfered with the profit that stood to be made. The report stated that by withdrawing federal services to the tribes and eliminating the reservation system the government would save millions of dollars every year. Without any Indian lands to administer, the BIA, the oldest bureau in the federal government could be shut down. This rearrangement would allow the large corporate structure which operated in convert with the federal government to quickly grab up the natural resources. The last vestige of Indian country would disappear into the history books, which could then proudly proclaim that "the American Indian has finally become fully assimilated into the mainstream of American society." It all sounded like a twist on the "final solution" idea proposed by another government just a few years earlier.

The next year the government put these plans into action and passed what is referred to as the Termination Act, which allowed them to begin removing the tribes' status as political entities. The process of dismantling 200 years of a relationship between the U.S. Government and the American Indians lurched into motion like a giant steam roller. But when the government began to look at closing down the reservations, they ran into an interesting problem: the Indian reservations were full of Indians!

The political leaders in Washington then put their collective heads together and dreamed up another scheme—they would reduce the reservation populations by relocating Indians to urban areas. Of course, this would all be done under the guise of helping the Indians. So by 1958 the decision had been made to establish eight relocation centers in major U.S. cities. Four of those centers were set up in California cities: Los Angeles, San Francisco, San Jose, and Oakland.

The BIA had the responsibility of running an employment assistance program for relocated Indians. Unfortunately the program was really a carrot on a stick to entice the Indians on the reservations, where many lived in great poverty. The BIA sent agents to the reservations to talk to the unemployed young men and women and even the older unemployed family men. The agents offered to help the Indians find work in a "meaningful job." The hitch was that the jobs weren't on or near the reservations as the Indians hoped, but often more than a thousand miles away from their homes and families.

The Indians that signed up for the program were given bus tickets to whichever center they had chosen. For instance, say a young Indian man chose the Oakland center. When he and his family arrived they immediately reported to the relocation office, which found them an apartment, usually in a ghetto. Every morning the young man checked into the relocation office where he was instructed to sit down and wait until called. He sat in a waiting room with a small television set and a bunch of old magazines while an "employment assistance officer" tried to line up a job interview. He was told that if he didn't report to the office each day his subsistence allowance would be cut off. In the meantime, his wife and kids locked themselves in their apartment, because they were afraid to go out by themselves into the crime-ridden streets. When the BIA found a job for their Indian "client," he was cut off from BIA services after his first paycheck. Many of the jobs were temporary. It didn't take long for the Indian to realize he had been trapped.

After the BIA "cut the cord" with the relocated Indians, those who had been given only temporary jobs had to turn to city, county, and state agencies. But the agencies seldom wanted anything to do with the Indians. They were considered the responsibility of the federal government, not local agencies. It was a terrible dilemma to be told, "You're an Indian, you go to the federal government for help." Or, as one Indian declared, "It's damn tough to go around to these different agencies looking for help and they pretend you don't exist."

In a hearing for the Committee on Urban Indians, sponsored by the National Council of Indian Opportunity in the late spring of 1969, an attorney testified to this problem by stating, "Discrimination is implicit in most of the programs for urban areas." Needy urban Indians found themselves in a new type of entrapment—too poor to go back to the reservation and too "Indian" to receive the benefits of society.

For some, the transition was simply too much to take. The government provided the bus ticket from the reservation to the city, but many Indians hitch-hiked back, more bitter than ever about what they felt was another government trick.

For others who stayed, the adjustment from reservation life to an urban existence proved to be chaotic at best. The pressures of adapting and the frustration of dealing with the agencies were too much for many young Indians trapped in the cities. In one eighteen-month period, there were four suicides reported among Indians in the Bay Area. One year in San Francisco, my own sister was counted among the despairing numbers who could not cope with the urban trap. She slipped a plastic bag over her head and filled it full of a greaseless cooking spray.

9.3 OAKLAND BLACK PANTHER PARTY FOR SELF-DEFENSE, TEN POINT PLAN

Source: Ten Point Plan, Black Panther Party, October 1966.

EDITORS' INTRODUCTION

The Black Panther Party, originally the Black Panther Party for Self-Defense, was formed in 1966 and disbanded in 1976. In May 1967, the group famously staged a march on the California State Capitol in Sacramento, demonstrating in support of their claimed right to bear arms. The symbol of the party, the crouching black panther, drew from the Lowndes County (Mississippi) Freedom Organization, which had fought for the right of African Americans to vote. Drawing from the ideological teachings of Malcolm X, and a symbol of the Black Power movement of the late 1960s and 1970s, the party coalesced under the leadership of such figures as Huey P. Newton, Bobby Seale, and Eldridge Cleaver, and had a strong association with Angela Davis. Alongside the North Oakland Neighborhood Anti-Poverty Center, the group worked on behalf of African American causes, such as sickle-cell anemia and poverty. The Black Panther Party caught on in cities throughout the country, and even inspired the founding of modern groups with similar ideals. By the time of the party's disbanding in the 1970s, police forces around the country had grown significantly more integrated.

OAKLAND BLACK PANTHER PARTY FOR SELF-DEFENSE, TEN POINT PLAN (1966)

Black Panther Party: Platform and Program

What We Want
What We Believe

1. *We want freedom. We want power to determine the destiny of our Black Community.*

We believe that black people will not be free until we are able to determine our destiny.

2. *We want full employment for our people.*

We believe that the federal government is responsible and obligated to give every man employment or a guaranteed income. We believe that if the white American businessmen will not give full employment, then the means of production should be taken from the businessmen and placed in the community so that the people of the community can organize and employ all of its people and give a high standard of living.

3. *We want an end to the robbery by the CAPITALIST of our Black Community.*

We believe that this racist government has robbed us and now we are demanding the overdue debt of forty acres and two mules. Forty acres and two mules was promised 100 years ago as restitution for slave labor and mass murder of black people. We will accept the payment as currency which will be distributed to our many communities. The Germans are now aiding the Jews in Israel for the genocide of the Jewish people. The Germans murdered six million Jews. The American racist has taken part in the slaughter of over twenty million[1] black people; therefore, we feel that this is a modest demand that we make.

4. *We want decent housing, fit for shelter of human beings.*

We believe that if the white landlords will not give decent housing to our black community, then the housing and the land should be made into cooperatives so that our community, with government aid, can build and make decent housing for its people.

5. *We want education for our people that exposes the true nature of this decadent American society. We want education that teaches us our true history and our role in the present-day society.*

We believe in an educational system that will give to our people a knowledge of self. If a man does not have knowledge of himself and his position in society and the world, then he has little chance to relate to anything else.

6. *We want all black men to be exempt from military service.*

We believe that Black people should not be forced to fight in the military service to defend a racist government that does not protect us. We will not fight and kill other people of color in the world who, like black people, are being victimized by the white racist government of America. We will protect ourselves from the force and violence of the racist police and the racist military, by whatever means necessary.

7. *We want an immediate end to POLICE BRUTALITY and MURDER of black people.*

We believe we can end police brutality in our black community by organizing black self-defense groups that are dedicated to defending our black community from racist police oppression and brutality. The Second Amendment to the Constitution of the United States gives a right to bear arms. We therefore believe that all black people should arm themselves for self-defense.

8. *We want freedom for all black men held in federal, state, county and city prisons and jails.*

We believe that all black people should be released from the many jails and prisons because they have not received a fair and impartial trial.

9. *We want all black people when brought to trial to be tried in court by a jury of their peer group or people from their black communities, as defined by the Constitution of the United States.*

We believe that the courts should follow the United States Constitution so that black people will receive fair trials. The 14th Amendment of the U.S. Constitution gives a man a right to be tried by his peer group. A peer is a person from a similar economic, social, religious, geographical, environmental, historical and racial background. To do this the court will be forced to select a jury from the black community from which the black defendant came. We have been, and are being tried by all-white juries that have no understanding of the "average reasoning man" of the black community.

10. *We want land, bread, housing, education, clothing, justice and peace. And as our major political objective, a United Nations-supervised plebiscite to be held throughout the black colony in which only black colonial subjects will be allowed to participate for the purpose of determining the will of black people as to their national destiny.*

When in the course of human events, it becomes necessary for one people to dissolve the political bands which have connected them with another, and to assume, among the powers of the earth, the separate and equal station to which the laws of nature and nature's God entitle them, a decent respect to the opinions of mankind requires that they should declare the causes which impel them to the separation.

We hold these truths to be self evident, that all men are created equal; that they are endowed by their Creator with certain unalienable rights; that among these are life, liberty, and the pursuit of happiness. *That, to secure these rights, governments are instituted among men, deriving their just powers from the consent of the governed; that, whenever any form of government becomes destructive of these ends, it is the right of the people to alter or to abolish it, and to institute a new government, laying its foundation on such principles, and organizing its powers in such form, as to them shall seem most likely to effect their safety and happiness.* Prudence, indeed, will dictate that governments long established should not be changed for light and transient causes; and, accordingly, all experience hath shown, that mankind are more disposed to suffer, while evils are

sufferable, than to right themselves by abolishing the forms to which they are accustomed. *But, when a long train of abuses and usurpations, pursuing invariable the same object, evinces a design to reduce them under absolute despotism, it is their right, it is their duty, to throw off such government, and to provide new guards for their future security.*

NOTE

1. In March 1972, the platform was revised to include the number of fifty million.

9.4 ADDRESS TO THE NATION ON THE CIVIL DISTURBANCES IN LOS ANGELES, CALIFORNIA (1992)

President George H. W. Bush

Source: *Public Papers of the Presidents of the United States, George Bush, 1992–93*, Book I— January to July 31, 1992 (Washington, D.C.: United States Government Printing Office, 1993).

EDITORS' INTRODUCTION

On April 29, 1992, a jury in Simi Valley, California acquitted four Los Angeles police officers in the brutal beating of African American Rodney King. Millions of Americans who saw the widely broadcast videotape of the incident, which took place in March 1991, were surprised at the verdict; thousands of Los Angelinos even took to the streets in anger. Violence eventually erupted and engulfed the city for the better part of a week, resulting in 53 deaths and approximately $1 billion in property damage, making it one of the most costly civil disturbances in American history. Other small riots and protests took place in cities across the United States, with notable acts of violence in San Francisco, Seattle, and Atlanta.

On the third day of rioting, May 1, 1992, President George H. W. Bush addressed the nation from the Oval Office at the White House. In his comments, excerpted in this document, President Bush noted the urgent need to restore order and for further investigation by the United States Department of Justice into the violation of Rodney King's civil rights. He also recounted the inspiring story of how four African Americans came to the aid of a beaten white truck driver (Reginald Denny) and helped get him safely to a hospital. In his concluding remarks, President Bush harkened back to John Winthrop's "A Model of Christian Charity" sermon **[see Document 2.3]** in reminding Americans of their special place in the world.

ADDRESS TO THE NATION ON THE CIVIL DISTURBANCES IN LOS ANGELES, CALIFORNIA (1992)

May 1, 1992
Tonight I want to talk to you about violence in our cities and justice for our

citizens, two big issues that have collided on the streets of Los Angeles. First, an update on where matters stand in Los Angeles.

Fifteen minutes ago I talked to California's Governor Pete Wilson and Los Angeles Mayor Tom Bradley. They told me that last night was better than the night before; today, calmer than yesterday. But there were still incidents of random terror and lawlessness this afternoon.

In the wake of the first night's violence, I spoke directly to both Governor Wilson and Mayor Bradley to assess the situation and to offer assistance. There are two very different issues at hand. One is the urgent need to restore order. What followed Wednesday's jury verdict in the Rodney King case was a tragic series of events for the city of Los Angeles: Nearly 4,000 fires, staggering property damage, hundreds of injuries, and the senseless deaths of over 30 people.

To restore order right now, there are 3,000 National Guardsmen on duty in the city of Los Angeles. Another 2,200 stand ready to provide immediate support. To supplement this effort I've taken several additional actions. First, this morning I've ordered the Justice Department to dispatch 1,000 Federal riot-trained law enforcement officials to help restore order in Los Angeles beginning tonight. These officials include FBI SWAT teams, special riot control units of the U.S. Marshals Service, the Border Patrol, and other Federal law enforcement agencies. Second, another 1,000 Federal law enforcement officials are on standby alert, should they be needed. Third, early today I directed 3,000 members of the 7th Infantry and 1,500 marines to stand by at El Toro Air Station, California. Tonight, at the request of the Governor and the Mayor, I have committed these troops to help restore order. I'm also federalizing the National Guard, and I'm instructing General Colin Powell to place all those troops under a central command.

What we saw last night and the night before in Los Angeles is not about civil rights. It's not about the great cause of equality that all Americans must uphold. It's not a message of protest. It's been the brutality of a mob, pure and simple. And let me assure you: I will use whatever force is necessary to restore order. What is going on in L.A. must and will stop. As your President I guarantee you this violence will end.

Now let's talk about the beating of Rodney King, because beyond the urgent need to restore order is the second issue, the question of justice: Whether Rodney King's Federal civil rights were violated. What you saw and what I saw on the TV video was revolting. I felt anger. I felt pain. I thought: How can I explain this to my grandchildren?

Civil rights leaders and just plain citizens fearful of and sometimes victimized by police brutality were deeply hurt. And I know good and decent policemen who were equally appalled.

I spoke this morning to many leaders of the civil rights community. And they saw the video, as we all did. For 14 months they waited patiently, hopefully. They waited for the system to work. And when the verdict came in, they felt betrayed. Viewed from outside the trial, it was hard to understand how the verdict could possibly square with the video. Those civil rights leaders with whom I met were stunned. And so was I, and so was Barbara, and so were my kids.

But the verdict Wednesday was not the end of the process. The Department of Justice had started its own investigation immediately after the Rodney King incident and was monitoring the State investigation and trial. And so let me tell you what actions we are taking on the Federal level to ensure that justice is served.

Within one hour of the verdict, I directed the Justice Department to move into high gear on its own independent criminal investigation into the case. And next, on Thursday, five Federal prosecutors were on their way to Los Angeles. Our Justice Department has consistently demonstrated its ability to investigate fully a matter like this. [...]

We owe it to all Americans who put their faith in the law to see that justice is served. But as we move forward on this or any other case, we must remember the fundamental tenet of our legal system. Every American, whether accused or accuser, is entitled to protection of his or her rights.

In this highly controversial court case, a verdict was handed down by a California jury. To Americans of all races who were shocked by the verdict, let me say this: You must understand that our system of justice provides for the peaceful, orderly means of addressing this frustration. We must respect the process of law whether or not we agree with the outcome: There's a difference between frustration with the law and direct assaults upon our legal system.

In a civilized society, there can be no excuse, no excuse for the murder, arson, theft, and vandalism that have terrorized the law-abiding citizens of Los Angeles. Mayor Bradley, just a few minutes ago, mentioned to me his particular concern, among others, regarding the safety of the Korean community. My heart goes out to them and all others who have suffered losses.

The wanton destruction of life and property is not a legitimate expression of outrage with injustice. It is itself injustice. And no rationalization, no matter how heartfelt, no matter how eloquent, can make it otherwise.

Television has become a medium that often brings us together. But its vivid display of Rodney King's beating shocked us. The America it has shown us on our screens these last 48 hours has appalled us. None of this is what we wish to think of as American. It's as if we were looking in a mirror that distorted our better selves and turned us ugly. We cannot let that happen. We cannot do that to ourselves. [...]

Among the many stories I've seen and heard about these past few days, one sticks in my mind, the story of one savagely beaten white truck driver, alive tonight because four strangers, four black strangers, came to his aid. Two were men who had been watching television and saw the beating as it was happening, and came out into the street to help; another was a woman on her way home from work; and the fourth, a young man whose name we may never know. The injured driver was able to get behind the wheel of his truck and tried to drive away. But his eyes were swollen shut. The woman asked him if he could see. He answered, "No." She said, "Well, then I will be your eyes." Together, those four people braved the mob and drove that truck driver to the hospital. He's alive today only because they stepped in to help.

It is for every one of them that we must rebuild the community of Los Angeles, for these four people and the others like them who in the midst of this nightmare acted with simple human decency.

We must understand that no one in Los Angeles or any other city has rendered a verdict on America. If we are to remain the most vibrant and hopeful Nation on Earth we must allow our diversity to bring us together, not drive us apart. This must be the rallying cry of good and decent people.

For their sake, for all our sakes, we must build a future where, in every city across this country, empty rage gives way to hope, where poverty and despair give way to opportunity. After peace is restored to Los Angeles, we must then turn again to the underlying causes of such tragic events. We must keep on working to create a climate of understanding and tolerance, a climate that refuses to accept racism, bigotry, anti-Semitism, and hate of any kind, anytime, anywhere.

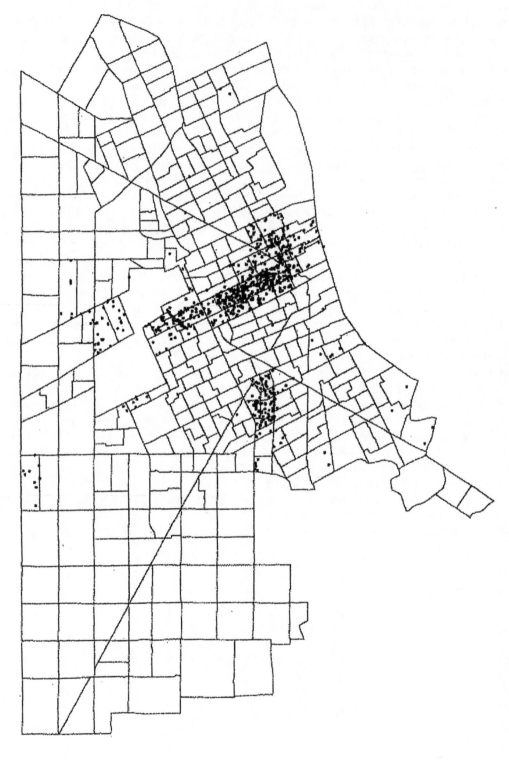

Illustration IX.1 "Map 7.1(a). Black Population in Detroit, 1940. 1 Dot = 200." Illustration for Essay 9.1.

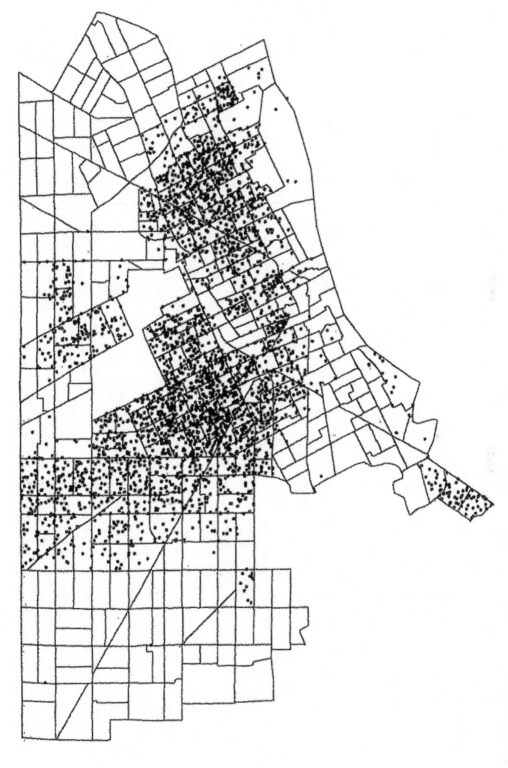

Illustration IX.2 "Map 7.1(d). Black Population in Detroit, 1970. 1 Dot = 200." Illustration for Essay 9.1.

PART X

POSTINDUSTRIAL CITIES

EDITORS' INTRODUCTION TO PART X

It is too early to fully understand the city of the early twenty-first century. However, skilled observers note some themes that are beginning to define the era. Although some pundits heralded the election of Barack Obama as the beginning of a "post-race" America, nothing could be further from the truth. It is clear from a modern vantage point that race is the most visceral category of analysis within both the nation's history and present.

Urban environmental concerns continued. The nation mourned when the city of Flint, Michigan was found to have lead and Legionnaire's in its public water system due to government mismanagement. California cities faced continued wildfires and air pollution difficulties. Increased building has exacerbated the risk of flash flooding.

Twenty-first century cities continued the theme of cities as playgrounds. Those dwelling outside the city popped in on weekends for entertainment, and left as soon as the fun was over. The larger the city the less likely it was to house a middle class—the very poor and the very rich lived side by side in major urban centers.

The election of Donald J. Trump in 2016 surprised many Americans. Trump ran on a platform of making America "great again," although it was unclear what time period his platform was lauding. He held large rallies before and after his election; in the stadiums a mostly white crowd was visible. Rally goers, urged by the president, chanted "build that wall," in reference to Trump's supposition that a large wall be built over the entirety of the U.S.–Mexico border. Trump made no bones about his anti-immigrant stance and he had a history of making anti-Muslim statements. He issued distasteful statements regarding his ability to touch women sexually, because of his long-term fame, and his extra-marital dalliances with a porn star and a Playboy model became fodder for tabloid and traditional journalists. After the Trump election, seeking to understand the Trump appeal, some journalists and writers took better care to learn about the stories of his supporters, many hailing from largely white communities affected by the loss of employment opportunities in their areas.

The economic base of the nation had undergone dramatic transformation during the second half of the twentieth century. Accompanying the decentralization of the population with migration to the suburbs was the establishment of numerous factories, warehouse/distribution centers, regional malls, and freestanding retail outlets outside of the city. Owners of these businesses were able to take advantage of the nation's new highway system and less expensive land further from large cities. They also benefited from their proximity to the growing suburbs. By the 1970s, transformation in the global economy resulted in mass deindustrialization in the United States. The loss of well-paying manufacturing jobs led to high levels of unemployment and underemployment in former industrial centers. Particularly hard hit were the Midwest, Middle Atlantic States, and parts of the Northeast known as nation's "rust belt." In place of bustling industry, service, retail, and knowledge-based economies emerged. Many cities in the Southeast and West that had bypassed the nine-teenth and twentieth century model of industrial economic development fared better and even witnessed overall growth in the 1980s and 1990s.

The essays in this part explore the nature of postindustrial urbanization. In his essay, "Inventing Modern Las Vegas," the late Hal Rothman examines how a small desert oasis became the prototype twenty-first century city by building upon the gaming and tourist industry. In Aaron Shkuda's essay, New York artists transform spaces abandoned by industry within the central city, creating a vibrant community in which the arts flourished. However the gentrification of SoHo area led to rents that even the most affluent artists could not afford. SoHo went from a spatial challenge—what to do with all of those mas-sive loft spaces?—to sought after real estate. Were the artists too successful in their quest to create an urban community? The essay by Chloe Taft asks if a casino can replace the factory as a reliable base for jobs, as residents yearned it would do in Bethlehem, Pennysl-vania. Once home to the mighty Bethlehem Steel, the city and its residents had staked their future on the promise that the casino industry could now support their families.

Seeking a better life, African Americans once again chose to migrate. In **Document 10.1**, Patrick Sisson demonstrates how a 'reverse Great Migration' was changing American cities. The modern migrants wondered if life could be improved by heading south. Much can be learned from **Document 10.2**, a selection from the United States Department of Justice's 2015 report on the Ferguson, Missouri Police Department. After the shooting of black teenager Michael Brown, the name of this St. Louis suburb—Ferguson—came to stand for the racial injustice and danger that remained in our communities. The death of Michael Brown was unfortunately just one of the bloody incidents against unarmed blacks, the majority of them young men, in this period. Two years before Ferguson, in 2012, Tray-von Martin lost his life to neighborhood watch member George Zimmerman. Martin had been passing by Zimmerman's home on his way back from buying a snack. Zimmerman was acquitted of murder in 2013. What do you make of the strong language in the Fer-guson report? What will bring change to our communities and greater safety to urban dwellers in the streets?

The early twenty-first century also saw a variety of mass shooting incidents that rocked individual cities and the nation as a whole. The public school, once seen as the bastion of safety and democracy, became the target of gunmen. The Newtown Shootings of 2012 left twenty eight dead and two injured at the Sandy Hook Elementary School in Connecticut. At the Marjory Stoneman Douglas High School in Parkland, Florida, seventeen students and staff were murdered and seventeen injured in February 2018. The students at the school took it upon themselves to speak out for gun control.

One of the mass shootings occurred in a Philadelphia synagogue in October 2018; it was the most deadly anti-Semitic crime in the nation's history up to that time. Using an AR-15 and at least three handguns, the assailant killed at least eleven members of the con-gregation, and wounded four police officers and two others.

Shooters wielding guns took lives, yet the gun lobby, led by the National Rifle Associ-ation, prevented legislation calling for more stringent background checks for gun purchas-ing, bans on assault-style rifles, and prohibitions on large bullet magazines. Americans did choose to imprison a record number of its population—and a greater percentage than any other nation in the world. In **Essay 10.4**, Todd R. Clear and Natasha A. Frost conclude that the United States was willing to launch a great social experiment on mass incarcer-ation. The imprisonment of so many Americans changed life in our cities, towns, and rural areas, pulling many citizens away from their homes and families for prolonged periods, placing them under great scrutiny by the parole system when or if they did return, and often keeping them from earning a living or voting upon release.

ESSAY 10.1

Inventing Modern Las Vegas

Hal Rothman

Source: Hal Rothman, *Neon Metropolis: How Las Vegas Started the Twenty-First Century* (New York: Routledge, 2003).

EDITORS' INTRODUCTION

Las Vegas is like no other place in the United States. A desert city, initially made infamous by the investments and influence of a wide cast of characters including Benjamin "Bugsy" Siegel, Meyer Lansky, and Howard Hughes, it came to be associated with popular entertainers such as Frank Sinatra and the Rat Pack, Elvis Presley, Wayne Newton, Celine Dion, and the quirky acrobats of Cirque du Soleil. The Las Vegas Strip is the heart of a sprawling gaming, entertainment, and recreation metropolis surrounded by an inhospitable desert. During the 1990s, the region was one of the fasting growing in the United States. In that decade, the city's population doubled to almost 500,000 residents. Las Vegas enjoys an international reputation as a tourist destination, fueled by the highly successful "Only Vegas" advertising campaign from the Las Vegas Convention and Visitors Authority that helped draw nearly forty million people to the region in 2007. With its glitzy casinos, extravagant theme resort hotels, amusement rides, and simulations of other world travel destinations — notably New York City, Venice, and Egypt — Las Vegas defies easy categorization.

This postindustrial, postmodern city is a new type of place that scholars are struggling to define. Like Los Angeles, the city of Las Vegas has a short history compared to municipalities in the East, South, and Midwest. Los Angeles has been the quintessential symbol of cities coming of age in the twentieth century. In *The City: Los Angeles and Urban Theory at the End of the Twentieth Century* (1996), Edward W. Soja and Allen J. Scott write that, "the historical geography of Los Angeles invites continuing debate between those who see in it the achievement of some sort of urban utopia and the American Dream, and those who see little more than the dystopia nightmares of 'Hell Town' grown to gargantuan proportions."[i] Las Vegas shares this oversized personality and beguiling reputation. Its economy centers on activities that are, or at least at one time were, frowned upon or outright illegal.

In the following essay, the late historian Hal Rothman (1959–2007) explores how Las Vegas went from being a seasonal outpost and railroad depot in the middle of nowhere to "a paradigm of the postindustrial city." Rothman writes, "Las Vegas anticipated the transformation of American culture not out of innate savvy, but as a result of a lack of other options in the city."[ii] Cities as diverse as Detroit and New Orleans now face a similar dearth of options and have no other choice but to adopt Las Vegas' once suspect gaming industry model.

---

i Edward W. Soja and Allen J. Scott, *The City: Los Angeles and Urban Theory at the End of the Twentieth Century* (Berkeley: University of California Press, 1996), 1–2.

ii Hal Rothman, *Neon Metropolis: How Las Vegas Started the Twenty-First Century* (New York: Routledge, 2003), 31, 323.

Hal Rothman was a professor and chair of the department of history at the University of Nevada, Las Vegas. He was the author or editor of over a dozen books on the American West and a frequent commentator, writer, and guest for newspapers and television. As one of the guiding members of the American Society for Environmental History (ASEH), he served as editor of *Environmental History* and its predecessor *Environmental History Review*. In addition to *Neon Metropolis*, his works include *On Rims and Ridges: The Los Alamos Area Since 1880* (Lincoln: University of Nebraska, 1992), *Devil's Bargains: Tourism in the Twentieth Century American West* (Lawrence: University of Kansas Press, 1998), *Saving the Planet: The American Response to the Environment in the Twentieth Century* (Chicago: Ivan R. Dee, 2000), *LBJ's Texas White House: "Our Heart's Home"* (College Station: Texas A&M Press, 2001), and *Blazing Heritage: A History of Wildfire in the National Parks* (New York: Oxford University Press, 2007).

INVENTING MODERN LAS VEGAS (2003)

The numbers are there, but they don't mean much. How do you explain a town that began as a railroad land auction in 1905, reached eight thousand in 1940, and topped one million people in 1995? There's no precedent for Las Vegas, no way to put its experience into the framework of other American cities. Distinct from the American whole, away from the arrows of progress and prosperity, Las Vegas was an insignificant part of the great government-industry matrix that defined the twentieth century. No set of circumstances led to Las Vegas. It didn't have fertile land or rich mineral veins; railroads didn't meet, highways didn't cross there. Banks didn't seek out Las Vegas, developers didn't fashion it into the next paradise, corporations didn't come to the desert to establish new headquarters, and people certainly didn't come looking for the little oasis to put down roots. Las Vegas's attractiveness was lost on Americans until after World War II and to the mainstream until well after 1975.

The reasons are obvious. Las Vegas was nowhere, a "miserable dinky little oasis town," the mobster Meyer Lansky supposedly called it, and without transportation that made it easy to reach or air-conditioning to make the stay bearable, Las Vegas's appeal was as seasonal as any ski resort. Before 1945, it had little to recommend it. Las Vegas had no markets, no hinterland to colonize. Even today, nearby St. George and southern Utah, heavily Mormon, look north to Salt Lake City; Kingman, Arizona, is a highway crossroads of its own; Flagstaff is fast becoming a suburb of Phoenix; and Barstow occupies its own dystopic universe. Las Vegas did not even have enough water to make it prey for Los Angeles. At its twentieth-century birth, Las Vegas was podunk, weak, and dependent, an inconsequential speck on the map.

The new town was typical of the small-town West. Modern Las Vegas began atop the remains of a nineteenth-century Mormon settlement that left only a few cantankerous ranchers. It started as a railroad town, a repair shop for the San Pedro, Los Angeles, and Salt Lake Railroad. Like so many other places in the West, its sustenance came from the rails, and when they prospered, as they did with the opening of the silver mines in Bullfrog and Rhyolite before 1910, so did the town. By 1910, Fremont Street, the heart of the old downtown, was paved, guttered, and flagged with sidewalks, and ten miles of local dirt road had been oiled to reduce the dust. The company built sixty-four workers' cottages and offered easy terms to workers who wanted to build their own. When the railroad's fortunes dipped, so did the town's. A track washout in 1910 sent the population spiking downward from twelve hundred to eight hundred. Only an upsurge in regional fortunes redirected the number upward. A pattern that typified the rural West in this period and ever after defined Las Vegas was set: the town was dependent on decisions made in other places.

Las Vegas's circumstances mirrored the history of the state. Nevada has always been a colony, dependent on the whims and needs of other larger, more powerful states some adjacent like California, others farther away. Shoehorned into the Union to guar-antee Abraham Lincoln's reelection in 1864, Nevada enjoyed the privilege of state-hood at the cost of its dignity and, some said, its independence. [...]

For two decades, Las Vegas was a simple small western town. Its main industry was the Union Pacific, which bought out the San Pedro, Los Angeles, and Salt Lake in 1921, kept the maintenance shop, and became master of the railroad town, responsible for its infrastructure as well as for its open social climate. Las Vegas had all the virtues and vices of such places. It was tough, raw, and sometimes mean. The rules of high-tone America not only did not apply, they simply didn't exist. Like many similar towns, Las Vegas did not explicitly forbid prostitution. As long as it was confined to one square block, block 16 of the original town plat, "quasi-legal" best defined its status. Railroad fiat restricted gambling, legal in Nevada until Progressive reformers barred it in 1910 in a prohibition that lasted until 1931 and alcohol to the same area. Illegal but only in a tech-nical sense, such activities were part of the compact the railroad made when it created towns that functioned like the port cities of yore. The railroad brought life and it tacitly condoned behavior at odds with Victorian norms. Railroad companies well understood the advantages and drawbacks of the rails, and towns that grew up along them made accommodation, even in the most moralistic of times.

Las Vegas's circumstances were typical of the rural West and even more characteristic of railroad towns. The railroad provided a capital regime; it was the only consistent source of funding for the town, and its goals determined those of the city. Much like the cattle trade of the nineteenth century, the rails brought a rowdy element with plenty of cash and a feel-ing of mobility. Workers lived in Las Vegas, but travelers passed through, and the sense of movement along the rails freed people from place and time. Vice flourished and became an integral part of local commerce. Although still considered not quite proper, it was recognized as necessary. Catering to other people's desires proved so lucrative that even the most upright small-town burghers held their noses and

looked away, as they had in the cattle towns. The accommodation made life palatable. Without vice there wasn't enough business to eke out a living.

This condition reflected a larger theme in the state's history. While Nevada liked to bill itself as the Old West, where the rules of modern civilization didn't apply, it was equally true that the state had few choices. Neither of its two nineteenth-century industries, mining and railroads, encouraged stability. Mining exploded on the landscape, peaked in great rushes, then left huge visible scars as testimony to its transience. The railroad epitomized nineteenth-century mobility, defying the rooted ideals of the time. Its reputation in American folklore for encouraging transi-ence and license and freedom inspired gen-erations of songwriters and other artists. The state embraced these industries because it had no other choice. If Nevadans seemed more willing to mind their own business than most, this incipient libertarianism was a product of the limits of its land and infra-structure in a harsh climate.

One-owner towns had their drawbacks for the people who lived in them. Even though they allowed locals considerable autonomy and leeway, outside power main-tained tremendous control. Early Las Vegas was wise to heed and placate its masters. When it didn't, disaster resulted. After the Union Pacific purchase in 1921, the new owners laid off sixty workers, earning the ire of the town. The next year, an oppor-tunity arose for railroad workers to pay back their new overlords; workers shut Las Vegas down during the national railroad strike in 1922. The new masters were not amused. In retribution, the Union Pacific signed the town's death warrant: it moved the maintenance shop and three hundred jobs to Caliente, about 125 miles track toward Utah. The railroad regime ended as arbitrarily as it had started, and Las Vegas was consigned to the fate of other small western towns. It had to adapt—or dimin-ish, wither, and finally go under. The period just following the railroad's depart-ure was the bleakest in modern Las Vegas's short history. The whistle-stop easily could have become a ghost town.

Only California and its imperial need for water saved the city. Since the remarkable fiction that created modern Los Angeles, the City of Angels became a vacuum for every drop of water it could collect. Southern California's growth demanded ever more water and threatened its neighbors near and far, paralyzing even distant states like Colorado. Largely to prevent California from taking all the water in the Colorado River, the other river states sued for peace. The result was ratification in 1927 of the Colorado Compact, which adjudicated the waters of the Colorado River on a state-by-state basis, and the decision to construct the Boulder Dam, now Hoover Dam, the largest public works project of its time, in Black Canyon about thirty miles from Las Vegas.

The dam was the signal event in the history of southern Nevada with ramifications far beyond the region. Beginning in 1931, construction lasted nearly four years, which meant four years of paychecks to almost five thousand workers at the height of the Depression. When Franklin D. Roosevelt dedicated the dam on September 30, 1935, the 760–foot concrete face presided over a technological miracle: a holding tank for all the water in the river, distributed by legal agreement between haves and havenots. The dam created life, an economy, infrastructure, business, and even tourism. Secretary of the Interior Dr. Ray Lyman Wilbur decided he wanted no part of the sinful railroad town of Las Vegas for the project. A stern moralist, Wilbur preferred the dry style of the Coolidge administration that preceded his tenure. Although Wilbur built a government town called Boulder City, dry and free of gambling, the road to the dam led through Las Vegas. Wilbur's puritanism had inadvertently given Las Vegas a new future.

The synergy the dam created was tremendous. Its success paved the way for the Bureau of Reclamation to become the pre-eminent federal agency of the 1930s and a powerful engine of federal spending until the 1970s. After Boulder Dam, the Bureau of Reclamation engaged in forty-year orgy of dam building until it controlled the distribution of most of the water west of the Mississippi River and created legions of dependent local oligarchies in the small-town and mini-city West. As the dam revived Las Vegas, it also provided a new master, one that carried other federal beneficiaries in tow.

Las Vegas was entirely typical of other western towns in the 1930s. The region's economy survived or thrived based on the size of the federal contribution. ... There was one way that Las Vegas could stand apart from the multitude of similar towns. It possessed a sense of itself as a place out of time, left over from an older western past. A certain amount of the Old West was considered ribald by 1930s standards, but Las Vegas wasn't really sinful, its symbolism seemed to say. It just hadn't changed while everyone else had, and so held a convenient place in memory that allowed it—and you, when you visited—to get away with things that you couldn't at home. In a society quick to condemn aberrant behavior yet nostalgic for its lost roots, ribald could be packaged as individual freedom.

This tradition became the crux of the vaunted Nevada individualism, the most appealing and vexing characteristic of the state then and now. Nevada was and is wide open, a dream for anyone who was ever a sophomore in college and entranced by Ayn Rand, even for a moment. In their rugged self-image, Nevadans pride themselves on having real freedom, not the namby-pamby eighteenth-century Paul Revere—style freedom within the constraints of the community, but the right to do what you want, whenever you want, wherever you want, and with whomever you want. Fusing its rugged history with economic necessity, Nevada put as few constraints on the individual as possible. Your property is *your* property more in Nevada than in any other state in the union; you can carry a concealed weapon with less red tape than in most places, and the concept of self-defense—your right to protect yourself—is carried further in Nevada law than elsewhere in the nation. The desert alone was not the sole attraction for James "Bo" Gritz, the survivalist who negotiated the surrender at Ruby Ridge in Idaho. Nor is it accident that within a mile of the state capitol in Carson City, legal houses of prostitution flourish. Nevada is the home of the Sagebrush Rebellion, an attempt to privatize most federal lands in the West under the pretext of furthering private property rights. Nevada still sells this same nostalgia. All of this individualism pulls on the nation's emotions in an age when we're oppressed by institutions and information and told that the self is all there is. But this romanticism embodies a difficult paradox: with ideals like these, it's hard to run a modern society.

The next capital regime, federal dollars, illustrated the perils of colonial existence. Lacking industry or infrastructure, Las Vegas depended first and foremost on outside money. Almost as an afterthought, the state permitted activities that were regarded as scandalous. Southern Nevadans especially recognized the perils of dependence. An arbitrary change in federal policy could threaten not only individual livelihood, but the economic viability of the entire region. Before air-conditioning, attracting newcomers to a town where summer temperatures routinely topped 110 degrees was a difficult task without the lure of easy prosperity.

As a result, Las Vegas shaped itself to the needs of the outside. In the West of the 1930s and 1940s, this was not unusual. Oklahoma City, Richmond, California, and countless communities did the same. Only Las Vegans recognized that their opportunity to capitalize was time-bound, and that long-term sustenance required other strategies. Southern Nevada especially welcomed the federal money and encouraged those dollars to stay. At the same time, its people looked for new ways to diversify their income base. [...]

As World War II ended, a little red sports car came up Highway 91 from Los Angeles, and from it emerged a strong-jawed if ragged-looking man with hard eyes. Benjamin "Bugsy" Siegel, a mobster and close associate of underworld leader Meyer Lansky, inaugurated the next capital regime in Las Vegas. A vicious and probably psychotic thug and hit man, Siegel had been flirting with Hollywood before he came to Las Vegas. He didn't understand why he hadn't been cast in movies; he was handsome, he thought, rugged-looking, and a good actor to boot. He should be in film. But his real business called, and Siegel headed down the road.

His arrival was part of a larger plan. Lansky and his associates eyed Las Vegas as early as 1941, but in most accounts Siegel receives credit for envisioning the complicated relationship between gambling and status that turned the Flamingo Hotel into Las Vegas's first national destination. Siegel transformed Las Vegas from a western, institution-free center of vice into a world-renowned spectacle of gambling, entertainment, and fun by blending the themes of Monte Carlo, Miami Beach, and Havana with the resortlike character of the hotels that preceded the Flamingo on Highway 91. Siegel had a bizarre idea of class, but in the process of painting it onto the dinky little oasis, he inaugurated an era in which the capital to fund gaming resorts, the newest dominant industry in Las Vegas, came first from the pockets of organized crime and later from legitimate money the underworld could control. [...]

Locals did not object to this seemingly nefarious involvement in what was becoming the primary local industry. There was only one other significant source of capital in postwar Las Vegas, the Nevada Test Site. Cold War spending in support of above-ground testing between 1951 and 1963 and underground testing afterwards provided as many as nine-thousand jobs. Although certainly significant, such spending only went so far: it provided jobs for the most specialized workforce in the area, offered a considerable number of well-paying but dangerous jobs, and became the baseline for the regional economy. But federal spending after 1945 was only the starting point. In southern Nevada, the need for capital was so great that almost everyone looked the other way when it came to mob dollars. Even the strait-laced Mormon culture welcomed the newcomers. The mobster's arrival opened a new pipeline to the capital for which Las Vegans thirsted. Siegel's well-known association with Murder Incorporated, the sensationalized mob killers from 1930s New York, did not scare away locals. Anyone with money to invest was welcome, even Benny Siegel.

Lansky was perhaps the shrewdest of the mobsters, carefully covering his tracks.

When Siegel purchased the El Cortez in 1945, his investors included locals as well as gangsters Lansky, Gus Greenbaum, an Arizona bookmaker, Davie Berman, the mob boss of Minneapolis, and his ne'er-do-well brother Chickie, and Israel "Icepick Willie" Alderman, who ran typical 1930s gaming road-houses called "carpet joints" in Minneapolis, and Moe Sedway, a Siegel associate from Los Angeles. The purchase of the El Cortez initiated a pattern that marked two decades of Las Vegas development. In every subsequent purchase or development of a resort on the Strip, "connected" illegal gamblers, who became legal in Nevada, participated. In nearly every new casino in the 1940s and 1950s, a visible relationship between locals and newcomers effectively linked outside capital with respectability. Locals who could easily be licensed or individuals with ties to organized crime but no significant criminal record held visible and often sizable percentages of new casinos. Most of these "owners" appeared to have recently come into money. Who truly owned their percentage was not a good question to ask. [...]

The mob and its strange habits with money created the Las Vegas of myth, the town where, as Debbie Reynolds observed, "nobody got killed who didn't deserve it." Las Vegas became a world of shadowy individual investment, usually hidden and always untaxed, with deliveries of the skim, paper bags, and briefcases full of money to distant cities. These individuals held "points" in Las Vegas, percentage investments that were not on the record but that returned monthly profits skimmed off the top of the casino's profits and never recorded in their ledgers, taxed, or made known to aboveground stockholders. Insidious and nefarious to be sure, most of these investments were also small-time, amounting to as little as a few thousand dollars a month in profit. On paper, Jack Entratter, the head of the Sands in the early 1960s, ostensibly owned 12 percent of the operation. A former headwaiter at the Copacabana in Miami Beach who had become a player and philanthropist in Las Vegas—the social hall in the oldest synagogue in town, Temple Beth Sholom, was constructed with his donation and named for

him—Entratter owned 2 percent himself. The other 10 points he held for various people, including the real power at the Sands, an old associate of Lansky's named Vincent "Jimmy Blue Eyes" Alo. The mythic Las Vegas was a personal world where everyone knew everyone else and all knew who buttered their figurative bread. [...]

In the open political and cultural climate of southern Nevada, Las Vegas became the center of gaming in the Western Hemisphere. With the rise of Fidel Castro in Cuba and the closure of the Havana casinos, only one location in North America provided legal big-time gambling. Combined with improvements such as the expansion of McCarran Airport in 1963, Las Vegas took advantage of the growing affluence and changing cultural mores of American society. In Nevada, gaming masked its social cost. Despite the reality that many casino employees gambled their pay-checks, most of casinos' winnings came from visitors. The industry consistently produced positive numbers for the state economy.

This new importance led to a much greater demand for capital than had existed during the 1950s. Until 1963, when the Fremont Casino skimming scandal was derailed by illegal Federal Bureau of Investigation wire-taps, Las Vegas was a small-time operator's paradise. Accustomed to seeing their occupation as risky, the individuals who ran casinos operated as fly-by-nights. Skimming was endemic. A piece of the profit went in the celebrated "three for the hotel, one for the government, and one for the boys" formula, and the real powers, mob bosses in other cities, received it in paper bags. They looked at the short-term profit that could be put in their pockets as the best profit, almost instinctively feeling that the idyllic moment could not last. They believed that their run of luck would soon end. The laws would change, the moralists would come out of the woodwork, the police would crack down, and they'd be on the run again, without their increasingly expensive tangible assets, the larger and larger casino hotels along the Strip.

When the hammer fell, as it did repeatedly, its impact was usually negligible. Americans were increasingly willing to experiment with self-indulgence. In a world where leisure and recreation were becoming more important, gambling ceased to be a moral violation and began its road toward acceptance as a legitimate recreational pastime, a journey completed sometime in the 1990s. The new emphasis on gambling as a form of entertainment rather than a tawdry pastime put pressure on operators to cater to a broader audience. To get Mom and Pop America to Sin City demanded that operators see the openness of Las Vegas as more than a moment that would soon end. It also required a lot more money. [...]

The financial markets still eschewed gaming resorts. The only legitimate source of such capital in southern Nevada was a local bank, the Bank of Las Vegas, founded in 1954 and reorganized as the Valley Bank in 1964. An arm of the empire of Walter Cosgriff of the Continental Bank of Utah, the only non-Mormon financial institution of significance in the Beehive State, the Bank of Las Vegas mirrored Cosgriff's willingness to loan money outside of the conventional channels of midcentury America. In the 1950s, the Bank of Las Vegas became a primary local source of capital, but despite its significance and that of banker E. Parry Thomas, growth still outstripped available funding. Casinos lined up for money from Thomas's bank, but the capital needed to transform Las Vegas into a first-class resort would have to come from somewhere else.

Again, the mob was at the center of the story. The Teamsters' Central States, Southeast, and Southwest Areas Pension Fund, run by Allen Dorfman, the stepson of mobster Paul "Red" Dorfman and an associate of the Chicago mob, provided the source. In the early 1950s, the Teamsters boss Jimmy Hoffa hand-picked the younger Dorfman, then a college physical education instructor, to handle the Teamsters' insurance to repay a favor to his stepfather. In 1967, as Hoffa prepared to go to jail, he gave Dorfman complete control of pension fund loans. [...]

Early Teamsters pension fund forays into Las Vegas had little to do with gaming. In 1958 *Las Vegas Sun* publisher Herman "Hank" Greenspun, one of the few American newspaper publishers to challenge Senator Joseph McCarthy's reign of terror and loudly critical of the influence of organized crime on his adopted state, received $250,000 from the pension fund for a golf course. Teamsters money funded other developments. On April 14, 1959, the one-hundred-bed Sunrise Hospital opened, built by the Paradise Development Company, whose officers included Moe Dalitz, casino executive Allard Roen, who had been indicted in the United Dye and Chemical stock fraud case, and two young Las Vegas businessmen, Irwin Molasky and Mervin Adelson. Hoffa ensured its profitability by delivering the Teamsters union health care contracts to the new hospital.

Subsequent construction by the Paradise Development Company, especially the 1967 Boulevard Mall, drew accolades from the community. With access to capital for developing noncasino projects, the company effectively planned the future of nonresort Las Vegas by turning Maryland Parkway, a two-lane road that paralleled the Strip about two miles to the east, into the main commercial thoroughfare for the growing city. Nearly everyone in the city with any kind of aspiration, workers and executives alike, came to live in the area east of the new commercial center. The enclosed Boulevard Mall, the first modern shopping center in Las Vegas, capped this process. With its completion, Las Vegans needed only a little self-deception to believe that their city had amenities for its residents to match those of the resorts that catered to visitors.

This was the most complicated dimension of mob rule in southern Nevada. In a colony lacking internal capital, in the middle of substantial growth, and dominated by an industry that the mainstream would not fund, Las Vegas hungered for fresh capital, no matter what its origins. Largely invisible to the public, unconventional financing helped shape the direction of the city. Teamsters pension fund money invested in social projects, albeit profitable ones like the hospital and the mall, made that capital even more palatable. To most of greater Las Vegas, which had grown from roughly 8,000 in 1940 to 269,000 in 1967 and was comprised of casino workers who regarded legalized gaming as the solution to legal woes they experienced elsewhere, the hospital and mall were community assets. Similar developments continued to normalize Las Vegas, offering people a sense of typicality that had been hard to sustain in the 1950s. For that, Las Vegans were grateful, and they were usually willing to overlook the unusual origins of the money that financed their normalcy. [...]

By 1966, the pension fund had become the dominant source of development capital in southern Nevada. The rising cost of resort development, particularly after Caesars Palace, demanded more than $100 million in development capital. The traditional means of capital formation, stock offerings and bonds, were still blocked. Wall Street was not ready, leaving gambling's lucrative rewards to the pension fund and the organized crime bosses who ran it. That made Las Vegas beholden not to conventional financial powers in America, but to the parasitic forces that preyed upon it. People in gaming were not bothered by the prospect of silent and powerful control. In the 1960s, Las Vegas's veneer of typicalty was thin. Although Las Vegans insisted that behind the glitz, they lived in a "normal" town, their definition of normal was quite at odds with the one held by the rest of the nation. [...]

The transformation of Las Vegas from a mob-dominated gambling town to corporate-owned modern resort began with two related events. The first was the arrival of reclusive billionaire Howard R. Hughes at a suite atop the Desert Inn in Las Vegas in his typically bizarre fashion on the eve of Thanksgiving, 1966. Hughes had been a frequent visitor to Las Vegas in the 1950s, living there for a year, often talking of bringing his entire business empire to Nevada. In 1966, the billionaire was ferried from his private railroad car and hustled upstairs to the floor of penthouse suites reserved for the high rollers on whom the casino depended. After a few weeks, the management of the Desert Inn sought to persuade Hughes to leave; they'd expected an increase in gambling as a result of the presence of the world's richest man and were sorely disappointed. Hughes had so far cost them money.

They couldn't put the high rollers they needed in the hotel because Hughes insisted on having the entire floor. Gamble or leave, they told Hughes's representatives.

Instead of doing either, Hughes bought the place for about $13 million and remained cloistered in the penthouse for four years. The purchase was the first in a buying spree that included the Frontier, for which Hughes paid $14 million, the Sands, $14.6 million, Castaways, $3 million, the $17 million Landmark and its nearly $9 million Teamsters pension fund loan, and the Silver Slipper. All of Hughes's purchases had been Lansky-dominated casinos. Hughes added a television station, airlines, small airport facilities, one hundred residential lots at the Desert Inn Country Club, and thousands of acres of undeveloped land, including more than twenty thousand acres called "Husite," where Hughes promised the federal government a guided missile base in return for the nearly free land. Hughes made overtures to purchase Caesars Palace, the Riviera, and the Dunes in Las Vegas as well as Harrah's in Reno and Lake Tahoe, but an antitrust suit halted negotiations. Before the Nixon administration received a bribe and overruled Justice Department objections to Hughes's purchase of Harold's Club in Reno and the Landmark Hotel, the tycoon controlled about one-seventh of the state's gaming revenue, one-quarter of that in Las Vegas, and more than one-third of the revenue generated on the Strip. [...]

Hughes served as a harbinger of a new era, the first set of truly deep pockets to seek to make Las Vegas his own. He arrived at the ideal moment for a newcomer, exactly as the fortunes of his predecessors began to give way. The first generation of mob impresarios, men such as Meyer Lansky and Jimmy Alo, were aging, and some grew tired of the constant federal surveillance and other hassles that accompanied a move to the legitimate American economy. Selling out to Hughes, whom they regarded as the quintessential sucker, seemed a good idea. They took their profit and departed.

In some ways, Hughes was more like the gangsters he replaced than the corporate America that revered him. Gaming was a natural for Hughes. He was a confirmed risk-taker who flaunted rules all his life, he was beholden to no one, and even more important, owed no one. Hughes was the sole stockholder of Hughes Tool Company, meaning that only he had to pass gaming commission investigations. A man of his stature and wealth had little problem manipulating regulatory bodies in a state with weak government. As was the case with the development of the Flamingo and its peers, Hughes's capital was private and personal. The reclusive and idiosyncratic billionaire's vast empire had no public association with organized crime. A forerunner of the new Las Vegas whose patterns resembled the old, Hughes's interest helped legitimize investment in the gaming industry.

The second change made the mobsters who sold out wince. In 1967, at the behest of William F. Harrah and Baron and Conrad Hilton, with the support of Nevada governor Paul Laxalt, the state passed the Corporate Gaming Act, which eliminated the requirement that each stockholder had to pass a Gaming Control Board background check. Governor Grant Sawyer had fought this law while in office, believing it would only institutionalize organized crime, but Laxalt had no such qualms. Passage of the law opened the door for an infusion of corporate capital and raised the stakes in gaming. Corporations could now invest, inaugurating a new capital regime that brought Las Vegas closer to the primary avenues of capital formation. [...]

In this climate, organized crime suddenly became financially obsolete. Hotel chains pioneered the way, and financial markets slowly changed their view of gaming. In a few seconds, Wall Street could muster a great deal more money than organized crime ever could. The $269 million of Teamsters pension fund money in late-1960s Las Vegas might have remained the largest investment in southern Nevada, but it ceased to represent the growth sector of gaming capital. In an instant, the passage of the revised Corporate Gaming Act redistributed power in Las Vegas away from mob-controlled dollars and toward Wall Street. [...]

Clearing the mob out was easier said than done. In 1979, after a nearly three-year battle to rid the Aladdin of James Tamer, an affiliate of the Lebanese underworld, and Sorkis Webbe, its legal counsel, the Gaming Commission suspended the Aladdin's state gaming license. Later the Gaming Commission gave the Aladdin a sell-or-close order. On August 6, 1979, gaming control agents entered the Aladdin casino and sealed the slot machines and the tables. It was a sad fate for the hotel where Elvis and Priscilla married. Even though Judge Harry Claiborne, who was later impeached by the Senate, issued an injunction a few hours later and the casino reopened, never before had a mob casino been shut down simply for being a mob casino. The closure was revolutionary. A little more than a decade after the Corporate Gaming Act, Nevada state government was making unprecedented efforts to rid its primary industry of organized crime.

The 1980s completed the process of excising the mob. The arrival of FBI agent Joe Yablonsky as special agent in charge in Las Vegas led to a half-decade of vigorous prosecution. The city became tense, and city leaders screamed that Yablonsky pursued a vendetta against them. Senator Paul Laxalt, a close confidant of President Ronald Reagan, squawked so loudly about Yablonsky that it attracted attention to corruption in Las Vegas. A scandal at the Tropicana led to further prosecutions, and the mob's hold, always tenuous, convulsed and released. [...]

Throughout the 1970s, national banks generally shied away from Las Vegas, but large profits in Atlantic City persuaded a few East Coast and California banks that Las Vegas might be a legitimate investment. Through the Del Webb Company, the Sahara received $135 million in 1979 from New York banks for improvements to the resort, $25 million more than the hotel requested. At about the same time, Aetna Insurance Company loaned Caesars World, the parent corporation of Caesars Palace, $60 million. Soon after, First Interstate Bank developed a sizeable casino and gaming loan portfolio. By 1980 the state's five dominant gaming entities, Harrah's, the MGM, Del Webb, the Hilton, and Caesars World, were all publicly traded corporations.

Las Vegas was yet again transformed by the nearly unlimited capital that public financing could generate. Impresario Steve Wynn, a protégé of Parry Thomas, raised the ante of casino financing, laying the foundation of a new and presumably competition-proof Las Vegas. Large-scale funding meant that Las Vegas could become more than the mecca of glitz and excess. Once its capital came from the mainstream, its attractions could be shaped to the tastes of the mainstream audience. Las Vegas promised a luxury experience at a middle-class price; now it could offer that price to the entire middle class. The gradual easing of the stigma of gaming and the willingness to merge gaming with conventional postwar attractions on the scale of Disneyland increased Las Vegas's reach. Not only did gamblers come to the transformed desert town, so did people who wanted to see the spectacle and have a vacation in a classic but updated sense of the word. Sin City became more palatable and maybe even marginally less sinful. [...]

The combination of widespread credit, the new availability of cash, and the great stock run-up of the 1990s extended the market for gaming and leisure. In the late 1970s, consumer interest rates were deregulated and companies located in states that permitted high interest rates could export them to customers in states with lower ceilings. The credit card revolution began. Within a few years, anyone with halfway decent credit and the prospect of paying back at least part of what they borrowed received offers of credit cards with limits that sometimes exceeded their annual income. With credit, people could truly attain the be-all and end-all of post-1960s culture: they could have whatever they wanted now and pay for it later, if at all. Cash flow was no longer a barrier to a weekend in Las Vegas. [...]

In a 1994 cover story, *Time* magazine declared that Las Vegas had become an All-American city, the new American hometown. The rest of the nation had become more like its former capital of sin, Kurt Andersen of the magazine averred, granting Las Vegas a leading role in the service economy that has become, for better and worse, the future of the nation. What this glitzy and superficial analysis failed to note was that at the same time, Las Vegas had become a lot more like the rest of the nation.

Las Vegas had solved one of the major problems of the transition from industrial to postindustrial economy. In this mecca of gaming, unskilled individuals with barely a high school education could still earn a middle-class income. The Culinary Union helped keep wages high, and some hotels provided wages and benefits that exceeded union contract in order to discourage unionization. Las Vegas had become the "Last Detroit" in the way it provided solid pay for unspecialized work; for anyone with a modicum of skill and grace, it was an easy place to do well in service positions.

The transformation was completed by the way in which the Las Vegas experience became a part of the business of professional leisure. By the 1990s ITT-Sheraton, Hilton, and other major hotel chains owned major casino-hotels. Graduates of Wharton Business School made decisions, and the gaming industry developed a hierarchy that resembled the army's. Special training was required before anyone received the opportunity to lead. There was even a glass ceiling in gaming, but its defining trait wasn't gender: dealers could no longer work their way off the floor to management positions. In the large resorts, the upward mobility that being "connected" once ensured disappeared. Pit boss was now as high as a dealer or floor worker could expect to go. The management positions were filled by MBAs, professional businesspeople who did not truly understand the gaming industry. The personal side of gaming, where a floor manager recognized and took care of regular patrons, disappeared as gaming became an industry like any other. [...]

As the twenty-first century gathers momentum, Las Vegas is finally sharing greater commonality with the rest of the nation. It depends on the same sources of capital that other communities do and has accepted many of the same rules and regulations. It's not only that the rest of the nation normalized the behaviors that used to make Las Vegas exceptional; in its hierarchy, distribution of wealth and status, demography, and stratification of its labor force, Las Vegas has become more like the rest of the nation as well. Once a pariah, Las Vegas has become a paradigm of the postindustrial economy. As gaming spreads throughout the nation—usually run by Las Vegas companies—the colony is being transformed. Las Vegas has become a colonizer, exporting its version of the new economy to New Orleans, Missouri, Detroit, and elsewhere. Las Vegas has always reflected America onto itself. It has always been the mirror people held up to their faces to see what they hoped for and, equally, what they feared. As it became normative, the entire historical equation of the city was thrown on its head. Las Vegas is the first city of the new century, the one that owes its allegiance to the shape of the new universe, to the signs and symbols of a culture of entertainment.

ESSAY 10.2

Artist Organizations, Political Advocacy, and the Creation of a Residential SoHo

Aaron Shkuda

Source: Aaron Shkuda, *The Lofts of SoHo: Gentrification, Art, and Industry in New York, 1950–1980* (Chicago: University of Chicago, 2016), 92–106.

EDITORS' INTRODUCTION

SoHo, the subject of urban planner Chester Rapkin's *The South Houston Industrial Area* (1963) study, is synonymous with the concept of gentrification. Gentrification is the act of redeveloping a portion of the urban landscape, often once the space of the poor or working-class, according to the style specifications of the middle or upper classes. In the process of gentrification, commercial aspects of the area may arise where they had withered, or change to suit the tastes of a wealthier clientele. Gentrification may displace industry or alter the commerce of a neighborhood, and gentrification ultimately may even displace the initial group of gentrifiers themselves. Once sought after, a particular street or urban neighborhood may prove less affordable. Gentrification has garnered criticism for exacerbating and even driving displacement of persons of color from cities. Writer Ta-Nehisi Coates argues that "'gentrification' is but a more pleasing name for white supremacy." Gentrification may accelerate the movement of the urban poor.

American cities have provided homes to the very rich and the very poor. Wealthy Americans obtain housing in key physical locations in the cities and have the means to secure the largest and highest quality apartments and homes. Cities feature some of the most exclusive clubs, social scenes, and entertainment offerings, and rich people seek access to these upscale urban amenities. Immigrants, many of whom historically were without financial means upon first arriving in the nation, cluster in cities due to cities' roles as ports and over-ground transportation hubs. The middle class may not be able to afford housing in the most central or sought after areas of the city, and may choose to avoid overcrowded areas inhabited by the urban poor. Thus the middle classes often use their moderate finances to refashion dwellings within an impoverished area to their tastes or may secure housing outside of the city.

City neighborhoods continuously evolve. Areas that are today considered slums may have housed the wealthy in the past. Larger homes are sliced up into smaller rental units over time. Some urban dwellers bring their creativity and resiliency to create strong neighborhoods in areas that were once devoted to industrial spaces.

In New York and other American cities, artists led urban change by settling in marginal or industrial neighborhoods and carving out new opportunities for housing, creative space, and vibrant neighborhood life within the buildings, streets, and sidewalks there. Before the artists devoted attention to SoHo, the floors of the industrial lofts, supported by aging cast iron beams, were literally collapsing. Factories were no longer dependent on the steam engines that made multiple story buildings practical. Modern industry needed the elongated one-floor factories now being built on the edges of the city. Trucks moved raw and finished materials more expeditiously than train cars. Trucks allowed factories to disperse over a wider area, and linked highway access with premium industrial sites. The outdated physical spaces south of Houston Street in New York City were in line to be destroyed in the name of progress by the planned but ultimately scrapped Lower Manhattan Expressway. What was unneeded by industry provided creative fodder for artists. Requiring access to large spaces in which to create art, and seeking affordable spaces in which to live, artists worked together over time to build the loft culture of SoHo. The section of New York evolved from a busy industrially-focused area to a setting for artist workshops, artist lofts, and art galleries.

In his book *The Rise of the Creative Class*, urban theorist Richard Florida posits that areas like SoHo, which house the "creative class," increase the livability of a neighborhood and bring considerable financial vitality to the city as a whole. The artists' work within SoHo provided so much attention and uplift to the Lower Manhattan neighborhood that it ultimately became unaffordable for all but the most financially successful artists. Redecorating, coupled with the energy of the art gallery scene, and the artists' fight to change laws vis-à-vis the once-illegal loft housing brought other New Yorkers to the area. The gentrified streets soon became home to some of the most expensive housing in the city.

Historian Aaron Shkuda is the project manager of the Princeton-Mellon Initiative in Architecture, Urbanism, and the Humanities at Princeton University. Formerly he was the American Council of Learned Society's New Faculty Fellow at Carnegie Mellon University and served as Assistant Director of a residential humanities program at Stanford University. Shkuda authored "Housing the 'Front Office to the World': Urban Planning for the Service Economy in Battery Park City, New York," *Journal of Planning History*, August 2014.

ARTISTIC ORGANIZATIONS, POLITICAL ADVOCACY, AND THE CREATION OF THE RESIDENTIAL SOHO (2016)

In February 1961, SoHo artists faced a threat that almost ended their nascent colony. This peril was not an economic downturn, the prospect of a highway, or even the early stages of gentrification. Instead, the culprits were some of the most mundane elements of urban governance: zoning ordinances and building codes. These types of regulations are meant to protect residents, and it was the issue of resident safety that caused an acute crisis in the SoHo artist community. In late 1960 and early 1961, a series of fires broke out in industrial lofts below Houston Street, leading to the deaths of four people, including three firefighters. Though none of the fires occurred in lofts where artists lived, these blazes led the New York City Fire Department and the New York City Department of Buildings to launch a series of inspections of SoHo structures.[1]

Although both agencies initially reacted to a series of code violations in industrial buildings, they soon made a surprising discovery: artists living illegally in these structures. The *New York Herald-Tribune* reported that city officials found at least 128 illegal apartments in the area containing "beatniks, complete with beards" living with "mattresses on the floor and works on Zen Buddhism," along with vermin and cockroaches. In turn, Deputy Assistant Fire Chief Thomas J. Hartnett wondered how anyone could stand living in this section of Manhattan, asking, "How do they get their milk delivered?"[2]

This "discover" of SoHo residents reveals an important element of the neighbourhood's early history: that the very idea of living in a loft was completely novel. Whereas lofts are now ubiquitous in urban areas worldwide, hardly any people considered living in former industrial space before the 1960s. Similarly, few observers saw artists as people with the power to transform neighbourhoods or develop real estate, as demonstrated by the *Herald-Tribune's* use of the word *beatniks*, the derogatory term for bohemians of that era, to describe SoHo residents; in that writer's view, they did not even rise to the level of artist. Local building and zoning laws made no allowance for people who wanted to live in industrial buildings. As a result, when they encountered loft residents for the first time, city officials did not celebrate the possible rebirth of a struggling industrial area at the hands of artists. Instead, they threatened them with eviction.

In response to the spectre of eviction, artists organized themselves politically, forming lobbying organizations and using public demonstrations and boycotts to advocate for their housing needs. SoHo artists threw the entire weight of the New York art world behind their cause. Well-known artists such as Willem de Kooning and Isamu Noguchi, as well as curators and gallery owners, spoke out in favour of loft residents. Through their advocacy, SoHo residents worked to redefine the role of the artist in society in the minds of local leaders. They argued that affordable housing for up-and-coming artists was crucial to New York's future because artists were the backbone of its cultural economy, as well as the people who gave the city its reputation as the world's leading creative and artistic center.

In making these arguments, SoHo artists placed the arts at the center of the debate about how to redevelop cities at a time of urban crisis. By finding value and beauty in outdated industrial structures, they also reclaimed property viewed as obsolete eyesores by urban renewal advocates. By pioneering new uses for lofts, SoHo residents created powerful arguments against slum clearance, particularly in industrial and commercial areas.

SoHo artists also shifted the terms of the ongoing debates over neighborhood preservation and rehabilitation. Although meeting the housing needs of lower-income populations in central cities had long been a preoccupation of policy makers, artists looked to demonstrate that they were a unique group—relatively poor people with distinct housing needs but who also had the power to drive the city's economy and give it its unique identity. They urged city leaders to help bolster one of the few things New York still had going for it—its reputation for the arts—by allowing artists to live in the manner that best suited them: in converted industrial lofts with room to live and work affordably.

Though they fought to change zoning laws, rather than against slum clearance, artists developed powerful arguments that pushed the debate over the future of urban neighborhoods beyond the renewal/community defense paradigm that had dominated discourse up to that point. Unlike antirenewal protesters, who mainly focused on preserving their neighborhoods, SoHo artists posited a new future for their community. They argued that their efforts would revitalize an area shaped by deindustrialization and urban renewal. At the same time, SoHo artists placed the arts at the center of a debate over the future of their neighborhood. To SoHo artists, urban culture could do for SoHo what other urban development schemes could not: create a vibrant neighborhood that helped drive the city's economy and identity. Much like the backers of the project such as Manhattan's Lincoln Center, SoHo artists were staking out a place for culture in the city. The same New York artistic culture that could help the United States compete with the Soviet Union for cultural dominance globally could also help breathe life into moribund industrial neighborhoods.[3]

In the end, artist grounds in SoHo achieved goals that were both modest and significant. Their advocacy led to changes in two regulations that allowed only a limited number of artists to live legally in a loft. Yet these laws were the first to make it legal for anyone to live in such a structure and the first to give government sanction to anyone, artists or otherwise, to live in any former industrial space. Moreover, these policies indicated that more New Yorkers were starting to support an argument made by SoHo activists: that artists had a unique power to reinvigorate neighborhoods long ago left for dead. Thanks to the artist advocacy, policy makers began to connect artist housing and urban vitality, a link that would become the foundations of theories of creative place making and the creative class several decades later. Through their actions and words, SoHo artists made the case that art could be a force for urban change.

Fires, Illegality, and Evictions: The Early Years of SoHo Lofts

SoHo artists learned quickly that their tenancy in lofts was vulnerable. After the series of fatal loft fires in late 1960, Fire Commissioner Edward F. Cavanagh Jr. promised increased inspection and fire code enforcement in Lower Manhattan and SoHo. Previous inspections had shown that buildings in this area often did not contain sprinklers or other fire-prevention systems. Although the existence of an artist community in SoHo seemed to be far from his mind, the fire commissioner promised to conduct a more extensive survey of code violations in three thousand Lower Manhattan structures.[4]

Fire Commissioner Cavanagh had reason to worry about the safety of loft buildings. Although cast-iron columns gave SoHo lofts their unique open floor plans, they could also be a safety hazard. Because each column rested on the one below it, a single stack of columns running from the basement to the roof supported the whole building. Even under normal conditions, cast-iron columns were in danger of collapsing or cracking. Building owners had to worry about industrial equipment shifting or knocking out a column. The risk of fire was even more troubling. Cast-iron columns were unable to withstand rapid temperature changes. A column that grew too hot too fast from a building fire, or too cold from the water used to put out that fire, could snap, collapsing the building. In addition, weak brick walls, older timber beams, and open elevator shafts meant that the overwhelming majority of SoHo buildings were not fire resistant.[5]

Public concern over fire safety in loft buildings grew after a man living on the second floor of a five-story commercial building at 275 Canal Street (near Broadway) died in a fire in February 1960, prompting another promise of inspections by Fire Commissioner Cavanagh. Although the tenant in this case was not an artist, and it appeared that he had been living in the building legally, the New York Fire Department paid increasing attention to residential units in Lower Manhattan. Cavanagh said, "nearly twenty persons, including two firemen" had been killed in fires in Lower Manhattan in the previous two years.[6]

SoHo residents faced a genuine threat of eviction as a result of these inspections. In 1961, well-known painter Romare Bearden claimed that he was the first artist evicted from his loft. At that time, a local artist group reported that one hundred or more artists had been evicted in the past year. Although it is unclear how many loft tenants were evicted from their homes, there was a risk of the entire residential population facing eviction.[7]

Even if they were not faced with eviction, living illegally created a variety of nuisances that made residing in SoHo difficult. Although some SoHo residents never thought twice about the legal status of their homes, others avoided placing houseplants near their windows that could attract the attention of city officials. Some even had movable beds and living room furniture that could be whisked out of sight at a moment's notice if an inspector came calling. Without a legal residential population, neighborhood residents did not have regular garbage service, and they had to walk to Greenwich Village to buy groceries. These peculiarities of SoHo living gave artists additional incentives to legalize their homes.

Organizing to Save Their Homes: The Beginnings of SoHo Artist Advocacy

A coalition of Lower Manhattan artists formed the Artist Tenant Association (ATA), an organization of "painters who have been told to vacate their studios in antiquated, low-rent commercial buildings that have not met fire department regulations." The group's goals included working with city and state officials to amend building and zoning codes to allow for loft residences. The ATA kicked off its existence with a meeting at Greenwich Village's Judson Memorial Church on April 6, 1961.[8]

Although the bulk of the lofts that artists turned into homes were in SoHo, the artists who joined the ATA lived all over Lower Manhattan, and some resided as far away as Midtown. In addition, unlike the bulk of SoHo artists, some of the leading ATA figures had connections to Greenwich Village. Chair James Gahagan was active in the Provincetown Painters in Cape Cod in the 1950s, essentially a northern satellite of Greenwich Village, while member Robert Henry studied at the Hoffmann School of Fine Arts, an institution that played a central role in shaping artistic production in the Village at midcentury.[9]

Although the ATA's concerns were practical—their first aim was to prevent evictions from lofts—they soon framed the issue of artist housing within the ongoing debates over deindustrialization and the city's need to strengthen its economy in a time of urban decline. Through the ATA, SoHo artists contended that some of the area's underutilized industrial space was best used as a center of housing for artists who contributed to New York's economy and status as a leading cultural center. They argued that New York City would become a "cultural wasteland" if city leaders continued to evict artists from unique structures. ATA members warned that without artist housing in SoHo, artists would follow the many businesses and residents who had left New York City for the suburbs or cities farther west. The organization's leadership even went so far as to telegraph "the Mayors of Hoboken and San Francisco 'asking for asylum' if their 'cruel persecution' forced them to become 'refugees.'"[10]

In addition, SoHo artists worked to rehabilitate the image of the loft dweller from the subversive outsider to important economic actor. Downtown artist Tom Hannan worried that the image of artists as beatniks prevented their grievances from being taken seriously. He said, "Artists are one of the few groups with a single identity. Because we're creative, people think we're all nuts. They call us 'beatniks' or 'kooks' and they think we don't take baths. There is a tremendous moral, middle-class anti-artist attitude in this town. Nobody wants to get involved with us." In response, the ATA worked to create an image of artists as hardworking, family-orientated contributors to New York's cultural and economic life. For example, Jim Gahagan stated in an interview with the New York Times that the five thousand to seven thousand artists living in Manhattan lofts were hardly degenerates. He countered, "We're Bohemians, but we're not Beatniks. We may be isolated from the social, economic, even the political values the rest of the country operates under, but we aren't isolated from people. We put up with substandard housing, we do part-time labor and a lot of other things. Most of us earn less than a thousand a year from our painting and sculpture, but we wouldn't change the situation." The article argued that artists who were "pioneering in what is unquestionably the most built up city of earth," were by and large "models of tranquillity and respectability by comparison with those, say, of some television and advertising people. A fairly high percentage not only are married but have children." He even tried dispelling the myth of the decadent "loft party," which was described as possessing "all the orgiastic aspects of rush-hour dash for a commuter train." Aside from providing evidence that artists were respectable economic contributors to society, be referring to artists as "pioneers" in the most built-up city on earth, the article implied that artists had the power to drive real estate development without the teardowns and other costs associated with urban renewal.[11]

In addition, the ATA argued that the city should encourage loft housing because artists made important contributions to New York's economy. In their public statements, the ATA highlighted the "big business" of art in New York, saying that a significant portion of the $500 million that Americans paid for art each year was spent in two hundred New York City galleries. SoHo artists also made explicit connections between Lower Manhattan artists and the well-known New York school of abstract expressionist painting. Even though only a few SoHo artists were part of this movement, they claimed that their inability to live in lofts threatened a school that brought cultural attention, and a good deal of profits from the sale and exhibition of art, to the city. Artist Basil King said, "Do you know what the New York School is? The New York School is the colony of artists they're talking about all over the world. Everywhere you go, you hear people saying The New York School... The New York School... But this is what the New York School is. It's just a bunch of painters painting in lofts."[12]

However, ATA members faced a challenge: when they spoke of the economic contributions of the New York artists, the relationship of a group of relatively low-income artists in SoHo to the more lucrative formal art world was not immediately apparent. To better connect artist housing in SoHo to the New York art world, the ATA enlisted well-known artists, patrons of the arts, and representatives of the city's museum and gallery communities to their cause. In May 1961, New York art patron Eleanor Roosevelt supported the ATA's cause through a press release that read, "I find it hard to believe that the Administration and people of this great city, once they are informed of the situation, would stand idly by and allow artists to be dispersed." Metropolitan Museum of Art director James J. Rorimer asked the city to intervene to help local artists because "it is the work of the artist that contributes to the soul of the nation." In May 1961, the ATA organized a rally that drew three hundred "artists and art patrons," including *Art News* editor Alfred M. Frankfurter, sculptor Isamu Noguchi, abstract expressionist painter Willem de Kooning, and art critic Clement Greenberg, to a meeting at Washington Irving High School in Greenwich Village. De Kooning criticized the city for cracking down on artist lofts as well as Greenwich Village coffeehouses. Greenberg and de Kooning's presence lent an aura of authenticity to the Lower Manhattan artist's cause, and he likened the health of the arts to the economic and cultural well-being of the city. Fittingly, Greenberg also remarked to the press that he had put on a good suit to avoid being labeled as a beatnik.[13]

"Artist in Residence"—The Beginning of Loft Policy

The ATA's advocacy efforts eventually captured the attention of Mayor Robert Wagner, who called for a policy allowing some of the artists to legally convert industrial lofts into homes and studios. The *New York Times* reported that the mayor took action after reading about their protests in the newspaper and grew concerned about their "charge that mass evictions were threatening New York's continued existence as a center of artistic life." At the urging of the mayor, Fire Commissioner Cavanagh met with representatives from the ATA in May 1961.[14]

However, SoHo artists still had a difficult time convincing city officials that their need for housing, and their contributions to the city's economy, were more important than the safety issues associated with living in industrial buildings. Cavanagh was still focused on the legal concerns associated with artists living in lofts. As the fire commissioner put it, "The loft-dwellers don't have a foot to stand on. The rules say what kind of building you can live in. I'd be indicted for maladministration if I don't carry out the rules. I'd like to leave them alone. I'm not afraid to live in a loft building and I know they're not." He remarked to the press that he liked art as much as the next person, but said, "I'd like to see it in a wholesome, safe atmosphere. It doesn't have to be wholesome even, as long as it's safe."[15] Despite meetings with Fire Commissioner Cavanagh and attention from Mayor Wagner, the ATA was not able to reach a satisfactory agreement with the city, leaving the threat of loft evictions in place.

In response to the continuing indifference to the artists' plight, in June 1961 the ATA organized an artists' strike. The organization enlisted its artists and art dealer supporters to remove their artworks from galleries and museums until the city and state legalized loft housing for Lower Manhattan artists. In addition to Kooning, famous artists who pledged their support for the strike included Jasper Johns, Ad Reinhardt, Robert Motherwell, Alex Katz and Fairfield Porter.[16]

The ATA also pledged to enlist as many of the city's four hundred galleries as possible to cement the connections between SoHo artists and the city's cultural economy in the minds of policy makers. The ATA requested that its members not participate as artists in any public activity in New York, including exhibiting, appearing on TV or radio, or lecturing. It also asked that participants not send their work to any gallery or museum in New York, nor show their work in studios, nor attend exhibitions at galleries or museums and to withdraw works on loan or consignment if possible. Finally, the ATA asked that artists encourage colleagues living outside of New York not to send or show anything in the city. SoHo artists sought to remind the public that the art they made in their loft studios ended up for sale in galleries, and unless city leaders took action to legalize loft residencies, the economic benefits of gallery sales might be lost.[17]

The threat of an artists' strike led to an agreement that created the first legal protections for artists living in loft buildings. On August 15, 1961, ATA chair James Gahagan and Robert Bobrick, the organization's counsel, met with city officials, including buildings commissioner Peter Reidy, acting fire commissioner George Mand, housing assistant to the mayor Hortense Gable, and acting city administrator Maxwell Lehman. The goal of the meeting was to reach an agreement in advance of the ATA's September 11 strike deadline.[18]

As a result of this meeting, a policy agreed on by Mayor Wager on August 15 and announced to the press on August 22 spelled out the conditions under which artists could use loft buildings in Lower Manhattan. The agreement allowed artists to live in commercially zoned buildings as long as there were two means of egress and no businesses that created excessive fire hazards, such as those that manufactured paint and plastics. The artist also had to send a letter notifying the commissioner of buildings that he or she was occupying the premises. In addition, artist tenants were required to place an eight-by-ten-inch sign on their loft's exterior that read A.I.R. The letters should for "Artist in Residence."

Each sign also indicated to first responders where to find residents in case of an emergency and to buildings department inspectors where they should focus their inspections to ensure artist studio residences were safe.[19]

The agreement between the ATA and the city was significant news. Local papers and national art journals such as *Art News* reported on it. *Art News* wrote, "For the first time, New York artists, most of them vanguard, have joined together as a political pressure group in order to influence the legislation to their own advantage, with the formation this summer of the Artist Tenants Association." The periodical reported on the notable artists who signed onto the ATA's pledge and quoted Mayor Wagner as saying, "The artist working in New York is assured of the city's continuing interest in his welfare and in his work."[20]

Wagner's policy was the first public action that recognized the right of the artists to live in lofts. The mayor developed the policy for practical reasons. Never a public figure who relished conflict, Wagner probably saw the action as a way to avoid evicting artists and help a population in need with a little effort or expenditure. Yet, aside from these practical issues, the action was also an indication that the mayor, as well as other public officials, recognized the unique housing needs of artists and their importance to the city's economy and image as a center for the arts.

However, this arrangement was temporary and incomplete. The policy was not rooted in stature; it was only an informal agreement between artist groups and Mayor Wagner regarding which city laws would be enforced. Consequently, its application was spotty at best. Only three months after the policy was announced, four artists were threatened with eviction for not bringing their lofts up to the commercial building code. Jim Gahagan responded, saying, "For 50 years, these buildings were used for commercial purposes without sprinkler systems. Now that artists live in them, the Fire Dept. demands that the landlord install sprinkler systems. If the Fire Dept. is going to throw industrial and factory code at the artists, then they can never comply."

Moreover, he claimed that having to install sprinkler systems would lead to prohibitively high rent, violating the spirit of the agreement between the ATA and the city.[21] Efforts to legalize loft living, it seemed, would have to continue.

Zoning Change, Loft Value and Postindustrial Artist SoHo

While these early policy changes demonstrated that artists were garnering more political support, government actions legalizing loft residencies were incomplete and temporary, leaving artists vulnerable to eviction. The Artist in Residence program was never truly a success. According to the ATA, in the years between 1961 and 1963, fewer than one tenth of Lower Manhattan artists applied for and obtained A.I.R status. This was due in part to the difficulties involved in becoming an official artist in residence and the continuing fears among some artists that registering with the city and displaying a sign alerting the world to their presence would have made their residences a target for theft, as well as for unscrupulous building inspectors looking to extract bribes. These concerns, and the fact that the state regulations allowed only two loft residences per building, served to keep A.I.R. enrollment down. More important, the city's agreement with the ATA only applied to structures that were zoned for commercial use. When, in 1963, the city rezoned the area south of Houston Street as an M1–5 light industrial zone, the city stopped accepting A.I.R. applications in SoHo.[22]

Consequently, the ATA began its grassroots organizing afresh. It once again organized a coalition to support its efforts, but one that now included politicians and housing advocates in addition to artists, critics, and curators, indicating that a wider group of influential people was paying attention to the issue. In February 1964, the ATA organized a meeting in Greenwich Village's Judson Memorial Church at which two hundred of its members gave their support to a state bill that would amend the State Multiple Dwelling Law to allow for artist loft residences. McNeil Mitchell, a Greenwich Village Republican, and Assembly member Alfred A.

Lama, a Brooklyn Democrat-Liberal, sponsored the legislation. The bill itself came as a result of ATA members working directly with representatives from the state legislature. The group reported that it was collaborating with State Senator Mitchell to change the Multiple Dwelling Law as early as December 1962.[23]

The involvement of Mitchell and Lama gives some indication of how policy makers viewed artist tenants. The duo was best known for the Mitchell-Lama Limited-Profit Housing Companies Law, which encouraged the construction of middle-income housing in the city through the provision of state-backed mortgages for such projects.[24] Thus, at this juncture, it is likely that city and state leaders viewed artists at least in part as a moderate-income group whose housing needs local leaders could meet through appropriate policy.

The next target of artist advocacy was the New York State Multiple Dwelling Law. In spite of the decision by the mayor's office to ignore the city's zoning ordinance to let artists live in commercial buildings, the New York City Department of Buildings still had to enforce the state laws governing residential structures. This meant holding artists and their landlords to the state laws governing buildings containing multiple dwellings, including the safety standards of apartment buildings.

To push for changes to this law, the ATA staged a multipart protest that combined public demonstrations by rank-and-file artists and a boycott by better-known members of the New York art community. On Friday, April 3, 1964, the ATA's previously threatened artist strike became a reality, and eighty New York galleries closed to protest "recent enforcement of commercial zoning regulations" that prevented artists from living in lofts. Artists argued that without legislation allowing them to live in SoHo, they would be forced to leave the city, taking the economic contributions of art gallery sales with them. As loft resident and sculptor Ron Westerfield put it, "This is the end of the line for New York artists. If we have to get out of the lofts, we'll be finished."[25]

On April 3, the ATA also launched its most public protest to date, organizing a march attended by one thousand artists at City Hall. The march was meant to highlight the $500 million in revenue the arts community brought to the city each year, economic activity that was threatened by the lack of legalized loft housing. While the march was going on, recently elected ATA chair Jean Pierre Merle met with representative of the City Planning Commission and the Department of Buildings, as well as the city councilman at large Paul O'Dwyer of Manhattan, about the zoning changes that would legalize artist residences in Lower Manhattan.[26]

Thanks to these protests, city leaders began to take artists, their housing needs, and their ability to contribute to the city's economy more seriously. Artists' protests and advocacy were increasingly effective, as ATA members began to work directly with policy makers on legislation legalizing loft residences, demonstrating the growing acceptance of their vision for Lower Manhattan. In April 1964, the ATA met with a committee comprising members of the New York City Planning Commission, Buildings Department, City Administrator's Office, and Office of Cultural Affairs for the purpose of "studying the present problem, arriving at an equitable solution, and planning future housing."[27]

In May 1964, local leaders put their support for artists, their housing needs, and economic contributions into policy by amending the New York State Multiple Dwelling Law to permit "certified artists" to live in New York lofts. The non-profit group Volunteer Lawyers for the Arts remarked that the amendment represented "the first official public policy statement enunciating a commitment to prevent the exodus of artists from New York City." The law demonstrated that the ATA's arguments connecting artists' ability to love in SoHo lofts with New York's status as the world's cultural capital were beginning to take hold. SoHo artists helped pass the legislation by working with their connections in the state legislature, most notably State Senator Mitchell. The drafters of the law reasoned that the large amount of space artists require, combined with the fact

that "financial remunerations to be obtained from pursuit of a career in the visual fine arts are general small," made it difficult for artists to work in New York in light of the city's high housing costs. Therefore, the state has to act to keep artists living and working in New York by legalizing loft residences.[28]

However, the 1964 amendment to the Multiple Dwelling Law did not unambiguously support artists' housing. There were tensions in the law itself between the desire to preserve industry and the impulse to encourage loft conversions as a form of housing development. The amendment required buildings to be classified as entirely industrial or entirely residential. It did not allow for the typical conversion pattern in SoHo, in which industries occupied larger and more commercially viable lower floors while artists lived in relatively cramped upper stories. The law required that loft residences adhere to residential fire and safety codes that were, in the opinion of the Volunteer Lawyers for the Arts, "economically prohibitive." The policy also made it legal for "a person engaged in the visual fine arts, such as painting and sculpture on a professional fine arts basis," to live in a loft. Artists doing so had to be certified by "an art academy, association or society, recognized by the municipal office of cultural affairs or the state council on the arts." This definition appeared overly restrictive to some and untenable to others, as the New York City Department of Cultural Affairs did not have a mechanism for determining who was an artist and in fact did not put one in place until 1971, when a more comprehensive SoHo zoning resolution required it.[29]

Moreover, although the state changed the Multiple Dwelling Law to allow for certified artists to live in commercial and residential buildings, the law applied only to districts with specific city zoning designations (M1 and C8), which limited the number of loft buildings in which artists could live legally. The city also refused to accept any further registrations to the A.I.R. program in these areas. The ATA asked the city to survey the neighbourhoods that allowed for loft studio residences and those that did not in order to determine the availability and demand, but negotiations soon broke down. The ATA staged a protest at the reopening of the Museum of Modern Art as a result of this decision, but no further action from the city was forthcoming.[30] New York was so adamant in its decision not to expand areas where artist housing would be allowed, or to accept further A.I.R. applications, that, according to the ATA, only 286 artists were registered to legally live in loft buildings by 1967.[31]

Artists and Urban Development

As the piecemeal nature of the loft policy and problems with its enforcement indicate, the city and state leaders had not adequately addressed the issue of loft housing in New York. Likely, they did not fully understand the demand for, and the particular legal and physical barriers to, loft living among artists. During this time of debates over urban renewal, when policy makers were increasingly aware of the challenges keeping industrial businesses in the city, they were also reluctant to enact any policy that could threaten the industrial businesses still housed in lofts.

Policy makers worried that increasing the ability of artists to live legally in lofts could develop into a zero-sum game. If too many artists lived in lofts, they could conceivably take up the spaces where job-producing industrial businesses could locate. If loft policy were too restrictive, artists might leave the city, and industrial loft space might remain vacant anyway, harming both industrial business owners and the city's cultural economy.

Artist advocates understood the political balancing act, and from the beginning of their legalization efforts, they argued that the benefits that loft conversions brought to the city were good for industry as well as the economy as a whole. Members of the ATA stressed that artists were able to upgrade urban neighbourhoods, achieving many of the goals of urban renewal without most of the costs. A 1962 ATA publication stated, "With artists' ingenuity they transformed vacant, rundown light manufacturing

lofts at their own expense into safe, adequate studios. In this process they have improved property, eliminated fire hazards, and solved their own living problems without relying on Federal, State or City funds."[32] Moreover, artists were able to achieve this upgrading of SoHo's built environment and stabilization of its economy without affecting its industrial tenants, who were operating under the threat of urban renewal.

Others noted artists' dual role as potential urban renewal victims and people with the ability to generate many of the goals of slum clearance with few of the costs. A 1964 article in the *Nation* on loft advocacy in Lower Manhattan observed that many local artists been pushed out of affordable housing by government-sponsored redevelopment projects. Because of their need for "extravagant amounts of space by slide-rule criteria" and their low incomes, artists "naturally gravitate to the older sections of town, where more expansive accommodations of an earlier age are standing in slow dissolution," exactly the types of locations that were frequent targets of urban renewal projects. Once in these older sections of town, "they produce, in effect, lively oases in a neighborhood of slums" and since "no community was ever blighted by painters and sculptors, they have an instinct for renewal." This instinct was particularly important in a time of white flight and suburbanization, as when "everyone is going to the suburbs... artists are urban creatures" who often bring great benefits to urban neighborhoods.[33]

Thus, much like the advocates of urban renewal projects in and around SoHo, artists sought to convince city leaders that by upgrading SoHo lofts, they were improving New York's economy by producing new houses, creating new jobs, and preserving old ones. Yet, unlike advocates for projects such as highways and housing developments, SoHo artists developed a way to upgrade the area's industrial built environment while avoiding the human and economic costs of urban renewal. Artists' ceaseless efforts to change laws to secure legal recognition of their right to turn deserted industrial lofts into their living as well as work spaces played a key, if initially unanticipated, role in pioneering new strategies for urban renewal.

Yet, carrying this argument forward, it is not hard to see where conflict could emerge. If artists' actions resulted in eliminating slums and upgrading neighbourhoods, they were also helping to increase the value of local property. If this pattern continued, it would not be long before this increase in the cost of area lofts became an issue, both for artists and the industries with which they shared space. In anticipation of this potential conflict, artists had to demonstrate that they were adding to the city's cultural economy without detracted from its industrial one. They did so by reasoning that by renting vacant portions of industrial buildings, they allowed building owners to stay financially afloat and businesses employing the city's minority populations to stay in business. Even those who purchased loft buildings could argue that they were putting money into the pockets of industrial building owners, who might have other neighborhood enterprises or prefer to use these funds to relocate to a more efficient building.

Both policy makers and artists realized that the balance between artist housing and industry remained precarious. Industry saved SoHo from the urban renewal wrecking ball, allowing artists to cultivate new methods of upgrading loft buildings and adding value to these structures. Yet, a very real possibility existed that residential and industrial uses would soon come into conflict, resulting in industry being pushed from SoHo in much the same way that urban renewal advocated intended.

In the coming years, this risk of this conflict would be exacerbated by another factor that would shape SoHo's development: the growth of an art gallery district downtown. Soon after the first policies that legalized loft housing, art dealers and some SoHo artists began to see the benefits of spacious and inexpensive loft space for the display and sale of art. With art galleries came visitors, and businesses catering to visitors soon followed. In time, a thriving retail scene developed, making SoHo a more attractive place to live but also providing another potentially profitable use for loft space, further threatening the remaining industry in the neighborhood.

NOTES

1. "Violations Found before Loft Fire," *NYT*, November 22, 1960, 37; "Warning by Cavanagh," *NYT*, 21 February 21, 1961, 41.
2. "No Beatnik Pads in Loft Bldgs.," *NYH-T*, February 27, 1961, 1.
3. Klemek, *Transatlantic Collapse of Urban Renewal*, 132; Zipp, *Manhattan Projects*, 22.
4. "Violations Found before Loft Fire."
5. Rapkin, *South Houston Industrial Area*, 147–50.
6. "Warning by Cavanagh."
7. "Art: The Angry Dwellers," *Newsweek*, May 29, 1961.
8. "Artists Organize to Save Lofts as Studios Despite Fire Hazard," *NYT*, April 6, 1961, 122.
9. "List of ATA A.I.R.s," Artist Tenants Association Records 1959–1976, Archives of American Art, Smithsonian Institute, Washington DC (hereafter cited as *ATA Records*), Box 1 Folder 6; "Gahagan, Peter" and "Henry, Robert," in Hastings-Falk, *Who Was Who in Art*, 2: 1230, 1534.
10. "Artists of the City Unite to Save Their Garrets, Seek Public's Aid Against Fire Department," *NYH-T*, May 9, 1961, 25.
11. "City Artists Facing New, Lofty Problem," *NYWT&S*, November 14, 1962, 3; "Portrait of the Loft Generation," *NYT*, January 7, 1962, 207.
12. "A portrait of the Artist as a Loft-Dweller," *NYP*, March 13, 1961, 63; "Art is Lofty—600 March at City Hall to Save Studios" *NYH-T*, April 4, 1964; "Artist-Tenants Association Press Release" and "Artists Tenants Association Newsletter, December 28, 1962," both Getty Research Institute, Irving Sandler Papers, 2000.M.43, Box 48, Folder 2.
13. "Artists Unite to Save Garrets"; "Eases Stand on Artists Lofts," *NYP*, May 10, 1961, 15; "Art: Angry Dwellers."
14. "Cavanagh Assures Artists on Housing," *NYT*, May 10, 1961, 35. At the meeting, Cavanagh said there had been no mass evictions of artists from Lower Manhattan and that only seven of seventy-one buildings inspected on the west side of Greenwich Village had been ordered vacated.
15. Ibid.; "Portrait of Artist as Loft-Dweller."
16. "Artists and New York Settle Housing Dispute," *Art News* 60, no. 5 (September 1961): 3.
17. "Artists May Strike to Save Lofts," *NYT*, June 3, 1961, 1; "Untitled Timeline of ATA Actions Towards Legalized Artist Housing

in SoHo [1964]," Box 1, Folder 6, ATA Records.

18. "Artists Meet with City Officials on Dispute over Loft Studios," *NYT*, August 16, 1961, 35.

19. "Artists Tenants Association Agreement with City, 1961," Box 1, Folder 15, SAA Records.

20. "Strike over Lofts Put Off by Artists as Formula is Set," *NYT*, August 23, 1961, 35; "Artists and New York Settle Housing Dispute."

21. "Artists Say City Breaks Loft Pact," *NYP*, December 1, 1961, 4.

22. "Untitled Timeline of ATA Actions"; "Untitled 24 Page History."

23. "Artists Tenants Association Newsletter, December 28, 1962"; "Artists to Picket in Loft Protest," *NYT*, February 29, 1964, 23.

24. "Mitchell-Lama," in K. Jackson, *Encyclopedia of New York City*, 765.

25. Ibid.; "Art Notes: Fighting City Hall," *NYT*, March 29, 1964, X20.

26. "1,000 Artists March to Protest Zoning Rules on Loft Studios," *NYT*, April 4, 1964, 29; "Art is Lofty"; "Lofty Debate," *NYDN*, April 4, 1964, 17.

27. "Untitled Timeline of ATA Actions."

28. Volunteer Lawyers for the Arts, *Housing for Artists*, 15–17, B-1[e].

29. Ibid., 15–19, 24–26. Another issue was the amendment's restrictive definition of "artist." In response, a 1968 amendment to article 7-B of the Multiple Dwelling Law (the section covering loft housing) expanded this definition to persons engaged in "the performing or creative arts," allowing filmmakers, musicians, and other fine artists to gain legal access to converted lofts.

30. "Untitled Timeline of ATA"; "Negotiations with the City, Begun after Our April 3 Demonstration Have Collapsed! (7/6/64)" Box 1, Folder 6, ATA Records.

31. "A.T.A on A.I.R," May 1967, Box 1, Folder 1, ATA Records.

32. "Message from the Artists Tenants Association, New York City" and "Artist-Tenants Association Statement [1962–3?];" Getty Research Institute, Irving Sandler Papers, 2000.M.43, Box 48, Folder 2.

33. "Victims of the Clean State," *Nation*, August 10, 1964, 43.

ESSAY 10.3

The Postindustrial Factory

Chloe E. Taft

Source: Chloe E. Taft, *From Steel to Slots: Casino Capitalism in the Postindustrial City* (Cambridge: Harvard University Press, 2016), 96–112.

EDITORS' INTRODUCTION

In Bethlehem, Pennsylvania, the steel industry came to a close and the large factories dominating the city and constituting much of its employment base shut their doors. Deindustrialization hit the community hard. In place of Bethlehem Steel, once the city's primary employer, came the casino industry. Where products had rolled out of the steel factories, day and night, the casino industry did not produce a tangible product, but offered a unique form of entertainment. Patrons brought in their hard-won cash in hopes of walking out with more cash.

The casino offered its unique brand of "casino capitalism," rather than the union-dominated, benefits-heavy steel industry of the earlier era. Certainly, the taxes gained from the new industry benefited Bethlehem, the region, and the state as a whole. But legislators had to weigh the casino's business needs with the desire to garner tax revenue for the region. Bethlehem was on its way to becoming a "company town" based around casinos the way it had been based around steel. But the rules of this new society seem different than those of the past.

The new jobs were service economy jobs—card dealers, waitresses, hotel workers. The jobs were lower wage, with a reliance on tips. Part-time work and/or irregular shifts predominated. Benefits fell. The Bethlehem casino was not unionized at the time this essay was written. Note the way in which the casino workers interviewed by Taft reflect on their experience by drawing on the tradition of American individualism. Some appear to prefer the freedom the new jobs provide. What do you make of this reaction? Casino workers have options to work in other American communities, and even overseas. But such work requires relocation. The casino jobs resemble the so-called "gig economy" work that is commanding a larger piece of the job market.

Even though gambling has moved online, the casino industry has invested millions of dollars in highly place-based entities. In other words, the physical location of casinos proves very important. These gaming centers rely on easy access to highways and airports, and do better in heavily settled corridors where many Americans live. Although the "product" produced inside casinos may be amorphous, the connection with a particular place is undeniable and even old-school. In an increasingly internet reliant world, it is hard to imagine any other industry filling up the spaces left by the steel mills as thoroughly as the casino industry did.

Chloe E. Taft is a Mellon Postdoctoral Associate in the Integrated Humanities in the American Studies Program at Yale University. The dissertation on which *From Steel to Slots* is based was awarded the Dissertation Prize from the Urban History Association in 2015 and the Society for American City and Regional Planning History John Reps Prize 2015. Taft is also the author of "Chinatown Buses at a Steeltown Casino: Global Flows in a Risk Economy," in Stephen Fan, ed., *Sub-Urbanisms: Casino Urbanization, Chinatowns, and the Contested American Land-scape* (New London, CT: Lyman Allyn Art Museum, 2014) and "Spectral Shorelines" in Martha Bayne, ed., *Rust Belt Chicago: An Anthology* (Cleveland, OH: Belt Publishing, 2017).

THE POSTINDUSTRIAL FACTORY (2016)

Las Vegas Sands Corp. CEO Sheldon Adelson likes to tell how he flitted from job to job as a young man, working his way up from nothing. He sold anti-freeze, advertisements, mortgages. He twice amassed a multimillion dollar fortune and then lost it before hitting the jackpot with the Vegas-based Comdex computer industry trade convention in 1979. Only then did Adelson re-brand himself as an "entrepreneur," and a highly successful one at that, instead of as a drifter with a short attention span.[1] His vision of the "self-made self" permeates popular job search literature in the postindustrial economy, including *What Color Is Your Parachute?* And *I Could Do Anything If I Only Knew What It Was*, urging readers to "stop waiting for luck and start creating it."[2] Mobility, adaptability, and identifying one's most transferable skills have become prime assets for both employability and job creation in everything from finance to retail.

The casino industry within which Adelson thrives is no exception. The ethos of individual risk-taking is not only central to the excitement that casinos market to their customers. Corporations also instill these postindustrial norms to their employees. While Bethlehem Steel's worksites post-World War II were regimented by union rules, new social structures (or the lack thereof) have ushered in an era of irregular schedules, high turnover, and fragile benefits. Rather than lament their insecurity and vulnerability in service industry positions, however, many employees portray workplace volatility as an advantage. As such, the casino industry is part of a broader realignment of expectations for postindustrial employment. Stability and mobility are not necessarily perceived as distinct workplace paradigms that define the before-and-after of deindustrialization. Rather, as casino employees make sense of their work, stability and mobility begin to resemble and reinforce one another.

The casino industry's arrival in Bethlehem was part of a series of changes that have restructured the economy over the past four decades. As a number of manufacturing jobs has declined precipitously, the global growth of "gaming" as a profitable business reflects the steady rise of the service, entertainment, and finance sectors. When Bethlehem Steel closed its local plant in 1998, casino gambling was still illegal in Pennsylvania. The idea of opening a casino on the site was not yet a feasible consideration. But on a national scale, the climate had been evolving. Before the late 1970s, casinos in Las Vegas were run by small, private, and largely unregulated companies. With the Nevada Corporate Gaming Acts of 1967 and 1969, however, casino corporations took steps into respectable society. The improved transparency and government oversight that came with the decision to allow publicly traded corporations to own casinos increased access to legitimate financing and boosted investor confidence.[3] Harrah's Entertainment became the first "pure casino" company to be traded on the New York Stock Exchange in 1973, and with the legalization of gambling in Atlantic City in 1976 the value of casino stocks jumped. Indeed, as politicians and developers in New Jersey tried to convince voters to support in-state gambling, they touted the risk of this new investment—mostly its potential upside—as being similar to the promise of the stock market. In the flurry of state attempts to legalize casinos in the 1980s—as was the case in Pennsylvania decades later—advocates cast critics' attacks on gaming's immorality as overly emotional and provincial compared to the perceived rationality of fiscal arguments.[4]

The rise of casino stocks also coincided with a broader economic shift toward riskier financial dealings. Critics coined the term "casino capitalism" in 1986 to refer to the post-World War II transformation away from industrial production and toward a less stable economic order based on speculative financial markets. Closely aligned with neo-liberal economic reforms that began to accelerate in the 1970s, this "new economy" is marked by flexible labor markets, economic deregulation, and the decentralization of global markets, particularly through advances in information technology. As in a casino full of flashing digital slot machines, profit is no longer based on production of durable goods, but is tied to abstract investments in profit itself. Neoliberal policy shifts emphasize the logic of the idealized "free market," where businesses and investors are unencumbered by government oversight or taxes, as being critical for economic growth. This logic supports the increased privatization of services, the decimation of the welfare state, and the elevation of the individual responsibility rather than collective action as guiding principles. The ideal, unfettered mobility of capital on a global scale also promises to make profit less reliant on particular places. In other words, it codifies the dismantling of the social contract.[5]

The new-economy paradigm extends into workplace expectations, amplifying the insecurity that Arnold Strong and other Bethlehem steel-workers found once the plant gates were locked behind them. My conversations across classes in Bethlehem suggested that a world-view based on faith in individual agency, free-market logic, and accepting precarious employment as a natural market condition is broadly adopted.[6] Compared to a planned career at the Steel, the postindustrial expectation is that all work is by definition temporary. Offshoring and job consolidation are routine. Loyalty to a single firm, a hallmark of the postwar period that was reinforced by union seniority rules and benefits, is perceived in the contemporary world-view to be misguided and expectations of job security or social protections to be ignorant. Those who will prosper in this economy, the story goes, will be free agents who embrace mobility, adaptability, and risk. Indeed, the decisions steelworkers made as the Bethlehem plant shut down in the 1990s were by that time understood as high-stakes gambles. Many chose to leave families behind and transfer to other plants, often at the risk of facing another layoff on arrival. Others bet on not being called to transfer while they rode out the wait list on layoff, again hoping to maximize pension returns. For some, a decision to just get out early, cut their losses, and move on, would in retrospect have been the safest bet.[7]

Kevin Engel was among those steel-workers who made a successful transition from the industrial plant to a postindustrial cubicle. Rather than reflect an unbridgeable gap between the "culture of the hands" and the "culture of the mind," Kevin occupies a hybrid culture, making much of the fact that he was able to find another job because he could "talk both languages"—steel plant and office. Kevin began work as an electronics technician at the Steel in 1963, his associate's degree augmented, like most steelwork, by on-the-job training as well as his early interest in computers. He spent the last seventeen years of his Steel career as a union official before he was laid off in 1997. Although he was eligible for his pension, Kevin chose to get certified in computer systems engineering and go on the job market for the first time in thirty-five years. First, he said, he had to develop "the right mindset." "I went to a number of interviews, and as you go to interviews you learn, and you learn how to modify your resume and so forth. And I never put any years on so they didn't know how old I was." In 2000, nearly age sixty, Kevin was hired by a local financial institution and worked there in the information technology department for another decade.

Kevin said the biggest difference between the two jobs was the dress code—from rolling in grease to wearing a tie—and working with mostly women. But he preferred to stress the similarities. "It sounds like I went from steelworker to banker. Because of my working with the union, I worked with people at the senior management level in dealing with grievances. So to move over into the banking industry I dealt with lots of senior management, and I was able to speak their language, and we got along pretty good." Just as he waved off the too-neat narrative (so appealing to an outside ethnographer) that he embodied the transition from manufacturing to finance, Kevin said his job choice had nothing to do with forecasting the future. "I just rolled with the punches. If the Bethlehem Steel in any way would have continued, I would have been here," he said, looking out at the blast furnaces that loom over the arts center where we sat. Indeed, Kevin still identifies most readily as a Steel employee, albeit a highly skilled one, speaking with deference about his ability to work with bankers, never quite losing a trained sense of workplace hierarchy.

Although Kevin landed on his feet with his post-Steel career, in the meantime he worries about his son, who more readily embraces the gamble of modern employment. He was laid off from his high-paying job—in risk management—a few years ago. Kevin thinks his son should have stuck with a lower-paying position instead of hopping from company to company during waves of consolidation, but he knows from his second career that the days of keeping one job for thirty-seven years are over. "The only way to get ahead in a bank, you got to quit and go to another bank," he explained. "The banking industry seems to be a big circle. You keep moving." While for some, including former industrial workers, this sort of mobility is freeing, it teeters on a fundamentally precarious financial future.

The adaptations that workers make to the loss of a social contract, whether forced by necessity or readily embraced, suggest that the narrative of crisis that has defined deindustrialisation primarily as a period of rupture may oversimplify the subsequent lived experience of postindustrialism. On an institutional level, social protections most visible in the form of the union contract have been replaced by emphases on individual risk, a model for which the casino industry seems an apt representative. But culturally, rather than adopt the volatile language of "casino capitalism," dealers and other casino workers continue to actively invoke the language and actions of the industrial workplaces in ways that make new economic structures locally legible and suture discontinuities in their postindustrial experiences. By envisioning the casino as a "postindustrial factory," not only in architectural design but also in terms of its labor and production, area residents use the history of the site to make sense of and solidify a tenuous present.

A Long-Term Temporary Solution

Tim Deluca trains casino dealers at the local community college branch just down the street from the Sands in the former Bethlehem Steel plant office building. He likes to emphasize that dealer certification from the college—which involved ten to fourteen weeks of training in two table games—is valid not only in the state of Pennsylvania, but can be transferred anywhere in the world, from a Las Vegas mega-resort to a cruise ship.[8] "As long as you have this trade, you'll always be able to have a job somewhere," he said. "If you're portable and you can travel, you'll always be able to make ends meet here. And I'm a perfect example of that." Tim started his career in 1985 in Atlantic City. In 2003 he left to continue his college education and the following year landed in Las Vegas working for Sands at The Venetian. After several promotions, Tim was laid off in 2008. A year later, when Sands opened the Bethlehem property, Tim's former boss called and offered him a position back east as a shift manager, the first step into executive management. Then in 2010 Tim was laid off again, so he began teaching at Bethlehem's community college for temporary income. He said he could get back into the industry any time, but he was waiting for the right opportunity. He at one point had his eye on Pennsylvania's eleventh casino that opened in 2012 in nearby Valley Forge, but his fantasy is of the Florida sunshine. If casino gambling is legalized in South Beach (as is periodically discussed by the state's legislature), he said he'd hop on a plane and start over yet again where it's warmer.

As the links between capital and community are reshaped through deindustrialization, relocation is increasingly accepted as a condition of advancement or even employment. Beyond retraining, a primary purpose of federal Trade Readjustment Allowance funds, for example, is to support moving expenses for the unemployed. And yet the social networks, community roots, families, or home mortgages that keep individuals tied to place are easily overlooked when data on jobs and capital are thought of in abstract, impersonal terms.[9] Much as the Sands Casino Bethlehem's opening ceremony and its architectural design blurred narratives of past and future, the casino also is a site through which to explore how residents vacillate between and ultimately fuse the interpretive poles of fixed place and mobile capital in the ways they make sense of and define postindustrial work.

Dealers and slot attendants at the Bethlehem casino range from eighteen years old to post-retirement age. Many of the younger employees have come straight out of associate's degrees, BAs, or aborted college plans. Several dealers I spoke with glowed with the anticipation of being able to use the community college's dealing certificate as a ticket out of Lehigh Valley. While 89 percent of the dealers trained in 2010 and 2011 were hired full time by the Sands, some have found jobs at other Pennsylvania casinos.[10] When we first talked in 2011, Matt Bednarik, a twenty-three-year-old mixed martial arts aficionado, was three days from starting work at the Sands dealing blackjack and roulette, but already he was thinking of his next move. In what is called "chasing tips" in the industry, he and some friends planned to apply to the new Valley Forge Casino set to open four months later. They believed its novelty would at least temporarily mean bigger crowds, which they translated into more tip income. After a year or two there, maybe the economy would pick up and Matt would finally have the impetus to finish his degree and find a job working with computers, which he said are his real passion. But if not, then Matt thought he'd check out Atlantic City, which at the same time was barely hanging on as the second largest gambling jurisdiction in the country and would in 2012 be surpassed in revenue by Pennsylvania.

This notion of the casino industry as what one trainee called "a long-term temporary solution" is a common refrain among dealers in Bethlehem. For many of the younger casino employees, dealing is the latest in a chain of short-term jobs that they were eager to leave for various reasons—the sixty-hour week at the online bookstore warehouse, the part-time, no-benefit work at the big-box home improvement store, the hot and dangerous steel job in Reading.[11] Twenty-three-year-old Nicholas Garcia initially gambled his career choice on a high school suitability exam. "My top three jobs were carpenter in residential construction, law enforcement, military. I went for my first bet," he explained. Nicholas entered an associate's program in construction, but when he couldn't find an internship with a skilled carpenter to complete his four-year degree, he briefly tried his "second bet" in law enforcement before abandoning his college plans. A few months into his new job dealing blackjack and craps, Nicholas still thought about returning to carpentry if the market for new homes recovered.

Dealer Mei Lung, meanwhile, saw working at the casino as the only opportunity to protect her house from foreclosure and stave off bankruptcy in a difficult economic climate. Mei's income as a realtor was decimated by the recession in 2008, a blow exacerbated by her husband's layoff from a nearby pharmaceutical company that outsourced its IT work to India and Argentina. A lawyer in China before she emigrated fifteen years earlier, Mei models the gamble many immigrants make when they leave the social networks of their home countries.[12] While she kept her real estate license active just in case, she was hesitant to imagine a near-term return to financial stability for her family of four. For now, she said, she had no choice but to deal.

Regardless of whether dealers perceive the "long-term temporary solution" of the casino floor as a career progression or a step down, for many an underlying need for work simmers beneath the surface. Amid a regional unemployment rate that four years post-recession still hovered around 9 percent, the full-time, entry-level jobs that dealers sought through community college training program where I met many of them started pay at roughly $40,000 a year (hourly base of $4.75 plus around $15 per hour in tips) and offered benefits after three months of employment. Bartenders and cocktail waitresses could earn twice as much. Many employees also touted the HMO health benefits the casino offered, noting that they required lower employee contribution than at many other area businesses given at Las Vegas Sands Corps.'s scale and bargaining power.

As a reflection of the free-market logic that values mobility, flexibility, and individual responsibility, the Sands Casino in many ways exemplifies broader transitions experienced in the postindustrial workplace. Julia Krause spends three days a week at the casino working as a part-time slots attendant. She weaves between the more than 3,000 slot machines that ring the casino floor, following the periodic cacophony of electronic bells and clanging digital coins to pay out jackpots and hope for tips from the lucky winners. Hired by the Sands at the age of seventy-five, Julia had been laid off at the Steel in 1992 after spending thirty-two years as a nurse in the plant and corporate dispensaries. Active and seeming much younger than her years, she said she went back to work on opening day in 2009 not simply to supplement her fixed income, but because she loves the excitement of the casino environment. "I almost feel like, oh, my God, this is my home again," she said of returning to the steel plant. Only now, she calls it "the fun house."

Julia often contemplates how expectations for employment have shifted from one industry to the other. She and her husband receive social security and what's left of their Steel pensions and thus are not fully dependent on her Sands' income. Still, her enthusiasm for the new economic model the casino represents was striking. "If everybody had the rules of the casino industry, we'd still have Bethlehem Steel, we'd still have most car industries, and the school district would be in good shape," she told me from the kitchen table of her home in and upscale North Side neighbourhood.

To illustrate her point about more efficient fiscal management, she explained how the casino offered employees only one paid holiday each year (Christmas) and gave them a certain number of "flex days" to use as they saw fit, rather than providing designated vacation or sick days. "It's really an interesting concept after working at Bethlehem Steel being an exempt employee, getting eight weeks vacation, getting sick days. If you're out for three months sick [at the Steel] you still get paid. And this whole thing was so new to me, and I found it very interesting." At the pro-labor apogee of the steelworkers' contracts in the early 1980s, union employees had eleven paid holidays in addition to vacation time. Senior steelworkers could earn thirteen-week sabbatical every fifth year to help compensate for the physically demanding and dangerous work they performed each day.[13] In contrast, the flex days and the "flextime" found at the casino and other postindustrial workplaces simulate the neoliberal deregulation of the marketplace, where an employee is free to determine the most advantageous use of his or her time. And yet, as Julia also noted, many of the employee protections (excessive or not) gained at the Steel through nationwide union negotiations are absent. Her curiosity about the casino's business model is in some ways a luxury compared to those who depend on these jobs for their livelihoods, but her buy-in employment sans safety net is nonetheless a remarkable example of a widespread shift in postindustrial worker expectations.

When Adelson tore down the old Rat Pack's Sands Casino in Las Vegas and built The Venetian in 1999, he replaced the union casino on the Strip with a nonunion property. The Vegas of the mid-1960s had depended on loans from Teamsters' pension funds as the major source of development capital when Wall Street was still unwilling to invest.[14] Las Vegas, sometimes called the "Last Detroit" or the "River Rouge of gambling," became a hotbed for union organizing. Indeed, Las Vegas Sands Corp. is one of the only two major nonunion casino operators in the city.[15] By the 1990s, Las Vegas Sands had become embroiled in bitter disputes with the Culinary Union, a powerful group representing hotel and restaurant workers. Adelson eventually filed a suit against Vegas picketers in 1999, claiming that the sidewalk in front of The Venetian was private property and not protected by the First Amendment. The United States Supreme Court refused to hear the case in 2002, in effect upholding a denial on The Venetian's claim, but appeals related to the case dragged on more than thirteen years later.[16]

This shaky premise to deny free speech endures in deed terms set forth by Las Vegas Sands in Bethlehem. The corporation offered central parcels of land west of the casino to not-for-profit ArtsQuest for the Steel-Stacks arts center, to the local PBS station for a new office, and to the City of Bethlehem for the performance pavilion and visitor center. The terms of the deal state that this land cannot be used for union organizing or for promoting themes "considered offensive by a reasonable casino operator." Although such clauses are typical of pseudo-public spaces like shopping malls, it was not lost on Bethlehem residents that the land under question is physically part of a former steel plant that hosted bitter labor battles and union gains through much of the twentieth century. Pressure from a small but vocal band of free speech advocates led to assurances from the city that it would not enforce the restrictions. The clause remains, however, in the art center's agreement, including for outside space billed—perhaps appropriately signaling this broader shift in expectations—as a "21st Century Town Square."[17]

Some residents are wary of ruffling corporate feathers over the clause since Las Vegas Sands has been generous in other ways, including donating the land, and because the in-progress nature of the brownfield development promises more contracts for the union construction crews that built the casino and other complexes on the site. Others fear Bethlehem will again become a "company town," where a high-powered corporation will "get to call the shots on what's best for the public interest."[18] Although Sands holds the economic clout, the relative strengths of the citizens' interests in the land remain culturally unsettled.

Meanwhile, as Julia noted, dealers and other employees at the Sands Casino Bethlehem are not unionized, although security guards have moved to organize against Sands' objections. In Las Vegas, the corporation offers wages and medical benefits a nudge above what other casino corporations offer their employees as prophylaxis against collective bargaining.[19] The security guards in Bethlehem are likewise among the highest paid in the state, earning between $12 and $14 an hour in 2015, but they say they want to organize less for the pay than for job stability and a voice in grievance procedures.[20] Union affiliations appear to have limited cachet among Bethlehem dealers, though, when they think about what job security means. Even in Las Vegas, dealers have generally not organized, in part because they fear having to give a cut of their tips to the union. They tend to view themselves as individual entrepreneurs and often move from one property to another.[21] Those dealers who have successfully formed unions at other casinos in recent years, however, have gained vacation, sick leave, and some protections against at-will terminations.[22]

In any case, the service jobs created by the casino industry, including those on the former factory side in Bethlehem, simply do not compare when it comes to the benefits and wages offered by the unionized steel mills in the second half of the twentieth century. In contrast to the Steel, where most training took place on the job, at the Sands dealers must pay for their own training before they can be hired, and required licensing fees are deducted from their paychecks.[23] Perhaps the most striking aspect of the casino's employment model is that just as it has in a sense "outsourced" retirement benefits from corporate-contribution pensions to employee-funded accounts, it also has outsourced employee's salaries to the consumers to the extent that dealers make three-quarters of their income from tips.

Like many service jobs, nonunionized casino positions also require one to work varied shifts and lack contract rules to protect from layoffs. Taking this trend of normalized instability to an extreme, Revel Atlantic City, a mega-casino resort that opened in 2012 in neighboring New Jersey, announced that dealers, waiters, and cocktail waitresses would be hired on four- to six-year contracts, requiring those employees to reapply for their own jobs at the end of the term. These conditions were a direct reversal of the seniority rules upheld by the union employers of an earlier era like the Steel to add predictability to the workplace. In addition, an unusually large percentage of Revel's initial hires were part-time, meaning they did not receive benefits. The local union called Revel's plan "unconscionable" for undermining employees' abilities to plan long term. Although no other casino had yet to adopt a similar approach, the head of the New Jersey Economic Development Authority seemed unfazed by this harbinger of increased insecurity. "In today's economic climate," she said simply, "people don't have lifetime contracts."[24] The temporary long-term solution of postindustrial work is economically and socially a fundamental break from the nation's manufacturing heyday.

It's All in Gaming

Still, many casino workers have found ways to reconcile their tenuous employment with the idealized vision of entrepreneurial self-achievement that Adelson himself claims. As an adherent to a postindustrial compromise that ultimately naturalizes instability, Rachel Moretti is among those who make sense of economic insecurity by reading opportunity into the cracks. Rachel, now in her late forties, had worked for eighteen years at an off-track betting establishment in New York City before it went bankrupt and she lost her job in 2010. "Of course I was very upset about losing my job, still am," she said. "But I was kind of happy about leaving that behind." Rachel had grown tired of the verbal abuse of patrons who were losing large sums of money, and she saw the layoff as an opportunity to start fresh and build up enough capital to open her own business.[25] After eight months without a job and with bills piling up, however, Rachel said she needed to be realistic. Having worked so long in off-track betting, "I have a very specific kind of skill really. It doesn't really transfer," she said. "I figure let me try this and get my benefits back, turn a little revenue again, but keep my dream alive so I don't have to feel too sad by going back into something I felt like was a bonus I could stop." Much as Matt hopes to one day find a job working with computers, and Nicholas's true passion is carpentry, Rachel has been forced to put her dream of opening an ice cream shop on hold as she sought a job dealing at Sands.

What's most surprising in this all-too-familiar tale of recession-fueled job loss and dreams deferred is her rereading of the situation as an opportunity rather than a setback. Burying her initial dismay, Rachel performed an interpretive flip, seeing her layoff as freeing and job security as imprisonment:

> The horse racing, it was a very good salary, I had my pension, I had my benefits. So I was really tied in. So I wasn't really able to pursue another dream right then because I wouldn't leave that job. But now I feel like the rug was ripped out from me, I'm not as afraid anymore to pursue it. So I think that I really want to pursue something else so I don't have to stay with the gambling industry. That's the honest answer. But the truth is I need to turn some revenue, so I figured I have—this is my best shot at getting benefits and a salary.

Having absorbed the ethos of self-created opportunity, economic insecurity became a dream enabler rather than a structural impediment. The increasingly elusive pension and good benefits for which steelworkers and others had fought so long in the industrial workplace are now perceived as traps that hold one back in an ever-changing postindustrial world. And yet, caught between the entrepreneurial framework and the need for financial and personal security, Rachel found that true freedom remains difficult to attain.

The tension between free-market individualism and expectations of the social contract's collective protections continues to shape both corporate structures and employee and public relations to them. The success of Sands' risk-based business model and reliance on flexible labor in many ways seems exemplary of the freewheeling postindustrial economy. But pure reflections of "casino capitalism" are not easily realized, and even the gaming industry is no exception. Free-market ideals emphasize reducing government oversight and cutting corporate taxes, thus removing the state as a barrier to unrestrained capital growth. As in other jurisdictions worldwide where gambling is legal, however, casinos in Pennsylvania are both highly regulated and heavily taxed. The taxes on gambling profits and the licensing fees that Pennsylvania reaps from casinos have helped offset perennial budget cuts to social services, including police, education, and state pensions. At the same time that it compels the industry to help rebuild social safety nets, the state has effectively levied a new, semi-privatized tax on consumers whose lost wagers at the slots or table games comprise those revenues. Instead of embracing a strictly laissez-faire attitude, the Pennsylvania Gaming Control Board also dictates most casino operating procedures, such as the gaming equipment used, staffing levels, and CPR training for employees. But because of the state's clear interest in the casino's profitability, many regulations, such as those awarding intentional monopolies and limited licenses, nonetheless directly benefit the gaming corporations. From a business and policy perspective, the state's casinos thus complicate, but ultimately complement, idealized understandings of neoliberal economies as free markets absent state interventions.[26]

Meanwhile, despite the free-market emphasis on unfettered capital mobility, place-based loci of economic activity like the casino floor and the Steel site, and the ways such space are imagined and occupied, remain relevant as material and cultural touchstones. The 2012 and 2013 legalization of online gambling in Delaware, Nevada, and New Jersey notwithstanding, the casino industry still depends primarily on physical proximity to consumers and face-to-face interactions that cannot be outsourced. Sands' revenues and hires in Bethlehem skyrocketed in 2010 when Pennsylvania legalized table games and the casino could replace its video blackjack dealers with human ones.[27] Casinos carefully select their locations based on regulatory and demographic advantages that are linked to place. Bethlehem's proximity to New York and New Jersey was integral to its early success.

In the end, though, the entertainment product manufactured in the casino remains essentially about deriving money from money, a fungibility that distances it from other geographic particularities. Such emphases on abstract market transactions invoke conceptions of universal economic orders that to some extent contradict the individualized focus on self-making, personal responsibility, and hard work that self-help books and entrepreneurs like Adelson stress. At the Sands Casino, "luck" is institutionalized in such a way as to bridge the gap between self-controlled decision making and omnipotent forces. Julia picked the time and day of her first shift as a slots attendant, for instance, via a multistep process in which she and her coworkers first selected envelopes that contained different numbers. The numbers determined the order in which they could choose their timeslots. "So they can't say, well they have favorites, or that they did anything. It's all in gaming," she said with a chuckle. She felt lucky she picked high enough to have Mondays off so she could continue to play golf with her women's league. By creating these kinds of internal structures based on individualized luck, the casino industry effectively distances itself from expectations for more interventionist social protections or collective commitments.

While Julia admires what she sees as efficiencies in Sands' policies and operating procedures compared to those at the Steel, their impartiality—both toward employees and players—comes into question when one considers how "luck" is nonetheless created and controlled by the corporate structures in place. For example, casinos closely track individual gamblers—particularly regulars and high rollers—to determine each person's "theoretical win," the amount he or she could walk away with at the end of the day based on average bets, games played, the house's statistical advantage, and a number of other factors. Players whose wins far exceed expectations are not seen as "lucky"; they are rather targeted for extra surveillance or simply asked to leave.

Employees likewise soon learn that regardless of who pulls the lever or who rolls the dice, when "it's all in gaming" the odds are generally stacked in favor of the house. Workers are employed "at will," and turnover is relatively high (roughly 20 percent among dealers).[28] In addition to "chasing tips" and moving to other casino properties, dealers face strict firing policies for infractions. Many other dealers find they can't cut it in the casino environment. New dealers are invariably assigned to work at least six months on the late shift, from eleven o'clock at night to seven in the morning. Others grow tired of the cigarette smoke or buckle under the stress of dealing to high rollers and calming irate players who are down on their luck. More senior employees gain some flexibility to determine their schedules and, being a new casino in a new market, there is real opportunity for internal advancement. But as a result, Sands Casino rarely stopped hiring new dealers in its first five years of the table-game operation. While high turnover may undercut the benefits of workforce stability, thanks to a constant stream of new trainees seeking jobs it also helps keep payrolls low.

Even if company gains come at worker's expense, dealers nonetheless frequently associate their own economic stability with the corporation's profitability. Mei worked part-time at a smaller casino in the Poconos before coming the Sands. In the Poconos, she said, the business seemed less organized, less corporate, and there were fewer players compared to Bethlehem. Indeed, it regularly ranks as one of Pennsylvania's least profitable casinos. In contrast, "Here [at the Sands] they have a lot. They're just very busy. You just feel safe," she said. Her analysis of economic security extended into the built environment. She described the Poconos casino as "like a home" in its scale.

Rather than associate its low ceiling and lodge-like porte-cochère with comfort though, she said the impersonal warehouse expanse of the Sands with double the casino floor space was more assuring that it would be a lasting and profitable business.[29]

While Mei measures her financial safety through a local comparison, Nicholas takes a global view. "I wanted something reliable in an emerging industry," he explained, "and the fact that the Sands just introduced table games the previous summer, it seemed like a really great up-and-coming employment opportunity." He was particularly struck by Sands' presence in Asia, where it reaps more than 85 percent of its net revenues from hugely successful mega-resorts in Macau and Singapore. (Bethlehem accounts for less than 4 percent.)[30] Las Vegas Sands Corp.'s market cap (or total value of the company based on its outstanding shares) reached $87 billion in 2014. It is not only the largest gaming company and largest real-estate developer in the world, but it is the largest foreign investor in China ever.[31] "Seeing that was a nice reassurance that even though it's in a different country, it's one big entity that's got a lot of opportunity, and a lot of opportunity for growth. I see it as very stable." Nicholas turns a more cynical interpretation of capital mobility on its head. Rather than associate globalization with an absence of local commitments, he interprets it as a marker of job stability. It is these inverted expectations of the meanings of postindustrial security that led insiders like Tim Deluca to negate the association of the casino industry and its brand of risk with volatility. "The fact that gambling is the product offered is not a gamble, because you're always going to produce revenue," he said. "Believe it or not, people will always gamble. You build it, they'll come."

A Postindustrial Factory

For area residents, it is clear that Bethlehem's casino physically occupies an economic space that vacillates between past and future, place-based production and mobile capital, often blurring what have been considered distinct cultural categories and interpretive poles. The casino industry is simultaneously stable and volatile, material and abstract in its profit and employment structures. The Sands Casino makes architectural and cultural references to place and community history even as its future-orientated business model is increasingly replicated in other jurisdictions that pass gaming legislation. As the debate over the casino license revealed, some see the casino's local theming as proof of Sands' commitment to the Bethlehem community, while others, like Nicholas, prefer to emphasize the corporation's international reach as evidence of its economic stability. Moreover, some of the contradictions that the casino encapsulates coexist uneasily, such as the frameworks of the entrepreneurial self-interest and remnants of social protections. Stakeholders nonetheless interpret these tensions in ways to provide a postindustrial narrative that makes culturally and locally legible the economic transition and social upheaval that the decline of the Steel represented.

Rather than narrate the betrayal and disjuncture that deindustrialization ushered in, casino inside Tim Deluca, for one, likes to stress the continuities between the two economic eras. "You went from one factory, a steel mill, and not you have—what is it, twenty years later—you have another factory. It's the casino," he explained.

The steel mill produced something. Now the casino offers a product, but they don't produce anything but revenue. So they produce revenue for the casino, they produce revenue for the employees, and they produce revenue for the community, without putting a product out in the street to sell.... The tables are your production line, the chips are your assets that you use to facilitate your production, and your dealers are your line workers. And that's the factor.

Amid strong (if exaggerated) local and national sentiments that "America doesn't make anything anymore," Tim's analogy offers a narrative of smooth transition to cleaner forms of production. Like Bethlehem Steel, the Sands Casino Bethlehem reaps profits while providing job and benefits for hundreds of area residents and contributing significant tax revenues and charitable gifts to the community. Tim might have added that the Steel's proximity to railroads and ore mines likewise is replaced by the casino factory's highway access to the raw material of gamblers' money in nearby New York and New Jersey. Indeed, here postindustrialism, rather than reflecting rupture with an earlier economic order, instead represents its epitome—production so efficient that the physical product becomes superfluous. Those who have recalibrated their expectations, as many dealers have, to a worldview in line with neoliberal economic reforms embrace that intangibility, which for so many ravaged by deindustrialization remains a source of anxiety and discomfort.[32]

NOTES

1. Connie Bruck, "The Brass Ring: A Multi-billionaire's Relentless Quest for Global Influence," *New Yorker*, June 30, 2008, 43.
2. Carrie M. Land, *A Company of One: Insecurity, Independence, and the New World Order of White-Collar Unemployment* (Ithaca, NY: ILR Press, 2011), 45–61, Richard Nelson Bolles, *What Color Is Your Parachute?: A Practical Manual for Job-Hunters and Career-Changers*, rev. ed. (Berkeley, CA: Ten Speed Press, 2013) (first published in 1970, this book is updated annually); Barbara Sher and Barbara Smith, *I Could Do Anything If I Only Knew What It Was: How to Discover What You Really Want and How to Get It* (New York: Delacorte Press, 1994).
3. Previously, each individual shareholder of the casino corporation would have had to apply for a gaming license from the state of Nevada.
4. John Dombrink and William N. Thompson, *The Last Resort: Success and Failure in Campaigns for Casinos* (Reno: University of Nevada Press, 1990), 2, 33.
5. See Susan Strange, *Casino Capitalism* (Oxford: B. Blackwell, 1986); David Harvey, *A Brief History of Neoliberalism* (Oxford: Oxford University Press, 2005); Jane L. Collins and Victoria Mayer, *Both Hands Tied: Welfare Reform and the Face to the Bottom in the Low-wage Labor Market* (Chicago: University of Chicago Press, 2010); Jeffrey J. Sallaz, *The Labor of Luck: Casino Capitalism in the United States and South Africa* (Berkeley: University of California Press, 2009).

6. See Lane, *A Company of One*, 4; Jennifer M. Silva, *Coming Up Short: Working Class Adulthood in an Age of Uncertainty* (Oxford: Oxford University Press, 2013), 145–146.

7. Jill Schennum, "Bethlehem Steelworkers: Reshaping the Industrial Working Class" (PhD diss., City University of New York, 2011), 202–207, 232. Schennum also notes that seniority, once a benefit, is now devalued as age becomes a liability rather than an asset. "Reshaping the Working Class: Bethlehem Steelworkers in Postindustrial Work" (paper presented at the annual meeting for the American Studies Association, Washington, DC, November 21–24, 2013).

8. Pennsylvania regulations require dealers to have a certificate from a state approved dealer training program. In addition to passing an extensive background check, Pennsylvania requires dealers to have a letter of intent to hire from the casino and CPR certification to get a state license. At Northampton Community College, Sands provided the tables and other equipment to train dealers and under-wrote some start-up costs, but NCC runs the program independently.

9. Gregory Pappas, *The Magic City: Unemployment in a Working-Class Community* (Ithaca, NY: Cornell University Press, 1989), 62; John R. Logan and Harvey L. Molotch, *Urban Fortuned: The Political Economy of Place* (Berkeley: University of California Press, 1987), 40–43.

10. Pam Thoma, NCC Dealer Training School, e-mail message to author, June 20, 2012.

11. See also Silva, *Coming Up Short*.

12. Katherine S. Newman, *Falling from Grace: Downward Mobility in the Age of Affluence* (Berkeley: University of California Press, 1999); Alejandro Portes and Min Zhou, "The New Second Generation: Segmented Assimilation and Its Variants." *Annals of the American Academy of Political Social Science* 530 (November 1993): 74–96.

13. Jack Metzgar, *Striking Steel: Solidarity Remembered* (Philidelphia: Temple University Press, 2000), 43, 135–136. Despite the number of paid holidays, which included United Nationals Day from 1979 until 1983, many workers preferred work holidays at double-time pay. In 1983, the United Steelworkers ratified its first concessionary contract, which included giving up United Nation's Day, the thirteen-week sabbatical, and one week of vacation.

14. Hal Rothman, *Neon Metropolis: How Las Vegas Started the Twenty-first Century* (New York: Routledge, 2002), 16–18.

15. The other nonunion operator is Stations Casino. Rothman, *Neon Metropolis*, 63–88; Arnold M. Knightly, "Workers' Paradise: Tips Can Help Companies Deal With Unions," *Las Vegas Business Press*, August 18, 2008; Mike Davis, "Class Struggle in Oz," in *The Grit Beneath the Glitter: Tales from the Real Las Vegas*, ed. Hal K. Rothman and Mike Davis (Berkeley: University of California Press, 2002), 183–184.

16. In 2015, aspects of the case were still ongoing: Venetian Casino Resort, LLC, National Labor Relations Board, No. 12–1021 (D.C. Cir. 2015), http://law.justia.com/cases/federal/apellate-courts/cadc/12-1021/12-1021-2015-07-10.html. The MGM Grand was the first big casino to open nonunion in 1993 and similarly claimed its sidewalks as private property when Culinary Union members picketed in 1994. Ultimately, MGM Grand changed course to become a union property.

17. Steve Esack, "Free Speech Rally to Protest Sands Casino," *Morning Call*, November 16, 2012. Many Community organizers only joined the free speech co-alition after being assured anonymity. They feared losing charitable donations from Las Vegas Sands, what some activists called "hush money."

18. Nicole Radzievich, "No Labor, Anti-Casino Activities at SteelStacks," *Morning Call*, June 27, 2011; Lynn Olanoff, "Free Speech Concerns Still Linger at Bethlehem's SteelStacks," *Express-Times*, September 22, 2012.

19. See, for example, "Raises Won't Deter Union," *Las Vegas Review-Journal*, February 27, 2008. The industry as a whole took a similar approach in the 1960s and early 1970s. In addition to high wages and benefits, dealers and others were given clearer work rules and grievance procedures. James P. Kraft, *Vegas at Odds: Labor Conflict in a Leisure Economy, 1960–1985* (Baltimore: Johns Hopkins University Press, 2010), 91–92.

20. Matt Assad, "Sands Ordered to Accept Guard Union," *Morning Call*, June 1, 2012; Matt Assad, "Sands Casino Guards Join New Force in Attempt to Unionize," *Morning Call*, October 10, 2015. Although most of Atlantic City's twelve casinos have union contracts in place, Pennsylvania, as a new gaming market, has yet to see the impact. Since opening, only a few of the eleven casinos have been unionized, beginning with their food and beverage workers and security guards.

21. Kraft, *Vegas at Odds*, 73–95; Sallaz, *The Labor of Luck*, 65, 215–216. According to Sallaz, the Culinary Union's success is tied to a contractual promise to *not* organize dealers or help other unions that try to do so (267n57). He notes several failed attempts to unionize until 2007, three decades after the first casinos opened. Ellen Mutari and

Deborah M. Figart, "Transformations in Casino Gaming and the Unionization of Atlantic City's Dealers," *Review of Radical Political Economics* 40, no. 3 (Summer 2008): 258–265.

22. In 2010 dealers at Wynn Las Vegas approved the resort's first contract, a ten-year deal, three years after they voted for union representation. The initial impetus for organizing was a new policy that split a portion of dealers' tips with their supervisors, although the contract did not reverse the policy. Chris Sierotylas, "Wynn Dealers Approve 10-Year Contract," *Las Vegas Review-Journal*, November 2, 2010. Dealers at Caesars Palace voted in favour of the union in 2007 and agreed on a contract in 2012. The dealers in Las Vegas were organized by the Transport Workers Union. The United Auto Workers Union has organized dealers in Atlantic City and elsewhere. Steve Green, "Caesars Palace, Union Finally Agree on Contract Terms for Dealers," *Vegas INC.*, July 11, 2012.

23. Sands requires that dealers know blackjack and one other table game. NCC offers courses in: roulette, craps, baccarat, and mini/midi baccarat, Pai Gow tiles, Pai Gow poker, and poker. The cost of two courses in 2012 at NCC was between $1,300 and $1,800. A dealer's license costs $350 and must be renewed every three years.

24. Ronda Kaysen, "The Casino the State Saved," *New York Times*, January 3, 2012; Emily Previti, "Revel's Original Estimate of 5,500 Full-time Employees Will Now Be 38 Percent Part-Timers," PressofAtlanticCity.com, February 15, 2012. According to Las Vegas Sands, 6 percent of all positions at the Bethlehem casino resort were part-time in 2013. Lynn Olanoff, "Sands Casino Bethlehem: We Must Add Amenities to Remain Competitive," *Express-Times*, October 15, 2013.

25. See also Ruth Milkman, *Farewell to the Factory: Auto Workers in the Late Twentieth Century* (Berkeley: University of California Press, 1997).

26. See also David Harvey, *The New Imperialism* (Oxford: Oxford University Press, 2003), 26–31. Natasha Dow Schüll argues that gambling regulations "function primarily to streamline and protect commercial gambling revenue, serving the interests of business and government rather than those of consumers." *Addiction by Design: Machine Gambling in Las Vegas* (Princeton, NJ: Princeton University Press, 2012), 298.

27. Sands announced plans in 2015 for a "stadium" of 150 hybrid gaming stations–personal electronic tables that play against a live dealer in the middle. The model decreases the dealer-to-player ratio. Matt Assad, "Sands Casino Plans Expansion," *Morning Call*, April 7, 2015. Initial forays into online gambling require patrons to be located within the state in which the activity is legal, as confirmed by geo-location technology. In New Jersey, part of the business model is to give online gamblers bonus credits they can only spend in the state's physical casinos.

28. Lynn Olanoff, "Sands Casino Resort Bethlehem Looking to Hire 100 Full-Time Dealers," *Express-Times*, August 7, 2014.

29. This contradicts some casino design experts who suggest low ceilings and greater intimacy are more attractive to gamblers. See Bill Friedman, *Designing Casinos to Dominate the Competition: The Friedman International Standards of Casino Design* (Reno, NV: Institute for the Study of Gambling and Commercial Gaming, 2000) Compared to casinos in Las Vegas or Atlantic City, Sands Bethlehem is still relatively small.

30. According to the LVS 10-K for the year ended December 31, 2014, 88 percent of Las Vegas Sands' $14,583,849,000 in net revenue came from Macau and Singapore, and just over 3 percent came from Bethlehem. http://www.sec.gov/Archives/edgar/data/1300514/000130051415000005/lvs-20141231x10k.htm.

31. Steven Bertoni, "Comeback Billionaire: How Adelson Dominates Chinese Gambling and U.S. Politics," *Forbes*, March 12, 2012, 1. By the end of 2014 LVS's market cap had dropped to $56 billion largely in response to government scrutiny of high rollers in Macau.

32. Arlie Russell Hochschild, *The Managed Heart: Commercialization of Human Feeling* (Berkeley: University of California Press, 1983). Later works that examine emotional labor in the service industry include: Robin Leidner, *Fast Food, Fast Talk: Service Work and the Routinization of Everyday Life* (Berkeley: University of California Press, 1993); Katherine S. Newman, *No Shame in My Game: The Working Poor in the Inner City* (New York: Knopf and the Russell Sage Foundation, 1999); Rachel Sherman, *Class Acts: Service and Inequality in Luxury Hotels* (Berkeley: University of California Press, 2007). Although emotional labor is often feminized, 58 percent of all workers at Sands Bethlehem in 2015 were men. Pennsylvania Gaming Control Board, *2014–2015 Gaming Diversity Report* (Harrisburg, PA: PGCB, 2015), 14, http://gamingcontrolboard.pa.gov/files/communications/2014–2015_Gaming_Diversity_Report.pdf.

ESSAY 10.4

The Punishment Imperative

Todd R. Clear and Natasha A. Frost

Source: Todd R. Clear and Natasha A. Frost, *The Punishment Imperative: The Rise and Failure of Mass Incarceration in America* (New York: New York University Press, 2014), 17–44.

EDITORS' INTRODUCTION

Mass incarceration has transformed American cities. The United States has the highest percentage of imprisonment in the world. The Prison Policy Report concluded in mid-2017 that "The American criminal justice system holds more than 2.3 million people in 1,719 state prisons, 102 federal prisons, 901 juvenile correctional facilities, 3,163 local jails, and 76 Indian Country jails as well as in military prisons, immigration detention facilities, civil commitment centers, and prisons in the U.S. territories." One in five of these persons is held on a drug related offense. When comparing to percentage of overall population, whites are underrepresented in the imprisoned percentages, while blacks are overrepresented.[i]

The Pew Center on the States concludes that 1 in 55 adults were on parole, probation, or in prison or jail in 2018. This means that millions of adults are either absent from American communities entirely, or face curtailed freedoms due to their involvement with the parole and probation systems. Due to voting restrictions for those convicted of felonies, and the disproportionate imprisonment rates of Americans of different racial backgrounds, people of color are disenfranchised at a higher rate than white Americans.[ii] A recent effort seeks to correct the voting restrictions on convicted felons in some states.

Contemporary scholarship has begun to examine why the United States has built such an extensive system of incarceration. How did the system come to be, and in what ways does it alter American urban communities? Scholars examine the history of the criminal justice system in the United States, the policies and procedures which led to the current level of imprisonment, and the belief systems propelling this phenomenon. Beyond sheer size, the quality of life American prisoners experience behind bars proves challenging. Heather Ann Thompson's Pulitzer Prize winning work, *Blood in the Water: The Attica Prison Uprising of 1971 and Its Legacy* traces the story of 1,300 prisoners who took matters into their own hands and protested conditions within the New York prison.[iii] In modern prisons, inmates may worry about physical safety and withstanding prolonged periods in solitary confinement.

---

i. Peter Wagner and Bernadette Rabuy, "Mass Incarceration: The Whole Pie 2017." March 14, 2017. Accessed at https://www.prisonpolicy.org/reports/pie2017.html

ii. Pew Charitable Trusts, "1 in 55 U.S. Adults is on Probation of Parole," October 31, 2018 accessed at https://www.pewtrusts.org/en/research-and-analysis/articles/2018/10/31/1-in-55-us-adults-is-on-probation-or-parole. Also see Pew Charitable Trusts, Public Safety Performance Project, "One in 31 Adults are Behind Bars, on Parole or Probation." Accessed at: http://www.pewtrusts.org/en/about/news-room/press-releases/0001/01/01/one-in-31-us-adults-are-behind-bars-on-parole-or-probation

iii. See Heather Ann Thompson, "Why Mass Incarceration Matters: Rethinking Crisis, Decline and Transformation in the Postwar United States," *Journal of American History* (December 2010).

Michelle Alexander's *The New Jim Crow: Mass Incarceration in the Age of Colorblindness* riveted readers with its assertion that the United States replaced its former system of legal racial separation—Jim Crow—with a new caste system, built out of the bricks and two-by-fours of the criminal justice edifice. Americans of color face a series of challenges due to the structure of the mass incarceration system, challenges that belie our constitutional claim of equality for all.

Historian Elizabeth Hinton discovers that the roots of today's American justice system lay in Lyndon Baines Johnson's Great Society. Hinton's assertion shocks, as the Great Society also birthed the Voting Rights Act and the Civil Rights Act. How could mass incarceration stem from the same set of ideas? Yet the Great Society set out to curtail urban disorder and introduced new levels of federal oversight into American lives. The 1965 Law Enforcement Assistance Act encouraged the militarization of urban police forces. Social Services grew interdependent with anti-crime forces. Black America, urbanized in the wake of the first and second great migrations, found itself in a swirl of local, state, and federal programs and government interaction with daily life. Under subsequent presidencies, perhaps most notably that of Richard Nixon and Ronald Reagan, these government processes solidified and normalized. Control of urban populations became *de riguer* practice and a central concern of American political rhetoric.

Todd R. Clear and Natasha A. Frost contend that approximately 7 percent of Americans can expect to be imprisoned in their lifetimes.[iv] The effect of mass incarceration on our communities cannot be overstated. But the rate of imprisonment effected some communities, and some groups within communities, at higher rates than others. In recent decades, the rate of incarceration has outpaced population growth and the growth in criminal acts. Politicians assert pro-law and order stances to gain votes.

Todd R. Clear serves as Provost, Rutgers University, Newark, and was previously dean of the School of Criminal Justice at Rutgers University. He published *Imprisoning Communities* (New York: Oxford University Press, 2009) and co-authored *What is Community Justice? Case Studies of Restorative Justice and Community Supervision* (New York: Sage, 2012). Clear founded *Criminology & Public Policy*, a popular journal in the field. He has served as president of the American Society of Criminology and other organizations.

Natasha A. Frost serves as Associate Dean for Northeastern University's Graduate Studies in the College of Social Sciences and Humanities and Professor in the School of Criminology and Criminal Justice, where she previously was Associate Dean. She has published *The Punitive State: Crime, Punishment, and Imprisonment across the United States* (New York: LFB Scholarly Publishing, 2006) and co-edited *Contemporary Issues in Crime and Justice Policy* (Belmont, CA: American Society of Criminology, 2010). Frost serves on the executive board of the American Society of Criminology and has published in a wide variety of journals, including *Criminology & Public Policy*.

THE PUNISHMENT IMPERATIVE (2014)

The Contours of Mass Incarceration

As the United States' prison and jail population approached, and then, in midyear 2002, exceeded the two million mark for the first time,[1] commentators—both expert and otherwise—no longer found it sufficient to refer to incarceration in the United States as simply incarceration: incarceration became mass incarceration. How else could one convey the enormity of the size of the America's incarcerated population? More than one in one hundred Americans were behind bars,[2] and, at the beginning of the new millennium,

---

iv. Todd R. Clear and Natasha A. Frost, *The Punishment Imperative: The Rise and Failure of Mass Incarceration in America* (New York: New York University Press, 2014), 17.

5.6 million Americans had served time in prison.[3] At these rates, almost 7 percent of the U.S. population could have expected to be imprisoned in their lifetime.[4] We did not simply have a lot of people in prisons and jails; we literally had *millions* of people in prisons and jails. We had earned the distinction of having the highest incarceration rate in the world, a rate that far exceeded the incarceration rates of our closest allies. With just under ten million people incarcerated in prisons and jails worldwide, America incarcerated more than one-fifth of the world's total prison population.[5] By any measure, these numbers were staggering.

Most scholars came to agree that, on the basis of its incarceration rate alone, America could fairly be described as the most punitive nation in the world.[6] The United States' incarceration rate of 756 inmates per 100,000 residents far exceeds the incarceration rates of other Western democracies, which generally have rates of less than 200 inmates per 100,000 residents.[7] Our incarceration rate has been the highest among Western industrialized countries since at least the mid-1990s.[8] In the fifteen years since we achieved that status, the number of people incarcerated across the United States has grown by more than a million, and we now incarcerate more people than any other nation in the world, in terms of both the absolute number of people in prison and the incarceration rate per one hundred thousand people.[9] [...] The United States leads the world in incarceration (followed by Russia, Rwanda, St. Kitts & Nevis, and Cuba) and has an incarceration rate that is more than four times that of several comparable European nations.[10]

Since 1980, we have seen the U.S. prison population increase by over 373 percent, from 319,598 prisoners in 1980 to 1,543,206 at year-end 2010, and the jail population increase by 324 percent, from 183,988 inmates in 1980 to 748,728 in 2010.[11] At year-end 2010, the overall incarceration rate had reached 731 inmates per 100,000 residents.[12] It might be tempting to think that we had turned to incarceration in lieu of community approaches to punishment—in other words, that we no longer

trusted probation and parole to supervise offenders in the community—but we had seen exponential growth across those domains as well.[13] While there were just over one million probationers in 1980, by 2010 that number had grown by 284 percent, to more than four million. Parole had likewise seen unprecedented growth from a parole population of 220,000 in 1980 to one of close to 841,000 in 2010.[14] [...]

So it was not just prisons and jails that had been affected by relentless growth. The Punishment Imperative had significantly impacted the size of the population under all types of correctional supervision. As astounding as it might sound, the 2.3 million people incarcerated in prisons and jails account for less than one-third of the total correctional population. When the population under any form of correctional supervision (probation, parole, or jail/prison) is counted, the numbers are even more staggering, with one in every thirty-one adults across the United States in prison or jail or on probation or parole.[15] In other words, as 2010 drew to a close, more than 7.25 million Americans were currently living under some form of correctional supervision.[16] By way of comparison, in 1980, prisons and jails across the country housed just over five hundred thousand people, and under two million (1,840,000) people were under correctional supervision.[17] To put the growth in perspective, in 2010, we had *half a million more people* in prison or jail alone than we had under any form of correctional supervision just thirty years before.

Of course this unprecedented growth in corrections came with quite a hefty price tag. In 2006, jurisdictions across the United States spent more than $68 billion on corrections.[18] Although the $68 billion spent on corrections was less than the more than $98 billion spent on policing, between 1982 and 2006, corrections expenditures grew more substantially than expenditures for any other criminal justice function. Direct expenditures on corrections grew from just over $9 billion in 1982 to over $68 billion in 2006 (an increase of 660 percent). By way of comparison, over the same period, direct judicial expenditures increased by 503 percent and direct policing expenditures increased by 420 percent.[19] The vast majority of correctional dollars spent—close to 90 percent—went toward sustaining mass incarceration. With a national average annual price tag of almost $29,000 per person per year of incarceration, it cost taxpayers at least ten times more to incarcerate a person than it would have cost to maintain him or her under supervision in the community.[20] The additional costs might have constituted a worthy investment if demonstrable benefits in terms of public safety could have been claimed, but research had repeatedly demonstrated that prison was no more effective than community supervision (at least in terms of crime prevention). As emphasized in a report issued by the Pew Center on the States, "serious, chronic and violent offenders belong behind bars, for a long time, and the expense of locking them up is justified many times over. But, for hundreds of thousands of lower-level inmates, incarceration costs taxpayers more than it saves in prevented crime."[21]

So who goes to prison? Prison population trend data, which suggest that over half of the current prison population is made up of violent offenders, exaggerate the extent to which we lock up serious violent offenders [...]. First, the offense-type classifications (violent, property, drug, and public order) used to calculate these population trend figures can include both very serious and far less serious offenses. Within each of these offense classifications, crime seriousness could be scored on a continuum, with offenses falling at both ends of the spectrum. "Violent offenses," for example, include very serious crimes like murder, rape, and armed robbery, but also presumably far less serious offenses like criminal endangerment, intimidation, and a whole host of "other" violent offenses. In other words, the types of offenses classified as violent offenses are perhaps more appropriately labeled something else. A similarly wide range of offenses is captured by the category "public order offenses," with crimes ranging from presumably quite serious weapons offenses at the high end of the spectrum to morals and decency charges and liquor law violations at the low end.

The same can be said of each of the other two broad categories of offenses (property and drug offenses). These broad classifications capture a very wide range of behaviors. Penal code reform rarely stems from the "average" case, however; when legislators write new laws, they are almost always reacting to extreme and highly publicized cases, and newspapers cover the most newsworthy cases.

These prison population trend figures also mask the fact that hundreds of thousands of inmates have been sent to prison each year for relatively low-level offenses and cycle through the system from year to year. Those serving time for violent offenses tend to stay in prison a lot longer than those serving time for public order offenses, and thus the population of violent offenders counted in these trends builds over time while the population of property, drug, and public order offenders tends to turn over more rapidly.[22] For those released in 2003, the average (median) time served for inmates released following admission for a violent offense was thirty-one months, while the average time served for inmates released following admission for a property (fourteen months), drug (fifteen months), or public order (thirteen months) offense was substantially lower.[23] Prison admissions data tell a quite different story. Using the same broad classifications of offenses, the most recently available data on prison admissions suggest that in 2003, just under 27 percent of all admissions were for violent offenses, about 30 percent were for property offenses, 32 percent were for drug offenses, and just over 11 percent were for public order offenses.[24] In other words, in terms of who is going to prison, more than two-thirds (over 70 percent) of those entering prisons each year were convicted of a nonviolent crime.

The absolute size of the prison population versus the number going into and coming out of prisons is often referred to as the distinction between stock and flow. The stock prison population is a count of the total number of prisoners incarcerated at any given point in time, while the flow refers to the movement of persons into and out of prisons (e.g., the absolute number of admissions and releases in a set time period). The distinction between stock and flow is helpful to the development of a more complete understanding of the dynamics of incarceration. At year-end 2008, the stock prison population stood at 1,610,446. In that same year, there were 739,132 prison admissions and 735,454 prison releases—together these admission and release figures represent the flow into and out of prison, respectively.[25] Until recently, in each year since the early 1970s, more prisoners were admitted to prison than had been released, and therefore the stock prison population continually increased. Moreover, the number of prisoners released in 2008 is just slightly lower than the number of prisoners admitted—although some of those released in 2008 might have served less than one year in prison, most of those released were probably not admitted in that same year. In other words, all prisoners contribute to the stock prison population—but do so for varying amounts of time. Inmates sentenced to serve long sentences (for example, serious violent offenders) contribute to the stock population for much longer than those serving relatively short sentences (like low-level drug offenders convicted of possession-only offenses). Stock prison population figures will always reflect larger numbers of violent long-term inmates than measures of the flow into and out of prison because low-level, nonviolent offenders cycle in and out of prison much more quickly.

[…] It is crucial to acknowledge that America's grand penal experiment extended well beyond mass incarceration. As prison, jail, probation, and parole populations expanded, so did a whole host of alternative methods of coercive social control. The alternatives—often described as intermediate sanctions—were designed to be more restrictive than probation but less confining than prison. Intermediate sanctions were intended to reduce or limit the use of incarceration, reserving the loss of liberty for use as a punishment of last resort.[26] Virtually all of these new and innovative alternatives to incarceration, though, became add-ons to

incarceration and, as Stanley Cohen noted many years ago, the net of punitive social control only widened.[27] The widening of the net of social controlled others to argue that there had been both an overt punitive strategy, focusing on "control through confinement," and a more covert strategy, focused on "control through surveillance."[28] Indeed it may very well be the case that growth in control through surveillance did as much as, if not more than, growth in confinement to increase the punitive reach of the justice system.[29] It can certainly be argued that growth in surveillance and other ostensibly community-based sanctions served to fuel growth in incarceration.[30] With enhanced surveillance came an enhanced ability to detect failure and an increased chance of incarceration as a result of those failures (and with debatable implications for public safety).[31]

The Distribution of Incarceration across Places

Although the national story—and indeed the headline—should be of unrelenting growth in prison populations for close to four decades, that growth did not distribute evenly across places. Controlling for the state population, some states had incarceration rates that were as much as five times higher than other states. At year-end 2010, for example, imprisonment rates (measured as the number of prisoners per one hundred thousand residents) ranged from a low of 148 in Maine to a high of 867 in Louisiana.[32] Given the wide range in incarceration rates across states, those states that managed to maintain fairly low rates of incarceration tended to look more like some of our Western European allies than they did their fellow (and sometimes geographically neighboring) states. Although all states experienced fairly substantial prison population growth through much of the period of prison expansion, in recent years, growth has continued unabated in a few states, slowed in others, and reversed course *in at least half of the states.*[33]

There have also been some fairly prominent regional patterns to prison population growth—although these patterns become less clear when the focus is shifted to something other than the sheer numbers of people in prison.[34] Southern states certainly led the way in imprisonment rates: at year-end 2010, five southern states (Louisiana, Mississippi, Texas, Oklahoma, and Alabama) each had imprisonment rates higher than six hundred prisoners per one hundred thousand residents. At the other end of the continuum, the low-imprisonment-rate states (those maintaining imprisonment rates of less than 250 per 100,000) were primarily northern states—with Nebraska, a decidedly midwestern state, the only non-northern state in that category.[35] A number of explanations have been offered for these relatively stable regional patterns, mostly having to do with race dynamics, but regardless of the cause, growth did not distribute evenly across places.[36]

Nor did growth distribute evenly over time. The most rapid growth occurred through the 1980s and continued well into the 1990s. Although growth has slowed since 2000, slowing growth was still growth. During the nearly forty years of sustained expansion in the use of prisons, several generations of Americans had known nothing but prison population growth. People born after 1973 had never known a time when the number of people incarcerated in this country was not rising. At no time in their lives had there been declines—let alone meaningful declines—in rates of imprisonment. High rates of imprisonment had assumed the status of social fact for these young Americans. And if high rates of incarceration were now social fact for an entire generation or two, nowhere was this more pronounced than in the places—and among the people—most impacted by these seemingly permanently high rates of incarceration.

The Concentration of Incarceration

Without question, growth in incarceration over the period concentrated among young black males from impoverished inner-city neighborhoods. Although an increasing number of Americans could claim prison experience, demographically, some—most notably young black males—were far more likely to have felt the consequences of mass incarceration. More than half of the adult prisoners are under thirty-five years old and almost nine in ten are under forty-five. Over 90 percent are men, and nearly half are African American.[37] Co-occurrence of these demographic characteristics concentrates incarceration even further: incarceration rates for black males are at least five times higher than for white males across every age group. Of black men in their late twenties, one in eight is currently behind bars.[38] Well more than half of all black high school dropouts born between 1965 and 1999 have been in (or will go to) prison, and overall, one in five black males can expect to be imprisoned sometime during adulthood.[39] These numbers are so staggering that it has become impossible to talk about incarceration without talking about its disparate impact on minority communities.

Why has incarceration concentrated so heavily in poor, inner-city communities that tend to be disproportionately comprised of minority populations? As is often the case, the answer to that seemingly simple question is complicated and multifaceted. Overly simplistic answers with a singular focus—like blacks commit more crime, or the criminal justice system is overtly or covertly racist—are woefully inadequate. A coalignment of factors, including disproportionate offending rates, the concentration of policing in inner-city communities, and (sometimes blatant) disparities in criminal justice outcomes across races all have contributed to black rates of incarceration that are more than five times higher than rates for whites.[40] Differential selection of blacks for criminal justice processing operates by moving blacks through the system at slightly higher rates at each and every stage of the system. The effect at each decision point might be small, but the overall effect, when all these small effects are added up, has been substantial.[41]

Understanding Growth in Prison Populations

Prior to the 1970s, prison populations across the United States had been remarkably stable, hovering at around one hundred prisoners per one hundred thousand population for most of the previous century [...]. Indeed, consistency in incarceration rates over time had been so remarkable, and so seemingly impervious to fluctuations in crime, that some of the most prominent criminologists of our time suggested that imprisonment might be a self-regulating process.[42] In the mid-1970s, Alfred Blumstein and his colleagues argued that stable incarceration rates since the early 1900s suggested that society required a stable amount of punishment in order to function as a society. Drawing from the work of sociologist Emile Durkheim, they postulated that societies use punishment to affirm behavioral norms, and that a more or less standard amount of incarceration was needed in order to do so. Their point was that while actual crimes leading to incarceration might shift fairly substantially from one era to another, the rate of incarceration would stay relatively constant within a fairly narrow range of about one hundred prisoners per one hundred thousand citizens. At the time Blumstein and his colleagues wrote, their thesis—which has come to be known as the "stability of punishment thesis"—was borne out by data on the U.S. incarceration rate through most of the first three-quarters of the twentieth century. Until the early 1970s, the incarceration rate had indeed remained remarkably consistent over time despite some quite remarkable shifts in the nature and scope of the crime problem.

Unfortunately for Blumstein and his colleagues, despite notable stability of punishment until 1970, the decade prior to the 1970s had been one of notable social turmoil and increasing distrust of government. Through the turbulent 1960s, the efficacy of punishment was frequently called into question, and there was a real push to develop alternatives to incarceration in the form of community-based sanctions. Prominent scholars of punishment publishing in the years preceding the era of relentless prison population growth not only failed to see it coming but, in some instances, they actually predicted that the end of imprisonment might be near. In the 1940s, Hermann Mannheim proclaimed, "The days of

imprisonment as a method of mass treatment of lawbreakers are over."[43] A quarter-century later, in a tribute to Mannheim, the late Norval Morris, one of the most preeminent penologists of our time, "confidently predicted that, before the end of this century, prison in [its current] form will become extinct, though the word may live on."[44] Morris was not alone in his sense that the prison was an institution with a foreshortened life expectancy. Historian David J. Rothman, who wrote several of the more influential accounts of the history of penal institutions, offered the following observation at the end of the now-classic *Discovery of the Asylum*, originally published in 1971:

> We still live with many of these institutions, accepting their presence as inevitable. Despite a personal revulsion, we think of them as always having been with us, and therefore as always to be with us. We tend to forget that they were the invention of one generation to serve very special needs, not the only possible reaction to social problems. In fact, since the Progressive era, we have been gradually escaping from institutional responses, and one can foresee the period when incarceration will be used still more rarely than it is today.[45]

All indications seemed to suggest that the prison was an institution that was fast outgrowing its utility. The predictions of these prominent scholars, which also preceded the era of unrelenting prison population growth, made some sense in the context of the time in which they were made. In the 1960s, amid social turmoil and increasing distrust of government, there had indeed been a movement toward decarceration (albeit, in hindsight, the decarceration movement was short-lived).

In 1972 prison populations across the United States began their steep and rapid climb and continued that ascent for more than a generation [...]. To be sure, toward the end of that period, some states began to experience small declines in the size of their prison populations, and in others growth slowed. But even as growth slowed, until 2010, overall prison populations continued to climb and our incarceration rates continued to grow. This is true even though, for at least the last fifteen years of that period, crime rates were not only falling but were doing so perhaps more dramatically than at any other time in our modern history.[46]

Partitioning Prison Population Growth

Although we witnessed almost unrelenting growth in prison populations since the 1970s, there is some evidence suggesting that the growth was driven by different factors at different times over the period. Franklin Zimring, for example, proposed that we think about prison population expansion in terms of three distinct phases of growth.[47] According to Zimring, most of the early growth in prison populations was best explained by an increasing risk of imprisonment. Beginning in the mid-1970s and continuing through the mid-1980s, imprisonment risk increased quite dramatically—meaning that those convicted of crimes were more likely to be sentenced to prison than they ever had been previously. This dramatic increase in imprisonment risk was inspired in part by the growing sense that the system had been too soft and its rehabilitative orientation misguided. Proponents of this perspective argued that in a rational cost-benefit analysis, crime actually paid, and therefore the payoff of crime needed to be addressed. The basic premise of deterrence—that people will avoid crime if the consequences are noxious enough— emphasized the importance of making punishment more certain and more severe to make offending less appealing, and this type of thinking resonated with the American public. As renowned political scientist James Q. Wilson noted in a widely read article published in *Atlantic Monthly* in the early 1980s,

> The average citizen hardly needs to be persuaded that crimes will be committed more frequently if, other things being equal, crime becomes more profitable than other ways of spending one's time. Accordingly, the average citizen thinks it obvious that one major reason why crime has increased is that people have discovered they can get away with it. By the same token, a good way to reduce crime is to make its consequences to the would-be

offender more costly (by making penalties swifter, more certain, or more severe).[48]

During this early phase of the Punishment Imperative, the likelihood of imprisonment generally increased for everyone but especially for those low-level offenders who previously would never have received a prison sentence in the first place.

Toward the middle of the 1980s, we entered the second phase, during which prison population growth was driven largely by policies and practices associated with the increasingly ubiquitous War on Drugs. Here the focus shifted from increasing the likelihood of imprisonment for all offenders, including relatively low-level offenders, to vastly increasing the likelihood of imprisonment for drug offenders more specifically. A series of federal legislative initiatives targeting drug offenders passed in the mid- to late 1980s all but ensured that the majority of offenders entering federal prisons would be drug offenders. Not only did the likelihood of receiving a sentence to imprisonment increase dramatically for drug offenders over this period, but so too did the length of sentence they could expect to serve. So while early prison population growth was driven by our inclination to send more and more people to prison, by the mid-1980s we were increasingly becoming concerned with extending the length of time that they would stay there. Although many were affected by this shift, the focus of these initiatives was on drug offenders who, by this time, had been increasingly vilified. From the mid-1980s through at least the early 1990, drug offenders were far more likely to be sent to prison and once there could expect to stay much longer than they ever had previously.

The third and final phase—which started in the early to mid-1990s and presumably persisted until very recently—shifted focus back to the more general offender population and emphasized increasing lengths of stay over increasing the likelihood of imprisonment. Zimring characterized the transition to the third phase as a "shift in emphasis from 'lock 'em up' to 'throw away the key'" and hypothesized that much of the more recent growth in incarceration could be attributed to increasingly long sentences.[49] [...] Truth-in-sentencing legislation that required that violent offenders serve at least 85 percent of their sentence was the centerpiece legislation of this most recent era, but a wide array of mandatory sentencing laws targeting all types of offenders meant that virtually everyone sent to prison would be serving sentences that were at least slightly longer than they had been previously. When upwards of half a million people are admitted to prison each year, even very small changes in the average time a prisoner can expect to serve results in quite dramatic increases in the prison population.

Although Zimring did not empirically test his thesis regarding the three distinct phases of imprisonment growth, in a series of studies, Alfred Blumstein and Allen Beck isolated growth across each of the various stages of the criminal justice process.[50] Along the crime-punishment continuum, there are really four processing stages that might contribute to increasing prison populations: (1) crime, (2) arrests, (3) sentencing, and (4) time served. First, and most obviously, increasing crime might lead to increasing use of imprisonment. Indeed, the perception that crime had been spiraling out of control has often been cited as one of the driving forces behind increasing punitiveness.[51] And, while there certainly were some quite substantial increases in crime in the period immediately preceding the Punishment Imperative, there has been some debate about the magnitude of those actual increases given changes in the way in which crime was recorded over the same period.[52] A change in the number of *arrests* might also affect prison population size with or without a concomitant increase in crime. In fact, one might expect changes in arrest patterns to have a bigger effect than changes in crime. Only those offenders who are arrested can ultimately be sanctioned by the criminal justice system, so changes in offending will have little effect if the police do not meet that challenge of increasing crime with more arrests. Holding crime constant, increases in arrests would indicate

that the police have become more effective in apprehending offenders, increasing the supply of offenders for the criminal justice system to sanction.

There are also two distinct processes associated with the sanctioning phase that could have contributed to prison population growth: commitments to prison and length of stay. The size of the prison population ultimately depends upon how many people go to prison and how long they stay (a truism recently referred to as the "Iron Law of Prison Populations").[53] A sudden increase in the number of persons sent to prison (e.g., commitments to prison) will have a pretty immediate effect on the size of the prison population while a sudden change in the length of time that they stay (e.g., time served) will have a delayed, but equally profound, effect over time.

Scholars have demonstrated that virtually all growth in prison populations over several decades could be attributed to the two sanctioning phases of the system: commitments to prison once convicted and length of stay once admitted. Eighty-eight percent of the growth in prison populations between 1980 and 1996 has been attributed to increasing commitments to prison and increasing lengths of stay.[54] The remaining 12 percent predominantly resulted from increases in crime, and particularly drug crime. Only one-half of 1 percent of the growth over that period could be explained by increasing police effectiveness at the arrest stage. Blumstein and Beck, the scholars who generated these estimates, provided empirical support for Zimring's thesis about the importance of the War on Drugs to prison population growth when they reported that virtually all of the early-stage growth in crime could be explained by drug offenses. When drug offenses were removed from the equation, changes during the two sanctioning phases accounted for more than 99 percent of the prison population growth.

In later work,[55] Blumstein and Beck extended their earlier analysis to 2001 and partitioned the period into two separate eras of growth (with 1992 as the break point). Again they found that increases in the early offense and apprehension phases explained very little prison population growth over either period, although those increases did explain some in the earlier period, and the sanctioning phases explained most of the growth in prison population. Crucially, increases in commitments contributed more to growth in the early period (1980–1992) and increases in length of stay contributed more to growth in the later period (1992–2001). Blumstein and Beck's empirical partitioning of prison population growth ultimately aligned quite nicely with Zimring's thesis that prison population growth might best be understood if parsed into three distinct eras.

Economists Steven Raphael and Michael Stoll similarly demonstrated that increasing lengths of stay account for a substantial portion of prison population growth, reporting that growth in average time served could explain roughly one-third of prison population growth.[56] Like Blumstein and Beck, Raphael and Stoll reported that changes in rates of criminal offending explained relatively little (at most 17 percent) of the growth in imprisonment between 1980 and 2005. Crucially, in their analysis of average time served, they controlled for the fact that the massive influx of relatively low-level offenders in the 1980s and 1990s will have disproportionately impacted the overall average time served (driving it downward). Those low-level offenders—who were now disproportionately represented in the prison population—served relatively short prison sentences, making it appear as though the average time served had actually changed little over time. Raphael and Stoll, however, estimated the average time served for "like" offenders and found that "prisoners today are serving longer sentences than comparable prisoners in years past, a fact that is missed in simple comparisons of the overall average release rate or the aggregate time-served distribution."[57] According to Raphael and Stoll, "collectively, changes in who goes to prison … and for how long … explain 80–85% of prison expansion over the last twenty-five years."[58] The increasingly sophisticated work of criminologists and economists has helped us to better understand the complicated dynamics of prison population growth. When changes in offending patterns could explain so little of the prison population growth, it became more and more clear that prison population growth had been driven primarily by policy choices.

The Relationship between Crime and Punishment

Work partitioning prison population growth has suggested that crime—or, more precisely, change in crime—has had a negligible impact on prison population growth, and few scholars today argue that changes in crime rates, or trends in crime over time, can adequately explain changes in the level of imprisonment. Even a quick glance at trends over the past forty years illustrates the complex and often contradictory nature of the relationship between crime and incarceration [...].

In the fifteen-year period before the incarceration rate began to rise, the crime rate doubled. Over the next decade or so, the crime rate had two accelerations and three declines, ending at about 50 percent higher than it started. The incarceration rate increased about 50 percent as well. In the decade that followed (the early eighties to the early nineties), crime rates fell and then rose again, ending up where they started that period, while incarceration rates almost tripled. Since the last crime peak in 1994, crime rates have steadily fallen for well over a decade. Incarceration rates over the same period grew by two-thirds. Thus, there has been no straightforward relationship between incarceration and crime—during a generation-long growth of imprisonment, crime rates first increased, then fluctuated quite erratically, and have since dropped rather substantially.[59]

It seems crucial to note that in studies of the relationship between crime and imprisonment, crime might be conceived of as both an *input* of imprisonment and an *output* of imprisonment—making the nature of the relationship between crime and imprisonment difficult to model statistically [...]. Crime is quite obviously an input for prisons (ostensibly only those accused and convicted of crimes are sentenced to prison),[60] and indeed it is in some ways a truism that the size of the prison population depends upon crime—after all, without crime there would be no imprisonment (or at least very little). Most obviously, as an explanatory variable, crime clearly might explain some of the variation in imprisonment rates over time. In times of increasing crime, for example, one might expect increasing imprisonment.

Although few studies examine the relationship between crime and imprisonment singularly, most empirical work specifies crime as one among many factors potentially explaining variation in imprisonment rates. Empirical research has demonstrated that, broadly speaking, crime rates—particularly violent crime rates—tend to explain some of the variation in imprisonment rates across states and over time. In a study attempting to explain variation in imprisonment rates across states, Greenberg and West broke the crime rate down into its two component parts (violent and property crime) and additionally included a measure of drug arrests.[61] They found that violent crime and drug arrest rates each significantly predicted imprisonment rates, but property crime rates did not, and noted that "although growth in crime was not a major cause of higher prison populations, imprisonment rates have been higher, and have grown faster, in states with higher levels of victimizing crime, especially violent crime."[62] They concluded that their findings support the conclusion that imprisonment rates are neither "entirely determined" by nor "entirely unrelated" to crime rates. In other words, crime rates—particularly violent crime rates—explain some, but certainly nothing like all, of the variation in state imprisonment rates.

But variation in crime might also be an output of prisons. When crime is specified as a potential outcome, one might predict that imprisonment would either reduce crime or increase crime. To the extent that imprisonment deters, rehabilitates, or effectively incapacitates criminal offenders, imprisonment might be expected to reduce crime. To the extent that imprisonment

weakens informal social control or disrupts important networks, imprisonment might be expected to increase crime.[63] Scholars of penology have long argued that prisons do little to improve the lot of those offenders sent to them for punishment and might actually be criminogenic—increasing the likelihood of future offending upon release rather than decreasing it. [...] We currently release large numbers of prisoners (more than seven hundred thousand each year) into communities with very little support, almost no material resources (financial or otherwise), and few if any educational credentials or marketable skills. Given the stigma of a criminal conviction and of having served a term of incarceration, these former offenders are quite likely to find themselves in a far worse position following a stint in prison than they had been prior to entering prison. To be sure, when prison populations grow, rates of prison releases also grow, with the attendant consequence of increased crime that results from increases in prisoner reentry.

A sizeable body of research has tried to estimate the impact of the size of the prison population on state and national levels of crime.[64] The theory is that prison incapacitates those who are locked up, and the more people who are in capacitated, the less the crime. This research has produced a range of estimates of incapacitation effects. Very high estimates, on the order of 187 crimes prevented per year of incarceration, have been based on self-reports of criminal activity by people who were incarcerated.[65] Much more moderate effects, on the order of a 1 percent drop in crime for every 10 percent increase in the size of the prison population, have been derived from observations of the national relationship between the rate of incarceration and the rate of crime over time.[66] In general, smaller estimates of incapacitation effects are provided by more recent models, more sophisticated models, and models using smaller geo-spatial units of analysis.[67] Indeed, a recent state-level panel study of incarceration between the years 1978 and 2004 found that, after accounting for reverse causality and the lagged effects of reentry rates, incarceration had actually increased rates of violent crime.[68]

In studies of the net effect of the size of the stock population of prisoners at any given time on crime rates (through incapacitation), incarceration is usually thought of as something that happens to individuals, changing the way in which offenders are free to act in the community. But recently, the idea has arisen among scholars that incarceration is not just a process operating on individuals who go to prison but is also a social process with impact at the community level.[69] By and large, convicted criminal offenders are not simply removed from communities never to return again. Rather, these offenders typically cycle through prison (often more than once in their lifetimes). The removal of people from communities to prison and their eventual return back to the community from prison has been referred to as reentry cycling—or, more recently, prison cycling.[70] The effects of that social process known as prison cycling are typically presented as unforeseen collateral consequences of a crime-control policy that tends to exacerbate the very social problems that are thought to undermine a community's public safety.[71] It may therefore be that the effect of the stock population of prisoners on suppressing crime rates is counteracted by the community-level impact of prison cycling: that the flow in and out of prison has a different impact on crime than the stay in prison. In other words, it might be the case that in the communities that are most differentially impacted by sustained high rates of prison cycling, incarceration actually backfires and ultimately ends up increasing crime in those communities [...].[72]

Penologist David Garland has made the point that crime and imprisonment are assuredly related to one another, but not in any simple or straightforward manner.[73] A cursory understanding of this relationship is that it is almost certainly reciprocal, changes in each producing changes in the other. The precise nature of these changes has not been empirically identified. Indeed, empirical work assessing the effect of either crime on imprisonment or imprisonment on crime has often produced conflicting results. When crime has been specified as an explanatory variable, some find

that crime—particularly violent crime—predicts imprisonment and others find no significant relationship. Similarly, when crime is specified as an outcome variable, some find that imprisonment reduces crime, some find that it increases crime, and others find no significant relationship between imprisonment and crime.[74]

If Not Crime, Then What?

In recent years, scholars have increasingly tried to understand incarceration as more than just a response to crime and as more than simply the end result of a collection of related policies that have been adopted largely in isolation. Although explanations for unabated prison population growth are many and varied, there are some dominant themes that occur across many of the more influential attempts to explain that growth. Central among these themes is the idea that the American sociopolitical culture is unique, producing a strong trend of control-oriented policies that emphasize the prison and "tough" responses to crime as salient political platforms and acceptable cultural starting points for crime policy.[75] [...] For now, we turn briefly to a historical development in crime policy whose influence on prison population growth cannot be overstated and should not be ignored. The framing of the crime problem as requiring an all-out "war" in response has had lasting consequences. The various war metaphors that have been used to characterize the necessary response to crime problems for at least the past four decades are important in that they served to legitimize the anything-goes approach that drove penal policy over that period. These wars also notably contributed to the increasing racial divide in punishment.

The Wars on Crime and on Drugs

There is no way to write about the Punishment Imperative without explicitly addressing the centrality of race and of the ongoing wars on crime and on drugs. The seeds for the wars on crime and then on drugs were certainly planted in the decade immediately preceding the buildup, and as has been noted by several before us, the framing of the crime problem was implicitly (and at times explicitly) racialized.[76]

The United States has a fairly long and storied history of crime wars. In fact, our crime wars have long outlasted any of our military wars, which, relatively speaking, have tended to be short-lived. Even the protracted Vietnam War, spanning more than fifteen years, seems fleeting by comparison to our ongoing crime wars. Before we launched the most recent War on Terror in the aftermath of the 9/11 attacks in 2001, we fought a protracted War on Drugs, and before that a prolonged War on Crime. All told, we have been fighting crime-related wars for close to half a century now—none of which have we won and all of which we continue to fight to varying degrees today. In other words, with the debut of each new crime-related war, we have supplemented rather than replaced the previous, yet-to-be-won (and, some would argue, unwinnable) crime-related war.

The earliest of these wars, the War on Crime, which was first initiated in the mid-1960s following what appeared to be a fairly dramatic increase in crime, has continued unabated for well over forty years now. Although labeled somewhat generically, at its inception, the War on Crime was quite specifically a war on violent crime and was the first in the series of wars that would virtually guarantee the supply of prisoners who would drive up prison populations over the next four decades. The War on Crime was initially launched following the release of the landmark 1967 report, *The Challenge of Crime in a Free Society*, authored by the President's Commission on Law Enforcement and the Administration of Justice (hereafter 1967 Crime Commission).[77] The 1967 Crime Commission report detailed the crime-related challenges facing the United States and laid the foundations of a crime-control strategy for beginning to address them. According to the report, the challenges were daunting and the task monumental. An ambitious agenda for the future, a road map for a War on Crime, was laid out in seven propositions:

First, society must seek to prevent crime before it happens by assuring all Americans a stake in the benefits and responsibilities of American life, by

strengthening law enforcement, and by reducing criminal opportunities. Second, society's aim of reducing crime would be better served if the system of criminal justice developed a far broader range of techniques with which to deal with individual offenders. Third, the system of criminal justice must eliminate existing injustices if it is to achieve its ideals and win the respect and cooperation of all citizens. Fourth, the system of criminal justice must attract more people and better people—police, prosecutors, judges, defense attorneys, probation and parole officers, and corrections officials with more knowledge, expertise, initiative, and integrity. Fifth, there must be much more operational and basic research into the problems of crime and criminal administration, by those both within and without the system of criminal justice. Sixth, the police, courts, and correctional agencies must be given substantially greater amounts of money if they are to improve their ability to control crime. Seventh, individual citizens, civic and business organizations, religious institutions, and all levels of government must take responsibility for planning and implementing the changes that must be made in the criminal justice system if crime is to be reduced.[78]

According to the President's Crime Commission, when it came to crime very little had been going well—virtually every facet of current crime prevention and control strategies had to be reassessed and the approach going forward would have to be multifaceted and comprehensive. In the three hundred pages that followed, the commission offered a litany of recommendations for waging a crime war covering everything from strengthening families to addressing underlying social problems to improving detection and eliminating disparities. Commemorating the fortieth anniversary of the publication of *The Challenge of Crime in a Free Society*, Thomas Feucht and Edwin Zedlewski describe its impact in the following way:

The President's Crime Commission thrust "ordinary street crime" irreversibly into policy discussions and provided the framework for the Federal Government to take new responsibility for fighting crime and enhancing public safety in neighborhoods and communities across the country. No one was under the illusion that crime could easily be banished. In fact, when Johnson accepted the

Challenge of Crime report in 1967, he cautioned that the war on crime would take generations to wage.[79]

President Johnson couldn't have been more accurate. More than forty years later, the War on Crime that was launched with the publication of that report in many ways wages on.

Not long after the launch of the War on Crime, the emphasis shifted from violent crime to drug crime—a type of crime that had been largely ignored by the 1967 Crime Commission.[80] Although President Nixon can be credited with turning the focus to drugs beginning in his 1968 campaign for office, the War on Drugs was really launched in earnest under the Reagan administration in the early 1980s. The subsequent administrations, at least through Republican George H. W. Bush and Democrat William Jefferson Clinton, ensured that the War on Drugs would continue unabated long after the core problems identified as substantiating the War on Drugs—primarily the emergence of crack cocaine and the violence associated with the drug trade—had waned. Although the precise reasons for the shift have proven difficult to isolate with any precision, several have argued that drugs offered a convenient avenue through which to shift the conversation about the nature of the crime problem (and those responsible for it)—and simultaneously offered a convenient diversion from the reality that the War on Crime had seen limited success in the fifteen years since it was launched with the publication of the 1967 Crime Commission report.

The vast majority of legislation associated with the War on Drugs has targeted the supply side of the equation—targeting those who manufacture, distribute, and possess illegal drugs. Very little of the drug war legislation has focused on addressing the underlying problem of drug addiction that fuels the drug markets. Indeed, from its inception, the focus of the War on Drugs has been predominantly on enforcement of drug laws, with far less funding going to prevention or treatment. In recent testimony before a subcommittee in Congress, criminologist Peter Reuter, a noted expert on drugs and crime, explained that "total expenditures for drug control, at all levels of government, totaled close to $40 billion in 2007" with approximately three-quarters (70–75 percent) of those funds going toward enforcement.[81] The impact of the enforcement-heavy War on Drugs has been profound, and its impact on inner-city minority communities, devastating. In 1980, the number of people incarcerated for drug offenses was small in both absolute and proportional terms—the growth has been exponential. The population incarcerated for drug offenses grew from less than fifty thousand drug offenders in 1980 to more than five hundred thousand in 2007.[82] In the 1970s, before the start of the War on Drugs, people in prison for drug crimes constituted about 5 percent of the total number of the prison population. By 2010, they represented close to 20 percent of the total population. At the federal level—where the drug war has been fought most prominently, *more than half* of all incarcerated offenders are serving time for drug offenses.[83] Given the dynamics of incarceration explained above, as longer sentences for violent crime kick in, the proportion of people behind bars for drug crimes decreases, even though the number actually going to prison for drug offenses remains high.[84]

[...] Suffice it to say, for now, that perhaps no series of crime control initiatives have contributed to the racialization of the crime problem and ensured the disparate impact of incarceration than those policies most closely associated with the War on Drugs. That said, although drugs (and particularly the policies associated with the War on Drugs) were central to the most precipitous period of prison population buildup, they were certainly not solely responsible for it. [...] The experiment was grand and the approach was multifaceted. Even without the War on Drugs, we would have seen unprecedented growth in the use of imprisonment. Sweeping changes in sentencing policy and correctional practice all but ensured that we would see prison populations reach astounding proportions.

NOTES

1. Paige M. Harrison and Jennifer C. Karberg, "Prison and Jail Inmates at Midyear 2002" (Washington, DC: Bureau of Justice Statistics, 2003).

2. Pew Center on the States, "1 in 100: Behind Bars in America 2008" (Washington, DC: Pew Charitable Trusts, 2008).
3. Thomas P. Bonczar, "Prevalence of Imprisonment in the U.S. Population, 1974–2001" (Washington, DC: Bureau of Justice Statistics, 2003).
4. Ibid.
5. Roy Walmsley, "World Prison Population, 8th Edition" (London: International Centre for Prison Studies, 2009).
6. See though Roger Matthews, "The Myth of Punitiveness," *Theoretical Criminology*, 9/2 (2005), 175–201.
7. Walmsley, "World Prison Population, 8th Edition."
8. William J. Chambliss, *Power, Politics, and Crime* (Boulder, CO: Westview, 2001), xiv, 173.
9. Adam Liptak, "Inmate Count in U.S. Dwarfs Other Nations," *New York Times*, April 23, 2008, A1.
10. Walmsley, "World Prison Population, 8th Edition."
11. Paul Guerino, Paige M. Harrison, and William J. Sabol, "Prisoners in 2010" (Washington, DC: Bureau of Justice Statistics, 2011).
12. Lauren Glaze, "Correctional Populations in the United States, 2010" (Washington, DC: Bureau of Justice Statistics, 2011), Heather C. West and William J. Sabol, "Prisoners in 2007" (Washington, DC: Bureau of Justice Statistics, 2008).
13. Lauren Glaze and Thomas P. Bonczar, "Probation and Parole in the United States, 2010" (Washington, DC: Bureau of Justice Statistics, 2011).
14. Ibid.
15. Pew Center on the States, "One in 31: The Long Reach of Corrections" (Washington, DC: Pew Charitable Trusts, 2009).
16. Glaze, "Correctional Populations in the United States, 2010."
17. Lauren E. Glaze and Thomas P. Bonczar, "Probation and Parole in the United States: 2007 Statistical Tables" (Washington, DC: Bureau of Justice Statistics, 2009).
18. Bureau of Justice Statistics, "Justice Expenditure and Employment Extracts" (Washington, DC: Bureau of Justice Statistics, 2008).
19. Ibid.
20. Pew Center on the States, "One in 31: The Long Reach of Corrections."
21. Ibid., 2.
22. Todd R. Clear and James Austin, "Reducing Mass Incarceration: Implications of the Iron Law of Prison Populations," *Harvard Law and Policy Review*, 3 (2009), 307–24.
23. Thomas P. Bonczar, "Table 8. State Prison Releases, 2003: Time Served in Prison, by Offense and Release Type" (Washington, DC: Bureau of Justice Statistics, 2007).
24. Thomas P. Bonczar, "Table 1. State Prison Admissions, 2003: Offense, by Type of Admission" (Washington, DC: Bureau of Justice Statistics, 2007).
25. William J. Sabol, Heather C. West, and Matthew Cooper, "Prisoners in 2008" (Washington, DC: Bureau of Justice Statistics, 2009).
26. Norval Morris and Michael H. Tonry, *Between Prison and Probation: Intermediate Punishments in a Rational Sentencing System* (New York: Oxford University Press, 1990), 283.
27. Stanley Cohen, *Visions of Social Control: Crime, Punishment, and Classification* (New York: Polity Press, 1985), x, 325.
28. Katherine Beckett and Steve Herbert, *Banished: The New Social Control in Urban America* (New York: Oxford University Press, 2010).
29. Diana Gordon, *The Justice Juggernaut: Fighting Street Crime, Controlling Citizens* (New Brunswick, NJ: Rutgers University Press, 1990).
30. Beckett and Herbert, *Banished: The New Social Control in Urban America*.
31. Joan Petersilia, "Understanding California Corrections: A Policy Research Program Report" (Berkeley: California Policy Research Center, 2006).
32. Guerino, Harrison, and Sabol, "Prisoners in 2010."
33. Ibid.
34. Natasha A. Frost, *The Punitive State: Crime, Punishment, and Imprisonment across the United States* (New York: LFB Scholarly Publications, 2006).
35. Guerino, Harrison, and Sabol, "Prisoners in 2010."
36. Stephanie Bontrager, William Bales, and Ted Chiricos, "Race, Ethnicity, Threat, and the Labeling of Convicted Felons," *Criminology*, 43/3 (2005), 589–622.
37. Paige M. Harrison and Allen J. Beck, "Prisoners in 2005" (Washington, DC: U.S. Department of Justice, Bureau of Justice Statistics, 2006).
38. Ibid., 10.
39. Bruce Western, *Punishment and Inequality in America* (New York: Russell Sage Foundation, 2006), 25–27.
40. Michael Tonry, *Punishing Race: A Continuing American Dilemma* (New York: Oxford University Press, 2011).
41. Samuel Walker, Cassia Spohn, and Miriam Delone, *The Color of Justice: Race, Ethnicity, and Crime in America* (4th edition Belmont, CA: Wadsworth, 2008).
42. Alfred Blumstein and Jacqueline Cohen, "A Theory of the Stability of Punishment," *Journal of Criminal Law, Criminology, and Police Science*, 63 (1973), 198–207, Alfred

Blumstein, Jacqueline Cohen, and Daniel Nagin, "The Dynamics of a Homeostatic Punishment Process," *Journal of Criminal Law and Criminology*, 67 (1977), 317–34, Alfred Blumstein and S. Moitra, "An Analysis of the Time-Series of the Imprisonment Rate in the States of the United States: A Further Test of the Stability of Punishment Hypothesis," *Journal of Criminal Law and Criminology*, 70 (1979), 376–90.

43. Hermann Mannheim, "American Criminology and Penology in War Time," *Sociological Review*, 34 (1942), 222–34, at 222, cited in Michael Tonry, "Has the Prison a Future?" in Michael Tonry (ed.), *The Future of Imprisonment* (New York: Oxford University Press, 2004), 3–24, at 3.

44. Norval Morris, "Prison in Evolution," in Tadeusz Grygier, Howard Jones, and John C. Spencer (eds.), *Criminology in Transition: Essays in Honour of Hermann Mannheim* (London: Tavistock, 1965), 268, cited in Tonry, "Has the Prison a Future?" 3.

45. David J. Rothman, *The Discovery of the Asylum: Social Order and Disorder in the New Republic* (revised edition Boston: Little, Brown, 1990/1971), at 295.

46. Franklin E. Zimring, *The Great American Crime Decline* (Studies in Crime and Public Policy) (New York: Oxford University Press, 2007), xiv, 258.

47. Franklin E. Zimring, "Imprisonment Rates and the New Politics of Criminal Punishment," *Punishment & Society*, 3 (2001), 161–66.

48. James Q. Wilson, "Thinking about Crime: The Debate over Deterrence," *Atlantic Monthly*, 252/3 (1983), 72–88.

49. Zimring, "Imprisonment Rates and the New Politics of Criminal Punishment," 162.

50. Alfred Blumstein and Allen J. Beck, "Population Growth in U.S. Prisons, 1980–1996," in Michael Tonry and Joan Petersilia (eds.), *Prisons* (Chicago: University of Chicago Press, 1999), 17–61, Alfred Blumstein and Allen J. Beck," Reentry as a Transient State between Liberty and Recommitment," in Jeremy Travis and Christy Visher (eds.), *Prisoner Reentry and Crime in America* (New York: Cambridge University Press, 2005), 50–79.

51. David Garland, *The Culture of Control: Crime and Social Order in Contemporary Society* (Chicago: University of Chicago Press, 2001), xiii, 307.

52. Bert Useem, Raymond V. Liedka, and Anne Morrison Piehl, "Popular Support for the Prison Build-Up," *Punishment & Society*, 5/1 (2003), 5–32.

53. Clear and Austin, "Reducing Mass Incarceration: Implications of the Iron Law of Prison Populations."

54. Blumstein and Beck, "Population Growth in U.S. Prisons, 1980–1996."

55. Blumstein and Beck, "Reentry as a Transient State between Liberty and Recommitment."

56. Steven Raphael and Michael A. Stoll, "Why Are So Many Americans in Prison?" in Steven Raphael and Michael A. Stoll (eds.), *Do Prisons Make Us Safer? The Benefits and Costs of the Prison Boom* (Washington, DC: Russell Sage Foundation, 2 009), 27–72.

57. Ibid.

58. Ibid., 65.

59. Zimring, *The Great American Crime Decline.*

60. Although most people incarcerated in prisons have been convicted, those incarcerated in jails and other detention facilities have often not. See Sharon Dolovich, "Confronting the Costs of Incarceration. Foreward: Incarceration American-Style," *Harvard Law and Policy Review*, 3 (2009), 237–59.

61. David H. Greenberg and Valerie West, "State Prison Populations and Their Growth, 1971–1991," *Criminology* 39/3 (2001), 615–54.

62. Ibid., 638.

63. See Todd R. Clear, "Backfire: When Incarceration Increases Crime," *Journal of the Oklahoma Criminal Justice Research Consortium*, 3 (1996), 1–10, Todd R. Clear, "The Problem with 'Addition by Subtraction': The Prison-Crime Relationship in Low-Income Communities," in Marc Mauer and Meda Chesney-Lind (eds.), *Invisible Punishment: The Collateral Consequences of Mass Imprisonment* (New York: New Press, 2002), 181–93, Todd R. Clear et al., "Coercive Mobility and Crime: A Preliminary Examination of Concentrated Incarceration and Social Disorganization," *Justice Quarterly*, 20/1 (2003), 33–64, Jeffrey Fagan, "Crime, Law, and the Community: Dynamics of Incarceration in New York City," in Michael Tonry (ed.), *The Future of Imprisonment* (New York: Oxford University Press, 2004), 27–59, James P. Lynch and William J. Sabol, "Assessing the Effects of Mass Incarceration on Informal Social Control in Communities," *Criminology & Public Policy*, 3/2 (2004), 267–94, James P. Lynch and William J. Sabol, "Effects of Incarceration on Informal Social Control in Communities," in Mary Patillo, David F. Weiman, and Bruce Western (eds.), *Imprisoning America: The Social Effects of Mass In carceration* (New York: Russell Sage Foundation, 2004), 135–64, Dina Rose and Todd R. Clear, "Incarceration, Social Capital, and Crime: Implications for Social Disorganization Theory," *Criminology*, 36 (1998), 441–80.

64. Tomislav Kovandzic and Lynne Vieraitis, "The Effect of County-Level Prison Population Growth on Crime Rates," *Criminology*

& *Public Policy*, 5/2 (2006), 213–44, Steven Levitt, "The Effect of Prison Population Size on Crime Rates: Evidence from Prison Over-Crowding Litigation," *Quarterly Journal of Economics*, 111 (1996), 319–51, Raymond V. Liedka, Anne Morrison Piehl, and Bert Useem, "The Crime Control Effects of Incarceration: Does Scale Matter?" *Criminology & Public Policy*, 5/2 (2006), 245–76, Thomas B. Marvell and Carlisle E. Moody, "Prison Population Growth and Crime Reduction," *Journal of Quantitative Criminology*, 10/2 (1994), 109–40, Thomas B. Marvell and Carlisle E. Moody, "The Impact of Prison Growth on Homicide," *Homicide Studies*, 1 (1997), 205–33, Lynne Vieraitis, Tomislav Kovandzic, and Thomas B. Marvell, "The Criminogenic Effects of Imprisonment: Evidence from State Panel Data, 1974–2002," *Criminology & Public Policy*, 6/3 (2007), 589–622.

65. Edwin Zedlewski, "Making Confinement Decisions: Research in Brief" (Washington, DC: U.S. Department of Justice, 1987).

66. Western, *Punishment and Inequality in America*.

67. For a review, Don Stemen, "Reconsidering Incarceration: New Directions for Reducing Crime" (New York: VERA Institute of Justice, 2007).

68. Robert DeFina and Lance Hannon, "For Incapacitation, There Is No Time Like the Present: The Lagged Effects of Prisoner Reentry on Property and Violent Crime Rates," *Social Science Research*, 39 (2010), 1004–1014.

69. Donald Braman, *Doing Time on the Outside: Incarceration and Family Life in America* (Ann Arbor: University of Michigan Press, 2004), Rose and Clear, "Incarceration, Social Capital, and Crime: Implications for Social Disorganization Theory," Robert J. Sampson and Charles Loeffler, "Punishment's Place: The Local Concentration of Mass Incarceration," *Daedalus*, 139/3 (2010), 20–31.

70. Natasha A. Frost and Todd R. Clear, "Coercive Mobility," in Francis T. Cullen and Pamela Wilcox (eds.), *Oxford Handbook of Criminological Theory* (New York: Oxford University Press, 2012), 691–708.

71. See Todd R. Clear, "The Impacts of Incarceration on Public Safety," *Social Research: An International Quarterly of the Social Sciences*, 74/2 (2007), 613–30, Marc Mauer and Meda Chesney-Lind (eds.), *Invisible Punishment: The Collateral Consequences of Mass Imprisonment* (New York: New Press, 2003), x, 355.

72. See Clear 1996 for one of the earliest expressions of this idea and Rose and Clear 1998 for a more fully articulated theory.

73. David Garland, *Punishment and Modern Society: A Study in Social Theory* (Studies in Crime and Justice) (Chicago: University of Chicago Press, 1990), 312.

74. It should be noted that each of these findings needs qualification as research rarely demonstrates that imprisonment reduces all types of crime. Levitt (1996), for example, found that imprisonment overall reduced both violent and property crimes, but that in an analysis of individual crime types only robbery and burglary were significantly reduced.

75. Garland, *The Culture of Control: Crime and Social Order in Contemporary Society*. James Q. Whitman, *Harsh Justice: Criminal Punishment and the Widening Divide between America and Europe* (New York: Oxford University Press, 200 3), viii, 311, [10] of plates. John Hagan, *Who Are the Criminals? The Politics of Crime Policy from the Age of Roosevelt to the Age of Reagan*(Princeton, NJ: Princeton University Press, 2010).

76. Michelle Alexander, *The New Jim Crow: Mass Incarceration in the Age of Colorblindness* (New York: New Press, 2010), Katherine Beckett, *Making Crime Pay: Law and Order in Contemporary American Politics* (New York: Oxford University Press, 1997), vi, 158, Christian Parenti, *Lockdown America: Police and Prisons in the Age of Crisis* (New York: Verso, 1999), xiii, 290.

77. President's Commission on Law Enforcement and Administration of Justice, "The Challege of Crime in a Free Society," ed. President's Commission on Law Enforcement and Administration of Justice (Washington, DC: United States Government Printing Office, 1967).

78. Ibid., vi.

79. Thomas E. Feucht and Edwin Zedlewski, "The 40th Anniversary of the Crime Report," *NIJ Journal*, 257 (2007), 20–23.

80. See Ted Gest, *Crime and Politics: Big Government's Erratic Campaign for Law and Order* (New York: Oxford University Press, 2001), chapter 6, for a lengthy discussion.

81. Peter Reuter, "Assessing U.S. Drug Policy and Providing a Base for Future Decisions: Statement to the U.S. Congress, Joint Economic Committee, Hearing, June 18, 2008," *Illegal Drugs: Economic Impact, Societal Costs, Policy Responses* (Washington, DC: U.S. Congress, Joint Economic Committee, 2008).

82. Ibid.

83. Guerino, Harrison, and Sabol, "Prisoners in 2010."

84. Clear and Austin, "Reducing Mass Incarceration: Implications of the Iron Law of Prison Populations."

DOCUMENTS FOR PART X

10.1 "HOW A 'REVERSE GREAT MIGRATION' IS RESHAPING U.S. CITIES," *CURBED* (2018)

Patrick Sisson

Source: *Curbed*, July 31, 2018, accessed at www.curbed.com/2018/7/31/17632092/black-chicago-neighborhood-great-migration.

EDITORS' INTRODUCTION

The First Great Migration took place approximately 1914–1930, and the Second Great Migration from 1940–1970. Millions of black southerners followed job opportunities and the promise of better living for their families in northern cities. But the promise did not reveal itself to every family. In recent years black Americans are again employing migration as a tool to seek a better life, and are moving elsewhere, including to the South.

Sisson's article demonstrates how creating the American Dream can be complicated by the intersectionality of race, class, and regional differences. We often think about the experience of the migrant, but what about those who are left behind?

"HOW A 'REVERSE GREAT MIGRATION' IS RESHAPING U.S. CITIES," *CURBED* (2018)

Alden Loury remembers when buying his home felt like achieving the American dream. A black journalist from Chicago, Loury and his wife were able to purchase a home for $165,000 in 2005 in Auburn Gresham, a predominantly black neighborhood on the city's south side, where he grew up.

"I felt great," he told Curbed. "I was back in my neighborhood. I knew the streets and the places I went to as a kid were still here."

For Loury, who grew up in public housing as well as an apartment in a three-flat, buying a bungalow in his old neighborhood was a big deal. His timing, of course, meant coping with the impact of the Great Recession, which started in 2008 and caused the value of his new home to plummet. He and his wife dutifully paid the mortgage, waiting for the cycle of boom and bust to play itself out.

But recovery, for Loury's home and much of the surrounding neighborhood, never really came. By 2015, when most parts of Chicago had recovered, Auburn Gresham and other predominantly black communities on the city's south and southwest side were still dealing with lower home values and a thinning population.

Even after sinking money into repairs, including a new roof and windows, Loury estimated the market value of his home never went far above $70,000, based on Redfin data and sales prices for similar properties in the neighborhood. Banks weren't interested in refinancing. Eventually, the Lourys realized that it didn't make sense to keep sinking money into a home and mortgage that would never recover, and in 2015, they decided to take the hit and walk away.

"Even when you're doing the right thing, you're susceptible to this reality that these communities aren't valued," says Loury, who eventually moved to Bronzeville, another Chicago neighborhood. "We couldn't escape that, despite our best efforts. What does that say for someone who's on housing assistance, or chronically underemployed? That doesn't speak well for the potential for success."

"Even when you're doing the right thing, you're susceptible to this reality that these communities aren't valued."

Loury, who has long studied demographic change in the city and was the director of research and evaluation at the Metropolitan Planning Council, says his experience exemplifies a trend that's reshaping Chicago: a large-scale migration of African-Americans to nearby suburbs and other cities, seeking better housing and economic opportunities, and in turn, changing the neighborhoods they leave behind.

Experts from the Urban Institute predict that by 2030, Chicago's African-American population will shrink to 665,000 from a post-war high of roughly 1.2 million. This movement, which some demographers have labeled "black flight," or a "reverse Great Migration," is reshaping neighborhoods like the one where Loury grew up.

As Loury wrote in a *Chicago Sun-Times* op-ed earlier this month, the recent economic downturn put further pressure on historically under-resourced black neighborhoods in Chicago, increasing foreclosures and depressing real estate values. That has just added additional reasons for African-Americans to move away from these neighborhoods in search of a better economic future, leaving these places further devoid of people and resources.

William Lee, a *Chicago Tribune* reporter who grew up in the South Shore neighborhood, wrote in an editorial that the exodus "has folks like myself, left behind on the South Side, feeling like life after the rapture, with relatives, good friends and classmates vanishing and their communities shattering."

While local leaders and city government have repeatedly talked about helping neighborhoods recover, this exodus isn't something the city has specifically articulated as an issue, says Loury. And that's a problem.

"They're missing the boat," he says. "These communities are losing real assets.

It's a loss you shouldn't stand by and watch. It's a problem for cities to wake up and pay attention to."

Seeking better opportunities outside the city

This isn't a shift unique to Chicago. According to William H. Frey, a senior fellow at the Brookings Institution's Metropolitan Policy Program, the black population in U.S. cities has steadily declined for decades. The percentage of African Americans living in urban cores shrunk from 47 to 41.7 percent between 1990 and 2017, according to Frey's analysis of census data, while the black population of the central cities in the nation's 100 largest metropolitan areas declined by 300,000 between 2000 and 2010. By 2010, a majority of African Americans nationwide lived in the suburbs.

Brookings Institution analysis of Census Bureau data

This is a shift happening everywhere, says Loury, especially northern cities such as Baltimore, Cleveland, St. Louis, and Detroit. It's even impacting Sunbelt metros such as Atlanta, which is seeing a huge boom in African-American migration, but mostly in the surrounding suburbs.

But Chicago stands out.

"There's no place with close to that amount of African-American population loss," Loury says. "It's staggering."

Brookings's Frey doesn't believe that the shift is about displacement as much as it's about chasing new possibilities. Younger black families have the opportunity to move to the suburbs to an extent that other generations, facing stricter redlining and segregation, could not.

Table 10.1 Black Americans Increasingly Shifting to Suburbs

Region	1990	2000	2010	2017
Urban Core	46.9%	45.8%	42.5%	41.7%
Mature Suburbs	18.1%	19.6%	22.1%	23.1%
Outer Suburbs	7.5%	7.8%	9.2%	9.7%
All Others	27.5%	26.8%	26.2%	25.4%

To get a better sense of where Chicagoans have been going, and why, Loury took a deep dive into Census data from 2005 to 2015, analyzing where African-Americans from Cook County (which contains Chicago) resettled. According to his analysis, 38 percent moved within the 14-county metro area around Chicago. The most popular destinations were in northwest Indiana, followed by a ring of suburban counties surrounding the city, including DuPage and Lake County.

The rest moved outside the metro area; a significantly higher percentage of the low-income African-Americans who left Chicago in recent decades moved to other urban areas within Illinois, such as Springfield and Rockford. Others, often those with more resources, moved out of state; the most popular destinations were Atlanta, Houston, Dallas, Minneapolis-St. Paul, and Milwaukee.

According to Professor William Sampson, a sociologist at Chicago's DePaul University who studies race, housing, and poverty, part of the shift is driven by black retirees taking northern dollars south and "living like kings and queens." He surmises that the rate of migration back south has played a big role in changing demographics and political shifts in states like Georgia, where democrat Stacey Abrams is in the running to become the nation's first female African-American governor.

Loury's analysis of migration patterns backs up what others are seeing nationwide. The suburbs of Atlanta, Houston, Washington, DC, and Dallas experienced the largest increases in black population in the U.S. between 2000 and 2010, according to a Brookings analysis of census data.

Demographic data shows the growth of wealthy African-American households in southern metro areas, especially in Georgia. *Nielsen*

The movement of African Americans to southern cities such as Atlanta has led to some calling this a reverse Great Migration, a reference to the large-scale migration of African Americans from the Jim Crow South to jobs in northern cities in the early half of the 20th century. The Great

Table 10.2 Top 10 Metro Areas for African-American Households Earning $100,000 or More

Top 10 Cities in 2000	Percent making $100K	Top 10 Cities in 2015	Percent making $100K
Washington, D.C.	3	Washington, D.C.	7.2
Atlanta, GA	1.8	Baltimore, MD	5.1
Detroit, MI	1.7	Norfolk, VA	3.9
Baltimore, MD	1.6	Atlanta, GA	3.6
New York, NY	1.5	Richmond-Petersburg, VA	3.5
Richmond-Petersburg, VA	1.4	Baton Rouge, LA	3.4
Chicago, IL	1.3	Memphis, TN	3.4
Memphis, TN	1.3	New York, NY	3.1
Jackson, MS	1.1	Columbus, GA	3
Columbia, SC	1.1	Augusta, GA	2.9

Migration helped make Chicago a capital of the country's African-American community. At some points during the 1920s, 1930s, and 1940s, more than 1,000 new arrivals a week came through booming areas such as Bronzeville, many of them hoping to work in the heavy industry and steel plants on the city's southeast side.

"People left the South for opportunity," Corey Brooks, pastor of the New Beginnings Church on the South Side, told *The Globe and Mail*. "Now it's the direct opposite. People are leaving Chicago to go south to look for better opportunities and a better lifestyle."

More vital to Chicago and other cities losing their black populations is the question of causation. The combined population of the city's Austin, Englewood, and West Englewood neighborhoods, all traditionally majority African-American, fell from 189,000 to 136,000 between 2000 and 2015. Loury has found that African Americans across the economic spectrum are making the move, not just those in the upper and middle classes.

"People left the South for opportunity, Now it's the direct opposite. People are leaving Chicago to go south to look for better opportunities and a better lifestyle."

"A lot of people who have been caught in this exodus, if you will, have been struggling economically," he says. "If there's one thing I'll rest my hat on, if there's one factor at play here, it's about job opportunities and a lack thereof."

His hypothesis is that moving out of the city is based on a number of factors: employment, housing, education, and concerns about safety and gun violence are the ones that leap out at him.

Paying attention to neighborhoods on the precipice

This move out of the city in search of opportunity is both a result and a cause of economic insecurity, according to Sampson. As upwardly mobile members of the community leave in search of opportunity, and a shift to a service economy has steadily eroded the city's traditional manufacturing and industrial job base, concentrated poverty has crept into formerly mixed-income areas.

Changing demographics have led to shifting economic fortunes; a 2015 study by Nielsen found that just 2.1 percent of black households in Chicago earned more than $100,000 a year, the 21st highest in the U.S. In 2000, Chicago ranked seventh on that metric.

According to both Sampson and Loury, this outflux from specific neighborhoods has created a vicious cycle, especially for small businesses and entrepreneurs; as income and customers leave, it's harder and harder to make the business case to stay.

"This has killed neighborhoods such as Chatham, an epicenter of working and middle class Black Chicago," says Sampson. "As middle income blacks started leaving back in the '80s, from neighborhoods such as Chatham, they've been replaced by working class and poor residents. Chicago used to have one of the largest numbers of middle-income African Americans in the country. Now, there's no heart to hold these communities together."

Loury says he often runs up against pushback when he tries to raise questions about the African-American exodus from the city. Why is he trying to distract from positive news? Englewood, for example, is seeing a raft of new investments, Bronzeville is gaining population, and the city's tech industry is expanding.

Perhaps it's a question of awareness of the issue. According to urbanist Pete Saunders, few in Chicago realize "how economically isolated parts of the city have become." As these demographic trends play out, the majority-minority city is headed toward being smaller, whiter, and wealthier.

"The response to this overall population loss has been pretty lukewarm," Loury says. "I don't think it's been widely acknowledged by many, at least in the halls of power. They're indifferent, and I find that troubling."

10.2 INVESTIGATION OF THE FERGUSON POLICE DEPARTMENT (2015)

Source: United States Department of Justice, Civil Rights Division, *Investigation of the Ferguson Police Department*, March 4, 2015, 1, 5–6, 15–16, and 24–28. See www.justice.gov/sites/default/files/opa/press-releases/attachments/2015/03/04/ferguson_police_department_report.pdf.

EDITORS' INTRODUCTION

There were many incidents involving police departments with high proportions of white officers and neighborhoods with mostly black residents in the first part of the twentieth century. A significant number of these conflicts led to organized protests and a commitment to rethink police policies and procedures and to reconsider economic inequities within American communities. The events that unfolded in Ferguson, Missouri—an area outside of St. Louis—on August 2014 had resonance for citizens of Ferguson and elsewhere. In March, 2015, the federal government issued a report detailing constitutional violations within Ferguson and called for significant reforms.

On August 9, 2014, Michael Brown, who was unarmed, had been shot and killed by white police officer Darren Wilson. Brown was a black eighteen-year-old, and his death rattled many residents in the vicinity, the larger community, and the nation. Wilson suspected Brown of committing a theft from a local market just moments before the two interacted. After an altercation between Wilson and Brown, who was standing outside the window of Wilson's police vehicle (and may or may not have reached inside the vehicle), Wilson fired two shots at Brown, and an on-foot chase ensued. Wilson shot Brown again when both men stopped the chase. Onlookers disagreed as to whether Brown moved towards Wilson before he was shot, and were conflicted on the position of his hands. Following Brown's death, organized demonstrations and civil unrest played out in the streets of Ferguson.

Officer Wilson was not indicted by the St. Louis County grand jury for the shooting, and this legal decision led to renewed outbreaks of fire and looting within Ferguson. Street demonstrations by the predominantly black residents of Ferguson persisted for weeks. The Missouri National Guard came into assist the Ferguson Police. The slogan "Hands up, don't shoot" became emblematic of the incident, whether or not the words "don't shoot" were really uttered by Brown before his death. The tensions in Ferguson, Missouri have garnered international attention and seem of even more historical importance when placed beside other racial conflicts, many involving the police, of the period.

INVESTIGATION OF THE FERGUSON POLICE DEPARTMENT, UNITED STATES DEPARTMENT OF JUSTICE, CIVIL RIGHTS DIVISION, MARCH 4, 2015

Report Summary

[...]

Community Distrust

Since the August 2014 shooting death of Michael Brown, the lack of trust between the Ferguson Police Department and a significant portion of Ferguson's residents, especially African Americans, has become undeniable. The causes of this distrust and division, however, have been the subject of debate. Police and other City officials, as well as some Ferguson residents, have insisted to us that the public outcry is attributable to "outside agitators" who do not reflect the opinions of "real Ferguson residents." That view is at odds with the facts we have gathered during our investigation. Our investigation has shown that distrust of the Ferguson Police Department is longstanding and largely attributable to Ferguson's approach to law enforcement. This approach results in patterns of unnecessarily aggressive and at times unlawful

policing; reinforces the harm of discriminatory stereotypes; discourages a culture of accountability; and neglects community engagement. In recent years, FPD has moved away from the modest community policing efforts it previously had implemented, reducing opportunities for positive police-community interactions, and losing the little familiarity it had with some African American neighborhoods. The confluence of policing to raise revenue and racial bias thus has resulted in practices that not only violate the Constitution and cause direct harm to the individuals whose rights are violated, but also undermine community trust, especially among many African Americans. As a consequence of these practices, law enforcement is seen as illegitimate, and the partnerships necessary for public safety are, in some areas, entirely absent.

Restoring trust in law enforcement will require recognition of the harms caused by Ferguson's law enforcement practices, and diligent, committed collaboration with the entire Ferguson community. At the conclusion of this report, we have broadly identified the changes that are necessary for meaningful and sustainable reform. These measures build upon a number of other recommended changes we communicated verbally to the Mayor, Police Chief, and City Manager in September so that Ferguson could begin immediately to address problems as we identified them. As a result of those recommendations, the City and police department have already begun to make some changes to municipal court and police practices. We commend City officials for beginning to take steps to address some of the concerns we have already raised. Nonetheless, these changes are only a small part of the reform necessary. Addressing the deeply embedded constitutional deficiencies we found demands an entire reorientation of law enforcement in Ferguson. The City must replace revenue-driven policing with a system grounded in the principles of community policing and police legitimacy, in which people are equally protected and treated with compassion, regardless of race.

[...]

FERGUSON LAW ENFORCEMENT PRACTICES VIOLATE THE LAW AND UNDERMINE COMMUNITY TRUST, ESPECIALLY AMONG AFRICAN AMERICANS

Ferguson's strategy of revenue generation through policing has fostered practices in the two central parts of Ferguson's law enforcement system—policing and the courts—that are themselves unconstitutional or that contribute to constitutional violations. In both parts of the system, these practices disproportionately harm African Americans. Further, the evidence indicates that this harm to African Americans stems, at least in part, from racial bias, including racial stereotyping. Ultimately, unlawful and harmful practices in policing and in the municipal court system erode police legitimacy and community trust, making policing in Ferguson less fair, less effective at promoting public safety, and less safe.

Ferguson's Police Practices

FPD's approach to law enforcement, shaped by the City's pressure to raise revenue, has resulted in a pattern and practice of constitutional violations. Officers violate the Fourth Amendment in stopping people without reasonable suspicion, arresting them without probable cause, and using unreasonable force. Officers frequently infringe on residents' First Amendment rights, interfering with their right to record police activities and making enforcement decisions based on the content of individuals' expression.

FPD's lack of systems to detect and hold officers responsible for misconduct reflects the department's focus on revenue generation at the expense of lawful policing and helps perpetuate the patterns of unconstitutional conduct we found. FPD fails to adequately supervise officers or review their enforcement actions. While FPD collects vehicle-stop data because it is required to do so by state law, it collects no reliable or consistent data regarding pedestrian stops, even though it has the technology to do so. In Ferguson, officers will sometimes make an arrest without writing a report or even obtaining an incident number, and hundreds of reports can pile up for months without supervisors reviewing them. Officers' uses of force frequently go unreported, and are reviewed only laxly when reviewed at all. As a result of these deficient practices, stops, arrests, and uses of force that violate the law or FPD policy are rarely detected and often ignored when they are discovered.

FPD Engages in a Pattern of Unconstitutional Stops and Arrests in Violation of the Fourth Amendment

FPD's approach to law enforcement has led officers to conduct stops and arrests that violate the Constitution. We identified several elements to this pattern of misconduct. Frequently, officers stop people without reasonable suspicion or arrest them without probable cause. Officers rely heavily on the municipal "Failure to Comply" charge, which appears to be facially unconstitutional in part, and is frequently abused in practice. FPD also relies on a system of officer-generated arrest orders called "wanteds" that circumvents the warrant system and poses a significant risk of abuse. The data show, moreover, that FPD misconduct in the area of stops and arrests disproportionately impacts African Americans.

[...]

FPD Engages in a Pattern of First Amendment Violations

FPD's approach to enforcement results in violations of individuals' First Amendment rights. FPD arrests people for a variety of protected conduct: people are punished for talking back to officers, recording public police activities, and lawfully protesting perceived injustices.

Under the Constitution, what a person says generally should not determine whether he or she is jailed. Police officers cannot constitutionally make arrest decisions based on individuals' verbal expressions of disrespect for law enforcement, including use of foul language. *Buffkins v. City of Omaha*, 922 F.2d 465, 472 (8th Cir. 1990) (holding that officers violated the Constitution when they arrested a woman for disorderly conduct after she called one an "asshole," especially since "police officers are expected to exercise greater restraint in their response than the average citizen"); *Copeland v. Locke*, 613 F.3d 875, 880 (8th Cir. 2010) (holding that the First Amendment prohibited a police chief from arresting an individual who pointed at him and told him "move the f*****g car," even if the comment momentarily distracted the chief from a routine traffic stop); *Gorra v. Hanson*, 880 F.2d 95, 100 (8th Cir. 1989) (holding that arresting a person in retaliation for making a statement "constitutes obvious infringement" of the First Amendment). As the Supreme Court has held, "the First Amendment protects a significant amount of verbal criticism and challenge directed at police officers." City of Houston, Tex. v. Hill, 482 U.S. 451, 461 (1987) (striking down as unconstitutionally overbroad a local ordinance that criminalized interference with police by speech).

In Ferguson, however, officers frequently make enforcement decisions based on what subjects say, or how they say it. Just as officers reflexively resort to arrest immediately upon noncompliance with their orders, whether lawful or not, they are quick to overreact to challenges and verbal slights. These incidents—sometimes called "contempt of cop" cases—are propelled by officers' belief that arrest is an appropriate response to disrespect. These arrests are typically charged as a Failure to Comply, Disorderly Conduct, Interference with Officer, or Resisting Arrest.

For example, in July 2012, a police officer arrested a business owner on charges of Interfering in Police Business and Misuse of 911 because she objected to the officer's detention of her employee. The officer had stopped the employee for "walking unsafely in the street" as he returned to work from the bank. According to FPD records, the owner "became verbally involved," came out of her shop three times after being asked to stay inside, and called 911 to complain to the Police Chief. The officer characterized her protestations as interference and arrested her inside her shop. The arrest violated the First Amendment, which "does not allow such speech to be made a crime." Hill, 482 U.S. at 462. Indeed, the officer's decision to arrest the woman after she tried to contact the Police Chief suggests that he may have been retaliating against her for reporting his conduct.

Officers in Ferguson also use their arrest power to retaliate against individuals for using language that, while disrespectful, is protected by the Constitution. For example, one afternoon in September 2012, an officer stopped a 20-year-old African-American man for dancing in the middle of a residential street. The officer obtained the man's identification and ran his name for warrants. Finding none, he told the man he was free to go. The man responded with profanities. When the officer told him to watch his language and reminded him that he was not being arrested, the man continued using profanity and was arrested for Manner of Walking in Roadway.

In February 2014, officers responded to a group of African-American teenage girls "play fighting" (in the words of the officer) in an intersection after school. When one of the schoolgirls gave the middle finger to a white witness who had called the police, an officer ordered her over to him. One of the girl's friends accompanied her. Though the friend had the right to be present and observe the situation—indeed, the offense reports include no facts suggesting a safety concern posed by her presence—the officers ordered her to leave and then attempted to arrest her when she refused. Officers used force to arrest the friend as she pulled away. When the first girl grabbed an officer's shoulder, they used force to arrest her, as well.

The ordinance on interfering with arrest, detention, or stop, Ferguson Mun. Code § 29–17, does not actually permit arrest unless the subject uses or threatens violence, which did not occur here. Another code provision the officer may have relied on, § 29–19, is likely unconstitutionally overbroad because it prohibits obstruction of government operations "in any manner whatsoever." See Hill, 482 U.S. at 455, 462, 466 (invalidating ordinance that made it unlawful to "in any manner oppose, molest, abuse, or interrupt any policeman in the execution of his duty"). Officers charged the two teenagers with a variety of offenses, including: Disorderly Conduct for giving the middle finger and using obscenities; Manner of Walking for being in the street; Failure to Comply for staying to observe; Interference with Officer; Assault on a Law Enforcement Officer; and Endangering the Welfare of a Child (themselves and their schoolmates) by resisting arrest and being involved in disorderly conduct. This incident underscores how officers' unlawful response to activity protected by the First Amendment can quickly escalate to physical resistance, resulting in additional force, additional charges, and increasing the risk of injury to officers and members of the public alike.

These accounts are drawn entirely from officers' own descriptions, recorded in offense reports. That FPD officers believe criticism and insolence are grounds for arrest, and that supervisors have condoned such unconstitutional policing, reflects intolerance for even lawful opposition to the exercise of police authority. These arrests also reflect that, in FPD, many

officers have no tools for de-escalating emotionally charged scenes, even though the ability of a police officer to bring calm to a situation is a core policing skill.

FPD officers also routinely infringe on the public's First Amendment rights by preventing people from recording their activities. The First Amendment "prohibit[s] the government from limiting the stock of information from which members of the public may draw." *First Nat'l Bank v. Belloti*, 435 U.S. 765, 783 (1978). Applying this principle, the federal courts of appeal have held that the First Amendment "unambiguously" establishes a constitutional right to videotape police activities. *Glik v. Cunniffe*, 655 F.3d 78, 82 (1st Cir. 2011); see also *ACLU v. Alvarez*, 679 F.3d 583, 600 (7th Cir. 2012) (issuing a preliminary injunction against the use of a state eavesdropping statute to prevent the recording of public police activities); *Fordyce v. City of Seattle*, 55 F.3d 436, 439 (9th Cir. 1995) (recognizing a First Amendment right to film police carrying out their public duties); *Smith v. City of Cumming*, 212 F.3d 1332, 1333 (11th Cir. 2000) (recognizing a First Amendment right "to photograph or videotape police conduct"). Indeed, as the ability to record police activity has become more widespread, the role it can play in capturing questionable police activity, and ensuring that the activity is investigated and subject to broad public debate, has become clear. Protecting civilian recording of police activity is thus at the core of speech the First Amendment is intended to protect. *Cf. Branzburg v. Hayes*, 408 U.S. 665, 681 (1972) (First Amendment protects "news gathering"); *Mills v. Alabama*, 384 U.S. 214, 218 (1966) (news gathering enhances "free discussion of governmental affairs"). "In a democracy, public officials have no general privilege to avoid publicity and embarrassment by preventing public scrutiny of their actions." *Walker v. City of Pine Bluff*, 414 F.3d 989, 992 (8th Cir. 2005).

In Ferguson, however, officers claim without any factual support that the use of camera phones endangers officer safety. Sometimes, officers offer no rationale at all.

Our conversations with community members and review of FPD records found numerous violations of the right to record police activity. In May 2014, an officer pulled over an African-American woman who was driving with her two sons. During the traffic stop, the woman's 16-year-old son began recording with his cell phone. The officer ordered him to put down the phone and refrain from using it for the remainder of the stop. The officer claimed this was "for safety reasons." The situation escalated, apparently due to the officer's rudeness and the woman's response. According to the 16 year old, he began recording again, leading the officer to wrestle the phone from him. Additional officers arrived and used force to arrest all three civilians under disputed circumstances that could have been clarified by a video recording.

In June 2014, an African-American couple who had taken their children to play at the park allowed their small children to urinate in the bushes next to their parked car. An officer stopped them, threatened to cite them for allowing the children to "expose themselves," and checked the father for warrants. When the mother asked if the officer had to detain the father in front of the children, the officer turned to the father and said, "you're going to jail because your wife keeps running her mouth." The mother then began recording the officer on her cell phone. The officer became irate, declaring, "you don't videotape me!" As the officer drove away with the father in custody for "parental neglect," the mother drove after them, continuing to record. The officer then pulled over and arrested her for traffic violations. When the father asked the officer to show mercy, he responded, "no more mercy, since she wanted to videotape," and declared "nobody videotapes me." The officer then took the phone, which the couple's daughter was holding. After posting bond, the couple found that the video had been deleted.

A month later, the same officer pulled over a truck hauling a trailer that did not have operating tail lights. The officer asked for identification from all three people inside, including a 54-year-old white man in the passenger seat who asked why. "You have to have a reason. This is a violation of my Fourth Amendment rights," he asserted. The officer, who characterized the man's reaction as "suspicious," responded, "the reason is, if you don't hand it to me, I'll arrest you." The man provided his identification. The officer then asked the man to move his cell phone from his lap to the dashboard, "for my safety." The man said, "okay, but I'm going to record this." Due to nervousness, he could not open the recording application and quickly placed the phone on the dash. The officer then announced that the man was under arrest for Failure to Comply. At the end of the traffic stop, the officer gave the driver a traffic citation, indicated at the other man, and said, "you're getting this ticket because of him." Upon bringing that man to the jail, someone asked the officer what offense the man had committed. The officer responded, "he's one of those guys who watches CNBC too much about his rights." The man did not say anything else, fearing what else the officer might be capable of doing. He later told us, "I never dreamed I could end up in jail for this. I'm scared of driving through Ferguson now." The Ferguson Police Department's infringement of individuals' freedom of speech and right to record has been highlighted in recent months in the context of large-scale public protest. In November 2014, a federal judge entered a consent order prohibiting Ferguson officers from interfering with individuals' rights to lawfully and peacefully record public police activities. That same month, the City settled another suit alleging that it had abused its loitering ordinance, Mun. Code § 29–89, to arrest people who were protesting peacefully on public sidewalks.

The Ferguson Police Department's infringement of individuals' freedom of speech and right to record has been highlighted in recent months in the context of large-scale public protest. In November 2014, a federal judge entered a consent order prohibiting Ferguson officers from interfering with individuals' rights to lawfully and peacefully record public police activities. That same month, the City settled another suit alleging that it had abused its loitering ordinance, Mun. Code § 29–89, to arrest people who were protesting peacefully on public sidewalks.

Despite these lawsuits, it appears that FPD continues to interfere with individuals' rights to protest and record police activities. On February 9, 2015, several individuals were protesting outside the Ferguson police station on the six-month anniversary of Michael Brown's death. According to protesters, and consistent with several video recordings from that evening, the protesters stood peacefully in the police department's parking lot, on the sidewalks in front of it, and across the street. Video footage shows that two FPD vehicles abruptly accelerated from the police parking lot into the street. An officer announced, "everybody here's going to jail," causing the protesters to run. Video shows that as one man recorded the police arresting others, he was arrested for interfering with police action. Officers pushed him to the ground, began handcuffing him, and announced, "stop resisting or you're going to get tased." It appears from the video, however, that the man was neither interfering nor resisting. A protester in a wheelchair who was live streaming the protest was also arrested. Another officer moved several people with cameras away from the scene of the arrests, warning them against interfering and urging them to back up or else be arrested for Failure to Obey.

The sergeant shouted at those filming that they would be arrested for Manner of Walking if they did not back away out of the street, even though it appears from the video recordings that the protesters and those recording were on the sidewalk at most, if not all, times. Six people were arrested during this incident. It appears that officers' escalation of this incident was unnecessary and in response to derogatory comments written in chalk on the FPD parking lot asphalt and on a police vehicle.

FPD's suppression of speech reflects a police culture that relies on the exercise of police power—however unlawful—to stifle unwelcome criticism. Recording police activity and engaging in public protest are fundamentally democratic enterprises because they provide a check on those "who are granted substantial discretion that may be misused to deprive individuals of their liberties." Glik, 655 F.3d at 82. Even profane backtalk can be a form of dissent against perceived misconduct. In the words of the Supreme Court, "[t]he freedom of individuals verbally to oppose or challenge police action without thereby risking arrest is one of the principal characteristics by which we distinguish a free nation from a police state." Hill, 482 U.S. at 463. Ideally, officers would not encounter verbal abuse. Communities would encourage mutual respect, and the police would likewise exhibit respect by treating people with dignity. But, particularly where officers engage in unconstitutional policing, they only exacerbate community opposition by quelling speech.

REFERENCES AND SUGGESTED BIBLIOGRAPHY

*Books may overlap categorization and are generally listed under one heading.

I. Overview Works

Anthologies

Binder, Frederick and David M. Reimers. *The Way We Lived: Essays and Documents in American Social History, Volume I: 1607–1877*. Second Edition. Lexington, KY: D.C. Heath, 1993.

Callow, Alexander B., Jr., ed. *American Urban History: An Interpretive Reader with Comments*. Third Edition. New York: Oxford University Press, 1982.

Chudacoff, Howard P. and Judith E. Smith. *The Evolution of American Urban Society*. Sixth Edition. Upper Saddle River, NJ: Pearson Prentice Hall, 2005.

Jackson, Kenneth and Stanley K. Schultz, eds. *Cities in American History*. New York: Knopf, 1972.

Kantor, Paul and Dennis R. Judd. *American Urban Politics in a Global Age: The Reader*. Fifth Edition. White Plains, NY: Pearson Longman, 2008.

Mohl, Raymond. *The Making of Urban America*. Wilmington, DE: SR Books, 1997.

Sennett, Richard, ed. *Classic Essays on the Culture of Cities*. Upper Saddle River, NJ: Pearson Prentice Hall, 1969.

Sennett, Richard and Stephan Thernstrom. *Nineteenth-Century Cities: Essays in the New Urban History*. New Haven, CT: Yale University Press, 1969.

Theory

Abrahamson, Mark. *Urban Enclaves: Identity and Place in America*. New York: St. Martin's Press, 1996.

Anderson, Benedict. *Imagined Communities: Reflection on the Origins and Spread of Nationalism*. New York: Verso, 1983.

Boyer, M. Christine. *The City of Collective Memory: Its Historical Imagery and Architectural Entertainments*. Cambridge, MA: MIT Press, 1996.

———. *CyberCities*. Princeton, NJ: Princeton Architectural Press, 1996.

Channing, Edward. *A History of the United States*. New York: Macmillan Company, 1922.

Durkheim, Emile. *The Division of Labor in Society*. New York: Free Press, 1984.

Frey, William H. *Diversity Explosion: How Racial Demographics Are Remaking America*. Washington, D.C.: Brookings Institute Press, 2018.

Ghent Urban Studies Team. *Post Ex Sub Dis: Urban Fragmentations and Constructions*. Rotterdam: 010 Publishers, 2002.

Hall, Sir Peter. *Cities in Civilization*. New York: Pantheon Books, 1998.

Harvey, David. *The Condition of Postmodernity: An Enquiry into the Origins of Cultural Change*. Cambridge, MA: Blackwell, 1990.

Hozic, Aida. *Hollyworld: Space, Power, and Fantasy in the American Economy*. Ithaca, NY: Cornell University Press, 2001.

Lears, T.J. Jackson. *No Place of Grace: Antimodernism and the Transformation of American Culture, 1880–1920*. New York: Pantheon Books, 1981.

Levine, Lawrence W. *Highbrow/Lowbrow: The Emergence of Cultural Hierarchy in America*. Cambridge, MA: Harvard University Press, 1988.

Marsh, Margaret, "Old Forms, New Visions: New Directions in United States Urban History," *Pennsylvania History* 59, no. 1 (1992): 21–40.

Marx, Leo. *The Machine in the Garden: Technology and the Pastoral Ideal in America*. New York: Oxford University Press, 1964.

Mumford, Lewis. *The Culture of Cities*. New York: Harcourt, Brace & Company, 1938.

Sassen, Saskia. *Cities in a World Economy*. New York: Pine Forge Press, 2006.

———. *The Global City: New York, London, Tokyo*. Princeton, NJ: Princeton University Press, 2001.

Sennett, Richard. *The Fall of Public Man*. New York: W. W. Norton, 1976.

Smith, Henry Nash. *Virgin Land: The American West as Symbol and Myth*. Cambridge, MA: Harvard University Press, 1978.

Soja, Edward. *The City: Los Angeles and Urban Theory at the End of the Twentieth Century*. Berkeley: University of California Press, 1998.

———. *Postmetropolis: Critical Studies of Cities and Regions*. Oxford: Wiley-Blackwell, 2000.

———. *Thirdspace: Journeys to Los Angeles and Other Real-and-Imagined Places*. Oxford: Wiley-Blackwell, 1996.

Sorkin, Michael, ed. *Variations on a Theme Park: The New American City and the End of Public Space*. New York: Hill and Wang, 1992.

Strong, Josiah. *Our Country: Its Possible Future and Its Present Crisis*. New York: Baker & Taylor, 1885.

Trachtenberg, Alan. *The Incorporation of America: Culture and Society in the Gilded Age*. New York: Hill and Wang, 1982.

Turner, Frederick Jackson. *The Frontier in American History*. Tucson: University of Arizona Press, 1986.

White, Morton and Lucia White. *The Intellectual Versus the City: From Thomas Jefferson to Frank Lloyd Wright*. Cambridge, MA: Harvard University Press and MIT Press, 1962.

Wiebe, Robert H. *The Search for Order, 1877–1920*. New York: Hill and Wang, 1967.

Zukin, Sharon. *The Culture of Cities*. Cambridge, MA: Blackstone Publishers, 1995.

———. *Landscapes of Power: From Detroit to Disney World*. Berkeley: University of California Press, 1991.

Urban Overviews and General U.S. History

Bender, Thomas. *Community and Social Change in America*. Piscataway, NJ: Rutgers, 1978.

Fishman, Robert. *Urban Utopias in the Twentieth Century*. Boston, MA: MIT Press, 1982.

Gillette, Howard, Jr. and Zane L. Miller, eds. *American Urbanism: Historiographical Review*. New York: Greenwood Press, 1987.

Goldfield, David. *Cotton Fields and Skyscrapers: Southern City and Region, 1607–1980*. Baton Rouge: Louisiana State University Press, 1982.

——— and Blaine A. Brownell. *Urban America: A History*. Second Edition. Boston, MA: Houghton Mifflin, 1990.

Green, Constance McLaughlin. *American Cities in the Growth of the Nation*. New York: John De Graff, 1957.

———. *The Rise of Urban America*. New York: Harper & Row, 1965.

Hall, Peter (Sir). *Cities in Civilization*. New York: Pantheon Books, 1998.

Hofstadter, Richard and Michael Wallace. *American Violence: A Documentary History*. New York: Vintage Books, 1970.

Howells, Frederic C. *The City: The Hope of Democracy*. New York: Charles Scribner's Sons, 1906.

Jacobs, Jane. *The Death and Life of Great American Cities*. New York: Vintage Books, 1961.

Kleniewski, Nancy. *Cities, Change & Conflict: A Political Economy of Urban Life*. Belmont, CA: Thompson/Wadsworth, 2006.

Kotkin, Joel. *A City: A Global History*. New York: Modern Library, 2005.

Macionis, John J. and Vincent N. Parrillo. *Cities and Urban Life*. Upper Saddle River, NJ: Pearson/Prentice Hall, 2007.

Monkonnen, Eric. *America Becomes Urban: The Development of U.S. Cities and Towns, 1780–1980*. Berkeley: University of California Press, 1990.

Mumford, Lewis. *The City in History: Its Origins, Its Transformations, and Its Prospects*. New York: Harcourt Brace, 1961.

Palen, John J. *The Urban World*. New York: McGraw Hill, 1997.

Schlesinger, Arthur. *Paths to the Present*. New York: MacMillan, 1949.

———. *The Rise of the City*. New York: MacMillan, 1933.

Warner, Sam Bass, Jr. *The Urban Wilderness: A History of the American City*. New York: Harper & Row, 1972.

II. Urban History by Time Period

Colonial

Bonomi, Patricia U. *Under the Cope of Heaven: Religion, Society, and Politics in Colonial America.* New York: Oxford University Press, 1986.

Bridenbaugh, Carl. *Cities in Revolt: Urban Life in America, 1743–1776.* New York: Knopf, 1955.

———. *Cities in the Wilderness: The First Century of Urban Life in America, 1625–1742.* New York: Oxford University Press, 1938, rev. 1966.

Bushman, Richard. "Family Security in the Transition from Farm to City, 1750–1850," *Journal of Family History*, vol. 6 (1981): 238–252.

Cronon, William. *Changes in the Land: Indians, Colonists, and the Ecology of New England.* New York: Hill and Wang, 1983.

Deetz, James. *In Small Things Forgotten: The Archeology of Early American Life.* New York: Anchor, 1977.

Demos, John. *A Little Commonwealth: Family Life in Plymouth Colony.* New York: Oxford University Press, 1970.

Fries, Sylvia Doughty. *The Urban Ideal in Colonial America.* Philadelphia, PA: Temple University Press, 1977.

Hart, Emma. *Building Charleston: Town and Society in the Eighteenth Century British Atlantic World.* Charlottesville: University of Virginia, 2010.

Lemisch, Jessie. "Jack Tar in the Street: Merchant Seamen and the Politics of Revolutionary America," *William and Mary Quarterly*, 3rd Series, vol. 25 (1968): 371–407.

Lemon, James. *The Best Poor Man's Country: Early Southeastern Pennsylvania.* Baltimore, MD: Johns Hopkins University Press, 2002.

Lockridge, Kenneth A. *A New England Town: The First Hundred Years.* New York: W. W. Norton, 1970.

Maier, Pauline. "Boston and New York in the Eighteenth Century," *Proceedings of the American Antiquarian Society*, vol. 91, Part 2 (Oct. 21, 1981): 177–195.

Nash, Gary. *The Urban Crucible; Social Change, Political Consciousness, and the Origins of the American Revolution.* Cambridge, MA: Harvard University Press, 1979.

Reps, John W. *Town Planning in Frontier America.* Princeton, NJ: Princeton University Press, 1969.

Teaford, Jon C. *The Municipal Revolution in America: Origins of Modern Urban Government, 1650–1825.* Chicago, IL: University of Chicago Press, 1975.

Ulrich, Laurel Thatcher. *A Midwife's Tale: The Life of Martha Ballard.* New York: Alfred A. Knopf, 1990.

Weber, David J. *The Spanish Frontier in North America.* Brief Edition. New Haven, CT: Yale University Press, 2009.

Nineteenth Century

Allen, Robert C. *Horrible Prettiness: Burlesque and American Culture.* Chapel Hill: University of North Carolina Press, 1991.

Badger, R. Reid. *The Great American Fair: The World's Columbian Exposition and American Culture.* Chicago, IL: Nelson Hall, 1979.

Bender, Thomas. *Towards an Urban Vision: Ideas and Institutions in Nineteenth Century America.* Baltimore, MD: Johns Hopkins University Press, 1991.

Blumin, Stuart M. *The Emergence of the Middle Class: Social Experience in the American City, 1760–1900.* Cambridge: Cambridge University Press, 1989.

———. *An Urban Threshold: Growth and Change in a Nineteenth-Century American Community.* Chicago, IL: University of Chicago Press, 1984.

Boyer, Paul. *Urban Masses and Moral Order in America, 1820–1920.* Cambridge, MA: Harvard University Press, 1978.

Bridges, Amy. *A City in the Republic: Antebellum New York and the Origins of Machine Politics.* Cambridge: Cambridge University Press, 2008.

Brown, Julie K. *Contesting Images: Photography and the World's Columbian Exposition.* Tucson: University of Arizona Press, 1.

Burg, David F. *Chicago's White City of 1893*. Lexington: University Press of Kentucky, 1976.

Cohen, Patricia Cline, Timothy J. Gilfoyle, and Helen Lefkowitz Horowitz. *The Flash Press: Sporting Male Weeklies in 1840s New York*. Chicago, IL: University of Chicago Press, 2008.

Cronon, William. *Nature's Metropolis: Chicago and the Great West*. New York: W. W. Norton & Company, 1991.

Dilworth, Richardson, ed. *The City in American Political Development*. New York: Routledge, 2009.

Ebner, Michael and Eugene Tobin, eds. *The Age of Urban Reform: New Perspectives on the Progressive Era*. Port Washington, NY: Kennikat Press, 1977.

Ethington, Phillip. *The Public City: The Political Construction of Urban Life in San Francisco, 1850–1900*. New York: Cambridge University Press, 1994.

Feldberg, Michael. *The Turbulent Era: Riot and Disorder in Jacksonian America*. New York: Oxford University Press, 1980.

Flanagan, Maureen. *Seeing with Their Hearts: Chicago and the Vision of the Good City, 1871–1933*. Princeton, NJ: Princeton University Press, 2002.

Gamber, Wendy. *The Boardinghouse in Nineteenth Century America*. Baltimore, MD: Johns Hopkins University Press, 2007.

Gilfoyle, Timothy. *City of Eros: New York City, Prostitution and the Commercialization of Sex, 1790–1920*. New York: W. W. Norton, 1994.

———. *A Pickpocket's Tale: The Underworld of Nineteenth-Century New York*. New York: W. W. Norton, 2006.

Ginzberg, Lori D. *Women and the Work of Benevolence: Morality, Politics, and Class in the 19th-Century United States*. New Haven, CT: Yale University Press, 1990.

Goldfield, David R. *Urban Growth in the Age of Sectionalism: Virginia, 1847–1861*. Baton Rouge: Louisiana State University Press, 1977.

Harris, Neil, Wim de Wit, James Gilbert, and Robert W. Rydell. *Grand Illusions: Chicago's World's Fair of 1893*. Chicago, IL: Chicago Historical Society, 1993.

Lebsock, Suzanne. *The Free Women of Petersburgh: Status and Culture in a Southern Town, 1784–1860*, New York: W. W. Norton, 1984.

Miller, Zane. *Boss Cox's Cincinnati: Urban Politics in the Progressive Era*. Columbus: Ohio State University Press, 2000.

Monkonnen, Eric. *Police in Urban America, 1860–1920*. Cambridge: Cambridge University Press, 2004.

Johnson, Paul. *A Shopkeeper's Millennium: Society and Revivals in Rochester, New York, 1815–1837*. New York: Hill and Wang, 1978.

Rosenberg, Charles E. *The Cholera Years: The United States in 1832, 1849, and 1866*. Chicago, IL: University of Chicago Press, 1962, 1987.

Ryan, Mary P. *Cradle of the Middle Class: The Family in Oneida County, New York, 1790–1865*. New York: Cambridge University Press, 1981.

Smith, Carl. *Urban Disorder and the Shape of Belief: The Great Chicago Fire, the Haymarket Bomb, and the Model Town of Pullman*. Chicago, IL: University of Chicago Press, 1995.

Stansell, Christine. *City of Women: Sex and Class in New York, 1780–1860*. New York: Knopf, 1982, 1986.

Trachtenberg, Alan. *The Incorporation of America: Culture and Society in the Gilded Age*. New York: Hill and Wang, 1982, 2007.

Wade, Richard. *The Urban Frontier: The Rise of Western Cities, 1790–1830*. Cambridge, MA: Harvard, 1959.

———. "Urban Life in Western America, 1790–1830," *AHR* LXIV (1957): 14–30.

Warner, Sam Bass. *The Private City: Philadelphia in Three Periods of Growth*. Philadelphia: University of Pennsylvania Press, 1968.

Wilentz, Sean. *Chants Democratic: New York City and the Rise of the American Working Class, 1788–1850*. New York: Oxford University Press, 1984.

Late Nineteenth to Twenty-First Century

Benson, Susan Porter. *Counter Cultures: Saleswomen, Managers, and Customers in American Department Stores, 1890–1940*. Urbana: University of Illinois Press, 1986.

Bergreen, Laurence. *Capone: The Man and the Era*. New York: Touchstone, 1994.

Biles, Roger. *Big City Boss in Depression and War: Mayor Edward J. Kelly of Chicago*. Dekalb, IL: Northern Illinois University Press, 1984.

———. *Richard J. Daley: Politics, Race, and the Governing of Chicago*. DeKalb, IL: Northern Illinois University Press, 1995.

Bloom, Nicholas Dagen. *Suburban Alchemy: 1960s New Towns and the Transformation of the American Dream*. Columbus: Ohio State University Press, 2001.

Clear, Todd and Natasha Frost. *The Punishment Imperative: The Rise and Failure of Mass Incarceration in America*. New York: New York University Press, 2014.

Cohen, Lizabeth. *A Consumer's Republic: The Politics of Mass Consumption in Postwar America*. New York: Vintage Books, 2003.

Conn, Steven. *Americans Against the City: Anti-Urbanism in the Twentieth Century*. New York: Oxford University Press, 2014.

Davis, Allen F. *Spearheads for Reform: The Social Settlements the Progressive Movement, 1890–1914*. New York: Oxford University Press, 1967.

Davis, Mike. *City of Quartz: Excavating the Future in Los Angeles*. New York: Vintage Books, 1992.

———. *The Ecology of Fear: Los Angeles and the Imagination of Disaster*. New York: Metropolitan Books, 1998.

Dolgon, Corey. *End of the Hamptons: Scenes from the Class Struggle in America's Paradise*. New York: New York University Press, 2005.

Findlay, John M. *Magic Lands: Western Cityscapes and American Culture after 1940*. Berkeley: University of California Press, 1992.

Gans, Herbert. *The Levittowners: Ways of Life and Politics in a New Suburban Community*. New York: Pantheon, 1967.

———. *The Urban Villagers: Group and Class Life of Italian Americans*. New York: Free Press, 1962.

Gelfand, Mark I. *A Nation of Cities: The Federal Government and Urban America, 1933–1965*. New York: Oxford University Press, 1975.

Jackson, Kenneth. *The Ku Klux Klan in the City*. New York: Oxford University Press, 1967.

Kessner, Thomas. *Fiorello H. LaGuardia and the Making of Modern New York*. New York: Penguin Books, 1989.

Miller, James. *Democracy is in the Streets: From Port Huron to the Siege of Chicago*. New York: Simon & Schuster, 1987.

Mowry, George E. *The Urban Nation, 1920–1960*. New York: Hill and Wang, 1965.

Palen, John J. *The Suburbs*. New York: McGraw Hill, 1995.

Pritchett, Wendell. *Brownsville, Brooklyn: Blacks, Jews, and the Changing Face of the Ghetto*. Chicago, IL: University of Chicago Press, 2002.

Riordan, William. *Plunkitt of Tammany Hall: A Series of Very Plain Talks on Very Practical Politics*. New York: Dutton, 1983.

Rosen, Ruth. *The Lost Sisterhood: Prostitution in America, 1900–1918*. Baltimore, MD: Johns Hopkins University Press, 1982.

Rothman, Hal. *Neon Metropolis: How Las Vegas Started the Twentieth Century*. New York: Routledge, 2003.

Self, Robert O. *American Babylon: Race and the Struggle for Postwar Oakland*. Princeton, NJ: Princeton University Press, 2005.

Straus, Emily. *Death of a Suburban Dream: Race and Schools in Compton, California*. Philadelphia: University of Pennsylvania Press, 2014.

Sugrue, Thomas J. *The Origins of the Urban Crisis: Race and Inequality in Postwar Detroit*. Princeton, NJ: Princeton University Press, 1996.

Taft, Chloe. *From Steel to Slots: Casino Capitalism in the Postindustrial City*. Cambridge, MA: Harvard University Press, 2016.

Teaford, Jon C. *Cities of the Heartland: The Rise and Fall of the Industrial Midwest*. Bloomington: Indiana University Press, 1993.

———. *The Rough Road to Renaissance: Urban Revitalization in America, 1940–1985*. Baltimore, MD: Johns Hopkins University Press, 1990.

———. *The 20th-Century American City: Problem, Promise, & Reality*. Baltimore, MD: Johns Hopkins University Press, 2016.

Wilder, Craig Steven. *A Covenant with Color: Race and Social Power in Brooklyn*. New York: Columbia University Press, 2000.

Wilson, William Julius. *The Declining Significance of Race: Blacks and Changing American Institutions*. Chicago, IL: University of Chicago Press, 1978.

————. *When Work Disappears: The World of the New Urban Poor*. New York: Vintage Books, 1996.

III. Urban History by Topic and Place

Architecture and Space

Gutman, Marta. *A City for Children: Women, Architecture, and the Charitable Landscapes of Oakland, 1850–1950*. Chicago, IL: University of Chicago Press, 2014.

Hayden, Dolores. *The Power of Place: Urban Landscapes as Public History*. Cambridge, MA: MIT Press, 1995.

Rybczynski, Witold. *Home: A Short History of an Idea*. New York: Penguin, 1987.

Stilgoe, John R. *Outside Lies Magic: Regaining History and Awareness in Everyday Places*. New York: Walker and Company, 1998.

Downtowns

Fogelson, Robert. *Downtown: Its Rise and Fall, 1880–1950*. New Haven, CT: Yale University Press, 2001.

Isenberg, Alison. *Downtown America: A History of the Place and the People that Made It*. Chicago, IL: University of Chicago Press, 2004.

Environment see Urban Environmental

Gay and Lesbian Urban History and Related Works

Chauncey, George. *Gay New York: Gender, Urban Culture, and the Making of the Gay Male World, 1890–1940*. New York: Basic Books, 1994.

Duberman, Martin. *Stonewall*. New York: St. Martins Press, 1993.

Krahulik, Karen Chistel. *Provincetown: From Pilgrim Landing to Gay Resort*. New York: New York University Press, 2005.

Yoshino, Kenji. *Covering: The Hidden Assault on our Civil Rights*. New York: Random House, 2006.

Highways see Suburban and Planning

Housing

Bauman, John F. *Public Housing, Race, and Renewal: Urban Planning in Philadelphia, 1920–1974*. Philadelphia, PA: Temple University Press, 1987.

————, Roger Biles, and Kristin Szylvian. *From Tenements to the Taylor Homes: In Search of an Urban Housing Policy in Twentieth Century America*. College Station: Pennsylvania State University Press, 2000.

Cowie, Jefferson and Joseph Heathcott. *Beyond the Ruins: The Meanings of Deindustrialization*. Ithaca, NY: Cornell University Press, 2003.

Hunt, D. Bradford. *Blueprint for Disaster: The Unraveling of Chicago Public Housing*. Chicago, IL: University of Chicago Press, 2009.

Venkatesh, Sudhir Alladi. *American Project: The Rise and Fall of a Modern Ghetto*. Cambridge, MA: Harvard University Press, 2000.

Wright, Gwendolyn. *Moralism & the Model Home: Domestic Architecture and Cultural Conflict in Chicago, 1873–1913*. Chicago, IL: University of Chicago Press, 1985.Immigration

Antin, Mary. *The Promised Land*. New York: Penguin Books, 1997.

Antler, Joyce. *The Journey Home: How Jewish Women Shaped Modern America*. New York: Schocken Books, 1997.

Barton, Josef. *Peasants and Strangers: Italians, Rumanians, and Slovaks in an American City, 1890–1950*. Cambridge, MA: Harvard University Press, 1975.

Bayor, Ronald H. *Neighbors in Conflict: The Irish, Germans, Jews, and Italians of New York City, 1929–1941*. Baltimore, MD: Johns Hopkins University Press, 1978.

Binder, Frederick M. and David Reimers. *All the Nations Under Heaven: An Ethnic and Racial History of New York City*. New York: Columbia University Press, 1995.

Bodnar, John. *The Transplanted: A History of Immigrants in Urban America*. Bloomington: Indiana University Press, 1985.

Bodnar, John, Roger D. Simon, and Michael P. Weber. *Lives of Their Own: Blacks, Italians, and Poles in Pittsburgh, 1900–1960*. Urbana: University of Illinois Press, 1982.

Conzen, Kathleen Neils. *Immigrant Milwaukee, 1836–1860: Accommodation and Community in a Frontier City*. Cambridge, MA: Harvard University Press, 1976.

Daniels, Roger and Otis L. Graham. *Debating American Immigration, 1882–Present*. New York: Roman and Littlefield, 2001.

Diner, Hasia. *Erin's Daughters in America: Irish Immigrant Women in the Nineteenth Century* Baltimore, MD: Johns Hopkins University Press, 1983.

———. *Hungering for America: Italian, Irish, & Jewish Foodways in the Age of Migration*. Cambridge, MA: Harvard University Press, 2001.

Dinnerstein, Leonard and David M. Reimers. *Ethnic Americans: A History of Immigration*. New York: Columbia University Press, 1999.

Ewen, Elizabeth. *Immigrant Women in the Land of Dollars: Life and Culture on the Lower East Side, 1890–1925*. New York: Monthly Review Press, 1985.

Gabaccia, Donna R. *From the Other Side: Women, Gender and Immigrant Life in the U.S., 1820–1990*. Bloomington: Indiana University Press, 1994.

———. *From Sicily to Elizabeth Street: Housing and Social Change Among Italian Immigrants, 1880–1930*. Albany: State University of New York Press, 1984.

Jacobson, Matthew Frye. *Whiteness of a Different Color: European Immigrants and the Alchemy of Race*. Cambridge, MA: Harvard University Press, 1998.

Kessner, Thomas. *The Golden Door; Italian and Jewish Immigrant Mobility in New York City, 1880–1915*. New York: Oxford University Press, 1977.

Meagher, Timothy J. *Inventing Irish America: Generation, Class, and Ethnic Identity in a New England City, 1880–1928*. Notre Dame, IN: University of Notre Dame Press, 2001.

Miller, Thomas. *Immigrants and the American City*. New York: New York University Press, 1993.

Powers, Vincent E. *Invisible Immigrants: The Pre-Famine Irish Immigrant Community in Worcester, MA from 1826–1860*. New York: Garland, 1989.

Reimers, David M. *Still the Golden Door: The Third World Comes to America*. New York: Columbia University Press, 1985.

———. *Unwelcome Strangers: American Identity and the Turn Against Immigration*. New York: Columbia University Press, 1998.

Riis, Jacob. *How the Other Half Lives: Studies Among the Tenements of New York*. New York: Scribner & Sons, 1890.

Takaki, Ronald. *A Different Mirror: A History of Multicultural America*. Boston, MA: Little, Brown and Company, 1993.

———. *Strangers from a Different Shore: A History of Asian Americans*. New York: Penguin, 1998.

Labor in Urban Settings

Barrett, James R. *Work and Community in the Jungle: Chicago's Packinghouse Workers, 1894–1922*. Urbana: University of Illinois Press, 1987.

Blewett, Mary H. *The Last Generation: Work and Life in the Textile Mills of Lowell, Massachusetts, 1910–1960*. Amherst: University of Massachusetts Press, 1990.

Brecher, Jeremy. *Strike*. Boston, MA: South End Press, 1972.

Cohen, Lizabeth. *Making a New Deal: Industrial Workers in Chicago, 1919–1939*. New York: Cambridge University Press, 1990.

Dawley, Alan. *Class and Community: The Industrial Revolution in Lynn*. Cambridge, MA: Harvard University Press, 1976.

Dublin, Thomas. *Women at Work: The Transformation of Work and Community in Lowell, Massachusetts, 1826–1860*. New York: Columbia University Press, 1979.

Faue, Elizabeth. *Community of Suffering and Struggle: Women, Men, and the Labor Movement in Minneapolis, 1915–1945*. Chapel Hill: University of North Carolina Press, 1991.

Gerstle, Gary. *Working-Class Americanism: The Politics of Labor in a Textile City, 1914–1960*. New York: Cambridge University Press, 1989.

Green, Hardy. *On Strike at Hormel: The Struggle for a Democratic Labor Movement*. Philadelphia: Temple University Press, 1990.

Green, James. *Death in the Haymarket: A Story of Chicago, the First Labor Movement, and the Bombing that Divided Gilded Age America*. New York: Pantheon Books, 2006.

Hareven, Tamara, and Randolph Langenbach. *Amoskeag: Life and Work in an American Factory City*. New York: Pantheon, 1978.

Jones, Jacqueline. *American Work: Four Centuries of Black and White Labor*. New York: W. W. Norton, 1998.

———. *The Dispossessed: America's Underclasses from the Civil War to the Present*. New York: Basic Books, 1992.

———. *Labor of Love, Labor of Sorrow: Black Women, Work, and Family from Slavery to the Present*. New York: Vintage Books, 1985.

Kessler-Harris, Alice. *Out to Work: A History of Wage Earning Women in the United States*. New York: Oxford University Press, 1982.

Lichtenstein, Nelson. *The Most Dangerous Man in Detroit: Walter Reuther and the Fate of American Labor*. New York: Basic Books, 1995.

Meyerowitz, Joanne. *Women Adrift: Independent Wage Earners in Chicago, 1880–1930*. Chicago, IL: University of Chicago Press, 1988.

Orleck, Annelise. *Storming Caesar's Palace: How Black Mothers Fought Their Own War on Poverty*. Boston, MA: Beacon Press, 2005.

Peiss, Kathy. *Cheap Amusements: Working Women and Leisure in Turn of the Century New York*. Philadelphia, PA: Temple University Press, 1986.

Rosenzweig, Roy. *Eight Hours For What We Will: Workers and Leisure in an Industrial City, 1870–1920*. Cambridge: Cambridge University Press, 1983.

Ross, Robert. *Slaves to Fashion: Poverty and Abuse in the New Sweatshops*. Ann Arbor: University of Michigan Press, 2004.

Smith, Carl. *Urban Disorder and the Shape of Belief: The Great Chicago Fire, the Haymarket Bomb, and the Model Town of Pullman*. Chicago, IL: University of Chicago Press, 1995.

Tentler, Leslie Woodcock. *Wage-Earning Women: Industrial Work and Family Life in the United States, 1900–1930*. New York: Oxford University Press, 1979.

Trotter, Joe William, Jr. *Black Milwaukee: The Making of an Industrial Proletariat, 1915–1945*. Urbana: University of Illinois Press, 1985.

Native Americans

Jaffee, David. *People of the Wachusett: Greater New England in History and Memory, 1630–1860*. Ithaca, NY: Cornell University Press, 1999.

LeGrande, James. *Indian Metropolis: Native Americans in Chicago, 1945–1975*. Urbana: University of Illinois Press, 2005.

Thrush, Coll. *Native Seattle: Histories from the Crossing-Over Place*. Seattle: University of Washington, 2007.

Novels

Algren, Nelson. *The Man with the Golden Arm*. New York: Doubleday & Company, Inc., 1949.

———. *Never Come Morning*. New York: Four Walls Eight Windows, 1987.

Angelou, Maya. *I Know Why the Caged Bird Sings*. New York: Bantam Books, 1993.

Arnow, Harriette. *The Dollmaker*. New York: Macmillan Publishing, 1954.

Bell, Thomas. *Out of This Furnace*. Pittsburgh, PA: University of Pittsburgh Press, 1941.

Bellow, Saul. *Adventures of Augie March*. New York: Penguin Books, 1984.

Brown, Claude. *Manchild in the Promised Land*. New York: Touchstone, 1995.

Cahan, Abraham. *The Rise of David Levinsky*. New York: Harper & Row, 1960.

Dreiser, Theodore. *Jennie Gerhardt*. New York: Penguin Books, 1994.

———. *Sister Carrie*. New York: Bantam Books, 1992.

———. *The Titan*. New York: Meridian Classic, 1984.

Gelernter, David. *1939: The Lost World of the Fair*. New York: Avon, 1995.

Lewis, Sinclair. *Babbitt*. New York: Harcourt, Brace, & Co., 1922.

Lehan, Richard. *The City in Literature: An Intellectual and Cultural History*. Berkeley: University of California Press, 1998.

Masters, Edgar Lee. *Spoon River Anthology*. New York: Dover, 1992.

Niles, Blair. *Strange Brother*. London: Liveright Press, 1931.

Norris, Frank. *The Pit: The Epic of Wheat*. New York: Penguin Books, 1994.

Petry, Ann. *The Street*. Boston, MA: Houghton Mifflin, 1974.

Simon, Kate. *Bronx Primitive: Portraits in a Childhood*. New York: Penguin, 1982.

Sinclair. Upton. *The Jungle*. New York: Penguin, 1985.

West, Dorothy. *The Living is Easy*. New York: The Feminist Press, 1948.

Wilson, Sloan. *Man in Grey Flannel Suit*. New York: Simon & Schuster, 1955.

Wright, Richard. *Black Boy (American Hunger)*. New York: HarperPerennial, 1993.

———. *Native Son*. New York: Harper & Row Publishers, 1966.

Yates, Richard. *Revolutionary Road*. New York: Vintage Books, 2008.

Yezerska, Aniza. *The Bread Givers*. New York: Persea Books, 2003.

Planning History, Planning Practice, and Urban Infrastructure

Abrams, Charles. *The City is the Frontier*. New York: Harper & Row, 1965.

Bluestone, Barry. *Constructing Chicago*. New Haven, CT: Yale University Press, 1993.

Boyer, M. Christine. *Dreaming the Rational City: The Myth of American City Planning*. Cambridge: MIT Press, 1986.

Bruegmann, Robert. *Sprawl: A Compact History*. Chicago, IL: University of Chicago Press, 2005.

Fairfield, John D. *The Mysteries of the Great City: The Politics of Urban Design, 1877–1937*. Columbus: Ohio State University Press, 1993.

Gilfoyle, Timothy. *Millennium Park: Creating a Chicago Landmark*. Chicago, IL: University of Chicago Press, 2006.

Gillette, Howard, Jr. *Between Justice and Beauty: Race, Planning, and the Failure of Urban Policy in Washington, D.C.* Philadelphia: University of Pennsylvania Press, 2006.

Hirsch, Arnold R. and A. Lee Leveret, "The Katrina Conspiracies: The Problem of Trust in Rebuilding an American City," *Journal of Urban History*, vol. 35, no. 2 (January 2009): 207–219.

Hood, Clifton. *722 Miles: The Building of the Subways and How They Transformed New York*. New York: Simon & Schuster, 1993.

Jacobs, Jane. *The Death and Life of Great American Cities*. New York: Vintage Books, 1961.

Kunstler, James Howard. *The Geography of Nowhere: The Rise and Decline of America's Man-Made Landscape*. New York: Touchstone, 1993.

———. *Home From Nowhere: Remaking our Everyday World for the 21st Century*. New York: Simon & Schuster, 1996.

Leazes, Francis J. and Mark T. Motte. *Providence, the Renaissance City*. Boston, MA: Northeastern University Press, 2004.

Levy, John D. *Contemporary Urban Planning*. Eighth Edition. Englewood Cliffs, NJ: Pearson, Prentice Hall, 2009.

Mayer, Harold and Richard C. Wade. *Chicago: Growth of a Metropolis*. Chicago, IL: University of Chicago Press, 1969.

McShane, Clay. *Asphalt Nation: How the Automobile Took Over American and How We Can Take It Back*. Berkeley: University of California Press, 1998.

Molotch, Harvey and John J. Logan. *Urban Fortunes: The Political Economy of Place*. Berkeley: University of California Press, 1987.

Platt, Harold L. *The Electric City: Energy and the Growth of the Chicago Area, 1880–1930*. Chicago, IL: University of Chicago Press, 1991.

Rosenzweig, Roy and Elizabeth Blackmar. *The Park and the People: A History of Central Park*. New York: Henry Holt, 1992.

Rybczynski, Witold. *A Clearing in the Distance: Frederick Law Olmsted and America in the 19th Century*. New York: Simon & Schuster, 1999.

Smith, Carl. *The Plan of Chicago: Daniel Burnham and the Remaking of the American City*. Chicago, IL: University of Chicago Press, 2006.

Poverty

Adams, Jane. *Twenty Years at Hull-House*. New York: Signet Classic, 1981.

Katz, Michael. *In The Shadow of the Poorhouse: A Social History of Welfare in America*. New York: Basic Books, 1986.

Levenstein, Lisa. *A Movement Without Marches: African American Women and the Politics of Poverty in Postwar Philadelphia*. Chapel Hill: University of North Carolina Press, 2009.

Pleck, Elizabeth. *Black Migration and Poverty in Boston, 1865–1900*. New York: Academic Press, 1979.

Thernstrom, Stephan. *The Other Bostonians: Poverty and Progress in the American Metropolis, 1880–1970*. Cambridge, MA: Harvard University Press, 1973.

———. *Poverty and Progress: Social Mobility in a Nineteenth-Century City*. Cambridge, MA: Harvard University Press, 1964.

Traverso, Susan. *Welfare Politics in Boston, 1910–1940*. Amherst: University of Massachusetts, 2003.

Venkatesh, Sudhir Alladi. *Off the Books: The Underground Economy of the Urban Poor*. Cambridge, MA: Harvard University Press, 2006.

Wilson, William Julius. *When Work Disappears: The World of the New Urban Poor*. New York: Vintage Books, 1996.

Primary Documents

Boller, Paul F., Jr. and Ronald Story. *A More Perfect Union: Documents in US History Volume II; Since 1865*. Third Edition. Boston, MA: Houghton Mifflin, 1992.

Marcus, Robert D. and David Burner. *America Firsthand. Volume II: From Reconstruction to the Present*. New York: St. Martins, 1992.

Rock, Howard B. *The New York City Artisan, 1789–1825: A Documentary History*. Albany: State University of New York Press, 1989.

Still, Bayard. *Urban America: A History with Documents*. Boston, MA: Little Brown, 1974.

Smith, Wilson, ed. *Cities of Our Past and Present: A Descriptive Reader*. New York: John Wiley & Sons, 1964.

Wade, Richard C. *Cities in American Life*. Boston, MA: Houghton Mifflin, 1971.

Race and Identity in Urban Areas

Anderson, Elijah. *Against the Wall: Poor, Young, Black, and Male*. Philadelphia: University of Pennsylvania Press, 2008.

———. *Streetwise: Race, Class, and Change in an Urban Community*. Chicago, IL: University of Chicago Press, 1990.

Ardizzone, Heidi and Earl Lewis. *Love on Trial: An American Scandal in Black and White*. New York: W. W. Norton, 2002.

Baldwin, Davarian L. *Chicago's New Negroes: Modernity, the Great Migration, and Black Urban Life*. Chapel Hill: University of North Carolina Press, 2007.

Boehm, Lisa Krissoff. *Making a Way out of No Way: African American Women and the Second Great Migration*. Jackson: University Press of Mississippi, 2009.

Boyle, Kevin. *Arc of Justice: A Saga of Race, Civil Rights, and Murder in the Jazz Age*. New York: Henry Holt, 2004.

Clark-Lewis, Elizabeth. *Living In, Living Out: African American Domestics and the Great Migration*. New York: Kodnasha America, 1994.

Connolly, N.D.B. *A World More Concrete: Real Estate and the Remaking of Jim Crow South Florida*. Chicago, IL: University of Chicago, 2016.

Douglas, Davison M. *Jim Crow Moves North: The Battle Over Northern School Desegregation, 1865–1954*. New York: Cambridge University Press, 2005.

Frey, William H. "The New Great Migration: Black American's Return to the South, 1865–2000." Center on Urban and Metropolitan Policy, Brookings Institution, May 2004.

Gillette, Howard, Jr. *Between Justice and Beauty: Race, Planning, and the Failure of Urban Policy in Washington, D.C.* Philadelphia: University of Pennsylvania Press, 2006.

Gottlieb, Peter. *Making Their Own Way: Southern Blacks' Migration to Pittsburgh, 1916–1930*. Urbana: University of Illinois Press, 1987.

Green, Adam. *Selling the Race: Culture, Community, and Black Chicago, 1940–1955*. Chicago, IL: University of Chicago Press, 2009.

Gregory, James N. *The Southern Diaspora: How the Great Migrations of Black and White Southerners Transformed America*. Chapel Hill: University of North Carolina Press, 2005.

Grossman, James R. *Land of Hope: Chicago, Black Southerners, and the Great Migration*. Chicago, IL: University of Chicago Press, 1991.

Harrison, Alferdteen, ed. *Black Exodus: The Great Migration from the American South*. Jackson: University Press of Mississippi, 1991.

Hirsch, Arnold R. *Making the Second Ghetto: Race & Housing in Chicago, 1940–1960*. New York: Cambridge University Press, 1990.

Jacoby, Tamar. *Someone Else's House: American's Unfinished Struggle for Integration*. New York: Free Press, 1998.

Jaffe, Harry S. and Tom Sherwood. *Dream City: Race, Power, and the Decline of Washington, D.C.* New York: Simon & Schuster, 1994.

Jelks, Randal Maurice. *African Americans in the Furniture City: The Struggle for Civil Rights in Grand Rapids*. Urbana: University of Illinois Press, 2006.

Kotlowitz, Alex. *There Are No Children Here: The Story of Two Boys Growing Up in the Other America*. New York: Anchor Books, 1991.

LeBlanc, Adrian Nicole. *Random Family: Love, Drugs, Trouble and Coming of Age in the Bronx*. New York: Scribner, 2003.

Lemann, Nicholas. *The Promised Land: The Great Black Migration and How it Changed America*. New York: Vintage Books, 1992.

Lewis, Earl. *In Their Own Interests: Race, Class and Power in Twentieth-Century Norfolk, Virginia*. Berkeley: University of California Press, 1993.

Marks, Carole. *Farewell—We're Good and Gone: The Great Black Migration*. Bloomington: Indiana University Press, 1989.

Patillo, Mary. *Black on the Block: The Politics of Race and Class in the City*. Chicago, IL: University of Chicago Press, 2007.

Perales, Monica. *Smeltertown: Making and Remembering a Southwest Border Community*. Chapel Hill: University of North Carolina Press, 2010.

Phillips, Kimberley L. *AlabamaNorth: African-American Migrants, Community, and Working-Class Activism in Cleveland, 1915–1945*. Urbana: University of Illinois Press, 1999.

Pruitt, Bernadette. "The African American Experience in Slavery and Freedom: Black Urban History Revisited." *Journal of Urban History* 33, no. 6 (September 2007): 1033–1047.

Rodriguez, Richard. *Brown: The Last Discovery of America*. New York: Viking, 2002.

———. *Hunger of Memory: An Autobiography*. New York: Bantam Books, 1992.

Santiago, Esmeralda. *When I Was Puerto Rican*. New York: Vintage Books, 1993.

Sitkoff, Harvard. *The Struggle for Black Equality, 1954–1992*. New York: Hill and Wang, 1993.

Strauz, A.K. Sandoval. "Latino Landscapes: Postwar Cities and the Transnational Origins of a New Urban America." *The Journal of American History* (December 2014): 804–826.

Takaki, Ronald. *A Different Mirror: A History of Multicultural America*. Boston, MA: Little, Brown and Company, 1993.

———. *Strangers from a Different Shore: A History of Asian Americans*. New York: Penguin, 1998.

Tolnay, Stewart E. "The Great Migration and Changes in the Northern Black Family, 1940–1990." *Social Forces* 75 (June 1997): 1213–1238.

Trent, Alexander J. "The Great Migration in Comparative Perspective: Interpreting the Urban Origins of Southern Black Migrants to Depression-Era Pittsburgh." *Social Science History* 22 (Fall 1998): 349–376.

Trotter, Joe William, Jr., ed. *The Great Migration in Historical Perspective: New Dimensions of Race, Class, and Gender*. Bloomington: Indiana University Press, 1991.

———, Earl Lewis, and Tera W. Hunter. *The African American Urban Experience*. New York: Palgrave Macmillan, 2004.

Tuttle, William M. *Race Riot: Chicago in the Red Summer of 1919*. New York: Athenaeum, 1970.

Religion

Bonomi, Patricia U. *Under the Cope of Heaven: Religion, Society, and Politics in Colonial America*. New York: Oxford University Press, 1986.

Orsi, Robert A., ed. *Gods of the City: Religion and the American Urban Landscape*. Bloomington: Indiana University Press, 1999.

———. *The Madonna of 115th Street: Faith and Community in Italian Harlem, 1880–1950*. New Haven, CT: Yale University Press, 1985.

Specific Cities and Regional Urban Histories

Boston

Binford, Henry. *The First Suburbs: Residential Communities on the Boston Periphery, 1815–1860*. Chicago, IL: University of Chicago Press, 1985.

Conzen, Michael and George K. Lewis. *Boston: A Geographical Portrait*. Cambridge, MA: Ballinger, 1976.

Gans, Herbert. *The Urban Villagers: Group and Class Life of Italian Americans*. New York: Free Press, 1962.

Handlin, Oscar. *Boston's Immigrants, 1790–1880*. Cambridge, MA: Harvard University Press, 1941.

Knights, Peter R. *Yankee Destinies: The Lives of Ordinary Nineteenth-Century Bostonians* Chapel Hill: North Carolina University Press, 1991.

Kreiger, Alex and David Cobb, with Amy Turner, eds. *Mapping Boston*. Cambridge, MA: MIT Press, 1999.

MacDonald, Michael Patrick. *All Souls: A Family Story from Southie*. Boston, MA: Beacon Press, 2007.

O'Connor, Thomas. *The Hub: Boston Past and Present*. Boston, MA: Northeastern University Press, 2001.

Thernstrom, Stephan. *The Other Bostonians: Poverty and Progress in the American Metropolis, 1880–1970*. Cambridge, MA: Harvard University Press, 1973.

Traverso, Susan. *Welfare Politics in Boston, 1910–1940*. Amherst: University of Massachusetts, 2003.

Warner, Sam Bass, Jr. *Streetcar Suburbs: The Process of Growth in Boston, 1870–1900*. Cambridge, MA: Harvard University Press, 1962.

Buffalo

Yans-McLaughlin, Virginia. *Family and Community: Italian Immigrants in Buffalo, 1880–1930*. Urbana: University of Illinois Press, 1982.

Chicago

Bluestone, Daniel. *Constructing Chicago*. New Haven, CT: Yale University Press, 1991.

Boehm, Lisa Krissoff. *Popular Culture and the Enduring Myth of Chicago*. New York: Routledge, 2004.

Cohen, Lizabeth. *Making a New Deal: Industrial Workers in Chicago, 1919–1939*. New York: Cambridge University Press, 1990.

Conzen, Michael and Diane Dillon. *Mapping Manifest Destiny: Chicago and the American West*. Chicago, IL: Newberry Library, 2008.

Cronon, William. *Nature's Metropolis: Chicago and the Great West*. New York: W. W. Norton, 1991.

Einhorn, Robin. *Property Rules: Political Economy in Chicago, 1833–1872*. Chicago, IL: University of Chicago Press, 1991.

Findling, John E. *Chicago's Great World Fairs*. Manchester: Manchester University Press, 1994.

Gilbert, James. *Perfect Cities: Chicago's Utopias of 1893*. Chicago, IL: University of Chicago Press, 1991.

Ginger, Ray. *Altgeld's America: The Lincoln Ideal Versus Changing Realities*. New York: Markus Wiener Publishing, 1958.

Helgeson, Jeffrey. *Crucibles of Black Empowerment: Chicago's Neighborhood Politics from the New Deal to Harold Washington*. Chicago, IL: University of Chicago Press, 2014.

Hoy, SueEllen. *Good Hearts: Catholic Sisters in Chicago's Past*. Urbana: University of Illinois Press, 2006.

Kirkland, Joseph. *The Story of Chicago*. Chicago, IL: Dibble Publishing Company, 1892.

Larson, Erik. *The Devil in the White City: Murder, Magic, and Madness at the Fair That Changed America*. New York: Vintage Books, 2003.

Mayer, Harold M. and Richard C. Wade. *Chicago: Growth of a Metropolis*. Chicago, IL: University of Chicago Press, 1969.

Meyerowitz, Joanne J. *Women Adrift: Independent Wage Earners in Chicago, 1880–1930*. Chicago, IL: University of Chicago Press, 1988.

Miller, Donald L. *City of the Century: The Epic of Chicago and the Making of America*. New York: Simon & Schuster, 1996.

Miller, Ross. *America Apocalypse: The Great Fire and the Myth of Chicago*. Chicago, IL: University of Chicago Press, 1990.

Pacyga, Dominic. *Slaughterhouse: Chicago's Union Stock Yard and the World It Made*. Chicago, IL: University of Chicago Press, 2015.

Royko, Mike. *Boss: Richard J. Daley of Chicago*. New York: E.P Dutton and Company, Inc., 1971.

Ruth, David E. *Inventing the Public Enemy: The Gangster in American Culture, 1918–1934*. Chicago, IL: University of Chicago Press, 1996.

Rydell, Robert W. *All the World's a Fair: Visions of Empire at American International Expositions, 1876–1916*. Chicago, IL: University of Chicago Press, 1984.

———. *World of Fairs: The Century-of-Progress Expositions*. Chicago, IL: University of Chicago Press, 1993.

Sawislak, Karen. *Smoldering City: Chicagoans and the Great Fire, 1871–1874*. Chicago, IL: University of Chicago Press, 1995.

Smith, Carl J. *Chicago and the American Literary Imagination, 1880–1920*. Chicago, IL: University of Chicago Press, 1984.

———. *Urban Disorder and the Shape of Belief: The Great Chicago Fire, the Haymarket Bomb, and the Model Town of Pullman*. Chicago, IL: University of Chicago Press, 1995.

Terkel, Studs. *Chicago*. New York: Pantheon Books, 1986.

Dallas

Hill, Patricia Evridge. *Dallas: The Making of a Modern City*. Austin: University of Texas Press, 1996.

Detroit

Babson, Steve, with Ron Alpern, Dave Elsila, and John Reville. *Working Detroit*. Detroit, MI: Wayne State University Press, 1986.

Chafets, Ze'ev. *Devil's Night and Other True Tales of Detroit*. New York: Vintage Books, 1991.

Meier, August, and Elliott Rudwick. *Black Detroit and the Rise of the UAW*. New York: Oxford University Press, 1979.

Sugrue, Thomas J. *The Origins of the Urban Crisis: Race and Inequality in Postwar Detroit*. Princeton, NJ: Princeton University Press, 1996.

Thomas, June Manning. *Redevelopment and Race: Planning a Finer City in Postwar Detroit.* Baltimore, MD: Johns Hopkins University Press, 1997.

Thomas, Richard W. *Life is For Us What We Make It: Building Black Community in Detroit, 1915–1945.* Bloomington: Indiana University Press, 1992.

Thompson, Heather Ann. *Whose Detroit? Politics, Labor, and Race in a Modern American City.* Ithaca, NY: Cornell University Press, 2001.

Widick, B.J. *Detroit: City of Race and Class Violence.* Detroit, MI: Wayne State University Press, 1989.

Wolcott, Virginia. *Remaking Respectability: African American Women in Interwar Detroit.* Chapel Hill: University of North Carolina Press, 2001.

Durham

Brown, Leslie. *Upbuilding Black Durham: Gender, Class, and Black Community Development in the Jim Crow South.* Chapel Hill: University Press of North Carolina, 2008.

Houston

Melosi, Martin and Joseph Pratt. *Energy Metropolis: An Environmental History of Houston and the Gulf Coast.* Pittsburgh, PA: University of Pittsburgh Press, 2007.

Platt, Harold L. *City Building in the New South: The Growth of Public Services in Houston, Texas, 1830–1920.* Philadelphia, PA: Temple University Press, 1983.

Los Angeles

Avila, Eric. *Popular Culture in the Age of White Flight: Fear and Fantasy in Suburban Los Angeles.* Los Angeles: University of California Press, 2004.

Gottlieb, Robert. *Reinventing Los Angeles: Nature and Community in the Global City.* Cambridge, MA: MIT Press, 2007.

Hise, Greg. *Magnetic Los Angeles: Planning the Twentieth Century Metropolis.* Baltimore, MD: Johns Hopkins University Press, 1999.

Soja, Edward. *The City: Los Angeles and Urban Theory at the End of the Twentieth Century.* Berkeley: University of California Press, 1998.

Straus, Emily. *The Making of the American School Crisis: Compton, California and the Death of the Suburban Dream.* Brandeis University Dissertation, 2006.

Miami

Shell-Weiss, Melanie. *Coming to Miami: A Social History.* Gainesville: University Press of Florida, 2009.

Minneapolis

Faue, Elizabeth. *Community of Suffering and Struggle: Women, Men, and the Labor Movement in Minneapolis, 1915–1945.* Chapel Hill: University of North Carolina Press, 1991.

The Midwest/Middle America

Atherton, Lewis. *Main Street on the Middle Border.* Bloomington: Indiana University Press, 1954.

Bloom, Stephen G. *Postville: A Clash of Cultures in Heartland America.* New York: Harcourt, Inc, 2000.

Jelks, Randal Maurice. *African Americans in the Furniture City: The Struggle for Civil Rights in Grand Rapids.* Urbana: University of Illinois Press, 2006.

Kotlowitz, Alex. *The Other Side of the River: A Story of Two Towns, a Death, and America's Dilemma*. New York: Doubleday, 1998.

Lynd, Robert and Helen. *Middletown: A Study in Contemporary American Culture*. New York: Harcourt Brace, 1929.

———. *Middletown in Transition*. New York: Harcourt Brace, 1937.

New York City

Abu-Lughod, Janet L. *From Urban Village to East Village: The Battle for New York's Lower East Side*. Oxford: Blackwell, 1994.

Bender, Thomas. *New York Intellect: A History of Intellectual Life in New York City, From 1750 to the Beginning of Our Time*. Baltimore, MD: Johns Hopkins University Press, 1987.

———. *The Unfinished City: New York and Metropolitan Idea*. New York: New York University Press, 2002.

Binder, Frederick M. and David Reimers. *All the Nations Under Heaven: An Ethnic and Racial History of New York City*. New York: Columbia University Press, 1995.

Blackmar, Elizabeth. *Manhattan for Rent, 1750–1850*. Ithaca, NY: Cornell University Press, 1989.

Burrow, Edwin G. and Mike Wallace. *Gotham: A History of New York City to 1898*. New York: Oxford University Press, 1999.

Day, Jared N. *Urban Castles: Tenement Housing and Landlord Activism in New York City, 1890–1943*. New York: Columbia University Press, 1999.

Douglas, Ann. *Terrible Honesty: Mongrel Manhattan in the 1920s*. New York: The Noonday Press, Farrar, Straus, and Giroux, 1995.

Gilfoyle, Timothy J. *City of Eros: New York City, Prostitution, and the Commercialization of Sex, 1790–1920*. New York: W. W. Norton &Company, 1992.

Gronowicz, Anthony. *Race and Class Politics in New York Before the Civil War*. Boston, MA: Northeastern University Press, 1998.

Hammack, David C. *Power and Society: Greater New York at the Turn of the Century*. New York: Russell Sage, 1982.

Henkin, David M. *City Reading: Written Words and Public Spaces in Antebellum New York*. New York: Columbia University Press, 1998.

Hood, Clifton. *In Pursuit of Privilege: A History of New York City's Upper Class and the Making of a Metropolis*. New York: Columbia University Press, 2017.

Kessner, Thomas. *Fiorello H. LaGuardia and the Making of Modern New York*. New York: Penguin Books, 1989.

Mandelbaum, Seymour J. *Boss Tweed's New York*. New York: J. Wiley, 1965.

Mele, Christopher. *Selling the Lower East Side: Culture, Real Estate, and Resistance in New York City*. Minneapolis: University of Minnesota Press, 2000.

Mollenkopf, John Hull. *A Phoenix in the Ashes: The Rise and Fall of the Koch Coalition in New York City Politics*. Princeton, NJ: Princeton University Press, 1992.

——— and Manuel Castells, eds. *Dual City: Restructuring New York*. New York: Russell Sage, 1991.

Osofsky, Gilbert. *Harlem: The Making of a Ghetto*. New York: Harper & Row, 1963.

Page, Max. *The Creative Destruction of Manhattan, 1900–1940*. Chicago, IL: University of Chicago Press, 1999.

Rieder, Jonathan. *Canarsie: The Jews and Italians of Brooklyn Against Liberalism*. Cambridge, MA: Harvard University Press, 1985.

Rosenzweig, Roy and Elizabeth Blackmar. *The Park and the People: A History of Central Park*. Ithaca, NY: Cornell University Press, 1992.

Sanjek, Roger. *The Future of All of Us: Race and Neighborhood Politics in New York City*. Ithaca, NY: Cornell University Press, 1998.

Sayre, Wallace and Herbert Kaufman. *Governing New York City: Politics in the Metropolis*. New York: Russell Sage, 1960.

Scherzer, Kenneth. *The Unbounded Community: Neighborhood Life and Social Structure in New York City, 1830–1875*. Durham: Duke University Press, 1992.

Schneider, Robert. *Voice of the City: Vaudeville and Popular Culture in New York*. New York: Oxford University Press, 1989.

Shkuda, Aaron. *The Lofts of SoHo: Gentrification, Art, and Industry in New York, 1950–1980*. Chicago, IL: University of Chicago, 2016.

Stansell, Christine. *City of Women: Sex and Class in New York, 1780–1860*. New York: Knopf, 1986.

Still, Bayrd. *Mirror for Gotham: New York as Seen by Contemporaries from Dutch Days to the Present*. New York: New York University Press, 1956.

Taylor, William R., ed. *Inventing Times Square: Commerce and Culture at The Crossroads of the World*. Baltimore, MD: Johns Hopkins University Press, 1991.

Wallace, Mike. *A New Deal for New York*. New York: Bell and Weiland, 2002.

Wilentz, Sean. *Chants Democratic: New York City and the Rise of the American Working Class, 1788–1850*. New York: Oxford University Press, 1984.

Philadelphia

Baumann, John F. *Public Housing, Race, and Renewal: Urban Planning in Philadelphia, 1920–1974*. Philadelphia: Temple University Press, 1987.

Hershberg, Theodore. *Philadelphia: Work, Space, Family, and Group Experience in the 19th Century*. New York: Oxford University Press, 1981.

Levenstein, Lisa. *A Movement Without Marches: African American Women and the Politics of Poverty in Postwar Philadelphia*. Chapel Hill: University of North Carolina Press, 2009.

Warner, Sam Bass, Jr. *The Private City: Philadelphia in Three Periods of Its Growth*. Philadelphia: University of Pennsylvania, 1968.

Pittsburgh

Bodnar, John, Roger Simon and Michael P. Weber. *Lives of Their Own: Blacks, Italians, and Poles in Pittsburgh, 1900–1960*. Urbana: University of Illinois Press, 1982.

Serrin, William. *Homestead: The Glory and Tragedy of an American Steel Town*. New York: Random House, 1992.

Washington, D.C.

Gillette, Howard, Jr. *Between Justice and Beauty: Race, Planning, and the Failure of Urban Policy in Washington, D.C.* Philadelphia: University of Pennsylvania Press, 2006.

Jaffe, Harry S. and Tom Sherwood. *Dream City: Race, Power, and the Decline of Washington, D.C.* New York: Simon & Schuster, 1994.

San Francisco/Silcon Valley/Oakland

Lemke-Santangelo, Gertrude. *Abiding Courage: African American Migrant Women and the East Bay Community*. Chapel Hill: University of North Carolina Press, 1996.

Matthews, Glenna. *Silicon Valley, Women, and the California Dream: Gender, Class and Opportunity in the Twentieth Century*. Palo Alto, CA: Stanford University Press, 2003.

Pellow, David Naguib and Lisa Sun-Hee Park. *The Silicon Valley of Dreams: Environmental Justice, Immigrant Workers, and the High-Tech Global Economy*. New York: New York University Press, 2002.

Self, Robert. *American Babylon: Race and the Struggle for Postwar Oakland*. Princeton, NJ: Princeton University Press, 2005.

St. Louis

Sandweiss, Eric. *St. Louis: The Evolution of an American Urban Landscape*. Philadephia, PA: Temple Universty Press, 2001.

Tulsa

Ellsworth, Scott. *Death in a Promised Land: The Tulsa Race Riot of 1921*. Baton Rouge: Louisiana State University Press, 1982.

Suburbia and Consumerism

Avila, Eric. *Popular Culture in the Age of White Flight: Fear and Fantasy in Suburban Los Angeles*. Los Angeles: University of California Press, 2004.

Binford, Henry. *The First Suburbs: Residential Communities on the Boston Periphery, 1815–1860*. Chicago, IL: University of Chicago Press, 1985.

Cohen, Lizabeth. *A Consumer's Republic: The Politics of Mass Consumption in Postwar America*. New York: Vintage Books, 2004.

Duany, Andres, Elizabeth Plater-Zyberk, and Jeff Speck. *Suburban Nation: The Rise of Sprawl and the Decline of the American Dream*. New York: North Point Press, 2000.

Fishman, Robert. *Beyond Suburbia: The Rise of the Technoburb*. New York: Basic Books, 1987.

Fishman, Robert. *Bourgeois Utopias: The Rise and Fall of Suburbia*. New York: Basic Books, 1987.

Fogelson, Robert M. *Bourgeois Nightmares: Suburbia, 1870–1930*. New Haven, CT: Yale University Press, 1995.

Frantz, Douglas and Catherine Collins. *Celebration U.S.A.: Living in Disney's Brave New Town*. New York: Henry Holt, 1999.

Garreau, Joel. *Edge City: Life on the New Frontier*. New York: Anchor Books, 1991.

Halberstam, David. *The Fifties*. New York: Fawcett Columbine, 1993.

Hayden, Dolores. *Building Suburbia, Green Fields and Urban Growth, 1820–2000*. New York: Vintage Books, 2004.

Hudnut, William H. *Halfway to Everywhere: A Portrait of America's First-Tier Suburbs*. Washington, D.C.: Urban Land Institute, 2003.

Jackson, Kenneth. *Crabgrass Frontier: The Suburbanization of the United States*. New York: Oxford University Press, 1987.

Kelly, Barbara, ed. *Suburbia Re-Examined*. Westport, CT: Greenwood, 1989.

Lewis, Tom. *Divided Highways: Building the Interstate Highways, Transforming American Life*. New York: Penguin, 1999.

Low, Setha. *Behind the Gates: Life, Security, and the Pursuit of Happiness in Fortress America*. New York: Routledge, 2003.

Marsh, Margaret. *Suburban Lives*. Piscataway, NJ: Rutgers University Press, 1990.

Marshall, Alex. *How Cities Work: Suburbs, Sprawl and the Roads Not Taken*. Austin: University of Texas Press, 2000.

May, Elaine Tyler. *Homeward Bound: American Families in the Cold War Era*. New York: HarperCollins, 1988.

Meyerowitz, Joanne. *Not June Cleaver: Women and Gender in Postwar America*. Philadelphia: Temple University Press, 1994.

Nicolaides, Becky. *My Blue Heaven: Life and Politics in the Suburbs of Los Angeles*. Chicago, IL: University of Chicago Press, 2002.

Rome, Adam. *The Bulldozer in the Countryside: Suburban Sprawl and the Rise of American Environmentalism*. Cambridge: Cambridge University Press, 2001.

Ross, Andrew. *The Celebration Chronicles: Life, Liberty and the Pursuit of Property Value in Disney's New Town*. New York: Ballantine Books, 1999.

Warner, Sam Bass. *Streetcar Suburbs: The Process of Growth in Boston, 1870–1920*. Cambridge, MA: Harvard University Press, 2004.

Wiese, Andrew. *Places of Their Own: African American Suburbanization in the Twentieth Century*. Chicago, IL: University of Chicago Press, 2005.

Urban Environmental

Burnstein, Daniel Eli. *Next to Godliness: Confronting Dirt and Despair in Progressive Era New York City*. Urbana: University of Illinois Press, 2006.

Cronon, William. *Changes in the Land: Indians, Colonists, and the Ecology of New England* New York: Hill and Wang, 1983.

———. *Nature's Metropolis: Chicago and the Great West*. New York: W. W. Norton, 1991.

Cumbler, John. *Reasonable Use: The People, the Environment, and the State, New England, 1790–1930*. New York: Oxford University Press, 2001.

Elkind, Sarah S. *Bay Cities and Water Politics: The Battle for Resources in Boston and Oakland*. Kansas City: University of Kansas Press, 1998.

Melosi, Martin V. *The Sanitary City: Urban Infrastructure in America from the Colonial Times to the Present*. Baltimore, MD: Johns Hopkins University Press, 2000.

Needham, Andrew. *Power Lines: Phoenix and the Making of the Modern Southwest*. Princeton, NJ: Princeton University Press, 2014.

Pellow, David Naguib and Lisa Sun-Hee Park. *The Silicon Valley of Dreams: Environmental Justice, Immigrant Workers, and the High-Tech Global Economy*. New York: New York University Press, 2002.

Steinberg, Theodore. *Acts of God: The Unnatural History of Natural Disaster in America*. New York: Oxford University Press, 2000.

———. *Nature Incorporated: Industrialization and the Waters of New England*. Amherst: University of Massachusetts Press, 1991.

Stradling, David. *Smokestacks and Progressives: Environmentalists, Engineers, and Air Quality in America, 1881–1951*. Baltimore, MD: Johns Hopkins University Press, 2002.

Sze, Julie. *Noxious New York: The Racial Politics of Urban Health and Environmental Justice*. Cambridge, MA: MIT Press, 2007.

Tarr, Joel. *The Search for the Ultimate Waste Sink: Urban Pollution in Historical Perspective*. Akron: Ohio University Press, 1996.

Young, Paula Lee, ed. *Meat, Modernity, and the Rise of the Slaughterhouse*. Dover, NH: University of New Hampshire Press/University of New England, 2008.

White Southern Migration

Arnow, Harriette. *The Dollmaker*. New York: Macmillan Publishing, 1954.

Berry, Chad, ed. *The Hayloft Gang: The Story of the National Barn Dance*. Urbana: University of Illinois Press, 2008.

———. *Southern Migrants, Northern Exiles*. Urbana: University of Illinois Press, 2000.

Gregory, James N. *The Southern Diaspora: How the Great Migrations of Black and White Southerners Transformed America*. Chapel Hill: University of North Carolina Press, 2005.

Women and the City

Boehm, Lisa Krissoff. *Making a Way out of No Way: African American Women and the Second Great Migration*. Jackson: University Press of Mississippi, 2009.

Deutsch, Sarah. *Women and the City: Gender, Space, and Power in Boston, 1870–1940*. New York: Oxford University Press, 2000.

Jones, Jacqueline. *American Work: Four Centuries of Black and White Labor*. New York: W. W. Norton, 1998.

———. *The Dispossessed: America's Underclasses from the Civil War to the Present*. New York: Basic Books, 1992.

———. *Labor of Love, Labor of Sorrow: Black Women, Work, and Family from Slavery to the Present*. New York: Vintage Books, 1985.

Kessler-Harris, Alice. *Out to Work: A History of Wage Earning Women in the United States*. New York: Oxford University Press, 1982.

Kunzel, Regina. *Fallen Women, Problem Girls: Unmarried Mothers and the Professionalization of Social Work, 1890–1945*. New Haven, CT: Yale University Press, 1995.

Lebsock, Suzanne. *The Free Women of Petersburgh: Status and Culture in a Southern Town, 1784–1860*. New York: W. W. Norton, 1984.

Lemke-Santangelo, Gertrude. *Abiding Courage: African American Migrant Women and the East Bay Community*. Chapel Hill: University of North Carolina Press, 1996.

Levenstein, Lisa. *A Movement Without Marches: African American Women and the Politics of Poverty in Postwar Philadelphia*. Chapel Hill: University of North Carolina Press, 2009.

Matthews, Glenna. *Silicon Valley, Women, and the California Dream: Gender, Class and Opportunity in the Twentieth Century*. Stanford, CA: Stanford University Press, 2003.

Meyerowitz, Joanne. *Women Adrift: Independent Wage Earners in Chicago, 1880–1930*. Chicago, IL: University of Chicago Press, 1988.

Muncy, Robyn. *Creating a Female Dominion in American Reform, 1890–1935*. New York: Oxford University Press, 1991.

Orleck, Annelise. *Storming Caesar's Palace: How Black Mothers Fought Their Own War on Poverty*. Boston, MA: Beacon Press, 2005.

Peiss, Kathy. *Cheap Amusements: Working Women and Leisure in Turn of the Century New York*. Philadelphia, PA: Temple University Press, 1986.

Rosen, Ruth. *The Lost Sisterhood: Prostitution in America, 1900–1918*. Baltimore, MD: Johns Hopkins University Press, 1983.

Stansell, Christine. *City of Women: Sex and Class in New York, 1780–1860*. New York: Knopf, 1986.

Wolcott, Virginia. *Remaking Respectability: African American Women in Interwar Detroit*. Chapel Hill: University of North Carolina Press, 2001.

Working Class/Radical America/Mass Culture

Avrich, Paul. *The Haymarket Tragedy*. Princeton, NJ: Princeton University Press, 1984.

Kasson, John F. *Amusing the Million: Coney Island at the Turn of the Century*. New York: Hill and Wang, 1978.

Kessler-Harris, Alice. *Out to Work: A History of Wage-Earning Women in the United States*. New York: Oxford University Press, 1982.

Lamphere, Louise. *From Working Daughters to Working Mothers: Immigrant Women in a New England Industrial Community*. Ithaca, NJ: Cornell University Press, 1987.

Nasaw, David. *Children of the City: At Work and At Play*. New York: Oxford University Press, 1985.

———. *Going Out: The Rise and Fall of Public Amusement*. New York: Basic Books, 1993.

Painter, Nell Irvin. *Standing at Armageddon: The United States, 1877–1919*. New York: W. W. Norton, 1987.

Reiss, Steven A. *City Games: The Evolution of American Urban Society and the Rise of Sports*. Urbana: University of Illinois Press, 1991.

COPYRIGHT INFORMATION

Part I: Definitions and Perspectives

ESSAYS

1.1 Steven H. Corey and Lisa Krissoff Boehm, "Examining America's Urban Landscape: From Social Reform to Social History, and Back." Copyright © 2010 and 2019 by Steven H. Corey and Lisa Krissoff Boehm.

1.2 Arthur M. Schlesinger, Sr., "The City in American Civilization," from *Paths to the Present* (1949). Copyright © 1949 by Arthur Schlesinger, used with the permission of the Wylie Agency, LLC.

1.3 Herbet J. Gans, "Urbanism and Suburbanism as Ways of Life: A Revaluation of Definitions," from *People, Plans, and Policies* (1991). Copyright © 1991by Columbia University Press. Reprinted with permission of Columbia University Press.

1.4 William Frey, "Melting Pot Cities and Suburbs," from *Diversity Explosion: How Racial Demographics Are Remaking America* (2018). Copyright © 2015, 2018 by The Brookings Institution. Reprinted with permission of William Frey and the Brookings Institution.

DOCUMENTS

1.1 John H. Griscom, "The Sanitary Condition of the Laboring Population of New York," from John H. Griscom, *The Sanitary Condition of the Laboring Population of New York. With Some Suggestions for Improvement* (New York: Harper & Brothers, 1845). Public domain.

1.2 Jane Addams and Ellen Gates Starr, "Hull-House, A Social Settlement," from Jane Addams and Ellen Gates Starr, *Hull-House, A Social Settlement at 225 Halsted Street, Chicago: An Outline-Sketch*, 1894. Courtesy of the Newberry Library, Chicago, Illinois. Public domain.

1.3 W.E.B. DuBois, "The Environment of the Negro" from W.E.B. DuBois, *The Philadelphia Negro: A Social Study* (Philadelphia: The University of Pennsylvania Press, 1899). Public domain.

ILLUSTRATIONS

1.1 "Senator Tillman's Allegorical Cow" from *The Congressional Record*: The Proceedings and Debates of the *Sixty-Third* Congress, *First Session* (Washington, DC: Government Printing Office) 50-Part 6 (October 1913). Public domain.

1.2 Ernest W. Burgess, "Urban Areas" from Robert E. Park, Ernest W. Burgess, and Roderick D. McKenzie, *The City* (Chicago: The University of Chicago Press, 1925). Public domain.

Part II: Pre-Columbian and European Foundations

ESSAYS

2.1 Lisa Krissoff Boehm and Steven Corey. "Pre-Colonial and Seventeenth-Century Native American Settlements," from Lisa Krissoff Boehm and Steven H. Corey, *America's Urban History* (New York: Routledge, 2015), Copyright © 2015 by Lisa Krissoff Boehm and Steven H. Corey.

2.2 David J. Weber, "Frontier and Frontier Peoples Transformed," from David J. Weber, *The Spanish Frontier in North America*, Brief Edition (2009). Copyright © 2009 by Yale University Press. Reprinted with permission of Yale University Press.

2.3 Emma Hart, "To Plant in Towns": Charles Towne at the Founding of Carolina," from Emma Hart, *Building Charleston: Town and Society in the Eighteenth- Century British Atlantic World* (Charlottesville: University of Virginia, 2010 and Columbia: University of South Carolina, 2015). Copyright © 2010 by the Rector and Visitors of the University of Virginia. Reprinted with Permission from Copyright Clearance Center (Copyright.com).

DOCUMENTS

2.1 "The 'Lost' Native American City of Etzanoa," excerpted from Jerry R. Craddock and John H. R. Polt, "Juan de Oñate in Quivira, 1601: the 'Relación cierta y verdadera' and the Valverde Interrogatory," University of California, Berkeley Cibola Project (2013). Open source at https://escholarship.org/uc/item/7162z2rp.

2.2 Henry Marie Brackenridge, "Envisioning Great American Indian Cities (1813)," from *Transactions of the American Philosophical Society,* Vol. 1, New Series (1818). Public domain.

2.3 John Winthrop, "A Model of Christian Charity (1630)," in Samuel Eliot Morison, ed., *Winthrop Papers*, Volume II, 1623–1630 (Boston: The Massachusetts Historical Society, 1931). Courtesy of the Massachusetts Historical Society, Boston, Massachusetts.

2.4 Benjamin Bullivant, "Philadelphia in 1697," from Benjamin Bullivant, *A Journall with Observations on my Travail from Boston in N.E. to N.Y. New Jersies & Philadelphia in Pennsylvania A.D. 1697*, as excerpted by Wayne Andrews, "The Travel Diary of Dr. Benjamin Bullivant," *New-York Historical Society Quarterly* 60, no. 1 (January 1956). Courtesy of the New-York Historical Society, New York, New York and the estate of Wayne Andrews.

2.5 "An Act for Establishing Ports and Towns (1705)," from William Waller Henning, *The Statutes at Large; Being a Collection of All the Laws of Virginia, From the First Session of the Legislature, in the Year 1619*, Volume III (Philadelphia; Printed for the Editor by Thomas Desilver, 1823). Public domain.

Part III: From British to American Cities

ESSAYS

3.1 Pauline Maier, "Boston and New York in the Eighteenth Century," *Proceedings of the American Antiquarian Society* 91, Part 2 (Oct. 21, 1981). Reprinted with permission of the American Antiquarian Society.

3.2 Benjamin Carp, "The Forgotten City," from Benjamin Carp, *Rebels Rising: Cities and the American Revolution* (2007). Copyright © 2007. Reprinted with permission of Oxford University Press.

3.3 Richard C. Wade, "Urban Life in Western America, 1790–1830," *The American Historical Review*, 64, no. 1 (October 1958). Reprinted with permission of Oxford University Press and the Estate of Richard C. Wade.

DOCUMENTS

3.1 "Conspiracy... For Burning the City of New-York (1741)," excerpted from Recorder of the City of New-York, *A Journal of the Proceeding in the Detection of the Conspiracy Formed by Some White People, in Conjunction with Negro and Other Slaves, For Burning the City of New-York in America, and Murdering the Inhabitants* (New-York: James Parker, at the New Printing-Office, 1744). Public domain.

ILLUSTRATIONS

Part IV: Ways of City Life, 1820s–1920s

ESSAYS

DOCUMENTS

4.4 Jacob Riis, "The Mixed Crowd" from *How the Other Half Lives: Studies Among the Tenements of New York* (1890). Public domain.

4.5 Theodore Dreiser, *Sister Carrie* (1900). Public domain.

4.6 "Triangle Shirtwaist Fire, New York City," from *The Ladies' Garment Worker*, April 1911. Permission of the Kheel Center at Cornell University.

4.7 John Hope Franklin and Scott Ellsworth, "Tulsa Race Riots," from *Tulsa Race Riots: A Report by the Oklahoma Commission to Study the Tulsa Race Riot of 1921*. Courtesy Research Division of the Oklahoma Historical Society, Oklahoma City, Oklahoma. Public domain.

4.8 Ku Klux Klan Initiation, Worcester, Massachusetts (1924). Reprinted with permission of the Worcester Telegram & Gazette Corp. and Gatehouse Media.

ILLUSTRATION

4.1 "The Pocket Book Dropper," *The National Police Gazette* May 27, 1848. Reprinted with Permission of the American Antiquarian Society.

Part V: Ways of Life 1820s–1920s

ESSAYS

5.1 Jessica Trounstine, "Challenging the Machine-Reform Dichotomy: Two Threats to Urban Democracy," in Richardson Dilworth, ed. *The City in American Political Development* (Routledge, 2009). Copyright © 2009 by Taylor & Francis. Reprinted with permission from Routledge/Taylor & Francis.

5.2 Lizabeth Cohen, "Workers Make a New Deal," (1990, 2008) from *Making a New Deal: Industrial Workers in Chicago, 1919–1939* (1990). Copyright ©1990 and 2008. Reprinted with permission of Cambridge University Press.

5.3. Nicholas Lemann, "Washington," from Nicholas Lemann, *The Promised Land: The Great Black Migration and How it Changed America* (1991). Copyright © 1991 by Nicholas Lemann. Reprinted with permission of Penguin Random House.

DOCUMENTS

5.1 "William Tweed's Confession," from Board of Aldermen, *Report of the Special Committee of the Board of Aldermen Appointed to Investigate the "Ring" Frauds Together with the Testimony Elicited During the Investigation*, Document No. 8, January 4, 1878 (New York: Martin B. Brown, 1878). Public domain.

5.2 Lincoln Steffens, "Philadelphia: Corrupt and Contented," from *McClure's Magazine* XXI (July 1903). Public domain.

5.3 Lyndon Baines Johnson, "The Great Society," *Public Papers of the Presidents of the United States: Lyndon B. Johnson, 1963–64*. Volume I (Washington, D.C.: Government Printing Office, 1965). Public domain.

5.4 United States Department of Labor, Office of Policy Planning and Research (Daniel Patrick Moynihan), "The Negro Family and the Case for National Action," (Washington, D.C., March 1965). Public domain.

5.5 "President Arrives in Alabama, Briefed on Hurricane Katrina," from Press Release, Office of the Press Secretary, President George W. Bush. September 2, 2005. https://georgewbush-whitehouse.archives.gov/news/releases/2005/09/20050902-2.html. Public domain.

5.6 Will Wilkinson, "Why Does Donald Trump Demonize Cities?" originally published in *The Washington Post* March 17, 2017. Reprinted with permission of Will Wilkinson and the Niskanen Center.

6.3. "Demolished and Tilted By the Earthquake, Homes on Howard Street at 17th, 1906. (544–7961) Kelly and Chadwick." San Francisco Earthquake of 1906. Courtesy of the American Antiquarian Society.

6.4. "Smog, Salt Lake City, Utah, November 11, 1950." Public domain.

Part VII: Transversing and Transforming Urban Space: Transportation and Planning

ESSAYS

7.1 Sam Bass Warner, Jr., "From Walking City to the Implementation of the Street Railways," from *Streetcar Suburbs: The Process of Growth in Boston, 1870–1920*, Second Edition, Harvard University Press. Copyright © 1962, 1978 by the President and Fellows of Harvard College.

7.2 Marta Gutman, "The Landscape of Charity in California: First Imprints in San Francisco," from *A City for Children: Women, Architecture, and the Charitable Landscapes of Oakland, 1850–1950* (2014). Copyright © 2014 by the University of Chicago Press. Reprinted with permission of the University of Chicago Press.

7.3 Clifton Hood, "The Subway and the City," from *722 MILES: The Building of the Subways and How They Transformed New York*. Copyright © 1993 by Clifton Hood. Abridged by permission of Simon & Schuster, Inc.

7.4 Robert Fogelson, "Wishful Thinking: Downtown and the Automotive Revolution," from *Downtown: Its Rise and Fall, 1880–1950*. Copyright © 2001 by Robert M. Fogelson. Reprinted with permission of Yale University Press.

7.5 D. Bradford Hunt, "Planning a Social Disaster," from *Blueprint for Disaster: The Unraveling of Chicago Public Housing* (2009). Copyright © 2009 by The University of Chicago Press. Reprinted with permission of The University of Chicago Press.

DOCUMENTS

7.1 *National Interstate and Defense Highways Act (1956)*. Public domain.

7.2 Walter D. Moody, *Wacker's Manual of the Plan of Chicago* (Chicago: Chicago Plan Commission, 1913). Original accessed at the Newberry Library, Chicago, Illinois. Public domain.

7.3 *The Housing Act of* (1949). Public domain.

7.4 Toni Randolph, Southdale Mall, Edina Minnesota (2006). Reprinted with permission of Minnesota Public Radio.

7.5 Jane Jacobs, "The Use of Sidewalks: Assimilating Children," from *The Death and Life of Great American Cities* (Random House/Vintage, 1961). Copyright © 1961, 1989 by Jane Jacobs. Reprinted with permission from Copyright Clearance Center (Copyright.com).

7.6 Congress for the New Urbanism, *Charter of the New Urbanism* (1996). Reprinted with permission of the Congress for the New Urbanism.

ILLUSTRATIONS

Transportation Revolution Photo Essay

7.1 "Clic-Clack De Omnibus," Street Scene, 1835. Courtesy of the American Antiquarian Society.

7.2 "Whitehall, South, and Staten Island Ferries and Revenue Barge Office, New York." Circa 1850s–1860s. Courtesy of the American Antiquarian Society.

7.3 Trolley Wayfinder, "Bird's Eye View of Trolley Routes in New England," New England Street Railway Club, 1907. Courtesy of the American Antiquarian Society.

7.4 Horsecar, New York City, 1908. Courtesy of the American Antiquarian Society.

7.5 Norfolk, Virginia, Granby Street, c. 1915. Courtesy of the Library of Congress.

9.2 N.B.D. Connolly, "Bargaining and Hoping," from *A World More Concrete: Real Estate and The Remaking of Jim Crow South Florida*. Copyright © 2016 by the University of Chicago Press. Reprinted with permission of the University of Chicago Press.

9.3 Monica Perales, "Making a Border City," from *Smeltertown: Making and Remembering a Southwest Border Community*. Copyright © 2010 by University of North Carolina Press. Reprinted with permission of University of North Carolina Press.

9.4 A.K. Sandoval-Strausz, "Latino Landscapes: Postwar Cities and the Transnational Origins of a New Urban America," *The Journal of American History* (December 2014). Reprinted with permission of the *Journal of American History* via Copyright Clearance Center (Copyright.com).

DOCUMENTS

9.1 Watts Riots (1965). Public domain.

9.2 Adam Fortunate Eagle, "Urban Indians (1964–1969)," from *Alcatraz! Alcatraz!* (California: Heyday Books, 1992). Reprinted with permission of Adam Fortunate Eagle.

9.3 Oakland Black Panther Party for Self-Defense, "Ten Point Plan (1966)." Public domain.

9.4 President George H. W. Bush, "Address to the Nation on the Civil Disturbances in Los Angeles, California" (1992). Public domain.

Part X: Postindustrial Cities

ESSAYS

10.1 Hal Rothman, "Inventing Modern Las Vegas," from *Neon Metropolis: How Las Vegas Started the Twenty-First Century* (Routledge, 2003). Copyright © 2003. Reprinted with permission of Taylor & Francis/Routledge.

10.2 Aaron Shkudka, "Artist Organizations, Political Advocacy, and the Creation of a Residential SoHo," from *The Lofts of SoHo: Gentrification, Art, and Industry in New York, 1950–1980*. Copyright © 2016 by the University of Chicago Press. Reprinted with permission of the University of Chicago Press.

10.3 Chloe Taft, "The Postindustrial Factory," from *From Steel to Slots: Casino Capitalism in the Postindustrial City*. Copyright © 2016 by Harvard University Press. Reprinted with permission of Harvard University Press.

10.4 Todd Clear and Natasha A. Frost, "The Punishment Imperative," from *The Punishment Imperative: The Rise and Failure of Mass Incarceration in America* (2014). Copyright © 2014 by New York University Press. Reprinted with permission of New York University Press.

DOCUMENTS

10.1 Patrick Sisson, "How a 'reverse Great Migration' is reshaping U.S. cities" *Curbed*, July 31, 2018, accessed at www.curbed.com/2018/7/31/17632092/black-chicago-neighborhood-great-migration. Reprinted with Permission of Vox Media.

10.2 "Investigation of the Ferguson Police Department," from United States Department of Justice, Civil Rights Division, *Investigation of the Ferguson Police Department*, March 4, 2014, accessed at www.justice.gov/sites/default/files/opa/press-releases/attachments/2015/03/04/ferguson_police_department_report.pdf. Public domain.

ILLUSTRATIONS

10.1 A First Responder Looks at 9-11. Photograph by Andrew Boss, 2001. Reprinted with permission of Andrew Boss.

INDEX

Page locators in *italics* refer to illustrations, photographs and images.